LEGAL RESPONSES TO TERRORISM

Second Edition

LEGAL RESPONSES TO TERRORISM

Second Edition

Wayne McCormack
Professor of Law
University of Utah

 LexisNexis®

Library of Congress Cataloging-in-Publication Data

McCormack, Wayne.
Legal Responses to Terrorism / Wayne McCormack.—2nd ed.
p. cm.
Includes bibliographical references and index.
ISBN 978–1–4224–2501–5 (hard cover)
1. War on Terrorism, 2001—Law and legislation—United States. 2. Terrorism—United States—Cases. 3. Terrorism—Prevention. I. Title.
KF9430.M3 2008
345.73'02–dc22
2008018284

> **NOTE TO USERS**
> To ensure that you are using the latest materials available in this area, please be sure to periodically check the LexisNexis Law School web site for downloadable updates and supplements at www.lexisnexis.com/lawschool.

Editorial Offices
744 Broad Street, Newark, NJ 07102 (973) 820-2000
201 Mission St., San Francisco, CA 94105-1831 (415) 908-3200
www.lexisnexis.com

MATTHEW◆BENDER

PREFACE

I believe that teaching materials should be balanced. Because this book may fail my own test without my knowing it, I should provide here a disclosure statement of my beliefs on this subject. As I was assembling the first edition in 2004, I assumed that the excesses of the Bush Administration would be pulled back, that cooler heads would prevail, and that the "Ship of State would right itself" in due course. I thought my task was merely to provide background on the various tools for confronting terrorism. I thought the notion of a "war" on a concept would dissipate in the face of both military and political realities. I thought that controls on military action, criminal prosecutions, and intelligence gathering would contribute to a balanced approach to an ongoing problem and would take us out of the crisis mode that threatened the very stability of our government.

I was wrong. In my innate optimism, I did not anticipate that the "war on terror" would become an all-out assault on the Rule of Law. Prisoner abuse turns out to have been a conscious strategy fueled by "legal opinions" that were travesties. Detentions without hearings became commonplace. Renditions of prisoners from one foreign country to another where they would be mistreated were frequent and authorized by the President himself. The National Security Agency was authorized to spy on U.S. citizens, at least when they were communicating with a person suspected to have terrorist ties but maybe in other undisclosed circumstances. Congress was then enlisted to ratify detentions and surveillance operations without judicial oversight. As I had said before, it was up to We the People to say when enough is enough, and Congress failed to say it for Us.

I don't know whether the book has a different tone now or whether I just feel differently about it. It has become necessary for those of us in the law schools to take on the responsibility of providing the navigational tools to get the Ship of State back on course.

I have added one note on the ethics of government lawyers. Rather than emphasizing the lapses of those in political positions, that note spends more ink on praising courageous military lawyers who have challenged detentions and mistreatment of prisoners to the detriment of their careers. I know that there were professionals in the Department of Justice who likewise challenged the excesses of the Bush Administration within the scope of their jobs, and they will remain unsung heroes.

In the fall of 2001, the United States had an opportunity unique in all of human history. One nation clearly dominated the world in both power and prestige. Almost the entire globe was of one mind to confront the cowardice of attacks on civilians. There was even an awareness within the decision elites of the world that something needed to be done to address the globalization of labor and the movement of capital. The good will of the entire world was focused on the United States and its leadership.

That good will provided an opportunity to reshape how the world goes about its political business but instead the leadership of the U.S. squandered that good will and that opportunity. Now we in the legal profession must go about the sometimes dreary but always challenging job of doing our job. Our job is the Rule of Law, and it is to that task that this book is now directed.

Table of Contents

Table of Contents

Table of Contents

Table of Contents

Table of Contents

Table of Contents

Table of Contents

Chapter 1

INTRODUCTION: DEFINITIONS AND STRUCTURES

The word "terrorism" evokes many images for each person who hears it. Perhaps the only consistent themes are that no image is positive and all are violent. A single mention of the word might set my mind loose on a kaleidoscopic rampage from Munich Olympic Village, to the Achille Lauro, to a masked gunman in the cockpit of an airplane in Athens, to guerillas in the jungles of Colombia, to a sidewalk café bomb in Spain, and ultimately to fully loaded airplanes flying into the World Trade Center Towers.

Notice that other themes could be lurking in the list above. All but the last incident occurred outside the United States. Most, but not all, involved Middle Eastern Islamist fundamentalists. Many were linked to demands for a Palestinian or Basque homeland, or a radical Colombian regime. Very few involve people such as Timothy McVeigh who acted out of sheer malice for his home government or other lone killers who may have been motivated by a variety of psychological compulsions.

As a lawyer, you may be asked to advise on the legality of various responses to international terrorism. Is it lawful to invade another country to pursue suspected terrorists? to track down a suspected terrorist and kill her? to capture one and imprison him secretly? or hand him off to another country with the prospect that he will be mistreated (tortured)? to capture one and treat her with aggressive interrogation methods that some would consider inhumane or torturous? to spy on your own citizens or resident aliens to gather information about terrorist plots? As an advisor on any of these questions of law, you will have also an interest in whether each of these actions is wise or likely to be effective. In other words, as a legal advisor you should also be viewed as a repository of wisdom on the available policy choices.

The dominant purposes of this course are to determine what should be the appropriate responses of the United States and the international community to international terrorism. More generally, the themes are about governmental responses to crisis.

An important starting point is to reduce some of the confusion surrounding the term "terrorism" itself. When faced with conduct to which we want to respond, whether punitively or preventively, the human mind naturally wants to define the unacceptable conduct so that we can distinguish it from acceptable behavior. When searching for a definition within the chaotic nature of terrorism, however, it is easy to be lured off our path into uncharted waters because some of the above themes could be red herrings leading us on wild goose chases. (Obviously, this mixing of metaphors is intentional to emphasize that chaotic events can cause chaotic thinking, which can lead in turn to unfortunate responses.)

§ 1.01 UNDERSTANDING TERRORISM

The one consistent theme in terrorism is violence against civilians. But not all violence against civilians is considered terrorism — most is simply criminal conduct. Some violence against civilians committed by official representatives of a government would be considered a war crime or genocide under international law, but it might also be considered terrorism.

[A] Defining Terrorism

Questions we will ask repeatedly are what difference does the terrorist label make for legal doctrine? is there a crime of being a terrorist? is terrorism an act of warfare? The question of legal consequences goes hand in glove with the question of what constitutes terrorism — you can't punish what you can't define. Which doesn't mean that you couldn't punish the constituent acts of terrorism such as bombing or murder.

Three common elements can be isolated in most actions labeled as terrorism: the terrorist appears in civilian clothing, attacks civilian targets, and blends back into civilian populations. But many people classify state-uniformed "death squads" and the like as terrorist activities. And many experts will not call an action terrorism unless the perpetrator has some kind of political motivation.

The U.S. Department of State is mandated by federal law, 8 U.S.C. § 1189, to designate "foreign terrorist organizations" based on three criteria: that it is a foreign organization, that it engages in terrorist activity, and that its terrorist activity threatens the security of U.S. nationals or the national security of the U.S. The definition of terrorism used for this purpose is that contained in a separate statute which requires an annual report to Congress of terrorism developments, 22 U.S.C. § 2656f(d):

> premeditated, politically motivated violence perpetrated against noncombatant targets by subnational groups or clandestine agents.

Similarly, the federal criminal code defines terrorism in 18 U.S.C. § 2331 as

> violent acts or acts dangerous to human life that are a violation of the criminal laws [and] appear to be intended
>
> (i) to intimidate or coerce a civilian population;
>
> (ii) to influence the policy of a government by intimidation or coercion; or
>
> (iii) to influence the policy of a government by mass destruction, assassination, or kidnapping.

Another definition used in the criminal code is at 18 U.S.C. § 2332b:

> an offense that
>
> (A) is calculated to influence or affect the conduct of government by intimidation or coercion, or to retaliate against government conduct; and
>
> (B) is a violation of [one or more of 39 listed criminal offenses].

Various authors have provided their own definitions. Professor Heymann describes terrorism as combining elements of crime and armed combat. It is different from normal crime because of its purposes (crime is usually motivated by greed, jealousy, anger, or power) and different from legitimate combat because of its clandestine and unauthorized character. His definition of terrorism thus is "an illegal form of clandestine warfare that is carried out by a sub-state group to change the policies, personnel, structure, or ideology of a government, or to influence the actions of another part of the population — one with enough self-identity to respond to selective violence." PHILLIP HEYMANN, TERRORISM AND AMERICA 9 (1998).

"Terrorism is the deliberate and systematic murder, maiming, and menacing of the innocent to inspire fear for political ends." CHRISTOPHER HARMON, TERRORISM TODAY 1 (2000).

"[T]errorism, . . . is simply the contemporary name given to, and the modern permutation of, warfare deliberately waged against civilians with the purpose of destroying their will to support either political leaders or policies that the agents of such violence find objectionable." CALEB CARR, THE LESSONS OF TERROR 6 (2003).

Terrorism is the "peacetime equivalent of war crimes: acts that would, if carried out by a government in war, violate the Geneva Convention." ALEX P. SCHMID & RONALD D. CRELINSTEN, WESTERN RESPONSES TO TERRORISM 13 (1993).

The international community has been edging ever closer to defining and outlawing terrorism. Although numerous UN Security Council resolutions have condemned terrorism, international conventions create commitments to eliminate certain practices such as bombing or aircraft piracy without attempting to define terrorism. For example, the Convention for Suppression of Terrorist Financing states that a person

> commits an offence within the meaning of this Convention if that person by any

means, directly or indirectly, unlawfully and wilfully, provides or collects funds with the intention that they should be used or in the knowledge that they are to be used, in full or in part, in order to carry out:

(a) An act which constitutes an offence within the scope of and as defined in one of the treaties listed in the annex; or

(b) Any other act intended to cause death or serious bodily injury to a civilian, or to any other person not taking an active part in the hostilities in a situation of armed conflict, when the purpose of such act, by its nature or context, is to intimidate a population, or to compel a Government or an international organization to do or to abstain from doing any act.

An ad hoc Committee of the General Assembly has been at work since 1996 on a draft Comprehensive Convention Against Terrorism, in which the working definition as of 2002 is this:

Any person commits an offence within the meaning of this Convention if that person, by any means, unlawfully and intentionally causes

(a) Death or serious bodily injury to any person; or

(b) Serious damage to public or private property, including a place of public use, a State or government facility, a public transportation system, an infrastructure facility or the environment; or

(c) Damage to property, places, facilities, or systems referred to in paragraph 1(b), resulting or likely to result in major economic loss

when the purpose of such act, by its nature or context, is to intimidate a population, or to compel a Government or an international organization to do or abstain from doing any act.

In some versions of the draft, the last clause is printed at the end of, as if part of, subsection (b). If placed there, then (a) would stand alone without a requirement of political motivation and thus cover virtually any act of violence.

From this welter of definitions, at least we can delineate some common features. Generally, a terrorist

1. is a civilian or subnational group who

2. uses violence

3. against civilians

4. for political motivations.

The first element, civilian or clandestine status, is relevant because such persons may blend back into civilian populations, thus making it difficult if not impossible to attack them without endangering other civilians. Members of a uniformed official agency may claim authority of the nation and may be acting pursuant to military orders, in which case their actions are proscribed by the laws of war or other international law, and most observers would not use the label of terrorism for their actions; some commentators nevertheless insist that officially sanctioned violence against civilians is still terrorism even when committed by uniformed troops.

The fourth element, political motivation, at first glance could seem irrelevant to the question of whether someone is deliberately targeting civilians with violence. The motivation, however, may distinguish the terrorist from the ordinary serial murderer, although again there are many instances in which the distinction can become blurred. Another relevance of this distinction may be relevant if international law attempts to distinguish between crimes against humanity or genocide (which may lack a discernible political motivation) and some future definition of terrorism. We will explore these topics in more depth below.

[B]   Describing the Terrorist Groups

The most famous (or infamous) terrorist groups active in the world today are al Qaeda, Hezbollah and its related groups, FARC (Revolutionary Armed Forces of Colombia), ETA (Basque Fatherland and Liberty — Spain), and Aum Shinrikyo (Japan). The IRA (Irish Republican Army) and Shining Path (Peru) arguably have cooled their level of activity over the past several years. Other groups come and go. The purely political ideologues of the 1960s and 1970s, such as the Red Brigade (Brigate Russo — Italy) and Baader-Meinhoff (Germany) have all but disappeared.

As of April 2007, the State Department designated 42 "Foreign Terrorist Organizations" (FTO) (http://www.state.gov/s/ct/rls/crt/2006/82738.htm) and provided background information on 43 "Other Groups of Concern." Designation as an FTO carries at least these legal consequences:

1.   It is a crime to knowingly provide material support or resources to a designated FTO.

2.   Representatives and certain members of a designated FTO can be denied visas or excluded from the United States.

3.   U.S. financial institutions must block funds of designated FTOs and their agents and must report suspicious transactions to the U.S. Department of the Treasury.

Christopher Harmon, a faculty member at the Marine Corps Command and Staff College, contends that "Terrorism is always political, even when it also evinces other motives, such as the religious, the economic, or the social. . . . If terrorism is best defined by its calculated abuse of the innocent for political purposes, there is reason to survey the political objectives which prompt such actions by militants of the modern day." He describes organizations with political agendas of anarchism, communism, neofascism, national separation, religion, and pro-state terrorism. With this variety of political motivations, can we even conclude that political objectives are a defining characteristic of terrorism? Harmon concedes that "Individual terrorists may find the clandestine struggle so appealing that it almost becomes an end in itself, a way of life. But while such nihilism is present by degrees in anyone willing to maim and murder the innocent, it is a mistake to think that nihilism, rather than purpose, is the essence of the typical contemporary terrorist organization."

Why do motivations matter? One answer is that motivation may distinguish the terrorist from the common criminal or serial killer. With this in mind, how would you characterize Theodore Kaczynski, the Unabomber? The Unabomber Manifesto decried technology and the industrial society, proposing a revolution that would smash the factories and even burn the books to prevent future regeneration of technology, but was he organized enough to warrant being treated as a terrorist rather than mere psychopath? Most authors consider Timothy McVeigh to be a terrorist because he acted out of malice for the government, but there is no known indication that he had an alternative in mind that would qualify as a political agenda.

What distinguishes the "terrorist" from the ordinary street criminal with ties to an international criminal organization? Take, for instance, a murder committed on the streets of an American city by a drug dealer who knows in some vague way that his livelihood is linked to a well-organized and well-funded cartel in Colombia or Afghanistan. Is this an act of terrorism? Is it an act of war? Is the U.S. justified in invading Colombia because there are organized criminals there who carry out violence on U.S. civilians? This has been the theme of several fictional books and movies, carrying the message that U.S. involvement in Colombia would be permissible only with the permission of the Colombian government, certainly the correct answer under international law.

Islamist fundamentalist groups have taken center stage in the global concern with terrorism over the past 30 years, but they neither invented terrorism nor are the only purveyors of it today. The term "fundamentalist" can be taken to refer either to a desire to return to basic fundamentals or to a belief that the adherent is caught up in a cosmic struggle between good and evil. Many fundamentalists will share these and more characteristics. For a good summary of the concept of fundamentalism, see http://religiousmovements.lib.virginia.edu/nrms/fund.html.

It is worth recalling that fundamentalist beliefs have spawned terrorist activities in many centuries, including the Spanish Inquisition and conflicts in Northern Ireland, and have contributed to other reigns of terror such as the KKK. For an excellent depiction of fundamentalism in the three principal monotheistic religions, see KAREN ARMSTRONG, THE BATTLE FOR GOD (2000).

[C] What Produces a Terrorist?

Who Becomes a Terrorist and Why is the name of a study conducted by the staff of the Library of Congress in 1999 (LC Study), attempting to determine from the available literature whether a psychological profile could be built of the typical terrorist. Although some gross generalizations were available, the basic conclusion was that profiling a terrorist would not make it possible to pick out the terrorist from a crowd. Identifying the terrorist is not the only reason for studying the psychology. Another desirable goal would be to find mechanisms of dissuading vulnerable young people from entering the trade. Study of the terrorist phenomenon with a sympathetic eye to understanding may eventually yield results in both prevention and response.

> The orderly and systematic analysis of terrorist motivation could provide valuable clues about strategies for responding to terrorism in terms of both protection and mitigation activities (antiterrorism) and for direct action involving preemption, interdiction, or retribution (counter-terrorism).

Thomas F. Ditzler, *Malevolent Minds: The Teleology of Terrorism, in* FATHALI MODHADDAM & ANTHONY MARSELLA, UNDERSTANDING TERRORISM 188 (2004).

Terrorist foot-soldiers tend to be in their twenties while the leaders are somewhat older (nothing surprising in that), about 80% are male (although the LC Study goes on at some length about the single-mindedness and ferocity of the few women terrorists), and most feel that they have a political injury (perhaps ethnic or religious in nature) to redress. Obviously, there are millions of oppressed males in their twenties who do not turn to terrorism, so a further question is what psychological forces can combine to produce the violence of terrorism.

From a psychological standpoint, there are a number of hypotheses about why someone turns to terrorism. The three cited in the LC Study are labeled frustration-aggression, negative identity, and narcissistic rage. What the hypotheses share are that an individual with either very low self-esteem or highly inflated views of self (and often these are found in the same person) may be so frustrated with society that violence seems the only method of releasing the pressure on his psyche. The LC Study cautions against making too much of this type of oversimplified psycho-profile.

"[T]he terrorist is not diagnosably psychopathic or mentally sick. Contrary to the stereotype that the terrorist is a psychopath or otherwise mentally disturbed, the terrorist is actually quite sane, although deluded by an ideological or religious way of viewing the world. . . . A member who exhibits traits of psychopathy or any noticeable degree of mental illness would only be a liability for the group." Nevertheless, it is possible to generalize that terrorist groups attract persons who are "action-oriented, aggressive persons who are stimulus-hungry and seek excitement." As the study points out, this description could apply to many persons who go into law enforcement; there are even people who enter more sedentary professions and seek their adrenaline rushes from rock-climbing or snow-boarding.

Despite these claims, there are many people who believe the modern terrorist is bent simply on killing for the sake of killing. After the school massacre at Breslan, Russia, one commentator said that terrorists were damaging many of their own causes. "But that's the idea. Because the death cult is not really about the cause it purports to serve. It's about the sheer pleasure of killing and dying." David Brooks, *Death Cult on the Fringe of the Muslim World Is Beyond Reason*, N.Y. TIMES, Sept. 7, 2004 at A23. Maybe it would be as difficult to generalize about the psychological condition of those who commit terrorist acts as it would be to generalize about the psychology of any other form of criminal behavior. Nevertheless, any glimmer of understanding the terrorist psychology should be helpful in crafting responses to it.

One factor that is often emphasized is the religious fanaticism of many recent terrorists. Some authors link this with the increasing fatality levels of the past two decades. In the 1970s and 1980s, the prevailing belief was that "Terrorists want a lot of people watching, not a lot of people dead." The LC Study then notes a new trend in the 1990s, "the emergence of religious fundamentalists and new religious groups espousing the rhetoric of mass-destruction terrorism." (*LC Study* at 6.) "The actions of terrorist organizations are based on a subjective interpretation of the world rather than objective reality." It is possible that the emergence of religion-based interpretations of reality ease the leaders' ability to instill fervor and lack of remorse in their followers.

A predominant characteristic of terrorists is the belief that they are right. Most report feeling no remorse over killing innocent civilians, including children, because it was the right thing to do. At least, that is, until they are confronted with pictures or descriptions of the lives of those they have killed. Because the psychological profiling excludes psychopaths or sociopaths, the speculation is that this lack of remorse can be instilled by consistent "brainwashing" emphasizing the wrongs that have been done to the ethnic or religious group with which the terrorist group identifies. Many terrorists will be disaffected from society before they contact a terrorist group. At first, the newcomer may be just curious or seeking like-minded comrades. Over time, the iteration of deeply felt injustices links the novitiate into taking further steps. Usually, full membership will require training and tests, perhaps even to the point of killing before full induction.

The terrorist's background and personal makeup can be combined to think of the "psychosocial" setting of the terrorist's worldview. This permits analyzing the worldview itself for a number of purposes. For example, to consider the likelihood that a terrorist organization may negotiate, we might look to this matrix developed from the analyses of Bruce Hoffman of the RAND Corporation:

Motivation	Context	Negotiate?
Rational	Political	High
Psychological	Personal	No
Cultural	Group	No

Ditzler, *Malevolent Minds* at 201.

In this framework, the rational terrorists with specific political objectives may "sound a lot like legitimate military authorities planning an operation or even business executives developing an advertising campaign" except that they choose illegal means of targeting civilian populations to accomplish their goals. One might expect to be able to negotiate compromises with such a group because the weighing of costs and benefits is part of the formulation of their strategy, and obtaining partial benefits at reduced costs may look attractive. One aspect to which we in the West must be alert is that our rationality may be different from the rationality of someone from another setting. For example, it may be perfectly rational for either an Israeli or Palestinian to sabotage peace negotiations by an extreme act if the actor does not like any of the proposed solutions for a peaceful settlement.

For Hoffman's "psychological" terrorist with a personal orientation to the world, "the impetus to commit acts of violence is often related to a profound sense of failure or inadequacy for which the perpetrator may seek redress through revenge." This person may possess elements of what many of us would think of as psychosis, although the LC Study insists that no terrorist group would trust the psychotic to be a member. This may be the category in which we could differentiate most cleanly between the terrorist and the criminal. The "lone wolf" seeking to ameliorate some deep personal pain does not easily fit the common-sense definition of terrorist because he or she is not acting pursuant to the direction of, or in complicity with, an organized group. Timothy McVeigh to many people is a terrorist, but without a group identity he does not represent an ongoing threat that will continue after his capture. The psychological terrorist may, on the other hand, be part of a group that represents a significant threat. "For these terrorists, the attraction to terrorism is typically based on the psychic benefits of group affiliation." And what if the whole group is bound to terrorism as a way of life?

> Hoffman noted that if these groups achieve any meaningful progress toward their espoused goals, they often adopt increasingly radicalized positions characterized by increasingly nonachievable goals. The development of these goals may become necessary for the organization, because the attainment of true success would threaten their continuing need to exist.

Ditzler, *Malevolent Minds* at 202. Assuming that these observations are accurate, then it is easy to see why this category gets a "will not negotiate" rating in the Hoffman chart.

The third category is the "culturally motivated" terrorist with a strong "group" identity. "According to Hoffman, the motivation for these groups to commit violent acts typically derives from an almost primordial fear of cultural extermination or the loss of cultural identity." Ditzler concentrates on religious fundamentalists in this category and finds again an extreme lack of ability or willingness to negotiate. "In a world of absolute truth . . . there is no room for dissent and no room for theological doubt." "In this worldview, the failure to respond to the utmost of one's ability would be tantamount to an acceptance of damnation." Racial/ethnic/cultural groups without the overlay of religion could be viewed in similar light with examples ranging from Nazi Germany through the Serbian atrocities in Kosovo and Hutu-Tutsi atrocities in Rwanda.

If the "cultural" group were to achieve an autonomous homeland, would the group then be persuaded to give up the terrorist methodology? Authors differ on this issue, some asserting that the successful terrorist will produce a tyrannical regime. Nevertheless, the group presumably would have no further incentive to attack transnationally so to some extent there would be a type of negotiated settlement in place. If that were to happen, then the chart might be revised to reflect a type of "negotiation" with the "cultural" terrorist, who then takes on many of the characteristics of a "political" terrorist.

No human can ever completely understand the motivations and character of another human being. Even harder is attempting to understand the motivations and character of a group of people, each of whom may come into an enterprise with unique expectations and assumptions. This section has emphasized the importance of coming to some minimal understanding of the motivations of terrorists and terrorist organizations for several reasons. First, in many definitions of terrorism, motivation is itself a critical factor. Second, the more one knows the thought patterns of an adversary, the better one is equipped to confront that adversary. For example, understanding some of the cultural background and motivations of a terrorist may be critically important to interrogation of a captive, a factor that we will consider in the final chapter of this book when we think about torture. Finally, considering the motivations and expectations of a terrorist organization may lead to some modifications of foreign policy that would alleviate the tensions motivating some terrorist acts.

Some psychiatrists and philosophers would say that "Motivation is a stream with many tributaries," meaning that any single act may be prompted by many motivating factors. In this context, the political motivation of a terrorist may be either pre-hoc or post-hoc, motivated by the past or motivated to the future. The political motivation may come from anger and frustration with what has happened in the past and thus could not be addressed, if at all, by anything other than an abject apology or reparations, neither of which is likely to be politically viable in the face of continued violence. Or the motivation may be forward looking, such as a set of objectives that could be addressed by hard-headed negotiation in an international setting. Once again, it is important to realize that one individual is likely to carry multiple motivations and that a group is even more complex.

§ 1.02   INTERLOCKING GOVERNMENTAL CONTROLS

Our next task is to understand the framework of responses available to us. There is an interlocking set of "communities" devoted to public safety within government today. Similarly, there are interlocking legal controls or restraints that operate both on the individual or group who contemplates terrorist action and on the government agencies attempting to respond. Although the political world and the popular press tend to lump all responses to terrorism together under the heading of "counter-terrorism," that label is more appropriately used for prosecutorial and military-type responses while preventive measures are more aptly characterized as "anti-terrorism." The difference corresponds roughly to prevention versus reaction.

[A]   Options — Force and Nonforce

One obvious starting point in analyzing the options available for addressing terrorism is to assess the relative merits of options that involve force or violence against those that employ less forceful or nonviolent means.[1] In the latter category are at least diplomatic and economic sanctions as well as counter-propaganda measures. Some preventive measures that depend on gathering intelligence about a group and its plans could have forceful aspects.

Diplomatic measures include the kind of pressure that is brought to bear by committees of the UN or by appeals to public sentiment. Some governments are not the least bit swayed by being publicly censured or castigated. The next step then would be imposition of economic sanctions, which are also of limited effectiveness. A country that is under a trade embargo may be able to obtain goods or services from other sources. And when economic sanctions are effective, they often operate to hurt the poorest members of the target country rather than the ruling elite.

In the realm of force, there is the issue of "targeted killing" dealt with by the Israeli Supreme Court in *Public Committee Against Torture v. Government of Israel, infra* § 9.03. Israel's "Operation Wrath of God" was the subject of Steven Spielberg's film *Munich*.

The U.S. killed five persons in Yemen by firing a Hellfire missile from a Predator drone at a car occupied by Qaed Salim Sinan al-Harithi, the reputed senior al Qaeda operative in Yemen.[2] Also killed in the attack was Kamal Derwish, a U.S. citizen, allegedly the recruiter for the Lackawanna cell (*see* § 2.05 *infra*).[3]

Curiously enough, the U.S. killing of a U.S. citizen and three other unknown persons has received very little comment. Anna Lindh, then Swedish Foreign Minister, commented: "If the USA is behind this with Yemen's consent, it is nevertheless a summary execution that violates human rights. If the USA has conducted the attack without Yemen's permission it is even worse. Then it is a question of unauthorised use

---

[1] Two opinion pieces set out starkly contrasting views on this general theme. Jay Bookman, *Power Found in U.S. Ideals, Not Weapons*, Cox News Service, Sept. 11, 2006; Haim Watzman, *When You Have to Shoot First*, N.Y. Times, July 28, 2005.

[2] http://www.cbsnews.com/stories/2002/11/04/attack/main527971.shtml.

[3] http://www.pbs.org/wgbh/pages/frontline/shows/sleeper/inside/derwish.html.

of force." http://www.guardian.co.uk/usa/story/0,12271,834311,00.html. The asserted justification for targeted killings flows from the concept of armed conflict and warfare. Jeffrey Addicott, *The Yemen Attack: Illegal Assassination or Lawful Killing?*, *available at* http://jurist.law.pitt.edu/forum/forumnew68.php ("Since we are at war with al-Qa'eda, any legal analysis of the use of violence against that enemy turns on how violence is employed. In short, the United States must exercise violence lawfully in accordance with the rules associated with the law of armed conflict.")

The choices among violent and nonviolent options are properly the subject of international relations courses, but it is important for the lawyer to recognize that there are options. Otherwise, it may be too easy to assume that extreme situations require extreme counter measures — that a time of crisis removes legal constraints that would otherwise operate.

[B]   Structure of U.S. Public Safety

The U.S. government, unlike many governments in history or even in the world today, has divided and separated various units which deal with aspects of public safety. The three principal divisions with which we will be concerned are protective services, law enforcement, and the military. In a rather loose or rough sense, their functions could be thought to form a spectrum of prevention, prosecution, and warfare. There are many other agencies involved in public safety, primarily those that deal with public health and response to emergencies.

The division of public safety into different units could be analogized to how individuals deal with their own home safety. Think about the steps you take to guard against intrusions on your own space. First, you lock your doors. This is a phenomenon of relatively recent vintage itself, and there are many societies in the world today that still do not have locking doors. If this is not enough, and you have the money, you install an electronic security system, and maybe you have that system wired to call armed guards at a signal of intrusion, or maybe you even go so far as to build a gated community with guards at the entrance. All these are progressive steps of increasingly aggressive preventive measures that you can take on your own or in conjunction with immediate neighbors. Second, if you have been the subject of an intrusion, you may want to apprehend and punish the intruder. In early stages of society, this might have been done by the individual acting alone, but for many centuries this function has been turned over to law enforcement agencies. Whether the purpose is to disempower the specific intruder or to deter others, punishment is the province of communal groups. Finally, if the community feels threatened as a group by some outside group, it may move to the level of armed conflict between politically defined groups. Again, in more "primitive" societies these conflicts were often less deadly and widespread than is likely to be the case today, but the concept of an organized military response that operates across more or less defined borders between recognized political groups is ancient.

These three steps reflect roughly the three divisions of prevention, enforcement, and military action. Each stage carries not only its own culture and modes of operation, but it also is constrained by a set of limiting rules. The civil liberties implications of prevention (such as limits on demonstrations or searching persons entering an airport) may differ somewhat from the civil liberties aspects of criminal law enforcement. The limitations on military action are among the most elusive of legal concepts because they arise rather infrequently and because the enforcement mechanisms for those limits themselves are somewhat tenuous.

At the state or local level, "public safety" agencies typically are thought to consist of police, fire, and emergency medical services. These are the groups that are assembled to plan and coordinate response to minor emergencies, such as an urban fire or a multi-car crash. When a major event is contemplated, however, whether a planned event such as a Super Bowl, or a natural disaster such as an earthquake or hurricane, other agencies must be brought to the table. Managers of the utility and infrastructure systems, transportation coordinators, public health agencies, and medical care providers all become part of any team that is planning for a major event. The Federal Emergency Management Agency (FEMA) was created in 1979 and charged with developing, coordinating, and funding emergency management using both federal and state resources to plan for response to either human-triggered or natural disasters and emergencies.

The principal federal civilian agencies devoted to combating terrorism, other than the intelligence agencies, are three. The lead prosecutorial office is the Counterterrorism Section of the Department of Justice, which was originally part of the Criminal Division and was moved in 2006 to a new National Security Division within DOJ. The investigative services of the FBI are structurally part of the DOJ as well. In the Department of State, the lead is taken by its Office of the Coordinator for Counterterrorism, and in the Department of Treasury by the Office of Terrorism and Financial Intelligence.

[C] Security and Law Enforcement

Prevention means information. Information means loss of privacy. The more information government acquires, the more safe we can feel and the less privacy we will have in our daily lives. So how safe do we want to be? American political and constitutional traditions include a healthy distrust of government, complete with innumerable references from the Framing to the McCarthy era about the need to keep government agents away from private information. The Bill of Rights stems in large part from that basic proposition.

A corollary of this tradition is a distaste for government secrecy. In interesting fashion, the concern for personal privacy links with the concern about government secrecy because we cannot challenge what we do not know. The more secrets government retains, the more likely some of those secrets will involve matters about individuals that we would rather not have residing in government files.

Three preliminary observations may be helpful:

1. Security is different from law enforcement.

Security planning uses a risk-threat formula to allocate available resources to a given situation. Risk refers to the potential for harm at a particular location (e.g., an event at a stadium, a nuclear reactor), and threat refers to likely attempts to cause harm. Threat analysis requires information about persons, groups, and political interests that are traditionally part of "protected" freedom.

Law enforcement most often seeks information about past wrongdoing, using sanctions for past wrongs as deterrence of future misconduct. Its connection to "protected" interests should be secondary. Only in rare instances, such as the Unabomber case, should inquiry into political agendas be necessary for solving past crimes. These also may be instances in which capturing a serial criminal directly prevents future crimes.

2. The committed, resourceful terrorist can beat any security system.

Security includes both interdiction of threats and physical methods of reducing risks, such as locking doors, screening persons at entry points, deploying high-tech devices, and the like. Even with unlimited resources, physical security can never anticipate nor forestall the imaginative miscreant because the miscreant has the advantages of time and anonymity. Security planners must therefore deal with the reality of making a reasonable allocation of resources to security versus other public needs.

3. Prevention necessarily implies invasions of privacy.

Prevention relies on information. Information threatens privacy and freedom of expression much more directly than traditional law enforcement. Post 9/11, the blurring of separation between security and law enforcement means that civil liberties issues will be raised even more frequently by the increased use of intelligence gathering tools.

The typical criminal investigation with which most of us are familiar begins with a civilian's lodging a complaint with a police officer. When your bicycle is stolen, the insurance company wants to know the "case number" assigned when you report it to the police. More serious crimes become the subject of investigation because a child is reported kidnaped, or a body is found under suspicious circumstances, or a white collar crime is suspected because someone has lost money. Once the "case" is initiated, investigating officers search for clues to what happened with regard to that incident by assembling a profile of the victim, searching for motives and opportunities for the crime, marshaling physical evidence at the scene, and the like. All of these aspects of an investigation have the objective of assembling a virtually complete picture of what happened at some point in the past. Only in the situation of an active serial criminal (e.g., Hillside Strangler, Son of Sam, Unabomber, Maryland Sniper), are the investigators likely to be consciously concerned about hastening to prevent a future crime.

The investigation of a reported crime may produce "probable cause" to believe that a certain person committed the crime, so that search warrants can be issued for that person's house or other premises. In some situations, there might even be probable cause to conduct electronic surveillance (such as a wiretap on the suspect's telephone) because evidence of the past crime might be transmitted either as part of evading detection or planning a future similar crime. Probable cause showings in the typical investigation, thus, are focused on information related to past events.

By contrast, the emphasis in most terrorism investigations is on preventing future crimes on the basis of a suspicion that someone (whether identified or unknown) is likely to be contemplating violent action. This suspicion will not be based on evidence gathered in the context of a past crime so much as on the basis of rumors, reports from members of the public about their neighbors or friends, or just something an investigator reads in the newspaper. A search warrant or wiretap warrant would not even be possible until the "conspiracy" has been cemented through some overt act in furtherance of the conspiracy. In the investigation leading to *United States v. Sarkissian, infra* § 5.01, FBI agents were monitoring plotters who managed to place dynamite in a suitcase that was checked as luggage on a cross-country flight. We might fault the FBI agents for not moving in before the dynamite was checked as luggage, but are we really being realistic? How did the agents even have knowledge that the conspiracy was under way given that there was no probable cause to believe that a crime had been committed? It would have been difficult to obtain a search warrant prior to the dynamite's being packed in the suitcase and, by that time, as Sherlock Holmes would have said, "the game was afoot."

Another feature of intelligence gathering is that it most often works by assembling massive amounts of information, each piece of which may be seemingly innocent, until a malevolent pattern emerges. Modern high-tech artwork offers analogies that might be helpful in understanding the process. Think of the pictures, usually in children's books, that ask you to "find the __ " buried in an elaborate drawing. In this instance, all the irrelevant information is masking the one piece of critical information. The converse can be produced by taking hundreds or thousands of utterly innocent pictures, reducing them to miniature scale, and reassembling them into a pattern, something like a mosaic, that produces an image totally unrelated to the component pictures. In this instance, the critical piece of information exists only as a pattern produced by assembling all the innocent images.

Lest you think we are getting carried away with Robert Ludlum or Tom Clancy fiction, the art analogies are not perfect examples, but they reflect the very real difficulty of assembling information about innocent-seeming persons or events to put together a pattern that could alert officials to something nefarious. One FBI agent in Phoenix had been alerted prior to 9/11 to a pattern of "persons of interest" taking courses in "aviation training." He wrote a memo which was slowly wending its way through channels at the time of the incident. Other agents had noticed the presence in the U.S. of persons who were on terrorist "watch lists." Zacarias Moussaoui had been arrested for visa violations but agents had decided they did not have sufficient probable cause even under FISA for an order to search his computer.

The 9/11 Commission[4] was critical of the lack of follow-up on these and other leads, although not nearly as critical as some politicians and public commentators have been. *See* 9/11 COMMISSION REPORT at 266–77. But how were agents to know that these were the critical pieces of information out of the many thousands of bits that were flowing through their offices at the time? How many other odd bits of information had agents noticed which turned out not to fit any pattern or to constitute patterns no more nefarious than their component parts? How many thousands of suspicions can government agents investigate without destroying the essence of a free society and thus doing some of what the terrorists seek?

The Supreme Court noticed this difficulty during the lull between the turbulence of the 1960s and the beginning of the terrorism expansion in the 1970s. *United States v. U.S. Dist. Court*, 407 U.S. 297 (1972):

> National security cases . . . often reflect a convergence of First and Fourth Amendment values not present in cases of "ordinary" crime. Though the investigative duty of the executive may be stronger in such cases, so also is there greater jeopardy to constitutionally protected speech. "Historically the struggle for freedom of speech and press in England was bound up with the issue of the scope of the search and seizure power," *Marcus v. Search Warrant*, 367 U.S. 717, 724 (1961). History abundantly documents the tendency of Government — however benevolent and benign its motives — to view with suspicion those who most fervently dispute its policies. Fourth Amendment protections become the more necessary when the targets of official surveillance may be those suspected of unorthodoxy in their political beliefs. The danger to political dissent is acute where the Government attempts to act under so vague a concept as the power to protect "domestic security."

> [S]ecurity surveillance may involve different policy and practical considerations from the surveillance of "ordinary crime." The gathering of security intelligence is often long range and involves the interrelation of various sources and types of information. The exact targets of such surveillance may be more difficult to identify than in surveillance operations against many types of crime specified in Title III. Often, too, the emphasis of domestic intelligence gathering is on the prevention of unlawful activity or the enhancement of the Government's preparedness for some possible future crisis or emergency. Thus, the focus of domestic surveillance may be less precise than that directed against more conventional types of crime.

In addition to the mere difficulty of intervention, there are very real political dynamics at work. The unfulfilled conspiracy will not result in very much of a prison sentence, so the conspirators can be back out and at work in relatively short order. Moreover, the headlines for arrests in an inchoate conspiracy will be smaller and shorter in duration than the headlines announcing arrests in a completed act of violence. Finally, prevention, as we have said before, operates on information. Acquiring information about politically-motivated conspiracies may produce massive amounts of information about "protected" political expression, something that the public and many law enforcement agencies are reluctant to countenance.

These are some of the factors that make prevention a more delicate exercise than

---

[4] FINAL REPORT OF THE NATIONAL COMMISSION ON TERRORIST ATTACKS UPON THE UNITED STATES [hereafter 9/11 COMMISSION REPORT or 9/11 REPORT].

enforcement investigation. After 9/11, the U.S. shifted strategy to emphasize prevention over enforcement. More than ever before, the public became aware of the operation of the intelligence services.

[D]   The Intelligence Community

Because intelligence services have been somewhat difficult for the public to understand, because they came in for heavy criticism following 9/11, and because a "major reorganization" has been undertaken, a quick discussion of the structure of the Intelligence Community (IC) of the United States is in order. By both Executive Order and statute, the Intelligence Community is defined as consisting of the eight intelligence agencies within the Department of Defense (DIA, NSA, NRO, NIMA, and the IA's of the four uniformed services), the CIA, and portions of five executive departments (State, Treasury, Homeland Security, Energy, and FBI).

The Director of National Intelligence, created in 2004, is formally responsible for coordination of all intelligence activities of the U.S. Until recently, under the National Security Act, 50 U.S.C. § 401 *et seq.*, the CIA was formally the lead agency for coordination of all intelligence. The reality, of course, is that coordination of such secretive organizations is not easy to achieve from what would be viewed as a co-equal agency. In practice, each President has had preferences with regard to which agency he or she will consider the most reliable and thus the strongest within that particular administration. *See* 9/11 COMMISSION REPORT at 86. For that reason, Presidents have tended to rely on the National Security Council and National Security Advisor to bring vertical pressure or control to the IC. The informal power structures thus were within the political choices of the President. Amendments to the IC structure in 2004, including creation of a Director of National Intelligence, may or may not affect the actual operation of the IC.

The Intelligence Community has its own website. The definition page describes the general mission and links to documents such as the National Security Act and Executive Order 12,333.

> The IC is a federation of executive branch agencies and organizations that work separately and together to conduct intelligence activities necessary for the conduct of foreign relations and the protection of the national security of the United States. These activities include:
>
> - Collection of information needed by the President, the National Security Council, the Secretaries of State and Defense, and other Executive Branch officials for the performance of their duties and responsibilities;
> - Production and dissemination of intelligence;
> - Collection of information concerning, and the conduct of activities to protect against, intelligence activities directed against the U.S., international terrorist and international narcotics activities, and other hostile activities directed against the U.S. by foreign powers, organizations, persons, and their agents;
> - Special activities;
> - Administrative and support activities within the U.S. and abroad necessary for the performance of authorized activities; and
> - Such other intelligence activities as the President may direct from time to time

http://www.intelligence.gov/1-definition.shtml.

There are many interesting assessments available on the internet of the U.S. Intelligence effort. In 1996, there was a presidential review of intelligence operations that resulted in enhancing the role of the Defense Department. The Federation of American Scientists did an analysis of the IC budget following the 1996 review. Although the details of the number of personnel and actual dollar amounts are secret, FAS extrapolated from public information to reach some estimates for each agency. http://www.fas.org/irp/commission/budget.htm.

Some important features can be observed from a quick glance at that analysis. The National Security Agency, with almost 40,000 employees, spent about $4 billion in 1996. That is less than $100,000 per employee for the agency that has all the high-tech electronic communications intercepts and code-breaking gadgetry. By contrast, the National Reconnaissance Office, with very few employees, spent more than $6 billion working through a variety of independent contractors to run a variety spy satellites and mapping programs. Neither of these agencies is involved in placing agents on the ground or running infiltration operations.

About 80% of the total intelligence budget of the U.S. is in the Defense Department, which first emphasized technological intelligence to track and identify military targets and then shifted that technology to monitoring communications traffic. That factor, plus budget cuts at the end of the Cold War, plus the fact that most CIA personnel were trained in the ways of Soviet intelligence rather than the distinctly different culture of terrorist organizations, all combined by the late 1990s to leave the U.S. less than adequately prepared to infiltrate or monitor terrorist organizations. 9/11 REPORT at 86–91.

On 9/11, Jane's (the primary private analyst of military capability) published a statement regarding the "chronic underfunding of HUMINT" in the U.S. intelligence community:

> One possible contributing factor to this failure of the intelligence and security system could be the lack of resources the U.S. has devoted to human intelligence (HUMINT) capabilities throughout the past decade. While national technical means continued to receive high levels of funding for . . . eavesdropping technologies, human-based intelligence capabilities have withered. Areas such as analysis, linguist skills, cultivation of agent networks, and "trade-craft" . . . have suffered a lack of resources of late. This shortfall has been exacerbated by the growing demand that increased emphasis on technical intelligence has placed on the people who must process the vast amounts of resulting data and prioritise it.

http://www.janes.com/security/international_security/news/jdw/jdw010911_1_n.shtml.

The 9/11 Commission also commented, somewhat less bluntly, on the impact of the Cold War on U.S. intelligence resources:

> During the Cold War, intelligence agencies did not depend on seamless integration to track and count the thousands of military targets — such as tanks and missiles — fielded by the Soviet Union and other adversary states. Each agency concentrated on its special mission, acquiring its own information and sharing it via formal, finished reports. The Department of Defense had given birth to and dominated the main agencies for technical collection of intelligence.

9/11 REPORT at 407. The Commission commented that the end of the Cold War also meant budget cuts, that the CIA had become highly risk averse and had no personnel trained for infiltrating terrorist organizations, and that the "intelligence community's confederated structure left open the question of who really was in charge of the entire U.S. intelligence effort." *Id.* at 93.

The Commission made specific recommendations addressing the structure of the Intelligence Community:

> The United States has the resources and the people. The government should combine them more effectively, achieving unity of effort. We offer five major recommendations to do that:

- unifying strategic intelligence and operational planning against Islamist terrorists across the foreign-domestic divide with a National Counter-terrorism Center;

- unifying the intelligence community with a new National Intelligence Director;

- unifying the many participants in the counterterrorism effort and their knowledge in a network-based information-sharing system that transcends traditional governmental boundaries;

- unifying and strengthening congressional oversight to improve quality and accountability; and

- strengthening the FBI and homeland defenders.

Id. at 399–400.

When bills were introduced in Congress to implement these recommendations, political controversy arose over whether the new NID would have full budgetary and personnel control over the existing units within the Department of Defense. The Commission's recommendation for a Director of National Intelligence to sit above the Director of Central Intelligence was designed to relieve the DCI of some of the office's conflicting job descriptions by assuming overall coordination of the Intelligence Community. On December 17, 2004, Congress passed a bill incorporating most elements of the Commission recommendations. The NID is to have some degree of involvement with the funding and deployment of intelligence resources in the Department of Defense, and also to have consultation authority with domestic agencies such as the FBI. National Security Intelligence Reform Act of 2004, Pub. L. 108-458.

Addressing the issues of human intelligence directly, Congress had this to say in section 101(b) of the Act:

It is the sense of Congress that

(1) the human intelligence officers of the intelligence community have performed admirably and honorably in the face of great personal dangers;

(2) during an extended period of unprecedented investment and improve-ments in technical collection means, the human intelligence capabilities of the United States have not received the necessary and commensurate priorities;

(3) human intelligence is becoming an increasingly important capability to provide information on the asymmetric threats to the national security of the United States;

(4) the continued development and improvement of a robust and empowered and flexible human intelligence work force is critical to identifying, understand-ing, and countering the plans and intentions of the adversaries of the United States; and

(5) an increased emphasis on, and resources applied to, enhancing the depth and breadth of human intelligence capabilities of the United States intelligence community must be among the top priorities of the Director of National Intelligence.

On a more substantive plane, the Commission's recommendation to "unify across the foreign-domestic divide" would run counter to the mandate of EO 12333 issued by President Ronald Reagan on Dec. 4, 1981. The key elements of the "foreign-domestic divide" were summarized in this statement of the CIA:

Collection within the United States of foreign intelligence not otherwise obtainable shall be undertaken by the FBI or, when significant foreign intelligence is sought, by other authorized agencies of the Intelligence Commu-nity, provided that no foreign intelligence collection by such agencies may be undertaken for the purpose of acquiring information concerning the domestic activities of United States persons.

http://www.cia.gov/cia/information/eo12333.html#2.3.

EO 12,333 was based on some of the work of the so-called "Church Commission," which held hearings and issued reports from 1973–1976 primarily on the activities of the CIA. Although a major focus of the recommendation for a foreign-domestic divide was the protection of civil liberties of U.S. persons, another aspect was the belief that the accumulation of too much power in one place could make that agency inefficient by reducing the need for it to justify its actions to other agencies.

These are critical issues for the structure and control of intelligence gathering, which will in turn dictate legal arguments over the validity of investigatory techniques. Therefore, lawyers concerned with national security and civil liberties issues will need to monitor these political arguments closely.

As lawyers involved in various ways in the struggle against terrorism, we must be aware of the difficulties of gathering reliable intelligence about terrorist groups and their actions. These difficulties raise many issues, including:

1. If military action in another country should be contemplated, as in the instances of Afghanistan and Iraq, what confidence level will you demand for intelligence data on which invasions might be based?

2. If it were decided that the use of deadly force against a known terrorist were appropriate, what confidence level would you demand before sending out a team to kill such a person? (Mossad experienced serious fallout from killing a person that they mistakenly believed to be involved in the Munich Olympic incident.)

3. Preventive security measures, such as screening at airports or special events, necessarily rise and fall with the level of threat reported at any time by the intelligence community. What level of intrusion into the privacy of citizens and visitors are you willing to endure to regulate security measures? (And bear in mind that tightening our borders can result in "reprisal" difficulties at entry points into other countries.)

4. What level of intelligence data should we be willing to share with other countries? and under what restrictions?

[E]   The International Framework

The previous section looked at the communities which provide the basic mechanisms for response to terrorism within the United States. The U.S. as a whole, however, is part of a larger community, the international body of law that is developing with respect to terrorism.

"One person's terrorist is another's freedom fighter." For many years, this deceptively ominous statement stalled the world's debates over outlawing terrorism. As numerous authors have pointed out, this is an almost silly argument because universal law criminalizes attacks on civilian populations without regard to the political motivations of the actor. The difficulty is not whether there could be justification for an attack on civilians because legally there cannot be, yet the nations of the world have been at odds for decades over the definition of terrorism and whether it constitutes a crime under international law. The difficulty is not in justifying violence against civilians but more in determining by what process to respond to an attack against civilians, a question that usually depends on the degree of affiliation by the actor with a nation-state or "sub-national" organization.

International law and organizations are creating cooperative efforts to deal with the transborder aspects of large criminal organizations without promoting intrusion into the internal affairs of any one nation. The United Nations Secretary-General established a Counter-Terrorism Implementation Task Force in July 2005 to coordinate efforts of a number of UN agencies. The Security Council has been active on this front since the fall of the Soviet Union:

> In the 1990s, its actions took the form of sanctions against States considered to have links to certain acts of terrorism: Libya (1992); Sudan (1996) and the Taliban (1999 — expanded to include Al-Qaida in 2000 by resolution 1333). In resolution 1269 of 1999, the Security Council called on countries to work together to prevent and suppress all terrorist acts; a precursor to the intensification of its counter-terrorism work since 2001 9/11.

> Prior to 11 September 2001, the Security Council had established a strong counter-terrorism tool: the 1267 Committee — made up of all Council members — established in 1999 by resolution 1267 and tasked with monitoring the sanctions against the Taliban (and subsequently Al-Qaida as of 2000).

> In 2001, following the September 11 terrorist attacks against the US, the Security Council established a Counter Terrorism Committee also comprising all members of the Security Council, under resolution 1373. This resolution obliges Member States to take a number of measures to prevent terrorist activities and to criminalize various forms of terrorist actions, as well as to take measures that assist and promote cooperation among countries including adherence to international counter-terrorism instruments. Member States are required to report regularly to the Counter Terrorism Committee on the measures they have taken to implement resolution 1373.

http://www.un.org/terrorism/securitycouncil.shtml

The UN lists 13 International Conventions dealing with terrorism. Most of the conventions call on member states to criminalize terrorist acts (usually defined as violence which cuts across national borders without military authority) and require extradition or trial of alleged perpetrators. *See* http://untreaty.un.org/English/Terrorism.asp. On the UN's role generally, see JANE BOULDEN & THOMAS G. WEISS, TERRORISM AND THE UN: BEFORE AND AFTER SEPTEMBER 11 (2004).

The UN Security Council Counter-Terrorism Committee was established following adoption of Sec. Council Resolution 1373, which condemned the acts of 9/11 and expressed that the Security Council "decides . . . that all states shall . . . take the necessary steps to prevent the commission of terrorist acts" and "shall ensure that . . . terrorist acts are established as serious criminal offences in domestic laws." Res. 1373 is the first directive of a UN agency requiring that member states take affirmative steps with regard to terrorism. The Security Council claims the power to direct action by declaring that "such acts constitute a threat to international peace and security." One troubling problem is that the Resolution does not define "terrorism" and only refers obliquely to the only existing UN definition, which is found in the Convention of Financing of Terrorism.

The United Nations Sixth (Legal) Committee has been debating a Draft Comprehensive Convention on International Terrorism since 1996. The principal components of the Convention would require that all signatories criminalize terrorist acts and agree to prosecute or extradite alleged perpetrators found within their borders. This is the same mechanism found in the prior Conventions dealing with air piracy, bombings, and financing of terrorism.

The Lawyer's Committee on Nuclear Policy reported the 2001 deliberations of the Sixth Committee in these terms:

> The Coordinator, Richard Rowe (Australia), reported that the outcome of the treaty would depend heavily on the decision for Article 18 on the exemption of armed forces from the scope of the treaty. Rowe proposed a draft that he prepared at the end of the October 2001 session, which exempted the activities of "armed forces . . . inasmuch as they are governed by other rules of

international law." Meanwhile, the Organization of the Islamic Conference proposed changes, which would exempt the activities of "parties during an armed conflict, including in situations of foreign occupation . . . in conformity with international law." The OIC wants to ensure that the "armed struggle against foreign occupation . . . shall not be considered a terrorist crime," and [to] prevent certain oppressed groups, like the Palestinians, from being more criminalized under the treaty than a state's armed forces.

http://www.lcnp.org/global/terrorismconvention.htm.

On March 6, 2008, the Ad Hoc Committee concluded its 12th session without reaching agreement. According to one observer,

> The most problematic issues may be summarized as:
>
> 1. Whether the definition of terrorism should include State-sponsored terrorism and acts of State terrorism. Some delegations (including Cuba, Iraq, Iran, Lebanon, Libya, Pakistan, Syria, and Sudan) previously have expressed the view that State, and State-sponsored, terrorism should be included in the definition. Other delegations have countered that State and State-sponsored terrorism already are subject to international conventions (including the Prohibition of the Use of Force under Article 2(4) of the UN Charter);
>
> 2. Whether the activities of armed forces should fall under the scope of the Convention. Some delegations (including the EU states, Canada, China, and Japan) wish to exclude military activities from the Convention, arguing that military activity is already subject to international conventions and treaties;
>
> 3. . . . ;
>
> 4. The legitimacy of armed struggle against foreign occupation, aggression, or colonialism. Some delegations consider such armed struggle to be aimed self-determination and believe that the Convention should in no way hinder any people's legitimate right to self-determination, whilst others argue that the Convention should identify any act that falls beyond the defined parameters of armed conflict as terrorism.

World Federalist Movement — Institute for Global Policy, *ReformtheUN.Org*, *available at* http://www.reformtheun.org/index.php/eupdate/3879.

The Coordinator of the Ad Hoc Committee observed that:

> Some . . . delegations stressed the need for the comprehensive convention to provide for a clear legal definition of terrorism. It was added that such a definition should establish a clear distinction between acts of terrorism covered by the convention and the legitimate struggle of peoples in the exercise of their right to self-determination or against foreign occupation. Furthermore, some speakers considered that the comprehensive convention should include provisions relating to military activities not covered by international humanitarian law, and apply to individuals in a position to control or direct such military activities. The point was also made that the conclusion of the convention should not be at the risk of undermining the principle that terrorism cannot be justified for *whatever* purposes.

The dispute over whether insurgency against an occupation force can be considered terrorism, and the related question of how to label misbehavior by uniformed forces, can be most easily seen in the two principal competing versions of article 18 as they stood in 2002:

Texts Relating to article 18 of the Draft Comprehensive Convention

Text circulated by the Coordinator for discussion:

1. Nothing in this Convention shall affect other rights, obligations and responsibilities of States, peoples and individuals under international law, in particular the purposes and principles of the Charter of the United Nations, and international humanitarian law.

2. The activities of armed forces during an armed conflict, as those terms are understood under international humanitarian law, which are governed by that law, are not governed by this Convention.

3. The activities undertaken by the military forces of a State in the exercise of their official duties, inasmuch as they are governed by other rules of international law, are not governed by this Convention.

4. Nothing in this article condones or makes lawful otherwise unlawful acts, nor precludes prosecution under other laws.

Text proposed by the Member States of the Organization of the Islamic Conference:

1. Nothing in this Convention shall affect other rights, obligations and responsibilities of States, peoples and individuals under international law, in particular the purposes and principles of the Charter of the United Nations, and international humanitarian law.

2. The activities of the parties during an armed conflict, including in situations of foreign occupation, as those terms are understood under international humanitarian law, which are governed by that law, are not governed by this Convention.

3. The activities undertaken by the military forces of a State in the exercise of their official duties, inasmuch as they are in conformity with international law, are not governed by this Convention.

4. Nothing in this article condones or makes lawful otherwise unlawful acts, nor precludes prosecution under other laws.

International law, found from custom as well as from the various conventions regarding use of force, has given rise to a heading of "universal jurisdiction" for any nation to prosecute offenses against the law of nations. This power was first used in relation to piracy and slave trade, but it could be a source of law with regard to terrorism as well.

In addition to these steps, the UN has been an integral part of prosecuting war crimes and genocide. It formed ad hoc tribunals for the trial of crimes committed in Rwanda and Yugoslavia. At the same time, it promoted the drafting and eventual adoption of the International Criminal Court, a multinational body asserting jurisdiction over offenses against the law of nations in the categories of war crimes, crimes against humanity, and genocide. The ICC would not be expected to assert jurisdiction over an act of terrorism unless it formed part of a "systematic and continuous" pattern by a state actor.

Thus, international law is becoming an increasing presence in regard to the behavior of persons formally affiliated with a nation-state (a state actor) and is promoting cooperation and assistance among the nations for dealing with non-state-actors such as terrorists and drug lords. All of these issues and developments will be given more extensive treatment in later chapters.

§ 1.03 TERRORIST CELLS AND CONSPIRACY LAW

Conspiracy classically is defined as "a combination of two or more persons to achieve an unlawful object or to achieve a lawful object by unlawful means." In the context of terrorism, this definition raises intriguing possibilities right from the start.

The most successful terrorist organizations carefully hide the "cells" from each other. In the classic business enterprise, members of the various departments feed information to their managers who then share it with the CEO and other managers to make the entire enterprise flow as smoothly as possible. The employees in a department will know as much or as little about the activities of employees in other departments as their managers have time or inclination to share, plus whatever information is shared in informal settings such as meetings, social occasions, or rumor mill. If an investigator, say a journalist doing a story on the company, asks questions about how an employee's work fits into the overall business plan, the employee may draw upon both fact and rumor to provide as complete a picture as possible.

In a clandestine operation, it becomes important that the members of each "department," usually known as "cells," know as little as possible about each other. This is so that an investigator who manages to capture or "turn" one cell member will not thereby be able to learn anything about the other cells.

Everyone who has ever read a spy novel will recognize that the lieutenants will even insulate themselves from the cell members by a series of "cutouts," anonymous or pseudonymous individuals who themselves know nothing of either the cells or the lieutenants. In a highly sophisticated operation such as al Qaeda or the Medellin Cartel of the 1980s, only the ruling elite or inner circle will know each other. This is why it has seemed so important to the U.S. to locate the al Qaeda leadership. But the classic hierarchical model is not fully adequate to describe this type of operation, and as we will discuss below, it is not necessarily true that "cutting off the head" will cause the "body to die."

In 1929, the British courts promulgated the metaphor of "wheels" and "chains" to describe two distinct types of conspiracy: "There may be one person . . . round whom the rest revolve. The metaphor is the metaphor of the centre of a circle and the circumference. There may be a conspiracy of another kind, where the metaphor would be rather that of a chain; A communicates with B, B with C, C with D, and so on to the end of the line of conspirators." *Rex v. Meyrick and Ribuffi*, 21 Crim. App. R. 94 (1929); *see* Jerome Campane, *Chains, Wheels, and the Single Conspiracy, Pt. I*, FBI LAW ENFORCEMENT BULL., Aug. 1981 at 24 and Pt. II, Sept. 1981 at 24; Note, *Federal Treatment of Multiple Conspiracies*, 57 COLUM. L. REV. 387 (1975).

Assume in a chain that Cell 4 has been successful in carrying out a terrorist act. Cell 1 provided money with which Cell 2 purchased materials, which Cell 3 assembled and delivered to a designated place for Cell 4 to use in the act. All of this was orchestrated by the elite group outside the chain. Nobody else had any idea of the identity of the members of Cell 4 or their precise plans. Can the members of the other cells be prosecuted for conspiracy?

In the wheel model, the question is whether each of the spokes of the wheel may be involved in a single conspiracy with each other even though they do not know each other's identity. In the chain, persons far removed from each other because of the presence of intermediaries may similarly be engaged in a single conspiracy. The element of secrecy in clandestine schemes was recognized by the U.S. Supreme Court when it declared that "the law rightly gives room for allowing the conviction of those discovered upon showing sufficiently the essential nature of the plan and their connections with it, without requiring evidence of knowledge of all its details or the participation of others." *Blumenthal v. United States*, 332 U.S. 539, 557 (1947).

There are limits, both constitutional and otherwise, on the application of these models. In *Kotteakos v. United States*, 328 U.S. 750 (1946), the hub of the conspiracy dealt with each of the spokes separately. The Supreme Court acknowledged that the person at the hub may have thought of the entire enterprise as a single scheme, but without something more to tie the individual transactions together (a rim around the spokes), "there was no drawing of all together in a single, overall comprehensive scheme." A wheel may have spokes each of which itself is a chain (the "chain-wheel"). In *United States v. Perez*, 489 F.2d 51 (5th Cir. 1973), the defendants were involved in multiple instances of fake traffic accidents in which doctors and lawyers concocted fraudulent reports for submission to insurance companies. Each chain included several persons (one driver and a pedestrian or two drivers and a passenger, doctor, lawyer, and "recruiter" who set up each accident), each chain of which reported back to the central organizer. The court considered that none of the participants could rationally have believed that the scheme would work if there were not others out doing the same thing because otherwise the risks would not be worth the payoff to professionals such as the doctors and lawyers. This inference of knowledge was sufficient to form a rim around the spokes to complete the wheel.

In the electronic world, we have developed another metaphor for exchange of information and services. We are growing accustomed to the language of "networks," and this is convenient for describing a more fluid type of organizational structure. In a network, cells are free to communicate with others and to move money or weapons or training services among various cells. The loose configuration means that a cell can change location or the nature of its operations without needing clearance from a central leadership. It also means that if one cell were eliminated, then the network could either grow a replacement cell or call on another cell to perform the functions of that one.

The growth of "al Qaeda in Iraq" and "al Qaeda of Mesopotamia" show that one organization can spawn a movement that has little, if any, direct contact with the parent organization. As some observers put it, the successful entrepreneur will franchise the name out to others. In the case of social movements, the franchisee may not pay a fee in material goods but simply in tribute to the principles of the franchisor. There can be conflicts between branches of a movement and the original entrepreneur such that the franchise would not be freely granted, but it is difficult to prevent a new entrant from picking up the name or modifying the principles.

These organizational structures, or formation of movements, should be borne in mind when we come to the question of punishing someone for providing material support to a terrorist organization. It is not always obvious what the organization is or how it receives support.

§ 1.04 SELECTED READINGS

General Readings on Terrorism:

- CALEB CARR, THE LESSONS OF TERROR (2002)
- CHRISTOPHER C. HARMON, TERRORISM TODAY (2000)
- BRUCE HOFFMAN, INSIDE TERRORISM (1998)
- PHILLIP B. HEYMANN, TERRORISM AND AMERICA (1998)
- LIBRARY OF CONGRESS, WHO BECOMES A TERRORIST AND WHY (1999)
- LOUISE RICHARDSON, WHAT TERRORISTS WANT (2006)
- JESSICA STERN, THE ULTIMATE TERRORISTS (1999)
- MARC SAGEMAN, UNDERSTANDING TERROR NETWORKS (2004)
- UNDERSTANDING TERRORISM (Fathali M. Moghaddam & Anthony J. Marsella eds., 2004)

Books Particular to al Qaeda:

- JOHN COOLEY, UNHOLY WARS (2002)
- ROHAN GUNARATNA, INSIDE AL QAEDA (2002)

Islamist Fundamentalism:

- MARY HABECK, KNOWING THE ENEMY (2006)
- JESSICA STERN, TERROR IN THE NAME OF GOD (2003)
- MICHAEL SCHEUER, THROUGH OUR ENEMIES EYES (2006)

Islamic Law and Democracy:

- NOAH FELDMAN, AFTER JIHAD (2003)
- M. CHERIF BASSIOUNI, THE ISLAMIC CRIMINAL JUSTICE SYSTEM (1982)
- M. Cherif Bassiouni & Gamal M. Badr, *The Shari'ah: Sources, Interpretation, and Rule Making*, 1 UCLA J. ISLAMIC & NEAR E.L. 135 (2002)
- Michael S. Doran, *The Saudi Paradox*, 83 FOREIGN AFFAIRS 35 (2004)
- Khaled Abou El Fadl, *Constitutionalism and the Islamic Sunni Legacy*, 1 UCLA J. ISLAMIC & NEAR E.L. 67 (2002)

Chapter 2
U.S. LAW AND GLOBALIZED TERRORISM

Very few Americans had anything more than hazy impressions about terrorist organizations prior to 9/11. Through the 1970s and 1980s we knew that a variety of Palestinian organizations, such as the PLO and Hamas, were active and had replaced the more ideological leftist organizations of the 1960s and early 1970s. Most of us still did not consider these organizations to be a significant threat on our soil even after the first World Trade Center bombing in 1993 and attacks on U.S. installations in Lebanon and Somalia. After U.S. embassies in Kenya and Tanzania were bombed in 1998, Americans gradually started becoming aware of a more significant and well-organized international regime of terrorist organizations.

It is surprising to many people to find that U.S. law enforcement agencies operate overseas — the FBI, CIA, and various components of the military cooperate (or compete in some instances) in tracking suspected criminal activities and plans around the world. That includes most dramatically the tracking and apprehension of persons suspected of complicity in terrorist activities. When a suspect is apprehended in another country, the U.S. agents have several choices of what to do with that person. The U.S. may formally seek extradition of that person to the U.S. for trial, may ask the host nation to hand that person over informally (rendition), or the U.S. agents might risk violation of the host nation's law by clandestinely spiriting the suspect out of the country.

The story of U.S. involvement with terrorism really begins with the post-Civil War statutes aimed at the Ku Klux Klan. There are perhaps some lessons for the international community to be gained from the experience of U.S. federalism, and we will look at some of those developments later. For now, we will focus on the prosecutions and statutes involving "international terrorism" beginning with prosecutions of airplane hijackers and bombers in the 1980s.

§ 2.01 U.S. STATUTES RELATED TO TERRORISM

The U.S. passed statutes dealing with Aircraft Piracy and Hostage-Taking in response to, or in conjunction with, treaty obligations entered into during the 1970s. The Omnibus Diplomatic Security and Antiterrorism Act of 1986 produced what is now 18 U.S.C. § 2332, which sets penalties for murder or manslaughter in the case of anyone who "kills a national of the United States, while such national is outside the United States."

The first "material support" statute, 18 U.S.C. § 2339A, was adopted in 1994. The Antiterrorism and Effective Death Penalty Act of 1996 (AEDPA) produced what is now 18 U.S.C. § 2332b, "acts of terrorism transcending national boundaries" and the prohibition on material support to designated organizations in 18 U.S.C. § 2339B.

To become familiar with the statutory scheme, you should read and become familiar with the following principal statutes.

General Federal Criminal Law

There are ample federal statutes criminalizing actions such as murder, destruction of property, and other violent actions that touch federal interests. Because of U.S. constitutional limitations on the power of the federal government, all of these have some jurisdictional base that ties either to interstate commerce or to governmental interests. The basic civil rights criminal provisions are included for comparison.

18 U.S.C. §§ 1111, 1114, 1119 (Murder)

18 U.S.C. § 844 (Unlawful use of explosive materials)

18 U.S.C. § 956 (Conspiracy to commit violence in a foreign country)

18 U.S.C. §§ 242, 245 (Civil rights)

U.S. Statutes Based on Extraterritoriality and International Conventions

Many U.S. statutes carry their own statement of extraterritorial jurisdiction, while others refer to the general statement in section 7 of the Criminal Code. A number of other statutes carry out the obligation under international conventions to criminalize actions such as aircraft piracy regardless of where the event occurred.

18 U.S.C. § 7 (Extraterritorial jurisdiction in general)

18 U.S.C. § 32 (Destruction of aircraft — including threats)

18 U.S.C. § 2340 (Torture)

U.S. Statutes Referring to "Terrorism"

In recent years, attempts have been made to define crimes that are based on more general concepts of terrorism. The following are the principal U.S. statutes in this regard.

18 U.S.C. § 2331 (Terrorism Definitions)

18 U.S.C. § 2332 (Terrorist Homicide)

18 U.S.C. § 2332b (Terrorism Transcending National Boundaries)

18 U.S.C. § 2339A (Providing Material Support to Terrorists)

18 U.S.C. § 2339B (Providing Material Support to Terrorist Organizations)

18 U.S.C. § 2339D (Receiving Training from Terrorist Organization)

Section 2332 (dealing with homicide of a U.S. national) states that

> No prosecution for any offense described in this section shall be undertaken by the United States except on written certification of the Attorney General or the highest ranking subordinate of the Attorney General with responsibility for criminal prosecutions that, in the judgment of the certifying official, such offense was intended to coerce, intimidate, or retaliate against a government or a civilian population.

If the concern was over diplomatic officials, why apply it to any U.S. national? For that matter, why the need for a special statute applying to homicide of a U.S. national in the first place? On this issue, consider whether the United States could have a general statute punishing murder of anyone anywhere. Would international law prevent the U.S. from asserting adjudicative jurisdiction over the murder of a foreign national by a foreign national in a foreign country? To go further, what is the point of the AG certification of a political motivation for the crime? 18 U.S.C. § 1113 applies the same penalties to anyone who commits murder or manslaughter on an officer or employee of the U.S. government while in the course of his or her duties.

§ 2.02 EXTRATERRITORIAL JURISDICTION AND APPREHENSION OF DEFENDANTS

[A] Abduction for Trial in the United States

United States v. Yunis is the earliest example in which the United States pursued and prosecuted an incident of international political terrorism taking place outside our borders. As you read *Yunis*, be alert to the multiple interactions between U.S. domestic law and customary international law, to the jurisdictional bases for prosecution in the United States, and to implications for investigation and enforcement of U.S. penal laws in incidents occurring abroad.

UNITED STATES v. YUNIS
288 U.S. App. D.C. 129; 924 F.2d 1086 (D.C. Cir. 1991)

MIKVA, CHIEF JUDGE.

Appellant Fawaz Yunis challenges his convictions on conspiracy, aircraft piracy, and hostage-taking charges stemming from the hijacking of a Jordanian passenger aircraft in Beirut, Lebanon. He appeals from orders of the district court denying his pretrial motions relating to jurisdiction, illegal arrest, alleged violations of the Posse Comitatus Act, and the government's withholding of classified documents during discovery. Yunis also challenges the district court's jury instructions as erroneous and prejudicial.

Although this appeal raises novel issues of domestic and international law, we reject Yunis' objections and affirm the convictions.

I. BACKGROUND

On June 11, 1985, appellant and four other men boarded Royal Jordanian Airlines Flight 402 ("Flight 402") shortly before its scheduled departure from Beirut, Lebanon. They wore civilian clothes and carried military assault rifles, ammunition bandoleers, and hand grenades. Appellant took control of the cockpit and forced the pilot to take off immediately. The remaining hijackers tied up Jordanian air marshals assigned to the flight and held the civilian passengers, including two American citizens, captive in their seats. The hijackers explained to the crew and passengers that they wanted the plane to fly to Tunis, where a conference of the Arab League was under way. The hijackers further explained that they wanted a meeting with delegates to the conference and that their ultimate goal was removal of all Palestinians from Lebanon.

After a refueling stop in Cyprus, the airplane headed for Tunis but turned away when authorities blocked the airport runway. Following a refueling stop at Palermo, Sicily, another attempt to land in Tunis, and a second stop in Cyprus, the plane returned to Beirut, where more hijackers came aboard. These reinforcements included an official of Lebanon's Amal Militia, the group at whose direction Yunis claims he acted. The plane then took off for Syria, but was turned away and went back to Beirut. There, the hijackers released the passengers, held a press conference reiterating their demand that Palestinians leave Lebanon, blew up the plane, and fled from the airport.

An American investigation identified Yunis as the probable leader of the hijackers and prompted U.S. civilian and military agencies, led by the Federal Bureau of Investigation (FBI), to plan Yunis' arrest. After obtaining an arrest warrant, the FBI put "Operation Goldenrod" into effect in September 1987. Undercover FBI agents lured Yunis onto a yacht in the eastern Mediterranean Sea with promises of a drug deal, and arrested him once the vessel entered international waters. The agents transferred Yunis to a United States Navy munitions ship and interrogated him for several days as the vessel steamed toward a second rendezvous, this time with a Navy aircraft carrier. Yunis was flown to Andrews Air Force Base from the aircraft carrier, and taken from there to Washington, D.C. In Washington, Yunis was arraigned on an original indictment charging him with conspiracy, hostage taking, and aircraft damage. A grand jury subsequently returned a superseding indictment adding additional aircraft damage counts and a charge of air piracy.

Yunis filed several pretrial motions, among them a motion to suppress statements he made while aboard the munitions ship. In *United States v. Yunis (Yunis I)*, 859 F.2d 953 (D.C. Cir. 1988), this court reversed a district court order suppressing the statements, and authorized their introduction at trial. We revisited the case on a second interlocutory appeal relating to discovery of classified information, reversing the district court's disclosure order. *United States v. Yunis (Yunis II)*, 276 U.S. App. D.C. 1, 867 F.2d 617 (D.C. Cir. 1989).

Yunis admitted participation in the hijacking at trial but denied parts of the government's account and offered the affirmative defense of obedience to military orders, asserting that he acted on instructions given by his superiors in Lebanon's Amal Militia. The jury convicted Yunis of conspiracy, 18 U.S.C. § 371 (1988), hostage taking, 18 U.S.C. § 1203 (1988), and air piracy, 49 U.S.C. App. § 1472(n) (1988). However, it acquitted him of three other charged offenses that went to trial: violence against people on board an aircraft, 18 U.S.C. § 32(b)(1) (1988), aircraft damage, 18 U.S.C. § 32(b)(2) (1988), and placing a destructive device aboard an aircraft, 18 U.S.C. § 32(b)(3) (1988). The district court imposed concurrent sentences of five years for conspiracy, thirty years for hostage taking, and twenty years for air piracy. Yunis appeals his conviction and seeks dismissal of the indictment.

II. Analysis

Yunis argues that the district court lacked subject matter and personal jurisdiction to try him on the charges of which he was convicted, that the indictment should have been dismissed because the government seized him in violation of the Posse Comitatus Act and withheld classified materials useful to his defense, and that the convictions should be reversed because of errors in the jury instructions. We consider these claims in turn.

A. *Jurisdictional Claims*

Yunis appeals first of all from the district court's denial of his motion to dismiss for lack of subject matter and personal jurisdiction. *See United States v. Yunis*, 681 F. Supp. 896 (D.D.C. 1988). Appellant's principal claim is that, as a matter of domestic law, the federal hostage taking and air piracy statutes do not authorize assertion of federal jurisdiction over him. Yunis also suggests that a contrary construction of these statutes would conflict with established principles of international law, and so should be avoided by this court. Finally, appellant claims that the district court lacked personal jurisdiction because he was seized in violation of American law.

1. Hostage Taking Act

The Hostage Taking Act provides, in relevant part:

(a) Whoever, whether inside or outside the United States, seizes or detains and threatens to kill, to injure, or to continue to detain another person in order to compel a third person or a governmental organization to do or to abstain from any act . . . shall be punished by imprisonment by any term of years or for life.

(b)(1) It is not an offense under this section if the conduct required for the offense occurred outside the United States unless

(A) the offender or the person seized or detained is a national of the United States;

(B) the offender is found in the United States; or

(C) the governmental organization sought to be compelled is the Government of the United States.

18 U.S.C. § 1203. Yunis claims that this statute cannot apply to an individual who is brought to the United States by force, since those convicted under it must be "found in the United States." But this ignores the law's plain language. Subsections (A), (B), and (C) of section 1203(b)(1) offer *independent* bases for jurisdiction where "the offense occurred outside the United States." Since two of the passengers on Flight 402 were U.S. citizens, section 1203(b)(1)(A), authorizing assertion of U.S. jurisdiction where "the offender or the person seized or detained is a national of the United States," is satisfied. The statute's jurisdictional requirement has been met regardless of whether or not Yunis was "found" within the United States under section 1203(b)(1)(B).

Appellant's argument that we should read the Hostage Taking Act differently to avoid tension with international law falls flat. Yunis points to no treaty obligations of the United States that give us pause. Indeed, Congress intended through the Hostage Taking Act to execute the International Convention Against the Taking of Hostages, which authorizes any signatory state to exercise jurisdiction over persons who take its nationals hostage "if that State considers it appropriate." International Convention Against the Taking of Hostages, *opened for signature* Dec. 18, 1979, art. 5, para. 1, 34 UN GAOR Supp. (No. 39), 18 I.L.M. 1456, 1458. *See* H.R. Conf. Rep. No. 1159, 98th Cong., 2d Sess. 418 (1984), *reprinted in* 1984 U.S. Code Cong. & Admin. News 3710, 3714.

Nor is jurisdiction precluded by norms of customary international law. The district court concluded that two jurisdictional theories of international law, the "universal principle" and the "passive personal principle," supported assertion of U.S. jurisdiction to prosecute Yunis on hijacking and hostage-taking charges. Under the universal principle, states may prescribe and prosecute "certain offenses recognized by the community of nations as of universal concern, such as piracy, slave trade, attacks on or hijacking of aircraft, genocide, war crimes, and perhaps certain acts of terrorism," even absent any special connection between the state and the offense. *See* RESTATEMENT (THIRD) OF THE FOREIGN RELATIONS LAW OF THE UNITED STATES §§ 404, 423 (1987) [hereinafter RESTATEMENT]. Under the passive personal principle, a state may punish non-nationals for crimes committed against its nationals outside of its territory, at least where the state has a particularly strong interest in the crime. *See id.* at § 402 comment g; *United States v. Benitez*, 741 F.2d 1312, 1316 (11th Cir. 1984) (passive personal principle invoked to approve prosecution of Colombian citizen convicted of shooting U.S. drug agents in Colombia).

Relying primarily on the Restatement, Yunis argues that hostage taking has not been recognized as a universal crime and that the passive personal principle authorizes assertion of jurisdiction over alleged hostage takers only where the victims were seized because they were nationals of the prosecuting state. Whatever merit appellant's claims may have as a matter of international law, they cannot prevail before this court. Yunis seeks to portray international law as a self-executing code that trumps domestic law whenever the two conflict. That effort misconceives the role of judges as appliers of international law and as participants in the federal system. Our duty is to enforce the Constitution, laws, and treaties of the United States, not to conform the law of the land to norms of customary international law. *See* U.S. Const. art. VI. As we said in *Committee of U.S. Citizens Living in Nicaragua v. Reagan*, 859 F.2d 929 (D.C. Cir. 1988): "Statutes inconsistent with principles of customary international law may well lead to international law violations. But within the domestic legal realm, that inconsistent statute simply modifies or supersedes customary international law to the extent of the inconsistency." *Id. at 938. See also Federal Trade Comm'n. v. Compagnie de Saint-Gobain-Pont-a-Mousson*, 205 U.S. App. D.C. 172, 636 F.2d 1300, 1323 (D.C. Cir. 1980) (U.S. courts "obligated to give effect to an unambiguous exercise by Congress of its jurisdiction to prescribe even if such an exercise would exceed the limitations imposed by international law").

To be sure, courts should hesitate to give penal statutes extraterritorial effect absent a clear congressional directive. Similarly, courts will not blind themselves to potential violations of international law where legislative intent is ambiguous. *See Murray v. The Schooner Charming Betsy*, 6 U.S. (2 Cranch) 64, 118, 2 L. Ed. 208 (1804) ("An act of congress ought never to be construed to violate the law of nations, if any other possible construction remains. . . . "). But the statute in question reflects an unmistakable congressional intent, consistent with treaty obligations of the United States, to authorize prosecution of those who take Americans hostage abroad no matter where the offense occurs or where the offender is found. Our inquiry can go no further.

2. Antihijacking Act

The Antihijacking Act provides for criminal punishment of persons who hijack aircraft operating wholly outside the "special aircraft jurisdiction" of the United States, provided that the hijacker is later "found in the United States." 49 U.S.C. App. § 1472(n). Flight 402, a Jordanian aircraft operating outside of the United States, was not within this nation's special aircraft jurisdiction. *See* 49 U.S.C. App. § 1301. Yunis urges this court to interpret the statutory requirement that persons prosecuted for air piracy must be "found" in the United States as precluding prosecution of alleged hijackers who are brought here to stand trial. But the issue before us is more fact-specific, since Yunis was indicted for air piracy while awaiting trial on hostage-taking and other charges; we must determine whether, once arrested and brought to this country on those other charges, Yunis was subject to prosecution under the Antihijacking Act as well.

The Antihijacking Act of 1974 was enacted to fulfill this nation's responsibilities under the Convention for the Suppression of Unlawful Seizure of Aircraft (the "Hague Convention"), which requires signatory nations to extradite or punish hijackers "present in" their territory. Convention for the Suppression of Unlawful Seizure of Aircraft, Dec. 16, 1970, art. 4, para. 2, Dec. 16, 1970. This suggests that Congress intended the statutory term "found in the United States" to parallel the Hague Convention's "present in [a contracting state's] territory," a phrase which does not indicate the voluntariness limitation urged by Yunis. Moreover, Congress interpreted the Hague Convention as requiring the United States to extradite or prosecute "offenders in its custody," evidencing no concern as to how alleged hijackers came within U.S. territory. From this legislative history we conclude that Yunis was properly indicted under section 1472(n) once in the United States and under arrest on other charges.

The district court correctly found that international law does not restrict this statutory jurisdiction to try Yunis on charges of air piracy. Aircraft hijacking may well be one of the few crimes so clearly condemned under the law of nations that states may assert universal jurisdiction to bring offenders to justice, even when the state has no territorial connection to the hijacking and its citizens are not involved. *See* . . . Randall, *Universal Jurisdiction under International Law*, 66 Tex. L. Rev. 785, 815–34 (1988). But in any event we are satisfied that the Antihijacking Act authorizes assertion of federal jurisdiction to try Yunis regardless of hijacking's status vel non as a universal crime. Thus, we affirm the district court on this issue.

3. Legality of Seizure

Yunis further argues that even if the district court had jurisdiction to try him, it should have declined to exercise that jurisdiction in light of the government's allegedly outrageous conduct in bringing him to the United States. This claim was rejected by the district court before trial.

Principally, Yunis relies on *United States v. Toscanino*, 500 F.2d 267 (2d Cir. 1974), in which the court held that due process requires courts to divest themselves of personal jurisdiction acquired through "the government's deliberate, unnecessary and unreasonable invasion of the accused's constitutional rights." *Id.* at 275. *Toscanino* establishes, at best, only a very limited exception to the general rule (known as the "*Ker-Frisbie* doctrine") that "the power of a court to try a person for crime is not impaired by the fact that he had been brought within the court's jurisdiction by reason of a 'forcible abduction.'" *Frisbie v. Collins*, 342 U.S. 519, 522, 72 S. Ct. 509 (1952) (citing, *inter alia*, *Ker v. Illinois*, 119 U.S. 436, 7 S. Ct. 225, 30 L. Ed. 421 (1886)). *Toscanino's* rule has, moreover, been limited to cases of "torture, brutality, and similar outrageous conduct," *United States ex rel. Lujan v. Gengler*, 510 F.2d 62, 65 (2d Cir.), and the Supreme Court has since reaffirmed the *Ker-Frisbie* doctrine.

Even assuming, arguendo, that a district court could correctly dismiss a case otherwise properly before it for the reasons given in *Toscanino*, we find no merit in

Yunis' claim. In *Yunis I*, we reviewed the facts of Operation Goldenrod in some detail, including the deception used to arrest Yunis, his injuries and hardships while in custody, and the delay between his arrest and arraignment in the United States. The court sought to determine whether or not these circumstances voided Yunis' waiver of Fifth and Sixth Amendment rights; we concluded that while the government's conduct was neither "picture perfect" nor "a model for law enforcement behavior," the "discomfort and surprise" to which appellant was subjected did not render his waiver invalid. *Yunis I*, 859 F.2d at 969. Similarly, we now find nothing in the record suggesting the sort of intentional, outrageous government conduct necessary to sustain appellant's jurisdictional argument. *Cf. Sami v. United States*, 199 U.S. App. D.C. 173, 617 F.2d 755, 774 (D.C. Cir. 1979) (finding "no shocking behavior characterized by abduction or brutality which would support an actionable constitutional claim").

B. *Posse Comitatus Act*

Next, Yunis appeals from the district court's denial of his motion to dismiss on the basis of the government's alleged violation of the Posse Comitatus Act, 18 U.S.C. § 1385 (1988), which establishes criminal penalties for willful use of "any part of the Army or the Air Force" in law enforcement, unless expressly authorized by law. Despite the Posse Comitatus Act's express limitation to the Army and Air Force, appellant seeks dismissal of the indictment on the grounds that the Navy played a direct role in Operation Goldenrod.

We cannot agree that Congress' words admit of any ambiguity. By its terms, 18 U.S.C. § 1385 places no restrictions on naval participation in law enforcement operations; an earlier version of the measure would have expressly extended the bill to the Navy, but the final legislation was attached to an Army appropriations bill and its language was accordingly limited to that service. Reference to the Air Force was added in 1956, consistent with reassignment of Army aviation responsibilities to that new branch of the military. Nothing in this history suggests that we should defy the express language of the Posse Comitatus Act by extending it to the Navy, and we decline to do so.

Furthermore, some courts have taken the view that the Posse Comitatus Act imposes no restriction on use of American armed forces abroad, noting that Congress intended to preclude military intervention in domestic civil affairs. *See Chandler v. United States*, 171 F.2d 921, 936 (1st Cir. 1948); *D'Aquino v. United States*, 192 F.2d 338, 351 (9th Cir. 1951). And even if these difficulties could be overcome, a remedial problem would remain, as dismissal of all charges against Yunis might well be an inappropriate remedy if violations of the Posse Comitatus Act were found.

Nor is Yunis helped by 10 U.S.C. § 375 (1988), which requires the Secretary of Defense to issue regulations prohibiting "direct participation" by military personnel in a civilian "search, seizure, arrest, or other similar activity" unless expressly authorized by law. Reliance on this provision faces the same remedial hurdle as direct reliance on the Posse Comitatus Act: Under the *Ker-Frisbie* doctrine, outright dismissal of the charges against Yunis would not be an appropriate remedy for legal violations relating to his arrest. Nor would a violation of the regulations at issue amount to a constitutional violation, making application of an exclusionary rule or similar prophylactic measures inappropriate.

In any event, we agree with the district court that no governmental illegality occurred. Regulations issued under 10 U.S.C. § 375 require Navy compliance with the restrictions of the Posse Comitatus Act, but interpret that Act as allowing "indirect assistance" to civilian authorities that does not "subject civilians to the exercise of military power that is regulatory, proscriptive, or compulsory in nature." The regulations are consistent with judicial interpretations of the Posse Comitatus Act; in fact, they incorporate one of three tests employed to identify violations.

The district court found that Navy personnel played only a "passive" role in housing, transporting, and caring for Yunis while he was in the custody of the FBI, and that "none of the Navy's activities constituted the exercise of regulatory, proscriptive, or compulsory military power." Nor did the Navy's participation in Operation Goldenrod violate either of the other judicial tests for violations of the Posse Comitatus Act: The Navy's role did not amount to "direct active involvement in the execution of the laws," and it did not "pervade the activities of civilian authorities." We see no error in this assessment of the record, and accordingly conclude that no violation of military regulations occurred.

C. *Discovery Claim*

Yunis appeals from the district court's denial of his motion to dismiss on the basis that pre-trial discovery provisions of the Classified Information Procedures Act (CIPA), 18 U.S.C. App. (1988), infringe upon procedural protections guaranteed him by the Fifth and Sixth Amendments. In light of our holding in *Yunis II* that CIPA "creates no new rights of or limits on discovery" of classified material, but only requires courts to consider secrecy concerns when applying general discovery rules, we find no merit in this claim. [CIPA is considered in § 5.02 *infra*.]

Yunis also objects to the district court's refusal to order the government to produce records of conversations between Flight 402 and the Beirut control tower. After *ex parte, in camera* review of classified materials relevant to Yunis' various discovery requests, the trial court ordered disclosure of numerous documents, including "all audio or video tapes and/or transcripts of conversations between defendant and all airport authorities covering the period of the alleged hijacking. . . . " Upon the government's motion for reconsideration, however, the court narrowed this disclosure order by excluding materials, including tapes and transcripts of conversations with airport authorities, that "do not help the defendant's cause." Yunis subsequently renewed his request for conversations between Yunis and the Beirut tower, claiming that these transcripts were "vital to understand what outside influence or 'orders' were being transmitted to the hijackers by person(s) not on the plane." Relying on its earlier rulings, the district court denied the request. Yunis now appeals from that denial.

To prevail on a discovery request for classified information, a defendant must make a threshold showing that the requested material is relevant to his case. If this "low hurdle" is successfully jumped, the court must determine whether or not the government has asserted a "colorable" claim to privilege. If the government has asserted such a claim, the defendant must show that the information would be helpful to his defense. We never have had occasion to adopt a rule to guide trial courts when all these showings are made, and we do not do so here; other circuits, however, have endorsed a balancing approach. *See United States v. Sarkissian*, 841 F.2d 959, 965 (9th Cir. 1988); *United States v. Smith*, 780 F.2d 1102, 1110 (4th Cir. 1985).

Having ourselves reviewed *in camera* the government's classified submissions to the district court, we find very little in them that is both responsive to the discovery request at issue and relevant in any way to Yunis' trial. We certainly agree with the court below that they reveal no information within the scope of Yunis' discovery request that would have helped him at trial. Moreover, *Yunis II* establishes that the government has at least a colorable interest in avoiding release of information that might reveal "the time, place, and nature of the government's ability to intercept the conversations at all." Under these circumstances, the district court properly declined to order the government to release classified information responsive to Yunis' discovery request.

D. *Jury Instructions*

Lastly, Yunis challenges the district court's instructions to the jury insofar as they relate to intent requirements of the federal hostage taking, hijacking, and conspiracy statutes and to appellant's affirmative defense of obedience to military orders.

1. Intent Requirements

Yunis claims that the Antihijacking Act, 49 U.S.C. App. § 1472(n), and the Hostage Taking Act, 18 U.S.C. § 1203, make specific intent an element of the offenses they establish, and that the district court erred in failing to adopt jury instructions offered by the defense that would have made this clear. In appellant's view, the trial judge's instruction that Yunis could be convicted on these counts only if he acted "intentionally, deliberately and knowingly" was inadequate.

49 U.S.C. App. § 1472(n) suggests no specific intent requirement on its face, criminalizing any "unlawful" hijacking of an aircraft. Nor do judicial interpretations of related statutes support appellant's position. In fact, courts have interpreted a companion provision criminalizing domestic hijacking, 49 U.S.C. App. § 1472(i), as requiring only general criminal intent, even though (unlike section 1472(n)) it specifies that hijackers must act with "wrongful intent." *See United States v. Castaneda-Reyes*, 703 F.2d 522, 525 (11th Cir.); *United States v. Busic*, 592 F.2d 13, 21 (2d Cir. 1978); *United States v. Bohle*, 445 F.2d 54, 60 (7th Cir. 1971). In light of these decisions, and absent any encouragement from Congress, we decline Yunis' invitation to graft a specific intent requirement onto the Antihijacking Act.

Yunis' claim that the Hostage Taking Act requires specific intent also fails. The statutory language suggests no intent requirement other than that the offender must act with the purpose of influencing some third person or government through the hostage taking, a point on which the jury received proper instructions. Nor are we aware of any legislative history suggesting that Congress meant to impose a specific intent requirement. Thus, we conclude that the trial judge's instructions on this count of the indictment accorded with law.

We find no merit in Yunis' objection (not raised at trial) that the district court failed to instruct the jury that specific intent is a necessary element of the crime of conspiracy. True, "the specific intent required for the crime of conspiracy is in fact the intent to advance or further the unlawful object of the conspiracy." *United States v. Haldeman*, 181 U.S. App. D.C. 254, 559 F.2d 31, 112 (D.C. Cir. 1976) (footnote omitted). But the jury received instructions that the government "must show beyond a reasonable doubt that the conspiracy was knowingly formed and that the defendant willfully participated in the unlawful plan with the intent to advance or further some object or purpose of the conspiracy." We discern no defect in this instruction.

2. Obedience to Military Orders

The final issues before us concern jury instructions relating to Yunis' affirmative defense of obedience to military orders. Yunis and the government agree on the elements of this common law defense, which are established by several civilian court decisions of rather ancient vintage and by military practice. These precedents generally accord with a formulation approved by the Court of Military Appeals in *United States v. Calley*, 22 C.M.A. 534, 48 C.M.R. 19, 22 U.S.C.M.A. 534 (1973):

> The acts of a subordinate done in compliance with an unlawful order given him by his superior are excused and impose no criminal liability upon him unless the superior's order is one which a man of ordinary sense and understanding would, under the circumstances, know to be unlawful, or if the order in question is actually known to the accused to be unlawful.

Id. at 542.

Appellant does not disagree with the district court's jury instructions on the general elements of this affirmative defense. Instead, Yunis claims that the district court erred as a matter of law when it instructed the jury that Yunis could prevail on this defense only if the Amal Militia — to which Yunis belonged and which, he claimed, ordered the hijacking — is a "military organization." The court further instructed the jury that it could find that the Amal Militia is a military organization only if the group has a hierarchical command structure and "conducts its operations in accordance with the laws and customs of war," and if its members have a uniform and carry arms openly.

Yunis disputes the district court's position that members of a legitimate military organization must have a uniform. Since the hijackers wore civilian clothes and there was evidence that members of the Amal Militia often dressed this way, appellant concludes that the instruction was prejudicial to his defense. Yunis argues that the relevance of uniforms to the ultimate factual question of whether or not the Amal Militia is a military organization is itself a factual question for the jury, not a question of law. He notes that U.S. courts have not developed any test for determining whether or not defendants who invoke the obedience defense actually belong to bona fide military organizations. But the government responds that courts have not developed such a test simply because the issue has not arisen in U.S. courts; heretofore, the defense has been raised only by members of the United States armed forces. In the government's view, the district court properly adapted its instructions on the obedience defense when faced with novel factual circumstances.

We agree that the district court did not commit legal error when it looked beyond domestic precedents to give jurors guidance in evaluating the Amal Militia's military credentials. Moreover, we find that the test of a bona fide military organization adopted by the district court reflects international practice, providing assurance that Yunis did not suffer from parochial projection of American norms onto the issue of whether he should be treated as a soldier for purposes of the obedience defense.

Specifically, the district court's uniform instruction finds sufficient support in international agreements that bear on the question. *See* Geneva Convention Relative to the Treatment of Prisoners of War, art. 4(A)(2); Hague Convention No. IV Respecting the Law and Customs of War on Land, art. 1. The Geneva Convention, signed by 167 nations including the United States and Lebanon, establishes "having a fixed and distinctive signal recognizable at a distance" as one of four necessary conditions that qualify the members of a militia for treatment as prisoners of war. The Hague Convention No. IV, to which the United States and forty-two other nations are parties, uses having "a fixed distinctive emblem recognizable at a distance" as a test for whether militiamen and members of volunteer corps have the rights and responsibilities of national armies. At oral argument, counsel for appellant disavowed reliance on the district court's substitution of "uniform" for "signal" or "emblem," and we agree that this free interpretation of the treaty language did not prejudice the defense.

Yunis' second objection to the district court's "military organization" test relates to the instruction, tracking language found in article 4 of the Geneva Convention and chapter I of the annex to the Hague Convention No. IV, that militias must "conduct [their] operations in accordance with the laws and customs of war" to qualify as military organizations. Appellant alleges that this instruction must be considered in tandem with the trial judge's statement to the jury that the hijacking of Flight 402 violated international law. Together, he says, these instructions directed the jury to conclude that the defense of obedience to military orders was unavailable to Yunis because no organization could have given the instruction to hijack Flight 402 without violating "the laws and customs of war."

We disagree with appellant's reading of the record, however, and find that when the district court's instructions are considered as a whole, it is highly improbable that a reasonable juror would have understood them to direct a verdict on the affirmative defense. In the first place, appellant ignores the trial judge's charge to the jury that it was responsible for determining, based on the evidence, whether or not the Amal Militia is a military organization. So too, the court told jurors that if they found that Yunis was a soldier in a military organization under the definition given them, they would then have to address the issue of whether or not Yunis knew that his orders were illegal. Both of these instructions contradict appellant's suggested reading, leading us to conclude that the jury would not have understood the question of whether or not the Amal Militia is a military organization to be foreclosed.

Appellant's interpretation becomes even more attenuated in light of the government's closing argument, during which the prosecution told jurors that they would have to determine whether the Amal Militia is "a military organization that *basically* plays by the rules." This statement framed the issue correctly, albeit informally, providing additional assurance that any ambiguity arising from the court's juxtaposition of the illegality instruction and the adherence to international law instruction did not prejudice Yunis' defense. Because the jury instructions, read as a whole and in light of the evidence and arguments at trial, leave us confident that no prejudicial error occurred, we find that the district court acted within the scope of its discretion.

III. Conclusion

For the foregoing reasons, the convictions are *Affirmed.*

NOTES AND QUESTIONS

1. Bases of Personal Jurisdiction. The court discusses two bases of extraterritorial application of U.S. law, the "passive personal principle" (nationality of the victim) and "universal jurisdiction." In *United States v. Layton,* 509 F. Supp. 212 (N.D. Cal. 1981), the court described five different bases of extraterritorial jurisdiction; in addition to the two in *Yunis,* the *Layton* court stated that jurisdiction could be based on the nationality of the offender, effects felt within the prosecuting nation, or "protective jurisdiction" to address harms to interests or possessions of the prosecuting nation.

RESTATEMENT (THIRD) OF FOREIGN RELATIONS LAW OF THE UNITED STATES § 402:

Subject to § 403, a state has jurisdiction to prescribe law with respect to:

(1)(a) conduct that, wholly or in substantial part, takes place within its territory;

(b) the status of persons, or interests in things, present within its territory;

(c) conduct outside its territory that has or is intended to have substantial effect within its territory;

(d) the activities, interests, status, or relations of its nationals outside as well as within its territory; and

(e) certain conduct outside its territory by persons not its nationals that is directed against the security of the state or against a limited class of other state interests.

Does the Restatement authorize "universal" jurisdiction? Are the other four headings of extraterritorial jurisdiction framed by the Restatement in the same way that they are by the courts?

2. Choice of Law. The RESTATEMENT, and many of the courts, refer to this issue as jurisdiction to prescribe or to apply its law. Are we not really more concerned with jurisdiction to adjudicate or punish? Think back to your Civil Procedure class and the difference between "long-arm jurisdiction" and choice of law.

3. Statutory Basis. 18 U.S.C. § 7 defines "special maritime and territorial jurisdiction of the United States" to include such areas as the high seas, vessels and vehicles registered in the U.S. or owned by U.S. citizens, military installations within the U.S., and diplomatic or consular properties overseas. Of particular note for some of our purposes are subsections 7 and 8:

(7) Any place outside the jurisdiction of any nation with respect to an offense by or against a national of the United States.

(8) To the extent permitted by international law, any foreign vessel during a voyage having a scheduled departure from or arrival in the United States with respect to an offense committed by or against a national of the United States.

Subsection 8 is the only provision limited by the language "to the extent permitted by international law." Although some of the special statutes related to terrorism refer back to 18 U.S.C. § 7, most of them also carry their own jurisdictional statements. The combination can make for very confusing efforts to parse the statutes.

4. Prisoner Treatment. Yunis made an argument that he could not be subject to a U.S. prosecution because of the circumstances of his capture abroad. In *Yunis I*, the court described his capture and interrogation this way:

Investigation of this crime by American law enforcement officials eventually focused on Yunis as the probable leader of the hijackers. Accordingly, the FBI — in concert with other federal agencies — developed "Operation Goldenrod." With the aid of an informant in the Middle East, Operation Goldenrod sought to lure Yunis into international waters to effect his arrest. The plan succeeded on September 13, 1987, when Yunis boarded a yacht manned by FBI agents in the eastern Mediterranean — allegedly drawn there by the promise of a profitable drug transaction. Yunis was promptly arrested by means of a "take down": agents on either side of Yunis grabbed his arms and kicked his feet out from under him, so that he ended up face down on the deck of the boat. He was handcuffed and shackled and then told that he was under arrest and was being taken to America to stand trial for the 1985 hijacking. The yacht proceeded to a prearranged rendezvous with an American munitions ship (the USS Butte) of the United States' Sixth Fleet. Yunis and two agents on the yacht boarded a transfer boat, which was then hoisted up the side of the Butte. In the process, the mechanical hoist failed and the boat's occupants were left swaying in midair as the Butte's crew completed the operation by hand. During this time, Yunis evidently grew seasick and either experienced dry heaves or vomited over the side of the boat.

Once on board the Butte, Yunis was taken to a small room that was to be his living quarters for the next four days, as the Butte made its way westward across the Mediterranean. The room was small — eight by ten feet — and poorly ventilated, as a malfunctioning vent evidently blew hot air into the room; the room's estimated temperature was 85 degrees. Although there were no windows, a hatch door (which at all times remained open) gave out onto a deck area, with some exposure to the ocean. In this room, a naval doctor examined Yunis and found him to be in good health, aside from his seasickness. During the examination, an FBI agent who was fluent in Arabic served as interpreter, since Yunis speaks very little English. The doctor did not notice any problem with Yunis' wrists, and Yunis did not complain about them at this time. However, it was later established by x-rays (after Yunis reached the United States) that both wrists had been fractured, apparently when the FBI agents first arrested him by means of the "take down."

When the doctor concluded his exam, he prescribed rest and clear liquids to alleviate Yunis' seasickness. The doctor then left Yunis' room, and FBI Special Agent Thomas Hansen, who was in charge of investigating the 1985 hijacking, began to talk to Yunis — communicating through the FBI interpreter. At the outset, Yunis was told that when he reached the United States he "would be appointed an attorney and would be formally charged . . . [and then] would go through a number of legal proceedings which may terminate in a trial." Agent Hansen further informed Yunis that "from this point forward, he would be afforded all the rights of a citizen of the United States and that he didn't have to be concerned with the fact that he wasn't an American, that now those rights would apply to him." The agents then gave Yunis a form, on which the warnings required under *Miranda v. Arizona*, were written in Arabic. Yunis was asked to read these warnings; thereafter, agent Hansen read the warnings aloud in English and the FBI interpreter translated each warning orally into Arabic. Both agents subsequently testified that Yunis was repeatedly asked whether he understood what had just been read to him and that Yunis answered affirmatively.

After thus informing Yunis of the constitutional rights that are afforded American citizens, agent Hansen asked Yunis "whether he was, knowing these rights, was he willing to talk to Agent Droujinsky [the interpreter] and myself about the hijacking. . . . He said yes. And then I requested that he sign the form." Between the time that agent Hansen initiated the conversation and the time that Yunis agreed to answer questions about the hijacking, nine minutes elapsed.

Yunis did sign the form and then, in response to agent Hansen's questions, began to recount the hijacking — how he was assigned to lead the 1985 hijacking by officials of Lebanon's Amal militia (of which he was then a member), how he and his accomplices arrived at Beirut Airport and boarded the Royal Jordanian airliner, and so on. After about half an hour of interrogation, Yunis said he felt sleepy, and agent Hansen proposed that they go out on the deck for some fresh air. Once outside, however, Yunis felt nauseous. Accordingly, agent Hansen told Yunis he could lie down in his room, and the first interrogation session ended.

In the afternoon, Yunis again experienced seasickness and vomited once. The naval doctor returned to examine Yunis in the early evening. During the examination, Yunis experienced dry heaves; the doctor once again prescribed clear liquids and rest. Not long thereafter, agent Hansen and the interpreter asked Yunis if he wished to resume talking, and Yunis consented. Neither at this time nor during any of the seven subsequent interrogation sessions on board the Butte did agent Hansen readminister the Miranda warnings. This second period of questioning was conducted out on the deck, rather than in the room. After talking for about forty minutes, Yunis indicated that he was again feeling seasick, and the session ended. Before Yunis went to sleep, he was given a scopolamine patch, which gradually releases medication through the skin behind the ear to mitigate nausea.

Early the following morning, Yunis ate a substantial breakfast but again became sick to his stomach and experienced dry heaves. The naval doctor again examined him, and on this occasion Yunis specifically complained that his wrists were bothering him. The doctor found Yunis' wrists "mildly swollen and . . . the right wrist had a bit of a bruise on th[e] inner part of the wrist." The injury was treated with ice packs and by keeping the wrists elevated.

Later that morning, agent Hansen and his interpreter returned, and Yunis agreed to resume the narrative of the hijacking. After half an hour, however, Yunis again complained that he was dizzy, and the session ended. By afternoon, the scopolamine patch had evidently begun to work. For the remainder of his journey on the Butte, Yunis appeared more animated and did not noticeably suffer from motion sickness. Accordingly, the interrogation sessions grew longer.

All told, Yunis answered questions during nine sessions aboard the Butte for a total of twelve hours. He not only described the full saga of the hijacking but also gave details about other events in Lebanon and the Middle East. At the end of the fourth day on the Butte, agent Hansen presented Yunis with a written confession (in Arabic), which distilled the salient details from Yunis' narrative. Yunis asked why he should sign it. As agent Hansen later testified at the suppression hearing:

"I indicated to him that by signing it, it would be a matter of record indicating exactly what he told us. And that we could not change what he had said to us and conversely he could not change what he had said to us. And again, just like anything else, he did not have to sign it, but if he cared to do so, it was up to him. He said he would sign it, which he did."

The general issue of interrogation techniques is taken up in Chapter 9. For now we are concerned with abduction from other countries, so we will look at an incident that required the use of a little more force than did the capture of Yunis — the invasion of Panama.

UNITED STATES v. NORIEGA
117 F.3d 1206 (11th Cir. 1997)

KRAVITCH, SENIOR CIRCUIT JUDGE.

Manuel Antonio Noriega appeals: (1) his multiple convictions stemming from his involvement in cocaine trafficking; and (2) the district court's denial of his motion for a new trial based on newly discovered evidence. In attacking his convictions, Noriega asserts that the district court should have dismissed the indictment against him due to his status as a head of state and the manner in which the United States brought him to justice. Noriega also contends that the district court committed two reversible evidentiary errors. Alternatively, he seeks a new trial based on his discovery of: (1) the government's suppression of its pact with a non-witness; and/or (2) certain allegations, lodged after his conviction, that a group associated with the undisclosed, cooperating non-witness bribed a prosecution witness. We affirm Noriega's convictions and the district court's order denying his new trial motion.

I.

On February 4, 1988, a federal grand jury for the Southern District of Florida indicted Manuel Antonio Noriega on drug-related charges. At that time, Noriega served as commander of the Panamanian Defense Forces in the Republic of Panama. Shortly thereafter, Panama's president, Eric Arturo Delvalle, formally discharged Noriega from his military post, but Noriega refused to accept the dismissal. Panama's legislature then ousted Delvalle from power. The United States, however, continued to acknowledge Delvalle as the constitutional leader of Panama. Later, after a disputed presidential election in Panama, the United States recognized Guillermo Endara as Panama's legitimate head of state.

On December 15, 1989, Noriega publicly declared that a state of war existed between Panama and the United States. Within days of this announcement by Noriega, President George Bush directed United States armed forces into combat in Panama for the stated purposes of "safeguarding American lives, restoring democracy, preserving the Panama Canal treaties, and seizing Noriega to face federal drug charges in the United States." *United States v. Noriega*, 746 F. Supp. 1506, 1511 (S.D. Fla. 1990). The ensuing military conflagration resulted in significant casualties and property loss among Panamanian civilians. Noriega lost his effective control over Panama during this armed conflict, and he surrendered to United States military officials on January 3, 1990. Noriega then was brought to Miami to face the pending federal charges.

Following extensive pre-trial proceedings and a lengthy trial, a jury found Noriega guilty of eight counts in the indictment and not guilty of the remaining two counts. The district court entered judgments of conviction against Noriega upon the jury's verdict and sentenced him to consecutive imprisonment terms of 20, 15 and five years, respectively. Noriega timely appealed his convictions. During the pendency of that appeal, Noriega filed in district court a motion for a new trial based on newly discovered evidence. This court deferred further consideration of Noriega's initial appeal while the district court heard Noriega's new trial motion. When the district court denied that motion, Noriega took a second, timely appeal. Both matters now are properly before this court.

II.

At trial, the government presented the testimony of numerous witnesses as well as documentary evidence to prove Noriega's guilt. Noriega, through both cross-examination and defense witness testimony, fervently contested the veracity of the witnesses and the significance of the documents offered by the government. Under the defense theory of the case, Noriega's subordinates used his name in their drug-trafficking schemes, but Noriega had no personal connection to the alleged offenses. "The facts set out below are those which the jury might reasonably have found from the evidence properly admitted at trial."

From the early 1970s to 1989, Noriega secured progressively greater dominion over state military and civilian institutions in Panama, first as his nation's chief of military intelligence and later as commander of the Panamanian Defense Forces. In the early 1980s, Noriega's position of authority brought him into contact with a group of drug traffickers from the Medellin area of Colombia (the "Medellin Cartel"). Various Medellin Cartel operatives met with Noriega's associates and, later, with Noriega personally, regarding the Medellin Cartel's desire to ship cocaine through Panama to the United States. Eventually, Noriega and the Medellin Cartel reached the first of a series of illicit agreements. Thereafter, from 1982 through 1985, with Noriega's assistance, the Medellin Cartel transported significant quantities of cocaine through Panama to the United States. It also utilized its relationship with Noriega to move ether for cocaine processing and substantial cash proceeds from drug sales from the United States to or through Panama.

Noriega and his associates personally met with Medellin Cartel leaders in Colombia, Panama and Cuba regarding the transhipping arrangement, unofficial asylum for Medellin Cartel members fleeing prosecution and a botched plan to operate a cocaine processing laboratory in the Darien region of Panama. The Medellin Cartel directed large cash payments to Noriega in connection with its drug, ether and cash shipments through Panama. During this period, Noriega opened secret accounts in his name and the names of his family members with the Bank of Credit and Commerce International ("BCCI") in Panama. Noriega's associates made large, unexplained cash deposits into these accounts for him. In 1988, Noriega transferred approximately $20,000,000 of his amassed fortune to banks in Europe. The government ultimately located more than $23,000,000 of funds traceable to Noriega in financial institutions outside of Panama.

III.

Noriega challenges his convictions on five distinct grounds: the first three relate to the district court's decision to exercise jurisdiction over this case and the final two concern evidentiary rulings by the district court. Noriega does not contend that the record contains insufficient evidence to support the jury's verdicts of guilt and the resultant judgments of conviction entered by the district court.

A.

Noriega raised two of his three quasi-jurisdictional appellate claims via a pre-trial motion to dismiss the indictment which the district court denied.

1.

Noriega first argues that the district court should have dismissed the indictment against him based on head-of-state immunity. He insists that he was entitled to such immunity because he served as the de facto, if not the de jure, leader of Panama. The district court rejected Noriega's head-of-state immunity claim because the United States government never recognized Noriega as Panama's legitimate, constitutional ruler.

The Supreme Court long ago held that "the jurisdiction of courts is a branch of that which is possessed by the nation as an independent sovereign power. The jurisdiction of the nation within its own territory is necessarily exclusive and absolute. It is susceptible of no limitation not imposed by itself." *The Schooner Exchange v. M'Faddon*, 11 U.S. (7 Cranch) 116, 136, 3 L. Ed. 287 (1812). The Court, however, ruled that nations, including the United States, had agreed implicitly to accept certain limitations on their individual territorial jurisdiction based on the "common interest impelling [sovereign nations] to mutual intercourse, and an interchange of good offices with each other. . . . " Chief among the exceptions to jurisdiction was "the exemption of the person of the sovereign from arrest or detention within a foreign territory."

The principles of international comity outlined by the Court in *The Schooner Exchange* led to the development of a general doctrine of foreign sovereign immunity which courts applied most often to protect foreign nations in their corporate form from civil process in the United States. To enforce this foreign sovereign immunity, nations concerned about their exposure to judicial proceedings in the United States:

> followed the accepted course of procedure [and] by appropriate representations, sought recognition by the State Department of [their] claim of immunity, and asked that the [State] Department advise the Attorney General of the claim of immunity and that the Attorney General instruct the United States Attorney for the [relevant district] to file in the district court the appropriate suggestion of immunity. . . .

Ex Parte Republic of Peru, 318 U.S. 578, 581 (1943) (citations omitted). As this doctrine emerged, the "Court consistently deferred to the decisions of the political branches — in particular, those of the Executive Branch — on whether to take jurisdiction over actions against foreign sovereigns and their instrumentalities."

In 1976, Congress passed the Foreign Sovereign Immunities Act ("FSIA"), 28 U.S.C. §§ 1602–1611. The FSIA . . . codified the State Department's general criteria for making suggestions of immunity, and transferred the responsibility for case-by-case application of these principles from the Executive Branch to the Judicial Branch. Because the FSIA addresses neither head-of-state immunity, nor foreign sovereign immunity in the criminal context, head-of-state immunity could attach in cases, such as this one, only pursuant to the principles and procedures outlined in *The Schooner Exchange* and its progeny. As a result, this court must look to the Executive Branch for direction on the propriety of Noriega's immunity claim. *See Kadic v. Karadzic*, 70 F.3d 232, 248 (2d Cir. 1995) (questioning viability of head-of-state immunity doctrine in light of FSIA, but noting that, even if still operative, doctrine was inapplicable because Executive Branch had not recognized defendant as head of state).

Generally, the Executive Branch's position on head-of-state immunity falls into one of three categories: the Executive Branch (1) explicitly suggests immunity; (2) expressly declines to suggest immunity; or (3) offers no guidance. Some courts have held that absent a formal suggestion of immunity, a putative head of state should receive no immunity. The Executive Branch has not merely refrained from taking a position on this matter; to the contrary, by pursuing Noriega's capture and this prosecution, the Executive Branch has manifested its clear sentiment that Noriega should be denied head-of-state immunity. Noriega has cited no authority that would empower a court to grant head-of-state immunity under these circumstances. Moreover, given that the record indicates that Noriega never served as the constitutional leader of Panama, that Panama has not sought immunity for Noriega and that the charged acts relate to Noriega's private pursuit of personal enrichment, Noriega likely would not prevail even if this court had to make an independent determination regarding the propriety of immunity in this case.

2.

Noriega next contends his conviction should be reversed because he alleges he was brought to the United States in violation of the Treaty Providing for the Extradition of Criminals, May 25, 1904, United States of America-Republic of Panama, 34 Stat. 2851 ("U.S.-Panama Extradition Treaty"). The Supreme Court's decision in *United States v. Alvarez-Machain*, 504 U.S. 655 (1992), forecloses this argument. In *Alvarez-Machain*, the Court considered the issue of "whether a criminal defendant, abducted to the United States from a nation with which it has an extradition treaty, thereby acquires a defense to the jurisdiction of this country's courts." In answer, the Court stated: "We hold that he does not, and that he may be tried in federal district court for violations of the criminal law of the United States."

In reaching this decision, the Court considered whether the treaty at issue expressly barred abductions. It determined that the treaty's provision that " 'neither Contracting Party shall be bound to deliver up its own nationals . . . ' [fails] to specify the only way in which one country may gain custody of a national of the other country for purposes of prosecution." *Id.* at 663–64 (quoting Extradition Treaty, May 4, 1978, United States of America-United Mexican States, 31 U.S.T. 5059 ("U.S.-Mexico Extradition Treaty")). The Court also rejected the argument that, by entering into an extradition treaty with Mexico, the United States impliedly agreed to seek custody of persons in Mexico only via extradition. ("To infer from this Treaty and its terms that it prohibits all means of gaining the presence of an individual outside of its terms goes beyond established precedent and practice.")

The article of the U.S.-Panama Extradition Treaty upon which Noriega relies for his extradition treaty claim contains almost the same language as the provision of the U.S.-Mexico Extradition Treaty at issue in *Alvarez-Machain*. Noriega contends that *Alvarez-Machain* is distinguishable despite the near identity of the relevant clauses because, at the time the United States entered into the U.S.-Panama Extradition Treaty, it knew or should have known that Panama's constitution prohibited the extradition of its nationals. This bald assertion, even if accepted, does not save Noriega's claim. A clause in Panama's constitution regarding the extradition of Panamanians, at most, informs the United States of the hurdles it will face when pursuing such extraditions in Panama; such a provision says nothing about the treaty signatories' rights to opt for self-help (i.e., abduction) over legal process (i.e., extradition).

Under *Alvarez-Machain*, to prevail on an extradition treaty claim, a defendant must demonstrate, by reference to the express language of a treaty and/or the established practice thereunder, that the United States affirmatively agreed not to seize foreign nationals from the territory of its treaty partner. Noriega has not carried this burden, and therefore, his claim fails.

3.

In his pre-trial motion, Noriega also sought the dismissal of the indictment against him on the ground that the manner in which he was brought before the district court (i.e., through a military invasion) was so unconscionable as to constitute a violation of substantive due process. Noriega also argued that to the extent the government's actions did not shock the judicial conscience sufficiently to trigger due process sanctions, the district court should exercise its supervisory power to decline jurisdiction. The district court rejected Noriega's due process argument, and it declared Noriega's alternative supervisory power rationale non-justiciable. On appeal, Noriega offers no substantive argument regarding the due process prong of this claim, but rather discusses only his alternative supervisory power theory. Because, however, the due process and supervisory power issues are intertwined, we discuss them both.

Noriega's due process claim "falls squarely within the [Supreme Court's] *Ker-Frisbie* doctrine, which holds that a defendant cannot defeat personal jurisdiction by asserting the illegality of the procurement of his presence." Noriega has not alleged that the government mistreated him personally, and thus, he cannot come within the purview of the caveat to *Ker-Frisbie* recognized by the Second Circuit in *United States v. Toscanino*, 500 F.2d 267 (2d Cir. 1974), were this court inclined to adopt such an exception. Further, whatever harm Panamanian civilians suffered during the armed conflict that preceded Noriega's arrest cannot support a due process claim in this case. *See United States v. Payner*, 447 U.S. 727, 737 n.9 (1980) (holding that even where government's conduct toward third parties "was so outrageous as to offend fundamental canons of decency and fairness, the fact remains that the limitations of the Due Process Clause . . . come into play only when the Government activity in question violates some protected right of the defendant" (internal quotations omitted)).

NOTES AND QUESTIONS

1. ***United States v. Alvarez-Machain.*** *United States v. Alvarez-Machain*, 504 U.S. 655 (1992), discussed in the *Noriega* case, is one of several incidents that have produced friction between the U.S. and Mexico. The opinions in the case contain stark contrasts in perceptions of the executive and judicial roles in response to international criminal behavior.

The Supreme Court described the abduction of Alvarez-Machain as follows:

> Respondent, Humberto Alvarez-Machain, is a citizen and resident of Mexico. He was indicted for participating in the kidnap and murder of United States Drug Enforcement Administration (DEA) special agent Enrique Camarena-Salazar and a Mexican pilot working with Camarena, Alfredo Zavala-Avelar. The DEA believes that respondent, a medical doctor, participated in the murder by prolonging Agent Camarena's life so that others could further torture and interrogate him. On April 2, 1990, respondent was forcibly kidnaped from his medical office in Guadalajara, Mexico, to be flown by private plane to El Paso, Texas, where he was arrested by DEA officials. The District Court concluded that DEA agents were responsible for respondent's abduction, although they were not personally involved in it.

The torture and murder of Camerena was particularly debilitating to the morale of DEA and other federal agents, so there was a substantial amount of pressure on the executive branch to pursue this prosecution. Mexico officially protested the abduction of Alvarez-Machain as a violation of both international law and the extradition treaty, and simultaneously requested extradition of two individuals from the U.S. whom Mexico wanted to prosecute for kidnapping of Alvarez-Machain. The lower courts dismissed the indictment on the basis of the treaty violation, but the Supreme Court held that the treaty did not specifically bar abductions. In response to arguments that prosecution under these circumstances would damage U.S. interests by being perceived as a violation of international law or treaty expectations, the Court held that these concerns were for the executive branch to deal with in pursuit of its diplomatic functions.

Justice Stevens in dissent pointed out that Mexico had already tried and sentenced several other conspirators in the Camerena incident, and had asserted its interest in prosecuting Alvarez-Machain. Justice Stevens' response to the majority's assertion of executive diplomatic prerogatives emphasized the independent role of the judicial function:

> As the Court observes at the outset of its opinion, there is reason to believe that respondent participated in an especially brutal murder of an American law enforcement agent. That fact, if true, may explain the Executive's intense interest in punishing respondent in our courts. Such an explanation, however,

provides no justification for disregarding the Rule of Law that this Court has a duty to uphold. That the Executive may wish to reinterpret the Treaty to allow for an action that the Treaty in no way authorizes should not influence this Court's interpretation. Indeed, the desire for revenge exerts "a kind of hydraulic pressure . . . before which even well settled principles of law will bend," but it is precisely at such moments that we should remember and be guided by our duty "to render judgment evenly and dispassionately according to law, as each is given understanding to ascertain and apply it."

The significance of this Court's precedents is illustrated by a recent decision of the Court of Appeal of the Republic of South Africa. Based largely on its understanding of the import of this Court's cases — including our decision in *Ker* — that court held that the prosecution of a defendant kidnaped by agents of South Africa in another country must be dismissed. *S v. Ebrahim*, S. Afr. L. Rep. (Apr.–June 1991). The Court of Appeal of South Africa — indeed, I suspect most courts throughout the civilized world — will be deeply disturbed by the "monstrous" decision the Court announces today. For every nation that has an interest in preserving the Rule of Law is affected, directly or indirectly, by a decision of this character. As Thomas Paine warned, an "avidity to punish is always dangerous to liberty" because it leads a nation "to stretch, to misinterpret, and to misapply even the best of laws." To counter that tendency, he reminds us: "He that would make his own liberty secure must guard even his enemy from oppression; for if he violates this duty he establishes a precedent that will reach to himself."

Michael J. Glennon, *International Kidnapping: State-sponsored Abduction: A Comment on* United States v. Alvarez-Machain, 86 A.J.I.L. 746 (1992):

[The] Supreme Court confronted what the Permanent Court of International Justice termed in *The Lotus* to be "the first and foremost restriction imposed by international law upon a State: . . . that — failing the existence of a permissive rule to the contrary — it may not exercise its power in any form in the territory of another State." Contrary to popular criticism, the Court did not challenge that proposition. But it did apply, without adequate analysis, an antiquated doctrine that permits a defendant to be tried regardless of the unlawfulness of the seizure. In so doing, it ignored altogether the issue of presidential constitutional power to conduct such seizures.

2. *United States v. Rezaq*. *United States v. Rezaq*, 134 F.2d 1121 (D.C. Cir. 1998):

Rezaq is Palestinian, and was, at the time of the hijacking, a member of a Palestinian terrorist organization, which planned and ordered the hijacking. On the evening of November 23, 1985, Rezaq boarded Air Egypt Flight 648 in Athens. He was accompanied by two other hijackers; one of his confederates, named Salem, was the leader of the operation, and the name of the other is unknown. Shortly after the plane took off, the three produced weapons, announced that they were seizing the plane, and demanded that the captain fly it to Malta. A gun battle ensued between the hijackers and an Egyptian plainclothes sky marshal stationed on the plane, as a result of which Salem was killed and the sky marshal was wounded.

Rezaq then took charge of the hijacking. After the plane arrived in Malta, he separated the Israeli and American passengers from the others, and moved them to the front of the plane. He released a number of Egyptian and Filipino female passengers, as well as two wounded flight attendants. He then demanded that the aircraft be refueled; when the authorities refused, he announced that he would shoot a passenger every fifteen minutes until his demand was met.

Rezaq carried out his threat. He first shot Israeli national Tamar Artzi. Although he shot her twice, once in the head, she survived. Fifteen minutes later, he shot her companion, Nitzan Mendelson, also an Israeli; Ms. Mendelson died of her injuries nine days later. Rezaq then shot Patrick Baker, an American, but only succeeded in grazing his head. Two or three hours later, Rezaq shot Scarlett Rogenkamp — a United States citizen and an employee of the United States Air Force — in the head, killing her. Some time later, he shot Jackie Pflug, also an American, in the head, injuring her very seriously. Rezaq shot his victims near the front door of the plane, and either threw them or let them fall onto the tarmac; this may explain why three of the five were able to survive, either by escaping (Artzi and Baker), or by feigning death (Pflug).

In the evening of November 24th — about a day after the hijacking began — Egyptian commandos stormed the plane. The operation seems to have been a singularly incompetent one. The commandos fired indiscriminately, and set off an explosive device of some kind, as a result of which the aircraft burst into flames. Fifty-seven passengers were killed, as was the third hijacker. Rezaq was injured, and was taken, with a multitude of injured passengers, to a hospital. There, he was identified as the hijacker by passengers, members of the crew, and several of his victims.

The authorities in Malta charged Rezaq with murder, attempted murder, and hostage taking. He pled guilty, and was sentenced to 25 years' imprisonment. For reasons unclear, Maltese authorities released him some seven years later, in February 1993, and allowed him to board a plane to Ghana. Rezaq's itinerary was to carry him from there to Nigeria, and then to Ethiopia, and finally to Sudan. Ghanaian officials detained Rezaq for several months, but eventually allowed him to proceed to Nigeria. When Rezaq's plane landed in Nigeria, Nigerian authorities placed him in the custody of FBI agents, who transported him on a waiting aircraft to the United States.

Rezaq argued that the Hi-Jacking Act's application to one who is "found in the United States" must mean something other than brought before the court involuntarily because that would make the provision a nullity. The court said that requiring the defendant to be present before the court is not meaningless because "at a minimum, it confirms the rule, issuing from the Confrontation Clause of the Sixth Amendment and from the Due Process Clause, that a defendant ordinarily may not be tried in absentia." Ordinarily? When might a defendant be tried *in absentia*?

3. Unconscionable Exception. The *Noriega* court expresses doubts about the *Toscanino* "unconscionable conduct" exception to *Ker-Frisbie*, and the *Yunis* court questions whether an exception should result in dismissal of an indictment. Assume that U.S. agents savagely beat a person in their custody while overseas, either attempting to get information about additional suspects or just because they are angry. What do you think a court should do about this? Are U.S. agents held to the same levels of propriety while acting abroad that they should be while on home soil? Should there be different standards for dealing with suspected terrorists? The "prisoner abuse" scandals of 2003–04 will be considered in Chapter 9.

UNITED STATES v. YOUSEF
927 F. Supp. 673 (S.D.N.Y. 1996)

DUFFY, DISTRICT JUDGE.

Defendants, Ramzi Ahmed Yousef, ("Yousef"), Abdul Hakim Murad ("Murad"), and Wali Khan Amin Shah, ("Shah"), are charged with conspiring and attempting to damage, destroy and bomb numerous United States commercial airliners operating in East Asia routes, all but one of which had some United States city as a scheduled stop. Defendants are also alleged to have been responsible for the detonation of a bomb in the Greenbelt Theater in Manila, Philippines, on or about December 1, 1994. Defendant Yousef is charged with the detonation of another bomb on December 11, 1994, aboard Philippine Airlines Flight 434 bound for Tokyo, Japan, which exploded while the airplane was in flight, causing the death of one passenger, Haruki Ikegami, and injuring several others. Both of these explosions are included as overt acts in the conspiracy to blow up the United States airliners, and the explosion aboard the Philippines airliner is charged as a separate count in the indictment.

The specific violations with which these Defendants are charged include: conspiring and attempting to destroy aircraft in foreign air commerce within the special aircraft jurisdiction of the United States, in violation of 18 U.S.C. §§ 32(a)(1), (2), (7) & 371 (Counts Twelve, Thirteen and Fourteen); conspiring to kill a national of the United States with malice aforethought, in violation of 18 U.S.C. § 2332(b) and (d) (Count Fifteen); conspiring to use a weapon of mass destruction in relation to the conspiracy charged in Count Fifteen of the indictment in violation of 18 U.S.C. § 2332a (Count Sixteen); using and carrying an improvised explosive device in relation to the conspiracy charged in Counts Twelve and Fifteen, in violation of 18 U.S.C. § 924(c) and 2 (Counts Seventeen and Eighteen); Defendant Yousef is charged with placing and causing the detonation of a bomb aboard a Philippines airliner, in violation of 18 U.S.C. § 32(b) (Count Nineteen); and finally, Defendant Shah is charged with attempting to escape from the custody of the United States in violation of 18 U.S.C. § 751(a) (Count Twenty).

All three Defendants have made various pretrial motions. Yousef moves for (1) dismissal of the indictment because of the alleged mistreatment he suffered while in the custody of unidentified individuals in Pakistan and Pakistani law enforcement agents; (2) dismissal of Count Nineteen of the Indictment, which charges the unlawful placing of a bomb aboard a Philippines airliner, based on jurisdictional "principles of both domestic and international law."

Defendant Murad also moves for dismissal of the indictment for lack of jurisdiction, arguing that the charged offenses did not occur in the "special aircraft jurisdiction" of the United States and that the indictment does not specify the particular United States citizens or property which were the target of the alleged conspiracy.

Defendant Shah moves for dismissal of the indictment alleging that the prosecution of a non-citizen for these extraterritorial crimes in the United States violates the Fifth and Sixth Amendments of the United States Constitution, federal statutory law, and provisions of international law and extradition treaties to which the United States is a party.

For the following reasons, Defendants' motions are denied.

Yousef's Motion to Dismiss the Indictment

Yousef argues that his abduction in Pakistan and the United States' direction of or acquiescence in his alleged torture and interrogation warrant dismissal of the indictment based on the Second Circuit decision in *United States v. Toscanino*, 500 F.2d 267 (2d Cir. 1974). Yousef argues that under the holding in Toscanino, jurisdiction over him was acquired as a result of a deliberate, unnecessary and unreasonable invasion of his rights. However, contrary to Yousef's arguments, *Toscanino* does not stand for the proposition that such allegations must result in dismissal of an indictment. *See United States ex rel. Lujan v. Gengler*, 510 F.2d 62, 66 (absent a set of incidents like that posited by the Court of Appeals as being present in *Toscanino*, not every violation by prosecution or police is so egregious that it requires nullification of the indictment).

The court in *Toscanino* merely remanded to the District Court for an evidentiary hearing to be held only if the defendant "offers some credible supporting evidence, including specifically evidence that the action was taken by or at the direction of United States officials." *Id.* at 281. On remand, Toscanino's only evidence of his torture and coercive interrogation was his own affidavit, which failed to show participation by United States officials. The trial court, therefore refused to hold an evidentiary hearing and denied the motion to vacate the conviction and dismiss the indictment.

Like the trial court in the original case, subsequent courts have interpreted the Second Circuit decision in *Toscanino* narrowly, and generally have refused to dismiss indictments either because of the defendant's failure to establish abusive activity or the defendant's failure to establish United States involvement in the offensive conduct. *See United States v. Yunis*, 681 F. Supp. 909, 919 (D.D.C. 1988) ("Although most circuits have acknowledged the exception carved out by *Toscanino*, it is highly significant that no court has ever applied it to dismiss an indictment.")

Yousef has failed to meet the requirements of *Toscanino*. Yousef's affidavit does not sufficiently allege that United States agents participated in his alleged abduction and torture in Pakistan. In his affidavit in support of this motion, Yousef alleges that he was subject to months of torture at the hands of unidentified individuals in Pakistan who were somehow under the direction of United States officials. Yousef maintains that he was abducted from his relatives' home in Pakistan sometime at the end of November 1994, and remained in the custody of these original abductors and other Pakistan officials until he was surrendered to United States law enforcement agents on February 8, 1995. It was during these months that Yousef allegedly suffered the torture.

Yousef maintains that a United States official was present during a period of his interrogation when he was taken to a desert jail cell in Pakistan some days after his alleged abduction, but before his arrest and surrender to United States officials in Islamabad on February 8, 1995. According to Yousef, the torture which he suffered while in the desert consisted of forced intake of drugs to keep him awake and the denial of rest except at meal times. Yousef does not claim that he was tortured or otherwise mistreated during his period of custody in Islamabad, from February 7 to February 8, 1995, or after his transfer to United States agents.

Yousef's allegations of a period of over two months of torture appear incredible, given that there is no record of his arrest by anyone until February 7, 1995 in Islamabad. Additionally, a passport issued in the name of "Ali Muhammad Baloch"[1] with Yousef's picture, was found in Yousef's possession at the time of his arrest and contained date stamps that tend to show that Yousef departed Pakistan on January 31, 1995, entered Bangkok, Thailand on February 1, 1995 and departed Bangkok on February 5, 1995. This passport, therefore, belies his claim that he was in custody in Pakistan between the period of November 1994 and February 7, 1995.

Yousef does not allege a sufficient factual basis for his assertion that a United States official was present during his alleged torture. Yousef alleges that he heard English being spoken during the desert interrogation and that he later recognized the voice as belonging to an FBI agent who questioned him in Islamabad as the same FBI agent who participated in the desert interrogation with unidentified Pakistanis. Yousef has not identified which FBI agent's voice he now claims he recognized as the one present in the desert. Nor has he stated what role this FBI agent played in the alleged torture.

Two FBI agents did in fact question Yousef in Islamabad. However, these agents, Legal Attache Ralph Paul Horton and Special Agent Bradley J. Garret, were not in Pakistan until February 4, 1995 and February 7, 1995 respectively. Moreover, according to Legal Attache Horton, who at the time was responsible for all FBI personnel entering Pakistan, no FBI agent was in Pakistan investigating the Yousef matter during this period prior to his arrival.

In *United States v. Lira*, 515 F.2d 68 (2d Cir.), the Circuit Court affirmed the denial of a motion to dismiss an indictment where the defendant's allegations of United States involvement were based on the defendant's overhearing English being spoken during his interrogation. The District Court held that the defendant's allegations were not sufficient "evidence that American agents were present at or privy to [defendant's]

---

[1] [Court's Footnote 2] Baloch is an acknowledged alias of Yousef, as evidenced by Yousef's own use of this name in signing a rights waiver form.

interrogation or that the persons overheard to speak English were Americans, much less Government agents."

Since no FBI agent was in Pakistan during the period of alleged torture, Yousef's allegations of voice recognition appear to be baseless and do not allege sufficient United States involvement under Toscanino and Lira.

Moreover, the United States request for Yousef's extradition is not sufficient United States involvement to warrant a dismissal of the indictment. As stated in Lira, "the DEA can hardly be expected to monitor the conduct of representatives of each foreign government to assure that a request for extradition or expulsion is carried out in accordance with American constitutional standards." This same principle must apply to other United States law enforcement agencies as well. Thus, a request to extradite is not sufficient United States involvement to warrant dismissal of the indictment.

Yousef's motion to dismiss the indictment because of the United States involvement in the alleged torture suffered while in Pakistan is denied.

Extraterritorial Jurisdiction

Each Defendant has made various arguments as to why this court should not exercise extraterritorial jurisdiction over the crimes charged in the Indictment. All Defendants argue that this court does not have subject matter jurisdiction to try them for the conspiracy or the attempt to blow up United States civil aircraft in the "special aircraft jurisdiction" of the United States in violation of 18 U.S.C. §§ 32(a)(1), (2), (7) & 371 (Counts Twelve, Thirteen and Fourteen). Defendant Yousef challenges jurisdiction for the actual bombing of the Philippine aircraft in violation of 18 U.S.C. § 32(b) (Count Nineteen). All Defendants also attack the propriety of any other count which relies on these counts.

Defendants' various jurisdictional arguments rely on either constitutional due process principles, statutory interpretation and other domestic law, or international law. While the form of each Defendants' argument differs, in substance each Defendant challenges the assertion of extraterritorial jurisdiction by United States courts where the offenses charged did not occur on United States soil, did not involve United States citizens as defendants, or did not result in the death or injury of a United States citizen.

Jurisdiction is based primarily on Section 32 of Title 18, which states in relevant part:

(a) Whoever willfully

(1) sets fire to, damages, destroys, disables, or wrecks any aircraft in the special aircraft jurisdiction of the United States or any civil aircraft used, operated, or employed in interstate, overseas, or foreign air commerce;

(2) places or causes to be placed a destructive device or substance in, upon, or in proximity to, or otherwise makes or causes to be made unworkable or unusable or hazardous to work or use, any such aircraft, or any part or other materials used or intended to be used in connection with the operation of such aircraft, if such placing or causing to be placed or such making or causing to be made is likely to endanger the safety of any such aircraft; . . .

(7) attempts to do anything prohibited under paragraphs (1) through (6) of this subsection;

shall be fined under this title or imprisoned not more than twenty years, or both.

(b) Whoever wilfully

(3) places or causes to be placed on a civil aircraft registered in a country other than the United States while such aircraft is in service, a device or substance which is likely to destroy that aircraft, or to cause damage to that aircraft which renders that aircraft incapable of flight or which is likely to

endanger that aircraft's safety in flight; . . .

shall, if the offender is later found in the United States, be fined under this title or imprisoned not more than twenty years, or both.

Defendants have been charged under Section 32(a)(1), (2), and (7) in conjunction with the federal conspiracy statute, 18 U.S.C. § 371, with conspiring to bomb eleven United States airliners operating in East Asia. Defendant Yousef has also been charged in a separate count for violation of section 32(b)(3) for the actual bombing of the Philippines airliner. Had the prosecution for the Philippines airliner bombing been brought separately, the argument that "this case has far more nexus to the Philippines than it does to the United States," may have been more persuasive. However, this prosecution alleges that the Philippines airliner bombing was just one step in the overall plot to sabotage United States airliners. As such, the Philippines airliner bombing is alleged to have been part of Defendants' continuous course of conduct in relation to the overall bombing plot. Correctly construed, therefore, it becomes apparent that this court has the authority to assert extraterritorial jurisdiction over the three Defendants for the crimes charged in this indictment consistent with the statutory jurisdictional requirements of Section 32, principles of international law, and the United States Constitution. Not only does this court have the authority to exercise extraterritorial jurisdiction in this case, but, under treaty obligations of the United States, it is required to do so.

Section 32, adopted as part of the Aircraft Sabotage Act, was enacted in 1984 to fulfill this country's responsibilities under the Montreal Convention for the Suppression of Unlawful Acts against the Safety of Civil Aviation, ("the Montreal Convention"), which came into effect on January 26, 1973. A principal purpose of the act was to provide federal jurisdiction over individuals who were accused of committing crimes involving aircraft sabotage and over whom the courts would not otherwise have jurisdiction under domestic law.

Traditional notions of jurisdiction provided that a country's jurisdiction extended internationally over vessels or aircraft flying that country's flag based on a "floating or flying territory" rationale. *See* RESTATEMENT (THIRD) § 402, Reporter's Note 4. This traditional concept was codified in some respects in the Aircraft Sabotage Act.

Section 32(a) proscribes destruction, bombing, and endangering the safety of any aircraft in the "special aircraft jurisdiction of the United States or any civil aircraft used, operated or employed in interstate, overseas or foreign air commerce." There are therefore two possible avenues for establishing jurisdiction under this section. The term "special aircraft jurisdiction" is defined to include "a civil aircraft of the United States" while that aircraft is in flight.

The indictment details a bombing plan by Defendants that targeted United States-flagged commercial airlines, all but one of which were bound for various cities in the United States. As part of the evidence in this case, the government will present a computer printout which it contends contains the specific flight numbers and itineraries for the aircraft involved. All the aircraft involved are from the fleets of well-known United States airline companies, which according to the government, were registered under chapter 441, making them "civil aircraft of the United States." Since the indictment alleges that the bombs were scheduled to explode while these civil aircraft were in flight, the allegations satisfy the "special aircraft jurisdiction" provision.

As part of the overt acts listed in the indictment, the government alleges that Defendants were in possession of a letter that specifically threatened United States civilians. Additionally, all of the aircraft targeted in the alleged plot were United States carriers, and all but one were scheduled to make stops in the United States. At the very least, some members of the flight crew assigned to the various flights were United States nationals. The indictment therefore sufficiently alleges that United States nationals and other United States interests were targets of the alleged conspiracy.

Defendant Yousef challenges jurisdiction over Count Nineteen of the indictment, which concerns the Philippines airliner bombing. Section 32(b)(3), provides for criminal punishment of persons who place aboard a civil aircraft registered in a country other than the United States while that aircraft is in service, any device or substance which is likely to destroy or otherwise damage or endanger the aircraft's safety, provided the saboteur is later "found in the United States." 18 U.S.C. § 32(b)(3). Philippines Airlines Flight 434 was a civil aircraft registered outside the United States, which was en route from the Philippines to Tokyo, Japan when a bomb exploded on board, causing the death of one passenger, Haruki Ikegami, and injuring several others.

Yousef argues that he was not properly "found" within the United States as that term is used in section 32(b). Yousef argues that the sole reason he was present in the United States was because the government brought him to the United States to stand trial for the other charges in the indictment related to the bombing of the World Trade Center. Yousef argues that the government knowingly delayed indicting him on the airliner bombing plot until he was brought to the United States, in order to establish his presence in the United States for purposes of this count of the indictment. Therefore, according to Yousef, he was not present within the United States voluntarily, and jurisdiction cannot be asserted over him pursuant to Section 32(b).

The question of whether a defendant is "found" within the United States for purposes of establishing jurisdiction for aircraft-related crimes, where the defendant was brought to the United States to stand trial on other charges, was considered in *United States v. Yunis*, 288 U.S. App. D.C. 129, 924 F.2d 1086, 1089 (D.C. Cir. 1984). There, the court held that jurisdiction was properly established under the Antihijacking Act, 49 U.S.C. § 1472(n), where the defendant was "found" within the United States as a result of his having been brought within the jurisdiction to stand trial for other charges contained in the same indictment.

Defendant Yousef was surrendered to United States officials by the Pakistani government pursuant to an extradition request made by the United States. Yousef was then returned to the Southern District of New York and subsequently indicted for the airliner bombing plot. These circumstances are at least as compelling as the facts presented in Yunis. The circumstances by which Yousef was "found" within the United States satisfy the statutory jurisdictional requirements.

Defendants Yousef and Shah argue that this court does not have jurisdiction based on principles of international law. Yousef argues that the only international law principle of jurisdiction applicable in this prosecution is that of universal jurisdiction. Yousef argues that "while courts have discussed universality as a basis of jurisdiction, in practice, it has never been used as the sole basis for the United States to assert jurisdiction over a defendant."

The issue of exercising extraterritorial jurisdiction over a criminal prosecution based on universal jurisdiction was also discussed in *United States v. Yunis, supra.* Yousef attempts to distinguish *Yunis* from this case by arguing that in *Yunis*, the presence of two United States citizens aboard the hijacked plane provided an "independent basis for jurisdiction" over the defendant.

The *Yunis* court did not decide that universal jurisdiction was insufficient as the sole basis for jurisdiction under the Antihijacking Act, but rather that the decision to exercise jurisdiction was bolstered by the fact that two of the passengers were United States citizens. The *Yunis* court held that the defendant had been "found" in the United States and therefore the prosecution satisfied the statutory jurisdictional requirements.

Endorsing the exercise of universal jurisdiction in the prosecution of an aircraft-related crime, the court stated that "aircraft hijacking may well be one of the few crimes so clearly condemned under the law of nations that states may assert universal jurisdiction to bring offenders to justice, even when the state has no territorial connection to the hijacking and its citizens are not involved."

The court in *Yunis* cited to the RESTATEMENT (THIRD) OF FOREIGN RELATIONS LAW to support exercise of universal jurisdiction in a criminal prosecution related to crimes involving aircraft. Section 404 states, "[a] state has jurisdiction to define and prescribe punishment for certain offenses recognized by the community of nations as of universal concern, such as piracy, slave trade, attacks on or hijacking of aircraft, genocide, war crimes, and perhaps certain acts of terrorism, even where none of the other bases of jurisdiction indicated in § 402 is present."

The disregard for human life which would accompany the placing of a bomb aboard an airplane with the intent for that bomb to explode while the airplane is in flight and fully occupied with people, or otherwise sabotaging that plane, is at least as heinous a crime of international concern as hijacking a plane. The same rationale that supports jurisdiction under the Antihijacking Act also supports jurisdiction under the Aircraft Sabotage Act, regardless of where the alleged crimes occurred.

Moreover, contrary to Yousef's arguments, there is an additional basis for jurisdiction in this case. The indictment alleges that the bombing aboard the Philippines airliner was not an isolated incident, but part of a continuing course of conduct related to the alleged conspiracy to blow up United States airliners in East Asia. As discussed above, jurisdiction is properly alleged for those counts related to the conspiracy to blow up United States airliners, and therefore, jurisdiction is proper for acts committed in the continuous course of conduct of that conspiracy.

The exercise of extraterritorial jurisdiction in this case is reasonable, since the crimes charged have a "substantial, direct, and foreseeable effect" in the United States and clearly affect United States interests, as would be required by principles of international law. The alleged crimes clearly had intended effects on the United States and its citizens, although they were committed abroad. The fact that the planned consequences of the plot did not come to fruition, and thereby did not directly injure any United States citizen, does not wrest jurisdiction over the prosecution from this court.

The fact that the Philippines airliner bombing is a part of the continuous course of conduct charged against the defendants squelches Shah's argument that the prosecution of the defendants in the United States does not have a "territorial nexus or other direct nexus to the U.S.," rendering the prosecution "arbitrary and fundamentally unfair," and in violation of the Fifth and Sixth Amendments. Any constitutionally required nexus to the United States is clearly present.

Yousef, Murad, and Shah also challenge this court's jurisdiction under Counts Twelve, Seventeen, and Eighteen, on the grounds that the statutes upon which these counts rely do not contain specific grants of extraterritorial jurisdiction. Extraterritorial jurisdiction over a conspiracy charge depends on whether extraterritorial jurisdiction exists as to the underlying substantive crime. Since this court has jurisdiction over the substantive Section 32 charges, jurisdiction over the conspiracy charged in Count Twelve is also proper.

The charge contained in Count Fifteen, a violation of Section 2332, which proscribes conspiracy to kill United States citizens abroad, clearly applies extraterritorially. Because the charges regarding the use and carrying of bombs charged in Counts Seventeen and Eighteen arise directly from the conspiracy offenses charged in Counts Twelve and Fifteen, this Court has jurisdiction over Counts Seventeen and Eighteen as well.

Conclusion

I find that exercising extraterritorial jurisdiction over Defendants Yousef, Murad, and Shah for the crimes charged in the indictment is consistent with the statutory requirements, principles of domestic and international law, and the United States

Constitution. Defendants' motions to dismiss the indictment and its various counts for lack of jurisdiction are therefore denied.

NOTES AND QUESTIONS

1. WTC I. Ramzi Ahmed Yousef is the bridge to our consideration of terrorist actions on U.S. soil. His name appears as a key player in the cases stemming from the first bombing of the World Trade Center. *United States v. Salameh, see infra* § 2.03. He fled the U.S. after that bombing and was active in a series of bombings of airliners and theaters in the Philippines during 1994.

2. International Conventions. Jurisdiction under the hostage and aircraft statutes, which themselves carry out treaty obligations under various international conventions, does not depend on showing a political motivation for the action. The nations signing these conventions have declared that these particularly dangerous actions are universally condemned regardless of the motivation. The rationales are similar to the reasons underlying the Torture Convention. Given that, could any nation exercise universal jurisdiction over a hostage-taker or an aircraft bomber? If so, then is the jurisdictional requirement of a U.S. victim necessary? Should these acts of violence be considered "terrorism" only if they carry a political motivation? So once again we should explore the questions of how to define a terrorist and whether the terrorist label really matters.

3. Congressional Power. Professor Bradley argues that the exercise of extraterritorial jurisdiction, even if based on universal jurisdiction, is still an exercise of judicial power to be delineated by Congress under the "Define and Punish" clause, not an exercise of international law. Thus, it is not particularly problematic for American criminal cases, although it may be a bit more problematic in civil cases. Curtis Bradley, *Universal Jurisdiction and U.S. Law*, 2001 U. Chi. L. Rev. 323.

[B]　Extraordinary Renditions

When U.S. agents apprehend a suspected terrorist in another country, one of the choices available is to hand that person off to a third country which can imprison or otherwise disable that person from committing a harmful act. The process of handing a person off to another country pursuant to that country's criminal processes is known as "rendition." Beginning in the 1990s, the CIA handed a number of suspected terrorists off to other countries. This process became known as "extraordinary rendition" — extraordinary because the accused never set foot in the U.S.

This practice came to light in 2005. Some persons were allegedly sent to countries in which they would be severely mistreated, if not actually tortured. The Convention Against Torture article 3 provides:

> No State Party shall expel, return, or extradite a person to another State where there are substantial grounds for believing that he would be in danger of being subjected to torture.

The torture issue is explored in Chapter 9 (*see El-Masri v. United States, infra* § 9.01[B]2 and *Arar v. Ashcroft, infra* § 9.02).

Among the incidents that upset both U.S. civil libertarians and some European nations were the apprehension of suspects in Europe and their rendition to other nations where they were allegedly mistreated. These incidents are explored in a report from a special committee of the European Union, to which one answer was that of Michael Scheuer below.

At the recommendation of the special committee, the European Parliament adopted this resolution on February 14, 2007:

EUROPEAN PARLIAMENT RESOLUTION
on the alleged use of European countries by the CIA for the
transportation and illegal detention of prisoners

The European Parliament:

2. Considers that after 11 September 2001, the so-called 'war on terror' — in its excesses — has produced a serious and dangerous erosion of human rights and fundamental freedoms;

3. Is convinced that the rights of the individual and full respect for human rights contribute to security; considers it necessary that in the relationship between the need for security and the rights of individuals, human rights must always be fully respected, ensuring that suspected terrorists are tried and sentenced while due process is observed;

8. Calls on the Council and the Member States to issue a clear and forceful declaration calling on the U.S. Administration to put an end to the practice of extraordinary arrests and renditions, in line with the position of Parliament;

9. Deplores the fact that the governments of European countries did not feel the need to ask the U.S. administration for clarifications regarding the existence of secret prisons outside U.S. territory;

15. Stresses the serious and rigorous work undertaken by the judicial authorities of Italy, Germany and Spain concerning the allegations which fall within the remit of the Temporary Committee, and invites the judicial authorities in other Member States to act similarly on the basis of the substantial information made available by the Temporary Committee;

18. Recognises that some information in this report, including the existence of secret CIA prisons, comes from official or unofficial U.S. sources, demonstrating the vitality and self-policing inherent in the U.S. democracy;

36. Recalls that the programme of extraordinary rendition is an extra-judicial practice which contravenes established international human rights standards and whereby an individual suspected of involvement in terrorism is illegally abducted, arrested and/or transferred into the custody of U.S. officials and/or transported to another country for interrogation which, in the majority of cases, involves *incommunicado* detention and torture;

39. Condemns extraordinary rendition as an illegal instrument used by the United States in the fight against terrorism; condemns, further, the acceptance and concealing of the practice, on several occasions, by the secret services and governmental authorities of certain European countries.

Michael F. Scheuer
Former Chief, bin Laden Unit, CIA
Statement before the House Committee on Foreign Affairs
April 17, 2007

The Rendition Program

The CIA's Rendition Program began in late summer, 1995. I authored it, and then ran and managed it against al-Qaeda leaders and other Sunni Islamists from August, 1995, until June, 1999.

A.) There were only two goals from the program:

1.) Take men off the street who were planning or had been involved in attacks on U.S. or its allies.

2.) Seize hard-copy or electric documents in their possession when arrested; Americans were never expected to read them.

3.) Interrogation was never a goal under President Clinton. Why?

— Because it would be a foreign intelligence or security service without CIA present or in control.

— Because the take from the interrogation would be filtered by the service holding the individual, and we would never know if it was complete or distorted.

— Because torture might be used and the information might be simply what an individual thought we wanted to hear.

B.) The Rendition Program was initiated because President Clinton, and Messrs. Lake, Berger, and Clarke requested that the CIA begin to attack and dismantle AQ. These men made it clear that they did not want to bring those captured to the U.S. and hold them in U.S. custody.

1.) President Clinton and his national security team directed the CIA to take each captured al-Qaeda leader to the country which had an outstanding legal process for him. This was a hard-and-fast rule which greatly restricted CIA's ability to confront al-Qaeda because we could only focus on al-Qaeda leaders who were wanted somewhere. As a result many al-Qaeda fighters we knew were dangerous to America could not be captured.

2.) CIA warned the president and the National Security Council that the U.S. State Department had and would identify the countries to which the captured fighters were being delivered as human rights abusers.

3.) In response, President Clinton et al. asked if CIA could get each receiving country to guarantee that it would treat the person according to its own laws. This was no problem and we did so.

— I have read and been told that Mr. Clinton, Mr. Burger, and Mr. Clarke have said since 9/11 that they insisted that each receiving country treat the rendered person it received according to U.S. legal standards. To the best of my memory that is a lie.

C.) After 9/11, and under President Bush, rendered al-Qaeda operatives have most often been kept in U.S. custody. The goals of the program remained the same, although Mr. Bush's national security team wanted to use U.S. officers to interrogate captured al-Qaeda fighters.

1.) This decision by the Bush administration allowed CIA to capture al-Qaeda fighters we knew were a threat to the United States without on all occasions being dependent on the availability of another country's outstanding legal process. This decision made the already successful Rendition Program even more effective.

D.) The following particulars about the Rendition Program may be of interest to you.

1.) From its start until today, the Program was focused on senior al-Qaeda leaders and not aimed at the rank-and-file members. With only limited manpower to conduct the Rendition Program, CIA wanted to inflict as much damage on al-Qaeda as possible and therefore focused on senior leaders, financiers, terrorist operators, field commanders, strategists, and logisticians.

2.) To the best of my knowledge, not a single target of rendition has ever been kidnapped by CIA officers. The claims to the contrary by the Swedish government regarding Mr. Aghiza and his associate, and those by the Italian government regarding Abu Omar, are either misstatements or lies by those governments.

— Indeed, it is passing strange that European leaders are here today to complain about very successful and security enhancing U.S. Government counterterrorism operations, when their European Union (EU) presides over the earth's single largest terrorist safe haven, and has done so for a quarter century. The EU's policy of easily attainable political asylum and its prohibition against deporting wanted or convicted terrorists to country's with the death penalty have made Europe a major, consistent, and invulnerable source of terrorist threat to the United States.

3.)   Each and every target of a rendition was vetted by a battery of lawyers at CIA and not infrequently by lawyers at the National Security Council and the Department of Justice. For each rendition target, I, and then my successors as the chief of the bin Laden/al-Qaeda operations, had to prepare and present a written brief citing and explaining the intelligence information that made the rendition target a threat to the United States and/or its allies. If the brief persuaded the lawyers, the operation went ahead. If the brief was insufficient, the lawyers disapproved and no operation was conducted against that target until additional reliable evidence was collected.

—   Let me be very explicit and precise on this point. Not one single al-Qaeda leader has ever been rendered on the basis of any CIA officer's "hunch" or "guess" or "caprice." There are scurrilous accusations that became fashionable after the Washington Post's correspondent Dana Priest revealed information that damaged U.S. national security and, as a result, won a journalism prize for abetting America's enemies, and when such lamentable politicians as Senators McCain, Rockefeller, Graham, and Levin following Ms. Priest's lead and began to attack the men and women of CIA who had risked their lives to protect America under the direct orders of two U.S. presidents and with the full knowledge of the intelligence committees of the United States Congress. Both Ms. Priest and the gentlemen just mentioned have behaved disgracefully, and ought to publicly apologize to the CIA's men and women who have executed the Rendition Program.

4.)   To proceed, the Rendition Program has been the single most effective counter-terrorism operation ever conducted by the United States government. Americans are safer today because of the program, but that degree of safety will ebb as the Senators just mentioned slowly but surely destroy the program. If there are those in this Congress, in the media, in this country, or in Europe who believe that we would be safer if Khalid Shaykh Muhammed, Abu Zubaydah, Mr. Hambali, Ibn Shaykh al-Libi, Khalid bin Attash, and several dozen other senior al-Qaeda leaders were still free and on the street, then the educational systems and the reservoirs of common sense on both sides of the Atlantic are in much more dilapidated shape than I thought.

5.)   On the issue of how rendered al-Qaeda leaders have been treated in prison, I am unable to speak with authority about the conditions these men found in the Middle Eastern prison they were delivered to at President Clinton's direction. I would not, however, be surprised if their treatment was not up U.S. standards, but this is a matter of no concern as the Rendition Program's goal was to protect America and the rendered fighters delivered to Middle Eastern governments are now either dead or in places from which they cannot harm America. Mission accomplished, as the saying goes.

—   Under President Bush, the rendered al-Qaeda fighters held in U.S. custody have been treated according to guidelines that were crafted by U.S. government lawyers, approved by the Executive Branch, and briefed to and permitted by at least the four senior members of the two congressional intelligence oversight committees.

6.)   Finally, I will close by saying that mistakes may well have been made during my tenure as the chief of CIA's bin Laden operations, and, if there were errors, they are my responsibility. Intelligence information is not the equivalent of courtroom-quality evidence, and it never will be. But I will again stress that no rendition target was ever approved or captured without a written brief composed of intelligence information that persuaded competent U.S. government legal authorities. If mistakes were made, I can only say that that is tough, but war is a tough and confusing business, and a well-supported chance to take action and protect Americans should always trump other considerations, especially pedantic worries about whether or not the intelligence data is air tight.

— To destroy the Rendition Program because of a mistake or two or more would be to sacrifice the protection of Americans to venal and prize-hungry reporters like Ms. Priest, grandstanding politicians like those mentioned above, and effete sanctimonious Europeans who take every bit of American protection offered them while publicly damning and seeking jail time for those who risk their lives to provide the protection. If the Rendition Program is halted, we will truly be able to say, by paraphrasing the late film actor John Wayne, that War is tough, but it is a lot tougher if you are deliberately stupid.

On July 20, 2007, President Bush signed an Executive Order authorizing C.I.A. detention and interrogation of suspected terrorists or "an alien detainee who could assist in detecting, mitigating, or preventing terrorist attacks." The matter of rendition to third countries should be reconsidered in conjunction with interrogation methods. *See* § 9.01, *infra*.

I hereby determine that a program of detention and interrogation approved by the Director of the Central Intelligence Agency fully complies with the obligations of the United States under Common Article 3, provided that:

(i) the conditions of confinement and interrogation practices of the program do not include:

(A) torture, as defined in section 2340 of title 18, United States Code;

(B) any of the acts prohibited by section 2441(d) of title 18, United States Code, including murder, torture, cruel or inhuman treatment, mutilation or maiming, intentionally causing serious bodily injury, rape, sexual assault or abuse, taking of hostages, or performing of biological experiments;

(E) willful and outrageous acts of personal abuse done for the purpose of humiliating or degrading the individual in a manner so serious that any reasonable person, considering the circumstances, would deem the acts to be beyond the bounds of human decency, such as sexual or sexually indecent acts undertaken for the purpose of humiliation, forcing the individual to perform sexual acts or to pose sexually, threatening the individual with sexual mutilation, or using the individual as a human shield; or

(F) acts intended to denigrate the religion, religious practices, or religious objects of the individual.

§ 2.03 WORLD TRADE CENTER I

We will read three terrorism conspiracy cases, two of which involve the New York cells responsible for the first World Trade Center bombing and various other criminal plots. You might try to diagram the structure of these "conspiracies" to see how well they conform to the models, an exercise which will then be useful in assessing whether it is fair to introduce evidence of activity by one person when the other "co-conspirators" had no idea who he was or what he was doing. At what point does the evidence get too far removed from the inferential knowledge of each defendant? or becomes overwhelmingly lopsided in light of what a particular defendant should have known?

The first bombing of the World Trade Center, claimed by the "Islamic Group" of Sheikh Abdel Rahman ("the blind Sheikh" of Brooklyn) occurred in February 1993 and resulted in three separate prosecutions.[2] Ramzi Yousef, the alleged mastermind of that specific incident, fled the U.S. but was brought back after capture in Pakistan for trial on other charges (see § 2.02[A], above). The four defendants in the *Salameh* case below were tried for various levels of involvement in a conspiracy to "bomb structures used in interstate commerce" and related charges. Sheikh Rahman and a number of others were then prosecuted for somewhat more peripheral connections to this incident and for a more broad-reaching charge of "seditious conspiracy" consisting of "levying war against the United States."

Conspiracy cases consistently refer to the concept of vicarious liability known as the Pinkerton Doctrine. *Pinkerton v. United States*, 328 U.S. 640 (1946), established several propositions regarding the law of conspiracy. One of the most important is the proposition that a person may be convicted of conspiracy without knowing the details of what others are planning to do. Agreement to commit a *category* of offense may produce liability for all members of the conspiracy when any one of the members commits an overt act of the type contemplated. "An overt act of one partner may be the act of all without any new agreement specifically directed to that act."

Pinkerton also confirms that conspiracy is an offense separate and apart from the "substantive" crimes contemplated. Thus, there is no double jeopardy involved in prosecution for the agreement as well as for the criminal act. And, thirdly, conspiracy is an inchoate offense that is punishable even if no physical harm ever occurs to a victim. "For two or more to confederate and combine together to commit or cause to be committed a breach of the criminal laws, is an offense of the gravest character, sometimes quite outweighing, in injury to the public, the mere commission of the contemplated crime. It involves deliberate plotting to subvert the laws, educating and preparing the conspirators for further and habitual criminal practices. And it is characterized by secrecy, rendering it difficult of detection, requiring more time for its discovery, and adding to the importance of punishing it when discovered."

UNITED STATES v. SALAMEH
152 F.3d 88 (2d Cir. 1998)

Before MESKILL, MCLAUGHLIN, and CALABRESI, CIRCUIT JUDGES.

PER CURIAM.

Following a lengthy jury trial, defendants were convicted of various crimes related to the bombing of the World Trade Center Complex in New York City. Defendants now appeal, asserting a congeries of arguments. For the reasons that follow, we affirm the judgment of the district court but remand for re-sentencing and decline to exercise jurisdiction over certain post-trial motions pending before the district court.

BACKGROUND

On April 24, 1992, Ahmad Mohammad Ajaj departed from his home in Houston, Texas, and traveled to the Middle East to attend a terrorist training camp, known as "Camp Khaldan," on the Afghanistan-Pakistan border. There he learned how to construct homemade explosive devices. During his time in Pakistan, Ajaj met Ramzi Ahmed Yousef. Together the two plotted to use their newly acquired skills to bomb targets in the United States.

In the fall of 1992, after formulating a terrorist plan, Ajaj and Yousef traveled to New York under assumed names. Ajaj carried with him a "terrorist kit" that he and Yousef had assembled in Pakistan. The kit included, among other things, handwritten notes Ajaj had taken while attending explosives courses, manuals containing formulae

---

[2] On October 26, 2005, a state jury found the Port Authority of New York to have been negligent in failing to take measures to secure the basement parking facility of the World Trade Center. Plaintiffs persuaded the jury that the property owner was alerted by experts to security concerns and failed to respond adequately.

and instructions for manufacturing bombs, materials describing how to carry-off a successful terrorist operation, videotapes advocating terrorist action against the United States, and fraudulent identification documents.

On September 1, 1992, Ajaj and Yousef, using false names and passports, arrived at John F. Kennedy International Airport in New York. At customs, INS inspectors discovered that Ajaj's passport had been altered and, consequently, they searched his belongings. Upon discovery of the "terrorist kit," Ajaj became belligerent. The INS seized Ajaj's "terrorist kit" and placed him under arrest. Ajaj was later indicted in the United States District Court for the Eastern District of New York for passport fraud. He pled guilty and was sentenced to six months' imprisonment.

During Ajaj's encounter with the INS inspectors, he denied that he was traveling with Yousef, who proceeded unmolested to the secondary inspection area where he presented an Iraqi passport and claimed political asylum. Yousef was arrested for entering the United States without a visa. Eventually he was released on his own recognizance.

Once in New York, Yousef assembled a team of trusted criminal associates, including Mohammed Salameh, Nidal Ayyad, Mahmoud Abouhalima and Abdul Rahman Yasin. Together, the conspirators implemented the bombing plot that Ajaj and Yousef had hatched overseas. Ayyad and Salameh opened a joint bank account into which they deposited funds to finance the bombing plot. Some of that money was later used by Salameh to rent a storage shed in Jersey City, New Jersey, where the conspirators stored chemicals for making explosives. Yousef also drew on that account to pay for materials described in Ajaj's manuals as ingredients for bomb making.

The first target of the conspirators' plot was the World Trade Center. Ayyad used his position as an engineer at Allied Signal, a large New Jersey chemical company, to order the necessary chemical ingredients for bomb making, and to order hydrogen tanks from ALG Welding Company that would enhance the bomb's destructive force. Abouhalima obtained "smokeless powder," which the conspirators used to make explosives. Smokeless powder, and all the other chemicals procured by the conspirators for the bomb, were stored in the shed rented by Salameh.

Abouhalima helped Salameh and Yousef find a ground floor apartment at 40 Pamrapo Avenue in Jersey City. The apartment fit the specifications in Ajaj's manuals for an ideal base of operations. In the 40 Pamrapo apartment, Abouhalima, Salameh, Yousef and Yasin mixed the chemicals for the World Trade Center bomb, following Ajaj's formulae. Abouhalima also obtained a telephone calling card, which the conspirators used to contact each other and to call various chemical companies for bomb ingredients.

During this entire period, although Ajaj remained incarcerated, he kept in telephone contact with Yousef. By doing so, Ajaj stayed abreast of the conspirators' progress in carrying out the terrorist plot and attempted to get his "terrorist kit" into Yousef's hands. Because Ajaj was in jail and his telephone calls were monitored, Ajaj and Yousef spoke in code when discussing the bomb plot.

On February 23, 1993, Salameh rented a yellow van at DIB Leasing, a Ryder dealership in Jersey City. The conspirators loaded their homemade bomb into that van. On February 26, 1993, the conspirators drove the bomb-laden van into a below-ground parking lot on the B-2 level of the World Trade Center Complex and, using a timer, set the bomb to detonate. At 12:18 p.m., the bomb exploded, killing six people, injuring over a thousand others, and causing hundreds of millions of dollars in damage.

After the explosion, Ayyad took credit for the bombing on behalf of the conspirators by, among other things, writing an anonymous letter to the New York Times explaining that the attack was undertaken in retaliation for American support of Israel. The letter threatened future terrorist "missions."

Immediately after the bombing, Yousef, Abouhalima and Yasin fled the country.

Abouhalima was apprehended in Egypt prior to the trial and turned over to federal agents by Egyptian authorities, but Yousef and Yasin remained fugitives. Salameh arranged to flee as well, but was arrested the day before he planned to depart when he made the ludicrous mistake of going back to the Ryder truck rental office to get his rental deposit back. On March 1, 1993, Ajaj completed his term of imprisonment on the passport fraud conviction and was released. Approximately one week later, on March 9, Ajaj was taken into government custody on an INS detainer.

In September 1993, Ayyad, Abouhalima, Ajaj, Salameh, Yousef and Yasin were indicted in the United States District Court for the Southern District of New York (Duffy, J.), on various charges relating to their participation in the plot to bomb the World Trade Center. Yousef and Yasin were still fugitives at the time of trial. [Yousef was captured in Pakistan on or about February 8, 1995. He was tried and convicted in 1997. As of March 2005, Yasin remains a fugitive. He is an interesting character who may have severed his connections with terrorist organizations while living in Iraq for the last decade. *See* http://www.trackingthethreat.com/content/entities/ent1007.htm]

The trial lasted six months and involved over 1000 exhibits and the testimony of more than 200 witnesses. The defendants were convicted on all counts and each was sentenced to 240 years' imprisonment. Defendants now appeal their convictions and sentences, raising a variety of issues.

I. Suppression Motions

A. *Motions to Suppress Materials Seized from Ajaj*

1. Ajaj's Motion

Ajaj claims that Judge Duffy should have suppressed the terrorist materials seized from him at Kennedy Airport. He maintains that the materials were obtained and then held pursuant to an illegal grand jury subpoena. Ajaj's argument has no merit.

On October 6, 1992, Ajaj pled guilty in the United States District Court for the Eastern District of New York (Raggi, J.) to one count of passport fraud. After the guilty plea, Judge Raggi ordered the government to return Ajaj's belongings or to come forward with a reason for failing to do so.

On December 22, 1992, an Assistant United States Attorney for the Eastern District of New York served a grand jury subpoena on Ajaj calling for production of many of the terrorist materials seized at Kennedy Airport. Although the subpoena purported to be a subpoena *ad testificandum*, it was accompanied by a *duces tecum* rider that specified the materials Ajaj was ordered to produce. When Ajaj's counsel in the passport fraud case inquired whether the subpoena really sought Ajaj's testimony as well as the evidence listed in the rider, the government explained that the subpoena sought only the specified evidence. Ajaj did not move to quash the subpoena.

After Ajaj learned that the government was planning to introduce the terrorist materials in the World Trade Center bombing trial, he moved to suppress the materials held pursuant to the grand jury subpoena. Ajaj argued that the subpoena was illegal since: (1) Ajaj could not have been under investigation when the subpoena was issued because it was issued after the completion of the passport fraud case but before the World Trade Center was bombed; and (2) the subpoena was a subpoena *ad testificandum*, not a subpoena *duces tecum*. Judge Duffy denied Ajaj's motion to suppress, finding that the use of the subpoena was proper. Ajaj renews his claim on appeal.

It is "improper for the government to use a grand jury subpoena 'for the sole or dominant purpose of preparing for trial.'" *United States v. Sasso*, 59 F.3d 341, 351 (2d Cir. 1995). However, "where there [is] some proper dominant purpose for the postindictment subpoena . . . the government is not barred from introducing evidence obtained thereby."

Ajaj failed to present any proof that the government misused the grand jury subpoena. He maintains that the subpoena had no legitimate purpose because in December 1992, when the subpoena was issued, his passport fraud prosecution was over and the World Trade Center had not yet been bombed. He therefore posits that he could not have been under investigation when the subpoena was issued and therefore that the sole purpose of the subpoena was to circumvent Judge Raggi's order for the return of the materials.

The government presented evidence that demonstrated a proper purpose for the grand jury subpoena. It consisted primarily of an affidavit from the Assistant United States Attorney who prepared the subpoena, explaining that the materials seized from Ajaj were used in a joint FBI-NYPD investigation of terrorism. The affidavit further noted that the subpoena was not connected to the Eastern District passport fraud case. This evidence established that the subpoena had a proper purpose.

2. Abouhalima's Motion

Judge Duffy admitted some of the materials seized from Ajaj into evidence against all the defendants. Abouhalima argues that the admission of Ajaj's terrorist materials violated Federal Rule of Evidence 403, and his rights under the First Amendment of the Constitution.

a. Rule 403

The trial judge admitted the following terrorist materials seized from Ajaj into evidence against all the defendants: (1) a videotape of the bombing of an American embassy which also provided instruction on how to make explosives and timing devices; (2) Ajaj's handwritten notebooks on how to make explosives (including urea nitrate) and improvised weapons; (3) a videotape containing a chemistry lesson on manufacturing explosives; (4) manuals on catalysts, detonators and other bomb ingredients; (5) a document entitled "Facing the enemies of God — terrorism is a religious duty and force is necessary," which urged acts of terrorism against the enemies of Islam; and (6) a book entitled "Rapid Destruction and Demolition," which described the destruction of buildings and contained a formula for using explosives to accomplish this end.

In addition, Judge Duffy admitted copies of: (1) "Facing the enemies of God"; and (2) "Rapid Destruction and Demolition" that were recovered from Abouhalima's residence. The copy of "Rapid Destruction and Demolition" found in Abouhalima's residence bore his fingerprint on the page containing the formula for destroying buildings with explosives. Abouhalima argues that Judge Duffy should not have admitted these terrorist materials because they were highly prejudicial and lacked probative value. He is incorrect.

Under Rule 403, relevant evidence may be excluded when its probative value is "substantially outweighed by the danger of unfair prejudice, confusion of the issues, or misleading the jury, or by considerations of undue delay, waste of time, or needless presentation of cumulative evidence." A district court is obviously in the best position to do the balancing mandated by Rule 403. We will second-guess a district court "only if there is a clear showing that the court abused its discretion or acted arbitrarily or irrationally." To avoid acting arbitrarily, the district court must make a "conscientious assessment" of whether unfair prejudice substantially outweighs probative value.

Although it does not bear directly on the charged elements of a crime, evidence offered to prove motive is commonly admitted. In addition, evidence that provides background information necessary to the jury's understanding of the nature of the conspiratorial agreement properly is admitted "to furnish an explanation of the understanding or intent with which certain acts were performed."

Where a defendant is a member of a conspiracy, all the evidence admitted to prove that conspiracy, even evidence relating to acts committed by co-defendants, is admissible against the defendant.

The record amply demonstrates that Judge Duffy made a "conscientious assessment" of the proffered evidence and properly determined that unfair prejudice did not substantially outweigh the probative value of these materials. Before admitting any materials, Judge Duffy scrupulously reviewed each item and heard extensive argument from counsel. Having heard both sides, Judge Duffy excluded a number of the materials seized from Ajaj as unduly prejudicial. The materials that were admitted established the existence of the conspiracy to bomb American targets and demonstrated the defendants' intent and motivation to use violence to protest American foreign policy in the Middle East.

For example, the documents seized from Ajaj provided instruction on: (1) constructing bombs; (2) mixing explosives; and (3) using bombs to destroy buildings. Specific pages of these materials contained formulae for the same explosives that were used to construct the World Trade Center bomb, and Ajaj's and Yousef's fingerprints were found on those pages. Moreover, traces of those same explosives were found in the homes of, and on objects linked to, Yousef, Abouhalima, Salameh and Ayyad. Thus, the terrorist materials provided circumstantial proof of a connection among the conspirators and their familiarity with bomb making and the use of explosives.

In addition, the copies of "Facing the enemies of God," and "Rapid Destruction and Demolition," that were recovered from Abouhalima's residence linked the conspirators. The copy of "Rapid Destruction and Demolition" seized from Abouhalima bore his fingerprint on the page containing the formula for destroying buildings with explosives. Under the circumstances, the fact that Ajaj and Abouhalima both possessed the same documents was probative of their relationship as co-conspirators.

The materials possessed by both Ajaj and Abouhalima bristled with strong anti-American sentiment and advocated violence against targets in the United States. These same themes were expressed in a letter attributed to another co-conspirator, Ayyad, that was sent to the New York Times in the aftermath of the bombing. The materials, in addition to establishing a link between the co-conspirators, evidenced the conspiracy's motive and intent to bomb targets in the United States. In addition, the materials provided the jury with background and "an explanation of the understanding or intent with which certain acts were performed."

Furthermore, the materials had probative value in light of their similarity to the actual bombing. As Judge Duffy recognized, one videotape admitted in evidence showed a man driving a truck into a building that was flying an American flag. The building was then demolished in an explosion. The videotape thus closely resembled the actual events at the World Trade Center and provided further evidence of motive and intent.

The sulphurous anti-American sentiments expressed in the terrorist materials no doubt threatened to prejudice the jury against the defendants. However, Judge Duffy did not abuse his discretion by concluding that the significant probative value of this evidence was not substantially outweighed by the danger of unfair prejudice.

b. First Amendment

Abouhalima argues also that the admission of Ajaj's terrorist materials violated Abouhalima's First Amendment rights. Ajaj's possession of the terrorist materials, Abouhalima contends, was used as the basis for an inference that Abouhalima and the other conspirators engaged in criminal acts. It is difficult to comprehend this argument since it is beyond cavil that "the First Amendment . . . does not prohibit the evidentiary use of speech to establish the elements of a crime or to prove motive or intent." Neither Ajaj nor Abouhalima was prosecuted for possessing or reading terrorist materials. The materials seized from Ajaj were used appropriately to prove the existence of the bombing conspiracy and its motive. Moreover, any prejudicial effect they might have had was ameliorated by the trial court's instruction that mere possession of the literature is not illegal and that the defendants' political beliefs were not on trial.

B. Motion to Suppress Contents of the Storage Shed

At trial, the government introduced homemade nitroglycerine and large quantities of bomb making ingredients seized from a storage shed (the "Shed"), at the Space Station storage facility in Jersey City (the "Space Station"). Salameh argues that Judge Duffy should have suppressed this evidence. Salameh is wrong.

On March 5, 1993, a Magistrate Judge in the District of New Jersey issued a search warrant for the Shed. Probable cause for the warrant was based upon an affidavit of FBI Special Agent Eric Pilker.

Before trial, Salameh moved to suppress the evidence from the Shed on the ground that Pilker's affidavit did not establish probable cause for the search. Salameh also requested a hearing to test alleged misstatements in Pilker's affidavit. Judge Duffy denied the motion to suppress as well as the requested hearing, finding that: (1) Salameh lacked standing to contest the search; (2) there was probable cause for the search warrant; and (3) even if the warrant was not supported by probable cause, the search was proper because it was conducted in good faith reliance on the search warrant. Because we agree that there was both probable cause and good faith, we need not and do not address the standing argument.

1. Probable Cause

In deciding whether probable cause exists for a search warrant, a judge must determine whether "there is a fair probability that contraband or evidence of a crime will be found in a particular place." "Only the probability, and not the prima facie showing, of criminal activity is the standard of probable cause." In assessing the proof of probable cause, the government's affidavit in support of the search warrant must be read as a whole, and construed realistically.

Pilker's affidavit in support of the search warrant stated that an explosion had occurred at the World Trade Center, and that an FBI explosives expert had determined that it was caused by a bomb. The affidavit also related that the expert knew from examining an auto part recovered at the crime scene that the part belonged to whatever vehicle carried the bomb. Using the part's vehicle identification number, investigators traced it to a yellow Ford Econoline 350 van registered in Alabama to the Ryder Truck Rental Company and leased by Mohammad Salameh from a rental office in Jersey City for a one-week period beginning three days before the explosion.

Elsewhere in the affidavit, Pilker related that a Space Station employee informed the FBI that storage shed number 4344 was under lease to "Kamil Ibrahim." The employee told the FBI that on February 25, 1993, one day before the bombing, he observed "Kamil Ibrahim," along with other males, making numerous trips to the Shed using a yellow Ryder van. Moreover, the same Space Station employee stated that on March 4, 1993, less than one week after the bombing, he entered the Shed and observed containers marked "sulfuric acid," "nitric acid" and "urea." A forensic chemist at the Bureau of Alcohol, Tobacco and Firearms informed the FBI that those three substances could be combined to produce a powerful bomb.

Finally, the affidavit described that, when renting the Ryder van, Salameh had given a telephone number that belonged to someone named Jodie Hadas at 34 Kensington Avenue, Apt. 4, in Jersey City. When investigators searched that apartment on March 4, 1993, they found tools, wiring and manuals concerning antennae, circuitry and electromagnetic devices. A law enforcement bomb technician advised the FBI that these items indicated that a bomb maker lived in that apartment.

Cumulatively, this evidence provided ample probable cause to believe that the Shed contained evidence of the World Trade Center bombing.

II. PROCEDURAL MOTIONS

A. Abouhalima — Severance

Abouhalima argues that the district court deprived him of a constitutionally fair trial by denying his pretrial motion for a severance. Specifically, Abouhalima first claims that absent severance, he was harmed by the admission and the subsequent "spillover" effect of "holy war" literature and video tapes that were seized from Ajaj at Kennedy Airport in September 1992 [the six items listed above].

Next, Abouhalima argues that through the joinder, he was prejudiced by Salameh's closing argument, where Salameh purportedly asserted a defense antagonistic to his own. In this regard, as part of his defense, Abouhalima refused to concede either that a bomb had caused the World Trade Center explosion, or that he had any association with Yousef. Salameh, on the other hand, conceded not only the existence of a bomb, but argued that he was an unwitting dupe of Yousef, who had masterminded the bombing. Because the government had characterized Yousef as Abouhalima's close associate, Abouhalima avers that Salameh's summation undermined his defense of not knowingly participating in the conspiracy.

We find no basis for reversal. "There is a preference in the federal system for joint trials of defendants who are indicted together." "It would impair both the efficiency and the fairness of the criminal justice system to require . . . that prosecutors bring separate proceedings, presenting the same evidence again and again, requiring victims and witnesses to repeat the inconvenience (and sometimes trauma) of testifying, and randomly favoring the last-tried defendants who have the advantage of knowing the prosecution's case beforehand." *Richardson v. Marsh*, 481 U.S. 200, 210 (1987).

1. Ajaj's Holy War Materials

The admission of Ajaj's "holy war" materials did not result in prejudicial spillover as to Abouhalima. Therefore, the district court did not err in denying severance. A defendant's claim that he was prejudiced by the admission of evidence at a joint conspiracy trial is insupportable when the evidence would have been admissible against him in a separate trial alone as a member of the conspiracy. "Prejudice" occurs in joint trials when proof inadmissible against a defendant becomes a part of his trial solely due to the presence of co-defendants as to whom its admission is proper. This is an unlikely occurrence when all the defendants are charged under the same conspiracy count.

In the present case, Ajaj and Abouhalima were alleged to have participated in a common plan or scheme and were tried under the same conspiracy count. As we have already discussed in connection with co-appellant Ayyad, the materials seized from Ajaj at Kennedy Airport were properly admitted as background evidence to establish the nature and scope of the conspiracy and to establish the motive and intent of the conspirators, namely, a desire to use violence to effect change in American foreign policy in the Middle East. Additionally, the materials were admissible to link Abouhalima to the conspiracy, as two of the terrorist publications seized from Ajaj were identical to the publications found in Abouhalima's apartment. Because each of the items would have been admitted against Abouhalima had he been tried alone, they were properly admitted against Abouhalima in the joint trial and there is no prejudicial "spillover." Consequently, Abouhalima has not shown that the district court erred in denying his pretrial motion for a severance, let alone an abuse of discretion and a miscarriage of justice.

2. Salameh's Summation

We find no prejudice to Abouhalima arising from Salameh's summation. " 'Mutually antagonistic' or 'irreconcilable' defenses may be so prejudicial in some circumstances as to mandate severance." In order to make a showing of "mutually antagonistic" or "irreconcilable defenses," the defendant must make a factual demonstration that "acceptance of one party's defense would tend to preclude the acquittal of [the] other." However, "mutually antagonistic defenses are not prejudicial per se. Moreover, Rule 14 does not require severance even if prejudice is shown; rather, it leaves the tailoring of the relief to be granted, if any, to the district court's sound discretion." *Zafiro v. United States*, 506 U.S. 534, 538–39 (1993) (where two co-defendants both claim they are innocent and each accuses the other of the crime, district court did not err in denying motion for severance).

Throughout the trial in this case, all four defendants challenged the government's case without attempting to accuse one another. Unlike Abouhalima, during summation Salameh abandoned his trial strategy of disputing that a bomb had caused the explosion and argued that he was nothing more that an unwitting dupe of Yousef, who had masterminded the bombing. While the defense asserted by Salameh was, in the end, inconsistent with Abouhalima's defense, at no time did Salameh argue or suggest that Abouhalima was involved in the bombing, or directly contradict Abouhalima's defense strategy. Salameh and Abouhalima both claimed to be innocent of the charges and neither's claim of innocence required the jury to find the other guilty.

B. Abouhalima — Involuntariness of Statement

Abouhalima made two incriminating remarks during his post-arrest interview. Specifically, shortly after being taken into United States' custody [in Egypt], Abouhalima was informed that he was under arrest for his participation in the World Trade Center bombing. Once FBI agents advised him of his constitutional rights, they interviewed him about the apartment at 40 Pamrapo. During the interview, Abouhalima asked an officer whether he knew an individual by the name of "Rashid." Yousef's nickname was "Rashed." Abouhalima also corrected an FBI agent's pronunciation of "Pamrapo."

Abouhalima now argues that we should direct the district court on remand to reconsider Abouhalima's motion to suppress his post-arrest remarks. Specifically, Abouhalima asserts that his comments were given involuntarily and without a valid Miranda waiver because they followed ten days of incarceration and torture in Egypt.

In the present case, while it is reasonable that Egyptian incarceration and torture, if true, would likely weaken one's mental state, one's mental state does not become part of the calculus for the suppression of evidence unless there is an allegation that agents of the United States engaged in some type of coercion. Because Abouhalima does not contend that federal agents either mentally or physically coerced his remarks during that interrogation, there is no basis for inquiry into a possible constitutional violation. "Only if we were to establish a brand new constitutional right — the right of a criminal defendant to confess to his crime only when totally rational and properly motivated — could respondent's present claim be sustained." *Colorado v. Connelly*, 479 U.S. 157, 166 (1986).

C. Elements of the Charged Conspiracy

Abouhalima next assails the district court's denial of his request to charge concerning the intent required to be convicted of the conspiracy. Specifically, in Abouhalima's request to charge, he averred that, based on the conspiracy as charged in the indictment, the government was required to prove specific knowledge and intent to bomb the World Trade Center. The district court disagreed and instead instructed the jury that for purposes of unlawful intent, the object of the conspiracy "is not restricted to a particular building." Abouhalima argues that the district court's instruction was error because it invited the jury to convict him without finding the mental element of the crime charged. Furthermore, Abouhalima asserts that the indictment's repeated references to the World Trade Center and the government's repeated references to that complex during opening statements and summation required the government to prove a specific conspiracy to bomb the World Trade Center.

It is well settled that the essential elements of the crime of conspiracy are: (1) that the defendant agreed with at least one other person to commit an offense; (2) the defendant knowingly participated in the conspiracy with the specific intent to commit the offenses that were the objects of the conspiracy; and (3) that during the existence of the conspiracy, at least one of the overt acts set forth in the indictment was committed by one or more of the members of the conspiracy in furtherance of the objectives of the conspiracy.

The indictment does not charge the defendants with conspiring to bomb the World Trade Center. The indictment alleges that the defendants conspired "to commit offenses against the United States." Four objectives of the conspiracy, each a separate bombing violation, are alleged as follows: (i) to bomb buildings used in or affecting interstate and foreign commerce, (ii) to bomb property and vehicles owned by the United States, (iii) to transport explosives interstate for the purpose of bombing buildings, vehicles, and other property, and (iv) to bomb automobiles used in interstate commerce. The World Trade Center bombing is not listed as an object of the conspiracy, but merely as one of 31 overt acts alleged to have been committed in furtherance of the conspiracy. Consequently, because the World Trade Center bombing is not alleged as an objective of the conspiracy, the district court did not err in refusing to charge the jury that specific knowledge and intent was required with respect to that bombing.

Consistent with the indictment, the government argued to the jury that the defendants engaged in a conspiracy to bomb buildings, vehicles and property in the United States and the World Trade Center bombing was one act committed in furtherance of the overall conspiracy.

Aside from the unprecedented nature of Abouhalima's argument, those multiple references to the World Trade Center bombing were due to the fact that most of the substantive crimes charged in the indictment stemmed from that bombing. In any event, the proof at trial demonstrated that the conspiracy encompassed considerably more than just the bombing of the World Trade Center, including: (1) the existence of additional chemicals recovered from the Shed after the bombing; (2) the modified timing device found in Ayyad's home; and (3) Ayyad's continuing attempts to procure additional explosive chemicals after the bombing. The most definitive proof of the broad scope of the conspiracy and the defendants' intent to commit additional bombings after the World Trade Center was the letter sent to the New York Times claiming responsibility for the bombing and the similar draft letter retrieved from an erased file on Ayyad's computer disk, both of which speak to future acts of terrorism.

The government is not required to demonstrate that the defendant agreed to all of the conspiracy's objectives, as long as the defendant shared "some knowledge of the [conspiracy's] unlawful aims and objectives."

III. SUFFICIENCY OF THE EVIDENCE

Ajaj

Ajaj argues that the government presented insufficient evidence to establish his guilt on the counts for which he was convicted. As an initial matter, Ajaj argues that the government failed to prove his membership in the conspiracy that bombed the World

Trade Center. Ajaj contends that the government's evidence fails to prove that Ajaj agreed to the "essential nature of the plan," that is, to bomb a populated structure in an urban area. In the alternative, Ajaj argues that his incarceration before the construction and detonation of the World Trade Center bomb constituted a withdrawal from the conspiracy as a matter of law, shielding him from criminal liability for the offenses later committed by his co-conspirators.

With respect to the conviction under Count One for conspiracy, the government's argument at trial that Ajaj not only agreed to the essential nature of the plan but was one of the conspiracy's architects enjoyed solid evidentiary support. The government established that in April 1992, Ajaj surreptitiously traveled from the United States to Pakistan to attend Camp Khaldan, a terrorist training camp. Ajaj, once in the Middle East, made contact with Yousef and they together plotted to bomb targets in the United States. The presence of both of their fingerprints in the terrorist manuals indicated that Ajaj and Yousef studied the materials, assimilating knowledge that Yousef later applied directly to the construction of the World Trade Center bomb.

The government demonstrated that after completing their training, Ajaj and Yousef jointly prepared to enter the United States illegally. Ajaj and Yousef carefully created false identities for themselves in the names of "Khurram Khan" and "Azan Mohammad," respectively. They collected false passports, identification cards and bank, education and medical records to support their false identities.

Ajaj's participation in the conspiracy continued even after his incarceration on the passport fraud conviction. Ajaj stayed abreast of the conspiracy's progress through telephone conversations with Yousef. The government's evidence went far beyond proving Ajaj's mere association with terrorists and suspicious circumstances. The possibility that the government's evidence at trial is subject to alternative inferences consistent with Ajaj's innocence does not vitiate the reasonableness of the jury verdict

Abouhalima

Abouhalima argues that the evidence presented at trial does not support a finding that he was a participant in the conspiracy to bomb the World Trade Center, but instead shows only that he knew the other defendants in this case and was present when they were taking some of the actions that furthered the conspiracy. Contrary to Abouhalima's claims, however, the government presented more than enough evidence from which the jury could have concluded beyond a reasonable doubt that Abouhalima was a knowing member of the conspiracy and was guilty, either directly or on a *Pinkerton* theory, on all of the substantive counts with which he was charged.

First, there was testimony that Abouhalima helped Salameh and Yousef find the apartment at 40 Pamrapo. And the evidence that 40 Pamrapo was intended to and did serve as a bomb factory was strong. The apartment had bluish stains on the walls and rust on the inside door knob and hinges of the back bedroom door, both consistent with the fumes generated by mixing explosives such as urea nitrate and nitroglycerine. Most important, samples of these two chemicals were found in scrapings taken from various items in the apartment.

Second, a receipt entered into evidence showed that Abouhalima was the purchaser of a refrigerator that bore Yousef's fingerprint and contained traces of nitroglycerine.

Third, there was testimony that, in the weeks preceding the bombing, Abouhalima, a limousine driver, made several unsuccessful attempts to secure the use of a van from his employer.

Fourth, one of Abouhalima's dress shoes, recovered from his apartment after the bombing, was found to have a burn that contained high levels of sulfate ions.

Fifth, in addition to the shoe, a copy of "Rapid Destruction and Demolition" was discovered at Abouhalima's home. Abouhalima's fingerprint was recovered from a page in this publication providing a formula for making explosives that could be used to destroy buildings.

Sixth, there was evidence that Abouhalima purchased a can of "Hodgdon" brand smokeless powder, a substance similar to that used in the detonator of the bomb planted at the World Trade Center.

Seventh, the government offered telephone records for a calling card that belonged to Abouhalima. These revealed that Abouhalima was in frequent contact with the other defendants. Moreover, the card was used to make various calls to chemical companies and garden supply stores.

Eighth, a gas station attendant identified Abouhalima as the driver of a Lincoln Town Car (to which Abouhalima had access in the course of his employment as a limousine driver) that accompanied the Ryder van carrying Salameh and Yousef (and presumably also the bomb) early in the morning of the day on which the bomb was detonated. The attendant stated that Abouhalima paid to fill the gas tanks of both vehicles.

Finally, on the day following the bombing, Abouhalima made arrangements to flee the country. On March 2, 1993, leaving his family behind, Abouhalima traveled from the United States to the Sudan without any luggage and with only a one-way ticket. The jury was entitled to infer consciousness of guilt from the facts surrounding this flight.

All of this evidence was more than sufficient, when taken together, to establish beyond a reasonable doubt that Abouhalima was a knowing and active participant in the conspiracy to bomb the World Trade Center; that he, himself, committed at least some of the substantive offenses in the indictment; and, to the extent that he did not directly participate in the substantive acts, that he was nonetheless liable under the *Pinkerton* doctrine.

NOTES AND QUESTIONS

1. Inchoate Crimes. Why did the prosecution bother to charge a conspiracy to bomb buildings other than the WTC? Understanding terrorism investigations will be aided by articulating how prevention of future violence relates to investigation and prosecution of completed offenses. This will become an explicit topic when we come to investigation of terrorist financing.

2. Grand Jury Subpoena. Ajaj was served with a grand jury subpoena for materials in his possession after his plea on the passport fraud and before the WTC bombing. As the next case shows, an FBI investigation of the Brooklyn groups was underway at this time but the FBI had severed relations with their main informant within the group. The subpoena was issued just six weeks before the WTC bombing. A grand jury subpoena is not reviewed by a judge unless the recipient moves to quash. When we consider some of the controversy over FISA Court orders under the PATRIOT Act amendments, the presence of grand jury subpoenas as an option will be relevant.

3. Co-conspirator Evidence. The Ajaj materials were introduced into evidence against all defendants. They were highly inflammatory, but the court holds their prejudicial character did not outweigh their probative value on motive and intent. Why does the jury need to know about motive? How does showing motive differ from showing that a person has a bad attitude?

4. Forensics and Expense. The discussion of the motion to suppress seized evidence displays some of the forensic techniques of law enforcement. Government spends millions of dollars on tracing minute details of a completed crime. Again, it will be helpful to articulate how pursuing the details of a completed crime relates to prevention of future harm. Any bombing incident will present you with an opportunity to reflect on this connection.

5. Prisoner Treatment. What do you think of the almost cavalier treatment of alleged torture of Abhouhalima at the hands of Egyptian agents? The practice of obtaining a captive from a foreign nation informally rather than through extradition is known as rendition. It is one of the principal tools in the investigative arsenal as nations attempt to cooperate in the suppression of terrorism. Should U.S. courts be more sensitive to potential abuses in these situations?

6. Interlocking Conspiracies. Finally, the *Salameh* opinion provides details of an investigation that should be borne in mind for future cases. The plot in this case is connected to the Rahman case that we consider next. Ramzi Yousef, who figures prominently in the WTC bombing, was later captured after a series of bombings in the Phillipines and returned to the U.S. for trial on air piracy charges unrelated to the WTC plot. His prosecution was considered earlier at § 2.02[A].

UNITED STATES v. RAHMAN
189 F.3d 88 (2d Cir. 1999)

[Editor's Note: This opinion is quite lengthy. The factual summary is reprinted here in some detail because it shows the methods of operation for a terrorist plot, for government infiltration of the group, and for subsequent investigation. Thus, it will serve as a referent for future discussions of investigative techniques.]

Before: NEWMAN, LEVAL, and PARKER, CIRCUIT JUDGES.

CONTENTS

PER CURIAM.

INTRODUCTION

These are appeals by ten defendants convicted of seditious conspiracy and other offenses arising out of a wide-ranging plot to conduct a campaign of urban terrorism. Among the activities of some or all of the defendants were rendering assistance to those who bombed the World Trade Center, see *United States v. Salameh*, 152 F.3d 88 (2d Cir. 1998) (affirming convictions of all four defendants), planning to bomb bridges and tunnels in New York City, murdering Rabbi Meir Kahane, and planning to murder the President of Egypt. We affirm the convictions of all the defendants. We also affirm all of the sentences, with the exception of the sentence of Ibrahim El-Gabrowny, which we remand for further consideration.

BACKGROUND

Defendants-Appellants Sheik Omar Abdel Rahman, El Sayyid Nosair, Ibrahim El-Gabrowny, Clement Hampton-El, Amir Abdelgani ("Amir"), Fares Khallafalla, Tarig Elhassan, Fadil Abdelgani ("Fadil"), Mohammed Saleh, and Victor Alvarez (collectively "defendants") appeal from judgments of conviction entered on January 17, 1996, following a nine-month jury trial in the United States District Court for the Southern District of New York (Michael B. Mukasey, District Judge).

The defendants were convicted of the following: seditious conspiracy (all defendants); soliciting the murder of Egyptian President Hosni Mubarak and soliciting an attack on American military installations (Rahman); conspiracy to murder Mubarak (Rahman); bombing conspiracy (all defendants found guilty except Nosair and El-Gabrowny); attempted bombing (Hampton-El, Amir, Fadil, Khallafalla, Elhassan, Saleh, and Alvarez); two counts of attempted murder and one count of murder in furtherance of a racketeering enterprise (Nosair); attempted murder of a federal officer (Nosair); three counts of use of a firearm in relation to a crime of violence (Nosair); possession of a firearm with an obliterated serial number (Nosair); facilitating the bombing conspiracy by shipping a firearm in interstate commerce and using and carrying a firearm in relation to a crime of violence (Alvarez); two counts of assault on a federal officer (El-Gabrowny); assault impeding the execution of a search warrant (El-Gabrowny); five counts of possession of a fraudulent foreign passport, and one count of possession with intent to transfer false identification documents (El-Gabrowny).

I. THE GOVERNMENT'S CASE

At trial, the Government sought to prove that the defendants and others joined in a seditious conspiracy to wage a war of urban terrorism against the United States and forcibly to oppose its authority. The Government also sought to prove various other counts against the defendants, all of which broadly relate to the seditious conspiracy. The Government alleged that members of the conspiracy (acting alone or in concert) took the following actions, among others, in furtherance of the group's objectives: the attempted murder of Hosni Mubarak, the provision of assistance to the bombing of the World Trade Center in New York City on February 26, 1993, and the Spring 1993 campaign of attempted bombings of buildings and tunnels in New York City. In addition, some members of the group were allegedly involved in the murder of Rabbi Meir Kahane by defendant Nosair.

The Government adduced evidence at trial showing the following: Rahman, a blind Islamic scholar and cleric, was the leader of the seditious conspiracy, the purpose of which was "jihad," in the sense of a struggle against the enemies of Islam. Indicative of this purpose, in a speech to his followers Rahman instructed that they were to "do jihad with the sword, with the cannon, with the grenades, with the missile . . . against God's enemies." Rahman's role in the conspiracy was generally limited to overall supervision and direction of the membership, as he made efforts to remain a level above the details of individual operations. However, as a cleric and the group's leader, Rahman was entitled to dispense "fatwas," religious opinions on the holiness of an act, to members of the group sanctioning proposed courses of conduct and advising them whether the acts would be in furtherance of jihad.

According to his speeches and writings, Rahman perceives the United States as the primary oppressor of Muslims worldwide, active in assisting Israel to gain power in the Middle East, and largely under the control of the Jewish lobby. Rahman also considers the secular Egyptian government of Mubarak to be an oppressor because it has abided Jewish migration to Israel while seeking to decrease Muslim births. Holding these views, Rahman believes that jihad against Egypt and the United States is mandated by the Qur'an. Formation of a jihad army made up of small "divisions" and "battalions" to carry out this jihad was therefore necessary, according to Rahman, in order to beat back these oppressors of Islam including the United States.

Although Rahman did not arrive in the United States until 1990, a group of his followers began to organize the jihad army in New York beginning in 1989. At that time, law enforcement had several of the members of the group under surveillance. In July 1989, on three successive weekends, FBI agents observed and photographed members of the jihad organization, including (at different times), Nosair, Hampton-El, Mahmoud Abouhalima, Mohammad Salameh, and Nidal Ayyad (the latter three of whom were later convicted of the World Trade Center bombing, shooting weapons, including AK-47's, at a public rifle range on Long Island. Although Rahman was in Egypt at the time, Nosair and Abouhalima called him there to discuss various issues including the progress of their military training, tape-recording these conversations for distribution among Rahman's followers. Nosair told Rahman "we have organized an encampment, we are concentrating here."

On November 5, 1990, Rabbi Meir Kahane, a former member of the Israeli parliament and a founder of the Jewish Defense League, gave a speech at the Marriot East Side Hotel in New York. Kahane was a militant Zionist, who advocated expelling Arabs from Israel. The content of this speech was a plea to American Jews to emigrate and settle in Israel. Nosair and possibly Salameh and Bilal Alkaisi, another member of the group, attended the speech. After the speech, as Kahane stood talking with the crowd, two shots were fired and Kahane was hit in the neck and chest.

Nosair, whom witnesses observed with a gun in hand immediately after the shooting, then ran toward the rear door of the room, trailed by one of the onlookers. At the door, 70-year-old Irving Franklin sought to impede Nosair's flight. Nosair shot Franklin in the leg, and fled the room. Outside the hotel Nosair encountered uniformed postal police officer Carlos Acosta. Acosta tried to draw his weapon and identify himself, but before he could fire, Nosair fired two shots at him. The first of these shots hit Acosta in the chest but was deflected into his shoulder by a bullet-proof vest he was wearing, and the second just missed Acosta's head. Despite being shot, Acosta returned fire, hitting Nosair in the neck. Nosair fell to the ground, dropping his weapon, a .357 caliber magnum revolver, at his side. Acosta recovered the weapon and detained Nosair. Ballistics testing showed that the weapon recovered from Nosair was the weapon that fired projectiles found in the room in which Kahane and Franklin had been shot, as well as in the area Acosta had been shot.

Subsequent to these events, law enforcement personnel executed search warrants for Nosair's home, car, and work lockers. Among the items seized in these searches was a handwritten notebook, in which Nosair stated that to establish a Muslim state in the Muslim holy lands it would be necessary:

> to break and destroy the morale of the enemies of Allah. (And this is by means of destroying) (exploding) the structure of their civilized pillars. Such as the touristic infrastructure which they are proud of and their high world buildings which they are proud of and their statues which they endear and the buildings in which they gather their heads (leaders).

While Nosair was at the prison ward of Bellevue Hospital following the shooting,

Nosair stated in response to a question from a treating physician that he had no choice but to kill Kahane, and that it was his "duty." After Nosair was moved from Bellevue to Rikers Island, he began to receive a steady stream of visitors, most regularly his cousin El-Gabrowny, and also Abouhalima, Salameh, and Ayyad. During these visits, as well as subsequent visits once Nosair was at Attica,[3] Nosair suggested numerous terrorist operations including the murders of the judge who sentenced him and of Dov Hikind, a New York City Assemblyman, and chided his visitors for doing nothing to further the jihad against the oppressors. Nosair also tape recorded messages while in custody, including one stating:

> God the Almighty . . . will facilitate for the believers to penetrate the lines no matter how strong they are, and the greatest proof of that [is] what happened in New York. God the Almighty enabled His extremely brave people, with His great power, to destroy one of the top infidels. They were preparing him to dominate, to be the Prime Minister some day. They were preparing him despite their assertion that they reject his agenda . . . and that he is a racist.

During Nosair's state trial in 1991, an FBI informant, Emad Salem, began to befriend various of Rahman's followers in an attempt to infiltrate the jihad organization.[4] At that trial, Salem met El-Gabrowny, Nosair's cousin, who was raising money to aid in Nosair's defense. Salem, accompanied by El-Gabrowny, also met with Nosair. El-Gabrowny introduced Salem as "a new member in the family."

As a result of these contacts, Salem traveled to Detroit with Rahman and others to attend a conference on the Islamic economy. During this trip, Salem, seeking to ingratiate himself to Rahman, informed Rahman of his prior service in the Egyptian military during the 1973 conflict with Israel. Rahman told Salem that this was not jihad because he had been paid to fight by an infidel government. Rahman also told Salem that he could make up for this, however, by assassinating Mubarak, a "loyal dog to the Americans."

Before the Nosair trial ended, Salem was invited for dinner at El-Gabrowny's house. During dinner, El-Gabrowny indicated he was concerned about being bugged by the FBI, turned up the television, and then discussed construction of high-powered explosives with Salem. Salem testified that after this dinner at El-Gabrowny's house, bombing became a frequent topic of conversation between them. By early 1992, Rahman had also welcomed Salem into the group. Rahman specifically praised Salem for attempting to restart paramilitary training with the group, noting that there would come a day when the training would be needed.

Mohammad Saad, the cousin of Sattar and a participant in the jihad group, developed a plan to get Nosair out of jail and confided the plan to Salem. Salem repeated the plan to El-Gabrowny, who cautioned them to slow down and await the outcome of Nosair's appeal. After being badgered by Nosair to take action, El-Gabrowny met with Salem and told him that he was in touch with "underground people" who could help them construct bombs. El-Gabrowny instructed Salem on the superiority of remote detonators rather than timers, describing to Salem how a remote detonator could assist in bombing Dov Hikind.

In June 1992 El-Gabrowny visited Nosair again in prison. Upon his return, he instructed Salem and Shinawy that Nosair wanted to see them. Salem testified that,

---

[3] [Court's Footnote 3] Nosair was eventually acquitted of the murder of Kahane in New York state court, but was found guilty of weapons charges, and was sentenced to a term of 7 1/3 to 22 years' imprisonment, and was transferred to Attica. The visits by members of the group continued when Nosair moved to Attica as did Nosair's calls to arms.

[4] [Court's Footnote 4] Salem was one of the Government's key witnesses at trial. The Government acknowledges that Salem is a braggart who often told tall tales of his past. However, by 1993 Salem was regularly tape recording his conversations with the group members and those tapes served to corroborate much of his testimony at trial.

when they made the visit, Nosair berated them for not proceeding with bombing plans and directed Shinawy to seek a fatwa from Rahman approving the bombings. On the way home from the visit, Shinaway told Salem that the planned operation would involve twelve bombs. Shinawy also explained that they would need guns in case they encountered police during the deployment, indicating that his source for firearms was Hampton-El.

Two days later Salem went to El-Gabrowny's house and found Shinawy already there. The three agreed that they would try to secure a "safehouse" for constructing bombs, and El-Gabrowny committed to attempt to obtain detonators from Afghanistan. A few days later, Shinawy summoned Salem to the Abu Bakr Mosque where he introduced Salem to Hampton-El. Salem and Shinaway explained to Hampton-El that they were making bombs but that they were having trouble getting detonators. Hampton-El said that he had access to "ready-made bombs" for $900 to $1,000 apiece. He also offered to obtain a handgun for Salem. A few days later Shinaway gave Salem a handgun presumably from Hampton-El.

In early July 1992, a rift developed between Salem and the FBI, and it was agreed that Salem's undercover investigation would be terminated. To explain his disappearance, Salem told El-Gabrowny that he needed to go to Spain for a while to take care of a problem in his jewelry business.

In late 1992, the paramilitary training resumed, led by Siddig Ali and Hampton-El on weekends between October 1992 and February 1993. Defendants Amir and Fadil Abdelgani and Elhassan all participated in the training camp, as did Abdo Haggag, an Egyptian spy who testified for the Government during the trial. The purpose of the training was to teach the participants jihad tactics. There was talk that jihad was needed in Bosnia, and that some of the trainees might go there. [None of the trainees ever went to Bosnia.] As Siddig Ali later explained to Salem, the training was meant to prepare the trainees for jihad wherever it was needed. During training, Siddig Ali reported to Rahman, and Rahman offered his insights into the training.

In the midst of this training, Hampton-El sought detonators and "clean" guns from Garrett Wilson, a cooperating witness for the U.S. Naval Investigative Service, who testified for the Government at trial. Hampton-El explained that he wanted to train a group of people in "commando tactics" and discussed training techniques and bomb identification.

During this time, Ramzi Yousef (another compatriot who was later convicted of the World Trade Center bombing) arrived in the United States. Rahman was making numerous calls to overseas numbers, including a Pakistan number which Yousef had inscribed in a bomb making pamphlet. Rahman, Salameh, and Yousef also made several calls to the same number in Pakistan in November. Nosair, speaking with his wife from prison, said, "And what will happen in New York, God willing, it will be . . . because of my prayers."

In January 1993, Rahman appeared at a conference in Brooklyn, and voiced his beliefs in violent jihad. Rahman further stated that being called terrorists was fine, so long as they were terrorizing the enemies of Islam, the foremost of which was the United States and its allies. While building the World Trade Center bomb, the builders kept in close phone contact with El-Gabrowny and Rahman. Salameh and Yousef repeatedly called El-Gabrowny at home and at the Abu Bakr Mosque and Rahman at home. In December 1992 and January 1993, El-Gabrowny visited Nosair at Attica and later arranged for the World Trade Center bombers to visit Nosair in the weeks preceding the bombing (Abouhalima visited Nosair on January 2 and February 7, and Salameh visited him on February 13).

On February 24, 1993, Salameh rented a van to be used in the World Trade Center bombing. As identification, he used a New York license bearing his own name and El-Gabrowny's address. As Ayyad was making arrangements to purchase the hydrogen gas to be used in the World Trade Center bomb, he called El-Gabrowny. On February

26, 1993, the World Trade Center complex was bombed, causing six deaths and massive destruction.

On March 4, 1993, federal agents executed a search warrant for El-Gabrowny's home. Salameh's use of El-Gabrowny's address when renting the van used in the bombing provided the basis for the warrant. The warrant allowed a search for explosives and related devices. The search of El-Gabrowny's home revealed, among other things, stun guns and taped messages from Nosair urging fighting and jihad in response to the Jewish immigration to Israel. Just prior to executing the search warrant, the agents encountered El-Gabrowny as he left the building and then, seeing them, started back toward it. The agents stopped and frisked him. El-Gabrowny became belligerent and assaulted two agents. On his person, the agents found five fraudulent Nicaraguan passports and birth certificates with pictures of Nosair and his wife and children.

After the bombing of the World Trade Center, Salem again began working for the FBI as an informant. In March of 1993, President Mubarak was scheduled to visit New York. Certain members of Rahman's group saw this visit as an opportunity to assassinate him, in the words of Siddig Ali, "to execute the desire of the Sheik." Siddig Ali described the plan to Abdo Mohammed Haggag, an Abdel Rahman confidant who later cooperated with the Egyptian and United States authorities. Nothing came of this plan because Haggag secretly gave the Egyptian government information about the plot, and the New York part of Mubarak's trip to the United States was canceled.

Siddig Ali then proposed a new round of bombings. In late April 1993, he became friendly with Salem, who was, by that point, tape recording his conversations for the FBI. Salem agreed to assist Siddig Ali in putting together the bombs but stated that he would have no part in deploying them. After contemplating bombing a U.S. armory, Siddig Ali proposed bombing the United Nations complex. When initially discussing this plan with Salem, he stated that Rahman had approved the attack on the United Nations, and had called it not merely permissible, but a "must" and a "duty." Siddig Ali invited Salem to discuss these matters directly with Rahman, but reminded him that because of the surveillance, to use caution in so doing. Caution, as defined by Siddig Ali, included phrasing statements in a broad and general manner, and assuring that Rahman was insulated from active involvement in the plot.

Salem met with Siddig Ali again on May 12, pretending that he had surveyed locations for use as a bomb-making safehouse and that he had settled on a garage in Queens that was renting for $1,000 a month. This safehouse was actually rented by the FBI, and the FBI installed videocameras and surveillance equipment in the safehouse before members of the group began using it.

Taking Siddig Ali up on his earlier invitation, Salem had a private conversation with Rahman on the night of May 23, 1993. At the bidding of Siddig Ali, Salem began the conversation by pledging allegiance to Rahman. Salem then told Rahman that he and Siddig Ali were planning to "do a job." Salem explicitly asked Rahman about the United Nations. Rahman replied that bombing the United Nations was "not illicit, however will be bad for Muslims." Rahman instead told Salem to "Find a plan, find a plan . . . to inflict damage on the American army itself." Salem then asked about a strike on the FBI headquarters in New York. Rahman told him to "wait for a while," and to "plan carefully."

Salem recounted this conversation to Siddig Ali, who stated that when he had discussed the United Nations issue with Rahman, Rahman had been in favor of the plan. Subsequently, in discussing the plan to bomb the United Nations with Hampton-El, Siddig Ali told him that he had received an "official fatwa" from Rahman regarding the plan. Siddig Ali also told Khallafalla and Amir Abdelgani the same thing, stating that Rahman's approval was necessary whenever one did something "basically unlawful," which would be wrong unless the "mission [was] under the flag of God and his messenger."

As a result of the failure of the plan to execute Mubarak, there was some speculation by members of the group that Siddig Ali was an informer. Siddig Ali and Salem conversed one day with Rahman about the issue. Rahman voiced his suspicions that Siddig Ali was the informer. Ironically, Salem secretly tape recorded this conversation for the Government. During the conversation, Rahman revealed that Abouhalima, one of the World Trade Center bombers, was supposed to have fled to Sudan, not to Egypt, where he was subsequently arrested after the bombing. After the discussion, Siddig Ali told Salem that Rahman had ordered that they be circumspect when discussing their plans with him so that he would not be incriminated.

On May 27, 1993, Siddig Ali introduced Salem to Amir Abdelgani and Fares Khallafalla near the Medina Mosque. The four then traveled to the safehouse where they discussed the bombing plans. At that time Siddig Ali indicated he wanted to bomb the United Nations and the Lincoln and Holland Tunnels. Siddig Ali outlined the proposed plan for three explosions five minutes apart, sometimes sketching on a piece of cardboard. The cardboard was later recovered at the safehouse.

Over the next few days, Siddig Ali and Amir Abdelgani (once accompanied by Salem) drove together to the Lincoln and Holland tunnels, the United Nations, and the Federal Building in Manhattan to scout the targets and examine traffic conditions. During one of these scouting trips, Amir suggested that they consider bombing the diamond district in Manhattan because that would be like "hitting Israel itself." At the United Nations, Siddig Ali noted that a bomb detonated at the entrance would topple the building. The men later gathered at the safehouse to discuss the operation.

On May 30, 1993, Hampton-El met with Siddig Ali and Salem at Hampton-El's safehouse, which he used for conducting business. Siddig Ali and Salem explained that they needed detonators, and Hampton-El said he would try to locate some for them. The three discussed the plan to blow up the United Nations and the tunnels. On June 4, 1993, Siddig Ali arranged to go with Salem to meet Mohammed Saleh. Siddig Ali explained to Salem that Saleh was an important supporter of jihad activities who might assist in the bombing campaign. Saleh was the owner of two gasoline stations in Yonkers, New York. During dinner at Saleh's house, Siddig Ali explained the bombing plan to Saleh, noting the different targets on a piece of paper. Salem was asked by Siddig Ali to eat the piece of paper once Siddig Ali felt that Saleh understood the plan. During dinner, Saleh agreed to help purchase military equipment.

Over the next few weeks, Siddig Ali brought Alvarez and Elhassan into the group. Various members of the group began to collect the items they believed were needed to prepare the bombs. The group also met frequently to refine the bombing plan. On June 13, 1993, Salem and Khallafalla purchased two timers for the bombs in Chinatown. On June 15 and 18, Hampton-El left messages for Siddig Ali indicating that he was still searching for detonators. On June 19, Amir Abdelgani, Khallafalla, Salem, Alvarez, and Siddig Ali met at Siddig Ali's house to discuss the details of the plan, including the number of people and bombs needed to carry it out. Siddig Ali indicated that they needed fertilizer, fuel, and stolen cars.

Amir, Alvarez, and Salem attempted on the evening of June 19 to buy stolen cars to deliver the bombs and to use as getaway cars during the bombing. Although they located a source for stolen cars, they did not have sufficient funds to purchase the cars. That same day, Elhassan met with a friend who was an engineer to discuss the feasibility of blowing up the tunnels and to determine where the weakest points of the tunnels were located.

On June 21, 1993, the group met at the Mosque and drove to the safehouse. Amir, Siddig Ali, and Elhassan discussed a method of communicating at the tunnels so that both of them would blow up at the same time, and planned their escapes after the bombing. Amir and Siddig Ali advised everyone that, if they were caught, not to talk until their lawyers were present. That evening Alvarez tried again, unsuccessfully, to obtain cars for the operation.

On June 22, 1993, after buying five 55-gallon steel barrels from a Newark drum business, Siddig Ali and Amir went to Saleh's gas station to get fuel for the bombs. Saleh agreed over the phone to provide the fuel. Belhabri, Saleh's employee, filled two of the drums with $140 worth of diesel fuel. Saleh agreed to keep two of the empty barrels in his garage. Siddig Ali and Amir did not pay for the fuel, but Belhabri made out a receipt on which he recorded the license plate of the van. Siddig Ali wrote a phony signature on the receipt.

The next day, June 23, Amir returned to Saleh's gas station with Fadil to fill the remaining three 55-gallon drums with diesel fuel. They met Saleh who called his employee at the other station to tell him to wait for the two so that they could get fuel before the station closed. Amir called Siddig Ali and asked if he could tell Fadil the bombing plan since Amir thought that Fadil would eventually catch on. Siddig Ali gave him permission to tell Fadil. Amir and Fadil obtained fuel. When Belhabri wrote out a receipt, Amir objected and called Saleh who then told Belhabri not to put the license number on the receipt but just to write "Sudanese." Belhabri provided $151 worth of fuel. At the same time, Siddig Ali and Salem were purchasing more fertilizer for the bombs.

Later in the day, Alvarez gave Siddig Ali a 9mm semi-automatic rifle with an empty 25-round magazine. Siddig Ali and Salem took the gun from Alvarez's apartment in New Jersey to the safehouse. A little after 8 p.m. that evening, Amir and Fadil arrived at the safehouse with the fuel. Amir then washed down the van so that there would be no traces left of the fuel. For the next hour, Amir, Fadil, Siddig Ali, and Salem discussed the bombing plan. At one point, Fadil was asked whether he would participate, and he responded that he had to perform an Istikhara prayer (a prayer seeking divine intervention to guide one's decision in a course of action). After going to the Mosque to pray, Fadil met Elhassan and Alvarez, and they drove back to the safehouse.

Back at the safehouse, Amir began mixing the fuel and the fertilizer, and watched a videotape showing the tunnels that had been shot earlier in the day by Siddig Ali and Salem. Elhassan, Alvarez, and Fadil then returned, joined Amir, and began stirring the fuel and fertilizer together. They discussed the timers and the placement of bombs. At about 2 a.m. on the morning of June 24, FBI agents raided the safehouse and arrested the defendants, seizing the fuel and fertilizer mixture and the cardboard diagram Siddig Ali had periodically used to sketch the bombing plan.

A few hours before arrests were made at the safehouse, FBI agents arrested Saleh at his apartment in Yonkers. At FBI headquarters, Saleh denied having sold fuel to the men but said that Salem had come to his station demanding fuel on two occasions. About a week later on July 5, 1993, Saleh called one of his employees from prison and instructed him to tell Belhabri to destroy the two receipts documenting the fuel given to the Abdelganis and Siddig Ali. Saleh said that it would be "dangerous" for Belhabri if he failed to follow these instructions.

II. The Defense Case

The defendants presented their case for two months, calling 71 witnesses. Hampton-El, Elhassan, Alvarez, and Fadil Abdelgani each testified on his own behalf. The specific defenses put forth by the individual defendants will be set out below as they become relevant to particular claims on appeal. Siddig Ali, among others, was charged in the same indictment as the defendants but was not part of the trial because he pleaded guilty to all counts with which he was charged and cooperated, to a degree, with the Government.

III. Verdicts and Sentences

The jury trial in the case ran from January 9, 1995, to October 1, 1995. The jury returned verdicts finding defendants guilty on all submitted charges, except that Nosair and El-Gabrowny obtained not guilty verdicts on the Count Five bombing conspiracy charges. The defendants were sentenced as follows: Rahman and Nosair, life imprisonment; El-Gabrowny, 57 years; Alvarez, Hampton-El, Elhassan, and Saleh, 35 years; Amir Abdelgani and Khallafalla, 30 years; Fadil Abdelgani, 25 years.

DISCUSSION

I. CONSTITUTIONAL CHALLENGES

A. Seditious Conspiracy Statute and the Treason Clause

Defendant Nosair (joined by other defendants) contends that his conviction for seditious conspiracy, in violation of 18 U.S.C. § 2384, was illegal because it failed to satisfy the requirements of the Treason Clause of the U.S. Constitution, Art. III, § 3.

Article III, Section 3 provides, in relevant part:

> Treason against the United States, shall consist only in levying War against them, or in adhering to their Enemies, giving them Aid and Comfort. No Person shall be convicted of Treason unless on the Testimony of two Witnesses to the same overt Act, or on Confession in open Court.

The seditious conspiracy statute provides:

> If two or more persons in any State or Territory, or in any place subject to the jurisdiction of the United States, conspire to overthrow, put down or to destroy by force the Government of the United States, or to levy war against them, or to oppose by force the authority thereof, or by force to prevent, hinder or delay the execution of any law of the United States, or by force to seize, take, or possess any property of the United States contrary to the authority thereof, they shall each be fined under this title or imprisoned not more than twenty years, or both.

18 U.S.C. § 2384.

Nosair contends that because the seditious conspiracy statute punishes conspiracy to "levy war" against the United States without a conforming two-witness requirement, the statute is unconstitutional. He further claims that because his conviction for conspiracy to levy war against the United States was not based on the testimony of two witnesses to the same overt act, the conviction violates constitutional standards.

It is undisputed that Nosair's conviction was not supported by two witnesses to the same overt act. Accordingly the conviction must be overturned if the requirement of the Treason Clause applies to this prosecution for seditious conspiracy. The plain answer is that the Treason Clause does not apply to the prosecution. The provisions of Article III, Section 3 apply to prosecutions for "treason." Nosair and his co-appellants were not charged with treason. Their offense of conviction, seditious conspiracy, differs from treason not only in name and associated stigma, but also in its essential elements and punishment.

Seditious conspiracy by levying war includes no requirement that the defendant owe allegiance to the United States, an element necessary to conviction of treason. *See* 18 U.S.C. § 2381 (defining "allegiance to United States" as an element of treason). Nosair nevertheless maintains that "the only distinction between the elements of seditious conspiracy under the levy war prong and treason by levying war is that the former requires proof of a conspiracy while the latter requires proof of the substantive crime."

Nosair's suggestion that the statutory definition of treason added the requirement of allegiance is mistaken. The reference to treason in the constitutional clause necessarily incorporates the elements of allegiance and betrayal that are essential to the concept of treason. The functions of the Clause are to limit the crime of treason to betrayals of allegiance that are substantial, amounting to levying war or giving comfort to enemies, and to require sufficiently reliable evidence. Treason, in other words, may not be found on the basis of mere mutterings of discontent, or relatively innocuous opposition. The fact that the Treason Clause imposes its requirements without mentioning the require-ment of allegiance is not a basis for concluding that treason may be prosecuted without allegiance being proved. That any conviction for treason under the laws of the United States requires a betrayal of allegiance is simply implicit in the term "treason." Nosair was thus tried for a different, and lesser, offense than treason.

B. Seditious Conspiracy Statute and the First Amendment

Rahman, joined by the other appellants, contends that the seditious conspiracy statute is an unconstitutional burden on free speech and the free exercise of religion in violation of the First Amendment. First, Rahman argues that the statute is facially invalid because it criminalizes protected expression and that it is overbroad and unconstitutionally vague. Second, Rahman contends that his conviction violated the First Amendment because it rested solely on his political views and religious practices.

1. Facial Challenge

As Section 2384 proscribes "speech" only when it constitutes an agreement to use force against the United States, Rahman's generalized First Amendment challenge to the statute is without merit.

It remains fundamental that while the state may not criminalize the expression of views — even including the view that violent overthrow of the government is desirable — it may nonetheless outlaw encouragement, inducement, or conspiracy to take violent action. The prohibitions of the seditious conspiracy statute are much further removed from the realm of constitutionally protected speech than those at issue in *United States v. Dennis* and its progeny [*see* § 6.02 *infra*]. To be convicted under Section 2384, one must conspire to use force, not just to advocate the use of force. We have no doubt that this passes the test of constitutionality.

2. Application of Section 2384 to Rahman's Case

Rahman also argues that he was convicted not for entering into any conspiratorial agreement that Congress may properly forbid, but "solely for his religious words and deeds" which, he contends, are protected by the First Amendment. In support of this claim, Rahman cites the Government's use in evidence of his speeches and writings.

There are two answers to Rahman's contention. The first is that freedom of speech and of religion do not extend so far as to bar prosecution of one who uses a public speech or a religious ministry to commit crimes. Numerous crimes under the federal criminal code are, or can be, committed by speech alone [citing statutes based on conspiracy, procuring, or inducing]. All of these offenses are characteristically committed through speech. Notwithstanding that political speech and religious exercise are among the activities most jealously guarded by the First Amendment, one is not immunized from prosecution for such speech-based offenses merely because one commits them through the medium of political speech or religious preaching. Of course, courts must be vigilant to insure that prosecutions are not improperly based on the mere expression of unpopular ideas. But if the evidence shows that the speeches crossed the line into criminal solicitation, procurement of criminal activity, or conspiracy to violate the laws, the prosecution is permissible.

The evidence justifying Rahman's conviction for conspiracy and solicitation showed beyond a reasonable doubt that he crossed this line. His speeches were not simply the expression of ideas; in some instances they constituted the crime of conspiracy to wage war on the United States and solicitation of attack on the United States military installations, as well as of the murder of Egyptian President Hosni Mubarak.

Words of this nature — ones that instruct, solicit, or persuade others to commit crimes of violence — violate the law and may be properly prosecuted regardless of whether they are uttered in private, or in a public speech, or in administering the duties of a religious ministry. The fact that his speech or conduct was "religious" does not immunize him from prosecution under generally-applicable criminal statutes. *See* [*Empl. Div. of Oregon v.*] *Smith*, 494 U.S. 872, 879 (1990).

Rahman also protests the Government's use in evidence of his speeches, writings, and preachings that did not in themselves constitute the crimes of solicitation or conspiracy. He is correct that the Government placed in evidence many instances of Rahman's writings and speeches in which Rahman expressed his opinions within the protection of the First Amendment. However, while the First Amendment fully protects Rahman's right to express hostility against the United States, and he may not be prosecuted for so speaking, it does not prevent the use of such speeches or writings in evidence when relevant to prove a pertinent fact in a criminal prosecution. The Government was free to demonstrate Rahman's resentment and hostility toward the United States in order to show his motive for soliciting and procuring illegal attacks against the United States and against President Mubarak of Egypt.

Furthermore, Judge Mukasey properly protected against the danger that Rahman might be convicted because of his unpopular religious beliefs that were hostile to the United States. He explained to the jury the limited use it was entitled to make of the material received as evidence of motive. He instructed that a defendant could not be convicted on the basis of his beliefs or the expression of them — even if those beliefs favored violence. He properly instructed the jury that it could find a defendant guilty only if the evidence proved he committed a crime charged in the indictment.

III. PRETRIAL AND TRIAL CHALLENGES

. . . .

D. Sufficiency of the Evidence

The following defendants challenge the sufficiency of the evidence on the following charges: Rahman challenges the sufficiency of the evidence on all counts of conviction; El-Gabrowny, Hampton-El, and Fadil Abdelgani challenge the sufficiency of the evidence supporting their seditious conspiracy convictions; Hampton-El and Alvarez contend that the proof supporting their attempted bombing convictions was insufficient; and Nosair attacks the sufficiency of the evidence supporting his three convictions for racketeering (the murder of Meir Kahane and the shootings of Irving Franklin and Carlos Acosta).

1. Standard of Review

[O]ne may be proven guilty of conspiracy even if one does not know all the other members or all the details of the conspiracy's operation. Once an unlawful agreement is shown, to show membership, the Government need provide only "some evidence from which it can reasonably be inferred that the person charged with conspiracy knew of the existence of the scheme alleged in the indictment and knowingly joined and participated in it."

2. Rahman

Rahman argues that the evidence presented by the Government was insufficient to support a conviction for any of the counts with which he was charged. Rahman asserts that he had limited contact with most of the other defendants, that he was physically incapable, due to his blindness, of participating in the "operational" aspects of the conspiracies, and that there was little direct evidence of his knowledge of many of the events in question. We find Rahman's claims unavailing.

a. Seditious Conspiracy and Bombing Conspiracy

First, we find ample evidence in the record to support the jury's finding that there was indeed a conspiracy to "levy war" against the United States. While there is no evidence that Rahman personally participated in the performance of the conspiracy, when conspiracy is charged, the Government is not required to show that the defendant personally performed acts in its furtherance: it is sufficient for the defendant to join in the illegal agreement. The evidence showed that Rahman was in constant contact with other members of the conspiracy, that he was looked to as a leader, and that he accepted that role and encouraged his co-conspirators to engage in violent acts against the United States.

Although Rahman did advise against making the United Nations a bombing target because that would be bad for Muslims, he advised Salem to seek a different target (U.S. military installations) for the bombings, and to plan for them carefully. In that same conversation, he also warned Salem to be careful around Siddig Ali, who he suspected was a traitor. Rahman then sought out the traitor in his group, having a long discussion with Salem and Siddig Ali over who was the traitor. This evidence shows that a reasonable trier of fact could have found that Rahman was a member of the conspiracy and that he was in fact its leader.

As to the bombing conspiracy count, there is clear evidence to support a reasonable conclusion that there was a conspiracy of which Rahman was a member, and that the conspirators had taken overt acts "to effect the object" thereof. The conspirators had, among other things: (1) scouted the Lincoln and Holland Tunnels; (2) contributed rent for a place to make the bombs; (3) purchased fuel oil, fertilizer, and timers from which to make the bombs; and (4) begun mixing the fuel and fertilizer.

b. Conspiracy and Solicitation to Murder Mubarak

Rahman also claims that there is insufficient evidence to support his convictions for soliciting Salem, Siddig Ali, and Haggag, to murder Mubarak, and for being a member of a conspiracy to do such. Rahman had made clear to Siddig Ali that he wanted Mubarak killed, and had already issued a fatwa regarding such. Rahman told Haggag that killing Mubarak did not require an additional fatwa, and that Haggag and "the people with training" should carry out the assassination.

In furtherance of this conspiracy, Siddig Ali made contacts with an individual at the Sudanese mission to the UN seeking to get information regarding Mubarak's itinerary, and made plans for the assassination. In May 1993, both Haggag and Siddig Ali sought to take credit for proposing the plan when Rahman was questioning them over who was the traitor in the group.

c. Solicitation to Bomb a Military Installation

With regard to the conviction for solicitation to bomb a military installation, the test is met again based on Rahman's status as leader of the group, combined with the fact that he specifically told Salem to target military bases. Thus a reasonable trier of fact could find Rahman guilty of such solicitation.

3. Nosair

Nosair argues that the evidence was insufficient to show that the murder of Kahane (or any of the specific charges levied under the RICO statute, including the attempted murder of Acosta and Franklin) was done with the statutorily required motive — to maintain or increase his position within a racketeering enterprise. Nosair bases his claim on a narrow construction of the term "Jihad Organization," which the indictment defined as being equivalent to the charged seditious conspiracy. Thus, Nosair claims that the murder of Kahane, a private Israeli citizen, could not further the goals of an organization whose primary purpose was to levy war on the United States. We find this reading of the indictment flawed. According to the indictment, the Jihad Organization, the RICO enterprise in question, was "opposed to nations, governments, institutions and individuals that did not share the group's particular radical interpretation of Islamic law," and an objective of this group was "to carry out, and conspire to carry out, acts of terrorism — including bombings, murders, and the taking of hostages — against various governments and government officials, including the United States government and its officials." Thus, the murder of Kahane did not "stray" from the purposes of the Jihad organization, and in fact was entirely consonant therewith.

Nosair, in a message taped from Rikers Island, stated "God the Almighty enabled His extremely brave people, with His great power, to destroy one of the top infidels." Nosair told his physician, in response to a question about the murder, "I had no choice, it was my duty." Nosair sought to use the murder to inspire his compatriots to take other action, thus using it to increase his position in the organization. Thus, a reasonable inference that the murder was in furtherance of his membership can be made, and his statement that it was his "duty" to murder Kahane leads to an inference that the murder was motivated by a desire to maintain or elevate his position in the organization.

4. Fadil Abdelgani

Fadil Abdelgani concedes that there was sufficient evidence for the jury to convict him of the conspiracy to bomb and attempted bombing charges. However, he alleges that there was not sufficient evidence to support the guilty verdict for seditious conspiracy for which he received twenty years' imprisonment. We disagree.

The Government persuasively counters that a jury could reasonably infer that Fadil knew of the group's overriding purpose of forcibly opposing the United States based on his participation in the 1992 training camp and on the time he spent with Amir and other group members in the safehouse on June 23 while the plot was discussed. Fadil's participation in the attempted bombing itself also justifies an inference that he agreed to forcibly oppose the United States; the bombing plan was to disable major commercial activity of the United States (by disabling the tunnels) and to hit at the Government itself by bombing the United Nations. Fadil's alleged lack of knowledge of Nosair or Rahman and the details of some of the other overt acts of the conspiracy is not fatal to the Government's position. The case law of this Court holds that to be guilty of conspiracy a defendant need not know every detail of the conspiracy or know of the identities of all of the other conspirators.

5. El-Gabrowny

El-Gabrowny claims there was insufficient evidence for the jury to convict him of seditious conspiracy. El-Gabrowny claims that the jury's verdict was based on circumstantial evidence and that he was simply found guilty "by association." The claim is unavailing. In his brief on appeal, El-Gabrowny focuses on the evidence that was not presented at trial and the acts in which he was not involved. El-Gabrowny notes that no tapes were produced in which he discusses plans to bomb buildings or any violent acts. He argues that he had nothing to do with the Kahane murder or the Spring 1993 bombing plots (during which time he was in prison).

El-Gabrowny routinely engaged in discussions with Salem about building bombs, and in June 1992 offered to attempt to obtain detonators from Afghanistan. He also indicated he would try to acquire a safehouse for the construction of bombs, and that he was in touch with "underground people" who could assist in a bombing. He was in constant contact with Nosair, and evidence seized from his house indicated that he shared Nosair's views on the duty to perform jihad. El-Gabrowny encouraged Salem and others to visit Nosair in prison at which time Nosair advocated that they begin jihad and plan to bomb buildings. El-Gabrowny frequently communicated with the World Trade Center bombers during the months, weeks, and days prior to the bombing. Salameh used El-Gabrowny's address on the driver's license that he used to rent the van that was used in the bombing. Upon his arrest, El-Gabrowny was carrying forged passports for Nosair and his family which were apparently meant to be used as part of the planned jailbreak of Nosair.

6. Alvarez

Alvarez claims that there was insufficient evidence to show a "substantial step" to support the attempted bombing charge. In this case, given the large number of steps taken by the defendants in preparation for the bombing, we find that they had moved beyond "mere preparation." The defendants had: recruited sufficient participants to carry out the plan; contributed money to rent a safehouse in which to build the bombs; reconnoitered the potential targets of the bombs, by driving through and videotaping the tunnels and discussing the structure of the tunnels with an engineer; purchased, or attempted to purchase, what they believed to be the necessary components for the bombs, including actually purchasing oil, fertilizer, timers, and barrels in which to mix the explosives; attempted to find stolen cars in which to carry the bombs; and obtained a submachine gun to assist in carrying out the plan. Given the nature and scope of the proposed plan, namely, that it was to be a coordinated explosion of massive bombs designed to destroy large targets, we believe that the defendants had moved beyond "mere preparation," and had in fact taken numerous "substantial steps" which were "strongly corroborative of their criminal purpose." We therefore reject Alvarez's claim.

7. Hampton-El

Hampton-El challenges the sufficiency of evidence against him on the seditious conspiracy and attempted bombing charges. As to both charges, he argues that he did not have the requisite intent. He asserts that the Government did not prove that he intended to "join Siddig Ali and his minions" to oppose the authority of the U.S. by force or to levy war against the U.S. nor did the Government prove that he specifically intended to bring about the bombing by aiding and abetting in the safehouse operation. [The Government did not seek to prove at trial that Hampton-El was guilty as a principal of the attempt.]

a. Seditious Conspiracy

At trial Hampton-El testified that he did not know any specifics of the operations of Siddig Ali, Salem, or the others, and that he "did not mean it," when he agreed to try to find detonators and weapons for them. We find sufficient evidence to support a finding of intent to join the conspiracy beyond a reasonable doubt based on the following evidence: Hampton-El co-led the shooting training in 1989 and the paramilitary training in 1992 of jihad group members, some of whom were involved in the World Trade Center bombing, and some of whom were involved in the spring 1993 bombing attempt; from 1989 to 1993, he was closely aligned with [others attempting to obtain detonators]; on May 30, 1993, he discussed the spring 1993 bombing plot with Siddig Ali and Salem, said the attack "takes a lot of courage," and agreed to try to find detonators for them; and he contacted Mustafa Assad after meeting with Siddig Ali and Salem, met with Assad who is known to have been a bomb builder, and then told Siddig Ali that his source was working on the request.

The jury was not obliged to accept Hampton-El's claim that after the May 30, 1993, meeting with Siddig Ali and Salem, he deliberately distanced himself from the bombing plan because he did not want to be involved in violence against the United States. In numerous phone calls to Siddig Ali after the meeting, several of which Hampton-El initiated, he assured Siddig Ali that he was continuing to look for detonators and that he expected to obtain them soon. Hampton-El also frequently called his source for the detonators, Assad, during this time period.

The evidence was sufficient to permit a jury to find beyond a reasonable doubt that Hampton-El was continuously involved with group members throughout the life of the conspiracy, that he actively sought out detonators for Siddig Ali and Salem, and that he joined in the seditious conspiracy to make war on the United States.

b. Attempted Bombing

The evidence was also sufficient to show that Hampton-El aided and abetted the attempt to bomb by his efforts to find detonators. To be found guilty as an aider and abettor, a defendant must know of the criminal venture, have joined the criminal venture, shared in it, and contributed to it by some act. [A] reasonable trier of fact could have found that Hampton-El did know of the scheme after the May 30, 1993, meeting at his apartment with Siddig Ali and Salem. At that time, Salem testified, and the intelligible portions of the tape corroborate, that Hampton-El was informed that they planned to bomb the United Nations and the tunnels, and that Hampton-El agreed to help find detonators. He then sought out the detonators. Thus, the jury's verdict finding Hampton-El guilty of attempted bombing was reasonable and supported by sufficient evidence.

E. Government Overinvolvement

Defendants Khallafalla and Saleh argue that their conviction violated the Due Process Clause by reason of the Government's "overinvolvement" in the conspiracy. According to defendants, the Government impermissibly lent direction, technical expertise, and critical resources to the bombing plot through Salem, an informant. We reject this claim because the Government's conduct was within acceptable bounds.

The Supreme Court has suggested that in an extreme case, Government involvement in criminal activity might be "so outrageous that due process principles would absolutely bar the Government from invoking judicial processes to obtain a conviction." Such an argument might in principle prevail even where, as here, the defendants went not entrapped by the Government.[5] However, only Government conduct that " 'shocks the conscience' " can violate due process. The paradigm examples of conscience-shocking conduct are egregious invasions of individual rights. *See, e.g., Rochin* [*v. California*], 342 U.S. at 172 (breaking into suspect's bedroom, forcibly attempting to pull capsules from his throat, and pumping his stomach without his consent). Especially in view of the courts' well-established deference to the Government's choice of investigatory methods, the burden of establishing outrageous investigatory conduct is very heavy.

The Government's behavior, and in particular the role of Salem, does not shock the conscience. Undercover work, in which a Government agent pretends to be engaged in criminal activity, is often necessary to detect criminal conspiracies. If such work is to succeed, the undercover agent must have "something of value to offer" the conspirators. Supplying such a resource "can hardly be said to violate" due process. In *Schmidt*, we found that United States Marshals did not violate due process when they posed as hit men, accepted a prisoner's solicitation to murder two guards during an escape, and then conducted a controlled breakout. In this case, Salem's contribution to the criminal conduct was proportionately far smaller: the defendants were already actively advancing a conspiracy, and they already had substantial resources and technical expertise.

---

5 [Court's Footnote 16] Entrapment requires proof that the Government induced commission of the charged crime, and that the defendant lacked a predisposition to engage in such criminal conduct. The evidence at trial established that both Khallafalla and Saleh joined the conspiracy at the bidding of Siddig Ali. There was no Government inducement, and hence no entrapment.

There is no evidence that the criminal conspiracy would have foundered without the Government's entry. The jihad organization had, after all, already bombed the World Trade Center without Salem's help. Moreover, as in *Schmidt*, the entry of the Government informant was intended not only to gather evidence, but also to prevent further death and destruction. Such conduct is not outrageous, and it does not violate due process.

NOTES AND QUESTIONS

1. Treason. The relationship between seditious conspiracy and treason will come up again when we consider prosecutions for "material support of terrorist organizations" and the constitutional right of association in Chapter 3. Why should treason be limited to those who "owe allegiance" to the United States and who would be considered to owe such allegiance? Does this cast a different light on controversies over the Pledge of Allegiance, such as religious objections to saying the Pledge, or is that a red herring?

2. Breadth of Conspiracy. The breadth of a conspiracy charge depends on how broadly the defendants can be shown to have agreed, either explicitly or tacitly. Only slightly tongue in cheek, can you imagine bringing every gang member in Los Angeles to trial for "conspiracy to intimidate the population of Los Angeles and thus to interfere with their rights to use public thoroughfares?" If that works, then how about sweeping in every kid wearing baggy pants and a black puffy jacket? Before you think your author is getting carried away with politically incorrect fantasy, look at the injunctions against gang-style loitering that were upheld in *Gallo v. Acuna*, 14 Cal. 4th 1090, 929 P.2d 596, 60 Cal. Rptr. 2d 277 (1997); and *City of New York v. Lenny Andrews, a/k/a Bloody Pimp*, 186 Misc. 2d 533, 719 N.Y.S.2d 442 (S. Ct. 2000).

NOTE ON ISLAMIC LAW AND TERMINOLOGY

Salameh introduces the concepts of jihad and fatwa to our study. As part of exploring appropriate responses to violence against civilian populations, it is natural to want to understand some of the motivations of those who engage in violence for political/ethnic/religious/cultural reasons. This Note is offered with great trepidation knowing that selective reading can cause gross misunderstanding of concepts that are central to the tenets of any faith system. To pursue the subject on your own, you can find much more simply by searching on the words "Shari'ah," "fatwa," or "jihad" on the web. It is also important to note that, although the acts of Islamist fundamentalists are a principal focus of terrorism concerns in the world today, these groups neither invented the technique nor have a monopoly on its use.

Shari'ah (sometimes transliterated as Shari'a) is the concept of Islamic law that corresponds to the Talmud in Hebrew law. Because neither Judaism nor Islam recognizes a separation of church and state, but rather sets out principles for all purposes, theological and behavioral principles are blended into a single code. Shari'ah is based on the Qu'ran (truth as revealed to the Prophet Muhammad), the Sunnah (words and deeds of the Prophet), and various secondary sources depending on the particular school of Shari'ah. It is promulgated and interpreted by jurists, persons with special training in the law who have created four distinct "schools" with slightly differing interpretations.

With respect to jihad, the following two pieces present competing views:

> Islamic jurisprudence divides the inhabitants of Dar al-Harb (known as harbis) into two: People of the Book (Ahl al-Kitab) and polytheists. People of the Book, defined in the Qur'an as Christians, Jews, and Sabeans, have a distinct status in Muslim eyes because they follow a genuine — if incomplete — revelation from a genuine prophet. They may live undisturbed under Muslim rule so long as they accept a subordinate status (that of the dhimmi) which entails paying a tribute (jizya) and suffering a wide range of disabilities. As for polytheists, the law requires Muslims to offer them the choice of Islam or death,

though this was rarely followed after the initial Muslim conquest of Arabia. Instead, Muslims generally treated all harbis as People of the Book. The jurists first sanctioned the inclusion of Zoroastrians in this category; Muslim conquerors of the Indian subcontinent extended it to Hindus as well, thereby effectively eliminating the category of polytheists.

The belief that jihad should continue until Dar al-Islam covers the entire world does not imply that the jurists expect Muslims to wage non-stop war. The Prophet Muhammad made a peace agreement with the Meccans in 630, the Treaty of Hudaybiya, and several of the early caliphs made peace treaties with the Byzantine Empire (some of which even required them to pay tribute to the Byzantines). Although there is no mechanism for recognizing a non-Muslim government as legitimate, the jurists built on these precedents to allow the negotiation of truces and peace treaties of limited duration. The jurists provide for military prudence, permitting the withdrawal of badly outnumbered or overpowered forces. And some jurists added an intermediate category, Dar al-'Ahd (Abode of Covenant) or Dar al-Sulh (Abode of Peace), for those countries where non-Muslim rulers govern non-Muslim subjects.

The jurists understand jihad not as an obligation of each individual Muslim but as a general obligation of the Muslim community. Only in emergencies, when Dar al-Islam comes under unexpected attack, do they expect all Muslims to participate in jihad warfare. Under normal circumstances, the failure of the community to fulfill the obligation of jihad is sinful; but an individual Muslim need not participate so long as other Muslims carry the burden. Shi'i writers make a further qualification, that offensive jihad is permissible only in the presence of the expected Imam — and thus not under current circumstances.

In contrast to this consensus view on a restricted doctrine of jihad, the prominent legal philosopher Ibn Taymiya (1268–1328) took a more activist position. He declared that a ruler who fails to enforce the Shari'a [Islamic law] rigorously in all its aspects, including the performance of jihad, forfeits his right to rule. A vigorous critic of the status quo, Ibn Taymiya strongly advocated, and personally participated in, jihad as warfare against the Crusaders and Mongols who occupied parts of Dar al-Islam. Ibn Taymiya developed his outlook by building on a long tradition of dissidents in Islamic history who directed jihad against rulers they deemed insufficiently Muslim, including the Kharijis of the seventh century and the Assassins of the eleventh century. Perhaps most important, he broke with the mainstream of Islam by his asserting that a professing Muslim who does not live by the faith is an unbeliever. Most jurists tolerated Muslim rulers who violated the Shari'a for the sake of the community, finding tyranny less bad than division or disorder, but Ibn Taymiya insisted on more. Ibn Taymiya and his associates are the most important intellectual precursors of contemporary Islamism.

Douglas E. Streusand, *What Does Jihad Mean?*, Middle East Q., Sept. 1997, *available at* http://www.ict.org.il/articles/jihad.htm.

The Islamic Revolution of Iran continues its triumphant march, despite the enemies' plots, and this year (1985) the Islamic Republic of Iran celebrates the sixth anniversary of the victory of the Revolution on Feb. 10, 1979. On this day, after a centuries-long night, the sun of Islam rose again in all its resplendent glory, and this historic event is celebrated in the Islamic Republic during the course of the "Ten-Day Dawn Celebrations."

It is said about Christianity that it has the distinction of not having any rule governing war. We, on the other hand, say that Islam has the distinction of having the law of jihad. If we look closely, we see that in Christianity there is no jihad because it has nothing at all. By which I mean that there is no Christian structure of society, no Christian legal system, and no Christian rules as to how a society is to be formed, for these to contain a law of jihad. There is no substance in Christianity; it contains no more than a few moral teachings that form a set of advice such as "tell the truth," "do not tell lies," "do not gobble up the wealth of others," and so on. Such things do not call for jihad? Islam however is a religion that sees it its duty and commitment to form an Islamic state. Islam came to reform society and to form a nation and government. Its mandate is the reform of the whole world.

Such a religion cannot be indifferent. It cannot be without a law of jihad. In the same way, its government cannot be without an army. While the scope of Christianity is extremely limited, that of Islam is extremely wide. While Christianity does not cross the frontiers of advice, Islam is a religion which covers all the activities of human life. It has laws which govern the society, economic laws, and political laws. It came to organize a state, to organize a government. Once this done, how can it remain without an army? How can it be without a law of jihad?

Council for Ten-Day Dawn Celebrations, *Jihad: The Holy War of Islam and Its Legitimacy in the Quran, available at* http://www.al-islam.org/short/jihad/.

In a similar vein, the term "fatwa" has different connotations to different adherents of Islam. In its most technical usage, it refers to a legal ruling by a religious lawyer or cleric with special qualifications to decide an issue. Because there is no central hierarchy or priesthood in Islam, however, various leaders can proclaim themselves qualified to issue fatwas. In the parlance of recent years, fatwas have been issued by various leaders for the purpose of calling on their followers to carry out violent acts against those who are thought to have committed a wrong against Islam. Sheikh Rahman and Osama bin Laden have both used the term in this fashion. Ayatollah Khomeini issued a fatwa, since declared inactive by the Iranian government, calling for the death of Salman Rushdie.

§ 2.04 THE EMERGENCE OF AL QAEDA

Among the many excellent depictions of the background of al Qaeda and Osama bin Laden, one of the most readable and accessible is the REPORT OF THE 9/11 COMMISSION. The underpinnings of U.S. support for the mujahideen in Afghanistan and the subsequent coalescing of the remnants of those forces into al Qaeda is probably familiar to most students. The training and weapons supplied by the CIA to confront the Soviets went to groups many of whom endorsed one or more of the views that the Middle East should never have been broken into separate nations after World War I, that the Muslim world should be reunited into a single Caliphate, and that the secular governments of most Arab nations were aligned with the nations of the West who were responsible for all the difficulties of the Middle East. The philosophical and historical bases of these views can be traced to the writings of Sayyid Qutb, the spokesperson for the Muslim Brotherhood who was executed by Egypt in 1966. *See* RONAN GUNARATNA, INSIDE AL QAEDA 114 (2002).

Two short quotes make the basic point.

When you decide to go to war against your current enemy, take a good, long look at the people behind you whom you choose as your friends, allies or mercenary fighters. Look well to see whether these allies already have unsheathed their knives — and are pointing them at your own back.

JOHN K. COOLEY, UNHOLY WARS 226 (2002).

To [many Muslim fundamentalists] the miracle victory over the Soviets was all the work of Allah — not the billions of dollars that America and Saudi Arabia poured into the battle, not the ten-year commitment of the CIA that turned an army of primitive tribesmen into techno-holy warriors. The consequence for America having waged a secret war and never acknowledging or advertising its role was that we set in motion the spirit of jihad and the belief in our surrogate soldiers that, having brought down one superpower, they could just as easily take on another.

GEORGE CRILE, CHARLIE WILSON'S WAR 521-22 (2002).

In 1993, al Qaeda made its existence known with attacks on U.S. forces serving as part of a UN peace-keeping mission in Somalia. The "Embassy Bombings" in Kenya and Tanzania on August 7, 1998 resulted in a wide-ranging conspiracy indictment in the Southern District of New York.

UNITED STATES v. BIN LADEN
(bill of particulars)
92 F. Supp. 2d 225 (S.D.N.Y. 2000)

MEMORANDUM AND ORDER

SAND, DISTRICT JUDGE.

Defendants are charged with numerous offenses arising out of their alleged involvement with an international terrorist organization led by Defendant Usama bin Laden ("bin Laden"). Presently before the Court are four motions, filed by Defendants Wadih El Hage ("El Hage"), Mamdouh Mahmud Salim ("Salim"), Mohamed Sadeek Odeh ("Odeh"), and Khalfan Khamis Mohamed ("K.K. Mohamed") seeking an order compelling the Government to file a bill of particulars that is responsive to over 150 separate requests for information. For the reasons set forth below, those motions are granted in part and denied in part. The Government is ordered to file a bill of particulars, but that bill need only be responsive to those specific requests that we identify below.

I. BACKGROUND

The indictment presently before the Court charges the 15 named Defendants with 267 discrete criminal offenses. Eleven of the Defendants (all except Salim, Khaled Al Fawwaz ("Al Fawwaz"), Ali Mohammed, and El Hage) are charged with 229 counts of murder as well as nine other substantive offenses,[6] based on the August, 1998 bombings of the United States embassies in Nairobi, Kenya and Dar es Salaam, Tanzania. Defendant El Hage is charged with twenty counts of perjury before a federal grand jury and three counts of making false statements to special agents of the Federal Bureau of Investigation ("FBI").

Each of the Defendants is also charged with participating in at least five distinct criminal conspiracies; El Hage and Ali Mohamed are accused of participating in six. Although each conspiracy is charged under a different provision of the federal criminal code, the allegations overlap to a significant degree. The six conspiracies are, for the most part, alleged to have had the same four criminal objectives: (1) murder of United States nationals; (2) killing of United States military personnel serving in Somalia and on the Saudi Arabian peninsula; (3) killing of United States nationals employed at the United States Embassies in Kenya and Tanzania; and (4) concealment of the conspirators' activities through the use of front companies, false identity and travel documents, coded correspondence, and by providing false information to authorities. All but one of the conspiracies are alleged to have been furthered by the commission of the same set of 144 overt acts.

---

[6] [Court's Footnote 1] In a prior opinion, this Court ordered two of those substantive offenses (two counts of maiming) as well as two of the murder counts to be dismissed for lack of jurisdiction. See United States v. bin Laden, 92 F. Supp. 2d [189] (S.D.N.Y. 2000). [The dismissed counts were based on the murder or maiming of persons other than U.S. nationals or employees on the embassy premises. The court merely held that §§ 114 & 1114 evidenced no congressional intent to claim U.S. jurisdiction for murder or maiming of a non-national by a non-national within a federal enclave overseas.]

In a section labeled, "Background," the Indictment explains that the charges arise out of the Defendants' alleged involvement with a vast, international terrorist network known as "al Qaeda," or "the Base." According to the Indictment, al Qaeda emerged in 1989, under the leadership of bin Laden and his two chief military commanders, Defendant Muhammad Atef ("Atef") and the now-deceased, Abu Ubaida al Banshiri ("Abu Ubaidah"), replacing a predecessor organization known as "mekhtab al khidemat," or the "Services Organization." Members of al Qaeda "pledged an oath of allegiance (called a 'bayat') to bin Laden and al Qaeda." The group was allegedly headquartered in Afghanistan from 1989 until 1991, at which time it re-located to the Sudan, ultimately returning to Afghanistan in 1996. According to the Indictment, al Qaeda functioned both on its own and in conjunction with other groups — such as the "al Jihad" organization in Egypt, Sheik Omar Abdel Rahman's "Islamic Group," the Iranian terrorist group, Hezballah, and the Sudanese National Islamic Front — that shared its strong opposition to the United States and a willingness to use violent, terrorist tactics in furtherance of their shared goals.

The Indictment's core factual allegations are set forth in a 31-page section that appears under the heading "Overt Acts." Without re-stating the entire litany of acts alleged therein, it is fair to say that the basic pattern that emerges is one in which al Qaeda, over a period of at least ten years, is said to have organized, financed, inspired, and generally facilitated a variety of violent attacks against United States personnel and property abroad. Some of the overt acts set forth in the Indictment, such as detonation of the explosives that destroyed the American embassies, are plainly violent acts in and of themselves. But many of the overt acts alleged consist of seemingly non-criminal conduct — such as writing letters, traveling, and engaging in business transactions — which, according to the Indictment, facilitated the violent attacks and thereby constitute overt acts in furtherance of the charged conspiracies.

A. The Organization

The Indictment alleges that beginning at least in 1989, al Qaeda established "training camps" and "guesthouses" in various areas around the world, including Afghanistan, Pakistan, the Sudan, Somalia, and Kenya. Al Qaeda members and the members of affiliated groups allegedly received military and intelligence training in those camps under the direction of Defendant Ali Mohamed and others. Defendant Salim allegedly managed some of the camps in Afghanistan and Pakistan.

The camps were allegedly operated under the auspices of a series of business established by bin Laden, Salim, and others. The businesses were used to engage in activities such as purchasing land, warehouses, and equipment for the camps; and for transporting currency and weapons to al Qaeda members "in various countries throughout the world."

Assistance from American citizens was allegedly essential to al Qaeda's operation. Two of the Defendants, Ali Mohamed and El Hage, both American citizens, are accused of assisting the organization by traveling "throughout the Western world to deliver messages and engage in financial transactions for the benefit of al Qaeda . . . ." According to the Indictment, Ali Mohamed and El Hage exchanged messages with each other, and with other co-conspirators, through letters and visits, regarding al Qaeda activities and the whereabouts of al Qaeda leaders.

B. The Fatwahs and Declarations of Jihad

In addition to providing military and intelligence training, obtaining weapons, establishing base camps, and coordinating the work of various members around the globe, al Qaeda allegedly facilitated violent attacks on United States interests by providing religious authority for those attacks. From time to time, according to the Indictment, bin Laden would issue rulings on Islamic law, called "fatwahs," which purported to justify al Qaeda's violent activities. [The earliest bin Laden fatwas urged that U.S. military forces in Somalia and the Arabian Peninsula should be attacked.]

Finally, in February, 1998 bin Laden issued another fatwah, eliminating the distinction between military and civilian personnel and stating that "Muslims should kill Americans — including civilians — anywhere in the world where they can be found." A few months later, in May, 1998, bin Laden endorsed a fatwah characterizing the United States Army as "the 'enemies of Islam'" and declaring a "jihad" against the United States "and its followers." That same month, according to the Indictment, bin Laden held a press conference, attended by Defendants Atef and Al-'Owhali, in which he reiterated his "intention to kill Americans."

C. The Violent Attacks

1. Somalia

Under the leadership of Defendants Atef, Fazul Abdullah Mohamed ("F.A. Mohamed"), Odeh, and the now deceased, Abu Ubaidah, al Qaeda allegedly provided military training and assistance in its camps to Somali tribes opposed to the UN peacekeeping mission in that country. On October 3 and 4, 1993, the Indictment alleges, those persons they trained "participated in an attack on United States military personnel serving in Somalia as part of Operation Restore Hope, which attack resulted in the killing of 18 United States Army personnel . . . ."

2. The East African Bombings

The Indictment includes roughly parallel allegations with respect to the bombings in Kenya and Tanzania. During the spring and early summer of 1998, al Qaeda members and other co-conspirators began to congregate in both Nairobi and Dar es Salaam. One of the first tasks for each group was to purchase a truck and make necessary alterations to prepare the truck for use with a bomb. Defendant Sheikh Ahmed Salim Swedan ("Swedan") is charged with purchasing both trucks, assisted in Nairobi by Msalam and assisted in Dar es Salaam by Defendant Ahmed Khalfan Ghailani ("Ghailani").

During the first week in August, final preparations were made. Defendants Al-'Owhali and F.A. Mohammed, along with Azzam, made those preparations at a villa in Nairobi; Defendants Fadhil, K.K. Mohamed, and Msalam, along with an unindicted co-conspirator identified only as "CS-2" made preparations in Dar es Salaam. On the night before the bombings, pursuant to the advice of an unidentified "al Qaeda member," Defendants Odeh, Msalam, and Ghailani left Nairobi under assumed names and traveled to Karachi, Pakistan. Early the next morning, claims of responsibility were sent by fax to London, England for further distribution by unidentified co-conspirators.

Finally, on August 7, 1998, separated in time by only ten minutes, the two bombs were detonated. In Nairobi, they were allegedly detonated by Azzam and F.A. Mohammed, accompanied by Al-'Owhali; in Dar es Salaam, they were detonated by an unindicted co-conspirator, identified by the Government as "Ahmed the German." In the immediate aftermath of the bombing, Defendant F.A. Mohammed allegedly cleaned out the villa in Nairobi where preparations had been made and traveled to the Comoros Islands.

Also in the aftermath of the bombing, Defendant El Hage — who had testified about al Qaeda before a federal grand jury upon his return to the United States from Kenya approximately one year earlier — was subpoenaed to appear before a federal grand jury investigating the bombings. On both occasions, El Hage was also interviewed by special agents of the FBI. The Indictment accuses Mr. El Hage of making a wide variety of false statements both to the FBI agents and to the grand jury, in both 1997 and 1998.

D. Procedural History

On September 16, 1998, following his testimony before the Grand Jury, Defendant El Hage was arrested by federal authorities. He was incarcerated pursuant to certain special conditions of confinement, which federal regulations authorize for particularly dangerous detainees. In this case, those conditions have included periods of solitary confinement, as well as severe restrictions on the Defendants' access to visitors and to the telephone. Defendants Odeh and Al-'Owhali were next brought into federal custody, and first appeared before the Court on October 8, 1998. Salim first appeared on December 21, 1998, after having been arrested in Germany on September 6, 1998. Ali Mohamed first appeared on May 27, 1999 and K.K. Mohamed was arraigned before this Court on October 8, 1999. Since being brought into federal custody, each of those Defendants has also been incarcerated pursuant to the particulary restrictive conditions described above.

The process of preparing for a trial in this case has been unusually protracted. The complexity of the charges, the voluminous discovery that needs to be exchanged, the location of many relevant documents and witnesses in various countries around the world, special procedures for handling classified material, the need to translate literally thousands of documents, and the potential availability of capital punishment for some of the Defendants have combined to require an extraordinary amount of work on the part of all parties involved. Despite everyone's best efforts, it is anticipated at this time that the earliest possible date that this case could be ready for trial is September 5, 2000 — almost two years after the first Defendant was brought into custody and incarcerated under restricted conditions. Trial of the guilt phase of this case, excluding jury selection and deliberation, is expected to last at least six months.

Four of the Defendants — El Hage, Salim, Odeh, and K.K. Mohamed — now move for an order requiring the Government to file a bill of particulars. Together, the Defendants have requested more than 150 specific items of information that they wish to be included in that bill. The Defendants contend that the filing of a bill of particulars responsive to those requests is necessary to permit them to prepare a defense and to prevent prejudicial surprise at trial. The Government, on the other hand, in addition to challenging the appropriateness of a bill of particulars that includes the types of information requested by the Defendants, contends that it need not file a bill of particulars because the extensive detail included in the Indictment, the voluminous discovery it has provided to date,[7] and the additional disclosures provided in its response to Mr. El Hage's bail application more than adequately apprise the Defendants of the charges that they must be prepared to answer.

[The court denied all but a few of the requests for more particular allegations.]

NOTES AND QUESTIONS

1. *United States v. bin Laden.* *United States v. bin Laden (severance)*, 109 F. Supp. 2d 211 (S.D.N.Y. 2000). Six of the persons indicted in the Somalia attacks and Embassy bombings were slated to be tried jointly. Three (El Hage, Salim, and Ali Mohamed), called themselves the "non-bombing defendants" because they were charged only with conspiracy, moved to sever their trials from the "bombing defendants" who were charged with both conspiracy and the substantive offenses. Their principal argument related to graphic photographs and details from the bombings that they claimed would not be admissible against them in a mere conspiracy trial. The judge responded:

The moving Defendants anticipate that the jury will erroneously consider the

---

[7] [Court's Footnote 14] To date, the Government has provided hundreds of thousands of pages of documents, dozens of audio and video tapes, transcripts and translations of these materials, hundreds of crime scene and other photographs, several dozen laboratory reports reflecting forensic tests of thousands of items and numerous other FBI Reports.

graphic bombing evidence against them even though it might be inadmissible. They argue that notwithstanding any cautionary instruction this Court might provide, the jurors will simply be unable to compartmentalize the evidence and consider it only against those Defendants as to whom it is admissible and they argue (somewhat differently) that, even if the jurors can compartmentalize the evidence, they will be so inflamed by the graphic bombing evidence that they will ignore what the moving Defendants claim is a relative lack of evidence establishing the existence of, and moving Defendants' participation in, the charged conspiracies. We are not convinced, at this stage of the case, that either form of anticipated prejudicial spillover is so likely as to constitute "a serious risk" that the jury will not make "a reliable judgment about guilt or innocence." Multi-defendant trials are quite common in the federal system, and many involve evidence that is admissible against one defendant, but not against another. Federal courts, quite routinely, have found juries able to follow and abide by appropriate cautionary instructions.

2. *United States v. El-Hage*. *United States v. El-Hage*, 213 F.3d 74 (2d Cir. 2000). El Hage was held in solitary confinement with very limited access to counsel, friends, or family. In response to his claims that he was a loyal U.S. citizen with a stable family and not a threat to flee, the Government produced affidavits regarding his involvement with the al Qaeda. "Defendant was one of bin Laden's trusted associates, privy to al Qaeda's secrets and plans, served as bin Laden's personal secretary, traveled on his American passport on bin Laden's behalf, moved bin Laden's money, and worked in bin Laden's factories in the Sudan — factories which served as a cover for the procurement of chemicals and weapons."

Defendant Wadih El-Hage appeals from an order [denying] defendant's motion to be released on bail, his application for rescission or for substantial modification of the Special Administrative Measures (S.A.M.) of his confinement. Pretrial detention is authorized by statute. Under 18 U.S.C. § 3142(e) a person may be detained before trial if it is found that no condition or combination of conditions of an indicted defendant "will reasonably assure the appearance of the [defendant] . . . and the safety of any other person and the community." Due process limits how long an accused may be detained in prison without a trial. But exactly how long such detention may extend before violating due process limits — the issue we face on this appeal — has not been fixed in the law. The 30–33 months of pretrial detention served or contemplated to be served before the conclusion of a trial in this case is extraordinary, and justified only by the unprecedented scope of violence that the conspiracy of which defendant was allegedly a part inflicted on innocent victims, by the extraordinarily complex and difficult preparation needed to present this case, and, more particularly, because the lengthy delay in bringing defendant to trial may not be laid at the government's doorstep.

3. Penalty Phase. Several defendants in the "embassy bombing" case eventually pleaded guilty, offered differing levels of cooperation, and were sentenced to various terms in prison. El-Hage and three other defendants were convicted after trial and sentenced to life imprisonment. In failing to come to a unanimous recommendation for the death penalty, the jury noted that some of its members believed that life imprisonment was a worse punishment than death.

§ 2.05   9/11 AND FOLLOW-UP PROSECUTIONS

A great deal of political ink has been spilled over the question of whether the airplane assaults of 9/11 should have been foreseen and thwarted. Detailed investigations after the fact isolated 20 hijackers who planned to be on board the aircraft, but only 19 made it. The alleged "20th hijacker" was Zacarias Moussaoui, who was already in custody for visa violations and whose computer was not tapped into until after the incidents. One

FBI agent in Phoenix had noticed the prevalence of young Arab males taking flying lessons without wanting to learn how to take-off or land. His memo was working its way through the system at the time of the incident.

The three most senior al Qaeda associates whom the U.S. has disclosed that it is holding are Khalid Sheikh Mohammed (aka KSM or Mukhtar), Riduan Isamuddin (aka Hambali), and Zein al Abideen Mohamed Hussein (aka Abu Zubaydah). These three are in military custody at Guantánamo.

Hambali and KSM illustrate the inter-connectedness of al Qaeda with other groups. Hambali was the leader of Jemaal Islamiya, worked closely with bin Laden until his capture in August 2003, and is credited with the bombing of the Bali night club in 2002.

KSM is widely regarded, and self-proclaimed, as the "mastermind" of the 9/11 plot as well as numerous other actions. He is the uncle of Ramzi Yousef, who was the mastermind of the 1993 WTC bombing working with the Sheikh Rahman group in New York. KSM was also involved with several other groups before affiliating with al Qaeda and claims to have maintained some autonomy by not "swearing allegiance to bin Laden." He was captured by Pakistani ISI forces on March 2, 2003 and turned over to U.S. authorities who interrogated him in an undisclosed location with "harsh" methods (*see* pages 452 & 522, *infra*). Time magazine reported on March 24, 2003 (http://www.time.com/time/nation/article/0,8599,436061,00.html):

> Mohammed's cooperation has improved investigators' understanding of al-Qaeda's command-and-control structure. Sources say he has explained that at any time, the organization has open-ended plans for as many as two dozen attacks — mostly ideas proposed by field operatives and sanctioned and financed by Osama bin Laden's inner circle.

Moussaoui is the only person who has been charged in U.S. courts with direct participation in the 9/11 attacks. He allegedly was to have been one of the hijackers but did not make the flight because he was already in custody for violations of immigration laws. Eventually, he was charged in the Eastern District of Virginia with six conspiracy counts: to commit a terrorist act, to commit air piracy, to destroy aircraft, to use weapons of mass destruction, to murder U.S. employees, and to destroy property. The tortured progress of attempting to bring his case to trial went on for years before the trial began in early 2006. The essential difficulty was that the defendant wanted access to witnesses in government custody but as to whom the government claimed a national security need for secrecy. We will take up the problems of the Classified Information Procedure Act in the next chapter. During his trial, he abruptly decided to plead guilty and was sentenced to life in prison. He then attempted to withdraw his guilty plea and appealed the denial of that motion to the Fourth Circuit. As of January, 2008, the Fourth Circuit has yet to rule on his appeal.

Another alleged 9/11 conspirator, Abdelghani Mzoudi, allegedly part of the "Hamburg cell," was tried and acquitted in a German court after both sides sought and were denied access to information from witnesses who were in U.S. custody at undisclosed locations. The German judge commented that "You were acquitted not because the court is convinced of your innocence, but because the evidence was not enough to convict you."[8]

In the wake of 9/11, federal agencies were subjected to harsh criticism for failing to prevent the attacks. Breaking up terrorist cells would seem to be what the public and politicians want. But how does a federal agent know which of the thousands of tips and leads to follow? For that matter, how does an agency "break up a cell?" Should there be some proof that the Lackawanna defendants planned to do something? They pleaded

---

[8] *See* BBC News, Feb. 5, 2004, *available at* http://news.bbc.co.uk/2/hi/europe/3460875.stm, Feb. 5, 2004; Washington Post, Feb. 5, 2004, *available at* http://www.washingtonpost.com/wp-dyn/articles/A15504-2004Feb5.html.

guilty to going to an al Qaeda training camp while al Qaeda was a "designated foreign terrorist organization." Does this interfere with their rights of association under the first amendment? Should there be more required before we throw people into prison? All these issues are explored in Chapter 3 below.

As a practical matter, there is also the question of when and how to move on a group of plotters.

§ 2.06 SELECTED READINGS

- M. Cherif Bassiouni, *Universal Jurisdiction for International Crimes: Historical Perspectives and Contemporary Practice*, 42 VA. J. INT'L LAW 81 (2001)

- Curtis Bradley, *Universal Jurisdiction and U.S. Law*, 2001 U. CHI. L. REV. 323

- Jonathan A. Bush, *How Did We Get Here? Foreign Abduction After Alvarez-Machain*, 45 STAN. L. REV. 939 (1993)

- James D. Fry, *Terrorism As A Crime Against Humanity and Genocide: The Backdoor to Universal Jurisdiction*, 7 UCLA J. INT'L L. & FOR. AFFAIRS 169 (2002)

- Michael J. Glennon, *International Kidnapping: State-sponsored Abduction: A Comment on United States v. Alvarez-Machain*, 86 A.J.I.L. 746 (1992)

- Douglas Kash, *Abducting Terrorists Under PDD-39: Much Ado About Nothing New*, 13 AM. U. INT'L L. REV. 139 (1997)

- Henry A. Kissinger, *The Pitfalls of Universal Jurisdiction*, 80 FOREIGN AFFAIRS, 86 (2001)

- Mark A. Summers, *The International Court of Justice's Decision in Congo v. Belgium: How Has It Affected the Development of a Principle of Universal Jurisdiction That Would Obligate All States to Prosecute War Criminals?* 21 BOSTON U. INT'L L.J. 63 (2003)

- Kristin Berdan Weissman, *Extraterritorial Abduction: The Endangerment of Future Peace*, 27 U.C. DAVIS L. REV. 460 (1994)

- Adam W. Wenger, *Extraterritorial Jurisdiction Under International Law: The Yunis Decision as a Model for the Prosecution of Terrorists in U.S. Courts*, 22 LAW & POLICY IN INT'L BUS. 409 (1991)

Chapter 3

MATERIAL SUPPORT OF TERRORISM

At the end of this chapter is a section highlighting some of the more significant conspiracy and "material support" prosecutions. The development of law in this area has been rapid but has left a couple of questions yet to be resolved by the Supreme Court. The principal question is whether a person donating money to a terrorist enterprise can be prosecuted even when he or she does not intend to advance the violent or unlawful portions of the group's activities. Terrorist organizations often have humanitarian activities (if for no reason other than to win adherents) but money given for those purposes frees up money for violent purposes. Two facts, that money is different from mere speech and that "money is fungible," lie at the heart of the developments traced in this chapter.

The *Salameh* case in Chapter 2 included charges of seditious conspiracy, which sounds much like treason, and Sheikh Rahman raised first amendment defenses that sound much like the concerns of the Framers with regard to treason itself. The Second Circuit pointed out that treason is a crime which applies only to those who have a duty of allegiance to the United States. The court also intimated that there could be a variety of other crimes with similar elements going by different names and questioned whether the constitutional restraints on treason prosecutions (such as two witnesses to the same overt act) would apply to those crimes.

In the Anti-Terrorism and Effective Death Penalty Act of 1996 (AEDPA), Congress created the offenses of "material support" for terrorists or for designated terrorist organizations. These offenses raise similar first amendment concerns to those of treason and conspiracy.

There are subtle differences among material support, conspiracy, and aiding and abetting an attempt. One way to understand the statutes, which also bears on the approach of the courts to the first amendment interests, is to focus on the scienter elements in the statutes. The principal statutory scheme consists of these principal steps:

- 18 U.S.C. § 2339A (providing material support to terrorists)
- 18 U.S.C. § 2339B (providing material support to a designated foreign terrorist organization [FTO])
- 8 U.S.C. § 1189 (designation of FTO by Secretary of State)

The material support statutes are a logical outgrowth of statutes that prohibit "trading with the enemy." In modern times, that concept has been extended to doing business with countries on designated embargo lists. The International Emergency Economic Powers Act, 50 U.S.C. § 1701-07, authorizes the President to exercise broad powers to "deal with any unusual and extraordinary threat, which has its source in whole or substantial part outside the United States, to the national security, foreign policy, or economy of the United States, if the President declares a national emergency with respect to such threat." Specific requirements and prohibitions apply to each nation so designated. Although the statute requires a finding of national emergency, prohibitions on trade may last for extended periods, as is the case with Cuba. Willful violations of regulatory orders under this statute are punishable as crimes.

The material support statutes are closely linked to statutes outlawing money laundering and structuring transactions to evade currency reporting requirements. Money laundering and structuring statutes criminalize apparently benign conduct that could be either a precursor to a known mischief (usually drug trafficking) or a method of covering up a completed offense. In similar fashion, the material support statutes represent an effort to enhance the preventive effectiveness of law enforcement by providing mechanisms to intercede in terrorist planning before an actual attack occurs. Government lawyers describe them as rough corollaries to laws against driving with an open container of alcohol in the car. The progression is something like this: Society wants to minimize automobile fatalities, so we make it a crime to kill someone with an automobile while intoxicated. To make that even more unlikely, we make it a crime to drive while intoxicated whether anyone is injured or not. This gives law enforcement power to prosecute an act before the substantive harm occurs. To extend out even further, most states prohibit driving with an open container of alcohol in the car. That is about the limit to which we can go because driving with a sealed container has sufficient social value that people are unwilling to outlaw that act.

In the "alcohol in the car scenario," recognize that not every drunk driver would kill someone. Further, not everyone with an open container in the car will drive while intoxicated. Yet, in both instances, the precursor conduct is criminalized because the threat of harm outweighs the social utility of the precursor conduct. Another striking example is presented by statutes and ordinances that limit the sale of pseudophedrine and other active ingredients that are precursors for making methamphetamine.

Similarly, prosecution of completed terrorist acts is not deemed sufficient to address the problem. If there were a completed crime, then investigators would (as happened after 9/11) start tracing backwards from that crime to find who supplied the money or other support and thus formed part of the conspiracy. To start that chain of investigation before the completed harm, the material support statutes create a precursor crime so that tracking and reporting requirements can be triggered at an earlier stage. The money laundering and financial reporting statutes move yet one more step out from the completed harm.

A major difference between the material support statutes and the alcohol-in-the-car scenario is that the social utility argument may be encountered much earlier when we are talking about interests of privacy and association. Particularly given the social interest in promoting charitable giving and political activism, there will be constitutional arguments to be made in almost every prosecution of this type.

Examples of proposed legislation that could go too far in reaction to the activities of animal rights groups are collected in STEVEN BEST & ANTHONY NOCELLA II, TERRORIST OR FREEDOM FIGHTERS: REFLECTIONS ON THE LIBERATION OF ANIMALS (2004). One example is a proposed Texas bill that would define an "animal rights or ecological terrorist organization as two or more persons organized for the purpose of supporting any politically motivated activity intended to obstruct or deter any person from participating in any activity involving animals." Another set of proposals would criminalize the photographing or videotaping of animal facilities.

To simplify matters, we will start with a case in which the constitutional arguments did not appear on the surface and move from there into more overt realms of political association.

§ 3.01 TREASON AND RELATED OFFENSES

[A] Trading with the Enemy

UNITED STATES v. LINDH
212 F. Supp. 2d 541 (E.D. Va. 2002)

T. S. ELLIS, III, DISTRICT JUDGE.

John Phillip Walker Lindh ("Lindh") is an American citizen who, according to the ten-count Indictment filed against him in February 2002, joined certain foreign terrorist organizations in Afghanistan and served these organizations there in combat against Northern Alliance and American forces until his capture in November 2001. In seven threshold motions, Lindh sought dismissal of certain counts of the Indictment on a variety of grounds, including lawful combatant immunity and selective prosecution.

All motions were denied following extensive briefing and oral argument. Recorded here are the reasons underlying those rulings.

I.

The Indictment's allegations may be succinctly summarized. In mid-2001, Lindh attended a military training camp in Pakistan run by Harakat ul-Mujahideen ("HUM"), a terrorist group dedicated to an extremist view of Islam.[1] After receiving several weeks of training, Lindh informed HUM officials that "he wished to fight with the Taliban in Afghanistan." Thus, in May or June 2001, he traveled from Pakistan into Afghanistan "for the purpose of taking up arms with the Taliban," eventually arriving at a Taliban recruiting center in Kabul, Afghanistan — the Dar ul-Anan Headquarters of the Mujahideen. On his arrival, Lindh presented a letter of introduction from HUM and advised Taliban personnel "that he was an American and that he wanted to go to the front lines to fight."

While at the Dar ul-Anan Headquarters, Lindh agreed to receive additional and extensive military training at an al Qaeda training camp. He made this decision "knowing that America and its citizens were the enemies of bin Laden and al-Qaeda and that a principal purpose of al-Qaeda was to fight and kill Americans." In late May or June 2001, Lindh traveled to a bin Laden guest house in Kandahar, Afghanistan, where he stayed for several days, and then traveled to the al Farooq training camp, "an al Qaeda facility located several hours west of Kandahar. He reported to the camp with approximately twenty other trainees, mostly Saudis, and remained there throughout June and July. During this period, he participated fully in the camp's training activities, despite being told early in his stay that "bin Laden had sent forth some fifty people to carry out twenty suicide terrorist operations against the United States and Israel." As part of his al Qaeda training, Lindh participated in "terrorist training courses in, among other things, weapons, orientating, navigation, explosives and battlefield combat." This training included the use of "shoulder weapons, pistols, and rocket-propelled grenades, and the construction of Molotov cocktails." During his stay at al Farooq, Lindh met personally with bin Laden, "who thanked him and other trainees for taking part in jihad." He also met with a senior al Qaeda official, Abu Mohammad Al-Masri, who inquired whether Lindh was interested in traveling outside Afghanistan to conduct operations against the United States and Israel. Lindh declined Al-Masri's offer in favor of going to the front lines to fight. It is specifically alleged that Lindh swore allegiance to jihad in June or July 2001.

When Lindh completed his training at al Farooq in July or August 2001, he traveled to Kabul, Afghanistan, where he was issued an AKM rifle "with a barrel suitable for long range shooting." Armed with this rifle, Lindh, together with approximately 150 non-Afghani fighters, traveled from Kabul to the front line at Takhar, located in Northeastern Afghanistan, where the entire unit was placed under the command of an Iraqi named Abdul Hady. Lindh's group was eventually divided into smaller groups that fought in shifts againt Northern Alliance troops in the Takhar trenches, rotating every one to two weeks. During this period, Lindh "carried various weapons with him, including the AKM rifle, an RPK rifle he was issued after the AKM rifle malfunctioned, and at least two grenades." He remained with his fighting group following the September 11, 2001 terrorist attacks, "despite having been told that bin Laden had ordered the [September 11] attacks, that additional terrorist attacks were planned, and that additional al Qaeda personnel were being sent from the front lines to protect bin Laden and defend against an anticipated military response from the United States." Indeed, it is specifically alleged that Lindh remained with his fighting group from October to December 2001, "after learning that United States military forces and

---

[1] [Court's Footnote 2] On October 8, 1997, HUM was designated by the Secretary of State as a foreign terrorist organization, pursuant to Section 219 of the Immigration and Nationality Act.

United States nationals had become directly engaged in support of the Northern Alliance in its military conflict with Taliban and al Qaeda forces."

In November 2001, Lindh and his fighting group retreated from Takhar to the area of Kunduz, Afghanistan, where they ultimately surrendered to Northern Alliance troops. On November 24, 2001, he and the other captured Taliban fighters were transported to Mazar-e-Sharif, and then to the nearby Qala-i-Janghi (QIJ) prison compound. The following day, November 25, Lindh was interviewed by two Americans — Agent Johnny Micheal Spann from the Central Intelligence Agency (CLA) and another government employee. Later that day, it is alleged that Taliban detainees in the QIJ compound attacked Spann and the other employee, overpowered the guards, and armed themselves. Spann was shot and killed in the course of the uprising and Lindh, after being wounded, retreated with other detainees to a basement area of the QIJ compound. The uprising at QIJ was eventually suppressed on December 1, 2001, at which time Lindh and other Taliban and al Qaeda fighters were taken into custody by Northern Alliance and American forces.

Following his capture, Lindh was interrogated, transported to the United States, and ultimately charged in this district with the following offenses in a ten-count Indictment:

(i) conspiracy to murder nationals of the United States, including American military personnel and other governmental employees serving in Afghanistan following the September 11, 2001 terrorist attacks, in violation of 18 U.S.C. § 2332(b)(2) (Count One);

(ii) conspiracy to provide material support and resources to HUM, a foreign terrorist organization, in violation of 18 U.S.C. § 2339B (Count Two);

(iii) providing material support and resources to HUM, in violation of 18 U.S.C. § 2339B and 2 (Count Three);

(iv) conspiracy to provide material support and resources to al Qaeda, a foreign terrorist organization, in violation of 18 U.S.C. § 2339B (Count Four);

(v) providing material support and resources to al Qaeda, in violation of 18 U.S.C. § 2339B and 2 (Count Five);

(vi) conspiracy to contribute services to al Qaeda, in violation of 50 U.S.C. § 1705(b) (Count Six);

(vii) contributing services to al Qaeda, in violation of 50 U.S.C. § 1705(b) (Count Seven);

(viii) conspiracy to supply services to the Taliban, in violation of 50 U.S.C. § 1705(b) (Count Eight);

(ix) supplying services to the Taliban, in violation of 50 U.S.C. § 1705(b) (Count Nine); and

(x) using and carrying firearms and destructive devices during crimes of violence, in violation of 18 U.S.C. §§ 924(c)(1)(A), 924(c)(1)(B)(ii) and 2 (Count Ten).

At issue are threshold motions to dismiss filed by the defense.

III.

Lindh claims that Count One of the Indictment should be dismissed because, as a Taliban soldier, he was a lawful combatant entitled to the affirmative defense of lawful combatant immunity.[2]

---

[2] [Court's Footnote 16] Lindh makes no claim of lawful combatant immunity with respect to the Indictment's allegations that he was a member or soldier of al Qaeda. Instead, Lindh focuses his lawful combatant immunity argument solely on the Indictment's allegations that he was a Taliban member. This focus is understandable as there is no plausible claim of lawful combatant immunity in connection with al Qaeda membership. Thus, it appears that Lindh's goal is to win lawful combatant immunity with respect to the

Lawful combatant immunity, a doctrine rooted in the customary international law of war, forbids prosecution of soldiers for their lawful belligerent acts committed during the course of armed conflicts against legitimate military targets. Belligerent acts committed in armed conflict by enemy members of the armed forces may be punished as crimes under a belligerent's municipal law only to the extent that they violate international humanitarian law or are unrelated to the armed conflict. This doctrine has a long history, which is reflected in part in various early international conventions, statutes and documents. But more pertinent, indeed controlling, here is that the doctrine also finds expression in the Geneva Convention Relative to the Treatment of Prisoners of War ("GPW"), to which the United States is a signatory. Significantly, Article 87 of the GPW admonishes that combatants "may not be sentenced . . . to any penalties except those provided for in respect of members of the armed forces of the said Power who have committed the same acts." Similarly, Article 99 provides that "no prisoner of war may be tried or sentenced for an act which is not forbidden by the law of the Detaining Power or by international law, in force at the time the said act was committed." These Articles, when read together, make clear that a belligerent in a war cannot prosecute the soldiers of its foes for the soldiers' lawful acts of war.

The inclusion of the lawful combatant immunity doctrine as a part of the GPW is particularly important here given that the GPW, insofar as it is pertinent here, is a self-executing treaty to which the United States is a signatory. It follows from this that the GPW provisions in issue here are a part of American law and thus binding in federal courts under the Supremacy Clause. This point, which finds support in the cases, is essentially conceded by the government. Moreover, the government does not dispute that this immunity may, under appropriate circumstances, serve as a defense to criminal prosecution of a lawful combatant.

The GPW sets forth four criteria an organization must meet for its members to qualify for lawful combatant status:

i. the organization must be commanded by a person responsible for his subordinates;

ii. the organization's members must have a fixed distinctive emblem or uniform recognizable at a distance;

iii. the organization's members must carry arms openly; and

iv. the organization's members must conduct their operations in accordance with the laws and customs of war.

[I]t appears that the Taliban lacked the command structure necessary to fulfill the first criterion, as it is manifest that the Taliban had no internal system of military command or discipline. Similarly, it appears the Taliban typically wore no distinctive sign that could be recognized by opposing combatants; they wore no uniforms or insignia and were effectively indistinguishable from the rest of the population. The requirement of such a sign is critical to ensure that combatants may be distinguished from the non-combatant, civilian population. Accordingly, Lindh cannot establish the second criterion. Next, although it appears that Lindh and his cohorts carried arms openly in satisfaction of the third criterion for lawful combatant status, it is equally apparent that members of the Taliban failed to observe the laws and customs of war. Thus, because record evidence supports the conclusion that the Taliban regularly targeted civilian

---

Taliban allegations and then to dispute factually the Indictment's allegations that he was a member of al Qaeda.

Also worth noting is that the government has not argued here that the Taliban's role in providing a home, a headquarters, and support to al Qaeda and its international terrorist activities serve to transform the Taliban from a legitimate state government into a terrorist institution whose soldiers are not entitled to lawful combatant immunity status. Put another way, the government has not argued that al Qaeda controlled the Taliban for its own purposes and that so-called Taliban soldiers were accordingly merely agents of al Qaeda, not lawful combatants.

populations in clear contravention of the laws and customs of war, Lindh cannot meet his burden concerning the fourth criterion.

In sum, the President's determination that Lindh is an unlawful combatant and thus ineligible for immunity is controlling here (i) because that determination is entitled to deference as a reasonable interpretation and application of the GPW to Lindh as a Taliban; (ii) because Lindh has failed to carry his burden of demonstrating the contrary; and (iii) because even absent deference, the Taliban falls far short when measured against the four GPW criteria for determining entitlement to lawful combatant immunity.

IV.

Lindh argues that Counts Six through Nine of the Indictment should be dismissed because they charge violations of regulations that were promulgated in excess of the statutory authority provided by the parent legislation, the International Economic Emergency Powers Act ("IEEPA"). Specifically, these four counts charge Lindh with "Contributing Services to al Qaeda," "Supplying Services to the Taliban," and conspiracy to do each of these, all in violation of the "Regulations." Simply put, Lindh contends that IEEPA does not authorize the promulgation of the Regulations to proscribe the conduct alleged in the Indictment. More particularly, Lindh argues that IEEPA cannot be construed to authorize promulgation of any regulations prohibiting his voluntary and noncommercial donation of services to the Taliban and al Qaeda.

The IEEPA is a relatively recent addition to this country's arsenal of sanctions to be used against hostile states and organizations in times of national emergency. For much of the twentieth century, this country's sanctions programs were governed by the Trading with the Enemy Act (hereafter "TWEA"), enacted in 1917. As amended in 1933, TWEA granted the President broad authority "to investigate, regulate, . . . prevent or prohibit . . . transactions" in times of war or declared national emergencies. Congress changed this statutory scheme in 1977 to limit TWEA's application to periods of declared wars, but created IEEPA to provide the President similar authority for use during other times of national emergency. Specifically, the language of IEEPA vests the President with the power to prescribe regulations to

> regulate, direct and compel, nullify, void, prevent or prohibit any acquisition, holding, withholding, use, transfer, withdrawal, transportation, importation or exportation of, or dealing in, or exercising any right, power, or privilege with respect to, or transactions involving, any property in which any foreign country or a national thereof has any interest by any person.

In January 1995, President Clinton, exercising his IEEPA authority, issued Executive Order 12947, declaring a national emergency to deal with the extraordinary threat posed by foreign terrorists who disrupt the Middle East peace process. Thereafter, the Treasury Department, via the Office of Foreign Assets Control ("OFAC"), promulgated, *inter alia*, 31 C.F.R. § 595.204, which, in relevant part, repeated the mandate of Executive Order 12947 regarding the prohibition on "the making or receiving of any contribution of funds, goods, or services" to or for the benefit of terrorists designated in, or pursuant to, the Executive Order.

In July 1999, again drawing upon his IEEPA authority, President Clinton issued Executive Order 13129, declaring a national emergency to deal with the threat posed by the Taliban. Specifically, the President found that the actions of the Taliban in Afghanistan in allowing territory there to be used as a safehaven and base of operations for Usama bin Laden and al Qaeda constituted an unusual and extraordinary threat to the national security and foreign policy of the United States. Presidents Clinton and Bush subsequently determined, in June 2000 and in June 2001, that the national emergency with respect to the Taliban would continue.

Despite the breadth of the Regulations and Executive Orders issued pursuant to

IEEPA, Lindh asserts that IEEPA does nothing more than permit the President to freeze the assets of a foreign state or foreign national and prohibit certain international financial transactions during times of a declared national emergency. Lindh argues, moreover, that neither the plain meaning of IEEPA, nor its legislative history, indicate that it provides a basis for the wide-ranging regulations here in issue. Thus, Lindh argues, the Regulations he is charged with violating exceed IEEPA's statutory grant of power.

The straightforward question presented, therefore, is whether the Regulations are within the scope of IEEPA. The IEEPA language in issue is as follows:

the President may, under such regulations as he may prescribe, by means of instructions, licenses, or otherwise

(A) investigate, regulate, or prohibit

(i) any transactions in foreign exchange,

(ii) transfers of credit or payments between, by, through or to any banking institution, to the extent that such transfers or payments involve any interest of any foreign country or a national thereof,

(iii) the importing or exporting of currency or securities; and

(B) investigate, regulate, direct and compel, nullify, void, prevent or prohibit, any acquisition, holding, withholding, use, transfer, withdrawal, transportation, importation or exportation of, or dealing in, or exercising any right, power, or privilege with respect to, or transactions involving, any property in which any foreign country or a national thereof has any interest;

by any person, or with respect to any property, subject to the jurisdiction of the United States.

On the question presented — whether the statute authorizes issuance of the Regulations — the statute's plain language is dispositive. Specifically, the dispositive language authorizes regulation and prohibition of the "use . . . , or dealing in, or exercising any right, power, or privilege with respect to, . . . any property" in which any "foreign country or national" has an interest. This sweeping language provides ample authority for the issuance of the Regulations and also easily reaches Lindh's alleged conduct. This conduct — which includes, for example, attending Taliban and al Qaeda training camps, using and transporting Taliban and al Qaeda weapons and ammunition, and using Taliban and al Qaeda transportation and residence facilities — plainly involves "use" of Taliban and al Qaeda "property." And, given the breadth of the common dictionary meanings of "use," "dealing," "transactions" and "property," there is similarly no doubt that Lindh's provision of combatant services to the Taliban and al Qaeda also falls within the IEEPA and the Regulations.

Lindh seeks to avoid the result reached here by arguing that IEEPA concerns only commercial or economic conduct. In support, he cites the statute's title and the fact that many cases involving IEEPA and TWEA address solely economic or commercial activity. This argument, while not implausible, is again contradicted by the statute's sweeping broad language. As noted, the plain dictionary meanings of statutory terms like "transaction," "dealing," "use," and "property" do not limit their use to commercial transactions; these terms are sufficiently broad to cover the conduct alleged here, including the donations of combatant services.

Lindh also argues unpersuasively that the D.C. Circuit's decision in *American Airways Charters, Inc. v. Regan*, 746 F.2d 865, 871-74, 241 U.S. App. D.C. 132 (D.C. Cir. 1984) precludes the result reached here. There, the court held that under the TWEA the Executive Branch could require a license before execution of a transaction reaching assets of a designated Cuban national, but that it lacked the authority to condition the bare formation of an attorney-client relationship on advance governmental approval. This decision is easily distinguishable from the instant case; it is rooted in constitutional due process concerns arising from the formation of the attorney-client relationship and the ability of a person to choose his or her counsel; it does not address the IEEPA's scope or the question whether that scope is ample authorization for the Regulations in issue.

V.

Lindh next argues that Counts Eight and Nine of the Indictment, which charge Lindh with providing and conspiring to provide prohibited services to the Taliban, should be dismissed because he is the victim of impermissible selective prosecution, in violation of his right to equal protection under the Fifth Amendment. Specifically, Lindh argues (i) he is the first to be prosecuted or criminally investigated under [the Taliban regulations] despite the fact that others appear to have violated these Regulations; and (ii) his selection for prosecution under the Regulations is based on his exercise of First Amendment rights. Should dismissal not be apparent on the existing record, Lindh seeks an evidentiary hearing to demonstrate the validity of his claim.

Significantly, claims of selective prosecution are not easily established. Such a claim "is not a defense on the merits to the criminal charge itself, but an independent assertion that the prosecutor has brought the charge for reasons forbidden by the Constitution."

To be sure, the allegations in the Complaint and the Indictment chronicle Lindh's conversion to Islam, his religious studies in Yemen and Pakistan, his voluntary association with the Taliban, and his oath of allegiance to jihad. Yet, none of this proves, as Lindh suggests, that the government prosecuted him because of his religious association. Instead, these allegations do nothing more than provide a chronology and context to explain how Lindh came to be on the battle front in Afghanistan and to supply services and support to the Taliban and al Qaeda. Discriminatory purpose cannot be inferred from a recitation of historical facts that merely provide context for criminal charges. Here, nothing in the Complaint or the Indictment suggests that Lindh's religious reasons for providing services to the Taliban motivated the government's decision to charge him with the offenses set out in Counts Eight and Nine. To the contrary, the serious offenses with which he is charged, *i.e.*, conspiracy to murder U.S. nationals and aiding foreign terrorist states and organizations, are manifestly the reasons for his prosecution, not his religious affiliation. Given the gravity of the allegations, there is every reason to believe that Lindh would have been prosecuted even had he been, say, a Presbyterian, a Scientologist, or an atheist.

VI.

Lindh also seeks dismissal of Counts Two through Nine of the Indictment on freedom of association, overbreadth, and vagueness grounds.

Lindh's First Amendment argument, distilled to its essence, is that he has a constitutional right to associate with foreign individuals and groups and that Counts Two through Nine impermissibly infringe this right by criminalizing this association. The statutes and regulations on which the Counts rest amount, in his view, to the government's attempt to impose on him guilt by association.

This argument is specious. Lindh is not accused of merely associating with a disfavored or subversive group whose activities are limited to circulating inflammatory political or religious material exhorting opposition to the government. Far from this, Lindh is accused of joining groups that do not merely advocate terror, violence, and murder of innocents; these groups actually carry out what they advocate and those who join them, at whatever level, participate in the groups' acts of terror, violence, and murder. There is, in other words, a clear line between First Amendment protected activity and criminal conduct for which there is no constitutional protection.

The most apposite authority on the issue is *Humanitarian Law Project v. Reno*, 205 F.3d 1130, 1133–34 (9th Cir. 2000), where a Ninth Circuit panel squarely rejected a constitutional challenge to the "material support or resources" prohibition of Section

2339B. There, the court resisted any analogy to cases based on association alone, noting that Section 2339B and related laws do "not prohibit being a member of one of the designated groups or vigorously promoting and supporting the political goals of the group." Rather, "plaintiffs are even free to praise the groups for using terrorism as a means of achieving their ends." What is prohibited by the statute is, in the court's words, "the act of giving material support." For this act, the court went on,

> there is no constitutional right to facilitate terrorism by giving terrorists the weapons and explosives with which to carry out their grisly missions. Nor, of course, is there a right to provide resources with which terrorists can buy weapons and explosives.

Unable to distinguish *Humanitarian Law Project,* Lindh argues instead that he is not a member of al Qaeda's "personnel" as defined by Section 2339B. Lindh maintains that providing "personnel" to HUM and al Qaeda could in certain instances amount to nothing more than the mere act of being physically present among members of a designated organization, obtaining information and training from such members, or simply being a member. Put differently, according to Lindh, allowing a prosecution under Section 2339B for providing "personnel" to a terrorist organization presents a constitutionally unacceptable risk that a mere bystander, sympathizer, or passive member will be convicted on the basis of association alone. This argument founders on the plain meaning of the term "personnel," which means "a body of persons usually employed (as in a factory, office, or organization)," or "a body of persons employed in some service." Thus, in Section 2339B, providing "personnel" to HUM or al Qaeda necessarily means that the persons provided to the foreign terrorist organization work under the direction and control of that organization. One who is merely present with other members of the organization, but is not under the organization's direction and control, is not part of the organization's "personnel." This distinction is sound; one can become a member of a political party without also becoming part of its "personnel;" one can visit an organization's training center, or actively espouse its cause, without thereby becoming "personnel." Simply put, the term "personnel" does not extend to independent actors. Rather, it describes employees or employee-like operatives who serve the designated group and work at its command or, in Lindh's case, who provide themselves to serve the organization.

Lindh also argues that Section 2339B and the IEEPA Regulations are facially unconstitutionally overbroad, as Section 2339B's prohibition of providing "personnel" penalizes mere association and the IEEPA Regulations' ban on the provision of "services" sweeps a substantial amount of protected conduct within its prohibitions. As noted, the term "personnel" entails more than mere presence. Indeed, a person can circulate a pamphlet or give a speech in support of an organization without also working within the organization's body of "personnel." So construed, and when any potential overbreadth is "judged in relation to the statute's plainly legitimate sweep," there is no danger, let alone a substantial one, that Section 2339B will be applied to infringe upon legitimate rights of association.

In support of his vagueness argument, Lindh relies principally on the Ninth Circuit's decision in *Humanitarian Law Project,* 205 F.3d at 1137–38, where the Ninth Circuit concluded that the district court did not abuse its discretion in issuing a limited preliminary injunction on vagueness grounds regarding the term "personnel." The Ninth Circuit stated, "it is easy to see how someone could be unsure about what [Section 2339B] prohibits with the use of the term 'personnel,' as it blurs the line between protected expression and unprotected conduct." The court observed that someone who advocates the cause of a terrorist organization "could be seen as supplying them with personnel," particularly since "having an independent advocate frees up members to engage in terrorist activities instead of advocacy." In response to the government's argument that "personnel" should be construed to extend only to a person's service "under the direction or control" of the terrorist organization, the Ninth Circuit declined to do so on the ground that it was "not authorized to rewrite the law so it will pass constitutional muster," and upheld the preliminary injunction in issue.

As already noted, the plain meaning of "personnel" is such that it requires, in the context of Section 2339B, an employment or employment-like relationship between the persons in question and the terrorist organization. The Ninth Circuit's vagueness holding in *Humanitarian Law Project* is neither persuasive nor controlling. The term is aimed at denying the provision of human resources to proscribed terrorist organizations, and not at the mere *independent* advocacy of an organization's interests or agenda. Thus, the term "personnel" in Section 2339B gives fair notice to the public of what is prohibited and the provision is therefore not unconstitutionally vague.

NOTES AND QUESTIONS

1. Pleas and Waivers. Following the district court's decision on the various motions to dismiss, Lindh entered into a plea agreement with the government by which he pleaded guilty to Count 9 (supplying services to the Taliban) and to an additional charge of carrying explosives in the commission of a felony. He accepted a 20-year sentence and agreed to cooperate with the government in its investigations. As part of the plea agreement, the government agreed not to treat him as an enemy combatant subject to military detention.

Media coverage of Lindh's transfer to Guantánamo showed him naked, apparently dirty and bruised. The plea agreement waives claims of mistreatment by U.S. agents and specifically states that Lindh does not allege "intentional mistreatment" by U.S. agents. Waiver of civil claims against the police is typical in plea agreements, but a remaining question is whether there really is any substantive "law" constraining the behavior of agents outside the U.S. If an action were brought on behalf of someone captured and interrogated outside the country, what law would apply?

2. Multiple Offenses. If there had been no plea bargain, what elements of "material support" might Lindh have been shown to have provided to al Qaeda or the Taliban? If the government had been required to prove these same elements in support of the charge of carrying explosives in the commission of a felony, is there a problem of compounding offenses from the same behavior? There is a discussion of the international law of cumulative charging and sentencing in the *Akayesu* case, *infra* § 6.02[B].

The court points out that the government did not charge that providing material support to the Taliban was the same as providing material support to al Qaeda. Placing yourself in the position of a prosecutor, if the Taliban were not itself on the list of embargoed regimes, what evidence would you have wanted to show the connection between the Taliban and al Qaeda, and to show Lindh's knowledge of that connection? This question will help set us up for later questions about accumulation of evidence for civilian criminal trials based on behavior in foreign countries, which leads to the issue of using the military justice system for these purposes.

3. *United States v. Khan.* A number of defendants were accused of multiple preparations for "violent jihad" in *United States v. Khan*, 309 F. Supp. 2d 789 (E.D. Va. 2004). The defendants used paintball and toy car remote controls in their preparation and training in the hills of Virginia. The defendants were preparing to assist, and some went to train with, the Lashkar-e-Taiba (LET or LT), a group warring against India in the Kashmir. This constituted a conspiracy to violate a slightly arcane federal statute, the Neutrality Act, 18 U.S.C. § 960, even though they never got to engage in action. In addition, some were charged with preparing to assist the Taliban and by inference al Qaeda. The judge disagreed with the inference of assistance to al Qaeda. "Although Khan's fighting on behalf of the Al-Qaeda's protector, the Taliban, would certainly benefit Al-Qaeda, such assistance does not fit the statutory definition of material support or resources."

4. Hamdi. Yaser Hamdi was picked up at the same time under similar circumstances as Lindh, was transported to Guantánamo, and was then transferred to military custody in South Carolina. Why might Lindh have been treated differently?

Why was Lindh not charged with treason? How close did this prosecution come to intruding upon Lindh's right of association?

[B]   Treason and Political Freedom

Excerpt from *United States v. Rahman*, § 2.03, *supra*:

In the late colonial period, as today, the charge of treason carried a "peculiar intimidation and stigma" with considerable "potentialities . . . as a political epithet." *See* William Hurst, *Treason in the United States (Pt. II)*, 58 HARV. L. REV. 395, 424–25 (1945).

At the time of the drafting of the Constitution, furthermore, treason was punishable not only by death, but by an exceptionally cruel method of execution designed to enhance the suffering of the traitor. *See* 4 WILLIAM BLACKSTONE, COMMENTARIES *92 (observing that the punishment for treason is "terrible" in that the traitor is "hanged by the neck, then cut down alive," that "his entrails [are then] taken out, and burned, while he is yet alive," "that his head [is] cut off," and that his "body [is then] divided into four parts"). In contrast, lesser subversive offenses were penalized by noncapital punishments or less brutal modes of execution. *See id.* at *94–*126. The Framers may have intended to limit the applicability of the most severe penalties — or simply the applicability of capital punishment for alleged subversion — to instances of levying war against, or adhering to enemies of, the United States. Today treason continues to be punishable by death, while seditious conspiracy commands a maximum penalty of twenty years imprisonment.

In recognition of the potential for political manipulation of the treason charge, the Framers may have formulated the Treason Clause as a protection against promiscuous resort to this particularly stigmatizing label, which carries such harsh consequences. It is thus possible to interpret the Treason Clause as applying only to charges denominated as "treason."

The Supreme Court has identified but not resolved the question whether the clause applies to offenses that include all the elements of treason but are not branded as such. *Compare Ex Parte Quirin*, 317 U.S. 1, 38 (1942) (suggesting, in dictum, that citizens could be tried for an offense against the law of war that included all the elements of treason), *with Cramer v. United States*, 325 U.S. 1, 45 (1945) (noting in dictum that the Court did not "intimate that Congress could dispense with [the] two-witness rule merely by giving the same offense another name") The question whether a defendant who engaged in subversive conduct might be tried for a crime involving all the elements of treason, but under a different name and without the constitutional protection of the Treason Clause, therefore remains open. And we need not decide it in this case, because the crime of which Nosair was convicted differs significantly from treason, not only in name and punishment, but also in definition.

———

The law of treason has not been widely studied in a very long time, but it may offer us some interesting insights. The Framers were so concerned about the potential misuses of treason charges that this is the only "crime" which is given special treatment in the Constitution. Article III, section 3 provides:

Treason against the United States, shall consist only in levying War against them, or in adhering to their Enemies, giving them Aid and Comfort. No Person shall be convicted of Treason unless on the Testimony of two Witnesses to the same overt Act, or on Confession in open Court.

The Treason Clause builds extremely high barricades against prosecution for this "heinous" crime, so the question becomes whether those barricades can be circumvented by creating other crimes, or by calling the traitor something else such as an "enemy combatant." To be flippant, could we avoid restrictions on prosecution for treason by calling it jaywalking?

Article III's "peculiar phraseology observable in the definition of" treason, and "the equally stringent feature" requiring two eyewitness' testimony of the same overt act, have been said to flow from the Framers' discomfort with "abuses . . . under the tyrannical reigns of the Tudors and the Stuarts." *Charge to Grand Jury — Treason*, 30 Fed. Cas. No. 18,271, at 1035 (S.D.N.Y. 1861). In particular, the Framers were reacting to the concept of "constructive treason" by which anyone who spoke in support of, or was friendly with those who expressed, resistance to policies of the Crown could be accused of treason. Indeed, it is not likely that even the Tudors and Stuarts would have had an easy time of tossing a citizen into jail indefinitely on the mere say-so of a military officer. That they did so on occasion led directly to our constitutional language preventing the possibility.

Is it possible to square this history with the "enemy combatant" concept employed by the Supreme Court in *Quirin* and leading to military incarceration of U.S. citizens? The answer is "not very easily," and the lessons to be learned are not very clear. The Treason Clause creates two categories of treason: levying war against the United States, and providing aid and comfort to the enemy. In the first there must be an armed assemblage and the second requires an enemy.

Chief Justice Marshall gave us our first instruction in the operation of the Treason Clause in *Ex parte Bollman*, 8 U.S. (4 Cranch) 75 (1807), dealing with some of the alleged conspirators in the Burr escapade.

> To constitute that specific crime for which the prisoners now before the court have been committed, war must be actually levied against the United States. However flagitious may be the crime of conspiring to subvert by force the government of our country, such conspiracy is not treason. To conspire to levy war, and actually to levy war, are distinct offences. The first must be brought into operation by the assemblage of men for a purpose treasonable in itself, or the fact of levying war cannot have been committed. [Even] the actual enlistment of men to serve against the government does not amount to levying war.

> It is not the intention of the court to say that no individual can be guilty of this crime who has not appeared in arms against his country. On the contrary, if war be actually levied, that is, if a body of men be actually assembled for the purpose of effecting by force a treasonable purpose, all those who perform any part, however minute, or however remote from the scene of action, and who are actually leagued in the general conspiracy, are to be considered as traitors. But there must be an actual assembling of men for the treasonable purpose, to constitute a levying of war.

> Crimes so atrocious as those which have for their object the subversion by violence of those laws and those institutions which have been ordained in order to secure the peace and happiness of society, are not to escape punishment because they have not ripened into treason. The wisdom of the legislature is competent to provide for the case; and the framers of our constitution, . . . must have conceived it more safe that punishment in such cases should be ordained by general laws, . . . than that it should be inflicted under the influence of those passions which . . . a flexible definition of the crime, or a construction which would render it flexible, might bring into operation. It is therefore more safe as well as more consonant to the principles of our constitution, . . . that crimes not clearly within the constitutional definition, should receive such

punishment as the legislature in its wisdom may provide.

> To complete the crime of levying war against the United States, there must be an actual assemblage of men for the purpose of executing a treasonable design. In the case now before the court, a design to overturn the government of the United States in New-Orleans by force, . . . if carried into execution, would have been treason, and the assemblage of a body of men for the purpose of carrying it into execution would amount to levying of war against the United States; but no conspiracy for this object, no enlisting of men to effect it, would be an actual levying of war.

Marshall distinguished strongly between treason and conspiracy: "However flagitious may be the crime of conspiring to subvert by force the government of our country, such conspiracy is not treason." It must be remembered, however, that the Burr escapade did not involve a foreign enemy, so there was no occasion for him to deal with the offense of providing aid and comfort to the enemy.

Marshall went on to deal with our very question. Although "to complete the crime of levying war against the United States, there must be an actual assemblage of men for the purpose of executing a treasonable design," he expressed the view that the legislature could define other offenses to which the strictures of the Treason Clause would not apply. The Framers were concerned about the passions that the thought of treason would engender, but they could have been comfortable with the thought that "crimes not clearly within the constitutional definition, should receive such punishment as the legislature in its wisdom may provide."

In a number of cases stemming from the Civil War, the judges expanded Marshall's view of conspiracy to state that there could be no such concept as an accessory to treason because an act was either treason or not. *United States v. Greathouse*, 26 Fed. Cas. No. 15,254 (C.C. Cal. 1863). They consistently recognized the differences between the two kinds of treason, the first depending on whether the defendant has taken up arms, the second consisting of providing material support to a recognized enemy. It is familiar ground that President Lincoln attempted to use the military courts for prosecution of Southern sympathizers, leading eventually to the opinion in *Ex parte Milligan*, § 8.02, *infra*.

After the War, in *Thorington v. Smith*, 75 U.S. (8 Wall.) 1 (1869), the Court dealt with the question of whether debts payable in Confederate currency were still valid as between two individuals (and, thus, payable in U.S. currency after the war ended). Chief Justice Chase distinguished among different levels of *de facto* governments. At one extreme would be a solidly established actual government such that "adherents to it in war against the government *de jure* do not incur the penalties of treason." The government of the Confederacy, he argued, was sufficiently established that it obtained "actual supremacy, however unlawfully gained, in all matters of government within its military lines."

> That supremacy did not justify acts of hostility to the United States. How far it should excuse them must be left to the lawful government upon the re-establishment of its authority. But it made obedience to its authority, in civil and local matters, not only a necessity but a duty. Without such obedience, civil order was impossible.

By this language, Chase was implying that there could be no prosecution for providing aid and comfort to the enemy by a person residing within the military control of the Confederacy. As we know, there were no such prosecutions.

World War I produced the seminal case for all of First Amendment law, *Schenck v. United States*, 249 U.S. 47 (1919). Schenck and his cohorts were convicted of conspiracy to violate the Espionage Act of 1917, which made it unlawful to "cause insubordination . . . in the military and naval forces of the United States, and to obstruct the recruiting and enlistment service of the United States." Justice Holmes' famous opinion for the Court, after using the analogy of "falsely shouting fire in a crowded theater," stated:

> The question in every case is whether the words used are used in such circumstances and are of such a nature as to create a clear and present danger that they will bring about the substantive evils that Congress has a right to prevent. It is a question of proximity and degree. When a nation is at war many things that might be said in time of peace are such a hindrance to its effort that their utterance will not be endured so long as men fight and that no Court could regard them as protected by any constitutional right. It seems to be admitted that if an actual obstruction of the recruiting service were proved, liability for words that produced that effect might be enforced. The statute of 1917 in § 4 punishes conspiracies to obstruct as well as actual obstruction. If the act, (speaking, or circulating a paper,) its tendency and the intent with which it is done are the same, we perceive no ground for saying that success alone warrants making the act a crime.

Before *Schenck* was decided, Congress had already responded to the emerging level of dissension regarding U.S. entry into the war in Europe by passing the 1918 amendments to the Espionage Act. Under the amendments, it was unlawful to "urge, incite, or advocate" actions that could disrupt the war. In *Abrams v. United States*, 250 U.S. 616 (1919), the majority of the Court found that an intent to disrupt the war effort was sufficient to uphold conviction under the statute. Justice Holmes, joined by Brandeis, dissented with the famous "marketplace of ideas" analysis. The combination of opinions sounds as if the majority were treating the statute as if it were a finding by Congress of "clear and present danger." It seems that in this stage, Congress and the Court had accepted Chief Justice Marshall's invitation to Congress to define non-treason offenses.

The only World War II case in the Supreme Court on the subject of Treason was *Cramer v. United States*, 325 U.S. 1 (1945), a follow-up to *Quirin*. One of the eight German saboteurs, Thiel, had a friend in the U.S. named Cramer, who was German by birth and a naturalized U.S. citizen. Thiel contacted Cramer in New York, met with him twice in public places, and gave Cramer some money to hold for him. Cramer testified that he suspected Thiel was here as a propagandist for the German government, but there was no evidence that Cramer suspected anything of the violent intentions of the saboteurs. Cramer was convicted of treason. The basic question presented to the Supreme Court was whether an overt act in furtherance of treason needed to be done with intent by the defendant of furthering enemy action against the government, or whether an innocent overt act could be treasonous because of its role in the enemy's plan.

Justice Jackson's majority opinion in *Cramer* canvassed the history of treason prosecutions from English law through the colonial era. The Framers built protections against treason prosecutions to guard against two dangers: "(1) perversion by established authority to repress peaceful political opposition; and (2) conviction of the innocent as a result of perjury, passion or inadequate evidence." The critical passage for definition of criminal behavior is this:

> Thus the crime of treason consists of two elements: adherence to the enemy; and rendering him aid and comfort. A citizen intellectually or emotionally may favor the enemy and harbor sympathies or convictions disloyal to this country's policy or interest, but so long as he commits no act of aid and comfort to the enemy, there is no treason. On the other hand, a citizen may take actions which do aid and comfort the enemy — making a speech critical of the government or opposing its measures, profiteering, striking in defense plants or essential work, and the hundred other things which impair our cohesion and diminish our strength — but if there is no adherence to the enemy in this, if there is no intent to betray, there is no treason.

Applying these thoughts to the evidence, Jackson pointed out that the prosecution had "withdrawn" the safekeeping of money as an overt act to be submitted to the jury. That left only the two meetings with Thiel that were corroborated by eyewitness testimony. These could not be said to have shown either furtherance of a scheme sufficient to prove either aid or adherence to the enemy. By contrast, the money transaction, if proved by the requisite testimony, would have made "a quite different case." Finally, Justice Jackson addressed the Government's arguments for relaxing the standards related to treason:

> The Government has urged that our initial interpretation of the treason clause should be less exacting, lest treason be too hard to prove and the Government disabled from adequately combating the techniques of modern warfare. But the treason offense is not the only nor can it well serve as the principal legal weapon to vindicate our national cohesion and security. In debating this provision, Rufus King observed to the Convention that the "controversy relating to Treason might be of less magnitude than was supposed; as the legislature might punish capitally under other names than Treason." His statement holds good today. Of course we do not intimate that Congress could dispense with the two-witness rule merely by giving the same offense another name. But the power of Congress is in no way limited to enact prohibitions of specified acts thought detrimental to our wartime safety.

Congress, with the assistance of many subsequent administrations, has accepted this invitation by enacting many statutes that relate to providing aid and comfort to those who threaten the public safety of the United States. Perhaps the most directly relevant are those that criminalize "providing material support to terrorists" (§ 2339A) and "providing material support or resources to designated terrorist organizations" (§ 2339B). There are also crimes, such as what John Walker Lindh pleaded guilty to, defined as violations of Presidential directives blocking trading with, or providing services to, regimes designated in time of national emergency, most of which are punishable under § 1705. Given the history of the Treason Clause, and particularly Justices Marshall's and Jackson's invitations to Congress, there can be little doubt about the validity of these statutes, except insofar as they might in some situations be subject to first amendment restrictions.

§ 3.02   THE COMMUNIST CONSPIRACY AND THE RIGHT OF ASSOCIATION

Whitney v. California, 274 U.S. 357 (1927). Ms. Whitney was convicted of criminal syndicalism under a state statute that defined the offense "as any doctrine, advocating [or] teaching unlawful methods of terrorism as a means of accomplishing a change in industrial ownership or control, or effecting any political change." Although Whitney was a delegate to the state Communist Labor Party convention, at which most members favored violence as a means of securing political change, she argued that she did not favor violence and in fact had attempted to forestall violence as a method of political change. The Supreme Court said that she was raising issues of fact which had been found against her and which an appellate court could not reconsider. The Court also reiterated the familiar formula that acting in concert was a greater threat to the public order than the expressions or acts of individuals acting separately.

Justices Brandeis and Justice Holmes concurred but added some warning thoughts:

> The felony which the statute created is a crime very unlike the old felony of conspiracy or the old misdemeanor of unlawful assembly. The mere act of assisting in forming a society for teaching syndicalism, of becoming a member of it, or assembling with others for that purpose is given the dynamic quality of crime. There is guilt although the society may not contemplate immediate promulgation of the doctrine. Thus the accused is to be punished, not for attempt, incitement or conspiracy, but for a step in preparation, which, if it

threatens the public order at all, does so only remotely. The novelty in the prohibition introduced is that the statute aims, not at the practice of criminal syndicalism, nor even directly at the preaching of it, but at association with those who propose to preach it.

The right of free speech, the right to teach and the right of assembly are, of course, fundamental rights. These may not be denied or abridged. But, although the rights of free speech and assembly are fundamental, they are not in their nature absolute. Their exercise is subject to restriction, if the particular restriction proposed is required in order to protect the state from destruction or from serious injury, political, economic or moral. That the necessity which is essential to a valid restriction does not exist unless speech would produce, or is intended to produce, a clear and imminent danger of some substantive evil which the state constitutionally may seek to prevent has been settled.

Those who won our independence believed that the final end of the state was to make men free to develop their faculties, and that in its government the deliberative forces should prevail over the arbitrary. They valued liberty both as an end and as a means. They believed liberty to be the secret of happiness and courage to be the secret of liberty. They believed that freedom to think as you will and to speak as you think are means indispensable to the discovery and spread of political truth; that without free speech and assembly discussion would be futile; that with them, discussion affords ordinarily adequate protection against the dissemination of noxious doctrine; that the greatest menace to freedom is an inert people; that public discussion is a political duty; and that this should be a fundamental principle of the American government. They recognized the risks to which all human institutions are subject. But they knew that order cannot be secured merely through fear of punishment for its infraction; that it is hazardous to discourage thought, hope and imagination; that fear breeds repression; that repression breeds hate; that hate menaces stable government; that the path of safety lies in the opportunity to discuss freely supposed grievances and proposed remedies; and that the fitting remedy for evil counsels is good ones.

Fear of serious injury cannot alone justify suppression of free speech and assembly. Men feared witches and burnt women. It is the function of speech to free men from the bondage of irrational fears. To justify suppression of free speech there must be reasonable ground to fear that serious evil will result if free speech is practiced. There must be reasonable ground to believe that the danger apprehended is imminent. There must be reasonable ground to believe that the evil to be prevented is a serious one. Every denunciation of existing law tends in some measure to increase the probability that there will be violation of it. Condonation of a breach enhances the probability. Expressions of approval add to the probability. Propagation of the criminal state of mind by teaching syndicalism increases it. Advocacy of law-breaking heightens it still further. But even advocacy of violence, however reprehensible morally, is not a justification for denying free speech where the advocacy falls short of incitement and there is nothing to indicate that the advocacy would be immediately acted on. The wide difference between advocacy and incitement, between preparation and attempt, between assembling and conspiracy, must be borne in mind. In order to support a finding of clear and present danger it must be shown either that immediate serious violence was to be expected or was advocated, or that the past conduct furnished reason to believe that such advocacy was then contemplated.

Those who won our independence by revolution were not cowards. They did not fear political change. They did not exalt order at the cost of liberty. To courageous, self-reliant men, with confidence in the power of free and fearless reasoning applied through the processes of proper government, no danger flowing from speech can be deemed clear and present, unless the incidence of the evil apprehended is so imminent that it may befall before there is opportunity for full discussion. If there be time to expose through discussion the falsehood and fallacies, to avert the evil by the processes of education, the remedy to be applied is more speech, not enforced silence. Only an emergency can justify repression. Such must be the rule if authority is to be reconciled with freedom. Such, in my opinion, is the command of the Constitution. It is therefore always open to Americans to challenge a law abridging free speech and assembly by showing that there was no emergency justifying it.

Dennis v. United States, **341 U.S. 494 (1951).** Several leaders of the American Communist Party were convicted of violating the federal Smith Act:

Sec. 2. (a) It shall be unlawful for any person

(1) to knowingly or willfully advocate, abet, advise, or teach the duty, necessity, desirability, or propriety of overthrowing or destroying any government in the United States by force or violence, or by the assassination of any officer of any such government;

(3) to organize or help to organize any society, group, or assembly of persons who teach, advocate, or encourage the overthrow or destruction of any government in the United States by force or violence; or to be or become a member of, or affiliate with, any such society, group, or assembly of persons, knowing the purposes thereof.

Sec. 3. It shall be unlawful for any person to attempt to commit, or to conspire to commit, any of the acts prohibited by the provisions of this title.

The majority opinion for the Supreme Court stated that it accepted the "clear and present danger" test as amplified by Brandeis and Holmes in *Whitney* but found that the circumstances of the U.S. in the 1940s met the test in this fashion:

If Government is aware that a group aiming at its overthrow is attempting to indoctrinate its members and to commit them to a course whereby they will strike when the leaders feel the circumstances permit, action by the Government is required. Certainly an attempt to overthrow the Government by force, even though doomed from the outset because of inadequate numbers or power of the revolutionists, is a sufficient evil for Congress to prevent. The damage which such attempts create both physically and politically to a nation makes it impossible to measure the validity in terms of the probability of success, or the immediacy of a successful attempt. In the instant case the trial judge charged the jury that they could not convict unless they found that petitioners intended to overthrow the Government "as speedily as circumstances would permit." This does not mean, and could not properly mean, that they would not strike until there was certainty of success. What was meant was that the revolutionists would strike when they thought the time was ripe. We must therefore reject the contention that success or probability of success is the criterion.

The mere fact that from the period 1945 to 1948 petitioners' activities did not result in an attempt to overthrow the Government by force and violence is of course no answer to the fact that there was a group that was ready to make the attempt. The formation by petitioners of such a highly organized conspiracy, with rigidly disciplined members subject to call when the leaders, these petitioners, felt that the time had come for action, coupled with the inflammable nature of world conditions, similar uprisings in other countries, and the touch-and-go nature of our relations with countries with whom petitioners were in the very least ideologically attuned, convince us that their convictions were justified on this score. And this analysis disposes of the contention that a conspiracy to advocate, as distinguished from the advocacy itself, cannot be constitutionally restrained, because it comprises only the preparation. It is the existence of the conspiracy which creates the danger. If the ingredients of the reaction are present, we cannot bind the Government to wait until the catalyst is added.

Justice Jackson concurred on this basis:

> The authors of the clear and present danger test never applied it to a case like this, nor would I. What really is under review here is a conviction of conspiracy. The Constitution does not make conspiracy a civil right. The basic rationale of the law of conspiracy is that a conspiracy may be an evil in itself, independently of any other evil it seeks to accomplish. Having held that a conspiracy alone is a crime and its consummation is another, it would be weird legal reasoning to hold that Congress could punish the one only if there was "clear and present danger" of the second.

Justices Black and Douglas dissented.

Following *Dennis*, the government attempted a few more prosecutions for violation of the Smith Act and found essentially that the Court was not so receptive as it was initially. In *Yates v. United States*, 354 U.S. 298, 324 (1957), Justice Harlan recast the holding of *Dennis*:

> The essence of the *Dennis* holding was that indoctrination of a group in preparation for future violent action, as well as exhortation to immediate action, by advocacy found to be directed to "action for the accomplishment" of forcible overthrow, to violence "as a rule or principle of action," and employing "language of incitement," is not constitutionally protected when the group is of sufficient size and cohesiveness, is sufficiently oriented towards action, and other circumstances are such as reasonable to justify apprehension that action will occur.

Scales v. United States, 367 U.S. 203, 228 (1961), further limited the Smith Act in ways that will be relevant in the cases below, implying that the limitations were required by the first amendment. The Court held that "active" participation in group with "guilty knowledge and intent" could be punished but not "merely an expression of sympathy with the alleged criminal enterprise, unaccompanied by any significant action in its support or any commitment to undertake such action."

McCarthyism in its extreme form died from the weight of its own intolerance and the misdeeds of its principal proponent. Senator McCarthy was censured by the Senate in 1954 and died in 1957. Nevertheless, the "red scare" continued to occupy a central place in the politics of the United States throughout much of the Cold War era. Prosecutions of communist sympathizers, however, became very rare. The Supreme Court then found that it was a threat from another quarter that would cause it to rethink much of its first amendment lore.

BRANDENBURG v. OHIO
395 U.S. 444, 89 S. Ct. 1827, 23 L. Ed. 2d 430 (1969)

PER CURIAM.

The appellant, a leader of a Ku Klux Klan group, was convicted under the Ohio Criminal Syndicalism statute for "advocat[ing] the duty, necessity, or propriety of crime, sabotage, violence, or unlawful methods of terrorism as a means of accomplishing industrial or political reform" and for "voluntarily assembl[ing] with any society, group, or assemblage of persons formed to teach or advocate the doctrines of criminal syndicalism." Ohio Rev. Code Ann. § 2923.13.

The Ohio Criminal Syndicalism Statute was enacted in 1919. From 1917 to 1920, identical or quite similar laws were adopted by 20 States and two territories. In 1927, this Court sustained the constitutionality of California's Criminal Syndicalism Act, the text of which is quite similar to that of the laws of Ohio. *Whitney v. California*. The

Court upheld the statute on the ground that, without more, "advocating" violent means to effect political and economic change involves such danger to the security of the State that the State may outlaw it. But *Whitney* has been throughly discredited by later decisions. *See Dennis v. United States.* These later decisions have fashioned the principle that the constitutional guarantees of free speech and free press do not permit a State to forbid or proscribe advocacy of the use of force or of law violation except where such advocacy is directed to inciting or producing imminent lawless action and is likely to incite or produce such actions. A statute which fails to draw this distinction impermissibly intrudes upon the freedoms guaranteed by the First and Fourteenth Amendments. It sweeps within its condemnation speech which our Constitution has immunized from governmental control.

Measured by this test, Ohio's Criminal Syndicalism Act cannot be sustained. The Act punishes persons who "advocate or teach the duty, necessity, or propriety" of violence "as a means of accomplishing industrial or political reform;" or who publish or circulate or display any book or paper containing such advocacy; or who "justify" the commission of violent acts "with intent to exemplify, spread or advocate the propriety of the doctrines of criminal syndicalism;" or who "voluntarily assemble" with a group formed "to teach or advocate the doctrines of criminal syndicalism." Neither the indictment nor the trial judge's instructions to the jury in any way refined the statute's bald definition of the crime in terms of mere advocacy not distinguished from incitement to imminent lawless action.

Accordingly, we are here confronted with a statute which, by its own words and as applied, purports to punish mere advocacy and to forbid, on pain of criminal punishment, assembly with others merely to advocate the described type of action. Such a statute falls within the condemnation of the First and Fourteenth Amendments. The contrary teaching of *Whitney v. California* cannot be supported, and that decision is therefore overruled.

JUSTICE BLACK, concurring:

I agree with the views expressed by Mr. Justice Douglas in his concurring opinion in this case that the "clear and present danger" doctrine should have no place in the interpretation of the First Amendment. I join the Court's opinion, which, as I understand it, simply cites *Dennis v. United States*, but does not indicate any agreement on the Court's part with the "clear and present danger" doctrine on which *Dennis* purported to rely.

JUSTICE DOUGLAS, concurring:

While I join the opinion of the Court, I desire to enter a caveat. Though I doubt if the "clear and present danger" test is congenial to the First Amendment in time of a declared war, I am certain it is not reconcilable with the First Amendment in days of peace. I see no place in the regime of the First Amendment for any "clear and present danger" test, whether strict and tight as some would make it, or free-wheeling as the Court in *Dennis* rephrased it.

When one reads the opinions closely and sees when and how the "clear and present danger" test has been applied, great misgivings are aroused. First, the threats were often loud but always puny and made serious only by judges so wedded to the status quo that critical analysis made them nervous. Second, the test was so twisted and perverted in *Dennis* as to make the trial of those teachers of Marxism an all-out political trial which was part and parcel of the cold war that has eroded substantial parts of the First Amendment.

Action is often a method of expression and within the protection of the First Amendment. Suppose one tears up his own copy of the Constitution in eloquent protest to a decision of this Court. May he be indicted? Suppose one rips his own Bible to shreds to celebrate his departure from one "faith" and his embrace of atheism. May he be indicted? The line between what is permissible and not subject to control and what may be made impermissible and subject to regulation is the line between ideas and overt acts.

The example usually given by those who would punish speech is the case of one who falsely shouts fire in a crowded theatre. This is, however, a classic case where speech is brigaded with action. They are indeed inseparable and a prosecution can be launched for the overt acts actually caused. Apart from rare instances of that kind, speech is, I think, immune from prosecution. Certainly there is no constitutional line between advocacy of abstract ideas as in *Yates* and advocacy of political action as in *Scales*. The quality of advocacy turns on the depth of the conviction; and government has no power to invade that sanctuary of belief and conscience.

NOTES AND QUESTIONS

1. **Membership and Association.** Prior to *Brandenburg*, the Court had already declared in a number of cases that mere membership in the Communist Party could not be penalized. In the process, there developed a distinct first amendment "right of association." *Scales v. United States*, 367 U.S. 203 (1961), upheld a conviction for membership in the Communist Party only upon a finding of specific intent to engage in illegal action. *Noto v. United States*, 367 U.S. 290 (1961), overturned a similar conviction in which the specific intent was lacking. Both cases read the statute's criminalizing of membership as if it included an element of intent to act.

2. *NAACP v. Alabama ex rel. Patterson.* *NAACP v. Alabama ex rel. Patterson*, 357 U.S. 449 (1958), unanimously declared that the state could not seek membership lists because disclosure would negatively impact the now-recognized right of association. Through the 1980s and 1990s, the Court elaborated on the right of association in a number of situations dealing with regulation of political parties and the electoral process. The scope of constitutional protection for election campaign giving, campaign reforms, and the like are all beyond the scope of the discussion here, but it is safe to say that the right of association is now firmly entrenched in the first amendment.

3. *NAACP v. Claiborne Hardware.* *NAACP v. Claiborne Hardware*, 458 U.S. 886 (1982), is cited frequently in the cases below on material support of terrorism. The Court overturned a state court judgment against the NAACP on behalf of merchants who had been damaged by a boycott of their businesses. Although some aspects of the boycott may have been unlawful, neither the organization nor its members could be held liable without a showing of direct participation in the unlawful activity. "Civil liability may not be imposed merely because an individual belonged to a group, some members of which committed acts of violence. For liability to be imposed by reason of association alone, it is necessary to establish that the group itself possessed unlawful goals and that the individual held a specific intent to further those illegal goals." *Id.* at 920.

4. *Buckley v. Valeo.* *Buckley v. Valeo*, 424 U.S. 1 (1976), dealt with the validity of the Federal Election Campaign Act of 1971. Among other things, FECA limited individual contributions to federal campaigns and attempted to limit campaign expenditures by individuals or groups, as well as expenditures by candidates themselves. The Supreme Court started with the proposition that all these activities carried first amendment protection as part of the political process and under the right of association. "In a republic where the people are sovereign, the ability of the citizenry to make informed choices among candidates for office is essential." The expenditure limitations were struck down on that basis. With regard to the contribution limitations, the Court found that the claim of freedom of expression was lessened: "A contribution serves as a general expression of support for the candidate and his views, but does not communicate the underlying basis for the support." The Court went on to hold that, although the contribution limits "impinge on protected associational freedoms," they

were warranted by a "sufficiently important interest" in "limit[ing] the actuality and appearance of corruption resulting from large individual financial contributions." These basic propositions were revalidated in *McConnell v. FEC*, 540 U.S. 93 (2003), while also recognizing that some expenditures could actually be counted as contributions toward a particular campaign when the expenditures were closely coordinated with the campaign itself (a controversy erupted in the 2004 presidential campaigns over the question of whether official campaign committees were collaborating with smear tactics of apparently independent groups).

§ 3.03   DESIGNATED FOREIGN TERRORIST ORGANIZATIONS AND THE RIGHT OF ASSOCIATION

What must the government prove to make out a conspiracy case while avoiding impact on the freedom of association? Providing material support "knowing or intending that they are to be used in preparation for, or in carrying out, a violation of" a specified statute differs from providing material support to a "foreign terrorist organization" designated by the Secretary of State. The designation places everyone on notice that mere support of this organization is unlawful, but does that really change the impact of the right of association? In other words, doesn't the Constitution require knowledge of imminent violent or fraudulent behavior before we can punish support of an organization?

Material support prosecutions raise constitutional issues of the right of association, vagueness and overbreadth of the statutes, and due process regarding the methods for designation of foreign terrorist organizations. The following cases address all these issues.

[A]   Prohibiting Material Support

HUMANITARIAN LAW PROJECT v. RENO [HLP I][3]
205 F.3d 1130 (9th Cir. 2000)

KOZINSKI, CIRCUIT JUDGE.

We consider whether Congress may, consistent with the First Amendment, prohibit contributions of material support to certain foreign terrorist organizations.

I

The Antiterrorism and Effective Death Penalty Act of 1996, known among the cognoscenti as AEDPA, authorizes the Secretary of State to "designate an organization as a foreign terrorist organization . . . if the Secretary finds that (A) the organization is a foreign organization; (B) the organization engages in terrorist activity . . . ; and (C) the terrorist activity of the organization threatens the security of United States nationals or the national security of the United States."

Pursuant to those guidelines, the Secretary had, as of October 1997, designated 30

---

[3] In UNDERSTANDING THE LAW OF TERRORISM (Matthew Bender 2007), I provided this explanation of the numbering system of the *HLP* cases:

> In my casebook, LEGAL RESPONSES TO TERRORISM (Matthew Bender 2005), I adopted a numbering system for these cases based on only the court of appeals decisions. Because the Ninth Circuit numbered them differently, and other courts used that numbering system, my earlier approach can create confusion. Accordingly, I am repenting and using the court's numbering of the decisions here. My apologies to students who will have to work with different numbers for a while.

Then in December 2007 the Ninth Circuit shifted to the system of numbering only the court of appeals opinions. Therefore, I will revert to that system, which once again means that the numbering in the casebook and the "Understanding" book will be different.

organizations as foreign terrorist organizations. Two such entities are the Kurdistan Workers' Party ("PKK") and the Liberation Tigers of Tamil Eelam ("LTTE"). Plaintiffs, six organizations and two United States citizens, wish to provide what they fear would be considered material support to the PKK and LTTE. Plaintiffs claim that such support would be directed to aid only the nonviolent humanitarian and political activities of the designated organizations. Being prohibited from giving this support, they argue, infringes their associational rights under the First Amendment. Because the statute criminalizes the giving of material support to an organization regardless of whether the donor intends to further the organization's unlawful ends, plaintiffs claim it runs afoul of the rule set forth in cases such as *NAACP v. Claiborne Hardware Co.*, 458 U.S. 886, 102 S. Ct. 3409 (1982). That rule, as succinctly stated in *Claiborne Hardware*, is "for liability to be imposed by reason of association alone, it is necessary to establish that the group itself possessed unlawful goals and that the individual held a specific intent to further those illegal aims." Plaintiffs further complain that AEDPA grants the Secretary unfettered and unreviewable authority to designate which groups are listed as foreign terrorist organizations, a violation of the First and Fifth Amendments. Lastly, plaintiffs maintain that AEDPA is unconstitutionally vague.

Plaintiffs sought a preliminary injunction barring enforcement of AEDPA against them. The district court denied the injunction, for the most part. However, it agreed with plaintiffs that AEDPA was impermissibly vague, specifically in its prohibition on providing "personnel" and "training." The court therefore enjoined the enforcement of those prohibitions. Each side appeals its losses.

II

A. Plaintiffs try hard to characterize the statute as imposing guilt by association, which would make it unconstitutional under cases such as *Claiborne Hardware*. But *Claiborne Hardware* and similar cases address situations where people are punished "by reason of association alone" — in other words, merely for membership in a group or for espousing its views. AEDPA authorizes no such thing. The statute does not prohibit being a member of one of the designated groups or vigorously promoting and supporting the political goals of the group. Plaintiffs are even free to praise the groups for using terrorism as a means of achieving their ends. What AEDPA prohibits is the act of giving material support, and there is no constitutional right to facilitate terrorism by giving terrorists the weapons and explosives with which to carry out their grisly missions. Nor, of course, is there a right to provide resources with which terrorists can buy weapons and explosives.

B. Plaintiffs also insist that AEDPA is unconstitutional because it proscribes the giving of material support even if the donor does not have the specific intent to aid in the organization's unlawful purposes. They rely on *American-Arab Anti-Discrimination Comm. v. Reno*, 70 F.3d 1045 (9th Cir. 1995) [deportation allegedly based on membership in subversive groups], where we declared that "the government must establish a 'knowing affiliation' and a 'specific intent to further those illegal aims' " in order to punish advocacy. But advocacy is far different from making donations of material support. Advocacy is always protected under the First Amendment whereas making donations is protected only in certain contexts. Plaintiffs here do not contend they are prohibited from advocating the goals of the foreign terrorist organizations, espousing their views or even being members of such groups. They can do so without fear of penalty right up to the line established by *Brandenburg v. Ohio*.

C. Plaintiffs make a separate First Amendment argument based on the fact that the terrorist organizations in question also engage in political advocacy. Pointing to cases such as *Buckley v. Valeo*, plaintiffs argue that providing money to organizations engaged in political expression is itself both political expression and association.[4] However, the cases equating monetary support with expression involved organizations whose overwhelming function was political advocacy. *Buckley* is the quintessential example where the contributions were made to candidates for political office for the purpose of helping them engage in electioneering. Under those circumstances, money, and the things money can buy, do indeed serve as a proxy for speech and demonstrate one's association with the organization. However, even in *Buckley*, the Court treated limits on donations differently from limits on candidates' expenditures of personal funds. While the First Amendment protects the expressive component of seeking and donating funds, expressive *conduct* receives significantly less protection than pure speech. The government may thus regulate contributions to organizations that engage in lawful — but non-speech related — activities. And it may certainly regulate contributions to organizations performing unlawful or harmful activities, even though such contributions may also express the donor's feelings about the recipient.

Contrary to plaintiffs' argument, the material support restriction here does not warrant strict scrutiny because it is not aimed at interfering with the expressive component of their conduct but at stopping aid to terrorist groups. Intermediate scrutiny applies where, as here, "a regulation . . . serves purposes unrelated to the content of expression."

When we review under the intermediate scrutiny standard, we must ask four questions: Is the regulation within the power of the government? Does it promote an important or substantial government interest? Is that interest unrelated to suppressing free expression? And, finally, is the incidental restriction on First Amendment freedoms no greater than necessary?

Here all four questions are answered in the affirmative. First, the federal government clearly has the power to enact laws restricting the dealings of United States citizens with foreign entities; such regulations have been upheld in the past over a variety of constitutional challenges. *See, e.g., Regan v. Wald*, 468 U.S. 222, 244 (1984) (restrictions on travel to Cuba did not violate Fifth Amendment); *Teague v. Regional Comm'r of Customs*, 404 F.2d 441, 445 (2d Cir. 1968) (upholding regulations "designed to limit the flow of currency to specified hostile nations" despite the fact that regulations "impinged on first amendment freedoms"). Second, the government has a legitimate interest in preventing the spread of international terrorism, and there is no doubt that that interest is substantial. Third, this interest is unrelated to suppressing free expression because it restricts the actions of those who wish to give material support to the groups, not the expression of those who advocate or believe the ideas that the groups supports.

So the heart of the matter is whether AEDPA is well enough tailored to its end of preventing the United States from being used as a base for terrorist fundraising. Because the judgment of how best to achieve that end is strongly bound up with foreign policy considerations, we must allow the political branches wide latitude in selecting the means to bring about the desired goal. Plaintiffs argue that the prior statutory scheme, which allowed the donation of humanitarian assistance to those who were not directly involved in terrorist activity, was properly tailored and the current statutory scheme is therefore overbroad. But the fact that the prior statutory scheme was narrower tells us nothing about whether the current scheme is overbroad, because we don't know how well the prior scheme worked. Presumably Congress thought that it did not work well enough and so decided to broaden it. Moreover, the Supreme Court has held that the

---

[4] [Court's Footnote 1] What is at issue here is the right of Americans to express their association with foreign political groups through donations. The political advocacy of the PKK and LTTE directed toward their own governments is not protected by our First Amendment. *Cf. United States v. Verdugo-Urquidez*, 494 U.S. 259 (1990) (refusing to extend constitutional protection to Mexican citizen).

government need not select the least restrictive or least intrusive means of accomplishing its purpose.

Congress explicitly incorporated a finding into the statute that "foreign organizations that engage in terrorist activity are so tainted by their criminal conduct that any contribution to such an organization facilitates that conduct." It follows that all material support given to such organizations aids their unlawful goals.[5] Indeed, as the government points out, terrorist organizations do not maintain open books. Therefore, when someone makes a donation to them, there is no way to tell how the donation is used. Further, as amicus Anti-Defamation League notes, even contributions earmarked for peaceful purposes can be used to give aid to the families of those killed while carrying out terrorist acts, thus making the decision to engage in terrorism more attractive. More fundamentally, money is fungible; giving support intended to aid an organization's peaceful activities frees up resources that can be used for terrorist acts. We will not indulge in speculation about whether Congress was right to come to the conclusion that it did. We simply note that Congress has the fact-finding resources to properly come to such a conclusion. Thus, we cannot say that AEDPA is not sufficiently tailored.

D. Plaintiffs also argue that the statute violates their First and Fifth Amendment rights by giving the Secretary "unfettered discretion" to limit their right to associate with certain foreign organizations, and by insulating her decisions from judicial review. AEDPA does not grant the Secretary unfettered discretion in designating the groups to which giving material support is prohibited. The statute authorizes the Secretary to designate only those groups that engage in terrorist activities. This standard is not so vague or indeterminate as to give the Secretary unfettered discretion. For example, the Secretary could not, under this standard, designate the International Red Cross or the International Olympic Committee as terrorist organizations. Rather, the Secretary must have reasonable grounds to believe that an organization has engaged in terrorist acts — assassinations, bombings, hostage-taking and the like — before she can place it on the list. This standard is sufficiently precise to satisfy constitutional concerns. And, because the regulation involves the conduct of foreign affairs, we owe the executive branch even more latitude than in the domestic context.

Plaintiffs argue that any decision the Secretary makes in designating an organization is essentially unreviewable. However, 8 U.S.C. § 1189(b) provides for judicial review of the Secretary's decision in the United States Court of Appeals for the District of Columbia Circuit. Although plaintiffs complain that the review is ineffectual because of the degree of deference accorded to the Secretary's decision, that is a necessary concomitant of the foreign affairs power. In any event, that challenge must be raised in an appeal from a decision to designate a particular organization.

E. Finally, Plaintiffs challenge AEDPA on vagueness grounds. In the district court, they alleged that "foreign terrorist organization" and "material support," as defined in AEDPA, were void for vagueness. The district court agreed in part, finding that two of the components included within the definition of material support, "training" and "personnel," were impermissibly vague. It enjoined the prosecution of any of the plaintiffs' members for activities covered by these terms. The district court did not abuse its discretion in doing so.

When a criminal law implicates First Amendment concerns, the law must be

---

[5] [Court's Footnote 4] Plaintiffs argue that this finding is undercut by other portions of the statute that allow the donation of unlimited amounts of medicine and religious items. We see things differently. Congress is entitled to conclude that respect for freedom of religion militates in favor of allowing religious items to be donated to foreign organizations, even though doing so may incidentally aid terrorism. Further it could also rationally decide that the humanitarian value of providing medicine to such organizations outweighs the risk that the medicine would be sold to finance terrorist activities. Congress is entitled to strike such delicate balances without giving up its ability to prohibit other types of assistance which would promote terrorism.

"sufficiently clear so as to allow persons of 'ordinary intelligence a reasonable opportunity to know what is prohibited.'" It is easy to see how someone could be unsure about what AEDPA prohibits with the use of the term "personnel," as it blurs the line between protected expression and unprotected conduct. Someone who advocates the cause of the PKK could be seen as supplying them with personnel; it even fits under the government's rubric of freeing up resources, since having an independent advocate frees up members to engage in terrorist activities instead of advocacy. But advocacy is pure speech protected by the First Amendment.

In order to keep the statute from trenching on such advocacy, the government urges that we read into it a requirement that the activity prohibited be performed "under the direction or control" of the foreign terrorist organization. While we construe a statute in such a way as to avoid constitutional questions, we are not authorized to rewrite the law so it will pass constitutional muster. This is especially true in the case of an interlocutory appeal from a preliminary injunction, because of the deferential standard of review applicable in such situations.

The term "training" fares little better. Again, it is easy to imagine protected expression that falls within the bounds of this term. For example, a plaintiff who wishes to instruct members of a designated group on how to petition the United Nations to give aid to their group could plausibly decide that such protected expression falls within the scope of the term "training." The government insists that the term is best understood to forbid the imparting of skills to foreign terrorist organizations through training. Yet, presumably, this definition would encompass teaching international law to members of designated organizations. The result would be different if the term "training" were qualified to include only military training or training in terrorist activities. Because plaintiffs have demonstrated that they are likely to succeed on the merits of their claim with respect to the terms "training" and "personnel," we conclude that the district court did not abuse its discretion in issuing its limited preliminary injunction.[6]

The judgment of the district court is AFFIRMED.

HUMANITARIAN LAW PROJECT v. UNITED STATES DOJ [HLP II]
352 F.3d 382 (9th Cir. 2003)

[On remand, the district court entered a permanent injunction against enforcement of the "personnel" and "training" provisions. The Government appealed and the Ninth Circuit held that those issues were foreclosed by its prior opinion. In addition to its vagueness arguments, HLP added an argument that due process would not allow conviction of its supporters without a showing of intent to further unlawful purposes.]

We are called upon to analyze a statute that presumes that a person acts with guilty intent whenever that person provides material support to a designated organization. We believe that serious due process concerns would be raised were we to accept the argument that a person who acts without knowledge of critical information about a designated organization presumably acts consistently with the intent and conduct of that designated organization. At oral argument, the government told us that it could convict a person under § 2339B if he or she donates support to a designated organization *even if he or she does not know the organization is so designated.* That is, according to the government, it can convict an individual who gives money to a designated organization that solicits money at their doorstep so long as the organization identifies itself by name. It is no defense, according to the government, that the organization describes to the donor only its humanitarian work to provide basic services

---

[6] [Court's Footnote 5] The government invites us to cure any possible vagueness problems with the statute by including the term "knowingly" in it. However, the term "knowingly" modifies the verb "provides," meaning that the only scienter requirement here is that the accused violator have knowledge of the fact that he has provided something, not knowledge of the fact that what is provided in fact constitutes material support.

to support victims displaced and orphaned by conflict, or to defend the cultural and linguistic rights of ethnic minorities. And, the government further contends, it is no defense that a donor contributes money solely to support the lawful, humanitarian purposes of a designated organization. But we believe that to attribute the intent to commit unlawful acts punishable by life imprisonment to persons who acted with innocent intent — in this context, without critical information about the relevant organization — contravenes the Fifth Amendment's requirement of "personal guilt."

[The court then discusses several of the Communist Party cases for the proposition that punishing mere support of the organization without intent to promote its unlawful purposes would violate due process.].

[W]e are to "construe [a criminal] statute in light of the fundamental principle that a person is not criminally responsible unless 'an evil-meaning mind' accompanies 'an evil-doing hand.'" Because criminal offenses requiring no *mens rea* have a "generally disfavored status," Congressional silence on whether a statute requires *mens rea* does not "justify dispensing with an intent requirement."

It is a question of statutory construction, whether § 2339B requires the government to prove that a person who provides "material support" to a designated organization knew of such designation or knew of the unlawful activities that caused it to be so designated. The language of § 2339B does not in any way suggest that Congress intended to impose strict liability on individuals who donate "material support" to designated organizations. It is significant that Congress used the term "knowingly" to modify "providing material support or resources to a foreign terrorist organization." Indeed, the Supreme Court and our circuit have construed Congress' inclusion of the word "knowingly" to require proof of knowledge of the law and an intent to further the proscribed act.

In *United States v. X-Citement Video*, [513 U.S. 64 (1999)], the Court read 18 U.S.C. § 2252, which prohibits "knowingly" transporting, shipping, receiving, distributing, or reproducing a visual depiction of a minor engaging in sexually explicit conduct, to require that the defendant also know the minor's age. The Court applied the knowledge requirement to the minor's age even though the "natural grammatical reading [of the statute], adopted by the Ninth Circuit, suggests that the term 'knowingly' modifies only the surrounding verbs[.]" The Court also held that the harsh penalties attached to the statute favored construing the statute to require specific intent. Finally, the Court concluded that an alternative reading of the statute would criminalize otherwise innocent conduct.

Applying these principles, we believe that when Congress included the term "knowingly" in § 2339B, it meant that proof that a defendant knew of the organization's designation as a terrorist organization or proof that a defendant knew of the unlawful activities that caused it to be so designated was required to convict a defendant under the statute.

Like *X-Citement Video* and *Staples*, the maximum fifteen-year penalty under § 2339B is a severe penalty for punishing someone who acted with an innocent intent. Charitable contributions made to organizations are not "inherently dangerous," as are grenades, firearms and corrosive liquids.

The one statement in the Congressional Record that refers to an intent requirement in § 2339B was made by Senator Hatch, who cosponsored AEDPA. In introducing the Senate Conference Report to the Senate, Senator Hatch stated: "this bill also includes provisions making it a crime to *knowingly provide material support to the terrorist functions* of foreign groups designated by a Presidential finding to be engaged in terrorist activities. I am convinced we have crafted a narrow but effective designation provision which meets these obligations while safeguarding the freedom to associate, which none of us would willingly give up." 142 Cong. Rec. S3354 (daily ed. April 16, 1996) (statement of Sen. Hatch) (emphasis added).

Without the knowledge requirement described above, a person who simply sends a check to a school or orphanage in Tamil Eelam run by the LTTE could be convicted under the statute, even if that individual is not aware of the LTTE's designation or of any unlawful activities undertaken by the LTTE. Or, according to the government's interpretation of § 2339B, a woman who buys cookies from a bake sale outside of her grocery store to support displaced Kurdish refugees to find new homes could be held liable so long as the bake sale had a sign that said that the sale was sponsored by the PKK, without regard to her knowledge of the PKK's designation or other activities. Furthermore, the legislative history contains no indication that Congress intended to impose strict liability on persons who provide "material support" to designated organizations.

In light of the text of § 2339B, the Court's longstanding principles interpreting the word "knowingly" to indicate Congress' intent to include a *mens rea* requirement, and the due process concern earlier discussed, we read § 2339B to require proof of knowledge, either of an organization's designation or of the unlawful activities that caused it to be so designated. Thus, to sustain a conviction under § 2339B, the government must prove beyond a reasonable doubt that the donor had knowledge that the organization was designated by the Secretary as a foreign terrorist organization or that the donor had knowledge of the organization's unlawful activities that caused it to be so designated.

NOTES AND QUESTIONS

1. Providing "Personnel." What did John Walker Lindh provide to the Taliban? "personnel" in the form of himself? "training" in the sense that he received training? The Statement of Facts in the *Lindh* case recited that he "willfully and unlawfully supplied and attempted to supply services to the Taliban." Is providing "services" different from supplying "personnel?" In responding to the defendant's motion to dismiss the indictment, the *Lindh* court stated:

> the plain meaning of "personnel" is such that it requires, in the context of Section 2339B, an employment or employment-like relationship between the persons in question and the terrorist organization. The Ninth Circuit's vagueness holding in *Humanitarian Law Project* is neither persuasive nor controlling. The term is aimed at denying the provision of human resources to proscribed terrorist organizations, and not at the mere independent advocacy of an organization's interests or agenda. Thus, the term "personnel" in Section 2339B gives fair notice to the public of what is prohibited and the provision is therefore not unconstitutionally vague.

United States v. Lindh, 212 F. Supp. 2d 541, 574 (E.D. Va. 2002).

2. Receiving Training. According to CNN, http://www.cnn.com/2003/LAW/11/07/ virginia.jihad (November 7, 2003):

> Three members of what government prosecutors called a "Virginia jihad network" were sentenced [to] 11 1/2 years each for travelling to Pakistan and seeking military training at a terrorist training camp. U.S. District Judge Leonie Brinkema rejected a government argument for stiffer sentences for both men. The judge said that she disagreed that their effort to obtain training constituted providing military services, as the prosecution contended. She said they were "absorbing resources, not providing them." She noted they gave no money or other materials to the cause.

If the defendants were "absorbing resources, not providing them," then of what were they guilty? Apparently, they intended to fight with the Taliban against U.S. forces but were captured before they got the chance. Does this constitute "conspiracy" to provide material support? In recently enacted 18 U.S.C. § 2339D, Congress has now specifically criminalized the receipt of training from a designated terrorist organization. Might there be a constitutional problem with this provision?

3. *United States v. Khan.* In *United States v. Khan*, 309 F. Supp. 2d 789 (E.D. Va. 2004) (*see* § 3.01[A], Note 5, *supra*). Judge Brinkema found that training could be a violation of the material support statute under active circumstances. The charges in *Khan* included provision of material support on the basis of supplying personnel who received training. Noting the *HLP II* holding, the court pointed out that the government had since interpreted the statute to apply only when the training went toward supplying personnel who would act on behalf of the organization in a directed capacity. "The conspiracy alleged in Count 5 was not to provide 'personnel' who would speak on behalf of LET, or provide moral support, or simply receive training, but to provide personnel who, after receiving training, would serve that organization as soldiers, recruiters, and procurers of supplies. Indeed, the evidence shows that the conspirators did much more than just receive training from LET — they returned to the United States, recruited co-conspirators, and purchased technology for LET to use in its attacks on India."

4. Zakat. Another note regarding Muslim religious practice and tradition is in order before we go further on the financial issues. Shari'ah mandates that Muslims practice the giving of alms, known as "zakat." Zakat is to be calculated not on the basis of income, as is tithing in most Christian denominations, but instead on the basis of accumulated wealth. It is usually calculated at 2.5% per year of cash, jewelry, and similar items over a minimum value. You can find many references on the web to zakat and organizations purporting to collect and distribute it. The giving of money to groups that represent their objectives to be humanitarian aid therefore becomes a hot-button issue in the tracking of Islamist fundamentalist groups.

HUMANITARIAN LAW PROJECT v. DOJ (HLP III)
393 F.3d 902 (9th Cir. 2004)

With respect to the appellants' First Amendment challenge to sections 302 and 303 of the Antiterrorism and Effective Death Penalty Act of 1996, we affirm the district court's order dated October 2, 2001, for the reasons set out in [HLP I. HLP II is vacated.] In light of Congress's recent amendment to the challenged statute, the Intelligence Reform and Terrorism Prevention Act of 2004, Pub. L. No. 108-458, 118 Stat. 3638, we affirm the judgment in part, as set forth above, vacate the judgment and injunction regarding the terms "personnel" and "training," and remand to the district court for further proceedings, if any, as appropriate. We decline to reach any other issue urged by the parties.

HUMANITARIAN LAW PROJECT v. MUKASEY (HLP IV)
509 F.3d 1122 (9th Cir. 2007)

PREGERSON, CIRCUIT JUDGE.

We are once again called upon to decide the constitutionality of sections 302 and 303 of the Antiterrorism and Effective Death Penalty Act ("AEDPA") and its 2004 amendment, the Intelligence Reform and Terrorism Prevention Act ("IRTPA").

OVERVIEW

Plaintiffs are six organizations, a retired federal administrative law judge, and a surgeon. The Kurdistan Workers Party, a.k.a Partiya Karkeran Kurdistan ("PKK"), and the Liberation Tigers of Tamil Eelam ("LTTE") engage in a wide variety of unlawful and lawful activities. Plaintiffs seek to provide support only to nonviolent and lawful activities of PKK and LTTE. This support would help Kurds living in Turkey and Tamils living in Tamil Eelam in the Northern and Eastern provinces of Sri Lanka to achieve self-determination.[7]

---

[7] [Court's Footnote 1] Plaintiffs who support PKK want: (1) to train members of PKK on how to use

In *HLP I*, we determined that AEDPA section 2339B is a content-neutral regulation of conduct subject to intermediate scrutiny. Further, we rejected Plaintiffs's licensing scheme argument and held that the discretion accorded to the Secretary of State to designate a group as a foreign terrorist organization is not "unfettered" "because the regulation involves the conduct of foreign affairs" for which the courts "owe the executive branch even more latitude." Finally, we agreed with Plaintiffs that AEDPA's prohibitions on providing "personnel" and "training" to designated foreign terrorist organizations were unconstitutionally vague because these prohibitions could be read to criminalize conduct protected by the First Amendment.

After the case went back to the district court, the government moved to dismiss and both parties sought summary judgment in their favor. The district court re-affirmed its prior decision in an unpublished order. *Humanitarian Law Project v. Reno*, 2001 U.S. Dist. LEXIS 16729 (C.D. Cal. Oct. 3, 2001). The district court entered a permanent injunction against enforcing AEDPA's prohibition on providing "personnel" and "training" to designated organizations.

On December 3, 2003, we affirmed the district court's holding that the terms "training" and "personnel" were void for vagueness. (*HLP II*). A majority of the panel also read into the statute a mens rea requirement holding that, "to sustain a conviction under § 2339B, the government must prove beyond a reasonable doubt that the donor had knowledge that the organization was designated by the Secretary as a foreign terrorist organization or that the donor had knowledge of the organization's unlawful activities that caused it to be so designated." The parties sought, and we granted, *en banc* review of *HLP II. Humanitarian Law Project v. United States Dep't of Justice*, 382 F.3d 1154 (9th Cir. 2004).

On December 17, 2004, three days after the en banc panel heard oral argument, Congress passed the Intelligence Reform and Terrorism Prevention Act ("IRTPA") which amended AEDPA. Because of the amendments to AEDPA contained in IRTPA, the en banc panel, on December 21, 2004, "vacate[d] the judgment and injunction [of the *HLP II* panel] regarding the terms 'personnel' and 'training,' and remanded [this case] to the district court for further proceedings." (*HLP III*). The en banc panel also affirmed the district court's rulings on the rest of Plaintiffs' First Amendment challenges "for the reasons set out in [*HLP I*]." On April 1, 2005, we remanded Plaintiffs' separate challenge to the term "expert advice or assistance" to the district court to consider IRTPA's impact on the litigation.

On July 25, 2005, the district court granted in part and denied in part the summary judgment motions in the consolidated cases. *See Humanitarian Law Project v. Gonzales*, 380 F. Supp. 2d 1134 (C.D. Cal. 2005) ("*DC-HLP III*"). The district court held that the terms "training" and "service" are unconstitutionally vague. With respect to the term "expert advice or assistance," the district court held that the "other specialized knowledge" part of the definition is void for vagueness, but that the "scientific" and "technical" knowledge part of the definition was not vague. The district court also held that the newly-added definition of "personnel" found in AEDPA section 2339B(h) cured the vagueness of that term. The district court rejected the rest of Plaintiffs' challenges and granted partial summary judgment for the government. Both parties timely appealed.

---

humanitarian and international law to peacefully resolve disputes, (2) to engage in political advocacy on behalf of Kurds who live in Turkey, and (3) to teach PKK members how to petition various representative bodies such as the United Nations for relief.

Plaintiffs who support LTTE want: (1) to train members of LTTE to present claims for tsunami-related aid to mediators and international bodies, (2) to offer their legal expertise in negotiating peace agreements between the LTTE and the Sri Lankan government, and (3) to engage in political advocacy on behalf of Tamils who live in Sri Lanka.

Discussion

A. Specific Intent

In their prior appeals, Plaintiffs argued that section 2339B(a) violates their Fifth Amendment due process rights because that section does not require proof of mens rea to convict a person for providing "material support or resources" to a designated foreign terrorist organization. In *HLP II*, we read the statute to require that the donor of the "material support or resources" have knowledge "either of an organization's designation or of the unlawful activities that caused it to be so designated."

In December 2004, Congress revised AEDPA to essentially adopt our reading of section 2339B to include a knowledge requirement. Thus, post-IRTPA, to convict a person for providing "material support or resources" to a designated foreign terrorist organization, the government must prove that the donor defendant "ha[d] knowledge that the organization is a designated terrorist organization, that the organization has engaged or engages in terrorist activity, or that the organization has engaged or engages in terrorism." 18 U.S.C. § 2339B(a).

Plaintiffs argue that IRTPA does not sufficiently cure section 2339B's *mens rea* deficiency. They contend that section 2339B(a) continues to violate due process because it does not require the government to prove that the donor defendant acted with specific intent to further the terrorist activity of the designated organization. Plaintiffs urge us to invalidate the statute or, alternatively, to read a specific intent requirement into the statute.

As amended, section 2339B(a) complies with the "conventional requirement for criminal conduct — awareness of some wrongdoing." Thus, a person with such knowledge is put on notice that "providing material support or resources" to a designated foreign terrorist organization is unlawful. Accordingly, we hold that the amended version of section 2339B comports with the Fifth Amendment's requirement of "personal guilt."

As the district court correctly observed, Congress could have, but chose not to, impose a requirement that the defendant act with the specific intent to further the terrorist activity of the organization, a requirement clearly set forth in sections 2339A and 2339C of the statute, but left out of section 2339B.

Because there is no Fifth Amendment due process violation, we affirm the district court on this issue.

B. Vagueness

Plaintiffs argue that the amended definition is impermissibly vague because the statute fails to notify a person of ordinary intelligence as to what conduct constitutes "material support or resources." Specifically, Plaintiffs argue that the prohibitions on providing "training," "expert advice or assistance," "service," and "personnel" to designated organizations are vague because they are unclear and could be interpreted to criminalize protected speech and expression.

Vague statutes are invalidated for three reasons: "(1) to avoid punishing people for behavior that they could not have known was illegal; (2) to avoid subjective enforcement of laws based on 'arbitrary and discriminatory enforcement' by government officers; and (3) to avoid any chilling effect on the exercise of First Amendment freedoms."

1. "Training"

In *HLP I*, we held that the term "training" under AEDPA was unconstitutionally vague. At the time of Plaintiffs' initial challenge in 1998, AEDPA provided no definition of the term "training." After we issued our opinion in *HLP I* in 2000, Congress amended the statute and defined the term "training" as "instruction or teaching designed to impart a specific skill, as opposed to general knowledge." On remand, Plaintiffs argued to the district court that the term "training" as defined by IRTPA remains unconstitutionally vague. Plaintiffs contended that persons of ordinary intelligence must discern whether the topic they wish to teach to members of designated organizations amounts to "teaching designed to impart a specific skill," which is criminalized, or "general knowledge," which is not. Specifically, Plaintiffs contended that they must guess whether training PKK members in how to use humanitarian and international human rights law to seek peaceful resolution of ongoing conflict amounts to teaching a "specific skill" or "general[ized] knowledge."

Because we find it highly unlikely that a person of ordinary intelligence would know whether, when teaching someone to petition international bodies for tsunami-related aid, one is imparting a "specific skill" or "general knowledge," we find the statute's proscription on providing "training" void for vagueness. *See HLP I* (finding the term "training" impermissibly vague because "a plaintiff who wishes to instruct members of a designated group on how to petition the United Nations to give aid to their group could plausibly decide that such protected expression falls within the scope of the term 'training' ").

Even if persons of ordinary intelligence could discern between the instruction that imparts a "specific skill," as opposed to one that imparts "general knowledge," we hold that the term "training" would remain impermissibly vague. As we previously noted in *HLP I*, limiting the definition of the term "training" to the "imparting of skills" does not cure unconstitutional vagueness because, so defined, the term "training" could still be read to encompass speech and advocacy protected by the First Amendment. *See HLP I* (finding "training" void for vagueness because "it is easy to imagine protected expression that falls within the bounds of this term").

For the foregoing reasons, we reject the government's challenge and agree with the district court that the term "training" remains impermissibly vague because it "implicates, and potentially chills, Plaintiffs' protected expressive activities and imposes criminal sanctions of up to fifteen years imprisonment without sufficiently defining the prohibited conduct for ordinary people to understand."

2. *"Expert Advice or Assistance"*

The district court previously invalidated the undefined term "expert advice or assistance" on vagueness grounds. The district court reasoned that the prohibition against providing "expert advice or assistance" could be construed to criminalize activities protected by the First Amendment. IRTPA defines the term "expert advice or assistance" as imparting "scientific, technical, or other specialized knowledge." 18 U.S.C. § 2339A(b)(3).

The government argues that the ban on "expert advice or assistance" is not vague. The government relies on the Federal Rules of Evidence's definition of expert testimony as testimony based on "scientific, technical, or other specialized knowledge." Fed. R. Evid. 702. The government argues that this definition gives a person of ordinary intelligence reasonable notice of conduct prohibited under the statute. Plaintiffs contend that the definition of "expert advice or assistance" is vague as applied to them because they cannot determine what "other specialized knowledge" means.

We agree with the district court that "the Federal Rules of Evidence's inclusion of the phrase 'scientific, technical, or other specialized knowledge' does not clarify the term 'expert advice or assistance' for the average person with no background in law."

At oral argument, the government stated that filing an amicus brief in support of a foreign terrorist organization would violate AEDPA's prohibition against providing "expert advice or assistance." Because the "other specialized knowledge" portion of the ban on providing "expert advice or assistance" continues to cover constitutionally protected advocacy, we hold that it is void for vagueness. *See* NAACP v. Button, 371 U.S. 415, 432–33 (1963) (noting that vagueness and overbreadth depend on "the danger of tolerating, in the area of First Amendment freedoms, the existence of a penal statute sU.S.C.eptible of sweeping and improper application").

The portion of the "expert advice or assistance" definition that refers to "scientific" and "technical" knowledge is not vague. Unlike "other specialized knowledge," which covers every conceivable subject, the meaning of "technical" and "scientific" is reasonably understandable to a person of ordinary intelligence. *See* Houghton Mifflin Reading Spelling and Vocabulary Word Lists (5th Grade) (including "technical" as a fifth-grade vocabulary word); *see also* Tennessee Department of Education Third Grade Science Vocabulary (including "scientific method" on third-grade vocabulary list).

3. "Service"

IRTPA amended the definition of "material support or resources" to add the prohibition on rendering "service" to a designated foreign terrorist organization. There is no statutory definition of the term "service." Plaintiffs argue that proscribing "service" is vague because each of the other challenged provisions could be construed as a provision of "service." The district court agreed.

We adopt the district court's holding and its reasoning. The term "service" presumably includes providing members of PKK and LTTE with "expert advice or assistance" on how to lobby or petition representative bodies such as the United Nations. "Service" would also include "training" members of PKK or LTTE on how to use humanitarian and international law to peacefully resolve ongoing disputes. Thus, we hold that the term "service" is impermissibly vague because "the statute defines 'service' to include 'training' or 'expert advice or assistance,'" and because "'it is easy to imagine protected expression that falls within the bounds' of the term 'service.'"

4. "Personnel"

In *HLP I*, we concluded that "personnel" was impermissibly vague because the term could be interpreted to encompass expressive activity protected by the First Amendment. We stated that, "[i]t is easy to see how someone could be unsure about what AEDPA prohibits with the use of the term 'personnel,' as it blurs the line between protected expression and unprotected conduct." We observed that "[s]omeone who advocates the cause of the PKK could be seen as supplying them with personnel. . . . But advocacy is pure speech protected by the First Amendment."

As stated above, in 2004, Congress added a limitation to the ban on providing "personnel." Section 2339B(h) clarifies that section 2339B(a) criminalizes providing "personnel" to a foreign terrorist organization only where a person, alone or with others, "[work]s under that terrorist organization's direction or control or . . . organize[s], manage[s], supervise[s], or otherwise direct[s] the operation of that organization." Section 2339B(h) also states that the ban on "personnel" does not criminalize the conduct of "[i]ndividuals who act entirely independently of the foreign terrorist organization to advance its goals or objectives."

As amended by IRTPA, AEDPA's prohibition on providing "personnel" is not vague because the ban no longer "blurs the line between protected expression and unprotected conduct." Unlike the version of the statute before it was amended by IRTPA, the prohibition on "personnel" no longer criminalizes pure speech protected by the First Amendment. Section 2339B(h) clarifies that Plaintiffs advocating lawful causes of PKK and LTTE cannot be held liable for providing these organizations with "personnel" as long as they engage in such advocacy "entirely independently of th[ose] foreign terrorist organization[s]."

Because IRTPA's definition of "personnel" provides fair notice of prohibited conduct to a person of ordinary intelligence and no longer punishes protected speech, we hold that the term "personnel" as defined in IRTPA is not vague.

C. Overbreadth

Plaintiffs argue that the terms "training," "personnel," "expert advice or assistance" and "service" are substantially overbroad. The district court rejected Plaintiffs' challenge. We affirm.

A statute is facially overbroad when its application to protected speech is "substantial, not only in an absolute sense, but also relative to the scope of the law's plainly legitimate applications."

We have previously held that AEDPA's prohibition against providing "material support or resources" to a designated organization "is not aimed at interfering with the expressive component of [Plaintiffs'] conduct but at stopping aid to terrorist groups."

Section 2339B(a)'s ban on provision of "material support or resources" to designated foreign terrorist organizations undoubtably has many legitimate applications. For instance, the importance of curbing terrorism cannot be underestimated. Cutting off "material support or resources" from terrorist organizations deprives them of means with which to carry out acts of terrorism and potentially leads to their demise. Thus, section 2339B(a) can legitimately be applied to criminalize facilitation of terrorism in the form of providing foreign terrorist organizations with income, weapons, or expertise in constructing explosive devices.

Were we to restrain the government from enforcing section 2339B(a) that prohibits individuals in the United States from providing "material support or resources" to foreign terrorist organizations, we would potentially be placing our nation in danger of future terrorist attacks.

Moreover, although Plaintiffs may be able to identify particular instances of protected speech that may fall within the statute, those instances are not substantial when compared to the legitimate applications of section 2339B(a).

Thus, because section 2339B is not aimed at expressive conduct and because it does not cover a substantial amount of protected speech, we hold that the prohibition against providing "material support or resources" to a foreign terrorist organization is not facially overbroad.

D. Licensing Scheme

IRTPA added section 2339B(j), an entirely new section. Section 2339B(j) allows the Secretary of State, with the concurrence of the Attorney General, to grant approval for individuals and organizations to carry out activities that would otherwise be considered providing "material support or resources" to designated foreign terrorist organizations. 18 U.S.C. § 2339B(j). Section 2339B(j) states that no one can be prosecuted under the terms " 'personnel,' 'training,' or 'expert advice or assistance' if the provision of that material support or resources to a foreign terrorist organization was approved by the Secretary of State with the concurrence of the Attorney General." The exception limits the scope of discretion by providing only that the "Secretary of State may not approve the provision of any material support that may be used to carry out terrorist activity."

Plaintiffs argue that this provision constitutes an unconstitutional licensing scheme. We disagree.

Courts may entertain pre-enforcement facial challenges to a licensing scheme where the law has a "close enough nexus to expression, or to conduct commonly associated with expression, to pose a real and substantial threat of the identified censorship risks."

We recognize that it is possible for the Secretary to exercise his or her discretion in a way that discriminates against the donor of "material support or assistance." For example, the Secretary could conceivably exempt from prosecution a person who teaches peacemaking skills to members of Hezbollah, but deny Plaintiffs immunity from prosecution if they teach the same peacemaking skills to PKK. However, when evaluating the constitutionality of a licensing scheme, we look at how closely the prior restraint, *on its face*, regulates constitutionally protected activity. Here, even though it is possible for the Secretary to refuse to exercise his or her discretion to exempt from prosecution a disliked speaker, any such power is incidental. The statute does not give the Secretary "*substantial* power to discriminate based on the content or viewpoint of speech" or the identity of the speaker.

Moreover, in Plaintiffs' case, any potential for content or viewpoint-based discrimination or discrimination based on the identity of the speaker is significantly reduced because the government is enjoined from enforcing those provisions of the statute we hold vague. Thus, because Plaintiffs are already immune from prosecution for protected speech, the danger that the Secretary can base his or her exercise of discretion on Plaintiffs' identity or the content or viewpoint of Plaintiffs' message is almost non-existent.

CONCLUSION

For the foregoing reasons, the judgment of the district court is AFFIRMED.

[B]   The Designation Process

PEOPLE'S MOJAHEDIN ORGANIZATION OF IRAN v. DEPARTMENT OF STATE [PMOI II]
327 F.3d 1238 (D.C. Cir. 2003)

SENTELLE, CIRCUIT JUDGE.

The People's Mojahedin Organization of Iran ("PMOI" or "Petitioner") seeks review of 1999 and 2001 decisions of the Secretary of State ("Respondent") designating Petitioner as a foreign terrorist organization. After review of Petitioner's various claims that the designation violates constitutional and statutory rights of Petitioner, we conclude that the Secretary acted according to law and in full compliance with the requirements of the Constitution. We therefore deny the petitions for the reasons set forth more fully below.

I. BACKGROUND

We note at the outset that this is PMOI's third petition to this court to review designations of the PMOI as a foreign terrorist organization. *See People's Mojahedin Org. of Iran v. Dep't. of State*, 182 F.3d 17, 337 U.S. App. D.C. 106 (D.C. Cir. 1999) ("*PMOI*"); *Nat'l Council of Resistance of Iran v. Dep't. of State*, 251 F.3d 192, 346 U.S. App. D.C. 131 (D.C. Cir. 2001) ("*NCOR*").

[The State Department's 2003 "Patterns of Global Terrorism" lists six groups under the umbrella heading of the "MEK" and describes them this way:

[Mujahedin-e Khalq Organization (MEK or MKO) a.k.a. The National Liberation Army of Iran (NLA, the militant wing of the MEK), the People's Mujahedin of Iran (PMOI), National Council of Resistance (NCR), the National Council of Resistance of Iran (NCRI), Muslim Iranian Student's Society (front organization used to garner financial support)

[The MEK philosophy mixes Marxism and Islam. Formed in the 1960s, the organization was expelled from Iran after the Islamic Revolution in 1979, and its primary support came from the former Iraqi regime of Saddam Hussein since the late 1980s. The MEK's history is filled with anti-Western attacks as well as terrorist attacks on the interests of the clerical regime in Iran and abroad. The

MEK now advocates the overthrow of the Iranian regime and its replacement with the group's own leadership.

[During the 1970s, the MEK killed U.S. military personnel and U.S. civilians working on defense projects in Tehran and supported the takeover in 1979 of the U.S. Embassy in Tehran. In 1981, the MEK detonated bombs in the head office of the Islamic Republic Party and the Premier's office, killing some 70 high-ranking Iranian officials, including chief Justice Ayatollah Mohammad Beheshti, President Mohammad-Ali Rajaei, and Premier Mohammad-Javad Bahonar. Near the end of the war with Iran during 1980–88, Baghdad armed the MEK with military equipment and sent it into action against Iranian forces. In 1991, it assisted the Government of Iraq in suppressing the Shia and Kurdish uprisings in southern Iraq and the Kurdish uprisings in the north. Coalition aircraft bombed MEK bases during Operation Iraqi Freedom, and the Coalition forced the MEK forces to surrender in May 2003. The future of the MEK forces remains undetermined with Coalition forces.]

[Section 1189] empowers the Secretary of State to designate an entity as a "foreign terrorist organization." Two features distinguish this procedure from other administrative proceedings governed by the Administrative Procedure Act ("APA"). First, the [statute] does not express any right of the aggrieved party to comment on the administrative record or to present evidence for inclusion in that record. Secondly, and most pertinent to the present review, the statute expressly states that the Secretary is to consider the classified information in making a designation and that classified information is not subject to disclosure under the Act except to a reviewing court *ex parte* and *in camera*. A designation under the Act persists for two years, and the Secretary may re-designate a foreign organization as a foreign terrorist organization for succeeding two-year periods.

In order for the Secretary to designate a foreign organization as a foreign terrorist organization, he must make three findings based on the administrative record, that:

    A. the organization is a foreign organization;

    B. the organization engages in terrorist activity; and

    C. the terrorist activity or terrorism of the organization threatens the security of United States nationals or the national security of the United States.

An organization designated as a foreign terrorist organization must seek judicial review of the designation in this court under § 1189(b). That section empowers us only to "hold unlawful and set aside" designations that we find to be

    (A) arbitrary, capricious, an abuse of discretion, or otherwise not in accordance with law;

    (B) contrary to constitutional right, power, privilege, or immunity;

    (C) in excess of statutory jurisdiction, authority, or limitation, or short of statutory right;

    (D) lacking substantial support in the administrative record taken as a whole or in classified information submitted to the court [*in camera* and *ex parte*], or

    (E) not in accord with the procedures required by law.

The Secretary has made successive designations of Petitioner as a foreign terrorist organization in 1997, 1999, and 2001. Following the 1997 designation, Petitioner sought review in a proceeding that generated our opinion in *PMOI*. In that petition, the PMOI argued that the procedure for designation violated its due process rights to notice and hearing. We easily disposed of any constitutional claim, holding that "[a] foreign entity without property or *presence in* this country has no constitutional rights under the due process clause." We then proceeded to consider the rights of the organization under the statute. This consisted principally of determining the legal sufficiency of the Secretary's administrative record to support the three findings under § 1189(a)(1). As to the first, that the petitioner was a foreign organization, there was no dispute; it was. As to the third, that "the terrorist activity of the organization threatens the security of United States nationals or the national security of the United States" we held that to present a nonjusticiable question. Such questions concerning the foreign policy decisions of the Executive Branch present political judgments, "decisions of a kind for which the Judiciary has neither aptitude, facilities nor responsibilities and have long been held to belong in the domain of political power not subject to judicial intrusion or inquiry."

That left us solely with the question of the sufficiency of the administrative record to support the Secretary's determination that "the organization engages in terrorist activity." We found that record sufficient.

When the Secretary re-designated the PMOI as a foreign terrorist organization in October of 1999, the organization again petitioned this court for review. One item in the 1999 designation differed from the 1997 designation. In 1999 the Secretary's designation included a finding that the National Council of Resistance of Iran, which claimed to be an organization independent of the PMOI, was an alias for the other organization and that the National Council was therefore a foreign terrorist organization as well — indeed, the same foreign terrorist organization. The Secretary's finding that the NCOR and the PMOI were one and the same made a material difference in the result of our review on the constitutional question. Whereas [PMOI] did not have property or presence in the United States and was therefore not entitled to assert due process rights under the Constitution, . . . the National Council did have such presence or property and was therefore entitled to assert that claim. We therefore considered the merits of the due process claim. We held that the statute, as applied by the Secretary, did not provide "the fundamental requirement of due process," that is, "the opportunity to be heard at a meaningful time and in a meaningful manner."

Based on our holding that the designees had not received the process they were due, we remanded the question to the Secretary for reconsideration. We directed that on remand the Secretary should provide the petitioners "the opportunity to file responses to the nonclassified evidence against them, to file evidence in support of their allegations that they are not terrorist organizations," and provide them "an opportunity to be meaningfully heard" on the issues before the Secretary. After the remand, the Secretary provided the PMOI with an opportunity to respond to the unclassified evidence, considered all material submitted by the PMOI along with both the unclassified and classified material in file, and reentered the 1999 designation on September 24, 2001, followed by a new two-year designation on October 5, 2001.

II. ANALYSIS

A. *Due Process and Sufficiency of Evidence*

Petitioner raises several arguments. First, it contends that its redesignation as a terrorist organization is unconstitutional under the Due Process Clause because the statute permitted the Secretary to rely upon secret evidence — the classified information that respondents refused to disclose and against which PMOI could therefore not effectively defend. We reject this contention. As noted above, that statute authorizes designation of a foreign terrorist organization when the Secretary finds three elements. As to the first, that is that the organization is a foreign organization, there is not and cannot be any dispute.

As to the second element, the PMOI advances a colorable argument: that the Secretary was able under § 1189(a)(3)(B) to "consider classified information in making [this designation]" and that the classified information was not "subject to disclosure" except to the court *ex parte* and *in camera* for purposes of this judicial review. Petitioner contends that this violates the due process standard set forth in *Abourezk v. Reagan*, 785 F.2d 1043, 1061 (D.C. Cir. 1986), "that a court may not dispose of the merits of a case on the basis of *ex parte, in camera* submissions." While colorable, this argument will not carry the day.

Granted, petitioners argue that their opportunity to be heard was not meaningful, given that the Secretary relied on secret information to which they were not afforded access. In the context of another statutory scheme involving classified information, we noted the courts are often ill-suited to determine the sensitivity of classified information. *United States v. Yunis* ("Things that did not make sense to [a judge] would make all too much sense to a foreign counter intelligence specialist."). The Due Process Clause requires only that process which is due under the circumstances of the case. We have already established in *NCOR* the process which is due under the circumstances of this sensitive matter of classified intelligence in the effort to combat foreign terrorism. The Secretary has complied with the standard we set forth therein, and nothing further is due.

However, even if we err in describing the process due, even had the Petitioner been entitled to have its counsel or itself view the classified information, the breach of that entitlement has caused it no harm. This brings us to Petitioner's statutory objection. Petitioner argues that there is not adequate record support for the Secretary's determination that it is a foreign terrorist organization under the statute. However, on this element, even the unclassified record taken alone is quite adequate to support the Secretary's determination. Indeed, as to this element — that is, that the organization engages in terrorist activities — the People's Mojahedin has effectively admitted not only the adequacy of the unclassified record, but the truth of the allegation. By its own admission, the PMOI has

> (1) attacked with mortars the Islamic Revolutionary Prosecutor's Office; (2) assassinated a former Iranian prosecutor and killed his security guards; (3) killed the Deputy Chief of the Iranian Joint Staff Command, who was the personal military adviser to Supreme Leader Khamenei; (4) attacked with mortars the Iranian Central Command Headquarters of the Islamic Revolutionary Guard Corps and the Defense Industries Organization in Tehran; (5) attacked and targeted with mortars the offices of the Iranian Supreme Leader Khamenei, and of the head of the State Exigencies Council; (6) attacked with mortars the central headquarters of the Revolutionary Guards; (7) attacked with mortars two Revolutionary Guards Corps headquarters; and (8) attacked the headquarters of the Iranian State Security Forces in Tehran.

Were there no classified information in the file, we could hardly find that the Secretary's determination that the Petitioner engaged in terrorist activities is "lacking substantial support in the administrative record taken as a whole," even without repairing to the "classified information submitted to the court."

To summarize, the Secretary did not deprive Petitioner of any process to which it was constitutionally entitled. Even if the record supported a finding of violation of due process, such a violation would be harmless as the unaffected portion of the record is ample to support the determination made.

The remaining element under § 1189(a)(1) is that "the terrorist activity or terrorism of the organization threatens the security of United States nationals or the national security of the United States." The thrust of Petitioner's argument is that its allegedly terrorist acts were not acts of terrorism under the statute, because they do not meet the requirement of subsection (C). Petitioner argues that the attempt to overthrow the despotic government of Iran, which itself remains on the State Department's list of state sponsors of terrorism, is not "terrorist activity," or if it is, that it does not threaten the security of the United States or its nationals. We cannot review that claim. In *PMOI* we expressly held that that finding "is nonjusticiable." As we stated in that decision, "it is beyond the judicial function for a court to review foreign policy decisions of the Executive Branch." Even if we differed with the analysis of the prior panel of this court, which we do not, we are bound by its decision. In short, we find neither statutory nor due process errors in the Secretary's designation of petitioner as a foreign terrorist organization.

B. *Petitioner's Other Claims*

Petitioner raises several other arguments to the effect that the designation violates its constitutional rights. Those warranting separate discussion fall under the general heading of First Amendment claims. Petitioner's argument that its First Amendment rights have been violated rests on the consequences of the designation. Petitioner argues that by forbidding all persons within or subject to the jurisdiction of the United States from "knowingly providing material support or resources," 18 U.S.C. § 2339B(a)(1), to it as a designated foreign terrorist organization, the statute violates its rights of free speech and association guaranteed by the First Amendment. We disagree.

As the Ninth Circuit held in *Humanitarian Law Project v. Reno*, the statute "is not aimed at interfering with the expressive component of [the organization's] conduct but at stopping aid to terrorist groups." It is conduct and not communication that the statute controls. We join the Ninth Circuit in observing that "there is no constitutional right to facilitate terrorism by giving terrorists the weapons and explosives with which to carry out their grisly missions.[8] Nor, of course, is there a right to provide resources with which terrorists can buy weapons and explosives."

III. Conclusion

For the reasons set forth above, we conclude that in the designation and redesignation of the People's Mojahedin of Iran as a foreign terrorist organization, the Secretary of State afforded all the process that the organization was due, and that this designation violated neither statutory nor constitutional rights of the Petitioner. We therefore deny the petitions for review.

Edwards, Circuit Judge, concurring.

I concur in the judgment denying the petitions for review. I find it unnecessary, however, to reach the constitutional due process challenge to the Secretary's use of classified evidence to designate petitioner.

The public, unclassified administrative record, including petitioner's own submissions to the Secretary, contains more than enough evidence to support the determination that petitioner engages in terrorist activity. The Government followed the procedures that we required in [*NCOR*]. Petitioner offered a wealth of submissions to the Secretary, which the public record now includes. Not only is there enough evidence in the public record to support the Secretary's determination that petitioner engaged in the acts alleged, there appears to be no dispute over the facts supporting that determination. Therefore, I find it unnecessary to reach petitioner's constitutional due process challenge to the Secretary's use of secret, classified material to bolster its determination.

In sum, because there is substantial, unrefuted evidence in the public, unclassified

---

[8] [Court's Footnote 2] Although not raised by either party, at the instruction of the court the parties addressed the possibility that the 1999 designation was moot. Both parties agree, as does the court, that a realistic possibility exists of prosecutions under 18 U.S.C. § 2339A-2339C for crimes related to the terrorist designation of the PMOI during the period of that designation so that this controversy escapes mootness under the "collateral consequences" exception.

record for the designation of petitioner as a foreign terrorist organization, I agree that the petition for review should be denied.

NOTES AND QUESTIONS

1. *United States v. Rahmani.* *United States v. Rahmani*, 209 F. Supp. 2d 1045 (C.D. Cal. 2002), *rev'd sub nom.* *United States v. Afshari*, 426 F.3d 1150 (9th Cir. 2005), § 3.03[C] *infra.* The D.C. Circuit's footnote reference to mootness and the possibility of prosecutions for material support during the hiatus of the 1999 designation was far from idle speculation. Shortly after the D.C. Circuit's second opinion (what it called *NCOR*), a district court in California dismissed an indictment against several fund-raisers for Mujahedin-e Khalq ("MEK"), an alleged alter ego of NCOR and PMOI.

The trial judge stated that the situation presented "this somewhat provocative question:"

> If the procedure whereby an organization is designated by the Secretary of State as "terrorist" violates the Due Process Clause of the United States Constitution, may such *designation nevertheless be utilized as a predicate in a criminal prosecution against individuals* for providing material support to that designated terrorist organization?

He then proceeded to hold the statute unconstitutional on its face despite these two arguments of the Government:

> First, the government argues that invalidating Section 1189 would have serious negative consequences on this country's counter-terrorism efforts. National security is certainly a matter of grave concern and responsibility. When weighed against a fundamental constitutional right which defines our very existence, the argument for national security should not serve as an excuse for obliterating the Constitution. The moral strength, vitality and commitment proudly enunciated in the Constitution is best tested at a time when forceful, emotionally moving arguments to ignore or trivialize its provisions seek a subordination of time honored constitutional protections. Such protections should not be dispensed with where the Secretary has not shown how the MEK is a national security threat.

> The government also cites numerous cases where the Supreme Court found statutes unconstitutional but, nevertheless, upheld actions that occurred under the unconstitutional scheme. The government seems to be saying that the result in *NCRI [NCOR]*, wherein the D.C. Circuit found the MEK's designation unconstitutional but, nevertheless, upheld such designation, is legally support-able. The cases cited by the government are distinguishable from the instant case in one critical respect — they are all civil cases. Where, as here, a criminal defendant is charged with crimes that could result in as much as 15 years imprisonment or more, this court will not abdicate its duty to ensure that the prosecution of such charges comports with due process.

That decision was then reversed by the Ninth Circuit in *United States v. Afshari* after the D.C. Circuit held that the designation was constitutional on the basis of the publicly disclosed information.

2. **Due Process and Designation.** In the second round [*NCOR*], the D.C. Circuit had this to say about the whether the due process violation warranted setting aside the designations:

> We recognize that a strict and immediate application of the principles of law which we have set forth herein could be taken to require a revocation of the designations before us. However, we also recognize the realities of the foreign policy and national security concerns asserted by the Secretary in support of those designations. We further recognize the timeline against which all are operating: the two-year designations before us expire in October of this year.

We therefore do not order the vacation of the existing designations, but rather remand the questions to the Secretary with instructions that the petitioners be afforded the opportunity to file responses to the nonclassified evidence against them, to file evidence in support of their allegations that they are not terrorist organizations, and that they be afforded an opportunity to be meaningfully heard by the Secretary upon the relevant findings. While not within our current order, we expect that the Secretary will afford due process rights to these and other similarly situated entities in the course of future designations.

Is national security a sufficient answer to the due process violation? What if the public record did not have sufficient grounds for determining that the organization was engaged in terrorist activity? Would the use of classified information then be a sufficient basis for the imposition of penalties on the organization? And, if the answer to that is yes because the organization is not going to jail, what about the individuals who provide funding? That final question is addressed by the Ninth Circuit in *Ashfari*.

3. Secret Evidence. The D.C. Circuit seems remarkably cavalier in *PMOI II* about its holding in *Abourezk* regarding the use of secret evidence. We will return to that question after the next case.

4. "Money is Fungible." The Ninth Circuit held, in *HLP I*, that providing resources for humanitarian aid would itself support the violent acts of the organization, so there is no functional difference between the two. In *HLP II*, the court then added a scienter requirement that the defendant must know either that the organization was designated or that support was provided with knowledge that it would be used for terrorist purposes. Can I give money to an apparent charitable organization without being concerned about the possible uses of that money, even if it turns out that the donee is a clandestine front group for a designated organization?

NOTE ON FINANCIAL TRANSACTIONS AND HAWALA

Tracking of financial transactions to curtail the flow of money to terrorist organizations is complicated in many ways. Charitable giving and the practice of zakat is one aspect of the problem. Hawala or hundi is another. Hawala is the practice of informally transferring value across borders without sending money. It originated in India but is essentially the same as the Chinese "chop" system of prior centuries. In these and other guises, informal value transfer creates a vast international unregulated and untaxed banking system. An excellent description is provided by Interpol at http://www.interpol.int/Public/FinancialCrime/MoneyLaundering/hawala/default.asp.

Suppose that Adam is working in America but has relatives including his father Benny in Balaysia to whom he wishes to send money. Doing so through formal banks would be expensive (as much as a 5% commission rate) and may be impracticable because Adam does not trust the banks in Balaysia or because Benny may have reasons for not wanting to appear in a bank. Adam can go to a storefront business (Store) that sells a variety of merchandise from Balaysia and also provides money transfer services. Adam gives Store hard currency and asks that money be delivered to Benny. Store calls a cooperating counterpart in Balaysia (Business), who delivers equivalent cash (minus a 1% commission) in Balaysian currency to Benny or sets up a line of credit for goods that Benny can obtain from Business.

Store now owes Business money, which will be covered when Business and Store exchange commodities that each wants from the other's country, or when Store decides to risk sending a courier with a satchel of cash. Store will sell goods from Balaysia that are desired in America and vice versa. The net effect is the transfer of value without the use of monitorable banking or other regulated financial institutions. And pertinent to the terrorism investigation is the possibility that some of the profit margin in these transactions (and the tax savings from unreported transactions) will end up in the hands of persons or organizations with terrorist designs.

Immigrant workers are not the only users of the hawala system and hawala is not the only method of transferring money across borders. It is instructive, however, to realize that current estimates are that immigrant workers alone sent $150 billion (yes, billion) out of the U.S. in 2004, some through regulated financial institutions but much not. How much of that ended up in the hands of terrorist organizations would be purest speculation. Other sources of funds for terrorist organizations include the very wealthy who can transfer huge sums in a single transaction by time-honored methods known to embezzlers such as overpayment for goods or services. *Boim* and *In re Terrorist Attacks* involved allegations of a third method, the provision of money to charities which have links to terrorist organizations.

Thus far, we have seen in action units of the Department of Justice, Department of Defense, and the State Department. Money laundering and financial monitoring are areas in which all counter-terrorism agencies of the federal government take an active interest. The Office of Foreign Asset Control (OFAC) within the Department of Treasury issues blockage and asset freezing orders under IEEPA, the statute under which Lindh was prosecuted. The next case deals more explicitly with activity of OFAC, but first we need to take note of another aspect of our current topic, the use of secret information.

NOTE ON SECRET INFORMATION AND THE WAR ANALOGY

The government claim for secrecy of information in these cases leads eventually to the analogy and terminology of "war" that will be considered later. The cases on use of classified information in criminal trials considered in Chapter 5 proceeded on the assumption that a criminal defendant had an absolute right to know the evidence against him. *Ex parte in camera* submissions were allowed in those cases only to allow the judge to make a decision on what would be disclosed to the defendant or a jury, not for the purpose of forming part of the basis for conviction. If a criminal defendant cannot be convicted on the basis of unknown evidence, then deprivation of property through an administrative designation would seem to be subject to the same due process requirements (even if it were only a temporary deprivation by freezing of assets).

Moreover, if the information is accurate, then it is already known to the organization's representatives and there should be no reason to withhold it from them. Right? Yet the government's asserted interest in withholding secret information from the organization is the same as the claim of need for secrecy of intelligence results during wartime. "If I tell you what I know about you, then you will know how I learned it and can then change your operations to keep future information away from me."

This leads to the perfectly understandable desire on the part of anti- and counter-terrorism specialists to use information acquired through incredibly difficult, and dangerous, methods to shut down terrorist organizations without destroying the intelligence networks by which the information was acquired.

But is proceeding by secret evidence an acceptable practice in a free and open society? That is the heart of several of the civil liberties issues presented in counter-terrorism. In the criminal cases in the previous chapter, the fact-finder would not get the classified information unless the trial were closed to the public and the defendant also received the information. In the designation process, however, neither the organization nor the potential donor knows what the classified information is.

To carry the analogy to wartime further, in succeeding chapters we will consider what rules of engagement apply to the known terrorist. Must government agents attempt to capture her and place her on trial? Is it permissible to shoot to kill as in a military engagement?

HOLY LAND FOUNDATION v. ASHCROFT
333 F.3d 156 (D.C. Cir. 2003)

SENTELLE, CIRCUIT JUDGE.

In December 2001, the Office of Foreign Asset Control ("OFAC") designated Holy Land Foundation ("HLF") as a "Specially Designated Global Terrorist" ("SDGT") pursuant to an Executive Order issued under the International Emergency Economic Powers Act, 50 U.S.C. § 1701 et seq. ("IEEPA"). This designation was accompanied by an order blocking all of the organization's assets. HLF brought an action in the district court challenging this designation and before us now appeals the lower court's decision which affirmed OFAC's actions and dismissed the complaint in substantial part. For the reasons explained below, we hereby affirm the district court's dismissal in part, and order summary judgment for the government.

I. BACKGROUND

The IEEPA authorizes the President to declare a national emergency when an extraordinary threat to the United States arises that originates in substantial part in a foreign state. Such a declaration clothes the President with extensive authority set out in 50 U.S.C. § 1702. Under that section he may investigate, regulate, or prohibit transactions in foreign exchange, banking transfers, and importation or exportation of currency or securities by persons or with respect to property, subject to the jurisdiction of the United States. Of further special concern to the Holy Land Foundation, he may

> investigate, block during the pendency of an investigation, regulate, direct and compel, nullify, void, prevent or prohibit, any acquisition, holding, withholding, use, transfer, withdrawal, transportation, importation or exportation of, or dealing in, or exercising any right, power, or privilege with respect to, or transactions involving, any property in which any foreign country or a national thereof has any interest by any person, or with respect to any property, subject to the jurisdiction of the United States. . . .

In 1995, the President issued Executive Order 12,947 pursuant to the IEEPA. Exec. Order No. 12,947. That order designated certain terrorist organizations, including the Palestinian organization Hamas, as "Specially Designated Terrorists," or SDTs, and blocked all of their property and interests in property. The order also allowed for additional designations if an organization or person is found to be "owned or controlled by, or to act for or on behalf of" an SDT.

In 2001, as part of his response to the attacks of September 11, the President issued Executive Order 13,224, similar to Order 12,947, pursuant to the IEEPA. Order 13,224 designated specified terrorist organizations, again including Hamas, as "Specially Designated Global Terrorists," or SDGTs, and blocked all of their property and interests in property subject to the jurisdiction of the United States. That order also allowed for additional SDGTs to be designated if organizations or persons are found to "act for or on behalf of" or are "owned or controlled by" designated terrorists, or they "assist in, sponsor, or provide . . . support for," or are "otherwise associated" with them.

HLF was originally established as the Occupied Land Fund and incorporated as a tax-exempt organization in California in 1989. In 1991 it changed its corporate name to the Holy Land Foundation for Relief and Development and moved to Texas. It describes itself as "the largest Muslim charity in the United States." In December 2001, OFAC, a division of the Department of the Treasury, acting pursuant to the IEEPA and the two Executive Orders, designated HLF as both an SDT and an SDGT and blocked all of its assets. The designations were based on information supporting the proposition that HLF was closely linked to Hamas. Soon thereafter, HLF filed a complaint in district court challenging its designations as a terrorist organization and the seizure of its assets, and alleging that its rights under the First, Fourth, and Fifth Amendments, its right to free exercise of religion, and its rights under the Administrative Procedure Act ("APA"), had all been violated. HLF also filed a motion for a preliminary injunction, seeking to enjoin the government from blocking or freezing its assets. In support of the motion, HLF attached exhibits purportedly showing that it was not linked to Hamas and therefore not a terrorist organization. Subsequently, in May 2002, the OFAC redesignated HLF as an SDT and an SDGT, and filed with the district court an administrative record which included HLF's motion for a preliminary injunction with attached exhibits.

II. The District Court's Opinion

The Holy Land Foundation attempted to supplement the record before the district court by the addition of exhibits attached to its opposition to the defendants' motion to dismiss. The government moved *in limine* to strike the supplemental material. The district court granted the government's motion, holding that APA review "must ordinarily be confined to the administrative record." The court then commenced a detailed review of the administrative record and reiterated the evidence on which the Treasury Department relied in making its determination to designate HLF as an SDGT. It found that the record contained "ample evidence that (1) HLF has had financial connections to Hamas since its creation in 1989; (2) HLF leaders have been actively involved in various meetings with Hamas leaders; (3) HLF funds Hamas-controlled charitable organizations; (4) HLF provides financial support to the orphans and families of Hamas martyrs and prisoners; (5) HLF's Jerusalem office acted on behalf of Hamas; and (6) FBI informants reliably reported that HLF funds Hamas." The court concluded, based on the substantial evidence in the record, Treasury's determination that HLF acts for or on behalf of Hamas was not arbitrary and capricious, and therefore, upheld the agency's reasonable determination.

III. Analysis

As a first matter, we reject HLF's claim that its designation exceeded Treasury's authority under the APA, and affirm the district court's dismissal of that claim. The district court correctly reviewed the actions of the Treasury Department under the highly deferential "arbitrary and capricious" standard. The district court noted that this standard does not allow the courts to undertake their own factfinding, but to review the agency record to determine whether the agency's decision was supported by a rational basis.

HLF attacks the reasonableness of this determination by contending that Treasury relied on hearsay evidence to reach its conclusion. This argument is unavailing as it is clear that the government may decide to designate an entity based on a broad range of evidence, including intelligence data and hearsay declarations.

Nor was the designation in any other way so egregiously unfair as to violate any constraints due process may place upon the substance of the agency's decision. Additionally, HLF was accorded all the administrative process it was due when it was redesignated as an SDGT. Even if Treasury's initial designation arguably violated HLF's due process rights, HLF's funds are blocked currently by a redesignation which Treasury applied in accordance with the requirements we outlined in *[NCOR]*.

As we stated in *NCOR*, we do not require an agency to provide procedures which approximate a judicial trial; therefore, HLF has no right to confront and cross-examine witnesses. Additionally, the notice "need not disclose the classified information to be presented *in camera* and *ex parte* to the court under the statute. This is within the privilege and the prerogative of the executive, and we do not intend to compel a breach in the security which that branch is charged to protect." The IEEPA expressly authorizes *ex parte* and *in camera* review of classified information in "any judicial review of a determination made under this section [that] was based on classified information."

HLF argues that the government violated its First Amendment rights of freedom of association and freedom of speech and its right to equal protection under the Fourteenth

Amendment. HLF argued below that the government had violated its First Amendment rights by prohibiting it from making any humanitarian contributions by blocking its assets. The district court dismissed these claims, ruling that HLF failed to state a claim because "there is no constitutional right to facilitate terrorism." As set forth in other portions of this opinion, the law is established that there is no constitutional right to fund terrorism. The ample record evidence (particularly taking into account the classified information presented to the court *in camera*) establishing HLF's role in the funding of Hamas and of its terrorist activities is incontrovertible. HLF has had every opportunity to come forward with some showing that that evidence is false or even that its ties to Hamas had been severed. HLF's presentations at the administrative stage did not reach this goal. Even following the district court's judgment, while HLF attempted to supplement the record on appeal, the supplementary material could not have defeated the proposition established by the record evidence that Holy Land was a funder of the terrorist organization Hamas.

In addition to the classified evidence that we have reviewed, all evidence from the government that is unclassified and otherwise discoverable is in the record before us, as is the evidence HLF produced in an effort to create a genuine factual dispute. HLF had every opportunity and incentive to produce the evidence sufficient to rebut the ample evidence supporting the necessary conclusion that it was a funder of Hamas but could not do so. Thus, we review an adequate record and conclude that there is no substantial question as to the material facts necessary to support the district court's judgment.

IV. THE [RELIGION] CLAIM

Similar reasoning supports a grant of summary judgment for the government on HLF's claim that the designation and blocking order substantially burden its exercise of religion.

Even accepting the dubious proposition that a charitable corporation not otherwise defined can exercise religion as protected in the First Amendment, preventing such a corporation from aiding terrorists does not violate any right contemplated in the Constitution. No one on behalf of Holy Land Foundation has forwarded the proposition that the fomenting and spread of terrorism is mandated by the religion of Islam. At most they argue a right to charitable giving as a pillar of that religion. Acting against the funding of terrorism does not violate the free exercise rights protected by the First Amendment. There is no free exercise right to fund terrorists. The record clearly supports a conclusion that HLF did. [B]ased on the evidence already in the record, summary judgment for the government is warranted.

V. CONCLUSION

Therefore, we uphold the district court's affirmance of the Treasury Department's decision to designate HLF as an SDGT and to block its assets. We also affirm the district court's dismissal [or summary judgment] of HLF's due process [and first amendment] claims on the basis of the administrative record.

NOTES AND QUESTIONS

1. Classified Information. According to the D.C. Circuit, due process has been satisfied by the administrative record coupled by the organization's ability to submit counter-information. In that view, there is no right of either the organization or criminal defendants to obtain the classified information on which the agency relied. But in *PMOI* the court noted its own holding in *Abourezk* that government cannot take negative action toward a person's rights on the basis of secret evidence. Is it constitutional to "take" (seize or freeze) money that was donated for charitable purposes on the basis of secret evidence? Is this different from the CIPA and related cases considered in Chapter 5? How? Even if this result is constitutional, is it wise?

What should be the answer with respect to using classified information to form the basis of a designation resulting in a criminal prosecution? This question still implicates a fundamental policy choice for a free society.

2. *United States v. Sattar.* *United States v. Sattar*, 272 F. Supp. 2d 348 (S.D.N.Y. 2003). Sheikh Rahman's lawyer, Lynne Stewart, and their interpreter were charged with violating prison regulations and also violating § 2339B by using their consultations with the Sheikh to pass messages to and from the Islamic Group. They moved to dismiss the indictment for many of the same reasons covered by the Ninth Circuit in *HLP* and by Judge Takasugi in *Rahmani*. Specifically, they challenged the portion of the statute that prohibits provision of "communication devices" and the court agreed that their use of telephones could not be the basis of a criminal charge. "[B]y criminalizing the mere use of phones and other means of communication the statute provides neither notice nor standards for its application such that it is unconstitutionally vague as applied." The court also agreed with the Ninth Circuit that the "personnel" provision was unconstitutionally vague.

With regard to the due process issue of designation, the district court preferred the holdings of the D.C. Circuit to that of Judge Takasugi. The heart of the matter was that the defendants were accused of providing support to a designated organization, regardless of whether that designation was proper. "The element of the offense is the designation of IG as an FTO, not the correctness of the determination."

3. Charitable Actions. Criminalizing support to an FTO regardless of the propriety of the designation adds a powerful arrow in the quiver of the government investigators and prosecutors. It is, as described above, the equivalent of prohibiting driving with an open container of alcohol in the car. The prosecution is not required to prove that the alcohol is being used improperly nor is the "material support" prosecutor required to prove that the funds are being used in support of terrorism. It is the act itself that is outlawed, not the purpose of the act. This answer is fine with respect to the alcohol because of the limited social utility of the act, but is it satisfactory when the act is involvement with what the defendant believes to be a political or charitable organization?

[C] *Mens Rea* of Material Support

UNITED STATES v. AL-ARIAN
308 F. Supp. 2d 1322 (M.D. Fla. 2004)

[Sami Al-Arian has been an Assistant Professor at the University of South Florida since 1986, participating actively in conferences and courses dealing with Arab or Middle Eastern Studies. He was instrumental in formation of a group known as World and Islamic Studies Enterprise (WISE), with which USF co-sponsored several conferences. In November 1994, a PBS documentary alleged that Al-Arian was the "head of the Islamic Jihad terrorist group's domestic support network." From that point on, Al-Arian and USF have been embroiled in political and legal disputes over his employment, including an investigation of academic freedom charges by the American Association of University Professors (AAUP). Finally, the Department of Justice indicted Al-Arian along with a number of others. The opinion here relates to a series of pretrial motions by the defendants.]

MOODY, DISTRICT JUDGE.

I. BACKGROUND

A. Factural and Procedural Background

This is a criminal action against alleged members of the Palestinian Islamic Jihad-Shiqaqi Faction (the "PIJ") who purportedly operated and directed fundraising and other organizational activities in the United States for almost twenty years. The PIJ is a foreign organization that uses violence, principally suicide bombings, and threats of violence to pressure Israel to cede territory to the Palestinian people. On February 19, 2003, the government indicted the Defendants in a 50 count indictment that included counts for: (1) conspiracy to commit racketeering; (2) conspiracy to commit murder, maim, or injure persons outside the United States; (3) conspiracy to provide material support to or for the benefit of foreign terrorists [among others].

Count 1 of the Indictment alleges a wide ranging pattern of racketeering activity beginning in 1984 lasting through February 2003, including murder, extortion, and money laundering. The Indictment details some 256 overt acts, ranging from soliciting and raising funds[9] to providing management, organizational, and logistical support for the PIJ. The overt act section of the Indictment details numerous suicide bombings and attacks by PIJ members causing the deaths of over 100 people, including 2 American citizens, and injuries to over 350 people, including 7 American citizens. These same overt acts (or parts of them) support the remaining counts of the Indictment.

B. Statutory Background

Center stage in the motions are two statutes: [AEDPA and IEEPA].

On October 8, 1997, the Secretary designated PIJ as a FTO under AEDPA. Neither Congress nor the Secretary revoked the PIJ's designation at any time, and the PIJ has not sought judicial review of its designations as a FTO.

The second statute central to these motions is IEEPA. Under IEEPA, the President is granted the authority "to deal with any unusual and extraordinary threat . . . to the national security, foreign policy, or economy of the United States, if the President declares a national emergency with respect to such threat." 50 U.S.C. § 1701(a). The President's authority includes the power to investigate, regulate, or prohibit financial transactions. Section 1705(b) makes it unlawful to willfully violate or attempt to violate any executive order or regulation issued pursuant to IEEPA and provides for imprisonment of up to 10 years for such a violation.

On January 23, 1995, pursuant to IEEPA, President Clinton issued Executive Order 12947 (the "Executive Order"). The Executive Order declared a national emergency with respect to the Middle East peace process that threatened the United States' national security, foreign policy, and economy. The Executive Order prohibited financial transactions with any specially designated terrorist ("SDT"). The annex to the Executive Order designates the PIJ as a SDT.[10]

The Secretary of the Treasury promulgated regulations that make it unlawful to "deal in property or interests in property of a . . . [SDT], including the making or receiving of any contribution of funds, goods, or services to or for the benefit of a [SDT]." The regulations interpret this prohibition to include charitable contributions or "donation[s] of funds, goods, services, or technology to relieve human suffering, such as food, clothing, or medicine."[11]

Not all transactions with a SDT are banned or are criminal. For example, the regulations make clear that there is no liability for a charitable contribution if the

---

[9] [Court's Footnote 5] An example of a soliciting or fundraising act is contained in Overt Act 130. In that overt act, the government claims that Defendant Al-Arian wrote a letter to a gentleman in Kuwait requesting additional money so that the PIJ could engage in more bombings and provide financial assistance to the families of recent suicide bombers who belonged to the PIJ.

[10] [Court's Footnote 14] Fathi Shiqaqi, co-defendant Awda, and co-defendant Shallah were designated SDTs.

[11] [Court's Footnote 16] Services is also broadly interpreted and includes legal, accounting, public relations, educational, or other services to a SDT. However, [regulations] allow for legal and emergency medical services, including legal services to a SDT regarding its designation.

contribution is made "without knowledge or reason to know that the donation or contribution is destined to or for the benefit of a [SDT]." In addition, the regulations exempt certain transactions from the ban, including transactions that: (a) are licensed or authorized; (b) involve personal communications that do not transfer anything of value; (c) involve some types of information and informational materials; or (d) are incidental to travel.

IEEPA itself does not explicitly or implicitly provide for judicial review of an executive order, but it does provide a procedure for court review of classified information. The regulations provide a process for administrative review of a designation of an organization as an SDT. Courts have held that judicial review of a designation under IEEPA or its regulations exists and that the Administrative Procedures Act governs that review. *See, e.g., Holy Land Foundation for Relief and Development v. Ashcroft*, 333 F.3d 156 (D.C. Cir. 2003). There are no limitations on judicial review like those contained in AEDPA.

II. DISCUSSION

Defendants' motions raise a host of statutory construction and constitutional issues purportedly on which this Court should dismiss or strike Counts 1 through 4 (or parts of Counts 1 through 4).

A. Statutory Construction and Constitutional Issues

1. Statutory Construction of AEDPA and IEEPA

a. First Amendment, Overbreadth, and Vagueness Background

Defendants assert that Counts 1 through 4 are unconstitutional because they do not require either: (a) a specific intent to further the unlawful activities of the PIJ; or (b) an intent to incite and a likelihood of imminent disorder.

As a corollary to their First Amendment argument, Defendants also claim that the doctrines of overbreadth and vagueness invalidate AEDPA or IEEPA in whole or in part. Defendants assert that the statutes sweep so broadly that they include substantial amounts of constitutionally protected advocacy within their prohibitions. Similarly, Defendants argue that the material terms of each statute are so broadly defined that a person is incapable of knowing when otherwise protected activity becomes criminal. In support of Defendants' position, Defendants cite to two Ninth Circuit opinions where that court twice concluded that portions of AEDPA are unconstitutionally vague as applied to the plaintiffs in that case. Defendants argue that the same hypothetical utilized by the Ninth Circuit indicates that other sections of AEDPA and IEEPA are similarly vague and unconstitutional.

The government responds that the Indictment alleges that Defendants engaged in criminal conduct and activities, not protected speech or association. The government asserts that the Indictment alleges that Defendants conspired with the PIJ and assisted the PIJ in the accomplishment of unlawful activities, including, but not limited to, murder, extortion, and money laundering. According to the government, speech is utilized in the Indictment to show Defendants' agreement to participate in the conspiracy, and their role, motive, and intent, all of which is allowable under the First Amendment. The government argues that AEDPA and IEEPA need not contain a specific intent to further unlawful activities or be limited to situations where a defendant intends to incite and a likelihood of imminent disorder, because the statutes and the Indictment are aimed at conduct and not speech or association. The government also cites to the Ninth Circuit's *Humanitarian [HLP I and HLP II]* cases, where the Ninth Circuit twice applied this analysis and concluded that AEDPA did not violate the First Amendment rights of the plaintiffs in those cases.

The government also opposes the Defendants' contentions that AEDPA and IEEPA are overbroad or vague. The government relies on the presence of "knowingly" or "willfully" *mens rea* requirements in the statutes to remove protected speech from the prohibited conduct covered under both statutes. Similarly, the government argues that the statutes in the vast number of applications cover only unprotected conduct and only in remote hypothetical situations do AEDPA and IEEPA even come close to impinging upon protected speech. The government cites to a line of Supreme Court cases, which have held in such circumstances that courts should not use the overbreadth and vagueness doctrines to invalidate statutes.

The broader this Court interprets AEDPA and IEEPA, the more likely that the statutes receive a higher standard of review and are unconstitutional. For example, if this Court interprets AEDPA and IEEPA as requiring a specific intent to further the illegal activities of the FTO or SDT, then no constitutional problems exist. Similarly, if this Court interprets AEDPA's and IEEPA's prohibitions broadly and does not impose a specific intent *mens rea* requirement, it will likely be forced to perform a vagueness analysis and find portions of AEDPA and IEEPA unconstitutional, as did the Ninth Circuit in the *Humanitarian* cases.

b. Standards for Interpreting a Statute

If an ambiguity exists or an absurd result occurs, this Court is to resort to the canons of statutory construction to determine the meaning of a statutory provision by focusing on the broader, statutory context. *See United States v. X-Citement Video, Inc.*, 513 U.S. 64 (1999). First, courts are to interpret statutes in a manner that avoids constitutional difficulty. Second, courts interpret criminal statutes to include broadly applicable *scienter* requirements.

In *X-Citement Video*, the Supreme Court faced almost the same statutory interpretation issues faced in this case. There, the Supreme Court considered the Protection of Children Against Sexual Exploitation Act, [which] made it unlawful for any person to "knowingly" transport, ship, receive, distribute, or reproduce a visual depiction involving a "minor engaging in sexually explicit conduct." The Ninth Circuit had interpreted "knowingly" to only modify the surrounding verbs, like transport or ship. Under this construction, whether a defendant knew the minority of the performer(s) or even knew whether the material was sexually explicit was inconsequential. The Supreme Court reversed, concluding that, while the Ninth Circuit's construction of Section 2252 complied with the plain meaning rule, the construction caused absurd results. Under the Ninth Circuit's construction, the Court noted that a Federal Express courier who knew that there was film in a package could be convicted even though the courier had no knowledge that the film contained child pornography. To avoid such results, the Court utilized the canons of statutory construction to imply a "knowing" requirement to each element, including the age of the performers and the sexually explicit nature of the material. The Court stated that in criminal statutes "the presumption in favor of a scienter requirement should apply to each of the statutory elements that criminalize otherwise innocent conduct."

c. Statutory Construction of AEDPA

This Court agrees with the Ninth Circuit in *HLP I* that a purely grammatical reading of the plain language of § 2339B(a)(1) makes it unlawful for any person to knowingly furnish any item contained in the material support categories to an organization that has been designated a FTO. And like *HLP II*, this Court agrees that this construction renders odd results and raises serious constitutional concerns. For example under *HLP I*, a donor could be convicted for giving money to a FTO without knowledge that an organization was a FTO or that it committed unlawful activities, and without an intent that the money be used to commit future unlawful activities. [Similarly, a bank teller who cashes the donor's check for a FTO could also be guilty despite a similar lack of knowledge.]

HLP II attempted to correct this odd result and accompanying constitutional concerns by interpreting "knowingly" to mean that a person knew: (a) an organization was a FTO; or (b) an organization committed unlawful activities, which caused it to be designated a FTO. But, *HLP II*'s construction of § 2339B only cures some of the Fifth Amendment concerns. First, *HLP II* fails to comply with *X-Citement Video*'s holding that a *mens rea* requirement "should apply to each of the statutory elements that criminalize otherwise innocent conduct." *HLP II* implies only a *mens rea* requirement to the FTO element of § 2339B(a)(1) and not to the material support element. Under *HLP II*'s construction, a cab driver could be guilty for giving a ride to a FTO member to the UN, if he knows that the person is a member of a FTO or the member or his organization at sometime conducted an unlawful activity in a foreign country. Similarly, a hotel clerk in New York could be committing a crime by providing lodging to that same FTO member under similar circumstances as the cab driver. Because the *HLP II*'s construction fails to avoid potential Fifth Amendment concerns, this Court rejects its construction of § 2339B.

Second, the *HLP II* construction does not solve the constitutional vagueness concerns of § 2339B(a)(1), which can be avoided by implying a *mens rea* requirement to the "terial support or resources" element of § 2339B(a)(1). If this Court accepted the *HLP II* construction, it would likely have to declare many more categories of "material support" (in addition to "training" and "personnel" determined to be unconstitutionally vague in the *HLP* cases) unconstitutionally vague for impinging on advocacy rights, including "financial services," "lodging," "safe houses," "communications equipment," "facilities," "transportation" and "other physical assets." Using the Ninth Circuit's vagueness example on "training," the statute could likewise punish other innocent conduct, such as where a person in New York City (where the United Nations is located) gave a FTO member a ride from the airport to the United Nations before the member petitioned the United Nations. Such conduct could be punished as providing "transportation" to a FTO under § 2339B. The end result of the Ninth Circuit's statutory construction in *HLP II* is to render a substantial portion of § 2339B unconstitutionally vague.[12]

This Court concludes that it is more consistent with Congress's intent, which was to prohibit material support from FTOs to the "fullest possible basis," to imply a *mens rea* requirement to the "material support" element of § 2339B(a)(1). Therefore, this Court concludes that to convict a defendant under § 2339B(a)(1) the government must prove beyond a reasonable doubt that the defendant knew that: (a) the organization was a FTO or had committed unlawful activities that caused it to be so designated; and (b) what he was furnishing was "material support." To avoid Fifth Amendment personal guilt problems, this Court concludes that the government must show more than a defendant knew something was within a category of "material support" in order to meet (b). In order to meet (b), the government must show that the defendant knew (had a specific intent) that the support would further the illegal activities of a FTO.[13]

---

[12] [Court's Footnote 31] Other examples of innocent conduct that could be prohibited include the same person allowing the FTO member to spend the night at his house, cashing a check, loaning the member a cell phone for use during the stay, or allowing the member to use the fax machine or laptop computer in preparing the petition. And, the additional phrase "expert advice or assistance" added by the Patriot Act in 2002 could also fail as unconstitutionally vague.

[13] [Court's Footnote 33] This Court's conclusion is consistent with the Seventh Circuit's decision in *Boim v. Quranic Literacy Inst.*, 291 F.3d 1000 (7th Cir. 2002). In *Boim*, the Seventh Circuit considered whether a violation of § 2339B could serve as a basis for civil liability under Section 2333. The Seventh Circuit held that to succeed on a Section 2333 claim, plaintiff must prove that the defendant knew about the unlawful activities of the FTO and intended to help in those unlawful activities. This Court's construction of § 2339B avoids the

This Court does not believe this burden is that great in the typical case.[14] Often, such an intent will be easily inferred. For example, a jury could infer a specific intent to further the illegal activities of a FTO when a defendant knowingly provides weapons, explosives, or lethal substances to an organization that he knows is a FTO because of the nature of the support. Likewise, a jury could infer a specific intent when a defendant knows that the organization continues to commit illegal acts and the defendant provides funds to that organization knowing that money is fungible and, once received, the donee can use the funds for any purpose it chooses. That is, by its nature, money carries an inherent danger for furthering the illegal aims of an organization. Congress said as much when it found that FTOs were "so tainted by their criminal conduct that any contribution to such an organization facilitates that conduct."

This opinion in no way creates a safe harbor for terrorists or their supporters to try and avoid prosecution through utilization of shell "charitable organizations" or by directing money through the memo line of a check towards lawful activities. This Court believes that a jury can quickly peer through such facades when appropriate. This is especially true if other facts indicate a defendant's true intent, like where defendants or conspirators utilize codes or unusual transaction practices to transfer funds. Instead, this Court's holding works to avoid potential constitutional problems and fully accomplish congressional intent.

d. Construction of IEEPA, the Executive Order, and the Regulations

Section 1705(b) makes it unlawful to "willfully" violate or attempt to violate any regulation or order issued pursuant to IEEPA.

While no court has construed the criminal prohibition contained in IEEPA, this Court concludes that a conviction under IEEPA in these circumstances requires similar proof of intent similar to that required under AEDPA. In other words, this Court concludes that to criminally convict a defendant for violating IEEPA the government must prove a defendant: (a) knew either that an organization was a SDT or committed unlawful activities that caused it to be designated as a SDT; and (b) had a specific intent that the contribution be used to further the unlawful activities of the SDT.

This Court's conclusion is based on the plain language of Section 1705(b), which criminalizes only "willfully" committed violations of the Executive Order and the regulations interpreting the Executive Order. The Supreme Court has interpreted "willfully" in criminal statutes to "differentiate between deliberate and unwitting conduct" and means an act "undertaken with a bad purpose . . . [the person need not be aware of the specific law or rule that his conduct may be violating. But he must act to do something that the law forbids.]"

While knowledge of IEEPA, the Executive Order, or the regulations thereunder is not necessary to support a conviction, some "bad purpose" must be demonstrated by the government. This Court concludes that a "bad purpose" cannot be demonstrated by proof of knowledge of past unlawful activity alone. The government must show some additional intent to further future unlawful activity to support criminal liability.

This Court's interpretation of § 1705(b) is not contrary to the intent of the Executive Order or its regulations. First, IEEPA contains a separate civil penalty provision that penalizes violations that are not willful. It makes sense that the regulations punish some unlawful transactions by a civil penalty only, while punishing worse transgressions both civilly and criminally. Second, the regulations themselves contain

---

anomaly of civil liability being more narrow than criminal liability based on the same statutory language.

[14] [Court's Footnote 34] Indeed, Congress recently added 18 U.S.C. § 2339C, which criminalized raising funds with the specific intent that the funds will be or are used to cause the death or serious bodily injury of a civilian with the purpose of intimidating the population or compelling a government to do or abstain from doing any act.

an exception for charitable contributions, if the contribution is made without knowledge or reason to know that it was made to or for the benefit of a SDT. Such an exception reinforces this Court's interpretation of a requirement of proof of a specific intent because it shows that the administering agency interprets the prohibition to not reach purely innocent or unwitting conduct.

Finally, this Court is concerned that without such a *scienter* requirement the prohibitions in the Executive Order may be unconstitutionally vague or violate the Fifth Amendment's requirement of personal guilt. By requiring a specific intent to further the illegal activities of the SDT, this Court avoids considering whether the regulations are unconstitutionally vague or violate the Fifth Amendment's requirement of personal guilt.

2. First Amendment

Given this Court's construction of the *mens rea* requirements of AEDPA and IEEPA, little remains to be said of Defendants' First Amendment challenges to Counts 3 and 4. This Court will address two points raised by Defendants as to the Indictment in general.

First, this Court agrees with the government that the Indictment does not criminalize "pure speech." Instead, the overt acts section of the Indictment utilizes the speech of Defendants to show the existence of the conspiracies, the Defendants' agreement to participate in them, their level of participation or role in them, and the Defendants' criminal intent. It is well established that the government can use speech to prove elements of crimes such as motive or intent. The fact that Defendants' speech is contained in the overt act section of the Indictment is of little consequence. The reason that an overt act can include even protected speech is that it is the agreement that is punishable in a conspiracy charge and not the overt act itself. Therefore, this Court denies Defendants' motion to dismiss on "pure speech" grounds.

Second, this Court declines Defendants' invitation to heighten the level of First Amendment protection given to seeking and donating funds. The Supreme Court has repeatedly considered the issue and determined that such activities are more like expressive conduct than pure speech. This Court agrees with the Seventh Circuit in *Boim v. Quaranic Literacy* that the *Buckley* standard applies to determine the constitutionality of a regulation prohibiting contributions to foreign organizations.[15] In *Boim*, the plaintiffs claimed defendant was liable to them under 18 U.S.C. § 2333 because the defendant violated § 2339B. Section 2333 provided a civil remedy to U.S. nationals injured by acts of international terrorism. The defendant challenged Section 2333 and 2339B's constitutionality on First Amendment grounds. The Seventh Circuit held that *Buckley*'s contribution analysis applied and concluded that Section 2333 (based on a violation of § 2339B) did not violate the First Amendment. The Seventh Circuit reasoned that *Buckley* applied because both speech and association components are implicated by regulations that restrict or prohibit a person's ability to contribute or fundraise on behalf of an organization.

Under *Buckley* and its progeny, a regulation of fundraising is constitutional if it is closely drawn to further a sufficiently important government interest. This Court

---

[15] [Court's Footnote 41] This Court disagrees with the Ninth Circuit that intermediate scrutiny under *United States v. O'Brien* applies to whether a prohibition on fundraising and contribution is constitutional under the First Amendment. The Ninth Circuit opinion provides no reason on why *Buckley*'s contribution analysis should not apply to other forms of contributions. This Court sees no basis for a difference in constitutional analysis between political contributions and other forms of contributions. Both have a speech and an associational component. However, as a practical matter, it may be easier for the government to regulate contributions to foreign groups because of the strength of the governmental interests at stake in cases similar to this one.

concludes that AEDPA, IEEPA, and the other statutes at issue in this case easily meet this analysis.

The Supreme Court has termed the protection of the foreign policy interests of the United States to be of great importance. Likewise, other courts have concluded that the government's interest in stopping the spread of global terrorism is "paramount" or "substantial." This Court agrees and would conclude that stopping the spread of terrorism is not just a sufficiently important governmental interest, but is a compelling governmental interest.

Similarly, a congressional decision to stop the spread of global terrorism by preventing fundraising and prohibiting support is closely drawn to further this interest. This Court's construction of AEDPA and IEEPA (requiring proof of a specific intent to further the unlawful activities of a SDT or FTO) reinforces this Court's conclusion that the prohibitions in AEDPA and IEEPA are closely drawn to further the governmental interest. Therefore, this Court denies Defendants' motion to dismiss on First Amendment grounds.

3. Procedural Due Process: PIJ's FTO Designation under AEDPA and SDT Designation under IEEPA

Defendants argue that Counts 3 and 4 of the Indictment should be dismissed because the PIJ was denied due process under AEDPA and IEEPA when it was designated, respectively, a FTO and a SDT. Defendants rely primarily on the Supreme Court's opinion in *United States v. Mendoza-Lopez*, and a district court decision in *United States v. Rahmani*, in support of their argument. The government argues that *Mendoza-Lopez* is inapplicable to this case because these Defendants lack standing to challenge the PIJ's designation and that *Rahmani* is seriously flawed. This Court concludes for those and additional reasons Defendants may not collaterally attack the designations of the PIJ under AEDPA or IEEPA.

[The Ninth Circuit reversed *Rahmani* in *United States v. Ashfari*, see *infra* § 3.03[C].]

4. Ex Post Facto

Finally, Defendants argue that Counts 1 through 4 attempt to punish the Defendants for conduct that was not criminal when it took place in violation of the *ex post facto* clause of the Constitution. Defendants argue that this Court should strike any overt act or reference to an act that occurred prior to PIJ's designation as a FTO (October 8, 1997) or prior to PIJ's designation as a SDT (January 23, 1995). Alternatively, Defendants argue that this Court should strike any act prior to the respective designation date from Counts 3 and 4. The government responds that the Defendants' conduct in this case has always been unlawful and that the PIJ's designation as a SDT and a FTO provided additional bases for criminal liability. The government also responds that conduct prior to either designation date is relevant to Counts 3 and 4 because Defendants are charged with being in conspiracies that continued after the conduct was criminalized and acts prior to the designation dates go to the existence of a conspiracy, the parties' agreement, and Defendants' purpose, motive, and intent.

Neither of Defendants' arguments are well taken. Defendants are correct only to the extent that the *ex post facto* clause prohibits the enactment by Congress of a statute that punishes an act which was innocent when committed. However, Counts 1 and 2 of the Indictment seek to punish Defendants for violating 18 U.S.C. §§ 1962(d) and 1956(a)(1). Both statutes were enacted (1970 and 1948 respectively) well prior to any act alleged in the Indictment. As to Counts 3 and 4, the Eleventh Circuit has held that the *ex post facto clause* was not violated when a conspiracy continues after the effective date of a statute making that action illegal. The Indictment alleges overt acts in furtherance of the conspiracy after 1995 and 1997. Therefore, this Court denies

Defendants' motions to dismiss or strike on *ex post facto* grounds.

NOTE

On December 5, 2005, the jury in Tampa acquited al-Arian of the conspiracy charges and hung on the material support charges. Consistent with the opinion above, the trial court instructed the jury that it should acquit on material support unless the defendants intended for their money to go to unlawful purposes. To repeat the scienter language, "to convict a defendant under § 2339B(a)(1) the government must prove beyond a reasonable doubt that the defendant knew that: (a) the organization was a FTO or had committed unlawful activities that caused it to be so designated; and (b) what he was furnishing was 'material support.' To avoid Fifth Amendment personal guilt problems, this Court concludes that the government must show more than a defendant knew something was within a category of 'material support' in order to meet (b). In order to meet (b), the government must show that the defendant knew (had a specific intent) that the support would further the illegal activities of a FTO."

In April 2006 Al-arian pleaded guilty to conspiracy to provide material support and agreed to be deported. He was sentenced to 57 months but given credit for time served, leaving 19 months to serve before being deported. Then, however, he was sentenced to 14 months civil contempt for refusing to testify in other trials. In December 2007, the civil contempt was lifted and he is due to be released in June 2008.

UNITED STATES v. HAMMOUD
381 F.3d 316 (4th Cir. 2004) (en banc)
[reaffirmed except as to sentence, 405 F.3d 1034 (4th Cir. 2005)]

WILKINS, CHIEF JUDGE.

Mohammed Hammoud appeals the sentence imposed following his convictions of numerous offenses, all of which are connected to his support of Hizballah, a designated foreign terrorist organization (FTO).

I. FACTS

The facts underlying Hammoud's convictions and sentence are largely undisputed. We therefore recount them briefly.

A. Hizballah

Hizballah is an organization founded by Lebanese Shi'a Muslims in response to the 1982 invasion of Lebanon by Israel. Hizballah provides various forms of humanitarian aid to Shi'a Muslims in Lebanon. However, it is also a strong opponent of Western presence in the Middle East, and it advocates the use of terrorism in support of its agenda. Hizballah is particularly opposed to the existence of Israel and to the activities of the American government in the Middle East. Hizballah's general secretary is Hassan Nasserallah, and its spiritual leader is Sheikh Fadlallah.

B. Hammoud

In 1992, Hammoud, a citizen of Lebanon, attempted to enter the United States on fraudulent documents. After being detained by the INS, Hammoud sought asylum. While the asylum application was pending, Hammoud moved to Charlotte, North Carolina, where his brothers and cousins were living. Hammoud ultimately obtained permanent resident status by marrying a United States citizen.

At some point in the mid-1990s, Hammoud, his wife, one of his brothers, and his cousins all became involved in a cigarette smuggling operation. The conspirators purchased large quantities of cigarettes in North Carolina, smuggled them to Michigan, and sold them without paying Michigan taxes. This scheme took advantage of the fact that Michigan imposes a tax of $7.50 per carton of cigarettes, while the North Carolina tax is only 50 [cents]. It is estimated that the conspiracy involved a quantity of cigarettes valued at roughly $7.5 million and that the state of Michigan was deprived of $3 million in tax revenues.

In 1996, Hammoud began leading weekly prayer services for Shi'a Muslims in Charlotte. These services were often conducted at Hammoud's home. At these meetings, Hammoud — who is acquainted with both Nasserallah and Fadlallah, as well as Sheikh Abbas Harake, a senior military commander for Hizballah — urged the attendees to donate money to Hizballah. Hammoud would then forward the money to Harake. The Government's evidence demonstrated that on one occasion, Hammoud donated $3,500 of his own money to Hizballah.

Based on these and other activities, Hammoud was charged with various immigration violations, sale of contraband cigarettes, money laundering, mail fraud, credit card fraud, and racketeering. Additionally, Hammoud was charged with conspiracy to provide material support to a designated FTO and with providing material support to a designated FTO, both in violation of 18 U.S.C.A. § 2339B. The latter § 2339B charge related specifically to Hammoud's personal donation of $3,500 to Hizballah.

At trial, one of the witnesses against Hammoud was Said Harb, who grew up in the same Lebanese neighborhood as Hammoud. Harb testified regarding his own involvement in the cigarette smuggling operation and also provided information regarding the provision of "dual use" equipment (such as global positioning systems, which can be used for both civilian and military activities) to Hizballah. The Government alleged that this conduct was part of the conspiracy to provide material support to Hizballah. Harb testified that Hammoud had declined to become involved in providing equipment because he was helping Hizballah in his own way. Harb also testified that when he traveled to Lebanon in September 1999, Hammoud gave him $3,500 for Hizballah.

C. Conviction and Sentence

The jury convicted Hammoud of 14 offenses: money laundering and conspiracy to commit money laundering (18 U.S.C. § 1956(a)(1), (h)); transportation of contraband cigarettes (18 U.S.C. § 2342); and providing material support to a designated FTO (18 U.S.C. § 2339B).

Applying the 2002 Guidelines Manual, the presentencing report (PSR) recommended that the base offense level correspond to the amount of tax evaded in the cigarette smuggling operation. The PSR recommended several upward adjustments to this base offense level. Most significantly, the PSR recommended a 12-level enhancement for committing a terrorist act, see id. § 3A1.4(a). Ultimately, the PSR recommended assignment of an adjusted offense level of 46, which required a sentence of life imprisonment.

Hammoud filed objections to the PSR, in which he challenged the factual basis for several of the upward adjustments. Hammoud also challenged the terrorism enhancement under *Apprendi [v. New Jersey*, 530 U.S. 466 (2000)], maintaining that the enhancement was invalid without a jury finding that he possessed the requisite mental state. Hammoud made similar arguments against the enhancements for his leadership role and obstruction of justice.

The district court conducted a sentencing hearing at which it rejected all of Hammoud's sentencing challenges. The court therefore concluded that the guidelines provided for a sentence of life imprisonment. Because none of the offenses of conviction carried a statutory maximum of life imprisonment, the district court imposed the maximum sentence on each count and ordered all sentences to be served consecutively. This resulted in the imposition of a sentence of 155 years.

We begin by addressing Hammoud's numerous challenges to his convictions for providing (and conspiring to provide) material support to a designated FTO. We then consider Hammoud's claim that *Blakely* [*v. Washington*, 124 S. Ct. 2531 (2004)], operates to invalidate his sentence.

II. CONSTITUTIONALITY OF 18 U.S.C.A. § 2339B

A. *Freedom of Association*

Hammoud first contends that § 2339B impermissibly restricts the First Amendment right of association. Hammoud concedes (at least for purposes of this argument) that Hizballah engages in terrorist activity. But, he also notes the undisputed fact that Hizballah provides humanitarian aid to citizens of Lebanon. Hammoud argues that because Hizballah engages in both legal and illegal activities, he can be found criminally liable for providing material support to Hizballah only if he had a specific intent to further the organization's illegal aims. Because § 2339B lacks such a specific intent requirement, Hammoud argues that it unconstitutionally restricts the freedom of association. *Cf. United States v. Al-Arian*, 329 F. Supp. 2d 1294 (M.D. Fla. 2004) (construing § 2339B as requiring proof of specific intent to further illegal activity because less stringent interpretation would raise constitutional questions regarding freedom of association and "due process requirements of personal guilt").

It is well established that "the First Amendment . . . restricts the ability of the State to impose liability on an individual solely because of his association with another." Therefore, it is a violation of the First Amendment to punish an individual for mere membership in an organization that has legal and illegal goals. Any statute prohibiting association with such an organization must require a showing that the defendant specifically intended to further the organization's unlawful goals. Hammoud maintains that because § 2339B does not contain such a specific intent requirement, his conviction violates the First Amendment.[16]

Hammoud's argument fails because § 2339B does not prohibit mere association; it prohibits the conduct of providing material support to a designated FTO. Therefore, cases regarding mere association with an organization do not control. Rather, the governing standard is found in *United States v. O'Brien*, 391 U.S. 367 (1968), which applies when a facially neutral statute restricts some expressive conduct. Such a statute is valid

> if it is within the constitutional power of the Government; if it furthers an important or substantial governmental interest; if the governmental interest is unrelated to the suppression of free expression; and if the incidental restriction on alleged First Amendment freedoms is no greater than is essential to the furtherance of that interest.

[T]he Government's interest in curbing terrorism is unrelated to the suppression of free expression. Hammoud is free to advocate in favor of Hizballah or its political objectives — § 2339B does not target such advocacy. [T]he incidental effect on expression caused by § 2339B is no greater than necessary. In enacting § 2339B and its sister statute, 18 U.S.C. § 2339A, Congress explicitly found that "foreign organizations that engage in terrorist activity are so tainted by their criminal conduct that any

---

[16] [Court's Footnote 3] Hammoud relies in part on cases holding that a donation to a political advocacy group is a proxy for speech. *See, e.g., Buckley v. Valeo*, 424 U.S. 1, 16–17 (1976) (per curiam). Hizballah is not a political advocacy group, however. Therefore, while providing monetary support to Hizballah may have an expressive component, it is not the equivalent of pure political speech. *See Humanitarian Law Project v. Reno*, 205 F.3d 1130, 1134–35 (9th Cir. 2000) (rejecting argument that material support prohibition is subject to strict scrutiny review under *Buckley* and similar cases).

contribution to such an organization facilitates that conduct." As the Ninth Circuit reasoned

> it follows that all material support given to [foreign terrorist] organizations aids their unlawful goals. Indeed, . . . terrorist organizations do not maintain open books. Therefore, when someone makes a donation to them, there is no way to tell how the donation is used. Further, . . . even contributions earmarked for peaceful purposes can be used to give aid to the families of those killed while carrying out terrorist acts, thus making the decision to engage in terrorism more attractive. More fundamentally, money is fungible; giving support intended to aid an organization's peaceful activities frees up resources that can be used for terrorist acts.

Humanitarian Law Project, 205 F.3d at 1136. In light of this reasoning, the prohibition on material support is adequately tailored to the interest served and does not suppress more speech than is necessary to further the Government's legitimate goal. We therefore conclude that § 2339B does not infringe on the constitutionally protected right of free association.

B. Overbreadth

Hammoud next argues that § 2339B is overbroad. A statute is overbroad only if it "punishes a substantial amount of protected free speech, judged in relation to the statute's plainly legitimate sweep." The overbreadth must be substantial "not only in an absolute sense, but also relative to the scope of the law's plainly legitimate applications." It is also worth noting that when, as here, a statute is addressed to conduct rather than speech, an overbreadth challenge is less likely to succeed.

Hammoud argues that § 2339B is overbroad because (1) it prohibits mere association with an FTO, and (2) it prohibits such plainly legitimate activities as teaching members of an FTO how to apply for grants to further the organization's humanitarian aims. As discussed above, § 2339B does not prohibit mere association with an FTO and therefore is not overbroad on that basis. Regarding Hammoud's second overbreadth argument, it may be true that the material support prohibition of § 2339B encompasses some forms of expression that are entitled to First Amendment protection.[17] *Cf. Humanitarian Law Project*, 205 F.3d at 1138 (holding that "training" prong of material support definition is vague because it covers such forms of protected expression as "instructing members of a designated group on how to petition the United Nations to give aid to their group"). Hammoud has utterly failed to demonstrate, however, that any overbreadth is substantial in relation to the legitimate reach of § 2339B.

C. Vagueness

Hammoud next argues that the term "material support" is unconstitutionally vague. As noted above, the term "material support" is specifically defined as a number of enumerated actions. Hammoud relies on *Humanitarian Law Project*, in which the Ninth Circuit ruled that two components of the material support definition — "personnel" and "training" — were vague. The possible vagueness of these prongs of the material support definition does not affect Hammoud's conviction, however, because he was specifically charged with providing material support in the form of currency. *See United States v. Rahman*, 189 F.3d 88, 116 (2d Cir. 1999) (per curiam) (rejecting vagueness challenge because allegedly vague term was not relevant to Appellant's conviction). There is nothing at all vague about the term "currency."

---

[17] [Court's Footnote 4] A defendant who is prosecuted because his protected speech is incidentally covered by a broader ban on unprotected activity may bring an as-applied challenge. Hammoud is not such a defendant for the reasons previously articulated.

D. Designation of an FTO

Hammoud's final challenge to the constitutionality of § 2339B concerns his inability to challenge the designation of Hizballah as an FTO. Section 2339B(g)(6) defines "terrorist organization" as "an organization designated as a terrorist organization under [8 U.S.C. § 1189]." Section 1189(a)(8) explicitly prohibits a defendant in a criminal action from challenging a designation. Hammoud argues that his inability to challenge the designation of Hizballah as an FTO is a violation of the Constitution.

Here, Congress has provided that the fact of an organization's designation as an FTO is an element of § 2339B, but the validity of the designation is not. Therefore, Hammoud's inability to challenge the designation is not a violation of his constitutional rights. *See United States v. Bozarov*, 974 F.2d 1037, 1045–46 (9th Cir. 1992) (holding that defendant's inability to challenge administrative classification did not violate due process because the validity of the classification was not an element of the offense).

Affirmed.

GREGORY, CIRCUIT JUDGE, dissenting.

I . . . dissent from the judgment. I believe the majority incorrectly concludes that AEDPA's "material support" provision, 18 U.S.C. § 2339B, is constitutional as applied in this case. As the Ninth Circuit has held, a strict textual reading of § 2339B(a)(1)'s plain language raises serious due process concerns. *See* [*HLP II*][18] ("We believe that serious due process concerns would be raised were we to accept the argument that a person who acts without knowledge of critical information about a designated organization presumably acts consistently with the intent and conduct of that designated organization.").

Unlike the Ninth Circuit, however, I do not believe that these constitutional infirmities can be cured by reading the statutory term "knowingly" as a scienter requirement meaning only that the defendant had knowledge of the organization's designation as a foreign terrorist organization ("FTO"), or that he or she knew of the organization's unlawful activities that caused it to be so designated.

Instead, I would follow the reasoning of *United States v. Al-Arian*, and conclude that to save the statute, one must apply the mens rea requirement to the entire "material support" provision such that the government must prove that the defendant (1) knew the organization was a FTO or knew of the organization's unlawful activities that caused it to be so designated and (2) knew what he or she was providing was "material support," i.e., the government must show that the defendant had a specific intent that the support would further the FTO's illegal activities. Because Hammoud was convicted of "material support" without the proper scienter requirement, violating his constitutional rights under the First and Fifth Amendments, I would hold that these constitutional violations constitute plain error and thus vacate his material support conviction.

I.

Hammoud and his *Amici Curiae*, the Center for Constitutional Rights, the National Coalition to Protect Political Freedom, the National Association of Criminal Defense Lawyers, and the National Lawyers Guild, raise a bevy of constitutional challenges to Hammoud's conviction under 18 U.S.C. § 2339B, including assertions that the "material support" provision is vague and overbroad in violation of the First Amendment, and that the statute violates the First and Sixth Amendments because the defendant cannot challenge the FTO designation. Moreover, Hammoud and Amici Curiae challenge

---

[18] [Court's Footnote 1] The Ninth Circuit and most other courts citing the *Humanitarian Law Project* cases use these Roman numeral designations, referring to the original district court case, *Humanitarian Law Project v. Reno*, 9 F. Supp. 2d 1176 (C.D. Cal. 1998), as "*Humanitarian Law Project I*." [The casebook will follow the more common practice of designating each of the Court of Appeals opinions as *HLP I* or *HLP II*.]

Hammoud's conviction on the basis that the statute lacks a specific intent requirement, which they contend is essential to avoid "guilt by association" in violation of the First and Fifth Amendments.

II.

Hammoud and *Amici Curiae* argue that the "material support" provision is unconstitutional because it penalizes association, in violation of the First Amendment, and fails to require the requisite specific intent, thus contravening the Fifth Amendment requirement of "personal guilt." They first frame these arguments by relying on the unimpeachable, but basic and preliminary, proposition that the Constitution protects individuals from being punished solely because of their association with a group.

Here, however, Hammoud and *Amici Curiae* also advance a legally independent — though somewhat interrelated to the First Amendment argument — Fifth Amendment Claim, which *HLP II* and the other cases noted above did not reach. Specifically, to pass Fifth Amendment scrutiny and to avoid a "personal guilt" problem, they argue that AEDPA's material support provision must include a scienter requirement, whereby the defendant must be found guilty of a specific intent to further the illegal aims of the association. Br. of Appellant at 25; Br. of *Amici Curiae* at 6 ("This statute is so sweeping that it would apply to a citizen who sent a human rights or constitutional law treatise to Hizballah to urge it to respect human rights and desist from committing terrorist acts."). Hammoud and *Amici Curiae* rely on more Communist Party cases to support their argument that AEDPA's "material support" provision is unconstitutional without such a specific intent requirement.

Hammoud and *Amici Curiae* assert that without a specific intent requirement, AEDPA's material support provision suffers the same fate. In this context, Amici Curiae posit that *HLP I*'s isolated focus on the First Amendment renders the prohibition on guilt by association a meaningless formality because under the Ninth Circuit's reasoning:

> Every anti-Communist law struck down by the Supreme Court for imposing guilt by association could have simply been rewritten to penalize dues payments to the Party. It would also lead to the anomalous result that while leaders of the NAACP could not be held responsible for injuries sustained during an NAACP-led economic boycott absent proof of specific intent, the NAACP's thousands of individual donors could have been held liable without any showing of specific intent.

While the Ninth Circuit's interpretation of "knowingly" is more advanced than the quasi-strict liability standard upon which Hammoud was convicted, I submit that such an interpretation of § 2339B's mental state requirement is still insufficient to withstand constitutional attack.

In *Al-Arian*, the court . . . disagreed with the Ninth Circuit's attempt to salvage the statute based on application of the statutory term "knowingly" in *HLP II*, stating that the Ninth Circuit's construction "only cures some of the Fifth Amendment concerns." The *Al-Arian* court . . . found that under the Ninth Circuit's construction:

> [A] cab driver could be guilty for giving a ride to a FTO member to the UN, if he knows that the person is a member of a FTO . . . . Similarly, a hotel clerk in New York could be committing a crime by providing lodging to that same FTO member under similar circumstances as the cab driver.[19]

I believe that § 2339B's "material support" provisions constitute a violation of the

---

[19] [Court's Footnote 12] Similarly, *Amici Curiae* properly recognize that the jury was not instructed that it had to find Hammoud intended the donation to be used for any violent, terrorist, or otherwise unlawful purpose, thus setting up the anomalous result that under § 2339B "Hammoud would be guilty even if it were stipulated that his support was intended to further only Hizballah's lawful activities . . . [while] an individual

Fifth Amendment when applied without the necessary specific intent requirement. Unlike the situation faced in *Al-Arian*, however, in Hammoud's case it is many days too late to apply a savings instruction — or to preliminarily enjoin the government from applying the "material support" provision as written, as in *HLP II* — therefore, I turn to the application and effect of the constitutional error in this case.

III.

For the reasons that follow, I would find that Hammoud satisfies [the] plain error standard and he should be granted a new trial on the "material support" charge.

[T]he Ninth Circuit's absurd construction of the statute in *X-Citement Video* is closely related to the absurd results, which necessarily follow from interpreting AEDPA's "material support" provisions without a scienter requirement. For the end result of applying "knowingly" as did the Ninth Circuit in *HLP II* "is to render a substantial portion of Section 2339B unconstitutionally vague."

IV.

For these reasons, I would hold that the jury instruction upon which Hammoud was convicted of providing material support to Hizballah violated his Fifth Amendment rights, and [was] "plain error," thus entitling him to a new trial. In recommending as much, I do not seek to give comfort to terrorist organizations, or to diminish the reality of clear and present threats posed by such groups. To the contrary, I seek to uphold the Constitution in a manner that does not harken back to a bleaker era of American history when characters were impugned, and individuals indicted, convicted and punished based on little more than suspicion, association and fear, without the "personal guilt" which is the hallmark of our criminal justice system. In applying AEDPA's material support provisions with the requisite scienter requirement, we may help insure that juries are not driven to findings of guilt by mere fear of the unknown, but instead arrive at the just result only after interrogation of the government's case to determine whether criminal intent is present.

I respectfully dissent.

NOTES AND QUESTIONS

1. Mens Rea. As we have already seen, the Ninth Circuit decided to review *HLP II* en banc, but before any decision was reached by the en banc panel, Congress amended § 2339B to provide that

> To violate this paragraph, a person must have knowledge that the organization is a designated terrorist organization, that the organization has engaged or engages in terrorist activity, or that the organization has engaged or engages in terrorism.

Does the amended statute satisfy the requirements of the original panel in *HLP II*? Does it satisfy the requirements of Judges Gregory and Moody? If not, then does the statute become unconstitutional or would a court construe it to add additional elements of *mens rea* even after revision by Congress? In *HLP IV*, the Ninth Circuit held that specific intent to promote violence was not constitutionally required.

2. Judicial "Activism." Judges Gregory and Moody both emulate a number of other judges who have engaged in verbal hand-wringing while issuing decisions counter to Government arguments. Why do you suppose they feel the need to engage in this explanation of what they view to be their judicial duty? In a speech to the Federalist Society on November 14, Attorney General Ashcroft criticized some "activist" federal

---

who gave a donation to a non-designated group intending that it be used for terrorist activity would not be guilty."

judges. "The danger I see here is that intrusive judicial oversight and second-guessing of presidential determinations in these critical areas can put at risk the very security of our nation in a time of war." He probably was referring most directly to the opinion of Judge Robertson of the District of Columbia in *Hamdan v. Rumsfeld*, § 8.04[B] below, in which the judge did not seem as abashed as some of the others.

3. Payment and Support. Judges Gregory and Moody both think it would be "absurd" to punish the cabbie, bank teller, or hotel manager who provided services to a representative of an FTO. Is that truly so absurd? If the services are provided by a sympathizer with full awareness of the FTO objectives, does Judge Moody's statement regarding the inference of intent render these examples less absurd and more just a matter of evidence and inference? Isn't providing weapons just as bad whether the provider is paid or not?

4. Sentencing. The Supreme Court vacated the Fourth Circuit's decision for reconsideration of Hammoud's sentence in light of *United States v. Booker*, 543 U.S. 220 (2004). The Fourth Circuit then directed that his sentence be reduced but reinstated all the substantive portions of its opinion. 405 F.3d 1034 (4th Cir. 2005).

UNITED STATES v. AFSHARI
392 F.3d 1031 (9th Cir. 2004)

KLEINFELD, CIRCUIT JUDGE.

We review the constitutionality of a statute prohibiting financial support to organizations designated as "terrorist."

The issue here is the constitutionality of the crime charged in the indictment, that from 1997 to 2001, Rahmani and others knowingly and willfully conspired to provide material support to the Mujahedin-e Khalq ("MEK"),[20] a designated terrorist organization, in violation of 18 U.S.C. § 2339B(a)(1).

According to the indictment, the defendants solicited charitable contributions at the Los Angeles International Airport for the "Committee for Human Rights," gave money and credit cards to the MEK, and wired money from the "Committee for Human Rights" to an MEK bank account in Turkey. They did all this after participating in a conference call with an MEK leader, in which they learned that the State Department had designated the MEK as a foreign terrorist organization. The MEK leader told them to continue to provide material support despite the designation. All told, according to the indictment in this case, the money they sent to the MEK amounted to at least several hundred thousand dollars.

The MEK was founded in the 1960s as an Iranian Marxist group seeking to overthrow the regime then ruling Iran. It participated in various terrorist activities against the Iranian regime and against the United States, including the taking of American embassy personnel as hostages in 1979. After the Iranian regime fell and was replaced by a clerical, rather than a Marxist, regime, MEK members fled to France. They later settled in Iraq, along the Iranian border. There they carried out terrorist activities with the support of Saddam Hussein's regime, as well as, if the indictment is correct, the money that the defendants sent them.

The MEK, since first being designated a terrorist organization, has developed a convoluted litigation history in the United States Court of Appeals for the District of Columbia. Because this history is important to the outcome of this case, we will briefly review the relevant parts.

The MEK was first designated a terrorist organization in 1997. The D.C. Circuit upheld this designation because the MEK was a "foreign entity without . . . presence in this country" and thus "had no constitutional rights under the due process clause."

---

[20] [Court's Footnote 1] The MEK is also known as the People's Mojahedin Organization for Iraq, or PMOI, and has a variety of other aliases. [See introduction to *PMOI II*, § 3.03[B], *supra*.]

Therefore, the MEK was not entitled to notice and a hearing. It also found the administrative record sufficient to establish that the MEK "engages in terrorist activity." In the process of designating MEK a terrorist organization in 1999, the State Department determined that another organization, the National Council of Resistance of Iran, was an "alias" of the MEK. When reviewing the 1999 designation, the D.C. Circuit held that the second organization had a presence in the United States and, based on that presence, that both organizations were entitled to "the opportunity to be heard at a meaningful time and in a meaningful manner." Nat'l Council of Resistance of Iran v. Dep't of State, 251 F.3d 192, 346 U.S. App. D.C. 131 (D.C. Cir. 2001).

The D.C. Circuit remanded the 1999 designation to the State Department with the instructions that both organizations be given an opportunity "to file evidence in support of their allegations that they are not terrorist organizations." Instead, the MEK submitted evidence showing that it was responsible for numerous assassinations of Iranian officials and mortar attacks on Iranian government installations. Upon reviewing this redesignation, the D.C. Circuit noted that any procedural due process error that might have existed was harmless because the MEK had "effectively admitted" that it was a terrorist organization. People's Mojahedin Org. of Iran v. Dep't of State, 327 F.3d 1238, 356 U.S. App. D.C. 101 (D.C. Cir. 2003).

For purposes of reviewing a motion to dismiss an indictment, we assume the truth of what the indictment alleges. Thus, we take it as true that the defendants knew that they were furnishing assistance to a designated "terrorist" organization, having been informed of the designation in a conference call with an MEK leader.

The district court dismissed the indictment on the ground that the terrorist designation statute was unconstitutional. We . . . reverse.

I. Challenging the Designation

[Section] 1189(a)(1) sets out a carefully articulated scheme for designating foreign terrorist organizations. To make the designation, the Secretary has to make specific findings that "the organization is a foreign organization"; that "the organization engages in terrorist activity";[21] and that "the terrorist activity of the organization threatens the security of United States nationals or the national security of the United States."

The designated organization is entitled to judicial review of the Secretary's action in the United States Court of Appeals for the District of Columbia.

The district court found that it was a facially unconstitutional restriction on judicial

---

[21] [Court's Footnote 7] 8 U.S.C. § 1182(a)(3)(B)(ii). As used in this Act, the term "terrorist activity" means any activity which is unlawful under the laws of the place where it is committed . . . and which involves any of the following:

(I)   The highjacking or sabotage of any conveyance . . . .

(II)   The seizing or detaining, and threatening to kill, injure, or continue to detain, another individual in order to compel a third person . . . to do or abstain from doing any act as an explicit or implicit condition for the release of the individual seized or detained.

(III)   A violent attack upon an internationally protected person . . . or upon the liberty of such a person.

(IV)   An assassination.

(V)   The use of any

      (a)   biological agent, chemical agent, or nuclear weapon or device, or

      (b)   explosive or firearm . . . ,

        with intent to endanger, directly or indirectly, the safety of one or more individuals or to cause substantial damage to property.

(VI)   A threat, attempt, or conspiracy to do any of the foregoing.

22 U.S.C. § 2656f(d)(2): [T]he term "terrorism" means premeditated, politically motivated violence perpetrated against noncombatant targets by subnational groups or clandestine agents.

review of the designation for Congress to assign such review exclusively to the D.C. Circuit. We reject that position.

Many administrative determinations are reviewable only by petition to the correct circuit court, bypassing the district court, and that procedure has generally been accepted. Many are reviewable only in the D.C. Circuit, or the Federal Circuit, and those restrictions have also been generally accepted. The congressional restriction does not interfere with the opportunity for judicial review, as the MEK's extensive litigation history shows. And this scheme avoids the awkwardness of criminalizing material support for a designated organization in some circuits but not others, as varying decisions in the different regional circuits might.

II. DUE PROCESS CLAIM

The defendants' central argument is that § 2339B denies them their constitutional rights because it prohibits them from collaterally attacking the designation of a foreign terrorist organization. This contention was recently rejected by the Fourth Circuit en banc. *United States v. Hammoud*, 381 F.3d 316 (4th Cir. 2004) (en banc). We, too, reject it.

The defendants are right that § 1189(a)(8) prevents them from contending, in defense of the charges against them under 18 U.S.C. § 2339B, that the designated terrorist organization is not really terrorist at all. No doubt Congress was well aware that some might be of the view that "one man's terrorist is another man's freedom fighter." Congress clearly chose to delegate policymaking authority to the President and Department of State with respect to designation of terrorist organizations, and to keep such policymaking authority out of the hands of United States Attorneys and juries. Under § 2339B, if defendants provide material support for an organization that has been designated a terrorist organization under § 1189, they commit the crime, and it does not matter whether the designation is correct or not.

The question then is whether due process prohibits a prosecution under § 2339B when the court vested with the power to review and set aside the predicate designation determines that the designation was obtained in an unconstitutional or otherwise erroneous manner, but nevertheless declines to set it aside. The D.C. Circuit did not vacate the designation [but] remanded to the Secretary of State with instructions that MEK be afforded due process rights. [The remand] was, in any event, harmless because the MEK proudly proclaimed its own terrorist activities.

Defendants further claim that the Due Process Clause prevents a designation found to be unconstitutional from serving as a predicate for the charge of providing material support to a designated terrorist organization, even if the designation has never been set aside. There are several reasons why this argument lacks force.

First, the Supreme Court, in *Lewis v. United States*, 445 U.S. 55 (1980), the Supreme Court held that a prior conviction could properly be used as a predicate for a subsequent conviction for a felon in possession of a firearm, even though it had been obtained in violation of the Sixth Amendment right to counsel. The Court held that it was proper to prohibit a collateral attack on the predicate during the criminal hearing because the felon-in-possession statute made no exception "for a person whose outstanding felony conviction ultimately might turn out to be invalid for any reason." The Court noted that the prohibition on collateral attack was proper because a convicted felon could challenge the validity of the conviction before he purchased his firearm.

The defendants attempt to distinguish *Lewis* from this § 2339B prosecution because the defendant in *Lewis* had the ability to challenge his predicate, whereas here the defendants, themselves, are prohibited from challenging the designation. But this does not change the principle that a criminal proceeding may go forward, even if the predicate was in some way unconstitutional, so long as a sufficient opportunity for judicial review of the predicate exists. Here there was such an opportunity, which the MEK took advantage of each time it was designated a foreign terrorist organization.

Second, the D.C. Circuit declined to set aside the 1999 designation. It remanded the determination but carefully explained that it did not vacate the designation. After the remand, the D.C. Circuit upheld the redesignation; therefore, at all relevant times, the "foreign terrorist organization" designation had been in full force. This court and the D.C. Circuit are co-equal courts. We cannot reverse its decision. Additionally, the statute expressly provides that only the D.C. Circuit may review these designations, so it would be contrary to the statutory scheme for us to hold that the designation was invalid. We have already determined that any constitutional challenge against 8 U.S.C. § 1189 "must be raised in an appeal from a decision to designate a particular organization" and must be heard in the D.C. Circuit. *HLP I*, 205 F.3d at 1137.

Third, 18 U.S.C. § 2339B only requires that Rahmani, et al., had knowledge of the MEK's designation as a foreign terrorist organization. The Fourth Circuit, sitting en banc, held that a criminal defendant charged under this statute cannot bring a challenge to the validity of a designation of an organization as "terrorist." In a case where there was no indication that the designation was invalid (other than the defendant's would-be challenge), the Fourth Circuit wrote, "The *fact* of an organization's designation as an [terrorist organization] is an element of § 2339B, but the validity of the designation is not." Here, the MEK has been designated a terrorist organization throughout the relevant period, and that designation has never been set aside. According to the indictment, defendants had knowledge of this designation, they were told during a telephone conference call with an MEK leader in October 1997 that the MEK had been designated a foreign terrorist organization by the State Department.

Fourth, as discussed earlier, the D.C. Circuit ultimately held that the procedural due process violation it identified was harmless. When challenging the 1999 designation, the MEK admitted to numerous terrorist acts making an argument that amounted to a claim that the enemy of our enemy is our friend, a decision that is committed to the Executive Branch, not the courts. Due to this "admission," the D.C. Circuit held that, even if there were a due process violation, the MEK was not harmed by it.

Thus, defendants' new due process argument attacks a designation that withstood judicial review, that we have no authority to review, that defendants knew was in place throughout the period of the indictment, and that is supported by the MEK's own submission. Defendants suffered no deprivation of due process, and even if they had, it was harmless.

The defendants further attempt to distinguish *Lewis* . . . by relying on *United States v. Mendoza-Lopez*, 481 U.S. 828 (1987). In that case, the Supreme Court held that a prosecution under 8 U.S.C. § 1326 for illegal reentry does not comport with due process if there is no judicial review of whether the predicate deportation proceeding violated the alien's rights. It is not at all clear from *Mendoza-Lopez* that the Supreme Court meant that the due process problem is in the *later* proceeding. The Court held that "where a determination made in an administrative proceeding is to play a critical role in the subsequent imposition of a criminal sanction, there must be *some* meaningful review of the administrative proceeding." Nothing in *Mendoza-Lopez* appears to require that this review be had by the defendant in the subsequent criminal proceeding.

Furthermore, it is obvious in *Lewis* and *Mendoza-Lopez* that the opportunity to seek review would be in the hands of the defendants themselves because it was *their* rights at issue in the hearing that created the predicate in the later criminal proceeding. But here, the defendants' rights were not directly violated in the earlier designation proceeding. The predicate designation was against the MEK, not the defendants. Section 1189 provides for the organizations to seek review of the predicate designation, and that review was had in this case. Therefore, due process does not require another review of the predicate by the court adjudicating the instant § 2339B criminal proceeding.

Our holding is further supported by our decision in *United States v. Bozarov*, 974 F.2d 1037 (9th Cir. 1992). In *Bozarov*, we held that a defendant charged with exporting items listed under the Export Administration Act without a license did not have a due process right to collaterally attack the listing in his criminal proceeding. We held, however, that Bozarov had standing to challenge the constitutionality of the Export Act in his criminal proceeding. This was because the Export Act explicitly provided that all actions taken by the Secretary of Commerce under it were "not subject to judicial review," including a denial of the license that was a predicate for a violation of the criminal provision. If a defendant were not allowed to challenge the Export Act in that proceeding, there would be *no* arbiter of the constitutionality of the Export Act. In contrast, Congress has explicitly provided that the D.C. Circuit is the arbiter of the constitutionality of any designation under § 1189. Thus, there is no constitutional need for the defendants to challenge the predicate designation in this proceeding.

As we noted in another case where we rejected a defendant's right to challenge an export listing in a subsequent criminal proceeding, the defendants' argument here "is analogous to one by a defendant in a drug possession case that his conviction cannot stand because no specific showing has been made that the drug is a threat to society. . . . [A] showing that the drug possessed by the individual defendant has a 'detrimental effect on the general welfare' [is not] an element of the offense." *United States v. Mandel*, 914 F.2d 1215 n. 11 (9th Cir. 1990). Likewise, the element of the crime that the prosecutor must prove in a § 2339B case is the predicate fact that a particular organization *was* designated at the time the material support was given, not whether the government made a correct designation. Our position is consistent with that of the Fourth Circuit, which held that a defendant's inability to challenge the designation was not a violation of his constitutional rights, since the *validity* of the designation is not an element of the crime. Rather, the element is the *fact* of an organization's designation as a "foreign terrorist organization."

III. FIRST AMENDMENT CLAIM

The defendants argue that (1) they have a First Amendment right to contribute to organizations that are not terrorist; (2) the statutory scheme denies them the opportunity to challenge the "foreign terrorist organization" designation; so therefore (3) it deprives them of their First Amendment right to make contributions to non-terrorist organizations.

This argument is mistaken because what the defendants propose to do is not to engage in speech, but rather to provide material assistance. The statute says "knowingly provides material support or resources to a foreign terrorist organization." The indictment charges them with sending money to the MEK.

The defendants argue that they seek to express their political views, not by supporting terrorism, but rather by supporting an organization that the State Department has mistakenly designated as terrorist. The due process part of this argument, that they are entitled to an opportunity in their criminal proceeding to relitigate whether the MEK is terrorist, is addressed above. Defendants also make a distinct free speech argument, however, based on *McKinney v. Alabama*, 424 U.S. 669 (1976).

McKinney holds that the First Amendment rights of a newsstand proprietor were violated by his conviction under a statute that prohibited him from selling an obscene magazine. What is similar to this case is that the obscenity of the magazine in *McKinney* was adjudicated, not in the criminal defendant's proceeding, but in a previous in rem proceeding against the magazine to which the newsstand proprietor was not a party. The Court held that a decision in another proceeding could not conclusively determine First Amendment rights to sell a magazine of persons who had no notice and opportunity to be heard in that proceeding. By analogy, the defendants in this case argue that they should be entitled to litigate the terrorism designation of the MEK in their criminal case.

The argument fails, however, because the cases are not analogous. The magazine in *McKinney* was speech, the money sent to the MEK is not. Though contributions of money given to fund speech receive some First Amendment protection,[22] it does not follow that all contributions of money are entitled to protection as though they were speech.

What is at issue here is not anything close to pure speech. It is, rather, material support to foreign organizations that the United States has deemed, through a process defined by federal statute and including judicial review by the D.C. Circuit, a threat to our national security. The fact that the support takes the form of money does not make the support the equivalent of speech. In this context, the donation of money could properly be viewed by the government as more like the donation of bombs and ammunition than speech. The "foreign terrorist organization" designation means that the Executive Branch has determined — and the D.C. Circuit, in choosing not to set aside the designation, has concluded that the determination was properly made — that materially supporting the organization is materially supporting actual violence.

Donations to designated foreign terrorist organizations are not akin to donations to domestic political parties or candidates. An organization cannot be designated unless it is foreign, so domestic associations are immune from the scheme. And in this case, there is no room for a vagueness challenge on the ground that the defendants were merely contributing what might arguably be in the nature of speech. The indictment charges them with sending money to the designated terrorist organization, not with providing instruction or advocacy.

We have already held that the strict scrutiny standard applicable to speech regulations does not apply to a prohibition against sending money to foreign terrorist organizations. That a group engages in politics and has political goals does not imply that all support for it is speech, or that it promotes its political goals by means of speech. Guns and bombs are not speech. Sometimes money serves as a proxy for speech, and sometimes it buys goods and services that are not speech. The government "may certainly regulate contributions to organizations performing unlawful or harmful activities, even though such contributions may also express the donor's feelings about the recipient." There is no First Amendment right "to facilitate terrorism by giving terrorists the weapons and explosives with which to carry out their grisly missions."

A less rigorous standard of review is applied to monetary contributions than to pure speech. Even giving money to perfectly legitimate political expression within the United States can be, and is, restricted by Congress, consistent with the Constitution.[23] *A fortiori*, contribution of money to organizations that the United States has determined engage in terrorist activities can be restricted by Congress. It would be anomalous indeed if Congress could prohibit the contribution of money for television commercials saying why a candidate would be a good or bad choice for political office, yet could not prohibit contribution of money to a group designated as a terrorist organization. Defendants are entitled under the First Amendment to publish articles arguing that the MEK is not really a terrorist organization, but they are not entitled to furnish bombs to the MEK, nor to furnish money to buy bombs and ammunition.

In *McConnell*, the Court found that "the prevention of corruption or its appearance

---

[22] [Court's Footnote 59] *See* McConnell v. FEC, 540 U.S. 93 (2003); Buckley v. Valeo, 424 U.S. 1 (1976) [campaign contributions].

[23] [Court's Footnote 67] *See McConnell*, 540 U.S. 93; *Buckley*, 424 U.S. 1, 20 ("[A] limitation upon the amount that any one person or group may contribute to a candidate or political committee entails only a marginal restriction upon the contributor's ability to engage in free communication.").

constitutes a sufficiently important interest to justify political contribution limits." The interest in protecting our country from foreign terrorist organizations is a fortiori "a sufficiently important interest." "The federal government clearly has the power to enact laws restricting the dealings of United States citizens with foreign entities." "We must allow the political branches wide latitude in selecting the means to bring about the desired goal" of "preventing the United States from being used as a base for terrorist fundraising."

Conceivably the MEK developed its practices at a time when the United States supported the previous regime in Iran, and maintained its position while harbored by the Saddam Hussein Ba'ath regime in Iraq. Maybe the MEK's position will change, or has changed, so that its interest in overturning the current regime in Iran coincides with the interests of the United States. Defendants could be right about the MEK. But that is not for us, or for a jury in defendants' case, to say. The sometimes subtle analysis of a foreign organization's political program to determine whether it is indeed a terrorist threat is peculiarly within the expertise of the State Department and the Executive Branch. Juries could not make reliable determinations without extensive foreign policy education and the disclosure of classified materials. Nor is it appropriate for a jury in a criminal case to make foreign policy decisions for the United States. Leaving the determination of whether a group is a "foreign terrorist organization" to the Executive Branch, coupled with the procedural protections and judicial review afforded by the statute, is both a reasonable and a constitutional way to make such determinations. The Constitution does not forbid Congress from requiring individuals, whether they agree with the Executive Branch determination or not, to refrain from furnishing material assistance to designated terrorist organizations during the period of designation.

UNITED STATES v. AFSHARI
446 F.3d 915 (2006)

ORDER

The petition for rehearing and the petition for rehearing en banc are DENIED.

KOZINSKI, CIRCUIT JUDGE, with whom JUDGES PREGERSON, REINHARDT, THOMAS and PAEZ join, dissenting from denial of rehearing en banc:

It goes without saying that the United States government may prohibit donations to terrorist organizations. As we explained in [HLP I], money is fungible; if an organization engages in terrorism, it can channel money donated to it for humanitarian and advocacy purposes to promote its grisly agenda. At the same time, however, giving money to a political organization that is *not* engaged in terrorist activities is constitutionally protected. The determination of whether or not an organization is engaged in terrorism is therefore crucial, because it distinguishes activities that can be criminalized from those that are protected by the First Amendment.

This case concerns the manner in which this distinction is drawn. Because designating an organization as terrorist cuts off the First Amendment rights of individuals wishing to donate to that organization, the designation must meet certain constitutional standards. The Supreme Court has twice spoken to the question of how the government may go about turning what would otherwise be protected First Amendment speech into criminal conduct, the first time in *Freedman v. Maryland*, 380 U.S. 51 (1965), and the second time in *McKinney v. Alabama*, 424 U.S. 669 (1976). In both cases, the Court laid out strict rules that the government must follow, yet the designation in this case complies neither with *Freedman* nor with *McKinney*. The net result is that Rahmani is being criminally prosecuted, and almost certainly will be convicted, for contributing to an organization that has been designated as terrorist with none of the protections that are constitutionally required for such a designation. Worse, Rahmani will in all likelihood spend many years in prison for contributing to an organization whose designation the D.C. Circuit has held does not even meet the requirements of due process. Because I believe that the prosecution in this case runs contrary to two of our defining traditions — that of free and open expression, and that of justice and fair play — I respectfully dissent from the court's failure to correct the panel's errors by taking this case en banc.

The panel dismisses Rahmani's *First Amendment* arguments with conclusory statements that the money here is being given to a *terrorist* organization, and is therefore a completely unprotected form of expression. But this begs the question. If the designation process does not comply with constitutional standards, then the designation is invalid and Rahmani's donations are protected by the First Amendment. In order to determine whether that process was constitutional, we must rely on the guidance of *Freedman* and *McKinney*.

In *Freedman*, the Supreme Court struck down a Maryland censorship scheme in which theaters were banned — on penalty of criminal prosecution — from showing films designated as obscene:

> It is readily apparent that the Maryland procedural scheme does not satisfy [constitutional] criteria. *First*, once the censor disapproves the film, *the exhibitor must assume the burden of instituting judicial proceedings and of persuading the courts that the film is protected expression*. *Second*, once the Board has acted against a film, *exhibition is prohibited pending judicial review, however protracted*. Under the statute, appellant could have been convicted if he had shown the film after unsuccessfully seeking a license, even though no court had ever ruled on the obscenity of the film. *Third*, it is abundantly clear that the Maryland statute provides *no assurance of prompt judicial determination*.

Id. at 59–60 (emphasis added).

The procedure for designating a foreign terrorist organization has all of the deficiencies identified by the Supreme Court in *Freedman*, and then some. First, once the Secretary of State makes the designation, the prohibition on monetary contributions takes effect immediately, and "the burden of instituting judicial proceedings and of persuading the courts" that the designation was improper falls on the organization.

Second, monetary contributions to a designated organization are prohibited even while judicial review is pending. This procedural deficiency is particularly damaging to Rahmani, who made all her donations at least two years before the D.C. Circuit finally approved MEK's designation as a terrorist organization.

Third, "it is abundantly clear that the . . . statute provides no assurance of prompt judicial determination." To the contrary, the statute seems to discourage any judicial determination at all, giving the organization only 30 days to challenge its designation. What's more, the panel concedes that the D.C. Circuit has found foreign entities have no due process rights: "MEK was a 'foreign entity without . . . presence in this country' and thus 'had no constitutional rights under the due process clause.' Therefore, the MEK was not entitled to notice and a hearing." In other words, the only entity that is statutorily eligible to challenge the terrorist designation — the organization being designated — will ordinarily be unable to bring any kind of meaningful challenge.

Even when an organization can avail itself of the full "judicial review" prescribed by the statute, such review comes nowhere near what *Freedman* requires. The statute uses "APA-like language," barring the D.C. Circuit from overturning the Secretary's designation unless, for example, it lacks substantial evidence or is arbitrary and capricious. As the D.C. Circuit noted, under the statute's judicial review provisions, the designated organization "does not have the benefit of meaningful adversary proceedings . . . other than procedural shortfalls so obvious a Secretary of State is not likely to commit them." But *Freedman* explicitly requires a "*judicial* determination in an *adversary* proceeding" on the merits, not merely a court's cursory check that the agency followed its own procedures.

As in *Freedman*, the only possible conclusion is that the terrorist organization designation scheme "fails to provide adequate safeguards against undue inhibition of protected expression," and therefore is an invalid prior restraint.

No "judicial determination" upheld MEK's designation on its merits until two years *after* Rahmani made her allegedly criminal monetary contributions. The panel thus condones a uniquely unconstitutional (and oxymoronic) practice: an *ex post facto prior restraint*. The simple fact is that Rahmani is being prosecuted — and will surely be sent to prison for up to 10 years — for giving money to an organization that no one other than some obscure mandarin in the bowels of the State Department had determined to be a terrorist organization. The panel has simply overruled *Freedman* — without so much as mentioning it.

The panel's opinion also contravenes *McKinney v. Alabama*. *McKinney* involved a criminal defendant charged with selling a magazine that had previously been declared obscene in a separate in rem action. The Supreme Court, in an opinion by Justice Rehnquist, held that the defendant had a right to argue *at his own trial* that the magazine was not actually obscene and was thus protected by the First Amendment. *McKinney* thus stands for the proposition that a criminal defendant has an individual right to challenge the exclusion of what would otherwise be protected speech from the protection of the First Amendment.

The *McKinney* portion of the panel's opinion is premised on the fact that the organization was properly designated as a terrorist organization, and that the designation had already been subject to judicial review. The panel states:

> What is at issue here is not anything close to pure speech. It is, rather, material support to foreign organizations that the United States has deemed, *through a process defined by federal statute and including judicial review by the D.C. Circuit*, a threat to our national security. . . . The "foreign terrorist organization" designation means that the Executive Branch has determined — *and the D.C. Circuit*, in choosing not to set aside the designation, *has concluded that the determination was properly made* — that materially supporting the organization is materially supporting actual violence.

426 F.3d at 1160 (emphasis added). But, as described above, the D.C. Circuit explicitly concluded that the designation in this case was *not* "properly made." Thus, the panel's argument — the very foundation of its attempt to distinguish this case from *McKinney* — is entirely beside the point.

Why does the panel ignore common sense and find this whole scheme constitutional? Because, it says, it "do[es] not have authority to reverse the decisions of a sister circuit," and "it would be contrary to the statutory scheme for us to hold that the designation was invalid." But the remedy Rahmani seeks requires neither: The D.C. Circuit's opinion in it *PMOI II*, which found the designation unconstitutional but remanded to the Secretary of State without setting the designation aside, said nothing about use of the designation in criminal prosecutions; thus, there is nothing to "reverse." Nor is there a need to strike down the designation; the designation, and the many civil consequences that flow from it, need not be disturbed. The panel need only hold that a designation found by the D.C. Circuit to be unconstitutional cannot form the basis of a criminal prosecution.

I can understand the panel's reticence to interfere with matters of national security, but the entire purpose of the terrorist designation process is to determine *whether* an organization poses a threat to national security. Under the Constitution, the State Department does not have carte blanche to label any organization it chooses a foreign terrorist organization and make a criminal out of anyone who donates money to it. Far too much political activity could be suppressed under such a regime.

In any event, our task in this case was simple. The D.C. Circuit had already done all of the hard work, examining MEK's designation and finding it to be constitutionally inadequate. All we had to do was take the next logical step and hold that this inadequate designation could not form the basis for a criminal prosecution. The Supreme Court hasn't hesitated to take a close look at the constitutionality of certain war on terror-related procedures — especially procedures that are still being tested and developed. We should be no less vigilant.

NOTES AND QUESTIONS

1. Interim Designation. The Ninth Circuit does not overtly address the vagueness-type dilemma questioned by Judge Takasugi and the D.C. Circuit's mootness footnote. During the interim between the second and third D.C. opinions, all the organizations covered by the umbrella of POMI or MEK were formally carried on the list of designated organizations, but that designation had been declared to be obtained in violation of due process. Given that finding, plus the importance of political association rights, would the individual defendants in *Ashfari* have been justified in believing that they could raise money for transmission to the organizations? Or is the designation sufficiently like the designation of a drug in the Ninth Circuit's analogy?

2. Intent and Utility. Does the *Ashfari* opinion fundamentally disagree with Judges Moody and Gregory? Both of the latter two would require that the Government show both knowledge of the designation *and* an intent to further unlawful purposes. *Ashfari* says that it is not necessary in a drug case to show that the drug is bad, so it is not necessary in a material support case to show that the money is intended to be used for bad purposes. In *HLP I*, the Ninth Circuit had pointed out the commingling and fungible nature of money so that one dollar for humanitarian purposes frees up another dollar for nefarious purposes. Who has the better of this argument? If Judges Moody and Gregory accept the commingling argument for purposes of the designation requirement, is their insistence on the donor's knowledge of bad purpose inconsistent with that?

The argument could be made that the right of association changes the equation because it is deserving of more consideration than any claim of right to take a drug. The argument would be that there is more social utility to the associational rights, something like the arguments preventing extension of our alcohol-driving analogy to driving with a closed container.

3. Questionable Activity. *POMI II* is a sufficient answer to the designation argument only because the publicly available evidence was sufficient to support a finding that the organization was involved in terrorist activity. What happens when that is not the case, when the finding would need support of undisclosed classified information? Does the ordinary citizen have a claim of associational right to contribute to such an organization? The Ninth Circuit says no, because the giving of money is not as strong an interest as stating support through pure speech or expressive activity. Consider the following examples of what someone in Ashfari's position might have done or might still want to do:

    a.   encourage others in the U.S. to donate money to MEK without collecting the funds himself. Is he guilty of conspiracy or does *Brandenburg* control?

    b.   encourage people in other countries to donate money to MEK. Does it matter whether those other countries are signatories to the Convention on Terrorist Financing?

    c.   receive messages from MEK leaders in other countries and passed them on through the internet. Is this a "providing of communication devices" punishable under § 2339B? *See United States v. Sattar*, § 3.03[B], Note 3, *supra*.

    d.   discuss with MEK leaders in other countries methods by which the organization could get itself off the designation list. Is this a providing of services that falls within *Lindh* or is it subject to the associational interests that prompted the holding in *HLP*?

See generally Rodney A. Smolla, *Terrorism and the Bill of Rights*, 10 WM. & MARY BILL RTS. J. 551 (2002).

§ 3.04   CONSPIRACY AND MATERIAL SUPPORT PROSECUTIONS

This section provides summaries of a sampling of significant terrorism prosecutions in recent years (beginning in 2002). With a couple of exceptions for appellate court opinions, the summaries do not include citations to authorities, but it is easy to get more details on each by Googling the name of the lead defendant (sometimes it helps to add the word terror to narrow the search or add the word "justice" to get the Department of Justice press release) or the common name of the conspiracy.[24]

al-Timimi — Ali al-Timimi was convicted in June 2005 and sentenced to life in prison for crimes that essentially amounted to inducing others to conspire to aid the Taliban.[25] He was a lecturer at an Islamic Center in Falls Church, Virginia. He allegedly induced others to engage in criminal conspiracies when he (1) "told [others] that the time had come for them to go abroad to join the mujahideen engaged in violent jihad in Afghanistan" and "advised" two persons "how to reach [a] training camp undetected," and (2) "told . . . others that they were obligated to help the Taliban in the face of an attack by the United States." In addition, he promulgated some highly inflammatory language about the wrongdoing of the U.S. to his followers.[26] These overt acts were

---

[24] A valuable service is provided by Professor Bobby Chesney of Wake Forest who keeps national security law teachers updated with regular e-mails of developments. Professor Chesney has published two articles that collect data on material support prosecutions. Robert M. Chesney, *Federal Prosecution of Terrorism-related Offenses: Conviction and Sentencing Data in Light of the "Soft-sentence" and "Data-reliability" Critiques*, 11 LEWIS & CLARK L. REV. 851 (2007); Robert M. Chesney, *Beyond Conspiracy? Anticipatory Prosecution and The Challenge of Unaffiliated Terrorism*, 80 SO. CAL. L. REV. 425 (2007).

The Department of Justice naturally attempts to extol its success rates in prosecuting terrorism cases. It has been argued, however, that some of its successes are not properly categorized as terrorism cases and that the sentences in many cases have been surprisingly lenient. Professor Chesney counters that these critiques are not as severe as might at first appear.

[25] He was convicted on all ten counts with which he was charged, which were:

Count 1: Inducing Others to Conspire to Use Firearms

Count 2: Soliciting Others to Levy War

Count 3: Inducing Others to Conspire to Levy War

Count 4: Attempting to Contribute Services to the Taliban

Count 5: Inducing Others to Aid the Taliban

Count 6: Inducing Others to Conspire to Violate the Neutrality Act

Counts 7–8: Inducing Others to Use Firearms

Counts 9–10: Inducing Others to Carry Explosives

[26] In the words of the indictment

On February 1, 2003, ALI AL-TIMIMI provided the following message to his followers:

> This morning, the world heard news about the crash of the space shuttle. There is no doubt that Muslims were overjoyed because of the adversity that befell their greatest enemy. Upon hearing the news, my heart felt certain good omens that I liked to spread to my brothers.

> First: The Name of the Shuttle: "Columbia" is the name of the shuttle, called after the name of "Columbus," the sailor who discovered the American Continent in 1492 after the fall of Grenada, the last Islamic stronghold in Andalusia. Historians know that, after discovering the two American Continents, the Romans (the Christians of Europe) exploited their wealth in order to be able to control the Islamic World. The Columbia crash made me feel, and God is the only One to know, that this is a strong signal that Western supremacy (especially that of America) that began 500 years ago is coming to a quick end, God Willing, as occurred to the shuttle.

> Second: The Shuttle Crew: The Israeli Ambassador to the UN described the Israeli astronaut

taken in the context of his knowledge that some of his audience owned assault-type weapons and were seriously considering going to paramilitary training camps in Pakistan to train as mujahadeen fighters in Islamist organizations.

"Paintball Jihadis" (Khan) [§ 3.01[A], Note 5, *supra*] — Several men prepared for jihad by training in the Virginia hills with paintball weapons. A few actually attempted to join LET or the Taliban as part of the group that met with Ali al-Timimi in Fairfax. They were charged with conspiracy, violation of the Neutrality Act, and material support. None had any contact with al Qaeda itself. The trial court refused to equate support of other groups with support of al Qaeda. "Although Khan's fighting on behalf of the al Qaeda's protector, the Taliban, would certainly benefit al Qaeda, such assistance does not fit the statutory definition of material support or resources." Khan actually traveled to Pakistan and trained with LET — he was sentenced to life plus 45 years. Another defendant went to Pakistan but returned after 9/11, claiming that he "would never be a terrorist" — he was sentenced to 65 years. In all, 10 people including al-Timimi were convicted in these cases.

Portland Seven — One member of the Portland "cell" pleaded guilty to conspiracy and testified that the seven formed a loose-knit group who gathered to talk about jihad and attempted to travel to Afghanistan in October 2001 and early 2002 to take up arms on behalf of the Taliban against the U.S. They called themselves "Katibat Al-Mawt" or "squad of death." One member of the group did make it and was killed by Pakistani forces. Some of the others were found guilty of conspiracy to levy war against the U.S. while others pleaded guilty to lesser firearms charges. They were sentenced to prison terms ranging from three years to 18 years.

Lackawanna Six — The Lackawanna Complaint alleged that members of the "cell" had trained at the al-Farooq training camp in Afghanistan in early 2001 and stayed at an al Qaeda safe house. There is nothing in the affidavit accompanying the charges that indicates any future plans other than the statement that two uncharged co-conspirators had communicated by e-mail with "information which law enforcement personnel interpret as referring to possible terrorist activity."

All six of those charged in the U.S. pleaded guilty to material support charges and were sentenced to prison terms of 10 years or less. One alleged member of the Lackawanna cell, Jaber A. Elbaneh, was imprisoned in Yemen but escaped and is still at large. Another, Ahmed Hijazi (aka Kamal Derwish), was in the car that was hit by a U.S. missile in Yemen in 2002.

Some defense attorneys complained that guilty pleas were coercively tainted by the

---

as someone carrying all the hopes and ambitions of the Israeli people. And so, God Willing, all these hopes and ambitions were burnt with the crash and the burning of the shuttle and one of its astronauts, the Israeli.

Third: The Crash Location: As soon as CNN announced the crash of the space shuttle nearby the city of Palestine, in Texas, I said to myself "God is Great." This way, God Willing, America will fall and disappear (nearby Palestine). The State of Texas is also the state of the foolish, obeyed President Bush the son. And so we hope, God Willing, similar to the crash of the shuttle on his state, his nation would fall upon his head due to his foolish policy.

Fourth: The President's Condolences to the American People: In the words that President Bush used to console his people, he referred to the Book of Isiah where there is a praise to God's creation, His stars and planets. I said to myself, Praise the Lord, in this same Book of Isiah there are news about the coming of Prophet Muhammad and a warning of the destruction of the Jews at the end of time. [A citation from the Koran follows].

And so, there are other signs that would take a long time to recount. For example, every time the Americans believe that they control the whole earth and the skies, and act as they wish, there comes a sign that reminds us that God, Almighty, is greater than his creatures, sitting on His Chair, handling everything, and that His angels act according to His commands. And so, he whoever will try to raise the Jews, who are a nation that God covered with humiliation and deserved God's wrath, will be afflicted with divine humiliation and wrath as much as he supports them. As I mentioned earlier, these are all ideas that came to me when I heard of the accident, and hopes that I wish God would fulfill, and God is the only One to know.

threat that the defendants could be subject to the "enemy combatant" designation and thus imprisoned without a trial. That prospect presumably would not be available after the Supreme Court decision in *Hamdi*, § 8.03[A].

al-Arian [§ 3.03[C], *supra*] — Sami al-Arian, the professor at University of South Florida who admittedly raised money for Palestinian Islamic Jihad, was tried for both conspiracy to murder and material support of PIJ. The jury acquited on the conspiracy and hung on the material support charges. In April 2006 Al-Arian pleaded guilty to conspiracy to provide material support and agreed to be deported. He was sentenced to 57 months but given credit for time served, leaving 19 months to serve before being deported. He is due to be deported in June 2008.

Hammoud [§ 3.03[C], *supra*] — Mohammed Hammoud, the cigarette smuggling conspirator, funneled some of the profits from his smuggling activities to Hezbollah. Among the interesting tidbits about Hammoud is that he tried three separate marriages as a route to obtaining U.S. residency. The third marriage was conducted while he was still married to the second — but no harm because she was also married to someone else. The INS detected the fraud in the first two but not in the third, although ultimately there were a number of people convicted of wide-ranging marriage fraud. There were a total of 18 people eventually tried in the smuggling and marriage fraud schemes. Hammoud was originally sentenced to 155 years but his sentence is being reviewed by the trial court under the standards of *United States v. Booker*.

Bly Training Camp — The following summary is from a press release of the U.S. Dept of Justice on September 25, 2007:

> Oussama Abdullah Kassir, an individual who is charged in the Southern District of New York with, among other things, conspiring to provide material support and resources to al Qaeda, has been extradited from the Czech Republic. The charges relate to his participation in an effort to establish a jihad training camp in Bly, Oregon, and his operation of several terrorist websites. Kassir was taken into FBI custody this morning in Prague.

> On Dec. 11, 2005, Kassir was arrested by Czech authorities, during a layover in Prague, as he was traveling from Stockholm, Sweden, to Beirut, Lebanon. The arrest was based on a criminal complaint filed in the Southern District of New York, and a corresponding arrest warrant on file with Interpol. Kassir was thereafter detained in Prague, awaiting extradition to the United States.

> Kassir conspired with Mustafa Kamel Mustafa and Haroon Rashid Aswat, and others, to establish a jihad training camp on a parcel of property located in Bly, Ore. The purpose of the Bly jihad training camp was to provide a place where Muslims could receive various types of training, including military-style jihad training, in preparation for a community of Muslims to move to Afghanistan. Once in Afghanistan, the men in the community would have gained enough familiarity with weapons at the Bly jihad training camp to fight jihad or to continue with additional jihad training in Afghanistan. In a letter faxed from one of the co-conspirators to another, the property in Bly was described as located in a "pro-militia and fire-arms state" that "looks just like Afghanistan," and the author stated that the group was "stock-piling weapons and ammunition."

Kassir is awaiting trial in the Southern District of New York. Aswat is in England under an extradition order that he has appealed to the European Court of Human Rights.

al-Masri — Abu Hamza al-Masri was born in Egypt, became radicalized, and went to fight with the mujahedin in Bosnia in the early 1990s, where he lost both hands and one eye. He was the Imam of the Finsbury Park Mosque in London until forced out by the government commission that monitors charities, when he then took to preaching in the streets. He was convicted in England of soliciting murder and inciting racial hatred. The U.S. is seeking his extradition to stand trial for the Bly conspiracy.

Abdi — Nuradin Abdi pleaded guilty to conspiracy to provide material support based on a trip to an Ethiopian training camp. He was initially arrested for attempting to obtain hand grenades to attack a shopping mall in Columbus, Ohio. In November 2007, he was sentenced to 10 years in prison.

Abujihaad — Hassan Abujihaad was indicted in Connecticut for conspiring to murder U.S. nationals abroad and for transmission of classified information. As a Navy enlisted man, he allegedly passed information on U.S. troop movements to agents of the Taliban prior to the U.S. invasion.

Aref — Yassin Aref may become the most controversial of terrorism convictions. He was sentenced in March 2007 to 15 years after conviction on both conspiracy and material support charges. He was initially targeted for an FBI sting operation when his name was found in a notebook in Iraq. A friend of Aref's, Hossain, who owned a pizza parlor in Albany was approached by an FBI informant with a plan to launder money through the pizza parlor accounts for eventual use by JEM (Jaish-e-Mohammed), a designated FTO operating in Pakistan. Aref was brought into the arrangement as a witness to the loan transactions as required by Islamic law. Supporters of both defendants claim that neither Hossain nor Aref spoke good English, failed to understand what was being transacted, and were entrapped. In addition, much of the prosecution evidence was based on wiretaps that were conducted under the NSA program before it was authorized by the August 2007 amendments to FISA.

Arnaout and BIF — Enaam Arnaout directed Benevolence International Foundation (BIF) operations in the United States. He pleaded guilty to RICO charges on the theory that he solicited donations from the public by purporting that BIF and its related overseas offices were part of a charitable organization involved solely in humanitarian work for the benefit of civilians when, in reality, a material portion of the donations received by BIF were being used to support Chechen and Bosnian insurgents. Although he was not convicted of a terrorism charge, the court allowed a sentencing enhancement for support of terrorist activities.

Awan — Khalid Awan was convicted in December 2006 of forwarding money to KCF (Khalistan Commando Force), a designated FTO promoting a Sikh homeland in northern India. He was sentenced to 13–18 years in prison. At sentencing, the judge noted that Awan was probably not as interested in the violent goals of the KCF as he was in being affiliated with the KCF leadership. His lack of specific intent was a factor in sentencing but not in the initial conviction.

al-Badawi — "When the Yemeni authorities released a convicted terrorist of Al Qaeda named Jamal al-Badawi from prison last October, American officials were furious. Mr. Badawi helped plan the attack on the American destroyer Cole in 2000, in which 17 American sailors were killed. But the Yemenis saw things differently. Mr. Badawi had agreed to help track down five other members of Al Qaeda who had escaped from prison, and was more useful to the government on the street than off." Robert F. Worth, *Yemen's Deals With Jihadists Unsettle the U.S.*, N.Y. TIMES, Jan. 28, 2008.

Brent — Mahmud Faruq Brent was sentenced in July 2007 to 15 years for attempting to provide his personal services to LET, a designated FTO operating out of Pakistan supporting Kashmir separation from India. He attended a training camp in Pakistan and returned home to Maryland to await orders.

Chiquita Banana — Chiquita Brands International pleaded guilty in March 2007 to making payments to both the right-wing AUC and the left-wing FARC, designated terrorist groups that operate in Colombia. Chiquita made the payments to obtain protection for its operations in South America. As part of its plea arrangement, it agreed to pay a $25 million fine.

FARC — An ICE sting operation has thus far netted seven convictions for offenses related to alien smuggling and the Revolutionary Armed Forces of Colombia (FARC). Jalal Sadat Moheisen (Sadat), a Palestinian national and resident of Bogota, Colombia, pleaded guilty in Miami to one count of conspiracy to provide material support to FARC. Nicolas Ricardo Tapasco Romero (Tapasco), 45, a former Colombian detective, pleaded guilty to one count of conspiracy to commit alien smuggling and two counts of bringing aliens to the United States for private financial gain. *See* USDOJ Press Release of November 13, 2007.

Fort Dix Plot — Six men were charged in May 2007 with conspiring to shoot up Fort Dix in New Jersey. The men had trained in the Pocono Mountains of Pennsylvania and obtained weapons. They are described by federal authorities as a "loose-knit" group with no apparent ties to any known terrorist organization. They became the subject of FBI investigation after taking a video of themselves to a store for transfer to DVD. The FBI then used informants to infiltrate and carry out a sting operation for purchase of weapons.

Gadahn — Adam Gadahn (aka Azzam al-Amriki) is the subject of a very rare prosecution for treason. The indictment alleges that he has frequently appeared in al Qaeda videos espousing anti-American sentiments and inciting others to join the jihadi cause. He is also charged with material support in the form of his services.

Hayat (the Lodi cell) — This father-son team from Lodi, California, were charged with material support. Allegedly, the son Hamid spent two years at al Qaeda training camps and the father Umer lied to investigating agents. Hamid was convicted in April 2006 and the jury hung on Umed, who eventually pleaded guilty and received a sentence of time served. Hamid was sentenced on his 25th birthday in September 2007 to 24 years in prison. His defense counsel described his client as engaging in "the idle chatter of a directionless young man with a sixth-grade education," and his supporters claim that his confession was coerced.

Holy Land Foundation — HLF began life as the Occupied Land Fund. It was based in Chicago originally but moved to Texas in the 1990s. In December 2001 it was declared an SDGT by the Treasury Department, and its assets were frozen by both the U.S. and the European Union. The criminal trial in Dallas resulted in a mistrial in October 2007 when the jury acquitted on some counts and failed to reach agreement on the rest.

Iqbal — The material support prosecution that most directly confronts first amendment values is that of Javed Iqbal, who was charged in New York in 2006 for operating a television rebroadcast service that carried the messages of Hezbollah station al Manar (the "Beacon").

Islamic American Relief Agency — The IARA, based in Columbia Missouri, was designated in 2004 by Treasury as an SDGT. The organization and five of its officers have been charged under IEEPA for funneling money to Iraqi insurgents as well as to al Qaeda and Sudanese groups.

Jabarah — Mohammed Mansour Jabarah trained with al Qaeda in 2000, came to the attention of bin Laden, who reportedly sent him to work with both Hambali (of Jemaah Islamiyah) and KSM. He plotted to bomb U.S. embassies in Singapore and Malaysia but fled when the plot was exposed. He was arrested in Oman, extradited to Canada, and agreed to come to the U.S. and plead guilty to conspiracy charges while cooperating with investigators. When he ceased cooperating and allegedly plotted to attack federal officials, he was sentenced to life in prison.

Lakhani — Hemant Lakhani is a 71-year-old with a history of commodities trading, including legal weapons deals. He was approached by an FBI informant who was working with a suspected terrorist in Dubai attempting to obtain Stinger missiles. Lakhani offered to obtain the Russian equivalent for $87,000 per missile. With the help of Russian agents, he was eventually arrested with a fake missile in hand and charged with both material support and illegal arms trading. His entrapment defense was rejected and he was sentenced to 47 years in prison. United States v. Lakhani, 480 F.3d 171 (3d Cir. 2007).

Padilla [§ 8.03[A], *infra*] — After spending almost four years in military detention,

Jose Padilla was finally charged in Florida with both material support and conspiracy to kill based on his attending al Qaeda training camps. He was convicted in August 2007 on both charges and sentenced to 17 years in prison.

Ressam — Ahmed Ressam was convicted on several counts involving illegal explosives and attempt to bomb an airport. He was arrested at the U.S. border crossing from Vancouver, Canada by an alert customs agent who inspected the trunk of his car after noticing that he was behaving very nervously. One count of his conviction was for carrying explosives in the commission of another felony, in this case lying to a federal official. The Ninth Circuit decided that the explosives were not carried to aid in the crime of lying, and that the statute did not contemplate the reverse. Therefore, the court vacated the sentence and remanded for resentencing on the other eight counts. The Supreme Court reversed and reinstated the conviction. *United States v. Ressam*, 2008 U.S. LEXIS 4316 (May 19, 2008).

Sabir — Rafiq Sabir was convicted in New York of attempting to provide material support by offering training in martial arts to a government informant whom he believed to be a representative of al Qaeda.

Shareef — Derrick Shareef pleaded guilty in November 2007 to one count of attempting to use a weapon of mass destruction. He was arrested when he tried to obtain hand grenades from an FBI agent, allegedly planning to use them to attack a suburban shopping mall. Shareef reportedly was once the roommate of Hassan Abujihaad.

Shorbagi — Mohamed Shorbagi, Imam of a mosque in Georgia, pleaded guilty to providing material support to Hamas and was sentenced to almost 8 years. Shorbagi raised money and funneled it through the Holy Land Foundation.

Siraj — Shahawar Matin Siraj on several explosives charges for plotting to bomb a subway station near Madison Square Garden during the Republican National Convention in 2004. He was sentenced to 30 years in prison. His entrapment defense was rejected despite his argument that the police informant was pushing the bombing, that he had no explosives and knew nothing about explosives.

Sattar [§ 3.03[B], Note 3, *supra*] — Sheikh Rahman's lawyer, Lynne Stewart, and their interpreter were charged with violating prison regulations and also violating § 2339B by using their consultations with the Sheikh to pass messages to and from the Islamic Group. The charges stemming from use of telephones and provision of services were dismissed by the trial judge on vagueness grounds. Stewart was convicted of defrauding the U.S. by violating prison regulations and conspiracy to provide material support in the form of making personnel (access to Rahman) available to the rest of the conspirators. She was disbarred and sentenced to 28 months in prison.

Maryland Tamil Tigers — Several defendants in Baltimore have pleaded guilty to conspiring to provide material support to the Tamil Tigers in the form of military equipment, along with money laundering charges. Thirunavukarasu Varatharasa was sentenced to five years and deported to Sri Lanka. Haji Subandi was sentenced to three years. Erick Wotulo, a retired Indonesian Marine Corps General, is awaiting sentencing.

NOTE

John Farmer, *A Terror Threat in the Courts*, N.Y. TIMES, Jan. 13, 2008:

> Over time, we may well transform the law of conspiracy to the point where an agreement alone is a crime. This would render thoughts punishable, reward government overreaching and erode our civil liberties. All because the criminal law is being used not primarily to punish crimes but for purposes of detaining people we are worried about.

> It is time to stop pretending that the criminal justice system is a viable primary option for preventing terrorism. The Bush administration should propose and Congress should pass legislation allowing for preventive detention in future terrorism cases like that of Mr. Padilla. It is the best way to ensure

both the integrity of our criminal law and the safety of our nation.

§ 3.05 SELECTED READINGS

- Sahar Aziz, *The Laws on Providing Material Support to Terrorist Organizations: The Erosion of Constitutional Rights or a Legitimate Tool for Preventing Terrorism?*, 9 Tex. F. on C.L. & C.R. 45 (2003)
- Robert Chesney, *Civil Liberties and the Terrorism Prevention Paradigm: The Guilt by Association Critique*, 101 Mich. L. Rev. 1409 (2003)
- Robert Chesney, *The Sleeper Scenario: Terrorism-Support Laws and the Demands of Prevention*, 42 Harv. J. Legis. 1 (2005)
- Randolph A. Jonakait, *A Double Due Process Denial: The Crime of Providing Material Support or Resources to Designated Foreign Terrorist Organizations*, 48 N.Y.L.S. L. Rev. 125 (2003)

Chapter 4
CIVIL ACTIONS

§ 4.01 CIVIL ACTIONS

There are four principal statutes under which injured persons can bring civil actions against state sponsors of terrorism or against private individuals. The Torture Victim Protection Act (TVPA) is codified as a note to the Alien Tort Statute (ATS), 28 U.S.C. § 1350. The civil version of the criminal "material support" statutes is sometimes known as the Anti-Terrorism Act (ATA) and is codified at 18 U.S.C. § 2333. The Foreign Sovereign Immunity Act (FSIA), 28 U.S.C. § 1605, withholds sovereign immunity for acts committed by designated terrorist states and for torts committed within the U.S.

Although it is tempting to downplay the role of civil lawsuits in light of more aggressive counter-terrorism actions of the government, bear in mind that some of the most severe blows struck at the Ku Klux Klan came from a series of lawsuits by which the Klan and its supporters lost most of their assets and thus much of their ability to function. The website of the Southern Poverty Law Center describes the evolution of its "Klanwatch" program into its current "Intelligence Project." http://www.splcenter.org/intel.

Prior to the 1990s, there was a serious question about the ability of an alien to sue another alien in U.S. courts for violations of humanitarian law. In *Filartiga v. Pena-Irala*, 630 F.2d 876 (2d Cir. 1980), the plaintiff citizens of Paraguay sued a Paraguayan official for torturing and killing their son and brother. The Alien Tort Statute, 28 U.S.C. § 1350, provided jurisdiction over suits "by an alien for a tort only, committed in violation of the law of nations or a treaty of the United States." Because Article III does not provide for diversity jurisdiction between two aliens, the statute would not be valid except to the extent that it applies to a suit that "arises under" federal law. Treaty law would be such law but treaties very seldom create private rights of action. Therefore, the question was whether the "law of nations" was federal law that would support subject matter jurisdiction. The Second Circuit held that "an act of torture committed by a state official against one held in detention violates established norms of the international law of human rights, and hence the law of nations."

Tel-Oren v. Libyan Arab Republic, 726 F.2d 774 (D.C. Cir. 1984), produced a badly splintered court in what Judge Edwards called "an area of the law that cries out for clarification by the Supreme Court." The *Tel-Oren* case was brought by survivors and representatives of victims of an attack on a bus in Israel in 1978. Two of the many defendants were Libya and the PLO, who were alleged to have acted in complicity in carrying out the attack. The three judges on the panel could agree on only a terse *per curiam* statement affirming the dismissal of the action by the district court. Each wrote a separate concurring opinion.

Judge Edwards argued that international law could supply the rule of decision for a claim of torture but not for murder. Libya was not alleged to have tortured anyone and would have enjoyed sovereign immunity at the time. The PLO was "not a recognized member of the community of nations" and thus was not subject to the rules and conventions on torture.

Judge Bork insisted international law did not recognize a private right of action for either torture or murder. Thus, unless Congress created a right of action, none would exist as a matter of federal law. Judge Edwards' response to this argument was that international law states the norms but leaves to each nation the methods of protection, whether through civil suit or otherwise.

Judge Robb would have declared the whole dispute to be a political question lacking in judicially manageable standards.

The Supreme Court did not accept Judge Edwards' plea for clarification, but

Congress did. The Torture Victims Protection Act, codified as a note to 18 U.S.C. § 1350, in 1991 explicitly created a civil action for official torture or "extrajudicial killing." The civil remedy usually known as the Anti-Terrorism Act, 18 U.S.C. § 2333, was added in 1992. In 1996, Congress adopted amendments to the Foreign Sovereign Immunity Act (FSIA). These are the principal statutes that form the basis for the civil suits in the following cases.

PRICE v. SOCIALIST PEOPLE'S LIBYAN ARAB JAMAHIRIYA
352 U.S. App. D.C. 284, 294 F.3d 82 (D.C. Cir. 2002)

EDWARDS, CIRCUIT JUDGE.

This case involves a lawsuit brought under the Foreign Sovereign Immunities Act ("FSIA") by two American citizens who sued the Socialist People's Libyan Arab Jamahiriya ("Libya") for torture and hostage taking. Plaintiffs' lawsuit seeks cover under a recent amendment to the FSIA which strips certain foreign states — including Libya of their sovereign immunity in American courts when they engage in such conduct. *See* 28 U.S.C. § 1605(a)(7).

In response to plaintiffs' suit, Libya moved to dismiss, claiming sovereign immunity and a lack of personal jurisdiction. The District Court denied the motion to dismiss and Libya now seeks review in this interlocutory appeal. Two central questions have been raised on appeal: first, whether plaintiffs have alleged facts that are legally sufficient to revoke Libya's immunity under the FSIA; and, second, whether the assertion of personal jurisdiction over Libya in the manner specifically authorized by the FSIA violates the Due Process Clause.

We hold, first, that plaintiffs have failed to state a claim for hostage taking adequate to abrogate sovereign immunity and establish subject matter jurisdiction. The allegations set forth in the complaint do not come close to satisfying the definition of "hostage taking" prescribed by the FSIA. In contrast to the hostage-taking claim, however, plaintiffs have at least intimated that they can allege facts that might state a proper claim for torture under the FSIA. Accordingly, we will remand the case to allow plaintiffs to attempt to amend their complaint in an effort to satisfy the statute's rigorous definition of torture. As a word of caution, we note that there is a question as to whether the complaint states a claim for relief upon which plaintiffs can recover; although this matter is not properly before us on interlocutory review, we are not foreclosing review of the issue in the District Court.

Finally, we hold that Libya, as a foreign state, is not a "person" within the meaning of the Due Process Clause. We therefore conclude that the Constitution imposes no limitation on the exercise of personal jurisdiction by the federal courts over Libya.

I. BACKGROUND

The facts and procedural history of this case are relatively straightforward. Plaintiffs Michael Price and Roger Frey, Americans who had been living in Libya in the employ of a Libyan company, were arrested in March of 1980 after taking pictures of various places in and around Tripoli. Libyan government officials apparently believed that these photographs constituted anti-revolutionary propaganda, because they would portray unfavorable images of life in Libya.

Price and Frey allege that, following their arrest, they were denied bail and kept in a "political prison" for 105 days pending the outcome of their trial. In their complaint, plaintiffs assert that they endured deplorable conditions while incarcerated, including urine-soaked mattresses, a cramped cell with substandard plumbing that they were forced to share with seven other inmates, a lack of medical care, and inadequate food. The complaint also asserts that the plaintiffs were "kicked, clubbed and beaten" by prison guards, and "interrogated and subjected to physical, mental and verbal abuse." The complaint contends that this incarceration was "for the purpose of demonstrating

Defendant's support of the government of Iran which held hostages in the U.S. Embassy in Tehran, Iran."

Ultimately, plaintiffs were tried and acquitted of the crimes with which they had been charged. After the verdict was announced, however, the Libyan government retained their passports for another 60 days while the prosecution pursued an appeal, which is permitted under the Libyan Code of Criminal Procedure. When this appeal was eventually rejected, plaintiffs were permitted to leave Libya.

On May 7, 1997, Price and Frey commenced a civil action against Libya in federal court. Their complaint asserted claims for hostage taking and torture and sought $ 20 million in damages for each man. Following receipt of process, Libya filed a motion to dismiss, arguing that (1) the grant of subject matter jurisdiction over plaintiffs' action was unconstitutional, (2) the court's exercise of personal jurisdiction was unconstitutional, and (3) plaintiffs had failed to state a claim on which relief could be granted. The District Court rejected each of these arguments, thus vitiating Libya's sovereign immunity defense and allowing the court to assert both subject matter jurisdiction over plaintiffs' claims and personal jurisdiction over the defendant. Libya now pursues an interlocutory appeal.

II. Discussion

On appeal, Libya has not renewed its constitutional attack on the court's subject matter jurisdiction. Instead, it claims that the District Court erred in not resolving certain disputed issues of fact, proceeding instead as if plaintiffs' factual allegations had already been established. Libya also argues that, even assuming that these facts were true, the plaintiffs have failed to make out a valid claim either for torture or hostage taking under the FSIA. Finally, Libya asserts that the Due Process Clause does not permit an American court to take jurisdiction over a foreign sovereign based on conduct that has no connection to the United States save for the nationality of the plaintiff.

A. Plaintiffs' Cause of Action

Before we address the issues arising under the FSIA and the Due Process Clause, we first want to make it clear that our decision today does not address or decide whether the plaintiffs have stated a *cause of action* against Libya. The parties appear to assume that a substantive claim against Libya arises under the FSIA, but this is far from clear. The FSIA is undoubtedly a jurisdictional statute which, in specified cases, eliminates foreign sovereign immunity and opens the door to subject matter jurisdiction in the federal courts. There is a question, however, whether the FSIA creates a federal cause of action for torture and hostage taking *against foreign states. See Roeder v. Islamic Republic of Iran*, 195 F. Supp. 2d 140, 171–73 (D.D.C. 2002).

The "Flatow Amendment" to the FSIA confers a right of action for torture and hostage taking against an "official, employee, or agent of a foreign state," *see Flatow v. Islamic Republic of Iran*, 999 F. Supp. 1, 12–13 (D.D.C. 1998), but the amendment does not list "foreign states" among the parties against whom such an action may be brought. While it is possible that such an action could be brought under the "international terrorism" statute, 18 U.S.C. § 2333(a), no such claim has been raised in this case.

The question relating to plaintiffs' cause of action has yet to be raised or addressed in the District Court, and it was neither briefed nor argued by the parties during this appeal. Therefore, although we flag the issue, we will leave its disposition to the District Court in the first instance following remand of this case. We will turn our attention now to the matters before us, i.e., the issues arising under the FSIA and the Due Process Clause.

B. The 1996 Amendments to the Foreign Sovereign Immunities Act

The FSIA provides a basis for asserting jurisdiction over foreign nations in the United States. *Argentine Republic v. Amerada Hess Shipping Corp.*, 488 U.S. 428, 443, 109 S. Ct. 683 (1989). The statute, which was originally enacted in 1976, confers immunity on foreign states in all cases that do not fall into one of its specifically enumerated exceptions. *See McKesson HBOC, Inc. v. Islamic Republic of Iran*, 271 F.3d 1101, 1105 (D.C. Cir. 2001). These exceptions were crafted in order to codify the "restrictive theory" of sovereign immunity, under which immunity is generally limited to a foreign state's public or governmental acts (*jure imperii*) but withheld from its private or commercial acts (*jure gestionis*).

The FSIA [provides] a list of specific circumstances in which that immunity is unavailable. These include cases in which the state has waived its immunity, cases based upon various forms of commercial activity, takings of property in violation of international law, and torts committed in the United States. The original FSIA was not intended as human rights legislation. *See* Jennifer A. Gergen, *Human Rights and the Foreign Sovereign Immunities Act*, 36 VA. J. INT'L L. 765, 771 (1996). *Thus, no matter how allegedly egregious a foreign state's conduct, suits that did not fit into one of the statute's discrete and limited exceptions invariably were rejected. See, e.g., Saudi Arabia v. Nelson*, 507 U.S. 349 (1993) (holding that a claim arising from the detention and torture of an American citizen in Saudi Arabia was not "based upon a commercial activity carried on in the United States"); *Smith v. Socialist People's Libyan Arab Jamahiriya*, 101 F.3d 239 (2d Cir. 1996) (holding that Libya retained its sovereign immunity for the bombing of Pam Am 103 over Lockerbie, Scotland); *Princz v. Fed. Republic of Germany*, 307 U.S. App. D.C. 102, 26 F.3d 1166 (D.C. Cir. 1994) (holding that plaintiff could not recover for slave labor performed at Nazi concentration camps, because Germany's conduct was not commercial activity causing a "direct effect in the United States" and did not constitute an implied waiver of sovereign immunity); *Siderman de Blake v. Republic of Argentina*, 965 F.2d 699 (9th Cir. 1992) (holding that Argentina was immune from liability for acts of torture committed by the ruling junta); *Tel-Oren v. Libyan Arab Republic*, 233 U.S. App. D.C. 384, 726 F.2d 774, 775 n.1 (D.C. Cir. 1984) (Edwards J., concurring) (FSIA precludes jurisdiction over Libya for armed attack on civilian bus in Israel); *cf. Amerada Hess*, 488 U.S. at 436 ("Immunity is granted in those cases involving violations of international law that do not come within one of the FSIA's exceptions.").

Under the original FSIA, therefore, terrorism, torture, and hostage taking committed abroad were immunized forms of state activity. Indeed, in *Nelson*, the Supreme Court recognized that conduct of the sort alleged in the present case — "wrongful arrest, imprisonment, and torture" — amounted to abuses of police power, and "however monstrous such abuse undoubtedly may be, a foreign's state's exercise of the power of its police has long been understood for purpose of the restrictive theory as peculiarly sovereign in nature." *See also* Mathias Reimann, *A Human Rights Exception to Sovereign Immunity: Some Thoughts on* Princz v. Federal Republic of Germany, 16 MICH. J. INT'L L. 403, 417–18 (1995) (observing that under the unamended FSIA "efforts to persuade the courts to recognize a human rights exception to sovereign immunity" had failed).

The mounting concern over decisions such as these eventually spurred the political branches into action. *See* John F. Murphy, *Civil Liability for the Commission of International Crimes as an Alternative to Criminal Prosecution*, 12 HARV. HUM. RTS. J. 1, 34 (1999). In 1996, as part of the comprehensive Antiterrorism and Effective Death Penalty Act ("AEDPA"), Congress amended the FSIA to add a new class of claims for which certain foreign states would be precluded from asserting sovereign immunity. Specifically, the amendment vitiates immunity in cases

> in which money damages are sought against a foreign state for personal injury
> or death that was caused by an act of torture, extrajudicial killing, aircraft

sabotage, hostage taking, or the provision of material support or resources-
. . . for such an act if such act or provision of material support is engaged in
by an official, employee, or agent of such foreign state while acting within the
scope of his or her office, employment, or agency[.]

28 U.S.C. § 1605(a)(7). In enacting this provision, Congress sought to create a judicial
forum for compensating the victims of terrorism, and in so doing to punish foreign states
who have committed or sponsored such acts and deter them from doing so in the future.
See Daliberti v. Republic of Iraq, 97 F. Supp. 2d 38, 50 (D.D.C. 2000); Molora Vadnais,
The Terrorism Exception to the Foreign Sovereign Immunities Act, 5 UCLA J. INT'L L.
& FOREIGN AFF. 199, 216 (2000).

*While such legislation had long been sought by victims' groups, it had been
consistently resisted by the executive branch. See* ALAN GERSON & JERRY ADLER, THE
PRICE OF TERROR 212–26 (2001). Executive branch officials feared that the proposed
amendment to FSIA might cause other nations to respond in kind, thus potentially
subjecting the American government to suits in foreign countries for actions taken in the
United States. Although these reservations did not prevent the amendment from
passing, they nevertheless left their mark in the final version of the bill.

Section 1605(a)(7) has some notable features which reveal the delicate legislative
compromise out of which it was born. First, not all foreign states may be sued. Instead,
only a defendant that has been specifically designated by the State Department as a
"state sponsor of terrorism" is subject to the loss of its sovereign immunity.
§ 1605(a)(7)(A). Second, even a foreign state listed as a sponsor of terrorism retains its
immunity unless (a) it is afforded a reasonable opportunity to arbitrate any claim based
on acts that occurred in that state, and (b) either the victim or the claimant was a U.S.
national at the time that those acts took place. § 1605(a)(7)(B). In the present case, Libya
has been designated as a sponsor of terrorism. *See Rein v. Socialist People's Libyan
Arab Jamahiriya*, 162 F.3d 748, 764 (2d Cir. 1998). Moreover, both plaintiffs are
American citizens, and Libya does not contend that it has been denied a chance to
arbitrate their claims.

If service of process has been made under § 1608, personal jurisdiction over a foreign
state exists for every claim over which the court has subject matter jurisdiction. *See* 28
U.S.C. § 1330(b). In turn, the statute automatically confers subject matter jurisdiction
whenever the state loses its immunity pursuant to § 1605(a)(7). Personal jurisdiction
determinations always have been made in this way under the FSIA. *See* JOSEPH W.
DELLAPENNA, SUING FOREIGN GOVERNMENTS AND THEIR CORPORATIONS 9 (1988) (commenting
on this "significant compression," whereby both "competence [subject matter jurisdic-
tion] and personal jurisdiction depend upon whether the foreign state is immune under
the substantive rules in the act"); *see also Harris v. VAO Intourist, Moscow*, 481 F.
Supp. 1056, 1065 (E.D.N.Y. 1979) (Weinstein, J.) (noting the way in which the FSIA
collapses subject matter jurisdiction, *in personam* jurisdiction, and sovereign immunity
into a single inquiry).

Under the original FSIA, however, it was generally understood that in order for
immunity to be lost, there had to be some tangible connection between the conduct of the
foreign defendant and the *territory* of the United States. In this way, the original
statute's immunity exceptions "prescribed the necessary contacts which must exist
before our courts can exercise personal jurisdiction."

When Congress passed the original FSIA, it was assumed that the exercise of
personal jurisdiction over foreign states under the statute always would satisfy the
demands of the Constitution. *See* Joseph W. Glannon & Jeffery Atik, *Politics and
Personal Jurisdiction: Suing State Sponsors of Terrorism under the 1996 Amendments
to the Foreign Sovereign Immunities Act*, 87 GEO. L.J. 675, 681–82 (1999). This
assumption proved accurate.

The antiterrorism amendments changed this statutory framework. Under

§ 1605(a)(7), the only required link between the defendant nation and the territory of the United States is the nationality of the claimant. Thus, § 1605(a)(7) now allows personal jurisdiction to be maintained over defendants in circumstances that do not appear to satisfy the "minimum contacts" requirement of the Due Process Clause.

C. Challenges to the Factual Underpinnings of an FSIA Complaint

[W]hen a foreign state defendant raises "a dispute over the factual basis of the court's subject matter jurisdiction under the FSIA," the trial court is required to "go beyond the pleadings and resolve any disputed issues of fact the resolution of which is necessary to a ruling upon the motion to dismiss." Libya still did not challenge the factual basis of plaintiffs' allegations. Instead, it wrote that, "even viewed in the light most favorable to the plaintiffs, the facts alleged in the complaint do not establish 'acts of torture' by Libya."

E. Torture

The FSIA's definition of torture derives from the meaning given that term in section 3 of the Torture Victim Protection Act of 1991 ("TVPA"). Section 3(b)(1) of the TVPA defines "torture" to include

> any act, directed against an individual in the offender's custody or physical control, by which *severe* pain or suffering (other than pain or suffering arising only from or inherent in, or incidental to, lawful sanctions), whether physical or mental, is intentionally inflicted on that individual *for such purposes* as obtaining from that individual or a third person information or a confession, punishing that individual for an act that individual or a third person has committed or is suspected of having committed, intimidating or coercing that individual or a third person, or for any reason based on discrimination of any kind.

(Emphases added). This definition, in turn, borrows extensively from the 1984 United Nations Convention Against Torture and Other Cruel, Inhuman or Degrading Treatment or Punishment ("Torture Convention"), which the United States signed in 1988 and ratified two years later. Indeed, the TVPA was passed in part to fulfill the Convention's mandate that ratifying nations take action to ensure that torturers are held legally accountable for their actions.

The drafters of the Convention, as well as the Reagan Administration that signed it, the Bush Administration that submitted it to Congress, and the Senate that ultimately ratified it, therefore all sought to ensure that "only acts of a certain gravity shall be considered to constitute torture." This understanding thus makes clear that torture does not automatically result whenever individuals in official custody are subjected even to direct physical assault. Not *all* police brutality, not *every* instance of excessive force used against prisoners, is torture under the FSIA.

As to the purposes for which abuse must be inflicted, it is clear from the text of the TVPA that the list of purposes provided was not meant to be exhaustive. Instead, this list was included in order to reinforce that torture requires acts both intentional and malicious, and to illustrate the common motivations that cause individuals to engage in torture. Moreover, this requirement ensures that, whatever its specific goal, torture can occur under the FSIA only when the production of pain is purposive, and not merely haphazard. In order to lose its sovereign immunity, a foreign state must impose suffering cruelly and deliberately, rather than as the unforeseen or unavoidable incident of some legitimate end.

[I]n light of the serious and far-reaching implications of the 1996 FSIA amendments, it is especially important for the courts to ensure that foreign states are not stripped of their sovereign immunity unless they have been charged with actual torture, and not mere police brutality.

In this case, plaintiffs' complaint offers no useful details about the nature of the kicking, clubbing, and beatings that plaintiffs allegedly suffered. As a result, there is no way to determine from the present complaint the severity of plaintiffs' alleged beatings — including their frequency, duration, the parts of the body at which they were aimed, and the weapons used to carry them out — in order to ensure that they satisfy the TVPA's rigorous definition of torture. In short, there is no way to discern whether plaintiffs' complaint merely alleges police brutality that falls short of torture. Thus, the facts pleaded do not reasonably support a finding that the physical abuse allegedly inflicted by Libya evinced the degree of cruelty necessary to reach a level of torture.

Furthermore, the present complaint says virtually nothing about the purpose of the alleged torture. Plaintiffs seemingly have left it for the courts to conjure some illicit purpose to fill in this pleading gap. Obviously this will not do.

In sum, plaintiffs' allegations of torture as presently stated are insufficient to survive defendant's motion to dismiss. Plaintiffs must allege more than that they were abused. They must demonstrate in their pleadings that Libya's conduct rose to such a level of depravity and caused them such intense pain and suffering as to be properly classified as torture. Although it is far from certain, their complaint hints that they might be able to state a proper claim for torture under the FSIA. Accordingly, we will remand the case to the District Court to allow plaintiffs to attempt to amend their complaint in an effort to satisfy TVPA's stringent definition of torture.

F. Hostage Taking

As with torture, the FSIA draws its definition of "hostage taking" from an exogenous legal source, here article 1 of the International Convention Against the Taking of Hostages. This provision reads as follows:

> Any person who seizes or detains and threatens to kill, to injure or to continue to detain another person *in order to compel a third party*, namely, a State, an international governmental organization, a natural or judicial person or a group of persons, *to do or abstain from doing any act as an explicit or implicit condition for the release of the hostage* commits the offense of taking hostages within the meaning of the Convention.

(Emphases added). Under no reasonable reading of the plaintiffs' complaint does their admittedly unpleasant imprisonment qualify as hostage taking so defined.

The Convention does not proscribe all detentions, but instead focuses on the intended purpose of the detention. In this case, the complaint asserts only that Libya incarcerated Price and Frey "for the purpose of demonstrating Defendant's support of the government of Iran which held hostages in the U.S. Embassy in Tehran, Iran." Such motivation does not satisfy the Convention's intentionality requirement. The definition speaks in terms of conditions of release; the defendant must have detained the victim in order to compel some particular result, specifically to force a third party either to perform an act otherwise unplanned or to abstain from one otherwise contemplated so as to ensure the freedom of the detainee. Accordingly, detention for the goal of expressing support for illegal behavior — even for behavior that would itself qualify as "hostage taking" — does not constitute the taking of hostages within the meaning of the FSIA.

In this case, the plaintiffs have suggested no demand for *quid pro quo* terms between the government of Libya and a third party whereby Price and Frey would have been released upon the performance or non-performance of any action by that third party. Indeed, even when read most favorably to them, their complaint points to no nexus between what happened to them in Libya and any concrete concession that Libya may have hoped to extract from the outside world. The one purpose that plaintiffs have alleged is plainly inadequate, and they have advanced no others. Their allegation thus falls short of the standard for hostage taking under § 1605(a)(7).

For these reasons, Libya cannot be stripped of its sovereign immunity based on plaintiffs' allegation of hostage taking. The District Court thus erred in refusing to dismiss this count. Accordingly, we reverse on this point.

G. Personal Jurisdiction

The last question that we face is whether the Due Process Clause is offended by the District Court's assertion of personal jurisdiction over Libya. If, on remand, plaintiffs can state a claim of torture under § 1605(a)(7) sufficient to survive a motion to dismiss, and if they have properly served process on the defendant, personal jurisdiction will be established under the FSIA.

The Due Process Clause requires that if the defendant "be not present within the territory of the forum, he have certain minimum contacts with it such that the maintenance of the suit does not offend 'traditional notions of fair play and substantial justice.'"

In the present case, it is undisputed that Libya has no connection with the District of Columbia or with the United States, except for the alleged fact that it tortured two American citizens in Libya. This would be insufficient to satisfy the usual "minimum contacts" requirement.

Implicit in Libya's argument is the claim that a foreign state is a "person" within the meaning of the Due Process Clause. In previous cases, we have proceeded *as if* this proposition were true, but we have never so held. Now, however, this assumption has been challenged. And, with the issue directly before us, we hold that foreign states are not "persons" protected by the Fifth Amendment.

Our conclusion is based on a number of considerations. [I]t is highly significant that in *South Carolina v. Katzenbach*, 383 U.S. 301, 323–24, 86 S. Ct. 803 (1966), the Court was unequivocal in holding that "the word 'person' in the context of the Due Process Clause of the Fifth Amendment cannot, by any reasonable mode of interpretation, be expanded to encompass the States of the Union." Therefore, absent some compelling reason to treat foreign sovereigns more favorably than "States of the Union," it would make no sense to view foreign states as "persons" under the Due Process Clause.

Indeed, we think it would be highly incongruous to afford greater Fifth Amendment rights to foreign nations, who are entirely alien to our constitutional system, than are afforded to the states, who help make up the very fabric of that system. The States are integral and active participants in the Constitution's infrastructure, and they both derive important benefits and must abide by significant limitations as a consequence of their participation. However, a "foreign State lies outside the structure of the Union." Given this fundamental dichotomy between the constitutional status of foreign states and States within the United States, we cannot perceive why the former should be permitted to avail themselves of the fundamental safeguards of the Due Process Clause if the latter may not.

It is especially significant that the Constitution does not limit foreign states, as it does the States of the Union, in the power they can exert against the United States or its government. Indeed, the federal government cannot invoke the Constitution, save possibly to declare war, to prevent a foreign nation from taking action adverse to the interest of the United States or to compel it to take action favorable to the United States. It would therefore be quite strange to interpret the Due Process Clause as conferring upon Libya rights and protections *against* the power of federal government.

In addition to text and structure, history and tradition support our conclusion. Never has the Supreme Court suggested that foreign nations enjoy rights derived from the Constitution, or that they can use such rights to shield themselves from adverse actions taken by the United States. This is not surprising. Relations between nations in the international community are seldom governed by the domestic law of one state or the other. And legal disputes between the United States and foreign governments are not mediated through the Constitution. *See Nat'l Council of Resistance of Iran v. Dep't of State*, 346 U.S. App. D.C. 131, 251 F.3d 192, 202 (D.C. Cir. 2001) (recognizing that "sovereign states interact with each other through diplomacy and even coercion in ways not affected by constitutional protections such as the Due Process Clause").

Rather, the federal judiciary has relied on principles of comity and international law to protect foreign governments in the American legal system. This approach recognizes the reality that foreign nations are external to the constitutional compact, and it preserves the flexibility and discretion of the political branches in conducting this country's relations with other nations.

An example of this approach is seen with respect to the right of access to the courts. Private individuals have "a constitutional right of access to the courts," that is, the "right to sue and defend in the courts." Foreign states also have been afforded the right to use the courts of the United States to prosecute civil claims "upon the same basis as a domestic corporation or individual might do." But the right of access enjoyed by foreign nations derives from "principles of comity," and it is "neither a matter of absolute obligation, on the one hand, nor of mere courtesy and good will, upon the other." This privilege is not to be denied lightly, because to do so "would manifest a want of comity and friendly feeling." Nonetheless, foreign nations do not have a *constitutional* right of access to the courts of the United States. Indeed, only nations recognized by and at peace with the United States may avail themselves of our courts, and "it is within the exclusive power of the Executive Branch to determine which nations are entitled to sue."

While we recognize that the present case implicates not the right of affirmative access to the courts, but rather its reverse — the right not to be haled into court — this does not change the analysis under the Due Process Clause. The personal jurisdiction requirement is not a structural limitation on the power of courts. Rather, "the personal jurisdiction requirement recognizes and protects an individual liberty interest. It represents a restriction on judicial power not as a matter of sovereignty, but as a matter of individual liberty." This makes sense, because "the requirement that a court have personal jurisdiction flows not from Art. III, but from the Due Process Clause." It is thus quite clear that the constitutional law of personal jurisdiction secures interests quite different from those at stake when a sovereign nation such as Libya seeks to defend itself against the prerogatives of a rival government. It therefore follows that foreign states stand on a fundamentally different footing than do private litigants who are compelled to defend themselves in American courts.

Unlike private entities, foreign nations are the juridical equals of the government that seeks to assert jurisdiction over them. If they believe that they have suffered harm by virtue of being haled into court in the United States, foreign states have available to them a panoply of mechanisms in the international arena through which to seek vindication or redress. These mechanisms, not the Constitution, set the terms by which sovereigns relate to one another.

Finally, it is worth noting that serious practical problems might arise were we to hold that foreign states may cloak themselves in the protections of the Due Process Clause. For example, the power of Congress and the President to freeze the assets of foreign nations, or to impose economic sanctions on them, could be challenged as deprivations of property without due process of law. The courts would be called upon to adjudicate these sensitive questions, which in turn could tie the hands of the other branches as they sought to respond to foreign policy crises. The Constitution does not command this.

In sum, we hold that the Fifth Amendment poses no obstacle to the decision of the United States government to subject Libya to personal jurisdiction in the federal courts. Our decision on this point reaches only an actual foreign government; we express no view as to whether other entities that fall within the FSIA's definition of "foreign state" including corporations in which a foreign state owns a majority interest — could yet be considered persons under the Due Process Clause.

NOTES AND QUESTIONS

1. Sources of Federal Law. The "Flatow Amendment" problem arises because of the distinction between subject matter jurisdiction and a cause of action. Although § 1605(a)(7) provides subject matter jurisdiction, the question is whether there is a source of law for a claim. The D.C. Circuit in *Price* left open the question of whether there is a source of law for a claim against a foreign state based on conduct occurring outside the U.S. On remand, the district court explained and resolved the issue in this fashion:

> By the 1990s, Congress had grown increasingly frustrated with the federal courts for having dismissed a number of actions, on subject matter jurisdiction grounds, that had been brought by American victims of abuse by foreign nations. In 1996, Congress addressed this problem by including within the Antiterrorism and Effective Death Penalty Act, 110 Stat. 1214 ("AEDPA"), an amendment to the FSIA revoking the foreign sovereign immunity of nations which sponsored terrorist acts. This amendment ("the state-sponsored terrorism exception") created a new exception under the FSIA for any foreign nation designated by the State Department as a sponsor of terrorism, if that nation either commits a terrorist act resulting in the death or personal injury of a U.S. national, or provides material support and resources to an individual or entity that commits such a terrorist act.

> Realizing that the new exception did not unambiguously explain the potential causes of action for which sovereign immunity had been waived, Congress acted swiftly to clarify the issue. On September 30, 1996, it passed an amendment to 28 U.S.C. 1605(a)(7), providing, in relevant part:

>> An official, employee, or agent of a foreign state designated as a state sponsor of terrorism designated under section 6(j) of the Export Administration Act of 1979 while acting within the scope of his or her office, employment, or agency shall be liable to a United States national or the national's legal representative for personal injury or death caused by acts of that official, employee, or agent for which the courts of the United States may maintain jurisdiction under section 1605(a)(7).

> (codified at 28 U.S.C. § 1605 note). This provision of law is commonly referred to as the "Flatow Amendment." [T]his Court has consistently interpreted the Flatow Amendment to provide a cause of action against foreign states for any act that would provide a court with jurisdiction under 28 U.S.C. § 1605(a)(7).

Price v. Socialist People's Libyan Arab Jamahiriya, 274 F. Supp. 2d 20 (D.D.C. 2003). The same question also was answered in the affirmative by the district court in *Pugh v. Socialist People's Libyan Arab Jamahiriya*, 290 F. Supp. 2d 54 (D.D.C. 2003) (*see* Note 5 after *Boim, infra*). That incident involved bombing of a UTA airliner bound from the Congo to Paris in which seven U.S. citizens were killed.

2. Foreign Tort Immunity. Section (a)(7) strips sovereign immunity for torture, hostage taking, extrajudicial death, and aircraft sabotage. Does this exhaust the list of torts for which a state ought to be held accountable? Why not plain police brutality that does not rise to the level of torture? Why not false imprisonment that does not carry the *quid pro quo* nature of hostage taking? Some allegations against Central and South American regimes in the 1960s to 1980s involved people who simply disappeared. Should extended secret detention be a violation?

3. *Rein v. Socialist People's Libyan Arab Jamahiriya.* *Rein v. Socialist People's Libyan Arab Jamahiriya*, 162 F.3d 748 (2d Cir. 1998), was the second try for representatives of the victims of the Pan Am Lockerbie bombing, which killed 259 persons, many of them U.S. citizens.

In 1994, some of the present plaintiffs brought suit against some of the present defendants, claiming that Libya and its agents were responsible for destroying Pan Am 103. Libya moved to dismiss for lack of jurisdiction under the FSIA or any other applicable law. The FSIA establishes that foreign states are generally immune from suit. But it gives the federal district courts jurisdiction over actions against such states when either §§ 1605–07 of the Act or relevant international agreements permit them to be sued. When the previous litigation was brought in 1994, no provision of the FSIA deprived Libya of sovereign immunity in suits of this sort. Accordingly, the [district court] dismissed the case for lack of subject matter jurisdiction [and the Second Circuit affirmed].

In 1996, the Antiterrorism and Effective Death Penalty Act ("AEDPA") amended the FSIA by adding what is now 28 U.S.C. § 1605(a)(7). Under this new section, foreign states that have been designated as state sponsors of terrorism are denied immunity from damage actions for personal injury or death resulting from aircraft sabotage. Shortly after passage of the AEDPA, the present plaintiffs filed (against the present defendants) substantially the same claims that had been previously dismissed.

Libya argues that § 1605(a)(7) is unconstitutional as a bill of attainder and as an ex post facto law. For a law to be unconstitutional as a bill of attainder, it must impose punishment. [A] finding of civil liability and the attendant imposition of compensatory damages does not suffice to make the retrospective application of a law invalid. Where a retroactive law is civil rather than criminal, it is only the imposition of punitive damages that might, in particular circumstances, raise a constitutional problem. But if it is only the possibility that punitive damages may be assessed that raises the question of the statute's being a bill of attainder or an ex post facto law, then those issues are not properly before us at this stage of the case. There has as yet been no trial on the merits and no finding of liability, let alone a punitive damage award.

The Second Circuit also dealt with an argument by Libya that Congress unconstitutionally delegated power to the Executive through the assignment of liability premised on designation of foreign states as sponsors of terrorism. Because the designation fell within an area of traditional executive discretion in foreign affairs, the delegation was not invalid even though it affected the subject matter jurisdiction of the federal judiciary.

BOIM v. HOLY LAND FOUNDATION FOR RELIEF AND DEVELOPMENT
511 F.3d 707 (7th Cir. 2007)

ROVNER, CIRCUIT JUDGE.

This lawsuit has its origins in the murder of David Boim more than ten years ago. David, a citizen of both Israel and the United States, was living with his parents in Israel when he was gunned down while waiting for a bus in the West Bank outside of Jerusalem. He was apparently shot at random by gunmen believed to be acting on behalf of the terrorist organization Hamas.

Section 2333 of the United States Criminal Code grants U.S. nationals injured by acts of international terrorism the right to sue for treble damages in federal court. David's parents, Stanley and Joyce Boim, on behalf of themselves and David's estate, filed suit under this statute against not only the two men believed to have shot David, but an array of individuals and organizations in the United States with alleged connections to Hamas. Broadly speaking, the Boims' theory as to the latter group of defendants was that in promoting, raising money for, and otherwise working on behalf of Hamas, these defendants had helped to fund, train, and arm the terrorists who had killed their son. In *Boim v. Quranic Literacy Inst.*, 291 F.3d 1000 (7th Cir. 2002) ("*Boim I*"), we sustained the viability of the Boims' complaint, concluding that liability under section 2333 attached not only to the persons who committed terrorist acts, but to all those individuals and organizations along the causal chain of terrorism.

[In *Boim I*, the district court had denied the defendants' motions to dismiss but had certified three questions for interlocutory appeal:

(1)   Does funding, *simpliciter*, of an international terrorist organization constitute an act of terrorism under 18 U.S.C. § 2331?

(2)   Does 18 U.S.C. § 2333 incorporate the definitions of international terrorism found in 18 U.S.C. §§ 2339A and 2339B?

(3)   Does a civil cause of action lie under 18 U.S.C. §§ 2331 and 2333 for aiding and abetting international terrorism?

The Seventh Circuit's answers to these questions are discussed below in its consideration of the current appeal.]

On remand, the district court found appellants Muhammad Abdul Hamid Khalil Salah ("Salah"), Holy Land Foundation for Relief and Development ("HLF"), and American Muslim Society ("AMS") liable to the Boims on summary judgment. Boim v. Quranic Literacy Inst., 340 F. Supp. 2d 885 (N.D. Ill. 2004). At the conclusion of a trial, a jury concluded that appellant Quranic Literacy Institute ("QLI") also was liable. The jury awarded damages of $ 52 million, which the district court trebled to $ 156 million. Salah, HLF, AMS, and QLI all appeal.[1]

Salah, HLF, and AMS contend that the criteria employed by the district court for imposing liability were incomplete or incorrect and that the evidence adduced below did not suffice to impose liability. QLI complains of the district court's refusal to continue the trial date after the court's summary judgment rulings left it as the sole defendant facing a trial on liability; it also contends that the district court erred in *sua sponte* entering partial summary judgment against QLI as to one aspect of liability.

We reverse the entry of partial summary judgment as to liability against defendants HLF, AMS, and Salah. As to HLF, we conclude that the district court erred in giving collateral estoppel effect to the District of Columbia Circuit's finding that HLF funds the terrorist activities of Hamas. As to AMS and Salah, we conclude that the district court erroneously relieved the Boims of the burden of showing that these defendants' actions were a cause in fact of David Boim's death. As to QLI, we conclude that the district court erred in sua sponte and without prior notice applying its summary judgment determination against the other defendants that Hamas was responsible for the murder of David Boim, to QLI, against whom the Boims did not seek summary judgment. However, the district court did not abuse its discretion when it denied QLI's request to continue the trial date.

In light of the errors in the summary judgment rulings below, we vacate the judgments entered against these four appellants and remand for further proceedings. On remand, the Boims will have to demonstrate an adequate causal link between the death of David Boim and the actions of HLF, Salah, and AMS. This will require evidence that the conduct of each defendant, be it direct involvement with or support of Hamas's terrorist activities or indirect support of Hamas or its affiliates, helped bring about the terrorist attack that ended David Boim's life. A defendant's conduct need not have been the sole or predominant cause of the attack; on the contrary, consistent with the intent of Congress that liability for terrorism extend the full length of the causal chain, even conduct that indirectly facilitated Hamas's terrorist activities might render a defendant liable for the death of David Boim. But the plaintiffs must be able to produce some evidence permitting a jury to find that the activities of HLF, Salah, and AMS contributed to the fatal attack on David Boim and were therefore a cause in fact of his death. Absent such proof, those appellants will be entitled to judgment in their

---

[1]   [Court's Footnote 1] The district court deemed a number of other defendants jointly and several liable for the judgment. No other defendants have appealed, however, and their liability consequently is not before us.

favor. As to QLI, which has not challenged the liability standard employed by the district court, the remand will be limited to the question of whether Hamas was responsible for the murder of David Boim. QLI will be given the opportunity (of which it was deprived by the district court's *sua sponte* summary judgment ruling) to attempt to demonstrate that there exists a dispute of material fact on this point.

I.

A.

The Boims moved to Israel from the United States in 1985 to pursue a more spiritual life. David was fifth of the Boim's seven children. In 1996, David was finishing his third year of high school and preparing to apply for college. He was an intelligent and determined student who dreamed of becoming a doctor. His classmates knew him as a warm, outgoing young man. "His trademark was his hug and his smile," recalled Yechiel Gellman, a friend and classmate. His mother described him as a peacemaker.

David studied in a yeshiva near Beit-El, a small West Bank village north of Jerusalem. By 3:30 p.m. on May 13, 1996, the school day had concluded. David and several of his classmates had gathered at a bus stop on a busy road between Jerusalem and Nablus. It was a hot, early-summer afternoon, and the boys were telling jokes and sharing stories as they awaited the bus that would carry them to Jerusalem, where they were taking a class to prepare them for their college entrance examinations. Shortly before 4:00 p.m., a car pulled off the road and stopped ten feet away from the assemblage of people at the bus stop; one or more of the car's occupants then opened fire. Gellman estimated that a total of thirty shots were fired; he could hear the bullets shrieking past his head. "[To] this day, I don't understand how I survived the shooting." He heard his friend Yair cry out, and he turned to see both Yair and David fall to the ground. David had been shot in the head. A passing dentist stopped and tried to revive him. He was subsequently evacuated by ambulance to a local hospital and then transferred to a second hospital for surgery. He died shortly after he was taken into the operating room. He was buried in Jerusalem that same evening after a service attended by his classmates and thousands of other mourners. "Part of me was taken away" the day he died, Joyce Boim would later testify. David was seventeen years old.

B.

The murder of David Boim was later attributed to two individuals: Amjad Hinawi and Khalil Tawfiq Al-Sharif. Both were apprehended by the Palestinian Authority in 1997 and then released pending trial. Al-Sharif killed himself in a suicide bombing at a shopping mall in Jerusalem later that same year. Hinawi was tried by a Palestinian Authority tribunal and convicted of participating in a terrorist attack and being an accomplice to Boim's murder. He was sentenced to ten years of hard labor.

Both Al-Sharif and Hinawi were believed to be members of the terrorist or "military" wing of Hamas.[2] Hamas is an organization that was founded in 1987 as an out-growth of the Muslim Brotherhood in Egypt. Its name is derived from an acronym for "Harakat al-Muqawama al-Islamiyya," which in English means the "Islamic Resistance Movement." Its charter, written in 1988, calls for the obliteration of the

---

[2] [Court's Footnote 3] We say "believed to be" because not all of the defendants have conceded that Al-Sharif and Hinawi were members of Hamas and that they murdered David Boim in furtherance of Hamas-sponsored terrorism. Although AMS/IAP concedes the point, one defendant's concession cannot bind another. Similarly, although a default judgment was entered against Hinwai, his default cannot bind the other defendants. As we further discuss, there is an array of problems with the evidence that the Boims have offered in order to establish that Al-Sharif and Hinawi were members of Hamas and that Hamas was responsible for David's murder.

State of Israel and the establishment of an Islamic republic in the area now comprising Israel, the West Bank, and the Gaza Strip. Soon after its founding, Hamas began to engage in terrorist attacks on both civilian and military targets. It was officially designated a terrorist organization by the United States Department of the Treasury's Office of Foreign Assets Control ("OFAC") on January 24, 1995. That designation made it illegal for a United States citizen or entity to engage in any transactions or dealings involving the property or interests of Hamas without license to do so. Hamas was subsequently deemed a foreign terrorist organization by the United States Secretary of State on October 8, 1997, a designation that made it illegal for anyone within the United States or subject to its jurisdiction to provide material support or resources to Hamas.

In addition to its military wing, Hamas has a political wing that advocates on behalf of the Palestinian people. Hamas also operates a network of social institutions known as Da'wa which provide medical care, schooling, and other services to Palestinians living in and around the Gaza Strip and the West Bank. Hamas's charitable endeavors have helped it to achieve a position of influence among the Palestinian people. That influence was evident in the 2006 election of Hamas candidates to governing positions within the Palestinian Authority.

C.

Pursuant to section 2333, Joyce and Stanley Boim sued a variety of individuals and organizations for their son's death. Joyce Boim would later testify that their aim was to keep "even one nickel" from Hamas that might be used for further terrorist acts like the murder of her son. In addition to Hinawi and Al-Sharif, to whom the murder of David Boim was directly attributed, the Boims' amended complaint named as defendants a variety of individuals and organizations with ties to Hamas. Among them are the four appellants:

1. Salah is a naturalized United States citizen who allegedly has served as the U.S.-based leader of Hamas's military wing. Salah was arrested at a Gaza checkpoint in January 1993 by Israeli military authorities and was subsequently charged with being an active member of, holding office in, and performing services for an illicit organization (Hamas), engaging in activity against the public order and undermining regional security, and providing shelter to terrorists. Salah ultimately pleaded guilty to these offenses and was incarcerated in Israel until his release in or around November 1997. In 1995, while he was incarcerated in Israel, the U.S. Treasury Department's OFAC added Salah to the government's list of specially designated terrorists. After he was released by the Israeli military authorities, Salah returned to the United States. In 2004, a grand jury in the Northern District of Illinois indicted Salah and others for: conspiring (beginning in 1988) to conduct and participate in the affairs of an enterprise (Hamas) through a pattern of criminal acts (including murder, kidnaping, hostage taking, money laundering, obstruction of justice, and forgery) in violation of the Racketeer Influenced and Corrupt Organizations Act, 18 U.S.C. § 1962(d) ("RICO"); knowingly providing and attempting to provide material support and resources to a foreign terrorist organization (Hamas) in violation of 18 U.S.C. § 2339B; and endeavoring to obstruct justice by giving false and misleading verified answers to interrogatories posed by the Boims in the instant civil litigation, in violation of 18 U.S.C. § 1503. The government dropped the material support charge shortly before trial. In February of this year, following a three-month trial, a jury acquitted Salah of the RICO conspiracy charge and convicted him of the obstruction charge. On July 11, 2007, the district court sentenced Salah to a prison term of twenty-one months on that charge.

2. HLF is an organization incorporated in the United States that the U.S. government has determined provided financial support to Hamas; it was effectively shut down by the government on that basis in 2001. HLF was incorporated as the Occupied Land Fund in California in 1989. It changed its name to HLF and relocated

to Texas in 1992. It is a not-for-profit organization which purported to fund humanitarian relief for Palestinian people in the West Bank, Gaza, and beyond. At one time, HLF described itself as the largest Muslim charity in the United States. As discussed in greater detail below, the government named HLF a specially designated terrorist organization and froze its assets in 2001 based on evidence that it supplied funds to Hamas and/or organizations affiliated with Hamas. In 2004, the government indicted HLF and seven of its principals for, inter alia, providing and conspiring to provide material support and resources to a foreign terrorist organization (Hamas) in violation of 18 U.S.C. § 2339B(a)(1). The indictment alleges that HLF channeled substantial financial support to Hamas through ostensibly charitable committees and organizations affiliated with Hamas. A two-month trial in the Northern District of Texas recently ended in a mistrial after the jury was unable to reach a verdict as to most of the charges, including those against HLF.

3. AMS is a now-defunct organization incorporated in the United States which did business as the Islamic Association of Palestine (IAP). Over time there have been multiple AMS/IAP entities at the local and national levels. The Boims' theory is that they all constituted a single entity, a proposition with which the district court agreed. We shall refer to this entity as AMS/IAP. AMS/IAP allegedly provided financial support to Hamas through HLF. IAP, which was headquartered in Chicago, described itself as a not-for-profit, grass-roots organization dedicated to advancing a just, comprehensive, and eternal solution to the cause of the Palestine people through political, social, and educational efforts. The U.S. government considers IAP to have acted as a front for Hamas in the U.S. by, for example, reprinting Hamas communiques in its periodical publications.

4. QLI is another U.S. organization that allegedly raised and laundered money for Hamas. QLI is an Illinois not-for-profit organization that was incorporated in 1990 and has operated in the Chicago area since that time. Ostensibly, its central endeavor was to undertake an authoritative translation into English of the principal texts of Islam. Salah worked for QLI beginning in the late 1980s or early 1990s and until 1993, when he was arrested in Israel. According to the plaintiffs, QLI aided Hamas and Salah in two ways: it gave cover to Salah by providing him with apparently legitimate employment while he was actually working on Hamas's behalf, and it helped to raise money for and funnel money to Hamas.

D.

Section 2333(a) permits U.S. nationals who have been injured "by reason of an act of international terrorism" to sue for their injuries in federal court and to recover treble damages. It is both a fair inference — and undisputed — that the murder of David Boim constitutes an act of international terrorism as so defined. It is equally plain that the individuals who themselves killed David — purportedly Hinawi and Al-Sharif — would be liable to the Boims under section 2333; and, indeed, a default judgment was entered against Hinawi below. (The Boims sued Al-Sharif's estate, but after they were unsuccessful in attempting service, the estate was dismissed from the suit.) We may also assume that Hamas, upon proof that Hinawi and Al-Sharif committed the murder at its behest or with its support, likewise would be liable to the Boims, although Hamas has not been named a defendant in this suit. But what has been vigorously disputed from the inception of this litigation is whether and under what circumstances persons and groups who allegedly have provided money and other support to Hamas (directly and indirectly) may also be liable for David's murder.

Salah, HLF, AMS, and QLI all moved to dismiss the Boims' complaint for failure to state a claim against them, and in *Boim I*, we affirmed the district court's decision not to do so. We concluded that section 2333 reflects an intent by Congress to allow a U.S. national injured by reason of international terrorism to recover from anyone along the causal chain of terrorism and that liability is not limited to those who commit the violent act that causes injury. Thus, to the extent that a third party had provided money or other support to a terrorist who engaged in a terrorist act, that party potentially could be held liable for the resulting injury along with the terrorist himself.

However, in response to the first of three questions the district court had certified for interlocutory review, we did reject the proposition that merely giving money to an organization engaged in terrorism, without more, would constitute an act of international terrorism sufficient to render the donor liable under section 2333.

> To say that funding simpliciter constitutes an act of terrorism is to give the statute an almost unlimited reach. Any act which turns out to facilitate terrorism, however remote that act may be from actual violence and regardless of the actor's intent, could be construed to "involve" terrorism. Without also requiring the plaintiffs to show knowledge of and intent to further the payee's violent criminal acts, such a broad definition might also lead to constitutional infirmities by punishing mere association with groups that engage in terrorism.

Thus, those injured by reason of the knowing and intentional financing of terrorist organizations and activities as proscribed by these two statutory provisions would be entitled to recover under section 2333, provided that causation can be shown as in traditional tort law. Financial support need not be substantial in order to qualify as material support; "even small donations made knowingly and intentionally in support of terrorism may meet the standard for civil liability under section 2333."[3]

Finally, we answered the last of the certified questions by holding that aiding and abetting an act of international terrorism would also support liability under section 2333. "The statute would have little effect if liability were limited to those who pull the trigger or plant the bomb because such persons are unlikely to have assets, much less assets in the United States, and would not be deterred by the statute." Thus, those who knowingly and intentionally aid terrorist acts by providing funds or other support to those who commit the acts could be held liable under the statute, consistent with "Congress' clearly expressed intent to cut off the flow of money to terrorists at every point along the causal chain of violence."

To establish a defendant's liability for aiding and abetting the terrorist acts of an organization like Hamas, the plaintiff would have to show that the defendant knew of Hamas's illegal activities, that the defendant desired to help those activities succeed, and that the defendant engaged in some act of helping the illegal conduct.

The jury found in favor of the Boims and against QLI on liability. It awarded damages of $ 52 million against all four defendants (QLI, HLF, IAP/AMS, and Salah). Those damages were subsequently trebled as provided in section 2333(a).

II. HOLY LAND FOUNDATION

A. Collateral Estoppel Based on DC Litigation Over IEEPA Designation

In litigation challenging the government's 2001 decision to name HLF a specially designated terrorist organization, the District of Columbia Circuit found that HLF had funded the terrorist activities of Hamas. As we have noted, the district court in this case gave that finding collateral estoppel effect and relied on that finding to hold HLF liable to the Boims on summary judgment. HLF contends that it was inappropriate for the

---

[3] [Court's Footnote 4] As we made clear, we were citing sections 2339A and 2339B and the conduct they criminalize solely to illustrate the types of activity that might qualify as acts of international terrorism for purposes of section 2333; we were not suggesting that the Boims would have to establish a violation of either of these two criminal statutes in order to prevail under section 2333. Indeed, section 2339B was not enacted until 1996, and Hamas was not designated a foreign terrorist organization to which section 2339B prohibits financial support until 1997, after David Boim was murdered.

court to grant the D.C. Circuit's finding collateral estoppel effect in the instant litigation. For the reasons that follow, we agree.

[The court reviewed the litigation and opinion of the D.C. Circuit in *HLF v. Ashcroft* at § 3.03[B] *supra.*]

It was the District of Columbia Circuit's resolution of HLF's First Amendment challenges to the blocking order that formed the springboard for the district court's invocation of collateral estoppel here. In particular, the district court relied upon the D.C. Circuit's finding that the "ample record evidence" before that court, including the classified evidence submitted in camera, proved "incontrovertibl[y]" that HLF funded Hamas and its terrorist activities. That language led the district court to conclude that HLF's provision of material support to Hamas was actually litigated in the prior action and was essential to the D.C. Circuit's decision to sustain the dismissal of HLF's First Amendment claims. The district court was also satisfied that HLF had been given a full and fair opportunity to litigate the subject of its financial support of Hamas in the prior litigation.

The district court acknowledged that the D.C. Circuit, in deeming HLF's role in funding terrorism incontrovertible, had in part relied on classified evidence presented to that court in camera. No one other than the government and the D.C. Circuit knew what that evidence was. However, in the district court's view, the secrecy shrouding that evidence "d[id] not vitiate the potential conclusive effect of the D.C. Circuit's judgment."

[A]lthough there undoubtedly is some factual overlap between the *Ashcroft* litigation and this case, the questions posed by the two suits are distinct. In *Ashcroft*, the issue posed by HLF's First Amendment challenge to the blocking order was whether it funded (directly or indirectly) Hamas's terrorist activities. Here, the question is whether HLF funded Hamas's terrorism knowingly — for example, realizing that it was giving money to charities controlled by Hamas, and that donations to such charities either would be diverted to terrorist ends or would free up other funds for terrorist activity — and intentionally. Furthermore, the litigation in the D.C. Circuit directly concerned the government's ability to further the national security and conduct the foreign policy of the United States by stopping the flow of funds from organizations in the United States to terrorist entities abroad by freezing those assets before they can leave this country. Nothing that this court, the district judge, or a jury might say in this case would affect HLF's designation as an SDT or SDGT or confine the government's ability to rely on that designation in the future. The validity of the designation is not at stake here. Instead, this suit looks backward to determine whether HLF knowingly and intentionally supported Hamas's terrorist activities in a way that had some causal connection with David's murder, which occurred before HLF was even designated an SDT and SDGT.

Because the questions presented by the *Ashcroft* litigation and this suit are not identical, HLF cannot be collaterally estopped from litigating here whether it knowingly provided financial (or other) support to Hamas with the intent to further Hamas's terrorist activities.

As we proceed to discuss below with respect to defendants AMS and Salah, the district court mistakenly believed that an organization or individual that contributed money or other support to Hamas with the intent to support its terrorist activities could be liable to the Boims even in the absence of proof that the money or support given to Hamas was a cause in fact of David's death, so long as the murder of David was foreseeable to the donor individual or organization. This misunderstanding of our opinion in *Boim I* requires the reversal of the partial summary judgments deeming AMS and Salah liable to the Boims. It constitutes a second basis for reversing the entry of partial summary judgment against HLF, as there has been no finding that HLF's financial support of Hamas was a cause in fact of David Boim's death.

III. American Muslim Society

Relying on *Boim I*, the district court stated that in order for AMS/IAP to be liable to the Boims, it must have (a) known about Hamas's illegal activities, (b) desired to help those activities succeed, and (c) engaged in some act of helping. These are the elements we identified as necessary to render a defendant liable for aiding and abetting an act of international terrorism committed by or on behalf of Hamas. In the [district] court's view, the undisputed facts established each of these three elements.

First, representatives of AMS/IAP had participated in the October 1993 Philadelphia meeting, which Hamas officials and representatives of HLS had also attended. The Watson memorandum [Assistant Director of the FBI Counterterrorism Division summarizing evidence for the OFAC designation] noted that the recurring theme of the discussions captured by FBI surveillance was how entities affiliated with and working for Hamas should operate in light of the Oslo Accord, in which Yassir Arafat and Yitzhak Rabin had recognized — on behalf of Palestinians and Israelis — the right of each to exist and had committed to negotiate a permanent settlement and means to improved relations. According to Agent Watson, participants in the Philadelphia meeting universally condemned the Accord and discussed ways in which they might undermine the Accord and continue to support Hamas inside what they referred to as the "Occupied Territories."

Second, IAP and AMS (and others within IAP umbrella) had contributed money to HLF and routinely and consistently encouraged others to donate to HLF and otherwise assisted HLF's fundraising. HLF, of course, had links to Hamas that had led the OFAC to conclude that it acted "for or on behalf of" Hamas. Taken in the context of other evidence, "this is strong evidence that IAP was supporting Hamas, consistent with the FBI surveillance reports."

Third, IAP and AMS had published and distributed pro-Hamas documents, including the Hamas charter and, more recently, documents that included an editorial by Khalid Amyreh advocating "martyrdom" operations, meeting death with death, and killing Jews. IAP had paid Amyreh for his materials, but denied that it necessarily published the editorial because it shared his views.

Fourth, when individuals with ties to Hamas were arrested and/or charged with supporting terrorism, IAP and AMS sought to rally public support for them. Following Salah's arrest in Israel, for example, IAP National and AMS held a number of events to garner public support for his release. The district court recognized that these activities were not against the law, "[b]ut all of this does tend to evidence a desire on the part of IAP to help Hamas succeed."

Fifth, IAP had held annual conferences, invited pro-Hamas speakers to participate in these gatherings, and paid their travel expenses. An IAP conference in 1989 had featured a veiled Hamas terrorist as a guest speaker.

What is strikingly absent from the district court's analysis is any consideration of a causal link between the assistance that the court found AMS/IAP to have given Hamas and the murder of David Boim. The court made no finding as to the existence of such a link, nor did it acknowledge that causation was a necessary element of the Boims' case.

Indeed, in its subsequent discussion of Salah's liability, the court appears to have said that no such causal link was required:

> The Seventh Circuit did not say that, to impose liability under § 2333, the Boims have to link Mr. Salah or any of the other defendants specifically to the attack that killed David Boim; rather, the court held that, to impose liability for aiding and abetting — that is, providing material support to[4] — a terrorist

---

[4] [Court's Footnote 14] [Footnote added by this court] Although providing material support to a terrorist organization would be one way to aid and abet that organization's terrorist activities, one could aid and abet

organization, the Boims need only show that the defendants knew of Hamas' illegal activities, that they desired to help those activities succeed, and that they engaged in some act of helping. The evidence shows that all three are true with respect to Mr. Salah and no reasonable jury could find otherwise.

The court added that Salah would be liable under civil conspiracy principles for acts in furtherance of a conspiracy to fund Hamas, even if those acts were committed after he ceased being an active participant (assuming that he did not withdraw from the conspiracy and disavow its aim). Thus, even if plaintiffs could not establish that Salah provided material support to Hamas (which, in the court's view, they had shown, though it did not expand on this point), Salah could still be liable to the Boims if their son's death was a reasonably foreseeable consequence "of the conspiracy that was Hamas."

The Boims defend the district court's silence as to causation (and in Salah's case, the court's apparent rejection of the need for proof of cause in fact) on the ground that our opinion in *Boim I* did not require it. In their view, all that need be shown is that it was foreseeable to the defendants that their support of Hamas might result in someone's death. This constitutes a profound misreading of our decision in *Boim I*.

Contrary to the district court's apparent impression, this court's opinion in *Boim I* did not relieve plaintiffs of the burden of showing causation in fact. We observed that the legislative history of the statute reveals an intent to codify general common law tort principles and to extend civil liability for acts of international terrorism to the full reaches of traditional tort law. We added that the statute itself reflects all of the elements of a traditional tort: a breach of duty (committing an act of international terrorism), an injury to the person, etc. of another, and causation (injured "by reason of").

What the statute does not do is identify the class of defendants who may be held liable, and this was the question that we proceeded to answer. We stated that the statute was clearly meant to reach not only those individuals who themselves commit the violent act that directly causes the injury, but rather extends to "anyone along the causal chain of terrorism." We added, however, that funding a terrorist organization by itself would not be enough to place someone in this causal chain. To say that funding alone sufficed would give the statute an almost unlimited reach. Rather, in addition to establishing funding (or some other act of supporting terrorism), the plaintiff would have to establish the defendant acted with knowledge of the terrorist activity and the intent to support that activity. Moreover, the statute bestows the right to sue on a person injured "by reason of "an act of international terrorism, and that language, we said, requires a showing of proximate causation, which in turn requires proof that the injury was foreseeable to the defendant." In the very least, the plaintiffs must be able to show that murder was a reasonably foreseeable result of making a donation."

Neither the aiding and abetting theory of liability, which we endorsed in *Boim I*, nor civil conspiracy, which the Boims pursued in their amended complaint on remand, obviates the need for a showing of cause in fact. Neither is an independent tort; each is simply a vehicle for spreading liability for a tortious act committed by another. So although the Boims might prevail by showing that a defendant aided and abetted someone else (e.g., HLF) in providing material support or resources to Hamas for its terrorist activities — for example, by hosting a fundraiser for HLF, knowing and intending that the funds raised would be funneled to Hamas to support terrorism — there still must be proof that the provision of material support or resources was in some way a cause of David Boim's death.

There are any number of ways in which the plaintiffs might be able to establish causation in fact. One way, of course, would be to establish a direct causal link between

---

the organization's terrorist acts in other ways as well. Lending material support to terrorist activity or a terrorist organization is actually a theory of liability that is separate and distinct from aiding and abetting an act of international terrorism, as our opinion in *Boim I* makes clear.

the defendants' acts and the murder of David Boim. The plaintiffs posited such a link in *Boim I*, theorizing that the defendants had channeled funds into a central pool of money that was used to train terrorists, buy their weapons, and so forth — and that the terrorists who killed David Boim had been trained and armed using those funds.

Nothing in *Boim I* demands that the plaintiffs establish a direct link between the defendants' donations (or other conduct) and David Boim's murder — that they funded in particular the terrorists who killed David Boim, for example — in view of the fact that money is fungible and the victims of terrorism are often killed or injured at random, as he was. For example, the Boims have pointed out that in his August 1995 statement, Salah wrote that in the early 1990s, he had helped to test and train terrorists, funneled money to Hamas for the purchase of weapons, and had coordinated with other Hamas leaders in rebuilding Hamas's infra-structure and command. If one were to credit Salah's statement, one reasonably might conclude that any number of terrorist acts subsequently committed by Hamas (and the resulting injuries) were in part caused by Salah's actions, even if Salah had no role in planning and executing a particular terrorist act. Similarly, if an individual or organization established a funding network in the United States designed to provide ongoing financial support for Hamas's terrorist activities, a factfinder might reasonably infer that the act of establishing that network was a cause of ensuing acts of Hamas terrorism, even if no line could be drawn linking a particular dollar raised to a particular terrorist act. As these hypotheticals suggest, the nature and significance of a defendant's action along with its chronological relationship to the terrorist act that injured the plaintiff would be important considerations in assessing whether the defendant caused the plaintiff's injury. Terrorist acts that follow within a reasonable time the donations and other support provided by a defendant to the perpetrators of those acts could be deemed to have been caused by those acts; and the more significant the support provided by a defendant, the more readily one might infer that support was a cause of later terrorist acts.

We add that a defendant's conduct need not be the sole circumstance responsible for a terrorist act in order to qualify as a cause in fact; it is enough that it be a cause of the act and the resulting harm. Alternatively, if the plaintiffs were able to show that by providing funding to Hamas's other activities, including the hospitals, schools, and other charitable missions that it sponsors, a donor frees up Hamas resources for, or otherwise makes possible, Hamas's terrorist activities, then proof that the defendants provided support to Hamas ostensibly for its humanitarian activities, but with the knowledge and intent that Hamas be able to conduct terrorism also, might support the inference that the defendants were a cause of terrorist activity of the kind that resulted in David Boim's death. But without some evidence of a causal link between a defendant's conduct and Boim's murder, proof that a defendant supported, aided and abetted, or conspired with Hamas (or an intermediary like HLF) will not suffice to render that defendant liable to the Boims.

None of this should be understood to rule out the possibility that relatively modest financial contributions to terrorists or other minor acts of support would be sufficient to render the donor liable for the injuries subsequently inflicted by terrorists. As we have noted, but-for causation does not demand a showing that the defendant's conduct was the sole cause of the plaintiff's injury; the conduct need only be one of the causes. A plaintiff might well be unable to show that a terrorist organization such as Hamas depended on a particular donor to support its terrorism, for example, or that one act of terrorism owed its existence to a specific donation. But a careful showing that many small donations collectively resulted in a cache of funds that in turn enabled a series of terrorist acts would permit a factfinder reasonably to infer a causal connection between the contribution made by a single donor and one of the terrorist acts made possible by that donor and others like him, even if a single donation would not by itself have been enough to cause that terrorist act.

We note that neither AMS/IAP nor any of the other appellants has challenged the amount of damages that the jury awarded to the Boims. Therefore, if the district court on remand concludes that the undisputed facts establish a causal link between a defendant's conduct and David Boim's murder, the court may reinstate the judgment as to that defendant. If the court finds that the evidence necessitates a trial as to cause in fact as to any defendant, then the judgment may be reinstated against any defendant whose conduct the jury determines to be a cause in fact of David's death.

IV. Mohammad Salah

The partial summary judgment entered against Salah is flawed for the same reasons that we have discussed as to AMS/IAP. Although there was a separate set of facts regarding Salah's links to Hamas (which Salah does not contest for purposes of this appeal), the district court relied on the same incomplete recitation of what would be necessary to establish a defendant's liability as an aider and abettor. The court stated that Salah would be liable for David Boim's death so long as he knew of Hamas's terrorist activities, desired to help those activities succeed, and engaged in some act of helping. The court did not insist on any proof of cause in fact or make any finding that Salah's actions in support of Hamas, and/or his participation in the undefined "conspiracy that was Hamas," had any causal nexus with David Boim's murder.

The court's statement that *Boim I* did not require a link to David Boim's death in particular, id., was correct insofar as a direct link between Salah's actions and the killing of David Boim need not be shown. We have mentioned above ways in which indirect causation might be proven. But *Boim I* certainly did not relieve the plaintiffs of establishing some form of causal link between a defendant's actions and David Boim's murder.

Salah was in Israeli custody in 1996 at the time of David Boim's murder and the plaintiffs have identified no evidence that he gave any sort of meaningful support to Hamas after January 1993 (when he was arrested), some forty months prior to the murder. The district court relied on conspiracy principles to say that Salah could be liable for acts post-dating his active involvement in the Hamas conspiracy so long as he did not renounce Hamas and withdraw from the conspiracy prior to David's killing.

There are at least two problems with this rationale. First, as we have discussed above, proof that Salah conspired with others in support of Hamas's terrorist aims and activities does not render Salah per se liable for all those injured by Hamas terrorists. Second, the plaintiffs' theory that Salah was a member of a Hamas-related conspiracy is not adequately supported. For its part, the district court simply pronounced Hamas a conspiracy without any discussion of the evidence that would support that pronouncement. Merely mouthing the word "conspiracy" is not enough to render a defendant liable for the acts of a third party, and certainly not on summary judgment.

So the partial summary judgment against Salah on liability must also be reversed. The evidentiary record before the district court must be re-examined on remand. Unless the plaintiffs can identify evidence that would permit a reasonable factfinder to find that Salah's actions on behalf of Hamas in some way caused or contributed to David Boim's death, Salah will be entitled to summary judgment.

V. Quranic Literacy Institute

Although a district court is not precluded from *sua sponte* granting summary judgment against a party, we have repeatedly warned that the court may not do so without first giving that party notice and the opportunity to respond. QLI was deprived of that opportunity.

For that reason, we vacate the judgment against QLI pending further proceedings in the district court. It is possible that the court's error as to QLI may prove to have been harmless, but that is a matter to be sorted out on remand. Our decision to vacate the judgment against QLI is without prejudice to the Boims seeking summary judgment on the question of Hamas's responsibility for David Boim's murder, provided that QLI is given the opportunity to respond of which it was deprived in the first instance. A jury finding that Hamas was responsible for David Boim's death would, again, call for reinstatement of the judgment against QLI. A jury finding to the contrary would, of course, compel the entry of judgment in favor of QLI.

VI.

We must briefly address the matter of a fees order entered against the defendants and/or their lawyers. On this record, the award of fees and expenses was defective, as the Boims all but concede.

VII.

Before concluding our opinion, we find it necessary to say a few words about potential hearsay problems presented by certain aspects of the Boims' case. In attempting to establish the defendants' links to terrorism, the Boims have relied heavily on out-of-court statements like the Watson memorandum, the contents of which are offered for the truth of the matters asserted therein. The district court relied on these documents in its summary judgment rulings, satisfied that the statements were fully admissible. Although portions of these statements may be admissible for limited purposes, the proscription against hearsay may render at least parts of these statements inadmissible for their truth. We direct the court on remand to undertake a careful evaluation of such statements to ensure that the Federal Rules of Evidence render them admissible for the purposes cited by the Boims. To aid in that evaluation, we note the potential problems posed by certain of the statements on which the Boims have relied.

Watson Memorandum. As we have noted, this memorandum was prepared by the Assistant Director of the FBI's Counterterrorism Division to document his recommendation that HLF be designated a terrorist organization by the Treasury Department's OFAC. The memorandum recounts at length the evidence that led Watson and his colleagues to conclude that HLF acted for or on behalf of Hamas. It primarily details the activities of HLF, naturally, but it also mentions the activities of Salah and representatives of AMS/IAP and makes a case for the notion that the activities of all of these defendants furthered the terrorist activities of Hamas. As the Watson memorandum set forth the basis for the government's decision to designate HLF an SDT, it was part of the administrative record before the court in the *Ashcroft* litigation.

We may assume, as the district court held, that the Watson memorandum, insofar as it embodies the results of the government's investigation into HLF's ties to Hamas, is admissible in this proceeding pursuant to Federal Rule of Evidence 803(8)(B) as a public report setting forth "matters observed pursuant to duty imposed by law as to which matters there was a duty to report."

[T]he Watson memorandum repeats a number of statements from informants and other individuals (in some instances unnamed) who, in contrast to Watson, were under no official duty to report the matters addressed in their statements. Rule 803(8) deems a public report admissible based on the notion that its official author knows what he is talking about and will state the facts accurately: "[i]n effect, it is presumed that public officials perform their tasks carefully and fairly, without bias or corruption, and this notion finds support in the scrutiny and risk of exposure that surround most government functions." 4 CHRISTOPHER B. MUELLER AND LAIRD C. KIRKPATRICK, FEDERAL EVIDENCE § 8:86, at 770–71 (3d ed. 2007). That presumption does not attach to the statements of third parties who themselves bear no public duty to report what they observe. Unless such statements have an independent basis for admission under the Rules, they must be excluded.

Websites attributed to Hamas. To show that the murder of David Boim was the work of Hamas, the Boims submitted the declaration of Dr. Ruven Paz, a former member of the Israeli security community who describes himself as an expert in terrorism and counter-terrorism, Islamic movements in the Arab and Islamic world, Palestinian Islamic groups, and Palestinian society and politics. Based on his review of various exhibits submitted in connection with this case, his independent research, and his knowledge of how Hamas and other Islamic terror organizations operate, Paz concluded that Hinawi and Al-Sharif had murdered David Boim, that Hinawi and Al-Sharif were members of Hamas at the time they killed Boim, and that Hamas itself had accepted responsibility for the murder.

Paz's reliance upon, and his recounting of, internet website postings demand a certain caution in evaluating his prospective testimony. Such postings would not be admissible into evidence for their truth absent proper authentication, and this would typically require some type of proof that the postings were actually made by the individual or organization to which they are being attributed — in this case, Hamas — as opposed to others with access to the website. Where, as here, the expert appears to be relying to a great extent on web postings to establish a particular fact, and where as a result the factfinder would be unable to evaluate the soundness of his conclusion without hearing the evidence he relied on, we believe the expert must lay out, in greater detail than Paz did, the basis for his conclusion that these websites are in fact controlled by Hamas and that the postings he cites can reasonably and reliably be attributed to Hamas.

There are other out-of-court statements that the Boims have relied upon directly or as the basis for witness testimony. We recognize that a case of this nature presents extraordinary challenges for a plaintiff and that resort to out-of-court statements will be necessary to show how international terrorist organizations and their accomplices operate. However, the Federal Rules of Evidence continue to govern, and the hearsay issues presented by such evidence demand careful attention and resolution.

VIII.

Our dissenting colleague parts ways with us in two respects. He believes that the undisputed facts show conclusively that Hamas was responsible for the murder of David Boim and that, contrary to our impression, the district court both required proof of and found that the acts of defendants AMS/IAP and Salah caused David's death.

With respect to Hamas's culpability for the murder, our point is not that an expert like Dr. Paz is foreclosed from relying on websites controlled by Hamas and/or Arab-language documents like Hinawi's judgment of conviction for information about who killed David Boim and whether they did so on Hamas's behalf. Our point is that when the plaintiffs rely solely on expert opinion to establish such facts, as the Boims have on appeal, the expert's declaration must reveal enough about his sources of information to permit the court to assess the reliability of his conclusions.

The notion that the district court both considered and found causation in fact simply cannot be squared with the record. One may search the district court's summary judgment decision from beginning to end and locate no such finding. Indeed, although our colleague believes that the court found causation, he cites no portion of the district court's opinion making such a finding. It is true, as Judge Evans points out, that the district court looked for and identified evidence that the defendants had engaged in some act of helping Hamas. But proof that a defendant helped Hamas, with knowledge of its terrorist activities and the intent that those activities succeed, is not the same thing as proof that the defendant's aid actually caused a particular injury. Causation remains a distinct element of proof that must be satisfied if the defendant is to be held liable for aiding and abetting Hamas's tortious acts. Otherwise, we would be saying that one who aids Hamas with the requisite knowledge and intent — whether by donating money to a Hamas-controlled school or by hosting a Hamas speaker at a conference — is automatically liable for any and all of Hamas's later terrorist acts, regardless of whether the aid played any role whatsoever in bringing those acts about. It may be that plaintiffs can demonstrate a causal link between the defendants' acts and the murder of David

Boim, but they have yet to identify such proof and the district court has yet to consider it.

IX.

The district court's task at this juncture is to apply the legal standards that we have discussed here to the parts of the case in which summary judgment was granted. Our key point here has been that knowledge, intent, and cause in fact must be proven, not assumed, with respect to each defendant.

Our basic point here has been that the statute does not demand an outright admission of responsibility for David Boim's murder (assuming that the terrorist act in question is that murder) or specific tracing of donations to Hamas or to the assassins (assuming that it is enough to show that the defendants aided and abetted a terrorist organization). Circumstantial evidence will also suffice. So far, however, that step has been skipped. On remand, the plaintiffs must demonstrate how (or show that there are no material issues of fact regarding how) the monetary donations from the defendant organizations supported the activities that grew to include the acts of terrorism. One way to do this, we suggested, would be to show that donations went into a central pool of funds that provided weapons and training for Hamas agents. Plaintiffs would need to show that Hinawi and Al-Sharif were affiliated with Hamas, but they would not otherwise have to show that funds from a particular defendant organization made their way to those two particular Hamas operatives. Another avenue would be to demonstrate that money from the defendant organizations went to Hamas for its charitable endeavors, and thereby freed up funds that Hamas could use for terrorist activities during the time period when David Boim was killed. These examples do not exhaust the possibilities. A comparable showing will, of course, have to be made as to defendant Salah as well.

Belief, assumption, and speculation are no substitutes for evidence in a court of law. However the plaintiffs might establish a line of proof connecting the defendants with the murder of David Boim, the law demands that they demonstrate such a nexus before any defendant may be held liable for David's death. We must resist the temptation to gloss over error, admit spurious evidence, and assume facts not adequately proved simply to side with the face of innocence and against the face of terrorism. Our endeavor to adhere to the dictates of law that this great nation has embodied since its founding must persevere, no matter how great our desire to hold someone accountable for the unspeakably evil acts that ended David Boim's life and created a lifetime of grief not only for the Boims but also for every other family scarred by terrorism.

X.

For the foregoing reasons, we VACATE the judgments entered against defendants-appellants HLF, AMS/IAP, Salah, and QLI and REMAND for further proceedings consistent with this opinion.

EVANS, CIRCUIT JUDGE, concurring in part and dissenting in part.

My review of this case causes me to conclude, as did Judge Keys, that the undisputed facts show that Hamas and its agents were responsible for the murder of David Boim. Furthermore, I cannot conclude that the judge failed to require a causal link between the defendants and the terrorist attack. For those reasons, I respectfully dissent, except as to the reversal of the judgment against the Holy Land Foundation. Given that the reader is probably suffering fatigue at this point, I will be brief. [But your editor nevertheless excised substantial portions of the opinion.]

The immediate cause-in-fact of the injury here was that two men gunned David down in what can only be considered a terrorist act. My first departure from the majority is in its apparent conclusion that the Boims failed to show that the two gunmen — Al-Sharif and Hinawi — and Hamas were in fact responsible for the murder, as AMS and IAP concede. I disagree with the majority's rejection of the expert opinion of Dr. Ruven Paz and the other evidence on which the district court relied in concluding that Hamas was, in fact, responsible for a murder it publicly took responsibility for. Dr. Paz is a former member of the Israeli security community who is an expert in terrorism in the Arab world and is fluent in Arabic. In reaching his conclusions, he analyzed many sources of data, including Web sites controlled by Hamas and documents related to Hinawi's trial and sentencing for Boim's murder. It seems particularly absurd for us to reject, as an underpinning for an expert opinion, what he believes to be the official verdict against Hinawi in this matter.

[T]he majority seems most concerned about . . . what needs to be proven to establish that in fact the defendants before us aided the terrorists. The majority refers to this requirement variously as cause-in-fact, direct cause, factual cause, causal chain, and causal link. No one would seriously dispute that there must be a causal link between the defendants and the terrorist act. A person or entity knowingly giving money to another terrorist group is not responsible for a murder committed by agents of Hamas.

But just what does "causal link" mean in this context, and how must one prove that the link exists between the defendants and Hamas? The majority wisely declines to set up an absurd requirement that the money given to Hamas by the defendants must be traced directly to, say, purchasing the gun used in the attack. Money, the majority recognizes, is fungible. At times, though, it seems that the majority is requiring a pretty clear trail leading from a defendant to the specific act which caused David's death.

The majority's bottom line, with which I do not disagree, assuming I read it correctly, seems to be that what must be shown is that the defendant established a funding network or provided "general support" for terrorist activities; if that is established, then the fact finder could infer that establishing the network was a cause of Hamas terrorism. That is especially true if the funding was within a reasonable time of the terrorist act and if it was significant.

As to the causal link, it seems to me that there is, at best, only a semantic difference between what the majority requires and what Judge Keys spent pages and pages examining. To reiterate, the majority says that what is required is, for instance, a funding network providing financial support of Hamas's terrorist activities, or other "general support" from which one can infer that the network was a cause of the acts of terrorism.

[Salah] contributed money to Hamas operatives for the purpose of carrying out terrorist activities. He provided money to a Hamas operative to buy weapons to be used in terrorist operations. In a statement he gave while in Israeli custody, he describes meetings with Hamas operatives regarding military operations. Salah's response to the Boims' evidence is not to offer facts which dispute it, but primarily to move to strike the evidence on various grounds and to contend that his statement was procured by torture. Judge Keys carefully considered Salah's arguments but concluded that the evidence was reliable. My review of the record convinces me that the standard the majority has articulated for a causal link has been met as to Salah.

AMS/IAP published and distributed pro-Hamas documents, including one which contained an editorial that advocated martyrdom operations, meeting death with death, and killing Jews. In addition, AMS/IAP published documents designed to garner public support for Marzook. IAP held annual conferences and invited pro-Hamas speakers and paid for their travel expenses, even including at one conference a veiled Hamas terrorist. There is a significant amount of evidence which shows that they contributed money to HLF and that they encouraged others to donate, knowing the money went to Hamas and its military activities.

The latter evidence loses its force, of course, because, in a part of the majority's opinion with which I agree, the grant of summary judgment against HLF has been over-turned. I agree that the district court erred in granting collateral estoppel effect to the decision in *Ashcroft*. Though if HLF is ultimately found to be liable, the evidence against AMS/IAP is strengthened as well. But I believe that, even without the evidence involving HLF, the Boims have shown AMS/IAP's "general support" for Hamas terrorist activities from which one can infer their actions were a cause of ensuing acts of Hamas terrorism.

Accordingly, I respectfully dissent from the court's decision as to all defendants except HLF. As to HLF, I join the majority opinion.

NOTES AND QUESTIONS

1. Fungible Money and Tort Causation. The cases under § 2339B have accepted that the defendant is guilty of a crime for providing $10,000 to a designated FTO for blankets and food because that frees up money that can be spent on weapons — regardless of whether any weapons actually are bought. The *Boim* court holds that for tort liability, you have to show that harm actually occurred. So does the plaintiff in a civil case have to show more than the prosecution in a criminal case?

Indeed, in several places, the court seems to accept the principle of § 2339B that money is fungible but seems nevertheless to insist on some tracking of a link between specific funds and specific acts. How do you read the following statements?

> [I]f the plaintiffs were able to show that by providing funding to Hamas's other activities, including the hospitals, schools, and other charitable missions that it sponsors, a donor frees up Hamas resources for, or otherwise makes possible, Hamas's terrorist activities, then proof that the defendants provided support to Hamas ostensibly for its humanitarian activities, but with the knowledge and intent that Hamas be able to conduct terrorism also, might support the inference that the defendants were a cause of terrorist activity of the kind that resulted in David Boim's death. But without some evidence of a causal link between a defendant's conduct and Boim's murder, . . . [t]he actual use to which the funds and other support that the defendants allegedly provided to Hamas and its intermediaries was put would be irrelevant.

If Congress has already made a legal determination of the facts described in the first sentence, then what is the point of the second sentence? Hasn't Congress made "the actual use to which the funds" were put irrelevant?

2. "Involvement" and Causation. The court decides that a person cannot be held liable for the actions of another unless "involved" in that conduct. A careful parsing of the statutes is necessary to set the context for this discussion. The source of law for a federal civil action is § 2333, which refers to "international terrorism," which is defined in § 2331 as an act that "involves" violence. The defendants' argument was that provision of money does not "involve" violence, to which the court responds that the statute "reaches beyond those persons who commit the violent act." At the other extreme, mere supplying of money is not enough to "involve" the donor. Are you satisfied that the court has provided a workable test in the middle ground?

What is the relevance of the criminal material support statues, § 2339A and § 2339B? Why not simply imply a private right of action from the criminal provisions? What is the point of the discussion about aiding and abetting in light of the previous holding that the defendant must be "involved" in the act?

3. *Pugh v. Socialist People's Libyan Arab Jamahiriya*. *Pugh v. Socialist People's Libyan Arab Jamahiriya*, 290 F. Supp. 2d 54 (D.D.C. 2003). This opinion addressed the question of personal jurisdiction over individual defendants in a § 2333 case. Libya was a defendant along with seven individual defendants in wrongful death actions arising from the bombing of a UTA flight over Africa in which seven U.S. citizens were killed. The State was subject to personal jurisdiction under the reasoning of *Price*, but the individual defendants claimed they had not contacts with the U.S. The district court responded:

> While the courts and legislatures have developed numerous approaches to

ascertaining whether a defendant meets the "minimum contacts" test, the single most important consideration is whether a defendant's "conduct and connection with the forum State are such that he should reasonably anticipate being haled into court there." Taking the factual allegations of the complaint as true for present purposes, the individual defendants in the instant action conspired to sabotage and succeeded in destroying a civilian commercial aircraft filled to capacity with innocent and unsuspecting passengers while in flight. As the plane they chose to destroy was on an international flight and expected to stop in several nations before reaching its final destination, the individual defendants could and should have reasonably postulated that passengers of many nationalities would be on board, from which they could also expect they might be haled into the courts of those nations whose citizens would die. Given the number of passengers on UTA Flight 772, and the international nature of the flight, it was also altogether foreseeable that some Americans would be aboard the plane, whose lives would be lost, and that the individual defendants would have to answer in some fashion in American courts for the consequences of their actions if their identities were ever discovered.

The interest of the United States in preventing and punishing international terrorism has been a matter of worldwide common knowledge for years. Congress has not been indifferent to providing judicial sanctions for terrorist acts committed abroad. Beginning at least five years before the UTA Flight 772 bombing, a succession of federal statutes had evinced an intent to assure the criminal prosecution of foreign individuals who committed terrorist acts overseas against U.S. persons or property.

These criminal statutes all contemplated the assertion by a United States court of jurisdiction over a foreign national for terrorist activities committed abroad, irrespective of the number and nature of that individual's other "contacts" with the United States. It logically follows that if federal courts may constitutionally exercise criminal jurisdiction over such individuals, the Constitution should be no bar to those same federal courts, in a civil action for damages, exercising civil in personam jurisdiction over those same individuals for the same acts.

Thus, in light of the pre-existing statutory authority providing for the criminal prosecution of those who carry out terrorist acts, and the defendants' intentional targeting of foreign nationals at the risk of killing Americans among them, defendants should have anticipated the possibility of being "haled into court" in the United States in some capacity. And because they should have anticipated as much, this Court concludes that it may constitutionally exercise personal jurisdiction over the individual defendants in their personal capacities without offending any "traditional notions of fair play and substantial justice."

IN RE TERRORIST ATTACKS ON SEPTEMBER 11, 2001
349 F. Supp. 2d 765 (S.D.N.Y. 2005)

RICHARD CONWAY CASEY, DISTRICT JUDGE.

Pursuant to 28 U.S.C. § 1407, on December 9, 2003 the Mulitidistrict Litigation Panel centralized six then-pending September 11-related cases before this Court "for coordinated or consolidated pretrial proceedings." Plaintiffs in these consolidated actions are more than three thousand survivors, family members, and representatives of victims, and insurance carriers seeking to hold responsible for the attacks the persons and entities that supported and funded al Qaeda. The complaints allege that over two hundred defendants directly or indirectly provided material support to Osama bin Laden and the al Qaeda terrorists. Generally, these defendants fall into one of several categories: al Qaeda and its members and associates; state sponsors of terrorism; and individuals and entities, including charities, banks, front organizations, terrorist organizations, and financiers who provided financial, logistical, and other support to al Qaeda.

The complaints assert subject matter jurisdiction under the Foreign Sovereign Immunities Act ("FSIA"), 28 U.S.C. § 1602 et seq.; and causes of action under the Torture Victim Protection Act ("TVPA"), 28 U.S.C. § 1350 note; the Antiterrorism Act ("ATA"), 18 U.S.C. § 2331 et seq.; the Alien Tort Claims Act ("ATCA"), 28 U.S.C. § 1350; the Racketeer Influenced and Corrupt Organizations Act ("RICO"), 18 U.S.C. § 1961 et seq.; theories of aiding and abetting, conspiracy, intentional infliction of emotional distress, negligence, survival, wrongful death, trespass, and assault and battery.

[The plaintiffs are labeled by the court as the Ashton and Burnett groups, the Federal Plaintiffs, and Federal Insurance plaintiffs. Neither the circumstances of the plaintiffs nor differences among their claims appear to be critically important in the court's analysis.]

I. [SOVEREIGN IMMUNITY] UNDER THE FSIA

Under the FSIA, a foreign state and its instrumentalities are presumed immune from United States courts' jurisdiction. *Saudi Arabia v. Nelson*, 507 U.S. 349, 355 (1993). The FSIA's exceptions to immunity provide the sole basis for obtaining subject matter jurisdiction over a foreign state and its instrumentalities in federal court.

[Some members of the Saudi royal family have been alleged to have ties to al Qaeda and bin Laden. Over the past few years, these claims seem to have dissipated. One theory is that, although radical Islamist groups would like to overthrow the Saudi royal family, some of its members either sympathized with these groups to some degree or paid them protection money to turn their attentions elsewhere. In the excerpts that follow, the court considers the allegations against the royal family and the Kingdom.]

Prince Sultan [was the full brother of King Fahd (died in 2005) and half-brother of King Adbullah. He was the third-highest member of the government before Fahd's death and became Crown Prince in 2005. He is now 82.]

Especially relevant here, Prince Sultan is the Chairman of the Supreme Council of Islamic Affairs, which was established in 1995 and is responsible for the Kingdom's Islamic policy abroad. Prince Sultan, as the head of the Special Committee of the Council of Ministers, which is a foreign policy advisory resource for King Saud, exercises authority over disbursements by the Special Committee. In the past, these disbursements, which are government funded, have included grants to Islamic charities.

The various complaints make substantially similar accusations against Prince Sultan. Prince Sultan is alleged to have met with Osama bin Laden after Iraq invaded Kuwait in the summer of 1990. At that meeting, which Prince Turki also attended, bin Laden purportedly offered his family's support to Saudi military forces. Plaintiffs allege that, at the time of the Gulf War, Prince Sultan "took radical stands against western countries and publicly supported and funded several Islamic charities that were sponsoring Osama bin Laden and al Qaeda operations." After the attacks of September 11, Prince Sultan allegedly advocated against granting the United States use of Saudi military bases to stage attacks against Afghanistan.

Prince Sultan allegedly made personal contributions, totaling $6,000,000 since 1994, to various Islamic charities that Plaintiffs claim sponsor or support al Qaeda. According to Plaintiffs, with respect to his alleged donations, "at best, Prince Sultan was grossly negligent in the oversight and administration of charitable funds, knowing they would be used to sponsor international terrorism, but turning a blind eye. At worse, Prince Sultan directly aided and abetted and materially sponsored al Qaeda and international terrorism."

Prince Turki . . . [f]rom 1977 until August 2001, was the Director of Saudi Arabia's

Department of General Intelligence ("DGI"). As such, Plaintiffs allege he was or should have been aware of the terrorist threat posed by Osama bin Laden, al Qaeda, and the Taliban. Prince Turki allegedly met with Osama bin Laden five times in the mid-1980s and mid-1990s. At one of those meetings, which Prince Sultan also attended, bin Laden allegedly offered the Saudis the use of his family's engineering equipment and suggested bolstering Saudi military forces with militants. In July 1998, Prince Turki is alleged to have met with members of the Taliban and representatives of bin Laden and agreed to not extradite bin Laden or close terrorist camps in exchange for bin Laden's protection of the Saudi Royal family. Prince Turki denies the allegations against him [and] states that [he met] with the Taliban to relay the official Saudi request that Osama bin Laden be extradited to Saudi Arabia for trial. The Taliban denied the Saudi request and Saudi Arabia subsequently suspended diplomatic relations with the Taliban in September 1998. Prince Turki denies facilitating money transfers to Osama bin Laden or al Qaeda, he denies offering material assistance to Osama bin Laden, his representatives, or al Qaeda in return for their not attacking Saudi Arabia, he denies promising or providing oil or financial assistance to the Taliban.

The Federal Plaintiffs claim that "more than any other factor, al Qaida's phenomenal growth and development into a sophisticated global terrorist network were made possible by the massive financial, logistical and other support it received from the Kingdom of Saudi Arabia, members of the Saudi Royal family, and prominent members of Saudi society." Further, the Federal Plaintiffs allege September 11 was "a direct, intended and foreseeable product of the Kingdom of Saudi Arabia's participation in al Qaida's jihadist campaign." Specifically, the Kingdom allegedly maintained and controlled several of the charities within al Qaeda's infrastructure. The Federal Plaintiffs claim Saudi Arabia knew the threat that these charities posed particularly to the United States, and did nothing to stop it. The Kingdom allegedly used its relationship with the Taliban to sustain al Qaeda in the mid-1990s. Finally, Plaintiffs allege that members of the Saudi Royal family provided support to al Qaeda in their official capacities as members of the Supreme Council of Islamic Affairs.

Torts Exception. In relevant part, the torts exception [to the FSIA] deprives a foreign sovereign of immunity in actions:

> in which money damages are sought against a foreign state for personal injury or death, or damage to or loss of property, occurring in the United States and caused by the tortious act or omission of that foreign state or of any official or employee of that foreign state while acting within the scope of his office or employment; except this [exception] shall not apply to—
>
>> (A) any claim based upon the exercise or performance or the failure to exercise or perform a discretionary function regardless of whether the discretion be abused.

28 U.S.C. § 1605(a)(5). Second Circuit law instructs that district courts must determine whether the defendant's alleged acts were tortious under the laws of New York and, if so, whether the defendant's acts were discretionary.

The FSIA's discretionary function exception replicates the discretionary function exception found in the Federal Tort Claims Act. Generally, acts are discretionary if they are performed at the planning level of government, as opposed to the operational level.

Plaintiffs exert much effort outlining the connections between al Qaeda and the Defendant charities that Prince Sultan and Prince Turki supported. Plaintiffs argue that the indirect nature of the Princes' contributions to al Qaeda is not fatal to their claims since they allegedly knew that funds they donated to the Defendant charities were being diverted to al Qaeda. The Court has reviewed the exhibits on which Plaintiffs rely and finds only a handful relate to Plaintiffs' arguments. Even construing these allegations and exhibits in the light most favorable to Plaintiffs, and drawing all inferences in their favor, none of these exhibits amount to admissible evidence that Prince Sultan or Prince

Turki knew the charities they supported were fronts for al Qaeda.

Alternatively, Plaintiffs argue that, since Osama bin Laden and al Qaeda made no effort to hide their hatred for the United States, Prince Sultan and Prince Turki had to have been aware that the United States was a target, making the atrocities of September 11, 2001 a foreseeable result of their actions. Unlike Hamas in *Boim*, none of the organizations the Princes are alleged to have supported in an official capacity were designated a sponsor of terrorism at the time of the alleged contributions. In fact, only BIF and certain branches of Al Haramain have since been designated.

Plaintiffs have not pleaded facts to suggest the Princes knew they were making contributions to terrorist fronts and provided substantial assistance or encouragement to the terrorists to satisfy *Boim* or New York law. The Court is not ruling as a matter of law that a defendant cannot be liable for contributions to organizations that are not themselves designated terrorists. But in such a case, there must be some facts presented to support the allegation that the defendant knew the receiving organization to be a solicitor, collector, supporter, front or launderer for such an entity. There must be some facts to support an inference that the defendant knowingly provided assistance or encouragement to the wrongdoer. Here, there are no such factual bases presented, there are only conclusions.

Plaintiffs argue that there is no discretion to conduct illegal activities and the so-called discretionary function exception to the tortious act exception should not apply to Prince Sultan or Prince Turki. The Court finds the discretionary function exception independently bars Plaintiffs' claims against Prince Sultan and Prince Turki. Both Princes are accused of donating money or recommending government grants to charities that allegedly supported al Qaeda. As the head of DGI, Prince Turki is also alleged to have attempted to protect Saudi Arabia from terrorism and to have implemented the Kingdom's foreign relations with the Taliban and Osama bin Laden.

There can be little doubt that, as the chairman of the Supreme Council of Islamic Affairs, charged with making recommendations to the Council of Ministers regarding requests for aid from Islamic organizations located abroad, and as the head of the Special Committee of the Council of Ministers, charged with deciding which grants should be made to Islamic charities, Prince Sultan's decisions were made at the planning level of government. Similarly, as the head of DGI, Prince Turki's decisions regarding the treatment of the Taliban and Osama bin Laden were judgments based on considerations of public policy.

There is no dispute that the Kingdom of Saudi Arabia is a foreign state within the meaning of the FSIA. In attempting to overcome the presumption of the Kingdom's sovereign immunity, Plaintiffs argue the merits of their claims against the charities. Based on news accounts that the Kingdom has dissolved its international charities and terrorist financing reports that implicate certain charities, Plaintiffs urge the Court to find that the Kingdom had previously willfully ignored the charities' support for terrorism.

In response, the Kingdom argues that Plaintiffs ignore Osama bin Laden's public targeting of the Kingdom. The 9/11 Commission Report: Final Report of the National Commission on Terrorist Attacks Upon the United States, 48, 373 (July 2004) (hereinafter "9/11 Report"). The Kingdom also submits it has worked with the United States to share information in the fight against terrorism. The U.S. State Department has not designated the Kingdom a state sponsor of terrorism. Additionally, the presidentially-appointed September 11 commission found no evidence of the Kingdom's funding or support for the September 11 terrorists. 9/11 Report, at 171.

The Court finds the Plaintiffs' allegations cannot overcome the discretionary function exception to the tortious acts exception.

II. Personal Jurisdiction

[Plaintiffs also sued a number of banks and individuals with various alleged ties to the financing of al Qaeda. Some had insufficient connection to New York unless they were alleged to be directly connected to 9/11 (specific jurisdiction) but others had sufficient ties to be subject to general jurisdiction of New York courts.]

III. Failure to State a Claim

A. Elements of Claims

Plaintiffs' claim that each Defendant provided material support to the al Qaeda terrorists who perpetrated the attacks on September 11, 2001. Under the ATA, material support includes money, financial services, lodging, training, safehouses, and false documentation or identification. 18 U.S.C. §§ 2339A(b), 2339B(g). Assuming such support is alleged, Plaintiffs will have to present a sufficient causal connection between that support and the injuries suffered by Plaintiffs. Proximate cause will support this connection. In light of al Qaeda's public acknowledgments of its war against the United States, the September 11 attacks may be the natural and probable consequence of knowingly and intentionally providing material support to al Qaeda.

Plaintiffs rely on theories of concerted action liability — conspiracy and aiding and abetting — in support of this causal link. "Concerted action liability under New York law is based on the principle that all those who, in pursuance of a common plan or design to commit a tortious act, actively take part in it, or further it by cooperation or request, or who lend aid or encouragement to the wrongdoer . . . are equally liable with him." To be liable under either conspiracy or aiding and abetting, however, the defendant "must know the wrongful nature of the primary actor's conduct," and the conduct must be tied to a substantive cause of action. Under a conspiracy theory, the Plaintiffs have to allege that the Defendants were involved in an agreement to accomplish an unlawful act and that the attacks of September 11 were a reasonably foreseeable consequence of that conspiracy.

B. Analysis of Claims Against the Moving Defendants

1. Al Rajhi Bank

Al Rajhi Bank was founded in 1987 and now has a network of nearly 400 branch offices throughout Saudi Arabia and seventeen worldwide subsidiaries. All the banking Defendants are alleged to have "provided essential support to the al Qaeda organization and operations. The banking Defendants in this lawsuit have acted as instruments of terror, in raising, facilitating and transferring money to terrorist organizations." Plaintiffs claim that Al Rajhi Bank is "the primary bank for a number of charities that serve as al Qaeda front groups," including Al Haramain, MWL, WAMY, SJRC, and IIRO. "Al Rajhi continues to maintain Al Haramain's accounts despite Al Haramain's designation on March 11, 2002 as terrorist organizations by both the United States and Saudi Arabian authorities."

The Burnett Plaintiffs also claim that Al Rajhi Bank has relationships with Hamas and other terrorists. Al Rajhi Bank chose Texas-based Infocom to host its website. Infocom has provided funding to Hamas and is owned and operated by Hamas leader and designated terrorist, Mousa Marzook.

Al Rajhi Bank argues that Plaintiffs offer no factual allegations in support of their conclusion that Al Rajhi Bank had to know that the charities it supported through Zakat and Hararm[5] payments were really fronts for al Qaeda. Al Rajhi Bank contends it had a legal and religious duty to make its charitable donations and any terrorist activity by the recipient charities was unknown to Al Rajhi Bank. Contrary to Plaintiffs' arguments, Al Rajhi Bank submits it did not have a duty, or a right, to inspect the Defendant charities' financial transactions to ascertain the ultimate destination of its donations. Al Rajhi Bank submits that SAMA did not implement any duty to investigate Zakat payments after its meeting with representatives of the National Security Council and Office of Foreign Assets Control.

New York law and the courts interpreting the ATA in *Boim* make very clear that concerted action liability requires general knowledge of the primary actor's conduct. Even with the opportunity to clarify their claims against Al Rajhi Bank, Plaintiffs do not offer facts to support their conclusions that Al Rajhi Bank had to know that Defendant charities WAMY, MWL, IIRC, and SJRC were supporting terrorism.

This Court, like Judge Robertson before it, has found no basis for a bank's liability for injuries funded by money passing through it on routine banking business. Finally, Plaintiffs' allegations that Al Rajhi Bank has connections to Hamas supporters fails to state a claim because Plaintiffs have not alleged any relationship between Hamas and al Qaeda or the terrorist attacks of September 11. Even accepting all the allegations against Al Rajhi Bank as true, Plaintiffs have failed to state a claim that would entitle them to relief. Accordingly, Al Rajhi Bank's motion to dismiss is granted in its entirety.

2. Saudi American Bank

Saudi American Bank is based in Rihadh, Saudi Arabia and was formed in 1980 pursuant to a royal decree to take over the then-existing branches of Citibank in Riyadh and Jeddah. It is the second largest bank in Saudi Arabia and has offices in the United States, based in New York.

The essence of Plaintiffs' claim is that through its relationships with other banks and support of the Saudi Binladin group's work in Sudan, Saudi American Bank provided material support to al Qaeda. It is not alleged to have done anything to directly support al Qaeda, Osama bin Laden, or their terrorist agenda. As the Court has stated before, there can be no bank liability for injuries caused by money routinely passing through the bank. Saudi American Bank is not alleged to have known that anything relating to terrorism was occurring through the services it provided.

3. Arab Bank

The Federal Plaintiffs claim Arab Bank is a financial institution headquartered in Egypt with branch offices throughout the world, including New York. Arab Bank claims it is actually a Jordanian bank headquartered in Amman, Jordan. Arab Bank allegedly has "long provided financial services and other forms of material support to terrorist organizations, including al Qaeda." Further, these Plaintiffs allege that the September 11 attacks were a "direct, intended and foreseeable product of Arab Bank's participation in al Qaeda's jihadist campaign." These claims are based on the allegation that Arab Bank has "long known that accounts it maintained were being used to solicit and transfer funds to terrorist organizations [and despite this knowledge] Arab Bank has continued to maintain those accounts."

Providing routine banking services, without having knowledge of the terrorist activities, cannot subject Arab Bank to liability. While claiming Arab Bank has ties with known Hamas fronts, the complaint does not contain any allegation of a connection between Hamas and Osama bin Laden, al Qaeda, or the September 11 attacks.

---

[5] [Court's Footnote 40] Under Islamic banking laws, Hararm is forbidden income that must be given away. The disposal of Hararm cannot be considered charitable giving.

6. Saudi Binladin Group

Based in Jeddah, Saudi Arabia, SBG is the successor to a construction company founded by Mohammed Binladin, the father of Osama bin Laden. It is now one of the largest engineering and construction companies in the Arab world and is managed by Osama bin Laden's half brothers, including defendants Bakr Binladin, who runs SBG, and Tariq Binladin, who holds a position on the board. Tariq Binladin allegedly had a prominent role at IIRO in 1990. Osama bin Laden purportedly used SBG to build an infrastructure in Afghanistan. After the Soviets withdrew from Afghanistan in 1989, Osama bin Laden returned to work with SBG in Jeddah. SBG allegedly continued to support Osama bin Laden after he relocated to Sudan in 1991. Plaintiffs claim Osama bin Laden's name is still listed on SBG corporate records. Defendants dispute this and argue he was formally removed from SBG's ownership documents in June 1993. Plaintiffs also claim that Osama bin Laden never "broke" with his family after he was exiled to Sudan and that SBG continued to provide him financial assistance and engineering support. Defendants also dispute this statement and argue that Bakr formally ostracized Osama from the family and the company in a February 1994 statement.

SBG has, at some point, had a close relationship with Osama bin Laden, but the complaints do not specify when or whether the relationship continues. While these allegations are certainly not sufficient to reach a jury, if Plaintiffs demonstrate that this Court has personal jurisdiction over SBG they are entitled the opportunity to develop these claims. SBG's motions to dismiss the Ashton and Burnett complaints for failure to state a claim are therefore denied without prejudice.

7. SAAR Network

Plaintiffs claim the SAAR Network is a network of "interrelated ostensible charities" that was established in the 1980s "to generate and surreptitiously transfer funds to terrorist organizations, including al-Qaeda." Several organizations within the SAAR Network, including SAAR Foundation, SAAR International, Safa Group, MarJac Poultry, Mar-Jac Holdings, Inc., Safa Trust, Inc. and Aradi, Inc., were established, funded or closely affiliated with Defendant Suleiman Abdul Aziz al Rajhi. By September 11, 2001, there were allegedly over one hundred entities in this network, "including the U.S. branches of MWL, IIRO and WAMY, [and the SAAR Network Defendants moving to dismiss here,] African Muslim Agency, Grove Corporate, Inc., Heritage Education Trust, International Institute of Islamic Thought, Mar-Jac Investment, Inc., Mena Corporation, Reston Investment, Inc., Sterling Charitable Gift Fund, Sterling Management Group, Inc., Success Foundation, and York Foundation." Allegedly, many of the entities are related by common management, few of them maintained a physical presence at their purported place of business, and they all "have long acted as fully integrated components of al Qaeda's logistical and financial support infrastructure."

Plaintiffs argue the Court has personal jurisdiction over the SAAR Network because it participated in the conspiracy that resulted in catastrophic effects in this district. After an ongoing investigation in the Eastern District of Virginia, federal authorities raided the offices of several of these Defendants in Herndon, Virginia in March 2002. The investigation has allegedly revealed that SAAR Network funds have been transferred to designated terrorists and al Qaeda operatives Youssef Nada and Ahmed Idris Nasreddin. Additionally, Plaintiffs claim that the investigation has revealed that SAAR Network entities have engaged in transactions with Bait Ul-mal, Inc. (BMI), which has transferred funds to terrorist organizations including al Qaeda, and materially supported the 1998 embassy bombings in Africa.

At this stage, the Court must accept as true Plaintiffs' allegations concerning the relationships of the SAAR Network. Defendants correctly argue, however, that Defendants have provided scant basis for linking these entities under the SAAR

Network title. Certain of these groups may be subject to personal jurisdiction in light of Plaintiffs' allegation that they purposefully directing its activities at the United States by transferring money to designated terrorists Youssef Nada and Ahmed Idris Nasreddin, particularly if they intended the money to support terrorism. Additionally, general jurisdiction could be appropriate for the SAAR Network entities having offices in Virginia. Accordingly, the SAAR Network's motion to dismiss is denied without prejudice. The parties are to engage in jurisdictional discovery to determine which of the Network's entities have a presence in Virginia and which entities transferred money to Nada and Nasreddin.

The Court's analysis of the SAAR Network's arguments in favor of 12(b)(6) dismissal depend on a predicate finding of which entities are subject to this Court's personal jurisdiction and which entities — and under what circumstances — transferred money to terror fronts. Accordingly, the SAAR Network's motion to dismiss is denied without prejudice. It may be renewed upon completion of personal jurisdiction discovery.

8. Adel A. J. Batterjee

Plaintiffs claim that Defendant Adel A. J. Batterjee is an associate of Osama bin Laden. On December 21, 2004, the U.S. Department of Treasury designated Mr. Batterjee as a Specially Designated Global Terrorist. Mr. Batterjee is the chairman of Al Shamal Islamic Bank, "an instrumental bank in Osama bin Laden's financial support network." Mr. Batterjee is also chairman of al-Bir Saudi Organization, whose United States branch, Defendant BIF [Benevolence International Foundation], is allegedly a "front for al Qaeda sponsorship." BIF is also a designated terrorist organization. The Saudi government closed Al-Bir in 1993 "at the same time it was closing other organizations for ties to terrorism." Mr. Batterjee then allegedly moved the charity's headquarters to Chicago in the name of BIF.

For substantially the same reasons the Court found it had personal jurisdiction over Mr. Batterjee, it denies his motion to dismiss for failure to state a claim. The allegations against him and his designation as a terrorist are sufficient to permit the inference that he provided support to al Qaeda directly or through Al Shamal Islamic Bank, BIF, or WAMY.

IV. CONCLUSION AND ORDER

[All motions were granted except for the following.] NCB's motions to dismiss for lack of subject matter and personal jurisdiction are denied without prejudice. The negligence claims against NCB are dismissed for failure to state a claim. The Saudi Binladin Group's motions to dismiss for lack of personal jurisdiction and failure to state a claim are denied without prejudice, but the TVPA and negligence claims against SBG are dismissed. The SAAR Network's motion to dismiss for lack of personal jurisdiction and failure to state a claim is denied without prejudice. Adel Batterjee's motion to dismiss the Burnett complaint is denied.

NOTES AND QUESTIONS

1. Tort Coverage. Referring back to the history set out at the beginning of this chapter, in light of all the statutory developments, are there still any significant gaps in tort coverage for acts of terrorism?

    a.   What about a terrorist killing by an alien in another country of another alien? Is there any reason why the U.S. courts should hear this case? The TVPA applies to actions "under actual or apparent authority, or color of law." What is the source of congressional power to enact federal law creating the right of action?

    b.   The court in *Terrorist Attacks* seems to read the note as if it applies only when the tort also fits the body of the ATCA as a violation of the "law of nations." If an act occurs as part of a "widespread and systematic" pattern of violence, then under the holdings of the ICTY and ICTR, it could violate international law without being imputed to the authority of the state.

c. What about an act that causes serious bodily harm but is neither a killing nor official torture? For example, many of the instances of beatings and rapes involved in Kosovo and Rwanda were violations of international law as crimes against humanity but were neither killings nor torture. Would they be cognizable in a U.S. civil court action?

2. Mens Rea for Torts. The *Terrorist Attacks* court holds that there is no claim for relief based upon giving money to a terrorist organization absent at least "general knowledge of the primary actor's conduct." The courts interpreting the material support statutes in criminal cases have struggled with whether a *mens rea* element is constitutionally required and whether it must include an intent to support the illegal behavior of the organization (as opposed, for example, to additional charitable activities of the organization). What would you require the plaintiff to prove in order to establish liability in a tort action? knowledge of some bad motive? knowledge of intent to kill? knowledge of the exact target of an attack?

3. PATH Liability. On October 26, 2005, the Port Authority of New York was found by a jury to have been negligent in failing to take measures to secure the basement parking facility of the World Trade Center prior to the 1993 bombing in which six people were killed and 1000 injured. This is a relatively straightforward property owner tort case in which the owner was allegedly alerted by experts to security concerns and failed to respond.

§ 4.02 SELECTED READINGS

· Hillel Sommer, *Providing Compensation for Harm Caused by Terrorism: Lessons Learned in the Israeli Experience*, 36 IND. L. REV. 335 (2003)

Chapter 5
INVESTIGATION, PROSECUTION, AND SECRETS

Ordinary criminal investigations begin after a completed crime has been discovered. The investigator knows what the crime was because the results are visible, and the focus will be on discovering who did it and collecting the evidence to prove that person's guilt. By contrast, an investigation aimed at preventing criminal harm must start from some other premise, perhaps a tip from an informant, or a set of rumors circulating in a given community, or maybe even a suspicion in the mind of an investigator looking at the aftermath of another completed crime.

In this chapter, we explore the operation of two statutes that appear frequently in terrorism investigations and prosecutions: the Foreign Intelligence Surveillance Act (FISA) and the Classified Information Procedures Act (CIPA). This chapter also sets us up for some of the principal controversies of the post-9/11 Bush Administration counter-terrorism strategy because FISA is both the statute most affected by the controversial provisions of the USA PATRIOT Act and the statute prohibiting domestic electronic surveillance without court order. In addition, CIPA is cited in a number of situations not because of its direct relevance but because it reflects general policy regarding judicial handling of government secrets.

The classic terrorism case, whether involving a completed act or a plot, will involve government surveillance (wiretaps and other electronic surveillance) carried out under FISA, seizure of dangerous material and arrest of the defendants (often without warrant under exigent circumstances), and the defendants; desire to obtain or introduce into evidence information that the government considers secret and subject to CIPA. Our study will begin by setting the context with a prototypical terrorist conspiracy investigation.

Running throughout these cases is a question of how a court itself is supposed to handle secret information, including the access of clerks and clerical personnel to information in the court's possession, but that issue can be left to the end of this chapter because it will be more understandable after we have some knowledge of the types and potential uses of classified information.

§ 5.01 FOREIGN INTELLIGENCE SURVEILLANCE ACT

Following World War II, as the U.S. and USSR faced off across the espionage divide, and as technology began to open new channels of information gathering, the U.S. Executive branch began routinely to claim the power to conduct electronic surveillance "in the interest of national security." Meanwhile, in cases discussed below, the Supreme Court held essentially that "wiretaps" and similar intrusions into zones of privacy were subject to the fourth amendment requirements of warrants based on probable cause, and also held that "domestic security" did not provide an adequate basis for warrantless wiretaps while hinting that the situation might be different with respect to foreign operatives.

Congress responded in 1978 by enacting FISA's procedures and standards to be met in conducting "foreign intelligence surveillance." The heart of the statutory scheme is the special court (FISC) consisting of sitting district judges designated by the Chief Justice to review applications for surveillance of foreign agents.

UNITED STATES v. SARKISSIAN
841 F.2d 959 (9th Cir. 1988)

SKOPIL, CIRCUIT JUDGE.

Sarkissian, Dadaian, and Hovsepian appeal their convictions for conspiracy to bomb, transportation of explosive materials, and possession of an unregistered firearm. They contend that (1) the government's warrantless search of a suitcase violated the fourth amendment; (2) the government was required to obtain wiretap authorization under Title III of the Omnibus Crime Control and Safe Streets Act of 1968 (Title III), not under the Foreign Intelligence Surveillance Act of 1978 (FISA); and (3) the district court erred in not disclosing the government's ex parte in camera submission of classified information. We affirm.

FACTS AND PROCEEDINGS BELOW

This case involves the Federal Bureau of Investigation's (FBI) attempt to prevent Armenian terrorists from bombing the Honorary Turkish Consulate in Philadelphia. On September 17, 1982, the FBI, as part of an ongoing investigation of Armenian terrorist groups, obtained authorization from the United States Foreign Surveillance Court (USFSC) to place a wiretap on Hovsepian's telephone in Santa Monica, California. The wiretap paid off from the start. Although defendants spoke in Armenian and used simple code words, FBI translators and investigators soon cracked the code. By late September the FBI knew that Hovsepian, Sarkissian, and others planned to take some type of violent action against the Honorary Turkish Consulate in Philadelphia and that they had a contact person in Boston. FBI Agent Maples, who headed the investigation in Los Angeles, believed that Hovsepian and others would act in early October.

Later intercepted phone calls convinced Maples that Hovsepian had postponed his plans. By October 19, Maples realized that Hovsepian's plans were on again; defendants were assembling a bomb. On October 21, the USFSC authorized a continuation of the surveillance. Shortly after 3:00 a.m. eastern daylight time (EDT), Maples discovered that one of Hovsepian's colleagues had missed a flight from Los Angeles but would take the next one, which would arrive at its destination at noon.

Maples and his agents continued the investigation through the early morning hours. He concluded that components of a bomb, if not an assembled bomb, were being transported from Los Angeles on an unidentified flight by an unidentified person or persons in unidentified luggage to an unidentified city. By checking the schedule of flights out of Los Angeles, Maples determined that the bomb's courier or couriers were probably on a Northwest Orient (NWO) flight due to arrive in Boston's Logan International Airport at noon EDT. He warned Boston's FBI office before 9:00 a.m. EDT of the danger.

At 9:10 a.m. EDT Maples discovered that the courier or couriers were "S. Tataian" and/or "V. Lopez." At 9:25 a.m. EDT Maples concluded that defendant Dadaian was probably one of the couriers. At 9:30 a.m. EDT he called Boston FBI agent Hildreth to warn that the suspect or suspects apparently were on a Trans World Airlines or NWO flight that would arrive at about 11:00 a.m. or noon EDT following stopovers in Minneapolis and New Jersey. Maples provided Hildreth with the names of four suspects. Between 9:45 and 10:00 a.m. EDT, Maples told Hildreth to disregard the names provided earlier. He advised Hildreth to focus on Dadaian who was on the NWO flight due to arrive at noon EDT. Maples gave Hildreth a general physical description of Dadaian.

Around 9:30 a.m. EDT the Boston FBI sent an agent to Logan Airport to to set up a command post. By 11:00 a.m. EDT fifty agents had assembled at the airport. The agents manned surveillance positions and established a search procedure that included a dog sniff and x-ray scan. After the NWO flight landed around 12:15 p.m. EDT, a Massachusetts state police officer boarded the plane and posed as a first class passenger. The officer spotted a man matching Dadaian's description and followed him to the baggage claim area.

A trained dog sniffed the fifty-seven pieces of luggage unloaded from the flight, but did not react to any of them. The agents then ran the luggage through the x-ray scanner and detected parts of a bomb in a suitcase labeled "V. Lopez." They opened the suitcase and found an unassembled bomb with five sticks of dynamite. The agents did not remove anything from the suitcase, but returned it to the baggage claim carousel. His suspicions aroused by activity around the airport, Dadaian never picked up the suitcase. The FBI arrested him several hours later.

At trial the defendants sought to suppress evidence from the suitcase search and FISA wiretap. The district court denied their suppression motions. The government also made an ex parte in camera submission of classified information. The court sealed the submission without allowing disclosure to the defendants. Defendants were found guilty of conspiracy to bomb, transportation of explosive materials, and possession of an unregistered firearm. They timely appealed.

DISCUSSION

A. Warrantless Search

A warrantless search of luggage requires exigent circumstances supported by probable cause. Defendants concede probable cause. The issue is whether there were exigent circumstances. Exigent circumstances include "those circumstances that would cause a reasonable person to believe that entry (or other relevant prompt action) was necessary to prevent physical harm to the officers or other persons." We view the exigency from the totality of circumstances known to the officer at the time of the warrantless intrusion.

We conclude there were exigent circumstances in this case. The FBI knew that a bomb or parts of a bomb were being carried in a suitcase or suitcases by a member or members of an Armenian terrorist group on a commercial flight to an international airport. *See United States v. Chadwick*, 433 U.S. 1, 15 n.9 (1977) (recognition of exigency created by placement of "some immediately dangerous instrumentality, such as explosives" in luggage); *United States v. Al-Azzawy*, 784 F.2d 890, 893 (9th Cir. 1985) (explosives in trailer); *United States v. Williams*, 626 F.2d 697, 703 (9th Cir. 1980) (bomb in car).

The FBI believed that defendants belonged to the Justice Commandoes of the Armenian Genocide (JCAG). Members of the JCAG were considered "armed and dangerous." An FBI report noted that "they have accomplished some 21 assassinations worldwide and numerous bombings of Turkish targets. JCAG members are known to carry concealed hanguns [sic], and to prefer 9mm browning hi-powered automatics, or .45 caliber colt combat commandos automatics." The FBI attributed three assassinations earlier in the year to the JCAG. One assassination occurred in Los Angeles on January 28, 1982, another in Boston on May 4, 1982, and a third in Ottawa, Canada on August 27, 1982. The JCAG often used bombing as a warning to be followed by an assassination attempt.

The Philadelphia FBI estimated heavy civilian casualties if the JCAG managed to detonate its bomb. The Honorary Turkish Consulate was located "in a highly populated area which has continuous activity at all hours of the day and night." A bomb composed of six sticks of dynamite would cause at least 100 casualties. A daytime explosion could inflict as many as 2,000 to 3,000 casualties. If a shoot out between the FBI and JCAG occurred, "people in the various residence units bordering on the site of the building would be expected to rush to the windows to see what was happening. If that occurs and the bomb was not able to be deactivated the minimal number of casualties would be substantially higher." We agree with the district court's finding that there was a "grave and imminent danger to persons and property."

Exigent circumstances alone, however, are insufficient. The government also bears the burden of showing that it could not have obtained a telephonic warrant under Fed. R. Crim. P. 41(c)(2). It must "attempt, in good faith, to secure a warrant or . . . present evidence explaining why a telephone warrant was unavailable or impractical."

Here, the government did not attempt to obtain a telephonic warrant. The record, however, contains evidence showing why it would have been impractical to do so. Probable cause to search arose almost three hours before the plane landed. By 9:25 a.m. EDT Maples had concluded that Dadaian was the bomb's courier. The plane was scheduled to land at noon EDT but actually landed around 12:15 p.m. EDT. Although the investigation preoccupied Maples throughout the early morning hours, after 10:00 a.m. EDT he did little but wait to "see what happened." Maples never considered trying to get a telephonic warrant. Though we find that troubling, we affirm.

The impracticality of obtaining a warrant compels that result. "Obtaining a telephonic warrant is not a simple procedure; 'among other things, a "duplicate original warrant" must be prepared in writing and read to the magistrate verbatim.' The only step that is saved is the trip to the magistrate's office." *United States v. Good*, 780 F.2d 773, 775 (9th Cir. 1986). Here, the procedure was complicated by the fact that the agents with the information were in Los Angeles. Fed. R. Crim. P. 41(a) requires that the warrant be issued by a judicial officer of the district where the property to be seized is located. Thus, the Los Angeles agents would have needed to locate a judicial officer in Boston, prepare a warrant, and then convince the judicial officer that probable cause existed. The district court found that no written summary of the necessary information was then in existence and that collecting and organizing the information would have been difficult.

The passage of time alone is not dispositive of whether the government had enough time to secure a warrant. In *Alvarez*, government agents had at least ninety minutes in which to get an arrest warrant. The agents made no attempt to secure the hotel where the drug deal was to occur or to monitor the suspect's movements before making a warrantless arrest. We refused to find exigent circumstances. "The agent's actions . . . were . . . fundamentally inconsistent with any true exigency." In *Echegoyen*, police officers waited approximately two and one-half to three hours before making their search. *United States v. Echegoyen*, 799 F.2d 1271, 1279 n.6. "The officers were faced with a potentially serious fire hazard and potentially dangerous drug traffickers in an isolated mountain community with little fire and police protection." We found exigent circumstances.

This case is closer to *Echegoyen* than to *Alvarez*. In extraordinary cases, the peril may be so great that law enforcement officers must be afforded sufficient latitude to direct their full attention to protecting lives and property. *See United States v. Jones*, 635 F.2d 1357, 1362 (8th Cir. 1980) ("The police were busily engaged in solving the problem, which they continued to believe was a dangerous one."); *Picariello*, 568 F.2d at 226 ("The emergency conditions . . . and the reasonable speed with which the agents acted substantiate a finding of exigent circumstances."); *United States v. Melville*, 309 F. Supp. 829, 832 (S.D.N.Y. 1970) (Police action to halt wave of bombings in New York and to secure explosives in apartment "cannot be judged in the calm of later philosophical review of what a phlegmatic analysis shows.").

The Boston FBI had to safeguard the people and property within the airport. The FBI set up a command post, contacted and coordinated efforts with the state police and a bomb expert, briefed the fifty agents assembled at the airport and assigned them to their posts, and set up a procedure to check for explosives. Uncertainty made the FBI's task more difficult. The FBI did not know the identity of the courier or couriers, whether the bomb was assembled or unassembled, whether the bomb was contained in one or more suitcases, and what the suitcase or suitcases looked like. Events rapidly unfolded. Here, the potentially violent consequences to the law enforcement agents and the public combined with the considerable amount of time required for the Los Angeles agents to gather the information and obtain a judicial officer's approval justify the warrantless search. Based on the totality of the circumstances, we conclude the time was insufficient to obtain a warrant.

B. FISA

Congress enacted FISA in 1978 "to establish procedures for the use of electronic surveillance in gathering foreign intelligence information." *Matter of Kevork*, 788 F.2d 566, 569 (9th Cir. 1986). The government generally must obtain judicial approval before it engages in such surveillance. A specially constituted court, the USFSC, hears the government's application. The Chief Justice of the Supreme Court designates seven United States District Court judges to serve on the court.

On Oct. 21, 1982 the USFSC authorized the FBI to continue its wiretap of Hovsepian's telephone. Defendants argue that by then the FBI's primary purpose for the surveillance had shifted from an intelligence investigation to a criminal investigation. They contend that (1) the FBI was required to obtain authorization under Title III, not FISA; and (2) the district court erred in not allowing a hearing on the issue. We disagree.

Defendants rely on the primary purpose test articulated in *United States v. Truong Dinh Hung*, 629 F.2d 908 (4th Cir. 1980). *Truong* held that the foreign intelligence exception to the warrant requirement applies "only when the surveillance is conducted 'primarily' for foreign intelligence reasons." One other court has applied the primary purpose test. *United States v. Duggan*, 743 F.2d 59, 77 (2d Cir. 1984). Another court has rejected it. *United States v. Falvey*, 540 F. Supp. 1306, 1313–14 (E.D.N.Y. 1982) (distinguishing *Truong*). A third court has declined to decide the issue. *Matter of Kevork*, 634 F. Supp. 1002, 1015 (C.D. Cal. 1985), *aff'd*, 788 F.2d 566 (9th Cir. 1986).

We also decline to decide the issue. We have generally stated that the purpose of the surveillance must be to secure foreign intelligence information. *United States v. Ott*, 827 F.2d 473, 475 (9th Cir. 1987); *Cavanagh*, 807 F.2d at 790–91 ("the purpose of the surveillance is not to ferret out criminal activity but rather to gather intelligence"). Regardless of whether the test is one of purpose or primary purpose, our review of the government's FISA materials convinces us that it is met in this case.

We refuse to draw too fine a distinction between criminal and intelligence investigations. "International terrorism," by definition, requires the investigation of activities that constitute crimes. That the government may later choose to prosecute is irrelevant. FISA contemplates prosecution based on evidence gathered through surveillance. "Surveillances . . . need not stop once conclusive evidence of a crime is obtained, but instead may be extended longer where protective measures other than arrest and prosecution are more appropriate." S. Rep. No. 701, 95th Cong., 2d Sess. 11.

FISA is meant to take into account "the differences between ordinary criminal investigations to gather evidence of specific crimes and foreign counterintelligence investigations to uncover and monitor clandestine activities . . . " *Id.* At no point was this case an ordinary criminal investigation. *See Badia*, 827 F.2d at 1461 (conspiracy to manufacture machine guns and silencers for "Omega-7," an anti-Castro group); *Duggan*, 743 F.2d at 78 (IRA attempt to buy parts for bombs and surface-to-air missiles); *Kevork*, 634 F. Supp. at 1015 (Armenian terrorist plot to assassinate Turkish diplomat); *Falvey*, 540 F. Supp. at 1314 (IRA arms smuggling).

C. Ex Parte In Camera Material

Defendants contend that the district court erred in not disclosing material submitted to the district court *ex parte* and *in camera*. They argue that (1) the court impermissibly balanced the parties' interests under the Classified Information Procedures Act (CIPA); (2) the court erred in accepting an *ex parte in camera* submission without requiring the filing of a public claim of privilege; and (3) the government failed to assert a formal claim to a state secret privilege under *United*

States v. Reynolds, 345 U.S. 1 (1953). We again disagree.

Congress passed CIPA to prevent the problem of "graymail," where defendants pressed for the release of classified information to force the government to drop the prosecution. CIPA permits "the trial judge to rule on questions of admissibility involving classified information before introduction of the evidence in open court. This procedure . . . permit[s] the government to ascertain the potential damage to national security of proceeding with a given prosecution before trial." CIPA creates a pretrial procedure for ruling upon the admissibility of classified information. *United States v. Smith*, 780 F.2d 1102, 1105 (4th Cir. 1985) (en banc). *See generally United States v. Collins*, 720 F.2d 1195, 1196–97 (11th Cir. 1983).

Defendants argue that CIPA forbids balancing national security concerns against defendant's need for documents. Their argument is meritless. Congress intended section 4 to clarify the court's powers under Fed. R. Crim. P. 16(d)(1) to deny or restrict discovery in order to protect national security. On issues of discovery, the court can engage in balancing.

Defendants next contend that the government must file a public claim of privilege before making an *ex parte in camera* submission. The clear language of the statute and its legislative history foreclose that contention. Section 4 allows the court to "permit the United States to make a request . . . in the form of a written statement to be inspected by the court alone." The legislative history emphasizes that "since the government is seeking to withhold classified information from the defendant, an adversary hearing with defense knowledge would defeat the very purpose of the discovery rules." Nowhere does CIPA require the government to file a public claim of privilege before making an *in camera ex parte* submission.

Defendants finally argue that the government failed to make a formal claim of state secret privilege under *Reynolds*. *Reynolds* requires "a formal claim of privilege, lodged by the head of the department which has control over the matter after actual personal consideration by that officer." We assume *arguendo* that the enactment of CIPA does not affect the validity of *Reynolds*. We have examined the government's sealed submission and conclude that it satisfies *Reynolds*.

The district court is *AFFIRMED*.

NOTES AND QUESTIONS

1. Timing and Prevention. *Sarkissian* presents a classic example of the difficulty of knowing when to intervene in a criminal plot. Can government agents create "exigent circumstances" for a warrantless search merely by waiting for the conspiracy to unfold until it reaches a danger point? How do you feel about the FBI's allowing a suitcase full of dynamite to be checked into the luggage hold of a public passenger plane bound from Los Angeles to Boston? On the other hand, would prosecution at an earlier stage have been viable?

2. Monitoring an Investigation. The Ninth Circuit says it is "troubled" by Agent Maple's waiting for three hours as events unfolded in Boston without attempting to obtain a search warrant. A somewhat optimistic version of investigative practice prior to 9/11 would have had a prosecutor from the U.S. Attorney's Office in Los Angeles involved as soon as the FBI agents learned of an active plot to use explosives. An affidavit could be drafted and amended as new information became available so that it was ready to go by fax from L.A. to Boston at a moment's notice. The Boston U.S. Attorney's Office could be prepared to take the affidavit to a magistrate, obtain a signature, and telephone or radio the authorization for search to the agents in the field. With this procedure in place, the warrant could have been issued well before the plane touched down in Boston, allowing special handling of all the luggage on the plane, and thus eliminating much of the danger to the public that the court finds to create exigent circumstances. (After 9/11, the Counter-Terrorism Section of Justice would coordinate any terrorist investigation out of Washington, but the rest of the scenario remains the same.)

This scenario would allow for an effective prosecution while decreasing some of the risk to the public. But, obviously, a procedure of this type entails time and expense, not to mention bureaucratic crossing of turf from FBI to Justice Department lawyers. How realistic do you think this scenario is? How much expense is the public willing to bear to maximize effective prosecutions while minimizing risks to public safety?

From a prosecutor's standpoint, this scenario raises two concerns: 1) Will a court accept the justification for a warrantless search. 2) Are agents flirting with danger by delaying intervention?

UNITED STATES v. DUGGAN
743 F.2d 59 (2d Cir. 1984)

KEARSE, CIRCUIT JUDGE.

The principal issues raised in this appeal by alleged agents of the Provisional Irish Republican Army ("PIRA") concern the constitutionality and proper application of the Foreign Intelligence Surveillance Act ("FISA" or the "Act"). [Defendants Andrew Duggan, Eamon Meehan, Gabriel Megahey, and Colm Meehan were convicted of[violations of various federal statutes dealing with interstate shipments of firearms and explosive devices. Each of the defendants received sentences ranging from two to seven years.]

On appeal, all of the defendants contend principally (1) that the district court erred in refusing to suppress evidence obtained through a wiretap pursuant to FISA on the grounds that (a) FISA is unconstitutionally broad and violates the probable cause requirement of the Fourth Amendment, and (b) the government failed to comply with FISA's prerequisites for wire surveillance; (2) that the district court erred in excluding their defense that their actions were taken in reasonable good faith reliance on the apparent authority of one Michael Hanratty, a government informant, to act as an agent of the Central Intelligence Agency ("CIA"); and (3) that the conduct of government agents was so outrageous as to deprive them of due process of law. In addition, Eamon and Colm Meehan contend that the district court erred in rejecting their proffered defense of insanity. We reject the defendants' contentions and affirm the convictions.

I. BACKGROUND

Although none of the defendants challenges the sufficiency of the proof to convict him, we summarize here so much of the trial evidence, taken in the light most favorable to the government, as is necessary to place defendants' major contentions in context. In general the evidence, presented largely through the testimony of Hanratty, videotapes of meetings between PIRA members and undercover law enforcement agents, and tape recordings of telephone conversations involving Megahey, showed defendants as part of a network of men working clandestinely on behalf of PIRA to acquire explosives, weapons, ammunition, and remote-controlled detonation devices in the United States to be exported to Northern Ireland for use in terrorist activities. Megahey, an Irish national who sought political asylum in the United States, was the leader and financier of PIRA operations in the United States. Duggan, an American citizen, was Megahey's assistant in contacting sellers of electronic equipment to be used in remote-controlled bombs and other sophisticated weaponry. Eamon Meehan, under the direction of Megahey, gathered and stored firearms and explosives; Eamon and his brother Colm — both aliens living illegally in the United States — secreted these materials in a shipment of goods bound for Northern Ireland.

A. *The Events*

1. PIRA Meets Hanratty

The events that culminated in the June 1982 arrests of the defendants began a year earlier, when Duggan, on the recommendation of an acquaintance, sought out Michael Hanratty, a seller of surveillance and countersurveillance equipment and other electronic items. At this first meeting, Duggan and an associate, Brendon Docherty, a/k/a Brendon Sloan ("Sloan"), identified themselves to Hanratty as members of PIRA, and explained that they sought to purchase equipment for use against the British in Northern Ireland. At a meeting that evening, Duggan, Sloan, and a third companion explained to Hanratty their political views and PIRA's equipment needs. Although Duggan and his associates inquired about the availability of a variety of equipment — including bullet proof vests, electronic tracking systems, and devices to detect the presence of electronic surveillance — their principal interest was in acquiring sophisticated remote-controlled explosive detonators, items that Hanratty could not supply.

Hanratty promptly informed the Federal Bureau of Investigation ("FBI") of these conversations and agreed to provide FBI agents with information gained from any future meetings, in particular the types of electronic equipment Duggan and his associates desired to purchase. Although the agents did not instruct Hanratty to initiate any further contact with Duggan's group, they requested that he attempt to introduce an undercover FBI agent into future dealings if the opportunity arose.

Over the next six months, Hanratty was contacted by Duggan and Sloan several times for the purchase of a variety of equipment that could be used as fusing mechanisms for bombs. In addition, Sloan asked Hanratty if he could supply surface-to-air missiles ("SAMs"), with which PIRA could shoot down British helicopters.

During these meetings Duggan and his associates frequently spoke of consulting their "money man" for the PIRA purchases. In January 1982, Hanratty was summoned by Duggan for his first meeting with the "money man" and was presented to Megahey. Megahey introduced himself as the leader of PIRA operations in the United States, and stated that all PIRA activities in the United States were conducted with his knowledge. Megahey said he had chosen to reveal himself to Hanratty because Hanratty had become a valuable asset to their organization, and he, *inter alia*, reminded Hanratty of the importance of acquiring certain previously ordered devices that were needed as safety mechanisms in the construction of remote-controlled bombs.

2. PIRA Meets the FBI

After Hanratty was introduced to Megahey, the government obtained from a judge of the United States Foreign Intelligence Surveillance Court ("FISA Court" and, generally, "FISA Judge") an order authorizing the FBI to conduct electronic surveillance of Megahey's home telephone. The surveillance was initiated on February 10, 1982, continued pursuant to a renewal order obtained on May 6, 1982, and terminated on June 21, 1982, the date of Megahey's arrest by the FBI. The wiretap intercepted several conversations between Megahey and Duggan concerning PIRA activities, and information from the wiretap led the FBI to conduct surveillance of the home of Eamon Meehan.

In March 1982, Hanratty obtained the bomb safety devices requested by Megahey and his associates and delivered them to Duggan under surveillance by the FBI. The switches had been microscopically marked by FBI laboratory personnel for future identification. Two months later these switches, along with weapons and explosive devices, were found hidden in a shipment of goods loaded by Eamon and Colm Meehan into a shipping container bound for Northern Ireland. Agents who had observed the

Meehans' activities secured the container, and caused it to be searched by United States Customs Service officials just before it was to be shipped to Northern Ireland.

In the meantime, two of Duggan's associates had reopened with Hanratty the question of obtaining SAMs. Hanratty told them he could not personally supply the missiles but said he knew of a possible source, a man he identified as "Luis." Hanratty described Luis as a Miami-based wheeler-dealer who supplied arms to Central American and other countries. Hanratty later gave the same story to Duggan in response to a question that Hanratty thought referred to Duggan's associates' inquiries about obtaining SAMs. Thereafter, Duggan and Megahey repeatedly asked Hanratty if he had been contacted by Luis.

On May 2, 1982, at the direction of the FBI, Hanratty introduced Duggan to "Enrique," supposedly one of Luis's lieutenants, played by FBI Special Agent Enrique Ghimenti. The FBI videotaped Duggan's discussion with Ghimenti, in which Duggan described himself as a "buffer" who located available weapons for others to purchase. Duggan told Ghimenti that although he was interested in purchasing hand grenades and automatic weapons, his top-priority was the purchase of SAMs. The session concluded with an agreement to arrange another meeting, to be attended by PIRA representatives more experienced in weapons and prices. Duggan later reported to Hanratty that the meeting had gone well, that he believed Enrique and Luis had access to the missiles PIRA sought, and that although Hanratty was not to be involved in the upcoming transactions, he would remain the contact for both sides.

The meeting with PIRA's technical specialists took place in New Orleans and was also videotaped. Duggan introduced his associates and then absented himself from the discussions. Duggan's associates told Enrique and two undercover FBI agents, playing the roles of Luis and his technical advisor, that they were the "provisionals . . . the Irish Republican Army," and stated that "what we want is a weapon which will take down . . . [British] helicopters, . . . warships of the sky." Ultimately, an agreement was reached for PIRA to buy five "Redeye" missiles for $50,000.

The transaction was never consummated, however, as Megahey repeatedly sought to assure himself that PIRA was not dealing with law enforcement agents. (Megahey commented to Enrique that "the only thing we can lose in this is if you're a policeman.") Megahey proposed to have the buyers and sellers exchange hostages until the deal was done and the weapons were in place, reasoning that law enforcement agents would not risk either the loss of their hostage's life or the loss of the missiles. The FBI rejected the hostage proposal, and the proposed purchase of the SAMs was cancelled.

Shortly after these negotiations fell through, the four defendants herein were arrested. They and several of their associates were indicted in a seven-count indictment charging the firearms, explosives, munitions, and conspiracy offenses described at the outset of this opinion.

II. FISA

Enacted in 1978, FISA generally allows a federal officer, if authorized by the President of the United States acting through the Attorney General (or the Acting Attorney General or the Deputy Attorney General) of the United States, to obtain from a judge of the specially created FISA Court an order "approving electronic surveillance of a foreign power or an agent of a foreign power for the purpose of obtaining foreign intelligence information." 50 U.S.C. § 1802(b).

FISA contains several definitions of "foreign power" and "agent of a foreign power." Most pertinently to this case, FISA defines "foreign power" to include "a group engaged in international terrorism or activities in preparation therefor."§ 1801(a)(4).

A federal officer making application for a FISA order approving electronic surveillance must include in his application "the identity, if known, or a description of the target of the electronic surveillance," "a statement of the facts and circumstances relied upon by the applicant to justify his belief that . . . the target of the electronic surveillance is a foreign power or an agent of a foreign power," and a certification by an executive branch designee of the President that the certifying official deems the information sought to be foreign intelligence information and that the purpose of the surveillance is to obtain foreign intelligence information, together with a statement of the basis for the certification that the information sought is the type of foreign intelligence information designated. When the target is a United States person [citizen or resident alien], the government is required to minimize the acquisition and retention of nonpublic available information and to prohibit its dissemination, consistent with the need of the United States to obtain, produce, and disseminate foreign intelligence information, and the application must set out what minimization procedures are proposed.

The FISA Judge is authorized to enter an order approving electronic surveillance if he finds, *inter alia*, that "on the basis of the facts submitted by the applicant there is probable cause to believe that —

> (A) the target of the electronic surveillance is a foreign power or an agent of a foreign power: *Provided*, That no United States person may be considered a foreign power or an agent of a foreign power solely upon the basis of activities protected by the first amendment to the Constitution of the United States."

§ 1805(a)(3).

Defendants mount two types of challenge with regard to FISA. First, they contend that the Act is unconstitutional on several grounds. In addition, they contend that even if FISA is not unconstitutional, its requirements were not met in this case.

A. *The Constitutionality of FISA*

Defendants contend that FISA is unconstitutional principally on the grounds that (1) it is so broad as to deprive certain persons of due process of law, (2) it violates the probable cause requirement of the Fourth Amendment, and (3) it deprives nonresident aliens of the equal protection of the law. We find no merit in these contentions.

1. The Scope of the Act

Defendants argue that FISA is impermissibly broad in several respects. They point out that foreign intelligence information includes "information with respect to a foreign power . . . that relates to . . . (A) the national defense or the security of the United States; or (B) the conduct of the foreign affairs of the United States." They also point to the definition of an agent of a foreign power as a person, other than a United States person, who

> acts for or on behalf of a foreign power which engages in clandestine intelligence activities in the United States contrary to the interests of the United States, when the circumstances of such person's presence in the United States indicate that such person *may* engage in such activities in the United States,

§ 1801(b)(1)(B) (emphasis added), and to the definition of an agent of a foreign power as any person who

> knowingly engages in clandestine intelligence gathering activities for or on behalf of a foreign power, which activities involve or *may* involve a violation of the criminal statutes of the United States,

§ 1801(b)(2)(A) (emphasis added). Defendants argue that the breadth of the above definitions gives the Act unlimited scope and permits the electronic surveillance of persons who "may" be engaging in activities that "may" violate United States law.

Interesting though these arguments may be in the abstract, they have no application to the case at hand. The information relayed by Hanratty to the FBI clearly portrayed Megahey as a member of a "group engaged in international terrorism or activities in preparation therefor;" Megahey was therefore an agent of a foreign power under. There is no suggestion in the record that Megahey was targeted because he was or may have been gathering intelligence. The sections of the Act relied upon by the defendants to show that the Act is impermissibly broad are simply irrelevant to this case. The sections and definitions plainly applicable to Megahey are explicit, unequivocal, and clearly defined.

Nor are we impressed by defendants' argument that insofar as § 1801(e)(2) defines foreign intelligence information as information that "relates to . . . (A) the national defense or the security of the United States; or (B) the conduct of the foreign affairs of the United States" it is impermissibly vague. Section 1801(e)(1)(B) defines foreign intelligence information as "information that relates to . . . the ability of the United States to protect against . . . international terrorism by a foreign power or an agent of a foreign power." Given the information provided by Hanratty, the government plainly had a basis under this section for describing the information sought by surveillance of Megahey, self-proclaimed leader of an international terrorist group, as foreign intelligence information. Thus, even if we thought § 1801(e)(2)'s concepts of national defense, national security, or conduct of foreign affairs to be vague, which we do not, we would find therein no basis for reversing the convictions of these defendants, whose circumstances were governed by an entirely different definition.

2. The Probable Cause Requirement of the Fourth Amendment

The Fourth Amendment provides that "no warrants shall issue, but upon probable cause. . . . " Defendants argue principally (1) that the Amendment applies to all proposed surveillances, including those in national security cases, and (2) that even if there were an exception for national security matters, it would not apply to terrorism cases where the objects of the terrorism are entirely outside of the United States. We reject these contentions.

Prior to the enactment of FISA, virtually every court that had addressed the issue had concluded that the President had the inherent power to conduct warrantless electronic surveillance to collect foreign intelligence information, and that such surveillances constituted an exception to the warrant requirement of the Fourth Amendment. The Supreme Court specifically declined to address this issue in *United States v. United States District Court* [*Keith, J.*], 407 U.S. 297 (1972) (hereinafter referred to as "*Keith*"), but it had made clear that the requirements of the Fourth Amendment may change when differing governmental interests are at stake, and it observed in *Keith* that the governmental interests presented in national security investigations differ substantially from those presented in traditional criminal investigations.

In *Keith*, the government argued that Title III of the Omnibus Crime Control and Safe Streets Act, 18 U.S.C. §§ 2510 *et seq.* ("Title III"), recognized the constitutional authority of the President to conduct domestic security surveillances without a warrant. The Court rejected this argument, noting that the legislative history made clear that Title III was not intended to legislate with respect to national security surveillances. The Court went on to hold that a warrant was required in *Keith* under the Fourth Amendment; but the implication of its discussion was that the warrant requirement is flexible and that different standards may be compatible with the Fourth Amendment in light of the different purposes and practical considerations of domestic national security surveillances. Thus, the Court observed

> that domestic security surveillance may involve different policy and practical considerations from the surveillance of "ordinary crime." The gathering of security intelligence is often long range and involves the interrelation of various sources and types of information. The exact targets of such surveillance may be more difficult to identify than in surveillance operations against many types of

crime specified in Title III. Often, too, the emphasis of domestic intelligence gathering is on the prevention of unlawful activity or the enhancement of the Government's preparedness for some possible future crisis or emergency. Thus, the focus of domestic surveillance may be less precise than that directed against more conventional types of crime.

Different standards [for surveillance involving domestic security] may be compatible with the Fourth Amendment if they are reasonable both in relation to the legitimate need of Government for intelligence information and the protected rights of our citizens. For the warrant application may vary according to the governmental interest to be enforced and the nature of citizen rights deserving protection.

Id. at 322–23.

Against this background, Congress passed FISA to settle what it believed to be the unresolved question of the applicability of the Fourth Amendment warrant requirement to electronic surveillance for foreign intelligence purposes, and to "remove any doubt as to the lawfulness of such surveillance." In constructing this framework, Congress gave close scrutiny to departures from those Fourth Amendment doctrines applicable in the criminal-investigation context in order

to ensure that the procedures established in [FISA] are reasonable in relation to legitimate foreign counterintelligence requirements and the protected rights of individuals. Their reasonableness depends, in part, upon an assessment of the difficulties of investigating activities planned, directed, and supported from abroad by foreign intelligence services and foreign-based terrorist groups. The differences between ordinary criminal investigations to gather evidence of specific crimes and foreign counterintelligence investigations to uncover and monitor clandestine activities have been taken into account. Other factors include the international responsibilities of the United States, the duties of the Federal Government to the States in matters involving foreign terrorism, and the need to maintain the secrecy of lawful counterintelligence sources and methods.

Senate Report 95-701, at 14–15, *reprinted in* 1978 U.S. Code Cong. & Ad. News 3973, 3983.

We regard the procedures fashioned in FISA as a constitutionally adequate balancing of the individual's Fourth Amendment rights against the nation's need to obtain foreign intelligence information. The governmental concerns are detailed in the passages quoted above from *Keith* and the legislative history of FISA, and those concerns make reasonable the adoption of prerequisites to surveillance that are less stringent than those precedent to the issuance of a warrant for a criminal investigation. Against this background, the Act requires that the FISA Judge find probable cause to believe that the target is a foreign power or an agent of a foreign power, and that the place at which the electronic surveillance is to be directed is being used or is about to be used by a foreign power or an agent of a foreign power; and it requires him to find that the application meets the requirements of the Act. These requirements make it reasonable to dispense with a requirement that the FISA Judge find probable cause to believe that surveillance will in fact lead to the gathering of foreign intelligence information.[1] Further, if the target is a United States person, the Act requires the FISA Judge to determine that the executive branch's certifications pursuant to § 1804(a)(7) are not clearly erroneous in light of the application as a whole, and to find that the application properly proposes to minimize the intrusion upon the target's privacy.

---

[1] [Court's Footnote 5] A fortiori we reject defendants' argument that a FISA order may not be issued consistent with the requirements of the Fourth Amendment unless there is a showing of probable cause to believe the target has committed a crime.

We conclude that these requirements provide an appropriate balance between the individual's interest in privacy and the government's need to obtain foreign intelligence information, and that FISA does not violate the probable cause requirement of the Fourth Amendment.

4. Equal Protection

In several respects FISA treats United States persons, who are defined principally to include United States citizens and resident aliens, differently from non-United States persons.

Although both the Fourth Amendment and the Equal Protection Clause afford protection to all aliens, nothing in either provision prevents Congress from adopting standards and procedures that are more beneficial to United States citizens and resident aliens than to nonresident aliens, so long as the differences are reasonable. In [*Mathews v.*] *Diaz*, the Supreme Court unanimously upheld a federal statute denying aliens the right to enroll in the Medicare program unless they had been admitted for permanent residence and had resided in the United States for five years. The Court noted that

> the fact that all persons, aliens and citizens alike, are protected by the Due Process Clause does not lead to the further conclusion that all aliens are entitled to enjoy all the advantages of citizenship. . . . [A] host of constitutional and statutory provisions rest on the premise that a legitimate distinction between citizens and aliens may justify attributes and benefits for one class not accorded to the other.

Thus, the Court recognized, as it had in the past, that it was appropriate that the political branches of government have the responsibility for regulating the relationship between the United States and aliens, since these matters implicate relations with foreign powers, and "a wide variety of classifications must be defined in the light of changing political and economic circumstances." Accordingly, the Court has adopted a stance of minimal scrutiny respecting federal regulations that contain alienage-based classifications.

In enacting FISA, Congress plainly perceived a need to treat nonresident aliens and United States persons differently. In discussing a provision in an earlier draft of the Act, which provided for a less strict probable cause standard for non-United States persons, Senate Report 95-604 observed that

> where there are compelling considerations of national security, alienage distinctions are clearly lawful. This Committee is aware that less intrusive investigative techniques may not be able to obtain sufficient information about persons visiting here only for a limited time; the additional showing required for United States citizens and permanent resident aliens, therefore, may simply not be possible.

We agree with the district court that the different treatment accorded nonresident aliens under FISA is rationally related to the "Act's purposes of attempting to protect the United States against various types of acts of foreign powers and to acquire information necessary to the national defense or the conduct of foreign affairs." In each instance, the distinctions are justified both by the greater likelihood that those engaged in the type of activities against which FISA seeks to protect the United States will be nonresident aliens, and by the need for the government to be able to act more quickly in situations where the target is unlikely to reside permanently in the United States.

B. *Compliance with the Requirements of FISA*

Defendants contend that, even if FISA is constitutional, the evidence derived from the wiretap should have been suppressed because the provisions of FISA were not complied with, in that (1) the surveillance was conducted as part of a criminal investigation, rather than a national security investigation; (2) the district court erred in failing to disclose the information contained in the FISA applications and orders; and (3) Duggan, although allegedly a "target" of the FISA surveillance, was not so named in the FISA applications. We reject each of these contentions.

1. The Alleged Use of FISA Surveillance To Conduct a Criminal Investigation

Defendants contend that the surveillance of Megahey's telephone was not authorized by FISA because the information was sought as part of a criminal investigation. We see no grounds for concluding that the requirements of FISA were not met.

FISA permits federal officials to obtain orders authorizing electronics surveillance "for the purpose of obtaining foreign intelligence information." The requirement that foreign intelligence information be the primary objective of the surveillance is plain not only from the language of § 1802(b) but also from the requirements in § 1804 as to what the application must contain. The application must contain a certification by a designated official of the executive branch that the purpose of the surveillance is to acquire foreign intelligence information, and the certification must set forth the basis for the certifying official's believe that the information sought is the type of foreign intelligence information described.

Once this certification is made, however, it is, under FISA, subjected to only minimal scrutiny by the courts. Congress deemed it a sufficient check in this regard to require the FISA Judge (1) to find probable cause to believe that the target of the requested surveillance is an agent of a foreign power; (2) to find that the application is complete and in proper form; and (3) when the target is a United States person, to find that the certifications are not "clearly erroneous." The FISA Judge, in reviewing the application, is not to second-guess the executive branch official's certification that the objective of the surveillance is foreign intelligence information. Further, Congress intended that, when a person affected by a FISA surveillance challenges the FISA Court's order, a reviewing court is to have no greater authority to second-guess the executive branch's certifications than has the FISA Judge.[2]

We see no basis for any suggestion in the present case that the application to the FISA Court did not meet the statutory requirement for certifying that the information sought was foreign intelligence information. At the time of the FISA application, the executive branch was aware that PIRA was an international terrorist organization and that Megahey played a leadership role in PIRA activities. In such circumstances, the foreign intelligence value of a FISA wiretap on Megahey's telephone would be plain: he would likely be a prime source of information relating to PIRA membership, goals, methods, and operations. The publicly filed government affidavits in this case make clear that the FISA surveillance was instituted as part of an investigation of international terrorism. Moreover, we have reviewed the *in camera* submissions to the FISA Judge, and we agree with the district court's finding that "the purpose of the surveillance in this case, both initially and throughout, was to secure foreign intelligence information and was not, as [the] defendants assert, directed towards criminal investigation or the institution of a criminal prosecution."

Finally, we emphasize that otherwise valid FISA surveillance is not tainted simply because the government can anticipate that the fruits of such surveillance may later be used, as allowed by § 1806(b), as evidence in a criminal trial. Congress recognized that in many cases the concerns of the government with respect to foreign intelligence will

---

[2] [Court's Footnote 6] FISA cannot, of course, give the government carte blanche to obtain a surveillance order in violation of a target's right to due process, and an application in which the requisite representations were fraudulently made would constitute such a violation. To be entitled to a hearing as to the validity of those presentations, the person challenging the FISA surveillance would be required to make "a substantial preliminary showing that a false statement knowingly and intentionally, or with reckless disregard for the truth, was included" in the application and that the allegedly false statement was "necessary" to the FISA Judge's approval of the application. Defendants have made no such showing here.

overlap those with respect to law enforcement. Thus, one Senate Report noted that

> intelligence and criminal law enforcement tend to merge in [the area of foreign counterintelligence investigations]. . . .
>
> Surveillances conducted under [FISA] need not stop once conclusive evidence of a crime is obtained, but instead may be extended longer where protective measures other than arrest and prosecution are more appropriate.

In sum, FISA authorizes surveillance for the purpose of obtaining foreign intelligence information; the information possessed about Megahey involved international terrorism; and the fact that domestic law enforcement concerns may also have been implicated did not eliminate the government's ability to obtain a valid FISA order.

2. The District Court's Refusal to Disclose the Substance of the FISA Applications

Defendant's contention that the district court erred in refusing to disclose the substance of the affidavits and certifications that accompanied the FISA applications need not detain us long. Section 1806(f) of FISA provides for *in camera, ex parte* review of the documents where the Attorney General has filed an affidavit stating that disclosure of the FISA applications and orders would harm the national security of the United States. The judge has the discretion to disclose portions of the documents, under appropriate protective procedures, only if he decides that such disclosure is "necessary to make an accurate determination of the legality of the surveillance." Such a need might arise if the judge's initial review revealed potential irregularities such as "possible misrepresentation of fact, vague identification of the persons to be surveilled or surveillance records which include . . . a significant amount of nonforeign intelligence information, calling into question compliance with the minimization standards contained in the order."

3. The Failure to Name Duggan as a Target of the Surveillance

Defendants contend that the fruits of the FISA surveillance should be suppressed because Duggan was not named as a target of the surveillance. The import of this argument is, apparently, that because Duggan is a United States person, the preconditions to granting an FISA order allowing surveillance of Duggan would have been more stringent than they were for surveillance of Megahey, a nonresident alien.

The identification requirement imposed by FISA is only that an application for surveillance identify the "target of the electronic surveillance." Once the proper preconditions are established with respect to a particular target, there is no requirement in FISA that all those likely to be overheard engaging in foreign intelligence conversations be named. The consequent differences between the prerequisites for surveillance for crime control purposes and those for surveillance for national security purposes under FISA are reflections of Congress's view of the differing governmental interests to be served.

IV. Appellants' Other Contensions

Defendants make a variety of other arguments, chiefly that (1) the district court should have instructed the jury that it should find the defendants not guilty if it found they had relied on the apparent authority of Hanratty as an agent of the CIA; (2) the conduct of the government in conducting the investigation was so outrageous that it deprived them of due process of law; and (3) the court erred in making various evidentiary rulings.[3] We find merit in none of them.

---

[3] [Court's Footnote 9] Among their other arguments, defendants assert that the district court should have suppressed the evidence, obtained through the search by customs officials at Port Newark, New Jersey, of the shipping container loaded with weapons and electronics equipment by Eamon and Colm Meehan. [S]ince the

A. *The Mistake of Law Defense*

Defendants contend that the district court erred in refusing to give their proposed jury instruction allowing them a defense for reasonable good faith reliance on apparent authority, based on their alleged mistaken belief that Hanratty had apparent authority to sanction their gun-running activities. We conclude that the court properly refused to give the instruction since defendants had failed to demonstrate a basis warranting submission of this requested charge to the jury.

The only evidence presented by defendants to justify their reliance on Hanratty's apparent authority is their testimony that Hanratty represented himself to be a CIA agent and showed Duggan and Megahey a white laminated card with "Central Intelligence Agency" printed on it, and their testimony that Sloan had "checked Hanratty out." No objective evidence was presented regarding Hanratty's purported CIA claim and there was no corroboration of defendant' claims about Hanratty's alleged assertions. The defendants knew Hanratty for only three weeks before they began dealing with him, they lacked personal knowledge of his claimed status, and they sought no independent verification that he was a CIA agent.

Nor was any reasonable legal basis shown for defendants' professed belief that Hanratty had authority to sanction such plainly unlawful activity as international trafficking in firearms and explosives. Indeed, Megahey acknowledged, on cross-examination, that he was aware that CIA operatives had been sought on criminal charges, despite their CIA background, for engaging in the same conduct the defendants attributed to Hanratty.

In sum, we agree with the district court that the defendants failed to establish that they were entitled to a jury instruction on any defense based on an exception to the general principle that a mistake of law is no defense.

B. *The "Outrageous Government Behavior" Defense*

Defendants argue that the behavior of the government in the investigation of this case was so outrageous and shocking as to deprive them of due process of law. They contend chiefly that Hanratty, the FBI informant, played on their emotional and psychological sensitivities to the situation in Northern Ireland in a successful effort to coerce them into committing unlawful acts. We find these contentions without merit.

The Supreme Court has noted the possibility that a due process violation grounded in outrageous government conduct might be available even if the defendant, because of his predisposition, could not establish an entrapment defense.

We have rarely sustained due process claims concerning government investigative conduct, stressing that the conduct involved must be "most egregious," and " 'so repugnant and excessive' as to shock the conscience." Thus, we have upheld against due process challenges drug convictions resulting from transactions initiated by government informants using government-supplied drugs, and convictions in the Abscam cases, where government operatives proposed various unlawful schemes.

[I]n this case Duggan has admitted that it was he who sought out Hanratty. Duggan was not introduced to undercover FBI agents until after he and Megahey repeatedly asked Hanratty about his gun-running acquaintance, "Luis"; and all other initiatives came from the defendants as well. The overwhelming evidence presented through tape, videotape, and the testimony of the government witnesses supports the district court's refusal to grant defendants' motion to dismiss on this due process argument.

We have considered all of defendants' remaining contentions and find them to be without merit.

---

containers were scheduled to be shipped from port imminently, the search was authorized under the border-search exception to the Fourth Amendment.

CONCLUSION

The judgments of conviction are affirmed.

NOTES AND QUESTIONS

1. FISA Structure. Several aspects of FISA, which is a complicated statutory scheme at first glance, may make the structure more clear:

a. Under FISA, agents do not even need a court order to engage in electronic surveillance of communications or premises of foreign powers if the Attorney General certifies that there is "no substantial likelihood that the surveillance will acquire the contents of any communication to which a United States person is a party."

b. To obtain a court order authorizing electronic surveillance of foreign agents, it is not necessary for the investigator to allege probable cause of a criminal violation; it is enough that there is probable cause to believe that the "target of the surveillance is a foreign power or agent of a foreign power," that "a significant purpose of the surveillance is to obtain" information helpful for protection of national security, and that acceptable "minimization procedures" are in place. Some observers believe that the order could be called a warrant, but the terminology helps distinguish it from a warrant based on probable cause to believe that a crime has been committed by a specified person.

c. If information acquired in a FISA surveillance is subsequently used in a criminal prosecution, the defendant may make a motion to suppress on the basis that the information was not lawfully acquired or that the surveillance did not conform to the court order. In this instance, the government may provide the court *ex parte* and *in camera* with "such materials relating to the surveillance as may be necessary to determine whether the surveillance was lawfully authorized and conducted.

d. Similar procedures and criteria apply with regard to physical searches of premises.

2. "Purpose" and the "Wall." Prior to the USA PATRIOT Act, passed in October 2001, the "purpose" language required that "the purpose" of the surveillance be acquisition of foreign intelligence information. In ruling on motions to suppress, trial courts frequently had to assess whether the purpose of the surveillance was truly for intelligence purposes rather than to obtain evidence for a prosecution. Under the minimization guidelines of the Justice Department, a "wall" was erected between intelligence and prosecution so that the transfer of information from an intelligence operation to prosecution required approval of higher officials. As the courts struggled with this issue, they were split on whether "the purpose" meant "sole purpose," "dominant purpose," or "any purpose." The 2001 change to "a significant purpose" was designed to resolve this controversy, but it also could have the effect of reducing the level of judicial review over the application. The FISA Court of Review opinion below addresses these issues.

It may be helpful at this stage to revisit the prosecutions in *Salameh* and *Rahman* with the fourth amendment issues in mind. *Sarkissian* and *Duggan* are both examples of how a FISA surveillance can generate evidence for a criminal prosecution.

3. *United States v. Isa.* Bearing in mind the "purpose" requirement, a tragic and interesting example is *United States v. Isa*, 923 F.2d 1300 (8th Cir. 1991), in which a FISA surveillance resulted in electronic taping of the target's murdering of his 16-year-old daughter. When the Attorney General decided to turn the tapes over to the state for prosecution of the murder, the U.S. sought a declaratory judgment in federal court of the legality under federal law of using that evidence in the state prosecution. The information on which the FISA order was based was presented to the court *ex parte* and *in camera* to prevent disclosure of the reasons for surveilling the target. The result of the federal court's ruling on the validity of the surveillance would then be to prevent public disclosure of that information in a subsequent state hearing to suppress the evidence.

4. DOJ and the FISA Court. The operations of the FISC are conducted in a highly secure controlled-access room within the building of the Justice Department in Washington, soon to be replaced by the court's own facility. Given the feeling of being "special" that is attached to appointment to this court, and the "glamor" of being on the inside of important proceedings, isn't there a significant likelihood that the judges will be "co-opted" to the point of view of the government in these proceedings? Most criticisms of the PATRIOT Act amendments to FISA have argued against its search and seizure provisions almost as if there were no judicial review of FBI requests for FISA orders. On the other hand, Article III judges tend to be fiercely proud of the independent status of the U.S. judiciary, and it is very difficult to know how these procedures will intrude into that feeling of independence.

5. *United States v. Cavanagh.* *United States v. Cavanagh*, 807 F.2d 787 (9th Cir. 1987), held that the FISA designation of judges is not unconstitutional even though they serve limited terms because they are still Article III judges and serve an Article III purpose.

IN RE SEALED CASE NO. 02-001
310 F.3d 717 (FIS Ct. Review 2002)

On Motions for Review of Orders of the United States Foreign Intelligence Surveillance Court

Before: GUY, SENIOR CIRCUIT JUDGE, PRESIDING; SILBERMAN and LEAVY, SENIOR CIRCUIT JUDGES.

PER CURIAM.

This is the first appeal from the Foreign Intelligence Surveillance Court to the Court of Review since the passage of the Foreign Intelligence Surveillance Act (FISA) in 1978. This appeal is brought by the United States from a FISA court surveillance order which imposed certain restrictions on the government. Since the government is the only party to FISA proceedings, we have accepted briefs filed by the American Civil Liberties Union (ACLU)[4] and the National Association of Criminal Defense Lawyers (NACDL) as *amici curiae*.

Not surprisingly this case raises important questions of statutory interpretation, and constitutionality. After a careful review of the briefs filed by the government and *amici*, we conclude that FISA, as amended by the Patriot Act, supports the government's position, and that the restrictions imposed by the FISA court are not required by FISA or the Constitution. We therefore remand for further proceedings in accordance with this opinion.

I.

The court's decision from which the government appeals imposed certain requirements and limitations accompanying an order authorizing electronic surveillance of an "agent of a foreign power" as defined in FISA. There is no disagreement between the government and the FISA court as to the propriety of the electronic surveillance; the court found that the government had shown probable cause to believe that the target is an agent of a foreign power and otherwise met the basic requirements of FISA. The government's application for a surveillance order contains detailed information to support its contention that the target, who is a United States

---

[4] [Court's Footnote 1] Joining the ACLU on its brief are the Center for Democracy and Technology, Center for National Security Studies, Electronic Privacy Information Center, and Electronic Frontier Foundation.

person, is aiding, abetting, or conspiring with others in international terrorism.[5] The FISA court authorized the surveillance, but imposed certain restrictions, which the government contends are neither mandated nor authorized by FISA. Particularly, the court ordered that

> law enforcement officials shall not make recommendations to intelligence officials concerning the initiation, operation, continuation or expansion of FISA searches or surveillances. Additionally, the FBI and the Criminal Division [of the Department of Justice] shall ensure that law enforcement officials do not direct or control the use of the FISA procedures to enhance criminal prosecution, and that advice intended to preserve the option of a criminal prosecution does not inadvertently result in the Criminal Division's directing or controlling the investigation using FISA searches and surveillances toward law enforcement objectives.

To ensure the Justice Department followed these strictures the court also fashioned what the government refers to as a "chaperone requirement"; that a unit of the Justice Department, the Office of Intelligence Policy and Review (OIPR) (composed of 31 lawyers and 25 support staff), "be invited" to all meetings between the FBI and the Criminal Division involving consultations for the purpose of coordinating efforts "to investigate or protect against foreign attack or other grave hostile acts, sabotage, international terrorism, or clandestine intelligence activities by foreign powers or their agents. If representatives of OIPR are unable to attend such meetings, "OIPR shall be apprized of the substance of the meetings forthwith in writing so that the Court may be notified at the earliest opportunity."

The opinion was issued after an oral argument before all of the then-serving FISA district judges and clearly represents the views of all those judges. We think it fair to say, however, that the May 17 opinion of the FISA court does not clearly set forth the basis for its decision. It appears to proceed from the assumption that FISA constructed a barrier between counterintelligence/ intelligence officials and law enforcement officers in the Executive Branch — indeed, it uses the word "wall" popularized by certain commentators (and journalists) to describe that supposed barrier. Yet the opinion does not support that assumption with any relevant language from the statute.

The "wall" emerges from the court's implicit interpretation of FISA. The court apparently believes it can approve applications for electronic surveillance only if the government's objective is *not* primarily directed toward criminal prosecution of the foreign agents for their foreign intelligence activity. But the court neither refers to any FISA language supporting that view, nor does it reference the Patriot Act amendments, which the government contends specifically altered FISA to make clear that an application could be obtained even if criminal prosecution is the primary counter mechanism.

Instead the court relied for its imposition of the disputed restrictions on its statutory authority to approve "minimization procedures" designed to prevent the acquisition, retention, and dissemination within the government of material gathered in an electronic surveillance that is unnecessary to the government's need for foreign intelligence information.

II.

The government makes two main arguments. The first, it must be noted, was not presented to the FISA court; indeed, insofar as we can determine it has never previously been advanced either before a court or Congress.[6] That argument is that the supposed

---

[5] [Court's Footnote 3] The bracketed information is classified and has been redacted from the public version of the opinion.

[6] [Court's Footnote 6] Since proceedings before the FISA court and the Court of Review are ex parte —

pre-Patriot Act limitation in FISA that restricts the government's intention to use foreign intelligence information in criminal prosecutions is an illusion; it finds no support in either the language of FISA or its legislative history. The government does recognize that several courts of appeals, while upholding the use of FISA surveillances, have opined that FISA may be used only if the government's primary purpose in pursuing foreign intelligence information is not criminal prosecution, but the government argues that those decisions, which did not carefully analyze the statute, were incorrect in their statements, if not incorrect in their holdings.

Alternatively, the government contends that even if the primary purpose test was a legitimate construction of FISA prior to the passage of the Patriot Act, that Act's amendments to FISA eliminate that concept. And as a corollary, the government insists the FISA court's construction of the minimization procedures is far off the mark both because it is a misconstruction of those provisions *per se*, as well as an end run around the specific amendments in the Patriot Act designed to deal with the real issue underlying this case. The government, moreover, contends that the FISA court's restrictions, which the court described as minimization procedures, are so intrusive into the operation of the Department of Justice as to exceed the constitutional authority of Article III judges.

The government's brief, and its supplementary brief requested by this court, also set forth its view that the primary purpose test is not required by the Fourth Amendment. The ACLU and NACDL argue, *inter alia*, the contrary; that the statutes are unconstitutional unless they are construed as prohibiting the government from obtaining approval of an application under FISA if its "primary purpose" is criminal prosecution.

The 1978 FISA

We turn first to the statute as enacted in 1978. It authorizes a judge on the FISA court to grant an application for an order approving electronic surveillance to "obtain foreign intelligence information" if "there is probable cause to believe that . . . the target of the electronic surveillance is a foreign power or an agent of a foreign power," and that "each of the facilities or places at which the surveillance is directed is being used, or is about to be used, by a foreign power or an agent of a foreign power." 50 U.S.C. § 1805(a)(3).

The definition of an agent of a foreign power, if it pertains to a U.S. person (which is the only category relevant to this case), is closely tied to criminal activity. The term includes any person who "knowingly engages in clandestine intelligence gathering activities . . . which activities involve or may involve a violation of the *criminal statutes* of the United States," or "knowingly engages in sabotage or international terrorism, or activities that are in preparation therefor." §§ 1801(b)(2)(A), (C) (emphasis added). International terrorism refers to activities that "involve violent acts or acts dangerous to human life that are a violation of the *criminal laws* of the United States or of any State, or that would be a *criminal violation* if committed within the jurisdiction of the United States or any State." § 1801(c)(1) (emphasis added). Sabotage means activities that "involve a violation of chapter 105 of [the criminal code], or that would involve such a violation if committed against the United States." § 1801(d). For purposes of clarity in this opinion we will refer to the crimes referred to in section 1801(a)–(e) as foreign intelligence crimes.

In light of these definitions, it is quite puzzling that the Justice Department, at some point during the 1980s, began to read the statute as limiting the Department's ability to obtain FISA orders if it intended to prosecute the targeted agents — even for foreign intelligence crimes. To be sure, section 1804, which sets forth the elements of an

---

not adversary — we can entertain an argument supporting the government's position not presented to the lower court.

application for an order, required a national security official in the Executive Branch — typically the Director of the FBI — to certify that "the purpose" of the surveillance is to obtain foreign intelligence information (amended by the Patriot Act to read "a significant purpose"). But as the government now argues, the definition of foreign intelligence information includes evidence of crimes such as espionage, sabotage or terrorism. Indeed, it is virtually impossible to read the 1978 FISA to exclude from its purpose the prosecution of foreign intelligence crimes, most importantly because, as we have noted, the definition of an agent of a foreign power — if he or she is a U.S. person — is grounded on criminal conduct.

The government argues persuasively that arresting and prosecuting terrorist agents of, or spies for, a foreign power may well be the best technique to prevent them from successfully continuing their terrorist or espionage activity. The government might wish to surveil the agent for some period of time to discover other participants in a conspiracy or to uncover a foreign power's plans, but typically at some point the government would wish to apprehend the agent and it might be that only a prosecution would provide sufficient incentives for the agent to cooperate with the government. Indeed, the threat of prosecution might be sufficient to "turn the agent." It would seem that the Congress actually anticipated the government's argument and explicitly approved it.

The origin of what the government refers to as the false dichotomy between foreign intelligence information that is evidence of foreign intelligence crimes and that which is not appears to have been a Fourth Circuit case decided in 1980. *United States v. Truong Dinh Hung*, 629 F.2d 908 (4th Cir. 1980). That case, however, involved an electronic surveillance carried out prior to the passage of FISA and predicated on the President's executive power. In approving the district court's exclusion of evidence obtained through a warrantless surveillance subsequent to the point in time when the government's investigation became "primarily" driven by law enforcement objectives, the court held that the Executive Branch should be excused from securing a warrant only when "the object of the search or the surveillance is a foreign power, its agents or collaborators," and "the surveillance is conducted 'primarily' for foreign intelligence reasons." Targets must "receive the protection of the warrant requirement if the government is primarily attempting to put together a criminal prosecution."

Several circuits have followed *Truong* in applying similar versions of the "primary purpose" test, despite the fact that *Truong* was not a FISA decision. (It was an interpretation of the Constitution, in the context of measuring the boundaries of the President's inherent executive authority, and we discuss *Truong's* constitutional analysis at length in Section III of this opinion.) In one of the first major challenges to a FISA search, *United States v. Duggan*, 743 F.2d 59 (2d Cir. 1984), the district court acknowledged that while Congress clearly viewed arrest and prosecution as one of the possible outcomes of a FISA investigation, surveillance under FISA would nevertheless be "appropriate only if foreign intelligence surveillance is the Government's primary purpose." The Second Circuit approved [the district court's] finding that the surveillance was not "directed towards criminal investigation or the institution of a criminal prosecution." Implicitly then, the Second Circuit endorsed the dichotomy. Two other circuits, the Fourth and the Eleventh, have similarly approved district court findings that a surveillance was primarily for foreign intelligence purposes without any discussion [of] the validity of the dichotomy. *See United States v. Pelton*, 835 F.2d 1067, 1075–76 (4th Cir. 1987); *United States v. Badia*, 827 F.2d 1458, 1464 (11th Cir. 1987).

Then, the First Circuit, seeing *Duggan* as following *Truong*, explicitly interpreted FISA's purpose wording in section 1804(a)(7)(B) to mean that "although evidence obtained under FISA subsequently may be used in criminal prosecutions, the investigation of criminal activity cannot be the primary purpose of the surveillance." *United States v. Johnson*, 952 F.2d 565, 572 (1st Cir. 1991). Notably, however, the Ninth Circuit has refused

to draw too fine a distinction between criminal and intelligence investigations.

"International terrorism," by definition, requires the investigation of activities that constitute crimes. That the government may later choose to prosecute is irrelevant. . . . FISA is meant to take into account "the differences between ordinary criminal investigations to gather evidence of specific crimes and foreign counterintelligence investigations to uncover and monitor clandestine activities."

United States v. Sarkissian, 841 F.2d 959, 964 (9th Cir. 1988).

Neither *Duggan* nor *Johnson* tied the "primary purpose" test to *actual* statutory language. It is almost as if *Duggan*, and particularly *Johnson*, assume that the government seeks foreign intelligence information (counterintelligence) for its own sake — to expand its pool of knowledge — because there is no discussion of how the government would use that information outside criminal prosecutions. That is not to say that the government could have no other use for that information. The government's overriding concern is to stop or frustrate the agent's or the foreign power's activity by any means, but if one considers the actual ways in which the government would foil espionage or terrorism it becomes apparent that criminal prosecution analytically cannot be placed easily in a separate response category. It may well be that the government itself, in an effort to conform to district court holdings, accepted the dichotomy it now contends is false.

In sum, we think that the FISA as passed by Congress in 1978 clearly did *not* preclude or limit the government's use or proposed use of foreign intelligence information, which included evidence of certain kinds of criminal activity, in a criminal prosecution.

Apparently to avoid running afoul of the primary purpose test used by some courts, the 1995 [Attorney General] Procedures limited contacts between the FBI and the Criminal Division in cases where FISA surveillance or searches were being conducted by the FBI for foreign intelligence (FI) or foreign counterintelligence (FCI) purposes. The procedures state that "the FBI and Criminal Division should ensure that advice intended to preserve the option of a criminal prosecution does not inadvertently result in either the fact or the appearance of the Criminal Division's *directing or controlling* the FI or FCI investigation toward law enforcement objectives." Although these procedures provided for significant information sharing and coordination between criminal and FI or FCI investigations, based at least in part on the "directing or controlling" language, they eventually came to be narrowly interpreted within the Department of Justice, and most particularly by OIPR, as requiring OIPR to act as a "wall" to prevent the FBI intelligence officials from communicating with the Criminal Division regarding ongoing FI or FCI investigations. Once prosecution of the target was being considered, the procedures, as interpreted by OIPR in light of the case law, prevented the Criminal Division from providing any meaningful advice to the FBI.

The Patriot Act and the FISA Court's Decision

The passage of the Patriot Act altered and to some degree muddied the landscape. In October 2001, Congress amended FISA to change "the purpose" language in 1804(a)(7)(B) to "a significant purpose." It also added a provision allowing "Federal officers who conduct electronic surveillance to acquire foreign intelligence information" to "consult with Federal law enforcement officers to coordinate efforts to investigate or protect against" attack or other grave hostile acts, sabotage or international terrorism, or clandestine intelligence activities, by foreign powers or their agents. § 1806(k)(1). And such coordination "shall not preclude" the government's certification that a significant purpose of the surveillance is to obtain foreign intelligence information, or the issuance of an order authorizing the surveillance. § 1806(k)(2). Although the Patriot Act amendments to FISA expressly sanctioned consultation and coordination between intelligence and law enforcement officials, in response to the first applications filed by

OIPR under those amendments, in November 2001, the FISA court for the first time adopted the 1995 Procedures, as augmented by the January 2000 and August 2001 Procedures, as "minimization procedures" to apply in all cases before the court.

The Attorney General interpreted the Patriot Act quite differently. On March 6, 2002, the Attorney General approved new "Intelligence Sharing Procedures" to implement the Act's amendments to FISA. The 2002 Procedures supersede prior procedures and were designed to permit the complete exchange of information and advice between intelligence and law enforcement officials. They eliminated the "direction and control" test and allowed the exchange of advice between the FBI, OIPR, and the Criminal Division regarding "the initiation, operation, continuation, or expansion of FISA searches or surveillance." On March 7, 2002, the government filed a motion with the FISA court, noting that the Department of Justice had adopted the 2002 Procedures and proposing to follow those procedures in all matters before the court. The government also asked the FISA court to vacate its orders adopting the prior procedures as minimization procedures in all cases and imposing special "wall" procedures in certain cases.

Unpersuaded by the Attorney General's interpretation of the Patriot Act, the court ordered that the 2002 Procedures be adopted, *with modifications*, as minimization procedures to apply in all cases. The court emphasized that the definition of minimization procedures had not been amended by the Patriot Act, and reasoned that the 2002 Procedures "cannot be used by the government to amend the Act in ways Congress has not."

Essentially, the FISA court took portions of the Attorney General's augmented 1995 Procedures — adopted to deal with the primary purpose standard — and imposed them generically as minimization procedures. In doing so, the FISA court erred. It did not provide any constitutional basis for its action — we think there is none — and misconstrued the main statutory provision on which it relied. The court mistakenly categorized the augmented 1995 Procedures as FISA minimization procedures and then compelled the government to utilize a modified version of those procedures in a way that is clearly inconsistent with the statutory purpose.

[T]he Patriot Act amendments clearly disapprove the primary purpose test. And as a matter of straightforward logic, if a FISA application can be granted even if "foreign intelligence" is only a significant — not a primary — purpose, another purpose can be primary. One other legitimate purpose that could exist is to prosecute a target for a foreign intelligence crime. We therefore believe the Patriot Act amply supports the government's alternative argument but, paradoxically, the Patriot Act would seem to conflict with the government's first argument because by using the term "significant purpose," the Act now implies that another purpose is to be distinguished from a foreign intelligence purpose.

In short, even though we agree that the original FISA did not contemplate the "false dichotomy," the Patriot Act actually did — which makes it no longer false. The addition of the word "significant" to section 1804(a)(7)(B) imposed a requirement that the government have a measurable foreign intelligence purpose, other than just criminal prosecution of even foreign intelligence crimes.

The important point is — and here we agree with the government — the Patriot Act amendment, by using the word "significant," eliminated any justification for the FISA court to balance the relative weight the government places on criminal prosecution as compared to other counterintelligence responses. If the certification of the application's purpose articulates a broader objective than criminal prosecution — such as stopping an ongoing conspiracy — and includes other potential non-prosecutorial responses, the government meets the statutory test.

III.

Having determined that FISA, as amended, does not oblige the government to demonstrate to the FISA court that its primary purpose in conducting electronic surveillance is *not* criminal prosecution, we are obliged to consider whether the statute as amended is consistent with the Fourth Amendment. The Fourth Amendment provides:

> The right of the people to be secure in their persons, houses, papers, and effects, against unreasonable searches and seizures, shall not be violated, and no Warrants shall issue, but upon probable cause, supported by Oath or affirmation, and particularly describing the place to be searched, and the persons or things to be seized.

Although the FISA court did not explicitly rely on the Fourth Amendment, it at least suggested that this provision was the animating principle driving its statutory analysis. The FISA court indicated that its disapproval of the Attorney General's 2002 Procedures was based on the need to safeguard the "privacy of Americans in these highly intrusive surveillances and searches," which implies the invocation of the Fourth Amendment.

Did Truong *Articulate the Appropriate Constitutional Standard?*

It will be recalled that the case that set forth the primary purpose test *as constitutionally required* was *Truong*. The Fourth Circuit thought that Keith's balancing standard implied the adoption of the primary purpose test. We reiterate that *Truong* dealt with a pre-FISA surveillance based on the President's constitutional responsibility to conduct the foreign affairs of the United States. Although *Truong* suggested the line it drew was a constitutional minimum that would apply to a FISA surveillance, it had no occasion to consider the application of the statute carefully. The *Truong* court, as did all the other courts to have decided the issue, held that the President did have inherent authority to conduct warrantless searches to obtain foreign intelligence information. It was incumbent upon the court, therefore, to determine the boundaries of that constitutional authority in the case before it. We take for granted that the President does have that authority and, assuming that is so, FISA could not encroach on the President's constitutional power. The question before us is the reverse, does FISA amplify the President's power by providing a mechanism that at least approaches a classic warrant and which therefore supports the government's contention that FISA searches are constitutionally reasonable.

The Fourth Circuit recognized that the Supreme Court had never considered the constitutionality of warrantless government searches for foreign intelligence reasons, but concluded the analytic framework the Supreme Court adopted in *Keith* — in the case of domestic intelligence surveillance — pointed the way to the line the Fourth Circuit drew. The Court in *Keith* had, indeed, balanced the government's interest against individual privacy interests, which is undoubtedly the key to this issue as well; but we think the *Truong* court misconceived the government's interest and, moreover, did not draw a more appropriate distinction that *Keith* at least suggested. That is the line drawn in the original FISA statute itself between ordinary crimes and foreign intelligence crimes.

It will be recalled that *Keith* carefully avoided the issue of a warrantless foreign intelligence search: "We have not addressed, and express no opinion as to, the issues which may be involved with respect to activities of foreign powers or their agents." But in indicating that a somewhat more relaxed warrant could suffice in the domestic intelligence situation, the court drew a distinction between the crime involved in that case, which posed a threat to national security, and "ordinary crime." It pointed out that "the focus of domestic surveillance may be less precise than that directed against more conventional types of crimes."

The main purpose of ordinary criminal law is twofold: to punish the wrongdoer and to deter other persons in society from embarking on the same course. The government's concern with respect to foreign intelligence crimes, on the other hand, is overwhelmingly to stop or frustrate the immediate criminal activity. As we discussed in the first section of this opinion, the criminal process is often used as part of an integrated effort to counter the malign efforts of a foreign power. Punishment of the terrorist or espionage agent is really a secondary objective; indeed, punishment of a terrorist is often a moot point.

Supreme Court's Special Needs Cases

The distinction between ordinary criminal prosecutions and extraordinary situations underlies the Supreme Court's approval of entirely warrantless and even suspicionless searches that are designed to serve the government's "special needs, beyond the normal need for law enforcement." *Vernonia School Dist. 47J v. Acton*, 515 U.S. 646, 653 (1995) (random drug-testing of student athletes).[7] Apprehending drunk drivers and securing the border constitute such unique interests beyond ordinary, general law enforcement. *Id.* at 654.

A recent case, *City of Indianapolis v. Edmond*, 531 U.S. 32 (2000), is relied on by both the government and *amici*. In that case, the Court held that a highway check point designed to catch drug dealers did not fit within its special needs exception because the government's "primary purpose" was merely "to uncover evidence of ordinary criminal wrongdoing." The Court rejected the government's argument that the "severe and intractable nature of the drug problem" was sufficient justification for such a dragnet seizure lacking any individualized suspicion. *Amici* particularly rely on the Court's statement that "the gravity of the threat alone cannot be dispositive of questions concerning what means law enforcement officers may employ to pursue a given purpose."

But by "purpose" the Court makes clear it was referring not to a subjective intent, which is not relevant in ordinary Fourth Amendment probable cause analysis, but rather to a programmatic purpose. The Court distinguished the prior check point cases *Martinez-Fuerte* (involving checkpoints less than 100 miles from the Mexican border) and *Sitz* (checkpoints to detect intoxicated motorists) on the ground that the former involved the government's "long-standing concern for the protection of the integrity of the border," and the latter was "aimed at reducing the immediate hazard posed by the presence of drunk drivers on the highways." The Court emphasized that it was decidedly not drawing a distinction between suspicionless seizures with a "non-law-enforcement primary purpose" and those designed for law enforcement. Rather, the Court distinguished general crime control programs and those that have another particular purpose, such as protection of citizens against special hazards or protection of our borders. The Court specifically acknowledged that an appropriately tailored road block could be used "to thwart an imminent terrorist attack." The nature of the "emergency," which is simply another word for threat, takes the matter out of the realm of ordinary crime control.

Conclusion

FISA's general programmatic purpose, to protect the nation against terrorists and espionage threats directed by foreign powers, has from its outset been distinguishable from "ordinary crime control." After the events of September 11, 2001, though, it is hard

---

[7] [Court's Footnote 32] The Court has also allowed searches for certain administrative purposes to be undertaken without particularized suspicion of misconduct. *See, e.g., New York v. Burger*, 482 U.S. 691, 702–04 (1987) (warrantless administrative inspection of premises of closely regulated business); *Camara v. Municipal Court*, 387 U.S. 523, 534–39 (1967) (administrative inspection to ensure compliance with city housing code).

to imagine greater emergencies facing Americans than those experienced on that date.

We acknowledge, however, that the constitutional question presented by this case — whether Congress's disapproval of the primary purpose test is consistent with the Fourth Amendment has no definitive jurisprudential answer. The Supreme Court's special needs cases involve random stops (seizures) not electronic searches. In one sense, they can be thought of as a greater encroachment into personal privacy because they are not based on any particular suspicion. On the other hand, wiretapping is a good deal more intrusive than an automobile stop accompanied by questioning.

Even without taking into account the President's inherent constitutional authority to conduct warrantless foreign intelligence surveillance, we think the procedures and government showings required under FISA, if they do not meet the minimum Fourth Amendment warrant standards, certainly come close. We, therefore, believe firmly, applying the balancing test drawn from *Keith*, that FISA as amended is constitutional because the surveillances it authorizes are reasonable.

NOTES AND QUESTIONS

1. Criticisms of PATRIOT. There are two aspects of FISA at stake in the *Sealed Case* opinions, the "wall" between intelligence and criminal investigators, and the degree of showing required before obtaining a surveillance or search order. Both elements run throughout discussions of the PATRIOT Act. For particularly searching criticisms, see DAVID COLE & JAMES X. DEMPSEY, TERRORISM AND THE CONSTITUTION (2002); RANETA LAWSON MACK & MICHAEL J. KELLY, EQUAL JUSTICE IN THE BALANCE (2004).

2. Breaches and Misrepresentations. The opinion reviewed in *Sealed Case* is reported as *In re All Matters Submitted to the Foreign Intelligence Surveillance Court*, 218 F. Supp. 611 (FISC 2002). The FISA Court was interpreting and approving Minimization Guidelines required by the statute in the light of what it perceived to be misrepresentations in prior cases. Beginning in March 2000 and running through the summer of 2001, the FBI had admitted to at least 75 breaches of the wall and misrepresentations to the court. Does the Court of Review too lightly pass off the "misrepresentations" as having resulted from confusion over the requirements?

Is the Court of Review persuasive in arguing that the minimization requirement does not provide authority to insist on a wall of separation between intelligence and criminal investigation? The "wall" erected by the FISA Court may have had more to do with avoiding direction of the investigation toward prosecutorial evidence than with ensuring that private noncriminal information remained private. It is on that ground that the Court of Review insisted that the lower court was delving too deeply into the organization of the Justice Department. These cases illustrate some level of independence of the judges from the executive branch, but is it enough? Is the lower court's involvement with oversight of the internal workings of the Justice Department troubling by intermingling the Judiciary and Executive? or is the Court of Review's deference more troubling?

3. Special Needs and Review. The FISA Court of Review allows the Attorney General's certification to satisfy the first particularity requirement of the Fourth Amendment — probable cause. If the certification stood alone, then this would seem to negate the neutral judicial requirement. But the court allows review for clear error to satisfy that element. What is it that ameliorates the Fourth Amendment requirements in this area? the severe threat of terrorism? the difficulty of investigation? or that the targets often have links to foreign powers and thus implicate foreign affairs?

4. Commentary. A rare academic approval of expanded investigatory powers argues that PATRIOT appropriately eliminates two barriers to investigative cooperation — the FISA wall and secrecy of grand jury testimony:

> Although the Patriot Act plainly expands the powers of those charged with responding to terrorist threats, it would be incorrect to view those powers as

wholly unregulated and discretionless. Indeed, the Patriot Act could be viewed as shifting the duties of regulation from the judicial branch to the legislative and executive branches. Given that questions of national security and privacy rights, and their appropriate balance, are among the most important policy issues confronting the nation, it would surely seem appropriate, and even preferable, that such debates take place openly, and in our elected branches.

Craig S. Lerner, *The USA PATRIOT Act: Promoting the Cooperation of Foreign Intelligence Gathering and Law Enforcement*, 11 GEO. MASON L. REV. 493, 495 (2003).

One commentator has argued that FISA should be abandoned entirely after the *Sealed Case* opinion:

> The USA PATRIOT Act has virtually eliminated the specialized intelligence-gathering function of FISA orders; they now can be used with the specific purpose of obtaining evidence to be used in criminal prosecutions, as long as this is not the sole purpose of such investigations. Additionally, prosecutors and intelligence officials may now consult over FISA warrant application and execution. A FISA warrant has become little more than a regular Title III warrant issued secretly with no required showing of probable cause of criminal activity. In view of these significant changes, the FISC retains little unique jurisdiction. The FISC's secret, perfunctory procedures no longer provide constitutionally adequate protection for surveillance targets who will be unknowingly investigated and prosecuted as a direct result of its orders, especially now that FISA surveillance may be used specifically for criminal — and not simply intelligence-gathering — investigations.

Nola K. Breglio, *Leaving FISA Behind: The Need To Return to Warrantless Foreign Intelligence Surveillance*, 113 YALE L.J. 179, 180 (2003). The argument continues that judicial review of unregulated warrantless surveillance under a "reasonableness" standard could be more effective than mere FISC review of certification that the target is an agent of a foreign power. Of course, one problem is that in that system, judicial review would occur only when a criminal prosecution occurs or when the target learns of the surveillance through some other means, if then.

Another commentary argues that the Court of Review misinterpreted the statutory framework:

> While the Court of Review was correct in allowing criminal and foreign intelligence investigators to collaborate during FISA investigations, the court's opinion goes too far in eroding restrictions on the government's use of FISA searches to the extent that it invites abuse of those searches. Even though the court recognized the Foreign Intelligence Surveillance Court's role in reviewing the government's purpose in seeking information under FISA, it diminished the FISC's ability to perform its oversight duties by applying a "measurable purpose' standard in reviewing applications for FISA searches and surveillances.

John E. Branch III, *Statutory Misinterpretation: The Foreign Intelligence Court of Review's Interpretation of the "Significant Purpose" Requirement of the Foreign Intelligence Surveillance Act*, 81 N.C.L. REV. 2075 (2003).

5. The NSA Surveillance Program. When it later came to light that the President had authorized electronic surveillance (wiretaps) of communications without FISA Court approval, the administration pointed to this sentence in the *Sealed Case* opinion:

> We take for granted that the President does have [inherent authority to conduct warrantless searches to obtain foreign intelligence information] and, assuming that is so, FISA could not encroach on the President's constitutional power.

That would seem to be a lot to take for granted. If the President has this inherent authority free of congressional control, then what is the point of FISA at all? Is it just a whimsical proceeding that need not be followed when the executive chooses not to do so?

This debate becomes especially critical in the torture controversy because the most controversial Justice Department memos asserted a similar inherent authority free of congressional control. The President clearly has inherent authority to conduct military operations but Congress has authority to define regulations for the governance of the armed forces and crimes against the law of nations. It may be that surveillance without congressional or judicial oversight could be permissible, but that is a momentous proposition to "take for granted."

MAYFIELD v. UNITED STATES
504 F. Supp. 2d 1023 (D. Or. 2007)

AIKEN, DISTRICT JUDGE.

Plaintiffs' Amended Complaint requests declaratory relief that the Foreign Intelligence Surveillance Act ("FISA"), as amended by the Patriot Act, is unconstitutional.

FACTUAL BACKGROUNDS

In brief, the facts as alleged by plaintiffs are as follows: On March 11, 2004, in Madrid, Spain, terrorists' bombs exploded on commuter trains, murdering 191 persons, and injuring another 1600 persons, including three United States citizens. Shortly after the bombings, the Spanish National Police ("SNP") recovered fingerprints from a plastic bag containing explosive detonators. The bag was found in a Renault van located near the bombing site.

On March 13, 2004, the SNP submitted digital photographs of the latent fingerprints lifted from the plastic bag to Interpol Madrid, which then transmitted the digital photographs to the FBI in Quantico, Virginia. On that same day, the Latent Print Unit of the FBI initiated an Automated Fingerprint Identification System ("AFIS") search in an attempt to match the latent prints received from Spain with known prints in the FBI computer system. The FBI was unable to locate a fingerprint match.

On March 14, 2004, the FBI requested and received from Spain higher resolution digital photographs of the eight latent prints and on March 15, 2004, another AFIS search was performed. The FBI technicians programmed the computer to return 20 candidates whose known prints had features in common with what was identified as Latent Finger Print #17 ("LFP #17"). On March 15, 2004, the computer produced 20 candidates that met the criteria. Each candidate was identified by an AFIS "score," a number that reflected a rank as to how closely the AFIS computer determined each candidate's fingerprint matched certain features of LFP #17.

Mayfield's AFIS "score" ranked #4 on the list of 20 candidates. Mayfield is an American citizen born in Oregon and reared in Kansas. He lives with his wife and three children in Aloha, Oregon, a suburb of Portland. Mayfield is 38 years old, a former Army officer with an honorable discharge, and a practicing Oregon lawyer. Prior to his arrest, he had not traveled outside the United States since 1994, and he had never been arrested for a crime. Plaintiffs allege that FBI examiners were aware of Mayfield's Muslim faith and that this knowledge influenced their examination of Mayfield's fingerprints. [3 reviews by examiners determined that there was a match]

On March 20, 2004, the FBI issued a formal report matching Mayfield's print to LFP #17. On March 21, 2004, FBI surveillance agents began to watch Mayfield and to follow Mayfield and members of his family when they traveled to and from the Bilal Mosque, the family's place of worship; to and from Mayfield's law office, his place of employment; to and from the children's school; and to and from family activities.

Plaintiffs allege that at some point after the wrongful fingerprint identification, the FBI applied to the Foreign Intelligence Security Court ("FISCH) for an order authorizing the FBI to place electronic listening devices ("bugs") in the "shared and intimate" rooms of the Mayfield family home; executed repeated "sneak and peek" searches of the Mayfield family home, occurring when the family was away from the home and performed "so incompetently that the FBI left traces of their searches behind, causing the Mayfield family to be frightened and believe that they had been burglarized;" obtained private and protected information about the Mayfields from third parties; executed "sneak and peek" searches of the law office of Brandon Mayfield; and placed wiretaps on Mayfield's office and home phones. The application for the FISA order before the FISC was personally approved by the U.S. Attorney General at the time, John Ashcroft.

On April 2, 2004, Mayfield's prints were sent by the FBI to Spain. Plaintiffs allege that by that date, the U.S. Government had already been advised by the Spanish Government that Moroccan immigrants were suspects in the Madrid bombing and had been taken into custody, and that the Spanish Government was not aware of any information connecting the Moroccans with Mayfield or anyone else in the United States.

The SNP examined the FBI's report and Mayfield's fingerprints, and concluded that there were dissimilarities in the comparison of the two prints for which there was no explanation. On April 13, 2004, the SNP provided a written report to the FBI explaining that they had compared LFP #17 to Mayfield's fingerprints, and concluded there was no match.

On April 21, 2004, the FBI sent one or more agents to Madrid to meet with their Spanish counterparts. Spanish authorities who met with the FBI agents "refused to validate" the FBI's conclusion that LFP #17 and Mayfield's print were a match.

Plaintiffs allege that DOJ and FBI employees "concocted false and misleading affidavits" in order to justify even more intrusive searches and ultimately to justify Mayfield's arrest as a "material witness." An FBI investigator, Werder, submitted a "concocted affidavit" to a federal judge of this court, which stated that Green, Wieners, and Massey considered LFP #17 a "100% positive identification" of Mayfield. Although the affidavits stated that "preliminary findings" of the SNP "were not consistent" with the FBI fingerprint analysis, no mention was made of Spain's April 13, 2004, report to the FBI that stated the SNP did not agree with the FBI's fingerprint match of LFP #17 and Mayfield.

The affidavit included "speculative and prejudicial narratives" focusing on Mayfield's religion and association with co-practitioners. Plaintiffs cite as an example, Werders's inclusion in his affidavit the fact that Mayfield attended a mosque and advertised his legal services in "Jerusalem Enterprises," or what are known as the "Muslim Yellow Pages," as evidence connecting Mayfield to the bombings as a material witness. Plaintiffs respond that the "Muslim Yellow Pages" also includes advertising by major companies such as Avis, Best Western and United Airlines. Plaintiffs allege that the affidavit submitted to this court was knowingly or recklessly false and misleading.

Due to Mayfield's protestations of innocence, and the issue of whether Mayfield's prints actually matched LFP #17, the Judge assigned to this matter ordered that LFP #17 be provided to a court-appointed expert witness for comparison to Mayfield's known fingerprints. That expert, Kenneth Moses, was selected by Mayfield and his defense attorneys. On May 19, 2004, Moses testified in the material witness proceeding that he had "compared the latent prints that were submitted on Brandon Mayfield, and [he] concluded that the latent print is the left index finger of Mr. Mayfield."

Based on these affidavits, broad search warrants were sought and issued. Mayfield's family home and law office were searched. Computer and paper files from his family home, including his children's homework, were seized. Mayfield was ultimately arrested and initially held in the lock down unit at the Multnomah County Detention Center. His family was not told where he was being held. He and his family were told, however, that he was being held as a primary suspect on offenses punishable by death, and that the

FBI had made a 100% match of his fingerprint with the Madrid train bombing fingerprint. Plaintiffs allege that leaks to the media by the FBI and DOJ led to local, national, and international headlines that Brandon Mayfield's fingerprints linked him to the Madrid bombings.

Mayfield was ultimately arrested and imprisoned from May 6, 2004, through May 20, 2004. On May 19, 2004, the SNP advised the FBI, and on May 20, 2004, news reports revealed, that Spain had matched the Madrid fingerprint with an Algerian, Ouhane Daoud. Mayfield was released from prison the following day.

DISCUSSION

Plaintiffs' Amended Complaint challenges the lawfulness of the physical searches, electronic eavesdropping and wiretapping performed pursuant to authorization from the FISC Court in Washington D.C., and the lawfulness of the government's continued retention of materials derived from those searches, eavesdropping, and wiretapping. Plaintiffs allege that 50 U.S.C. § 1804 (electronic surveillance under FISA) and 50 U.S.C. § 1823 (physical searches under FISA) violate the Fourth Amendment on their face. Specifically, plaintiffs allege that pursuant to FISA and in violation of the Fourth Amendment, they were subjected to secret surveillance and searches of their home, law office, vehicles, and communications.

Plaintiffs' Allegations

Plaintiffs request a declaration from this court that FISA, as amended by the Patriot Act, violates the Fourth Amendment because it:

a. permit[s] the federal government to perform covert physical searches and electronic surveillance and wiretaps of the home, office and vehicles of a person without first requiring the government to demonstrate to a court the existence of probable cause that the person has committed a crime;

b. permit[s] the federal government to perform covert physical searches and electronic surveillance and wiretaps of a person without first requiring the government to demonstrate to a court that the primary purpose of the searches and surveillance is to obtain foreign intelligence information; and

c. permit[s] the federal government to covertly collect, disseminate and retain information collected through covert physical searches and electronic surveillance without first requiring the government to demonstrate to a court the existence of probable cause that the person who is the target of physical searches and electronic surveillance has committed a crime, or, alternatively, that the primary purpose of the searches and surveillance [is] to obtain foreign intelligence information.

Prior to the Patriot Act, the government was required to certify that the primary purpose of its surveillance was to obtain foreign intelligence information. The Patriot Act now authorizes FISA surveillance and searches as long as a significant purpose of the surveillance and searches is the gathering of foreign intelligence. This amendment allows the government to obtain surveillance orders under FISA even if the government's primary purpose is to gather evidence of domestic criminal activity. The practical result of this amendment, objected to by plaintiffs, is that in criminal investigations, the government can now avoid the Fourth Amendment's probable cause requirement when conducting surveillance or searches of a criminal suspect's home or office merely by asserting a desire to also gather foreign intelligence information from the person whom the government intends to criminally prosecute. The government is now authorized to conduct physical searches and electronic surveillance upon criminal suspects without first proving to an objective and neutral magistrate that probable cause exists to believe that a crime has been committed. The government need only represent that the targeted individual was an agent of a foreign power (a representation that must be accepted unless "clearly erroneous") and that "a significant purpose" of the surveillance and search is to collect foreign intelligence.

Here, the government chose to go to the FISC, despite the following evidence: Mayfield did not have a current passport; he had not been out of the country since completing his military duty as a U.S. Army lieutenant in Germany during the early 1990s; the fingerprint identification had been determined to be "negative" by the SNP; the SNP believed the bombings were conducted by persons from northern Africa; and there was no evidence linking Mayfield with Spain or North Africa. The government nevertheless made the requisite showing to the FISC that Mayfield was an "agent of a foreign power." That representation, which by law the FISC could not ignore unless clearly erroneous, provided the government with sufficient justification to compel the FISC to authorize covert searches and electronic surveillance in support of a criminal investigation.

At issue here are two fundamental concerns: the safety of our nation and the constitutional rights of citizens. With the passage of the Patriot Act, these concerns are now placed in conflict. The court recognizes that a difficult balance must be struck in a manner that preserves the peace and security of our nation while at the same time preserving the constitutional rights and civil liberties of all Americans.

Prior to passage of the Patriot Act, the government would have been required to follow the traditional process and demonstrate probable cause to a "detached and neutral magistrate" that Mayfield had committed a crime. Therefore, prior to issuing a search warrant, the Fourth Amendment required that law enforcement have reasonable grounds to believe that the law was being violated. FISA does not contain this criminal standard of probable cause. Instead, FISA contains a "foreign intelligence standard" of probable cause which requires a showing that the target may be an agent of a foreign government and the place or facility to be searched is being used in furtherance of espionage or terrorist activities.

Significantly, a seemingly minor change in wording has a dramatic and significant impact on the application of FISA. A warrant under FISA now issues if "a significant purpose" of the surveillance is foreign intelligence. Now, for the first time in our Nation's history, the government can conduct surveillance to gather evidence for use in a criminal case without a traditional warrant, as long as it presents a non-reviewable assertion that it also has a significant interest in the targeted person for foreign intelligence purposes.

Since the adoption of the Bill of Rights in 1791, the government has been prohibited from gathering evidence for use in a prosecution against an American citizen in a courtroom unless the government could prove the existence of probable cause that a crime has been committed. The hard won legislative compromise previously embodied in FISA reduced the probable cause requirement only for national security intelligence gathering. The Patriot Act effectively eliminates that compromise by allowing the Executive Branch to bypass the Fourth Amendment in gathering evidence for a criminal prosecution.

After the Supreme Court's decision in *Keith*, and prior to the enactment of FISA, numerous federal appellate courts recognized our Nation's interest in security and affirmed warrantless surveillance authorized within the Executive Branch, because the purpose of the surveillance was foreign intelligence gathering. *See, e.g., United States v. Brown*, 484 F.2d 418, 426 (5th Cir. 1973); *United States v. Butenko*, 494 F.2d 593 (3d Cir. 1974); *United States v. Buck*, 548 F.2d 871 (9th Cir. 1977). The Third, Fifth and Ninth Circuits all held that warrantless surveillance could be conducted by the Executive Branch only if the purpose of this surveillance was to gather foreign intelligence. It was against this backdrop, in 1978, that Congress passed FISA, permitting the government to obtain an electronic surveillance order based upon probable cause that the prospective target was a "foreign power" or an "agent of a foreign power."

The decisions in *Katz* and *Keith* drew a line between surveillance conducted by law enforcement officials to investigate crime — which requires a traditional warrant based on probable cause — and surveillance conducted by intelligence officials to obtain foreign intelligence information. Notably, the primary purpose of the electronic surveillance and physical searching of Mayfield's home was to gather evidence to prosecute him for crimes. Mayfield was ultimately arrested to compel his testimony before a Grand Jury investigating his alleged involvement in the crimes of bombing places of public use, providing national support to terrorists and conspiracy to kill, kidnap, maim or injure persons or damage property in a foreign county. The government stipulated that it did not demonstrate to the FISC that its primary purpose in wiretapping, electronically eavesdropping, or physically searching Mayfield's home or law office was to gather foreign intelligence. "In the FISA applications, the government did not seek to establish, and under the terms of FISA was not required to establish, all of the requirements set forth in 18 U.S.C. § 2510 et seq. and Rule 41, Fed. R. Crim. P." Thus, FISA now permits the Executive Branch to conduct surveillance and searches of American citizens without satisfying the probable cause requirements of the Fourth Amendment. As plaintiffs allege, when proceeding pursuant to FISA, "there is no [need for] showing or finding that a crime has been or is being committed, as in the case of a search or seizure for law enforcement purposes." "Additionally, and with respect to the nexus to criminality required by the definitions of an 'agent of a foreign power,' the government need not show probable cause as to each and every element of the crime involved or about to be involved." When the FISC reviews a FISA search application, the government satisfies most FISA requirements simply by certifying that the requirements are met. The statute directs that the FISC is not to scrutinize such statements, but is to defer to the government's certification unless it is "clearly erroneous."

This procedure allows the government to avoid traditional Fourth Amendment judicial oversight used to obtain a surveillance order.

FISA also does not require particularity. The Fourth Amendment prohibits the government from conducting intrusive surveillance unless it first obtains a warrant describing with particularity the things to be seized as well as the place to be searched.

Finally, FISA authorizes surveillance terms up to 120-days. FISA's provisions relating to the duration of surveillance orders violates the Fourth Amendment requirements [of reasonableness] for criminal investigations.

The government does not refute plaintiffs' historical recitation of law leading up to the enactment of FISA. Similarly, the parties agree that when surveying the case law prior to *In re Sealed Case*, 310 F.3d 717 (FISA Ct. of Rev. 2003), every Article III court that had considered the issue directly concluded that to justify non-probable cause searches and electronic surveillance, the government's purpose, or at least its primary purpose, must have been the collection of foreign intelligence. Specifically, as originally drafted and implemented over its 24-year history, FISA applications were properly granted only when "the purpose" of the surveillance was foreign intelligence gathering.

In the history underlying *In re Sealed Case*, the government sought to conduct surveillance of an "agent of a foreign power." In granting the request, the FISC also addressed the new 2002 FISA Procedures. On May 17, 2002, the seven judges of the FISC issued a rare public and unanimous opinion ruling the Procedures improper.

The government filed the first ever appeal to the FISCR, a court that had never before met. The FISCR reversed the FISC's ruling and held the 2002 Procedures consistent with the Patriot Act, found the 2002 Procedures constitutionally reasonable, and held that they met Fourth Amendment standards. While the court permitted amicus briefs, only the government was allowed to appear and participate at oral argument. Moreover, only the government is allowed under FISA to seek Supreme Court review of a FISCR decision, which it declined to do. Even without the benefit of full adversarial proceedings, the FISCR conceded that "the constitutional question presented by this case — whether Congress' disapproval of the primary purpose test is consistent with the

Fourth Amendment — has no definitive jurisprudential answer."

The government cites *In re Sealed Case* as "highly persuasive" authority for this court and suggests that the Ninth Circuit would adopt the ruling. The government cites both *United States v. Cavanagh*, 807 F.2d 787 (9th Cir. 1987), and *United States v. Sarkissian*, 841 F.2d 959 (9th Cir. 1988), as evidence that the Ninth Circuit would follow the ruling of *In re Sealed Case*. Both Ninth Circuit cases were decided prior to the Patriot Act's amendments to FISA. Regardless, I disagree with the government's analysis and find those cases are not persuasive as to whether the Ninth Circuit would adopt the reasoning of *In re Sealed Case*. For example, in *Cavanagh* the court held that where "the purpose of the surveillance is to obtain foreign intelligence," FISA passes constitutional muster. In *Sarkissian*, the Ninth Circuit expressly declined to consider whether the primary purpose test was constitutionally required.

In this case, the court declines to adopt the analysis and conclusion reached by the FISCR in *In re Sealed Case*. Notably, the FISCR's two fundamental premises underlying its ruling are contradictory. FISCR determined both that FISA never contained a purpose requirement, and that in altering the purpose requirement, Congress did not undermine the validity of searches conducted pursuant to FISA. Regarding FISCR's second premise, FISCR found that the primary purpose test "generates dangerous confusion and creates perverse organizational incentives arising from the purported need to distinguish between intelligence gathering and criminal investigation." However, a provision of the Patriot Act, unchallenged by plaintiffs here, eliminates the DOJ "wall" and with it the "dangerous confusion" and "perverse organizational incentives" referred to and relied on by the FISCR. Moreover, to the extent the "primary purpose" test imposes any restraint on the sharing of FISA surveillance with criminal investigators, investigators are, of course, free to seek orders authorizing surveillance under Title III, and traditional search warrants that satisfy Fourth Amendment requirements. Finally, Title III includes predicate offenses for which surveillance is justified for virtually all terrorism and espionage-related offenses. 18 U.S.C. § 2516(1). As such, Title III provides a satisfactory alternative when criminal investigators cannot have access to FISA surveillance.

The FISCR also attempts, without merit, to distinguish the Supreme Court's "special needs" cases. "Special needs" cases are those where the Supreme Court has found it appropriate to carve out an exception to the Fourth Amendment's requirement of probable cause based upon an individualized suspicion of wrongdoing. In these cases, the Court found that special needs, beyond the normal need of law enforcement, might justify an otherwise unconstitutional search. Prior to the Patriot Act, FISA may have had as its "general programmatic purpose . . . to protect the nation against terrorism and espionage threats directed by foreign powers." After the Patriot Act, however, FISA surveillance, including the surveillance at bar, may have as its "programmatic purpose" the generation of evidence for law enforcement purposes — which is forbidden without criminal probable cause and a warrant.

Finally and perhaps most significantly, *In re Sealed Case* ignores congressional concern with the appropriate balance between intelligence gathering and criminal law enforcement. It is notable that our Founding Fathers anticipated this very conflict as evidenced by the discussion in the FEDERALIST PAPERS. Their concern regarding unrestrained government resulted in the separation of powers, checks and balances, and ultimately, the Bill of Rights. Where these important objectives merge, it is critical that we, as a democratic Nation, pay close attention to traditional Fourth Amendment principles. The Fourth Amendment has served this Nation well for 220 years, through many other perils. Title III, like the Supreme Court's pronouncements in *Katz* and *Berger*, recognizes that wiretaps are searches requiring fidelity to the Fourth Amendment.

Moreover, the constitutionally required interplay between Executive action, Judicial decision, and Congressional enactment, has been eliminated by the FISA amendments.

Prior to the amendments, the three branches of government operated with thoughtful and deliberate checks and balances — a principle upon which our Nation was founded. These constitutional checks and balances effectively curtail overzealous executive, legislative, or judicial activity regardless of the catalyst for overzealousness. The Constitution contains bedrock principles that the framers believed essential. Those principles should not be easily altered by the expediencies of the moment.

Despite this, the FISCR holds that the Constitution need not control the conduct of criminal surveillance in the United States. In place of the Fourth Amendment, the people are expected to defer to the Executive Branch and its representation that it will authorize such surveillance only when appropriate. The defendant here is asking this court to, in essence, amend the Bill of Rights, by giving it an interpretation that would deprive it of any real meaning. This court declines to do so.

For over 200 years, this Nation has adhered to the rule of law — with unparalleled success. A shift to a Nation based on extra-constitutional authority is prohibited, as well as ill-advised. In this regard, the Supreme Court has cautioned:

> The price of lawful public dissent must not be a dread of subjection to an unchecked surveillance power. Nor must the fear of unauthorized official eavesdropping deter vigorous citizen dissent and discussion of Government action in private conversation. For private dissent, no less than open public discourse, is essential to our free society.

Keith, 407 U.S. at 314.

Therefore, I conclude that 50 U.S.C. §§ 1804 and 1823, as amended by the Patriot Act, are unconstitutional because they violate the Fourth Amendment of the United States Constitution. Plaintiffs' Amended Complaint for declaratory relief is granted.

NOTES AND QUESTIONS

1. "Primary Purpose." *Mayfield* presents a fundamental issue that the Supreme Court may need to resolve. Is the Fourth Amendment warrant requirement applicable to investigations in which a purpose is criminal law enforcement along with other purposes? The court says that after Congress eliminated the requirement that the "primary purpose" of an investigation be international intelligence, the executive is now free to conduct a criminal investigation without independent judicial oversight and without particular description of the person or things to be seized.

> Prior to the Patriot Act, FISA may have had as its "general programmatic purpose . . . to protect the nation against terrorism and espionage threats directed by foreign powers." After the Patriot Act, however, FISA surveillance, including the surveillance at bar, may have as its "programmatic purpose" the generation of evidence for law enforcement purposes — which is forbidden without criminal probable cause and a warrant.

The court does not delve very far into whether it is established that the warrant requirement of the Fourth Amendment is more rigorous in a criminal context than in other contexts. The text of the Amendment does not refer to criminal matters and it could be argued that the warrant requirement applies whenever government seeks to search or seize items regardless of the use to which the information is to be put.

2. "Special Needs." The Government's position in *In re Sealed Case* and *Mayfield* is that FISA is premised on the special circumstances of foreign intelligence gathering, which takes the case out of the criminal warrant context. For example, it should be permissible for the Health Department to inspect restaurant kitchens on a routine basis without obtaining judicial permission. The *Mayfield* court refers to these as the "special needs" cases, which the Supreme Court has described this way:

> [T]he Fourth Amendment does not proscribe all searches and seizures, but only those that are unreasonable. What is reasonable, of course, "depends on all

of the circumstances surrounding the search or seizure and the nature of the search or seizure itself." Thus, the permissibility of a particular practice "is judged by balancing its intrusion on the individual's Fourth Amendment interests against its promotion of legitimate governmental interests."

In most criminal cases, we strike this balance in favor of the procedures described by the Warrant Clause of the Fourth Amendment. Except in certain well-defined circumstances, a search or seizure in such a case is not reasonable unless it is accomplished pursuant to a judicial warrant issued upon probable cause. We have recognized exceptions to this rule, however, "when special needs, beyond the normal need for law enforcement, make the warrant and probable-cause requirement impracticable." *Griffin v. Wisconsin*, 483 U.S. 868, 873 (1987). When faced with such special needs, we have not hesitated to balance the governmental and privacy interests to assess the practicality of the warrant and probable-cause requirements in the particular context. *See, e. g., Griffin v. Wisconsin* (search of probationer's home); *New York v. Burger*, 482 U.S. 691, 699–703 (1987) (search of premises of certain highly regulated businesses); *O'Connor v. Ortega* (work-related searches of employees' desks and offices); *New Jersey v. T. L. O.* (search of student's property by school officials); *Bell v. Wolfish* (body cavity searches of prison inmates).

Skinner v. Ry. Labor Executives' Ass'n, 489 U.S. 602, 619 (1989).

What are the distinguishing characteristics of the "special needs" cases? Is it the action of the target in placing his or her activities within the scope of government interest by running a business, going to school, or being imprisoned? Or is it the government interest independent of the actions of the individual, in which case the target's actions are not at issue?

§ 5.02   PATRIOT AND PRIVACY

[A]   USA Patriot

The USA PATRIOT Act (Uniting and Strengthening America by Providing Appropriate Tools Required to Intercept and Obstruct Terrorism) was passed on October 26, 2001, just six weeks after 9/11. It was a compendium of provisions that had been drafted and debated over the prior decade by various units within the federal government. It runs 130 pages in the Statutes at Large. It contains 156 sections, many of which contain several technical and detailed amendments to various other sections of existing law. Thus the Act contains hundreds of individual statutory changes, few of which could be understood without seeing how the amending language fit into pre-existing law.

It can be argued that PATRIOT did not have nearly the significance attached to it initially. Almost all terrorism-related litigation against the Government in the first three years after its passage involved either statutes that predated PATRIOT, such as the procedures for designation of foreign terrorist organizations, or administrative initiatives such as indefinite detention of "enemy combatants" and secret deportation proceedings.

1. *Intelligence Investigations*

In addition to the "significant purpose" change disputed between the *In re Sealed Case* and *Mayfield* courts, FISA as amended by PATRIOT permits "roving" surveillance of persons rather than site-specific surveillance.

2. *Gathering Records*

PATRIOT § 215 (50 U.S.C. § 1861) provides that either the FISA Court or a Magistrate Judge shall order third parties (such as internet service providers and libraries) to turn over records upon an FBI certification that the records are sought in connection with a foreign intelligence investigation. The third party is prohibited from disclosing to anyone that the records have been sought.

3. *Communication, Financial, and Credit Records*

As spelled out in *Doe v. Ashcroft* below, three separate statutes authorize FBI issuance of National Security Letters (NSL's) to electronic communication providers, financial institutions, and credit agencies. An NSL directs the recipient to provide specified types of information on certification by the agents that there is "reason to believe" that the target is a foreign agent and that the information is "relevant to" an intelligence investigation.

4. *Tracking Communications*

Prior federal law prohibited electronic eavesdropping on telephone conversations, face-to-face conversations, or computer and other forms of electronic communications without a court order, which was available only for investigation of specified crimes, and required notice to the parties to any conversations seized when the order expired. PATRIOT expands the "predicate crimes," allows delay of notice, and removes stored electronic communications from this protection (thus treating them as records susceptible to administrative demand, grand jury subpoena, or court order). Court orders authorizing trap-and-trace devices or pen registers (which record the source or destination of calls made to or from a particular telephone) are available on mere certification, rather than a finding of a court, that use of the device is likely to produce information relevant to the investigation of a crime.

5. *Tracking Money*

PATRIOT (1) requires many businesses in addition to banks and brokers to file Suspicious Activity Reports, (2) prohibits U.S. financial institutions from maintaining correspondent accounts for foreign shell banks, (3) establishes minimum new customer identification standards, particularly with respect to the identity of foreign customers, (4) prohibits banks from disclosing to a customer that information has been provided to an agency involved in an intelligence investigation or regulatory demand.

6. *Other Provisions*

PATRIOT authorizes extended detention of aliens pending a determination of whether a person is connected to terrorist activities; expands the Posse Comitatus Act exceptions; provides a standardized duration of "sneak and peek" warrants; permits nationwide and perhaps worldwide execution of warrants in terrorism cases; allows the Attorney General to collect DNA samples from prisoners convicted of any federal crime of violence or terrorism; lengthens the statute of limitations applicable to crimes of terrorism.

Some advocacy groups objected vociferously to various provisions of PATRIOT.

- The American Library Association complained particularly about the ability of investigators to acquire circulation records that would show which patrons have been reading which books and to pen registers that would show the websites accessed from library computers by public patrons. The ALA worried that this could become a concern of constitutional dimension through the first amendment. *See* http://www.ala.org/ala/oif/ifissues/fbiyourlibrary.htm. The 2006 amendments to FISA require approval at the national level of the FBI for any demand of records from a library, book sales records, book customer lists, firearms sales records, tax return records, educational records, or medical records.

- The American Civil Liberties Union objected to many aspects of PATRIOT under the general statement that "without a warrant and without probable cause, the FBI now has the power to access your most private" records. *See* http://www.aclu.org.

- The Electronic Privacy Information Center lobbied and litigated against provisions of PATRIOT having to do with interception of electronic communications.

  See http://www.epic.org/privacy/terrorism/usapatriot. Some of these issues have been addressed following disclosure of the NSA TSP surveillance program. *See* § 5.02[C] *infra*.

- PATRIOT split some segments of the conservative side of the political spectrum. The American Conservative magazine came out strongly against PATRIOT and what it viewed as the departure of Attorney General Ashcroft from his prior stands in favor of privacy.

  See http://www.amconmag.com/05_19_03/cover.html. The Gun Owners of America argued aggressively against PATRIOT and any extension of it. *See* http://gunowners.org.

One of the complaints of the advocacy groups is that it will be difficult to obtain judicial review of these provisions because the information collected through these devices may never be used in a prosecution. Instead, it could sit in government files for potential misuse at a future date or could be the basis for further investigations that ultimately result in prosecutions in which this information is neither incriminating nor exculpatory, so it is never introduced as evidence.

[B] Access to Third-Party Records

One hotly contested aspect of the PATRIOT Act was the expansion of the FBI's ability to request and FISA Court's ability to authorize, seizure of records from a third party without the knowledge of the person to whom the information pertained. This would apply, for example, to rental car agencies, banks, phone companies, and so forth. Special provisions, however, in other statutes apply to acquisition of records from banks and electronic communication companies (telephone and internet providers).

The acquisition of some records, however, had long been subject to the ability of the FBI to act without court order by issuing what is known as a National Security Letter (NSL). Although the NSL amounted to a request because there was no court order behind it, it appeared on its face to be a demand. In addition, the statutes barred the recipient from telling anyone about the letter so that the target of the investigation would not know that his or her records were being sought. When this system was challenged, the district court engaged in a lengthy review of the history and perceived defects in the statutory process. While the case was pending on appeal, Congress amended the statutes to cure some of the problems highlighted by the district court. The Second Circuit remanded and the district court once again declared the process unconstitutional.

DOE v. GONZALES
500 F. Supp. 2d 379 (S.D.N.Y. 2007)

MARRERO, DISTRICT JUDGE.

I. INTRODUCTION

This Court, in a lengthy decision dated September 28, 2004, granted Plaintiffs' motion for summary judgment and declared 18 U.S.C. § 2709 unconstitutional on its face, under the First and Fourth Amendments. Shortly after this Court's decision, a court in the District of Connecticut enjoined the Government from enforcing the nondisclosure requirement of § 2709(c) ("*Doe II*").

While appeals in *Doe I* and *Doe II* were pending, Congress passed the USA Patriot Improvement and Reauthorization Act of 2005, Pub. L. No. 109-177 (Mar. 9, 2006). The Reauthorization Act effectuated substantial changes to § 2709 and added several provisions relating to judicial review of NSLs which were codified at 18 U.S.C. § 3511.

As a result of these amendments, the Second Circuit remanded the *Doe I* appeal to enable this Court, if the parties were to continue the litigation in light of the amendments to the statute, to consider the validity of the revised § 2709(c) and the new procedures codified in § 3511.

The Court holds that §§ 2709 (c) and 3511(b) are facially unconstitutional. However, the statutory provisions governing hearings, proceedings, and judicial review of evidence related to a challenge to an NSL, §§ 3511(d) and (e) respectively, are constitutional. Accordingly, Plaintiffs' motion for summary judgment is GRANTED in part and DENIED in part, and the Government's cross-motion for dismissal or summary judgment is DENIED.

II. BACKGROUND

A. *Section 2709*

The FBI is authorized by § 2709 to issue NSLs requesting a range of information about an ECSP's [Electronic Communications Service Provider] subscribers and their telephone or internet activity. Section 2709(a) states that an ECSP "shall comply" with a request for "subscriber information and toll billing records information, or electronic communication transactional records" made by the FBI. 18 U.S.C. § 2709(a). Section 2709(b) requires that, in order for the FBI to request "the name, address, length of service, and local and long distance toll billing records" of a person or entity, the Director of the FBI, or his designee, must certify that such information is "relevant to an authorized investigation to protect against international terrorism or clandestine intelligence activities."

As the Court noted in *Doe I*, "the statute's reference to 'transactional records' creates ambiguity regarding the scope of the information required to be produced by the NSL recipient." That ambiguity is compounded because the NSL directs the recipient to determine for itself whether any information it maintains regarding the target of the NSL "may be considered . . . to be an electronic communication transaction record" in accordance with § 2709, but not "contents" of communications within the meaning of 18 U.S.C. § 2510(8). Such information might include the "to," "from," "date," and "time" fields of all emails sent or received, activity logs indicating dates and times that the target accessed the internet, the contents of queries made to search engines, and histories of websites visited. *See generally* Jonathan Zittrain, *Searches and Seizures in a Networked World*, 119 HARV. L. REV. F. 83 (2005). Information requested by NSLs issued pursuant to § 2709 can also reveal the identity of an internet user associated with a certain email address, Internet Protocol address, or screen name.

B. *DOE I*

The Court held that the nondisclosure provision of § 2709 was unconstitutional on its face, and because the Court could not sever § 2709(c) from the remainder of the statute, the Court enjoined the government from using § 2709 in any case as a means of gathering information.

C. *The Revised Nondisclosure Provision*

As indicated above, while the Government's appeals were pending before the Second Circuit, Congress enacted the Reauthorization Act. The Government contends that the revised § 2709(c) and the newly enacted § 3511 directly addresses the concerns raised by this Court in its *Doe I* decision and rectifies any constitutional deficiencies. Instead of a categorical, blanket prohibition on disclosure with respect to the issuance of any NSL, § 2709(c) now calls for a case-by-case determination of the need for a nondisclosure order to accompany an NSL. Specifically, the statute provides that a recipient of an NSL is barred from disclosing that the FBI "has sought or obtained access to information or records" under the NSL statute if the Director of the FBI, or his designee, "certifies" that disclosure "may result" in "a danger to the national security of the United States, interference with a criminal, counterterrorism, or counterintelligence investigation, interference with diplomatic relations, or danger to the life or physical safety of any person" (here collectively referred to as the "Enumerated Harms").

The newly enacted § 3511 provides an opportunity for judicial review of NSLs. Section 3511(a) explicitly allows the recipient of an NSL to petition a United States district court "for an order modifying or setting aside the request," which the court "may" grant "if compliance would be unreasonable, oppressive, or otherwise unlawful." Additionally, under § 3511(b), an NSL recipient may seek an order modifying or setting aside a nondisclosure requirement.

If a petition to modify or set aside the nondisclosure requirement is filed within one year of the NSL request, the reviewing court may grant such relief only if it finds that "there is no reason to believe" disclosure "may result" in one or more of the Enumerated Harms. Moreover, if one of several authorized senior FBI officials "certifies that disclosure may endanger the national security of the United States or interfere with diplomatic relations, such certification shall be treated as conclusive unless the court finds that the certification was made in bad faith."

If the petition to modify or set aside the nondisclosure requirement is filed one year or more after the NSL request was issued, the FBI must either terminate the nondisclosure requirement or re-certify that disclosure may result in one of the Enumerated Harms, in which case the court could grant the petition only in accordance with the standards described above. Additionally, if the court denies the petition, the NSL recipient is precluded from filing another petition for one year.

As § 3511 now explicitly permits challenges to NSLs, Plaintiffs do not renew their Fourth Amendment challenge. However, Plaintiffs contend that the amendments do not cure the statute's First Amendment deficiencies, and that it remains an unconstitutional prior restraint and a content-based restriction on speech because it (1) fails to provide constitutionally mandated procedural safeguards, (2) invests the FBI with unbridled discretion to suppress speech, (3) forecloses reviewing courts from applying a constitutionally mandated standard of review, and (4) authorizes the issuance of nondisclosure orders that are not narrowly tailored.

As the Second Circuit vacated this Court's prior decision in light of the Reauthorization Act, the Court must now consider whether the nondisclosure provision, with the judicial review now contemplated, still runs afoul of the First Amendment. For the reasons set forth below, the Court finds that it does.

D. The FBI's Use of NSLs

Doe I detailed the history of NSLs and the revisions embodied in the Patriot Act which expanded their usefulness as an investigatory tool. The Patriot Act expanded the government's authority to use NSLs under the four existing NSL statutes[8] and created a fifth category of NSLs.[9] However, at the time that *Doe I* was decided, little was

---

[8] [Court's Footnote 10] In addition to § 2709, which expanded the use of NSLs under the ECPA, the USA Patriot Act amended: Section 1114(a) (5) of the Right to Financial Privacy Act, 12 U.S.C. § 3414(a) (5) (permits FBI to obtain financial records); Section 626 of the Fair Credit Reporting Act, 15 U.S.C. § 1681u (permits FBI and certain other agencies to obtain a limited amount of information about an individual's credit history); Section 802 of the National Security Act, 50 U.S.C. § 436 (allows FBI to request information related to investigation of improper disclosure of classified information).

[9] [Court's Footnote 11] Section 627 of the Fair Credit Reporting Act, 15 U.S.C. § 1681v, allows the FBI to

publicly known about how NSLs were being used by the FBI under the new relaxed standards required for issuance after the Patriot Act.

As part of the Reauthorization Act, Congress directed the Department of Justice, Office of the Inspector General ("OIG"), to review the "effectiveness and use, including any improper or illegal use, or national security letters issued by the Department of Justice." In March, 2007, the OIG issued its first public report pursuant to this statute, entitled "A Review of the Federal Bureau of Investigation's Use of National Security Letters" (the "OIG Report"). The OIG Report addresses the FBI's use of NSLs for calendar years 2003 through 2005.

The OIG Report confirms that the Patriot Act transformed NSLs into a much more frequently employed investigatory tool. Specifically, it states that "the FBI issued approximately 8,500. NSL requests in CY 2000, the year prior to passage of the Patriot Act. After the Patriot Act, according to FBI data, the number of NSL requests increased to approximately 39,000 in 2003, approximately 56,000 in 2004, and approximately 47,000 in 2005."[10] While the number of NSL requests issued under each separate NSL provision is not publicly available, the report does indicate that "the overwhelming majority of the NSL requests sought telephone toll billing records information, subscriber information (telephone or e-mail), or electronic communication transactional records" under § 2709. In considering these statistics, it is important to distinguish between "NSLs" and "NSL requests" — a single NSL may contain multiple requests for information. The OIG Report specifies that "the 39,000 NSL requests in 2003 were contained in approximately 12,000 letters, and the 47,000 requests in 2005 were contained in approximately 19,000 letters."

While the OIG Report provides helpful background on how NSLs are actually used by the FBI, Plaintiffs emphasize that the report also details significant misuse of NSLs by the FBI, which Plaintiffs claim supports their argument that the statute, in its current form, is too susceptible to abuse to survive First Amendment scrutiny. Specifically, the OIG Report found that in addition to significantly under-reporting the number of NSL requests issued, the FBI: (1) under-reported violations arising from the use of NSLs; (2) sought information not permitted by the statute; (3) issued NSLs without proper authorization; (4) issued over 700 "exigent letters" requesting the type of information covered by § 2709 without following the process for obtaining an NSL; and (5) repeatedly failed to properly adhere to the FBI's own internal documentation requirements for the approval of an NSL. In summary, while noting the significant challenges and major structural changes the FBI was facing during the period covered and the lack of any misuse rising to the level of criminal misconduct, the OIG Report nonetheless concluded that "the FBI used NSLs in violation of applicable NSL statutes, Attorney General Guidelines, and internal FBI policies."

E. Placing NSLs Issued Under § 2709 in Context

As discussed at length in *Doe I*, the issuance of NSLs under § 2709 is just one of many investigatory tools the government uses to gather information. The Government stresses, as it did in *Doe I* arguments, that the nondisclosure provision in the revised § 2709 is not unique in requiring secrecy in the context of confidential investigations. However, a review of those other investigatory tools reveals that, in comparison to statutes which allow for the imposition of secrecy in other contexts, the revised § 2709, even with the limited judicial review contemplated in § 3511, remains a very broad and substantially onerous secrecy provision.

---

obtain full credit reports and all other consumer information in a consumer reporting agency's files.

[10] [Court's Footnote 13] The OIG Report notes, however, that the total number of NSL requests were under-reported by the FBI. The OIG estimated that "approximately 8,850 NSL requests, or 6 percent of NSL requests issued by the FBI during this period, were missing from the database."

1. Administrative Subpoenas

Several federal statutes authorizing administrative subpoenas, for example, "permit the investigating agency to apply for a court order to temporarily bar disclosure of the inquiry, generally during specific renewable increments or for an appropriate period of time fixed by the Court, where such disclosure could jeopardize the investigation." Significantly, these provisions generally both place the burden on the government to seek a court-issued nondisclosure order and specifically contemplate a time limit on any secrecy imposed.

2. Pen Registers, Wiretaps, and Foreign Intelligence Surveillance

In *Doe I*, the Court noted that there were only three federal statutes "arguably analogous" to § 2709 in terms of the breadth of its nondisclosure rules. The Court stated:

> First, communications firms are categorically barred, unless otherwise ordered by a court, from ever disclosing that a pen register or trap and trace device is in effect. Second, communications firms are categorically barred, subject to a similar exception "as may otherwise be required by legal process," from ever disclosing that a wiretap or electronic surveillance is in place. Third, recipients of a subpoena under FISA are categorically prohibited from ever disclosing to any person, "other than those persons necessary to produce" the records sought, that the subpoena was ever issued.

Addressing this point, the Government emphasizes that these three statutes — 18 U.S.C. § 3123(d) (2) (pen registers), 18 U.S.C. § 2511(2) (a)(ii) (wiretaps), and 50 U.S.C. § 1861(d) (Foreign Intelligence Surveillance Act ("FISA") subpoenas) — "permit the government to preserve the secrecy of its investigations by prohibiting disclosure by non-government actors, automatically and with no special procedural protections."

However, the Court's observation in *Doe I* highlights what still remains a relevant and critical distinction between these provisions and § 2709: those statutes generally "apply in contexts in which a court authorizes the investigative method in the first place," and indeed provide for judicial review safeguards not only prior to surveillance, but also after it has concluded. The lone exception is that certain FISA surveillance orders may be obtained solely based on a certification by the Attorney General that the surveillance meets the statutory requirements. See 334 F. Supp. 2d at 515 n.208 (noting that this exception may be justified because "the FISA orders are specifically limited to electronic surveillance of foreign governments and their agents" and consequently do not implicate the First Amendment rights of American citizens).[11]

Thus, while a telephone company may be prohibited from disclosing the existence of a wiretap on one of its customers, that wiretap cannot be legally installed in the first instance without an Article III judge determining, pursuant to application by the government, and in advance of the restraint on constitutional rights, that there is "probable cause" for the government to believe both that the target of the wiretap is engaged in illegal activity and that the wiretap will assist in obtaining communications concerning that activity, and also that the government has demonstrated to the court's satisfaction that normal investigative procedures have failed or are unlikely to succeed.

Moreover, both surveillance tools place durational limits on their use. Wiretaps are generally limited to no more than thirty-day periods, after which the government must

---

[11] [Court's Footnote 15] The Court notes that new legislation signed by President Bush on August 4, 2007 appears to expand the government's ability to conduct surveillance of American citizens under FISA without a warrant. See James Risen, Bush Signs Law to Widen Reach for Wiretapping, N.Y. Times, Aug. 6, 2007, at A1. Warrantless surveillance of phone calls and emails are authorized under the new legislation if the target is "reasonably believed" to be overseas, even if the target is communicating with an American citizen in the United States.

apply for an extension. Pen registers and trap-and-trace devices are limited to sixty-day periods, after which the government must apply for an extension.

The wording of both statutes, and in particular their use of the phrase "the existence of," implies that communications providers might be free to discuss wiretaps and pen registers, as well as their knowledge of underlying criminal investigations, after those investigations are completed. After that time, the government presumably has no interest in prohibiting the communications provider from revealing its role in the investigation, and it is unlikely that a permanent ban on disclosure could be justified under the First Amendment.

3. Secrecy in Grand Jury Proceedings

Federal Rule of Criminal Procedure 6(e) governs secrecy in grand jury proceedings. The "federal rules impose stringent secrecy requirements on certain grand jury participants, including the attorneys, court reporters, and grand jurors." However, witnesses called before the grand jury are not under an obligation of secrecy. ("[T]he theory of grand jury secrecy is that the witness is guaranteed against compulsory disclosure, the privilege must therefore be that of the witness, and rests upon his consent.")

III. Discussion

As the Court observed in *Doe I*, this case presents novel issues involving both the security of the nation and the rights of citizens under the First Amendment. The government's use of NSLs to obtain private information about activities of individuals using the internet is a matter of the utmost public interest. As the OIG Report evenhandedly documents, the NSL serves as a critical tool to enable the government to perform investigations and law enforcement functions vital to the nation's safety and security. But, as powerful and valuable as it may be as a means of surveillance, and as crucial the purpose it serves, the NSL nonetheless poses profound concerns to our society, not the least of which, as reported by the OIG, is the potential for abuse in its employment. Through the use of NSLs, the government can unmask the identity of internet users engaged in anonymous speech in online discussions. It can obtain an itemized list of all of the emails sent and received by the target of the NSL, and it can then seek information on individuals communicating with that person. It may even be able to discover the websites an individual has visited and queries submitted to search engines. In light of the seriousness of the potential intrusion into the individual's personal affairs and the significant possibility of a chilling effect on speech and association — particularly of expression that is critical of the government or its policies — a compelling need exists to ensure that the use of NSLs is subject to the safeguards of public accountability, checks and balances, and separation of powers that our Constitution prescribes.

Accordingly, the issue now before the Court is not whether, or under what circumstances, the government should possess the authority to issue NSLs. Rather, the more fundamental question is the extent of the authority that the First Amendment allows the government to exercise in keeping its use of NSLs secret, insofar as such secrecy inhibits freedom of speech.

As a prior restraint and content-based restriction, the amended statute is hence subject to strict scrutiny. The statute can survive strict scrutiny only if it is "narrowly tailored to promote a compelling government interest," and there are no "less restrictive alternatives [that] would be at least as effective in achieving the legitimate purpose that the statute was enacted to serve."

As *Doe I* also acknowledged, the government's asserted interest in seeking to impose a gag on NSL recipients — protecting the nation's security by preventing terrorism — is certainly compelling in appropriate circumstances. Thus, the Court must consider whether § 2709(c), in light of the judicial review now afforded by § 3511(b), constitutes a sufficiently narrowly tailored means of advancing the government's compelling interest in national security.

As was the case with the Court's initial decision, fundamentally this ruling is "about the process antecedent to the substance of any particular challenge." When a statute confers discretion on government officials to suppress speech, as § 2709(c) does, that discretion must be reasonably limited by objective criteria. Moreover, the government must exercise its discretion within a system that allows for "procedural safeguards designed to obviate the dangers of a censorship system." *Freedman v. Maryland*, 380 U.S. 51 (1965). Such safeguards must include an opportunity for meaningful judicial review. Finally, even where the government has demonstrated a compelling interest justifying the restriction of expression, any such restriction must be narrowly tailored both in scope and duration. As detailed below, the nondisclosure provision of § 2709(c), even with the safeguard of the judicial review afforded by § 3511(b), prescribes a process that is constitutionally deficient under the First Amendment in several respects.

D. Procedural Safeguards

Freedman involved a Maryland motion picture censorship statute that made it unlawful to exhibit a motion picture prior to obtaining the approval of the Maryland State Board of Censors (the "Board"), which was empowered to bar the exhibition of any film that it considered "obscene" or that, in its opinion, tended to "debase or corrupt morals or incite to crimes." Under the statute, a film exhibitor was required to submit the film to the Board for approval prior to showing it, and the exhibitor could appeal a disapproval to a Maryland state court.

The *Freedman* Court held that such a system "avoids constitutional infirmity only if it takes place under procedural safeguards designed to obviate the dangers of a censorship system." In particular, the Supreme Court held that the following safeguards are required: (1) any restraint in advance of judicial review may be imposed only for "a specified brief period," (2) any further restraint prior to "a final judicial determination on the merits" must be limited to "the shortest fixed period compatible with sound judicial resolution," and (3) the burden of going to court to suppress the speech and the burden of proof once in court must rest on the censoring government.

The third *Freedman* safeguard, the requirement that the government bear the burden both of initiating judicial review and, once in court, of justifying the prior restraint, is not satisfied by § 3511(b), which places the burden of challenging the nondisclosure order on the NSL recipient. [A]n NSL recipient will generally lack the incentive to challenge the nondisclosure order in court. Such a challenge would be time consuming and financially burdensome, and the NSL recipient's business does not depend on overturning the particular form of restriction on its speech. That NSL recipients generally have little or no incentive to challenge nondisclosure orders is suggested by empirical evidence. Although the FBI issued 143,074 NSL requests from 2003 to 2005 alone, the most recent year for which figures have been released, only two challenges have been made in federal court since the original enactment of the statute in 1986.

In light of these considerations, the Court concludes that the third Freedman procedural safeguard does apply to judicial review of the NSL statute. Accordingly, it is the government that must bear the burden of going to court to suppress the speech and that must bear the burden of proof once in court.

That the government bears the burden of justifying the need for nondisclosure to a court does not mean that the FBI must obtain the approval of a court prior to issuing an NSL with a nondisclosure order. In light of the first two *Freedman* protections, the FBI may issue a temporary nondisclosure order on its own in accordance with the standards set forth in § 2709(c), provided that, within a reasonable and brief period of time, it must either notify the NSL recipient that the order is no longer in effect, or justify to a court the need for a continued period of nondisclosure.

Allowing the FBI to issue nondisclosure orders for a limited period of time prior to any judicial oversight balances the strong First Amendment concerns at issue with the FBI's need to act quickly in conducting counterterrorism investigations. This balance also takes into account that, as described in the OIG Report, the FBI is now using NSLs as an information-gathering tool in the preliminary phase of its investigations. It allows the FBI measured discretion, sufficient but not greater than necessary, to issue NSLs with nondisclosure orders, without demanding that it immediately be required to produce evidence substantiating its assertion that disclosure might endanger national security.

E. Discretion

Plaintiffs argue that § 2709(c) violates the First Amendment because the standard governing the issuance of nondisclosure orders provides the FBI with unbridled discretion to suppress speech. Plaintiffs argue that a standard based on "a danger to national security," among other potential harms, is simply not susceptible to an objective test. They contend that the term "national security" is inherently vague, and they point out that it has been used in the past to "cloak many questionable executive practices." That the rubric of "national security" has been abused on occasion does not imply that the Court should presume the language of "national security" in § 2709(c) necessarily affords unfettered discretion to the FBI likely to result in abuse.

As the Court stated in *Doe I*, "[t]he high stakes here pressing the scales . . . compel the Court to strike the most sensitive judicial balance, calibrating by delicate increments toward a result that adequately protects national security without unduly sacrificing individual freedoms." In striking this balance, the Court finds that the FBI's discretion in certifying a need for nondisclosure of an NSL is broad but not inappropriately so under the circumstances. As detailed elsewhere in this opinion, the best protection against abuse of the FBI's discretion in certifying nondisclosure is to ensure that such discretion is checked by meaningful and reasonably expeditious judicial review.

F. Prescribing the Standard of Judicial Review

As the Court has already made clear, judicial review of the Reauthorization Act's nondisclosure requirement is subject to strict scrutiny. Section 3511(b) allows a reviewing court to modify or set aside the nondisclosure requirement of an NSL issued under § 2709 only "if it finds that there is no reason to believe that disclosure" will lead to one of the Enumerated Harms. 18 U.S.C. § 3511(b) (2). Moreover, if an authorized Justice Department or FBI official certifies that disclosure may "endanger the national security of the United States or interfere with diplomatic relations, such certification shall be treated as conclusive unless the court finds that the certification was made in bad faith." Id. The Court agrees with Plaintiffs that this standard is plainly at odds with First Amendment jurisprudence which requires that courts strictly construe content-based restrictions and prior restraints to ensure they are narrowly tailored to advance a compelling government interest. A court reviewing a statute implicating the First Amendment must review that statute in accordance with First Amendment doctrine.

G. Narrow Tailoring

Section 2709(c) prohibits an NSL recipient from "disclos[ing] to any person that the [FBI] has sought or obtained access to information or records under this section." This nondisclosure provision contains no time limit.

The Government asserts that the scope of the nondisclosure order is "as narrow as can reasonably be expected, and prohibits only minimal disclosure." To the contrary, NSL recipients are effectively barred from engaging in any discussion regarding their experiences and opinions related to the government's use of NSLs. It is perhaps telling that, in justifying the need for the nondisclosure provision of the NSL statute, the Government relies entirely on the possible harms to national security or diplomatic relations that could result from the disclosure of a particular NSL — i.e., revealing that a named individual was the target of an NSL. Arguably, guarding the secrecy of that particular detail may be defensible as promoting national security interests in a given case. The Government, however, provides no support for its argument that the much broader nondisclosure still permitted by § 2709(c) in all other circumstances serves a compelling government interest.

The Government again points to grand jury secrecy statutes and the nondisclosure requirements of related investigative tools — Fwiretaps, pen registers, and administrative subpoenas — and contends that case-by-case analysis with respect to the scope and duration of nondisclosure is not required in those contexts. But, as discussed at length above, these contexts differ substantially from present one; in particular, they all involve prior judicial oversight and limited duration.

H. Scope of 18 U.S.C. §§ 3511(d) and 3511(e)

In amending the NSL statute, Congress added two provisions intended to guide reviewing courts with respect to decisions to close hearings, seal documents, or review evidence ex parte and in camera. Upon review, the Court finds each section constitutional, provided that the attendant language as interpreted by the Court preserves the traditional role of the court in carefully examining the extent to which closure, sealing, and limited evidentiary access by the defendant is necessary.

IV. CONCLUSION

For the reasons stated above, the Court concludes that § 2709(c) is unconstitutional under the First Amendment because it functions as a licensing scheme that does not afford adequate procedural safeguards, and because it is not a sufficiently narrowly tailored restriction on protected speech. Because the Court finds that § 2709(c) cannot be severed from the remainder of the statute, the Court finds the entirety of § 2709 unconstitutional. Additionally, the Court concludes that § 3511(b) is unconstitutional under the First Amendment and the doctrine of separation of powers.

V. STAY OF JUDGMENT

As it did in *Doe I*, in light of the implications of its ruling and the importance of the issues involved, the Court will stay enforcement of its judgment pending appeal, or for the Government otherwise to pursue any alternate course of action, for 90 days. The stay is intended to give the Government the opportunity to move this Court, or the Court of Appeals, for whatever appropriate relief it may seek to maintain the confidentiality of any information implicated by the Court's ruling.

NOTES AND QUESTIONS

1. The Issues with NSLs. In an extremely long and heavily documented opinion in *Doe I* (56 pages and 268 footnotes), the court covered a number of potential problem areas with government acquisition of information. What is the heart of the matter from your point of view? the lack of judicial involvement before issuance of the demand? lack of notice to the generator of the information? the fundamental issue of anonymity in internet communications?

2. Judicial Review. This opinion could reflect a fundamental bias shared by much of the populace in favor of trusting courts more than investigators. Is that value one that should be or is enshrined in constitutional doctrine? What components would go into that value choice?

3. Privacy of Communications. In *Doe I*, the court pointed out that

> *Katz v. United States* held that the Fourth Amendment's privacy protections applied where the Government wiretapped a telephone call placed from a public phone booth. "The Government's activities in electronically listening to and recording the petitioner's words violated the privacy upon which he justifiably relied while using the telephone booth and thus constituted a 'search and seizure' within the meaning of the Fourth Amendment." The Supreme Court also stated that a person entering a phone booth who "shuts the door behind him" is "surely entitled to assume that the words he utters into the mouthpiece will not be broadcast to the world."

> Applying that reasoning to anonymous internet speech and associational activity is relatively straightforward. A person who signs onto an anonymous forum under a pseudonym, for example, is essentially "shut[ting] the door behind him," and is surely entitled to a reasonable expectation that his speech, whatever form the expression assumes, will not be accessible to the Government to be broadcast to the world absent appropriate legal process. To hold otherwise would ignore the role of the internet as a remarkably powerful forum for private communication and association.

How much weight should we give to the claimed right of anonymity by a speaker in public discourse? There are different types of doors on the internet. It may be easier to understand the claim of privacy when thinking about e-mail from one person directed specifically to another than to see the same claim for anonymity when posting material for public consumption on a website. In between these examples, there are chat rooms where the technology provides an appearance of anonymity but an ISP or the manager of the chat room may have full awareness of each speaker's identity. In truth, how reliable are our beliefs in privacy when using electronic communication? The technology that allows instant communication also allows identification of the speaker.

Technology aside, isn't the claim for anonymity in a public setting a little disingenuous? If I want to make a public statement, shouldn't I be willing to face the consequences of public disapproval? If not, then shouldn't I keep that communication private?

4. Sources and Methods. The "mosaic" argument recurs frequently in government attempts to prevent disclosure of its investigations, not only from public disclosure but even from disclosure to the individuals involved. The argument is noted in this case that even a perceptive federal judge might not grasp the significance of a single bit of information that would fit a central piece of a puzzle to a knowledgeable terrorist. This argument seems to resonate in the terrorism context in a little different way than it might with other organized crime elements. Should we assume or believe that terrorist organizations are more sophisticated or smarter than organizations such as, for example, the Medellin Cartel of the 1980s?

The Second Circuit's remand in this case was through a brief *per curiam* opinion. *Doe I v. Gonzales*, 449 F.3d 415 (2d Cir. 2006). One judge, however, took the occasion to comment on the government's continued insistence on secrecy.

> The government advanced the "mosaic theory" as one of the reasons to support a permanent ban on speech. That theory envisions thousands of bits and pieces of apparently innocuous information, which when properly assembled create a picture. At bottom the government's assertion is simply that antiterrorism investigations are different from other investigations in that they are derivative of prior or concurrent investigations. Thus, permanent nondisclosure is necessary because, implicitly in the government's view, all terrorism investigations are permanent and unending.

> The government's urging that an endless investigation leads logically to an endless ban on speech flies in the face of human knowledge and common sense: witnesses disappear, plans change or are completed, cases are closed, investi-

gations terminate. Further, a ban on speech and a shroud of secrecy in perpetuity are antithetical to democratic concepts and do not fit comfortably with the fundamental rights guaranteed American citizens. Unending secrecy of actions taken by government officials may also serve as a cover for possible official misconduct and/or incompetence.

Moreover, with regard to having something be secret forever, most Americans would agree with Benjamin Franklin's observation on our human inability to maintain secrecy for very long. He wrote "three may keep a secret, if two of them are dead." BENJAMIN FRANKLIN, POOR RICHARD'S ALMANACK 8 (Dean Walley ed., Hallmark 1967) (1732). In fact, what happened in the Connecticut case bears out Franklin's astute observation. While striving to keep the identities of the Connecticut plaintiffs secret, the government inadvertently revealed their identities through public court filings. This revelation was widely reported in the media. Thus, the case assumed the awkward posture where the identities of the Connecticut plaintiffs were published, yet the government continued to insist that the Connecticut plaintiffs may not identify themselves and that their identities must still be kept secret. This is like closing the barn door after the horse has already bolted.

5. _Muslim Community Association v. Ashcroft_, 459 F. Supp. 2d 592 (E.D. Mich. 2006). This case was filed in the Eastern District of Michigan in July 2003 to challenge the constitutionality of the original section 215 of PATRIOT, codified in FISA as 50 U.S.C. § 1861. The plaintiffs summarized their claims this way:

> To obtain a Section 215 order, the FBI need only assert that the records or personal belongings are 'sought for' an ongoing foreign intelligence, counterintelligence, or international terrorism investigation. The FBI is not required to show probable cause — or any reason — to believe that the target of the order is a criminal suspect or foreign agent. . . . The targets of Section 215 orders are never notified that their privacy has been compromised — even years later, and even if they are innocent. The law includes a gag provision that prohibits persons or entities served with Section 215 orders from ever disclosing, even in the most general terms, that the FBI has sought information from them.

The complaint went on to claim that the organizations "have a well-founded belief" that third parties have been ordered to divulge records regarding the organizations and their members. For example, some of the organizations have been associated with expressing support for Sami al-Arian and Rabih Haddad. As a result of that association and the known investigations into the activities of those two persons, "section 215 has caused some of plaintiffs' members and clients to be inhibited from publicly expressing their political views."

In October 2003, the government filed motions to dismiss on the basis of standing, ripeness, and failure to state a claim. As part of its submission to the court, the government filed an affidavit stating that no applications had been presented to the FISA Court under section 215 through September 18, 2003. In May 2004, the government submitted a letter clarifying that any filings after September 2003 would remain classified but would be irrelevant to the ACLU litigation in any event. The ACLU then responded in June that it had obtained information through a FOIA request indicating that at least one section 215 order had been sought as early as October 15, 2003. The government then responded with a letter to the court including an affidavit submitted in two forms, one with classified portions redacted for the public record and a complete version that was submitted to the court security officer to be available to the judge upon request.

On September 29, 2006, the district court denied the government's motion to dismiss on the basis of standing.

> Plaintiffs have alleged that their members are afraid to attend mosque, practice their religion, and express their opinions on religion and political issues.

Plaintiffs' members are afraid to obtain services from the human services organizations for fear that any information obtained by the organization can be obtained by the Government. Plaintiffs have shown threats of present injury sufficient to satisfy constitutional standing requirements on their First Amendment claims.

Because § 1861 had been altered substantially by Congress in 2005, the Government moved to dismiss on the basis of mootness. The plaintiffs asked for additional time to consult with their parties and to amend the complaint. No further developments have been reported.

NOTE ON INTERCEPTION OF ELECTRONIC COMMUNICATIONS

The Electronic Privacy Information Center (EPIC) vigorously criticized many aspects of PATRIOT. Among its specific concerns were these:

> The implications for online privacy are considerable. For example, the Act increases the ability of law enforcement agencies to authorize installation of pen registers and trap and trace devices (a pen register collects the outgoing phone numbers placed from a specific telephone line; a trap and trace device captures the incoming numbers placed to a specific phone line — a caller-id box is a trap and trace device), and to authorize the installation of such devices to record all computer routing, addressing, and signaling information. . . . Although the use of such devices requires a court order, it does not require a showing of probable cause. There is, in effect, no judicial discretion, as the court is required to authorize monitoring upon the mere certification by a government attorney that the "information likely to be obtained by such installation and use is relevant to an ongoing criminal investigation."

> By expanding the nature of the information that can be captured, the new law clearly expanded pen register capacities to the Internet, covering electronic mail, Web surfing, and all other forms of electronic communications. The fact that the provision prohibits the capture of "content" does not adequately take into account the unique nature of information captured electronically, which contains data far more revealing than phone numbers, such as URLs generated while using the Web (which often contain a great deal of information that cannot in any way be analogized to a telephone number). . . . Because Carnivore provides the FBI with access to the communications of all subscribers of a monitored Internet Service Provider (and not just those of the court-designated target), it raises substantial privacy issues for millions of law-abiding American citizens.

> Section 214 removes the pre-existing statutory requirement that the government prove the surveillance target is "an agent of a foreign power" before obtaining a pen register/trap and trace order under the FISA. Therefore, the government could obtain a pen register/trap and trace device "for any investigation to gather foreign intelligence information," without a showing that the device has, is or will be used by a foreign agent or by an individual engaged in international terrorism or clandestine intelligence activities. The amendment significantly eviscerates the constitutional rationale for the relatively lax requirements that apply to foreign intelligence surveillance. That laxity is premised on the assumption that the Executive Branch, in pursuit of its national security responsibilities to monitor the activities of foreign powers and their agents, should not be unduly restrained by Congress and the courts. The removal of the "foreign power" predicate for pen register/trap and trace surveillance upsets that delicate balance.

http://www.epic.org/privacy/terrorism/usapatriot.

Why is EPIC so concerned about "pen registers" and "trap and trace" devices?

Historically, these devices have merely recorded the numbers called from a particular telephone or the number calling that telephone. They do not record the content of a conversation. By using these devices on computer websites, does government acquire information about the user who accesses the website? Does it matter that government agents know I went online looking for information about C-4 explosives? I probably need to know much more about "cookies" and how the technology works before I can assess all the privacy implications of internet communications, but the central point is whether I have a privacy interest in what I read. Government lawyers have argued in response to the ALA concerns over library circulation records that there is no privacy interest in what a patron reads because the material is acquired in public view just as your grocery purchases are in public view at the checkout counter. What do you think of this line of argument?

In some sense, the internet is a publicly accessible bank of information similar to the open shelves of a library, but it is not a physical space that is normally observable by others. To pursue the library analogy, if government agents were posted near the shelves of a public library and observed who was looking at certain books, would this be a problem? If your answer is "yes," is it a problem of constitutional dimension or a problem of good practice?

The owner of a computer that is linked to the web can now ask for "intercept" of communications by "computer trespassers" (hackers). EPIC complains that this "permits wiretapping of the intruder's communications without any judicial oversight, in contrast to most federal communication-intercept laws that require objective oversight from someone outside the investigative chain." So what? Why should we be worried about the privacy of hackers?

Some of the concerns about PATRIOT have to do with what have been statutory limits on normal law enforcement investigative tools, specifically the new nationwide service of search warrants and the use of "sneak and peek" warrants. Again, why should we be concerned about removing some limits on the ability of investigators to protect the public safety? What aspects of privacy were protected by the prior limitations?

One recommendation of the 9/11 Commission contemplates a unified "network-based information system." This arose from the realization that the FBI and CIA did not easily share information, a barrier that once was built into law but eased by the PATRIOT Act. Is sharing of all intelligence data in one big database a good idea? How realistic is it to expect sharing? and what human could possibly assimilate and evaluate the billions of pieces of information that flow through the IC agencies in any given month?

[C] The NSA Surveillance Program

On December 16, 2005, the *New York Times* disclosed that the National Security Agency had been monitoring electronic communications without seeking FISA court approval, including communications where one party was in the U.S. The President in his next radio address put forward the usual justification of "inherent" power to protect against terrorism. In subsequent disclosures, the Justice Department pointed out that FISA prohibits intercept except as authorized "by statute," and claimed that the AUMF as interpreted in *Hamdi* could be such a statute. As the debate intensified, this surveillance came to be known as the "Terrorist Surveillance Program" (TSP).

Meanwhile, Attorney General Gonzales came under increasing fire during the first half of 2007 as a result of the OIG Report described in *Doe v. Gonzales*, the controversy over firing of eight U.S. Attorneys, and then ultimately further disclosures about TSP. In May 2007, former Deputy Attorney General James Comey described a tense scene in 2004 when he raced to the hospital sickbed of then-AG Ashcroft to get there ahead of Gonzales who wanted to have Ashcroft sign off on various controversial measures. Comey would not specify the nature of the dispute, saying that it was classified except that it involved "the program disclosed by the President."

In July, AG Gonzales testified further about the U.S. Attorney firings and was questioned about the TSP. In a follow-up letter to the committee chair on August 1, 2007, he provided this further explanation:

> In my public testimony, including on July 24th, . . . discussing only that particular aspect of the NSA activities that the President has publicly acknowledged, and that we have called the Terrorist Surveillance Program, as defined in the DNI's letter.
>
> In March 2004, when the presidential order was set to expire, the Department of Justice, under Acting Attorney General James Comey, refused to give its approval to the reauthorization of the order because of concerns about the legal basis of certain of these NSA activities. . . . In the spring of 2004, after a thorough reexamination of all these activities, Mr. Comey and the Office of Legal Counsel ultimately agreed that the President could direct the NSA to intercept international communications without a court order where the interceptions were targeted at al Qaeda or its affiliates. Other aspects of the NSA activities referenced in the DNI's letter did precipitate very serious disagreement. The nature of these disagreements has been the subject of oversight by the Intelligence Committees, including a closed hearing before the House Permanent Select Committee on Intelligence at which I recently testified.

Although this letter and the DNI letter seem to make it clear that there are more aspects of secret surveillance than what has been disclosed, Congress dropped the issue. In August 2007, it passed a 6-month amendment to FISA to allow surveillance without prior court approval. 50 U.S.C. § 1805a, 1805b (2008). That authorization expired February 16, 2008, but orders issued prior to that time remain valid for one year.

Regardless of whether Congress continues to authorize the surveillance of international electronic communications, the issue of the legality of what was done under the TSP does not entirely go away. First, there is the question of whether illegal activity took place for a number of years. Second, the arguments over "inherent presidential powers" will resonate for years to come and will be important to future crises. Third, as the dissenting judge in the 6th Circuit opinion below observes, the case cannot be moot because it could recur at any time. Finally, there apparently are elements of government surveillance that have not yet been disclosed and that could well be challenged in the future. For all these reasons, the legal basis of TSP needs to be examined.

AMERICAN CIVIL LIBERTIES UNION v. NATIONAL SECURITY AGENCY
493 F.3d 644 (6th Cir. 2007)

Before: BATCHELDER, GILMAN, and GIBBONS, CIRCUIT JUDGES. BATCHELDER, J., delivered the judgment of the court. GIBBONS, J., delivered a separate opinion concurring in the judgment only. GILMAN, J., delivered a separate dissenting opinion.

ALICE M. BATCHELDER, CIRCUIT JUDGE.

The United States National Security Agency ("NSA") appeals from the decision of the District Court for the Eastern District of Michigan that granted summary judgment against the NSA and imposed a permanent injunction. The plaintiffs are a collection of associations and individuals led by the American Civil Liberties Union, and they cross-appeal. Because we cannot find that any of the plaintiffs have standing for any of their claims, we must vacate the district court's order and remand for dismissal of the entire action.

I.

Sometime after the September 11, 2001, terrorist attacks, President Bush authorized the NSA to begin a counter-terrorism operation that has come to be known as the Terrorist Surveillance Program ("TSP"). Although the specifics remain undisclosed, it has been publicly acknowledged that the TSP includes the interception (i.e., wiretapping), without warrants, of telephone and email communications where one party to the communication is located outside the United States and the NSA has "a reasonable basis to conclude that one party to the communication is a member of al Qaeda, affiliated with al Qaeda, or a member of an organization affiliated with al Qaeda, or working in support of al Qaeda."

The plaintiffs in this action include journalists, academics, and lawyers who regularly communicate with individuals located overseas, who the plaintiffs believe are the types of people the NSA suspects of being al Qaeda terrorists, affiliates, or supporters, and are therefore likely to be monitored under the TSP. From this suspicion, and the limited factual foundation in this case, the plaintiffs allege that they have a "well founded belief" that their communications are being tapped. According to the plaintiffs, the NSA's operation of the TSP — and the possibility of warrantless surveillance — subjects them to conditions that constitute an irreparable harm.

The plaintiffs filed suit in the Eastern District of Michigan, seeking a permanent injunction against the NSA's continuation of the TSP and a declaration that two particular aspects of the TSP — warrantless wiretapping and data mining — violate the First and Fourth Amendments, the Separation of Powers Doctrine, the Administrative Procedures Act ("APA"), Title III of the Omnibus Crime Control and Safe Streets Act ("Title III"), and the Foreign Intelligence Surveillance Act ("FISA"). Both sides moved for summary judgment. The district court dismissed the data mining aspect of the plaintiffs' claim, but granted judgment to the plaintiffs regarding the warrantless wiretapping.

The NSA had invoked the State Secrets Doctrine[12] to bar the discovery or admission of evidence that would "expose [confidential] matters which, in the interest of national security, should not be divulged." The NSA argued that, without the privileged information, none of the named plaintiffs could establish standing. The district court applied the state secrets privilege, but rejected the NSA's argument, holding instead that three publicly acknowledged facts about the TSP — (1) it eavesdrops, (2) without warrants, (3) on international telephone and email communications in which at least one of the parties is a suspected al Qaeda affiliate — were sufficient to establish standing. Moreover, the district court found these three facts sufficient to grant summary judgment to the plaintiffs on the merits of their claims, resulting in a declaratory judgment and the imposition of an injunction. These three facts constitute all the evidence in the record relating to the NSA's conduct under the TSP.

This appeal presents a number of serious issues, none of which can be addressed until a determination is made that these plaintiffs have standing to litigate them. The "particular plaintiffs" to this action are a diverse group of associations and individuals, and it would require a rigorous undertaking to assure that each has standing to litigate. The conduct giving rise to the alleged injuries is undisputed: the NSA (1) eavesdrops, (2) without warrants, (3) on international telephone and email communications in which at least one of the parties is reasonably suspected of al Qaeda ties.

The plaintiffs' objection to this conduct is also undisputed, and they demand that the

---

[12] [Court's Footnote 2] The State Secrets Doctrine has two applications: a rule of evidentiary privilege, see *United States v. Reynolds*, 345 U.S. 1, 10 (1953), and a rule of non-justiciability, *see Tenet v. Doe*, 544 U.S. 1, 9 (2005). The present case implicates only the rule of state secrets evidentiary privilege. The rule of non-justiciability applies when the subject matter of the lawsuit is itself a state secret, so the claim cannot survive. *See id.* (espionage contract); *Weinberger v. Catholic Action Of Hawaii/ Peace Educ. Project*, 454 U.S. 139, 146–47 (1981) (storage of nuclear weapons); *Totten v. United States*, 92 U.S. 105 (1875) (espionage contract). If litigation would necessitate admission or disclosure of even the existence of the secret, then the case is non-justiciable and must be dismissed on the pleadings. Because the government has already acknowledged the existence of the warrantless wiretapping in this case, there is no risk of such disclosure and the rule of non-justiciability does not apply. The alleged data mining, which has not been publicly acknowledged, might fall within this rule. But, under the present analysis, a decision on this matter is unnecessary.

NSA discontinue it. The plaintiffs do not contend — nor could they — that the mere practice of wiretapping (i.e., eavesdropping) is, by itself, unconstitutional, illegal, or even improper. Rather, the plaintiffs object to the NSA's eavesdropping without warrants, specifically FISA warrants with their associated limitations and minimization requirements. According to the plaintiffs, it is the absence of these warrants that renders the NSA's conduct illegal and unconstitutional. But the plaintiffs do not — and because of the State Secrets Doctrine cannot — produce any evidence that any of their own communications have ever been intercepted by the NSA, under the TSP, or without warrants. Instead, they assert a mere belief, which they contend is reasonable and which they label a "well founded belief," that: their overseas contacts are the types of people targeted by the NSA; the plaintiffs are consequently subjected to the NSA's eavesdropping; the eavesdropping leads the NSA to discover (and possibly disclose) private or privileged information; and the mere possibility of such discovery (or disclosure) has injured them in three particular ways.

Notably, the plaintiffs do *not* allege as injury that they personally, either as individuals or associations, anticipate or fear any form of direct reprisal by the government (e.g., the NSA, the Justice Department, the Department of Homeland Security, etc.), such as criminal prosecution, deportation, administrative inquiry, civil litigation, or even public exposure. The injuries that these plaintiffs allege are not so direct; they are more amorphous and necessitate a pointed description.

The plaintiffs' primary alleged injury — the first of three — is their inability to communicate with their overseas contacts by telephone or email due to their self-governing ethical obligations. Under this claim, the *immediate* injury results directly from the plaintiffs' own actions and decisions, based on (1) their subjective belief that the NSA might be intercepting their communications, and (2) the ethical requirements governing such circumstances, as dictated by their respective professional organizations or affiliations. Relying on the district court's three facts, the plaintiffs allege their "well founded belief" that the NSA is intercepting their communications with overseas contacts, to the perceived detriment of those overseas contacts. The plaintiffs explain that they have an ethical duty to keep their communications confidential, which, under the circumstances, requires that they refrain from communicating with the overseas contacts by telephone or email, lest they violate that duty. The possibility that private communications may be revealed burdens the plaintiffs' pursuit of their chosen professions or organizational objectives — i.e., in order to comply with their ethical duties, the plaintiffs must refrain from communicating by telephone or email, and are instead required either to travel overseas to meet with these contacts in person or else refrain from communicating with them altogether.

The second alleged injury — and the only one expressly addressed by the district court — is the "chilling effect" on the overseas contacts' willingness to communicate with the plaintiffs by telephone or email. Under this claim, the *immediate* injury results directly from the actions of the overseas contacts who, the plaintiffs contend, fear that the NSA's discovery of otherwise private or privileged information (being communicated by telephone or email) will lead to some direct reprisal by the United States government, their own governments, or others. This fear causes the overseas contacts to refuse to communicate with the plaintiffs by telephone or email, and this refusal to communicate burdens the plaintiffs in the performance of their jobs or other lawful objectives, because, in order to pursue their chosen professions or organizational objectives, the plaintiffs must travel overseas to meet with these contacts in person. This injury manifests itself as both an added expense and an added burden.

The plaintiffs' third alleged injury is the NSA's violation of their legitimate expectation of privacy in their overseas telephone and email communications. Under this claim, the *immediate* injury comes directly from the actions of the NSA. The plaintiffs conclude that, because the NSA has conducted foreign electronic surveillance without obtaining FISA warrants (and presumably, without strict adherence to FISA's minimization requirements), the NSA has breached their legitimate expectation of privacy, thereby causing them injury.

This third kind of injury, unlike the other two, is direct and personal; under this theory, the NSA has directly invaded the plaintiffs' interest and proof of such invasion is all that is necessary to establish standing. If, for instance, a plaintiff could demonstrate that her privacy had actually been breached (i.e., that her communications had actually been wiretapped), then she would have standing to assert a *Fourth Amendment* cause of action for breach of privacy. In the present case, the plaintiffs concede that there is no single plaintiff who can show that he or she has actually been wiretapped. Moreover, due to the State Secrets Doctrine, the proof needed either to make or negate such a showing is privileged, and therefore withheld from discovery or disclosure.

The district court dismissed the data mining aspect of the plaintiffs' claim, finding that the plaintiffs could not establish a *prima facie* case without resorting to privileged information. A thorough review of the complaint, the district court opinion, and the arguments presented on appeal, makes it clear that the plaintiffs allege no separate injury in connection with the alleged data-mining aspect of the TSP. Therefore, this standing analysis applies equally, and the plaintiffs' cross-appeal must be dismissed for lack of jurisdiction.We hold that the plaintiffs do not have standing to assert their claims in federal court.

RONALD LEE GILMAN, CIRCUIT JUDGE, dissenting.

My colleagues conclude that the plaintiffs have not established standing to bring their challenge to the Bush Administration's so-called Terrorist Surveillance Program (TSP). A fundamental disagreement exists between the two of them and myself on what is required to show standing and whether any of the plaintiffs have met that requirement. Because of that disagreement, I respectfully dissent. Moreover, I would affirm the judgment of the district court because I am persuaded that the TSP as originally implemented violated the Foreign Intelligence Surveillance Act of 1978 (FISA).

I. ANALYSIS

A. *Procedural Posture*

This case comes to us in a relatively unique procedural posture. In the district court, the plaintiffs moved for partial summary judgment. They filed a statement of undisputed facts in support of that motion. The government then filed its own motion to dismiss or, in the alternative, a motion for summary judgment. In this motion, the government asserted that the plaintiffs could not establish standing and that the state-secrets privilege barred their claims. But the government did not contest the plaintiffs' statement of undisputed facts or provide its own statement of undisputed facts.

After reviewing the affidavits and related supporting material submitted in support of the plaintiffs' motion, the district court found that they had set forth the necessary facts to meet the prerequisites for standing. The court then considered the plaintiffs' claims on the merits and granted their motion as to all but their datamining claim.

Despite this procedural posture, the lead opinion asserts that the record presently before us contains only "three publicly acknowledged facts about the TSP-(1) it eavesdrops, (2) without warrants, (3) on international telephone and email communications in which at least one of the parties is a suspected al Qaeda affiliate." For the reasons both stated above and set forth below, I believe that this description significantly understates the material in the record presently before us.

B. Standing

1. Injury in fact

The position of the attorney-plaintiffs, in my opinion, is the strongest for the purpose of the standing analysis. This is not to say that the journalists and the scholars do not have standing. They might. But because only one plaintiff need establish standing, I will focus my discussion on the attorney-plaintiffs.

The attorney-plaintiffs assert a claim for the injuries flowing from the failure of the TSP to comply with FISA's requirements that "minimization procedures" be utilized to protect privileged communications-such as between attorneys and their clients-from interception or, if intercepted, from subsequent disclosure. Contrary to the lead opinion's characterization of the attorney-plaintiffs' assertions, the harm alleged here in fact "causes the plaintiffs to refrain from" potentially harmful conduct. I find that the distinction the lead opinion attempts to draw between a harm that *causes* an injury and a harm that *results* from an injury is ultimately unpersuasive. To my mind, the attorney-plaintiffs have articulated an actual or imminent harm flowing from the TSP.

On appeal, the government contends that any litigation about the TSP must be premised on the three general facts that the government has publicly disclosed: (1) the TSP exists, (2) it operates without warrants, and (3) it intercepts "only communications that originate or conclude in a foreign country, and only if there are reasonable grounds to believe that a party to the communication is affiliated with al Qaeda." According to the government, the plaintiffs cannot demonstrate that they were actually targets of the TSP and thus cannot show more than a "subjective chill" on their activities. The government asserts that the plaintiffs cannot establish standing because the state-secrets privilege prevents us from testing the plaintiffs' allegations that they have been or likely will be subject to surveillance under the TSP. Moreover, the government argues that the plaintiffs improperly seek to assert the rights of third parties, such as their overseas contacts, clients, and sources, who are not presently before the court.

The attorney-plaintiffs respond that they have suffered concrete, particularized injuries as a result of the TSP. Specifically, they contend that the TSP puts them in the position of abrogating their duties under applicable professional-responsibility rules if they communicate with clients and contacts via telephone or email. The TSP, in short, allegedly prevents them from doing their jobs. Specifically, the attorney-plaintiffs contend that they have had to travel internationally for face-to-face meetings at a significant expense in terms of time and money. They claim that their ability to conduct research and factfinding has been limited, if not entirely thwarted, as a result.

The attorney-plaintiffs, as part of their representation of clients accused of being enemy combatants or of providing aid to organizations designated as terrorist groups, declare that they have conducted internet research on terrorism, religion, politics, and human-rights issues in parts of the Middle East and South Asia. They further state that they have reviewed web sites where topics including jihad, kidnapping, and other terrorist acts are discussed. As part of their work on behalf of their clients, these attorneys have communicated with potential witnesses, experts, lawyers, and other individuals who live and work outside the United States about subjects such as terrorism, jihad, and al-Qaeda. The attorney-plaintiffs contend that because of the TSP, they have ceased telephone or email communications about substantive issues with their overseas contacts. This is because the TSP, unlike FISA, provides no minimization procedures to protect attorney-client communications.

[T]he attorney-plaintiffs here complain of specific present harms, not simply of some generalized fear of the future misuse of intercepted communications. The TSP forces them to decide between breaching their duty of confidentiality to their clients and breaching their duty to provide zealous representation. Neither position is tenable. The attorney-plaintiffs must travel to meet in person with clients and sources in order to avoid the risk of TSP surveillance. The attorney-plaintiffs have thus identified concrete harms to themselves flowing from their reasonable fear that the TSP will intercept privileged communications between themselves and their clients.

Finally, the concurring opinion would find that the state-secrets privilege prevents the attorney-plaintiffs from establishing an injury in fact. But this reading expands the reach of the privilege in ways that the caselaw does not support. Because the state-secrets privilege "operates to foreclose relief for violations of rights that may well have occurred by foreclosing the discovery of evidence that they did occur, it is a privilege not to be lightly invoked."

My colleagues believe that the attorney-plaintiffs must establish that they were actually subject to surveillance under the TSP, whereas I conclude that a demonstration of a reasonable, well-founded fear that has resulted in actual and particularized injury suffices.

In short, the critical question in this case is not whether the attorney-plaintiffs have actually been surveilled — because, as the lead opinion aptly notes, a wiretap by its nature is meant to be unknown to its targets — but whether the "reasonableness of the fear" of such surveillance is sufficient to establish that they have suffered actual, imminent, concrete, or particularized harm from the government's alleged unlawful action. I believe that the plaintiffs have established such an injury in fact. I therefore turn to the remaining factors in the Article III constitutional-standing analysis.

C. Mootness

[The case is not moot despite the congressional amendment to FISA because the government claims inherent authority to eavesdrop if the FISA authorization were withdrawn.]

D. Merits

Without expressing an opinion concerning the analysis of the district court, I would affirm its judgment because I conclude that the TSP violates FISA and Title III and that the President does not have the inherent authority to act in disregard of those statutes. The clearest ground for deciding the merits of this appeal is the plaintiffs' statutory claim, just as the clearest argument for standing is presented by the attorney-plaintiffs. This is not to say that the plaintiffs' other causes of action lack merit, but simply that this case can, and therefore should, be decided on the narrowest grounds possible.

1. The TSP violated FISA and Title III

Both FISA and Title III expressly prohibit electronic surveillance outside of their statutory frameworks. The language used is unequivocal. In enacting FISA, Congress directed that electronic surveillance conducted inside the United States for foreign intelligence purposes was to be undertaken only as authorized by specific federal statutory authority. The statute clearly states that chapter 119 and FISA "shall be the *exclusive means* by which electronic surveillance . . . and the interception of domestic wire, oral, and electronic communications may be conducted." *Id.* (emphasis added).

Congress has thus unequivocally declared that FISA and Title III are the exclusive means by which electronic surveillance is permitted. No other authorization can comply with the law. Congress further emphasized this point by criminalizing the undertaking of electronic surveillance not authorized by statute in two separate places in the U.S. Code. The government, however, contends that Congress authorized the TSP in the aftermath of the September 11, 2001 attacks by enacting the Authorization for Use of Military Force (AUMF). In addition, the government notes that "foreign intelligence gathering is . . . vital to the successful prosecution of war."

But FISA itself expressly and specifically restricts the President's authority even in times of war. The statute provides that "[n]otwithstanding any other law, the President, through the Attorney General, may authorize electronic surveillance without a court order under this subchapter to acquire foreign intelligence information for a period not to exceed fifteen calendar days following a declaration of war by the Congress." 50 U.S.C. § 1811. FISA thus limits warrantless electronic surveillance to the first 15 days following a declaration of war, a more formal action than even the enactment of an authorization for the use of force. This 15-day period of warrantless surveillance was enacted to permit "consideration of any amendment to this Act that may be appropriate during a wartime emergency." H.R. Conf. Rep. 95-1720, at 34, *reprinted at* 1978 U.S.C.C.A.N. 4048, 4063.

To be sure, Congress in 1978 likely did not contemplate a situation such as the one that arose with the attacks of September 11, 2001. But in the aftermath of those attacks, Congress has shown itself both willing and able to consider appropriate amendments to FISA. Congress has in fact amended FISA multiple times since September 11, 2001, increasing the President's authority by permitting "roving" wiretaps and expanding the permissible use of pen-register devices.

But Congress has never suspended FISA's application nor altered the 15-day limit on warrantless electronic surveillance. The Attorney General has in fact acknowledged that the Bush Administration has never sought an amendment to FISA that might have provided authorization for the TSP or a similar program because certain members of Congress allegedly informed the Administration that such an amendment would be "difficult, if not impossible" to obtain. Press Briefing by Alberto Gonzales, Att'y Gen., http://www.whitehouse.gov/news/releases/2005/12/20051219-1.html.

Yet the TSP is precisely the type of program that FISA was enacted to oversee. A senior Department of Justice official has conceded that the TSP involved warrantless electronic surveillance of communications into and out of the United States.

According to the government, the AUMF provides the authorization necessary to satisfy FISA's prohibition on electronic surveillance "except as authorized by statute. No reference to surveillance, however, is found in the AUMF. Instead, the government's argument rests on a general inference to be drawn from the AUMF; in other words, that the phrase "all necessary and appropriate force" encompasses electronic surveillance by implication. But this interpretation of the AUMF directly conflicts with the specific statutory language of both FISA and Title III."

FISA, as noted previously, includes explicit provisions for wartime usage. The government argues that if the AUMF has not implicitly repealed the exclusive-means provision, then the AUMF and FISA must be in conflict, and that the AUMF should trump FISA. This disregards the fact that shortly after enacting the AUMF, Congress amended certain provisions of FISA through its enactment of the USA PATRIOT Act, as described above. Congress thus saw no conflict between FISA and the AUMF. *Cf. Al-Marri v. Wright*, 487 F.3d 160 (4th Cir. Jun. 11, 2007) (concluding that Congress's enactment of the USA PATRIOT Act, with specific provisions relating to the detention of "terrorist aliens such as the plaintiff, "provides still another reason why we cannot assume that Congress silently empowered the President in the AUMF to order the indefinite military detention without any criminal process of civilian 'terrorist aliens' as 'enemy combatants' ").

In addition, the government's argument completely ignores two fundamental principles of statutory construction. The first relevant principle is that when interpreting potentially conflicting statutes, "a more specific statute will be given precedence over a more general one, regardless of their temporal sequence." FISA's provisions regarding wartime electronic surveillance are detailed and specific. The AUMF, in contrast, sweeps broadly, making no reference at all to electronic surveillance. To read the statutes as the government suggests would render FISA's provisions relating to wartime usage mere surplusage. Such a reading would run counter to the second relevant principle of statutory construction that requires courts to "give effect, if possible, to every clause and word of a statute."

Finally, the Supreme Court's more recent decision in *Hamdan v. Rumsfeld* clearly rejected the government's theory of the AUMF. The Court in *Hamdan* declined to read the AUMF as implicitly authorizing the President to override a provision in the Uniform Code of Military Justice (UCMJ) that sets forth the conditions for convening military commissions in lieu of courts-martial. "[T]here is nothing in the text or legislative history of the AUMF even hinting that Congress intended to expand or alter the authorization set forth in Article 21 of the UCMJ."

The same observation holds true in the present case. Nothing in the AUMF suggests that Congress intended to "expand or alter the authorization" set forth in FISA. Moreover, the text and the legislative history of FISA and Title III make quite clear that the TSP or a similar program can be authorized only through those two statutes. The TSP plainly violated FISA and Title III and, unless there exists some authority for the President to supersede this statutory authority, was therefore unlawful.

2. Inherent authority

The government's final defense is that the Constitution grants the President the "inherent authority" to "intercept the international communications of those affiliated with al Qaeda." A contrary position would, according to the government, "present a grave constitutional question of the highest order."

The Constitution divides the nation's war powers between the Executive and the Legislative Branches. In contrast to the government's suggestion, the President does not have *exclusive* war powers.

The Constitution expressly grants Congress the power to make laws in the context of national defense. Moreover, the Constitution requires the President to conform to duly enacted laws. The Supreme Court reiterated this principle in *Ex Parte Milligan*, 71 U.S. (4 Wall) 2, 18 L. Ed. 281 (1866), holding that the Habeas Corpus Act of 1863 barred the President from denying habeas corpus rights to a detainee who was captured outside the area of battle. More recently, the Court held in *Hamdan* that the President "may not disregard limitations that Congress has, in proper exercise of its own war powers, placed on his powers."

The Supreme Court fully addressed the question of the inherent authority of the President in *Youngstown*. There, the Court struck down President Truman's executive order to seize domestic steel-production facilities during the Korean war. In his famous concurring opinion, Justice Jackson described our tripartite system as one of "separateness but interdependence, autonomy but reciprocity." *Youngstown, 343 U.S. at 635* (Jackson, J., concurring). "Presidential powers are not fixed but fluctuate, depending upon their disjunction or conjunction with those of Congress." He then laid out the three so-called zones of presidential power as follows:

> 1. When the President acts pursuant to an express or implied authorization of Congress, his authority is at its maximum, for it includes all that he possesses in his own right plus all that Congress can delegate.

> 2. When the President acts in absence of either a congressional grant or denial of authority, he can only rely upon his own independent powers, but there is a zone of twilight in which he and Congress may have concurrent authority, or in which its distribution is uncertain. . . .

> 3. When the President takes measures incompatible with the expressed or implied will of Congress, his power is at its lowest ebb, for then he can rely only upon his own constitutional powers minus any constitutional powers of Congress over the matter.

When the President acts in Zone 3, "[c]ourts can sustain exclusive Presidential control in such a case only by disabling the Congress from acting upon the subject. Presidential claim to a power at once so conclusive and preclusive must be scrutinized with caution, for what is at stake is the equilibrium established by our constitutional system."

We must thus determine into which zone the TSP fits. From that determination, the program will stand or fall. The government argues that the TSP fits into Zone 1, where the President's authority is at its zenith. But this argument ignores Congress's clear directive that FISA and Title III constitute the exclusive means for undertaking electronic surveillance within the United States for foreign intelligence purposes. The result might not be what the President would prefer, but that does not give him license to "disregard limitations" that Congress has "placed on his powers." *Hamdan*, 126 S. Ct. at 2774 n.23. In light of FISA and Title III, I have no doubt that the TSP falls into Zone 3, where the President's authority is at its lowest ebb.

The government, however, turns to a case from the Foreign Intelligence Surveillance Court of Review as support for its argument that the President has "inherent constitutional authority to conduct warrantless foreign intelligence surveillance." *See In re Sealed Case*, 310 F.3d 717, 746 (For. Intel. Surv. Ct. Rev. 2002) (per curiam). To be sure, the *Sealed Case* court stated in dicta that "[w]e take for granted that the President does have" the "inherent authority to conduct warrantless searches to obtain foreign intelligence information." This dicta, however, is unpersuasive because the *Sealed Case* court relied on a Fourth Circuit decision from 1980 that dealt with a challenge to pre-FISA surveillance.

E. Plaintiffs' Datamining Cross-appeal

The plaintiffs raise a cross-appeal from the district court's grant of summary judgment to the government on the plaintiffs' datamining claim. After a careful review of the record, I conclude that the district court's analysis of this issue and of the preclusive effect of the state-secrets privilege is persuasive. I would therefore not disturb the district court's judgment on the plaintiffs' datamining claim.

II. Conclusion

The closest question in this case, in my opinion, is whether the plaintiffs have the standing to sue. Once past that hurdle, however, the rest gets progressively easier. Mootness is not a problem because of the government's position that it retains the right to opt out of the FISA regime whenever it chooses. Its AUMF and inherent-authority arguments are weak in light of existing precedent and the rules of statutory construction. Finally, when faced with the clear wording of FISA and Title III that these statutes provide the "exclusive means" for the government to engage in electronic surveillance within the United States for foreign intelligence purposes, the conclusion becomes inescapable that the TSP was unlawful. I would therefore affirm the judgment of the district court.

AL-HARAMAIN ISLAMIC FOUNDATION, INC. v. BUSH
507 F.3d 1190 (9th Cir. 2007)

McKeown, Circuit Judge.

Following the terrorist attacks on September 11, 2001, President George W. Bush authorized the National Security Agency ("NSA") to conduct a warrantless communications surveillance program. The program intercepted international communications into and out of the United States of persons alleged to have ties to Al Qaeda and other terrorist networks. Though its operating parameters remain murky, and certain details may forever remain so, much of what is known about the Terrorist Surveillance Program ("TSP") was spoon-fed to the public by the President and his administration.

After *The New York Times* first revealed the program's existence in late 2005, government officials moved at lightning-speed to quell public concern and doled out a series of detailed disclosures about the program. Only one day after *The New York Times'* story broke, President Bush informed the country in a public radio address that he had authorized the interception of international communications of individuals with known links to Al Qaeda and related terrorist organizations. Two days after President Bush's announcement, then-Attorney General Alberto Gonzales disclosed that the program targeted communications where the government had concluded that one party to the communication was a member of, or affiliated with, Al Qaeda. The Department of Justice followed these and other official disclosures with a lengthy white paper inwhich it both confirmed the existence of the surveillance program and also offered legal justification of the intercepts.

The government's plethora of voluntary disclosures did not go unnoticed. Al-Haramain Islamic Foundation, a designated terrorist organization, and two of its attorneys (collectively, "Al-Haramain") brought suit against President Bush and other executive branch agencies and officials. They claimed that they were subject to warrantless electronic surveillance in 2004 in violation of the Foreign Intelligence Surveillance Act, various provisions of the United States Constitution, and international law. The government countered that the suit is foreclosed by the state secrets privilege, an evidentiary privilege that protects national security and military information in appropriate circumstances.

Essential to substantiating Al-Haramain's allegations against the government is a classified "Top Secret" document (the "Sealed Document") that the government inadvertently gave to Al-Haramain in 2004 during a proceeding to freeze the organization's assets. Faced with the government's motions to dismiss and to bar Al-Haramain from access to the Sealed Document, the district court concluded that the state secrets privilege did not bar the lawsuit altogether. The court held that the Sealed Document was protected by the state secrets privilege and that its inadvertent disclosure did not alter its privileged nature, but decided that Al-Haramain would be permitted to file *in camera* affidavits attesting to the contents of the document based on the memories of lawyers who had received copies.

In light of extensive government disclosures about the TSP, the government is hard-pressed to sustain its claim that the very subject matter of the litigation is a state secret. Unlike a truly secret or "black box" program that remains in the shadows of public knowledge, the government has moved affirmatively to engage in public discourse about the TSP. Since President Bush's initial confirmation of the program's existence, there has been a cascade of acknowledgments and information coming from the government, as officials have openly, albeit selectively, described the contours of this program. Thus, we agree with the district court that the state secrets privilege does not bar the very subject matter of this action. After *in camera* review and consideration of the government's documentation of its national security claim, we also agree that the Sealed Document is protected by the state secrets privilege. However, we reverse the court's order allowing Al-Haramain to reconstruct the essence of the document through memory. Such an approach countenances a back door around the privilege and would eviscerate the state secret itself. Once properly invoked and judicially blessed, the state secrets privilege is not a half-way proposition.

Nonetheless, our resolution of the state secrets issue as applied to the Sealed Document does not conclude the litigation. Al-Haramain also claims that FISA preempts the common law state secrets privilege. We remand for determination of this claim, a question the district court did not reach in its denial of the government's motion to dismiss.

I. Factual Background[13]

On December 16, 2005, the New York Times reported that in the years following September 11, 2001, President Bush secretly authorized the NSA to conduct electronic surveillance on Americans and others without warrants. James Risen & Eric Lichtblau, *Bush Lets U.S. Spy on Callers Without Courts*, N.Y. Times, Dec. 16, 2005, at A1. The next day, President Bush confirmed in a radio address that he had authorized "the interception of international communications of people with known links to Al Qaeda and related terrorist organizations." George W. Bush, President's Radio Address (Dec. 17, 2005), http://www.whitehouse.gov/news/releases/2005/12/20051217.html (last visited Nov. 8, 2007). The President acknowledged that he reauthorized the program more than 30 times since September 11, 2001, but that the program was suspended in January 2007.

Then-Attorney General Alberto Gonzales, and other administration officials, also disclosed in public statements that the NSA, under the TSP, intercepted electronic information where the government had grounds to believe that one party to the communication was a member or agent of a terrorist organization affiliated with Al Qaeda. Attorney General Gonzales emphasized that the government had not engaged in "blanket surveillance," but instead attempted to hone in on individuals who had apparent links to Al Qaeda. The government stated that interception under the program took place only if there were reasonable grounds to believe that one party to the communication was a member or agent of Al Qaeda or an affiliated terrorist organization. The government did not obtain warrants for this surveillance, which took place outside the context of the Foreign Intelligence Surveillance Court ("FISC"). In January 2007, Attorney General Gonzales stated that this type of surveillance is now subject to the judicial jurisdiction of the FISC. Letter from Alberto Gonzales, Attorney General, to Patrick Leahy and Arlen Specter, Senators (Jan. 17, 2007), *available at* http://leahy.senate.gov/press/200701/1-17-07%20AG%20to%20PJL%20Re%20FISA%20Court.pdf.

Al-Haramain is a Muslim charity which is active in more than 50 countries. Its activities include building mosques and maintaining various development and education programs. The United Nations Security Council has identified Al-Haramain as an entity belonging to or associated with Al Qaeda. In February 2004, the Office of Foreign Assets Control of the Department of Treasury temporarily froze Al-Haramain's assets pending a proceeding to determine whether to declare it a "Specially Designated Global Terrorist" due to the organization's alleged ties to Al Qaeda. Ultimately, Al-Haramain and one of its directors, Soliman Al-Buthi, were declared "Specially Designated Global Terrorists."

In August 2004, during Al-Haramain's civil designation proceeding, the Department of the Treasury produced a number of unclassified materials that were given to Al-Haramain's counsel and two of its directors. Inadvertently included in these materials was the Sealed Document, which was labeled "TOP SECRET." Al-Haramain's counsel copied and disseminated the materials, including the Sealed Document, to Al-Haramain's directors and co-counsel, including Wendell Belew and Asim Ghafoor. In August or September of 2004, a reporter from *The Washington Post* reviewed these documents while researching an article. In late August, the FBI was notified of the Sealed Document's inadvertent disclosure. In October of 2004, the FBI retrieved all copies of the Sealed Document from Al-Haramain's counsel, though it did not seek out Al-Haramain's directors to obtain their copies. The Sealed Document is located in a Department of Justice Secured Compartmentalized Information Facility.

---

[13] [Court's Footnote 2] Pursuant to special procedures established by the Department of Justice, Litigation Security Section, the members of the panel reviewed the Sealed Document and the non-public classified versions of the pleadings and declarations. Our recitation of facts derives only from publicly-filed pleadings, including public versions of the declarations.

Al-Haramain alleges that after *The New York Times*' story broke in December 2005, it realized that the Sealed Document was proof that it had been subjected to warrantless surveillance in March and April of 2004. Though the government has acknowledged the existence of the TSP, it has not disclosed the identities of the specific persons or entities surveilled under the program, and disputes whether Al-Haramain's inferences are correct.

II. PROCEEDINGS IN THE DISTRICT COURT

In February 2006, Al-Haramain filed a complaint in the District of Oregon alleging violations of FISA, the First, Fourth, and Sixth Amendments to the United States Constitution, the doctrine of separation of powers, and the International Covenant on Civil and Political Rights. Al-Haramain sought damages and declaratory relief, alleging that the government engaged in electronic surveillance of Al-Haramain's private telephone, email, and other electronic communications without probable cause, warrants, or other prior authorization. Al-Haramain also provided a sealed copy of the Sealed Document to the district court.

The government moved to dismiss the case, or in the alternative, for summary judgment, on the basis of the state secrets privilege, asserting that the very subject matter of the action was a state secret.

The district court denied the government's motion to dismiss, finding that the existence of the TSP was not a secret, and that "no harm to the national security would occur if plaintiffs are able to prove the general point that they were subject to surveillance as revealed in the Sealed Document, without publicly disclosing any other information contained in the Sealed Document." *Al-Haramain Islamic Foundation, Inc. v. Bush*, 451 F. Supp. 2d 1215, 1224 (D. Or. 2006).

According to the district court, there was "no reasonable danger that the national security would be harmed if it is confirmed or denied that plaintiffs were subject to surveillance." The district court granted the government's motion to bar Al-Haramain from access to the Sealed Document on the basis that it was protected by the state secrets privilege. The court stated that it would, however, permit Al-Haramain-related witnesses to file *in camera* affidavits attesting from memory to the contents of the document to support Al-Haramain's assertion of standing and its prima facie case.

The district court sua sponte certified its order for interlocutory appeal.

ANALYSIS

I. THE STATE SECRETS PRIVILEGE

The state secrets privilege is a common law evidentiary privilege that permits the government to bar the disclosure of information if "there is a reasonable danger" that disclosure will "expose military matters which, in the interest of national security, should not be divulged." *United States v. Reynolds*, 345 U.S. 1, 10 (1953). The privilege is not to be lightly invoked.

Although *Reynolds* is widely viewed as the first explicit recognition of the privilege by the Supreme Court, *see* Amanda Frost, *The State Secrets Privilege and Separation of Powers*, 75 FORDHAM L. REV. 1931 (2007), the Supreme Court considered a form of the privilege — the nonjusticiability of certain state secrets cases — in *Totten v. United States*, 92 U.S. 105 (1875). *Totten* arose out of a contract between President Lincoln and a secret agent who was allegedly dispatched to spy on enemy troops. As the Court explained in a very short opinion, "[i]t may be stated as a general principle, that public policy forbids the maintenance of any suit in a court of justice, the trial of which would inevitably lead to the disclosure of matters which the law itself regards as confidential, and respecting which it will not allow the confidence to be violated." The court then barred suit regarding the contract, as "[t]he secrecy which such contracts impose precludes any action for their enforcement," and noted that "the existence of a contract of that kind is itself a fact not to be disclosed."

As the Supreme Court noted in a later case involving an alleged agreement for espionage services, "lawsuits premised on alleged espionage agreements are altogether forbidden." *Tenet v. Doe*, 544 U.S. 1 (2005). This conclusion has evolved into the principle that where the very subject matter of a lawsuit is a matter of state secret, the action must be dismissed without reaching the question of evidence.

More than 75 years passed before the Supreme Court directly addressed the state secrets privilege, observing that "[j]udicial experience with the privilege which protects military and state secrets has been limited in this country. English experience has been more extensive, but still relatively slight compared with other evidentiary privileges." *Reynolds*, 345 U.S. at 7 (footnotes omitted). In *Reynolds*, the Court addressed the privilege at length, analogizing to the policy and legal parameters of other privileges, such as the privilege against self-incrimination. *See id.* at 8–9.

These two cases — *Totten* and *Reynolds* — thus provide the foundation for our analysis. Although there is only a single state secrets evidentiary privilege, as a matter of analysis, courts have approached the privilege as both a rule of non-justiciability, akin to a political question, and as a privilege that may bar proof of a prima facie case.

Mirroring these applications of the state secrets privilege, on appeal the government argues that the state secrets privilege mandates the dismissal of Al-Haramain's claims for three reasons: (1) the very subject matter of the litigation is a state secret; (2) Al-Haramain cannot establish standing to bring suit, absent the Sealed Document; and (3) Al-Haramain cannot establish a prima facie case, and the government cannot defend against Al-Haramain's assertions, without resorting to state secrets.

II. The Subject Matter of the Litigation Is Not a State Secret

Based on the various public statements made by the President and members of his administration acknowledging the existence of the TSP, and Al-Haramain's purported knowledge that its members' communications had been intercepted, the district court rejected the government's contention that the subject matter of the litigation is a state secret.

We agree with the district court's conclusion that the very subject matter of the litigation — the government's alleged warrantless surveillance program under the TSP — is not protected by the state secrets privilege. Two discrete sets of unclassified facts support this determination. First, President Bush and others in the administration publicly acknowledged that in the months following the September 11, 2001, terrorist attacks, the President authorized a communications surveillance program that intercepted the communications of persons with suspected links to Al Qaeda and related terrorist organizations. Second, in 2004, Al-Haramain was officially declared by the government to be a "Specially Designated Global Terrorist" due to its purported ties to Al Qaeda. The subject matter of the litigation — the TSP and the government's warrantless surveillance of persons or entities who, like Al-Haramain, were suspected by the NSA to have connections to terrorists — is simply not a state secret.

Nor are we persuaded by the recent case of *El-Masri*. Khaled El-Masri, a German citizen of Lebanese descent, brought claims stemming from injuries allegedly received during his detention under the Central Intelligence Agency's ("CIA") "extraordinary rendition" program. *El-Masri*, 479 F.3d at 300. The government defended the suit on the basis of the state secrets privilege, but El-Masri argued that the state secrets privilege did not require dismissal of his claims because the CIA's program had been widely discussed in the press and in public fora, and acknowledged by administration officials. El-Masri maintained that the subject of his suit was only his particular rendition, not the renditions of other victims, and that the litigation posed no harm to national security because sufficient information had entered the public sphere to enable him to pursue his claims without compromising state secrets.

The Fourth Circuit upheld the government's assertion of the state secrets privilege and dismissed the action. To establish liability, El-Masri would be required to produce "evidence that exposes how the CIA organizes, staffs, and supervises its most sensitive intelligence operations." For example, to establish then-Director of the CIA George Tenet's liability, El-Masri would be "obliged to show in detail how the head of the CIA participates in such operations, and how information concerning their progress is relayed to him. Dismissal was proper because the information that was known to the public about the renditions program did not include "facts that are central to litigating [El-Masri's] action."

In contrast, we do not necessarily view the "subject matter" of a lawsuit as one and the same with the facts necessary to litigate the case. Because the Fourth Circuit has accorded an expansive meaning to the "subject matter" of an action, one that we have not adopted, *El-Masri* does not support dismissal based on the subject matter of the suit.

To be sure, a bright line does not always separate the subject matter of the lawsuit from the information necessary to establish a prima facie case. In some cases, there may be no dividing line. In other cases, the suit itself may not be barred because of its subject matter and yet ultimately, the state secrets privilege may nonetheless preclude the case from proceeding to the merits. In other circumstances, the decision on the state secrets privilege may need to await preliminary discovery. It is precisely because of this continuum of analysis that the courts, the parties, and the commentators tend to treat the "subject matter" issue as a separate threshold determination.

Al-Haramain's case does involve privileged information, but that fact alone does not render the very subject matter of the action a state secret. Accordingly, we affirm the district court's denial of dismissal on that basis.

III. THE GOVERNMENT'S INVOCATION OF THE STATE SECRETS PRIVILEGE

Although the very subject matter of this lawsuit does not result in automatic dismissal, we must still address the government's invocation of the state secrets privilege as to the Sealed Document and its assertion that Al-Haramain cannot establish either standing or a prima facie case without the use of state secrets. Our analysis of the state secrets privilege involves three steps. First, we must "ascertain that the procedural requirements for invoking the state secrets privilege have been satisfied." Second, we must make an independent determination whether the information is privileged. In deciding whether the privilege attaches, we may consider a party's need for access to the allegedly privileged information. *See Reynolds*, 345 U.S. at 11. Finally, "the ultimate question to be resolved is how the matter should proceed in light of the successful privilege claim."

With respect to the first step, *Reynolds* requires the government to make a "formal claim of privilege, lodged by the head of the department which has control over the matter, after actual personal consideration by that officer." The parties do not dispute that the procedural requirements for invoking the state secrets privilege have been met. The government formally lodged its claim of privilege through classified and unclassified declarations filed by then-Director of National Intelligence, John Negroponte, as Head of the United States Intelligence Community, and Lieutenant General Keith B. Alexander, Director, National Security Agency.

Next, we must determine whether the circumstances before us counsel that the state secrets privilege is applicable, without forcing a disclosure of the very thing that the privilege is designed to protect. Two claims of privilege are at issue, although they are intertwined and we refer generally to both under the rubric of the Sealed Document: (1) whether Al-Haramain was subject to surveillance and (2) the Sealed Document. This case presents a most unusual posture because Al-Haramain has seen the Sealed Document and believes that its members were subject to surveillance. The district court held, however, that "because the government has not officially confirmed or denied whether plaintiffs were subject to surveillance, even if plaintiffs know they were, this information remains secret. Furthermore, while plaintiffs know the contents of the [Sealed] Document, it too remains secret."

The district court also concluded that the government did not waive its privilege by inadvertent disclosure of the Sealed Document. Because Al-Haramain unwittingly knows the contents of the Sealed Document, its allegations and pleadings are founded on information that it believes is derived from the document without revealing the content of the document. This convoluted sentence and explication underscore the practical difficulty for us in writing about a privileged document, while being cautious not to disclose any national security information. Unlike the alleged spies in *Totten* and *Tenet*, who were knowing parties to a secret contract with the government, Al-Haramain is privy to knowledge that the government fully intended to maintain as a national security secret. Unlike the contract for secret services in *Totten*, which was "itself a fact not to be disclosed," the fact of the previously-secret surveillance program is "itself a fact [that has been] disclosed."

Despite this wrinkle, we read *Reynolds* as requiring an *in camera* review of the Sealed Document in these circumstances. "[T]he showing of necessity which is made will determine how far the court should probe in satisfying itself that the occasion for invoking the privilege is appropriate." Reynolds, 345 U.S. at 11. We reviewed the Sealed Document *in camera* because of Al-Haramain's admittedly substantial need for the document to establish its case.

Having reviewed it *in camera*, we conclude that the Sealed Document is protected by the state secrets privilege, along with the information as to whether the government surveilled Al-Haramain. We take very seriously our obligation to review the documents with a very careful, indeed a skeptical, eye, and not to accept at face value the government's claim or justification of privilege. Simply saying "military secret," "national security" or "terrorist threat" or invoking an ethereal fear that disclosure will threaten our nation is insufficient to support the privilege. Sufficient detail must be — and has been — provided for us to make a meaningful examination. The process of *in camera* review ineluctably places the court in a role that runs contrary to our fundamental principle of a transparent judicial system. It also places on the court a special burden to assure itself that an appropriate balance is struck between protecting national security matters and preserving an open court system. That said, we acknowledge the need to defer to the Executive on matters of foreign policy and national security and surely cannot legitimately find ourselves second guessing the Executive in this arena.

For example, at some level, the question whether Al-Haramain has been subject to NSA surveillance may seem, without more, somewhat innocuous. The organization posits that the very existence of the TSP, and Al-Haramain's status as a "Specially Designated Global Terrorist," suggest that the government is in fact intercepting Al-Haramain's communications. But our judicial intuition about this proposition is no substitute for documented risks and threats posed by the potential disclosure of national security information. Thus, we look to the government's filings, along with publicly available materials and relevant case law, to review the district court's privilege determination.

It is no secret that the Sealed Document has something to do with intelligence activities. Beyond that, we go no further in disclosure. The filings involving classified information, including the Sealed Document, declarations and portions of briefs, are referred to in the pleadings as *In Camera or Ex Parte* documents. Each member of the panel has had unlimited access to these documents.

We have spent considerable time examining the government's declarations (both publicly filed and those filed under seal). We are satisfied that the basis for the privilege is exceptionally well documented. Detailed statements underscore that disclosure of information concerning the Sealed Document and the means, sources and methods of intelligence gathering in the context of this case would undermine the government's intelligence capabilities and compromise national security. Thus, we reach the same conclusion as the district court: the government has sustained its burden as to the state secrets privilege.

We must next resolve how the litigation should proceed in light of the government's successful privilege claim. The privilege, once found to exist, "cannot be compromised by any showing of need on the part of the party seeking the information." The effect of the government's successful invocation of privilege "is simply that the evidence is unavailable, as though a witness had died, and the case will proceed accordingly, with no consequences save those resulting from the loss of evidence."

After correctly determining that the Sealed Document was protected by the state secrets privilege, the district court then erred in forging an unusual path forward in this litigation. Though it granted the government's motion to deny Al-Haramain access to the Sealed Document based on the state secrets privilege, the court permitted the Al-Haramain plaintiffs to file *in camera* affidavits attesting to the contents of the document from their memories.

The district court's approach — a commendable effort to thread the needle — is contrary to established Supreme Court precedent. If information is found to be a privileged state secret, there are only two ways that litigation can proceed: (1) if the plaintiffs can prove "the essential facts" of their claims "without resort to material touching upon military secrets," *Reynolds*, 345 U.S. at 11, or (2) in accord with the procedure outlined in FISA. By allowing *in camera* review of affidavits attesting to individuals' memories of the Sealed Document, the district court sanctioned "material touching" upon privileged information, contrary to *Reynolds*. Although FISA permits district court judges to conduct an *in camera* review of information relating to electronic surveillance, there are detailed procedural safeguards that must be satisfied before such review can be conducted. The district court did not address this issue nor do we here.

Moreover, the district court's solution is flawed: if the Sealed Document is privileged because it contains very sensitive information regarding national security, permitting the same information to be revealed through reconstructed memories circumvents the document's absolute privilege. That approach also suffers from a worst of both world's deficiency: either the memory is wholly accurate, in which case the approach is tantamount to release of the document itself, or the memory is inaccurate, in which case the court is not well-served and the disclosure may be even more problematic from a security standpoint. The state secrets privilege, because of its unique national security considerations, does not lend itself to a compromise solution in this case. The Sealed Document, its contents, and any individuals' memories of its contents, even well-reasoned speculation as to its contents, are completely barred from further disclosure in this litigation by the common law state secrets privilege.

IV. Absent the Sealed Document, Al-haramain Cannot Establish Standing

Al-Haramain cannot establish that it suffered injury in fact, a "concrete and particularized" injury, because the Sealed Document, which Al-Haramain alleges proves that its members were unlawfully surveilled, is protected by the state secrets privilege. At oral argument, counsel for Al-Haramain essentially conceded that Al-Haramain cannot establish standing without reference to the Sealed Document. When asked if there is data or information beyond the Sealed Document that would support standing, counsel offered up no options, hypothetical or otherwise. Thus, Al-Haramain has indicated that its ability to establish injury in fact hinges entirely on a privileged document. It is not sufficient for Al-Haramain to speculate that it might be subject to surveillance under the TSP simply because it has been designated a "Specially Designated Global Terrorist."

"[E]ven the most compelling necessity cannot overcome the claim of privilege if the court is ultimately satisfied that military secrets are at stake." *Reynolds*, 345 U.S. at 11. Because we affirm the district court's conclusion that the Sealed Document, along with data concerning surveillance, are privileged, and conclude that no testimony attesting to individuals' memories of the document may be admitted to establish the contents of the document, Al-Haramain cannot establish that it has standing, and its claims must be dismissed, unless FISA preempts the state secrets privilege.

V. FISA AND PREEMPTION OF THE STATE SECRETS PRIVILEGE

Under FISA, if an "aggrieved person" requests discovery of materials relating to electronic surveillance, and the Attorney General files an affidavit stating that the disclosure of such information would harm the national security of the United States, a district court may review *in camera* and ex parte the materials "as may be necessary to determine whether the surveillance of the aggrieved person was lawfully authorized and conducted." The statute further provides that the court may disclose to the aggrieved person, using protective orders, portions of the materials "where such disclosure is necessary to make an accurate determination of the legality of the surveillance." The statute, unlike the common law state secrets privilege, provides a detailed regime to determine whether surveillance "was lawfully authorized and conducted."

As an alternative argument, Al-Haramain posits that FISA preempts the state secrets privilege. The district court chose not to rule on this issue. Now, however, the FISA issue remains central to Al-Haramain's ability to proceed with this lawsuit. Rather than consider the issue for the first time on appeal, we remand to the district court to consider whether FISA preempts the state secrets privilege and for any proceedings collateral to that determination.

NOTES AND QUESTIONS

1. Standing. Both the Sixth Circuit and the Ninth Circuit accept the government's argument that without being able to show that their communications were intercepted, plaintiffs do not have standing to sue. By contrast, Judge Gilman in the Sixth Circuit says that a "well-founded belief" in being the target of surveillance is enough. Does that make anyone who has made an international telephone call a potential plaintiff? After all, how do I know that I haven't been speaking to suspected terrorists?

2. International Technology and FISA. As a practical matter, it is not clear that surveillance can be limited to international conversations and e-mail traffic. Our e-mails travel a variety of circuitous paths that often involve overseas communication nodes. Under the procedures described in *al-Haramain*, if I file a petition with FISA, can I find out whether I have been the subject of communication intercepts? Should I be able to? Or should it at least be necessary that the FISA Court will look at the government information *in camera* to determine whether I have been properly surveilled?

§ 5.03 CLASSIFIED INFORMATION PROCEDURES ACT

Investigation of terrorist plots will often involve information that the government does not wish disclosed. Among the possibilities are the following:

1. *Informants.* The courts have long recognized an "informer's privilege" so that government may be able to keep secret the identity of an informant who is lodged within a criminal scheme. Some of the best information leading to prosecutions of mafiosi, drug rings, and paramilitary groups has come from insiders. The informer's privilege may be invoked when the defendant challenges probable cause for a search or attempts to discover information that might shed light on the background of the investigation. It

does not mean that government may introduce anonymous testimony at trial. The Sixth Amendment right of confrontation means that, if the informer is to remain anonymous, conviction must be based on other admissible information developed from the informer's information.

2. *Hardware specifications.* Terrorists may get their hands on explosives, military equipment, or related hardware that the government does not want described in detail during trial. Can the prosecution introduce evidence that the defendant stole secret stuff without describing the things stolen? [One of the cases below deals with C-4 explosives. I went online to get information about C-4 and was unsuccessful. I wonder what federal databases now contain my attempts to gain information about this material. Ah, the hazards of being a diligent law professor.]

3. *Technology and investigative techniques.* High-tech industries have developed, often with government funding, some rather amazing abilities over the past few decades. The combination of sophisticated software to go with micro electronic devices allows eavesdropping on conversations in ways that most of us can only imagine. Satellites can pick up millions of telephone conversations while software filters those conversations for voice patterns or key words to isolate and record conversations that are of interest to an investigation. Other devices can monitor and record conversations taking place at great distances inside buildings and other structures. Infrared and similar devices can monitor human movements. Computers can break most codes, although concepts such as "one-time pads" and insider jargon may still baffle cryptography programs until behavior confirms what was communicated. Exactly how good all these devices are and what they can accomplish in many instances remain government-protected secrets.

4. *Government planning and foreign relations.* The earliest recognition of government secrets came in the form of the courts' noting that the executive branch should be allowed to keep secrets about other governments and about its own plans. "[The President] has his confidential sources of information. He has his agents in the form of diplomatic, consular, and other officials. Secrecy in respect of information gathered by them may be highly necessary, and the premature disclosure of it productive of harmful results. Indeed, so clearly is this true that the first President refused to accede to a request to lay before the House of Representatives the instructions, correspondence and documents relating to the negotiation of the Jay Treaty, a refusal the wisdom of which was recognized by the House itself and has never since been doubted." *United States v. Curtiss-Wright Export Corp.*, 299 U.S. 304 (1936).

Government secrets are protected by criminal sanctions under the espionage provisions of the criminal statutes. "The term 'classified information' means information which, at the time of a violation of this section, is, for reasons of national security, specifically designated by a United States Government Agency for limited or restricted dissemination or distribution." 18 U.S.C. § 798. Each agency is responsible for making its own determinations, but the classifications and procedures for handling classified documents are governed by Executive Order 12958. The three classifications provided in the EO are "Top Secret," "Secret," and "Confidential." Because the procedures for handling classified information can be quite elaborate and the persons entitled to handle it carefully controlled, one question that has arisen is how to handle this type of information when it must be disclosed to a judge.

At the outset, it is important to realize that very little will allow the government to rely on secret information in presenting its own evidence in a prosecution. As the next case illustrates, the Sixth Amendment's right to confront witnesses will allow hearsay testimony or summaries of secret information to be used in lieu of cross-examination of the most knowledgeable person only in recognized exceptions to the hearsay rule. Government secrecy may sometimes curtail the production of evidence and result in an acquittal, but that is just the price of protecting against tyranny. In a few rare instances, the right to a public trial may be compromised so that the public could be excluded from a portion of the trial in which secret information is placed before the factfinder. These issues are explored in the cases below.

The Classified Information Procedures Act (CIPA), 18 U.S.C. App. IV, adopted in 1980, stems from the proposition that a defendant is entitled to provide his or her best defense but that the government is also entitled to a national security privilege for classified information. The two competing interests are both of constitutional dimension and CIPA attempts to provide a framework for dealing with the conflict by allowing the trial judge to review the material in secret to attempt reaching an accommodation of both interests. In reading the cases, it may be helpful to compare the CIPA discussions of a national security privilege with assertion of an attorney-client privilege in ordinary civil litigation. The practice of *ex parte in camera* inspection of privilege claims is more routine in that setting, but the constitutional and institutional concerns in a CIPA case add significantly different dimensions.

CIPA § 4 addresses defense requests for discovery of information in classified documents. CIPA § 5 requires the defendant to give advance notice of intent to introduce classified information at trial. Both sections are subject to the procedural provisions of § 6, which allows the government to make an *in camera* disclosure to the judge of secret information seeking a ruling on admissibility and relevance. If the judge agrees that the information would not be helpful to the defense, that is the end of the matter. If the information would be helpful but a substantial equivalent can be obtained by redacting the secrets or providing a summary, then the judge can order disclosure in the appropriate form. Finally, if the information is necessary to the defense and the government refuses to allow its admission, dismissal of the prosecution would be the ultimate remedy.

UNITED STATES v. SMITH
780 F.2d 1102 (4th Cir. 1985) (en banc)

WIDENER, CIRCUIT JUDGE.

Richard Craig Smith has been indicted on five counts of espionage under 18 U.S.C. §§ 793(a), 794(a) and (c). Prior to trial, Smith gave notice to the government and to the court pursuant to 18 U.S.C.App. § 5 that he intended to disclose classified information as part of his defense. Following the procedures set out in the Classified Information Procedures Act (CIPA), the district court conducted a closed hearing to determine the use, relevance, or admissibility of the classified information the defendant proffered. At the conclusion of the hearing, the court ruled that part of the classified information Smith sought to introduce would be admissible at trial. The government invoked CIPA's provision allowing interlocutory appeals and sought a reversal of the district court's ruling allowing introduction of the classified information. A panel of this court upheld the district court's finding that the classified information in question could be introduced at trial. We vacated the panel decision and granted en banc review. We conclude that the district court applied an incorrect legal standard in ruling upon the introduction of the classified information, and accordingly vacate the order of the district court and remand.

Smith was employed by the Army Intelligence Security Command (INSCOM) between 1973 and 1980. He is here charged with unlawfully selling in 1982 and 1983 certain classified information to Victor I. Okunev, an agent of the Soviet Union. The indictment charges that Smith met with Okunev at the Soviet Commercial Compound in Tokyo, Japan, twice in November 1982 and once in February 1983. Smith allegedly gave Okunev classified information regarding five INSCOM double agent operations, for which he received $11,000 from Okunev.

In his defense, on account of the facts he relates just below, Smith argues that he believed he was working for the Central Intelligence Agency (CIA) when he turned over the information to Okunev. He claims that he was sought out by two men who claimed to be CIA agents, Ken White and Danny Ishida. White and Ishida sought

Smith's help in setting up a double agent project directed toward the Russians in Japan. Smith was to gain the confidence of the Soviets by supplying them with the details of eight INSCOM double agent operations. White and Ishida told Smith that this information would be of no real value to the Russians because those eight operations had been discontinued. Smith became convinced that White and Ishida were indeed working for the CIA and agreed to help them by supplying the specified information to the Russians.

Smith seeks to introduce at trial several pieces of classified information to support his defense that he thought he was working for the CIA when he sold the information to the Russians. Such proof may negate an essential element of the crimes charged, intent or reason to believe the information sold would be used to injure the United States or to the advantage of a foreign country. After a lengthy hearing, the district court ruled that Smith could introduce part of the classified information he relied upon in his defense. It found that certain classified information was relevant to Smith's defense and therefore was admissible at trial. For example, in a ruling not appealed from, the court found that details of the INSCOM operations White and Ishida allegedly gave to Smith to pass on to the Soviets were admissible because such information made the existence of White and Ishida more probable than otherwise would be the case.

The district court further found that CIPA was not intended to change the existing law of evidence regarding admissibility; and Congress did not intend to allow exclusion of evidence relevant to the defense simply because that evidence was classified. Because the evidence proffered was found to be relevant, it reasoned, it could be introduced at trial.

A panel of this court affirmed the district court's finding that the evidence in question was admissible. It concluded that the district court correctly applied the standards for judging relevance under Fed.R.Evid. 401 and 403. It rejected the government's argument that governmental privilege required that a balancing test similar to the one set out in *Roviaro v. United States*, 353 U.S. 53 (1957), should be applied here. The *Roviaro* standard as we view it is one that calls for balancing the public interest in protecting the information against the individual's right to prepare his defense. Its application results in a more strict rule of admissibility, and we think that standard should have been applied here.

In order to properly understand the troubling issue before us, we should review CIPA and the legislative history surrounding it. CIPA was enacted by Congress in an effort to combat the growing problem of graymail, a practice whereby a criminal defendant threatens to reveal classified information during the course of his trial in the hope of forcing the government to drop the criminal charge against him. Prior to the enactment of CIPA, the government had no method of evaluating such disclosure claims before trial actually began. Oftentimes it would abandon prosecution rather than risk possible disclosure of classified information.

CIPA established a pretrial procedure for ruling upon the admissibility of classified information.[14] A criminal defendant must notify the United States and the court if he reasonably expects to disclose classified information during his trial or during any pretrial proceeding. A defendant is forbidden from disclosing any such information absent the giving of notice. 18 U.S.C.App. § 5. The notice must specifically set out the classified information the defendant believes he will rely upon in his defense. A general statement of the areas the evidence will cover is insufficient.

Once the defendant gives notice of his intention to introduce classified information, the United States may request a hearing at which the court shall determine the "use,

---

[14] [Court's Footnote 7] The Act also provides a procedure by which the court can delete portions of classified documents to be discovered by a defendant. Substitutions are also permitted under certain circumstances. 18 U.S.C.App. § 4. No issues are raised here regarding Smith's discovery rights

relevance, or admissibility of classified information that would otherwise be made during the trial or pretrial proceeding." 18 U.S.C.App. § 6. Upon a determination by the court that the classified information is admissible, the United States may move to substitute either a statement admitting relevant facts that the classified information would tend to prove or a summary of the classified information instead of the classified information itself. 18 U.S.C.App. § 6(c)(1). The court shall grant the government's motion if the substitution will give the defendant substantially the same ability to make his defense as would the disclosure of the classified information. If the court denies a motion for a substitution, the Attorney General can submit an affidavit objecting to the disclosure of the classified information at issue. 18 U.S.C.App. § 6(e). Once such an affidavit is filed, the defendant is barred from disclosing the classified information. 18 U.S.C.App. § 6(e). The court then can dismiss certain counts of the indictment, find against the United States on issues relating to the classified information, strike testimony, or as a last resort dismiss the indictment. 18 U.S.C.App. § 6(e). The United States can take an interlocutory appeal from an adverse district court decision with respect to the disclosure of classified information. 18 U.S.C.App. § 7.

This appeal concerns the construction and meaning of § 6 of CIPA as it sets out the district court's role in deciding the use, relevance or admissibility of classified information as evidence. The legislative history is clear that Congress did not intend to alter the existing law governing the admissibility of evidence. Thus, the Conference Report provided "the conferees agree that, as noted in the report to accompany S. 1482 and H.R. 4736, nothing in the conference substitute is intended to change the existing standards for determining relevance and admissibility."[15] The circuits that have considered the matter agree with the legislative history cited that ordinary rules of evidence determine admissibility under CIPA. No new substantive law was created by the enactment of CIPA. Neither did the adoption of the Federal Rules of Evidence change the existing law on the subject where not addressed.

The district court correctly concluded that CIPA was merely a procedural tool requiring a pretrial court ruling on the admissibility of classified information. The court then looked at the two groups of classified information at a CIPA hearing and concluded that they were relevant to Smith's defense. Under the standards of Fed.R.Evid. 401, we find no error in the district court's conclusion as to some of the classified information it held should be admitted which would make Smith's account of the events more probable than without that evidence and hence relevant.

The relevance of some of the information is apparent when reviewing Smith's defense. He does not deny that he gave the classified information to the Soviets. He defends the charges against him solely on the grounds that he did not have the necessary intent or reason to believe the information would be used to harm the United

---

[15] [Court's Footnote 8] Should it be argued that our decision is contrary to the understanding of the House, we think a reading of the House Report in that light reads into the report a necessary inconsistency within the report itself, for the report provided that "the existing standards of use, relevance, and/or admissibility of information or materials in criminal trials not be affected." We think the "higher standard of admissibility" rejected in the House Report may only mean a higher standard of admissibility than that already required by existing law. Our construction of the legislative history is supported by the Conference Report we have mentioned in the text.

Like reasoning applies to the Senate Report. That report provides, " . . . on the question of a standard for admissibility of evidence at trial, the committee intends to retain current law." The Committee's later recital that the court should not balance the national security interest against the right of the defendant to obtain the information is entirely inconsistent with the committee's intent to retain existing law as to admissibility if it is read to forbid all balancing. Thus, we do not read into the Senate Report a necessary inconsistency, and construe it as we do the House Report to mean any balancing not already required by existing law.

The Conference Report notably leaves out all reference to such matter, and states, as we have noted in the text, that the existing standards for determining relevance and admissibility are unchanged. We follow the Conference Report.

States or to give advantage to a foreign nation. Instead, he claims that he thought he was aiding the United States by working for the CIA in setting up a double agent operation.

Not all relevant evidence is admissible at trial, however. Fed.R.Evid. 402. The government argues that even if the evidence in question is relevant it should be excluded under a privilege similar to the informer's privilege recognized by *Roviaro*. We believe that the district court committed an error of law in not applying such a privilege before ruling the relevant classified information admissible. Although evidence may be relevant, it yet may be inadmissible because of common law privileges with respect to the testimony. Fed.R.Evid. 501. Some such common law privileges include the attorney- client privilege, marital privilege, military or state secrets, and the informant's privilege.

Roviaro recognizes the existence of a qualified privilege to withhold the identity of persons who furnish information regarding criminal activity to law enforcement officials. Such a privilege is designed to protect and foster the interests of law enforcement by encouraging citizens to aid criminal justice without fear of public disclosure.

The privilege is a qualified one, however. The privilege ceases once the reasons for it cease, that is, once disclosure occurs to "those who would have cause to resent the communication." The privilege must also give way when the informant or the contents of his communication "is relevant and helpful to the defense of an accused, or is essential to a fair determination of a cause." The trial court is required to balance the public interest in nondisclosure against the defendant's right to prepare a defense. A decision on disclosure of such information must depend on the "particular circumstances of each case, taking into consideration the crime charged, the possible defenses, the possible significance of the informer's testimony, and other relevant factors."

The defendant in *Roviaro* was convicted of selling heroin to one John Doe and illegally transporting that heroin. Roviaro moved to learn the identity of John Doe. The motion was denied. At trial, prosecution witnesses described John Doe's part in the drug transaction but he was never produced or identified. The Court vacated the conviction after concluding that John Doe was a material witness to the defendant because of his participation in the crime. Because John Doe was the only other participant in the crimes charged, his testimony was "highly relevant and might have been helpful to the defense."

Dual interests arise from nondisclosure of informers and the information they possess. First, the public interest is served by nondisclosure because it encourages persons to come forward with information that can aid effective law enforcement. Second, the safety and security of the person supplying the information is best protected by nondisclosure of his identity to those who may cause him harm. Those interests must be balanced against a defendant's right to present his defense. The privilege must give way to the "fundamental requirements of fairness." The defendant must come forward with something more than speculation as to the usefulness of such disclosure. Disclosure is not required despite the fact that a criminal defendant may have no other means of determining what relevant information the informant possesses. Disclosure is only required after a court has determined that the informer's testimony is highly relevant. One of the most important factors to be considered is the materiality of the evidence to the defendant's particular defense.

The government's privilege does not give way simply because the defendant knows the informant's name or identity. Protection of the informant can justify nondisclosure of his address or location. When the informant's identity is known to the defendant but his location is not, the same balancing of the public interest in nondisclosure against the defendant's need for disclosure must occur. Defendant must still show that disclosure will significantly aid his defense.

The government has a substantial interest in protecting sensitive sources and methods of gathering information. The gathering of such information and the methods used resemble closely the gathering of law enforcement information. The confidentiality of sources and the methods used in both instances are critical. Persons who supply information to the government regarding matters taking place in foreign countries are likely to be located outside the United States. Their safety would immediately be placed in jeopardy if their identity were made public. Revealing such information absent an essential need by a defendant would also result in the drying up of a primary source of information to our intelligence community.[16]

Law enforcement domestic informers generally know who their enemies are; intelligence agents ofttimes do not. To give the domestic informer of the police more protection than the foreign informer of the CIA seems to us to place the security of the nation from foreign danger on a lower plane than the security of the nation from the danger from domestic criminals. In our opinion the national interest is as well served by cooperation with the CIA as with the domestic police.

As the Supreme Court has reasoned, albeit in the context of a civil action,

"The Government has a compelling interest in protecting both the secrecy of information to our national security and the appearance of confidentiality so essential to the effective operation of our foreign intelligence service." If potentially valuable intelligence sources come to think that the Agency will be unable to maintain the confidentiality of its relationship to them, many could well refuse to supply information to the Agency in the first place.

Even a small chance that some court will order disclosure of a source's identity could well impair intelligence gathering and cause sources to "close up like a clam." To induce some sources to cooperate, the Government must tender as absolute an assurance of confidentiality as it possibly can. "The continued availability of [intelligence] sources depends upon the CIA's ability to guarantee the security of information that might compromise them and even danger [their] personal safety."

CIA v. Sims, 471 U.S. 159, 175 (1985).

We find the privilege applicable here even though Smith has had access to the information he seeks to admit at trial. *Roviaro* speaks of protection from "those who would have cause to resent the communication." This is not the typical informant case where the criminal defendant is usually the one that would resent the communications. Here, a significant part of the risk of harm arises from disclosure to the public. The government's interest is still protectable although Smith may have had access to the information. The privilege is not extinguished by previous disclosure to the defendant alone. The government interest to be protected here includes disclosure of the information to the public. We therefore conclude that the privilege did not cease because Smith has had access to the information.

Smith argues that even if the government's *Roviaro* type privilege exists, in the government's exercise of that privilege it must follow the substitution procedure of § 6(c) of CIPA rather than seek exclusion of the evidence altogether. Adoption of Smith's argument would result in a substantive change in the law of evidence, exactly what Congress said CIPA was not designed to do. Had CIPA not been enacted, the

---

[16] [Court's Footnote 12] Much of the Bishop, Baldwin information sought to be disclosed here falls within our interpretation of such a government privilege. Smith seeks to introduce evidence relating to the details of the operation of the Bishop, Baldwin agency and the CIA's involvement in that operation. Included in this information are other operations of the CIA in the Far East, for example, which would seem to have no relevancy in this case under any standard. As well, when the balance of the details permitted by the district court to be proved are properly balanced against the public interest in nondisclosure, the admissibility of many of them is suspect as we discuss later in this opinion.

government could have raised its privilege at trial. The trial court then should have engaged in the balancing test of *Roviaro*. If it determined that the government's interest was superior, taking all proper factors into account, the evidence would not be disclosed. That is yet the law, but CIPA dictates that such a decision be made prior to trial.

The court decisions construing CIPA are consistent with our holding here. In *United States v. Pringle*, 751 F.2d 419 (1st Cir.1984), the defendants were convicted of possession and conspiracy to possess marijuana with the intent to import after a ship full of marijuana in their charge was seized. The defendants sought to have the government produce information regarding the surveillance, boarding and seizure of their ship. Instead of supplying the information, the government moved for a hearing under CIPA to prevent release of the material. Following an *in camera ex parte* examination of the material, the district court refused to require the release of the information to the defendants. The court of appeals affirmed after applying *Roviaro*. It agreed with the district court that the information "was not relevant to the determination of the guilt or innocence of the defendants, was not helpful to the defense and was not essential to a fair determination of the cause." The significance of *Pringle*, of course, is that it applied *Roviaro* as the standard in its construction of CIPA.

We find no CIPA case that has involved the issue now before us. We reject Smith's argument that several cases hold that relevancy is the only determination to be made by the trial court. In those cases, the trial court determined that the evidence was not relevant so that it did not need to go further and decide if that relevant evidence was admissible. *United States v. Wilson*, 732 F.2d 404, 412 (5th Cir.1984) (affirming the district court's holding that evidence was irrelevant and immaterial).

Our holding is also supported by the language used by Congress in § 6 of CIPA, requiring the district court to rule upon the use, relevance, or admissibility of classified information. Such language is consistent with existing law. Had Congress wished to allow all relevant classified information to be automatically admissible at trial, it would have so provided. The error of the district court here was in doing just that. It did not go further with its analysis than determine that the evidence was relevant. It should still have determined whether any relevant evidence was admissible in light of the applicable government privilege.

Having held that the district court erred by its failure to consider the government's privilege in arriving at its conclusion that the evidence in question was admissible at trial, we think it is not out of order to call to that court's attention some of the principles the cases have established, although we do not lay down at this time any rigid rule, for *Roviaro* requires that "[w]hether a proper balance renders nondisclosure erroneous must depend upon the particular circumstance of each case, taking into consideration the crime charged, the possible defense, the possible significance of the informer's testimony, and other relevant factors." A district court may order disclosure only when the information is at least "essential to the defense," "necessary to his defense," and neither merely cumulative nor corroborative, nor speculative. We do hold, however, that we equate the disclosure of the classified information sought in this case with the disclosure of the various kinds of information sought about informers in the cases construing *Roviaro*. The *Roviaro* standard of *admissibility* is at the least more restrictive than the ordinary rules of *relevancy* would indicate.

The judgment of the district court is vacated and the case is remanded for reconsideration not inconsistent with this opinion.

Vacated and Remanded.[17]

---

[17] [Court's Footnote 13] In applying its rule that relevance and admissibility are synonymous, the district court permitted Smith to introduce into evidence broad classes of classified information about Bishop, Baldwin, including evidence that Bishop, Baldwin was used as a CIA cover organization, that subsidiaries of Bishop, Baldwin were established for cover purposes, and that the CIA deposited funds into Bishop, Baldwin's account. It also permitted the defense to show the activities of a CIA agent known as Richard Cavanaugh,

BUTZNER, SENIOR CIRCUIT JUDGE, dissenting, with whom WINTER, CHIEF JUDGE, PHILLIPS, MURNAGHAN, and ERVIN, CIRCUIT JUDGES join:

For reasons set forth in the opinion of the panel, I believe the district court properly interpreted and applied the Classified Information Procedures Act, 18 U.S.C.App. 3, and its order should be affirmed. Two additional comments are prompted by the opinion of the en banc court.

Congress was aware of the government's desire to impress on pending legislation the standard of admissibility of classified evidence derived from *Roviaro v. United States*. An assistant attorney general testified:

> The "relevant and material" standard we propose for inclusion in S. 1482 is based on the standard adopted by the Supreme Court in *Roviaro v. United States*, for determining whether the defendant is entitled to obtain and disclose the identity of a government informant in a criminal case. Noting the important "public interest in effective law enforcement" served by the protection of the identity of informants, the Court in *Roviaro* ruled that disclosure of such sensitive information is not required unless the information "is relevant and helpful to the defense of an accused or is essential to a fair determination of a cause." Certainly a similar standard would be appropriate in cases involving national security matters, for the interest in protecting the confidentiality of classified information is equally, if not more, compelling than that in protecting the identities of law enforcement informants.

Testimony of Feb. 7, 1980, before Subcommittee on Criminal Justice of the Committee on the Judiciary, S. No. 96-57 at 18.

In testimony before a House Subcommittee, the assistant attorney general explicitly characterized the standard derived from *Roviaro* as an "important" difference between the House and the administration bills. Noting that the House bill did not include the *Roviaro* standard of "relevant and material," he testified at length on the reasons this omission should be rectified. The government's argument in this appeal is essentially a paraphrase of the assistant attorney general's testimony.

The Congress rejected the assistant attorney general's recommendation. Congressional intent not to incorporate the *Roviaro* standard is manifest from legislative history. The Senate Report states:

---

including double agent programs in the Far East not related to the current charges. Smith was permitted to show that Cavanaugh engaged in covert activities without prior authorization and that his "free lance style" offended his superiors. Smith was further permitted to show that the CIA began to terminate its relationship with Bishop, Baldwin due in part to an IRS investigation.

The broad range of proof the district court would have permitted concerning Bishop, Baldwin is centered around the activities of Cavanaugh. Yet, despite wide discovery permitted the defendant and the defendant's proffer of testimony of numerous witnesses acquainted with the intelligence community and even with Bishop, Baldwin and the United States Far East intelligence operations, Smith has failed to connect Cavanaugh to his double agent operation. In his lengthy proffer of testimony, Smith does not even claim that White and Ishida would testify that they worked for Cavanaugh. Yet he would ask the jury to infer that Cavanaugh directed his double agent operation and that he was left dangling because Cavanaugh was trying to protect himself.

Thus, the inferences Smith would ask the jury to draw are strained and of marginal relevance at best. Certainly they are no better than speculative and hence do not support the admission of the privileged information.

In its brief in this court, the government states that it has no objection if Smith shows that White and Ishida told him to communicate with them through a telephone number which was in fact a number of Bishop, Baldwin and that calls to that number were transmitted to CIA agents. These facts would seem to be admissible under the balancing test we have outlined in the text of the opinion. They would be essential to the defense, not merely cumulative, corroborative nor speculative. All the balance of the classified information held admissible by the district court under the heading "Bishop, Baldwin Information" we think is inadmissible and that the holding of the district court admitting the same was an abuse of discretion.

It should be emphasized, however, that the court should not balance the national security interests of the Government against the rights of the defendant to obtain the information. The sanctions against the Government are designed to make the defendant whole again.

S. Rep. No. 823, 96th Cong., 2d Sess. at 9, *reprinted in* 1980 U.S.Cong. and Ad.News 4294, 4303. We cannot accept the notion expressed in note 8 of the majority opinion that this unequivocal statement is inconsistent with congressional intent. It is clear from the text of the Act and its legislative history that the Congress intended the Executive, not the courts, to decide whether to expose relevant classified information subject to sanctions the Act provides. The Act does not incorporate the *Rovario* standard. It omitted the requirement that the evidence be "relevant and material," as urged by the Department of Justice's spokesman. Now the majority opinion embraces what the Congress rejected.

Smith is not seeking disclosure by the government of two items of classified evidence that are the subject of this appeal. He has no need to discover it. He possesses this evidence and seeks to introduce it in his defense. The district court has ruled that it is relevant and admissible.

The text of the statute, its legislative history, and cases interpreting it establish that the Act does not alter existing standards for determining relevance and admissibility of evidence. Existing standards apply *Roviaro* to requests for discovery of information known to the government but unknown to the defendant. Under existing standards which the Congress intended to leave intact, *Roviaro* did not exclude the introduction of relevant evidence known to the defendant. Consequently, the majority is unable to cite a case in which the informer's privilege was successfully invoked to bar a defendant from calling an informant as a witness when his identity and whereabouts were known to the defendant and his testimony was relevant.

If under existing standards *Roviaro* governed admissibility of evidence known to the defendant, there would be little need for the Act. A simple pretrial disclosure rule such as those required for alibi, insanity, or rape would suffice if the government was required to disclose to the court the necessary information to balance intelligently the defendant's needs against the interests of national security. The Act, however, was designed to shield the government from the necessity of explaining to the court at the hearing contemplated by § 6(a) the information that is ordinarily furnished by the government when a *Roviaro* request is denied under existing law.

The application of *Roviaro* to exclude relevant evidence known to the defendant, instead of confining its principles to discovery requests, significantly alters the existing standard for determining the admissibility of evidence in contravention of express congressional intent. This novel alteration of the standard is made at the cost of introducing confusion into a well drafted, straightforward procedure that at once protects national security and affords the defendant a fair trial. Contrary to the provisions of the Act, the court, in a hearing required by Section 6(a), will have to require the government to produce information in support of its claim that the interests of national security outweigh the defendant's need to introduce relevant evidence which he already possesses. Alternatively, the court will have to try and balance these interests without the information which *Roviaro* contemplates it should have.

Roviaro, of course, is still applicable to discovery requests. This is clearly explained in *United States v. Pringle*, 751 F.2d 419 (1st Cir.1984), on which the majority relies. There the court pointed out that none of the defendants "possessed classified information which they threatened to disclose. Quite to the contrary, they were seeking classified information which the government sought to protect." Consequently, the court held that the district court did not err in refusing discovery without convening a hearing under Section 6(a). It is apparent that *Pringle* dealt with a situation quite different from the issues raised in this appeal about the Section 6(a) hearing.

The majority opinion, for which there is no precedent, departs both from the procedure set out in the Act and from existing standards for determining the admissibility of evidence that the Congress intended to leave intact. Sadly, the departure is altogether needless. If a district court follows step by step the procedures established by the Act and adheres to the congressional admonition to apply existing standards for determining the admissibility of evidence, the government's interest in national security, which the district judge and all members of this court seek to protect, will be preserved. At the same time, the need of the defendant to present relevant evidence, which Congress recognized, will be addressed in the manner provided by the Act.

Section 6(c)(2) of the Act directs the district court to hold a hearing on a motion by the government for an alternative procedure for disclosure of classified information. Until this appeal is resolved, the district court cannot conduct a hearing pursuant to this section. Nevertheless, without a motion and without a hearing, the majority has decreed that two alternatives suggested by the government in its brief adequately serve the needs of the defendant.

Appellate pre-emption of the district judge's functions specified by Section 6(c)(2) is unauthorized by the Act, and it is prejudicial. It deprives the defendant of the hearing Congress intended him to have. As a predicate to one of its rulings, the majority misapprehends the reasons the defense seeks to introduce certain evidence and the basis for the district court's ruling. A hearing contemplated by Section 6(c)(2) would enable the district court to avoid such an error.

I respectfully dissent.

NOTES AND QUESTIONS

1. *United States v. Wilson.* *United States v. Wilson,* 732 F.2d 404 (5th Cir. 1984), cited in *Smith,* involved an attempted sale and export to Libya of 20 tons of C-4 explosives. Wilson introduced evidence of his prior relationship with the CIA and testified that, on the basis of continuing contacts with CIA agents, he believed his activities were authorized or at least would not be prosecuted. His professed belief was that he was being encouraged to ingratiate himself with the Qaddafi regime to bring back information to the U.S. The CIA sought to have a high-ranking official testify pseudonymously, and ultimately the judge settled on the compromise of an affidavit from the CIA personnel director stating that Wilson "was not asked or requested, directly or indirectly, to perform or provide any service, directly or indirectly, for [the] CIA."

Twenty years later, in response to Wilson's motion to vacate his sentence, the Government finally turned over information showing that there were "more than 80" contacts between him and CIA agents during the relevant time and that lawyers knew this at the time of trial. The district court judge was not pleased:

> The government discussed among dozens of its officials and lawyers whether to correct the testimony. No correction was made — not after trial, not before sentencing, not on appeal, and not in this review. Confronted with its own internal memoranda, the government now says that, well, it might have misstated the truth, but that it was Wilson's fault, it did not really matter, and it did not know what it was doing. Because the government knowingly used false evidence against him and suppressed favorable evidence, his conviction will be vacated. This opinion refers only to the part of the record that the government has reluctantly agreed may be made public. It does not attempt to recount even that limited range of data in its entirety; the governmental deceit mentioned here is illustrative — not exhaustive.

United States v. Wilson, 289 F. Supp. 2d 801 (S.D. Tex. 2003).

This was not exactly a CIPA case because it involved government submission of a substitute for live testimony in rebuttal of defense testimony. It may be interesting to note that Wilson remains in prison under other convictions for such offenses as attempted murder and retaliation against witnesses. It also bears mention that Justice Department lawyers dispute the District Judge's characterization of the proceedings.

2. *United States v. Fernandez.* *United States v. Fernandez*, 913 F.2d 148 (4th Cir. 1990), was part of the fallout of the Oliver North Iran-Contra scandal of 1984–86. Fernandez was CIA Station Chief in Costa Rica during the time that Congress prohibited use of U.S. funds for supplying the "Contras," paramilitary organizations attempting to overthrow the leftist government of Nicaragua from bases in El Salvador, Honduras, and Costa Rica. As part of the 1980 settlement with Iran of the hostage situation in that country, the U.S. sold Iran military equipment. Colonel North diverted proceeds of those sales to "private benefactors" who would help supply the Contras. When questioned about these activities, Fernandez allegedly lied and misled investigators by obfuscating the purpose of building an airstrip in Costa Rica. Fernandez wanted to introduce as part of his defense particulars of other CIA projects in the region and the U.S. objected under CIPA. The opinion of the Fourth Circuit is instructive for its omissions and difficulty of handling this type of case. In the excerpts below, classified material is identified as ****:

> The first category of classified information admitted by the trial judge concerned three intelligence projects undertaken jointly by the United States and Costa Rica: (1) ****, (2) ****, and (3) **** (collectively referred to as the "projects"). The district court agreed with Fernandez that classified information concerning these programs would corroborate his claim that the airstrip project was part of a larger Costa Rican effort to protect itself against a Nicaraguan invasion, which would in turn support the truth of his allegedly false statements about the origin and purpose of, and his involvement in, the airstrip project.

> The second category of classified material that the trial judge authorized for disclosure at trial concerned the location of CIA **** (collectively referred to as "locations" ****). At the CIPA hearing, Fernandez's attorney argued, and the district court agreed, that Fernandez needed to present the identity and location of these **** to the jury in order to demonstrate the CIA's extensive involvement in the resupply operation. One of the **** was located **** through their operations, were deeply involved in the private benefactor program. The identity and location of these **** were relevant because they would help paint a picture of massive CIA involvement in and knowledge of the resupply of the Contras. This picture, in turn, would support Fernandez's claim that he never made the allegedly false statements (which were never recorded or transcribed), and thus did not lie, and had no motive or intent to lie, concerning his knowledge of North's role in the Contra resupply operation or his knowledge of the nature of the supplies delivered in 1986.

> Following the district court's order authorizing the disclosure of information about the locations and the projects, the United States submitted a series of proposed substitutions under § 6(c) of CIPA. The government's proposed substitutions were introduced on July 12, and revised on July 14, 21, and 24. As explained below, the district court rejected these various substitution proposals over the course of several days as inadequate to "provide the defendant with substantially the same ability to make his defense as would disclosure of the specific classified information."

> In lieu of information about the **** projects in Costa Rica, the government offered on July 12 to acknowledge ****. The district court rejected these proposed substitutions because they failed to describe the nature and extent of the programs in operation at the same time as the airstrip. The court explained that the substitutions would undermine Fernandez's ability to show the seriousness with which the Costa Rican government took the Nicaraguan

threat, the substantial efforts the Costa Rican government took (in the form of the three projects) to address this threat, and the close relationship between the three projects and the airstrip.

The district court also rejected the substitution proposals concerning the locations of the ****. In place of the information about the location and activities of the CIA **** facilities, the government proposed on July 12 to acknowledge that ****. The court rejected these proposed substitutions as "insufficient" after reiterating its earlier determination that the identities of the **** were critical to Fernandez's defense.

Ultimately, the government refused to allow disclosure of the material, and the district court ordered the indictment dismissed. The Fourth Circuit affirmed on the basis that the classified material was critical to Fernandez's ability to present his case because the other projects would show that he had no reason to lie about the airstrip and that the CIA was fully knowledgeable of his activities.

3. Redaction and Precedent. The Fourth Circuit discloses a lot about Fernandez's defense while attempting to keep secret information out of its opinion. By contrast, the Ninth Circuit tells us nothing about the information that *Sarkissian* wanted, although we can guess that it had something to do with informants or wiretap tapes. If you were going to provide instructions to Courts of Appeals about how to report CIPA cases so that the legal profession could understand development of this area of the law, how would you describe the role of the reviewing court?

4. Defendant Knowledge. The D.C. Circuit in *Yunis* responded as follows to the argument that the defendant is handicapped in arguing materiality of classified material because he does not know what the material says: "Yunis was present during all the relevant conversations. It does not impose upon him any burden of absolute memory, omniscience, or superhuman mental capacity to expect some specificity as to what benefit he expects to gain from the evidence sought here." What if in fact Yunis was not present? How does a defendant who is the subject of a mistaken identity, and has no knowledge of the crime, defend himself? Secondly, is it proper to insist on "materiality" of the desired evidence rather than a mere "helpful to the defense" standard?

5. Balancing and Confrontation. The Ninth Circuit in *Sarkissian* cited cases from the Fourth Circuit and First Circuit to the effect that CIPA required balancing of the defendant's need for the information with the government's (or public's) harm if the information were disclosed. The D.C. Circuit in *Yunis* refused to adopt a balancing approach, and the Fourth Circuit in *Fernandez* had this to say about "balancing" interests:

> The judge emphasized that he reached this decision after weighing the interests of national security against the need to provide Fernandez with a fair trial. He concluded by emphasizing: "I believe that the identity of these **** is necessary for the defense, and would rule that your substitution would not be adequate." It was clearly within the district court's discretion to conclude that the government's vague, compressed descriptions about the CIA's general presence in the region and about its general familiarity with the resupply operations were no substitute for live testimony from witnesses and the introduction of actual documents detailing the CIA's intimate involvement with the resupply operation.

Is this "balancing" or is it placing a burden on the government to justify imposition on the right to confront witnesses? CIPA provides that the court will accept substitute material "if it finds that the statement or summary will provide the defendant with substantially the same ability to make his defense as would disclosure of the specific classified information." If the government has sole discretion whether to authorize disclosure, then should the court balance rather than simply deciding the question of whether the substituted material is a substantial equivalent of the actual material?

UNITED STATES v. MOUSSAOUI
382 F.3d 453 (4th Cir. 2004)

[Zacarias Moussaoui is the alleged "20th hijacker" who was supposed to have been on one of the planes on 9/11 but was already in jail on visa violations. He was prosecuted in the Eastern District of Virginia on six conspiracy counts: to commit a terrorist act, to commit air piracy, to destroy aircraft, to use weapons of mass destruction, to murder U.S. employees, and to destroy property. Moussaoui demanded to depose some members of the Al Qaeda organization who are in U.S. custody at undisclosed locations (presumably outside the U.S.). Probably the key deponent would have been Khalid Sheikh Muhammed (KSM), who is generally regarded as the mastermind of the 9/11 plot. The Government resisted on the ground that the identity of these persons as well as any information that they might possess was classified — that even disclosure of their identity or location would endanger national security.

[The District Judge rejected the Government's proposed substituted redactions and summaries, stating that Moussaoui must have the ability to find out what these persons know before it can then be determined whether that information could be disclosed at trial. The parties assumed that if the Government did not allow the depositions to occur, then the Court would have no further recourse than to dismiss the indictment. The Government stated that if the case were dismissed, Moussaoui could be remitted to military detention as an "enemy combatant," but that option may have been foreclosed by the Supreme Court in the *Hamdi* case, § 8.03[A].

[The Government first sought to appeal the Court's orders requiring the government to allow defense counsel to take depositions of these witnesses. That appeal was premised on the provisions of CIPA that allow interlocutory appeal of orders requiring "disclosure" of classified information. In July 2004, the Fourth Circuit held that the orders were not appealable because they were not really based on CIPA and the taking of the deposition would not by itself "disclose" classified information. The Government still refused to allow access to the witnesses and suggested that the trial judge should dismiss the indictment so that there would be a final appealable order. Instead, the judge imposed other sanctions, eliminating the possibility of the death penalty and excluding any evidence relating to the 9/11 plot.

[Following the opinion of the Fourth Circuit excerpted here, his case proceeded to trial. During the trial, he decided to plead guilty and was sentenced to life in prison. He then attempted to withdraw his guilty plea and appealed the denial of that motion to the Fourth Circuit. As of January, 2008, the Fourth Circuit has yet to rule on his appeal.]

Before WILKINS, CHIEF JUDGE, and WILLIAMS and GREGORY, CIRCUIT JUDGES. Affirmed in part, vacated in part, and remanded by published opinion. CHIEF JUDGE WILKINS announced the judgment of the court and wrote an opinion, in which JUDGE WILLIAMS concurs, and in which JUDGE GREGORY concurs except as to Part V.C. Judge Williams wrote a concurring opinion. JUDGE GREGORY wrote an opinion concurring in part and dissenting in part.

WILKINS, CHIEF JUDGE.

The Government appeals a series of rulings by the district court granting Appellee Zacarias Moussaoui access to certain individuals[18] ("the enemy combatant witnesses" or "the witnesses") for the purpose of deposing them pursuant to Federal Rule of Criminal Procedure 15; rejecting the Government's proposed substitutions for the depositions; and imposing sanctions for the Government's refusal to produce the witnesses. We are presented with questions of grave significance — questions that test the commitment of this nation to an independent judiciary, to the constitutional guarantee of a fair trial even to one accused of the most heinous of crimes, and to the

---

[18] [Court's Footnote 1] The names of these individuals are classified, as is much of the information pertinent to this appeal. We have avoided reference to classified material to the greatest extent possible.

protection of our citizens against additional terrorist attacks. These questions do not admit of easy answers.

For the reasons set forth below, we reject the Government's claim that the district court exceeded its authority in granting Moussaoui access to the witnesses. We affirm the conclusion of the district court that the enemy combatant witnesses could provide material, favorable testimony on Moussaoui's behalf, and we agree with the district court that the Government's proposed substitutions for the witnesses' deposition testimony are inadequate. However, we reverse the district court insofar as it held that it is not possible to craft adequate substitutions, and we remand with instructions for the district court and the parties to craft substitutions under certain guidelines. Finally, we vacate the order imposing sanctions on the Government.

I.

A. *Background Information*

Moussaoui was arrested for an immigration violation in mid-August 2001 and, in December of that year, was indicted on several charges of conspiracy related to the September 11 attacks. In July 2002, the Government filed a superceding indictment charging Moussaoui with six offenses: conspiracy to commit acts of terrorism transcending national boundaries, 18 U.S.C. § 2332b(a)(2), (c); conspiracy to commit aircraft piracy, 49 U.S.C. § 46502(a)(1)(A), (a)(2)(B); conspiracy to destroy aircraft, 18 U.S.C. §§ 32(a)(7), 34; conspiracy to use weapons of mass destruction, 18 U.S.C. § 2332a(a); conspiracy to murder United States employees, 18 U.S.C. §§ 1114, 1117; and conspiracy to destroy property, 18 U.S.C. § 844(f), (i), (n). The Government seeks the death penalty on the first four of these charges.

According to the allegations of the indictment, Moussaoui was present at an al Qaeda training camp in April 1998. The indictment further alleges that Moussaoui arrived in the United States in late February 2001 and thereafter began flight lessons in Norman, Oklahoma. Other allegations in the indictment highlight similarities between Moussaoui's conduct and the conduct of the September 11 hijackers. Each of the four death-eligible counts of the indictment alleges that the actions of Moussaoui and his coconspirators "result[ed] in the deaths of thousands of persons on September 11, 2001."

B. *Events Leading to this Appeal*

Simultaneously with its prosecution of Moussaoui, the Executive Branch has been engaged in ongoing efforts to eradicate al Qaeda and to capture its leader, Usama bin Laden. These efforts have resulted in the capture of numerous members of al Qaeda, including the witnesses at issue here: __ ("Witness A"), __ ("Witness B"), __ and __ ("Witness C"), __

Witness A was captured __. Shortly thereafter, Moussaoui (who at that time was representing himself in the district court) moved for access to Witness A, asserting that the witness would be an important part of his defense. Moussaoui's motion was supported by then-standby counsel, who filed a motion seeking pretrial access to Witness A and a writ of habeas corpus *ad testificandum* to obtain Witness A's trial testimony. The Government opposed this request.

The district court conducted a hearing, after which it issued an oral ruling granting access to Witness A ("the January 30 order"). The district court concluded that Witness A could offer material testimony in Moussaoui's defense; in particular, the court determined that Witness A had extensive knowledge of the September 11 plot and that his testimony would support Moussaoui's claim that he was not involved in the attacks. At a minimum, the court observed, Witness A's testimony could support an argument that Moussaoui should not receive the death penalty if convicted.

The district court acknowledged that Witness A is a national security asset and therefore denied standby counsel's request for unmonitored pretrial access and declined to order his production at trial. The court also determined, however, that the Government's national security interest must yield to Moussaoui's right to a fair trial. Accordingly, the court ordered that Witness A's testimony be preserved by means of a Rule 15 deposition (providing that court may order deposition of witness to preserve testimony for trial "because of exceptional circumstances and in the interest of justice"). In an attempt to minimize the effect of its order on national security, the district court ordered that certain precautions be taken. Specifically, the court directed that the deposition would be taken by remote video, with Witness A in an undisclosed location and Moussaoui, standby counsel, and counsel for the Government in the presence of the district court, __

[The Government's interlocutory appeal from that order was dismissed.] On July 14, 2003, the Government filed a pleading indicating that it would refuse to provide access to Witness A for the purpose of conducting a deposition. On August 29, the district court entered an order ("the August 29 order") granting access to Witnesses B and C for purposes of conducting Rule 15 depositions of those witnesses. The order imposed the same conditions as those applicable to Witness A. The court also directed the Government to file any proposed substitutions for the witnesses' testimony by September 5, and it directed standby counsel to file any response to the substitutions by September 12.

On September 8, the district court rejected the Government's proposed substitutions without requiring any response from the defense. The court stated that the Government's proposed substitutions for the deposition testimony of Witnesses B and C failed for the same reasons as the Government's proposed substitutions for the deposition testimony of Witness A. Following the rejection of its proposed substitutions, the Government informed the court that it would not comply with the August 29 order.

The district court then directed the parties to submit briefs concerning the appropriate sanction to be imposed for the Government's refusal to comply with the January 30 and August 29 orders. Standby counsel sought dismissal but alternatively asked the district court to dismiss the death notice. The Government filed a responsive pleading stating that "[t]o present the issue most efficiently to the Court of Appeals, and because [CIPA] prescribes dismissal as the presumptive action a district court must take in these circumstances, we do not oppose standby counsel's suggestion that the appropriate action in this case is to dismiss the indictment."

Noting that "[t]he unprecedented investment of both human and material resources in this case mandates the careful consideration of some sanction other than dismissal," the district court rejected the parties' claims that the indictment should be dismissed. Rather, the court dismissed the death notice, reasoning that Moussaoui had adequately demonstrated that the witnesses could provide testimony that, if believed, might preclude a jury from finding Moussaoui eligible for the death penalty. Further, because proof of Moussaoui's involvement in the September 11 attacks was not necessary to a conviction, and because the witnesses' testimony, if believed, could exonerate Moussaoui of involvement in those attacks, the district court prohibited the Government "from making any argument, or offering any evidence, suggesting that the defendant had any involvement in, or knowledge of, the September 11 attacks." In conjunction with this ruling, the district court denied the Government's motions to admit into evidence cockpit voice recordings made on September 11; video footage of the collapse of the World Trade Center towers; and photographs of the victims of the attacks.

The Government appealed, attacking multiple aspects of the rulings of the district court.

C. *Events Leading to Issuance of this Amended Opinion*

We issued our decision on April 22, 2004. *See United States v. Moussaoui*, 365 F.3d 292 (4th Cir. 2004). Moussaoui thereafter timely filed a petition for rehearing and suggestion for rehearing en banc (the Petition). On May 12, the Government submitted a letter to the court purporting to "clarify certain factual matters." Letter to Deputy Clerk from United States Attorney at 1 (May 12, 2004) [hereinafter "Letter"]. In particular, the Government referred to pages 50–51 of the classified slip opinion, where the court stated:

> " __ "

In response to the emphasized portion of the above quotation, the Government stated that

> members of the prosecution team, including FBI Special Agents assigned to the September 11 and other related investigations, __ have provided __ information __ consistent with the __ desire to maximize their own efforts to obtain actionable information __.

Based in part on the revelations in the May 12 letter, we directed the Government to file a response to the Petition. In particular, we directed the Government to provide answers to the following questions:

> (1) Why was the information in the May 12 Letter not provided to this court or the district court prior to May 12?

> (4) __ provided inculpatory of exculpatory information regarding Moussaoui?

> (5) In light of the information contained in the Letter and any other pertinent developments, would it now be appropriate to submit written questions to any of the enemy combatant witnesses?

> (9) If circumstances have changed such that submission of written questions is now possible, when did the circumstances change and why was neither this court nor the district court so informed at that time?

Underlying this order were concerns among the panel members that members of the prosecution team may have __ rendered the witnesses' statements less reliable.

D. *Additional Facts Contained in the Government's Submissions in Response to the Petition*

4. *Intelligence Community Use of Information*

__ the intelligence community is interested only in obtaining information that has foreign intelligence value; the intelligence community is not concerned with obtaining information to aid in the prosecution of Moussaoui. __ not create special __ reports for use by the prosecution, rather, the prosecution and the PESTTBOM team receive the same reports that are distributed to the intelligence community at large. Information is included in these reports only if __ the information to have foreign intelligence value.[19]

---

[19] [Court's Footnote 14] The Government's submissions indicate that those responsible for __ the witnesses record and pass on only information __ to have foreign intelligence value. Consequently, it is at least possible, albeit unlikely, that one of the witnesses has imparted significant exculpatory information related to Moussaoui that has not been included __. If so, there may be a due process problem under *Brady v. Maryland*, 373 U.S. 83, 83 S.Ct. 1194, 10 L.Ed.2d 215 (1963). *See United States v. Perdomo*, 929 F.2d 967, 971 (3d Cir.1991) (stating that prosecution is obligated under Brady to disclose all exculpatory information "in the possession of some arm of the state"). We need not consider this question, however, as there is no evidence before us that the Government possesses exculpatory material that has not been disclosed to the defense.

II.

Before turning to the merits, we consider the preliminary question of our jurisdiction. [18 U.S.C. § 3731 allows interlocutory appeals by the government from orders dismissing indictments or excluding evidence under certain circumstances.] The district court sanctioned the Government for refusing to produce the enemy combatant witnesses for depositions by dismissing the death notice and excluding specific items of evidence. Both aspects of the sanction are appealable under U.S.C. § 3731 — the latter under the text of the statute itself, and the former by liberal construction of the term "dismissing."

III.

With respect to the merits, the Government first argues that the district court erred in ordering the production of the enemy combatant witnesses for the purpose of deposing them. Within the context of this argument, the Government makes two related claims. First, the Government asserts that because the witnesses are noncitizens outside the territorial boundaries of the United States, there is no means by which the district court can compel their appearance on Moussaoui's behalf. Second, the Government maintains that even if the district court has the power to reach the witnesses, its exercise of that power is curtailed by the reality that the witnesses are in military custody in time of war, and thus requiring them to be produced would violate constitutional principles of separation of powers. We address these arguments seriatim.

A. *Process Power*

The Sixth Amendment guarantees that "[i]n all criminal prosecutions, the accused shall enjoy the right . . . to have compulsory process for obtaining witnesses in his favor." U.S. Const. amend. VI. The compulsory process right is circumscribed, however, by the ability of the district court to obtain the presence of a witness through service of process. The Government maintains that because the enemy combatant witnesses are foreign nationals outside the boundaries of the United States, they are beyond the process power of the district court and, hence, unavailable to Moussaoui.

The Government's argument rests primarily on the well established and undisputed principle that the process power of the district court does not extend to foreign nationals abroad. Were this the governing rule, Moussaoui clearly would have no claim under the Sixth Amendment. This is not the controlling principle, however.

The Government's argument overlooks the critical fact that the enemy combatant witnesses are __ of the United States Government.[20] Therefore, we are concerned not with the ability of the district court to issue a subpoena to the witnesses, but rather with its power to issue a writ of habeas corpus *ad testificandum* ("testimonial writ") to the witnesses' custodian.

B. *Person to be Served*

Ordinarily, a habeas writ must be served on a prisoner's immediate custodian — "the individual with day-to-day control over" the prisoner. Here, however, the immediate custodian is unknown. Under such circumstances, the writ is properly served on the prisoner's ultimate custodian. It would appear — at least the Government has not disputed — that the witnesses are in military custody. Therefore, Secretary of Defense Donald Rumsfeld is their ultimate custodian. Secretary Rumsfeld — who is indisputably within the process power of the district court — is thus a proper recipient of a testimonial writ directing production of the witnesses. __

---

[20] [Court's Footnote 15] The Government will neither confirm nor deny that the witnesses are __. However, it concedes, and we agree, that for purposes of this appeal we must assume that the witnesses are __.

IV.

The Government next argues that even if the district court would otherwise have the power to order the production of the witnesses, the January 30 and August 29 orders are improper because they infringe on the Executive's warmaking authority, in violation of separation of powers principles.[21]

A. *Immunity Cases*

We begin by examining the Government's reliance on cases concerning governmental refusal to grant immunity to potential defense witnesses. The Government argues that these cases stand for the proposition that the district court may be precluded from issuing certain orders that implicate the separation of powers. We reject this characterization of these cases.

The Self-Incrimination Clause of the Fifth Amendment guarantees that no person "shall be compelled in any criminal case to be a witness against himself." The circuit courts, including the Fourth Circuit, have uniformly held that district courts do not have any authority to grant immunity, even when a grant of immunity would allow a defendant to present material, favorable testimony. These holdings have been based on the facts that no power to grant immunity is found in the Constitution and that Congress reserved the statutory immunity power to the Attorney General. Because a district court has no power to grant immunity to compel the testimony of a potential witness who has invoked the privilege against self-incrimination, a defendant has no Sixth Amendment right to such testimony.

The circuits are divided with respect to the question of whether a district court can ever compel the government, on pain of dismissal, to grant immunity to a potential defense witness. The Fourth Circuit, consistent with the majority rule, has held that a district court may compel the government to grant immunity upon a showing of prosecutorial misconduct and materiality.

The Government claims that these "immunity cases" stand for the proposition that, under certain circumstances, legitimate separation of powers concerns effectively insulate the Government from being compelled to produce evidence or witnesses. In fact, the majority rule and the law of this circuit stand for precisely the opposite proposition, namely, that courts *will* compel a grant of immunity, *despite the existence of separation of powers concerns,* when the defendant demonstrates that the Government's refusal to grant immunity to an essential defense witness constitutes an abuse of the discretion granted to the Government by the Immunity Act. A showing of misconduct is necessary because, as explained above, a defendant has no Sixth Amendment right to the testimony of a potential witness who has invoked the Fifth Amendment right against self-incrimination; therefore, the defendant has no Sixth Amendment right that could outweigh the Government's interest in using its immunity power sparingly. Governmental abuse of the immunity power, however, vitiates this interest because when the Government's misconduct threatens to impair the defendant's right to a fair trial, it is proper for the district court to protect that right by compelling the Government to immunize the witness.

For these reasons, the analogy between this case and the immunity cases is inapt. The witnesses at issue here, unlike potential witnesses who have invoked their Fifth

---

[21] [Court's Footnote 18] Moussaoui asserts that we should not consider this argument because any conflict between the Governments' interests and Moussaoui's is of the Government's making. There is no question that the Government cannot invoke national security concerns as a means of depriving Moussaoui of a fair trial. That is not what the Government is attempting to do, however. The Government's claim is that separation of powers principles place the enemy combatant witnesses beyond the reach of the district court. If that is so (although we ultimately conclude it is not), then Moussaoui would not have an enforceable Sixth Amendment right to the witnesses' testimony.

Amendment rights, are within the process power of the district court, and Moussaoui therefore has a Sixth Amendment right to their testimony. As discussed below, this right must be balanced against the Government's legitimate interest in preventing disruption __ of the enemy combatant witnesses.

B. *Governing Principles*

The concept that the various forms of governmental power — legislative, executive, and judicial — should be exercised by different bodies predates the Constitution.

Separation of powers does not mean, however, that each branch is prohibited from *any* activity that might have an impact on another. Stated in its simplest terms, the separation of powers doctrine prohibits each branch of the government from "intrud-[ing] upon the central prerogatives of another." Such an intrusion occurs when one branch arrogates to itself powers constitutionally assigned to another branch or when the otherwise legitimate actions of one branch impair the functions of another.

This is not a case involving arrogation of the powers or duties of another branch. The district court orders requiring production of the enemy combatant witnesses involved the resolution of questions properly — indeed, exclusively — reserved to the judiciary. Therefore, if there is a separation of powers problem at all, it arises only from the burden the actions of the district court place on the Executive's performance of its duties.

The Supreme Court has explained on several occasions that determining whether a judicial act places impermissible burdens on another branch of government requires balancing the competing interests.

C. *Balancing*

1. *The Burden on the Government*

The Constitution charges the Congress and the Executive with the making and conduct of war. Thus, "[i]n accordance with [the] constitutional text, the Supreme Court has shown great deference to the political branches when called upon to decide cases implicating sensitive matters of foreign policy, national security, or military affairs." *Hamdi II,* 296 F.3d at 281.

The Government alleges — and we accept as true — that __ the enemy combatant witnesses is critical to the ongoing effort to combat terrorism by al Qaeda. The witnesses are __ al Qaeda operatives who have extensive knowledge concerning not just the September 11 attacks, but also other past attacks, future operations, and the structure, personnel, and tactics of al Qaeda. Their value as intelligence sources can hardly be overstated. And, we must defer to the Government's assertion that interruption __ of these witnesses will have devastating effects on the ability to gather information from them. __ it is not unreasonable to suppose that interruption __ could result in the loss of information that might prevent future terrorist attacks.

The Government also asserts that production of the witnesses would burden the Executive's ability to conduct foreign relations. The Government claims that if the Executive's assurances of confidentiality can be abrogated by the judiciary, the vital ability to obtain the cooperation of other governments will be devastated.

In summary, the burdens that would arise from production of the enemy combatant witnesses are substantial.

2. *Moussaoui's Interest*

The importance of the Sixth Amendment right to compulsory process is not subject to question — it is integral to our adversarial criminal justice system. [The judicial system itself, not just the defendant, needs all available evidence to ensure its full functioning and credibility.]

The compulsory process right does not attach to any witness the defendant wishes to call, however. Rather, a defendant must demonstrate that the witness he desires to have produced would testify "in his favor." Thus, in order to assess Moussaoui's interest, we must determine whether the enemy combatant witnesses could provide testimony material to Moussaoui's defense.

In the CIPA context,[22] we have adopted the standard articulated by the Supreme Court in *Roviaro v. United States*, 353 U.S. 53 (1957), for determining whether the government's privilege in classified information must give way. Under that standard, a defendant becomes entitled to disclosure of classified information upon a showing that the information "is relevant and helpful to the defense . . . or is essential to a fair determination of a cause."

Because Moussaoui has not had — and will not receive — direct access to any of the witnesses, he cannot be required to show materiality with the degree of specificity that applies in the ordinary case. Rather, it is sufficient if Moussaoui can make a "plausible showing" of materiality. However, in determining whether Moussaoui has made a plausible showing, we must bear in mind that Moussaoui *does* have access to the __ summaries.

[T]he Government argues that even if the witnesses' testimony would tend to exonerate Moussaoui of involvement in the September 11 attacks, such testimony would not be material because the conspiracies with which Moussaoui is charged are broader than September 11. Thus, the Government argues, Moussaoui can be convicted even if he lacked any prior knowledge of September 11. This argument ignores the principle that the scope of an alleged conspiracy is a jury question, and the possibility that Moussaoui may assert that the conspiracy culminating in the September 11 attacks was distinct from any conspiracy in which he was involved. Moreover, even if the jury accepts the Government's claims regarding the scope of the charged conspiracy, testimony regarding Moussaoui's non-involvement in September 11 is critical to the penalty phase. If Moussaoui had no involvement in or knowledge of September 11, it is entirely possible that he would not be found eligible for the death penalty.

We now consider the rulings of the district court regarding the ability of each witness to provide material testimony in Moussaoui's favor.

a. *Witness A*

The district court did not err in concluding that Witness A could offer material evidence on Moussaoui's behalf. __ Several statements by Witness A tend to exculpate Moussaoui. __ to undermine the theory (which the Government may or may not intend to advance at trial) that Moussaoui was to pilot a fifth plane into the White House. __ This statement is significant in light of other evidence __ This is consistent with Moussaoui's claim that he was to be part of a post-September 11 operation.

The Government argues that Witness A's statements are actually incriminatory of Moussaoui. It is true that Witness A has made some statements that arguably implicate Moussaoui in the September 11 attacks. __ On balance, however, Moussaoui has made a sufficient showing that evidence from Witness A would be more helpful than hurtful,

---

[22] [Court's Footnote 20] We adhere to our prior ruling that CIPA does not apply because the January 30 and August 29 orders of the district court are not covered by either of the potentially relevant provisions of CIPA: § 4 (concerning deletion of classified information from documents to be turned over to the defendant during discovery) or § 6 (concerning the disclosure of classified information by the defense during pretrial or trial proceedings). Like the district court, however, we believe that CIPA provides a useful framework for considering the questions raised by Moussaoui's request for access to the enemy combatant witnesses.

or at least that we cannot have confidence in the outcome of the trial without Witness A's evidence.

b. *Witness B*

There can be no question that Witness B could provide material evidence on behalf of Moussaoui. __ Witness B __ has indicated that Moussaoui's operational knowledge was limited, a fact that is clearly of exculpatory value as to both guilt and penalty. __ Thus, of all three witnesses, Witness B is of the greatest exculpatory value.

c. *Witness C*

The district court determined that Witness C could provide material evidence because he could support Moussaoui's contention that he was not involved in the September 11 attacks. We agree with the district court that a jury might reasonably infer, from Witness C__ that Moussaoui was not involved in September 11. We therefore conclude that Moussaoui has made a plausible showing that Witness C would, if available, be a favorable witness.

3. *Balancing*

Having considered the burden alleged by the Government and the right claimed by Moussaoui, we now turn to the question of whether the district court should have refrained from acting in light of the national security interests asserted by the Government. The question is not unique; the Supreme Court has addressed similar matters on numerous occasions. In all cases of this type — cases falling into "what might loosely be called the area of constitutionally guaranteed access to evidence" — the Supreme Court has held that the defendant's right to a trial that comports with the Fifth and Sixth Amendments prevails over the governmental privilege. Ultimately, as these cases make clear, the appropriate procedure is for the district court to order production of the evidence or witness and leave to the Government the choice of whether to comply with that order. If the government refuses to produce the information at issue — as it may properly do — the result is ordinarily dismissal.

For example, in *Roviaro*, the Supreme Court considered the conflict between the governmental interest in protecting the identity of a confidential informant and a defendant's right to present his case. The Court acknowledged the importance of the so-called informer's privilege but held that this privilege is limited by "the fundamental requirements of fairness. Where the disclosure of an informer's identity, or of the contents of his communication, is relevant and helpful to the defense of an accused, or is essential to a fair determination of a cause, the privilege must give way." The Court emphasized that the choice to comply with an order to disclose the identity of a confidential informant belongs to the Government.

In addition to the pronouncements of the Supreme Court in this area, we are also mindful of Congress' judgment, expressed in CIPA, that the Executive's interest in protecting classified information does not overcome a defendant's right to present his case. Under CIPA, once the district court determines that an item of classified information is relevant and material, that item must be admitted unless the government provides an adequate substitution. If no adequate substitution can be found, the government must decide whether it will prohibit the disclosure of the classified information; if it does so, the district court must impose a sanction, which is presumptively dismissal of the indictment.

In view of these authorities, it is clear that when an evidentiary privilege — even one that involves national security — is asserted by the Government in the context of its prosecution of a criminal offense, the "balancing" we must conduct is primarily, if not solely, an examination of whether the district court correctly determined that the information the Government seeks to withhold is material to the defense. We have determined that the enemy combatant witnesses can offer material testimony that is essential to Moussaoui's defense, and we therefore affirm the January 30 and August 29 orders, Thus, the choice is the Government's whether to comply with those orders or suffer a sanction.

V.

As noted previously, the Government has stated that it will not produce the enemy combatant witnesses for depositions (or, we presume, for any other purpose related to this litigation). We are thus left in the following situation: the district court has the power to order production of the enemy combatant witnesses and has properly determined that they could offer material testimony on Moussaoui's behalf, but the Government has refused to produce the witnesses. Under such circumstances, dismissal of the indictment is the usual course. Like the district court, however, we believe that a more measured approach is required. Additionally, we emphasize that no punitive sanction is warranted here because the Government has rightfully exercised its prerogative to protect national security interests by refusing to produce the witnesses.

Although, as explained above, this is not a CIPA case, that act nevertheless provides useful guidance in determining the nature of the remedies that may be available. Under CIPA, dismissal of an indictment is authorized only if the government has failed to produce an adequate substitute for the classified information, and the interests of justice would not be served by imposition of a lesser sanction. CIPA thus enjoins district courts to seek a solution that neither disadvantages the defendant nor penalizes the government (and the public) for protecting classified information that may be vital to national security.

A similar approach is appropriate here. Under such an approach, the first question is whether there is any appropriate substitution for the witnesses' testimony. Because we conclude, for the reasons set forth below, that appropriate substitutions are available, we need not consider any other remedy.

A. *Standard*

CIPA provides that the government may avoid the disclosure of classified information by proposing a substitute for the information, which the district court must accept if it "will provide the defendant with substantially the same ability to make his defense as would disclosure of the specific classified information." We believe that the standard set forth in CIPA adequately conveys the fundamental purpose of a substitution; to place the defendant, as nearly as possible, in the position he would be in if the classified information (here, the depositions of the witnesses) were available to him. Thus, a substitution is an appropriate remedy when it will not materially disadvantage the defendant.

B. *Substitutions Proposed by the Government*

The Government proposed substitutions for the witnesses' deposition testimony in the form of a series of statements derived from the __ summaries. The district court rejected all proposed substitutions as inadequate. The ruling of the district court was based on its conclusions regarding the inherent inadequacy of the substitutions and its findings regarding the specific failings of the Government's proposals. For the reasons set forth below, we reject the ruling of the district court that any substitution for the witnesses' testimony would be inadequate. We agree, however, with the assessment that the particular proposals submitted by the Government are inadequate in their current form.

First, the district court deemed the substitutions inherently inadequate because the

__ reports, from which the substitutions were ultimately derived, were unreliable.[23] This was so, the court reasoned, because the witnesses' __. The district court also complained that it cannot be determined whether the __ reports accurately reflect the witnesses' statements __. The court further commented that the lack of quotation marks in the __ reports made it impossible to determine whether a given statement is a verbatim recording or __.

The conclusion of the district court that the proposed substitutions are inherently inadequate is tantamount to a declaration that there could be no adequate substitution for the witnesses' deposition testimony. We reject this conclusion. The answer to the concerns of the district court regarding the accuracy of the __ reports is that those who are __ the witnesses have a profound interest in obtaining accurate information from the witnesses and in reporting that information accurately to those who can use it to prevent acts of terrorism and to capture other al Qaeda operatives. These considerations provide sufficient indicia of reliability to alleviate the concerns of the district court.

Next, the district court noted that the substitutions do not indicate that they are summaries of statements made over the course of several months. We agree with the district court that in order to adequately protect Moussaoui's right to a fair trial, the jury must be made aware of certain information concerning the substitutions. [A]t the very least the jury should be informed that the substitutions are derived from reports __ of the witnesses. The instructions must account for the fact that members of the prosecution team have provided information and suggested __. The jury should also be instructed that the statements were obtained under circumstances that support a conclusion that the statements are reliable.[24]

We reject the suggestion of the district court that the Government acted improperly in attempting to organize the information presented in the substitutions. Counsel rarely, if ever, present information to the jury in the order they received it during pretrial investigations. Indeed, organizing and distilling voluminous information for comprehensible presentation to a jury is a hallmark of effective advocacy. In short, while there may be problems with the *manner* in which the Government organized the substitutions, the fact that the Government has attempted such organization is not a mark against it.

The district court identified particular problems with the proposed substitutions for Witness A's testimony. For example, the court noted that the proposed substitutions failed to include exculpatory information provided by Witness A and incorporated at least one incriminatory inference not supplied by Witness A's statements. __ Our own review of the proposed substitutions for the testimony of Witnesses B and C reveals similar problems __. These problems, however, may be remedied as described below.

---

[23] [Court's Footnote 29] The court also deemed the substitutions inadequate because the use of substitutions would deprive Moussaoui of the ability to question the witnesses regarding matters that do not appear in the __ reports. In essence, the district court appears to have concluded that the substitutions are inadequate because they are not the same thing as a deposition. However, we have already determined that a proposed substitution need not provide Moussaoui with all the benefits of a deposition in order to be adequate.

[24] [Court's Footnote 31] Nothing in the Government's submissions in connection with the Petition contradicts our conclusion that those __ the witnesses have a profound interest in obtaining truthful information. To the contrary, we are even more persuaded that the __ process is carefully designed to elicit truthful and accurate information from the witnesses.

We emphasize that we have never held, nor do we now hold, that the witnesses' statements are in fact truthful, and the jury should not be so instructed. Instead, the jury should be informed that the circumstances were designed to elicit truthful statements from the witnesses. We offer no opinion regarding whether this instruction may include information regarding __.

C. *Instructions for the District Court*

1. *Submission of Questions by Moussaoui*

The Government's submissions in response to the Petition make clear that members of the prosecution team, __ have had some input __ the enemy combatant witnesses. Our review of the circumstances of this access indicates that the input by the prosecution team into the __ process has worked no unfairness on Moussaoui. Nevertheless, in order to provide Moussaoui with the fullest possible range of information from the witnesses, we direct the district court to provide Moussaoui with an opportunity to __ for __ discretionary use __ of the witnesses.[25]

2. *Substitutions*

For the reasons set forth above, we conclude that the district court erred in ruling that any substitution for the witnesses' testimony is inherently inadequate to the extent it is derived from the __ reports. To the contrary, we hold that the __ summaries (which, as the district court determined, accurately recapitulate the __ reports) provide an adequate basis for the creation of written statements that may be submitted to the jury in lieu of the witnesses' deposition testimony.

The compiling of substitutions is a task best suited to the district court, given its greater familiarity with the facts of the case and its authority to manage the presentation of evidence.[26] Nevertheless, we think it is appropriate to provide some guidance to the court and the parties.

First, the circumstances of this case — most notably, the fact that the substitutions may very well support Moussaoui's defense — dictate that the compiling of substitutions be an interactive process among the parties and the district court. Second, we think that accuracy and fairness are best achieved by compiling substitutions that use the exact language of the __ summaries to the greatest extent possible. We believe that the best means of achieving both of these objectives is for defense counsel to identify particular portions of the __ summaries that Moussaoui may want to admit into evidence at trial. The Government may then offer any objections and argue that additional portions must be included in the interest of completeness, as discussed below. If the substitutions are to be admitted at all (we leave open the possibility that Moussaoui may decide not to use the substitutions in his defense), they may be admitted only by Moussaoui. Based on defense counsel's submissions and the Government's objections, the district court could then compile an appropriate set of substitutions. We leave to the discretion of the district court the question of whether to rule on the admissibility of a particular substitution (e.g., whether a substitution is relevant) at trial or during pre-trial proceedings.

As previously indicated, the jury must be provided with certain information regarding the substitutions. While we leave the particulars of the instructions to the district court, the jury must be informed, at a minimum, that the substitutions are what the witnesses would say if called to testify; that the substitutions are derived from statements obtained

---

[25] [Court's Footnote 34] During the hearing regarding the Petition, defense counsel expressed concern over whether __ would result in the disclosure of trial strategy to the Government. The Government, in its June 16 filing, informs us that measures can be taken to avoid such disclosures. We leave the particulars of any such process to the discretion of the district court. At an absolute minimum, however, whatever process is adopted must ensure that the prosecution team is not privy to __ propounded by the defense, just as the defense was unaware or __ propounded by the prosecution team.

[26] [Court's Footnote 35] We note that the district court will not be drafting original language for submission to the jury. Instead, as we discuss further in the text, Moussaoui will designate portions of the __ summaries for submission; the Government will raise objections and cross-designate portions of the summaries it believes are required by the rule of completeness; and the district court will make rulings as necessary to compile an appropriate set of substitutions.

under conditions that provide circumstantial guarantees of reliability; that the substitutions contain statements obtained over the course of weeks or months; that members of the prosecution team have contributed to __ the witnesses; and, if applicable, that Moussaoui has __ to the witnesses.[27]

On rehearing, both parties acknowledged our holding that CIPA does not apply here but indicated their belief that once the district court has approved substitutions for the witnesses' testimony, CIPA comes into play, with the result that the Government may object to the disclosure of the classified information in the substitutions and request that the district court adopt an alternative form of evidence. We disagree.

It must be remembered that the substitution process we here order is a *replacement* for the testimony of the enemy combatant witnesses. Because the Government will not allow Moussaoui to have contact with the witnesses, we must provide a remedy adequate to protect Moussaoui's constitutional rights. Here, that remedy is substitutions. Once Moussaoui has selected the portions of the __ summaries he wishes to submit to the jury and the Government has been given an opportunity to be heard, the district court will compile the substitutions, using such additional language as may be necessary to aid the understanding of the jury. Once this process is complete, the matter is at an end — there are to be no additional or supplementary proceedings under CIPA regarding the substitutions.

VI.

In summary, the judgment of the court is as follows. The January 30 and August 29 orders are affirmed, as is the rejection of the Government's proposed substitutions by the district court. The order imposing sanctions on the Government is vacated, and the case is remanded for the compiling of substitutions for the deposition testimony of the enemy combatant witnesses.

Affirmed in Part, Vacated in Part, and Remanded

GREGORY, CIRCUIT JUDGE, concurring in part and dissenting in part.

I concur with my colleagues' conclusion that the witnesses at issue in this appeal could provide material, favorable testimony on Moussaoui's behalf. I further concur with their conclusion that the witnesses' overseas location does not preclude a finding that they are within the reach of the Compulsory Process Clause because they are, for purposes of this litigation, deemed to be __ of the United States. I wholeheartedly agree with my colleagues that the Government has an absolute right to refuse access to the witnesses on national security grounds; we shall not, indeed we must not, question the Government's determination that permitting the witnesses to be deposed would put our nation's security at risk. Further, as noted in the majority opinion, the district court correctly found that the proposed substitutions offered by the Government are not adequate to protect Moussaoui's right to a fair trial. However, as both the district court and the majority have recognized, the Government's refusal to comply with the district court's orders necessarily brings with it some consequences. The remedy proposed by the majority does not begin to vindicate Moussaoui's rights. Thus, it is in formulating the remedy for the Government's refusal to comply with the district court's order that I must part ways with the majority.

The __ summaries paint a complete, if disjointed, picture of the statements made by the witnesses to date; if the summaries are to be used as a substitution for the witnesses' testimony, they should be used in their entirety, subject to the district court's trial rulings on admissibility of any given passage to which either party objects, whether on

---

[27] [Court's Footnote 38] We are mindful of the fact that no written substitution will enable the jury to consider the witnesses' demeanor in determining their credibility. We believe that the instructions outlined above, plus any other instructions the district court may dean necessary in the exercise of its discretion, adequately address this problem.

hearsay grounds, as cumulative, as unduly prejudicial, or upon any other evidentiary basis.

Additionally, I disagree with the majority's decision to vacate the district court's order striking the Government's death notice at this juncture.[28]

Moussaoui's theory of the case, as we understand it, is that even though he is a member of al Qaeda who has pledged his allegiance to Osame bin Laden, and even though he was willing to engage in terrorist acts, and was indeed training to participate in terrorist acts, he was not involved in the terrorist acts that occurred on September 11, 2001, nor did he know of the plans before the attack took place. Instead, his participation was to involve later attacks, attacks that may or may not have been planned to occur in the United States or against this country's interests abroad.

Even if Moussaoui is permitted to admit substitutions derived from the __ summaries, those substitutions cannot be considered a functional equivalent of live (or deposition) testimony, nor are they adequate or sufficient to substitute for testimony. Because the summaries are not responses to the questions that Moussaoui would ask if given the opportunity to depose the witnesses, and because the jury will not be able to see the witnesses and judge their credibility, use of the summaries will necessarily place severe limits on the evidence Moussaoui can present in his defense, particularly during the penalty phase of a capital proceeding. The Government may argue that no one, other than Moussaoui himself, has stated he was not involved. Moussaoui has no access to those who could exonerate him from death eligibility, and the jury will not have any evidence upon which to base a finding in this regard except, possibly, for Moussaoui's own testimony, which he is not obligated to provide. Moussaoui will not be able to offer the most relevant evidence with which he might be able to avoid the death penalty.

After we issued our opinion, the Government filed a letter dated May 12, 2004, purporting to "clarify certain factual matters." In that letter, the Government stated that this court's opinion erroneously relied on a presumption that the Government's attorneys had not been privy to, nor had any input into, the __ witnesses at issue. Until now, no parallel access to the __ process has been available to Moussaoui.

The Government's May 12 letter, and its positions taken during the hearing before the panel on June 3, 2004, only serve to reinforce my conclusion that the district court was correct in holding that the death penalty should not be within the range of sentencing options available when, as here, the Defendant's ability to mount a defense is severely impaired. As the Government has made clear, the summaries of witness statements provided to the defense are not a complete account of the witnesses' responses __ the only __ responses passed to the prosecution, and subsequently provided to the defense, are those responses deemed __ to have actionable foreign intelligence value. Thus, as the majority acknowledges, it is certainly possible that the witnesses, __ may have provided information that, although exculpatory as to Moussaoui, was not passed on to the prosecution, and in turn to the defense team, because __ the information had no actionable foreign intelligence value.[29] As the majority further

---

[28] The majority leaves open the possibility that if the substitutions compiled by the district court are inadequate, or if the jury is not properly instructed as to the circumstances of the substitutions and their reliability, the death notice could be stricken and other sanctions could be imposed. In my view, however, Moussaoui's inability to question the witnesses critically impairs his ability to prepare a defense, particularly (though not solely) as to a potential death sentence. Accordingly, as explained more fully below, if Moussaoui must proceed to trial on the basis of substitutions rather than the witnesses' testimony, as we all agree he must, the death penalty should be removed from the range of possible sentences Moussaoui may face.

[29] [Court's Footnote 6] Although the prosecutorial function is to achieve justice, and as such prosecutors must seek out both inculpatory and exculpatory evidence, the Government makes clear that __. __ have no duty __ exculpatory evidence unless that evidence would have actionable foreign intelligence value. Accordingly, even though __ "have a profound interest in obtaining truthful information," they do not have an interest in ensuring that justice is achieved in this case.

recognizes, if __ have exculpatory evidence that they have not passed on to the prosecution, Moussaoui's due process rights may be implicated. The majority downplays this possibility, calling it unlikely, and states that it need not be further explored because "there is no evidence before us that the Government possesses exculpatory material that has not been disclosed to the defense." This conclusion is, at best, misguided. Because of the highly classified nature of the evidence at issue in this case, there is no way this court or Moussaoui could know whether an arm of the Government possesses exculpatory evidence that does not have foreign intelligence value; indeed, even the prosecution would not have access to any such evidence, __ distribute only those witness summaries that have foreign intelligence value. How there could ever be any evidence before us from which we could conduct a *Brady* analysis under these circumstances is a mystery.

Further, the reliability (or lack thereof) of the witnesses' statements poses real stumbling blocks to the admission of those statements. The Government admits that the summaries are simply accurate reflections of the witnesses' responses __. However, we do not have all of the witnesses' statements; instead, we are privy only to those portions of their statements that are deemed to have actionable foreign intelligence value. We do not have __ we do not have __ we do not know __. Although the Government assures us that the statements have some indicia of reliability __. Without this context, however, we have only the bare statement, which the jury may consider to be true __. This is a slim reed indeed upon which to base a jury verdict, especially where a man's life hangs in the balance.

I cannot disagree with the majority's statement that "[b]ecause the Government will not allow Moussaoui to have contact with the witnesses, this court must provide a remedy adequate to protect Moussaoui's constitutional rights." However, the majority's effort to craft such a remedy rings hollow. The entire process is cloaked in secrecy, making it difficult, if not impossible, for the courts to ensure the provision of Moussaoui's rights. Although the prosecution is laboring under the same constraints __ Moussaoui has constitutional rights, not extended to the prosecution, that are implicated by this procedure. Because the majority decrees that this so-called "remedy" will fulfill this court's obligation to protect Moussaoui's constitutional rights, today justice has taken a long stride backward.

Here, the reliability of a death sentence would be significantly impaired by the limitations on the evidence available for Moussaoui's use in proving mitigating factors (if he is found guilty). Although it has been repeated often enough to have the ring of cliche, death is different. It is the ultimate penalty, and once carried out, it is irrevocable. A sentence of death cannot be imposed unless the defendant has been accorded the opportunity to defend himself fully; it cannot be imposed without the utmost certainty, the fundamental belief in the fairness of the result. Because Moussaoui will not have access to the witnesses who could answer the question of his involvement, he should not face the ultimate penalty of death. Accordingly, I would uphold the district court's sanction to the extent that it struck the Government's death notice. On this basis, I must dissent.

NOTES AND QUESTIONS

1. Military Detention Option. Bear in mind that the Government also took the position prior to the *Hamdi* decision of the Supreme Court that it could, at any time, remand an accused terrorist such as Moussaoui to military custody as an "enemy combatant" with nothing more than a Presidential order. As of February 2005, at least two persons, al Maari and Padilla, remain in custody under these conditions.

2. Prosecutor Access to Information. The redacted version of the Fourth Circuit's opinion makes it extremely difficult to know who knows what about the interrogation of the three witnesses. Your author has edited out a great deal of even more unintelligible language to reduce your frustration in reading. My understanding of the situation is that interrogators were asking the questions in which they are interested, providing summaries of the answers that provide "actionable foreign intelligence information," and passing those summaries to the prosecution team. At some point, however, it appears that the prosecution team had access to the witnesses or at least was able to propound questions for them. Judge Gregory makes a strong argument that this procedure (a) is unfair because it is one-sided, (b) does not allow the defense to propound its own questions, and (c) is wholly inadequate as a substitute for jury observation of the witnesses. But he makes this argument only as applied to the death penalty. Is it not a complete argument against allowing the prosecution to proceed at all under these conditions?

The majority asserts that the interrogators of these witnesses have "a profound interest in obtaining accurate information from the witnesses and in reporting that information accurately to those who can use it." But do the interrogators have any interest in obtaining information exculpatory of someone such as Moussaoui? And does their interest substitute for questioning by someone with Moussaoui's own knowledge? In this regard, be alert to the explanation for why the defendant must be present at questioning of government witnesses in *Hamdan v. Rumsfeld*, § 8.04[B].

3. Balancing National Security and Prosecution. The majority states that "the 'balancing' we must conduct is primarily, if not solely, an examination of whether . . . the information the Government seeks to withhold is material to the defense." Is this balancing? Once this conclusion is reached, then what is the basis for not allowing the defense to have access to the witness?

All three judges reiterate that, in Judge Gregory's words, they "must not question the Government's determination that permitting the witnesses to be deposed would put our nation's security at risk." But that is not the question presented. The question is what to do with Moussaoui in light of the Government's refusal to accord him a constitutionally guaranteed right of access to witnesses. What might be lost if Moussaoui were set "free" to go about his business under heavy government surveillance?

4. Abdelghani Mzoudi. Abdelghani Mzoudi, an alleged key member of the "Hamburg cell" that provided support for the 9/11 hijackers, was acquitted in a German court for lack of evidence. The trial judge complained that both sides had sought and been denied evidence from witnesses in U.S. custody. "One of the main problems in this trial was that it was not possible to get files from intelligence services. . . . You are acquitted not because the court is convinced of your innocence, but because the evidence was not enough to convict you."

§ 5.04 PUBLIC TRIALS, THE JUDICIARY, AND CLASSIFIED INFORMATION

UNITED STATES v. GRUNDEN
United States Court of Military Appeals
2 M.J. 116 (1977)

FLETCHER, CHIEF JUDGE.

The appellant's court-martial resulted in his conviction of two specifications of failing to report contact with persons believed by him to be agents of governments hostile to the United States and one specification of attempted espionage, in violation of Articles 92 and 134, respectively, Uniform Code of Military Justice, 10 U.S.C. §§ 892 & 934. The appellant challenges the validity of his conviction on several grounds. We find it necessary for the resolution of this case to address only two: first, the failure of the military judge to sua sponte instruct the court members on evidence of uncharged misconduct; and, second, the denial of his right to a public trial. We find on both counts the judge erred.

The facts are not in dispute. The appellant, after a series of discussions with three individuals, each of whom worked covertly for the government, failed to report these conversations and ultimately attempted to communicate information relating to national defense, contrary to Air Force Regulation 205-37 and 18 U.S.C. § 793(d).

Throughout the proceedings the prosecution adduced numerous acts of misconduct, over defense objection, including possible earlier acts of espionage. The military judge, in an Article 39(a) session, subsequent to the presentment of evidence on the merits, accurately noted each act of uncharged misconduct. He correctly stated that he was required to instruct the court members as to the limited purpose of this evidence. Appellant's counsel requested that an uncharged misconduct instruction not be given. The judge considered the request and did not so instruct.

No evidence can so fester in the minds of court members as to the guilt or innocence of the accused as to the crime charged as evidence of uncharged misconduct. Its use must be given the weight of judicial comment, i.e., an instruction as to its limited use.[30]

This Court's statement in *United States v. Graves*, 23 U.S.C.M.A. 434, 437 (1975):

> Irrespective of the desires of counsel, the military judge must bear the primary responsibility for assuring that the jury properly is instructed on the elements of the offenses raised by the evidence as well as potential defenses and other questions of law. Simply stated, counsel do not frame issues for the jury; that is the duty of the military judge based upon his evaluation of the testimony related by the witnesses during the trial.

encases the judge's obligation to instruct. When evidence of uncharged misconduct is permitted, nothing short of an instruction will suffice.

As to the second error, the military judge during the preliminary Article 39(a) session, stated that because the trial on the espionage charges could delve into classified matters, certain procedures would be instituted. These included ascertaining that all court members and personnel would have the appropriate security clearances, and that the public would be excluded from portions of the trial. Thus, despite the objection of the defense counsel, and the trial judge's own assurances that he would "bend over backwards" to protect the appellant's rights, the public was excluded from virtually the entire trial as to the espionage charges.[31] During this portion of the trial, nine witnesses testified, only one of whom discussed classified matters at any length. Of the remaining eight witnesses one made less than 10 references to classified matters, three made only one reference, and the remaining four made no references. In excising the public from the trial, the trial judge employed an ax in place of the constitutionally required scalpel.

---

[30] [Court's Footnote 1] The basic legal tenet and the seven exceptions to that rule which permit the introduction of uncharged misconduct are set forth in paragraph 138g of the Manual for Courts-Martial, United States, 1969 (Rev.), as reiterated by this Court in *United States v. Janis*, 1 M.J. 395 (1976). The fact that this evidence was admissible under that test gives rise to the question of the need for an instruction.

[31] [Court's Footnote 2] The propriety or impropriety of the exclusion of the public from all or part of a trial cannot, as attempted by the government in this case, be reduced to solution by mathematical formulas. The logic and rationale governing the exclusion, not mere percentages of the total pages of the record, must be dispositive.

The dissenting judge has apparently adopted the government position that as over 60 percent of the total record was conducted in open session, there can be little or no question but that the trial judge exercised discretion in his exclusion of the public. Unfortunately what both the dissenting judge and the government have failed to do is to analyze what portions of the record are involved in this question. The "over 60 percent" figure which has been bandied about entails the preliminary procedural matters the entire trial on the merits as to the charge of which the appellant was acquitted, final instructions, and the sentencing phase of the trial. The fact that these portions of the trial were open to the public can have no bearing on the resolution of the propriety of the judge's exclusion of the public from virtually the entire trial as to the espionage matters. Further, simple examination of the record reveals that the "bulk of the closed session" did not contain numerous and repeated references to classified matters; in fact, as noted by the government in its pleadings, only two witnesses of the total of nine would fit into this category.

The right of an accused to a public trial is a substantial right secured by the Sixth Amendment to the Constitution of the United States. *In re Oliver*, 333 U.S. 257 (1948). Indeed, this Court has long held that an accused is, at the very least, entitled to have his friends, relatives, and counsel present regardless of the offense charged. *United States v. Brown*, 7 U.S.C.M.A. 251, 22 C.M.R. 41 (1956).[32] The improper exclusion of the public has been treated as error per se in recognition that to do otherwise is to place the defendant in the ironic position of having "to prove what the disregard of his constitutional right has made it impossible for him to learn."

As recognized in *Brown*, the right to a public trial is not absolute, and under exceptional circumstances, limited portions of a criminal trial may be partially closed over defense objection. In each instance the exclusion must be used sparingly with the emphasis always toward a public trial. Historical exceptions have evolved and expanded[33] which need not be discussed, for the stated basis for the exclusion of the public in this case was the fact that classified or security matters might be presented. Exclusion of the public on such a basis is provided for in paragraph 53e, Manual for Courts-Martial, United States, 1969 (Rev.) which provides in pertinent part that

> As a general rule, the public shall be permitted to attend open sessions of courts-martial. Unless otherwise limited by directives of the Secretary of a Department, the convening authority, the military judge, or the president of a special court-martial without a military judge may, for security or other good reasons, direct that the public or certain portions thereof be excluded from a trial. However, all spectators may be excluded from an entire trial, over the accused's objection, only to prevent the disclosure of classified information. The authority to exclude should be cautiously exercised, and the right of the accused to a trial completely open to the public must be weighed against the public policy considerations justifying exclusion.

Although the presentation of classified or security matters did not develop as an historical exception to the requirement of a public trial, this Court recognizes that, within carefully limited guidelines, partial exclusion of the public on such a basis can be justified. Military appellate courts have noted the necessity to require that court personnel and members have designated security clearances, and that questions of classified materials could properly be disposed of in closed sessions. Yet, in each instance the exclusion of the public was narrowly and carefully drawn. The blanket exclusion of the spectators from all or most of a trial, such as in the present case, has not been approved by this Court, nor could it be absent a compelling showing that such was necessary to prevent the disclosure of classified information. The simple utilization of the terms "security" or "military necessity" cannot be the talisman in whose presence the protections of the Sixth Amendment and its guarantee to a public trial must vanish.[34] Unless an appropriate balancing test is employed with examination and analysis of the need for, and the scope of any suggested exclusion, the result is, as here, unsupportable.

---

[32] [Court's Footnote 3] This Court is in full agreement with the concurrence of then Chief Judge Quinn that the right to a public trial is indeed required in a court-martial. To the extent that *United States v. Brown* implies a "military exception" to the right to a public trial for service personnel in reliance upon *Ex parte Quirin*, 317 U.S. 1 (1942), it is overruled.

[33] [Court's Footnote 6] *See, e.g.*, Note, *The Accused's Right to a Public Trial*, 42 NOTRE DAME LAWYER 499 (1967); Note, *The Right to a Public Trial in Criminal Cases*, 41 N.Y.U.L.R REV. 1138 (1966); Radin, *The Right to a Public Trial*, 6 TEMP. L.Q. 381 (1932). These traditional exceptions have been broadened to include limited exclusions to protect undercover policemen or agents, to ensure full and honest testimony by government witnesses, to protect airline hijacking profiles, and to preserve order.

[34] [Court's Footnote 9] This Court recognizes that the Supreme Court in *Parker v. Levy*, 417 U.S. 733, 743 (1974), acknowledged the uniqueness of the military society, and that it has reaffirmed that belief in recent decisions. Yet, this Court once again must state that analysis and rationale will be determinative of the propriety of given situations, and that the mere uniqueness of the military society or military necessity cannot be urged as the basis for sustaining that which reason and analysis indicate is untenable.

It is our decision that the balancing test employed by a trial judge in instances involving the possible divulgence of classified material should be as follows. His initial task is to determine whether the perceived need urged as grounds for the exclusion of the public is of sufficient magnitude so as to outweigh "the danger of a miscarriage of justice which may attend judicial proceedings carried out in even partial secrecy." This may be best achieved by conducting a preliminary hearing which is closed to the public at which time the government must demonstrate that it has met the heavy burden of justifying the imposition of restraints on this constitutional right. The prosecution to meet this heavy burden must demonstrate the classified nature, if any, of the materials in question. It must then delineate those portions of its case which will involve these materials.

It is acknowledged that special deference should be accorded matters of national security. Although the actual classification of materials and the policy determinations involved therein are not normal judicial functions, immunization from judicial review cannot be countenanced in situations where strong countervailing constitutional interests exist which merit judicial protection. Before a trial judge can order the exclusion of the public on this basis, he must be satisfied from all the evidence and circumstances that there is a reasonable danger that presentation of these materials before the public will expose military matters which in the interest of national security should not be divulged. The method used by the prosecution to satisfy this burden, as recognized in *United States v. Reynolds*, will vary depending upon the nature of the materials in question and the information offered. It is important to realize that this initial review by the trial judge is not for the purpose of conducting a de novo review of the propriety of a given classification decision. All that must be determined is that the material in question has been classified by the proper authorities in accordance with the appropriate regulations. The ultimate questions of whether these materials "relat[ed] to the national defense" and could be used to the injury of the United States or the advantage of a foreign country must remain for resolution by the jury. The sole purpose of this review is to protect an accused's right to a public trial by preventing circumvention of that right by the mere utterance of a conclusion or blanket acceptance of the government's position without a demonstration of a compelling need.

This Court appreciates full well that such a hearing may involve complex and delicate matters for resolution by the trial judge, yet, as recognized by the Supreme Court, these are matters that judicial officers must and should be equipped to properly determine. Similarly, we feel that objections to this procedure because of the possibility of "leaks" are insufficient to prohibit its use; adequate measures exist to insure the necessary confidentiality required when matters of national security are concerned.

The trial judge's determination that the prosecution has met its burden as to the nature of the materials does not complete his review in this preliminary hearing. He must further decide the scope of the exclusion of the public. The prosecution must delineate which witnesses will testify on classified matters, and what portion of each witness' testimony will actually be devoted to this area. Clearly, unlike the instant case, any witness whose testimony does not contain references to classified material will testify in open court. The witness whose testimony is only partially concerned with this area should testify in open court on all other matters. For even assuming a valid underlying basis for the exclusion of the public, it is error of "constitutional magnitude" to exclude the public from all of a given witness' testimony when only a portion is devoted to classified material.[35] The remaining portion of his testimony will be presented to the court members in closed session. This bifurcated presentation of a given witness'

---

[35] [Court's Footnote 19] *United States v. Clark*, 475 F.2d 240, 246 (2d Cir. 1973). The Second Circuit sustained the underlying basis for the exclusion in reliance upon its prior decision of *United States v. Bell*, 464 F.2d 667 (2d Cir. 1972) — prevention of the disclosure of airline skyjacking profiles because of a compelling need to protect the air traveling public. However, the court would not permit the total exclusion of the public in a hearing where only a portion of the testimony presented related to this profile, and the remainder, as here,

testimony is the most satisfactory resolution of the competing needs for secrecy by the government, and for a public trial by the accused. It will be incumbent upon the trial judge to sua sponte instruct the court members both as an introductory matter and in greater detail during his final instructions as to the underlying basis for the use of this bifurcated process. It is imperative that the court members determine whether the documents or information in question are violative of the espionage statute based solely upon the evidence presented. Neither the utilization of a particular document marking, nor the presentation of certain testimony in closed sessions can be, in and of itself, sufficient to sustain a conviction.

Applying the above criteria and procedures to the facts of the instant case it is abundantly clear that the military judge committed error of constitutional magnitude. His blanket exclusion of the public failed to satisfactorily balance the competing interests, and improperly denied the appellant his right to a public trial.

Reversal is required. The findings and sentence as approved by the United States Air Force Court of Military Review are set aside. The record of trial is returned to the Judge Advocate General of the Air Force. A rehearing may be ordered.

COOK, JUDGE, dissenting.

I disagree with both aspects of the majority opinion. As to the instruction on uncharged misconduct there is a vast difference between the failure of defense counsel to request an appropriate instruction as constituting a waiver of the trial judge's duty to instruct on issues for determination by the court members and an affirmative request by the defense that a particular instruction not be given. In my book, the latter instance represents defense-induced error which, except in the case of a manifest miscarriage of justice, will not be considered by an appellate court as a ground for reversal of an otherwise valid conviction.

As to the public trial issue, the principal opinion acknowledges that the right to a public trial is "not absolute." The fact that the trial judge held a preliminary hearing on the matter demonstrates to me that he was mindful of his responsibility to effect a sensitive accommodation between the accused's right to a public trial and the Government's need to protect classified information affecting national security. His declaration that he would "bend over backwards" to preserve the accused's right demonstrates to me that his criterion for exclusion of the public was at least as stringent as that contemplated by the majority. The question then is whether the judge disregarded his own declaration and, in fact, wielded "an ax in place of the . . . required scalpel," as the majority conclude.

Contrary to the majority's disdain of "mere percentages of the total pages of the record," as indicative of the scope of exclusion, in my opinion, that circumstance is very important to resolution of the issue. The defense brief represents that the trial was conducted "almost entirely in secret." However, Government counsel's analysis of the transcript of the record, with which I agree, indicates that over 60 percent of the proceedings were "open to the public," and that the "bulk of the closed session of the court-martial . . . contained numerous and repeated references to classified matters." In my opinion, therefore, the record does not reflect "blanket exclusion of the public," as the majority describe the trial judge's ruling, but rather it convinces me the trial judge was firmly committed to, and properly applied, the "logic and rationale governing the exclusion" of the public, which the majority posit as an appropriate standard for measuring the validity of the trial judge's ruling. I would affirm the determination by the Court of Military Review that the accused was not improperly denied the right to the

---

was devoted to a wide range of matters bearing on the defendant's innocence or guilt.

presence of the public at portions of his trial.

NOTES AND QUESTIONS

1. Military Justice. When we get to the Presidential Order authorizing military tribunals for alleged terrorists, some people will be interested in the question of whether military courts are "better" or "worse" for defendants than the civilian courts. *Grunden* will be an interesting example to bear in mind. The Court of Military Appeals in this case is so sensitive to the rights of the accused that it even allows what the dissent describes as a "defense-induced error" to result in reversal.

The U.S. Court of Military Appeals was renamed in 1994 to be the U.S. Court of Appeals for the Armed Forces, but it remains an Article I court. Its judges are appointed from civilian life for a term of five years.

2. Secrets and Juries. The court discusses a civilian court case in which the public was excluded from a portion of a trial involving classified information. How would a civilian court prevent jurors from disclosing secrets that are received in evidence during a closed proceeding? The members of the "jury" in a military trial can be selected with security classifications in mind and are already under the coverage of Official Secrets Act sanctions. This is one way in which the Presidential Order justifies use of military tribunals. But if the military courts are under the same obligation to provide a public trial, then what difference does this really make?

UNITED STATES v. SMITH
899 F.2d 564 (6th Cir. 1990)

MERRITT, CHIEF JUDGE.

The United States appeals the denial of a proposed protective order under a government secrecy statute known as the Classified Information Procedures Act, 18 U.S.C. app. IV (1988), an enabling statute delegating to the Chief Justice authority to issue regulations governing the security clearance of judicial employees in cases in which classified information is admitted. Section 4 of the regulations issued by the Chief Justice provides that "any problem of security involving court personnel or persons acting for the court shall be referred to the court for appropriate action." The issue presented on appeal is whether various police and intelligence agencies of the Executive Branch may, in accordance with their standard security clearance procedures, investigate Judicial Branch employees whom the court has designated to work on a criminal proceeding involving classified information. In light of the provision of section 4 in which the Judicial Branch retains authority to resolve "any problems of security" arising from the administration of the system of security clearances, we hold that such investigations do not violate the principle of separation of powers. We therefore reverse the decision below.

I

According to the indictment, Major Michael L. Smith transported and concealed stolen goods, possessed an unregistered silencer, and possessed a silencer without a serial number. The government alleges that Major Smith illegally obtained $60,000 worth of weapons which Army investigators discovered during a consent search of the major's house. According to the government, when he allegedly stole the weapons, Major Smith was a member of the "Intelligence Support Activity," an Army unit with classified, undisclosed duties. Because the prosecution and defense of this case is said to involve classified information relating to Smith's duties, the United States moved for protection of the information under [CIPA] § 3. The proposed protective order would require court employees, *e.g.*, law clerks and secretaries, to submit to government investigation and clearance before being permitted to handle any classified information.

District Judge Wiseman issued an order protecting the classified information. He did not, however, honor the government's request that the Executive Branch perform background investigations on all courtroom personnel. Instead, Judge Wiseman specified particular individuals, including a secretary and a law clerk, whom he designated as authorized to have access to classified information. Those designated individuals would, according to Judge Wiseman's order, be required to sign a memorandum of understanding, a document indicating that the signer understands the possible dangers to the United States posed by unauthorized release of classified information. When the designated security officer asked Judge Wiseman whether he should arrange for clearances for the personnel, the Judge said it would not be necessary.

The United States moved for reconsideration. It argued that the security regulations that Chief Justice Burger promulgated pursuant to section 9 of the Act[36] (hereinafter "Burger regulations") required Judge Wiseman to permit the Executive Branch to perform background checks on all courtroom personnel before the court received any classified information. Section 4 of the Burger regulations states that

> No person appointed by the court or designated for service therein shall be given access to any classified information in the custody of the court, unless such person has received a security clearance as provided herein and unless access to such information is necessary for the performance of an official function. . . .

> The court shall inform the court security officer or the attorney for the government of the names of court personnel who may require access to classified information. That person shall then notify the Department of Justice Security Officer, who shall promptly make arrangements to obtain any necessary security clearances and shall approve such clearances under standards of the Executive Branch applicable to the level and category of classified information involved. . . .

> Any problem of security involving court personnel or persons acting for the court shall be referred to the court for appropriate action.

In a comprehensive opinion designed to maintain the independence of the Judicial Branch, Judge Wiseman denied the motion. Finding that the "CIPA procedures-. . . invite executive officials into a court's chambers and authorize them to dictate to federal judges the manner in which they conduct their business," he held that section 4 of the Burger regulations violated the constitutionally-mandated separation of powers and the independence of the judiciary.

After Judge Wiseman denied the motion for reconsideration, the United States brought an interlocutory appeal to this Court pursuant to § 7(a) of the Act. That section provides that an interlocutory appeal may be taken "from a decision or order of a district court in a criminal case authorizing the disclosure of classified information. . . . " Because Judge Wiseman's order is said to have the effect of permitting the disclosure of classified information to putatively unauthorized persons, we have appellate jurisdiction under § 7(a).

II

Section 9 of the Act directed the Chief Justice of the United States — then Chief Justice Burger — to establish procedures ensuring the security of the classified information while a court is using it. Congress intended these procedures to be basic "housekeeping rules," covering "where safes are to be located, who is to have the combinations, *how many court employees can have access to the documents,* and the

---

[36] [Court's Footnote 2] The Chief Justice of the United States, in consultation with the Attorney General, the Director of Central Intelligence, and the Secretary of Defense, shall prescribe rules establishing procedures for the protection against unauthorized disclosure of any classified information in the custody of the United States district courts, courts of appeal, or Supreme Court.

like." H.R. Rep. No. 831, 96th Cong., 2d Sess., pt. 2, at 8 (1980) (emphasis added). Congress did not further delineate what procedures the Chief Justice should adopt with regard to background checks of personnel.

The Burger regulations explicitly provide that court personnel must undergo a security examination designed and conducted by Executive Branch personnel. On the question of who shall have the final authority to decide which judicial employees may see the classified information after the background check is performed, section 4 of the regulations states that "any problem of security involving court personnel or persons acting for the court shall be referred to the court for appropriate action." Because Judge Wiseman forbade the Department of Justice from engaging in the first step under the regulations, i.e., performing background checks, the only question ripe for review is whether the Executive Branch may constitutionally investigate the backgrounds of court personnel prior to their participation in a case involving classified information. Only if the Justice Department actually performed a security check on Judge Wiseman's court personnel and denied one or more of them clearance would the final authority issue require judicial resolution.

We analyze the separation of powers issue first by referring to the methods for protecting classified information employed by the special Foreign Intelligence Court and the Legislative Branch — the methods which Congress and Chief Justice Burger seemed to have had in mind in adopting the security provisions at issue here. We will explain those analogous procedures for the light they shed on the separation of powers question presented in the instant case. In the case of the Foreign Intelligence Court and the Legislative Branch, the Court and Congress respectively appear to retain final authority over the security clearance process after background checks are performed.

The legislative history of section 9 is sparse, and states only that Congress based that section on a similar provision under the Foreign Intelligence Surveillance Act. Congressional committees drafted and developed both provisions to delegate rulemaking authority for security procedures to a panel of the Chief Justice and three national security executive officials. The security procedures established by Chief Justice Burger for the special court created under the Surveillance Act "to hear applications for and grant orders approving electronic surveillance anywhere within the United States," provide, in pertinent part, that court personnel

> shall undergo appropriate background investigation by the Federal Bureau of Investigation under the standards established by Director of Central Intelligence Directive No. 1/14 . . . or successor directives as concurred in by the Attorney General. These personnel shall not have access to classified information unless they have received *a security clearance determined appropriate by the court* in consultation with the Attorney General and the Director of Central Intelligence. All court personnel having access to court records shall sign appropriate security agreements. If a question concerning the security clearance of court personnel is raised subsequent to appointment, *the matter shall be referred to the court* which may consult the Attorney General and the Director of Central Intelligence regarding its security significance before taking such action as it deems appropriate.

The security procedures promulgated pursuant to the Surveillance Act demonstrate that Congress, in analogous circumstances, has subjected the Judiciary, in this case the Surveillance Court, to security measures designed and administered by the Department of Justice.

The Legislative Branch also has delegated responsibility for safeguarding the flow of classified information. The Senate Resolution establishing the Select Committee on Intelligence states that employees of the Committee, or persons performing services for or at the Committee's request, cannot have access to classified information unless they agree to be bound by the Committee's confidentiality requirements. Further, before gaining access to classified materials, they must "receive an appropriate security clearance as determined by such committee in consultation with the Director of Central Intelligence."

It is evident from both Houses' method of protecting classified information that the Legislative Branch has determined that the participation of the Executive Branch in designing and administering security measures is not in itself an intrusion that rises to the level of an unconstitutional interference with its legislative function. In accommodating the interests of the Judicial and Executive Branches in the instant case, we are influenced by the accommodation offered by the legislative committees as well as that offered by the Surveillance Court under the Surveillance Act described above. In making this accommodation, the district courts retain the same level of protection that the Surveillance Court and legislative committees retain against the possibility of overly intrusive inquiries which the Executive might engage in pursuant to its investigation of courtroom personnel.

III

The accommodation of the interests of the three branches mentioned above has its roots in the historical deference paid to the Executive on issues of national security. For example, in *Totten v. United States*, 92 U.S. 105, 106 (1875), the Court recognized the power inherent in the Executive, through the President, to make contracts with secret agents to "enter the rebel lines and obtain information respecting the strength, resources, and movements of the enemy" in times of war. Recognizing the President's power to make such contracts, the Court stated that courts of justice — being open to the public — should not be used for trials

> which would inevitably lead to the disclosure of matters which the law itself regards as confidential, and respecting which it will not allow the confidence to be violated. On this principle, suits cannot be maintained which would require a disclosure of the confidences of the confessional, or those between husband and wife, or of communications by a client to his counsel for professional advice, or of a patient to his physician for a similar purpose. Much greater reason exists for the application of the principle to cases of contract for secret services with the government, as the existence of a contract of that kind is itself a fact not to be disclosed.

Similarly, by recognizing the need for secrecy in the area of foreign relations, the Court has deferred to the judgment of the Executive to preserve national security and to guard against the unwanted dissemination of political and military secrets:

> Even if courts could require full disclosure, the very nature of executive decisions as to foreign policy is political, not judicial. Such decisions are wholly confided by our Constitution to the political departments of the government, Executive and Legislative. They are delicate, complex, and involve large elements of prophecy. They are and should be undertaken only by those directly responsible to the people whose welfare they advance or imperil. They are decisions of a kind for which the Judiciary has neither aptitude, facilities nor responsibility and which has long been held to belong in the domain of political power not subject to judicial intrusion or inquiry.

Chicago & S. Air Lines v. Waterman Steamship Corp., 333 U.S. 103, 111 (1948); *see also United States v. Curtiss-Wright Export Corp.*, 299 U.S. 304, 320 (1936) ("Secrecy in respect of information gathered by [confidential sources of information] may be highly necessary, and the premature disclosure of it productive of harmful results.").

Clearly the indictment of Major Smith, a member of the "Intelligence Support Activity," for stealing weapons and ammunition from the United States Government, implicates the broad authority of the Executive Branch to exercise its discretion in matters that touch national security and foreign affairs.

IV

District Judge Wiseman's concerns about preserving the judiciary from unwarranted encroachment by co-equal branches are firmly rooted in the Constitution and Supreme Court precedents. Under no circumstances should the Judiciary become the hand-maiden of the Executive. The independence of the Judiciary must be jealously guarded at all times against efforts by prosecutors to erode its authority. The Constitution commands that the " 'judicial power of the United States' must be reposed in an independent Judiciary," "free from potential domination by other branches of government." However, the Supreme Court also has confirmed the government's "compelling interest in protecting both the secrecy of information important to our national security and the appearance of confidentiality." *Snepp v. United States*, 444 U.S. 507, 509 n.3 (1980). Although permissible measures taken to satisfy this compelling interest would not include those that cause "the encroachment or aggrandizement of one branch at the expense of the other," the requirement of the Burger regulations that courtroom personnel be subject to background checks before gaining access to classified information does not in itself threaten such a result. Such a requirement affecting law clerks, secretaries and bailiffs is not closely related to the deliberative process because these individuals do not and should not decide cases; thus it only mildly intrudes into the manner in which federal judges conduct business. *See In re United States Department of Justice*, No. 87-1205, slip. op. at 4 (4th Cir. Apr. 7, 1988) (unpublished disposition) (in issuing writ of *mandamus* that required security clearances for courtroom staff in civil case, court concluded that contempt or disclosure dilemma justified "minimally intrusive" requirement of routine security clearance). Under section 4 of the Burger regulations, district courts retain sufficient power to preclude the Executive from engaging in procedures that intrude upon both the judicial function and, potentially, the privacy interests of court personnel. Proper administration of the regulations is therefore consistent with the doctrine of separation of powers.

V

We therefore hold that the Executive Branch may conduct reasonable background investigations, subject to district court review, of judicial personnel before such personnel are cleared to work on a case involving classified information. The security clearance procedures established under the Burger regulations do not on their face, or as applied in this case so far, violate principles of separation of powers. Because the District Court precluded the Executive from performing any initial background checks in this case, the propriety of the checks themselves is not at issue.

§ 5.05 PREVENTION AND FREE EXPRESSION

One more aspect of the intersection between preventive safety measures and constitutional liberties is the degree to which attendance at public or semi-public events can be curtailed. Demonstrators and protestors may be disruptive, but the nature of some events demands accommodation of their ability to present their message. There is not room here to go into all the ramifications of public forum doctrine, but there are some good recent cases dealing primarily with rights of ingress and egress at government facilities and political gatherings. Security planners at a major public event will need to balance concerns over ingress and egress with the first amendment interests of those with dissident positions, while also considering available intelligence that may indicate the potential for disruption or even violence at the event.

UNITED STATES v. BAUGH
187 F.3d 1037 (9th Cir. 1999)

SCHROEDER, CIRCUIT JUDGE.

Pamela Baugh and other members of a group called Religious Witness with Homeless People ("RWHP") appeal their convictions for demonstrating without a permit on National Park property, in violation of 36 C.F.R. § 2.51(a). At the time of their arrest, the defendants were protesting the Park Service's plan to demolish the Wherry housing in the Presidio in San Francisco instead of using the units to house the homeless.

The defendants challenge the constitutional validity of the permit regulation and its implementing rules both facially and as applied to their protest. We do not reach the facial challenge, for we hold that the Park Service's application of the regulation to the defendants violated the defendants' First Amendment rights.

FACTS AND PROCEDURAL HISTORY

The demonstration for which the government arrested the defendants occurred on March 9, 1997. This was not the first time RWHP had protested the planned destruction of the housing that it wanted used to house the homeless. In past protests by the organization at the Presidio, after marching through the Wherry housing area, some RWHP members had trespassed into the housing and had refused to leave until they were arrested. On these occasions, the trespassing demonstrators were arrested both for demonstrating without a permit and for trespass, but were only prosecuted for trespass.

Park Police Lieutenant Kevin Hay learned of the March 9th demonstration a few days before. He telephoned Sister Bernie Galvin, executive director of RWHP, and asked her if the group wanted a permit. Lt. Hay told Sister Bernie that RWHP would receive a permit only if Sister Bernie promised that no trespassing into the units would occur at the march. Sister Bernie indicated that RWHP desired a permit but refused to promise that no trespassing would occur.

Although the earlier protests had taken place solely at the housing area, RWHP intended to convene on March 9th at the Visitor Center, in a different part of the Presidio, before going to the Wherry housing area to march. On March 9th, about 150 to 175 RWHP members gathered before the Visitor Center. Sister Bernie spoke to Lt. Hay two or three times at that location. He again made it clear that the permit would issue only if Sister Bernie would promise that none of the RWHP members would trespass into the housing units. Sister Bernie again refused to make this pledge.

Lt. Hay told Sister Bernie that the group would have to move to an area reserved for protestors known as the "First Amendment area" located 150 to 175 yards from the Visitor Center. Sister Bernie declined this option as well. She and other RWHP members believed that the designated area was located too far away from the Visitor Center to convey RWHP's message to Park Service officials and the public. Because of the Park Service's stance, the group gave up their march and decided instead to hold a prayer service where they stood: on the Visitor Center's lawn. Shortly after the inception of the prayer service, Lt. Hay made several announcements that the group would be arrested if it did not move to the First Amendment area. Although some RWHP demonstrators went to the First Amendment area or crossed the street, those who remained in front of the Visitor Center were promptly arrested.

The record contains some indication that the protestors may have caused some disruption of Visitor Center activities, but the Park Service did not arrest defendants for this reason. It arrested defendants solely for not having a permit to engage in their expressive activities. According to Lt. Hay's testimony, the Park Service might have permitted the demonstration to go forward at a location much closer to the Visitor Center than the so-called First Amendment area had Sister Bernie been willing to negotiate further. Sister Bernie, for her part, testified that she did not believe she possessed this option.

The defendants moved to quash their arrests on the grounds that the arrests violated the First Amendment and the district court denied the motion. The court held that 36 C.F.R. § 2.51 and the Park Service's implementing regulations were constitutional on their face and as applied to the defendants. On April 13, 1998, after a one-day bench trial, defendants were convicted of demonstrating without a permit in violation of § 2.51(a). The district court held that the no-trespassing condition imposed by the Park Service constituted a reasonable condition for the permit. The district court sentenced the defendants to ninety days of unsupervised probation and twelve hours of community service.

THE REGULATION AND ITS IMPLEMENTING RULES

The permit regulation presumptively allows expressive activities, provided the Park superintendent has issued a permit in advance. The regulation further specifies that the superintendent shall, without unreasonable delay, issue a permit upon a proper application unless certain conditions apply. One such condition is "it reasonably appears that the event will present a clear and present danger to the public health or safety." Another condition is the inability to accommodate the event in the applied-for location due to the nature of the event and considering such factors as damage to park resources or facilities, damage to a protected area's atmosphere of peace and tranquility, or disturbance of program activities or public use facilities.

The regulation also provides that the superintendent should designate on a map the locations available for public assemblies. These areas must be available for assemblies unless, *inter alia*, the activities would cause injury or damage to park resources; unreasonably interfere with interpretive, visitor service, or other program activities, or with the administrative activities of the National Park Service; substantially interfere with the operation of public use facilities; or present a clear and present danger to the public health and safety.

The compendium of implementing regulations designates three locations within the Presidio for which the Park Service will issue permits for First Amendment activities. If a group wishes to stage a special event, it may apply to the superintendent for the designation of an additional First Amendment area. If the criteria in the regulations are complied with, the superintendent will designate another specific location for the exercise of First Amendment activities. At trial, a Park Service official testified that he had the authority to issue floating permits to groups who applied and who wished to hold First Amendment activities that warranted such a permit.

THE CONSTITUTIONALITY OF THE REGULATION AS APPLIED

A march and other protest activities clearly constitute protected speech. *See Shuttlesworth v. City of Birmingham*, 394 U.S. 147, 152 (1969) (describing the privilege of citizens to assemble, parade, and discuss public questions in streets and parks). We have stressed that a public park, such as the Presidio, represents a "quintessential public forum." "Parks . . . have immemorially been held in trust for the use of the public and, time out of mind, have been used for purposes of assembly, communicating thoughts between citizens, and discussing public questions." (quoting *Hague v. CIO*, 307 U.S. 496, 515 (1939)).

The refusal of the Park Service to authorize any expressive activity in the Presidio absent the defendants' promise to keep out of certain areas constitutes a "prior restraint" that prevented expressive activity from occurring. Prior restraints on speech bear a heavy presumption of unconstitutionality because they "are the most serious and the least tolerable infringements on First Amendment rights." However, even prior restraints may be imposed if they amount to reasonable time, place, and manner restrictions on speech. To qualify as a permissible restriction, the regulation must be content neutral, narrowly tailored to serve a significant governmental interest, and leave open ample alternative channels for communication of the message.

We are not the first court to consider this regulatory scheme. The few decisions have not been uniform.

In *United States v. Kistner*, 68 F.3d 218 (8th Cir. 1995), the Eighth Circuit examined § 2.52, the companion regulation to § 2.51 that pertains to pamphleting and that contains similar language. The court held that the regulation did not violate the First Amendment on its face nor as applied to the defendant. The defendant in *Kistner* had been arrested for distributing religious pamphlets without a permit in Jefferson National Expansion Memorial, in St. Louis. The pro se defendant broadly argued that the latitude given to park officials by the regulation created a risk that the discretion would be exercised based on the content of speech *Kistner* rejected this argument, finding that the regulation contained guidelines for the issuance of the permit and that the record belied the defendant's contention that the park granted and denied permits based on content.

Two district courts, however, have found similar permit schemes to the one that confronts us unconstitutional on their face. *See Naturist Soc'y v. Fillyaw*, 858 F. Supp. 1559 (S.D. Fla. 1994); *United States v. Rainbow Family*, 695 F. Supp. 294 (E.D. Tex. 1988). Both courts held that the regulations were unduly vague and thus bestowed too much discretion upon park officials because, *inter alia*, the provisions in the regulations allowed park officials to deny permits if they perceived that the demonstration presented "a clear and present danger."

The regulation before us also authorizes denial of a permit on grounds of "clear and present danger." The government in part relies on this subsection to justify its refusal to issue RWHP a permit absent a promise not to trespass. We need not reach the issue of the facial constitutionality of § 2.51, however, because we hold that even if the regulation on its face created reasonable time, place, and manner constraints, the Park Service unconstitutionally applied the requirement when it refused to issue a permit for any expressive activity in this case.

The first criteria for a reasonable restriction on speech is that the restriction be content neutral, or "justified without reference to the content of the regulated speech." This requirement appears to have been met. Lt. Hay testified that the Park Service insisted on the promise of no trespassing out of a concern for preventing property damage and protecting the safety of protesters who might injure themselves by trespassing into the uninhabited Wherry houses. These concerns did not stem from the underlying content of RWHP's message. The government had a significant interest in protecting the Presidio's facilities and its users, including the protesters.

The critical question is whether the requirement that Sister Bernie promise that no trespassing would occur before the Park Service would issue RWHP a permit was sufficiently narrowly tailored to constitute a valid First Amendment restriction. A narrowly tailored requirement need not be the least restrictive means of furthering the Park Service's interests, but the restriction may not burden substantially more speech than necessary to further the interests. To do otherwise would be to burden substantially those seeking to express their political views. Organizers of protests ordinarily cannot warrant in good faith that all the participants in a demonstration will comply with the law. Demonstrations are often robust. No one can guarantee how demonstrators will behave throughout the course of the entire protest. Thus, the promise the Park Service sought would be illusory and meaningless at best.

We have held that a complete ban on First Amendment activity cannot be justified simply because past similar activity led to violence. *See Collins v. Jordan*, 110 F.3d 1363, 1371-72 (9th Cir. 1997). In *Collins*, this court disapproved of a San Francisco policy instituted in the days following the Rodney King verdict, to disperse demonstrations before the demonstrators acted illegally or posed any threat to other people or activities. We stated that "the generally accepted way of dealing with unlawful conduct that may be intertwined with First Amendment activity is to punish it after it occurs rather than to prevent the First Amendment activity from occurring in order to obviate the possible unlawful conduct." The Park Service, in lieu of restraining the expressive activity by refusing to issue the permit, should have issued the permit for the lawful expressive activity and then arrested the demonstrators if and when they trespassed.

The Supreme Court's decision in *Clark* [*v. Community for Creative Non-Violence*, 468 U.S. 288 (1984)], illustrates the point. In that case, a group wished to draw attention to the plight of homelessness by holding a day and night wintertime demonstration in Lafayette Park and on the Mall in Washington, D.C. The Park Service granted the group a permit to erect two symbolic tent cities. However, the Park Service refused to grant the group's request for a permit allowing the demonstrators to sleep in the tents. The Supreme Court held that the limitation the Park Service placed on the permit constituted a valid restriction on the manner of the demonstration. The Park Service in *Clark* issued the permit to allow a lawful demonstration to go forward. It did not withhold the right to any demonstration.

In this case, by failing to tailor the no-trespass condition narrowly to allow for lawful demonstrations, the Park Service also failed to leave open sufficient alternative means for the protestors to communicate their views. Lt. Hay ordered the demonstrators to a First Amendment area 150 to 175 yards away from the Visitor Center. The Park Service officials and the public to whom RWHP wished to communicate its message were at the Visitor Center. Such distancing of the demonstrators from the intended audience does not provide a reasonable alternative means for communication of RWHP's views. In *Bay Area Peace Navy*, we held that requiring a 75-yard security zone between demonstrators and the persons to whom they directed their message did not leave open ample alternative means of communicating the protesters' message. 914 F.2d at 1229. We stated that "an alternative is not ample if the speaker is not permitted to reach the 'intended audience.'" *Id.* (citation omitted); *see also Heffron v. International Soc'y for Krishna Consciousness, Inc.*, 452 U.S. 640, 655 (1981) ("The First Amendment protects the right of every citizen to 'reach the minds of willing listeners and to do so there must be opportunity to win their attention.'" (citation omitted)); *cf. Schenck v. Pro-Choice Network of W.N.Y.*, 519 U.S. 357, 377 (1997) (floating buffer zones prevent abortion protesters from communicating their message). Because RWHP was left with no alternative that allowed it to reach its intended audience, the Park Service's application of the permit regulations also failed to satisfy the final requirement for valid First Amendment restrictions.

The judgment is REVERSED with instructions to VACATE defendants' convictions and sentences.

SILVERMAN, CIRCUIT JUDGE, concurring.

On March 9, 1997, the defendants set out to get arrested at the Presidio to generate publicity for their cause. They admit that. They could have obtained the requisite permit if they would have agreed to comply with the permit. They admit that, too. They could have demonstrated in the First Amendment area of the Presidio without any permit whatsoever. That, also, is admitted. The problem is that if the defendants had agreed to comply with the permit or to hold their demonstration in the First Amendment area, they wouldn't have gotten themselves arrested, which is what they wanted to accomplish to begin with. It is in the context of this contrived, intentionally provoked controversy that the defendants attack both the facial constitutionality of 36 C.F.R. § 2.51(a) and the constitutionality of that section as applied.

Although I agree with the result reached by the majority, I write separately to express some sympathy for the situation faced by the officers of the Park Service in this case. Contrary to the main opinion's dramatic overstatement, the Park Service officers did not prohibit the defendants from engaging in "any expressive activity in the

Presidio" on the day in question. They could have expressed themselves to their hearts' content in the First Amendment area. The First Amendment area was not Siberia. It was located only 150 yards or so away, and in view of, the Visitors Center.

Likewise, the Park Service officers were ready, willing and able to issue a floating permit so that the defendants could conduct their demonstration elsewhere in the Presidio if they would have agreed to comply with it. And as the main opinion acknowledges, the denial of the permit was content-neutral, i.e., "did not stem from the underlying content of [the defendants'] message."

The Park Service certainly had plenty of reason to believe that the organizers of the demonstration *intended* to violate the very permit for which they were applying. As Sister Bernie testified, at the time Lt. Hays asked for an assurance that the permit would be complied with, "He had a copy of our press release that had gone out earlier which also indicated that we were going to do civil disobedience. * * * We couldn't agree to the condition of no civil disobedience and we found being relegated to a remote area where we indeed could not witness was simply unacceptable."

In retrospect, what the Park Service should have done is issue the permit, await its advertised violation, and then make the arrest. The Park Service should not have denied the permit just because it anticipated a violation. However, one certainly can understand why conscientious officers, concerned with the public safety and the protection of park property, would want to try to head off a 150-person trespass, if possible. Although it is difficult to articulate when threatened First Amendment activity might create such a clear and present danger to public safety that it can be prevented in advance, Sunday in the park with Sister Bernie was not such a case.

NOTES AND QUESTIONS

1. *Rowley v. McMillan.* In *Rowley v. McMillan*, 502 F.2d 1326 (4th Cir. 1974), the Fourth Circuit held unconstitutional a Secret Service attempt to prevent dissident members of the public from entering a gathering at which President Nixon was due to appear. The district court had granted a preliminary injunction for future appearances of the President to prevent the defendants from

> discriminatorily arresting or detaining, or keeping from the general public presence of the President, plaintiffs and others similarly situated, on account of their mode of dress or hair style, life style, peaceable expression of political (including dissenting) views, exercise of constitutional rights of free speech, petition for redress of grievances or right of association, without prior judicial authorization or without probable cause, or for any other cause not rationally necessary for the personal safety of the President.

The Government did not contest that the injunction accurately reflected constitutional standards but argued only that the case was moot, that the facts did not reflect Secret Service involvement in the decision to exclude plaintiffs, and that the officers involved should have immunity from damages.

Butler v. United States, 365 F. Supp. 1035 (D. Hawaii 1973), was a similar action arising from a visit by President Nixon to an Air Force base in Hawaii.

2. *Service Employees Local 660 v. City of Los Angeles.* *Service Employees Local 660 v. City of Los Angeles*, 114 F. Supp. 2d 966 (C.D. Cal. 2000). When the Democratic National Convention of 2000 was scheduled at the Staples Center in Los Angeles, the LAPD and Secret Service planned out a "secure zone" of about 12 square blocks around the facility. Entry into that zone was limited by pass, while "some 260 yards from the entrance to the Staples Center, a small 'protest' or 'demonstration' site has been designated for use during the convention." Plaintiffs included groups that wanted to picket closer to the event. The court found that the secure zone was not narrowly tailored, that the protest zone was too far removed to allow access to the speakers' intended audiences, and that the secure zone had to be reconfigured to allow reasonable access by the plaintiffs to those attending the event. Most pertinent to our concerns was this statement: "The government cannot infringe on First Amendment rights on the mere speculation that violence may occur."

3. *Madsen v. Women's Health Center.* *Madsen v. Women's Health Center*, 512 U.S. 753 (1994), is the principal abortion demonstration case. The Supreme Court upheld restrictions imposed by a state court on noise levels outside the clinic and a 36-foot buffer zone to allow unimpeded ingress, and egress to the clinic but struck down other provisions of the state court's order such as restrictions on personal contact with patrons and prohibition of "observable images."

4. Intelligence and Event Security. What can you as the lawyer advising security personnel do with information about the plans of a dissident group to disrupt an event? Does it matter how the information was gathered? For example, consider the differences among these modes of gathering intelligence in advance of an event:

    a. by undercover officers attending a meeting of a dissident group

        i. without misidentifying themselves in any way

        ii. pretending to be members of the group

    b. by surveillance pursuant to a FISA order

§ 5.06 SELECTED READINGS

[Note: It is difficult to find scholarly writings about FISA that are not criticisms of PATRIOT Act amendments. CIPA has been the subject of virtually no scholarly analysis or critique.]

- DAVID COLE & JAMES X. DEMPSEY, TERRORISM AND THE CONSTITUTION (2002)
- RONALD DANIELS, PATRICK MACKLEM & KENT ROACH, THE SECURITY OF FREEDOM: ESSAYS ON CANADA'S ANTI-TERRORISM BILL (2001)
- SAMUEL DASH, THE INTRUDERS: UNREASONABLE SEARCHES AND SEIZURES FROM KING JOHN TO JOHN ASHCROFT (2004)
- PHILLIP H. MELANSON, SECRECY WARS: NATIONAL SECURITY, PRIVACY, AND THE PUBLIC'S RIGHT TO KNOW (2001)
- JEFFREY ROSEN, THE NAKED CROWD: RECLAIMING SECURITY AND FREEDOM IN AN ANXIOUS AGE (2004)
- Nola K. Breglio, *Leaving FISA Behind: The Need To Return to Warrantless Foreign Intelligence Surveillance*, 111 YALE L.J. 179 (2003)
- Kelley Brooke Snyder, *A Clash of Values: Classified Information in Immigration Proceedings*, 88 VA. L. REV. 447 (2002)
- David Hard, *Note: The Fuss over Two Small Words: The Unconstitutionality of the USA PATRIOT Act Amendments to FISA Under the Fourth Amendment*, 71 GEO. WASH. L. REV. 291 (2003)
- Nathan C. Henderson, *Note: The Patriot Act's Impact on the Government's Ability to Conduct Electronic Surveillance of Ongoing Domestic Communications*, 52 DUKE L.J. 179 (2002)
- Craig S. Lerner, *The USA PATRIOT Act: Promoting the Cooperation of Foreign Intelligence Gathering and Law Enforcement*, 11 GEO. MASON L. REV. 493 (2003)
- Steven A. Osher, *Privacy, Computers and the Patriot Act: The Fourth Amendment Isn't Dead, But No One Will Insure It*, 54 FLA. L. REV. 521 (2002)
- Ronald J. Sievert, *War on Terrorism or Global Law Enforcement Operation?*, 78 NOTRE DAME L. REV. 307 (2003)
- Symposium, *Internet Surveillance, Privacy & the USA PATRIOT Act*, 72 GEO. WASH. L. REV. 1145 (2004)

· David Kris, *Modernizing the Foreign Intelligence Surveillance Act*, BROOKINGS INSTITUTE, Nov. 15, 2007, *available at* http://www.brookings.edu/papers/2007/1115_nationalsecurity_kris.aspx

Chapter 6
TOWARD AN INTERNATIONAL LAW OF TERRORISM

There are at least four reasons why a study of legal responses to international terrorism must include the international law of war and its offspring, international humanitarian law. One is that some aspects of terrorism essentially amount to illegal methods of warfare and can be treated as such by criminal processes that enforce the "customs and law of war." Second, international criminal law dealing with widespread violence against civilians (genocide and crimes against humanity) has been spawned from international enforcement of the law of war, and instances of this behavior may prompt calls for international military intervention (most recently, for example, in the Sudan). The third reason is that some nations, particularly the U.S. following 9/11, use the language of war and envision the use of military force in responding to terrorism. Finally, the law of war may be incorporated into the domestic law of a nation and serve as a limitation on how to deal with captives — this usage of the law of war is highlighted in the arguments regarding interrogation and executive detention by the U.S.

For all these reasons, we will spend some time with the law of war, then turn to international criminal enforcement and conventions regarding terrorism. The progression of legal concepts here flows from norms of behavior during time of warfare between nations, to international sanctions on atrocities committed during internal conflicts, to national and international sanctions on violence by civilians against civilians.

§ 6.01 INTERNATIONAL LAW OF ARMED CONFLICT

The rhetoric of a "war against terrorism" began immediately on September 11, 2001. It was difficult to argue against it at the time, although a few cautionary voices were heard. Some observers pointed out that military action against terrorist groups would not technically be a war and argued against immediate military action as a response. Others pointed out that this will be a war of ideas, not just weapons. Meanwhile, President Bush authorized the creation of military tribunals to deal with alleged terrorists under statutory authorization that allows military tribunals to punish violations of the "law of war." Thus, the laws and customs of war are very much a part of our study of responses to terrorism.

[A] The Language and History of War

In traditional international terms, it would not be possible for a nation to go to war with a group of individuals, criminal or otherwise. War traditionally is a status that exists between nations, not among individuals nor even between a nation-state and a group of individuals. Professor Paust says that the law of war applies in "armed conflict" with a "nation, state, belligerent, or insurgent group." The difference between the latter two is that the insurgent has not yet received "outside recognition by one or more states as a belligerent or a state." To the extent that insurgents gain enough power to move beyond the status of ordinary street criminals, then they may be engaged in an "armed conflict" with the state, but they do not partake of the protections of the law of war unless they organize and behave according to those rules. Jordan J. Paust, *War and Enemy Status After 9/11: Attacks on the Laws of War*, 28 YALE J. INT'L L. 325, 326 (2003).

Professor Feldman claims that the status of "war" is a bit more complicated than that. He notes that the distinction between "war" and "crime" has "practical consequences . . . for the pursuit and capture of international terrorists" because of

> a striking asymmetry: on the one hand, criminals generally may not be killed by their pursuers if they pose no immediate threat, but may be punished after capture; adversaries in war, on the other hand, may generally be killed in

pursuit without giving quarter, but generally cannot be punished after they are captured.

Noah Feldman, *Choices of Law, Choices of War*, 25 HARV. J. L. PUB. POLICY 457 (2002). Professor Feldman distinguishes between war and crime on the basis of four criteria, which he calls the identity factor (status of the actor as a state or recognized group), provenance (whether action originates from within or outside the state), intent (whether the actor is challenging the very existence of the governing regime), and scale (the scope of violent action).

Generally, in the international law regime discussed below, war must be defensive, carried out by persons identified by discernible insignia, and limited to military targets, sparing civilian populations to the extent possible. (The principal argument against the legality of nuclear weapons is that they can never be limited effectively to military targets without extensive destruction of human life. This is still under debate in the international community.)

Generally speaking, a terrorist is a person who *clandestinely* attacks *civilian* targets and *blends* back into a civilian population. Each of these three aspects defies the rules laid down by nations for the conduct of their affairs. We must be careful, however, not to use the language of war loosely because the "law of war" applies only in the context of "armed conflict," a term of art that refers to organized use of deadly force. Other law, primarily "international humanitarian law" (IHL) is developing from the law of war at least to govern "widespread and systematic" attacks on civilians.

The nations of the world have not agreed on a definition of terrorist because some have argued that clandestine attacks, with likely civilian casualties, are the only methods for "freedom fighters" to strike at an oppressive regime. The counter-argument is that the striking of civilian targets is neither essential to the freedom fighter nor warranted by the customs and usages of war. As the twentieth century drew to a close, systematic violence against civilians became more a matter of organized violence by national forces or militias against minority or subservient civilian populations than a matter of violence by insurgents against the civilians of a perceived aggressor or colonizer. Examples of the former included Yugoslavia (Bosnia & Kosovo), Rwanda, Somalia, Darfur. An example of the latter would be Iraq after 2003. As a result of that shift, most third-world countries have come to the view that systematic violence against civilians should be condemned by the international community, and attention has turned from the basic moral question to the technical definition.

[B]   International Law and Use of Force

1.   Historical Introduction to the Law of War

International law applies to "armed conflict." In recent decades, commentators have been abandoning the term "war" because of the need to deal with undeclared conditions of combat. Many students will be tempted to believe that it is also an oxymoron to speak of international "law" because the rules to be followed appear to be simply whatever the strongest wish to apply to the weaker. More prosaically, the rules of etiquette are set by the 500 pound gorilla at the dinner table. There is some truth to this observation, but the complete picture is much more complex. Over the last 4000 years, norms have been written down, and in the last few hundred years those norms have come to receive increasing levels of enforcement in various settings.

The "law of war" flows from self-imposed limitations on the use of force that have been promulgated by every known civilization. "As early as the Egyptian and Sumerian wars of the second millennium B.C.E., there were rules defining the circumstances under which war might be initiated. Among the Hittites of the fourteenth century B.C.E., a formal exchange of letters and demands generally preceded hostilities." 1 LEON FRIEDMAN, THE LAW OF WAR: A DOCUMENTARY HISTORY 3 (1972). The Hebrew

Torah, in the Book of Deuteronomy, written down somewhere around 500 B.C.E., contained mandates to spare noncombatants (with exceptions) and the "trees of the field." In China, Sun Tzu's *The Art of War*, also circa 500 B.C.E., prohibited injury to a wounded enemy and exhorted leaders that "All the soldiers taken must be cared for with magnanimity and sincerity so that they may be used by us." The Hindu *Book of Manu*, circa 200 C.E., contained lengthy, detailed proscriptions on hidden or poisoned weapons as well as on treatment of prisoners.

The seminal written work for Western development was provided by St. Augustine in various letters and essays before and around the time of the fall of Rome in 410 CE. Augustine is best known for distinguishing between *jus ad bellum* (law of going to war) and *jus in bello* (law during war). His two conditions for "just war" dictated by *jus ad bellum* were that it must be declared by a recognized authority and that it must be defensive (the origin of nonaggression). The three principal elements of *jus in bello* he said to be sparing noncombatants, limitations of military necessity and proportionality, and protection of the means of human survival (water, trees, etc).

Over the course of European history, heavily influenced by the writings of Christian clergy, rules for the conduct of warfare became ever more elaborate. Rules of warfare during the medieval period were expressed mostly in the codes of chivalry. Then, at the dawn of the age of colonialism, as European nations came into contact with other cultures that they wished to subdue, writers began to elaborate the "laws and customs" by which these other cultures were to be approached. The principal architect of what is now the international law of war was HUGO GROTIUS, ON THE LAW OF WAR AND PEACE (1625). In this series of three books, Grotius, a Dutch lawyer, set out the requirements for lawful use of military force and the limitations on the use of force.

The cynical may view all these mandates, and the many departures from them over the centuries, as nothing but self-aggrandizing sentiments that could be followed or not as the military commanders and their sovereigns chose. Certainly, human history is rampant with unjustified use of force and with extreme cruelty and barbarity to both civilians and combatants. Nevertheless, there are self-interested reasons for imposing limitations. "A commander does not kill his prisoners because he does not want his own men slaughtered if they fall into an enemy's hands. Civilian populations should not be eliminated after they have been conquered since they can work for, pay tribute to, or be conscripted into, the victorious army. Unrestrained warfare would jeopardize reconciliation and make later trade and peaceful intercourse impossible." FRIEDMAN at 4. In addition, Friedman points out that evolving standards of civilization (to which we might add increasing levels of globalized trade) have added levels of conscience to the human tension between violence and peace. Philosophical norms eventually do find their way into enforceable norms of law.

Fourteen separate Conventions adopted at the Hague in 1907 committed signatory nations to a variety of limitations on the use of force. Hague I ("Pacific Settlement of International Disputes") stated that "the Signatory Powers agree to use their best efforts to ensure the pacific settlement of disputes" and established a system of mediation and the Permanent Court of Arbitration for international disputes. Hague II ("Laws and Customs of War on Land") stated that "In view of the High Contracting Parties, these provisions, the wording of which has been inspired by the desire to diminish the evils of war so far as military necessities permit, are destined to serve as general rules of conduct for belligerents in their relations with each other and with populations." The other Conventions established conditions for conduct of military operations in specific settings, established conditions for treatment of prisoners, and prohibited certain kinds of weapons. Although the Hague Conventions were treated with attitudes approaching contempt in the initiation and conduct of World War I, it was the rules of these conventions that ultimately became the bases for prosecutions after World War II for violations of the "laws and customs of war."

The most visible enforcement mechanisms of current international law are one set for nations and one for individuals. The United Nations Security Council enforces rules of nonaggression by calling on member states to invoke sanctions against any state that violates the UN Charter's prohibition on aggression. That there are obvious political dimensions to the decisions of the Security Council does not take away the facial legitimacy of those decisions.

The second set of enforcement mechanisms, applying the law of war to individuals, begins with war crimes trials following World War II. The United States tried some German spies and saboteurs in military courts. *Johnson v. Eisentrager*, 339 U.S. 763 (1950). The United States also conducted military trials for vanquished Japanese commanders accused of allowing their troops to violate the "laws and customs of war." *In re Yamashita*, 327 U.S. 1 (1946).

The genesis of international enforcement of the law of war was the Treaty of London and the resulting Nuremberg trials of high-ranking Nazi officials. The trials at Nuremberg were intended to import the processes of law onto the international scene for dealing with war crimes. Prior to that time, "victor's justice" had been meted out at the national level. Gerry J. Simpson, *War Crimes: A Critical Introduction, in* TIMOTHY L.H. MCCORMACK & GERRY J. SIMPSON, THE LAW OF WAR CRIMES 5 (1997). The Nuremberg trials have been followed in more recent times by Ad Hoc Tribunals for Rwanda & Yugoslavia. *See* Christopher Blakesley, *Atrocity and Its Prosecution*, MCCORMACK & SIMPSON, THE LAW OF WAR CRIMES 189 (1997). These Tribunals are considered in § 6.02[B] below.

Until recently, the world held to a dichotomous distinction between the processes of warfare and those of the civilian criminal system. War was something that took place between nations, involved an effort to kill or capture enemy combatants, and thus provided no occasion for making considered judgments about the culpability of someone on the other side. The rules of engagement of a particular military action eliminate the soldier's need to inquire into the culpability of someone in uniform carrying arms. WILLIAM WINTHROP, MILITARY LAW AND PROCEDURE 778 (2d ed. 1920): "The State is represented in active war by its contending army, and the laws of war justify killing or disabling of members of the one army by those of the other in battle or hostile operations."

The exclusive focus on nation-state participation in international law has been modified by the emergence of additional organizations as world players, such as Regional Organizations (e.g., NATO, EU, OAS) and Non Governmental Organizations (e.g., Amnesty International, International Red Cross). Although these additional actors are participants in the development of international law, there are only a few instances of treaties that specifically recognize their role as legal actors.

More importantly, the lines between warfare and criminal processes have blurred because of changes in approach both by the enforcers of peace and the perpetrators of violence. The peacemakers have attempted to use processes patterned from criminal law to punish violations of respected rules of warfare, while the perpetrators of violence have acted on their own outside the confines of government and those same rules of warfare. The world's search for a new paradigm to deal with these phenomena has produced international commissions for prosecution of war crimes and calls for responses to terrorism.

2. The Basics of "Armed Attack" and Aggression

The starting point for international law is similar to the rules regarding assault between individuals. If you use force against another, you must have a justification. UN Charter Art. 2(4) sets out the basic rule of nonaggression: "All Members shall refrain in their international relations from the threat or use of force against the territorial integrity or political independence of any state, or in any other manner inconsistent with the Purposes of the United Nations." Articles 39–50 give the Security Council authority to determine when a nation is committing aggression and to call on Member nations to employ sanctions, ranging from diplomatic and economic sanctions to the use of military force against the aggressor.

Justifications for the use of force are implied in Article 51, which states that "Nothing in the present Charter shall impair the inherent right of individual or collective self-defense if an armed attack occurs against a Member of the United Nations." Recognition of the right of self-defense calls into play a network of doctrines regarding response to threats, proportional reprisals, protection of nationals, humanitarian intervention, and dealing with insurgents or belligerents.

First, there is the question of what constitutes aggression sufficient to justify self-defensive reaction. "Armed attack" under Art. 51 seems to imply the obvious, incursion of armed invaders with full military equipment (planes, tanks, etc) in the uniforms of the invading country into the recognized borders of another nation. In this event, the invaded country can use whatever force is necessary to defend itself including, at least if it declares war, invading the offending country to take the offensive.

Short of the obvious level of armed attack, however, there are a host of lesser incursions that might trigger the right of self-defense. Blockade of a nation's ports is traditionally regarded as an act of war. An embassy is generally regarded as part of the sovereign territory of the guest nation so that an attack on the embassy is an act of war. Attacks on military ships on the high seas, and arguably attacks on merchant vessels as well, are acts of war. And minor border skirmishes may trigger the right of reprisal as part of self-defense, and there will inevitably be questions raised as to whether the incursions were actually undertaken on behalf of the neighboring state or were instead private actions (by "irregulars" or terrorists). In all these instances of "minor" acts of war, the defending nation is limited to responding to the extent necessary to defend itself and in proportion to the actions of the aggressor. These rules of necessity and proportionality may be more frequently observed than one might think, for the simple reason that escalation of the conflict is undertaken only at risk of triggering "total war," in which all the military-industrial apparatus of the enemy nation is arrayed in an effort to obliterate the defensive capability of the enemy.

The issues of "armed attack" and appropriate responses are explored in the opinions of the International Court of Justice in *Nicaragua v. United States*, 1986 ICJ 14, excerpted below.

Second, to what extent may a nation respond to a perceived threat before the other nation can strike? The United Nations has never adopted language that specifically addresses this issue. Classic statements include language similar to that in the law related to individuals — one may take action when under a threat of imminent harm. The nuclear age, however, makes "imminence" a more delicate judgment than in earlier times.

Many observers believe that a majority of nations do not subscribe to the doctrine of anticipatory self-defense or preemptive strikes. Israel claimed anticipatory self-defense in its 1981 attack on an Iraq nuclear power plant, but skirted the issue in justifying its 1967 invasion of Egypt, Jordan, and Syria by claiming that other actions of those states essentially amounted to acts of war against Israel. The U.S. used a similar approach to justify its blockade of Cuba during the 1962 missile crisis by claiming that it was engaged in regional peacekeeping under Chapter VIII of the UN Charter. The U.S. has specifically invoked anticipatory self-defense with regard to Iraq, first in enforcing the "no-fly" zones by targeting Iraq installations that show "hostile intent" and then ultimately in the 2003 invasion based on reported stockpiles of weapons of mass destruction.

As one observer concluded prior to the 2003 invasion, "reluctance to rely on anticipatory self-defence even by the USA and Israel is not conclusive that they do not believe that it is legal, as it is natural for states to choose the strongest grounds to justify their claims, but it is strong evidence of the controversial nature of this justification for the use of force, as is the deliberate avoidance of the issue of the legality of anticipatory self-defence by the International Court of Justice in the Nicaragua case. States prefer to argue for an extended interpretation of armed attack and to avoid the fundamental doctrinal debate." CHRISTINE GRAY, INTERNATIONAL LAW AND THE USE OF FORCE 115 (2000).

Third, may one state invade the territory of another state to protect its nationals? The U.S. has claimed this right in its invasions of Panama (1989) and Grenada (1983), the hostage-rescue attempt in Iran (1980), and a few other instances. One of the most famous incidents of this type was the hostage rescue by Israeli forces at Entebbe in 1976. Grey points out that the pattern of allowing incursions into other states to rescue a nation's own citizens has been accepted by silence of the invaded state in most instances but that there is still not a widely accepted norm that would lead to the conclusion that this is a lawful practice. The options, however, are limited if the harboring state does not respond immediately to diplomatic demands.

Fourth, may one state or a collection of states invade another for humanitarian reasons? This rationale was probably unheard of until the late twentieth century. It has been the focus of a number of legal debates regarding the NATO intrusion into Kosovo, the most significant of which was expression of serious doubts about the matter by the International Court of Justice. In justifying invasion of Iraq in 2003, the Bush Administration repeatedly referred to the "brutal dictatorship" of Saddam Hussein as a political justification to the American people but did not seem to be arguing for humanitarian intervention as a matter of legal justification.

Fifth, and finally for our purposes, may a state invade the territory of another in pursuit of terrorists? The justification for U.S. invasion of Afghanistan in 2002 was that Afghanistan was "harboring" persons involved in the 9/11 attacks. Indeed, the links between al Qaeda and the Taliban may have been sufficient to consider one to be the agent of the other. Earlier justifications for limited strikes by Israel and the U.S. may have been more in the nature of "reprisals" than defensive actions. Most of those strikes were sharply limited by "necessity and proportionality" but they also seemed to be designed to punish the offending state. The UN Security Council in Resolution 188 stated in 1964 that it condemned reprisals in general.

Perhaps the closest corollary in international custom has been the use of military force to root out piracy and slave trading centers in the eighteenth and nineteenth centuries. There are several examples in recent decades of the U.S. government's seizing drug lords and bringing them to trial in this country. In the cases of a few individuals seized in Mexico and brought to the U.S. for trial, U.S. agents did not engage in an "armed attack" but the Mexican government objected to the perceived interference in its internal affairs. In the case of Manuel Noriega, we justified our actions by claiming that the prior government of Panama was the legitimate government and we were carrying out their wishes.

The International Court of Justice has decided a handful of cases regarding the justifications for military invasion of another country. The two most significant involve Nicaragua nd Yugoslavia.

CASE CONCERNING MILITARY AND PARAMILITARY ACTIVITIES IN AND AGAINST NICARAGUA (NICARAGUA v. UNITED STATES OF AMERICA)
1986 I.C.J. 14
International Court of Justice
June 27, 1986

[Nicaragua filed a petition with the ICJ regarding U.S. support of groups, known collectively as the Contras, who were engaged in violent conflict with the leftist government of Nicaragua. The source of the conflict was the ouster of the prior Samosa regime and its replacement by the leftist Sandinista regime in 1979. The U.S. initially was friendly to the new regime but eventually began to support the rebel forces from bases in Costa Rica, Honduras, and El Salvador. The U.S. objected to the jurisdiction of the ICJ on the ground that issues of the legality of an armed conflict were within the exclusive jurisdiction of the UN Security Council, but the court held that customary international law could also be a source of law. The U.S. did not participate in the proceedings after that decision. Ultimately, the court found that the U.S. was not sufficiently in control of the Contras to the point that the U.S. could be found responsible for the acts of the Contras. This issue of control of a guerilla force is important to understanding the opinions of the International Criminal Tribunals for Yugoslavia and Rwanda, which in turn become part of the international response to acts of terrorism.

[The U.S. support, however, was held to constitute interference in the internal affairs of Nicaragua in violation of international law, and the U.S. actions in mining harbors of Nicaragua was a direct act of aggression. The principal questions after that were whether the U.S. could claim a right to assist Costa Rica, Honduras, or El Salvador in their defense against border actions of Nicaragua, a claim that was also rejected by the court. The self-defense issues are relevant to the issue of armed intervention by the U.S. into Afghanistan and Iraq as part of a response to terrorism.]

110. [W]hether the United States Government at any stage devised the strategy and directed the tactics of the contras depends on the extent to which the United States made use of the potential for control inherent in [the dependence of the Contras on U.S. aid]. The Court already indicated that it has insufficient evidence to reach a finding on this point. It is *a fortiori* unable to determine that the contra force may be equated for legal purposes with the forces of the United States. This conclusion, however, does not of course suffice to resolve the entire question of the responsibility incurred by the United States through its assistance to the contras.

116. The Court does not consider that the assistance given by the United States to the contras warrants the conclusion that these forces are subject to the United States to such an extent that any acts they have committed are imputable to that State. It takes the view that the contras remain responsible for their acts, and that the United States is not responsible for the acts of the contras, but for its own conduct *vis-á-vis* Nicaragua, including conduct related to the acts of the contras. What the Court has to investigate is not the complaints relating to alleged violations of humanitarian law by the contras, regarded by Nicaragua as imputable to the United States, but rather unlawful acts for which the United States may be responsible directly in connection with the activities of the contras. The lawfulness or otherwise of such acts of the United States is a question different from the violations of humanitarian law of which the contras may or may not have been guilty. It is for this reason that the Court does not have to determine whether the violations of humanitarian law attributed to the contras were in fact committed by them.

[The Court examined two manuals allegedly authored and distributed by the CIA to the Contras. One was admittedly a CIA document but was somewhat ambiguous about the extent to which it promoted tactics such as torture or murder of civilians. The Court found that it could have had that effect.]

[Customary Law of Justification for Armed Conflict]

183. [T]he Court has next to consider what are the rules of customary international law applicable to the present dispute. . . . In this respect the Court must not lose sight of the Charter of the United Nations and that of the Organization of American States, notwithstanding the operation of the multilateral treaty reservation. Although the Court has no jurisdiction to determine whether the conduct of the United States constitutes a breach of those conventions, it can and must take them into account in ascertaining the content of the customary international law which the United States is also alleged to have infringed.

191. As regards certain particular aspects of the principle in question, it will be necessary to distinguish the most grave forms of the use of force (those constituting an armed attack) from other less grave forms. In determining the legal rule which applies

to these latter forms, the Court can again draw on the formulations contained in the Declaration on Principles of International Law concerning Friendly Relations and Co-operation among States in accordance with the Charter of the United Nations (General Assembly resolution 2625 (XXV)). As already observed, the adoption by States of this text affords an indication of their *opinio juris* as to customary international law on the question. Alongside certain descriptions which may refer to aggression, this text includes others which refer only to less grave forms of the use of force. In particular, according to this resolution:

> Every State has the duty to refrain from the threat or use of force to violate the existing international boundaries of another State or as a means of solving international disputes, including territorial disputes and problems concerning frontiers of States.

> States have a duty to refrain from acts of reprisal involving the use of force.

> Every State has the duty to refrain from any forcible action which deprives peoples referred to in the elaboration of the principle of equal rights and self-determination of that right to self-determination and freedom and independence.

> Every State has the duty to refrain from organizing or encouraging the organization of irregular forces or armed bands, including mercenaries, for incursion into the territory of another State.

> Every State has the duty to refrain from organizing, instigating, assisting or participating in acts of civil strife or terrorist acts in another State or acquiescing in organized activities within its territory directed towards the commission of such acts, when the acts referred to in the present paragraph involve a threat or use of force.

192. Moreover, in the part of this same resolution devoted to the principle of non-intervention in matters within the national jurisdiction of States, a very similar rule is found:

> Also, no State shall organize, assist, foment, finance, incite or tolerate subversive, terrorist or armed activities directed towards the violent overthrow of the regime of another State, or interfere in civil strife in another State.

211. The Court has recalled above (paragraphs 193 to 195) that for one State to use force against another, on the ground that that State has committed a wrongful act of force against a third State, is regarded as lawful, by way of exception, only when the wrongful act provoking the response was an armed attack. Thus the lawfulness of the use of force by a State in response to a wrongful act of which it has not itself been the victim is not admitted when this wrongful act is not an armed attack. In the view of the Court, under international law in force today — whether customary international law or that of the United Nations system — States do not have a right of 'collective' armed response to acts which do not constitute an 'armed attack.'

[Application of Law to Facts]

227. The Court will first appraise the facts in the light of the principle of the non-use of force. What is unlawful, in accordance with that principle, is recourse to either the threat or the use of force against the territorial integrity or political independence of any State. For the most part, the complaints by Nicaragua are of the actual use of force against it by the United States. Of the acts which the Court has found imputable to the Government of the United States, the following are relevant in this respect:

· the laying of mines in Nicaraguan internal or territorial waters in early 1984;

· certain attacks on Nicaraguan ports, oil installations and a naval base.

These activities constitute infringements of the principle of the prohibition of the use of force, defined earlier, unless they are justified by circumstances which exclude their unlawfulness, a question now to be examined.

228. As to the claim that United States activities in relation to the contras constitute a breach of the customary international law principle of the non-use of force, the Court finds that, subject to the question whether the action of the United States might be justified as an exercise of the right of self-defence, the United States has committed a prima facie violation of that principle by its assistance to the contras in Nicaragua, by 'organizing or encouraging the organization of irregular forces or armed bands . . . for incursion into the territory of another State,' and 'participating in acts of civil strife . . . in another State,' in the terms of General Assembly resolution 2625 (XXV). In the view of the Court, while the arming and training of the contras can certainly be said to involve the threat or use of force against Nicaragua, this is not necessarily so in respect of all the assistance given by the United States Government. In particular, the Court considers that the mere supply of funds to the contras, while undoubtedly an act of intervention in the internal affairs of Nicaragua, as will be explained below, does not in itself amount to a use of force.

229. The Court must thus consider whether, as the Respondent claims, the acts in question of the United States are justified by the exercise of its right of collective self-defence against an armed attack. For the Court to conclude that the United States was lawfully exercising its right of collective self-defence, it must first find that Nicaragua engaged in an armed attack against El Salvador, Honduras or Costa Rica.

230. As regards El Salvador, the Court has found that between July 1979 and the early months of 1981, an intermittent flow of arms was routed via the territory of Nicaragua to the armed opposition in that country. The Court was not however satisfied that assistance has reached the Salvadorian armed opposition, on a scale of any significance, since the early months of 1981, or that the Government of Nicaragua was responsible for any flow of arms at either period. Even assuming that the supply of arms to the opposition in El Salvador could be treated as imputable to the Government of Nicaragua, to justify invocation of the right of collective self-defence in customary international law, it would have to be equated with an armed attack by Nicaragua on El Salvador. As stated above, the Court is unable to consider that, in customary international law, the provision of arms to the opposition in another State constitutes an armed attack on that State. Even at a time when the arms flow was at its peak, and again assuming the participation of the Nicaraguan Government, that would not constitute such armed attack.

231. Turning to Honduras and Costa Rica, the Court has also stated that it should find established that certain transborder incursions into the territory of those two States, in 1982, 1983 and 1984, were imputable to the Government of Nicaragua. Very little information is however available to the Court as to the circumstances of these incursions or their possible motivations, which renders it difficult to decide whether they may be treated for legal purposes as amounting, singly or collectively, to an 'armed attack' by Nicaragua on either or both States.

232. The exercise of the right of collective self-defence presupposes that an armed attack has occurred; and it is evident that it is the victim State, being the most directly aware of that fact, which is likely to draw general attention to its plight. It is also evident that if the victim State wishes another State to come to its help in the exercise of the right of collective self-defence, it will normally make an express request to that effect. Thus in the present instance, the Court is entitled to take account, in judging the asserted justification of the exercise of collective self-defence by the United States, of the actual conduct of El Salvador, Honduras and Costa Rica at the relevant time, as indicative of a belief by the State in question that it was the victim of an armed attack by Nicaragua, and of the making of a request by the victim State to the United States for help in the exercise of collective self-defence.

233. The Court has seen no evidence that the conduct of those States was consistent with such a situation, either at the time when the United States first embarked on the activities which were allegedly justified by self-defence, or indeed for a long period

subsequently. So far as El Salvador is concerned, it appears to the Court that while El Salvador did in fact officially declare itself the victim of an armed attack, and did ask for the United States to exercise its right of collective self-defence, this occurred only on a date much later than the commencement of the United States activities which were allegedly justified by this request.

234. As to Honduras and Costa Rica, they also were prompted by the institution of proceedings in this case to address communications to the Court; in neither of these is there mention of armed attack or collective self-defence.

235. There is also an aspect of the conduct of the United States which the Court is entitled to take into account as indicative of the view of that State on the question of the existence of an armed attack. At no time, up to the present, has the United States Government addressed to the Security Council, in connection with the matters the subject of the present case, the report which is required by Article 51 of the United Nations Charter in respect of measures which a State believes itself bound to take when it exercises the right of individual or collective self-defence. This fact is all the more noteworthy because, in the Security Council, the United States has itself taken the view that failure to observe the requirement to make a report contradicted a State's claim to be acting on the basis of collective self-defence.

237. Since the Court has found that the condition *sine qua non* required for the exercise of the right of collective self-defence by the United States is not fulfilled in this case, the appraisal of the United States activities in relation to the criteria of necessity and proportionality takes on a different significance. As a result of this conclusion of the Court, even if the United States activities in question had been carried on in strict compliance with the canons of necessity and proportionality, they would not thereby become lawful. If however they were not, this may constitute an additional ground of wrongfulness.

241. It appears to the Court to be clearly established first, that the United States intended, by its support of the contras, to coerce the Government of Nicaragua in respect of matters in which each State is permitted, by the principle of State sovereignty, to decide freely; and secondly that the intention of the contras themselves was to overthrow the present Government of Nicaragua. The Court considers that in international law, if one State, with a view to the coercion of another State, supports and assists armed bands in that State whose purpose is to overthrow the government of that State, that amounts to an intervention by the one State in the internal affairs of the other, whether or not the political objective of the State giving such support and assistance is equally farreaching. It is for this reason that the Court has only examined the intentions of the United States Government so far as they bear on the question of self-defence.

242. The Court therefore finds that the support given by the United States, up to the end of September 1984, to the military and paramilitary activities of the contras in Nicaragua, by financial support, training, supply of weapons, intelligence and logistic support, constitutes a clear breach of the principle of non-intervention. The Court has however taken note that, with effect from the beginning of the United States governmental financial year 1985, namely 1 October 1984, the United States Congress has restricted the use of the funds appropriated for assistance to the contras to 'humanitarian assistance.' There can be no doubt that the provision of strictly humanitarian aid to persons or forces in another country, whatever their political affiliations or objectives, cannot be regarded as unlawful intervention, or as in any other way contrary to international law.

252. These violations cannot be justified either by collective self-defence, for which, as the Court has recognized, the necessary circumstances are lacking, nor by any right of the United States to take counter-measures involving the use of force in the event of intervention by Nicaragua in El Salvador, since no such right exists under the applicable international law. They cannot be justified by the activities in El Salvador attributed to

the Government of Nicaragua. The latter activities, assuming that they did in fact occur, do not bring into effect any right belonging to the United States which would justify the actions in question. Accordingly, such actions constitute violations of Nicaragua's sovereignty under customary international law.

256. It is also appropriate to recall the circumstances in which the manual of psychological operations was issued. When considering whether the publication of such a manual, encouraging the commission of acts contrary to general principles of humanitarian law, is unlawful, it is material to consider whether that encouragement was offered to persons in circumstances where the commission of such acts was likely or foreseeable. The Court has however found that at the relevant time those responsible for the issue of the manual were aware of, at the least, allegations that the behaviour of the contras in the field was not consistent with humanitarian law; it was in fact even claimed by the CIA that the purpose of the manual was to 'moderate' such behaviour. The publication and dissemination of a manual in fact containing the advice quoted above must therefore be regarded as an encouragement, which was likely to be effective, to commit acts contrary to general principles of international humanitarian law reflected in treaties.

DISSENTING OPINION OF JUDGE SCHWEBEL.

1. To say that I dissent from the Court's Judgment is to understate the depth of my differences with it. I agree with the Court's finding that the United States, by failing to make known the existence and location of the mines laid by it, acted in violation of customary international law (in relation to the shipping of third States); I agree that the CIA's causing publication of a manual advocating acts in violation of the law of war is indefensible; and I agree with some other elements of the Judgment as well. Nevertheless, in my view the Judgment misperceives and misconstrues essential facts — not so much the facts concerning the actions of the United States of which Nicaragua complains as the facts concerning the actions of Nicaragua of which the United States complains. It misconceives and misapplies the law — not in all respects, on some of which the whole Court is agreed, but in paramount respects: particularly in its interpretation of what is an 'armed attack' within the meaning of the United Nations Charter and customary international law; in its appearing to justify foreign intervention in furtherance of 'the process of decolonization'; and in nearly all of its holdings as to which Party to this case has acted in violation of its international responsibilities and which, because it has acted defensively, has not. And, I am profoundly pained to say, I dissent from this Judgment because I believe that, in effect, it adopts the false testimony of representatives of the Government of the Republic of Nicaragua on a matter which, in my view, is essential to the disposition of this case and which, on any view, is material to its disposition. The effect of the Court's treatment of that false testimony upon the validity of the Judgment is a question which only others can decide.

2. These are uncommonly critical words in a Court which rightly enjoys very great respect. Coming as they do from a Judge who is a national of a Party to the case, I am conscious of the fact that this opinion accordingly is long, not only for that reason but because the differences between the Court's views and mine turn particularly on the facts.

7. While United States pressure upon Nicaragua is essentially lawful, nevertheless questions about the legality of aspects of United States conduct remain. In my view, the fundamental question is this. Granting that the United States can join El Salvador in measures of collective self-defence (even if, contrary to Article 51 of the United Nations Charter, they were not reported to the United Nations Security Council, as, by their nature, covert defensive measures will not be), those measures must be necessary, and proportionate to the delicts — the actions tantamount to armed attack — of Nicaragua. And they must in their nature be fundamentally measures of self-defence.

8. By these standards, the unannounced mining by the United States of Nicaraguan ports was a violation of international law. That mining could affect and did affect third

States as against whom no rationale of self-defence could apply in these circumstances. As against Nicaragua, however, the mining was no less lawful than other measures of pressure.

9. Are United States support of the contras and direct United States assaults on Nicaraguan oil tanks, ports and pipelines, as well as other measures such as intelligence overflights, military and naval manoeuvres, and a trade embargo, unnecessary and disproportionate acts of self-defence? I do not believe so. Their necessity is, or arguably is, indicated by recurrent, persistent Nicaraguan failure to cease armed subversion of El Salvador. To the extent that proportionality of defensive measures is required, in their nature, far from being disproportionate to the acts against which they are a defence, the actions of the United States are strikingly proportionate. The Salvadoran rebels, vitally supported by Nicaragua, conduct a rebellion in El Salvador; in collective self-defence, the United States symmetrically supports rebels who conduct a rebellion in Nicaragua. The rebels in El Salvador pervasively attack economic targets of importance in El Salvador; the United States selectively attacks economic targets of military importance, such as ports and oil stocks, in Nicaragua. Even if it be accepted, arguendo, that the current object of United States policy is to overthrow the Nicaraguan Government — and that is by no means established — that is not necessarily disproportionate to the obvious object of Nicaragua in supporting the Salvadoran rebels who seek overthrow of the Government of El Salvador. To say, as did Nicaraguan counsel, that action designed to overthrow a government cannot be defensive, is evident error, which would have come as a surprise to Roosevelt and Churchill (and Stalin), who insisted on the unconditional surrender of the Axis Powers.

NOTES AND QUESTIONS

1. **Settlement with Nicaragua.** The ICJ announced on September 26, 1991, that Nicaragua had chosen to "discontinue" the proceedings. "The Sandinista regime and the Contras successfully concluded direct negotiations on a cease-fire in meetings held at Sapoá, Nicaragua, during June 1988. In February 1989, the five Central American presidents met once again in Costa del Sol, El Salvador, and agreed on a plan to support the disarming and dissolving of Contra forces in Honduras, as well as their voluntary repatriation into Nicaragua." Library of Congress, Country Studies, Nicaragua, *available at* http://countrystudies.us/nicaragua/18.htm.

2. **Assistance as Armed Attack.** One critical feature of the *Nicaragua* opinion is its holding that "the supply of arms and other support to [opposition] bands cannot be equated with armed attack." The concurring opinion of Judge Ruda elaborated further:

> I fully agree with this statement and others made by the Court in the same sense. It does not mean, however, that assistance to rebels in another country could not be considered illegal under other rules of international law, such as the obligation not to intervene in the internal affairs of another State and to refrain in international relations from the threat or use of force.

3. **International Humanitarian Law.** The reasons for considering international law of armed conflict and international humanitarian law as part of the law of terrorism become more clear as the law develops through these international courts. Common Article 3 of the Geneva Conventions of 1949 is described in the *Nicaragua* opinion as setting out minimum standards of humanitarian law applying to armed conflicts of both international and non-international character. This provision became a focal point for the question of whether international law could be applied to authorize criminal punishment for some of the gross abuses occurring in the former Yugoslavia and Rwanda in the early 1990s. Because much of the behavior in those situations fits some of the classic definitions of "terrorism," the use of Common Article 3 as a source of criminal law may become important in a number of situations. Therefore, we will consider it more thoroughly in the context of the International Criminal Tribunals for Yugoslavia and Rwanda.

4. Iran Hostages. In November 1979, the United States filed a petition in the ICJ against Iran for allowing the seizure and continued detention of hostages from the U.S. Embassy in Tehran. On May 24, 1980, the ICJ issued its opinion holding that, even if the Government of Iran were not responsible for the initial seizure of the embassy and its personnel, it had an obligation under various international multilateral conventions on the protection of diplomatic and consular personnel to secure the release of those held hostage and to return control of the premises to the U.S. http://www.icj-cij.org/icjwww/icases/iusir/iusir_ijudgment /iusir_iJudgment_19800524.pdf. The U.S. exerted pressure on Iran by freezing assets of Iran held in the U.S., such as billions of dollars in U.S. financial institutions. Release of the hostages was finally secured on the last day of President Carter's administration through a complicated Executive Agreement that was the subject of domestic litigation in *Dames & Moore v. Regan*, 453 U.S. 654 (1981). There could be an apparent inconsistency in the U.S. position in the *Iran* and *Nicaragua* cases regarding the ICJ jurisdiction to interpret and enforce multilateral treaties. But the Iranian situation did not involve an ongoing state of armed conflict. Does this make ICJ jurisdiction dependent on whether the parties decide to resort to armed force to resolve their disputes?

5. Non-territorial Aspirations. Many of the violence-prone religious-cultural groups in the Third Millennium are formed around religious fundamentalism. Few of these groups have a motivation to control any particular territory, although driving all Westerners from Muslim lands could be counted as a political objective. Does lack of a motivation to control certain territory make these groups something other than belligerents in character? This issue is important in the application of the label of "combatant" in Chapter 8.

CASE CONCERNING LEGALITY OF USE OF FORCE (YUGOSLAVIA v. BELGIUM) [NATO]
1999 I.C.J. 124

[Identical petitions were filed by Yugoslavia against each of the member nations of NATO. Yugoslavia made a "request for provisional measures," which is the rough equivalent of a motion for preliminary injunction.]

1. Whereas Yugoslavia defines the subject of the dispute as follows:

"The subject-matter of the dispute are acts of the Kingdom of Belgium by which it has violated its international obligation banning the use of force against another State, the obligation not to intervene in the internal affairs of another State, the obligation not to violate the sovereignty of another State, the obligation to protect the civilian population and civilian objects in wartime, the obligation to protect the environment, the obligation relating to free navigation on international rivers, the obligation regarding fundamental human rights and freedoms, the obligation not to use prohibited weapons, the obligation not to deliberately inflict conditions of life calculated to cause the physical destruction of a national group";

3. Whereas Yugoslavia states that the claims submitted by it to the Court are based upon the following facts:

The Government of the Kingdom of Belgium, together with the Governments of other Member States of NATO, took part in the acts of use of force against the Federal Republic of Yugoslavia by taking part in bombing targets in the Federal Republic of Yugoslavia. In bombing the Federal Republic of Yugoslavia military and civilian targets were attacked. Great number of people were killed, including a great many civilians. Residential houses came under attack. Numerous dwellings were destroyed. Enormous damage was caused to schools, hospitals, radio and television stations, cultural and health institutions and to places of worship. A large number of bridges, roads and railway lines were destroyed. Attacks on oil refineries and chemical plants have had serious environmental effects on cities, towns and villages in the Federal Republic of Yugoslavia. The use of weapons containing depleted uranium is having far-reaching consequences for human life. The above-mentioned acts are deliberately creating conditions calculated at the physical destruction of an ethnic group, in whole or in part. The Government of the Kingdom of Belgium is taking part in the training, arming, financing, equipping and supplying the so-called 'Kosovo Liberation Army.'

6. Whereas, in support of its request for the indication of provisional measures, Yugoslavia contends inter alia that, since the onset of the bombing of its territory, and as a result thereof, about 1,000 civilians, including 19 children, have been killed and more than 4,500 have sustained serious injuries; that the lives of three million children are endangered; that hundreds of thousands of citizens have been exposed to poisonous gases; that about one million citizens are short of water supply; that about 500,000 workers have become jobless; that two million citizens have no means of livelihood and are unable to ensure minimum means of sustenance; and that the road and railway network has suffered extensive destruction.

16. Whereas the Court is deeply concerned with the human tragedy, the loss of life, and the enormous suffering in Kosovo which form the background of the present dispute, and with the continuing loss of life and human suffering in all parts of Yugoslavia;

17. Whereas the Court is profoundly concerned with the use of force in Yugoslavia; whereas under the present circumstances such use raises very serious issues of international law;

18. Whereas the Court is mindful of the purposes and principles of the United Nations Charter and of its own responsibilities in the maintenance of peace and security under the Charter and the Statute of the Court;

19. Whereas the Court deems it necessary to emphasize that all parties appearing before it must act in conformity with their obligations under the United Nations Charter and other rules of international law, including humanitarian law;

48. Whereas, whether or not States accept the jurisdiction of the Court, they remain in any event responsible for acts attributable to them that violate international law, including humanitarian law; whereas any disputes relating to the legality of such acts are required to be resolved by peaceful means, the choice of which, pursuant to Article 33 of the Charter, is left to the parties;

49. Whereas in this context the parties should take care not to aggravate or extend the dispute;

50. Whereas, when such a dispute gives rise to a threat to the peace, breach of the peace or act of aggression, the Security Council has special responsibilities under Chapter VII of the Charter;

51. For these reasons,

THE COURT,

(1) By twelve votes to four,

Rejects the request for the indication of provisional measures submitted by the Federal Republic of Yugoslavia on 29 April 1999;

(2) By fifteen votes to one,

Reserves the subsequent procedure for further decision.

NOTES AND QUESTIONS

1. **ICJ Outcome.** On December 15, 2004, the ICJ dismissed the various actions challenging the use of force by NATO nations in the Yugoslav conflict. It found that Serbia and Montenegro did not exist between 1992 and 2000, when they were admitted

to the UN as a separate nation under the name of Yugoslavia. Therefore, there was no state party to appear before the court with regard to the time at which the armed intervention occurred. To Professor Eric Posner, this decision

> demonstrated just how incapable the court is of resolving disputes, and what little hope the new International Criminal Court has to do much better. First, there is no doubt that, in strictly legal terms, NATO's intervention violated international standards. . . . [T]he court was in an unenviable position: if it had held against the NATO states, they would surely have ignored the judgment. By holding in favor of these states, the court showed its irrelevance.

Eric A. Posner, *All Justice, Too, Is Local*, N.Y. TIMES, Dec. 30, 2004.

2. Multilateral Intervention. The ICJ statement that it was "profoundly concerned with the use of force in Yugoslavia; whereas under the present circumstances such use raises very serious issues of international law" has become a focal point for debate over the propriety of humanitarian intervention without Security Council authorization. The "serious issues" included whether NATO could act without UN sanction. In fact, the European nations came under heavy criticism for delaying action while they engaged in a long debate over whether to intervene in the bloodshed and "ethnic cleansing" taking place in the republics of the former Yugoslavia. There was very little thought given at the time to seeking Security Council intervention, at least partly because it was not clear that the attempts of these republics to break away from Yugoslavia created an "international" dispute rather than a civil war (i.e., an armed conflict not of an international character).

Arguments over the validity of NATO's bombing campaign also were pursued through the forum of the International Criminal Tribunal for Yugoslavia (ICTY) established by the UN Security Council. The work of the ICTY will be considered in the next section. For now, it is enough to know that the Tribunal has criminal jurisdiction over war crimes committed during the conflict. To assess the assertion that the NATO bombing was illegal both in its inception and in its targeting decisions, the Prosecutor appointed a committee to review the available evidence. The Committee report included this statement regarding the legality of the bombing in its inception:

> Allegations have been made that, as NATO's resort to force was not authorized by the Security Council or in self-defence, that the resort to force was illegal and, consequently, all forceful measures taken by NATO were unlawful. These allegations justify a brief discussion of the *jus ad bellum*. In brief, the *jus ad bellum* regulates when states may use force and is, for the most part, enshrined in the UN Charter. In general, states may use force in self defence (individual or collective) and for very few other purposes. In particular, the legitimacy of the presumed basis for the NATO bombing campaign, humanitarian intervention without prior Security Council authorization, is hotly debated. That being said, . . . the crime related to an unlawful decision to use force is the crime against peace or aggression. While a person convicted of a crime against peace may, potentially, be held criminally responsible for all of the activities causing death, injury or destruction during a conflict, the ICTY does not have jurisdiction over crimes against peace.
>
> The *jus in bello* regulates how states may use force. The ICTY has jurisdiction over serious violations of international humanitarian law as specified in Articles 2-5 of the Statute. These are *jus in bello* offences.
>
> The precise linkage between *jus ad bellum* and *jus in bello* is not completely resolved. There were suggestions by the prosecution before the International Military Tribunal at Nuremberg and in some other post World War II war crimes cases that all of the killing and destruction caused by German forces were war crimes because the Germans were conducting an aggressive war. The courts were unreceptive to these arguments.

www.un.org/icty/pressreal/nato061300.htm at ¶ 30–32.

3. Darfur. As of early 2008, a similar dispute is raging over the responsibility of other nations or the United Nations to act in the "internal" bloodbath occurring in Darfur in the Sudan. European nations and the U.S. have condemned the Sudanese government for massive human rights violations, either actively or passively allowing unofficial groups to massacre civilians. From the UN perspective, one question is whether the situation amounts to a threat to "international peace and security" and another is whether it would be in the long-term interests of the world community to promote regional solutions to problems of this type. The African Union has attempted to promote ceasefire and humanitarian aid to the region, but its troops have received heavy casualties. An excellent summary of the situation is provided by Human Rights Watch at http://hrw.org/reports/2007/sudan0907/.

4. Afghanistan. Shortly after 9/11, U.S. intelligence agencies identified al Qaeda as the perpetrator of the incidents and identified the Taliban regime in Afghanistan as harboring and fostering the operations of the organization. The U.S. Congress adopted this resolution:

> That the President is authorized to use all necessary and appropriate force against those nations, organizations, or persons he determines planned, authorized, committed, or aided the terrorist attacks that occurred on September 11, 2001, or harbored such organizations or persons, in order to prevent any future acts of international terrorism against the United States by such nations, organizations or persons.

PUB. LAW 107-40 [S.J. Res. 23] (Sept. 18, 2001).

The resolution was widely understood at the time to refer primarily to Afghanistan although, only one week after the incidents, it was not entirely clear which countries could be found to have been involved. In passing this resolution, Congress declined to act on this proposed language: "Congress hereby declares that a state of war exists between the United States of America and any entity determined by the President to have planned, carried out, or otherwise supported the attacks against the United States on September 11, 2001."

There are two theories under which the U.S. invaded Afghanistan. One is that Afghanistan "harbored" terrorists to the extent that the terrorists became essentially the agents of that government, thus moving from the class of mere criminal to agents of war. Because those agents violated the rules of war by taking aggression, by striking civilian targets, and by blending back into civilian populations, other nations were justified in using military force to retaliate and prevent further attack.

The second theory harkens back to the piracy and slave trading of the eighteenth and nineteenth Centuries. "From the Halls to Montezuma to the shores of Tripoli" salutes the actions of Marines who rooted out pirate strongholds located in other nations. Other nations of the world were never called on to decide whether our actions were legitimate. Similarly, the European-American nations were in disarray over whether it was legitimate to strike militarily against slave depots and slave trading ships within the boundaries of other nations. Suffice to say that time and history are on the side of the victors in those cases. Today there is near, but not complete, consensus that it is permissible to make "surgical" incursions into another country to root out a pirate or slave trader to an extent that would not be permissible with a "mere" criminal.

There has been virtually no dissent from the proposition that the U.S. was within its rights under international law to invade Afghanistan for the purpose of disrupting the activities of al Qaeda. Afghanistan had refused to turn over those responsible for what could be considered an "armed attack" on the U.S., an obligation that would exist regardless of whether those persons could be considered agents of the government of Afghanistan. In the process, the invasion went further by toppling the Taliban regime and installing a new regime friendly to the West. Is "overthrow of the government" of another nation illegal in the absence of finding that that government had engaged in an "armed attack" against the U.S.? Recall the ICJ's statement that funding and support of an armed band is not itself an armed attack.

In this regard, also bear in mind the political and cultural fallout of the widespread characterization of the Taliban regime as brutal and despotic (women in particular were brutalized under its power). For those who applaud the humanitarian response of bringing some degree of liberty to Afghanistan, there are others who view the U.S. intrusion as part of an ongoing "Crusade" against Islam.

5. Iraq. By contrast to Afghanistan, the U.S. invasion of Iraq has brought widespread criticism. *See* Arthur Schlesinger, Jr., *The Making of a Mess*, 51 N.Y. REVIEW OF BOOKS, Sept. 23, 2004, *reviewing* JAMES BAMFORD, A PRETEXT FOR WAR: 9/11, IRAQ, AND THE ABUSE OF AMERICA'S INTELLIGENCE NETWORKS (2004) *and* JAMES MANN, RISE OF THE VULCANS: THE HISTORY OF BUSH'S WAR CABINET (2004).

The initial arguments for the invasion were (1) humanitarian intervention, on the basis that the Saddam Hussein regime was a brutal dictatorship committing multiple crimes against its own people, (2) self-defense, on the basis that Iraq was harboring elements of al Qaeda engaged in an ongoing campaign against western nations, and (3) preemptive self-defense, on the basis that Iraq was attempting to acquire weapons of mass destruction (WMD) and would allow them to be used against the U.S.

As events unfolded, it became apparent that the WMD justification was based on faulty intelligence. The al Qaeda connection also proved to be unlikely. It is likely that prior to the invasion, Osama bin Laden had some degree of hostility toward Saddam Hussein along with other "secular" Arab leaders, but Iraq had harbored Abu Musab al-Zarqawi who had been sentenced to death by Jordan for various terrorist activities. Zarqawi may or may not have had links to bin Laden prior to the invasion, and intelligence sources differed on whether he was an associate of or a rival to bin Laden. After the invasion, elements of groups linked to al Qaeda, particularly Zarqawi and his associates, concentrated in Iraq and become principals in some of the insurgent resistance. Zarqawi has subsequently declared himself to be in alliance with al Qaeda.

The third justification, humanitarian intervention, seems forbidden in the absence of at least multilateral action of the NATO-Yugoslavia variety or more formal UN Security Council action. The official U.S. position became difficult to discern in the partisan politics of the 2004 presidential campaign. The Bush campaign combined humanitarian intervention with the preemptive self-defense rationale and made an argument for "exporting democracy." The Kerry campaign promoted the view that armed force, outside of imminent self-defense, should be employed only if it passed a "global test."

Although doubts about the legality of the Iraq invasion persist in both the academic and popular press, a widespread acceptance seems to be emerging from a number of sources, both Government and NGO, that the international community should have some role to play in bringing freedom and democracy to oppressed peoples. *See* NOAH FELDMAN, AFTER JIHAD (2003). Whether this rhetoric could develop into a full-blown justification for armed intervention in the affairs of another nation will have to await further developments.

Finally, a number of critics have argued that one effect of the Iraq invasion was to reduce the resources applied to the effort to apprehend Osama bin Laden. *See* Peter Bergen, *The Long Hunt for Osama*, ATLANTIC MONTHLY 88 (Oct. 2004); James Fallows, *Bush's Lost Year*, ATLANTIC MONTHLY 68 (Oct. 2004).

§ 6.02 DEVELOPING INTERNATIONAL CRIMINAL LAW

International action to control violence comes in two forms. One is cooperation among states, traditionally consisting of extradition of alleged offenders by one state for trial in another, and in recent years emerging as codified agreements to cooperate in the detection, apprehension, and prosecution of offenders. The other, and much more recent, phenomenon is collective action in the form of supranational tribunals.

We will look at these in reverse order, however, to form a more logical progression leading toward both international and American law related to terrorism. One outgrowth of prosecution of war crimes at the end of World War II has been international tribunals for atrocities in "internal" conflicts that yield a number of legal principles regarding criminal responsibility for attacks on civilian populations. These developments parallel the establishment of an International Criminal Court. If there develops an international crime of terrorism, which could evolve from the crimes of humanitarian law, then a number of implications would follow from the traditional approaches that include extradition of offenders. Some of this possibility is hinted in the *Pinochet* case at the end of this chapter.

American students may find familiar themes in trial of an offender under state law compared with definition and prosecution of crimes by the federal government. If you think that Utah is to the U.S. as the U.S. is to international bodies, then some of the lessons of American federalism can be transported to the international scene. Of course, some significant differences make the analogy far less than perfect.

Starting with Nuremberg, the international community began to impose individual criminal sanctions for serious violations of the law of war, genocide, and crimes against humanity. The first effort of this type under United Nations auspices was establishment of the International Criminal Tribunal for the Former Yugoslavia in 1993, followed closely by the International Criminal Tribunal for Rwanda in 1994. The UN, working through its International Law Commission, promulgated a convention to create a permanent international tribunal for prosecution of crimes against the law of war, genocide, and crimes against humanity, now known as the International Criminal Court (ICC).

[A]   World War II "War Crimes" Tribunals

We start our reading with the Judgment of the International Military Tribunal created for the purpose of trying Nazi war criminals by the victorious parties after World War II. The Charter of the IMT was adopted through the Treaty of London as a project of the four victorious powers (U.S., Britain, France, USSR). It lists three categories of crimes: crimes against peace (aggression), war crimes, and crimes against humanity. The IMT conducted one trial, known generally as the Trial of Major War Criminals. In addition to the trial of major leaders, the four occupying forces adopted Control Council Law No. 10, which repeated the definition of crimes and authorized each military authority to conduct trials of lower-level Nazi officials. Under this order, the U.S. conducted 12 additional trials in Germany.

Excerpts from the Major War Crimes Trial appear below. On the assumption that you are familiar with the atrocities of the Nazi regime, the excerpts omit recitation of the atrocities themselves and the specific evidence with respect to each defendant. Twenty-two persons were indicted and tried by the tribunal (two more were indicted but not tried, one committed suicide and the other was too frail). Twelve were sentenced to death, three to life imprisonment, four to prison ranging from 10 to 20 years, and three were acquitted. Ten of the twelve sentenced to death were hanged on October 16, 1946. (Hermann Göring committed suicide just three hours before the hanging. Martin Bormann was tried in absentia and sentenced to death but it was later discovered that he had died.) Rudolf Hess was the controversial deputy to Hitler who flew to England in 1941, ostensibly to negotiate a peace without Hitler's approval; he was sentenced to life in prison and for decades was the only inmate of Spandau Prison in Berlin until his death at the age of 93 in 1987. The three persons acquitted at Nuremberg were sentenced by other courts to work camps. Conversely, Alfred Jodl was hanged but posthumously found by a German court to be not guilty of violating international law.

INTERNATIONAL MILITARY TRIBUNAL (NUREMBERG)

Nuremberg, 30th September and 1st October, 1946

THE PRESIDENT: The judgment of the International Military Tribunal will now be read. I shall not read the title and the formal parts.

JUDGMENT

On the 8th August, 1945, the Government of the United Kingdom of Great Britain and Northern Ireland, the Government of the United States of America, the Provisional Government of the French Republic, and the Government of the Union of Soviet Socialist Republics entered into an Agreement establishing this Tribunal for the trial of War Criminals whose offences have no particular geographical location.

The Tribunal was invested with power to try and punish persons who had committed crimes against peace, war crimes and crimes against humanity as defined in the Charter

This Indictment charges the defendants with crimes against peace by the planning, preparation, initiation and waging of wars of aggression, which were also wars in violation of international treaties, agreements and assurances: with war crimes: and with crimes against humanity. The defendants are also charged with participating in the formulation or execution of a common plan or conspiracy to commit all these crimes. The Tribunal was further asked by the Prosecution to declare all the named groups or organisations to be criminal within the meaning of the Charter.

On the 17th November, 1945, the Tribunal decided to try the defendant Bormann in his absence under the provisions of Article 12 of the Charter. After argument, and consideration of full medical reports, and a statement from the defendant himself, the Tribunal decided on the 1st December, 1945, that no grounds existed for a postponement of the trial against the defendant Hess because of his mental condition. A similar decision was made in the case of the defendant Streicher.

The Trial [lasted 9 months and involved dozens of witnesses and thousands of documents].

Much of the evidence presented to the Tribunal on behalf of the Prosecution was documentary evidence, captured by the Allied armies in German army headquarters, Government buildings, and elsewhere. Some of the documents were found in salt mines, buried in the ground, hidden behind false walls and in other places thought to be secure from discovery. The case, therefore, against the defendants rests in a large measure on documents of their own making, the authenticity of which has not been challenged except in one or two cases.

LAW OF THE CHARTER

The making of the Charter was the exercise of the sovereign legislative power by the countries to which the German Reich unconditionally surrendered; and the undoubted right of these countries to legislate for the occupied territories has been recognised by the civilised world. The Charter is not an arbitrary exercise of power on the part of the victorious nations, but in the view of the Tribunal, as will be shown, it is the expression of international law existing at the time of its creation; and to that extent is itself a contribution to international law.

The Signatory Powers created this Tribunal, defined the law it was to administer, and made regulations for the proper conduct of the Trial. In doing so, they have done together what any one of them might have done singly; for it is not to be doubted that any nation has the right thus to set up special courts to administer law. With regard to the constitution of the court, all that the defendants are entitled to ask is to receive a fair trial on the facts and law.

The Charter makes the planning or waging of a war of aggression or a war in violation of international treaties a crime, and it is therefore not strictly necessary to consider whether and to what extent aggressive war was a crime before the execution of the London Agreement. But in view of the great importance of the questions of law involved, the Tribunal has heard full argument from the Prosecution and the Defence, and will express its view on the matter.

It was urged on behalf of the defendants that a fundamental principle of all law — international and domestic — is that there can be no punishment of crime without a pre-existing law. "*Nullum crimen sine lege. Nulla poena sine lege.*" It was submitted that ex post facto punishment is abhorrent to the law of all civilised nations, that no sovereign power had made aggressive war a crime at the time the alleged criminal acts were committed, that no statute had defined aggressive war, that no penalty had been fixed for its commission, and no court had been created to try and punish offenders.

In the first place, it is to be observed that the maxim *nullum crimen sine lege* is not a limitation of sovereignty, but is in general a principle of justice. To assert that it is unjust to punish those who in defiance of treaties and assurances have attacked neighbouring states without warning is obviously untrue, for in such circumstances the attacker must know that he is doing wrong, and so far from it being unjust to punish him, it would be unjust if his wrong were allowed to go unpunished.

This view is strongly reinforced by a consideration of the state of international law in 1939, so far as aggressive war is concerned. The General Treaty for the Renunciation of War of 27th August, 1928, more generally known as the Pact of Paris or the Kellogg-Briand Pact, was binding on sixty-three nations, including Germany, Italy and Japan at the outbreak of war in 1939. The first two Articles are as follows:

> Article I: The High Contracting Parties solemnly declare in the names of their respective peoples that they condemn recourse to war for the solution of international controversies and renounce it as an instrument of national policy in their relations to one another.

> Article II: The High Contracting Parties agree that the settlement or solution of all disputes or conflicts of whatever nature or of whatever origin they may be, which may arise among them, shall never be sought except by pacific means.

The question is, what was the legal effect of this Pact? The nations who signed the Pact or adhered to it unconditionally condemned recourse to war for the future as an instrument of policy, and expressly renounced it. In the opinion of the Tribunal, the solemn renunciation of war as an instrument of national policy necessarily involves the proposition that such a war is illegal in international law; and that those who plan and wage such a war, with its inevitable and terrible consequences, are committing a crime in so doing.

But it is argued that the Pact does not expressly enact that such wars are crimes, or set up courts to try those who make such wars. To that extent the same is true with regard to the laws of war contained in the Hague Convention. The Hague Convention of 1907 prohibited resort to certain methods of waging war. These included the inhumane treatment of prisoners, the employment of poisoned weapons, the improper use of flags of truce, and similar matters. Many of these prohibitions had been enforced long before the date of the Convention; but since 1907 they have certainly been crimes, punishable as offences against the laws of war; yet the Hague Convention nowhere designates such practices as criminal, nor is any sentence prescribed, nor any mention made of a court to try and punish offenders. For many years past, however, military tribunals have tried and punished individuals guilty of violating the rules of land warfare laid down by this Convention. In the opinion of the Tribunal, those who wage aggressive war are doing that which is equally illegal, and of much greater moment than a breach of one of the rules of the Hague Convention. In interpreting the words of the Pact, it must be remembered that international law is not the product of an international legislature, and that such international agreements as the Pact have to deal with general principles of law, and not with administrative matters of procedure. The law of war is to be found not only in treaties, but in the customs and practices of states which gradually obtained universal recognition, and from the general principles of justice applied by jurists and practiced by military courts. This law is not static, but by continual adaptation follows the needs of a changing world. Indeed, in many cases treaties do no more than express and define for more accurate reference the principles of law already existing.

The view which the Tribunal takes of the true interpretation of the Pact is supported by the international history which preceded it. In the year 1923 the draft of a Treaty of Mutual Assistance was sponsored by the League of Nations. In Article I the Treaty declared "that aggressive war is an international crime," and that the parties would "undertake that no one of them will be guilty of its commission." The draft treaty was submitted to twenty-nine States, about half of whom were in favour of accepting the text. The principal objection appeared to be in the difficulty of defining the acts which would constitute "aggression," rather than any doubt as to the criminality of aggressive war.

At the meeting of the Assembly of the League of Nations on the 24th September, 1927, all the delegations then present (including the German, the Italian and the Japanese), unanimously adopted a declaration concerning wars of aggression. The preamble to the declaration stated:

> The Assembly:
>
> Recognising the solidity which unites the community of nations;
>
> Being inspired by a firm desire for the maintenance of general peace;
>
> Being convinced that a war of aggression can never serve as a means of settling international disputes, and is in consequence an international crime.

All these expressions of opinion, and others that could be cited, so solemnly made, reinforce the construction which the Tribunal placed upon the Pact of Paris, that resort to a war of aggression is not merely illegal, but is criminal. The prohibition of aggressive war demanded by the conscience of the world, finds its expression in the series of pacts and treaties to which the Tribunal has just referred.

It is also important to remember that Article 227 of the Treaty of Versailles provided for the constitution of a special Tribunal, composed of representatives of five of the Allied and Associated Powers which had been belligerents in the first World War opposed to Germany, to try the former German Emperor "for a supreme offence against international morality and the sanctity of treaties." The purpose of this trial was expressed to be "to vindicate the solemn obligations of international undertakings, and the validity of international morality." In Article 228 of the Treaty, the German Government expressly recognised the right of the Allied Powers "to bring before military tribunals persons accused of having committed acts in violation of the laws and customs of war."

It was submitted that international law is concerned with the action of sovereign States, and provides no punishment for individuals; and further, that where the act in question is an act of state, those who carry it out are not personally responsible, but are protected by the doctrine of the sovereignty of the State. In the opinion of the Tribunal, both these submissions must be rejected. That international law imposes duties and liabilities upon individuals as well as upon States has long been recognised. In the recent case of *Ex Parte Quirin* (1942 317 U.S. 1), before the Supreme Court of the United States persons were charged during the war with landing in the United States for purposes of spying and sabotage. The late Justice Stone, speaking for the Court, said:

> From the very beginning of its history this Court has applied the law of war as including that part of the law of nations which prescribes for the conduct of war the status, rights and duties of enemy nations as well as enemy individuals.

It was also submitted on behalf of most of these defendants that in doing what they did they were acting under the orders of Hitler, and therefore cannot be held responsible for the acts committed by them in carrying out these orders. The Charter specially provides in Article 8:

> The fact that the defendant acted pursuant to order of his Government or of a superior shall not free him from responsibility, but may the considered in mitigation of punishment.

The provisions of this Article are in conformity with the law of all nations. That a soldier was ordered to kill or torture in violation of the international law of war has never been recognised as a defence to such acts of brutality, though, as the Charter here provides, the order may be urged in mitigation of the punishment. The true test, which is found in varying degrees in the criminal law of most nations, is not the existence of the order, but whether moral choice was in fact possible.

LAW AS TO THE COMMON PLAN OR CONSPIRACY

In the previous recital of the facts relating to aggressive war, it is clear that planning and preparation had been carried out in the most systematic way at every stage of the history.

Planning and preparation are essential to the making of war. In the opinion of the Tribunal aggressive war is a crime under international law. The Charter defines this offence as planning, preparation, initiation or waging of a war of aggression "or participation in a common plan or conspiracy for the accomplishment . . . of the foregoing." The Indictment follows this distinction. Count One charges the common plan or conspiracy. Count Two charges the planning and waging of war. The same evidence has been introduced to support both counts. We shall therefore discuss both counts together, as they are in substance the same. The defendants have been charged under both counts, and their guilt under each count must be determined.

The "common plan or conspiracy" charged in the Indictment covers twenty-five years, from the formation of the Nazi party in 1919 to the end of the war in 1945. The party is spoken of as "the instrument of cohesion among the defendants" for carrying out the purposes of the conspiracy the overthrowing of the Treaty of Versailles, acquiring territory lost by Germany in the last war and "lebensraum" in Europe, by the use, if necessary, of armed force, of aggressive war. The seizure of power by the Nazis, the use of terror, the destruction of trade unions, the attack on Christian teaching and on churches, the persecution of the Jews, the regimentation of youth — all these are said to be steps deliberately taken to carry out the common plan. It found expression, so it is alleged, in secret rearmament, the withdrawal by Germany from the Disarmament Conference and the League of Nations, universal military service, and seizure of the Rhineland. Finally, according to the Indictment, aggressive action was planned and carried out against Austria and Czechoslovakia in 1936–1938, followed by the planning and waging of war against Poland; and, successively, against ten other countries.

The Prosecution says, in effect, that any significant participation in the affairs of the Nazi Party or Government is evidence of a participation in a conspiracy that is in itself criminal. Conspiracy is not defined in the Charter. But in the opinion of the Tribunal the conspiracy must be clearly outlined in its criminal purpose. It must not be too far removed from the time of decision and of action. The planning, to be criminal, must not rest merely on the declarations of a party programme, such as are found in the twenty-five points of the Nazi Party, announced in 1920, or the political affirmations expressed in "Mein Kampf" in later years. The Tribunal must examine whether a concrete plan to wage war existed, and determine the participants in that concrete plan.

It is not necessary to decide whether a single master conspiracy between the defendants has been established by the evidence. But the evidence establishes with certainty the existence of many separate plans rather than a single conspiracy embracing them all. That Germany was rapidly moving to complete dictatorship from the moment that the Nazis seized power, and progressively in the direction of war, has been overwhelmingly shown in the ordered sequence of aggressive acts and wars already set out in this Judgment.

In the opinion of the Tribunal, the evidence establishes the common planning to prepare and wage war by certain of the defendants. It is immaterial to consider whether a single conspiracy to the extent and over the time set out in the Indictment has been conclusively proved. Continued planning, with aggressive war as the objective, has been established beyond doubt.

The argument that such common planning cannot exist where there is complete dictatorship is unsound. A plan in the execution of which a number of persons participate is still a plan, even though conceived by only one of them; and those who execute the plan do not avoid responsibility by showing that they acted under the direction of the man who conceived it. Hitler could not make aggressive war by himself. He had to have the co-operation of statesmen, military leaders, diplomats, and business men. When they, with knowledge of his aims, gave him their co-operation, they made themselves parties to the plan he had initiated. They are not to be deemed innocent because Hitler made use of them, if they knew what they were doing. That they were assigned to their tasks by a dictator does not absolve them from responsibility for their acts. The relation of leader and follower does not preclude responsibility here any more than it does in the comparable tyranny of organised domestic crime.

Count One, however, charges not only the conspiracy to commit aggressive war, but also to commit war crimes and crimes against humanity. But the Charter does not define as a separate crime any conspiracy except the one to commit acts of aggressive war. Article 6 of the Charter provides:

> Leaders, organisers, instigators and accomplices participating in the formulation or execution of a common plan or conspiracy to commit any of the foregoing crimes are responsible for all acts performed by any persons in execution of such plan.

In the opinion of the Tribunal these words do not add a new and separate crime to those already listed. The words are designed to establish the responsibility of persons participating in a common plan. The Tribunal will therefore disregard the charges in Count One that the defendants conspired to commit war crimes and crimes against humanity, and will consider only the common plan to prepare, initiate and wage aggressive war.

War Crimes and Crimes Against Humanity

The evidence relating to war crimes has been overwhelming, in its volume and its detail. It is impossible for this Judgment adequately to review it, or to record the mass of documentary and oral evidence that has been presented. The truth remains that war crimes were committed on a vast scale, never before seen in the history of war. They were perpetrated in all the countries occupied by Germany, and on the High Seas, and were attended by every conceivable circumstance of cruelty and horror. There can be no doubt that the majority of them arose from the Nazi conception of "total war," with which the aggressive wars were waged. For in this conception of "total war," the moral ideas underlying the conventions which seek to make war more humane are no longer regarded as having force or validity. Everything is made subordinate to the overmastering dictates of war. Rules, regulations, assurances and treaties all alike are of no moment, and so, freed from the restraining influence of international law, the aggressive war is conducted by the Nazi leaders in the most barbaric way. Accordingly, war crimes were committed when and wherever the Fuehrer and his close associates thought them to be advantageous. They were for the most part the result of cold and criminal calculation.

On some occasions, war crimes were deliberately planned long in advance. In the case of the Soviet Union, the plunder of the territories to be occupied, and the ill-treatment of the civilian population, were settled in minute detail before the attack was begun.

Similarly, when planning to exploit the inhabitants of the occupied countries for slave labour on the very greatest scale, the German Government conceived it as an integral part of the war economy, and planned and organised this particular war crime down to the last elaborate detail.

Other war crimes, such as the murder of prisoners of war who had escaped and been recaptured, or the murder of Commandos or captured airmen, or the destruction of the Soviet Commissars, were the result of direct orders circulated through the highest official channels.

The Tribunal proposes, therefore, to deal quite generally with the question of war crimes, and to refer to them later when examining the responsibility of the individual defendants in relation to them. Prisoners of war were ill-treated and tortured and murdered, not only in defiance of the well-established rules of international law, but in complete disregard of the elementary dictates of humanity. Civilian populations in occupied territories suffered the same fate. Whole populations were deported to Germany for the purposes of slave labour upon defence works, armament production and similar tasks connected with the war effort. Hostages were taken in very large numbers from the civilian populations in all the occupied countries, and were shot as suited the German purposes. Public and private property was systematically plundered and pillaged in order to enlarge the resources of Germany at the expense of the rest of Europe. Cities and towns and villages were wantonly destroyed without military justification or necessity.

Law Relating to War Crimes and Crimes Against Humanity

Article 6 of the Charter provides:

(b) War Crimes: namely, violations of the laws or customs of war. Such violations shall include, but not be limited to, murder, ill-treatment or deportation to slave labour or for any other purpose of civilian population of or in occupied territory, murder or ill-treatment of prisoners of war or persons on the seas, killing of hostages, plunder of public or private property, wanton destruction of cities, towns or villages. or devastation not justified by military necessity;

(c) Crimes against Humanity: namely, murder, extermination, enslavement, deportation, and other inhumane acts committed against any civilian population, before or during the war, or persecutions on political, racial or religious grounds in execution of or in connection with any crime within the jurisdiction of the Tribunal, whether or not in violation of the domestic law of the country where perpetrated.

As heretofore stated, the Charter does not define as a separate crime any conspiracy except the one set out in Article 6 (a), dealing with crimes against peace.

The Tribunal is of course bound by the Charter, in the definition which it gives both of war crimes and crimes against humanity. With respect to war crimes, however, as has already been pointed out, the crimes defined by Article 6, section (b), of the Charter were already recognised as war crimes under international law. They were covered by the Hague Convention of 1907, and the Geneva Convention of 1929. That violations of these provisions constituted crimes for which the guilty individuals were punishable is too well settled to admit of argument.

But it is argued that the Hague Convention does not apply in this case, because of the "general participation" clause in Article 2 of the Hague Convention of 1907. That clause provided:

The provisions contained in the regulations (Rules of Land Warfare) referred to in Article 1 as well as in the present Convention do not apply except between contracting powers, and then only if all the belligerents are parties to the Convention.

Several of the belligerents in the recent war were not parties to this Convention.

In the opinion of the Tribunal it is not necessary to decide this question. The rules of land warfare expressed in the Convention undoubtedly represented an advance over existing international law at the time of their adoption. But the Convention expressly stated that it was an attempt "to revise the general laws and customs of war," which it thus recognised to be then existing, but by 1939 these rules laid down in the Convention were recognised by all civilised nations, and were regarded as being declaratory of the laws and customs of war which are referred to in Article 6 (b) of the Charter.

A further submission was made that Germany was no longer bound by the rules of land warfare in many of the territories occupied during the war, because Germany had completely subjugated those countries and incorporated them into the German Reich, a fact which gave Germany authority to deal with the occupied countries as though they were part of Germany. In the view of the Tribunal it is unnecessary in this case to decide whether this doctrine of subjugation, dependent as it is upon military conquest, has any application where the subjugation is the result of the crime of aggressive war. The doctrine was never considered to be applicable so long as there was an army in the field attempting to restore the occupied countries to their true owners.

With regard to crimes against humanity, there is no doubt whatever that political opponents were murdered in Germany before the war, and that many of them were kept in concentration camps in circumstances of great horror and cruelty. The policy of terror was certainly carried out on a vast scale, and in many cases was organised and systematic. The policy of persecution, repression and murder of civilians in Germany before the war of 1939, who were likely to be hostile to the Government, was most ruthlessly carried out. The persecution of Jews during the same period is established beyond all doubt.

To constitute crimes against humanity, the acts relied on before the outbreak of war must have been in execution of, or in connection with, any crime within the jurisdiction of the Tribunal. The Tribunal is of the opinion that revolting and horrible as many of these crimes were, it has not been satisfactorily proved that they were done in execution of, or in connection with, any such crime. The Tribunal therefore cannot make a general declaration that the acts before 1939 were crimes against humanity within the meaning of the Charter, but from the beginning of the war in 1939 war crimes were committed on a vast scale, which were also crimes against humanity; and insofar as the inhumane acts charged in the Indictment, and committed after the beginning of the war, did not constitute war crimes, they were all committed in execution of, or in connection with, the aggressive war, and therefore constituted crimes against humanity.

NOTES AND QUESTIONS

1. Defining Crimes. The Nuremberg Tribunal operated under a "statute" created by the Treaty of London, which defined three categories of crimes: aggression, war crimes, and crimes against humanity. Could the Nazi defendants have been held liable for war crimes with respect to offenses against their own citizens? If not, then how does the international community have power to punish them for crimes against humanity with regard to their own citizens? This theme will be a dominant subject in the cases below dealing with Yugoslavia and Rwanda.

2. International Interests. The international interest in internal affairs, reflected in crimes against humanity, is similar to that of the international interest in terrorism. If the Nazi party rose to power on the basis of intimidation and violence in the streets of Germany, was it guilty from the beginning of terrorism? If so, was this a violation of international law? The realization that this kind of power and intimidation over one's own citizenry is an added impetus for protection of human rights and the interest of other nations in the internal affairs of an abusive regime.

3. Post-WWII Trials. The Nuremberg trials have been the subject of extensive commentary. A set of essays applying its principles in developing international criminal law is TIMOTHY McCORMACK & GERRY J. SIMPSON, THE LAW OF WAR CRIMES (1997). *See also* OSCAR SCHACHTER, INTERNATIONAL LAW IN THEORY AND PRACTICE (1991).

In addition to the IMT and the trials in Germany under the auspices of the Control Council, additional military tribunals were convened to prosecute Italian, Yugoslav, and Japanese officials. One early activity of the United Nations (formed in 1945) was to monitor these proceedings through its War Crimes Commission, which reported that the U.S. conducted a total of 809 trials of war crimes. Other nations were engaged in similar trials, both in military courts and in ordinary civilian courts. The most controversial of these trials was that of General Yamashita who commanded the Japanese forces overrun by American troops in the Philippines.

IN RE YAMASHITA
327 U.S. 1 (1946)

MR. CHIEF JUSTICE STONE delivered the opinion of the Court.

[The Court had before it both an application for leave to file a petition for writs of habeas corpus and prohibition under the Court's original jurisdiction and a petition for certiorari to review an order of the Supreme Court of the Commonwealth of the Philippines, denying petitioner's application to that court for writs of habeas corpus and prohibition.

[Yamashita was the Commanding General of Japanese forces in the Philippines. He surrendered to U.S. forces on Sept. 3, 1945, was charged with violations of the law of war on Sept. 25, brought to trial on Oct 8, and convicted on Dec. 7 by a military commission of five Army officers. He was sentenced to death by hanging. His Army defense team of six lawyers brought petitions before both the Philippine courts and the Supreme Court.]

In *Ex parte Quirin*, we had occasion to consider at length the sources and nature of the authority to create military commissions for the trial of enemy combatants for offenses against the law of war. We there pointed out that Congress, in the exercise of the power conferred upon it by Article I, § 8, cl. 10 of the Constitution to "define and punish . . . Offenses against the Law of Nations," of which the law of war is a part, had by the Articles of War recognized the "military commission" appointed by military command, as it had previously existed in United States Army practice, as an appropriate tribunal for the trial and punishment of offenses against the law of war. Article 15 [now Article 21, 10 U.S.C. § 821, preserves the practice of trial by military commission or tribunal for violations of the "law of war"].

We further pointed out that Congress, by sanctioning trial of enemy combatants for violations of the law of war by military commission, had not attempted to codify the law of war or to mark its precise boundaries. Instead, by Article 15 it had incorporated, by reference, as within the preexisting jurisdiction of military commissions created by appropriate military command, all offenses which are defined as such by the law of war, and which may constitutionally be included within that jurisdiction. It thus adopted the system of military common law applied by military tribunals so far as it should be recognized and deemed applicable by the courts, and as further defined and supplemented by the Hague Convention, to which the United States and the Axis powers were parties.

Finally, we held in *Ex parte Quirin*, as we hold now, that Congress by sanctioning trials of enemy aliens by military commission for offenses against the law of war had recognized the right of the accused to make a defense. It has not foreclosed their right to contend that the Constitution or laws of the United States withhold authority to proceed with the trial. It has not withdrawn, and the Executive branch of the government could not, unless there was suspension of the writ, withdraw from the courts the duty and power to make such inquiry into the authority of the commission as may be made by habeas corpus.

The Authority to Create the Commission. An important incident to the conduct of war is the adoption of measures by the military commander, not only to repel and defeat the enemy, but to seize and subject to disciplinary measures those enemies who, in their attempt to thwart or impede our military effort, have violated the law of war. The trial and punishment of enemy combatants who have committed violations of the law of war is thus not only a part of the conduct of war operating as a preventive measure against such violations, but is an exercise of the authority sanctioned by Congress to administer the system of military justice recognized by the law of war. That sanction is without qualification as to the exercise of this authority so long as a state of war exists — from its declaration until peace is proclaimed. The war power, from which the commission derives its existence, is not limited to victories in the field, but carries with it the inherent power to guard against the immediate renewal of the conflict, and to remedy, at least in ways Congress has recognized, the evils which the military operations have produced.

No writer on international law appears to have regarded the power of military tribunals, otherwise competent to try violations of the law of war, as terminating before the formal state of war has ended. In our own military history there have been numerous instances in which offenders were tried by military commission after the cessation of hostilities and before the proclamation of peace, for offenses against the law of war committed before the cessation of hostilities.

The extent to which the power to prosecute violations of the law of war shall be exercised before peace is declared rests, not with the courts, but with the political branch of the Government, and may itself be governed by the terms of an armistice or the treaty of peace. Here, peace has not been agreed upon or proclaimed. Japan, by her acceptance of the Potsdam Declaration and her surrender, has acquiesced in the trials of those guilty of violations of the law of war. The conduct of the trial by the military commission has been authorized by the political branch of the Government, by military command, by international law and usage, and by the terms of the surrender of the Japanese government.

The Charge. Neither Congressional action nor the military orders constituting the commission authorized it to place petitioner on trial unless the charge preferred against him is of a violation of the law of war. The charge is that petitioner "unlawfully disregarded and failed to discharge his duty as commander to control the operations of the members of his command, permitting them to commit brutal atrocities and other high crimes against people of the United States and of its allies and dependencies, particularly the Philippines; and he . . . thereby violated the laws of war."

Bills of particulars allege a series of acts committed by members of the forces under petitioner's command, during the period mentioned. The first item specifies the execution of "a deliberate plan and purpose to massacre and exterminate a large part of the civilian population of Batangas Province, and to devastate and destroy public, private and religious property therein, as a result of which more than 25,000 men, women and children, all unarmed noncombatant civilians, were brutally mistreated and killed, without cause or trial, and entire settlements were devastated and destroyed wantonly and without military necessity." Other items specify acts of violence, cruelty and homicide inflicted upon the civilian population and prisoners of war, acts of wholesale pillage and the wanton destruction of religious monuments.

It is not denied that such acts directed against the civilian population of an occupied country and against prisoners of war are recognized in international law as violations of the law of war. But it is urged that the charge does not allege that petitioner has either committed or directed the commission of such acts, and consequently that no violation is charged as against him. But this overlooks the fact that the gist of the charge is an unlawful breach of duty by petitioner as an army commander to control the operations of the members of his command by "permitting them to commit" the extensive and widespread atrocities specified. The question then is whether the law of war imposes on an army commander a duty to take such appropriate measures as are within his power to control the troops under his command for the prevention of the specified acts which are violations of the law of war and which are likely to attend the occupation of hostile territory by an uncontrolled soldiery, and whether he may be charged with personal responsibility for his failure to take such measures when violations result. That this was the precise issue to be tried was made clear by the statement of the prosecution at the opening of the trial.

It is evident that the conduct of military operations by troops whose excesses are unrestrained by the orders or efforts of their commander would almost certainly result in violations which it is the purpose of the law of war to prevent. Its purpose to protect civilian populations and prisoners of war from brutality would largely be defeated if the commander of an invading army could with impunity neglect to take reasonable measures for their protection. Hence the law of war presupposes that its violation is to be avoided through the control of the operations of war by commanders who are to some extent responsible for their subordinates.

[The Hague Conventions] plainly imposed on petitioner, who at the time specified was military governor of the Philippines, as well as commander of the Japanese forces, an affirmative duty to take such measures as were within his power and appropriate in the circumstances to protect prisoners of war and the civilian population. This duty of a commanding officer has heretofore been recognized, and its breach penalized by our own military tribunals. A like principle has been applied so as to impose liability on the United States in international arbitrations.

We do not make the laws of war but we respect them so far as they do not conflict with the commands of Congress or the Constitution. There is no contention that the present charge, thus read, is without the support of evidence, or that the commission held petitioner responsible for failing to take measures which were beyond his control or inappropriate for a commanding officer to take in the circumstances.[1] We do not here appraise the evidence on which petitioner was convicted. We do not consider what measures, if any, petitioner took to prevent the commission, by the troops under his command, of the plain violations of the law of war detailed in the bill of particulars, or whether such measures as he may have taken were appropriate and sufficient to discharge the duty imposed upon him. These are questions within the peculiar competence of the military officers composing the commission and were for it to decide.

The Proceedings before the Commission. The regulations prescribed by General MacArthur governing the procedure for the trial of petitioner by the commission directed that the commission should admit such evidence "as in its opinion would be of assistance in proving or disproving the charge, or such as in the commission's opinion would have probative value in the mind of a reasonable man," and that in particular it might admit affidavits, depositions or other statements taken by officers detailed for that purpose by military authority. The petitions in this case charged that in the course of the trial the commission received, over objection by petitioner's counsel, the deposition of a witness taken pursuant to military authority by a United States Army captain. It also, over like objection admitted hearsay and opinion evidence tendered by

---

[1] [Court's Footnote 4] In its findings the commission took account of the difficulties "faced by the accused, with respect not only to the swift and overpowering advance of American forces, but also to errors of his predecessors, weakness in organization, equipment, supply, training, communication, discipline and morale of his troops," and "the tactical situation, the character, training and capacity of staff officers and subordinate commanders, as well as the traits of character of his troops." It nonetheless found that petitioner had not taken such measures to control his troops as were "required by the circumstances." We do not weigh the evidence. We merely hold that the charge sufficiently states a violation against the law of war, and that the commission, upon the facts found, could properly find petitioner guilty of such a violation.

the prosecution. Petitioner argues as ground for the writ of habeas corpus, that Article 25 of the Articles of War prohibited the reception in evidence by the commission of depositions on behalf of the prosecution in a capital case, and that Article 38 prohibited the reception of hearsay and of opinion evidence.

We think that neither Article 25 nor Article 38 is applicable to the trial of an enemy combatant by a military commission for violations of the law of war. Petitioner, an enemy combatant, is . . . not a person made subject to the Articles of War, and the military commission before which he was tried, though sanctioned, and its jurisdiction saved, by Article 15, was not convened by virtue of the Articles of War, but pursuant to the common law of war. It follows that the Articles of War were not applicable to petitioner's trial and imposed no restrictions upon the procedure to be followed. The Articles left the control over the procedure in such a case where it had previously been, with the military command.

Petitioner further urges that by virtue of Article 63 of the Geneva Convention of 1929, he is entitled to the benefits afforded by the 25th and 38th Articles of War to members of our own forces. Article 63 provides: "Sentence may be pronounced against a prisoner of war only by the same courts and according to the same procedure as in the case of persons belonging to the armed forces of the detaining Power." Since petitioner is a prisoner of war, and as the 25th and 38th Articles of War apply to the trial of any person in our own armed forces, it is said that Article 63 requires them to be applied in the trial of petitioner. But we think examination of Article 63 in its setting in the Convention plainly shows that it refers to sentence "pronounced against a prisoner of war" for an offense committed while a prisoner of war, and not for a violation of the law of war committed while a combatant.

We cannot say that the commission, in admitting evidence to which objection is now made, violated any act of Congress, treaty or military command defining the commission's authority. From this viewpoint it is unnecessary to consider what, in other situations, the Fifth Amendment might require, and as to that no intimation one way or the other is to be implied.

We therefore conclude that the detention of petitioner for trial and his detention upon his conviction, subject to the prescribed review by the military authorities were lawful, and that the petition for certiorari, and leave to file in this Court petitions for writs of habeas corpus and prohibition should be, and they are

Denied.

MR. JUSTICE JACKSON took no part in the consideration or decision of these cases.

MR. JUSTICE MURPHY, dissenting.

The significance of the issue facing the Court today cannot be overemphasized. An American military commission has been established to try a fallen military commander of a conquered nation for an alleged war crime. The authority for such action grows out of the exercise of the power conferred upon Congress by Article I, § 8, cl. 10 of the Constitution to "define and punish . . . Offenses against the Law of Nations. . . . " The grave issue raised by this case is whether a military commission so established and so authorized may disregard the procedural rights of an accused person as guaranteed by the Constitution, especially by the due process clause of the Fifth Amendment.

The answer is plain. The Fifth Amendment guarantee of due process of law applies to "any person" who is accused of a crime by the Federal Government or any of its agencies. No exception is made as to those who are accused of war crimes or as to those who possess the status of an enemy belligerent. Indeed, such an exception would be contrary to the whole philosophy of human rights which makes the Constitution the great living document that it is. The immutable rights of the individual, including those secured by the due process clause of the Fifth Amendment, belong not alone to the members of those nations that excel on the battlefield or that subscribe to the democratic ideology. They belong to every person in the world, victor or vanquished, whatever may be his race, color or beliefs. They rise above any status of belligerency or outlawry. They survive any popular passion or frenzy of the moment. No court or legislature or executive, not even the mightiest army in the world, can ever destroy them. Such is the universal and indestructible nature of the rights which the due process clause of the Fifth Amendment recognizes and protects when life or liberty is threatened by virtue of the authority of the United States.

The failure of the military commission to obey the dictates of the due process requirements of the Fifth Amendment is apparent in this case. The petitioner was the commander of an army totally destroyed by the superior power of this nation. While under heavy and destructive attack by our forces, his troops committed many brutal atrocities and other high crimes. Hostilities ceased and he voluntarily surrendered. At that point he was entitled, as an individual protected by the due process clause of the Fifth amendment, to be treated fairly and justly according to the accepted rules of law and procedure. He was also entitled to a fair trial as to any alleged crimes and to be free from charges of legally unrecognized crimes that would serve only to permit his accusers to satisfy their desires for revenge.

A military commission was appointed to try the petitioner for an alleged war crime. The trial was ordered to be held in territory over which the United States has complete sovereignty. No military necessity or other emergency demanded the suspension of the safeguards of due process. Yet petitioner was rushed to trial under an improper charge, given insufficient time to prepare an adequate defense, deprived of the benefits of some of the most elementary rules of evidence and summarily sentenced to be hanged. In all this needless and unseemly haste there was no serious attempt to charge or to prove that he committed a recognized violation of the laws of war. He was not charged with personally participating in the acts of atrocity or with ordering or condoning their commission. Not even knowledge of these crimes was attributed to him. It was simply alleged that he unlawfully disregarded and failed to discharge his duty as commander to control the operations of the members of his command, permitting them to commit the acts of atrocity. The recorded annals of warfare and the established principles of international law afford not the slightest precedent for such a charge.

In my opinion, such a procedure is unworthy of the traditions of our people or of the immense sacrifices that they have made to advance the common ideals of mankind. The high feelings of the moment doubtless will be satisfied. But in the sober afterglow will come the realization of the boundless and dangerous implications of the procedure sanctioned today. No one in a position of command in an army, from sergeant to general, can escape those implications. Indeed, the fate of some future President of the United States and his chiefs of staff and military advisers may well have been sealed by this decision. But even more significant will be the hatred and ill-will growing out of the application of this unprecedented procedure.

War breeds atrocities. From the earliest conflicts of recorded history to the global struggles of modern times inhumanities, lust and pillage have been the inevitable by-products of man's resort to force and arms. Unfortunately, such despicable acts have a dangerous tendency to call forth primitive impulses of vengeance and retaliation among the victimized peoples. The satisfaction of such impulses in turn breeds resentment and fresh tension. Thus does the spiral of cruelty and hatred grow.

If we are ever to develop an orderly international community based upon a recognition of human dignity it is of the utmost importance that the necessary punishment of those guilty of atrocities be as free as possible from the ugly stigma of revenge and vindictiveness. Justice must be tempered by compassion rather than by vengeance. In this, the first case involving this momentous problem ever to reach this Court, our responsibility is both lofty and difficult. We must insist, within the confines of our proper jurisdiction, that the highest standards of justice be applied in this trial of an enemy commander conducted under the authority of the United States. Otherwise stark retribution will be free to masquerade in a cloak of false legalism. And the hatred and cynicism engendered by that retribution will supplant the great ideals to which this nation is dedicated.

This Court fortunately has taken the first and most important step toward insuring the supremacy of law and justice in the treatment of an enemy belligerent accused of violating the laws of war. Jurisdiction properly has been asserted to inquire "into the cause of restraint of liberty" of such a person. Thus the obnoxious doctrine asserted by the Government in this case, to the effect that restraints of liberty resulting from military trials of war criminals are political matters completely outside the arena of judicial review, has been rejected fully and unquestionably. This does not mean, of course, that the foreign affairs and policies of the nation are proper subjects of judicial inquiry. But when the liberty of any person is restrained by reason of the authority of the United States the writ of habeas corpus is available to test the legality of that restraint, even though direct court review of the restraint is prohibited. The conclusive presumption must be made, in this country at least, that illegal restraints are unauthorized and unjustified by any foreign policy of the Government and that commonly accepted juridical standards are to be recognized and enforced. On that basis judicial inquiry into these matters may proceed within its proper sphere.

At a time like this when emotions are understandably high it is difficult to adopt a dispassionate attitude toward a case of this nature. Yet now is precisely the time when that attitude is most essential. We live under the Constitution, which is the embodiment of all the high hopes and aspirations of the new world. And it is applicable in both war and peace. We must act accordingly. Indeed, an uncurbed spirt of revenge and retribution, masked in formal legal procedure for purposes of dealing with a fallen enemy commander, can do more lasting harm than all of the atrocities giving rise to that spirit. The people's faith in the fairness and objectiveness of the law can be seriously undercut by that spirit. The fires of nationalism can be further kindled. And the hearts of all mankind can be embittered and filled with hatred, leaving forlorn and impoverished the noble ideal of malice toward none and charity to all. These are the reasons that lead me to dissent in these terms.

MR. JUSTICE RUTLEDGE, dissenting.

Not with ease does one find his views at odds with the Court's in a matter of this character and gravity. Only the most deeply felt convictions could force one to differ. That reason alone leads me to do so now, against strong considerations for withholding dissent.

More is at stake than General Yamashita's fate. There could be no possible sympathy for him if he is guilty of the atrocities for which his death is sought. But there can be and should be justice administered according to law. In this stage of war's aftermath it is too early for Lincoln's great spirit, best lighted in the Second Inaugural, to have wide hold for the treatment of foes. It is not too early, it is never too early, for the nation steadfastly to follow its great constitutional traditions, none older or more universally protective against unbridled power than due process of law in the trial and punishment of men, that is, of all men, whether citizens, aliens, alien enemies or enemy belligerents. It can become too late.

The difference between the Court's view of this proceeding and my own comes down in the end to the view, on the one hand, that there is no law restrictive upon these proceedings other than whatever rules and regulations may be prescribed for their government by the executive authority or the military and, on the other hand, that the provisions of the Articles of War, of the Geneva Convention and the Fifth Amendment apply.

I cannot accept the view that anywhere in our system resides or lurks a power so unrestrained to deal with any human being through any process of trial. What military agencies or authorities may do with our enemies in battle or invasion, apart from proceedings in the nature of trial and some semblance of judicial action, is beside the point. Nor has any human being heretofore been held to be wholly beyond elementary procedural protection by the Fifth Amendment. I cannot consent to even implied departure from that great absolute.

It was a great patriot who said: "He that would make his own liberty secure must guard even his enemy from oppression; for if he violates this duty he establishes a precedent that will reach himself." 2 The Complete Writings of Thomas Paine (edited by Foner, 1945) 588.

NOTES AND QUESTIONS

1. Command Responsibility. Was it "fair" to hang General Yamashita for the actions of his troops if he really was unable to control them in the chaos of the Allied invasion? Did he perhaps bear some responsibility for years of propaganda that created the conditions of undisciplined patriotic fervor leading to this result?

2. Retribution and Fairness. Justices Murphy and Rutledge used strong language to express their outrage over the treatment of General Yamashita, while the more famous liberal Justices Douglas and Black were silent. Do you suspect that the Murphy and Rutledge reactions were prompted more by (1) military procedures, (2) the fairness of holding him responsible for the actions of his troops, or (3) the assertion of unilateral authority by the U.S. to execute a vanquished general? From the perspective of more than a half century later, and in the context of worldwide terrorism, what do you think of Justice Murphy's warning that vengeful action could create more fuel for a cycle of hate?

[B] International Criminal Tribunals for Yugoslavia (ICTY) and Rwanda (ICTR)

The ICTY was created by action of the UN Security Council in 1993, followed shortly by creation of the ICTR in 1994. The ICTY is based in The Hague and ICTR in Arusha, Tanzania. Each has multiple Trial Chambers composed of panels of judges, but both share the same Appellate Chamber. The judges of all Chambers are elected by the General Assembly.

The "statutes" of the tribunals define the crimes to be adjudicated. There are some subtle differences between the two statutes, and the Tribunals struggle with what law applies in some situations. Both Tribunals have developed elaborate procedures for protection of witnesses and for translation of testimony.

The first case to reach final conclusion in the ICTY was that of Dusko Tadic, a relatively obscure Serbian resident of Bosnia who was shown to have participated in some of the brutalities of 1992–94. Muslim and Croat residents were rounded up, imprisoned, and eventually either killed or expelled from the region as part of the ethnic cleansing of what dominant Serbian elements hoped would result in a Serbian addition to Yugoslavia. Because this is the first opinion of a tribunal instigated by the United Nations for war crimes, the Court goes into vast detail regarding the background of the incidents and the analysis of customary international law that creates individual criminal responsibility for atrocities against civilian populations.

This background and analysis is part of what may become international criminal responsibility for terrorism, as it sets the stage for finding that targeting of civilians by an organized group, whether affiliated with a government or not, is a subject of customary international law and thus enforceable either by international tribunals or under the universal jurisdiction of individual states. But the Trial Chamber and Appeals Chamber hold that the Geneva Conventions are not violated by the actions of someone who is not acting under the auspices of a nation-State. These discussions should be read with several questions in mind:

1. why is state involvement even under discussion in these cases? is it like the state action issue in the U.S.? why doesn't the federal government just prosecute anyone who harms another for racial reasons? why do we insist on either "under

color of state law" or "affecting interstate commerce?"

2. what do these opinions tell us about the nature of armed conflict when there are patterns of violence against civilians? can a "private" group not affiliated with or attempting to become a State be involved in "armed conflict"? are there separate legal regimes for "combatants" that are part of organized military groups and "others" who are not "pretenders to the throne" of a state?

PROSECUTOR v. TADIC
Int'l Crim. Tribunal for Yugoslavia, Trial Chamber
1997

OPINION AND JUDGMENT

I. INTRODUCTION

3. The International Tribunal is governed by its Statute ("Statute"), adopted by the Security Council.

4. The Statute grants competence to prosecute persons responsible for serious violations of international humanitarian law committed in the territory of the former Yugoslavia since 1991. Subject-matter jurisdiction is stated in Articles 2 to 5 of the Statute to consist of the power to prosecute persons responsible for "grave breaches" of the Geneva Conventions of 1949 (Article 2), [violations of] the laws or customs of war (Article 3), genocide (Article 4), and crimes against humanity when committed in armed conflict (Article 5), which are beyond any doubt part of customary international law.

B. Procedural Background

9. The accused was charged with individual counts of persecution, inhuman treatment, cruel treatment, rape, wilful killing, murder, torture, wilfully causing great suffering or serious injury to body and health, and inhumane acts alleged to have been committed in the Republic of Bosnia and Herzegovina. The accused was transferred to the International Tribunal on 24 April 1995, after the Federal Republic of Germany enacted the necessary implementing legislation for his surrender, and thereafter was detained in the United Nations detention unit in The Hague.

II. BACKGROUND AND PRELIMINARY FACTUAL FINDINGS

A. The Context of the Conflict

53. In order to place in context the evidence relating to the counts of the Indictment, especially Count 1, persecution, it is necessary to say something in a preliminary way about the relevant historical, geographic, administrative and military setting about which evidence was received.

1. Historical and Geographic Background

55. The area with which this trial is primarily concerned is north-western Bosnia and Herzegovina; more specifically, opstina (district) Prijedor, which includes the town of Prijedor and the town of Kozarac some 10 kilometres to its east.

56. For centuries the population of Bosnia and Herzegovina, more so than any other republic of the former Yugoslavia, has been multi-ethnic. For more than 400 years Bosnia and Herzegovina was part of the Ottoman Empire. Its western and northern borders formed the boundary with the Austro-Hungarian Empire or its predecessors; a military frontier along that boundary was established as early as the sixteenth century to protect the Hapsburg lands from the Ottoman Turks. The presence of this old military frontier is said to account for the presence there of much of its present-day Serb population, encouraged centuries ago to move into and settle on the frontier, forming there a loyal population base as a potential border defence force. The large Muslim population of Bosnia and Herzegovina owes its religion and culture, and hence

its identity, to the long Turkish occupation, during which time many Slavs adopted the Islamic faith. The third ethnic population living in Bosnia and Herzegovina, also sizeable, are the Croats, living principally in the south-west adjacent to Croatia's Dalmatian coast. Since all three population groups are Slav it is, no doubt, inaccurate to speak of three different ethnic groups; however, this appears to be accepted common usage.

[Here the Court engages in a lengthy review of the history and religious-ethnic strife of the region. The Balkan region has been fractured for so many centuries that it has produced the term "balkanization" to refer to a situation in which various entities are competing for the same political spoils in a chaotic fashion. Geographically, the region runs from the border of Hungary in the north to the border of Greece in the south. It includes what are now known as Slovenia, Croatia, Yugoslavia (Serbia and Montenegro), Bosnia-Herzegovina, Albania, Bulgaria, and Macedonia.

[Over the centuries, the region has been the dividing line between eastern and western empires. In the West, these have included Rome, the Holy Roman Empire, and Austro-Hungarian Empire. From the east have come the Persian, Turkish and Ottoman Empires. Similarly, it has been the meeting point of religions: Roman Catholic, Eastern Orthodox, and Muslim.

[In biological or genetic terms, it is at least arguable that all the long-term population of the region are of a single Slavic background, but the inhabitants identify themselves as ethnic Serb, Croat, or Muslim (and others not relevant here) more along cultural than biologic lines. Indeed, surnames are common to all groups and only the Muslim given names are distinctive from the other groups. Thus, it would be difficult to identify someone as belonging to one or other group by appearance or name alone without knowing the person's family and cultural history.

[At the end of World War II, much of the region was unified in the republic of Yugoslavia under Marshal Tito allied to some extent with the Soviet Union. As dissatisfaction with the USSR grew during the 1960s and 1970s, Yugoslavia began to be viewed as almost an independent buffer between east and west. Without the common unifier (or common enemy) of communism, the various ethnic groups began to assert their claims for nationhood. With the breakup of the Soviet Union in 1989, all hell broke loose in the Balkans.

[In elections in 1990, separatist parties won in Slovenia, Croatia, and Bosnia-Herzegovina. Slovenia and Croatia immediately declared independence. That left the Serbian majority in Yugoslavia in control of the Yugoslav National Army (JNA) but without political control of the rebellious areas. Slovenia was allowed to go its way but Serb JNA forces attempted to subdue Croatia. In bitter fighting through 1991 & the first half of 1992, Serbian Yugoslavia managed to annex the most Serbian portions of Croatia but the JNA was repelled from the rest of what became a new nation-state. Moving back across the border into Bosnia-Herzegovina, the JNA was welcomed by the Serbian sympathizers in the northern part of that republic.

[The following acronyms are used throughout the Court's opinion:

[JNA = Yugoslav National Army

[SDS = Serbian political party of Bosnia-Herzegovina

[SDA = Muslim political party of B-H

[HDZ = Croat political party of B-H

[TO = Territorial Defense

[In northern Bosnia-Herzegovina, Serb citizens formed SDS provisional governments, allied with the JNA troops, and embarked on a program of "ethnic cleansing" of the region.]

147. Immediately upon its formation, the ARK Crisis Staff began to make decisions about the treatment of non-Serbs. The President of the ARK Crisis Staff [stated] that

the largest percentage of non-Serbs acceptable in the territory designated as Greater Serbia was 2 percent. In order to secure this percentage he advocated on Radio Banja Luka a direct struggle, including the killing of non-Serbs. Similarly [another Serbian municipal official decided] not to allow any non-Serb women to give birth at Banja Luka Hospital. He also asserted that all mixed marriage couples should be divorced or that all mixed marriages should be annulled and that children of mixed marriages "were good only for making soap."

151. Generally the [non-Serb] men were taken to the Keraterm and Omarska camps and the women to the Trnopolje camp. For those held at camps in the area, the overwhelming majority of whom were non-Serbs, the situation was horrendous, with, as described below, brutal beatings, rapes and torture commonplace and the conditions of life appalling.

152. Whereas before the conflict opstina Prijedor contained approximately 50,000 Muslims and 6,000 Croats, only approximately 6,000 Muslims and 3,000 Croats remained after the cleansing and they endured very harsh conditions. They were required to perform dangerous and difficult work, had difficulties buying food, were harassed, and killings occurred on a continual basis.

154. After the take-over of Prijedor and the outlying areas, the Serb forces confined thousands of Muslim and Croat civilians in the Omarska, Keraterm and Trnopolje camps. The establishment of these camps was part of the Greater Serbia plan to expel non-Serbs from opstina Prijedor. Generally the camps were established and run either at the direction of, or in cooperation with, the Crisis Staffs, the armed forces and the police. During confinement, both male and female prisoners were subjected to severe mistreatment, which included beatings, sexual assaults, torture and executions. Members of paramilitary organizations and local Serbs were routinely allowed to enter the camps to abuse, beat and kill prisoners.

155. Perhaps the most notorious of the camps, where the most horrific conditions existed, was the Omarska camp. It was located at the former Ljubija iron-ore mine, situated some two kilometres to the south of Omarska village. The camp was in operation from 25 May 1992 until late August 1992 when the prisoners were transferred to Trnopolje and other camps. Omarska held as many as 3,000 prisoners at one time, primarily men, but also had at least 36 to 38 women. With little exception, all were Muslims or Croats. The only Serb prisoners sighted by any of the witnesses were said to have been there because they were on the side of the Muslims. The commander of the camp was Zeljko Meakic. The camp consisted of two large buildings, the hangar and the administrative building, and two smaller buildings, known as the "white house" and the "red house."

[Prisoners were regularly called out for interrogation, in the process of which many were severely beaten or killed.]

164. The calling-out of prisoners was not only for the purposes of interrogation. In the evening, groups from outside the camp would appear, would call out particular prisoners from their rooms and attack them with a variety of sticks, iron bars or lengths of heavy electric cable. Sometimes these weapons would have nails embedded in them so as to pierce the skin. On occasions knives would be used to slash a prisoner's body. The prisoners as a whole feared groups of men from outside the camp even more than they did the regular camp guards. These groups appeared to be allowed free access to the camp and their visits greatly increased the atmosphere of terror which prevailed in the camp. Frequently prisoners who were called out failed to return and witnesses who were their close relatives gave evidence that they had never been seen since, and were assumed to have been murdered.

165. Women who were held at Omarska were routinely called out of their rooms at night and raped. One witness testified that she was taken out five times and raped and after each rape she was beaten.

166. The white house was a place of particular horror. One room in it was reserved for brutal assaults on prisoners, who were often stripped, beaten and kicked and otherwise abused. Many died as a result of these repeated assaults on them. Prisoners who were forced to clean up after these beatings reported finding blood, teeth and skin of victims on the floor. Dead bodies of prisoners, lying in heaps on the grass near the white house, were a not infrequent sight. Those bodies would be thrown out of the white house and later loaded into trucks and removed from the camp.

167. The red house was another small building where prisoners were taken to be beaten and killed. When prisoners were required to clean the red house, they often found hair, clothes, blood, footwear and empty pistol cartridges. They also loaded onto trucks bodies of prisoners who had been beaten and killed in the red house.

[The Tribunal describes conditions and incidents at other camps in the region. In American courts, this evidence likely would have been excluded as prejudicial to the accused and not sufficiently connected to the offenses with which he was charged.]

C. The Accused

180. The accused, Dusko Tadic, was born on 1 October 1955 and grew up in Kozarac, living most of the time in the family home in the centre of the town. He came from a very prominent family of Serb ethnicity in Kozarac; his father was a decorated Second World War hero and well respected throughout the community.

181. Towards the end of 1990 or in the beginning of 1991 the accused opened a café in Kozarac, the Nipon café, attached to the family home on Marsala Tita Street in the centre of town. At first it was a popular bar visited by Muslims and Serbs alike from Kozarac and the surrounding area. Ninety percent of the inhabitants of Kozarac were Muslims prior to the conflict and the accused testified that most of his friends were Muslim.

185. The accused himself acknowledges that several Serbs and Muslims began to boycott his café in the belief that he wanted to "disturb relations between ethnic groups."

188. After the ethnic cleansing of Kozarac had been accomplished, the accused became the political leader of Kozarac. He became its representative to the Prijedor Municipal Assembly, which entrusted him with the task of re-establishing civilian control in Kozarac and he was in charge of population resettlement there.

III. Factual Findings

[The Court went into elaborate detail of witness testimony on the events in each paragraph of the Indictment. Given the chaotic nature of the times, it is not surprising that witnesses were confused and often unable to identify an assailant. Tadic, however, was known to many of the prisoners from prior life in town. This led to his being identified but also to some question of whether the identification was erroneously based on rumor or imagination. The specific incidents in which he was alleged to be involved included beatings of nine different prisoners, shooting of four civilians who were pulled out of a line of detainees in the street, and one particularly gruesome incident in which one prisoner was coerced into oral castration of another prisoner.

[The voluminous recitation of evidence is omitted, although it is worth emphasizing that Tadic maintained that his role was passive or even a tentative peacemaker. He insisted that he was not present at many of these events, and pointed out that he was fired from his municipal post for conflicts with the ruling SDS chiefs and eventually deserted from the military and fled to Germany.

[In brief, the Court found that Tadjic was present but not actively involved in many of the beatings, murders, and the sexual mutilation. Because bodies were disposed of in secrecy, the Court was unable to find beyond a reasonable doubt that persons who were beaten and disappeared had in fact died of their injuries, so the murder counts other than the shooting incident resulted in not guilty verdicts.

[U.S. students should note that the Court acts as fact-finder. There is no provision for jury in most continental systems, on which the procedure of the International Tribunal is based. The lengthy detailed recitation of evidence in the opinion may be similar to that of U.S. judges when making findings without a jury, but it is more technical in tone and structure than that of most U.S. judges. The structure of the opinion also reflects the "syllogistic" process of continental legal decisions.]

VI. Applicable Law

A. General Requirements of Articles 2, 3 & 5 of the Statute

B. Article 2 of the Statute

[The Geneva Conventions prohibit violence against "protected persons." Each of the four Conventions applies to a different category of "protected persons" (soldiers, naval personnel, prisoners of war, and civilians). A major legal question was presented by whether the inmates of the camps were harmed by forces of a party to an armed conflict other than the state of which they were nationals. If the camps were under the control of Yugoslavia, then the protected status would apply. If the camps were under control of persons of the same nationality as the inmates, then the matter would be one for domestic law. The situation thus was somewhat comparable to the question of whether the U.S. "controlled" the Contras in Nicaragua. The Court concluded on this issue that "since it cannot be said that any of the victims, all of whom were civilians, were at any relevant time in the hands of a party to the conflict of which they were not nationals, the accused must be found not guilty of the counts which rely upon" Article 2 of the ICTY Statute.]

C. Article 3 of the Statute

[All four of the Geneva Conventions contain what is known as "Common Article 3," a provision which applies in "armed conflict not of an international character." It requires that "persons taking no active part in the hostilities" be "treated humanely" without discrimination and defines certain prohibited acts, such as violence, torture, or hostage-taking.]

609. Article 3 of the Statute directs the Trial Chamber to the laws or customs of war, being that body of customary international humanitarian law [which] includes the regime of protection established under Common Article 3 applicable to armed conflicts not of an international character, as a reflection of elementary considerations of humanity, and which is applicable to armed conflicts in general.

617. For the purposes of the application of the rules of customary international humanitarian law contained in Common Article 3, this Trial Chamber finds, in the present case, that: (i) an armed conflict existed at all relevant times in relation to the alleged offences; (ii) each of the victims of the acts charged was a person protected by those provisions being a person taking no active part in the hostilities; and (iii) the offences charged were committed within the context of that armed conflict. Accordingly, the requirements of Article 3 of the Statute are met.

D. Article 5 of the Statute

618. The notion of crimes against humanity as an independent juridical concept, and the imputation of individual criminal responsibility for their commission, was first recognized in Article 6(c) of the Nürnberg Charter. The term "crimes against humanity," although not previously codified, had been used in a non-technical sense as far back as 1915 and in subsequent statements concerning the First World War and was hinted at in the preamble to the 1907 Hague Convention. Thus when crimes against humanity were included in the Nürnberg Charter, although it was the first technical use of the term, it was not considered a novel concept. Nevertheless a new category of crime was created.

623. [S]ince the Nürnberg Charter, the customary status of the prohibition against crimes against humanity and the attribution of individual criminal responsibility for their commission have not been seriously questioned. "It is by now a settled rule of customary international law that crimes against humanity do not require a connection to international armed conflict."

The meaning of "population"

644. The requirement in Article 5 of the Statute that the prohibited acts must be directed against a civilian "population" does not mean that the entire population of a given State or territory must be victimised by these acts in order for the acts to constitute a crime against humanity. Instead the "population" element is intended to imply crimes of a collective nature and thus exclude single or isolated acts which, although possibly constituting war crimes or crimes against national penal legislation, do not rise to the level of crimes against humanity. [T]he inclusion in Article 5 of the requirement that the acts "be 'directed against any civilian population' ensures that what is to be alleged will not be one particular act but, instead, a course of conduct."

Thus the emphasis is not on the individual victim but rather on the collective, the individual being victimised not because of his individual attributes but rather because of his membership of a targeted civilian population. This has been interpreted to mean, as elaborated below, that the acts must occur on a widespread or systematic basis, that there must be some form of a governmental, organizational or group policy to commit these acts and that the perpetrator must know of the context within which his actions are taken, as well as the requirement that the actions be taken on discriminatory grounds.

649. Clearly, a single act by a perpetrator taken within the context of a widespread or systematic attack against a civilian population entails individual criminal responsibility and an individual perpetrator need not commit numerous offences to be held liable. Although it is correct that isolated, random acts should not be included in the definition of crimes against humanity, that is the purpose of requiring that the acts be directed against a civilian population and thus "[e]ven an isolated act can constitute a crime against humanity if it is the product of a political system based on terror or persecution."

E. Individual Criminal Responsibility

676. As noted in the *Justice* case [an American military trial of Nazi judges], knowledge and intent can be inferred from the circumstances [in that case, knowledge that the courts were being used in furtherance of Nazi racial objectives]. In the *Mauthausen* case, the United States Military Tribunal, after finding all 61 accused guilty, stated in its special findings that the state of the camp where detainees were murdered *en masse* in gas chambers "was of such a criminal nature as to cause every official, governmental, military and civil, and every employee thereof, whether he be a member of the Waffen SS, Allgemeine SS, a guard, or civilian, to be culpably and criminally responsible." This finding was based on the determination that "it was impossible for a governmental, military or civil official, a guard or a civilian employee, of the Concentration Camp Mauthausen, to have been in control of, been employed in, or present in, or residing in, Mauthausen at any time during its existence, without having acquired a definite knowledge of the criminal practices and activities therein existing." Thus the court inferred knowledge on the part of the accused, and concluded that the staff of the concentration camp was guilty of the commission of a war crime based on this knowledge and their continued participation in the enterprise.

681. The remaining question for consideration is the amount of assistance that must be shown before one can be held culpable for involvement in a crime.

689. The Trial Chamber finds that aiding and abetting includes all acts of assistance by words or acts that lend encouragement or support, as long as the requisite intent is present. Under this theory, presence alone is not sufficient if it is an ignorant or

unwilling presence. However, if the presence can be shown or inferred, by circumstantial or other evidence, to be knowing and to have a direct and substantial effect on the commission of the illegal act, then it is sufficient on which to base a finding of participation and assign the criminal culpability that accompanies it.

690. Moreover, when an accused is present and participates in the beating of one person and remains with the group when it moves on to beat another person, his presence would have an encouraging effect, even if he does not physically take part in this second beating, and he should be viewed as participating in this second beating as well. This is assuming that the accused has not actively withdrawn from the group or spoken out against the conduct of the group.

691. However, actual physical presence when the crime is committed is not necessary; just as with the defendants who only drove victims to the woods to be killed, an accused can be considered to have participated in the commission of a crime based on the precedent of the Nürnberg war crimes trials if he is found to be "concerned with the killing." However, the acts of the accused must be direct and substantial.

692. In sum, the accused will be found criminally culpable for any conduct where it is determined that he knowingly participated in the commission of an offence that violates international humanitarian law and his participation directly and substantially affected the commission of that offence through supporting the actual commission before, during, or after the incident. He will also be responsible for all that naturally results from the commission of the act in question.

VII. LEGAL FINDINGS

693. The Trial Chamber has held, by a majority, that the Prosecution has failed to prove beyond reasonable doubt that the victims of the acts alleged in the Indictment were protected persons under the provisions of the Geneva Conventions. Accordingly, as found by the Appeals Chamber, Article 2 of the Statute proscribing grave breaches of those Conventions is inapplicable; therefore, the evidence will be assessed by considering Article 3 of the Statute and its invocation of Common Article 3 of the Geneva Conventions, and Articles 5 and 7, paragraph 1 of the Statute.

[The Tribunal then proceeds to discuss the law and facts again in relation to each of the 34 counts in the indictment, finding Tadic to have been present and supportive of a number of beatings, torture, and killings but not involved with others. With regard to persons who were beaten and never seen again, the court could not find beyond a reasonable doubt that they died of those wounds and thus acquitted on some charges of murder. With regard to mistreatment of dead bodies, the court decided that the statutes apply only to living persons.]

VIII. JUDGMENT

FOR THE FOREGOING REASONS, having considered all of the evidence and the arguments, THE TRIAL CHAMBER finds [the Accused guilty on 11 of the 34 counts in the indictment].

NOTES AND QUESTIONS

1. **"Protected Persons" and "Armed Conflict."** The discussion of who is protected under what circumstances is critical to our study of terrorism for several reasons. First, there is the question of whether clandestine actors can be held to have violated international law. Second, under what circumstances is a large-scale act of violence subject to the "law of war?" Third, by what constraints is a military force governed in its dealings with paramilitary or even less-organized groups, such as those engaged in resistance violence in Iraq? And, conversely, what law applies to those insurgents themselves?

The Trial Chamber decided that the Geneva Conventions did not apply to the situation in Bosnia because the Serbian militias were not under the "effective control" of Serbian Yugoslavia and therefore the situation was not an "international armed conflict." As a result, the civilian victims would not be considered "protected persons" under the Conventions. In other words, the Geneva Conventions apply to international armed conflicts, not to localized violence.

The Prosecutor appealed from this ruling on the ground that the conflict was international in scope because the Bosnian Serb militias had a "demonstrable link" to the forces of Yugoslavia.

2. Patterns of Violence and External Law. The dilemma of what to do about loosely organized mob violence has been around for millennia. As mentioned before, the U.S. experience with the KKK presented a similar phenomenon in the sense that it was not clear in early stages that California had a sufficient interest in what occurred in Alabama to trigger federal oversight of occurrences that were "local" to the state where they were occurring. Even today, federal statutes dealing with racial violence hinge on jurisdictional factors such as depriving a person of the use of public facilities or exercising a right connected to the federal government. This is roughly corollary to the question of when the international community should take oversight of violence that is contained within one nation-state.

If two rival gangs in Los Angeles are engaged in bloodshed without following the laws and customs of war, that is no business of the international community but is a problem to be dealt with by local authorities. If the United States Government is engaged in bloodshed against its own civilians, there may be sources of international humanitarian law that apply but not the Geneva Conventions (unless the situation rises to the level of a "Common Article 3" situation discussed later). In between these extremes, there is the possibility that one of the rival gangs is acting, as U.S. statutes put it, "under color of state law," in which case outsiders take an interest.

PROSECUTOR v. TADIC
ICTY Appeals Chamber (July 15, 1999)

IV. THE FIRST GROUND OF CROSS-APPEAL BY THE PROSECUTION: THE TRIAL CHAMBER'S FINDING THAT IT HAD NOT BEEN PROVED THAT THE VICTIMS WERE "PROTECTED PERSONS" UNDER ARTICLE 2 OF THE STATUTE (ON GRAVE BREACHES)

A. Submissions of the Parties

1. The Prosecution Case

68. In the first ground of the Cross-Appeal, the Prosecution challenges the Appellant's acquittal on [the] Counts of the Indictment which charged the Appellant with grave breaches under Article 2 of the Statute. The Appellant was acquitted on these counts on the ground that the victims referred to in those counts had not been proved to be "protected persons" under the applicable provisions of the Fourth Geneva Convention.

69. The Prosecution maintains that all relevant criteria under Article 2 of the Statute were met. Consequently, the Trial Chamber erred by relying exclusively upon the "effective control" test derived from the *Case concerning Military and Paramilitary Activities in and against Nicaragua (Nicaragua v. United States)* in order to determine the applicability of the grave breach provisions of the relevant Geneva Convention. The Prosecution submits that the Chamber should have instead applied the provisions of the Geneva Conventions and the relevant principles and authorities of international humanitarian law which, in its view, apply a "demonstrable link" test.

70. In distinguishing the present situation from the facts in Nicaragua, the Prosecution notes that *Nicaragua* was concerned with State responsibility rather than individual criminal responsibility. Further, the Prosecution asserts that the

International Court of Justice in *Nicaragua* deliberately avoided dealing with the question of which body of treaty rules was applicable. Instead the Court focused on the minimum yardstick of rules contained in Common Article 3 of the Geneva Conventions, which in the Court's view applied to all conflicts in *Nicaragua*, thus obviating the need for the Court to decide which body of law was applicable in that case.

71. The Prosecution submits that the Trial Chamber erred by not applying the provisions of the Geneva Conventions and general principles of international humanitarian law to determine individual criminal responsibility for grave breaches of the Geneva Conventions. In the Prosecution's submission, these sources require that there be a "demonstrable link" between the perpetrator and a Party to an international armed conflict of which the victim is not a national.

72. The Prosecution submits that the "demonstrable link" test is satisfied on the facts of the case at hand. In its view, the Army of the Serbian Republic of Bosnia and Herzegovina/Republika Srpska ("VRS") had a "demonstrable link" with the Federal Republic of Yugoslavia (Serbia and Montenegro) ("FRY") and the Army of the FRY ("VJ"); it was not a situation of mere logistical support by the FRY to the VRS.

73. In addition, the Prosecution submits that the Trial Chamber erred in finding that the only test relied upon in *Nicaragua* was the "effective control" test. The Court in *Nicaragua* also applied an "agency" test which, the Prosecution submits, is a more appropriate standard for determining the applicability of the grave breach provisions.

74. Were either the "effective control" test or the "agency" test to be adopted by the Appeals Chamber, the Prosecution submits that in any event both tests would be satisfied on the facts of this case. To support this contention, the Prosecution looks to the fact, inter alia, that after 19 May 1992, when the Yugoslav People's Army ("JNA") formally withdrew from Bosnia and Herzegovina, VRS soldiers continued to receive their salaries from the government of the FRY which also funded the pensions of retired VJ soldiers who had been serving with the VRS. The Prosecution looks to a number of additional factors in support of its contention that there was more than mere logistical support by the FRY after 19 May 1992. These factors include the structures and ranks of the VRS and VJ being identical, as well as the supervision of the VRS by the FRY after that date. From those facts, the Prosecution draws the inference that the FRY was exercising effective military control over the VRS.

2. The Defence Case

75. The Defence asserts that the Trial Chamber was correct in applying the "effective control" test derived from Nicaragua and submits that the "demonstrable link" test is incorrect. The Defence formulates the test which the Appeals Chamber should apply as "were the Bosnian Serbs acting as 'organs' of another State?" 99

76. The Defence submits that it is misleading to distinguish Nicaragua on the basis that the decision is concerned only with State responsibility. The Defence further argues that the Court in Nicaragua was concerned with the broader question of which part of international humanitarian law should apply to the relevant conduct.

77. On the facts of the present case there is no evidential basis for concluding that after 19 May 1992, the VRS was either effectively controlled by or could be regarded as an agent of the FRY government. The Defence's submission is that the FRY and the Republika Srpska coordinated with each other, solely as allies. For this reason, the VRS was not an organ of the FRY.

78. The Defence submits that the "demonstrable link" test is not the correct test to be applied under Article 2 of the Statute. The Defence argues that the test has no authority in international law and submits that it should also be rejected for policy reasons. If the Appeals Chamber were to accept the "demonstrable link" test, this could result in the undesirable outcome of a State being held responsible for the actions of another State or entity over which the State did not have any effective control. Further, the Defence submits that the test at issue introduces uncertainty into international law

as it is unclear what degree of link is necessary in order to satisfy the test.

79. The Defence concedes that if the correct test were the "demonstrable link" test, on the facts of this case the test would be satisfied. 100

B. Discussion

1. The Requirements for the Applicability of Article 2 of the Statute

80. Article 2 of the Statute embraces various disparate classes of offences with their own specific legal ingredients. The general legal ingredients, however, may be categorised as follows.

(i) The nature of the conflict. [T]he international nature of the conflict is a prerequisite for the applicability of Article 2.

(ii) The status of the victim. Grave breaches must be perpetrated against persons or property defined as "protected" by any of the four Geneva Conventions of 1949. To establish whether a person is "protected," reference must clearly be made to the relevant provisions of those Conventions.

81. In the instant case it therefore falls to the Appeals Chamber to establish first of all (i) on what legal conditions armed forces fighting in a prima facie internal armed conflict may be regarded as acting on behalf of a foreign Power and (ii) whether in the instant case the factual conditions which are required by law were satisfied.

82. Only if the Appeals Chamber finds that the conflict was international at all relevant times will it turn to the second question of whether the victims were to be regarded as "protected persons."

2. The Nature of the Conflict

83. The requirement that the conflict be international for the grave breaches regime to operate pursuant to Article 2 of the Statute has not been contested by the parties.

84. It is indisputable that an armed conflict is international if it takes place between two or more States. In addition, in case of an internal armed conflict breaking out on the territory of a State, it may become international (or, depending upon the circumstances, be international in character alongside an internal armed conflict) if (i) another State intervenes in that conflict through its troops, or alternatively if (ii) some of the participants in the internal armed conflict act on behalf of that other State.

85. In the instant case, the Prosecution claims that at all relevant times, the conflict was an international armed conflict between two States, namely Bosnia and Herzegovina ("BH") on the one hand, and the FRY on the other.

86. The Trial Chamber found the conflict to be an international armed conflict between BH and FRY until 19 May 1992, when the JNA formally withdrew from Bosnia and Herzegovina.

87. In the instant case, there is sufficient evidence to justify the Trial Chamber's finding of fact that the conflict prior to 19 May 1992 was international in character. The question whether after 19 May 1992 it continued to be international or became instead exclusively internal turns on the issue of whether Bosnian Serb forces — in whose hands the Bosnian victims in this case found themselves — could be considered as *de iure* or *de facto* organs of a foreign Power, namely the FRY.

3. The Legal Criteria for Establishing When, in an Armed Conflict Which is Prima Facie Internal, Armed Forces May Be Regarded as Acting On Behalf of a Foreign Power, Thereby Rendering the Conflict International

92. A starting point for this discussion is provided by the criteria for lawful combatants laid down in the Third Geneva Convention of 1949. Under this Convention, militias or paramilitary groups or units may be regarded as legitimate combatants if they form "part of [the] armed forces" of a Party to the conflict (Article 4A(1)) or "belong [to a] Party to the conflict" (Article 4A(2)) and satisfy the other four requirements

provided for in Article 4A(2).[2] It is clear that this provision is primarily directed toward establishing the requirements for the status of lawful combatants. Nevertheless, one of its logical consequences is that if, in an armed conflict, paramilitary units "belong" to a State other than the one against which they are fighting, the conflict is international and therefore serious violations of the Geneva Conventions may be classified as "grave breaches."

94. In other words, States have in practice accepted that belligerents may use paramilitary units and other irregulars in the conduct of hostilities only on the condition that those belligerents are prepared to take responsibility for any infringements committed by such forces. In order for irregulars to qualify as lawful combatants, it appears that international rules and State practice therefore require control over them by a Party to an international armed conflict and, by the same token, a relationship of dependence and allegiance of these irregulars vis-à-vis that Party to the conflict. These then may be regarded as the ingredients of the term "belonging to a Party to the conflict."

95. The Appeals Chamber thus considers that the Third Geneva Convention, by providing in Article 4 the requirement of "belonging to a Party to the conflict," implicitly refers to a test of control.

96. This conclusion, based on the letter and the spirit of the Geneva Conventions, is borne out by the entire logic of international humanitarian law. This body of law is not grounded on formalistic postulates. It is not based on the notion that only those who have the formal status of State organs, *i.e.*, are members of the armed forces of a State, are duty bound both to refrain from engaging in violations of humanitarian law as well as — if they are in a position of authority — to prevent or punish the commission of such crimes. Rather, it is a realistic body of law, grounded on the notion of effectiveness and inspired by the aim of deterring deviation from its standards to the maximum extent possible. It follows, amongst other things, that humanitarian law holds accountable not only those having formal positions of authority but also those who wield *de facto* power as well as those who exercise control over perpetrators of serious violations of international humanitarian law. Hence, in cases such as that currently under discussion, what is required for criminal responsibility to arise is some measure of control by a Party to the conflict over the perpetrators.[3]

97. It is nevertheless imperative to specify what degree of authority or control must be wielded by a foreign State over armed forces fighting on its behalf in order to render international an armed conflict which is *prima facie* internal. Indeed, the legal consequences of the characterisation of the conflict as either internal or international are extremely important. Should the conflict eventually be classified as international, it would *inter alia* follow that a foreign State may in certain circumstances be held responsible for violations of international law perpetrated by the armed groups acting on its behalf.

---

[2] [Court's Footnote 113] These four conditions are as follows:
  (a) that of being commanded by a person responsible for his subordinates;
  (b) that of having a fixed distinctive sign recognisable at a distance;
  (c) that of carrying arms openly; and
  (d) that of conducting their operations in accordance with the laws and customs of war.

[3] [Court's Footnote 116] *See also* the ICRC Commentary to Article 29 of the Fourth Geneva Convention (Jean Pictet (ed.), Commentary: IV Geneva Convention Relative to the Protection of Civilian Persons in Time of War, International Committee of the Red Cross, Geneva, 1958, First Reprint, 1994, p. 212):

> It does not matter whether the person guilty of treatment contrary to the Convention is an agent of the Occupying Power or in the service of the occupied State; what is important is to know where the decision leading to the unlawful act was made, where the intention was formed and the order given. If the unlawful act was committed at the instigation of the Occupying Power, then the Occupying Power is responsible; if, on the other hand, it was the result of a truly independent decision on the part of the local authorities, the Occupying Power cannot be held responsible.

98. International humanitarian law does not contain any criteria unique to this body of law for establishing when a group of individuals may be regarded as being under the control of a State, that is, as acting as *de facto* State officials. Consequently, it is necessary to examine the notion of control by a State over individuals, laid down in general international law, for the purpose of establishing whether those individuals may be regarded as acting as de facto State officials. This notion can be found in those general international rules on State responsibility which set out the legal criteria for attributing to a State acts performed by individuals not having the formal status of State officials.

99. In dealing with the question of the legal conditions required for individuals to be considered as acting on behalf of a State, *i.e.*, as *de facto* State officials, a high degree of control has been authoritatively suggested by the International Court of Justice in *Nicaragua*.

100. The issue brought before the International Court of Justice was whether a foreign State, the United States, because of its financing, organising, training, equipping and planning of the operations of organised military and paramilitary groups of Nicaraguan rebels (the so-called contras) in Nicaragua, was responsible for violations of international humanitarian law committed by those rebels. The Court held that a high degree of control was necessary for this to be the case. It required that (i) a Party not only be in effective control of a military or paramilitary group, but that (ii) the control be exercised with respect to the specific operation in the course of which breaches may have been committed. The Court went so far as to state that in order to establish that the United States was responsible for "acts contrary to human rights and humanitarian law" allegedly perpetrated by the Nicaraguan contras, it was necessary to prove that the United States had specifically "directed or enforced" the perpetration of those acts.

101. As is apparent, the issue brought before the International Court of Justice revolved around State responsibility; what was at stake was not the criminal culpability of the contras for serious violations of international humanitarian law, but rather the question of whether or not the contras had acted as *de facto* organs of the United States on its request, thus generating the international responsibility of that State.

103. [W]ith a view to limiting the scope of the test at issue, the Prosecution has contended that the criterion for ascertaining State responsibility is different from that necessary for establishing individual criminal responsibility. In the former case one would have to decide whether serious violations of international humanitarian law by private individuals may be attributed to a State because those individuals acted as *de facto* State officials. In the latter case, one would have instead to establish whether a private individual may be held criminally responsible for serious violations of international humanitarian law amounting to "grave breaches." Consequently, it has been asserted, the *Nicaragua* test, while valid within the context of State responsibility, is immaterial to the issue of individual criminal responsibility for "grave breaches." The Appeals Chamber, with respect, does not share this view.

104. What is at issue is not the distinction between the two classes of responsibility. What is at issue is a preliminary question: that of the conditions on which under international law an individual may be held to act as a de facto organ of a State. Logically these conditions must be the same both in the case: (i) where the court's task is to ascertain whether an act performed by an individual may be attributed to a State, thereby generating the international responsibility of that State; and (ii) where the court must instead determine whether individuals are acting as de facto State officials, thereby rendering the conflict international and thus setting the necessary precondition for the "grave breaches" regime to apply. In both cases, what is at issue is not the distinction between State responsibility and individual criminal responsibility. Rather, the question is that of establishing the criteria for the legal imputability to a State of acts performed by individuals not having the status of State officials. In the one case these acts, if they prove to be attributable to a State, will give rise to the international

responsibility of that State; in the other case, they will ensure that the armed conflict must be classified as international.

117. The principles of international law concerning the attribution to States of acts performed by private individuals are not based on rigid and uniform criteria. [I]f it is proved that individuals who are not regarded as organs of a State by its legislation nevertheless do in fact act on behalf of that State, their acts are attributable to the State. The rationale behind this rule is to prevent States from escaping international responsibility by having private individuals carry out tasks that may not or should not be performed by State officials, or by claiming that individuals actually participating in governmental authority are not classified as State organs under national legislation and therefore do not engage State responsibility. In other words, States are not allowed on the one hand to act *de facto* through individuals and on the other to disassociate themselves from such conduct when these individuals breach international law. The requirement of international law for the attribution to States of acts performed by private individuals is that the State exercises control over the individuals. The degree of control may, however, vary according to the factual circumstances of each case. The Appeals Chamber fails to see why in each and every circumstance international law should require a high threshold for the test of control. Rather, various situations may be distinguished.

118. One situation is the case of a private individual who is engaged by a State to perform some specific illegal acts in the territory of another State (for instance, kidnapping a State official, murdering a dignitary or a high-ranking State official, blowing up a power station or, especially in times of war, carrying out acts of sabotage). In such a case, it would be necessary to show that the State issued specific instructions concerning the commission of the breach in order to prove — if only by necessary implication — that the individual acted as a *de facto* State agent. A generic authority over the individual would not be sufficient to engage the international responsibility of the State. A similar situation may come about when an unorganised group of individuals commits acts contrary to international law. For these acts to be attributed to the State it would seem necessary to prove not only that the State exercised some measure of authority over those individuals but also that it issued specific instructions to them concerning the performance of the acts at issue, or that it *ex post facto* publicly endorsed those acts.

119. To these situations another one may be added, which arises when a State entrusts a private individual (or group of individuals) with the specific task of performing lawful actions on its behalf, but then the individuals, in discharging that task, breach an international obligation of the State (for instance, a private detective is requested by State authorities to protect a senior foreign diplomat but he instead seriously mistreats him while performing that task). In this case, by analogy with the rules concerning State responsibility for acts of State officials acting *ultra vires*, it can be held that the State incurs responsibility on account of its specific request to the private individual or individuals to discharge a task on its behalf.

120. One should distinguish the situation of individuals acting on behalf of a State without specific instructions, from that of individuals making up an organised and hierarchically structured group, such as a military unit or, in case of war or civil strife, armed bands of irregulars or rebels. Plainly, an organised group differs from an individual in that the former normally has a structure, a chain of command and a set of rules as well as the outward symbols of authority. Normally a member of the group does not act on his own but conforms to the standards prevailing in the group and is subject to the authority of the head of the group. Consequently, for the attribution to a State of acts of these groups it is sufficient to require that the group as a whole be under the overall control of the State.

121. This kind of State control over a military group and the fact that the State is held responsible for acts performed by a group independently of any State instructions, or

even contrary to instructions, to some extent equates the group with State organs proper. Under the rules of State responsibility, a State is internationally accountable for *ultra vires* acts or transactions of its organs. In other words it incurs responsibility even for acts committed by its officials outside their remit or contrary to its behest. Generally speaking, it can be maintained that the whole body of international law on State responsibility is based on a realistic concept of accountability, which disregards legal formalities and aims at ensuring that States entrusting some functions to individuals or groups of individuals must answer for their actions, even when they act contrary to their directives.

122. The same logic should apply to the situation under discussion. As noted above, the situation of an organised group is different from that of a single private individual performing a specific act on behalf of a State. In the case of an organised group, the group normally engages in a series of activities. If it is under the overall control of a State, it must perforce engage the responsibility of that State for its activities, whether or not each of them was specifically imposed, requested or directed by the State.

123. Despite these legal differences, the fact nevertheless remains that international law renders any State responsible for acts in breach of international law performed (i) by individuals having the formal status of organs of a State (and this occurs even when these organs act ultra vires or contra legem), or (ii) by individuals who make up organised groups subject to the State's control. International law does so regardless of whether or not the State has issued specific instructions to those individuals. Clearly, the rationale behind this legal regulation is that otherwise, States might easily shelter behind, or use as a pretext, their internal legal system or the lack of any specific instructions in order to disclaim international responsibility.

125. In cases dealing with members of military or paramilitary groups, courts have clearly departed from the notion of "effective control" set out by the International Court of Justice (i.e., control that extends to the issuance of specific instructions concerning the various activities of the individuals in question).

130. Precisely what measure of State control does international law require for organised military groups? Judging from international case law and State practice, it would seem that for such control to come about, it is not sufficient for the group to be financially or even militarily assisted by a State. This proposition is confirmed by the international practice concerning national liberation movements. Although some States provided movements such as the PLO, SWAPO or the ANC with a territorial base or with economic and military assistance (short of sending their own troops to aid them), other States, including those against which these movements were fighting, did not attribute international responsibility for the acts of the movements to the assisting States. *Nicaragua* also supports this proposition, since the United States, although it aided the contras financially, and otherwise, was not held responsible for their acts (whereas on account of this financial and other assistance to the contras, the United States was held by the Court to be responsible for breaching the principle of non-intervention as well as "its obligation . . . not to use force against another State." This was clearly a case of responsibility for the acts of its own organs).

131. In order to attribute the acts of a military or paramilitary group to a State, it must be proved that the State wields overall control over the group, not only by equipping and financing the group, but also by coordinating or helping in the general planning of its military activity. Only then can the State be held internationally accountable for any misconduct of the group. However, it is not necessary that, in addition, the State should also issue, either to the head or to members of the group, instructions for the commission of specific acts contrary to international law.

132. It should be added that courts have taken a different approach with regard to individuals or groups not organised into military structures. With regard to such individuals or groups, courts have not considered an overall or general level of control to be sufficient, but have instead insisted upon specific instructions or directives aimed

at the commission of specific acts, or have required public approval of those acts following their commission.

137. In sum, the Appeals Chamber holds the view that international rules do not always require the same degree of control over armed groups or private individuals for the purpose of determining whether an individual not having the status of a State official under internal legislation can be regarded as a de facto organ of the State.

141. It should be added that international law does not provide only for a test of overall control applying to armed groups and that of specific instructions (or subsequent public approval), applying to single individuals or militarily unorganised groups. The Appeals Chamber holds the view that international law also embraces a third test. This test is the assimilation of individuals to State organs on account of their actual behaviour within the structure of a State (and regardless of any possible requirement of State instructions). Such a test is best illustrated by reference to certain cases that deserve to be mentioned, if only briefly.

142. The first case is *Joseph Kramer et al.* (also called the *Belsen* case), brought before a British military court sitting at Luneburg (Germany). The Defendants comprised not only some German staff members of the Belsen and Auschwitz concentration camps but also a number of camp inmates of Polish nationality and an Austrian Jew "elevated by the camp administrators to positions of authority over the other internees." They were *inter alia* accused of murder and other offences against the camp inmates. According to the official report on this case:

> In meeting the argument that no war crime could be committed by Poles against other Allied nationals, the Prosecutor said that by identifying themselves with the authorities the Polish accused had made themselves as much responsible as the S.S. themselves. Perhaps it could be claimed that by the same process they could be regarded as having approximated to membership of the armed forces of Germany.

143. Another case is more recent. This is the judgement handed down by the Dutch Court of Cassation on 29 May 1978 in the *Menten* case. Menten, a Dutch national who was not formally a member of the German forces, had been accused of war crimes and crimes against humanity for having killed a number of civilians, mostly Jews, in Poland, on behalf of German special forces (SD or Einsatzkommandos). The court found that Menten in fact behaved as a member of the German forces and consequently was criminally liable for these crimes.

145. In the light of the above discussion, the following conclusion may be safely reached. In the case at issue, given that the Bosnian Serb armed forces constituted a "military organization," the control of the FRY authorities over these armed forces required by international law for considering the armed conflict to be international was overall control going beyond the mere financing and equipping of such forces and involving also participation in the planning and supervision of military operations. By contrast, international rules do not require that such control should extend to the issuance of specific orders or instructions relating to single military actions, whether or not such actions were contrary to international humanitarian law.

162. The Appeals Chamber therefore concludes that, for the period material to this case (1992), the armed forces of the Republika Srpska were to be regarded as acting under the overall control of and on behalf of the FRY. Hence, even after 19 May 1992 the armed conflict in Bosnia and Herzegovina between the Bosnian Serbs and the central authorities of Bosnia and Herzegovina must be classified as an international armed conflict.

5. The Status of the Victims

163. Having established that in the circumstances of the case the first of the two requirements set out in Article 2 of the Statute for the grave breaches provisions to be applicable, namely, that the armed conflict be international, was fulfilled, the Appeals

Chamber now turns to the second requirement, that is, whether the victims of the alleged offences were "protected persons."

(a) The Relevant Rules

164. Article 4(1) of Geneva Convention IV (protection of civilians), applicable to the case at issue, defines "protected persons" — hence possible victims of grave breaches — as those "in the hands of a Party to the conflict or Occupying Power of which they are not nationals." In other words, subject to the provisions of Article 4(2), the Convention intends to protect civilians (in enemy territory, occupied territory or the combat zone) who do not have the nationality of the belligerent in whose hands they find themselves, or who are stateless persons. In addition, as is apparent from the preparatory work, the Convention also intends to protect those civilians in occupied territory who, while having the nationality of the Party to the conflict in whose hands they find themselves, are refugees and thus no longer owe allegiance to this Party and no longer enjoy its diplomatic protection (consider, for instance, a situation similar to that of German Jews who had fled to France before 1940, and thereafter found themselves in the hands of German forces occupying French territory).

165. Thus already in 1949 the legal bond of nationality was not regarded as crucial and allowance was made for special cases. In the aforementioned case of refugees, the lack of both allegiance to a State and diplomatic protection by this State was regarded as more important than the formal link of nationality. In the cases provided for in Article 4(2), in addition to nationality, account was taken of the existence or non-existence of diplomatic protection: nationals of a neutral State or a co-belligerent State are not treated as "protected persons" unless they are deprived of or do not enjoy diplomatic protection. In other words, those nationals are not "protected persons" as long as they benefit from the normal diplomatic protection of their State; when they lose it or in any event do not enjoy it, the Convention automatically grants them the status of "protected persons."

166. This legal approach, hinging on substantial relations more than on formal bonds, becomes all the more important in present-day international armed conflicts. While previously wars were primarily between well-established States, in modern inter-ethnic armed conflicts such as that in the former Yugoslavia, new States are often created during the conflict and ethnicity rather than nationality may become the grounds for allegiance. Or, put another way, ethnicity may become determinative of national allegiance. Under these conditions, the requirement of nationality is even less adequate to define protected persons. In such conflicts, not only the text and the drafting history of the Convention but also, and more importantly, the Convention's object and purpose suggest that allegiance to a Party to the conflict and, correspondingly, control by this Party over persons in a given territory, may be regarded as the crucial test.

(b) Factual Findings

167. In the instant case the Bosnian Serbs, including the Appellant, arguably had the same nationality as the victims, that is, they were nationals of Bosnia and Herzegovina. However, it has been shown above that the Bosnian Serb forces acted as *de facto* organs of another State, namely, the FRY. Thus the requirements set out in Article 4 of Geneva Convention IV are met: the victims were "protected persons" as they found themselves in the hands of armed forces of a State of which they were not nationals.

169. Hence, even if in the circumstances of the case the perpetrators and the victims were to be regarded as possessing the same nationality, Article 4 would still be applicable. Indeed, the victims did not owe allegiance to (and did not receive the diplomatic protection of) the State (the FRY) on whose behalf the Bosnian Serb armed forces had been fighting.

170. It follows from the above that the Trial Chamber erred in so far as it acquitted the Appellant on the sole ground that the grave breaches regime of the Geneva Conventions of 1949 did not apply.

171. The Appeals Chamber accordingly finds that the Appellant was guilty of grave breaches of the Geneva Conventions on Counts 8, 9, 12, 15, 21 and 32.

NOTES AND QUESTIONS

1. Formalism and the Reach of Law. The logic of the Appeals Chamber presents a serious challenge:

> The Appeals Chamber . . . considers that the Third Geneva Convention, by providing in Article 4 the requirement of "belonging to a Party to the conflict," implicitly refers to a test of control. This conclusion, based on the letter and the spirit of the Geneva Conventions, is borne out by the entire logic of international humanitarian law. This body of law is not grounded on formalistic postulates. It is not based on the notion that only those who have the formal status of State organs, i.e., are members of the armed forces of a State, are duty bound both to refrain from engaging in violations of humanitarian law as well as — if they are in a position of authority — to prevent or punish the commission of such crimes. Rather, it is a realistic body of law, grounded on the notion of effectiveness and inspired by the aim of deterring deviation from its standards to the maximum extent possible. It follows, amongst other things, that humanitarian law holds accountable not only those having formal positions of authority but also those who wield de facto power as well as those who exercise control over perpetrators of serious violations of international humanitarian law. Hence, in cases such as that currently under discussion, what is required for criminal responsibility to arise is some measure of control by a Party to the conflict over the perpetrators.

What does the court mean by the statement that "this body of law is not grounded on formalistic postulates" when the court then proceeds to many pages of formalistic argument? If the court really meant to extend international humanitarian law to its fullest extent, then what is the point of asking whether there is State involvement in the actions at all? Isn't a person criminally responsible for atrocities, under the heading of crimes against humanity, regardless of whether he or she is involved with a State?

Perhaps this is where a difference between the Law of Armed Conflict (LOAC) and International Humanitarian Law (IHL) becomes critical. If a person is not connected to a State or a State pretender, then maybe the relevant body of law is not the law of war but IHL (crimes against humanity and genocide). On that understanding, the members of a "nonstate" group are not combatants but criminals.

2. Individual and State Responsibility. The court does not really explain its assertion in ¶ 104 that "what is at issue is not the distinction between State responsibility and individual criminal responsibility." It maintains that those two issues are to be governed by the same criteria. But why should that be so? IHL clearly applies to non-State actors, so why is the court so adamant that individual and State responsibility are the same? Again, the answer could be that the two issues are the same with regard to LOAC but not with regard to other international law (IHL).

3. LOAC and IHL. Assuming that the previous notes are correct and that the explanation for all this formalistic argumentation is to distinguish between application of LOAC and application of IHL, then why is that important? Maybe the explanation here is something like the explanation for the "state action" requirement in U.S. law. The federal government does not punish someone unless that person acts "under color of state law" or in violation of some federal interest such as regulation of interstate commerce.

4. LOAC and Internal Conflicts. Why does it matter that the conflict became internal after May 19, 1992? In an internal conflict, common article 3 would still apply and so wouldn't the concept of "war crimes"? Are there actually three categories in play

— international armed conflict (AC), internal AC, and no AC (which still leaves IHL applicable?).

5. Insurgents. Because the ICTY equates individual and state responsibility in an armed conflict, it is not the least bit clear what the court would say about atrocities committed by an insurgent group against civilians within its own borders. Such a group would not be under the control of a State, so would it not be subject to the law of war? Traditionally, when a group reaches sufficient strength to be considered a "belligerent," (i.e., having sufficient power to control some portion of the territory), then its members obtain combat immunity and POW status so long as they comply with LOAC themselves. Ingrid de Lupis, The Law of War 23–24 (1987). If they commit atrocities, then would they not be guilty of war crimes?

6. Non-state Combatants. Can a person who acts on behalf of a group without military pretensions be considered a combatant? The Bush Administration's idea of an "unlawful enemy combatant" appeared to be that anyone who was engaged in violent behavior without wearing a uniform of a nation-State could be declared a combatant and thus thrown into military prison. Eventually, the Military Commission Act of 2006, *infra* § 8.05[A], defined the term to mean "a person who has engaged in hostilities or who has purposefully and materially supported hostilities against the United States or its co-belligerents who is not a lawful enemy combatant." That raises the question whether "hostilities" is the same as "armed conflict." If it is, then the struggle with non-state terrorist organizations would not qualify in the view of the ICTY unless those groups were under some level of control of a State.

7. International Concern with Violence. Despite the formalism of the European opinion style, there is some policy reality behind the Tribunal's position. If a rebel group is not playing by the rules, then the international community can leave them to the tender mercies of the government under attack and not take an interest in their behavior, at least insofar as the Geneva Conventions are concerned. In this situation, then the government need not be concerned about application of the Geneva Conventions to its treatment of the rebels.

In the Yugoslavia situation, however, the armed bands were not attacking the government but were attacking civilians, allegedly with government acquiescence. Thus, the real policy question is at what stage does the international community take an interest in this situation? The answer of the ICTY is "when the perpetrators are under the control of the State."

All of this, however, is limited to application of those Conventions that depend upon the existence of a state of "armed conflict." Absent "armed conflict," the government forces are still subject to other Conventions such as those dealing with torture. The next question is whether crimes against humanity and genocide have been sufficiently incorporated into customary international law that they can be applied to non-state actors.

NOTE ON CRIMES AGAINST HUMANITY

Two additional grounds of appeal by the Prosecutor dealt with the Trial Chamber's reading of the Statute's definition of "crimes against humanity" to exclude both purely personal pursuits and actions not tinged with discrimination on the basis of race, sex, religion, or similar criteria.

The Trial Chamber held that a person does not commit a "crime against humanity" when acting for purely personal reasons separated from any "armed conflict" during which those actions occur. This is not exactly the same as a "color of law" argument, because it recognizes that even private persons are subject to the rules against commission of crimes against humanity. Although Tadic had been convicted for these crimes and thus the ruling had no bearing on the outcome, the Appeals Chamber nevertheless took up this issue as an "matter of general significance for the Tribunal's jurisprudence." (We can only wonder how vigorously did the Defence Team research and argue the opposite position?)

The Appeals Chamber decided that personal motivation is irrelevant to crimes against humanity. Even if the defendant were acting for reasons wholly unrelated to the armed conflict and even if there were no group-based discriminatory motivation behind those actions, the listed actions would still be criminal. The U.S. has faced this issue in its KKK statutes that criminalize conspiracies to deprive persons of civil rights and has imposed a group-based discriminatory intent requirement. The ICTY decision, however, must be read in light of the particular wording of its statute, which criminalizes certain actions when taken "in armed conflict . . . and directed against a civilian population."

Could Tadic have been considered a terrorist? Was he engaged in "armed conflict" subject to the laws and customs of war? or was he a civilian engaged in violence against fellow civilians? Should ordinary street thugs be subject to the processes of international criminal law? In the context of widespread civil unrest and bloodshed, perhaps so.

Both the Geneva Convention issue and the crimes against humanity issues were addressed by the Security Council in creating the Statute of the International Tribunal for Rwanda, to which we turn next.

PROSECUTOR v. AKAYESU
International Criminal Tribunal for Rwanda, Trial Chambre I
Case No. ICTR-96-4-T

JUDGEMENT

Rwanda is a small, very hilly country in the Great Lakes region of Central Africa. Before the events of 1994, it was the most densely populated country of the African continent (7.1 million inhabitants for 26,338 square kilometres) [about 100 miles square, slightly smaller than Maryland]. Ninety percent of the population lives on agriculture. Its per capita income is among the lowest in the world, mainly because of a very high population pressure on land.

[Colonial rule in the region began with Germany in 1897 and was taken over by Belgium in 1917. The native monarchy drew heavily on a type of caste system in which the Tutsi were like a nobility.]

The terms Hutu and Tutsi . . . referred to individuals rather than to groups. In those days, the distinction between the Hutu and Tutsi was based on lineage rather than ethnicity. Indeed, the demarcation line was blurred: one could move from one status to another, as one became rich or poor, or even through marriage. Both German and Belgian colonial authorities, if only at the outset as far as the latter are concerned, relied on an elite essentially composed of people who referred to themselves as Tutsi. . . . In the early 1930s, Belgian authorities introduced a permanent distinction by dividing the population into three groups which they called ethnic groups, with the Hutu representing about 84% of the population, while the Tutsi (about 15%) and Twa (about 1%) accounted for the rest. In line with this division, it became mandatory for every Rwandan to carry an identity card mentioning his or her ethnicity.

[Belgium established a "provisional government" and granted self-governance to the country in 1961. Over the next three decades, sporadic outbreaks of violence resulted in thousands of deaths and large-scale emigration of Tutsis to neighboring countries. Some of those exiles formed armed rebel forces such as the RPF. Following several assassinations, a transitional government attempted to negotiate new arrangements but the President was killed in a plane crash in April 1994. The Rwandan military seized control of the government and several moderate leaders (both Tutsi and sympathetic Hutus) were killed. The Tutsi exile forces then started moving across the border and mass violence erupted. Reliable estimates indicate that between April and the end of June 1994, as many as 500,000 to 1,000,000 were killed, mostly Tutsi and their Hutu sympathizers. The principal Hutu perpetrators were the MRND paramilitary militia and its youth subsidiary, the Interahamwe.

[Jean Paul Akayesu, a Rwandan citizen who was bourgmestre of Taba commune (something like chief executive of a U.S. county), was brought to trial on charges of participating in the violence.

[The principal differences between the ICTY Statute and the ICTR Statute are that the latter omitted "violations of the laws or customs of war" but specifically included "serious violations of Common Article 3." Thus, the ICTR has jurisdiction over Common Article 3, genocide, and crimes against humanity.]

1. INTRODUCTION

6. The Amended Indictment [stated, among other things]:

12. As bourgmestre, Jean Paul AKAYESU was responsible for maintaining law and public order in his commune. At least 2000 Tutsis were killed in Taba between April 7 and the end of June, 1994, while he was still in power. The killings in Taba were openly committed and so widespread that, as bourgmestre, Jean Paul AKAYESU must have known about them. Although he had the authority and responsibility to do so, Jean Paul AKAYESU never attempted to prevent the killing of Tutsis in the commune in any way or called for assistance from regional or national authorities to quell the violence.

12A. Between April 7 and the end of June, 1994, hundreds of civilians (hereinafter "displaced civilians") sought refuge at the bureau communal. The majority of these displaced civilians were Tutsi. While seeking refuge at the bureau communal, female displaced civilians were regularly taken by armed local militia and/or communal police and subjected to sexual violence, and/or beaten on or near the bureau communal premises. Displaced civilians were also murdered frequently on or near the bureau communal premises. Many women were forced to endure multiple acts of sexual violence which were at times committed by more than one assailant. These acts of sexual violence were generally accompanied by explicit threats of death or bodily harm. The female displaced civilians lived in constant fear and their physical and psychological health deteriorated as a result of the sexual violence and beatings and killings.

12B. Jean Paul AKAYESU knew that the acts of sexual violence, beatings and murders were being committed and was at times present during their commission. Jean Paul AKAYESU facilitated the commission of the sexual violence, beatings and murders by allowing the sexual violence and beatings and murders to occur on or near the bureau communal premises. By virtue of his presence during the commission of the sexual violence, beatings and murders and by failing to prevent the sexual violence, beatings and murders, Jean Paul AKAYESU encouraged these activities.

14. The morning of April 19, 1994, following the murder of Sylvere Karera, Jean Paul AKAYESU led a meeting in Gishyeshye sector at which he sanctioned the death of Sylvere Karera and urged the population to eliminate accomplices of the RPF, which was understood by those present to mean Tutsis. Over 100 people were present at the meeting. The killing of Tutsis in Taba began shortly after the meeting.

15. At the same meeting in Gishyeshye sector on April 19, 1994, Jean Paul AKAYESU named at least three prominent Tutsis who had to be killed because of their alleged relationships with the RPF. Later that day, Juvénal Rukundakuvuga was killed in Kanyinya. Within the next few days, Emmanuel Sempabwa was clubbed to death in front of the Taba bureau communal.

19. On or about April 19, 1994, Jean Paul AKAYESU took 8 detained men from the Taba bureau communal and ordered militia members to kill them. The militia killed them with clubs, machetes, small axes and sticks. The victims had fled from Runda

commune and had been held by Jean Paul AKAYESU.

20. On or about April 19, 1994, Jean Paul AKAYESU ordered the local people and militia to kill intellectual and influential people. Five teachers from the secondary school of Taba were killed on his instructions. The local people and militia killed them with machetes and agricultural tools in front of the Taba bureau communal.

30. In essence, the Defence case — insofar as the Chamber has been able to establish it — is that the Accused did not commit, order or participate in any of the killings, beatings or acts of sexual violence alleged in the Indictment. The Defence concedes that a genocide occurred in Rwanda and that massacres of Tutsi took place in Taba Commune, but it argues that the Accused was helpless to prevent them, being outnumbered and overpowered by one Silas Kubwimana and the Interahamwe. The Defence pointed out that, according to prosecution witness R, Akayesu had been so harassed by the Interahamwe that at one point he had had to flee Taba commune. Once the massacres had become widespread, the Accused was denuded of all authority and lacked the means to stop the killings.

31. The Defence claims that the Chamber should not require the Accused to be a hero, to have laid down his life — as, for example, did the bourgmestre of Mugina — in a futile attempt to prevent killings and beatings. The Defence alluded to the fact that General Dallaire, in charge of UNAMIR and 2,500 troops, was unable to prevent the genocide. How, then, was Akayesu, with 10 communal policemen at his disposal, to fare any better? Moreover, the Defence argue, no bourgmestre in the whole of Rwanda was able to prevent the massacres in his Commune, no matter how willing he was to do so.

3. GENOCIDE IN RWANDA IN 1994?

114. Even though the number of victims is yet to be known with accuracy, no one can reasonably refute the fact that widespread killings were perpetrated throughout Rwanda in 1994.

116. Consequently, in view of these widespread killings the victims of which were mainly Tutsi, the Chamber is of the opinion that the first requirement for there to be genocide has been met, the killing and causing serious bodily harm to members of a group.

117. The second requirement is that these killings and serious bodily harm, as is the case in this instance, be committed with the intent to destroy, in whole or in part, a particular group targeted as such.

118. In the opinion of the Chamber, there is no doubt that considering their undeniable scale, their systematic nature and their atrociousness, the massacres were aimed at exterminating the group that was targeted.

4. EVIDENTIARY MATTERS

151. The Interahamwe were the youth movement of the MRND. During the war, the term also covered anyone who had anti-Tutsi tendencies, irrespective of their political background, and who collaborated with the MRND youth.

5. FACTUAL FINDINGS

192. The Chamber finds that the allegations set forth in paragraph 12 cannot be fully established. The Accused did take action between 7 April and 18 April to protect the citizens of his commune. It appears that he did also request assistance from national authorities at the meeting on 18 April 1994. Accordingly, the Accused did attempt to prevent the killing of Tutsi in his Commune, and it cannot be said that he never did so.

193. Nevertheless, the Chamber finds beyond a reasonable doubt that the conduct of the Accused changed after 18 April 1994 and that after this date the Accused did not attempt to prevent the killing of Tutsi in the commune of Taba. In fact, there is

evidence that he not only knew of and witnessed killings, but that he participated in and even ordered killings. The fact that on one occasion he helped one Hutu woman protect her Tutsi children does not alter the Chamber's assessment that the Accused did not generally attempt to prevent the killings at all after 18 April. The Accused contends that he was subject to coercion, but the Chamber finds this contention greatly inconsistent with a substantial amount of concordant testimony from other witnesses. It is also inconsistent with his own pre-trial written statement. Witness C testified to having heard the accused say to an Interahamwe "I do not think that what we are doing is proper. We are going to have to pay for this blood that is being shed," a statement which indicates the Accused's knowledge of the wrongfulness of his acts and his awareness of the consequences of his deeds. For these reasons, the Chamber does not accept the testimony of the Accused regarding his conduct after 18 April, and finds beyond a reasonable doubt that he did not attempt to prevent killings of Tutsi after this date. Whether he had the power to do so is not at issue, as he never even tried and as there is evidence establishing beyond a reasonable doubt that he consciously chose the course of collaboration with violence against Tutsi rather than shielding them from it.

309. The Chamber finds that it has been proved beyond reasonable doubt that Akayesu released eight detained men of Runda commune whom he was holding in the bureau communal and handed them over to the Interahamwe. It has also been proved beyond reasonable doubt that Akayesu ordered the local militia to kill them. It has been proved beyond reasonable doubt that the eight refugees were killed by the Interahamwe in the presence of Akayesu. It has been proved beyond reasonable doubt that the eight refugees were killed because they were Tutsi.

313. The Chamber finds that it has been proved beyond reasonable doubt that on or about 19 April 1994, Akayesu ordered the local people and Interahamwe to kill "intellectual people." It has been proved beyond reasonable doubt that, after the killing of the refugees, Akayesu instructed the local people and Interahamwe near him at the bureau communal to "fetch the one who remains," a professor by the name of Samuel, and that consequent to this instruction, a certain professor by the name of Samuel was brought to the bureau communal. It has been proved beyond reasonable doubt that Samuel was then killed by the local people and Interahamwe with a machete blow to the neck. The Chamber finds that it has been proved beyond reasonable doubt that teachers from the commune of Taba were killed pursuant to the instructions of Akayesu.

314. The Chamber finds that it has been proved beyond reasonable doubt that the teachers were killed because they were Tutsi.

359. On the basis of consistent evidence and the facts confirmed by the Accused himself, the Chamber is satisfied beyond a reasonable doubt that the Accused was present in Gishyeshye, during the early hours of 19 April 1994, that he joined the crowd gathered around the body of a young member of the Interahamwe militia, and that he took that opportunity to address the people. Furthermore, on the basis of consistent evidence, the Chamber is satisfied beyond a reasonable doubt that on that occasion, the Accused, by virtue of his functions as bourgmestre and the authority he held over the population, did lead the crowd and the ensuing proceedings.

361. With regard to the allegation that the Accused urged the population, during the said gathering, to eliminate the accomplices of the RPF, after considering the weight of all supporting and corroborative evidence, the Chamber is satisfied beyond a reasonable doubt that the Accused clearly called on the population to unite and eliminate the sole enemy: accomplices of the Inkotanyi. The Chamber is satisfied beyond a reasonable doubt that the Accused was himself fully aware of the impact of his statement on the crowd and of the fact that his call to wage war against Inkotanyi accomplices could be construed as one to kill the Tutsi in general.

452. On the basis of the evidence set forth herein, the Chamber finds beyond a reasonable doubt that the Accused had reason to know and in fact knew that sexual

violence was taking place on or near the premises of the bureau communal, and that women were being taken away from the bureau communal and sexually violated. There is no evidence that the Accused took any measures to prevent acts of sexual violence or to punish the perpetrators of sexual violence. In fact there is evidence that the Accused ordered, instigated and otherwise aided and abetted sexual violence.

6. The Law

6.1 Cumulative Charges

461. In the amended Indictment, the accused is charged cumulatively with more than one crime in relation to the same sets of facts, in all but count 4. [ICT practice is to make sentences run concurrently for convictions based on the same facts.]

467. It is clear that the practice of concurrent sentencing ensures that the accused is not twice punished for the same acts. Notwithstanding this absence of prejudice to the accused, it is still necessary to justify the prosecutorial practice of accumulating criminal charges.

468. On the basis of national and international law and jurisprudence, the Chamber concludes that it is acceptable to convict the accused of two offences in relation to the same set of facts in the following circumstances: (1) where the offences have different elements; or (2) where the provisions creating the offences protect different interests; or (3) where it is necessary to record a conviction for both offences in order fully to describe what the accused did. However, the Chamber finds that it is not justifiable to convict an accused of two offences in relation to the same set of facts where (a) one offence is a lesser included offence of the other, for example, murder and grievous bodily harm, robbery and theft, or rape and indecent assault; or (b) where one offence charges accomplice liability and the other offence charges liability as a principal, *e.g.*, genocide and complicity in genocide.

469. Having regard to its Statute, the Chamber believes that the offences under the Statute — genocide, crimes against humanity, and violations of article 3 common to the Geneva Conventions and of Additional Protocol II — have different elements and, moreover, are intended to protect different interests. The crime of genocide exists to protect certain groups from extermination or attempted extermination. The concept of crimes against humanity exists to protect civilian populations from persecution. The idea of violations of article 3 common to the Geneva Conventions and of Additional Protocol II is to protect non-combatants from war crimes in civil war. These crimes have different purposes and are, therefore, never co-extensive.

6.3. Genocide (Article 2 of the Statute)

6.3.1. Genocide

494. The definition of genocide, as given in Article 2 of the Tribunal's Statute, is taken verbatim from Articles 2 and 3 of the Convention on the Prevention and Punishment of the Crime of Genocide (the "Genocide Convention"). It states:

> Genocide means any of the following acts committed with intent to destroy, in whole or in part, a national, ethnical, racial or religious group, as such: (a) Killing members of the group; (b) Causing serious bodily or mental harm to members of the group; (c) Deliberately inflicting on the group conditions of life calculated to bring about its physical destruction in whole or in part; (d) Imposing measures intended to prevent births within the group; (e) Forcibly transferring children of the group to another group.

498. Genocide is distinct from other crimes inasmuch as it embodies a special intent, . . . "the intent to destroy, in whole or in part, a national, ethnical, racial or religious group, as such."

512. [T]he Chamber holds that a national group is defined as a collection of people who

are perceived to share a legal bond based on common citizenship, coupled with reciprocity of rights and duties.

513. An ethnic group is generally defined as a group whose members share a common language or culture.

514. The conventional definition of racial group is based on the hereditary physical traits often identified with a geographical region, irrespective of linguistic, cultural, national or religious factors.

515. The religious group is one whose members share the same religion, denomination or mode of worship.

560. The mens rea required for the crime of direct and public incitement to commit genocide lies in the intent to directly prompt or provoke another to commit genocide.

6.4. Crimes against Humanity (Article 3 of the Statute)

565. Crimes against humanity are aimed at any civilian population and are prohibited regardless of whether they are committed in an armed conflict, international or internal in character.

567. The Chamber notes that, following the Nuremberg and Tokyo trials, the concept of crimes against humanity underwent a gradual evolution in the Eichmann, Barbie, Touvier and Papon cases.

568. In the *Eichmann* case, the accused, Otto Adolf Eichmann, was charged with offences under [Israeli] Nazi and Nazi Collaborators Law for his participation in the implementation of the plan known as the "Final Solution of the Jewish problem." The district court in the *Eichmann* case stated that crimes against humanity differs from genocide in that for the commission of genocide special intent is required. This special intent is not required for crimes against humanity. Eichmann was convicted by the District court and sentenced to death.

569. In the *Barbie* case, the accused, Klaus Barbie, who was the head of the Gestapo in Lyons from November 1942 to August 1944, during the wartime occupation of France, was convicted in 1987 of crimes against humanity for his role in the deportation and extermination of civilians. The French Court of Cassation, . . . held that:

> The fact that the accused . . . took part in the execution of a common plan to bring about the deportation or extermination of the civilian population during the war, or persecutions on political, racial or religious grounds, constituted not a distinct offence or an aggravating circumstance but rather an essential element of the crime against humanity, consisting of the fact that the acts charged were performed in a systematic manner in the name of a State practising by those means a policy of ideological supremacy.

577. Article 7 of the Statute of the International Criminal Court defines a crime against humanity as any of the enumerated acts committed as part of a widespread of systematic attack directed against any civilian population, with knowledge of the attack

578. The Chamber considers that Article 3 of the Statute confers on the Chamber the jurisdiction to prosecute persons for various inhumane acts which constitute crimes against humanity. This category of crimes may be broadly broken down into four essential elements, namely:

> (i) the act must be inhumane in nature and character, causing great suffering, or serious injury to body or to mental or physical health;

> (ii) the act must be committed as part of a wide spread or systematic attack;

> (iii) the act must be committed against members of the civilian population;

> (iv) the act must be committed on one or more discriminatory grounds, namely, national, political, ethnic, racial or religious grounds.

6.5. Violations of Common Article 3 and Additional Protocol II (Article 4 of the Statute)

599. Pursuant to Article 4 of the Statute, the Chamber shall have the power to prosecute persons committing or ordering to be committed serious violations of Article 3 common to the four Geneva Conventions of 12 August 1949 for the Protection of War Victims, and of Additional Protocol II thereto of 8 June 1977. [Common Article 3 applies during "armed conflicts not of an international character."] These violations shall include, but shall not be limited to:

a) violence to life, health and physical or mental well-being of persons, in particular murder as well as cruel treatment such as torture, mutilation or any form of corporal punishment;

b) collective punishments;

c) taking of hostages;

d) acts of terrorism;

e) outrages upon personal dignity, in particular humiliating and degrading treatment, rape, enforced prostitution and any form of indecent assault;

f) pillage;

g) the passing of sentences and the carrying out of executions without previous judgment pronounced by a regularly constituted court, affording all the judicial guarantees which are recognised as indispensable by civilised peoples;

h) threats to commit any of the foregoing acts.

601. The four 1949 Geneva Conventions and the 1977 Additional Protocol I thereto generally apply to international armed conflicts only, whereas Article 3 common to the Geneva Conventions extends a minimum threshold of humanitarian protection as well to all persons affected by a non-international conflict, a protection which was further developed and enhanced in the 1977 Additional Protocol II. In the field of international humanitarian law, a clear distinction as to the thresholds of application has been made between situations of international armed conflicts, in which the law of armed conflicts is applicable as a whole, situations of non-international (internal) armed conflicts, where Common Article 3 and Additional Protocol II are applicable, and non-international armed conflicts where only Common Article 3 is applicable. Situations of internal disturbances are not covered by international humanitarian law.

619. The norms set by Common Article 3 apply to a conflict as soon as it is an "armed conflict not of an international character." An inherent question follows such a description, namely, what constitutes an armed conflict? The Appeals Chamber in the *Tadic decision on Jurisdiction* held "that an armed conflict exists whenever there is . . . protracted armed violence between governmental authorities and organized armed groups or between such groups within a State. International humanitarian law applies from the initiation of such armed conflicts and extends beyond the cessation of hostilities until . . . in the case of internal conflicts, a peaceful settlement is reached."

625. It suffices to recall that an armed conflict is distinguished from internal disturbances by the level of intensity of the conflict and the degree of organization of the parties to the conflict. Under Additional Protocol II, the parties to the conflict will usually either be the government confronting dissident armed forces, or the government fighting insurgent organized armed groups.

626. The armed forces opposing the government must be under responsible command, which entails a degree of organization within the armed group or dissident armed forces. This degree of organization should be such so as to enable the armed group or dissident forces to plan and carry out concerted military operations, and to impose discipline in the name of a de facto authority. Further, these armed forces must be able to dominate a sufficient part of the territory so as to maintain sustained and concerted military operations. In essence, the operations must be continuous and planned. The

territory in their control is usually that which has eluded the control of the government forces.

627. In the present case, evidence has been presented to the Chamber which showed there was at the least a conflict not of a international character in Rwanda at the time of the events alleged in the Indictment. It has been shown that there was a conflict between, on the one hand, the RPF, under the command of General Kagame, and, on the other, the governmental forces, the FAR.

631. The duties and responsibilities of the Geneva Conventions and the Additional Protocols, hence, will normally apply only to individuals of all ranks belonging to the armed forces under the military command of either of the belligerent parties, or to individuals who were legitimately mandated and expected, as public officials or agents or persons otherwise holding public authority or de facto representing the Government, to support or fulfil the war efforts.

634. Thus it is clear from the above that the laws of war must apply equally to civilians as to combatants in the conventional sense. Further, the Chamber notes, in light of the above dicta, that the accused was not, at the time of the events in question, a mere civilian but a bourgmestre. The Chamber therefore concludes that, if so established factually, the accused could fall in the class of individuals who may be held responsible for serious violations of international humanitarian law, in particular serious violations of Common Article 3 and Additional Protocol II.

7. LEGAL FINDINGS

[Akayesu was found not guilty of war crimes because there was not a sufficient connection between him and the government forces. He was found guilty of crimes against humanity for murder or aiding and abetting murder as to incidents at which he was present during a period of armed conflict. He was found guilty of genocide and incitement to genocide. He was found guilty of crimes against humanity on the basis of torture incidents in which detainees were interrogated with threats to their lives or with physical beating. He was found guilty of crimes against humanity on the basis of sexual violence which he either specifically instigated or which took place in the government compound while he was present. In all, he was convicted on 9 of 15 counts.]

NOTES AND QUESTIONS

1. **Responsibility for Acts of Others.** If Akayesu is held responsible for murder and genocide based on his failure to "attempt to stop the killing," who else should be prosecuted on this basis? doctors? photographers and journalists? Belgian military officials? In the language of Anglo-American tort law, what gives rise to a duty to act? Harkening back to the *Yamashita* questions, is it fair to hold civilian leaders responsible for the acts of their citizens?

2. **International Criminal Law.** If "widespread and systematic" violence by civilians against fellow civilians is already criminal under international law, do we need a separate concept for terrorism? What would be the limits of the theories deployed in *Akayesu*?

3. **Genocide.** Would it be genocide to try to kill all Republicans in the U.S.? what about all Baptists? The ICTR states that the concept applies to groups that are "permanent and stable," but it also says that ethnicity is based on cultural identity. In the current literature, it appears that ethnic identity is a matter of some degree of choice by each individual. If I am free to think of myself as American, or Irish-American, or English, could I also have the choice of thinking of myself as Armenian? Or is the identity more a matter of what others think you are, in which case it is not a matter of your own choice but someone else's?

4. **Prisoner Abuse.** You should recall the *Akayesu* case when we come to the "prisoner abuse scandal" of Abu Ghraib and Guantánamo.

PROSECUTOR v. NAHIMANA
International Criminal Tribunal for Rwanda
Case No. ICTR-99-52-T

[The defendants in this proceeding were the publisher of a newspaper Kangura, the leadership of radio and television station RTLM, and leadership of the Hutu political group known as CDR. They were tried jointly for "direct and public incitement to commit genocide."]

3. Direct and Public Incitement to Commit Genocide

Jurisprudence

978. The Tribunal first considered the elements of the crime of direct and public incitement to commit genocide in the case of *Akayesu*, noting that at the time the Convention on Genocide was adopted, this crime was included "in particular, because of its critical role in the planning of a genocide." The *Akayesu* judgement cited the explanatory remarks of the delegate from the USSR, who described this role as essential, stating, "It was impossible that hundreds of thousands of people should commit so many crimes unless they had been incited to do so." He asked "how in these circumstances, the inciters and organizers of the crime should be allowed to escape punishment, when they were the ones really responsible for the atrocities committed."

979. The present case squarely addresses the role of the media in the genocide that took place in Rwanda in 1994 and the related legal question of what constitutes individual criminal responsibility for direct and public incitement to commit genocide. Unlike Akayesu and others found by the Tribunal to have engaged in incitement through their own speech, the Accused in this case used the print and radio media systematically, not only for their own words but for the words of many others, for the collective communication of ideas and for the mobilization of the population on a grand scale. In considering the role of mass media, the Chamber must consider not only the contents of particular broadcasts and articles, but also the broader application of these principles to media programming, as well as the responsibilities inherent in ownership and institutional control over the media.

980. To this end, a review of international law and jurisprudence on incitement to discrimination and violence is helpful as a guide to the assessment of criminal accountability for direct and public incitement to genocide, in light of the fundamental right of freedom of expression.

The International Military Tribunal at Nuremberg

Streicher

981. Characterized by the Tribunal in its *Akayesu* judgment as the "most famous conviction for incitement" and noted in the Tribunal's *Ruggiu* judgment as "particularly relevant" is the case of Julius Streicher, who was sentenced to death by the International Military Tribunal at Nuremberg for the anti-Semitic articles that he published in his weekly newspaper Der Stürmer. Known widely as "Jew-Baiter Number One," Julius Streicher was the publisher of Der Stürmer from 1923 to 1945 and served as its editor until 1933. In its judgement, the Nuremberg Tribunal quoted Streicher's own writing, articles he published, and a letter he published from one of the newspaper's readers, all calling for the extermination of Jews. The Nuremberg judgement found that although in his testimony at trial, Streicher denied any knowledge of mass executions of Jews, in fact he continually received information on the deportation and killing of Jews in Eastern Europe. However, the judgment does not explicitly note a direct causal link between Streicher's publication and any specific acts of murder. Rather it characterizes his work as a poison "injected in to the minds of thousands of Germans which caused them to follow the National Socialists' policy of Jewish persecution and extermination."

Although Streicher was found by the Nuremberg Tribunal not to have been within Hitler's inner circle of advisers or even connected to the formulation of policy, he was convicted of crimes against humanity for his incitement to murder and extermination of Jews, which was found to have constituted the crime of "persecution" as defined by the Charter of the International Military Tribunal.

Fritzsche

982. Also charged with incitement as a crime against humanity, Hans Fritzsche was acquitted by the International Military Tribunal. Head of the Radio Section of the Propaganda Ministry during the war, Fritzsche was well-known for his weekly broadcasts. In his defense, Fritzsche asserted that he had refused requests from Goebbels to incite antagonism and arouse hatred, and that he had never voiced the theory of the "master race." In fact, he had expressly prohibited the term from being used by German press and radio that he controlled. He also testified that he had expressed his concern over the content of the newspaper Der Stürmer, published by Julius Streicher, and that he had tried twice to ban it. In its judgement for acquittal, the Tribunal found that Fritzsche had not had control over the formulation of propaganda policies, that he had merely been a conduit to the press of directives passed down to him. With regard to the charge that had incited the commission of war crimes by deliberately falsifying news to arouse passions in the German people, the Tribunal found that although he had sometimes spread false news, it had not been established that he knew it to be false.

United Nations Conventions

[The United Nations Human Rights Committee interprets covenants in the context of "cases" that arise from action of signatory nations.]

983. International law protects both the right to be free from discrimination and the right to freedom of expression. The Universal Declaration of Human Rights provides in Article 7 that "All are entitled to equal protection against any discrimination . . . and against any incitement to such discrimination." Article 19 states: "Everyone has the right to freedom of opinion and expression." Both of these principles are elaborated in international and regional treaties, as is the relation between these two fundamental rights, which in certain contexts may be seen to conflict, requiring some mediation.

984. The International Covenant on Civil and Political Rights (ICCPR) provides in Article 19(2) that "Everyone shall have the right to freedom of expression," while noting in Article 19(3) that the exercise of this right "carries with it special duties and responsibilities" and may therefore be subject to certain necessary restrictions: "for respect of the rights or reputations of others," and "for the protection of national security or of public order (ordre public), or of public health or morals." In its interpretation of this language, in a General Comment on Article 19, the United Nations Human Rights Committee has stated, "It is the interplay between the principle of freedom of expression and such limitations and restrictions which determines the actual scope of the individual's right." The Committee also noted in its General Comment that permissible restrictions on the right to freedom of expression "may relate either to the interests of other persons or to those of the community as a whole."

985. By virtue of Article 20 of the ICCPR, certain speech not only may but in fact must be restricted. Article 20(2) provides that "Any advocacy of national, racial or religious hatred that constitutes incitement to discrimination, hostility or violence shall be prohibited by law." Similarly, Article 4(a) of the International Convention on the Elimination of all Forms of Racial Discrimination (CERD) requires States Parties to declare as an offence punishable by law "all dissemination of ideas based on racial superiority or hatred, incitement to racial discrimination, as well as all acts of violence or incitement to such acts against any race or group of persons of another colour or ethnic origin, and also the provision of any assistance to racist activities, including the financing thereof." Article 4(b) of CERD further requires the prohibition of organizations and all other organized propaganda activities that "promote and incite racial discrimination," and the recognition of participation in such organizations or activities as an offence punishable by law.

986. The jurisprudence on Article 19 of the ICCPR affirms the duty to restrict freedom of expression for the protection of other rights. In *Ross v. Canada*, the Human Rights Committee upheld the disciplinary action taken against a school teacher in Canada for statements he made that were found to have "denigrated the faith and beliefs of Jews and called upon true Christians to not merely question the validity of Jewish beliefs and teachings but to hold those of the Jewish faith and ancestry in contempt as undermining freedom, democracy and Christian beliefs and values." The Human Rights Committee noted in its views the finding of the Canadian Supreme Court that "it was reasonable to anticipate that there was a causal link between the expressions of the author and the poisoned atmosphere."

987. Another case from Canada, *J.R.T. and the W.G. Party v. Canada*, a complaint alleging a violation of the right to freedom of expression under Article 19, was declared inadmissible by the Human Rights Committee. The authors of the complaint had been precluded from using public telephone services after using them to circulate messages warning of the dangers of international Jewry leading the world into wars, unemployment and inflation and the collapse of world values and principles. The Human Rights Committee determined that the opinions being disseminated "clearly constitute the advocacy of racial or religious hatred which there is an obligation under art 20(2) to prohibit." In effect, it found that there was no scope to consider the complaint under the Article 19 right of a state to restrict freedom of expression because in this case the restriction was required under Article 20 of the ICCPR.

988. In *Robert Faurisson v. France* (1996), the Human Rights Committee considered the meaning of the term "incitement" in Article 20(2) of the ICCPR. The author of the complaint challenged as a violation of his right to freedom of expression under Article 19 of the ICCPR his conviction in France for publishing his view doubting the existence of gas chambers for extermination purposes at AU.S.C.hwitz and other Nazi concentration camps. The French government took the position that "by challenging the reality of the extermination of Jews during the Second World War, the author incites his readers to anti-semitic behaviour," arguing more generally that "racism did not constitute an opinion but an aggression, and that every time racism was allowed to express itself publicly, the public order was immediately and severely threatened." The Committee held in the case that the restriction on publication of these views did not violate the right to freedom of expression in Article 19 and in fact that the restriction was necessary under Art 19(3). "The restrictions placed on the author did not curb the core of his right to freedom of expression, nor did they in any way affect his freedom of research; they were intimately linked to the value they were meant to protect — the right to be free from incitement to racism or anti-semitism."

The European Convention on Human Rights

[The European Court of Human Rights hears cases arising from alleged violations of the European Covenant.]

991. At the regional level, the European Convention on Human Rights has given rise to extensive jurisprudence on the proper balancing of the right to freedom of expression, guaranteed by Article 10(1) of the Convention, and the right to restrict such freedom inter alia "in the interests of national security" and "for the protection of the reputation or rights of others," pursuant to Article 10(2) of the Convention. The approach to this balancing test, much like the one used for the ICCPR, review (i) whether the restrictions are prescribed by law; (ii) whether their aim is legitimate; and (iii) whether they can be considered necessary in a democratic society, taken to imply the existence of a "pressing social need" and an intervention "proportionate to the legitimate aims pursued."

992. A number of the European Court cases address the role of journalists, as well as editors and publishers, and their responsibility for the dissemination of views promoting discrimination. In *Jersild v. Denmark* [ECHR 1994], the Court overturned the conviction of a journalist for the Danish Broadcasting Corporation, based on his

interview of three "Greenjackets," members of a racist youth group in Denmark. The interview was broadcast on Sunday News Magazine, described by the Court as a "serious television programme intended for a well-informed audience, dealing with a wide range of social and political issues, including xenophobia, immigration and refugees." In the interview, the Greenjackets identified themselves as racist and made extremely offensive remarks about black people and immigrants. Together with them, the journalist who interviewed them was convicted by Denmark under its law prohibiting "dissemination of ideas based on racial superiority or hatred, incitement to racial discrimination, as well as acts of violence or incitement to such acts against any race or group of persons of another colour or ethnic origin. . . . " In the interview, the journalist had asked one or two questions suggesting that there were very accomplished black people and in the introduction the youth had been clearly identified as racist. The program was presented as an exploration of their thinking and background, but there was no explicit condemnation of them. [The ECHR held for the journalist with two dissents.

994. The European Court of Human Rights has also considered extensively in its jurisprudence the extent to which national security concerns justify restrictions on the right to freedom of expression. In a series of cases from Turkey, the Court has explored the extent to which Article 10 of the European Convention protects the right to express support for, and to disseminate expression of support for, political goals that are identified with violent means used in an effort to attain them. [Turkish authorities have prosecuted a number of journalists and local officials who have reported on or publicly discussed activities of the PKK, a Kurdish nationalist group that has engaged in terrorist tactics. The ECHR approach generally has been to allow objective reporting as well as criticism of the existing regime as long as there was no support expressed for terrorist activities or ethnic animosity.]

Discussion of General Principles

1000. A number of central principles emerge from the international jurisprudence on incitement to discrimination and violence that serve as a useful guide to the factors to be considered in defining elements of "direct and public incitement to genocide" as applied to mass media.

Purpose

1001. Editors and publishers have generally been held responsible for the media they control. In determining the scope of this responsibility, the importance of intent, that is the purpose of the communications they channel, emerges from the jurisprudence — whether or not the purpose in publicly transmitting the material was of a bona fide nature (e.g. historical research, the dissemination of news and information, the public accountability of government authorities). The actual language used in the media has often been cited as an indicator of intent. For example, in the Faurisson case, the term "magic gas chamber" was seen by the UN Human Rights Committee as suggesting that the author was motivated by anti-Semitism rather than pursuit of historical truth. In the Jersild case, the comments of the interviewer distancing himself from the racist remarks made by his subject were a critical factor for the European Court of Human Rights in determining that the purpose of the television program was the dissemination of news rather than propagation of racist views.

1002. In the Turkish cases on national security concerns, the European Court of Human Rights carefully distinguishes between language that explains the motivation for terrorist activities and language that promotes terrorist activities. Again, the actual language used is critical to this determination. The sensitivity of the Court to volatile language goes to the determination of intent, as evidenced by one of the questions put forward in a concurring opinion in this case: "Was the language intended to inflame or incite to violence?"

1003. In determining the scope of liability for editors and publishers, the content of a text is taken to be more important than its author. In Sürek (No.1), even letters from readers are treated without distinction as subject to liability. Moreover, publishers and editors are regarded as equally responsible on the grounds that they are providing a forum and that owners have "the power to shape the editorial direction. . . . " A critical distance was identified as the key factor in evaluating the purpose of the publication.

Context

1004. The jurisprudence on incitement highlights the importance of taking context into account when considering the potential impact of expression. In Faurisson, the Human Rights Committee noted that, in context, the impact of challenging the existence of gas chambers, a well-documented historical fact, would promote anti-Semitism. Similarly in the Zana case, the European Court of Human Rights considered the general statement made about massacres by the former mayor of Diyarbakir in the context of the fact that massacres were taking place at that time, which in the Court's view made the statement "likely to exacerbate an already explosive situation."

Causation

1007. In considering whether particular expression constitutes a form of incitement on which restrictions would be justified, the international jurisprudence does not include any specific causation requirement linking the expression at issue with the demonstration of a direct effect. In the Streicher case, there was no allegation that the publication Der Stürmer was tied to any particular violence. Much more generally, it was found to have "injected in to the minds of thousands of Germans" a "poison" that caused them to support the National Socialist policy of Jewish persecution and extermination. In the Turkish cases considered by the European Court of Human Rights, no specific acts of violence are cited as having been caused by the applicant's expression. Rather, the question considered is what the likely impact might be, recognizing that causation in this context might be relatively indirect.

1008. The Chamber notes that international standards restricting hate speech and the protection of freedom of expression have evolved largely in the context of national initiatives to control the danger and harm represented by various forms of prejudiced communication. The protection of free expression of political views has historically been balanced in the jurisprudence against the interest in national security. The dangers of censorship have often been associated in particular with the suppression of political or other minorities, or opposition to the government. The special protections developed by the jurisprudence for speech of this kind, in international law and more particularly in the American legal tradition of free speech, recognize the power dynamic inherent in the circumstances that make minority groups and political opposition vulnerable to the exercise of power by the majority or by the government. These circumstances do not arise in the present case, where at issue is the speech of the so-called "majority population," in support of the government. The special protections for this kind of speech should accordingly be adapted, in the Chamber's view, so that ethnically specific expression would be more rather than less carefully scrutinized to ensure that minorities without equal means of defence are not endangered.

1009. Similarly, the Chamber considers that the "wider margin of appreciation" given in European Court cases to government discretion in its restriction of expression that constitutes incitement to violence should be adapted to the circumstance of this case. At issue is not a challenged restriction of expression but the expression itself. Moreover, the expression charged as incitement to violence was situated, in fact and at the time by its speakers, not as a threat to national security but rather in defence of national security, aligning it with state power rather than in opposition to it. Thus there is justification for adaptation of the application of international standards, which have evolved to protect the right of the government to defend itself from incitement to violence by others against it, rather than incitement to violence on its behalf against others, particularly as in this case when the others are members of a minority group.

1010. Counsel for Ngeze has argued that United States law, as the most speech-protective, should be used as a standard, to ensure the universal acceptance and legitimacy of the Tribunal's jurisprudence. The Chamber considers international law, which has been well developed in the areas of freedom from discrimination and freedom of expression, to be the point of reference for its consideration of these issues, noting that domestic law varies widely while international law codifies evolving universal standards. The Chamber notes that the jurisprudence of the United States also accepts the fundamental principles set forth in international law and has recognized in its domestic law that incitement to violence, threats, libel, false advertising, obscenity, and child pornography are among those forms of expression that fall outside the scope of freedom of speech protection.[4] In *Virginia v. Black*,[5] the United States Supreme Court recently interpreted the free speech guarantee of the First Amendment of the Constitution to permit a ban on cross burning with intent to intimidate. The historical terrorization of African Americans by the Ku Klux Klan through cross burnings, in the Court's view, made the burning of a cross, as a recognized symbol of hate and a "true threat," unprotected as symbolic expression. Intimidation was held to be constitutionally proscribable "where a speaker directs a threat to a person or group of persons with the intent of placing the victim in fear of bodily harm or death." In the immigration context, adherents of National Socialism have been stripped of citizenship and deported from the United States on the basis of their anti-semitic writings.[6]

ICTR Jurisprudence

1011. The ICTR jurisprudence provides the only direct precedent for the interpretation of "direct and public incitement to genocide." In *Akayesu*, the Tribunal reviewed the meaning of each term constituting "direct and public incitement." With regard to "incitement," the Tribunal observed that in both common law and civil law systems, "incitement," or "provocation" as it is called under civil law, is defined as encouragement or provocation to commit an offence. The Tribunal cited the International Law Commission as having characterized "public" incitement as "a call for criminal action to a number of individuals in a public place or to members of the general public at large by such means as the mass media, for example, radio or television."

1015. In *Akayesu*, the Tribunal considered in its legal findings on the charge of direct and public incitement to genocide that "there was a causal relationship between the Defendant's speech to [the] crowd and the ensuing widespread massacres of Tutsis in the community." The Chamber notes that this causal relationship is not requisite to a finding of incitement. It is the potential of the communication to cause genocide that makes it incitement. As set forth in the Legal Findings on Genocide, when this potential is realized, a crime of genocide as well as incitement to genocide has occurred.

Charges Against the Accused

1017. The Chamber notes that the crime of direct and public incitement to commit genocide, like conspiracy, is an inchoate offence that continues in time until the completion of the acts contemplated. The Chamber accordingly considers that the publication of Kangura, from its first issue in May 1990 through its March 1994 issue, the alleged impact of which culminated in events that took place in 1994, falls within the temporal jurisdiction of the Tribunal to the extent that the publication is deemed to

---

   4 [Court's Footnote 1111] Brandenburg v. Ohio, 395 U.S. 444, 447 (1969); Chaplinsky v. New Hampshire, 315 U.S. 568, 572 (1941); Watts v. United States, 394 U.S. 705 (1969); Miller v. California, 413 U.S. 15 (1973); Gertz v. Robert Welch, Inc., 418 U.S. 323 (1974); Virginia State Board of Pharmacy v. Virginia Citizens Consumer Council, Inc., 425 U.S. 748, 771–73 & n. 24 (1976); Posadas de Puerto Rico Assocs. v. Tourism Co., 478 U.S. 328 (1986); NLRB v. Gissel Packing Co., 395 U.S. 575, 618 (1969); New York v. Ferber, 458 U.S. 747 (1982); F.C.C. v. Pacifica Foundation, 438 U.S. 726 (1978); Beauharnais v. Illinois, 343 U.S. 250, 251 (1952).

   5 [Court's Footnote 1112] 123 S. Ct. 1536 (2003).

   6 [Court's Footnote 1113] United States v. Sokolov, 814 F.2d 864 (1987); United States v. Ferenc Koreh, aff'd., 59 F.3d 431 (2d Cir., 1995).

constitute direct and public incitement to genocide. Similarly, the Chamber considers that the entirety of RTLM broadcasting, from July 1993 through July 1994, the alleged impact of which culminated in events that took place in 1994, falls within the temporal jurisdiction of the Tribunal to the extent that the broadcasts are deemed to constitute direct and public incitement to genocide.

1019. In its review of Kangura and RTLM, the Chamber notes that some of the articles and broadcasts highlighted by the Prosecution convey historical information, political analysis, or advocacy of an ethnic consciousness regarding the inequitable distribution of privilege in Rwanda. Barayagwiza's RTLM broadcast of 12 December 1993, for example, is a moving personal account of his experience of discrimination as a Hutu. Prosecution Expert Witness Alison Des Forges, in cross-examination, would not comment on the propriety of this particular broadcast, citing as her concern the repeated emphasis and priority given to ethnicity, rather than any single broadcast. She stated her view that undue emphasis on ethnicity and presentation of all issues in ethnic terms exacerbated ethnic tensions.

1020. The Chamber considers that it is critical to distinguish between the discussion of ethnic consciousness and the promotion of ethnic hatred. This broadcast by Barayagwiza is the the former but not the latter. While the impact of these words, which are powerful, may well have been to move listeners to want to take action to remedy the discrimination recounted, such impact would be the result, in the Chamber's view, of the reality conveyed by the words rather than the words themselves. A communication such as this broadcast does not constitute incitement. In fact, it falls squarely within the scope of speech that is protected by the right to freedom of expression. Similarly, public discussion of the merits of the Arusha Accords, however critical, constitutes a protected exercise of free speech.

1021. The Chamber considers that speech constituting ethnic hatred results from the stereotyping of ethnicity combined with its denigration. The Accused have maintained in their defence that certain communications made by them about the Tutsi population were simply true, for example the broadcast stating that 70% of the taxis in Rwanda were owned by people of Tutsi ethnicity. The accuracy of this statement was not established one way or the other by the evidence presented, but the statement is informational in nature. Its impact, if true, might well be to generate resentment over the inequitable distribution of wealth in Rwanda. However, this impact, in the Chamber's view, would be a result of the inequitable distribution of wealth in Rwanda, the information conveyed by the statement rather than the statement itself. If it were not true, the inaccuracy of the statement might then be an indicator that the intent of the statement was not to convey information but rather to promote unfounded resentment and inflame ethnic tensions. The RTLM broadcast stating about the Tutsi that "they are the ones who have all the money" differs from the statement about taxi ownership in that it is a generalization that has been extended to the Tutsi population as a whole. The tone of the broadcast is different and conveys the hostility and resentment of the journalist, Kantano Habimana. While this broadcast, which does not call on listeners to take action of any kind, does not constitute direct incitement, it demonstrates the progression from ethnic consciousness to harmful ethnic stereotyping.

1022. The Chamber also considers the context in which the statement is made to be important. A statement of ethnic generalization provoking resentment against members of that ethnicity would have a heightened impact in the context of a genocidal environment. It would be more likely to lead to violence. At the same time the environment would be an indicator that incitement to violence was the intent of the statement.

1024. The Chamber recognizes that some media are advocacy-oriented and considers that the issue of importance to its findings is not whether the media played an advocacy role but rather the content of what it was actually advocating. In cases where the media disseminates views that constitute ethnic hatred and calls to violence for informative or educational purposes, a clear distancing from these is necessary to avoid conveying an endorsement of the message and in fact to convey a counter-message to ensure that no harm results from the broadcast. The positioning of the media with regard to the message indicates the real intent of the message, and to some degree the real message itself. The editor of Kangura and the journalists who broadcast on RTLM did not distance themselves from the message of ethnic hatred. Rather they purveyed the message.

1025. The Accused have also cited in their defence the need for vigilance against the enemy, the enemy being defined as armed and dangerous RPF forces who attacked the Hutu population and were fighting to destroy democracy and reconquer power in Rwanda. The Chamber accepts that the media has a role to play in the protection of democracy and where necessary the mobilization of civil defence for the protection of a nation and its people. What distinguishes both Kangura and RTLM from an initiative to this end is the consistent identification made by the publication and the radio broadcasts of the enemy as the Tutsi population. Readers and listeners were not directed against individuals who were clearly defined to be armed and dangerous. Instead, Tutsi civilians and in fact the Tutsi population as a whole were targeted as the threat.

1028. The names published and broadcast were generally done so in the context of a threat that varied in explicitness. An official list of 123 names of suspects was published in Kangura No. 40 with an express warning to readers that the government was not effectively protecting them from these people and that they needed to organize their own self-defence to prevent their own extermination. This message classically illustrates the incitement of Kangura readers to violence: by instilling fear in them, giving them names to associate with this fear, and mobilizing them to take independent, proactive measures in an effort to protect themselves. In some instances, names were mentioned by Kangura without such an explicit call to action. The message was nevertheless direct. That it was clearly understood is overwhelmingly evidenced by the testimony of witnesses that being named in Kangura would bring dire consequences. François-Xavier Nsanzuwera called Kangura "the bell of death" (see paragraph 237). Similarly, RTLM broadcast a message of fear, provided listeners with names, and encouraged them to defend and protect themselves, incessantly telling them to "be vigilant," which became a coded term for aggression in the guise of self-defence.

1029. With regard to causation, the Chamber recalls that incitement is a crime regardless of whether it has the effect it intends to have. In determining whether communications represent an intent to cause genocide and thereby constitute incitement, the Chamber considers it significant that in fact genocide occurred. That the media intended to have this effect is evidenced in part by the fact that it did have this effect.

RTLM

1031. RTLM broadcasting was a drumbeat, calling on listeners to take action against the enemy and enemy accomplices, equated with the Tutsi population. The phrase "heating up heads" captures the process of incitement systematically engaged in by RTLM, which after 6 April 1994 was also known as "Radio Machete." The nature of radio transmission made RTLM particularly dangerous and harmful, as did the breadth of its reach. Unlike print media, radio is immediately present and active. The power of the human voice, heard by the Chamber when the broadcast tapes were played in Kinyarwanda, adds a quality and dimension beyond words to the message conveyed. In this setting, radio heightened the sense of fear, the sense of danger and the sense of urgency giving rise to the need for action by listeners. The denigration of Tutsi ethnicity was augmented by the visceral scorn coming out of the airwaves — the ridiculing laugh and the nasty sneer. These elements greatly amplified the impact of RTLM broadcasts.

1033. The Chamber has found beyond a reasonable doubt that Ferdinand Nahimana acted with genocidal intent. Accordingly, the Chamber finds Ferdinand Nahimana guilty of direct and public incitement to genocide under Article 2(3)(c), pursuant to Article 6(1) and Article 6(3) of the Statute.

CDR

1035. Jean-Bosco Barayagwiza was one of the principal founders of CDR and played a leading role in its formation and development. He was a decision-maker for the party. The killing of Tutsi civilians was promoted by the CDR, as evidenced by the chanting of "tubatsembatsembe" or "let's exterminate them," by Barayagwiza himself and by CDR members and Impuzamugambi in his presence at public meetings and demonstrations. The reference to "them" was understood to mean the Tutsi population. The killing of Tutsi civilians was also promoted by the CDR through the publication of communiqués and other writings that called for the extermination of the enemy and defined the enemy as the Tutsi population. The Chamber notes the direct involvement of Barayagwiza in this call for genocide. Barayagwiza was at the organizational helm of CDR. He was also on site at the meetings, demonstrations and roadblocks that created an infrastructure for the killing of Tutsi civilians. For these acts, the Chamber finds Jean-Bosco Barayagwiza guilty of direct and public incitement to genocide.

Kangura

1036. Many of the writings published in Kangura combined ethnic hatred and fear — mongering with a call to violence to be directed against the Tutsi population, who were characterized as the enemy or enemy accomplices. The Appeal to the Conscience of the Hutu and the cover of Kangura No. 26 are two notable examples in which the message clearly conveyed to the readers of Kangura was that the Hutu population should "wake up" and take the measures necessary to deter the Tutsi enemy from decimating the Hutu. The Chamber notes that the name Kangura itself means "to wake up other." What it intended to wake the Hutu up to is evidenced by its content, a litany of ethnic denigration presenting the Tutsi population as inherently evil and calling for the extermination of the Tutsi as a preventive measure. The Chamber notes the increased attention in 1994 issues of Kangura to the fear of an RPF attack and the threat that killing of innocent Tutsi civilians that would follow as a consequence.

1037. The Chamber notes that not all of the writings published in Kangura and highlighted by the Prosecution constitute direct incitement. A Cockroach Cannot Give Birth to a Butterfly, for example, is an article brimming with ethnic hatred but did not call on readers to take action against the Tutsi population.

1038. As founder, owner and editor of Kangura, Hassan Ngeze directly controlled the publication and all of its contents, for which he has largely acknowledged responsibility. The Chamber has found that Ngeze acted with genocidal intent. Ngeze used the publication to instill hatred, promote fear, and incite genocide. It is evident that Kangura played a significant role, and was seen to have played a significant role, in creating the conditions that led to acts of genocide. Accordingly, the Chamber finds Hassan Ngeze guilty of direct and public incitement to genocide.

Acts of Hassan Ngeze

1039. As set forth in paragraph 837, Hassan Ngeze often drove around with a megaphone in his vehicle, mobilizing the Hutu population to come to CDR meetings and spreading the message that the Inyenzi would be exterminated, Inyenzi meaning, and being understood to mean, the Tutsi ethnic minority. For these acts, which called for the extermination of the Tutsi population, the Chamber finds Hassan Ngeze guilty of direct and public incitement to genocide.

[C] International Criminal Court

The Statute of the International Criminal Court went into effect on 1 July 2002 with 139 signatory nations. The statute creates a court for prosecution of individuals who commit crimes in four categories: aggression, genocide, crimes against humanity, or war crimes. There are definitional elaborations for each of these categories except for the crime of aggression. The applicable law is stated to be the Statute itself, plus "applicable treaties and the principles and rules of international law, including the established principles of the international law of armed conflict" and "general principles of law derived by the Court from national laws."

The United States initially signed the document on 31 December 2000 (during the last weeks of the Clinton administration) and then withdrew its consent during the Bush administration. The U.S. government sent the following communique to the UN on 6 May 2002:

> This is to inform you, in connection with the Rome Statute of the International Criminal Court adopted on July 17, 1998, that the United States does not intend to become a party to the treaty. Accordingly, the United States has no legal obligations arising from its signature on December 31, 2000. The United States requests that its intention not to become a party, as expressed in this letter, be reflected in the depositary's status lists relating to this treaty.

The ICC is still in its formative stages. *See* http://www.icc-cpi.int/home.html. In 2004, the Prosecutor opened investigations into two situations in Africa at the behest of the governments of Uganda and the Congo.

In a related development, some nations have specifically asserted "universal jurisdiction" over offenses against international law, such as war crimes. The Center for Constitutional Rights, an American NGO, filed petitions in France and Germany seeking prosecution of Secretary of Defense Rumsfeld and others for the prisoner abuses at Abu Ghraib.

[D] Extradition and Universal Jurisdiction

International Conventions related to terrorism all proceed on the following structure: state parties agree to criminalize certain behavior, to cooperate in the apprehension of persons who commit that behavior, and then either to extradite or prosecute an accused person. Extradition arises only by operation of treaties and not by operation of general customary international law, although there is some reason to expect this to change under increasing pressure of international regimes.

One reason that it is important for states to agree to criminalize the defined behavior is that extradition hinges on the principle of "dual criminality," which permits extradition only if the alleged conduct would be criminal in both the requesting and requested states. Dual criminality does not require identity of all elements of the crime or of procedures for adjudication, it requires only that the specific alleged conduct would be criminal in both jurisdictions. The next case involves an effort by Spain to extradite the former Chilean President from Britain to stand trial in Spain. It is not an international prosecution but an effort by one state to prosecute for crimes committed in another state. Part of the conceptual difficulty with this situation is the question of what law is the prosecuting state to enforce? Of course, the political difficulties of Britain in this instance were that it felt caught between the Spain and Chile.

EX PARTE PINOCHET UGARTE (No. 3)
[2000] 1 AC 147, [1999] 2 All ER 97 (House of Lords 1999)

[Spain applied for extradition of Pinochet to prosecute him for crimes allegedly committed while he was President of Chile. The lower court held that the offenses were not extraditable for lack of "dual criminality" and that Pinochet had immunity as a head of state when the offenses were committed. The government appealed to the House of

Lords. The House held that Pinochet could be extradited only for acts committed after the date on which Chile ratified the Convention Against Torture in 1988. The House of Lords by tradition acts through an Appellate Committee of judges who each submits a separate opinion.]

Lord Browne-Wilkinson.

My Lords, as is well known, this case concerns an attempt by the Government of Spain to extradite Senator Pinochet from this country to stand trial in Spain for crimes committed (primarily in Chile) during the period when Senator Pinochet was head of state in Chile.

The Facts

On 11 September 1973 a right-wing coup evicted the left-wing regime of President Allende. The coup was led by a military junta, of whom Senator (then General) Pinochet was the leader. At some stage he became head of state. The Pinochet regime remained in power until 11 March 1990 when Senator Pinochet resigned.

There is no real dispute that during the period of the Senator Pinochet regime appalling acts of barbarism were committed in Chile and elsewhere in the world: torture, murder and the unexplained disappearance of individuals, all on a large scale. Although it is not alleged that Senator Pinochet himself committed any of those acts, it is alleged that they were done in pursuance of a conspiracy to which he was a party, at his instigation and with his knowledge. He denies these allegations. None of the conduct alleged was committed by or against citizens of the United Kingdom or in the United Kingdom.

In 1998 Senator Pinochet came to the United Kingdom for medical treatment. The judicial authorities in Spain sought to extradite him in order to stand trial in Spain on a large number of charges. Some of those charges had links with Spain. But most of the charges had no connection with Spain. The background to the case is that to those of left-wing political convictions Senator Pinochet is seen as an arch-devil: to those of right-wing persuasions he is seen as the saviour of Chile. It may well be thought that the trial of Senator Pinochet in Spain for offences all of which related to the State of Chile and most of which occurred in Chile is not calculated to achieve the best justice. Our job is to decide two questions of law: are there any extradition crimes and, if so, is Senator Pinochet immune from trial for committing those crimes. If, as a matter of law, there are no extradition crimes or he is entitled to immunity in relation to whichever crimes there are, then there is no legal right to extradite Senator Pinochet to Spain or, indeed, to stand in the way of his return to Chile. If, on the other hand, there are extradition crimes in relation to which Senator Pinochet is not entitled to state immunity then it will be open to the Home Secretary to extradite him. The task of this House is only to decide those points of law.

On 16 October 1998 an international warrant for the arrest of Senator Pinochet was issued in Spain. On the same day, a magistrate in London issued a provisional warrant ("the first warrant") under section 8 of the Extradition Act 1989. He was arrested in a London hospital on 17 October 1998. On 18 October the Spanish authorities issued a second international warrant. A further provisional warrant ("the second warrant") was issued by the magistrate at Bow Street Magistrates' Court on 22 October 1998 accusing Senator Pinochet of [torture and conspiracy to commit torture between 1 January 1988 and December 1992, taking of hostages and conspiracy to take hostages between 1 January 1982 and 31 January 1992, and conspiracy to commit murder between January 1976 and December 1992].

Outline of the Law

In general, a state only exercises criminal jurisdiction over offences which occur within its geographical boundaries. If a person who is alleged to have committed a crime in Spain is found in the United Kingdom, Spain can apply to the United Kingdom to extradite him to Spain. The power to extradite from the United Kingdom for an "extradition crime" is now contained in the Extradition Act 1989. That Act defines what constitutes an "extradition crime." For the purposes of the present case, the most important requirement is that the conduct complained of must constitute a crime under the law both of Spain and of the United Kingdom. This is known as the double criminality rule.

Since the Nazi atrocities and the Nuremberg trials, international law has recognised a number of offences as being international crimes. Individual states have taken jurisdiction to try some international crimes even in cases where such crimes were not committed within the geographical boundaries of such states. The most important of such international crimes for present purposes is torture which is regulated by the International Convention against Torture and other Cruel, Inhuman or Degrading Treatment or Punishment. The obligations placed on the United Kingdom by that Convention (and on the other 110 or more signatory states who have adopted the Convention) were incorporated into the law of the United Kingdom by section 134 of the Criminal Justice Act 1988. That Act came into force on 29 September 1988. Section 134 created a new crime under United Kingdom law, the crime of torture. As required by the Torture Convention "all" torture wherever committed worldwide was made criminal under United Kingdom law and triable in the United Kingdom.

No one has suggested that before section 134 came into effect torture committed outside the United Kingdom was a crime under United Kingdom law. Nor is it suggested that section 134 was retrospective so as to make torture committed outside the United Kingdom before 29 September 1988 a United Kingdom crime. Since torture outside the United Kingdom was not a crime under U.K. law until 29 September 1988, the principle of double criminality which requires an Act to be a crime under both the law of Spain and of the United Kingdom cannot be satisfied in relation to conduct before that date.

Torture [and Universal Jurisdiction]

Apart from the law of piracy, the concept of personal liability under international law for international crimes is of comparatively modern growth. The traditional subjects of international law are states not human beings. But consequent upon the war crime trials after the 1939–45 World War, the international community came to recognise that there could be criminal liability under international law for a class of crimes such as war crimes and crimes against humanity. In the early years state torture was one of the elements of a war crime. In consequence torture, and various other crimes against humanity, were linked to war or at least to hostilities of some kind. But in the course of time this linkage with war fell away and torture, divorced from war or hostilities, became an international crime on its own: *see Prosecutor v. Furundzija*, International Criminal Tribunal for the Former Yugoslavia, Case No. IT-95-17/1-T 10.

Moreover, the Republic of Chile accepted before your Lordships that the international law prohibiting torture has the character of *jus cogens* or a peremptory norm, i.e., one of those rules of international law which have a particular status. In the *Furundzija* case, at paragraphs 153 and 154, the tribunal said:

> Because of the importance of the values it protects, [the prohibition of torture] has evolved into a peremptory norm or *jus cogens*, that is, a norm that enjoys a higher rank in the international hierarchy than treaty law and even 'ordinary' customary rules. The most conspicuous consequence of this higher rank is that the principle at issue cannot be derogated from by states through international treaties or local or special customs or even general customary rules not endowed with the same normative force. . . . Clearly, the *jus cogens* nature of the prohibition against torture articulates the notion that the prohibition has now become one of the most fundamental standards of the

international community. Furthermore, this prohibition is designed to produce a deterrent effect, in that it signals to all members of the international community and the individuals over whom they wield authority that the prohibition of torture is an absolute value from which nobody must deviate.

The *jus cogens* nature of the international crime of torture justifies states in taking universal jurisdiction over torture wherever committed. International law provides that offences *jus cogens* may be punished by any state because the offenders are "common enemies of all mankind and all nations have an equal interest in their apprehension and prosecution:"

But there was no tribunal or court to punish international crimes of torture. Local courts could take jurisdiction. But the objective was to ensure a general jurisdiction so that the torturer was not safe wherever he went. For example, in this case it is alleged that during the Pinochet regime torture was an official, although unacknowledged, weapon of government and that, when the regime was about to end, it passed legislation designed to afford an amnesty to those who had engaged in institutionalised torture. If these allegations are true, the fact that the local court had jurisdiction to deal with the international crime of torture was nothing to the point so long as the totalitarian regime remained in power: a totalitarian regime will not permit adjudication by its own courts on its own shortcomings. Hence the demand for some international machinery to repress state torture which is not dependent upon the local courts where the torture was committed. In the event, over 110 states (including Chile, Spain and the United Kingdom) became state parties to the Torture Convention. But it is far from clear that none of them practised state torture. What was needed therefore was an international system which could punish those who were guilty of torture and which did not permit the evasion of punishment by the torturer moving from one state to another. The Torture Convention was agreed not in order to create an international crime which had not previously existed but to provide an international system under which the international criminal — the torturer — could find no safe haven.

The Torture Convention

Article 1 of the Convention defines torture as the intentional infliction of severe pain and of suffering with a view to achieving a wide range of purposes "when such pain or suffering is inflicted by or at the instigation of or with the consent or acquiescence of a public official or other person acting in an official capacity." Article 2(1) requires each state party to prohibit torture on territory within its own jurisdiction and article 4 requires each state party to ensure that "all" acts of torture are offences under its criminal law. Article 2(3) outlaws any defence of superior orders. Under article 5(1) each state party has to establish its jurisdiction over torture (a) when committed within territory under its jurisdiction (b) when the alleged offender is a national of that state, and (c) in certain circumstances, when the victim is a national of that state. Under article 5(2) a state party has to take jurisdiction over any alleged offender who is found within its territory. Article 6 contains provisions for a state in whose territory an alleged torturer is found to detain him, inquire into the position and notify the states referred to in article 5(1) and to indicate whether it intends to exercise jurisdiction. Under article 7 the state in whose territory the alleged torturer is found shall, if he is not extradited to any of the states mentioned in article 5(1), submit him to its authorities for the purpose of prosecution. Under article 8(1) torture is to be treated as an extraditable offence and under article 8(4) torture shall, for the purposes of extradition, be treated as having been committed not only in the place where it occurred but also in the state mentioned in article 5(1).

State Immunity

It is a basic principle of international law that one sovereign state (the forum state) does not adjudicate on the conduct of a foreign state. The foreign state is entitled to procedural immunity from the processes of the forum state. This immunity extends to both criminal and civil liability. State immunity probably grew from the historical immunity of the person of the monarch. In any event, such personal immunity of the head of state persists to the present day: the head of state is entitled to the same immunity as the state itself. The diplomatic representative of the foreign state in the forum state is also afforded the same immunity in recognition of the dignity of the state which he represents. This immunity enjoyed by a head of state in power and an ambassador in post is a complete immunity attaching to the person of the head of state or ambassador and rendering him immune from all actions or prosecutions whether or not they relate to matters done for the benefit of the state. Such immunity is said to be granted *ratione personae*.

The continuing partial immunity of the ambassador after leaving post is of a different kind from that enjoyed *ratione personae* while he was in post. Since he is no longer the representative of the foreign state he merits no particular privileges or immunities as a person. However in order to preserve the integrity of the activities of the foreign state during the period when he was ambassador, it is necessary to provide that immunity is afforded to his official acts during his tenure in post. If this were not done the sovereign immunity of the state could be evaded by calling in question acts done during the previous ambassador's time. Accordingly under article 39(2) the ambassador, like any other official of the state, enjoys immunity in relation to his official acts done while he was an official. This limited immunity, *ratione materiae*, is to be contrasted with the former immunity ratione personae which gave complete immunity to all activities whether public or private.

The question then which has to be answered is whether the alleged organisation of state torture by Senator Pinochet (if proved) would constitute an act committed by Senator Pinochet as part of his official functions as head of state. It is not enough to say that it cannot be part of the functions of the head of state to commit a crime. Actions which are criminal under the local law can still have been done officially and therefore give rise to immunity *ratione materiae*. The case needs to be analysed more closely.

I have doubts whether, before the coming into force of the Torture Convention, the existence of the international crime of torture as *jus cogens* was enough to justify the conclusion that the organisation of state torture could not rank for immunity purposes as performance of an official function. At that stage there was no international tribunal to punish torture and no general jurisdiction to permit or require its punishment in domestic courts. Not until there was some form of universal jurisdiction for the punishment of the crime of torture could it really be talked about as a fully constituted international crime. But in my judgment the Torture Convention did provide what was missing: a worldwide universal jurisdiction. Further, it required all member states to ban and outlaw torture. How can it be for international law purposes an official function to do something which international law itself prohibits and criminalises? Thirdly, an essential feature of the international crime of torture is that it must be committed "by or with the acquiesence of a public official or other person acting in an official capacity." As a result all defendants in torture cases will be state officials. Yet, if the former head of state has immunity, the man most responsible will escape liability while his inferiors (the chiefs of police, junior army officers) who carried out his orders will be liable. I find it impossible to accept that this was the intention.

For these reasons in my judgment if, as alleged, Senator Pinochet organised and authorised torture after 8 December 1988 [the date after which both Chile and the UK recognized torture as a crime wherever committed], he was not acting in any capacity which gives rise to immunity *ratione materiae* because such actions were contrary to international law, Chile had agreed to outlaw such conduct and Chile had agreed with the other parties to the Torture Convention that all signatory states should have jurisdiction to try official torture (as defined in the Convention) even if such torture were committed in Chile.

As to the charges of murder and conspiracy to murder, no one has advanced any reason why the ordinary rules of immunity should not apply and Senator Pinochet is entitled to such immunity.

For these reasons, I would allow the appeal so as to permit the extradition proceedings to proceed on the allegation that torture in pursuance of a conspiracy to commit torture was being committed by Senator Pinochet after 8 December 1988 when he lost his immunity.

LORD GOFF OF CHIEVELEY.

The central question in the appeal is whether Senator Pinochet is entitled as former head of state to the benefit of state immunity *ratione materiae* in respect of the charges advanced against him.

[I]f immunity *ratione materiae* was excluded [by the Torture Convention], former heads of state and senior public officials would have to think twice about travelling abroad, for fear of being the subject of unfounded allegations emanating from states of a different political persuasion. Preservation of state immunity is therefore a matter of particular importance to powerful countries whose heads of state perform an executive role, and who may therefore be regarded as possible targets by governments of states which, for deeply felt political reasons, deplore their actions while in office. But, to bring the matter nearer home, we must not overlook the fact that it is not only in the United States of America that a substantial body of opinion supports the campaign of the I.R.A. to overthrow the democratic government of Northern Ireland. It is not beyond the bounds of possibility that a state whose government is imbued with this opinion might seek to extradite from a third country, where he or she happens to be, a responsible Minister of the Crown, or even a more humble public official such as a police inspector, on the ground that he or she has acquiesced in a single act of physical or mental torture in Northern Ireland. The well known case of *Ireland v. United Kingdom* (1978) 2 E.H.R.R. 25 provides an indication of circumstances in which this might come about. [See Chapter 9 *infra*.]

Reasons such as these may well have persuaded possible state parties to the Torture Convention that it would be unwise to give up the valuable protection afforded by state immunity. Indeed, it would be strange if state parties had given up the immunity *ratione materiae* of a head of state which is regarded as an essential support for his immunity *ratione personae*. In practice state immunity is relevant in only two cases — where the offender is present in a third state, or where the offender is present in a state one of whose nationals was the victim, that state being different from the state where the offence was committed.

LORD HOPE OF CRAIGHEAD.

The crimes which are alleged in the Spanish request are murder on such a scale as to amount to genocide and terrorism, including torture and hostage-taking. The Secretary of State has already stated in his authority to proceed that Senator Pinochet is not to be extradited to Spain for genocide. So that part of the request must now be left out of account. But my impression is that the omission of the allegation of genocide is of little consequence in view of the scope which is given in Spanish law to the allegations of murder and terrorism.

Murder is a common law crime which, before it became an extraterritorial offence if committed in a convention country under section 4 of the Suppression of Terrorism Act 1978, could not be prosecuted in the United Kingdom if it was committed abroad except in the case of a murder committed abroad by a British citizen.

Section 134 of the Criminal Law Act 1988 did not come into force until 29 September 1988. But acts of physical torture were already criminal under English law. Among the various offences against the person which would have been committed by torturing would have been the common law offence of assault occasioning actual bodily harm. A conspiracy which was entered into in England to commit these offences in England was an offence at common law.

However none of these offences, if committed prior to the coming into force of section 134 of the Criminal Justice Act 1988, could be said to be extraterritorial offences against the law of the United Kingdom as there is no basis upon which they could have been tried extraterritorially in this country. The effect of section 134 of the Criminal Justice Act 1988 was to make acts of official torture, wherever they were committed and whatever the nationality of the offender, an extraterritorial offence in the United Kingdom. The section came into force two months after the passing of the Act on 29 September 1988, and it was not retrospective. As from that date official torture was an extradition crime because it was an extraterritorial offence against the law of the United Kingdom.

DISPOSITION:

Appeal allowed to extent that extradition to proceed for offences of torture and conspiracy to torture occurring after 8 December 1988.

NOTES AND QUESTIONS

1. Dual Criminality. Lord Browne-Wilkinson states: "No one has suggested that before section 134 came into effect torture committed outside the United Kingdom was a crime under United Kingdom law." Why not? As Lord Hope states, "torture and murder were crimes in the United Kingdom long before 1988." And dual criminality does not require that the requested nation assert extraterritorial jurisdiction over the alleged misconduct. So what would be the point of requiring that the requested nation criminalize conduct committed outside its borders? Lord Browne-Wilkinson's answer appears to be that the extraterritorial acts were not an extraditable crime because neither Spain nor the UK would have had jurisdiction until all three states ratified the Convention. Lord Hope's answer appears to be that the 1989 Act limited extradition to acts that would have been punishable in the UK, which acts committed in Chile would not have been until the 1988 Act proclaimed power to do so.

In other words, the problem is not whether the type of offense was a crime under English law, but whether the particular acts were punishable by both Britain and Spain. Murder and assault are not criminal under international jus cogens and thus not subject to universal jurisdiction, but torture is. In this sense, the Lords were struggling with the point in time at which torture became subject to either to universal jurisdiction or to the jurisdiction of Spain based on harms to its nationals. *See* DIANA WOODHOUSE, THE PINOCHET CASE (2000).

2. Universal Jurisdiction and U.S. Officials. The issue of defining and criminalizing Torture will be explored again in Chapter 9 in the specific context of the "prisoner abuse" scandal arising from the aggressive interrogation of detainees in Iraq and Guantánamo. For now, it is enough to note that Lord Goff's concern about a third country's prosecution of a government official for torture based on policies of interrogation has borne fruit in attempts to have U.S. officials prosecuted abroad.

[E]   International Conventions Related to Terrorism

The United Nations lists 12 separate Conventions dealing with terrorism. (http://untreaty.un.org/English/Terrorism.asp). The principal headings are aircraft crimes, protection of nuclear materials, hostage taking, and the most recent on financing of terrorism.

International concern over terrorism started with airplane hijackings in the 1960s. Although many of those incidents were just attempts by desperate persons to get "home" or conversely to flee to a perceived safer environment, some created dangerous situations as pilots were forced to divert their aircraft. These incidents also occasioned significant expense for the companies and countries involved. Even when the receiving country could make political mileage of the incident, it could prove costly. For example, if a hijacker diverted a plane from the U.S. to Cuba, the Cuban government would incur expenses in landing, refueling, and sending the plane on its way before it even experienced political costs associated with harboring someone who had committed what most countries would consider the crime of piracy.

As the phenomenon began to unfold, western nations enacted specific statutes criminalizing the offense of air piracy and attempted to extradite perpetrators. The host country, however, might be unwilling to extradite because it had promised safe haven to the hijacker as part of a deal in which the plane was allowed to land and the hijacker freed the crew and passengers. Reneging on that promise would then cause difficulties in future negotiations with hijackers. The first international treaty (convention) dealing with the issue attempted to meet the threat head-on by allowing the pilot ("aircraft commander") to subdue any person who threatened the safety of a flight. It also create an obligation on the part of a state to restore control of an aircraft to its crew and to send it on its way. Notably, however, the treaty specifically stated that "nothing in this Convention shall be deemed to create an obligation to grant extradition."

The attitude of the international community changed with the campaign of Palestinian hijackings beginning with El Al planes in 1968 and continuing through 1972 with hijackings of U.S. and British flag carriers. In some of those incidents, passengers and crew were killed. In most the hijackers were set free as part of negotiated deals, and in some instances the planes were blown up at the end of their usefulness. The 1970 Hague Convention dealing with aircraft hijacking and the 1971 Montreal Convention dealing with placing explosives on an airplane attempted to establish two central themes: signatory countries agreed to punish the proscribed offenses with "severe penalties" and a country having custody of an offender was required either to extradite or prosecute. (Almost as a sidenote, in order to define the offenses that were to be subject to "severe penalties," the Conventions described certain behaviors as criminal. Prior attempts to enact international criminal provisions had foundered, with the exception of the post-hoc definitions of war crimes in the Treaty of London.)

The 1972 Munich Olympics saw the kidnaping of the Israeli wrestling team and the botched rescue attempt at the Munich airport leaving 11 Israelis, 5 terrorists and one German policeman dead, much of which was displayed on international television. Then came the Achille Lauro, with the cold-blooded murder of a U.S. citizen in a wheelchair, and a series of kidnapings and murders of western diplomats in various African and Middle East countries. Two events prior to 9/11 touched U.S. interests or soil, the bombing of Pan Am 103 over Lockerbie, Scotland, and an attempted bombing of the World Trade Center, for which a number of associates of Osama bin Laden were convicted and bin Laden himself was indicted. The second millennium closed with a campaign of suicide bombings in Israel.

Meanwhile, the diplomatic wheels were turning out conventions: taking of hostages, piracy against maritime shipping, acts involving airports, control of nuclear devices and plastic explosives. Each of the conventions commits signatory nations to define the offenses as crimes within their own law, which in turn leads to a commitment either to extradite or to place the accused on trial. The loop is closed by stating that nobody can be tried if he or she has already been tried for the same offense unless the accusing nation finds that the first trial was essentially a sham.

No convention prior to the "Financing of Terrorism" in 1999 attempted to define terrorism. Instead, the conventions described "offenses" and committed signatory nations to criminalize those offenses. In many instances, there were exceptions to the description of offenses such as that the offense of placing an explosive on an aircraft did not apply to military or police aircraft. Another notable exception was that exploding a device in a public place did not constitute an offense under the convention if the perpetrator and victims were nationals of the same nation in which the acts occurred. It was only in these backhanded fashions that the international community addressed the phenomenon known as "terrorism."

In the Convention for the Suppression of Financing of Terrorism, it finally became necessary to define what the international community conceived to be terrorism:

Article 2

1. Any person commits an offence within the meaning of this Convention if that person by any means, directly or indirectly, unlawfully and wilfully, provides or collects funds with the intention that they should be used or in the knowledge that they are to be used, in full or in part, in order to carry out:

a. An act which constitutes an offence within the scope of and as defined in one of the treaties listed in the annex; or

b. Any other act intended to cause death or serious bodily injury to a civilian, or to any other person not taking an active part in the hostilities in a situation of armed conflict, when the purpose of such act, by its nature or context, is to intimidate a population, or to compel a Government or an international organization to do or to abstain from doing any act.

NOTES AND QUESTIONS

1. Drafting Issues. An apparently easy question that could provoke some much deeper thought is: What is a "situation of armed conflict" and why are persons engaged in it not protected by the Convention? Are the ordinary laws of war adequate for dealing with intentional harm to civilians during armed conflict?

What is the point of the mens rea requirement (purpose is to intimidate a population or coerce a government)? For that matter what is a population? What does it mean to describe the purpose of an act "by its nature or context?" Each of these points is discussed in the *Akayesu* opinion.

If a drug dealer lets it be known that his "troops" will conduct drive-by shootings in any neighborhood in which a snitch or informer might be living, is this terrorism?

With regard to the funding provision itself, do I commit an offense if I contribute money to an organization that is often described in the popular press as "having ties" or being the "political arm" of a group that does use violence? For example, Sinn Fein and the IRA. Or what about all the various factions of the PLO?

2. Money and Association. The U.S. Supreme Court held in *Buckley v. Valeo*, 424 U.S. 1 (1976), that contributing money to an election campaign is protected by the free expression clause of the First Amendment to the U.S. Constitution. In subsequent cases, this protection was extended to contributions to campaigns for political agenda other than partisan elections. The Court has also protected the freedom of association by which persons join organizations to carry out political objectives. Is there an argument that some of this activity could fall within the definition in the Convention yet also be protected by the U.S. Constitution? We will return to this question when we discuss U.S. statutes dealing with providing "material support" to terrorist organizations.

THE DRAFT COMPREHENSIVE CONVENTION ON INTERNATIONAL TERRORISM

The draft was proposed by India in 1996. It is significant that India would be the proponent because India is the leader of the Non-Aligned Movement. (India even refused to accept western aid following the December 2004 tsunami despite some criticism for that stance.) The draft has been in the process of review both by an ad hoc committee of the UN General Assembly and by the International Law Commission. To this date, no agreement has been reached, although the universal condemnation of terrorism by both General Assembly and Security Council appear to have taken away the thrust of the position that "one man's terrorist is another man's freedom fighter."

Despite unanimity on the condemnation of terrorism, there still remains some concern that an insurgent attacking only military targets of an occupying nation could be considered a terrorist and thus subject to international criminal sanctions and procedures. The difficulty is that the insurgent in that position would be considered a criminal under the law of the occupying force (e.g. the U.S. in Iraq), but the "developing" nations do not want to put that person in jeopardy of being apprehended and extradited or prosecuted by a third nation. The initial definition of terrorism in Article 2 is quite broad:

> Article 2(1). Any person commits an offence within the meaning of this Convention if that person, by any means, unlawfully and intentionally, does an act intended to cause:

> (a) Death or serious bodily injury to any person; or

> (b) Serious damage to a State or government facility, a public transportation system, communication system or infrastructure facility with the intent to cause extensive destruction of such a place, facility or system, or where such destruction results or is likely to result in major economic loss;

> when the purpose of such act, by its nature or context, is to intimidate a population, or to compel a Government or an international organization to do or abstain from doing any act.

The breadth of the definition, however, is ameliorated by the principal exclusion in Article 3:

> This Convention shall not apply where the offence is committed within a single State, the alleged offender is a national of that State and is present in the territory of that State and no other State has a basis . . . to exercise jurisdiction. . . .

In addition, the obligations of the States Party to the Convention have a number of exclusions and limitations depending on their interest in or connection to the offense. The thrust of the controversy to this point has been whether to tighten the basic definition, rely on the exclusions and limitations, or undertake some combination of both.

§ 6.03 SELECTED READINGS

Law of War:

- INGRID DETTER DE LUPIS, THE LAW OF WAR (1987)
- LEON FRIEDMAN, THE LAW OF WAR: A DOCUMENTARY HISTORY (1972)
- CHRISTINE GRAY, INTERNATIONAL LAW AND THE USE OF FORCE (2000)
- MICHAEL HOWARD, GEORGE ANDROPOULOS & MARK SHULMAN, THE LAWS OF WAR (1994)
- RICHARD I. MILLER, THE LAW OF WAR (1975)
- TIMOTHY L.H. MCCORMACK & GERRY J. SIMPSON (EDS.), THE LAW OF WAR CRIMES (1997)
- OSCAR SCHACHTER, INTERNATIONAL LAW IN THEORY AND PRACTICE (1991)
- Symposium, *The Changing Laws of War: Do We Need a New Legal Regime After September 11?* 79 NOTRE DAME L. REV. 1183 (2004)

International Criminal Law:

- CHRISTOPH SAFFERLING, TOWARDS AN INTERNATIONAL CRIMINAL PROCEDURE (2001)
- WILLIAM A. SCHABAS, AN INTRODUCTION TO THE INTERNATIONAL CRIMINAL COURT (2001)
- LYAL S. SUNGA, THE EMERGING SYSTEM OF INTERNATIONAL CRIMINAL LAW (1997)
- DIANA WOODHOUSE, THE PINOCHET CASE (2000)

Chapter 7
ALIENS AND ETHNIC PROFILING

§ 7.01   ALIEN DETENTIONS AND SECRECY

One aspect of PATRIOT that received vociferous critique was section 412, which authorized the Attorney General hold aliens suspected of terrorist connections for up to six months in renewable increments. In response to congressional inquiries about the use of PATRIOT powers, the Justice Department replied in May 2003 that it had not used the section 412 authorization because it had sufficient authority under existing law to hold aliens considered for deportation without bond.

Just prior to 9/11 and PATRIOT, the Supreme Court decided in *Zadvydas v. Davis*, 533 U.S. 678 (2001), that an alien who was subject to a removal order (deportation) but who had nowhere to go could be held in detention, according to the immigration statutes, only pursuant to the attempt to remove. Therefore, a detained alien would be entitled by due process to a hearing to determine whether removal was possible. The Court assumed that release into the U.S. would be required at some point because "an alien may be held in confinement until it has been determined that there is no significant likelihood of removal in the reasonably foreseeable future."

The internal tensions within the *Zadvydas* opinion, the difficulties it leaves for dealing with removable aliens who have nowhere to go, and the implications for detention of those with suspected terrorist connections are discussed in T. Alexander Aleinikoff, *Detaining Plenary Power: The Meaning and Impact of* Zadvydas v. Davis, 16 GEO. IMMIG. L.J. 365 (2002). The issue of indefinite detention of aliens suspected of terrorist connections was taken up by the British House of Lords in *A v. Home Secretary*, § 9.03 *infra*.

In the meantime, decades of institutional concern about the structure of the Immigration and Nationalization Service (INS) coalesced with terrorism-related concerns when the Department of Homeland Security was created and took over the enforcement of immigration laws. Previously, the INS had attempted to perform both service functions (visas, naturalization, etc) and enforcement (deportation, etc). The two functions were often in conflict and made for confusion. With the splitting of these functions, Homeland Security now has an agency known as Immigration and Customs Enforcement (ICE) with a subdivision Office of Detention and Removal.

ICE states that it houses over 260,000 detainees per year, averaging over 27,000 on any given day. It has announced that it is so overwhelmed with mandated detentions, fueled by pressure not to release anyone who might be a threat to public safety for any reason, that it has formed an Alternatives to Detention Unit (ATD).

[A]   Secret Deportation Proceedings

Exacerbating the fears that flow from detention and deportation decisions is that the government has taken the position that information about the use of these techniques, even frequency of their use, is classified and need not be disclosed to the public. The aura of secrecy that has always been part of law enforcement is thus heightened substantially as part of the shift toward prevention of terrorist activity. Two cases dealing with closure of deportation proceedings to the press and public resulted in conflicting holdings.

DETROIT FREE PRESS v. ASHCROFT
303 F.3d 681 (6th Cir. 2002)

DAMON J. KEITH, CIRCUIT JUDGE.

[Rabbi Haddad, whose situation is highlighted in the Muslim Community Association complaint, (§ 5.02[A]) was "subject to deportation, having overstayed his tourist visa. The Government further suspects that the Islamic charity Haddad operates supplies funds to terrorist organizations." For these reasons, he was declared a "special interest case" and his deportation hearing was closed to the public. Newspapers and Congressman Conyers joined to challenge the lack of public access.]

The primary issue on appeal in this case, is whether the First Amendment to the United States Constitution confers a public right of access to deportation hearings. If it does, then the Government must make a showing to overcome that right.

No one will ever forget the egregious, deplorable, and despicable terrorist attacks of September 11, 2001. These were cowardly acts. In response, our government launched an extensive investigation into the attacks, future threats, conspiracies, and attempts to come. As part of this effort, immigration laws are prosecuted with increased vigor. The issue before us today involves these efforts.

The political branches of our government enjoy near-unrestrained ability to control our borders. "These are policy questions entrusted exclusively to the political branches of our government." Since the end of the 19th Century, our government has enacted immigration laws banishing, or deporting, non-citizens because of their race and their beliefs. While the Bill of Rights jealously protects citizens from such laws, it has never protected non-citizens facing deportation in the same way. In our democracy, based on checks and balances, neither the Bill of Rights nor the judiciary can second-guess government's choices. The only safeguard on this extraordinary governmental power is the public, deputizing the press as the guardians of their liberty. "An informed public is the most potent of all restraints upon misgovernment." *Grosjean v. Am. Press Co.*, 297 U.S. 233, 250 (1936).

Today, the Executive Branch seeks to take this safeguard away from the public by placing its actions beyond public scrutiny. Against non-citizens, it seeks the power to secretly deport a class if it unilaterally calls them "special interest" cases. The Executive Branch seeks to uproot people's lives, outside the public eye, and behind a closed door. Democracies die behind closed doors. The First Amendment, through a free press, protects the people's right to know that their government acts fairly, lawfully, and accurately in deportation proceedings. When government begins closing doors, it selectively controls information rightfully belonging to the people. Selective information is misinformation. The Framers of the First Amendment "did not trust any government to separate the true from the false for us." *Kleindienst v. Mandel*, 408 U.S. 753, 773 (1972). They protected the people against secret government.

The Office of the Chief Immigration Judge, under the authorization of Attorney General John Ashcroft, designates certain cases to be special interest cases, conducted in secret, closed off from the public. Arguing that closure of these hearings was unconstitutional, plaintiffs in three separate cases sought an injunction against such action. The Government filed a motion to dismiss, arguing that closing special interest cases was not unconstitutional.

The district court granted the injunction, finding blanket closure of deportation hearings in "special interest" cases unconstitutional. For the reasons that follow, we affirm the district court's order granting Plaintiffs a preliminary injunction.

I. FACTS AND PROCEDURAL HISTORY

On September 21, 2001, Chief Immigration Judge Michael Creppy issued a directive (the "Creppy directive") to all United States Immigration Judges requiring closure of special interest cases. The Creppy directive requires that all proceedings in such cases be closed to the press and public, including family members and friends. The Record of the Proceeding is not to be disclosed to anyone except a deportee's attorney or representative, "assuming the file does not contain classified information." "This restriction on information includes confirming or denying whether such a case is on the docket or scheduled for a hearing."

The district court granted the Newspaper Plaintiffs' motion [for preliminary injunction]. Finding that the Newspaper Plaintiffs had a First Amendment right of access to the proceedings under *Richmond Newspapers Inc., v. Virginia*, 448 U.S. 555 (1980), and its progeny, the district court further declined to review the Government's actions under the highly deferential standard articulated in *Kleindienst v. Mandel*, 408 U.S. 753 (1972). The Government timely filed its notice of appeal. In the interim, on April 10, 2002, the Government obtained a temporary stay of the district court's order from this Court. On April 18, 2002, we dissolved the temporary stay and denied the Government's motion for stay pending this appeal.

III. ANALYSIS

A. *Likelihood of Success on the Merits*

1. The Effect of the Government's Plenary Power Over Immigration

The Government argues that the district court erred in ruling that the government's plenary power over immigration did not warrant deferential review. *See, e.g., Kleindienst v. Mandel*, 408 U.S. 753 (1972) (no First Amendment bar to excluding people because of their beliefs); *Wong Wing*, 163 U.S. at 237 (court cannot limit Congress from expelling "aliens whose race or habits render them undesirable as citizens"). We are unpersuaded by the Government's claim, which would require complete deference in all facets of immigration law, including non-substantive immigration laws that infringe upon the Constitution. We hold that the Constitution meaningfully limits non-substantive immigration laws and does not require special deference to the Government.

The Government's broad authority over immigration was first announced more than one-hundred years ago in *The Chinese Exclusion Case*, 130 U.S. 581 (1889). In that case, the Court recounted the strife following Chinese immigration to California after the gold rush of the mid-1800s. A convention of lawmakers in California had petitioned Congress to alleviate this "problem." The petition charged, among other things, that:

> the presence of Chinese laborers had a baneful effect upon the material interests of the State, and upon public morals; that their immigration was in numbers approaching the character of an Oriental invasion, and was a menace to our civilization.

Noting this plea against "existing and anticipated evils," the Court valued the "the well-founded apprehension — from the experience of years — that limitation to the immigration of certain classes from China was essential to the peace of the community on the Pacific Coast, and possibly the preservation of our civilization there." Adding that "it seemed impossible for them to assimilate with our people or to make any change in their habits or modes of living," the Court found that "if the government . . . considers the presence of foreigners of a different race in this country, who will not assimilate with us, to be dangerous to its peace and security," this "determination is conclusive upon the judiciary." This power was derived not from an express provision of the Constitution, but from powers incident to sovereignty.

Today, the Government seeks to expand upon the rule from this case. The Government argues that it has plenary authority over not only substantive immigration laws and decisions, but also non-substantive ones, like the Creppy directive. Therefore, whether or not there is a First Amendment right of access to deportation proceedings, the Government argues, it can implement any non-substantive policy infringing upon that right if it is "facially legitimate and bona fide."

Even *The Chinese Exclusion Case*, however, acknowledged that Congress's power over immigration matters was limited by "the constitution itself."

a. *The Government Interprets* Kleindienst *Too Broadly*

In *Kleindienst*, Ernest Mandel, a self-proclaimed "revolutionary Marxist" and Belgian citizen, sought entry into the United States to speak at a conference at Stanford University. Mandel applied for and was denied a non-immigrant visa under a blanket provision of the Immigration and Nationality Act, prohibiting the entrance of "anarchists" or "persons advocating the overthrow of the government." In excluding Mandel, the Attorney General declined to exercise his discretionary authority to waive this prohibition.

Several professors brought suit alleging a violation of their First Amendment rights. The Court stated the issue as this: "Whether the First Amendment confers upon the appellee professors, because they wish to hear, speak, and debate with Mandel in person, the ability to determine that Mandel should be permitted to enter the country or, in other words, to compel the Attorney General to allow Mandel's admission." The Court, while acknowledging that the professors' First Amendment rights were implicated, affirmed the decision denying Mandel a visa. The Court stated:

> Plenary congressional power to make policies and rules for exclusion of aliens has long been firmly established. In the case of an alien excludable under § 212(a)(28), Congress has delegated conditional exercise of this power to the Executive. We hold that when the Executive exercises this power negatively on the basis of a facially legitimate and bona fide reason, the courts will neither look behind the exercise of that discretion, *nor test it by balancing its justification against the First Amendment interests* of those who seek personal communication with the applicant.

Kleindienst differs from the present case in two important, and related, ways. First, *Kleindienst* involved a substantive immigration decision. The law and decision at issue determined who entered the United States. Here, the Creppy directive has no effect on the eventual outcome of the deportation hearings. Second, *Kleindienst*, although recognizing a constitutional right, did not give any weight to that right. It specifically declined to balance the First Amendment right against the government's plenary power, because the law was a substantive immigration law. Therefore, if the First Amendment limits non-substantive immigration laws, *Kleindienst* offers no authority that the Government's actions are entitled to deferential review — *Kleindienst* ignored the existence of the professors' First Amendment rights altogether. In a case such as this, where a non-substantive immigration law involving a constitutional right is at issue, the Supreme Court has always recognized the importance of that constitutional right, never deferring to an assertion of plenary authority.

b. *The Constitution, Including the First Amendment, Meaningfully Limits Non-Substantive Immigration Laws*

[T]he Supreme Court has applied non-deferential review to non-substantive immigration law. In *Zadvydas v. Davis*, 533 U.S. 678 (2001), two non-citizens were being held indefinitely beyond the normal statutory-removal period of ninety days, because no country would accept them. A post-removal-period statute authorized such detention. The issue, however, was whether the post-removal statute authorized a detention indefinitely, or for a period reasonably necessary to secure removal. The language of the statute set no such limit. The Court read an implicit reasonableness limit into the statute to avoid "serious constitutional problems." Significantly, the Court dismissed the government's argument that Congress's plenary power to create immigration law required deference to the political branches' decision-making.

The Government correctly notes that the Court in *Zadvydas* twice indicated that it might be deferential in situations involving terrorism. However, nothing in *Zadvydas* indicates that given such a situation, the Court would defer to the political branches' determination of who belongs in that "small segment of particularly dangerous individuals" without judicial review of the individual circumstances of each case, something that the Creppy directive strikingly lacks. The Court repeated the importance of strong procedural protections when constitutional rights were involved: "The Constitution may well preclude granting an administrative body the unreviewable authority to make determinations implicating fundamental rights."

Importantly, the Creppy directive does not apply to "a small segment of particularly dangerous" information, but a broad, indiscriminate range of information, including information likely to be entirely innocuous. Similarly, no definable standards used to determine whether a case is of "special interest" have been articulated. Nothing in the Creppy directive counsels that it is limited to "a small segment of particularly dangerous individuals." In fact, the Government so much as argues that certain non-citizens known to have no links to terrorism will be designated "special interest" cases. Supposedly, closing a more targeted class would allow terrorists to draw inferences from which hearings are open and which are closed.

While we sympathize and share the Government's fear that dangerous information might be disclosed in some of these hearings, we feel that the ordinary process of determining whether closure is warranted on a case-by-case basis sufficiently addresses their concerns. Using this stricter standard does not mean that information helpful to terrorists will be disclosed, only that the Government must be more targeted and precise in its approach. Given the importance of the constitutional rights involved, such safeguards must be vigorously guarded lest the First Amendment turn into another balancing test.

4. Strict Scrutiny

Under the standard articulated in *Globe Newspaper*, government action that curtails a First Amendment right of access "in order to inhibit the disclosure of sensitive information" must be supported by a showing "that denial is necessitated by a compelling governmental interest, and is narrowly tailored to serve that interest." Moreover, "the interest is to be articulated along with findings specific enough that a reviewing court can determine whether the closure order was properly entered." The Government's ongoing anti-terrorism investigation certainly implicates a compelling interest. However, the Creppy directive is neither narrowly tailored, nor does it require particularized findings. Therefore, it impermissibly infringes on the Newspaper Plaintiffs' First Amendment right of access.

a. *The Government Cites Compelling Interests*

We do not agree with the district court that the Government failed to demonstrate that there are compelling interests sufficient to justify closure. The Government contends that "closure of removal proceedings in special interest cases is necessary to protect national security by safeguarding the Government's investigation of the September 11 terrorist attack and other terrorist conspiracies."

Before the district court, the Government provided the affidavit of James S. Reynolds, Chief of the Terrorism and Violent Crimes Section, to explain the types of information that public access to removal proceedings would disclose. In his affidavit, Mr. Reynolds explained the rationale for prohibiting public access to the proceedings as follows:

1. "Disclosing the names of 'special interest' detainees . . . could lead to public identification of individuals associated with them, other investigative

sources, and potential witnesses . . . and terrorist organizations . . . could subject them to intimidation or harm. . . . "

2. "Divulging the detainees' identities may deter them from cooperating [and] . . . terrorist organizations with whom they have connection may refuse to deal further with them, . . . " thereby eliminating valuable sources of information for the Government and impairing its ability to infiltrate terrorist organizations.

3. "Releasing the names of the detainees . . . would reveal the direction and progress of the investigation . . . " and "official verification that a member [of a terrorist organization] has been detained and therefore can no longer carry out the plans of his terrorist organization may enable the organization to find a substitute who can achieve its goals. . . . "

4. "Public release of names, and place and date of arrest . . . could allow terrorist organizations and others to interfere with the pending proceedings by creating false or misleading evidence."

5. "The closure directive is justified by the need to avoid stigmatizing 'special interest' detainees, who may ultimately be found to have no connection to terrorism. . . . "

Although the district court specifically invited the Government to articulate any other basis for closing Haddad's deportation hearing, the Government provided the district court no other reasons for closure.

The Government certainly has a compelling interest in preventing terrorism. In addition to Mr. Reynold's affidavit, other affidavits have been provided that justify the Government's interest in closure. According to the additional affidavits, public access to removal proceedings would disclose the following information that would impede the Government's investigation:

"Bits and pieces of information that may appear innocuous in isolation," but used by terrorist groups to help form a "bigger picture" of the Government's terrorism investigation, would be disclosed. The Government describes this type of intelligence gathering as "akin to the construction of a mosaic," where an individual piece of information is not of obvious importance until pieced together with other pieces of information.

The identifications of the detainees, witnesses, and investigative sources would be disclosed. Terrorist groups could subject these individuals or their families to intimidation or harm and discourage them from cooperating with the Government.

Methods of entry to the country, communicating, or funding could be revealed. This information could allow terrorist organizations to alter their patterns of activity to find the most effective means of evading detection.

"Information that is *not* presented at the hearings also might provide important clues to terrorist, because it could reveal what the investigation has not yet discovered." The Government provides this example: "If the government discloses the evidence it has about a particular member of a terrorist organization, but fails to mention that the detainee is involved in an impending attack, the other members of the organization may be able to infer that the government is not yet aware of the attack."

Inasmuch as these agents' declarations establish that certain information revealed during removal proceedings could impede the ongoing anti-terrorism investigation, we defer to their judgment. These agents are certainly in a better position to understand the contours of the investigation and the intelligence capabilities of terrorist organizations. *Cf. CIA v. Sims*, 471 U.S. 159, 180 (1985) (stating that "it is the responsibility of the Director of Central Intelligence, not that of the judiciary, to weigh the variety of complex and subtle factors in determining whether the disclosure of information may lead to unacceptable risk of compromising the Agency's intelligence-gathering process.").

b. *The Creppy Directive Does Not Require Particularized Findings*

Although the Government is able to demonstrate a compelling interest for closure, the immigration judge, Defendant Hacker, failed to make specific findings before closing Haddad's deportation proceedings. *Press-Enterprise II* instructs that in cases where partial or complete closure is warranted, there must be specific findings on the record so that a reviewing court can determine whether closure was proper and whether less restrictive alternatives exist. Similarly, the Creppy directive fails this requirement.

c. *The Creppy Directive is Not Narrowly Tailored*

Finally, the blanket closure rule mandated by the Creppy directive is not narrowly tailored. The Government offers no persuasive argument as to why the Government's concerns cannot be addressed on a case-by-case basis. The Newspaper Plaintiffs argue, and the district court agreed, that the Creppy directive is ineffective in achieving its purported goals because the detainees and their lawyers are allowed to publicize the proceedings. According to the Newspaper Plaintiffs, to the extent that Haddad had discussed his proceedings (and disclosed documents) with family, friends and the media, the information that the Government seeks to protect is disclosed to the public anyway. We are not persuaded by the Government's argument in response that few detainees will disclose any information and that their disclosure will be less than complete public access. This contention is, at best, speculative and belies the Government's assertion that *any* information disclosed, even bits and pieces that seem innocuous, will be detrimental to the anti-terrorism investigation.

It is clear that certain types of information that the Government seeks to keep confidential could be kept from the public on a case-by-case basis through protective orders or in camera review — for example, the identification of investigative sources and witnesses. The Government, however, argues that it is impossible to keep some sensitive information confidential if any portion of a hearing is open or if the immigration court conducts a hearing to determine if closure is proper. Stated differently, the Government argues that there is sensitive information that would be disclosed if closure occurred on a case-by-case basis. First, the Government contends that the identities of the detainees would be revealed if closure occurred on a case-by-case basis, and such information would impede the anti-terrorism investigation. This information, however, is already being disclosed to the public through the detainees themselves or their counsel. Even if, as a result of the interim rule, a detainee remains silent, a terrorist group capable of sophisticated intelligence-gathering would certainly be made aware that one of its operatives, or someone connected to a particular terrorist plot, has disappeared into the Government's custody. Moreover, if a deportee does have links to terrorist organizations, there is nothing to stop that deportee from divulging the information learned from these proceedings once deported.

Next, the Government argues that open hearings would reveal the amount of intelligence that the Government does not possess. The Government argues that evidence concerning a particular detainee could be incomplete, and an incomplete presentation of evidence would permit terrorists groups to gauge how much the Government knows and does not know about their operations. The issue in a removal hearing is, however, narrowly focused and the Government has enormous control over what evidence it introduces. "To deport an overstay, the INS must convince the immigration judge by clear and convincing evidence that the alien was admitted as a non-immigrant for a specific period, that the period has elapsed, and that the alien is still in this country."

Here, the Government has detained Haddad and instituted removal proceedings based on his overstay of a tourist visa. Thus, the Government need only establish that Haddad obtained a visa, the visa has expired, and that he is still in the country. Very little information is required. The fact that the Government may have to contest the non-citizen's application for discretionary relief is similarly unavailing. At oral argument, it was brought to our attention that Haddad intends to apply for asylum, a form of discretionary relief available to non-citizens in deportations proceedings. We see no reason why, in making its case against the applicant's request for discretionary relief, the Government could not seek to keep confidential, pertinent information, as the need arises.

Finally, the Government seeks to protect from disclosure the bits and pieces of information that seem innocuous in isolation, but when pieced together with other bits and pieces aid in creating a bigger picture of the Government's anti-terrorism investigation, i.e., the "mosaic intelligence." Mindful of the Government's concerns, we must nevertheless conclude that the Creppy directive is over-inclusive. While the risk of "mosaic intelligence" may exist, we do not believe speculation should form the basis for such a drastic restriction of the public's First Amendment rights. Fittingly, in this case, the Government subsequently admitted that there was no information disclosed in any of Haddad's first three hearings that threatened "national security or the safety of the American people." Yet, all these hearings were closed. The only reason offered for closing the hearings has been that the presiding immigration judge was told do it by the chief immigration judge who in turn was told to do it by the Attorney General.

Furthermore, there seems to be no limit to the Government's argument. The Government could use its "mosaic intelligence" argument as a justification to close any public hearing completely and categorically, including criminal proceedings. The Government could operate in virtual secrecy in all matters dealing, even remotely, with "national security," resulting in a wholesale suspension of First Amendment rights. By the simple assertion of "national security," the Government seeks a process where it may, without review, designate certain classes of cases as "special interest cases" and, behind closed doors, adjudicate the merits of these cases to deprive non-citizens of their fundamental liberty interests.

This, we simply may not countenance. A government operating in the shadow of secrecy stands in complete opposition to the society envisioned by the Framers of our Constitution.

In sum, we find that the Government's attempt to establish a narrowly tailored restriction has failed. The Creppy directive is under-inclusive by permitting the disclosure of sensitive information while at the same time drastically restricting First Amendment rights. The directive is over-inclusive by categorically and completely closing all special interest hearings without demonstrating, beyond speculation, that such a closure is absolutely necessary.

Lastly, the public's interests are best served by open proceedings. A true democracy is one that operates on faith — faith that government officials are forthcoming and honest, and faith that informed citizens will arrive at logical conclusions. This is a vital reciprocity that America should not discard in these troubling times. Without question, the events of September 11, 2001, left an indelible mark on our nation, but we as a people are united in the wake of the destruction to demonstrate to the world that we are a country deeply committed to preserving the rights and freedoms guaranteed by our democracy. Today, we reflect our commitment to those democratic values by ensuring that our government is held accountable to the people and that First Amendment rights are not impermissibly compromised. Open proceedings, with a vigorous and scrutinizing press, serve to ensure the durability of our democracy.

NOTES AND QUESTIONS

1. Individuals and the Mosaic. Judge Keith acknowledges the Supreme Court's statement in *Zadvydas* that "it might be deferential in situations involving terrorism. However, nothing in *Zadvydas* indicates that given such a situation, the Court would defer to the political branches' determination of who belongs in that 'small segment of particularly dangerous individuals' without judicial review of the individual circumstances of each case, something that the Creppy directive strikingly lacks." But the judicial review of individual circumstances is precisely what the Government seeks to avoid in order to avoid the "mosaic" problem described in the Reynolds Affidavit. Is the Sixth Circuit simply unwilling to yield to the mosaic issue?

The *Zadvydas* dictum regarding an exception for indefinite detention of terrorism suspects was answered in the negative by the British House of Lords decision in *A v. Home Secretary*, § 9.03 *infra*.

2. *North Jersey Media Group, Inc. v. Ashcroft.* *North Jersey Media Group, Inc. v. Ashcroft*, 308 F.3d 198 (3d Cir. 2002):

> [W]e find ourselves in disagreement with the Sixth Circuit. . . . Deportation procedures have been codified for approximately 100 years but, despite their constant reenactment during that time, Congress has never explicitly guaranteed public access. Indeed, deportation cases involving abused alien children are mandatorily closed by statute, and hearings are often conducted in places generally inaccessible to the public. While INS regulations promulgated in 1964 create a rebuttable presumption of openness for most deportation cases, we conclude that a recently-created regulatory presumption of openness with significant statutory exceptions does not present the type of "unbroken, uncontradicted history" that *Richmond Newspapers* and its progeny require to establish a First Amendment right of access.

The Sixth Circuit stated, "The Government could use its 'mosaic intelligence' argument as a justification to close any public hearing completely and categorically, including criminal proceedings." The Third Circuit disagrees on the ground that a criminal proceeding would be subject to different standards than a deportation proceeding for reasons of tradition. What is the relevance of this issue, and which court has the better of the argument?

The Sixth Circuit responds point by point to each of the Government claims for secrecy and finds that information is already available to the public through the detainee himself. Does it matter whether the disclosure comes from the detainee or from another source? The next case touches the same arguments.

3. PATRIOT Detentions. Much of the criticism of detention of aliens from Arab countries has alluded to the PATRIOT Act's increase of the time that an alien could be detained for suspicion of visa violations without going before an immigration judge. The Justice Department, in response to inquiries from congressional committees, pointed out that it did not rely on the PATRIOT provisions because pre-existing law already allowed it to hold an alien for visa violations without bail when authorized by an immigration judge.

[B]   Secrecy of Detentions

CENTER FOR NATIONAL SECURITY STUDIES v. U.S. DEPARTMENT OF JUSTICE
331 F.3d 918 (D.C. Cir. 2003)

SENTELLE, CIRCUIT JUDGE.

Various "public interest" groups (plaintiffs) brought this Freedom of Information Act (FOIA) action against the Department of Justice (DOJ or government) seeking release of information concerning persons detained in the wake of the September 11 terrorist attacks, including: their names, their attorneys, dates of arrest and release, locations of arrest and detention, and reasons for detention. The government objected to release, and asserted numerous exceptions to FOIA requirements in order to justify withholding the information. The parties filed cross-motions for summary judgment. The district court ordered release of the names of the detainees and their attorneys, but held that the government could withhold all other detention information pursuant to

FOIA Exemption 7(A), which exempts "records or information compiled for law enforcement purposes . . . to the extent that the production" of them "could reasonably be expected to interfere with enforcement proceedings." 5 U.S.C. § 552(b)(7)(A) (2000).

Upon de novo review, we agree with the district court that the detention information is properly covered by Exemption 7(A); but we further hold that Exemption 7(A) justifies withholding the names of the detainees and their attorneys. We also reject plaintiffs' alternate theories that the First Amendment and the common law mandate disclosure of the contested information. We therefore affirm in part, reverse in part, and remand the case to the district court for the entry of a judgment of dismissal.

I. Background

A. *The Investigation*

Consistent with the mutual decision of the parties to seek resolution to this controversy on summary judgment, the facts are not in serious dispute. In the course of the post-September 11 investigation, the government interviewed over one thousand individuals about whom concern had arisen. The concerns related to some of these individuals were resolved by the interviews, and no further action was taken with respect to them. Other interviews resulted in the interviewees' being detained. As relevant here, these detainees fall into three general categories.

The first category of detainees consists of individuals who were questioned in the course of the investigation and detained by the INS for violation of the immigration laws (INS detainees). INS detainees were initially questioned because there were "indications that they might have connections with, or possess information pertaining to, terrorist activity against the United States including particularly the September 11 attacks and/or the individuals or organizations who perpetrated them." Based on the initial questioning, each INS detainee was determined to have violated immigration law; some of the INS detainees were also determined to "have links to other facets of the investigation." Over 700 individuals were detained on INS charges. As of June 13, 2002, only seventy-four remained in custody. Many have been deported. INS detainees have had access to counsel, and the INS has provided detainees with lists of attorneys willing to represent them, as required by 8 U.S.C. § 1229(b)(2) (2000). INS detainees have had access to the courts to file *habeas corpus* petitions. They have also been free to disclose their names to the public.

The second category of detainees consists of individuals held on federal criminal charges (criminal detainees). The government asserts that none of these detainees can be eliminated as a source of probative information until after the investigation is completed. According to the most recent information released by the Department of Justice, 134 individuals have been detained on federal criminal charges in the post-September 11 investigation; 99 of these have been found guilty either through pleas or trials. While many of the crimes bear no direct connection to terrorism, several criminal detainees have been charged with terrorism-related crimes, and many others have been charged with visa or passport forgery, perjury, identification fraud, and illegal possession of weapons. Zacarias Moussaoui, presently on trial for participating in the September 11 attacks, is among those who were detained on criminal charges.

The third category consists of persons detained after a judge issued a material witness warrant to secure their testimony before a grand jury, pursuant to the material witness statute, 18 U.S.C. § 3144 (2000) (material witness detainees). Each material witness detainee was believed to have information material to the events of September 11. The district courts before which these material witnesses have appeared have issued sealing orders that prohibit the government from releasing any information about the proceedings. The government has not revealed how many individuals were detained on material witness warrants. At least two individuals initially held as material witnesses are now being held for alleged terrorist activity.

The criminal detainees and material witness detainees are free to retain counsel and have been provided court-appointed counsel if they cannot afford representation, as required by the Sixth Amendment to the Constitution. In sum, each of the detainees has had access to counsel, access to the courts, and freedom to contact the press or the public at large.

B. *The Litigation*

To support its FOIA request, plaintiffs cited press reports about mistreatment of the detainees, which plaintiffs claimed raised serious questions about "deprivations of fundamental due process, including imprisonment without probable cause, interference with the right to counsel, and threats of serious bodily injury."

In response to plaintiffs' FOIA request, the government released some information, but withheld much of the information requested. As to INS detainees, the government withheld the detainees' names, locations of arrest and detention, the dates of release, and the names of lawyers. As to criminal detainees, the government withheld the dates and locations of arrest and detention, the dates of release, and the citizenship status of each detainee. The government withheld all requested information with respect to material witnesses. Although the government has refused to disclose a comprehensive list of detainees' names and other detention information sought by plaintiffs, the government has from time to time publicly revealed names and information of the type sought by plaintiffs regarding a few individual detainees, particularly those found to have some connection to terrorism.

FOIA Exemptions 7(A), 7(C), and 7(F) permit withholding information "compiled for law enforcement purposes" whenever disclosure:

> (A) could reasonably be expected to interfere with enforcement proceedings, . . . (C) could reasonably be expected to constitute an unwarranted invasion of personal privacy, . . . or (F) could reasonably be expected to endanger the life or physical safety of any individual.

As to Exemption 7(A), the declarations state that release of the requested information could hamper the ongoing investigation by leading to the identification of detainees by terrorist groups, resulting in terrorists either intimidating or cutting off communication with the detainees; by revealing the progress and direction of the ongoing investigation, thus allowing terrorists to impede or evade the investigation; and by enabling terrorists to create false or misleading evidence. As to Exemption 7(C), the declarations assert that the detainees have a substantial privacy interest in their names and detention information because release of this information would associate detainees with the September 11 attacks, thus injuring detainees' reputations and possibly endangering detainees' personal safety. Finally, as to Exemption 7(F), the government's declarations contend that release of the information could endanger the public safety by making terrorist attacks more likely and could endanger the safety of individual detainees by making them more vulnerable to attack from terrorist organizations. For these same reasons, the counterterrorism officials state that the names of the detainees' lawyers should also be withheld.

II. The FOIA Claims

A. *Names of Detainees*

Exemption 7(A) allows an agency to withhold "records or information compiled for law enforcement purposes, but only to the extent that the production of such law enforcement records or information . . . could reasonably be expected to interfere with enforcement proceedings."

In *CIA v. Sims*, 471 U.S. 159 (1985), the Supreme Court examined the CIA's claims that the names and institutional affiliations of certain researchers in a government-sponsored behavior modification program were exempt from disclosure under FOIA Exemption 3. The agency claimed that the information was protected from disclosure by a statute charging the CIA to prevent unauthorized disclosure of "intelligence sources and methods." In accepting the CIA Director's judgment that disclosure would reveal intelligence sources and methods, the Court explained that "the decisions of the Director, who must of course be familiar with 'the whole picture,' as judges are not, are worthy of great deference given the magnitude of the national security interests and potential risks at stake." The Court further held that "it is the responsibility of the Director of Central Intelligence, not that of the judiciary, to weigh the variety of subtle and complex factors in determining whether disclosure of information may lead to an unacceptable risk of compromising the Agency's intelligence-gathering process."

The same is true of the Justice Department officials in charge of the present investigation. In light of the deference mandated by the separation of powers and Supreme Court precedent, we hold that the government's expectation that disclosure of the detainees' names would enable al Qaeda or other terrorist groups to map the course of the investigation and thus develop the means to impede it is reasonable. A complete list of names informing terrorists of every suspect detained by the government at any point during the September 11 investigation would give terrorist organizations a composite picture of the government investigation, and since these organizations would generally know the activities and locations of its members on or about September 11, disclosure would inform terrorists of both the substantive and geographic focus of the investigation. Moreover, disclosure would inform terrorists which of their members were compromised by the investigation, and which were not. This information could allow terrorists to better evade the ongoing investigation and more easily formulate or revise counter-efforts. In short, the "records could reveal much about the focus and scope of the [agency's] investigation, and are thus precisely the sort of information exemption 7(A) allows an agency to keep secret."

As the district court noted, courts have relied on similar mosaic arguments in the context of national security. In *Sims*, for example, the Supreme Court cautioned that "bits and pieces" of data " 'may aid in piecing together bits of other information even when the individual piece is not of obvious importance in itself.' " Thus, "what may seem trivial to the uninformed, may appear of great moment to one who has a broad view of the scene and may put the questioned item of information in its proper context."

For several reasons, plaintiffs contend that we should reject the government's predictive judgments of the harms that would result from disclosure. First, they argue that terrorist organizations likely already know which of their members have been detained. We have no way of assessing that likelihood. Moreover, even if terrorist organizations know about some of their members who were detained, a complete list of detainees could still have great value in confirming the status of their members. For example, an organization may be unaware of a member who was detained briefly and then released, but remains subject to continuing government surveillance. After disclosure, this detainee could be irreparably compromised as a source of information.

More importantly, some detainees may not be members of terrorist organizations, but may nonetheless have been detained on INS or material witness warrants as having information about terrorists. Terrorist organizations are less likely to be aware of such individuals' status as detainees. Such detainees could be acquaintances of the September 11 terrorists, or members of the same community groups or mosques. These detainees, fearing retribution or stigma, would be less likely to cooperate with the investigation if their names are disclosed. Moreover, tracking down the background and location of these detainees could give terrorists insights into the investigation they would otherwise be unlikely to have. After disclosure, terrorist organizations could attempt to intimidate these detainees or their families, or feed the detainees false or misleading information. It is important to remember that many of these detainees have been released at this time and are thus especially vulnerable to intimidation or coercion. While the detainees have been free to disclose their names to the press or public, it is telling that so few have come forward, perhaps for fear of this very intimidation.

In support of this conclusion, we note that the Third Circuit confronted a similar issue involving the INS detainees when it considered the constitutionality of closed deportation hearings in *North Jersey Media Group, Inc. v. Ashcroft*, 308 F.3d 198 (3d Cir. 2002). The court was faced with the same Watson Declaration in evidence here and the same government prediction that harm would result from the disclosure of information about the INS detainees. That court acknowledged that the "representations of the Watson Declaration are to some degree speculative." The court concluded: "To the extent that the Attorney General's national security concerns seem credible, we will not lightly second-guess them." We think the Third Circuit's approach was correct and we follow it here. Inasmuch as the concerns expressed in the government's declarations seem credible — and inasmuch as the declarations were made by counter-terrorism experts with far greater knowledge than this Court — we hold that the disclosure of the names of the detainees could reasonably be expected to interfere with the ongoing investigation.

In upholding the government's invocation of Exemption 7(A), we observe that we are in accord with several federal courts that have wisely respected the executive's judgment in prosecuting the national response to terrorism. We realize that not all courts are in agreement. We do not find the Sixth Circuit's reasoning compelling, but join the Third, Fourth, and Seventh Circuits in holding that the courts must defer to the executive on decisions of national security. In so deferring, we do not abdicate the role of the judiciary. Rather, in undertaking a deferential review we simply recognize the different roles underlying the constitutional separation of powers. It is within the role of the executive to acquire and exercise the expertise of protecting national security. It is not within the role of the courts to second-guess executive judgments made in furtherance of that branch's proper role. The judgment of the district court ordering the government to disclose the names of the detainees is reversed.

B. *Identity of Counsel*

The government contends that a list of attorneys for the detainees would facilitate the easy compilation of a list of all detainees, and all of the dangers flowing therefrom. It is more than reasonable to assume that plaintiffs and *amici* press organizations would attempt to contact detainees' attorneys and compile a list of all detainees. As discussed above, if such a list fell into the hands of al Qaeda, the consequences could be disastrous.

C. *Other Detention Information*

As outlined above, plaintiffs sought the dates and locations of arrest, detention, and release for each of the detainees. Even more than disclosure of the identities of detainees, the information requested here would provide a complete roadmap of the government's investigation. Knowing when and where each individual was arrested would provide a chronological and geographical picture of the government investigation. Terrorists could learn from this information not only where the government focused its investigation but how that investigation progressed step by step. Armed with that knowledge, they could then reach such conclusions as, for example, which cells had been compromised, and which individuals had been cooperative with the United States. They might well be able to derive conclusions as to how more adequately [to] secure their clandestine operations in future terrorist undertakings. Similarly, knowing where each individual is presently held could facilitate communication between terrorist organizations and detainees and the attendant intimidation of witnesses and fabrication of evidence. As explained in detail above, these impediments to an ongoing law enforcement investigation are precisely what Exemption 7(A) was enacted to preclude. Accordingly, we affirm the district court and hold that the government properly withheld information about the dates and locations of arrest, detention, and release for each detainee.

III. Alternative Grounds

We turn now to plaintiffs' alternative grounds for seeking disclosure of the detainees' names and detention information. Although FOIA does not mandate disclosure, plaintiffs contend that disclosure is independently required by both the First Amendment and the common law right of access to government information.

We will not convert the First Amendment right of access to criminal judicial proceedings into a requirement that the government disclose information compiled during the exercise of a quintessential executive power — the investigation and prevention of terrorism. The dangers which we have catalogued above of making such release in this case provide ample evidence of the need to follow this course.

We also reject plaintiffs' final claim that disclosure is required by the common law right of access to public records. The Supreme Court held in *Nixon v. Warner Communications, Inc.*, 435 U.S. 589 (1978), that "the courts of this country recognize a general right to inspect and copy public records and documents, including judicial documents." Plaintiffs, citing several state court cases finding a common law right of access to arrest records, urge us to recognize a federal common law right to receive the information they seek. In response, the government claims that the common law right of access is limited to judicial records. Even if the common law right applies to executive records, the government contends, FOIA has displaced the common law right. While we question the government's first contention, we accept its second.

IV. Conclusion

For the reasons set forth above, we conclude that the government was entitled to withhold under FOIA Exemption 7(A) the names of INS detainees and those detained as material witnesses in the course of the post-September 11 terrorism investigation; the dates and locations of arrest, detention, and release of all detainees, including those charged with federal crimes; and the names of counsel for detainees. Finally, neither the First Amendment nor federal common law requires the government to disclose the information sought by plaintiffs.

Affirmed in part, reversed in part and remanded.

Tatel, Circuit Judge, dissenting.

Disregarding settled principles governing the release of government records under the Freedom of Information Act, this court holds that the government may keep secret the names of hundreds of persons whom it has detained in connection with its investigation of the September 11, 2001 terrorist attacks without distinguishing between information that can, in FOIA's words, "reasonably be expected to interfere" with the investigation and information that cannot. While the government's reasons for withholding *some* of the information may well be legitimate, the court's uncritical deference to the government's vague, poorly explained arguments for withholding broad categories of information about the detainees, as well as its willingness to fill in the factual and logical gaps in the government's case, eviscerates both FOIA itself and the principles of openness in government that FOIA embodies.

The government claims that the detainees have access to counsel and freedom to contact whomever they wish, but the public has a fundamental interest in being able to examine the veracity of such claims. Just as the government has a compelling interest in ensuring citizens' safety, so do citizens have a compelling interest in ensuring that their government does not, in discharging its duties, abuse one of its most awesome powers, the power to arrest and jail.

Invoking the "heightened deference to the judgments of the political branches with respect to matters of national security," the government refuses to identify the specific categories of information that would actually interfere with its investigation, but rather asks us simply to trust its judgment. This court obeys, declaring that "the judiciary is in an extremely poor position to second-guess the executive's judgment in this area of national security." But requiring agencies to make the detailed showing FOIA requires is not second-guessing their judgment about matters within their expertise. And in any event, this court is also in an extremely poor position to second-guess the legislature's judgment that the judiciary must play a meaningful role in reviewing FOIA exemption requests. Neither FOIA itself nor this circuit's interpretation of the statute authorizes the court to invoke the phrase "national security" to relieve the government of its burden of justifying its refusal to release information under FOIA.

The only argument that could conceivably support withholding innocent detainees' names is the assertion that disclosure of the names "*may* reveal details about the focus and scope of the investigation and thereby allow terrorists to counteract it." That Reynolds believes these harms *may* result from disclosure is hardly surprising — anything is possible. But before accepting the government's argument, this court must insist on knowing whether these harms "*could reasonably be expected to*" result from disclosure — the standard Congress prescribed for exemption under 7(A). Nothing in Reynolds's declaration suggests that these harms are in fact reasonably likely to occur.

Although I think it unreasonable to infer that all of the information plaintiffs seek in their FOIA request qualifies for exemption, the government may be able to point to more narrowly defined categories of information that might justify the inference. For example, while nothing in the record supports the government's contention that releasing the names of innocent detainees would harm the investigation, perhaps the government could justify withholding the places of arrest on the ground that such information might provide terrorist organizations with some insight into the government's investigative methods and strategy. I would therefore remand to allow the government to describe, for each detainee or reasonably defined category of detainees, on what basis it may withhold their names and other information.

NOTES AND QUESTIONS

1. Public Knowledge. The Sixth Circuit thought that a detainee's ability to communicate with the public was a good reason for opening deportation hearings. The D.C. Circuit thinks that the same ability is an argument for not requiring government disclosure of information to the public. The difference apparently lies in the manner in which information would become available pursuant to a FOIA request: "even if terrorist organizations know about some of their members who were detained, a complete list of detainees could still have great value in confirming the status of their members. For example, an organization may be unaware of a member who was detained briefly and then released, but remains subject to continuing government surveillance."

2. Individuals and the Government. Judge Tatel and the majority disagree about application of "deference" in the context of terrorism investigations. The heart of the difference seems to be Judge Tatel's view that "requiring agencies to make the detailed showing FOIA requires is not second-guessing their judgment about matters within their expertise." But it is a detailed showing that the Government says would be harmful to matters within its expertise. This is very similar to the disagreement between the Sixth and Third Circuits over the question of making individualized decisions on closing deportation hearings. Thus, the dilemma of how to monitor critical aspects of government behavior in a free society while still protecting the public from unknown risks is highlighted again by these differences of opinion.

NOTE ON MATERIAL WITNESS WARRANTS

Material witness warrants are an important tool of criminal procedure that are mostly beyond the scope of this book, but which along with grand jury subpoenas make some of the more controversial aspects of PATRIOT virtually irrelevant. A material witness warrant is issued by a judge or magistrate under conditions similar to an arrest warrant but the purpose is to secure that person's testimony rather than to hold the person for trial.

The Justice Department stated to Congress in May 2003 that less than 50 persons had been detained on material witness warrants "in the course of the September 11 investigation." Of those, all but about 5 were "detained for 90 days or less."

The D.C. Circuit in the FOIA case says that even material witness warrants allow the detainee to contact the press. That assumes, of course, that their custodians provide the mechanism to do so. The court notes that two former material witnesses were being held at that time "for alleged terrorist activity." Jose Padilla has been held incommunicado for extended periods of time without the filing of any charges against him, initially as a material witness then as an enemy combatant. Ali al Marri was originally charged with perjury, then detained as an enemy combatant. I do not know who is the other person to whom the court refers in this statement. Because the Government has refused to detail the number of persons held on material witness warrants and the length of time held, on the ground that grand jury proceedings are secret for several reasons, there are a number of advocacy groups expressing deep suspicion about abuse of the material witness warrant in this context.

In *United States v. Awadallah*, 349 F.3d 4 (2d Cir. 2003), Osama Awadallah was taken into custody in Los Angeles after his name and phone number were found on a gum wrapper in the car of one of the 9/11 hijackers. He was detained on a material witness warrant and flown to New York where he testified twice before a grand jury over the course of several weeks. He admitted knowing one of the hijackers but first denied knowing a second one whom he later remembered. Charged with perjury for the first statement, he moved to dismiss the indictment for abuse of the material witness statute. The district judge held that "no Congress has granted the government the authority to imprison an innocent person in order to guarantee that he will testify before a grand jury conducting a criminal investigation. Because Awadallah was unlawfully detained, his grand jury testimony must be suppressed. The indictment is therefore dismissed." The Second Circuit reversed, holding that obtaining grand jury testimony would be an appropriate use of the material witness statute:

> The district court noted (and we agree) that it would be improper for the government to use § 3144 for other ends, such as the detention of persons suspected of criminal activity for which probable cause has not yet been established. However, the district court made no finding (and we see no evidence to suggest) that the government arrested Awadallah for any purpose other than to secure information material to a grand jury investigation. Moreover, that grand jury was investigating the September 11 terrorist attacks. The particular governmental interests at stake therefore were the indictment and successful prosecution of terrorists whose attack, if committed by a sovereign, would have been tantamount to war, and the discovery of the conspirators' means, contacts, and operations in order to forestall future attacks.

See Robert Boyle, *The Material Witness Statute Post September 11: What It Should Not Include Grand Jury Witnesses*, 48 N.Y.L.S. L. Rev. 13 (2003).

§ 7.02   DETENTIONS AND ETHNIC PROFILING

Two early responses to 9/11 by the Justice Department had ethnic overtones. One was to interview many U.S. citizens or resident aliens who came from countries with terrorist ties in an effort to obtain information that could be assembled and analyzed to discern patterns related either to 9/11 itself or to future plots. The second initiative was to detain many aliens from those same countries who had overstayed their visas or otherwise violated immigration laws, some of whom eventually might be deportable. As a number of advocacy groups observed, most of the countries considered to be linked to terrorist planning were Arab nations and most of those detained were young Arab males. While not explicitly based on ethnicity, the practice resulted in a clearly disparate impact on Arab aliens.

In that setting, public opinion swung suddenly and visibly to acceptance of racial or ethnic profiling. One survey conducted in Detroit reported that 61% of Arab Americans believed that "extra scrutiny of people with Middle Eastern features or accents by law enforcement officials" was justified. *Arab Americans Expect Scrutiny, Feel Sting of Bias*, DETROIT FREE PRESS, Oct. 1, 2001, *available at* http://www.freep.com/news/nw/terror2001/poll1_20011001.htm.

Ethnic profiling has been a target of some scrutiny in legal academic writing for the past couple of decades. Academic commentary immediately after 9/11 showed a similar swing in emphasis. Noting that as of September 10, 2001, a strong consensus against racial profiling had been accepted by everyone from Jesse Jackson to John Ashcroft, Professors Gross and Livingston argued that harsh realities prompted a rethinking of the issues:

> The September 11 attacks and the threat of future terrorism clearly require an intensive investigation. Given the extremity of the threat and identity of the known terrorists, the government is justified in focusing that investigation on Middle Eastern men despite the fact that the public decision to do so has caused understandable pain and anxiety for many Arab Americans. But that should be only the beginning of our inquiry. In the end, what the Department of Justice does to those it seeks to interview, for what reasons and on what basis, are more important than the fact that they may have been initially selected for interviews in part because of their ethnicity or national origin.

Samuel R. Gross & Debra Livingston, *Racial Profiling Under Attack*, 102 COLUM. L. REV. 1413, 1437 (2002). Professor Harris now thinks that the earlier unacceptability of racial profiling should be reinstated, although he believes that a sophisticated form of "behavioral profiling" could be more effective without the stigma. David A. Harris, *New Risks, New Tactics: An Assessment of the Re-Assessment of Racial Profiling in the Wake of September 11, 2001*, 2004 UTAH L. REV. 913.

In only rare instances have courts been asked to address allegations of police discrimination in "stop and frisk" situations. Only when a very strong pattern of unjustified racial or ethnic discrimination has been shown have the courts been willing to step in and set out guidelines for control of police discretion. In one sense, the issues have involved questions of cause and effect — is a disparate stop pattern indicative of racial bias in the police or is it the result of higher likelihood of suspicious behavior among minority groups? In another sense, the cases reflect a reluctance to push the causation issue very aggressively out of fear that a police response would be to decrease law enforcement efforts in low-income, high-crime, predominantly minority neighborhoods. *See generally* RANDALL KENNEDY, RACE, CRIME AND THE LAW (1997).

The classic example of permissible racial segregation is that of separating prison inmates by race during a race riot. When the Supreme Court has cited this example, it has never had reason to speculate about the degree of evidence that would be required to support the conclusion of an emergency for this purpose. Perhaps it is safe to assume that in the context of a prison riot, we would know an emergency when we see it, but more troubling is whether we know a national emergency when we see it. The reason for the difficulty is that the greater the intrusion onto personal liberties, the greater the showing of emergency that should be expected.

[A] Japanese "Exclusion" and National Emergency

A consideration of race in the context of declared national emergency must begin with the Japanese cases of World War II. While the most notorious of the three Supreme Court cases is *Korematsu v. United States*, 323 U.S. 214 (1944), *Hirabayashi v. United States*, 320 U.S. 81 (1943), may be a closer precedent to what could happen again. Justice Jackson's dissent in *Korematsu* forecast the concern (while perhaps foreshadowing his role as chief prosecutor at Nuremberg) when he bemoaned the Court's war-time review of military judgments:

> [T]he Court for all time has validated the principle of racial discrimination in criminal procedure and of transplanting American citizens. The principle then lies about like a loaded weapon ready for the hand of any authority that can bring forward a plausible claim of an urgent need. (*Korematsu*, 323 U.S. at 246.)

> If the people ever let command of the war power fall into irresponsible and unscrupulous hands, the courts wield no power equal to its restraint. The chief restraint upon those who command the physical forces of the country, in the future as in the past, must be their responsibility to the political judgments of their contemporaries and to the moral judgements of history. *Korematsu*, 323 U.S. at 248.

Japanese exclusion came in three steps. First, there was a Presidential directive broadly authorizing military commanders to exclude persons from certain areas, primarily Hawaii and the Pacific Coast. The second step was an Act of Congress criminalizing violation of military orders issued under the President's authorization. Then the military commanders issued orders setting curfews, authorizing detention, and establishing relocation camps.

Hirabayashi upheld a curfew by which all persons of Japanese ancestry in certain areas were required to be in their residences from 8 p.m. to 6 a.m. The order was challenged on the grounds that it was beyond the war powers as well as racial discrimination, to which the Court responded that

> we cannot reject as unfounded the judgment of the military authorities and of Congress that there were disloyal members of that population, whose number and strength could not be precisely and quickly ascertained. We cannot say that the war-making branches of the Government did not have ground for believing that in a critical hour such persons could not readily be isolated and separately dealt with, and constituted a menace to the national defense and safety, which demanded that prompt and adequate measures be taken to guard against it.

Moving from curfew to detention, the Court upheld "temporary" relocation of thousands of persons of Japanese ancestry while recognizing that relocation carried a much greater impact than curfew:

> Compulsory exclusion of large groups of citizens from their homes, except under circumstances of direst emergency and peril, is inconsistent with our basic governmental institutions. But when under conditions of modern warfare our shores are threatened by hostile forces, the power to protect must be commensurate with the threatened danger.

Justice Black's opinion insisted that the Court was addressing only exclusion from the West Coast and was not concerned with "relocation centers" because the curfew was all that Korematsu was charged with violating. Then, when the validity of continued detention was considered in *Ex parte Endo*, 323 U.S. 283 (1944), the Court construed the EO and statute narrowly to find that detention would be authorized only by the exigencies of separating the loyal from the disloyal or as a voluntary measure of humanitarian aid to those excluded from coastal areas:

> The authority to detain a citizen or to grant him a conditional release as protection against espionage or sabotage is exhausted at least when his loyalty is conceded. If we held that the authority to detain continued thereafter, we would transform an espionage or sabotage measure into something else. That was not done by Executive Order No. 9066 or by the Act of March 21, 1942, which ratified it. What they did not do we cannot do. Detention which furthered the campaign against espionage and sabotage would be one thing. But detention which has no relationship to that campaign is of a distinct character.

Although the combination of *Korematsu* and *Endo* technically was to authorize exclusion while invalidating detention, as a practical matter one carried implication of the other. First, the burden was on the applicant to prove loyalty and, moreover, it was not clear where this person was to go when excluded from the home and community in which he or she had been born and raised. Even long after the military justification had ceased, inertia delayed the end of detention. The effect was that over 100,000 presumably loyal citizens spent the war years behind barbed wire in mostly desert encampments.

The aftermath of the program eventually led to a congressionally mandated Commission on Wartime Relocation and Internment of Civilians. The CWRIC described the subsequent remorse of many of the participants in the program (including Justices Douglas, Clark, and Warren) and summarized its own findings this way:

> The promulgation of Executive Order 9066 was not justified by military necessity, and the decisions which followed from it — detention, ending detention, and ending exclusion — were not driven by analysis of military conditions. The broad historical causes which shaped these decisions were race prejudice, war hysteria and a failure of political leadership. Widespread ignorance of Japanese Americans contributed to a policy conceived in haste and executed in an atmosphere of fear and anger at Japan. A grave injustice was done to American citizens and resident aliens of Japanese ancestry who, without individual review or any probative evidence against them, were excluded, removed and detained by the United States during World War II.

To what extent does *Korematsu* stand as precedent today? As thoroughly regretted and discredited as the Japanese exclusion program itself may be, the opinion has never been overruled and indeed is cited as the beginning of reviewing racial discrimination by government with strict scrutiny.

[B]   Ethnic Profiling in Law Enforcement

MARSHALL v. COLUMBIA LEA REGIONAL HOSPITAL
345 F.3d 1157 (10th Cir. 2003)

McCONNELL, CIRCUIT JUDGE.

This case involves troubling allegations regarding possible police misconduct by an officer in Hobbs, New Mexico. We are not in a position to judge the truth of those allegations at this early stage in the litigation, but we conclude that the district court acted prematurely in granting summary judgment on all claims.

In December, 1996, police officer Rodney Porter stopped Plaintiff-Appellant Jimmie Marshall, an African-American part-time resident of Hobbs, New Mexico, for an alleged traffic violation. Officer Porter arrested Marshall, administered field sobriety tests, and took him to the Columbia Lea Regional Hospital for a blood test. Among other legal claims, Mr. Marshall alleges that the traffic stop and arrest were made on account of his race and without probable cause, in violation of the Fourth Amendment and the Equal Protection Clause, and that the coerced blood test violated his rights under the Fourth Amendment and state tort law. The defendants are Officer Porter, who conducted the traffic stop and arrest, and Sergeant Walter Roye, who ordered the blood test. Plaintiff seeks damages and other appropriate relief under 42 U.S.C. § 1983.

In a pair of orders dated June 18, 2002, the district court granted summary judgment for the defendants as to all claims. For the reasons set forth below, we reverse the judgment of the district court insofar as it granted summary judgment in favor of the Hobbs Defendants on the Equal Protection claim and the Fourth Amendment blood-test claim, and remand for further proceedings on these and the related state law claims. With respect to the remaining claims against the Hobbs Defendants, as well as all claims asserted against the Medical Defendants, we affirm the district court's grant of summary judgment.

I. BACKGROUND

A. *Mr. Marshall's Arrest and Blood Test*

On December 26, 1996, Jimmie Marshall, an African-American self-employed electrician, was driving his gold Toyota pickup in Hobbs, New Mexico, when he noticed a police car parked by the side of the road with its lights off. According to Mr. Marshall, the police officer — later identified as Officer Rodney Porter — followed his pickup for several blocks. While Mr. Marshall was stopped at an intersection with his left-turn signal blinking, Officer Porter pulled up alongside the pickup and "gazed intently at [Marshall's] face," which Marshall infers was for the purpose of ascertaining his race. Officer Porter contends that Mr. Marshall failed to stop at the stop sign, which Mr. Marshall denies. Officer Porter then activated his emergency lights, but Mr. Marshall continued to drive for more than two miles before coming to a stop at his residence. Mr. Marshall claims that he evaded the officer for several miles because he was fearful to stop his vehicle outside of the presence of witnesses, on account of the reputation of the Hobbs Police Department for racist practices. At that time, Mr. Marshall did not know Officer Porter and did not have any information about him. In the criminal complaint filed as a result of the incident, Officer Porter stated that Mr. Marshall accelerated to 100 miles per hour, drove through a four-way stop, and weaved from lane to lane, which Marshall denies. However, Officer Porter made no mention of these allegations in the affidavit he filed in this case describing the events of December 26, 1996, nor were they mentioned in Defendants' later pleadings.

On the street in front of Mr. Marshall's residence, the two men emerged from their vehicles. Officer Porter had drawn his pistol. His first words were to accuse Mr. Marshall of being on crack, which Marshall has consistently denied. Defendants have proffered no evidence in support of this accusation. Officer Porter states that Mr. Marshall had the odor of alcohol on his breath, which Marshall does not deny, stating that he had imbibed one drink with his brother Alfred. Officer Porter arrested Mr. Marshall on various charges, including the traffic violation, driving under the influence, and resisting arrest. On the written citation form, in the space for indicating the gender of the person receiving the citation, Officer Porter wrote "B/M," presumably meaning black male.

After arresting Mr. Marshall, Officer Porter proceeded to search Marshall's truck. The search revealed a .40 caliber pistol under the driver's seat (apparently lawful), and Officer Porter claimed also to have found a small amount of a "green leafy substance," a contention Marshall denies. Mr. Marshall was taken to the city jail, where several sobriety tests were performed on him. Mr. Marshall passed two breathalyzer tests, but had difficulty completing the recitation of the alphabet (the "ABC test"). [He was eventually taken to the hospital for a blood test, which produced evidence of THC in his bloodstream.]

Later, he was charged in a criminal complaint with (i) possession of a controlled substance (marijuana), (ii) resisting, evading or obstructing a police officer, (iii) negligent use of a firearm (possession while intoxicated), (iv) reckless driving, (v) running a stop sign, and (vi) driving under the influence. In May of 1997, the Assistant District Attorney for Lea County entered a *nolle prosequi* because the evidence in Marshall's case was suppressed. The record does not contain any further information about that proceeding, or the legal basis for the suppression of the evidence.

B. *Officer Porter's Alleged Pattern of Misconduct*

Slightly more than a year before the events in question here, Officer Porter was forced to resign from the Midland, Texas, police force after an internal investigation uncovered evidence of serious misconduct. In response to Mr. Marshall's subpoena, Midland Police Chief John Urby provided documents from his department's internal investigation showing an extensive pattern of misconduct and violation of citizens' constitutional rights by Officer Porter when he was on the Midland force.

If admissible, the Midland documents provide evidence that in more than thirty cases, Officer Porter falsely charged arrestees with possession of narcotics, seriously mishandled narcotics evidence, or both. Further, in other cases, Officer Porter was accused of planting evidence on arrestees, as well as using evidence to barter for sexual favors. According to the documents, Officer Porter denied the charges until after failing a polygraph test, when he admitted mishandling evidence.

According to Mr. Marshall, a review of Officer Porter's arrest reports on cases where he had not logged in drug evidence

> shows that an overwhelming number of the suspects were black. Most of the rest were Hispanic surnamed. Virtually all were stopped for minor traffic violations such as seat belts, failing to signal a turn, failing to stop at a stop sign, or making a wide turn so as to touch the stripe of the other lane. Also, in many [cases] Porter either claimed to have secured consent or went ahead and conducted searches anyway.

He claims that this pattern closely resembles the facts of his own case, and establishes a *modus operandi* under which Officer Porter targets individuals on the basis of their race and subjects them to traffic stops, arrests, and searches for pretextual drug violations not based on any evidence.

In further support of his equal protection claim, Mr. Marshall presented evidence regarding several lawsuits alleging civil rights violations against African-American citizens of Hobbs pending at the time his complaint was filed. Mr. Marshall also provided newspaper articles dealing with the racial tensions between the Hobbs Police Department and its African-American citizens, including an incident involving Officer Porter in which an allegedly racially motivated arrest at a high school football game resulted in a riot

II. ANALYSIS

A. *Fourth Amendment Challenges to the Traffic Stop and Arrest*

The first issue raised in Mr. Marshall's appellate brief is the validity of the traffic stop and arrest under the Fourth Amendment. Mr. Marshall concedes that the "perceived" traffic violation "may have provided sufficient grounds for the initial stop," but maintains that "Officer Porter did not have justifiable reasons to arrest and seize the plaintiff/ appellant."

Whether or not Mr. Marshall failed to obey the stop sign, which is disputed, the actual "stop" did not occur until after Mr. Marshall had driven for two miles without responding to the police officer's emergency lights. This behavior violated N.M. Stat.

Ann. § 30-22-1 and constituted probable cause to support the stop, the citation, and the arrest.

B. *Equal Protection Claims*

That Mr. Marshall's stop and arrest were based on probable cause does not resolve his more troubling claim that he was targeted by Officer Porter on account of his race. In *Whren v. United States*, 517 U.S. 806, 813 (1996), the Supreme Court held that claims asserting selective enforcement of a law on the basis of race are properly brought under the Equal Protection Clause, and that the right to equal protection may be violated even if the actions of the police are acceptable under the Fourth Amendment. As the court noted in *United States v. Avery*, 137 F.3d 343, 352 (6th Cir. 1997), "the Equal Protection Clause of the Fourteenth Amendment provides citizens a degree of protection independent of the Fourth Amendment protection against unreasonable searches and seizures."

Racially selective law enforcement violates this nation's constitutional values at the most fundamental level; indeed, unequal application of criminal law to white and black persons was one of the central evils addressed by the framers of the Fourteenth Amendment. *See generally* WILLIAM NELSON, THE FOURTEENTH AMENDMENT: FROM POLITICAL PRINCIPLE TO JUDICIAL DOCTRINE 43–48 (1988); John Frank & Robert Munro, *The Original Understanding of "Equal Protection of the Laws,"* 1972 WASH. U.L.Q. 421, 445–46. In its modern form, however, racially selective law enforcement has only recently come to public attention, and state and federal law enforcement authorities are struggling to develop practical means for distinguishing between legitimate and illegitimate uses of race in the investigation and prevention of crime. *See generally* Samuel R. Gross & Debra Livingston, *Racial Profiling Under Attack*, 102 COLUM. L. REV. 1413 (2002); Albert W. Alschuler, *Racial Profiling and the Constitution*, 2002 U. CHI. LEGAL F. 163 (2002). Recently at the behest of President Bush, the Department of Justice promulgated guidelines designed to end racial profiling in federal law enforcement.

It is one thing for law enforcement administrators to identify the problem and to undertake administrative steps to eliminate the improper use of racial and ethnic stereotypes in law enforcement. It is more difficult to craft judicially manageable standards for determining liability under § 1983. Broad discretion has been vested in executive branch officials to determine when to prosecute, *United States v. Armstrong*, 517 U.S. 456, 464 (1996), and by analogy, when to conduct a traffic stop or initiate an arrest. Police officers and departments should not lightly be put to the expense and risk of trial on charges of racial discrimination that may be easy to make and difficult to disprove. Not only does litigation divert prosecutorial resources and threaten an excessive judicial interference with executive discretion, but it could induce police officers to protect themselves against false accusations in ways that are counterproductive to fair and effective enforcement of the laws. For example, police may be induced to direct their law enforcement efforts in race-conscious ways by focusing law enforcement on neighborhoods with relatively few low-income, minority persons. Perhaps for these reasons, the Supreme Court has held that "to dispel the presumption that a prosecutor has not violated equal protection, a criminal defendant must present 'clear evidence to the contrary.'" Claims of racially discriminatory traffic stops and arrests should be held to a similarly high standard.

Neither this Court nor the Supreme Court has set forth the standards of proof needed for a plaintiff to withstand a motion for summary judgment in a case of an alleged racially discriminatory stop and arrest by a single officer. In analogous contexts, however, the Court has "taken great pains to explain that the standard is a demanding one." *Armstrong*. In *Wade v. United States*, 504 U.S. 181, 186 (1992), the Court held that a defendant is not entitled to an evidentiary hearing on a claim of a prosecutor's racially discriminatory refusal to request a downward departure on the basis of "generalized allegations of improper motive." He must "make . . . a substantial threshold showing."

In *Armstrong*, the Court held that a defendant is not entitled to discovery on a claim that the prosecuting attorney singled him out for prosecution on the basis of his race unless he can show "that similarly situated individuals of a different race were not prosecuted."

The plaintiff must demonstrate that the defendant's actions had a discriminatory effect and were motivated by a discriminatory purpose. These standards have been applied to traffic stops challenged on equal protection grounds. *Chavez v. Ill. State Police*, 251 F.3d 612, 635–36 (7th Cir. 2001); *Farm Labor Org. Comm. v. Ohio State Highway Patrol*, 308 F.3d 523, 533–36 (6th Cir. 2002). The discriminatory purpose need not be the only purpose, but it must be a motivating factor in the decision.

In general, the absence of an overtly discriminatory policy or of direct evidence of police motivation results in most claims being based on statistical comparisons between the number of black or other minority Americans stopped or arrested and their percentage in some measure of the relevant population. This requires a reliable measure of the demographics of the relevant population, a means of telling whether the data represent similarly situated individuals, and a point of comparison to the actual incidence of crime among different racial or ethnic segments of the population. This case, however, is different, and perhaps more sU.S.C.eptible to traditional modes of proof before a jury. Here, Mr. Marshall seeks to prove the racially selective nature of his stop and arrest not by means of statistical inference but by direct evidence of Officer Porter's behavior during the events in question, Officer Porter's own statements and testimony (the credibility of which can be evaluated by a jury), and Officer Porter's alleged record of racially selective stops and arrests in drug cases under similar circumstances in Midland, Texas.

Viewing the evidence in the light most favorable to the nonmoving party, Mr. Marshall, and drawing reasonable inferences in his favor, we conclude that the court below erred in granting summary judgment on Mr. Marshall's equal protection claim. We will analyze each fact Marshall invokes in support of his claim, starting with the events surrounding the traffic stop itself.

Mr. Marshall testified that he did not fail to stop at the stop sign or commit any other traffic violation in Officer Porter's presence. This testimony was not sufficient to establish lack of probable cause for the ultimate stop and arrest two miles down the road, but if accepted as true by the trier of fact, would be evidence that the officer's initial decision to pull Mr. Marshall over was pretextual. Moreover, Mr Marshall testified — and Officer Porter did not dispute — that he was aware of the police car following him for several blocks before he came to the intersection where the alleged traffic violation occurred. Since drivers aware of being observed by the police tend to be particularly cautious about traffic regulations, this lends credence to his account of the events.

Second, Mr. Marshall testified, and Officer Porter did not deny, that the officer made eye contact with him while stopped at the intersection prior to activating his emergency lights. From these facts it might reasonably be inferred that Officer Porter was ascertaining Mr. Marshall's race.

The first words out of Officer Porter's mouth when he confronted Mr. Marshall after the stop were a cryptic accusation that Mr. Marshall was on crack. ("Is a few rocks worth all that?") Officer Porter reiterated this accusation during interrogation at the station house, and again at the hospital. [I]n the context of this case as a whole, a jury might reasonably infer from these exchanges that Officer Porter was acting on the basis of stereotype or prejudice rather than evidence.

The record also reflects that on the citation form, in the box designated for the gender of the cited driver, Officer Porter wrote "B/M," making a racial designation where none was called for. Possibly, this reflects unwritten police policy or has some other nondiscriminatory explanation, but the Hobbs Defendants have not suggested one. A jury might also think it significant — at least as it bears on Officer Porter's credibility — that the officer wrote on the original criminal complaint that Mr. Marshall accelerated to 100 miles per hour, drove through a four-way stop, and weaved from lane to lane, but later made no mention of these remarkable corroborating facts in his sworn affidavit in this case about what happened that day.

The record thus contains evidence — disputed, to be sure — that Mr. Marshall did not commit the traffic violation for which he was initially stopped, that Officer Porter ascertained Mr. Marshall's race before initiating the stop, that he made repeated accusations that Mr. Marshall was on crack with no apparent basis, that he made an apparently unnecessary note of Marshall's race, and that his account of the events changed dramatically between the date of the incident and the date of his affidavit. Other than to insist that Mr. Marshall committed the traffic violation and thus that there was probable cause for the stop and the arrest, the Defendants offer no nondiscriminatory explanation for these aspects of Officer Porter's conduct in this case.

It is a close question whether this is sufficient to require the Hobbs Defendants to go to trial on the allegations of racial discrimination. But there is more.

Mr. Marshall presented evidence regarding extensive alleged misconduct by Officer Porter during his prior employment as a police officer in Midland, Texas. In a memo terminating Officer Porter's employment, the Midland police chief stated that Porter had failed "to treat people fairly and equally under the law." If admissible, these documents, together with the other facts of record pertaining to the events of December 26, 1996, may be sufficient to create a triable issue on Mr. Marshall's claim of racially selective law enforcement.

Once the documents have been analyzed, the district court will be able to determine whether they establish a "pattern" of traffic stops and arrests that raises an inference of racial discrimination, or provide evidence that similarly situated individuals of a different race received differential treatment.

In their Reply in Support of Hobbs Defendants' Motion for Summary Judgment, the Hobbs Defendants raised certain objections to the admissibility of the Midland documents. As far as the record reveals, the district court never ruled on those objections. We therefore reverse the grant of summary judgment in favor of the Hobbs Defendants on the equal protection claims, and remand to the district court to determine the admissibility of the Midland documents and to reconsider the Hobbs Defendants' motion for summary judgment in light of this opinion.

NOTES AND QUESTIONS

1. Race and Criminal Justice. In addition to the *Whren* and *Armstrong* cases, the Supreme Court dealt cautiously with alleged racial disparities in the criminal justice system in *O'Shea v. Littleton*, 414 U.S. 488 (1974). Plaintiffs alleged a long-standing pattern of harsher bail and sentences for black defendants than for whites in the town of Cairo, Illinois, a pattern and practice that would be difficult to show on the record of any single case. They sought to enjoin disparate bail and sentencing by the judge and magistrate. Rather than going to the merits, which would have involved highly discretionary roles of the judiciary, the Court dismissed the action on the basis of standing because the plaintiffs could not show that they were likely to be arrested or convicted in the future.

Another instance of circumspect handling of racial claims in the criminal justice system was *McCleskey v. Kemp*, 481 U.S. 279 (1987), in which an elaborate statistical study tended to show that imposition of the death penalty in Georgia was imposed disproportionately on the basis of the race of the victim even more than on the basis of the race of the defendant. The Court emphasized the individual decisions of all the prosecutors and jurors in the system and refused to find that the death penalty was imposed through unconstitutional discriminatory intent or purpose.

By contrast, the Court has been much more willing to focus on claims of racial discrimination in the selection of a jury, a setting in which the record of a single case can be parsed to determine whether a pattern of racial disparity can be sufficient to infer intent on the part of the prosecutor. *Batson v. Kentucky*, 476 U.S. 79 (1986).

2. "Invalid Purpose" Detentions. Although traffic stops may seem far removed from terrorism investigations, most of the claims of racial profiling have arisen in that setting. The basic Fourth Amendment standard for a reasonable stop that then results in a consensual search is whether the original stop was "pretextual." The Tenth Circuit opinion in *Marshall* discusses the original stop on the basis of whether the officer actually observed a traffic violation. In *United States v. Guzman*, 864 F.2d 1512 (10th Cir. 1988), the court adopted a test that focused on whether the presence of an invalid purpose, such as suspicion that the driver could be a drug courier, prevented a stop from being lawful: "whether under the same circumstances a reasonable officer would have made the stop in the absence of the invalid purpose." The same court later abandoned that test for a more simple test that leaves out the invalid purpose: "a traffic stop is valid under the Fourth Amendment if the stop is based on an observed traffic violation or if the police officer has reasonable articulable suspicion that a traffic or equipment violation has occurred or is occurring." *United States v. Botero-Ospina*, 71 F.3d 783 (10th Cir. 1995) (en banc holding over three dissents). Attempting to carry those thoughts to the context of terrorism investigations, we can ask whether it is valid to detain and question Arab visa violators with greater frequency than visa violators of other ethnic groups. Is the violation a sufficient basis even in the presence of what might be thought to be an "invalid purpose?"

[C]   Federal Ethnic Profiling

1.   The Post-9/11 Investigation

In the wake of 9/11, the FBI questioned many recent immigrants and nonresident aliens. Some were detained on probable visa violations. Information about these detainees was kept from the public, and in many instances even from their families.

The Department of Justice's Office of Inspector General undertook a review of these detentions and the conditions of confinement.

> In the aftermath of the September 11 terrorist attacks, the Department of Justice used the federal immigration laws to detain aliens who were suspected of having ties to the attacks or terrorism in general. More than 750 aliens who had violated immigration laws were arrested and detained in connection with the FBI's investigation into the attacks, called PENTTBOM. While recognizing the difficult circumstances confronting the Department in responding to the terrorist attacks, we found significant problems in the way the September 11 detainees were treated.

The report concluded that delays in processing detainees couple with a blanket "no bond" policy based on ethnicity deprived many detainees of the ability to communicate with counsel or family members. The report also found "a pattern of physical and verbal abuse by some correctional officers . . . against some September 11 detainees, particularly during the first months after the attacks."

Attorney General Ashcroft responded to the OIG Report with this statement:

> The Justice Department believes that the Inspector General report is fully consistent with what courts have ruled over and over — that our actions are fully within the law and necessary to protect the American people. Our policy is to use all legal tools available to protect innocent Americans from terrorist attacks. We make no apologies for finding every legal way possible to protect the American public from further terrorist attacks.
>
> Detention of illegal aliens is lawful. We detained illegal aliens encountered during the 9/11 terrorist investigation until it was determined they were not involved in terrorist activity, did not have relevant knowledge of terrorist

activity, or it was determined that their removal was appropriate.

After reviewing the responses of the AG and INS, the DoJ Inspector General provided a follow-up analysis, which reported progress in improving the agencies' handling of the situation.

The DoJ Inspector General Report criticized a failure to distinguish between suspected terrorists and mere immigration violators. Why is this significant' Ted Bundy was stopped three times for traffic violations which led to his arrests for serial rape and murder. Other serial killers have been apprehended for similar violations. Criminal conspirators often commit minor violations in the course of their bigger conspiracies. If police are searching for a bank robber, shouldn't they be particularly alert to anyone driving recklessly, waving a pistol around, or wearing a mask on the street' What is wrong with picking up immigration violators to see if there is a terrorist lurking in their midst?

The Report also criticizes delays in processing and the conditions of confinement for many of the detainees. This general subject took on heightened importance with the disclosures of serious prisoner abuse at Guatánamo and Abu Ghraib, which we will consider in Chapter 9.

The Report also criticizes failure to provide access to lawyers or relatives. AG Ashcroft's statement and the government's position before the DC Circuit claim that secrecy was necessary to prevent terrorists from passing information to each other. How do we evaluate this fear?

2. The Federal Guidelines

Following some public criticism of FBI practices that included agents' attending mosques and taking notes on conversations or behavior, the Attorney General issued new "Guidelines on . . . Terrorism Enterprise Investigations" in May 2002. With regard to attending public events, the Guidelines stated:

> For the purpose of detecting or preventing terrorist activities, the FBI is authorized to visit any place and attend any event that is open to the public, on the same terms and conditions as members of the public generally. No information obtained from such visits shall be retained unless it relates to potential criminal or terrorist activity.

The Department of Justice issued general guidelines on racial profiling on June 17, 2003. *Guidance Regarding the Use of Race by Federal Law Enforcement Agencies, available at* http://www.usdoj.gov/crt/split/documents/guidance_on_race.htm. The Guidelines generally prohibit any federal law enforcement agency from using racial characteristics in routine investigations.

The DoJ Guidelines and similar state statutes allow racial or ethnic descriptions as part of the description of a known suspect. If a description of a suspect characterizes him as a "Hispanic male," the police are likely to stop and question a disproportionate number of Hispanic males as compared to Asian or white males in the same vicinity. Is this ethnic profiling? If not, what is the difference?

The Guidelines distinguish between "traditional law enforcement activities" and "national security and border integrity." For "traditional" activities, the Guidelines state:

> • In conducting activities in connection with a specific investigation, federal law enforcement officers may consider race and ethnicity only to the extent that there is trustworthy information, relevant to the locality or time frame, that links persons of a particular race or ethnicity to an identified criminal incident, scheme, or organization.

By contrast, for national security and border control, the Guidelines merely incorporate constitutional standards:

- In investigating or preventing threats to national security or other catastrophic events (including the performance of duties related to air transportation security), or in enforcing laws protecting the integrity of the nation's borders, federal law enforcement officers may not consider race or ethnicity except to the extent permitted by the Constitution and laws of the United States.

The Constitution prohibits consideration of race or ethnicity in law enforcement decisions in all but the most exceptional instances. Given the incalculably high stakes involved in such investigations, however, Federal law enforcement officers who are protecting national security or preventing catastrophic events (as well as airport security screeners) may consider race, ethnicity and other relevant factors to the extent permitted by our laws and the Constitution.

> *Example*: U.S. intelligence sources report that Middle Eastern terrorists are planning to use commercial jetliners as weapons by hijacking them at an airport in California during the next week. Before allowing men appearing to be of Middle Eastern origin to board commercial airplanes in California airports during the next week, Transportation Security Administration personnel, and other federal and state authorities, may subject them to heightened scrutiny.

These are very difficult "rules" to follow. At first glance, the example would seem to mean that ethnic identifiers can be considered only when there is a very specific threat at a specific place by a specific ethnically identifiable group. But the general statements indicate that ethnicity may be used to the extent of the Constitution. Because there are virtually no cases holding that preliminary screening and investigations are controlled by constitutional restraints, it is difficult to know the limits of using ethnicity in these contexts.

If there were any sanctions attached to the Guidelines, a person attempting to comply with them might complain that they were either vague or ambiguous. The Guidelines, however, are just that — guidelines — and do not seem to have any coercive force behind them.

It has been argued that ethnic profiling is inefficient because "an overwhelming number of 'suspects' will prove to be innocent, no matter what combination of factors is used to focus in on them." Although it could "turn out that in the case of terrorism, a particular segment of the population is in fact disproportionately represented among offenders," Professor Colb nevertheless worries that "future generations may judge us as harshly as we now judge the supporters of internment during World War II." Sherry F. Colb, *Racial Profiling and Terrorism, available at* http://writ.news.findlaw.com/colb/20011010.html (Oct. 10, 2001).

Some people would argue that focused questioning of Arab and Muslim males in the current environment could actually increase the incidence of terrorism. "Whether the targets are Muslim and Arab Americans or Blacks and Latinos, all victims of racial and ethnic profiling are left feeling humiliated, angry and distrustful of law enforcement. These feelings of anger and distrust add to tensions that often exist between ethnic minorities and law enforcement." Dan Salvin, Urban Voices, *Racial/Ethnic Profiling Is Still Wrong*.

There was a fear expressed even by such insiders as some former CIA employees in the lead-up to Gulf War II, that invading Iraq would actually produce more terrorists for the anti-American cause.

This area leaves us with any number of difficult policy issues to consider:

1. Are there constitutional or legal limitations on the use of ethnicity in a preliminary screening or investigation?

2. How specific must an ethnic-cultural threat be to trigger the permissible use of ethnicity as a screening device?

3. As a sheer pragmatic matter, setting morality or justice aside if one can do so, is there more to fear from passing up a chance to interdict a given threat or from alienating a segment of the population?

For critical discussions of these issues, see Liam Braber, *Korematsu's Ghost: A Post-September 11th Analysis of Race and National Security*, 47 VILL. L. REV. 451 (2002); David A. Harris, *New Risks, New Tactics: An Assessment of the Re-Assessment of Racial Profiling in the Wake of September 11, 2001*, 2004 UTAH L. REV. 913.

§ 7.03   SELECTED READINGS

· DAVID COLE, ENEMY ALIENS: DOUBLE STANDARDS AND CONSTITUTIONAL FREEDOMS IN THE WAR ON TERRORISM (2003)

· DAVID A. HARRIS, PROFILES IN INJUSTICE: WHY RACIAL PROFILING CANNOT WORK (2002)

· Robert M. Chesney, *Civil Liberties and the Terrorism Prevention Paradigm: The Guilt by Association Critique*, 101 MICH. L. REV. 1408 (2003)

· Gerald L. Neuman, *Terrorism, Selective Deportation and the First Amendment After* Reno v. AADC, 14 GEO. IMMIGR. L.J. 313 (2000)

· Natsu Taylor Smith, *For "Our" Security: Who Is an "American" and What Is Protected by Enhanced Law Enforcement and Intelligence Powers?"* 2 SEATTLE J. SOC. JUSTICE 24 (2003)

Chapter 8

THE MILITARY OPTION

Although the pen may be mightier than the sword, nevertheless the most powerful physical institution of humanity is the military. At an earlier point in this course, we looked at the international norms of warfare as part of the background for why and how terrorism could be controlled by international institutions. This chapter returns to the mechanisms for deploying and controlling the power of military force, which will take us back to international law because the law to be applied by military commissions and tribunals has been the "law of war" or Law of Armed Conflict (LOAC). Although LOAC was long enforced as part of international law, the U.S. government persuaded Congress to enact its own set of crimes for military commissions to apply to accused terrorists following the Supreme Court's decision in *Hamdan*.

The U.S. program of military detentions, both domestically and at places such as Guantánamo, hinges on the assertion that the U.S. is "at war" with terrorist organizations. The Bush Administration's original idea of an "unlawful enemy combatant" appeared to be that anyone who was thought to be connected with violent behavior without wearing a uniform of a nation-state could be declared a combatant and thrown into military prison. Eventually, the Military Commission Act defined the term to mean "a person who has engaged in hostilities or who has purposefully and materially supported hostilities against the United States or its co-belligerents who is not a lawful enemy combatant." That raises the question whether "hostilities" is the same as "armed conflict." At this point, the arguments harken back to the issues in the *Tadic* case when the ICTY decided that "armed conflict" existed only when a military-type group was under some level of control by a nation-state or had pretensions to take over the territory of its own state.

President Bush's order authorizing military commissions for the trial of suspected terrorists and collaborators was promulgated on November 13, 2001. It is patterned on the orders issued during World War II to deal with suspected spies in *Ex parte Quirin*, 317 U.S. 1 (1942). Similar orders were issued following WWII for war-crimes trials of both German and Japanese officials.

The order allowed the Secretary of Defense to establish a military commission for trial of "all offenses" alleged to be committed by any person who the President finds "is or was a member of the organization known as al Qaida" or "has engaged in, aided or abetted, or conspired to commit, acts of international terrorism, or acts in preparation therefor, that have caused, threaten to cause, or have as their aim to cause, injury to or adverse effects on the United States, its citizens, national security, foreign policy, or economy." The order did not purport to create new crimes but referred instead to "offenses triable by military commission" and "penalties under applicable law."

The order was first met with some skepticism but very little open criticism. Professor Paust (a former faculty member at the JAG School) was the earliest and most outspoken academic critic of the order. Jordan J. Paust, *Antiterrorism Military Commissions: Courting Illegality*, 23 MICH. J. INT'L L. 1 (2001). An early response to the criticisms was provided by Curtis A. Bradley and Jack L. Goldsmith, *The Constitutional Validity of Military Commissions*, 5 GREEN BAG 2d 249 (2002). Other scholarly exchanges are collected at the end of this chapter.

In early 2002, the administration made an initial decision to detain some captured Taliban and others captured in Afghanistan at Camp X-Ray at Guantánamo Bay, Cuba. As events unfolded, other suspected terrorists apprehended in various places around the world were taken to Guantánamo. Camp X-Ray was replaced by Camp Delta

No prosecutions were begun under the order until after the Supreme Court decided in *Rasul v. Bush*, § 8.03[A] *infra*, that alien military detainees were entitled to some determination of their status by a neutral decision maker. The first prosecution then was derailed by the D.C. District Court, affirmed by the Supreme Court in *Hamdan v. Rumsfeld*, § 8.04[B] *infra*. Those cases were followed by the Detainee Treatment Act of 2005, *infra*, and the Military Commission Act of 2006 (§ 8.04[B], Note 3 after *Hamdan*, *infra*), which authorized Combatant Status Review Tribunals, established crimes under U.S. law for the military commissions, and attempted to isolate both CSRT and Commission proceedings from habeas corpus review.

In addition to the legal maneuvering around the validity of the detentions, there has been a great deal of controversy about the treatment of prisoners. We will take up the prisoner abuse and torture issues in Chapter 9.

Meanwhile, the military intelligence community has been incorporated into the hunt for terrorists through mandates to cooperate with the CIA and domestic intelligence agencies. All of these activity causes us to question the wisdom of involving the military in domestic security. We will first look at the "posse comitatus" provisions that impede military involvement in domestic law enforcement, along with the concept of martial law, and then look at the history of military commissions in the United States. In the next section, we will look at the potential for use of military tribunals and military detentions in the terrorism context.

§ 8.01 DOMESTIC ROLE OF THE MILITARY

The "posse comitatus" statute prohibits employment of the military in civil law enforcement. The phrase (roughly translated as "power of the county") refers to the inherent discretion of civil authorities to call on the entire population to assist in maintaining order or apprehending criminals. The thrust of the statute is to exclude the military from that usage.

18 U.S.C. § 1385 (2003):

> Whoever, except in cases and under circumstances expressly authorized by the Constitution or Act of Congress, willfully uses any part of the Army or the Air Force as a posse comitatus or otherwise to execute the laws shall be fined under this title or imprisoned not more than two years, or both.

These provisions were extended to the Navy and Marines by 10 U.S.C. § 375, which also provides for the Secretary of Defense to promulgate regulations "to ensure that any [assistance to state and local authorities] does not include or permit direct participation . . . in a search, seizure, arrest, or other similar activity."

The statute was first adopted in 1875 as part of the end of Reconstruction, the immediate impetus being the presence of military troops as election monitors when civil authority had been restored. Although the sweep of the statute could be read as building a wall between military and civilian authorities, it has not been given that effect by subsequent Congresses. Indeed, Congress has authorized a wide array of military assistance to federal, state, or local authorities in pursuit of maintaining order or law enforcement, so long as military personnel are not directly engaged in searches or arrests. Courts have routinely upheld "passive" engagement of military personnel in support of civilian criminal investigations and have upheld "active" participation of military personnel in criminal enforcement when the offense concerns a military facility or activity.

The effect of the posse comitatus statute on the question of declaring martial law essentially is to preserve the power to make such a declaration in Congress. The military can be used to assist directly in civil law enforcement only when authorized by statute. This approach codifies, with some clarification, the results reached following the Civil War and Reconstruction. Prior to that time, the Judiciary Act of 1789 had authorized federal marshals to call on the military to serve as a posse whenever it was useful for execution of the law. William Winthrop, Military Law and Precedents 866–67 (reprint 1920).

In *Texas v. White*, 74 U.S. 700 (1868), the Supreme Court validated the occupation of

Southern states by federal military force following the Civil War. In *Ex parte Milligan*, 71 U.S. 2 (1866), the Court invalidated the trial of civilians by military tribunals in areas in which the civilian courts were open and operating. The combination of these cases could be read as permitting martial law in areas that are in a state of war but not allowing it elsewhere. As Colonel Winthrop points out, however, this would be an oversimplification. WINTHROP at 799.

To go further, we need to distinguish between military government and martial law. The former is the result of occupation of hostile territory, whether foreign or rebellious. The latter is a condition that provides a military complement to the civil authorities on home soil because of an emergency. Military government completely supplants civil government while martial law provides a type of self-defensive use of force commensurate with the necessity. The Supreme Court adopted this view in *Duncan v. Kahanamoku*, 327 U.S. 304 (1946), when it overturned a conviction by military tribunal in Hawaii during a time of declared martial law because the civilian courts were open and operating.

Duncan does not deny the possibility of using military presence to supplement or even replace some functions of civilian government in time of actual emergency. The examples cited in *Duncan* of martial law to quell civil disturbances stemming principally from labor disputes do not seem to have taken into account the *posse comitatus* statute. Given the tacit approval of the use of troops in those cases, so long as crimes were tried in the civilian courts, it is not clear how the Court would deal with this statutory argument. Some further insight might be gleaned from *Youngstown Sheet & Tube v. Sawyer*, 343 U.S. 579 (1952), in which the Court struck down President Truman's attempt to seize the steel mills to avert labor strife during the Korean War. Only the three dissenting Justices were impressed by the argument that there was any level of national emergency justifying unilateral seizure without congressional authorization.

In his classic concurrence analyzing separation of powers, Justice Jackson pointed out that the President is on strongest ground when he acts with congressional authorization, may or may not have constitutional powers when acting in congressional silence, and must have strong independent constitutional grounds when going against the will of Congress. To justify military force to perform civil law enforcement after passage of the posse comitatus legislation, the President would have to persuade a majority of the court that a genuine emergency existed sufficient to justify departure from specific congressional direction. After the experience of *Korematsu*, *Duncan*, and *Youngstown*, it is possible that little short of imminent invasion would justify unilateral action. As a practical matter, however, it would take some time before a court could intervene, by which time the presence of a genuine emergency would likely be known or dispelled.

Other than martial law as an emergency measure, some use of the military to assist civilian authorities in times of civil disturbance is also possible and its limits are found only in the statutes that prevent use of the military in direct search and arrest of offenders.

Although the posse comitatus statute seems to imply that the military can have no involvement in civilian law enforcement, another federal statute offers assistance to state governments in time of "insurrection." 10 U.S.C. § 331:

> Whenever there is an insurrection in any State against its government, the President may, upon the request of its legislature or of its governor if the legislature cannot be convened, call into Federal service such of the militia of the other States, in the number requested by that State, and use such of the armed forces, as he considers necessary to suppress the insurrection.

The "insurrection" statute amounts to a standing delegation from Congress of the power to make an exception to the posse comitatus statute when a state government requests assistance and the President finds that there is a need for military force to "suppress the insurrection." It does not, however, appear to be a standing delegation of the power to declare martial law. That power remains implicitly within Congress unless it cannot meet.

The authority of the President under the insurrection statute has come before the Supreme Court on only two occasions, and one of those did not involve insurrection. (One other insurrection case did not involve validity of a military call-out. With regard to Shea's Rebellion, the Court held that it had no power to determine which of the contending parties was the legitimate government of a state, that this is a question for the political branches. *Luther v. Borden*, 48 U.S. 1 (1849).) In *Martin v. Mott*, 25 U.S. (12 Wheat.) 19 (1827), a member of the New York militia had refused to answer the President's call to arms during the War of 1812. He was fined, his belongings were seized, and he brought a replevin action claiming that the President was without authority to order him into service prior to an actual invasion of the territory of the U.S. His first argument was that the fact of a military emergency should have been shown to the court, to which the Supreme Court seemed to respond that the President's determination was conclusive on the courts as well as on military personnel. The only reason to hedge with the phrase "seemed to respond" is that all the arguments put forth by the Court were addressed to the need for immediate unquestioning obedience by military personnel.

> [T]he authority to decide whether the exigency has arisen, belongs exclu-
> sively to the President, and that his decision is conclusive upon all other persons.
> We think that this construction necessarily results from the nature of the power
> itself, and from the manifest object contemplated by the act of Congress. The
> power itself is to be exercised upon sudden emergencies, upon great occasions
> of state, and under circumstances which may be vital to the existence of the
> Union.

> The argument is, that the power confided to the President is a limited power,
> and can be exercised only in the cases pointed out in the statute, and therefore
> it is necessary to aver the fact which bring the exercise within the purview of the
> statute. . . . When the President exercises an authority confided to him by law,
> the presumption that it is exercised in pursuance of law. Every public officer is
> presumed to act in obedience to his duty, until the contrary is shown; and, a
> fortiori, this presumption ought to be favourably applied to the chief magistrate
> of the Union. It is not necessary to aver, that the act which he may rightfully do,
> was so done. If the fact of the existence of the exigency were averred, it would
> be traversable, and of course might be passed upon by a jury; and thus the
> legality of the orders of the President would depend, not on his own judgment
> of the facts, but upon the finding of those facts upon the proofs submitted to a
> jury.

Whether those same arguments would hold when a court was faced with a more doubtful situation, one in which the presence of a military threat was less clear, could be a slightly different matter as we will see with *Youngstown Sheet & Tube*.

The *Prize Cases*, 67 U.S. 635 (1863), contained similar language seeming to grant the President unreviewable discretion to engage in acts of war. Several ships owned by foreign nationals and flagged by neutral countries had been seized while running a blockade against the Confederate states. The owners argued that the President lacked authority to enforce a blockade against neutrals, and the Court responded:

> Whether the President in fulfilling his duties, as Commander-in-chief, in
> suppressing an insurrection, has met with such armed hostile resistance, and a
> civil war of such alarming proportions as will compel him to accord to them the
> character of belligerents, is a question to be decided by him, and this Court must
> be governed by the decisions and acts of the political department of the
> Government to which this power was entrusted. "He must determine what
> degree of force the crisis demands." The proclamation of blockade is itself
> official and conclusive evidence to the Court that a state of war existed which

demanded and authorized a recourse to such a measure, under the circumstances peculiar to the case.

Again the word "seeming" is used in describing the Court's deference to the President to emphasize that there was no question about the state of armed conflict between the Union and Confederacy, and that the only significant arguments in the case had to do with the status of the contending sides under international law. Whether the President needed deference regarding the fact of armed conflict was hardly in issue.

The only twentieth century case citing the assistance statute is a federal court case dealing with property damage in D.C. during the riots following the 1968 assassination of Dr. Martin Luther King. Insurers who had paid out damage claims brought suit against the U.S. alleging that the government had been negligent in failing to call out the militia or use military force to suppress the riots. The district court simply pointed out that "the decision whether to use troops or the militia (National Guard) in quelling a civil disorder is exclusively within the province of the President. The Courts also have made it clear that presidential discretion in exercising those powers granted in the Constitution and in the implementing statutes is not subject to judicial review." *Monarch Ins. Co. v. District of Columbia*, 353 F. Supp. 1249 (D.D.C. 1973).

It is one thing to say that there is no constitutional duty on the part of the President to call out military force, but it would be quite another to say that the President lacked authority to call out military force unless an insurrection justified it to the satisfaction of a court. Common sense would indicate that a judge would be loathe to intervene in the face of any genuine threat of imminent violence, a position that needs little elaboration of a claim of deference to executive judgment.

The most extensive analysis of the posse comitatus and assistance statutes came in a series of cases arising out of the three-week occupation of Wounded Knee by members of the American Indian Movement in 1973. Various defendants were prosecuted for offenses such as trespass, assault, and interference with federal officers in the discharge of their duties. The defendants pointed to the involvement of military units in what could have been viewed as an ordinary law enforcement operation and asserted that this involvement violated the posse comitatus statute. This defense was relevant at least to the question of whether the federal officers were "lawfully engaged in the discharge of their duties."

The FBI and Bureau of Indian Affairs had closed off the town to prevent additional sympathizers from joining those dissidents already on the scene. As part of the control operation, military units assisted with advice, aerial reconnaissance and the loan of equipment. The district judges dealing with the defense of posse comitatus violation reached different conclusions with different standards for testing the validity of military involvement. To Judge Urbom, the statute would be violated if military personnel influenced the decisions of the civilian officers or actively maintained and operated the equipment provided. *United States v. Jaramillo*, 380 F. Supp. 1375 (D. Neb. 1974). Judge Nichol went "one step further" than Judge Ubrom and held that there was no evidence justifying submission of issues to the jury regarding the nature of the military involvement. *United States v. Banks*, 383 F. Supp. 368 (D.S.D. 1974). Judge Bogue provided a more nuanced analysis by concentrating on whether military personnel were "actively engaged in law enforcement." *United States v. Red Feather*, 392 F. Supp. 916 (D.S.D. 1975):

> Based upon the clear intent of Congress, this Court holds that the clause "to execute the laws," contained in 18 U.S.C. § 1385, makes unlawful the use of federal military troops in an active role of direct law enforcement by civil law enforcement officers. Activities which constitute an active role in direct law enforcement are: arrest; seizure of evidence; search of a person; search of a building; investigation of crime; interviewing witnesses; pursuit of an escaped civilian prisoner; search of an area for a suspect and other like activities. Such use of federal military troops to "execute the laws," or as the Court has defined

the clause, in "an active role of direct law enforcement," is unlawful under 18 U.S.C. § 1385.

Activities which constitute a passive role which might indirectly aid law enforcement are: mere presence of military personnel under orders to report on the necessity for military intervention; preparation of contingency plans to be used if military intervention is ordered; advice or recommendations given to civilian law enforcement officers by military personnel on tactics or logistics; presence of military personnel to deliver military materiel, equipment or supplies, to train local law enforcement officials on the proper use and care of such material or equipment, and to maintain such materiel or equipment; aerial photographic reconnaissance flights and other like activities.

In this sequence of cases, the judges took varying approaches to interpreting the phrase "use [military] forces . . . to execute the laws." Although there were constitutional concerns lurking in the background of the analyses, the focus was on whether Congress had authorized or prohibited the use of military force in domestic disturbances.

§ 8.02 MILITARY TRIBUNALS IN U.S. HISTORY

The Bush Military Tribunal Order was premised on *Ex parte Quirin*, which upheld military commissions to deal with alleged saboteurs on U.S. soil during World War II. *Quirin*, however, was sandwiched between two cases striking down use of military tribunals for civilians.

EX PARTE MILLIGAN
71 U.S. 2 (4 Wall.) (1866)

Mr. Justice Davis delivered the opinion of the court.

On the 10th day of May, 1865, Lambdin P. Milligan presented a petition to the Circuit Court of the United States for the District of Indiana, to be discharged from an alleged unlawful imprisonment. The case made by the petition is this: Milligan is a citizen of the United States; has lived for twenty years in Indiana; and, at the time of the grievances complained of, was not, and never had been in the military or naval service of the United States. On the 5th day of October, 1864, while at home, he was arrested by order of General Alvin P. Hovey, commanding the military district of Indiana; and has ever since been kept in close confinement.

On the 21st day of October, 1864, he was brought before a military commission, convened at Indianapolis, by order of General Hovey, tried on certain charges and specifications; found guilty, and sentenced to be hanged; and the sentence ordered to be executed on Friday, the 19th day of May, 1865.

On the 2d day of January, 1865, after the proceedings of the military commission were at an end, the Circuit Court of the United States for Indiana met at Indianapolis and empanelled a grand jury, who were charged to inquire whether the laws of the United States had been violated; and, if so, to make presentments. The court adjourned on the 27th day of January, having, prior thereto, discharged from further service the grand jury, who did not find any bill of indictment or make any presentment against Milligan for any offence whatever; and, in fact, since his imprisonment, no bill of indictment has been found or presentment made against him by any grand jury of the United States.

Milligan insists that said military commission had no jurisdiction to try him upon the charges preferred, or upon any charges whatever; because he was a citizen of the United States and the State of Indiana, and had not been, since the commencement of the late Rebellion, a resident of any of the States whose citizens were arrayed against the government, and that the right of trial by jury was guaranteed to him by the Constitution of the United States.

The prayer of the petition was, that under the act of Congress, approved March 3d, 1863, entitled, "An act relating to habeas corpus and regulating judicial proceedings in certain cases,"[1] he may be brought before the court, and either turned over to the proper civil tribunal to be proceeded against according to the law of the land or discharged from custody altogether.

The importance of the main question presented by this record cannot be overstated; for it involves the very framework of the government and the fundamental principles of American liberty.

During the late wicked Rebellion, the temper of the times did not allow that calmness in deliberation and discussion so necessary to a correct conclusion of a purely judicial question. Then, considerations of safety were mingled with the exercise of power; and feelings and interests prevailed which are happily terminated. Now that the public safety is assured, this question, as well as all others, can be discussed and decided without passion or the admixture of any element not required to form a legal judgment. We approach the investigation of this case, fully sensible of the magnitude of the inquiry and the necessity of full and cautious deliberation.

But it is said that this case is ended, as the presumption is, that Milligan was hanged in pursuance of the order of the President.

Although we have no judicial information on the subject, yet the inference is that he is alive; for otherwise learned counsel would not appear for him and urge this court to decide his case. It can never be in this country of written constitution and laws, with a judicial department to interpret them, that any chief magistrate would be so far forgetful of his duty, as to order the execution of a man who denied the jurisdiction that tried and convicted him; after his case was before Federal judges with power to decide

---

[1] [Footnote 2 from the statement of the case by the official reporter]

The first section authorizes the suspension, during the Rebellion, of the writ of habeas corpus, throughout the United States, by the President.

Two following sections limited the authority in certain respects.

The second section required that lists of all persons, being citizens of States in which the administration of the laws had continued unimpaired in the Federal courts, who were then held, or might thereafter be held, as prisoners of the United States, under the authority of the President, otherwise than as prisoners of war, should be furnished by the Secretary of State and Secretary of War to the judges of the Circuit and District Courts. These lists were to contain the names of all persons, residing within their respective jurisdictions, charged with violation of national law. And it was required, in cases where the grand jury in attendance upon any of these courts should terminate its session without proceeding by indictment or otherwise against any prisoner named in the list, that the judge of the court should forthwith make an order that such prisoner, desiring a discharge, should be brought before him or the court to be discharged, on entering into recognizance, if required, to keep the peace and for good behavior, or to appear, as the court might direct, to be further dealt with according to law. Every officer of the United States having custody of such prisoners was required to obey and execute the judge's order, under penalty, for refusal or delay, of fine and imprisonment.

The third section enacts, in case lists of persons other than prisoners of war then held in confinement, or thereafter arrested, should not be furnished within twenty days after the passage of the act, or, in cases of subsequent arrest, within twenty days after the time of arrest, that any citizen, after the termination of a session of the grand jury without indictment or presentment, might, by petition alleging the facts and verified by oath, obtain the judge's order of discharge in favor of any person so imprisoned, on the terms and conditions prescribed in the second section.

This act made it the duty of the District Attorney of the United States to attend examinations on petitions for discharge.

By proclamation, dated the 15th September following the President reciting this statute suspended the privilege of the writ in the cases where, by his authority, military, naval, and civil officers of the United States "hold persons in their custody either as prisoners of war, spies, or aiders and abettors of the enemy, . . . or belonging to the land or naval forces of the United States, or otherwise amenable to military law, or the rules and articles of war, or the rules or regulations prescribed for the military or naval services, by authority of the President, or for resisting a draft, or for any other offence against the military or naval service."

it, who, being unable to agree on the grave questions involved, had, according to known law, sent it to the Supreme Court of the United States for decision. But even the suggestion is injurious to the Executive, and we dismiss it from further consideration. There is, therefore, nothing to hinder this court from an investigation of the merits of this controversy.

The controlling question in the case is this: Upon the facts stated in Milligan's petition, and the exhibits filed, had the military commission mentioned in it jurisdiction, legally, to try and sentence him? Milligan, not a resident of one of the rebellious states, or a prisoner of war, but a citizen of Indiana for twenty years past, and never in the military or naval service, is, while at his home, arrested by the military power of the United States, imprisoned, and, on certain criminal charges preferred against him, tried, convicted, and sentenced to be hanged by a military commission, organized under the direction of the military commander of the military district of Indiana. Had this tribunal the legal power and authority to try and punish this man?

No graver question was ever considered by this court, nor one which more nearly concerns the rights of the whole people; for it is the birthright of every American citizen when charged with crime, to be tried and punished according to law. The power of punishment is, alone through the means which the laws have provided for that purpose, and if they are ineffectual, there is an immunity from punishment, no matter how great an offender the individual may be, or how much his crimes may have shocked the sense of justice of the country, or endangered its safety. By the protection of the law human rights are secured; withdraw that protection, and they are at the mercy of wicked rulers, or the clamor of an excited people. If there was law to justify this military trial, it is not our province to interfere; if there was not, it is our duty to declare the nullity of the whole proceedings.

The decision of this question does not depend on argument or judicial precedents, numerous and highly illustrative as they are. These precedents inform us of the extent of the struggle to preserve liberty and to relieve those in civil life from military trials. The founders of our government were familiar with the history of that struggle; and secured in a written constitution every right which the people had wrested from power during a contest of ages. By that Constitution and the laws authorized by it this question must be determined.

The provisions of that instrument on the administration of criminal justice are too plain and direct, to leave room for misconstruction or doubt of their true meaning. Those applicable to this case are found in that clause of the original Constitution which says, "That the trial of all crimes, except in case of impeachment, shall be by jury;" and in the fourth, fifth, and sixth articles of the amendments. The fourth proclaims the right to be secure in person and effects against unreasonable search and seizure; and directs that a judicial warrant shall not issue "without proof of probable cause supported by oath or affirmation." The fifth declares "that no person shall be held to answer for a capital or otherwise infamous crime unless on presentment by a grand jury, except in cases arising in the land or naval forces, or in the militia, when in actual service in time of war or public danger, nor be deprived of life, liberty, or property, without due process of law." And the sixth guarantees the right of trial by jury, in such manner and with such regulations that with upright judges, impartial juries, and an able bar, the innocent will be saved and the guilty punished.

Time has proven the discernment of our ancestors; for even these provisions, expressed in such plain English words, that it would seem the ingenuity of man could not evade them, are now, after the lapse of more than seventy years, sought to be avoided. Those great and good men foresaw that troublous times would arise, when rules and people would become restive under restraint, and seek by sharp and decisive measures to accomplish ends deemed just and proper; and that the principles of constitutional liberty would be in peril, unless established by irrepealable law. The history of the world had taught them that what was done in the past might be attempted in the future. The Constitution of the United States is a law for rulers and people, equally in war and in peace, and covers with the shield of its protection all classes of men, at all times, and under all circumstances. No doctrine, involving more pernicious consequences, was ever invented by the wit of man than that any of its provisions can be suspended during any of the great exigencies of government. Such a doctrine leads directly to anarchy or despotism, but the theory of necessity on which it is based is false; for the government, within the Constitution, has all the powers granted to it, which are necessary to preserve its existence; as has been happily proved by the result of the great effort to throw off its just authority.

Have any of the rights guaranteed by the Constitution been violated in the case of Milligan? and if so, what are they?

Every trial involves the exercise of judicial power; and from what source did the military commission that tried him derive their authority? Certainly no part of the judicial power of the country was conferred on them; because the Constitution expressly vests it "in one supreme court and such inferior courts as the Congress may from time to time ordain and establish," and it is not pretended that the commission was a court ordained and established by Congress. They cannot justify on the mandate of the President; because he is controlled by law, and has his appropriate sphere of duty, which is to execute, not to make, the laws; and there is "no unwritten criminal code to which resort can be had as a source of jurisdiction."

But it is said that the jurisdiction is complete under the "laws and usages of war."

It can serve no useful purpose to inquire what those laws and usages are, whence they originated, where found, and on whom they operate; they can never be applied to citizens in states which have upheld the authority of the government, and where the courts are open and their process unobstructed. This court has judicial knowledge that in Indiana the Federal authority was always unopposed, and its courts always open to hear criminal accusations and redress grievances; and no usage of war could sanction a military trial there for any offence whatever of a citizen in civil life, in nowise connected with the military service. Congress could grant no such power; and to the honor of our national legislature be it said, it has never been provoked by the state of the country even to attempt its exercise. One of the plainest constitutional provisions was, therefore, infringed when Milligan was tried by a court not ordained and established by Congress, and not composed of judges appointed during good behavior.

Why was he not delivered to the Circuit Court of Indiana to be proceeded against according to law? No reason of necessity could be urged against it; because Congress had declared penalties against the offences charged, provided for their punishment, and directed that court to hear and determine them. And soon after this military tribunal was ended, the Circuit Court met, peacefully transacted its business, and adjourned. It needed no bayonets to protect it, and required no military aid to execute its judgments. It was held in a state, eminently distinguished for patriotism, by judges commissioned during the Rebellion, who were provided with juries, upright, intelligent, and selected by a marshal appointed by the President. The government had no right to conclude that Milligan, if guilty, would not receive in that court merited punishment; for its records disclose that it was constantly engaged in the trial of similar offences, and was never interrupted in its administration of criminal justice. If it was dangerous, in the distracted condition of affairs, to leave Milligan unrestrained of his liberty, because he "conspired against the government, afforded aid and comfort to rebels, and incited the people to insurrection," the law said arrest him, confine him closely, render him powerless to do further mischief; and then present his case to the grand jury of the district, with proofs of his guilt, and, if indicted, try him according to the course of the common law. If this had been done, the Constitution would have been vindicated, the law of 1863 enforced, and the securities for personal liberty preserved and defended.

Another guarantee of freedom was broken when Milligan was denied a trial by jury.

The discipline necessary to the efficiency of the army and navy, required other and swifter modes of trial than are furnished by the common law courts; and, in pursuance of the power conferred by the Constitution, Congress has declared the kinds of trial, and the manner in which they shall be conducted, for offences committed while the party is in the military or naval service. Every one connected with these branches of the public service is amenable to the jurisdiction which Congress has created for their government, and, while thus serving, surrenders his right to be tried by the civil courts. All other persons, citizens of states where the courts are open, if charged with crime, are guaranteed the inestimable privilege of trial by jury.

It is claimed that martial law covers with its broad mantle the proceedings of this military commission. The statement of this proposition shows its importance; for, if true, republican government is a failure, and there is an end of liberty regulated by law. Martial law, established on such a basis, destroys every guarantee of the Constitution, and effectually renders the "military independent of and superior to the civil power."

It will be borne in mind that this is not a question of the power to proclaim martial law, when war exists in a community and the courts and civil authorities are overthrown. Nor is it a question what rule a military commander, at the head of his army, can impose on states in rebellion to cripple their resources and quell the insurrection. The jurisdiction claimed is much more extensive. The necessities of the service, during the late Rebellion, required that the loyal states should be placed within the limits of certain military districts and commanders appointed in them; and, it is urged, that this, in a military sense, constituted them the theatre of military operations; and, as in this case, Indiana had been and was again threatened with invasion by the enemy, the occasion was furnished to establish martial law. The conclusion does not follow from the premises. If armies were collected in Indiana, they were to be employed in another locality, where the laws were obstructed and the national authority disputed. On her soil there was no hostile foot; if once invaded, that invasion was at an end, and with it all pretext for martial law. Martial law cannot arise from a threatened invasion. The necessity must be actual and present; the invasion real, such ad effectually closes the courts and deposes the civil administration.

It is difficult to see how the safety of the country required martial law in Indiana. If any of her citizens were plotting treason, the power of arrest could secure them, until the government was prepared for their trial, when the courts were open and ready to try them. It was as easy to protect witnesses before a civil as a military tribunal; and as there could be no wish to convict, except on sufficient legal evidence, surely an ordained and established court was better able to judge of this than a military tribunal composed of gentlemen not trained to the profession of the law.

It follows, from what has been said on this subject, that there are occasions when martial rule can be properly applied. If, in foreign invasion or civil war, the courts are actually closed, and it is impossible to administer criminal justice according to law, then, on the theatre of active military operations, where war really prevails, there is a necessity to furnish a substituted for the civil authority, thus overthrown, to preserve the safety of the army and society; and as no power is left but the military, it is allowed to govern by martial rule until the laws can have their free course. As necessity creates the nule, so it limits its duration; for, if this government is continued after the courts are reinstated, it is a gross usurpation of power. Martial rule can never exist where the courts are open, and in the proper and unobstructed exercise of their jurisdiction. It is also confined to the locality of actual war. Because, during the late Rebellion it could have been enforced in Virginia, where the national authority was overturned and the courts driven out, it does not follow that it should obtain in Indiana, where that authority was never disputed, and justice was always administered. And so in the case of a foreign invasion, martial rule may become a necessity in one state, when, in another, it would be "mere lawless violence."

If the military trial of Milligan was contrary to law, then he was entitled, on the facts stated in his petition, to be discharged from custody by the terms of the act of Congress of March 3d, 1863.

But it is insisted that Milligan was a prisoner of war, and, therefore, excluded from the privileges of the statute. It is not easy to see how he can be treated as a prisoner of war, when he lived in Indiana for the past twenty years, was arrested there, and had not been, during the late troubles, a resident of any of the states in rebellion. If in Indiana he conspired with bad men to assist the enemy, he is punishable for it in the courts of Indiana; but, when tried for the offence, he cannot plead the rights of war; for he was not engaged in legal acts of hostility against the government, and only such persons, when captured, are prisoners of war. If he cannot enjoy the immunities attaching to the character of a prisoner of war, how can he be subject to their pains and penalties?

CHIEF JUSTICE CHASE, dissenting.

Four members of the court, concurring with their brethren in the order heretofore made in this cause, but unable to concur in some important particulars with the opinion which has just been read, think it their duty to make a separate statement of their views of the whole case.

We agree that [Milligan is entitled to be discharged from military custody by writ of habeas corpus].We do not doubt that the positive provisions of the act of Congress require such answers. We do not think it necessary to look beyond these provisions. In them we find sufficient and controlling reasons for our conclusions.

But the opinion which has just been read goes further; and as we understand it, asserts not only that the military commission held in Indiana was not authorized by Congress, but that it was not in the power of Congress to authorize it; from which it may be thought to follow, that Congress has no power to indemnify the officers who composed the commission against liability in civil courts for acting as members of it.

We cannot agree to this.

We agree in the proposition that no department of the government of the United States — neither President, nor Congress, nor the Courts — possesses any power not given by the Constitution.

We assent, fully, to all that is said, in the opinion, of the inestimable value of the trial by jury, and of the other constitutional safeguards of civil liberty. And we concur, also, in what is said of the writ of habeas corpus, and of its suspension, with two reservations: (1.) That, in our judgment, when the writ is suspended, the Executive is authorized to arrest as well as to detain; and (2.) that there are cases in which, the privilege of the writ being suspended, trial and punishment by military commission, in states where civil courts are open, may be authorized by Congress, as well as arrest and detention.

We think that Congress had power, though not exercised, to authorize the military commission which was held in Indiana.

The Constitution itself provides for military government as well as for civil government. And we do not understand it to be claimed that the civil safeguards of the Constitution have application in cases within the proper sphere of the former.

We by no means assert that Congress can establish and apply the laws of war where no war had been declared or exists.

Where peace exists the laws of peace must prevail. What we do maintain is, that when the nation is involved in war, and some portions of the country are invaded, and all are exposed to invasion, it is within the power of Congress to determine in what states or districts such great and imminent public danger exists as justifies the authorization of military tribunals for the trial of crimes and offences against the discipline or security of the army or against the public safety.

In Indiana, for example, at the time of the arrest of Milligan and his co-conspirators, it is established by the papers in the record, that the state was a military district, was the theatre of military operations, had been actually invaded, and was constantly threatened with invasion. It appears, also, that a powerful secret association, composed of citizens and others, existed within the state, under military organization, conspiring against the draft, and plotting insurrection, the liberation of the prisoners of war at various depots, the seizure of the state and national arsenals, armed cooperation with the enemy, and war against the national government.

We cannot doubt that, in such a time of public danger, Congress had power, under the Constitution, to provide for the organization of a military commission, and for trial by that commission of persons engaged in this conspiracy. The fact that the Federal courts were open was regarded by Congress as a sufficient reason for not exercising the power; but that fact could not deprive Congress of the right to exercise it. Those courts might be open and undisturbed in the execution of their functions, and yet wholly incompetent to avert threatened danger, or to punish, with adequate promptitude and certainty, the guilty conspirators.

In Indiana, the judges and officers of the courts were loyal to the government. But it might have been otherwise. In times of rebellion and civil war it may often happen, indeed, that judges and marshals will be in active sympathy with the rebels, and courts their most efficient allies.

We have confined ourselves to the question of power. It was for Congress to determine the question of expediency. And Congress did determine it. That body did not see fit to authorize trials by military commission in Indiana, but by the strongest implication prohibited them. With that prohibition we are satisfied, and should have remained silent if the answers to the questions certified had been put on that ground, without denial of the existence of a power which we believe to be constitutional and important to the public safety, — a denial which, as we have already suggested, seems to draw in question the power of Congress to protect from prosecution the members of military commissions who acted in obedience to their superior officers, and whose action, whether warranted by law or not, was approved by that upright and patriotic President under whose administration the Republic was rescued from threatened destruction.

We have thus far said little of martial law, nor do we propose to say much. What we have already said sufficiently indicates our opinion that there is no law for the government of the citizens, the armies or the navy of the United States, within American jurisdiction, which is not contained in or derived from the Constitution. And wherever our army or navy may go beyond our territorial limits, neither can go beyond the authority of the President or the legislation of Congress.

There are under the Constitution three kinds of military jurisdiction: one to be exercised both in peace and war; another to be exercised in time of foreign war without the boundaries of the United States, or in time of rebellion and civil war within states or districts occupied by rebels treated as belligerents; and a third to be exercised in time of invasion or insurrection within the limits of the United States, or during rebellion within the limits of states maintaining adhesion to the National Government, when the public danger requires its exercise. The first of these may be called jurisdiction under MILITARY LAW, and is found in acts of Congress prescribing rules and articles of war, or otherwise providing for the government of the national forces; the second may be distinguished as MILITARY GOVERNMENT, superseding, as far as may be deemed expedient, the local law, and exercised by the military commander under the direction of the President, with the express or implied sanction of Congress; while the third may be denominated MARTIAL LAW PROPER, and is called into action by Congress, or temporarily, when the action of Congress cannot be invited, and in the case of justifying or excusing peril, by the President, in times of insurrection or invasion, or of civil or foreign war, within districts or localities where ordinary law no longer adequately secures public safety and private rights.

We think that the power of Congress, in such times and in such localities, to authorize trials for crimes against the security and safety of the national forces, may be derived from its constitutional authority to raise and support armies and to declare war, if not from its constitutional authority to provide for governing the national forces.

We have no apprehension that this power, under our American system of government, in which all official authority is derived from the people, and exercised under direct responsibility to the people, is more likely to be abused than the power to regulate commerce, or the power to borrow money. And we are unwilling to give our assent by silence to expressions of opinion which seem to us calculated, though not intended, to cripple the constitutional powers of the government, and to augment the public dangers in times of invasion and rebellion.

MR. JUSTICE WAYNE, MR. JUSTICE SWAYNE, and MR. JUSTICE MILLER concur with me in these views.

NOTES AND QUESTIONS

1. Civil War. The opinion in *Milligan* was presaged by *Ex parte Merryman*, 17 F. Cas. 144 (C.C.D. Md. 1861). Merryman was arrested early in the Civil War as an alleged conspirator to sabotage rail lines and bridges in Maryland. He was placed in military custody under the same Lincoln orders later considered in *Milligan*. Chief Justice Taney, sitting in Circuit Court, issued an order to the military commander at Fort Baltimore requiring that Merryman be brought forward for the purpose of justifying his detention. The military commander refused and Taney declared that his "power has been resisted by a force too strong for me to overcome." At the time, there was active fighting in Baltimore, Merryman was almost certainly involved in sabotage with others who were still at large, the seat of government in D.C. was virtually cut off from its loyal states, and there was no hope of enforcing an order to release Merryman. Did the law change after the war was over. Is it too cynical to say that the Court merely waited until it became safe to issue its opinion in *Milligan*? For an excellent treatment of the Lincoln-Taney interaction, see WILLIAM H. REHNQUIST, ALL THE LAWS BUT ONE (1998).

If the government had made a return to the habeas petition in *Merryman* stating its evidence of his involvement in blowing up railroad bridges, and asserting an intent to conduct a trial (even a military trial in an active theater of combat might have been acceptable), then there would have been no violation. Perhaps the suspension of the writ by the President was really overkill. Could it be argued that there was no need for it because the judges and the people would have willingly accepted military law enforcement in the face of a genuine emergency, and the government could easily have made satisfactory returns to habeas corpus petitions until the emergency passed? One counter-argument gets into personal political issues because Lincoln knew that Taney was at least somewhat sympathetic to the Southern cause. Merryman was never tried by a military tribunal. He was held for much of the war and eventually released.

2. Judicial Courage. What level of courage on the part of the judges is required by these situations? As with Taney's order in *Merryman*, there is always the possibility that the President will disregard a court order, particularly one issued in the grey area between genuine emergency and lasting peace. In that instance, Justice Jackson's civics lecture has real bite. Once the court has ruled, if the President does not obey, the political will of the people must have the final say. In the midst of armed conflict, the public would most likely be inclined to go along with the President's wishes.

The opposite side of the courage coin is that the President will obey and disaster befall the community as a result of some person's wrongdoing made possible, or at least contributed to, by the court's ruling. This is probably the more frightening aspect, particularly because the judges will often have the feeling that they are acting without full awareness of the background risks involved. These themes are hinted, and sometimes laid out explicitly in the cases that follow.

EX PARTE QUIRIN
317 U.S. 1 (1942)

MR. CHIEF JUSTICE STONE delivered the opinion of the Court.

[Petitioners were eight alleged German saboteurs who arrived by submarine in two groups, one group landing in New Jersey on the night of June 13, 1942, and the other in Florida on June 17. One defendant (Dasch) went to the FBI, apparently at the urging of another (Burger). By June 27, all eight were in custody. Trial before a military commission began on July 8 and evidence was concluded by July 27. Defense counsel sought extraordinary habeas corpus relief first from the District Court and then from the Supreme Court, which heard arguments on July 29 and rendered a brief *per curiam* decision on July 31. The commission then announced its judgment of conviction and recommendation of the death penalty for all the defendants, six of whom were executed on August 8. The Court then issued a full opinion on October 29.]

All the petitioners were born in Germany; all have lived in the United States. All returned to Germany between 1933 and 1941. All except petitioner Haupt are admittedly citizens of the German Reich, with which the United States is at war. Haupt came to this country with his parents when he was five years old; it is contended that he became a citizen of the United States by virtue of the naturalization of his parents during his minority and that he has not since lost his citizenship. The Government, however, takes the position that on attaining his majority he elected to maintain German allegiance and citizenship, or in any case that he has by his conduct renounced or abandoned his United States citizenship. For reasons presently to be stated we do not find it necessary to resolve these contentions.

After the declaration of war between the United States and the German Reich, petitioners received training at a sabotage school near Berlin, Germany, where they were instructed in the use of explosives and in methods of secret writing. While landing [on U.S. shores] they wore German Marine Infantry uniforms or parts of uniforms. Immediately after landing they buried their uniforms. All had received instructions in Germany from an officer of the German High Command to destroy war industries and war facilities in the United States, for which they or their relatives in Germany were to receive salary payments from the German Government. They also had been paid by the German Government during their course of training at the sabotage school and had received substantial sums in United States currency, which were in their possession when arrested.

The President appointed a Military Commission and directed it to try petitioners for offenses against the law of war, [stating] that "all persons who are subjects, citizens or residents of any nation at war with the United States or who give obedience to or act under the direction of any such nation, and who during time of war enter or attempt to enter the United States . . . through coastal or boundary defenses, and are charged with committing or attempting or preparing to commit sabotage, espionage, hostile or warlike acts, or violations of the law of war, shall be subject to the law of war and to the jurisdiction of military tribunals."

The Proclamation also stated in terms that all such persons were denied access to the courts.

Petitioners' main contention is that the President is without any statutory or constitutional authority to order the petitioners to be tried by military tribunal for offenses with which they are charged; that in consequence they are entitled to be tried in the civil courts with the safeguards, including trial by jury, which the Fifth and Sixth Amendments guarantee to all persons charged in such courts with criminal offenses. In any case it is urged that the President's Order, in prescribing the procedure of the Commission and the method for review of its findings and sentence, and the proceedings of the Commission under the Order, conflict with Articles of War adopted by Congress, and are illegal and void.

The Government challenges each of these propositions. But regardless of their merits, it also insists that petitioners must be denied access to the courts, both because they are enemy aliens or have entered our territory as enemy belligerents, and because the President's Proclamation undertakes in terms to deny such access to the class of persons defined by the Proclamation, which aptly describes the character and conduct of petitioners. It is urged that if they are enemy aliens or if the Proclamation has force, no court may afford the petitioners a hearing. But there is certainly nothing in the Proclamation to preclude access to the courts for determining its applicability to the particular case. And neither the Proclamation nor the fact that they are enemy aliens forecloses consideration by the courts of petitioners' contentions that the Constitution and laws of the United States constitutionally enacted forbid their trial by military commission.

We are not here concerned with any question of the guilt or innocence of petitioners. Constitutional safeguards for the protection of all who are charged with offenses are not to be disregarded in order to inflict merited punishment on some who are guilty. But the detention and trial of petitioners — ordered by the President in the declared exercise of his powers as Commander in Chief of the Army in time of war and of grave public danger — are not to be set aside by the courts without the clear conviction that they are in conflict with the Constitution or laws of Congress constitutionally enacted.

Congress and the President, like the courts, possess no power not derived from the Constitution. But one of the objects of the Constitution, as declared by its preamble, is to "provide for the common defence."

The Constitution thus invests the President, as Commander in Chief, with the power to wage war which Congress has declared, and to carry into effect all laws passed by Congress for the conduct of war and for the government and regulation of the Armed Forces, and all laws defining and punishing offenses against the law of nations, including those which pertain to the conduct of war.

By the Articles of War, 10 U.S.C. §§ [801 et seq.], Congress has provided rules for the government of the Army. It has provided for the trial and punishment, by courts martial, of violations of the Articles by members of the armed forces and by specified classes of persons associated or serving with the Army. Arts. 1, 2. But the Articles also recognize the "military commission" appointed by military command as an appropriate tribunal for the trial and punishment of offenses against the law of war not ordinarily tried by court martial. And Article 15 [now Art. 21, 10 U.S.C. § 821] declares that "the provisions of these articles conferring jurisdiction upon courts martial shall not be construed as depriving military commissions . . . or other military tribunals of concurrent jurisdiction in respect of offenders or offenses that by statute or by the law of war may be triable by such military commissions . . . or other military tribunals." Article 2 includes among those persons subject to military law the personnel of our own military establishment. But this, as Article 12 provides, does not exclude from that class "any other person who by the law of war is subject to trial by military tribunals" and who under Article 12 may be tried by court martial or under Article 15 by military commission.

Similarly the Espionage Act of 1917, which authorizes trial in the district courts of certain offenses that tend to interfere with the prosecution of war, provides that nothing contained in the act "shall be deemed to limit the jurisdiction of the general courts-martial, military commissions, or naval courts-martial."

From the very beginning of its history this Court has recognized and applied the law of war as including that part of the law of nations which prescribes, for the conduct of war, the status, rights and duties of enemy nations as well as of enemy individuals. By the Articles of War, and especially Article 15, Congress has explicitly provided, so far as it may constitutionally do so, that military tribunals shall have jurisdiction to try offenders or offenses against the law of war in appropriate cases.

An important incident to the conduct of war is the adoption of measures by the military command not only to repel and defeat the enemy, but to seize and subject to disciplinary measures those enemies who in their attempt to thwart or impede our military effort have violated the law of war. It is unnecessary for present purposes to determine to what extent the President as Commander in Chief has constitutional power to create military commissions without the support of Congressional legislation. For here Congress has authorized trial of offenses against the law of war before such commissions. We are concerned only with the question whether it is within the constitutional power of the National Government to place petitioners upon trial before a military commission for the offenses with which they are charged. We must therefore first inquire whether any of the acts charged is an offense against the law of war cognizable before a military tribunal, and if so whether the Constitution prohibits the trial. We may assume that there are acts regarded in other countries, or by some writers on international law, as offenses against the law of war which would not be triable by military tribunal here, either because they are not recognized by our courts as violations of the law of war or because they are of that class of offenses constitutionally triable only by a jury. It was upon such grounds that the Court denied the right to proceed by military tribunal in *Ex parte Milligan.* But as we shall show, these petitioners were charged with an offense against the law of war which the Constitution does not require to be tried by jury.

It is no objection that Congress in providing for the trial of such offenses has not itself undertaken to codify that branch of international law or to mark its precise boundaries, or to enumerate or define by statute all the acts which that law condemns. An Act of Congress punishing "the crime of piracy, as defined by the law of nations" is an appropriate exercise of its constitutional authority, Art. I, § 8, cl. 10, "to define and punish" the offense, since it has adopted by reference the sufficiently precise definition of international law.[2] Similarly, by the reference in the 15th Article of War to "offenders or offenses that . . . by the law of war may be triable by such military commissions," Congress has incorporated by reference, as within the jurisdiction of military commissions, all offenses which are defined as such by the law of war and which may constitutionally be included within that jurisdiction. Congress had the choice of crystallizing in permanent form and in minute detail every offense against the law of war, or of adopting the system of common law applied by military tribunals so far as it should be recognized and deemed applicable by the courts. It chose the latter course.

Such was the practice of our own military authorities before the adoption of the Constitution,[3] and during the Mexican and Civil Wars.[4]

Rules of Land Warfare promulgated by the War Department for the guidance of the

---

[2] [Court's Footnote 6] By universal agreement and practice, the law of war draws a distinction between the armed forces and the peaceful populations of belligerent nations and also between those who are lawful and unlawful combatants. Lawful combatants are subject to capture and detention as prisoners of war by opposing military forces. Unlawful combatants are likewise subject to capture and detention, but in addition they are subject to trial and punishment by military tribunals for acts which render their belligerency unlawful. The spy who secretly and without uniform passes the military lines of a belligerent in time of war, seeking to gather military information and communicate it to the enemy, or an enemy combatant who without uniform comes secretly through the lines for the purpose of waging war by destruction of life or property, are familiar examples of belligerents who are generally deemed not to be entitled to the status of prisoners of war, but to be offenders against the law of war subject to trial and punishment by military tribunals. *See* WINTHROP, MILITARY LAW, 2d ed., pp. 1196–97, 1219–21.

[3] [Court's Footnote 9] On September 29, 1780, Major John Andre, Adjutant-General to the British Army, was tried by a "Board of General Officers" appointed by General Washington, on a charge that he had come within the lines for an interview with General Benedict Arnold and had been captured while in disguise and travelling under an assumed name. Major Andre was hanged on October 2, 1780.

[4] [Court's Footnote 10] During the Mexican War military commissions were created in a large number of instances for the trial of various offenses. During the Civil War the military commission was extensively used for the trial of offenses against the law of war. 2 WINTHROP, MILITARY LAWS AND PRECEDENTS (2d ed. 1896).

Army provides that "All war crimes are subject to the death penalty, although a lesser penalty may be imposed." Paragraph 8 (1940) divides the enemy population into "armed forces" and "peaceful population," and Paragraph 9 names as distinguishing characteristics of lawful belligerents that they "carry arms openly" and "have a fixed distinctive emblem." The definition of lawful belligerents by Paragraph 9 is that adopted by Article 1, Annex to Hague Convention No. IV of October 18, 1907. The preamble to the Convention declares:

> Until a more complete code of the laws of war has been issued, the High Contracting Parties deem it expedient to declare that, in cases not included in the Regulations adopted by them, the inhabitants and the belligerents remain under the protection and the rule of the principles of the law of nations, as they result from the usages established among civilized peoples, from the laws of humanity, and the dictates of the public conscience.

Our Government, by thus defining lawful belligerents entitled to be treated as prisoners of war, has recognized that there is a class of unlawful belligerents not entitled to that privilege, including those who, though combatants, do not wear "fixed and distinctive emblems." And by Article 15 of the Articles of War Congress has made provision for their trial and punishment by military commission, according to "the law of war."

By a long course of practical administrative construction by its military authorities, our Government has likewise recognized that those who during time of war pass surreptitiously from enemy territory into our own, discarding their uniforms upon entry, for the commission of hostile acts involving destruction of life or property, have the status of unlawful combatants punishable as such by military commission. This precept of the law of war has been so recognized in practice both here and abroad, and has so generally been accepted as valid by authorities on international law[5] that we think it must be regarded as a rule or principle of the law of war recognized by this Government by its enactment of the Fifteenth Article of War.

Specification 1 of the first charge is sufficient to charge all the petitioners with the offense of unlawful belligerency, trial of which is within the jurisdiction of the Commission, and the admitted facts affirmatively show that the charge is not merely colorable or without foundation.

As we have seen, entry upon our territory in time of war by enemy belligerents, including those acting under the direction of the armed forces of the enemy, for the purpose of destroying property used or useful in prosecuting the war, is a hostile and warlike act. It subjects those who participate in it without uniform to the punishment prescribed by the law of war for unlawful belligerents. It is without significance that petitioners were not alleged to have borne conventional weapons or that their proposed hostile acts did not necessarily contemplate collision with the Armed Forces of the United States. By passing our boundaries for such purposes without uniform or other emblem signifying their belligerent status, or by discarding that means of identification after entry, such enemies become unlawful belligerents subject to trial and punishment.

Citizenship in the United States of an enemy belligerent does not relieve him from the consequences of a belligerency which is unlawful because in violation of the law of war. Citizens who associate themselves with the military arm of the enemy government, and with its aid, guidance and direction enter this country bent on hostile acts, are enemy belligerents within the meaning of the Hague Convention and the law of war. It is as an

---

[5] [Court's Footnote 12] Authorities on International Law have regarded as war criminals such persons who pass through the lines for the purpose of (a) destroying bridges, war materials, communication facilities, etc.; (b) carrying messages secretly; (c) any hostile act. 2 WINTHROP, MILITARY LAW AND PRECEDENTS (2nd ed. 1896) 1224. These authorities are unanimous in stating that a soldier in uniform who commits the acts mentioned would be entitled to treatment as a prisoner of war; it is the absence of uniform that renders the offender liable to trial for violation of the laws of war.

enemy belligerent that petitioner Haupt is charged with entering the United States, and unlawful belligerency is the gravamen of the offense of which he is accused.

Nor are petitioners any the less belligerents if, as they argue, they have not actually committed or attempted to commit any act of depredation or entered the theatre or zone of active military operations. The . . . nature of the offense . . . is that each petitioner, in circumstances which gave him the status of an enemy belligerent, passed our military and naval lines and defenses or went behind those lines, in civilian dress and with hostile purpose. The offense was complete when with that purpose they entered — or, having so entered, they remained upon — our territory in time of war without uniform or other appropriate means of identification. For that reason, even when committed by a citizen, the offense is distinct from the crime of treason defined in Article III, § 3 of the Constitution, since the absence of uniform essential to one is irrelevant to the other.

Presentment by a grand jury and trial by a jury of the vicinage where the crime was committed were at the time of the adoption of the Constitution familiar parts of the machinery for criminal trials in the civil courts. But they were procedures unknown to military tribunals, which are not courts in the sense of the Judiciary Article, and which in the natural course of events are usually called upon to function under conditions precluding resort to such procedures. As this Court has often recognized, it was not the purpose or effect of § 2 of Article III, read in the light of the common law, to enlarge the then existing right to a jury trial. The object was to preserve unimpaired trial by jury in all those cases in which it had been recognized by the common law and in all cases of a like nature as they might arise in the future, but not to bring within the sweep of the guaranty those cases in which it was then well understood that a jury trial could not be demanded as of right.

[Petty offenses and criminal contempts] are instances of offenses committed against the United States, for which a penalty is imposed, but they are not deemed to be within Article III, § 2, or the provisions of the Fifth and Sixth Amendments relating to "crimes" and "criminal prosecutions." In the light of this long-continued and consistent interpretation we must conclude that § 2 of Article III and the Fifth and Sixth Amendments cannot be taken to have extended the right to demand a jury to trials by military commission, or to have required that offenses against the law of war not triable by jury at common law be tried only in the civil courts.

The fact that "cases arising in the land or naval forces" are excepted from the operation of the Amendments does not militate against this conclusion. Such cases are expressly excepted from the Fifth Amendment, and are deemed excepted by implication from the Sixth. *Ex parte Milligan.* It is argued that the exception, which excludes from the Amendment cases arising in the armed forces, has also by implication extended its guaranty to all other cases; that since petitioners, not being members of the Armed Forces of the United States, are not within the exception, the Amendment operates to give to them the right to a jury trial. But we think this argument misconceives both the scope of the Amendment and the purpose of the exception.

No exception is necessary to exclude from the operation of these provisions cases never deemed to be within their terms. An express exception from Article III, § 2, and from the Fifth and Sixth Amendments, of trials of petty offenses and of criminal contempts has not been found necessary in order to preserve the traditional practice of trying those offenses without a jury. It is no more so in order to continue the practice of trying, before military tribunals without a jury, offenses committed by enemy belligerents against the law of war.

[An 1806 statute] imposed the death penalty on alien spies "according to the law and usage of nations, by sentence of a general court martial." This enactment must be regarded as a contemporary construction of both Article III, § 2, and the Amendments as not foreclosing trial by military tribunals, without a jury, of offenses against the law of war committed by enemies not in or associated with our Armed Forces. It is a construction of the Constitution which has been followed since the founding of our Government. Such a construction is entitled to the greatest respect. It has not hitherto been challenged, and, so far as we are advised, it has never been suggested in the very extensive literature of the subject that an alien spy, in time of war, could not be tried by military tribunal without a jury. [The Court recites 26 examples from the Revolutionary War, War of 1812, and Civil War of persons executed after being found by military tribunals to be guilty of spying. One was released by President Madison apparently on the ground that he was a U.S. citizen.]

Petitioners, and especially petitioner Haupt, stress the pronouncement of this Court in the *Milligan* case, that the law of war "can never be applied to citizens in states which have upheld the authority of the government, and where the courts are open and their process unobstructed." Elsewhere in its opinion, the Court was at pains to point out that Milligan, a citizen twenty years resident in Indiana, who had never been a resident of any of the states in rebellion, was not an enemy belligerent either entitled to the status of a prisoner of war or subject to the penalties imposed upon unlawful belligerents. We construe the Court's statement as to the inapplicability of the law of war to Milligan's case as having particular reference to the facts before it. From them the Court concluded that Milligan, not being a part of or associated with the armed forces of the enemy, was a non-belligerent, not subject to the law of war save as — in circumstances found not there to be present, and not involved here — martial law might be constitutionally established.

The Court's opinion is inapplicable to the case presented by the present record. We have no occasion now to define with meticulous care the ultimate boundaries of the jurisdiction of military tribunals to try persons according to the law of war. It is enough that petitioners here, upon the conceded facts, were plainly within those boundaries, and were held in good faith for trial by military commission, charged with being enemies who, with the purpose of destroying war materials and utilities, entered, or after entry remained in, our territory without uniform — an offense against the law of war. We hold only that those particular acts constitute an offense against the law of war which the Constitution authorizes to be tried by military commission.

MR. JUSTICE MURPHY took no part in the consideration or decision of these cases.

NOTES AND QUESTIONS

1. The *Quirin* Aftermath. The eight defendants in *Quirin* had all lived in the United States before returning to Germany between 1933 and 1941. They claimed that they had no intention of following the orders they were given in Germany but went along with the German plan out of fear of retribution to their families if they failed to make at least a token gesture of compliance. Burger and Dasch's sentences were commuted from death to life imprisonment in 1948. Each served six years in prison and was deported to Germany in 1948. They reportedly lived out their lives as pariahs in Germany.

Haupt's father, who lived in Chicago, was convicted of treason and sentenced to life in prison for aiding his son with knowledge of the scheme. *Haupt v. United States*, 330 U.S. 631 (1947). Thiel's friend Cramer was first convicted of treason but his conviction was overturned for lack of evidence that he had knowledge of the conspiracy. *Cramer v. United States*, 325 U.S. 1 (1945).

2. The *Quirin* Precedent. Before attempting to apply *Quirin* to current settings, we should try to isolate what made *Quirin* different from *Milligan*.

    a.   wartime?

    b.   foreign power or "enemy government"?

    c.   foreign citizenry?

    d.   military theater of operations?

For further analysis of *Quirin* in the post-9/11 context, see A. Christopher Bryant & Carl Tobias, *Quirin Revisited*, 2003 Wis. L. Rev. 309; Carl Tobias, *Detentions, Military Commissions, Terrorism, and Domestic Case Precedent*, 76 So. Cal. L. Rev. 1371 (2003).

DUNCAN v. KAHANAMOKU
327 U.S. 304, 66 S. Ct. 606, 90 L. Ed. 688 (1946)

Mr. Justice Black delivered the opinion of the Court.

The petitioners in these cases were sentenced to prison by military tribunals in Hawaii. Both are civilians. The question before us is whether the military tribunals had power to do this. The United States district court for Hawaii in habeas corpus proceedings held that the military tribunals had no such power and ordered that they be set free. The circuit court of appeals reversed, and ordered that the petitioners be returned to prison. Both cases thus involve the rights of individuals charged with crime and not connected with the armed forces to have their guilt or innocence determined in courts of law which provide established procedural safeguards, rather than by military tribunals which fail to afford many of these safeguards. Since these judicial safeguards are prized privileges of our system of government we granted certiorari.

The following events led to the military tribunals' exercise of jurisdiction over the petitioners. On December 7, 1941, immediately following the surprise air attack by the Japanese on Pearl Harbor, the Governor of Hawaii by proclamation undertook to suspend the privilege of the writ of habeas corpus and to place the Territory under "martial law." Section 67 of the Hawaiian Organic Act,[6] authorizes the Territorial Governor to take this action "in case of rebellion or invasion, or imminent danger thereof, when the public safety requires it. . . . " His action was to remain in effect only "until communication can be had with the President and his decision thereon made known." The President approved the Governor's action on December 9th. The Governor's proclamation also authorized and requested the Commanding General, "during the . . . emergency and until danger of invasion is removed, to exercise all the powers normally exercised" by the Governor and by the "judicial officers and employees of this territory."

Pursuant to this authorization the commanding general immediately proclaimed himself Military Governor and undertook the defense of the Territory and the maintenance of order. On December 8th, both civil and criminal courts were forbidden to summon jurors and witnesses and to try cases. The Commanding General established military tribunals to take the place of the courts. These were to try civilians charged with violating the laws of the United States and of the Territory, and rules, regulations, orders or policies of the Military Government. Rules of evidence and procedure of courts of law were not to control the military trials. In imposing penalties the military tribunals were to be "guided by, but not limited to the penalties authorized by the courts martial manual, the laws of the United States, the Territory of Hawaii, the District of Columbia, and the customs of war in like cases." The rule announced was simply that punishment was to be "commensurate with the offense committed" and that the death penalty might be imposed "in appropriate cases." Thus the military authorities took over the government of Hawaii. They could and did, by simply

---

[6] [Court's Footnote 1] That the governor shall be responsible for the faithful execution of the laws of the United States and of the Territory of Hawaii within the said Territory, and whenever it becomes necessary he may call upon the commanders of the military and naval forces of the United States in the Territory of Hawaii, or summon the posse comitatus, or call out the militia of the Territory to prevent or suppress lawless violence, invasion, insurrection, or rebellion in said Territory, and he may, in case of rebellion or invasion, or imminent danger thereof, when the public safety requires it, suspend the privilege of the writ of habeas corpus, or place the Territory, or any part thereof, under martial law until communication can be had with the President and his decision thereon made known.

promulgating orders, govern the day to day activities of civilians who lived, worked, or were merely passing through there. The military tribunals interpreted the very orders promulgated by the military authorities and proceeded to punish violators. The sentences imposed were not subject to direct appellate court review, since it had long been established that military tribunals are not part of our judicial system. *Ex parte Vallandigham*, 1 Wall. 243. The military undoubtedly assumed that its rule was not subject to any judicial control whatever, for by orders issued on August 25, 1943, it prohibited even accepting of a petition for writ of habeas corpus by a judge or judicial employee or the filing of such a petition by a prisoner or his attorney. Military tribunals could punish violators of these orders by fine, imprisonment or death.

White, the petitioner in No. 15, was a stockbroker in Honolulu. Neither he nor his business was connected with the armed forces. On August 20, 1942, more than eight months after the Pearl Harbor attack, the military police arrested him. The charge against him was embezzling stock belonging to another civilian in violation of Chapter 183 of the Revised Laws of Hawaii. Though by the time of White's arrest the courts were permitted "as agents of the Military Governor" to dispose of some non-jury civil cases, they were still forbidden to summon jurors and to exercise criminal jurisdiction. On August 22nd, White was brought before a military tribunal designated as a "Provost Court." The "Court" orally informed him of the charge. He objected to the tribunal's jurisdiction but the objection was overruled. He demanded to be tried by a jury. This request was denied. His attorney asked for additional time to prepare the case. This was refused. On August 25th he was tried and convicted. The tribunal sentenced him to five years imprisonment. Later the sentence was reduced to four years.

Duncan, the petitioner in No. 14, was a civilian shipfitter employed in the Navy Yard at Honolulu. On February 24, 1944, more than two years and two months after the Pearl Harbor attack, he engaged in a brawl with two armed Marine sentries at the yard. He was arrested by the military authorities. By the time of his arrest the military had to some extent eased the stringency of military rule. Schools, bars and motion picture theatres had been reopened. Courts had been authorized to "exercise their normal jurisdiction." They were once more summoning jurors and witnesses and conducting criminal trials. There were important exceptions, however. One of these was that only military tribunals were to try "Criminal prosecutions for violations of military orders." As the record shows, these military orders still covered a wide range of day to day civilian conduct. Duncan was charged with violating one of these orders, which prohibited assault on military or naval personnel with intent to resist or hinder them in the discharge of their duty. He was, therefore, tried by a military tribunal rather than the territorial court, although the general laws of Hawaii made assault a crime. A conviction followed and Duncan was sentenced to six months imprisonment.

The petitioners contend that "martial law" as provided for by § 67 did not authorize the military to try and punish civilians such as petitioners and urge further that if such authority should be inferred from the Organic Act, it would be unconstitutional. We need decide the constitutional question only if we agree with the Government that Congress did authorize what was done here.

We note first that at the time the alleged offenses were committed the dangers apprehended by the military were not sufficiently imminent to cause them to require civilians to evacuate the area or even to evacuate any of the buildings necessary to carry on the business of the courts. In fact, the buildings had long been open and actually in use for certain kinds of trials. Our question does not involve the well-established power of the military to exercise jurisdiction over members of the armed forces, those directly connected with such forces, or enemy belligerents, prisoners of war, or others charged with violating the laws of war. *Ex parte Quirin*. We are not concerned with the recognized power of the military to try civilians in tribunals established as a part of a temporary military government over occupied enemy territory or territory regained from an enemy where civilian government cannot and does not function. For Hawaii since annexation has been held by and loyal to the United States. Nor need we here consider the power of the military simply to arrest and detain civilians interfering with a necessary military function at a time of turbulence and danger from insurrection or war. And finally, there was no specialized effort of the military, here, to enforce orders which related only to military functions, such as, for illustration, curfew rules or blackouts. For these petitioners were tried before tribunals set up under a military program which took over all government and superseded all civil laws and courts. If the Organic Act, properly interpreted, did not give the armed forces this awesome power, both petitioners are entitled to their freedom.

Since both the language of the Organic Act and its legislative history fail to indicate that the scope of "martial law" in Hawaii includes the supplanting of courts by military tribunals, we must look to other sources in order to interpret that term. We think the answer may be found in the birth, development and growth of our governmental institutions up to the time Congress passed the Organic Act.

People of many ages and countries have feared and unflinchingly opposed the kind of subordination of executive, legislative and judicial authorities to complete military rule which, according to the Government, Congress has authorized here. In this country that fear has become part of our cultural and political institutions. The story of that development is well known and we see no need to retell it all. But we might mention a few pertinent incidents. As early as the 17th Century our British ancestors took political action against aggressive military rule. When James I and Charles I authorized martial law for purposes of speedily punishing all types of crimes committed by civilians the protest led to the historic Petition of Right which in uncompromising terms objected to this arbitrary procedure and prayed that it be stopped and never repeated. When later the American colonies declared their independence one of the grievances listed by Jefferson was that the King had endeavored to render the military superior to the civil power.

In 1787, the year in which the Constitution was formulated, the Governor of Massachusetts Colony used the militia to cope with Shay's Rebellion. In his instructions to the Commander of the troops the Governor listed the "great objects" of the mission. The troops were to "protect the judicial courts . . . ," "to assist the civil magistrates in executing the laws . . . ," and to "aid them in apprehending the disturbers of the public peace. . . . " The Commander was to consider himself "constantly as under the direction of the civil officer, saving where any armed force shall appear and oppose . . . [his] marching to execute these orders." President Washington's instructions to the Commander of the troops sent into Pennsylvania to suppress the Whiskey Rebellion of 1794 were to the same effect. The troops were to see to it that the laws were enforced and were to deliver the leaders of armed insurgents to the regular courts for trial. The President admonished the Commanding General "that the judge can not be controlled in his functions. . . . " In the many instances of the use of troops to control the activities of civilians that followed, the troops were generally again employed merely to aid and not to supplant the civilian authorities.[7] The last noteworthy incident before the enactment of the Organic Act was the rioting that occurred in the spring of 1899 at the Coeur d'Alene mines of Shoshone County, Idaho. The President ordered the regular troops to report to the Governor for instructions and

---

[7] [Court's Footnote 18] After the passing of the Organic Act disturbances in the coal fields of West Virginia, a longshoremen's strike in Galveston and a packers' strike in Nebraska City, all led to criminal trials of civilians by military tribunals which were upheld by decisions of state and lower federal courts. All these cases rested on the ground that the Governor's determination of the existence of insurrection conclusively established that all the Governor had done was legal. The basis of these decisions was definitely held erroneous in *Sterling v. Constantin*, 287 U.S. 378, 401, where this Court said: "What are the allowable limits of military discretion, and whether or not they have been overstepped in a particular case, are judicial questions." As one commentator puts it, this Court "has knocked out the prop" on which these aforementioned cases Rested. WIENER, A PRACTICAL MANUAL OF MARTIAL LAW, 1940, p. 116.

to support the civil authorities in preserving the peace. Later the State Auditor as agent of the Governor, and not the Commanding General, ordered the troops to detain citizens without trial and to aid the Auditor in doing all he thought necessary to stop the riot. Once more, the military authorities did not undertake to supplant the courts and to establish military tribunals to try and punish ordinary civilian offenders.

Courts and their procedural safeguards are indispensable to our system of government. They were set up by our founders to protect the liberties they valued. *Ex parte Quirin.* Our system of government clearly is the antithesis of total military rule and the founders of this country are not likely to have contemplated complete military dominance within the limits of a territory made part of this country and not recently taken from an enemy. They were opposed to governments that placed in the hands of one man the power to make, interpret and enforce the laws. Their philosophy has been the people's throughout our history. For that reason we have maintained legislatures chosen by citizens or their representatives and courts and juries to try those who violate legislative enactments. We have always been especially concerned about the potential evils of summary criminal trials and have guarded against them by provisions embodied in the Constitution itself. *See Ex parte Milligan; Chambers v. Florida,* 309 U.S. 227. Legislatures and courts are not merely cherished American institutions; they are indispensable to our Government.

Military tribunals have no such standing. For as this Court has said before: " . . . the military should always be kept in subjection to the laws of the country to which it belongs, and that he is no friend to the Republic who advocates the contrary. The established principle of every free people is, that the law shall alone govern; and to it the military must always yield." Congress prior to the time of the enactment of the Organic Act had only once authorized the supplanting of the courts by military tribunals. Legislation to that effect was enacted immediately after the South's unsuccessful attempt to secede from the Union. Insofar as that legislation applied to the Southern States after the war was at an end it was challenged by a series of Presidential vetoes as vigorous as any in the country's history. And in order to prevent this Court from passing on the constitutionality of this legislation Congress found it necessary to curtail our appellate jurisdiction.[8] Indeed, prior to the Organic Act, the only time this Court had ever discussed the supplanting of courts by military tribunals in a situation other than that involving the establishment of a military government over recently occupied enemy territory, it had emphatically declared that "civil liberty and this kind of martial law cannot endure together; the antagonism is irreconcilable; and, in the conflict, one or the other must perish." *Ex parte Milligan.*

We believe that when Congress passed the Hawaiian Organic Act and authorized the establishment of "martial law" it had in mind and did not wish to exceed the boundaries between military and civilian power, in which our people have always believed, which responsible military and executive officers had heeded, and which had become part of our political philosophy and institutions prior to the time Congress passed the Organic Act. The phrase "martial law" as employed in that Act, therefore, while intended to authorize the military to act vigorously for the maintenance of an orderly civil government and for the defense of the Islands against actual or threatened rebellion or invasion, was not intended to authorize the supplanting of courts by military tribunals. Yet the Government seeks to justify the punishment of both White and Duncan on the ground of such supposed congressional authorization. We hold that both petitioners are now entitled to be released from custody.

Reversed.

MR. JUSTICE JACKSON took no part in the consideration or decision of these cases.

MR. JUSTICE MURPHY, concurring.

---

[8] [Court's Footnote 22] *Ex parte McCardle,* 6 Wall. 318. *See also* WARREN, THE SUPREME COURT IN UNITED STATES HISTORY, Vol. 2, at 464, 484.

The Court's opinion, in which I join, makes clear that the military trials in these cases were unjustified by the martial law provisions of the Hawaiian Organic Act. Equally obvious, as I see it, is the fact that these trials were forbidden by the Bill of Rights of the Constitution of the United States, which applies in both spirit and letter to Hawaii. Indeed, the unconstitutionality of the usurpation of civil power by the military is so great in this instance as to warrant this Court's complete and outright repudiation of the action.

Abhorrence of military rule is ingrained in our form of government. This supremacy of the civil over the military is one of our great heritages. It has made possible the attainment of a high degree of liberty regulated by law rather than by caprice. Our duty is to give effect to that heritage at all times, that it may be handed down untarnished to future generations.

The so-called "open court" rule of the *Milligan* case, to be sure, has been the subject of severe criticism, especially by military commentators. That criticism is repeated by the Government in these cases. It is said that the fact that courts are open is but one of many factors relevant to determining the necessity and hence the constitutionality of military trials of civilians. The argument is made that however adequate the "open court" rule may have been in 1628 or 1864 it is distinctly unsuited to modern warfare conditions where all of the territories of a warring nation may be in combat zones or imminently threatened with long-range attack even while civil courts are operating. Hence if a military commander, on the basis of his conception of military necessity, requires all civilians accused of crime to be tried summarily before martial law tribunals, the Bill of Rights must bow humbly to his judgment despite the unquestioned ability of the civil courts to exercise their criminal jurisdiction.

The argument thus advanced is as untenable today as it was when cast in the language of the Plantagenets, the Tudors and the Stuarts. It is a rank appeal to abandon the fate of all our liberties to the reasonableness of the judgment of those who are trained primarily for war. It seeks to justify military usurpation of civilian authority to punish crime without regard to the potency of the Bill of Rights. It deserves repudiation.

First. We may assume that the threat to Hawaii was a real one; we may also take it for granted that the general declaration of martial law was justified. But it does not follow from these assumptions that the military was free under the Constitution to close the civil courts or to strip them of their criminal jurisdiction, especially after the initial shock of the sudden Japanese attack had been dissipated.

Second. Delays in the civil courts and slowness in their procedure are also cited as an excuse for shearing away their criminal jurisdiction. It is said that the military "cannot brook a delay" and that "the punishment must be swift; there is an element of time in it, and we cannot afford to let the trial linger and be protracted." This military attitude toward constitutional processes is not novel. Civil liberties and military expediency are often irreconcilable. It does take time to . . . judge guilt or innocence according to accepted rules of law. But experience has demonstrated that such time is well spent. It is the only method we have of insuring the protection of constitutional rights and of guarding against oppression. The swift trial and punishment which the military desires is precisely what the Bill of Rights outlaws.

Third. It is further said that the issuance of military orders relating to civilians required that the military have at its disposal some sort of tribunal to enforce those regulations. [T]he mere fact that it may be more expedient and convenient for the military to try violators of its own orders before its own tribunals does not and should not furnish a constitutional basis for the jurisdiction of such tribunals when civil courts are in fact functioning or are capable of functioning. Constitutional rights are rooted deeper than the wishes and desires of the military.

Fourth. Much is made of the assertion that the civil courts in Hawaii had no jurisdiction over violations of military orders by civilians and that military courts were therefore necessary. Aside from the fact that the civil courts were ordered not to attempt to exercise such jurisdiction, it is sufficient to note that Congress on March 21, 1942, vested in the federal courts jurisdiction to enforce military orders with criminal penalties. It is undisputed that the federal court in Hawaii was open at all times in issue and was capable of exercising criminal jurisdiction.

Fifth. Objection is made to the enforcement in civil courts of military orders on the ground that it would subject the military to "all sorts of influences, political and otherwise, as happened in the cases on the east coast in both Philadelphia and Boston" and that "it is inconceivable that the Military Commander should be subjected for the enforcement of his orders to the control of other agents." This is merely a military criticism of the proposition that in this nation the military is subordinate to the civil authority. It does not qualify as a recognizable reason for closing the civil courts to criminal cases.

Sixth. Further objection is made that the holding of civil trials might interrupt vital work through the attendance as jurors of war workers. This also is too unmeritorious to warrant serious or lengthy discussion. War workers could easily have been excused from jury duty by military order if necessary.

Seventh. The final reason advanced relates to the testimony of military leaders that Hawaii is said to have a "heterogeneous population with all sorts of affinities and loyalties which are alien in many cases to the philosophy of life of the American Government," one-third of the civilian population being of Japanese descent. The court below observed that "Governmental and military problems alike were complicated by the presence in the Territory of tens of thousands of citizens of Japanese ancestry besides large numbers of aliens of the same race." The Government adds that many of the military personnel stationed in Hawaii were unaccustomed to living in such a community and that "potential problems" created in Hawaii by racially mixed juries in criminal cases have heretofore been recognized "although, on the whole, it has been found that members of such mixed juries have not acted on a racial basis."

Especially deplorable is this use of the iniquitous doctrine of racism to justify the imposition of military trials. Racism has no place whatever in our civilization. The Constitution as well as the conscience of mankind disclaims its use for any purpose, military or otherwise. It can only result, as it does in this instance, in striking down individual rights and in aggravating rather than solving the problems toward which it is directed. It renders impotent the ideal of the dignity of the human personality, destroying something of what is noble in our way of life. We must therefore reject it completely whenever it arises in the course of a legal proceeding.

The reasons here advanced for abandoning the "open court" rule of the *Milligan* case are without substance. To retreat from that rule is to open the door to rampant militarism and the glorification of war, which have destroyed so many nations in history. There is a very necessary part in our national life for the military; it has defended this country well in its darkest hours of trial. But militarism is not our way of life. It is to be used only in the most extreme circumstances. Moreover, we must be on constant guard against an excessive use of any power, military or otherwise, that results in the needless destruction of our rights and liberties. There must be a careful balancing of interests. And we must ever keep in mind that "The Constitution of the United States is a law for rulers and people, equally in war and in peace, and covers with the shield of its protection all classes of men, at all times, and under all circumstances." *Ex parte Milligan* 120–121.

Mr. Chief Justice Stone, concurring.

I take it that the Japanese attack on Hawaii on December 7, 1941, was an "invasion" within the meaning of § 67. But it began and ended long before these petitioners were tried by military tribunals in August 1942 and February 1944. I assume that there was danger of further invasion of Hawaii at the times of those trials. I assume also that there could be circumstances in which the public safety requires, and the Constitution permits, substitution of trials by military tribunals for trials in the civil courts. But the record here discloses no such conditions in Hawaii, at least during the period after February, 1942, and the trial court so found.

MR. JUSTICE BURTON, with whom MR. JUSTICE FRANKFURTER concurs, dissenting.

With the rest of this Court I subscribe unreservedly to the Bill of Rights. I recognize the importance of the civil courts in protecting individual rights guaranteed by the Constitution. I prefer civil to military control of civilian life and I agree that in war our Constitution contemplates the preservation of the individual rights of all of our people in accordance with a plan of constitutional procedure fitted to the needs of a self-governing republic at war.

Our Constitution expressly provides for waging war, and it is with the constitutional instruments for the successful conduct of war that I am concerned. I recognize here, as elsewhere, the constitutional direction that our respective branches of the Government do not exceed their allotted shares of authority. The courts, as well as our other agencies of the Government, accordingly owe a constitutional obligation not to invade the fields reserved either to the people, the States, or the other coordinate branches of the Government.

On December 7 and in the period immediately following, every inch of the Territory of Hawaii was like a frontier stockade under savage attack with notice that such attack would not be restrained by the laws of civilized nations. Measures of defense had to be taken on the basis that anything could happen. The relation of the Constitution of the United States to such a situation is important. Of course, the Constitution is not put aside. It was written by a generation fresh from war. The people established a more perfect union, in part, so that they might the better defend themselves from military attack. In doing so they centralized far more military power and responsibility in the Chief Executive than previously had been done. The Constitution was built for rough as well as smooth roads. In time of war the nation simply changes gears and takes the harder going under the same power.

The conduct of war under the Constitution is largely an executive function. Within the field of military action in time of war, the executive is allowed wide discretion. While, even in the conduct of war, there are many lines of jurisdiction to draw between the proper spheres of legislative, executive and judicial action, it seems clear that at least on an active battle field, the executive discretion to determine policy is there intended by the Constitution to be supreme. The question then arises: What is a battle field and how long does it remain one after the first barrage?

It is well that the outer limits of the jurisdiction of our military authorities is subject to review by our courts even under such extreme circumstances as those of the battle field. This, however, requires the courts to put themselves as nearly as possible in the place of those who had the constitutional responsibility for immediate executive action.

For this Court to intrude its judgment into spheres of constitutional discretion that are reserved either to the Congress or to the Chief Executive, is to invite disregard of that judgment by the Congress or by executive agencies under a claim of constitutional right to do so. On the other hand, this Court can contribute much to the orderly conduct of government, if it will outline reasonable boundaries for the discretion of the respective departments of the Government, with full regard for the limitations and also for the responsibilities imposed upon them by the Constitution.

It is important to approach the present cases with a full appreciation of the responsibility of the executive branch of the Government in Hawaii under the invasion which occurred on December 7, 1941. The question is not shall the Constitution apply under such circumstances? The question is with what authority has the Constitution and laws of this country vested the official representatives of the people upon whom are placed the responsibilities of leadership under those extraordinary circumstances?

The vital distinction is between conditions in "the theatre of actual military operations" and outside of that theatre. In this case Hawaii was not only in the theatre of operations, it was under fire. The actual presence of battle in a community creates a substantially different condition from that which exists in other parts of a nation at war.

Now that the war has been won and the safety of the Islands has been again assured, there is opportunity, in the calm light of peace, for the readjustment of sentences imposed upon civilians and military personnel during the emergency of war and which have not yet expired. It is important, however, that in reviewing the constitutionality of the conduct of our agencies of government in time of war, invasion and threatened invasion, we do not now make precedents which in other emergencies may handicap the executive branch of the Government in the performance of duties allotted to it by the Constitution and by the exercise of which it successfully defended the nation against the greatest attack ever made upon it.

One way to test the soundness of a decision today that the trial of petitioner White on August 25, 1942, and the trial of petitioner Duncan on March 2, 1944, were unconstitutional procedures, is to ask ourselves whether or not on those dates, with the war against Japan in full swing, this Court would have, or should have, granted a writ of habeas corpus, an injunction or a writ of prohibition to release the petitioners or otherwise to oust the provost courts of their claimed jurisdiction. Such a test emphasizes the issue. I believe that this Court would not have been justified in granting the relief suggested at such times. Also I believe that this Court might well have found itself embarrassed had it ordered such relief and then had attempted to enforce its order in the theatre of military operations, at a time when the area was under martial law and the writ of habeas corpus was still suspended, all in accordance with the orders of the President of the United States.

NOTES AND QUESTIONS

1. **The *Milligan* Precedent.** After *Duncan*, should we read *Milligan* as a constitutional holding or a statutory holding? Justice Black may have been a bit overly enthusiastic about what "our people have always believed" or about what "responsible military and executive officers had heeded," but his message is clearly stated that martial law does not itself close the civilian courts nor authorize diversion of civilian defendants to military tribunals. Is this essentially a statement about constitutional norms in the course of statutory interpretation?

2. **Martial Law and Tribunals.** How was it determined that Congress had authorized military tribunals for the saboteurs in *Quirin* but not for crimes, even committed on a military base, in *Duncan*? This is perhaps the most clearly visible reason for understanding the nature of the "law of war" with which we started this course.

Chief Justice Stone points out that there were no active hostilities in or around Hawaii in 1942, while Justice says that Hawaii was "under fire." How can there be such a difference in perception of the existence of "armed conflict" or "active hostilities?" Are courts really incapable of making the factual determinations necessary for this decision? If so, how does a military tribunal or an international tribunal determine when a state of armed conflict exist?

***Johnson v. Eisentrager*, 339 U.S. 763 (1950).** This was a habeas corpus petition brought in the D.C. district court on behalf of 21 German citizens who had been captured in China following Germany's surrender and before Japan's surrender. They were tried by U.S. military commission in China and convicted of spying on behalf of Japan in violation of the law of war. They were then transferred to a U.S. military prison in Germany. Justice Jackson for the Supreme Court first engaged in a lengthy discussion of the differences among citizens, resident aliens, resident enemy aliens, and nonresident aliens.

We are here confronted with a decision whose basic premise is that these prisoners are entitled, as a constitutional right, to sue in some court of the United States for a writ of habeas corpus. To support that assumption we must hold that a prisoner of our military authorities is constitutionally entitled to the writ, even though he (a) is an enemy alien; (b) has never been or resided in the United States; (c) was captured outside of our territory and there held in military custody as a prisoner of war; (d) was tried and convicted by a Military Commission sitting outside the United States; (e) for offenses against laws of war committed outside the United States; (f) and is at all times imprisoned outside the United States.

We have pointed out that the privilege of litigation has been extended to aliens, whether friendly or enemy, only because permitting their presence in the country implied protection. No such basis can be invoked here, for these prisoners at no relevant time were within any territory over which the United States is sovereign, and the scenes of their offense, their capture, their trial and their punishment were all beyond the territorial jurisdiction of any court of the United States.

But Justice Jackson then went on to an apparent review of the merits of the petitions by addressing the "lawful power of the commission to try the petitioner:

It is not for us to say whether these prisoners were or were not guilty of a war crime, or whether if we were to retry the case we would agree to the findings of fact or the application of the laws of war made by the Military Commission. The petition shows that these prisoners were formally accused of violating the laws of war and fully informed of particulars of these charges. As we observed in the *Yamashita* case, "If the military tribunals have lawful authority to hear, decide and condemn, their action is not subject to judicial review merely because they have made a wrong decision on disputed facts. Correction of their errors of decision is not for the courts but for the military authorities which are alone authorized to review their decisions. . . . We consider here only the lawful power of the commission to try the petitioner for the offense charged."

That there is a basis in conventional and long-established law by which conduct ascribed to them might amount to a violation seems beyond question. Breach of the terms of an act of surrender is no novelty among war crimes. "That capitulations must be scrupulously adhered to is an old customary rule, since enacted by Article 35 of the Hague Regulations. Any act contrary to a capitulation would constitute an international delinquency if ordered by a belligerent Government, and a war crime if committed without such order. Such violation may be met by reprisals or punishment of the offenders as war criminals." II OPPENHEIM, INTERNATIONAL LAW 433 (6th ed. rev., Lauterpacht, 1944). It being within the jurisdiction of a Military Commission to try the prisoners, it was for it to determine whether the laws of war applied and whether an offense against them had been committed.

The meaning and significance of *Eisentrager* is extensively debated in the military detention cases of 2004 considered in the next section.

§ 8.03 MILITARY DETENTIONS

[A] The 2004 Cases

The clearest example of departure from peace time norms in the "war on terrorism" is the military detention without trial of a U.S. citizen arrested by the FBI on U.S. soil and accused of planning to engage in a terrorist act on U.S. soil. His name is Jose Padilla, and he has been held in the Navy brig at Charleston, South Carolina, while habeas corpus proceedings test the validity of his detention. Another U.S. citizen held under slightly different circumstances was Yaser Hamdi, who was in military custody since he was picked up in Afghanistan in early 2002. And then there were the roughly 700 persons of various nationalities held at Guantánamo Bay, most of whom were captured in Afghanistan but some of whom may have been captured in other places under different circumstances.

In all three instances, the Government claimed that it could detain these persons as "enemy combatants" pursuant to the war powers of the President. In June 2004, the Supreme Court decided all three cases, rejecting the Government's underlying premise of near-unreviewable executive power. But the opinions need to be read carefully to determine precisely what was held in each instance.

The concepts involved in the "law of war" were introduced in Chapter 3. In short, the "law of war" applies at least during periods of "armed conflict" such that would trigger the Geneva Conventions. Under the law of war, a combatant in an international armed conflict possesses combat immunity for acts that do not violate the law of war, while a civilian would have no combat immunity unless he or she can fall within the definitions of eligibility for POW status under article 4 of Geneva III (GPW). And the law of war generally would not require recognition of combat immunity for violent acts during a period of insurrection or internal armed conflict. These concepts form part of the background for the question of how to deal with violent actors who are not connected with any entity claiming the status of a nation or state.

HAMDI v. RUMSFELD
542 U.S. 507 (2004)

O'CONNOR, J., announced the judgment of the Court and delivered an opinion, in which REHNQUIST, C.J, and KENNEDY and BREYER, JJ., joined. SOUTER, J., filed an opinion concurring in part, dissenting in part, and concurring in the judgment, in which GINSBURG, J., joined. SCALIA, J., filed a dissenting opinion, in which STEVENS, J., joined. THOMAS, J., filed a dissenting opinion.

JUSTICE O'CONNOR announced the judgment of the Court and delivered an opinion, in which THE CHIEF JUSTICE, JUSTICE KENNEDY, and JUSTICE BREYER join.

At this difficult time in our Nation's history, we are called upon to consider the legality of the Government's detention of a United States citizen on United States soil as an "enemy combatant" and to address the process that is constitutionally owed to one who seeks to challenge his classification as such. The United States Court of Appeals for the Fourth Circuit held that petitioner's detention was legally authorized and that he was entitled to no further opportunity to challenge his enemy-combatant label. We now vacate and remand. We hold that although Congress authorized the detention of combatants in the narrow circumstances alleged here, due process demands that a citizen held in the United States as an enemy combatant be given a meaningful opportunity to contest the factual basis for that detention before a neutral decisionmaker.

I

On September 11, 2001, the al Qaeda terrorist network used hijacked commercial airliners to attack prominent targets in the United States. Approximately 3,000 people were killed in those attacks. One week later, in response to these "acts of treacherous violence," Congress passed a resolution authorizing the President to "use all necessary and appropriate force against those nations, organizations, or persons he determines planned, authorized, committed, or aided the terrorist attacks" or "harbored such organizations or persons, in order to prevent any future acts of international terrorism against the United States by such nations, organizations or persons." Authorization for Use of Military Force ("the AUMF"). Soon thereafter, the President ordered United

States Armed Forces to Afghanistan, with a mission to subdue al Qaeda and quell the Taliban regime that was known to support it.

This case arises out of the detention of a man whom the Government alleges took up arms with the Taliban during this conflict. His name is Yaser Esam Hamdi. Born an American citizen in Louisiana in 1980, Hamdi moved with his family to Saudi Arabia as a child. By 2001, the parties agree, he resided in Afghanistan. At some point that year, he was seized by members of the Northern Alliance, a coalition of military groups opposed to the Taliban government, and eventually was turned over to the United States military. The Government asserts that it initially detained and interrogated Hamdi in Afghanistan before transferring him to the United States Naval Base in Guantánamo Bay in January 2002. In April 2002, upon learning that Hamdi is an American citizen, authorities transferred him to a naval brig in Norfolk, Virginia, where he remained until a recent transfer to a brig in Charleston, South Carolina. The Government contends that Hamdi is an "enemy combatant," and that this status justifies holding him in the United States indefinitely — without formal charges or proceedings — unless and until it makes the determination that access to counsel or further process is warranted.

In June 2002, Hamdi's father, Esam Fouad Hamdi, filed the present petition for a writ of habeas corpus under 28 U.S.C. § 2241 in the Eastern District of Virginia, naming as petitioners his son and himself as next friend. The elder Hamdi alleges in the petition that he has had no contact with his son since the Government took custody of him in 2001, and that the Government has held his son "without access to legal counsel or notice of any charges pending against him." Although his habeas petition provides no details with regard to the factual circumstances surrounding his son's capture and detention, Hamdi's father has asserted in documents found elsewhere in the record that his son went to Afghanistan to do "relief work," and that he had been in that country less than two months before September 11, 2001, and could not have received military training. The 20-year-old was traveling on his own for the first time, his father says, and "because of his lack of experience, he was trapped in Afghanistan once that military campaign began."

[T]he Government filed a response and a motion to dismiss the petition. It attached to its response a declaration from one Michael Mobbs (hereinafter "Mobbs Declaration"), who identified himself as Special Advisor to the Under Secretary of Defense for Policy. Mobbs . . . set forth what remains the sole evidentiary support that the Government has provided to the courts for Hamdi's detention. The declaration states that Hamdi "traveled to Afghanistan" in July or August 2001, and that he thereafter "affiliated with a Taliban military unit and received weapons training." It asserts that Hamdi "remained with his Taliban unit following the attacks of September 11" and that, during the time when Northern Alliance forces were "engaged in battle with the Taliban, . . . Hamdi's Taliban unit surrendered" to those forces, after which he "surrendered his Kalishnikov assault rifle" to them. The Mobbs Declaration also states that, because al Qaeda and the Taliban "were and are hostile forces engaged in armed conflict with the armed forces of the United States," "individuals associated with" those groups "were and continue to be enemy combatants." Mobbs states that Hamdi was labeled an enemy combatant "based upon his interviews and in light of his association with the Taliban." According to the declaration, a series of "U.S. military screening teams" determined that Hamdi met "the criteria for enemy combatants," and "a subsequent interview of Hamdi has confirmed that he surrendered and gave his firearm to Northern Alliance forces, which supports his classification as an enemy combatant."

The District Court found that the Mobbs Declaration fell "far short" of supporting Hamdi's detention. It criticized the generic and hearsay nature of the affidavit, calling it "little more than the government's 'say-so.'" It ordered the Government to turn over numerous materials for *in camera* review. The Fourth Circuit reversed, . . . [and]

stressed that, because it was "undisputed that Hamdi was captured in a zone of active combat in a foreign theater of conflict," no factual inquiry or evidentiary hearing allowing Hamdi to be heard or to rebut the Government's assertions was necessary or proper. Concluding that the factual averments in the Mobbs Declaration, "if accurate," provided a sufficient basis upon which to conclude that the President had constitutionally detained Hamdi pursuant to the President's war powers, it ordered the habeas petition dismissed. Relying on *Ex parte Quirin*, 317 U.S. 1 (1942), the court emphasized that "one who takes up arms against the United States in a foreign theater of war, regardless of his citizenship, may properly be designated an enemy combatant and treated as such."

We now vacate the judgment below and remand.

II

The threshold question before us is whether the Executive has the authority to detain citizens who qualify as "enemy combatants." There is some debate as to the proper scope of this term, and the Government has never provided any court with the full criteria that it uses in classifying individuals as such. It has made clear, however, that, for purposes of this case, the "enemy combatant" that it is seeking to detain is an individual who, it alleges, was " 'part of or supporting forces hostile to the United States or coalition partners' " in Afghanistan and who " 'engaged in an armed conflict against the United States' " there. We therefore answer only the narrow question before us: whether the detention of citizens falling within that definition is authorized.

The Government maintains that no explicit congressional authorization is required, because the Executive possesses plenary authority to detain pursuant to Article II of the Constitution. We do not reach the question whether Article II provides such authority, however, because we agree with the Government's alternative position, that Congress has in fact authorized Hamdi's detention, through the AUMF.

Our analysis on that point, set forth below, substantially overlaps with our analysis of Hamdi's principal argument for the illegality of his detention. He posits that his detention is forbidden by 18 U.S.C. § 4001(a). Section 4001(a) states that "no citizen shall be imprisoned or otherwise detained by the United States except pursuant to an Act of Congress." Congress passed § 4001(a) in 1971 as part of a bill to repeal the Emergency Detention Act of 1950, which provided procedures for executive detention, during times of emergency, of individuals deemed likely to engage in espionage or sabotage. Congress was particularly concerned about the possibility that the Act could be used to reprise the Japanese internment camps of World War II. The Government again presses two alternative positions. First, it argues that § 4001(a), in light of its legislative history and its location in Title 18, applies only to "the control of civilian prisons and related detentions," not to military detentions. Second, it maintains that § 4001(a) is satisfied, because Hamdi is being detained "pursuant to an Act of Congress" — the AUMF. Again, because we conclude that the Government's second assertion is correct, we do not address the first. In other words, for the reasons that follow, we conclude that the AUMF is explicit congressional authorization for the detention of individuals in the narrow category we describe (assuming, without deciding, that such authorization is required), and that the AUMF satisfied § 4001(a)'s requirement that a detention be "pursuant to an Act of Congress" (assuming, without deciding, that § 4001(a) applies to military detentions).

The AUMF authorizes the President to use "all necessary and appropriate force" against "nations, organizations, or persons" associated with the September 11, 2001, terrorist attacks. There can be no doubt that individuals who fought against the United States in Afghanistan as part of the Taliban, an organization known to have supported the al Qaeda terrorist network responsible for those attacks, are individuals Congress sought to target in passing the AUMF. We conclude that detention of individuals falling into the limited category we are considering, for the duration of the particular conflict in which they were captured, is so fundamental and accepted an incident to war as to be an exercise of the "necessary and appropriate force" Congress has authorized the President to use.

The capture and detention of lawful combatants and the capture, detention, and trial of unlawful combatants, by "universal agreement and practice," are "important incidents of war." The purpose of detention is to prevent captured individuals from returning to the field of battle and taking up arms once again.

There is no bar to this Nation's holding one of its own citizens as an enemy combatant. In *Quirin*, one of the detainees, Haupt, alleged that he was a naturalized United States citizen. We held that "citizens who associate themselves with the military arm of the enemy government, and with its aid, guidance and direction enter this country bent on hostile acts, are enemy belligerents within the meaning of . . . the law of war." While Haupt was tried for violations of the law of war, nothing in *Quirin* suggests that his citizenship would have precluded his mere detention for the duration of the relevant hostilities. Nor can we see any reason for drawing such a line here. A citizen, no less than an alien, can be "part of or supporting forces hostile to the United States or coalition partners" and "engaged in an armed conflict against the United States;" such a citizen, if released, would pose the same threat of returning to the front during the ongoing conflict.

In light of these principles, it is of no moment that the AUMF does not use specific language of detention. Because detention to prevent a combatant's return to the battlefield is a fundamental incident of waging war, in permitting the use of "necessary and appropriate force," Congress has clearly and unmistakably authorized detention in the narrow circumstances considered here.

Hamdi objects, nevertheless, that Congress has not authorized the *indefinite* detention to which he is now subject. The Government responds that "the detention of enemy combatants during World War II was just as 'indefinite' while that war was being fought." We take Hamdi's objection to be not to the lack of certainty regarding the date on which the conflict will end, but to the substantial prospect of perpetual detention. We recognize that the national security underpinnings of the "war on terror," although crucially important, are broad and malleable. As the Government concedes, "given its unconventional nature, the current conflict is unlikely to end with a formal cease-fire agreement." The prospect Hamdi raises is therefore not far-fetched. If the Government does not consider this unconventional war won for two generations, and if it maintains during that time that Hamdi might, if released, rejoin forces fighting against the United States, then the position it has taken throughout the litigation of this case suggests that Hamdi's detention could last for the rest of his life.

It is a clearly established principle of the law of war that detention may last no longer than active hostilities. *See* Article 118 of the Geneva Convention (III) Relative to the Treatment of Prisoners of War ("Prisoners of war shall be released and repatriated without delay after the cessation of active hostilities").

Hamdi contends that the AUMF does not authorize indefinite or perpetual detention. Certainly, we agree that indefinite detention for the purpose of interrogation is not authorized. Further, we understand Congress' grant of authority for the use of "necessary and appropriate force" to include the authority to detain for the duration of the relevant conflict, and our understanding is based on longstanding law-of-war principles. If the practical circumstances of a given conflict are entirely unlike those of the conflicts that informed the development of the law of war, that understanding may unravel. But that is not the situation we face as of this date. Active combat operations against Taliban fighters apparently are ongoing in Afghanistan. The United States may detain, for the duration of these hostilities, individuals legitimately determined to be Taliban combatants who "engaged in an armed conflict against the United States." If the record establishes that United States troops are still involved in active combat in Afghanistan, those detentions are part of the exercise of "necessary and appropriate force," and therefore are authorized by the AUMF.

Ex parte Milligan, 4 Wall. 2, 125 (1866), does not undermine our holding about the Government's authority to seize enemy combatants, as we define that term today. In that case, the Court made repeated reference to the fact that its inquiry into whether the military tribunal had jurisdiction to try and punish Milligan turned in large part on the fact that Milligan was not a prisoner of war, but a resident of Indiana arrested while at home there. That fact was central to its conclusion. Had Milligan been captured while he was assisting Confederate soldiers by carrying a rifle against Union troops on a Confederate battlefield, the holding of the Court might well have been different. The Court's repeated explanations that Milligan was not a prisoner of war suggest that had these different circumstances been present he could have been detained under military authority for the duration of the conflict, whether or not he was a citizen.

Quirin was a unanimous opinion. It both postdates and clarifies *Milligan*, providing us with the most apposite precedent that we have on the question of whether citizens may be detained in such circumstances. Brushing aside such precedent — particularly when doing so gives rise to a host of new questions never dealt with by this Court — is unjustified and unwise.

To the extent that Justice Scalia accepts the precedential value of *Quirin*, he argues that it cannot guide our inquiry here because "in *Quirin* it was uncontested that the petitioners were members of enemy forces," while Hamdi challenges his classification as an enemy combatant. But it is unclear why, in the paradigm outlined by Justice Scalia, such a concession should have any relevance. Justice Scalia envisions a system in which the only options are congressional suspension of the writ of habeas corpus or prosecution for treason or some other crime. He does not explain how his historical analysis supports the addition of a third option — detention under some other process after concession of enemy-combatant status — or why a concession should carry any different effect than proof of enemy-combatant status in a proceeding that comports with due process. To be clear, our opinion only finds legislative authority to detain under the AUMF once it is sufficiently clear that the individual is, in fact, an enemy combatant; whether that is established by concession or by some other process that verifies this fact with sufficient certainty seems beside the point.

Further, Justice Scalia largely ignores the context of this case: a United States citizen captured in a *foreign* combat zone. Because Justice Scalia finds the fact of battlefield capture irrelevant, his distinction based on the fact that the petitioner "conceded" enemy combatant status is beside the point. Justice Scalia can point to no case or other authority for the proposition that those captured on a foreign battlefield (whether detained there or in U.S. territory) cannot be detained outside the criminal process.

Moreover, Justice Scalia presumably would come to a different result if Hamdi had been kept in Afghanistan or even Guantánamo Bay. This creates a perverse incentive. Military authorities faced with the stark choice of submitting to the full-blown criminal process or releasing a suspected enemy combatant captured on the battlefield will simply keep citizen-detainees abroad. Indeed, the Government transferred Hamdi from Guantánamo Bay to the United States naval brig only after it learned that he might be an American citizen. It is not at all clear why that should make a determinative constitutional difference.

III

Even in cases in which the detention of enemy combatants is legally authorized, there remains the question of what process is constitutionally due to a citizen who disputes his enemy-combatant status. Hamdi argues that he is owed a meaningful and timely hearing and that "extra-judicial detention [that] begins and ends with the submission of an affidavit based on third-hand hearsay" does not comport with the Fifth and Fourteenth Amendments. The Government counters that any more process than was provided below would be both unworkable and "constitutionally intolerable." Our resolution of this dispute requires a careful examination both of the writ of habeas corpus, which Hamdi now seeks to employ as a mechanism of judicial review, and of the Due Process Clause, which informs the procedural contours of that mechanism in this instance.

A

Though they reach radically different conclusions on the process that ought to attend the present proceeding, the parties begin on common ground. All agree that, absent suspension, the writ of habeas corpus remains available to every individual detained within the United States. All agree suspension of the writ has not occurred here. Thus, it is undisputed that Hamdi was properly before an Article III court to challenge his detention under 28 U.S.C. § 2241. Further, all agree that § 2241 and its companion provisions provide at least a skeletal outline of the procedures to be afforded a petitioner in federal habeas review. Most notably, § 2243 provides that "the person detained may, under oath, deny any of the facts set forth in the return or allege any other material facts," and § 2246 allows the taking of evidence in habeas proceedings by deposition, affidavit, or interrogatories.

The simple outline of § 2241 makes clear both that Congress envisioned that habeas petitioners would have some opportunity to present and rebut facts and that courts in cases like this retain some ability to vary the ways in which they do so as mandated by due process. The Government recognizes the basic procedural protections required by the habeas statute, but asks us to hold that, given both the flexibility of the habeas mechanism and the circumstances presented in this case, the presentation of the Mobbs Declaration to the habeas court completed the required factual development. It suggests two separate reasons for its position that no further process is due.

B

First, the Government urges the adoption of the Fourth Circuit's holding below — that because it is "undisputed" that Hamdi's seizure took place in a combat zone, the habeas determination can be made purely as a matter of law, with no further hearing or factfinding necessary. This argument is easily rejected. [T]he circumstances surrounding Hamdi's seizure cannot in any way be characterized as "undisputed," as "those circumstances are neither conceded in fact, nor sU.S.C.eptible to concession in law, because Hamdi has not been permitted to speak for himself or even through counsel as to those circumstances." Further, the "facts" that constitute the alleged concession are insufficient to support Hamdi's detention. Under the definition of enemy combatant that we accept today as falling within the scope of Congress' authorization, Hamdi would need to be "part of or supporting forces hostile to the United States or coalition partners" and "engaged in an armed conflict against the United States" to justify his detention in the United States for the duration of the relevant conflict. The habeas petition states only that "when seized by the United States Government, Mr. Hamdi resided in Afghanistan." An assertion that one *resided* in a country in which combat operations are taking place is not a concession that one was "*captured* in a zone of active combat operations in a foreign theater of war," and certainly is not a concession that one was "part of or supporting forces hostile to the United States or coalition partners" and "engaged in an armed conflict against the United States." Accordingly, we reject any argument that Hamdi has made concessions that eliminate any right to further process.

C

The Government's second argument requires closer consideration. This is the argument that further factual exploration is unwarranted and inappropriate in light of the extraordinary constitutional interests at stake. Under the Government's most extreme rendition of this argument, "respect for separation of powers and the limited institutional capabilities of courts in matters of military decision-making in connection with an ongoing conflict" ought to eliminate entirely any individual process, restricting the courts to investigating only whether legal authorization exists for the broader detention scheme. At most, the Government argues, courts should review its determination that a citizen is an enemy combatant under a very deferential "some evidence" standard. Under this review, a court would assume the accuracy of the Government's articulated basis for Hamdi's detention, as set forth in the Mobbs Declaration, and assess only whether that articulated basis was a legitimate one.

In response, Hamdi emphasizes that this Court consistently has recognized that an individual challenging his detention may not be held at the will of the Executive without recourse to some proceeding before a neutral tribunal to determine whether the Executive's asserted justifications for that detention have basis in fact and warrant in law. He argues that the Fourth Circuit inappropriately "ceded power to the Executive during wartime to define the conduct for which a citizen may be detained, judge whether that citizen has engaged in the proscribed conduct, and imprison that citizen indefinitely," and that due process demands that he receive a hearing in which he may challenge the Mobbs Declaration and adduce his own counter evidence. The District Court, agreeing with Hamdi, apparently believed that the appropriate process would approach the process that accompanies a criminal trial. It therefore disapproved of the hearsay nature of the Mobbs Declaration and anticipated quite extensive discovery of various military affairs. Anything less, it concluded, would not be "meaningful judicial review."

Both of these positions highlight legitimate concerns. And both emphasize the tension that often exists between the autonomy that the Government asserts is necessary in order to pursue effectively a particular goal and the process that a citizen contends he is due before he is deprived of a constitutional right. The ordinary mechanism that we use for balancing such serious competing interests, and for determining the procedures that are necessary to ensure that a citizen is not "deprived of life, liberty, or property, without due process of law," is the test that we articulated in *Mathews v. Eldridge*, 424 U.S. 319 (1976). *Mathews* dictates that the process due in any given instance is determined by weighing "the private interest that will be affected by the official action" against the Government's asserted interest, "including the function involved" and the burdens the Government would face in providing greater process. The *Mathews* calculus then contemplates a judicious balancing of these concerns, through an analysis of "the risk of an erroneous deprivation" of the private interest if the process were reduced and the "probable value, if any, of additional or substitute safeguards." We take each of these steps in turn.

1

It is beyond question that substantial interests lie on both sides of the scale in this case. Hamdi's "private interest . . . affected by the official action," is the most elemental of liberty interests — the interest in being free from physical detention by one's own government. We have always been careful not to 'minimize the importance and fundamental nature' of the individual's right to liberty, and we will not do so today.

Nor is the weight on this side of the *Mathews* scale offset by the circumstances of war or the accusation of treasonous behavior, for "it is clear that commitment for *any* purpose constitutes a significant deprivation of liberty that requires due process protection," and at this stage in the *Mathews* calculus, we consider the interest of the *erroneously* detained individual. Indeed, as *amicus* briefs from media and relief organizations emphasize, the risk of erroneous deprivation of a citizen's liberty in the absence of sufficient process here is very real (noting ways in which "the nature of humanitarian relief work and journalism present a significant risk of mistaken military detentions"). Moreover, as critical as the Government's interest may be in detaining those who actually pose an immediate threat to the national security of the United States during ongoing international conflict, history and common sense teach us that an unchecked system of detention carries the potential to become a means for oppression and abuse of others who do not present that sort of threat. Because we live in a society in which "mere public intolerance or animosity cannot constitutionally justify the deprivation of a person's physical liberty," our starting point for the *Mathews v. Eldridge* analysis is unaltered by the allegations surrounding the particular detainee or the organizations with which he is alleged to have associated. We reaffirm today the fundamental nature of a citizen's right to be free from involuntary confinement by his own government without due process of law, and we weigh the opposing governmental interests against the curtailment of liberty that such confinement entails.

2

On the other side of the scale are the weighty and sensitive governmental interests in ensuring that those who have in fact fought with the enemy during a war do not return to battle against the United States. As discussed above, the law of war and the realities of combat may render such detentions both necessary and appropriate, and our due process analysis need not blink at those realities. Without doubt, our Constitution recognizes that core strategic matters of warmaking belong in the hands of those who are best positioned and most politically accountable for making them. *Youngstown Sheet & Tube Co. v. Sawyer* (acknowledging "broad powers in military commanders engaged in day-to-day fighting in a theater of war").

The Government also argues at some length that its interests in reducing the process available to alleged enemy combatants are heightened by the practical difficulties that would accompany a system of trial-like process. In its view, military officers who are engaged in the serious work of waging battle would be unnecessarily and dangerously distracted by litigation half a world away, and discovery into military operations would both intrude on the sensitive secrets of national defense and result in a futile search for evidence buried under the rubble of war. To the extent that these burdens are triggered by heightened procedures, they are properly taken into account in our due process analysis.

3

Striking the proper constitutional balance here is of great importance to the Nation during this period of ongoing combat. But it is equally vital that our calculus not give short shrift to the values that this country holds dear or to the privilege that is American citizenship. It is during our most challenging and uncertain moments that our Nation's commitment to due process is most severely tested; and it is in those times that we must preserve our commitment at home to the principles for which we fight abroad. See *United States v. Robel*, 389 U.S. 258, 264 (1967) ("It would indeed be ironic if, in the name of national defense, we would sanction the subversion of one of those liberties . . . which makes the defense of the Nation worthwhile").

With due recognition of these competing concerns, we believe that neither the process proposed by the Government nor the process apparently envisioned by the District Court below strikes the proper constitutional balance when a United States citizen is detained in the United States as an enemy combatant. That is, "the risk of erroneous deprivation" of a detainee's liberty interest is unacceptably high under the Government's proposed rule, while some of the "additional or substitute procedural safeguards" suggested by the District Court are unwarranted in light of their limited "probable value" and the burdens they may impose on the military in such cases.

We therefore hold that a citizen-detainee seeking to challenge his classification as an enemy combatant must receive notice of the factual basis for his classification, and a fair opportunity to rebut the Government's factual assertions before a neutral decisionmaker.

At the same time, the exigencies of the circumstances may demand that, aside from these core elements, enemy combatant proceedings may be tailored to alleviate their uncommon potential to burden the Executive at a time of ongoing military conflict. Hearsay, for example, may need to be accepted as the most reliable available evidence from the Government in such a proceeding. Likewise, the Constitution would not be offended by a presumption in favor of the Government's evidence, so long as that presumption remained a rebuttable one and fair opportunity for rebuttal were provided. Thus, once the Government puts forth credible evidence that the habeas petitioner meets the enemy-combatant criteria, the onus could shift to the petitioner to rebut that evidence with more persuasive evidence that he falls outside the criteria. A burden-shifting scheme of this sort would meet the goal of ensuring that the errant tourist, embedded journalist, or local aid worker has a chance to prove military error while giving due regard to the Executive once it has put forth meaningful support for its conclusion that the detainee is in fact an enemy combatant. In the words of *Mathews*, process of this sort would sufficiently address the "risk of erroneous deprivation" of a detainee's liberty interest while eliminating certain procedures that have questionable additional value in light of the burden on the *Government.*

We think it unlikely that this basic process will have the dire impact on the central functions of warmaking that the Government forecasts. The parties agree that initial captures on the battlefield need not receive the process we have discussed here; that process is due only when the determination is made to *continue* to hold those who have been seized. The Government has made clear in its briefing that documentation regarding battlefield detainees already is kept in the ordinary course of military affairs. Any factfinding imposition created by requiring a knowledgeable affiant to summarize these records to an independent tribunal is a minimal one. Likewise, arguments that military officers ought not have to wage war under the threat of litigation lose much of their steam when factual disputes at enemy-combatant hearings are limited to the alleged combatant's acts. This focus meddles little, if at all, in the strategy or conduct of war, inquiring only into the appropriateness of continuing to detain an individual claimed to have taken up arms against the United States. While we accord the greatest respect and consideration to the judgments of military authorities in matters relating to the actual prosecution of a war, and recognize that the scope of that discretion necessarily is wide, it does not infringe on the core role of the military for the courts to exercise their own time-honored and constitutionally mandated roles of reviewing and resolving claims like those presented here.

In sum, while the full protections that accompany challenges to detentions in other settings may prove unworkable and inappropriate in the enemy-combatant setting, the threats to military operations posed by a basic system of independent review are not so weighty as to trump a citizen's core rights to challenge meaningfully the Government's case and to be heard by an impartial adjudicator.

D

In so holding, we necessarily reject the Government's assertion that separation of powers principles mandate a heavily circumscribed role for the courts in such circumstances. Indeed, the position that the courts must forgo any examination of the individual case and focus exclusively on the legality of the broader detention scheme cannot be mandated by any reasonable view of separation of powers, as this approach serves only to *condense* power into a single branch of government. We have long since made clear that a state of war is not a blank check for the President when it comes to the rights of the Nation's citizens. *Youngstown Sheet & Tube.* Whatever power the United States Constitution envisions for the Executive in its exchanges with other nations or with enemy organizations in times of conflict, it most assuredly envisions a role for all three branches when individual liberties are at stake. Likewise, we have made clear that, unless Congress acts to suspend it, the Great Writ of habeas corpus allows the Judicial Branch to play a necessary role in maintaining this delicate balance of governance, serving as an important judicial check on the Executive's discretion in the realm of detentions. Thus, while we do not question that our due process assessment must pay keen attention to the particular burdens faced by the Executive in the context of military action, it would turn our system of checks and balances on its head to suggest that a citizen could not make his way to court with a challenge to the factual basis for his detention by his government, simply because the Executive opposes making available such a challenge. Absent suspension of the writ by Congress, a citizen detained as an enemy combatant is entitled to this process.

Because we conclude that due process demands some system for a citizen detainee to refute his classification, the proposed "some evidence" standard is inadequate. Any process in which the Executive's factual assertions go wholly unchallenged or are simply presumed correct without any opportunity for the alleged combatant to demonstrate otherwise falls constitutionally short. Aside from unspecified "screening" processes, and military interrogations in which the Government suggests Hamdi could have contested his classification, Hamdi has received no process. An interrogation by one's captor, however effective an intelligence-gathering tool, hardly constitutes a constitutionally adequate factfinding before a neutral decisionmaker. Plainly, the "process" Hamdi has received is not that to which he is entitled under the Due Process Clause.

There remains the possibility that the standards we have articulated could be met by an appropriately authorized and properly constituted military tribunal. Indeed, it is notable that military regulations already provide for such process in related instances, dictating that tribunals be made available to determine the status of enemy detainees who assert prisoner-of-war status under the Geneva Convention. In the absence of such process, however, a court that receives a petition for a writ of habeas corpus from an alleged enemy combatant must itself ensure that the minimum requirements of due process are achieved. Both courts below recognized as much, focusing their energies on the question of whether Hamdi was due an opportunity to rebut the Government's case against him. The Government, too, proceeded on this assumption, presenting its affidavit and then seeking that it be evaluated under a deferential standard of review based on burdens that it alleged would accompany any greater process.

IV

Hamdi asks us to hold that the Fourth Circuit also erred by denying him immediate access to counsel upon his detention and by disposing of the case without permitting him to meet with an attorney. Since our grant of certiorari in this case, Hamdi has been appointed counsel, with whom he has met for consultation purposes on several occasions, and with whom he is now being granted unmonitored meetings. He unquestionably has the right to access to counsel in connection with the proceedings on remand. No further consideration of this issue is necessary at this stage of the case.

The judgment of the United States Court of Appeals for the Fourth Circuit is vacated, and the case is remanded for further proceedings.

JUSTICE SOUTER, with whom JUSTICE GINSBURG joins, concurring in part, dissenting in part, and concurring in the judgment.

The plurality . . . accept[s] the Government's position that if Hamdi's designation as an enemy combatant is correct, his detention (at least as to some period) is authorized by an Act of Congress as required by § 4001(a), that is, by the Authorization for Use of Military Force. Here, I disagree and respectfully dissent. The Government has failed to demonstrate that the Force Resolution authorizes the detention complained of here even on the facts the Government claims. If the Government raises nothing further than the record now shows, the Non-Detention Act entitles Hamdi to be released.

The threshold issue is how broadly or narrowly to read the Non-Detention Act, the tone of which is severe: "No citizen shall be imprisoned or otherwise detained by the United States except pursuant to an Act of Congress." Should the severity of the Act be relieved when the Government's stated factual justification for incommunicado detention is a war on terrorism, so that the Government may be said to act "pursuant" to congressional terms that fall short of explicit authority to imprison individuals' With one possible though important qualification, the answer has to be no. For a number of reasons, the prohibition within § 4001(a) has to be read broadly to accord the statute a long reach and to impose a burden of justification on the Government.

[E]ven if history had spared us the cautionary example of the internments in World War II, even if there had been no *Korematsu*, and *Endo* had set no principle of statutory interpretation, there would be a compelling reason to read § 4001(a) to demand manifest authority to detain before detention is authorized. The defining character of American constitutional government is its constant tension between security and liberty, serving both by partial helpings of each. In a government of separated powers, deciding finally on what is a reasonable degree of guaranteed liberty whether in peace or war (or some condition in between) is not well entrusted to the Executive Branch of Government, whose particular responsibility is to maintain security. For reasons of inescapable human nature, the branch of the Government asked to counter a serious threat is not the branch on which to rest the Nation's entire reliance in striking the balance between the will to win and the cost in liberty on the way to victory; the responsibility for security will naturally amplify the claim that security legitimately raises. A reasonable balance is more likely to be reached on the judgment of a different branch, just as Madison said in remarking that "the constant aim is to divide and arrange the several offices in such a manner as that each may be a check on the other — that the private interest of every individual may be a sentinel over the public rights." The Federalist No. 51. Hence the need for an assessment by Congress before citizens are subject to lockup, and likewise the need for a clearly expressed congressional resolution of the competing claims.

Next, there is the Government's claim, accepted by the Court, that the terms of the Force Resolution are adequate to authorize detention of an enemy combatant under the circumstances described, a claim the Government fails to support sufficiently to satisfy § 4001(a) as read to require a clear statement of authority to detain. Since the Force Resolution was adopted one week after the attacks of September 11, 2001, it naturally speaks with some generality, but its focus is clear, and that is on the use of military power. It is fairly read to authorize the use of armies and weapons, whether against other armies or individual terrorists. But, like the statute discussed in *Endo*, it never so much as uses the word detention, and there is no reason to think Congress might have perceived any need to augment Executive power to deal with dangerous citizens within the United States, given the well-stocked statutory arsenal of defined criminal offenses covering the gamut of actions that a citizen sympathetic to terrorists might commit.

Even so, there is one argument for treating the Force Resolution as sufficiently clear to authorize detention of a citizen consistently with § 4001(a). Assuming the argument to be sound, however, the Government is in no position to claim its advantage.

Because the Force Resolution authorizes the use of military force in acts of war by the United States, the argument goes, it is reasonably clear that the military and its Commander in Chief are authorized to deal with enemy belligerents according to the treaties and customs known collectively as the laws of war. Accordingly, the United States may detain captured enemies, and *Ex parte Quirin* may perhaps be claimed for the proposition that the American citizenship of such a captive does not as such limit the Government's power to deal with him under the usages of war. Thus, the Government here repeatedly argues that Hamdi's detention amounts to nothing more than customary detention of a captive taken on the field of battle: if the usages of war are fairly authorized by the Force Resolution, Hamdi's detention is authorized for purposes of § 4001(a).

There is no need, however, to address the merits of such an argument in all possible circumstances. For now it is enough to recognize that the Government's stated legal position in its campaign against the Taliban (among whom Hamdi was allegedly captured) is apparently at odds with its claim here to be acting in accordance with customary law of war and hence to be within the terms of the Force Resolution in its detention of Hamdi. In a statement of its legal position cited in its brief, the Government says that "the Geneva Convention applies to the Taliban detainees." Hamdi presumably is such a detainee, since according to the Government's own account, he was taken bearing arms on the Taliban side of a field of battle in Afghanistan. He would therefore seem to qualify for treatment as a prisoner of war under the Third Geneva Convention, to which the United States is a party.

By holding him incommunicado, however, the Government obviously has not been treating him as a prisoner of war, and in fact the Government claims that no Taliban detainee is entitled to prisoner of war status. This treatment appears to be a violation of the Geneva Convention provision that even in cases of doubt, captives are entitled to be treated as prisoners of war "until such time as their status has been determined by a competent tribunal." The Government answers that the President's determination that Taliban detainees do not qualify as prisoners of war is conclusive as to Hamdi's status and removes any doubt that would trigger application of the Convention's tribunal requirement. But reliance on this categorical pronouncement to settle doubt is apparently at odds with the military regulation, adopted to implement the Geneva Convention, and setting out a detailed procedure for a military tribunal to determine an individual's status. One of the types of doubt these tribunals are meant to settle is whether a given individual may be, as Hamdi says he is, an "innocent civilian who should be immediately returned to his home or released." The regulation, jointly promulgated by the Headquarters of the Departments of the Army, Navy, Air Force, and Marine Corps, provides that "persons who have been determined by a competent tribunal not to be entitled to prisoner of war status may not be executed, imprisoned, or otherwise penalized without further proceedings to determine what acts they have committed and what penalty should be imposed." The regulation also incorporates the Geneva Convention's presumption that in cases of doubt, "persons shall enjoy the protection of the . . . Convention until such time as their status has been determined by a competent tribunal." Thus, there is reason to question whether the United States is acting in accordance with the laws of war it claims as authority.

Whether, or to what degree, the Government is in fact violating the Geneva Convention and is thus acting outside the customary usages of war are not matters I can resolve at this point. What I can say, though, is that the Government has not made out its claim that in detaining Hamdi in the manner described, it is acting in accord with the laws of war authorized to be applied against citizens by the Force Resolution. I conclude accordingly that the Government has failed to support the position that the Force Resolution authorizes the described detention of Hamdi for purposes of § 4001(a).

It is worth adding a further reason for requiring the Government to bear the burden of clearly justifying its claim to be exercising recognized war powers before declaring § 4001(a) satisfied. Thirty-eight days after adopting the Force Resolution, Congress passed the statute entitled Uniting and Strengthening America by Providing Appropriate Tools Required to Intercept and Obstruct Terrorism Act of 2001 (USA PATRIOT Act); that Act authorized the detention of alien terrorists for no more than seven days in the absence of criminal charges or deportation proceedings. It is very difficult to believe that the same Congress that carefully circumscribed Executive power over alien terrorists on home soil would not have meant to require the Government to justify clearly its detention of an American citizen held on home soil incommunicado.

Since the Government has given no reason either to deflect the application of § 4001(a) or to hold it to be satisfied, I need to go no further; the Government hints of a constitutional challenge to the statute, but it presents none here. I will, however, stray across the line between statutory and constitutional territory just far enough to note the weakness of the Government's mixed claim of inherent, extrastatutory authority under a combination of Article II of the Constitution and the usages of war. It is in fact in this connection that the Government developed its argument that the exercise of war powers justifies the detention, and what I have just said about its inadequacy applies here as well. Beyond that, it is instructive to recall Justice Jackson's observation that the President is not Commander in Chief of the country, only of the military.

There may be room for one qualification to Justice Jackson's statement, however: in a moment of genuine emergency, when the Government must act with no time for deliberation, the Executive may be able to detain a citizen if there is reason to fear he is an imminent threat to the safety of the Nation and its people (though I doubt there is any want of statutory authority). This case, however, does not present that question, because an emergency power of necessity must at least be limited by the emergency; Hamdi has been locked up for over two years.

Whether insisting on the careful scrutiny of emergency claims or on a vigorous reading of § 4001(a), we are heirs to a tradition given voice 800 years ago by Magna Carta, which, on the barons' insistence, confined executive power by "the law of the land."

Because I find Hamdi's detention forbidden by § 4001(a) and unauthorized by the Force Resolution, I would not reach any questions of what process he may be due in litigating disputed issues in a proceeding under the habeas statute or prior to the habeas enquiry itself. For me, it suffices that the Government has failed to justify holding him in the absence of a further Act of Congress, criminal charges, a showing that the detention conforms to the laws of war, or a demonstration that § 4001(a) is unconstitutional. I would therefore vacate the judgment of the Court of Appeals and remand for proceedings consistent with this view.

Since this disposition does not command a majority of the Court, however, the need to give practical effect to the conclusions of eight members of the Court rejecting the Government's position calls for me to join with the plurality in ordering remand on terms closest to those I would impose. Although I think litigation of Hamdi's status as an enemy combatant is unnecessary, the terms of the plurality's remand will allow Hamdi to offer evidence that he is not an enemy combatant, and he should at the least have the benefit of that opportunity.

It should go without saying that in joining with the plurality to produce a judgment, I do not adopt the plurality's resolution of constitutional issues that I would not reach. It is not that I could disagree with the plurality's determinations (given the plurality's view of the Force Resolution) that someone in Hamdi's position is entitled at a minimum to notice of the Government's claimed factual basis for holding him, and to a fair chance to rebut it before a neutral decision maker; nor, of course, could I disagree with the plurality's affirmation of Hamdi's right to counsel. On the other hand, I do not mean to imply agreement that the Government could claim an evidentiary presumption casting the burden of rebuttal on Hamdi, or that an opportunity to litigate before a military tribunal might obviate or truncate enquiry by a court on habeas.

Subject to these qualifications, I join with the plurality in a judgment of the Court vacating the Fourth Circuit's judgment and remanding the case.

JUSTICE SCALIA, with whom JUSTICE STEVENS joins, dissenting.

Petitioner, a presumed American citizen, has been imprisoned without charge or hearing in the Norfolk and Charleston Naval Brigs for more than two years, on the allegation that he is an enemy combatant who bore arms against his country for the Taliban. His father claims to the contrary, that he is an inexperienced aid worker caught in the wrong place at the wrong time. This case brings into conflict the competing demands of national security and our citizens' constitutional right to personal liberty. Although I share the Court's evident unease as it seeks to reconcile the two, I do not agree with its resolution.

Where the Government accuses a citizen of waging war against it, our constitutional tradition has been to prosecute him in federal court for treason or some other crime. Where the exigencies of war prevent that, the Constitution's Suspension Clause, allows Congress to relax the usual protections temporarily. Absent suspension, however, the Executive's assertion of military exigency has not been thought sufficient to permit detention without charge. No one contends that the congressional Authorization for Use of Military Force, on which the Government relies to justify its actions here, is an implementation of the Suspension Clause. Accordingly, I would reverse the decision below.

I

The very core of liberty secured by our Anglo-Saxon system of separated powers has been freedom from indefinite imprisonment at the will of the Executive. Blackstone stated this principle clearly:

> "Of great importance to the public is the preservation of this personal liberty: for if once it were left in the power of any, the highest, magistrate to imprison arbitrarily whomever he or his officers thought proper . . . there would soon be an end of all other rights and immunities. . . . To bereave a man of life, or by violence to confiscate his estate, without accusation or trial, would be so gross and notorious an act of despotism, as must at once convey the alarm of tyranny throughout the whole kingdom. But confinement of the person, by secretly hurrying him to gaol, where his sufferings are unknown or forgotten; is a less public, a less striking, and therefore a more dangerous engine of arbitrary government. . . .

> "To make imprisonment lawful, it must either be, by process from the courts of judicature, or by warrant from some legal officer, having authority to commit to prison; which warrant must be in writing, under the hand and seal of the magistrate, and express the causes of the commitment, in order to be examined into (if necessary) upon a *habeas corpus*. If there be no cause expressed, the gaoler is not bound to detain the prisoner. For the law judges in this respect, . . . that it is unreasonable to send a prisoner, and not to signify withal the crimes alleged against him."

1 W. BLACKSTONE, COMMENTARIES ON THE LAWS OF ENGLAND 132–133 (1765) (hereinafter Blackstone).

These words were well known to the Founders. Hamilton quoted from this very passage in THE FEDERALIST No. 84. The two ideas central to Blackstone's understanding — due process as the right secured, and habeas corpus as the instrument by which due process could be insisted upon by a citizen illegally imprisoned — found expression in the Constitution's Due Process and Suspension Clauses.

The gist of the Due Process Clause, as understood at the founding and since, was to force the Government to follow those common-law procedures traditionally deemed necessary before depriving a person of life, liberty, or property.

To be sure, certain types of permissible *non*criminal detention — that is, those not dependent upon the contention that the citizen had committed a criminal act — did not require the protections of criminal procedure. However, these fell into a limited number of well-recognized exceptions — civil commitment of the mentally ill, for example, and temporary detention in quarantine of the infectious. It is unthinkable that the Executive could render otherwise criminal grounds for detention noncriminal merely by disclaiming an intent to prosecute, or by asserting that it was incapacitating dangerous offenders rather than punishing wrongdoing.

These due process rights have historically been vindicated by the writ of habeas corpus. In England before the founding, the writ developed into a tool for challenging executive confinement. It was not always effective. [As a result, the Habeas Corpus Act of 1679 added additional protections.]

The writ of habeas corpus was preserved in the Constitution — the only common-law writ to be explicitly mentioned. Hamilton lauded "the establishment of the writ of *habeas corpus*" in his FEDERALIST defense as a means to protect against "the practice of arbitrary imprisonments . . . in all ages, [one of] the favourite and most formidable instruments of tyranny." THE FEDERALIST No. 84. Indeed, availability of the writ under the new Constitution (along with the requirement of trial by jury in criminal cases) was his basis for arguing that additional, explicit procedural protections were unnecessary.

II

The allegations here, of course, are no ordinary accusations of criminal activity. Yaser Esam Hamdi has been imprisoned because the Government believes he participated in the waging of war against the United States. The relevant question, then, is whether there is a different, special procedure for imprisonment of a citizen accused of wrongdoing *by aiding the enemy in wartime*.

A

Justice O'Connor, writing for a plurality of this Court, asserts that captured enemy combatants (other than those suspected of war crimes) have traditionally been detained until the cessation of hostilities and then released. That is probably an accurate description of wartime practice with respect to enemy *aliens*. The tradition with respect to American citizens, however, has been quite different. Citizens aiding the enemy have been treated as traitors subject to the criminal process.

The modern treason statute is 18 U.S.C. § 2381; it basically tracks the language of the constitutional provision. Other provisions of Title 18 criminalize various acts of warmaking and adherence to the enemy. The only citizen other than Hamdi known to be imprisoned in connection with military hostilities in Afghanistan against the United States *was* subjected to criminal process and convicted upon a guilty plea. *See United States v. Lindh*, 212 F. Supp. 2d 541 (E.D. Va. 2002).

B

There are times when military exigency renders resort to the traditional criminal process impracticable. English law accommodated such exigencies by allowing legislative suspension of the writ of habeas corpus for brief periods.

Our Federal Constitution contains a provision explicitly permitting suspension, but limiting the situations in which it may be invoked: "The privilege of the Writ of Habeas Corpus shall not be suspended, unless when in Cases of Rebellion or Invasion the public Safety may require it." Although this provision does not state that suspension must be effected by, or authorized by, a legislative act, it has been so understood, consistent with English practice and the Clause's placement in Article I.

The Suspension Clause was by design a safety valve, the Constitution's only "express provision for exercise of extraordinary authority because of a crisis," *Youngstown Sheet*

& Tube Co. v. Sawyer (Jackson, J., concurring). Very early in the Nation's history, President Jefferson unsuccessfully sought a suspension of habeas corpus to deal with Aaron Burr's conspiracy to overthrow the Government. During the Civil War, Congress passed its first Act authorizing Executive suspension of the writ of habeas corpus, to the relief of those many who thought President Lincoln's unauthorized proclamations of suspension unconstitutional. Later Presidential proclamations of suspension relied upon the congressional authorization. During Reconstruction, Congress passed the Ku Klux Klan Act, which included a provision authorizing suspension of the writ, invoked by President Grant in quelling a rebellion in nine South Carolina counties.

III

Of course the extensive historical evidence of criminal convictions and habeas suspensions does not *necessarily* refute the Government's position in this case. When the writ is suspended, the Government is entirely free from judicial oversight. It does not claim such total liberation here, but argues that it need only produce what it calls "some evidence" to satisfy a habeas court that a detained individual is an enemy combatant. Even if suspension of the writ on the one hand, and committal for criminal charges on the other hand, have been the only *traditional* means of dealing with citizens who levied war against their own country, it is theoretically possible that the Constitution does not *require* a choice between these alternatives.

I believe, however, that substantial evidence does refute that possibility. First, the text of the 1679 Habeas Corpus Act makes clear that indefinite imprisonment on reasonable suspicion is not an available option of treatment for those accused of aiding the enemy, absent a suspension of the writ. In the United States, this Act was read as "enforcing the common law," and shaped the early understanding of the scope of the writ.

Writings from the founding generation also suggest that, without exception, the only constitutional alternatives are to charge the crime or suspend the writ. President Lincoln, when he purported to suspend habeas corpus without congressional authorization during the Civil War, apparently did not doubt that suspension was required if the prisoner was to be held without criminal trial. In his famous message to Congress on July 4, 1861, he argued only that he could suspend the writ, not that even without suspension, his imprisonment of citizens without criminal trial was permitted.

Further evidence comes from this Court's decision in *Ex parte Milligan*. There, the Court issued the writ to an American citizen who had been tried by military commission for offenses that included conspiring to overthrow the Government, seize munitions, and liberate prisoners of war. The Court rejected in no uncertain terms the Government's assertion that military jurisdiction was proper "under the laws and usages of war:"

> It can serve no useful purpose to inquire what those laws and usages are, whence they originated, where found, and on whom they operate; they can never be applied to citizens in states which have upheld the authority of the government, and where the courts are open and their process unobstructed.

Milligan is not exactly this case, of course, since the petitioner was threatened with death, not merely imprisonment. But the reasoning and conclusion of *Milligan* logically cover the present case. The Government justifies imprisonment of Hamdi on principles of the law of war and admits that, absent the war, it would have no such authority. But if the law of war cannot be applied to citizens where courts are open, then Hamdi's imprisonment without criminal trial is no less unlawful than Milligan's trial by military tribunal.

IV

The Government argues that our more recent jurisprudence ratifies its indefinite imprisonment of a citizen within the territorial jurisdiction of federal courts. It places primary reliance upon *Ex parte Quirin*, a World War II case upholding the trial by military commission of eight German saboteurs, one of whom, Hans Haupt, was a U.S. citizen. The case was not this Court's finest hour. The Court upheld the commission and denied relief in a brief *per curiam* issued the day after oral argument concluded; a week later the Government carried out the commission's death sentence upon six saboteurs, including Haupt. The Court eventually explained its reasoning in a written opinion issued several months later.

Only three paragraphs of the Court's lengthy opinion dealt with the particular circumstances of Haupt's case. The Government argued that Haupt, like the other petitioners, could be tried by military commission under the laws of war. In agreeing with that contention, *Quirin* purported to interpret the language of *Milligan* quoted above (the law of war "can never be applied to citizens in states which have upheld the authority of the government, and where the courts are open and their process unobstructed") in the following manner:

> Elsewhere in its opinion . . . the Court was at pains to point out that Milligan, a citizen twenty years resident in Indiana, who had never been a resident of any of the states in rebellion, was not an enemy belligerent either entitled to the status of a prisoner of war or subject to the penalties imposed upon unlawful belligerents. We construe the Court's statement as to the inapplicability of the law of war to Milligan's case as having particular reference to the facts before it. From them the Court concluded that Milligan, not being a part of or associated with the armed forces of the enemy, was a non-belligerent, not subject to the law of war.

[E]ven if *Quirin* gave a correct description of *Milligan*, or made an irrevocable revision of it, *Quirin* would still not justify denial of the writ here. In *Quirin* it was uncontested that the petitioners were members of enemy forces. They were "*admitted* enemy invaders," and it was "undisputed" that they had landed in the United States in service of German forces. The specific holding of the Court was only that, "upon the *conceded* facts," the petitioners were "plainly within [the] boundaries" of military jurisdiction. But where those jurisdictional facts are *not* conceded — where the petitioner insists that he is *not* a belligerent — *Quirin* left the pre-existing law in place: Absent suspension of the writ, a citizen held where the courts are open is entitled either to criminal trial or to a judicial decree requiring his release.

V

It follows from what I have said that Hamdi is entitled to a habeas decree requiring his release unless (1) criminal proceedings are promptly brought, or (2) Congress has suspended the writ of habeas corpus. A suspension of the writ could, of course, lay down conditions for continued detention, similar to those that today's opinion prescribes under the Due Process Clause. But there is a world of difference between the people's representatives' determining the need for that suspension (and prescribing the conditions for it), and this Court's doing so.

The plurality finds justification for Hamdi's imprisonment in the Authorization for Use of Military Force. [The AUMF] is not remotely a congressional suspension of the writ, and no one claims that it is. Contrary to the plurality's view, I do not think this statute even authorizes detention of a citizen with the clarity necessary to satisfy the interpretive canon that statutes should be construed so as to avoid grave constitutional concerns; with the clarity necessary to comport with cases such as *Ex parte Endo* and *Duncan v. Kahanamoku* or with the clarity necessary to overcome the statutory prescription [of] § 4001(a). But even if it did, I would not permit it to overcome Hamdi's entitlement to habeas corpus relief. The Suspension Clause of the Constitution, which carefully circumscribes the conditions under which the writ can be withheld, would be a sham if it could be evaded by congressional prescription of requirements *other than the common-law requirement of committal for criminal prosecution* that render the writ, though available, unavailing.

Having found a congressional authorization for detention of citizens where none clearly exists; and having discarded the categorical procedural protection of the Suspension Clause; the plurality then proceeds, under the guise of the Due Process Clause, to prescribe what procedural protections *it* thinks appropriate.

Having distorted the Suspension Clause, the plurality finishes up by transmogrifying the Great Writ — disposing of the present habeas petition by remanding for the District Court to "engage in a factfinding process that is both prudent and incremental." This judicial remediation of executive default is unheard of. The role of habeas corpus is to determine the legality of executive detention, not to supply the omitted process necessary to make it legal. It is not the habeas court's function to make illegal detention legal by supplying a process that the Government could have provided, but chose not to. If Hamdi is being imprisoned in violation of the Constitution (because without due process of law), then his habeas petition should be granted; the Executive may then hand him over to the criminal authorities, whose detention for the purpose of prosecution will be lawful, or else must release him.

There is a certain harmony of approach in the plurality's making up for Congress's failure to invoke the Suspension Clause and its making up for the Executive's failure to apply what it says are needed procedures — an approach that reflects what might be called a Mr. Fix-it Mentality. The plurality seems to view it as its mission to Make Everything Come Out Right, rather than merely to decree the consequences, as far as individual rights are concerned, of the other two branches' actions and omissions. Has the Legislature failed to suspend the writ in the current dire emergency? Well, we will remedy that failure by prescribing the reasonable conditions that a suspension should have included. And has the Executive failed to live up to those reasonable conditions? Well, we will ourselves make that failure good, so that this dangerous fellow (if he is dangerous) need not be set free. The problem with this approach is not only that it steps out of the courts' modest and limited role in a democratic society; but that by repeatedly doing what it thinks the political branches ought to do it encourages their lassitude and saps the vitality of government by the people.

VI

Several limitations give my views in this matter a relatively narrow compass. They apply only to citizens, accused of being enemy combatants, who are detained within the territorial jurisdiction of a federal court. This is not likely to be a numerous group; currently we know of only two, Hamdi and Jose Padilla. Where the citizen is captured outside and held outside the United States, the constitutional requirements may be different. Moreover, even within the United States, the accused citizen-enemy combatant may lawfully be detained once prosecution is in progress or in contemplation. The Government has been notably successful in securing conviction, and hence long-term custody or execution, of those who have waged war against the state.

I frankly do not know whether these tools are sufficient to meet the Government's security needs, including the need to obtain intelligence through interrogation. It is far beyond my competence, or the Court's competence, to determine that. But it is not beyond Congress's. If the situation demands it, the Executive can ask Congress to authorize suspension of the writ — which can be made subject to whatever conditions Congress deems appropriate, including even the procedural novelties invented by the plurality today. To be sure, suspension is limited by the Constitution to cases of rebellion or invasion. But whether the attacks of September 11, 2001, constitute an "invasion," and whether those attacks still justify suspension several years later, are questions for Congress rather than this Court. If civil rights are to be curtailed during wartime, it must be done openly and democratically, as the Constitution requires, rather than by silent erosion through an opinion of this Court.

Many think it not only inevitable but entirely proper that liberty give way to security in times of national crisis — that, at the extremes of military exigency, *inter arma silent leges*. Whatever the general merits of the view that war silences law or modulates its voice, that view has no place in the interpretation and application of a Constitution designed precisely to confront war and, in a manner that accords with democratic principles, to accommodate it. Because the Court has proceeded to meet the current emergency in a manner the Constitution does not envision. I respectfully dissent.

JUSTICE THOMAS, dissenting.

The Executive Branch, acting pursuant to the powers vested in the President by the Constitution and with explicit congressional approval, has determined that Yaser Hamdi is an enemy combatant and should be detained. This detention falls squarely within the Federal Government's war powers, and we lack the expertise and capacity to second-guess that decision. As such, petitioners' habeas challenge should fail, and there is no reason to remand the case. The plurality reaches a contrary conclusion by failing adequately to consider basic principles of the constitutional structure as it relates to national security and foreign affairs and by using the balancing scheme of *Mathews v. Eldridge*. I do not think that the Federal Government's war powers can be balanced away by this Court. Arguably, Congress could provide for additional procedural protections, but until it does, we have no right to insist upon them. But even if I were to agree with the general approach the plurality takes, I could not accept the particulars. The plurality utterly fails to account for the Government's compelling interests and for our own institutional inability to weigh competing concerns correctly. I respectfully dissent.

I

"It is 'obvious and unarguable' that no governmental interest is more compelling than the security of the Nation." The national security, after all, is the primary responsibility and purpose of the Federal Government. But because the Founders understood that they could not foresee the myriad potential threats to national security that might later arise, they chose to create a Federal Government that necessarily possesses sufficient power to handle any threat to the security of the Nation.

The Founders intended that the President have primary responsibility — along with the necessary power — to protect the national security and to conduct the Nation's foreign relations. They did so principally because the structural advantages of a unitary Executive are essential in these domains. This is because "decision, activity, secrecy, and dispatch will generally characterise the proceedings of one man, in a much more eminent degree, than the proceedings of any greater number."

These structural advantages are most important in the national-security and foreign-affairs contexts. "Of all the cares or concerns of government, the direction of war most peculiarly demands those qualities which distinguish the exercise of power by a single hand." THE FEDERALIST No. 74 (A. Hamilton). Also for these reasons, John Marshall explained that "the President is the sole organ of the nation in its external relations, and its sole representative with foreign nations." To this end, the Constitution vests in the President "the executive Power," provides that he "shall be Commander in Chief of the" armed forces, and places in him the power to recognize foreign governments.

This Court has long recognized these features and has accordingly held that the President has *constitutional* authority to protect the national security and that this authority carries with it broad discretion.

Congress, to be sure, has a substantial and essential role in both foreign affairs and national security. But it is crucial to recognize that *judicial* interference in these domains destroys the purpose of vesting primary responsibility in a unitary Executive. Several points, made forcefully by Justice Jackson, are worth emphasizing. First, with respect to certain decisions relating to national security and foreign affairs, the courts simply lack the relevant information and expertise to second-guess determinations made by the President based on information properly withheld. Second, even if the courts could compel the Executive to produce the necessary information, such decisions are simply not amenable to judicial determination because "they are delicate, complex, and involve large elements of prophecy." Third, the Court has correctly recognized the primacy of the political branches in the foreign-affairs and national-security contexts.

To be sure, the Court has at times held, in specific circumstances, that the military acted beyond its warmaking authority. But these cases are distinguishable in important ways. In *Ex parte Endo*, the Court held unlawful the detention of an admittedly law-abiding and loyal American of Japanese ancestry. It did so because the Government's asserted reason for the detention had nothing to do with the congressional and executive authorities upon which the Government relied. Those authorities permitted detention for the purpose of preventing espionage and sabotage and thus could not be pressed into service for detaining a loyal citizen. And in *Youngstown*, Justice Jackson emphasized that "Congress had not left seizure of private property an open field but had covered it by three statutory policies inconsistent with the seizure."

I acknowledge that the question whether Hamdi's executive detention is lawful is a question properly resolved by the Judicial Branch, though the question comes to the Court with the strongest presumptions in favor of the Government. The plurality agrees that Hamdi's detention is lawful if he is an enemy combatant. But the question whether Hamdi is actually an enemy combatant is "of a kind for which the Judiciary has neither aptitude, facilities nor responsibility and which has long been held to belong in the domain of political power not subject to judicial intrusion or inquiry." That is, although it is appropriate for the Court to determine the judicial question whether the President has the asserted authority, we lack the information and expertise to question whether Hamdi is actually an enemy combatant, a question the resolution of which is committed to other branches.

II

Although the President very well may have inherent authority to detain those arrayed against our troops, I agree with the plurality that we need not decide that question because Congress has authorized the President to do so. The Authorization for Use of Military Force (AUMF), authorizes the President to "use all necessary and appropriate force against those nations, organizations, or persons he determines planned, authorized, committed, or aided the terrorist attacks" of September 11, 2001.

The plurality, however, qualifies its recognition of the President's authority to detain enemy combatants in the war on terrorism in ways that are at odds with our precedent. Thus, the plurality relies primarily on Article 118 of the Geneva Convention (III) Relative to the Treatment of Prisoners of War, for the proposition that "it is a clearly established principle of the law of war that detention may last no longer than active hostilities." It then appears to limit the President's authority to detain by requiring that the record establish that United States troops are still involved in active combat in Afghanistan because, in that case, detention would be "part of the exercise of 'necessary and appropriate force.'" But I do not believe that we may diminish the Federal Government's war powers by reference to a treaty and certainly not to a treaty that does not apply. Further, we are bound by the political branches' determination that the United States is at war. And, in any case, the power to detain does not end with the cessation of formal hostilities.

Accordingly, the President's action here is "supported by the strongest of presumptions and the widest latitude of judicial interpretation." The question becomes whether the Federal Government (rather than the President acting alone) has power to detain Hamdi as an enemy combatant. More precisely, we must determine whether the Government may detain Hamdi given the procedures that were used.

III

I agree with the plurality that the Federal Government has power to detain those that the Executive Branch determines to be enemy combatants. But I do not think that the plurality has adequately explained the breadth of the President's authority to detain enemy combatants, an authority that includes making virtually conclusive factual findings. In my view, the structural considerations discussed above, as recognized in our precedent, demonstrate that we lack the capacity and responsibility to second-guess this determination.

In a case strikingly similar to this one, the Court addressed a Governor's authority to detain for an extended period a person the executive believed to be responsible, in part, for a local insurrection. [*Moyer v. Peabody*, 212 U.S. 78 (1909).] In *Luther v. Borden*, 48 U.S. 1, 7 How. 1, 12 L. Ed. 581 (1849), the Court discussed the President's constitutional and statutory authority, in response to a request from a state legislature or executive, " 'to call forth such number of the militia of any other State or States, as may be applied for, as he may judge sufficient to suppress [an] insurrection.' "

In this context, due process requires nothing more than a good-faith executive determination. To be clear: The Court has held that an executive, acting pursuant to statutory and constitutional authority may, consistent with the Due Process Clause, unilaterally decide to detain an individual if the executive deems this necessary for the public safety *even if he is mistaken*.

The Government's asserted authority to detain an individual that the President has determined to be an enemy combatant, at least while hostilities continue, comports with the Due Process Clause. As these cases also show, the Executive's decision that a detention is necessary to protect the public need not and should not be subjected to judicial second-guessing. Indeed, at least in the context of enemy-combatant determinations, this would defeat the unity, secrecy, and dispatch that the Founders believed to be so important to the warmaking function.

Justice Scalia relies heavily upon *Ex parte Milligan*. I admit that *Milligan* supports his position. But because the Executive Branch there, unlike here, did not follow a specific statutory mechanism provided by Congress, the Court did not need to reach the broader question of Congress' power, and its discussion on this point was arguably dicta. More importantly, the Court referred frequently and pervasively to the criminal nature of the proceedings instituted against Milligan. In fact, this feature serves to distinguish the state cases as well.

Although I do acknowledge that the reasoning of these cases might apply beyond criminal punishment, the punishment-nonpunishment distinction harmonizes all of the precedent. And, subsequent cases have at least implicitly distinguished *Milligan* in just this way. Because the Government does not detain Hamdi in order to punish him, as the plurality acknowledges, *Milligan* and the New York cases do not control.

Accordingly, I conclude that the Government's detention of Hamdi as an enemy combatant does not violate the Constitution. By detaining Hamdi, the President, in the prosecution of a war and authorized by Congress, has acted well within his authority. Hamdi thereby received all the process to which he was due under the circumstances. I therefore believe that this is no occasion to balance the competing interests, as the plurality unconvincingly attempts to do.

NOTES AND QUESTIONS

1. Hamdi Ourcome. Hamdi was released from U.S. custody pursuant to an agreement with Saudi Arabian authorities to accept him into that country. Hamdi agreed to renounce U.S. citizenship, to reside in Saudi Arabia for at least 5 years, and to report any contacts from persons who he has reason to believe could be involved in hostile or terrorist actions. The agreement can be found at http://news.findlaw.com/hdocs/docs/hamdi/91704stlagrmnt.html.

2. Life Imprisonment and Criteria. The O'Connor plurality opinion is quite explicit that "individuals legitimately determined to be Taliban combatants" could be held without trial for the remainder of their lives if "active hostilities" continue so long. With four votes for that position coupled with Justice Thomas' position, there seems to be a majority of the Court willing to countenance indefinite detention without trial under some circumstances. The plurality just requires a determination by a competent tribunal of — what? combatant status? by what level of evidence? by what procedures? All of these questions are raised in the *Hamdan* case below with regard to noncitizens.

3. Executive Classifications. Perhaps some slightly tongue-in-cheek examples would clarify the problem of judicial review over executive findings related to national security. If the government's arguments for deference to the President were accepted, would there be anything to prevent the President from classifying a skinhead militant as an enemy combatant? If that worked, how about classifying a politically volatile dissident as an EC? If that worked, how about the President's next election campaign opponent? Obviously, there must be a stopping point but it could be argued that the stopping point should be a matter for citizen or political action rather than judicial action. Which position carries the best message for the democratic process?

4. Due Process and Habeas Corpus. The central point of disagreement between Justices O'Connor and Scalia concerns the interplay between Due Process and the Suspension Clause.

    a.   Justice Scalia asserts that, although there may be more latitude for executive detention of aliens, with regard to citizens the government's choice is criminal trial or suspension of habeas corpus. How does he read the Court's treatment of Haupt in the *Quirin* case? How would it be that Due Process means something different for citizens than for aliens? Although aliens may be treated differently for a number of government entitlements, doesn't the concept of fair procedures apply to both equally?

    b.   Justice O'Connor argues that the Suspension Clause is satisfied by the AUMF because the AUMF is a congressional determination triggering the traditional power of military detention of combatants, but that Due Process then requires that the detainee be found by some appropriate process to fit within the category of "enemy combatant."

    c.   Justice O'Connor argues that Justice Scalia is making up a third option (other than trial or suspension) in which "concession of enemy combatant status" satisfies the habeas corpus requirement. Justice Scalia in return argues that Justice O'Connor is aggrandizing the role of the courts to make a determination of status that should be made by someone else. Justice O'Connor is willing to allow the determination to be made by any "neutral decisionmaker" whether court or other. Who has the better of this argument?

5. Enemy Combatants. What is the definition of "enemy combatant" in the O'Connor scheme? If the Haupt example means that a U.S. citizen arrested in the U.S. can be an enemy combatant, then can the executive declare any alleged terrorist to be an enemy combatant? What would be the standards for reviewing that determination? Justice O'Connor's explanation of battlefield conditions says that the question is "the appropriateness of continuing to detain an individual claimed to have taken up arms against the United States." In what sense had Haupt "taken up arms" against the U.S.? Has any member of a terrorist organization "taken up arms" by engaging in a conspiracy to bomb either a military installation or a civilian target?

Perhaps the enemy combatant posture can be clarified by thinking of a range of persons and actions. At one extreme would be an Iraqi soldier in uniform wounded while firing a weapon at U.S. forces and then taken into custody. At the other extreme would be Jose Padilla, who was arrested by civilian authorities on U.S. soil while unarmed and having no more access to weapons than any other resident of the U.S. Where in this range of actions does a person become an enemy combatant?

a.   uniformed soldier on field of battle

b.   insurgent in civilian clothing firing weapon against uniformed invading force

c.   insurgent attacking either military or civilian units allied with invading force

d.   civilian attacking military installation on domestic soil of another country (the 9/11 plane flown into the Pentagon? does the target matter in this instance?)

e.   civilian attacking civilian targets on soil of another country (the 9/11 planes flown into the WTC or almost any act of international terrorism)

f.   civilian arrested on home soil allegedly intending to attack civilian targets (how distinguish Padilla from McVeigh?)

For an interesting and unfamiliar historical perspective, see Ingrid Brunk Wuerth, *The President's Power To Detain "Enemy Combatants:" Modern Lessons from Mr. Madison's Forgotten War*, 98 NW. U.L. REV. 1567 (2004).

RASUL v. BUSH
542 U.S. 466 (2004)

JUSTICE STEVENS delivered the opinion of the Court.

These two cases present the narrow but important question whether United States courts lack jurisdiction to consider challenges to the legality of the detention of foreign nationals captured abroad in connection with hostilities and incarcerated at the Guantánamo Bay Naval Base, Cuba.

Since early 2002, the U.S. military has held [petitioners' relatives, Kuwaitis and Australians] — along with, according to the Government's estimate, approximately 640 other non-Americans captured abroad — at the Naval Base at Guantánamo Bay. The United States occupies the Base, which comprises 45 square miles of land and water along the southeast coast of Cuba, pursuant to a 1903 Lease Agreement executed with the newly independent Republic of Cuba in the aftermath of the Spanish-American War. Under the Agreement, "the United States recognizes the continuance of the ultimate sovereignty of the Republic of Cuba over the [leased areas]," while "the Republic of Cuba consents that during the period of the occupation by the United States . . . the United States shall exercise complete jurisdiction and control over and within said areas." In 1934, the parties entered into a treaty providing that, absent an agreement to modify or abrogate the lease, the lease would remain in effect "so long as the United States of America shall not abandon the . . . naval station of Guantánamo."

In 2002, petitioners, through relatives acting as their next friends, filed various actions in the U.S. District Court for the District of Columbia challenging the legality of their detention at the Base. All alleged that none of the petitioners has ever been a combatant against the United States or has ever engaged in any terrorist acts. They also alleged that none has been charged with any wrongdoing, permitted to consult with counsel, or provided access to the courts or any other tribunal.

[T]he District Court dismissed for want of jurisdiction. The court held, in reliance on our opinion in *Johnson v. Eisentrager*, 339 U.S. 763 (1950), that "aliens detained outside the sovereign territory of the United States [may not] invoke a petition for a writ of habeas corpus." The Court of Appeals affirmed. We granted certiorari and now reverse.

Congress has granted federal district courts, "within their respective jurisdictions," the authority to hear applications for habeas corpus by any person who claims to be held "in custody in violation of the Constitution or laws or treaties of the United States." 28 U.S.C. §§ 2241(a), (c)(3). Habeas corpus is, however, "a writ antecedent to statute, . . . throwing its root deep into the genius of our common law." The writ appeared in English law several centuries ago, became "an integral part of our common-law heritage" by the time the Colonies achieved independence, and received explicit recognition in the Constitution, which forbids suspension of "the Privilege of the

Writ of Habeas Corpus . . . unless when in Cases of Rebellion or Invasion the public Safety may require it."

As it has evolved over the past two centuries, the habeas statute clearly has expanded habeas corpus "beyond the limits that obtained during the 17th and 18th centuries." But "at its historical core, the writ of habeas corpus has served as a means of reviewing the legality of Executive detention, and it is in that context that its protections have been strongest." As Justice Jackson wrote in an opinion respecting the availability of habeas corpus to aliens held in U.S. custody: "Executive imprisonment has been considered oppressive and lawless since John, at Runnymede, pledged that no free man should be imprisoned, dispossessed, outlawed, or exiled save by the judgment of his peers or by the law of the land. The judges of England developed the writ of habeas corpus largely to preserve these immunities from executive restraint."

Consistent with the historic purpose of the writ, this Court has recognized the federal courts' power to review applications for habeas relief in a wide variety of cases involving Executive detention, in wartime as well as in times of peace. The Court has, for example, entertained the habeas petitions of an American citizen who plotted an attack on military installations during the Civil War, *Ex parte Milligan*, and of admitted enemy aliens convicted of war crimes during a declared war and held in the United States, *Ex parte Quirin*, and its insular possessions, *In re Yamashita*.

The question now before us is whether the habeas statute confers a right to judicial review of the legality of Executive detention of aliens in a territory over which the United States exercises plenary and exclusive jurisdiction, but not "ultimate sovereignty."

Respondents' primary submission is that the answer to the jurisdictional question is controlled by our decision in *Eisentrager*. In that case, we held that a Federal District Court lacked authority to issue a writ of habeas corpus to 21 German citizens who had been captured by U.S. forces in China, tried and convicted of war crimes by an American military commission headquartered in Nanking, and incarcerated in the Landsberg Prison in occupied Germany. The Court of Appeals in *Eisentrager* had found jurisdiction, reasoning that "any person who is deprived of his liberty by officials of the United States, acting under purported authority of that Government, and who can show that his confinement is in violation of a prohibition of the Constitution, has a right to the writ." In reversing that determination, this Court summarized the six critical facts in the case:

> We are here confronted with a decision whose basic premise is that these prisoners are entitled, as a constitutional right, to sue in some court of the United States for a writ of *habeas corpus*. To support that assumption we must hold that a prisoner of our military authorities is constitutionally entitled to the writ, even though he (a) is an enemy alien; (b) has never been or resided in the United States; (c) was captured outside of our territory and there held in military custody as a prisoner of war; (d) was tried and convicted by a Military Commission sitting outside the United States; (e) for offenses against laws of war committed outside the United States; (f) and is at all times imprisoned outside the United States.

On this set of facts, the Court concluded, "no right to the writ of *habeas corpus* appears."

Petitioners in these cases differ from the *Eisentrager* detainees in important respects: They are not nationals of countries at war with the United States, and they deny that they have engaged in or plotted acts of aggression against the United States; they have never been afforded access to any tribunal, much less charged with and convicted of wrongdoing; and for more than two years they have been imprisoned in territory over which the United States exercises exclusive jurisdiction and control.

Because subsequent decisions of this Court have filled the statutory gap that had occasioned *Eisentrager*'s resort to "fundamentals," persons detained outside the territorial jurisdiction of any federal district court no longer need rely on the Constitution as the source of their right to federal habeas review. In *Braden v. 30th Judicial Circuit Court of Ky.*, 410 U.S. 484, 495 (1973), this Court held that the prisoner's presence within the territorial jurisdiction of the district court is not "an invariable prerequisite" to the exercise of district court jurisdiction under the federal habeas statute. Rather, because "the writ of habeas corpus does not act upon the prisoner who seeks relief, but upon the person who holds him in what is alleged to be unlawful custody," a district court acts "within [its] respective jurisdiction" within the meaning of § 2241 as long as "the custodian can be reached by service of process."

[*Braden* was preceded by] decisions of this Court in cases involving habeas petitioners "confined overseas (and thus outside the territory of any district court)," in which the Court "held, if only implicitly, that the petitioners' absence from the district does not present a jurisdictional obstacle to the consideration of the claim." [citing cases involving U.S. servicemen and civilians tried by courts-martial in other countries] Because *Braden* overruled the statutory predicate to *Eisentrager*'s holding, *Eisentrager* plainly does not preclude the exercise of § 2241 jurisdiction over petitioners' claims.

Application of the habeas statute to persons detained at the base is consistent with the historical reach of the writ of habeas corpus. At common law, courts exercised habeas jurisdiction over the claims of aliens detained within sovereign territory of the realm, as well as the claims of persons detained in the so-called "exempt jurisdictions," where ordinary writs did not run, and all other dominions under the sovereign's control. As Lord Mansfield wrote in 1759, even if a territory was "no part of the realm," there was "no doubt" as to the court's power to issue writs of habeas corpus if the territory was "under the subjection of the Crown."

In the end, the answer to the question presented is clear. Petitioners contend that they are being held in federal custody in violation of the laws of the United States. No party questions the District Court's jurisdiction over petitioners' custodians. Section 2241, by its terms, requires nothing more. We therefore hold that § 2241 confers on the District Court jurisdiction to hear petitioners' habeas corpus challenges to the legality of their detention at the Guantánamo Bay Naval Base.

In addition to invoking the District Court's jurisdiction under § 2241, [some of the petitioners] invoked the court's jurisdiction under 28 U.S.C. § 1331, the federal question statute, as well as § 1350, the Alien Tort Statute. The Court of Appeals, again relying on *Eisentrager*, held that the District Court correctly dismissed the claims founded on § 1331 and § 1350 for lack of jurisdiction, even to the extent that these claims "deal only with conditions of confinement and do not sound in habeas," because petitioners lack the "privilege of litigation" in U.S. courts.

As explained above, *Eisentrager* itself erects no bar to the exercise of federal court jurisdiction over the petitioners' habeas corpus claims. The courts of the United States have traditionally been open to nonresident aliens. And indeed, 28 U.S.C. § 1350 explicitly confers the privilege of suing for an actionable "tort . . . committed in violation of the law of nations or a treaty of the United States" on aliens alone. The fact that petitioners in these cases are being held in military custody is immaterial to the question of the District Court's jurisdiction over their nonhabeas statutory claims.

In the end, the answer to the question presented is clear. Petitioners contend that they are being held in federal custody in violation of the laws of the United States.[9] No party questions the District Court's jurisdiction over petitioners' custodians. Section

---

[9] [Court's Footnote 15] Petitioners' allegations — that, although they have engaged neither in combat nor in acts of terrorism against the United States, they have been held in Executive detention for more than two years in territory subject to the long-term, exclusive jurisdiction and control of the United States, without access to counsel and without being charged with any wrongdoing — unquestionably describe "custody in violation of the Constitution or laws or treaties of the United States."

2241, by its terms, requires nothing more. We therefore hold that § 2241 confers on the District Court jurisdiction to hear petitioners' habeas corpus challenges to the legality of their detention at the Guantánamo Bay Naval Base.

VI

Whether and what further proceedings may become necessary after respondents make their response to the merits of petitioners' claims are matters that we need not address now. What is presently at stake is only whether the federal courts have jurisdiction to determine the legality of the Executive's potentially indefinite detention of individuals who claim to be wholly innocent of wrongdoing. Answering that question in the affirmative, we reverse the judgment of the Court of Appeals and remand for the District Court to consider in the first instance the merits of petitioners' claims.

It is so ordered.

JUSTICE KENNEDY, concurring in the judgment.

The Court is correct, in my view, to conclude that federal courts have jurisdiction to consider challenges to the legality of the detention of foreign nationals held at the Guantánamo Bay Naval Base in Cuba. While I reach the same conclusion, my analysis follows a different course. In my view, the correct course is to follow the framework of *Eisentrager.*

The decision in *Eisentrager* indicates that there is a realm of political authority over military affairs where the judicial power may not enter. The existence of this realm acknowledges the power of the President as Commander in Chief, and the joint role of the President and the Congress, in the conduct of military affairs. A faithful application of *Eisentrager*, then, requires an initial inquiry into the general circumstances of the detention to determine whether the Court has the authority to entertain the petition and to grant relief after considering all of the facts presented. A necessary corollary of *Eisentrager* is that there are circumstances in which the courts maintain the power and the responsibility to protect persons from unlawful detention even where military affairs are implicated.

The facts here are distinguishable from those in *Eisentrager* in two critical ways, leading to the conclusion that a federal court may entertain the petitions. First, Guantánamo Bay is in every practical respect a United States territory, and it is one far removed from any hostilities. What matters is the unchallenged and indefinite control that the United States has long exercised over Guantánamo Bay. From a practical perspective, the indefinite lease of Guantánamo Bay has produced a place that belongs to the United States, extending the "implied protection" of the United States to it.

The second critical set of facts is that the detainees at Guantánamo Bay are being held indefinitely, and without benefit of any legal proceeding to determine their status. In *Eisentrager*, the prisoners were tried and convicted by a military commission of violating the laws of war and were sentenced to prison terms. Having already been subject to procedures establishing their status, they could not justify "a limited opening of our courts" to show that they were "of friendly personal disposition" and not enemy aliens. Indefinite detention without trial or other proceeding presents altogether different considerations. It allows friends and foes alike to remain in detention. It suggests a weaker case of military necessity and much greater alignment with the traditional function of habeas corpus. Perhaps, where detainees are taken from a zone of hostilities, detention without proceedings or trial would be justified by military necessity for a matter of weeks; but as the period of detention stretches from months to years, the case for continued detention to meet military exigencies becomes weaker.

In light of the status of Guantánamo Bay and the indefinite pretrial detention of the detainees, I would hold that federal-court jurisdiction is permitted in these cases. This approach would avoid creating automatic statutory authority to adjudicate the claims of persons located outside the United States, and remains true to the reasoning of

Eisentrager. For these reasons, I concur in the judgment of the Court.

JUSTICE SCALIA, with whom THE CHIEF JUSTICE and JUSTICE THOMAS join, dissenting.

The Court today holds that the habeas statute, 28 U.S.C. § 2241, extends to aliens detained by the United States military overseas, outside the sovereign borders of the United States and beyond the territorial jurisdictions of all its courts. This is not only a novel holding; it contradicts a half-century-old precedent on which the military undoubtedly relied, *Johnson v. Eisentrager*. This is an irresponsible overturning of settled law in a matter of extreme importance to our forces currently in the field. I would leave it to Congress to change § 2241, and dissent from the Court's unprecedented holding.

In abandoning the venerable statutory line drawn in *Eisentrager*, the Court boldly extends the scope of the habeas statute to the four corners of the earth. Part III of its opinion asserts that "a district court acts 'within [its] respective jurisdiction' within the meaning of § 2241 as long as 'the custodian can be reached by service of process.' "

The consequence of this holding, as applied to aliens outside the country, is breathtaking. It permits an alien captured in a foreign theater of active combat to bring a § 2241 petition against the Secretary of Defense. Over the course of the last century, the United States has held millions of alien prisoners abroad. A great many of these prisoners would no doubt have complained about the circumstances of their capture and the terms of their confinement. The military is currently detaining over 600 prisoners at Guantánamo Bay alone; each detainee undoubtedly has complaints — real or contrived — about those terms and circumstances. The Court's unheralded expansion of federal-court jurisdiction is not even mitigated by a comforting assurance that the legion of ensuing claims will be easily resolved on the merits. To the contrary, the Court says that the "petitioners' allegations . . . unquestionably describe 'custody in violation of the Constitution or laws or treaties of the United States.' " From this point forward, federal courts will entertain petitions from these prisoners, and others like them around the world, challenging actions and events far away, and forcing the courts to oversee one aspect of the Executive's conduct of a foreign war.

Today's carefree Court disregards, without a word of acknowledgment, the dire warning of a more circumspect Court in *Eisentrager*:

> "To grant the writ to these prisoners might mean that our army must transport them across the seas for hearing. This would require allocation for shipping space, guarding personnel, billeting and rations. It might also require transportation for whatever witnesses the prisoners desired to call as well as transportation for those necessary to defend legality of the sentence. The writ, since it is held to be a matter of right, would be equally available to enemies during active hostilities as in the present twilight between war and peace. Such trials would hamper the war effort and bring aid and comfort to the enemy. They would diminish the prestige of our commanders, not only with enemies but with wavering neutrals. It would be difficult to devise more effective fettering of a field commander than to allow the very enemies he is ordered to reduce to submission to call him to account in his own civil courts and divert his efforts and attention from the military offensive abroad to the legal defensive at home. Nor is it unlikely that the result of such enemy litigiousness would be conflict between judicial and military opinion highly comforting to enemies of the United States."

The Court gives only two reasons why the presumption against extraterritorial effect does not apply to Guantánamo Bay. First, the Court says (without any further elaboration) that "the United States exercises 'complete jurisdiction and control' over the Guantánamo Bay Naval Base [under the terms of a 1903 lease agreement], and may continue to exercise such control permanently if it so chooses [under the terms of a 1934 Treaty]." The Court does not explain how "complete jurisdiction and control" without sovereignty causes an enclave to be part of the United States for purposes of its domestic laws. Since "jurisdiction and control" obtained through a lease is no different in effect from "jurisdiction and control" acquired by lawful force of arms, parts of Afghanistan and Iraq should logically be regarded as subject to our domestic laws. Indeed, if "jurisdiction and control" rather than sovereignty were the test, so should the Landsberg Prison in Germany, where the United States held the *Eisentrager* detainees.

The second and last reason the Court gives for the proposition that domestic law applies to Guantánamo Bay is the Solicitor General's concession that there would be habeas jurisdiction over a United States citizen in Guantánamo Bay. "Considering that the statute draws no distinction between Americans and aliens held in federal custody, there is little reason to think that Congress intended the geographical coverage of the statute to vary depending on the detainee's citizenship." But the reason the Solicitor General conceded there would be jurisdiction over a detainee who was a United States citizen had *nothing to do* with the special status of Guantánamo Bay: "Our answer to that question, Justice Souter, is that citizens of the United States, because of their constitutional circumstances, may have greater rights with respect to the scope and reach of the Habeas Statute as the Court has or would interpret it." And *that* position — the position that United States citizens throughout the world may be entitled to habeas corpus rights — is precisely the position that this Court adopted in *Eisentrager*, even while holding that aliens abroad *did not have* habeas corpus rights.

To the extent the writ's "extraordinary territorial ambit" did extend to exempt jurisdictions, outlying dominions, and the like, that extension applied only to British *subjects*. Blackstone explained that the writ "runs into all parts of the king's dominions" because "the king is at all times entitled to have an account why the liberty of any of his *subjects* is restrained."

Departure from our rule of *stare decisis* in statutory cases is always extraordinary; it ought to be unthinkable when the departure has a potentially harmful effect upon the Nation's conduct of a war. The Commander in Chief and his subordinates had every reason to expect that the internment of combatants at Guantánamo Bay would not have the consequence of bringing the cumbersome machinery of our domestic courts into military affairs. Congress is in session. If it wished to change federal judges' habeas jurisdiction from what this Court had previously held that to be, it could have done so. And it could have done so by intelligent revision of the statute, instead of by today's clumsy, countertextual reinterpretation that confers upon wartime prisoners greater habeas rights than domestic detainees. The latter must challenge their present physical confinement in the district of their confinement, *see Rumsfeld v. Padilla*, whereas under today's strange holding Guantánamo Bay detainees can petition in any of the 94 federal judicial districts. The fact that extraterritorially located detainees lack the district of detention that the statute requires has been converted from a factor that precludes their ability to bring a petition at all into a factor that frees them to petition wherever they wish — and, as a result, to forum shop. For this Court to create such a monstrous scheme in time of war, and in frustration of our military commanders' reliance upon clearly stated prior law, is judicial adventurism of the worst sort. I dissent.

NOTES AND QUESTIONS

1. Law to Apply. Justice Stevens does not explore the "merits" of the Guantánamo detentions. "In the end, the answer to the question presented is clear. Petitioners contend that they are being held in federal custody in violation of the laws of the United States." Justice Scalia, however, says essentially that there is no law that protects these persons, making a distinction between citizens and noncitizens, much as he did in *Hamdi*. On remand in these cases, or in ruling on any future habeas corpus petitions, what law will apply to determine whether a detainee in U.S. military custody is being held "in violation of the Constitution or laws" of the U.S.? Consider these possibilities:

a. constitutional rights — It is not clear that an alien held in federal custody outside the U.S. would have constitutional rights other than perhaps some rights regarding conditions of confinement, or perhaps the due process right to a determination of status similar to that accorded to *Hamdi*. In one of the cases reviewed in *Rasul*, the D.C. Circuit stated: "We cannot see why, or how, the writ may be made available to aliens abroad when basic constitutional protections are not. This much is at the heart of *Eisentrager*. If the Constitution does not entitle the detainees to due process, and it does not, they cannot invoke the jurisdiction of our courts to test the constitutionality or the legality of restraints on their liberty." *Al Odah v. United States*, 355 U.S. App. D.C. 189 (D.C. Cir. 2003).

b.   statutory rights — An alien seeking admission to the U.S. may have claims to statutory rights under the immigration laws. Are there any statutes protecting the interests of the Guantánamo detainees?

c.   treaty rights — Are the Geneva Conventions self-executing or do they create rights on behalf of individuals? The Government argued in the lower courts that the Conventions created diplomatic remedies and not individual remedies, an argument repeated and addressed in *In re Guantánamo Detainees, Khalid v. Bush* and *Hamdan v. Rumsfeld* below.

d.   customary international law — Professor Paust argues that both treaties and customary international law entitle a person to freedom from "arbitrary" detention, which implies some level of judicial review over the propriety of detention. Jordan J. Paust, *Judicial Power to Determine the Status and Rights of Persons Detained Without Trial*, 44 HARV. INT'L L.J. 503 (2003).

2. Post-*Rasual* Proceedings. After the Supreme Court's decision, proceedings with respect to the Guantánamo detainees split into three tracks:

a.   Petitions for habeas corpus filed in various courts were transferred to the District of Columbia. Most were consolidated for initial motions.

b.   The military established "Combatant Status Review Tribunals" (CSRT) Guantánamo Bay to make determinations on the status of each detainee.

c.   Some detainees were brought before military commissions to answer charges of violations of the law of war. *See Hamdan v. Rumsfeld,* § 8.04[B] *infra.*

RUMSFELD v. PADILLA
542 U.S. 426 (2004)

CHIEF JUSTICE REHNQUIST delivered the opinion of the Court.

Respondent Jose Padilla is a United States citizen detained by the Department of Defense pursuant to the President's determination that he is an "enemy combatant" who conspired with al Qaeda to carry out terrorist attacks in the United States. We confront two questions: First, did Padilla properly file his habeas petition in the Southern District of New York; and second, did the President possess authority to detain Padilla militarily. We answer the threshold question in the negative and thus do not reach the second question presented.

Because we do not decide the merits, we only briefly recount the relevant facts. On May 8, 2002, Padilla flew from Pakistan to Chicago's O'Hare International Airport. As he stepped off the plane, Padilla was apprehended by federal agents executing a material witness warrant issued by the United States District Court for the Southern District of New York (Southern District) in connection with its grand jury investigation into the September 11th terrorist attacks. Padilla was then transported to New York, where he was held in federal criminal custody. On May 22, acting through appointed counsel, Padilla moved to vacate the material witness warrant.

Padilla's motion was still pending when, on June 9, the President issued an order to Secretary of Defense Donald H. Rumsfeld designating Padilla an "enemy combatant" and directing the Secretary to detain him in military custody. In support of this action, the President invoked his authority as "Commander in Chief of the U.S. armed forces" and the Authorization for Use of Military Force Joint Resolution, enacted by Congress on September 18, 2001.

That same day, Padilla was taken into custody by Department of Defense officials and transported to the Consolidated Naval Brig in Charleston, South Carolina. He has been held there ever since.

On June 11, Padilla's counsel, claiming to act as his next friend, filed in the Southern District a habeas corpus petition under 28 U.S.C. § 2241. The amended petition named as respondents President Bush, Secretary Rumsfeld, and Melanie A. Marr, Commander of the Consolidated Naval Brig.

The Government moved to dismiss, arguing that Commander Marr, as Padilla's immediate custodian, is the only proper respondent to his habeas petition, and that the District Court lacks jurisdiction over Commander Marr because she is located outside the Southern District.

The District Court issued its decision in December 2002. The court held that the Secretary's "personal involvement" in Padilla's military custody renders him a proper respondent to Padilla's habeas petition, and that it can assert jurisdiction over the Secretary under New York's long-arm statute, notwithstanding his absence from the Southern District. On the merits, however, the court accepted the Government's contention that the President has authority to detain as enemy combatants citizens captured on American soil during a time of war.

The Court of Appeals for the Second Circuit reversed. The court agreed with the District Court that Secretary Rumsfeld is a proper respondent, reasoning that in cases where the habeas petitioner is detained for "other than federal criminal violations, the Supreme Court has recognized exceptions to the general practice of naming the immediate physical custodian as respondent." Reaching the merits, the Court of Appeals held that the President lacks authority to detain Padilla militarily. The court concluded that neither the President's Commander-in-Chief power nor the AUMF authorizes military detentions of American citizens captured on American soil.

We granted the Government's petition for certiorari to review the Court of Appeals' rulings with respect to the jurisdictional and the merits issues, both of which raise important questions of federal law. The question whether the Southern District has jurisdiction over Padilla's habeas petition breaks down into two related subquestions. First, who is the proper respondent to that petition? And second, does the Southern District have jurisdiction over him or her? We address these questions in turn.

The federal habeas statute straightforwardly provides that the proper respondent to a habeas petition is "the person who has custody over [the petitioner]." The consistent use of the definite article in reference to the custodian indicates that there is generally only one proper respondent to a given prisoner's habeas petition. This custodian, moreover, is "the person" with the ability to produce the prisoner's body before the habeas court. We summed up the plain language of the habeas statute over 100 years ago in this way: "These provisions contemplate a proceeding against some person who has the *immediate custody* of the party detained, with the power to produce the body of such party before the court or judge, that he may be liberated if no sufficient reason is shown to the contrary."

In accord with the statutory language, longstanding practice confirms that in habeas challenges to present physical confinement — "core challenges" — the default rule is that the proper respondent is the warden of the facility where the prisoner is being held, not the Attorney General or some other remote supervisory official. No exceptions to this rule, either recognized or proposed, apply here.[10]

---

[10] [Court's Footnote 9] We have long implicitly recognized an exception to the immediate custodian rule in the military context where an American citizen is detained outside the territorial jurisdiction of any district court. *Braden v. 30th Judicial Circuit Court of Ky.*, 410 U.S. 484 (1973) (discussing the exception); *United*

We turn now to the second subquestion. District courts are limited to granting habeas relief "within their respective jurisdictions." 28 U.S.C. § 2241(a). We have interpreted this language to require "nothing more than that the court issuing the writ have jurisdiction over the custodian." Thus, jurisdiction over Padilla's habeas petition lies in the Southern District only if it has jurisdiction over Commander Marr. We conclude it does not.

The proviso that district courts may issue the writ only "within their respective jurisdictions" forms an important corollary to the immediate custodian rule in challenges to present physical custody under § 2241. Together they compose a simple rule that has been consistently applied in the lower courts, including in the context of military detentions: Whenever a § 2241 habeas petitioner seeks to challenge his present physical custody within the United States, he should name his warden as respondent and file the petition in the district of confinement.[11]

The dissent contends that the Court has made "numerous exceptions" to the immediate custodian and district of confinement rules, rendering our bright-line rule "far from bright." Yet the dissent cannot cite a single case in which we have deviated from the longstanding rule we reaffirm today — that is, a case in which we allowed a habeas petitioner challenging his present physical custody within the United States to name as respondent someone other than the immediate custodian and to file somewhere other than the district of confinement.[12]

The District of South Carolina, not the Southern District of New York, was the district court in which Padilla should have brought his habeas petition. We therefore reverse the judgment of the Court of Appeals and remand the case for entry of an order of dismissal without prejudice.

JUSTICE KENNEDY, with whom JUSTICE O'CONNOR joins, concurring.

Both Padilla's change in location and his change of custodian reflected a change in the Government's rationale for detaining him. He ceased to be held under the authority of the criminal justice system, and began to be held under that of the military detention system. Rather than being designed to play games with forums, the Government's removal of Padilla reflected the change in the theory on which it was holding him. Whether that theory is a permissible one, of course, is a question the Court does not reach today.

JUSTICE STEVENS, with whom JUSTICE SOUTER, JUSTICE GINSBURG, and JUSTICE BREYER, join, dissenting.

The petition for a writ of habeas corpus filed in this case raises questions of profound importance to the Nation. The arguments set forth by the Court do not justify avoidance of our duty to answer those questions. It is quite wrong to characterize the proceeding as a "simple challenge to physical custody," that should be resolved by

---

States ex rel. Toth v. Quarles, 350 U.S. 11(1955) (court-martial convict detained in Korea named Secretary of the Air Force as respondent); *Burns v. Wilson*, 346 U.S. 137 (1953) (court-martial convicts detained in Guam named Secretary of Defense as respondent).

[11] [Court's Footnote 16] As a corollary to the previously referenced exception to the immediate custodian rule, we have similarly relaxed the district of confinement rule when "Americans citizens confined overseas (and thus outside the territory of any district court) have sought relief in habeas corpus." In such cases, we have allowed the petitioner to name as respondent a supervisory official and file the petition in the district where the respondent resides. *Burns v. Wilson*, 346 U.S. 137 (1953) (court-martial convicts held in Guam sued Secretary of Defense in the District of Columbia); *United States ex rel. Toth v. Quarles*, 350 U.S. 11 (1955) (court-martial convict held in Korea sued Secretary of the Air Force in the District of Columbia).

[12] [Court's Footnote 18] *Demjanjuk v. Meese*, 251 U.S. App. D.C. 310, 784 F.2d 1114 (CADC 1986), on which the dissent relies, is similarly unhelpful: When, as in that case, a prisoner is held in an undisclosed location by an unknown custodian, it is impossible to apply the immediate custodian and district of confinement rules. That is not the case here, where the identity of the immediate custodian and the location of the appropriate district court are clear.

slavish application of a "bright-line rule" designed to prevent "rampant forum shopping" by litigious prison inmates. As the Court's opinion itself demonstrates, that rule is riddled with exceptions fashioned to protect the high office of the Great Writ. This is an exceptional case that we clearly have jurisdiction to decide.

All Members of this Court agree that the immediate custodian rule should control in the ordinary case and that habeas petitioners should not be permitted to engage in forum shopping. More narrowly, we agree that if jurisdiction was proper when the petition was filed, it cannot be defeated by a later transfer of the prisoner to another district.

It is reasonable to assume that if the Government had given Newman, who was then representing respondent in an adversary proceeding, notice of its intent to ask the District Court to vacate the outstanding material witness warrant and transfer custody to the Department of Defense, Newman would have filed the habeas petition then and there, rather than waiting two days. Under that scenario, respondent's immediate custodian would then have been physically present in the Southern District of New York carrying out orders of the Secretary of Defense. Surely at that time Secretary Rumsfeld, rather than the lesser official who placed the handcuffs on petitioner, would have been the proper person to name as a respondent to that petition.

The difference between that scenario and the secret transfer that actually occurred should not affect our decision, for we should not permit the Government to obtain a tactical advantage as a consequence of an *ex parte* proceeding. The departure from the time-honored practice of giving one's adversary fair notice of an intent to present an important motion to the court justifies treating the habeas application as the functional equivalent of one filed two days earlier.

At stake in this case is nothing less than the essence of a free society. Even more important than the method of selecting the people's rulers and their successors is the character of the constraints imposed on the Executive by the rule of law. Unconstrained Executive detention for the purpose of investigating and preventing subversive activity is the hallmark of the Star Chamber. Access to counsel for the purpose of protecting the citizen from official mistakes and mistreatment is the hallmark of due process.

Executive detention of subversive citizens, like detention of enemy soldiers to keep them off the battlefield, may sometimes be justified to prevent persons from launching or becoming missiles of destruction. It may not, however, be justified by the naked interest in using unlawful procedures to extract information. Incommunicado detention for months on end is such a procedure. Whether the information so procured is more or less reliable than that acquired by more extreme forms of torture is of no consequence. For if this Nation is to remain true to the ideals symbolized by its flag, it must not wield the tools of tyrants even to resist an assault by the forces of tyranny.

I respectfully dissent.

NOTES AND QUESTIONS

1. al-Marri. The majority in *Padilla* cites with approval the case of Ali al-Marri, who was indicted and preparing for trial in federal court in Illinois for credit fraud and making false statements to government agents, when he was suddenly made the subject of a Presidential finding of enemy combatant status and shipped off to a military jail in South Carolina. The Seventh Circuit held that the proper place for filing a writ of habeas corpus would be South Carolina, not the place of original criminal proceedings. *al-Marri v. Rumsfeld*, 360 F.3d 707 (7th Cir. 2004). He was eventually the subject of a stinging opinion by the Fourth Circuit. *See infra* § 8.05[B].

2. Reasons for Executive Detentions. If there were sufficient evidence, are there other reasons not to charge Padilla with a criminal offense in an ordinary civilian court proceeding? After all, John Walker Lindh was charged and pleaded guilty, as have a number of other alleged cell members and sympathizers. Hamdi could be prosecuted similarly to Lindh or he could be treated as a prisoner of war. What do you think of each of the following reasons for military detention?

a. *Indeterminate Duration of Hostilities.* If Hamdi were treated as a prisoner of war, when would he be repatriated and to what country? As a citizen of the U.S. engaged in warfare against the U.S., he might also be tried for treason but the Government's information presented to the district court created the strong impression that there were not two witnesses to the same overt act. If either Hamdi or Padilla were prosecuted for a criminal violation and sentenced to a few years in prison, how safe would you feel with them on the streets at the end of their sentence? Should this be a reason for avoiding the civilian justice system?

b. *Detention as Incentive To Talk.* The information presented by the Government in all three cases emphasized that government agents wanted to pump the detainees for further information about al Qaeda and other operatives who may still be at large. If they were treated as recalcitrant witnesses before a grand jury, for example, they could be imprisoned until they agreed to disclose. But the government argues that the mere fact of isolation creates a sense of dependency on the interrogator which is conducive to disclosure. Is this a reasonable constitutional argument? To what extent might the Supreme Court have been influenced by the disclosures of prisoner abuse made public while these cases were pending?

c. *Detention to Prevent Violent Acts.* Administrative detention to prevent violence has been discussed loosely in the past, particularly with respect to child molesters and the criminally insane. The Supreme Court has flatly rejected detention without at least a judicial finding of propensity to harm.

d. *Problems With the Civilian Criminal System.* The principal rights that Hamdi and Padilla would be able to claim if charged in the civilian criminal system are notice of charges, right to counsel, confrontation of witnesses, public trial by jury. How would these same rights fare in the military justice system if charges were brought? *See United States v. Grunden, supra.*

e. *The Mosaic Concern.* If Padilla were brought to trial, then the methods by which federal agents discovered his alleged plot would be much more likely to come out into public scrutiny.

Padilla v. Hanft, 423 F.3d 386 (4th Cir. 2005). Following the Supreme Court opinion, Padilla's attorneys filed a habeas corpus petition in South Carolina. The District Court, Judge Floyd, held that the AUMF did not authorize detention of Padilla, who was not captured on the battlefield (unlike Hamdi) and who was not charged with any violation of the law of war or any other crime but was merely held in preventive detention. Calling the situation a "law enforcement matter, not a military matter," the court ordered that Padilla be released in 45 days unless the Government decided to charge him with a crime. Government lawyers had already indicated in several settings that it would be impossible to assemble admissible evidence for a civilian prosecution.

The Fourth Circuit, Judge Luttig, diagreed. "Like Haupt [the U.S. citizen involved in *Quirin*], Padilla associated with the military arm of the enemy, and with its aid, guidance, and direction entered this country bent on committing hostile acts on American soil. Padilla thus falls within *Quirin's* definition of enemy belligerent, as well as within the definition of the equivalent term accepted by the plurality in *Hamdi*."

Padilla then petitioned for certiorari, at which point the Government decided to transfer him to civilian custody to face charges in federal court. Supreme Court Rules required a court order to allow transfer of custody, which the Fourth Circuit refused but the Supreme Court then granted. Ultimately, the Court denied certiorari, 547 U.S. 1062 (2006).

Justice Kennedy, for himself and two others, concurred in the denial of certiorari with these comments:

> In light of the previous changes in his custody status and the fact that nearly four years have passed since he first was detained, Padilla, it must be acknowledged, has a continuing concern that his status might be altered again. That concern, however, can be addressed if the necessity arises. Padilla is now being held pursuant to the control and supervision of the United States District Court for the Southern District of Florida, pending trial of the criminal case. In the course of its supervision over Padilla's custody and trial the District Court will be obliged to afford him the protection, including the right to a speedy trial, guaranteed to all federal criminal defendants. Were the Government to seek to change the status or conditions of Padilla's custody, that court would be in a position to rule quickly on any responsive filings submitted by Padilla. In such an event, the District Court, as well as other courts of competent jurisdiction, should act promptly to ensure that the office and purposes of the writ of habeas corpus are not compromised. Padilla, moreover, retains the option of seeking a writ of habeas corpus in this Court.

Justice Ginsburg dissented from the denial of certiorari on the ground that the case was one "capable of repetition yet evading review."

Subsequently, Padilla was tried in Florida and convicted of conspiracy to murder and material support for seeking to attend a training camp. The principal evidence against him was a form for training bearing his fingerprints. There was no evidence of any particular plans on his part to do anything. *See* Jenny S. Martinez, *The Real Verdict on Jose Padilla*, WASHINGTON POST, Aug. 17, 2007, at A23. David Cole provided this assessment:

> In the end, the prosecution succeeded, as the jury found Padilla guilty of attending the training camp and of one count of conspiracy to maim, murder or kidnap overseas. But given how weak the evidence was, the case could easily have come out the other way — and may not withstand appeal. If what the Administration says about Padilla is true, this should not have been a close case. But because the Administration obtained its evidence against him through unconstitutional means, it was never able to tell the jury what it really thinks Padilla was up to.

David Cole, *The Real Lesson of the Padilla Conviction*, THE NATION, Aug. 18, 2007, *available at* http://www.thenation.com/doc/20070827/cole.

[B]   Habeas Corpus in Iraq

MUNAF v. GREEN
482 F.3d 582 (D.C. Cir. 2007),
cert. granted Dec. 7, 2007 along with *Omar v. Geren*

SENTELLE, CIRCUIT JUDGE.

Mohammad Munaf, an American citizen, traveled to Iraq in 2005. In October 2006 he was convicted on kidnapping charges and sentenced to death by the Central Criminal Court of Iraq ("CCCI"). He is being held, in Iraq, by United States military personnel serving as part of the Multi-National Force-Iraq ("MNF-I"). Munaf sought a writ of habeas corpus in the United States District Court for the District of Columbia, naming the Secretary of the Army and others as respondents. Soon after Munaf's conviction by the Iraqi criminal court, the district court held that it lacked jurisdiction and dismissed the petition. *Mohammed v. Harvey*, 456 F. Supp. 2d 115 (D.D.C. 2006). Munaf appeals. Constrained by precedent, we hold that the district court does not have the power or authority to entertain Munaf's petition and we therefore affirm.

Our result is required by the Supreme Court's decision in *Hirota v. MacArthur*, 338

U.S. 197 (1948), as that decision has been applied by this court in *Flick v. Johnson*, 174 F.2d 983 (D.C. Cir. 1949), and interpreted by *Omar v. Harvey*, 479 F.3d 1 (D.C. Cir. 2007). In *Hirota*, Japanese citizens sought permission to file petitions for writs of habeas corpus directly in the United States Supreme Court. The petitioners were held in Japan, where they had been tried by a military tribunal authorized by General Douglas MacArthur acting as the Supreme Commander for the occupying Allied Powers. In a short per curiam opinion the Supreme Court concluded that the sentencing tribunal "[was] not a tribunal of the United States" and held that "[u]nder the foregoing circumstances the courts of the United States have no power or authority to review, to affirm, set aside or annul the judgments and sentences imposed on these petitioners."

Flick involved a habeas petition filed in the United States District Court for the District of Columbia by a German citizen held in Germany by American forces after he was convicted by a military tribunal. Relying on *Hirota*, we framed the jurisdictional question as follows: "Was the court which tried and sentenced Flick a tribunal of the United States? If it was not, no court of this country has power or authority to review, affirm, set aside or annul the judgment and sentence imposed on Flick." Finding that the military tribunal was not a U.S. court, we held that the district court lacked jurisdiction to review Flick's habeas petition.

Our recent decision in *Omar* involved a habeas petition filed on behalf of a United States citizen being held in Iraq by U.S. forces acting as part of the MNF-I. As in *Hirota* and *Flick*, *Omar* involved detention overseas and a multinational force. But unlike the petitioners in *Hirota* and *Flick*, Omar had not been charged or convicted by a non-U.S. court. We distinguished *Hirota* and *Flick* on this basis and went on to hold that the district court had jurisdiction to hear Omar's habeas claim.

Unlike *Omar*, the instant case is controlled by *Hirota* and *Flick*. The MNF-I is a multinational force, authorized by the United Nations Security Council, that operates in Iraq in coordination with the Iraqi government. The CCCI is an Iraqi criminal court of nationwide jurisdiction and is administered by the government of Iraq; it is not a tribunal of the United States. Accordingly, the district court has no power or authority to hear this case.

Munaf contends that *Hirota* and *Flick* do not control because, like Omar and unlike the petitioners in *Hirota* and *Flick*, Munaf is a United States citizen. *See, e.g., Johnson v. Eisentrager*, 339 U.S. 763, 769 (1950) (describing citizenship as "a head of jurisdiction and a ground of protection"). But Munaf's citizenship does not take his case out of the ambit of *Hirota* and *Flick*. *Hirota* did not suggest any distinction between citizens and noncitizens who were held abroad pursuant to the judgment of a non-U.S. tribunal. Indeed, Justice Douglas wrote a separate opinion criticizing the *Hirota* majority for seeming to foreclose habeas review even for American citizens held in such circumstances. In *Omar*, we held that "the critical factor in *Hirota* was the petitioners' convictions by an international tribunal." We explained that, because *Hirota* "articulates no general principle at all," the decision is controlling as a matter of precedent if the circumstances important to the Court's decision are present here. As in *Hirota*, Munaf's case involves an international force, detention overseas, and a conviction by a non-U.S. court. As we noted in *Omar*, conducting habeas proceedings in the face of such a conviction risks judicial second-guessing of a non-U.S. court's judgments and sentences, and we explained that *Hirota's* repeated references to the petitioners' sentences "demonstrate[] that the Court's primary concern was that the petitions represented a collateral attack on the final judgment of an international tribunal." Whether a habeas attack on a conviction by a non-U.S. court is not dependent on the petitioner's citizenship. In light of the precedent established by *Hirota*, specifically as interpreted in *Flick* and *Omar*, American citizenship cannot displace the fact of a criminal conviction in a non-United States court and permit the district court to exercise jurisdiction over Munaf's habeas petition.

Munaf also argues that he does not challenge his conviction by the Iraqi court but rather the lawfulness of his detention at the hands of United States military personnel. As with Munaf's citizenship argument, we do not think that *Hirota* and *Flick* can be distinguished on this ground. In *Hirota* and *Flick*, as in this case, U.S. forces who were operating as part of a multinational force detained the petitioners. And as in those cases, continued confinement is dependent on a conviction by a court not of the United States — specifically, a multinational tribunal in *Hirota* and *Flick* and, in this case, the CCCI, which is a foreign tribunal. The fact that the MNF-I is not an arm of the Iraqi government but rather cooperates with Iraq and its courts in matters of detention does not bring this case outside the scope of *Hirota*. Munaf states in his brief that "[e]ven if the Iraqi charges were dismissed tomorrow the United States does not suggest [Munaf] would be released." But the district court's jurisdiction to inquire into such matters is precisely the issue; if the charges were dismissed, and United States forces were to continue to hold Munaf, this would be a different case. Under *Omar* the district court arguably *would* have jurisdiction over Munaf's habeas claim.

One final point deserves emphasis. In holding that the district court lacks jurisdiction, we do not mean to suggest that we find the logic of *Hirota* especially clear or compelling, particularly as applied to American citizens. In particular, *Hirota* does not explain why, in cases such as this, the fact of a criminal conviction in a non-U.S. court is a fact of jurisdictional significance under the habeas statute. And as we acknowledged in *Omar*, the Supreme Court's recent decisions in *Hamdi v. Rumsfeld*, 542 U.S. 507 (2004), and *Rasul v. Bush*, 542 U.S. 466 (2004), are grounds for questioning *Hirota's* continued vitality. But we are not free to disregard *Hirota* simply because we may find its logic less than compelling. "If a precedent of [the Supreme] Court has direct application in a case, yet appears to rest on reasons rejected in some other line of decisions, the Court of Appeals should follow the case which directly controls, leaving to [the Supreme] Court the prerogative of overruling its own decisions."

For the reasons discussed above, the judgment of the district court is *Affirmed*.

RANDOLPH, CIRCUIT JUDGE, concurring in the judgment.

I believe the district court had jurisdiction over Munaf's habeas corpus petition. The critical considerations are that Munaf is an American citizen and that he is held by American forces overseas. *Hirota v. MacArthur*, 338 U.S. 197 (1948) (per curiam), in which the habeas petitioners were Japanese citizens held in Japan, therefore does not apply. There is a longstanding jurisdictional distinction between citizens and aliens detained outside the sovereign territory of the United States. In *Johnson v. Eisentrager*, 339 U.S. 763, 781 (1950), decided two years after *Hirota*, the Court held that it lacked jurisdiction to issue writs of habeas corpus for German prisoners held by the United States in Germany. But the Court stated that its holding did not apply to American citizens, to whom the "Court long ago extended *habeas corpus*" when they were held outside the United States. *See id.* at 769–70 (citing *Chin Yow v. United States*, 208 U.S. 8 (1908)).

It is hardly surprising then that eight of the nine Justices in *Rasul v. Bush*, 542 U.S. 466 (2004), explicitly agreed that American citizens held by American officials overseas could invoke habeas jurisdiction. For himself and four other Justices, Justice Stevens wrote that "[a]liens held at the [Guantánamo Bay Naval] base, no less than American citizens, are entitled to invoke the federal courts' authority under [28 U.S.C.] § 2241." Justice Scalia, joined by Chief Justice Rehnquist and Justice Thomas, stated that "[n]either party to the present case challenges the atextual extension of the habeas statute to United States citizens held beyond the territorial jurisdictions of the United States courts," "[a]nd *that* position — the position that United States citizens throughout the world may be entitled to habeas corpus rights — is precisely the position that this Court adopted in *Eisentrager* . . . even while holding that aliens abroad *did not have* habeas corpus rights." *Id.* at 497, 502 (Scalia, J., dissenting) (citation omitted).

It is true that *Omar v. Harvey*, 2007 U.S. App. LEXIS 2891 (D.C. Cir. Feb. 9, 2007), distinguished *Hirota* and *Flick* on the ground that in both cases the alien petitioners held overseas had been convicted by an international tribunal. But *Omar* did not speak to the jurisdictional issue confronting us here. To extend *Hirota* to habeas petitions filed by American citizens not only would contradict *Eisentrager* and the majority and dissenting opinions in *Rasul*, but also would constitute an unwarranted extension of an opinion that "articulates no general legal principle at all."

Habeas petitions test the legality of detention. The fact that the United States is holding Munaf because of his conviction by a foreign tribunal thus goes to the question whether he is entitled to the writ, not to the question whether the court has jurisdiction to consider the petition. As to the merits, I believe *Wilson v. Girard*, 354 U.S. 524 (1957), is conclusive. After Japan indicted a United States soldier for killing a Japanese woman in Japan, the soldier sought a writ of habeas corpus in the United States District Court for the District of Columbia to prevent his transfer to Japanese authorities. The district court denied the writ on the merits but issued a preliminary injunction against the soldier's transfer. Referring to a Security Treaty between the United States and Japan, the Supreme Court upheld the denial of the writ but reversed the grant of the injunction, reasoning that a "sovereign nation has exclusive jurisdiction to punish offenses against its laws committed within its borders, unless it expressly or impliedly consents to surrender its jurisdiction." In Munaf's case, the Congressional Authorization for Use of Military Force Against Iraq, in conjunction with United Nations Security Council Resolutions 1546 (June 8, 2004) and 1637 (Nov. 11, 2005), commands the same result.

§ 8.04   GUANTÁNAMO: MILITARY TRIBUNALS AND CONGRESS

Following the June 2004 Supreme Court cases, the treatment of military detainees split into three tracks. The military established "Combatant Status Review Tribunals" to make determinations on the status of each of the Guantánamo detainees. Meanwhile, some of those detainees continued to pursue their habeas corpus petitions. The third track was that some detainees were brought before military commissions for trial on charges.

[A]   The Guantánamo Detainees

At its peak, Guantánamo housed about 750 prisoners. By the first of 2008, there were less than 300 remaining and about a third of those were awaiting movement to some country willing to accept them. The rest have been released pursuant to findings that they were No Longer Enemy Combatants (NLEC) or Non Enemy Combatants (NEC).

The treatment of detainees at Guantánamo was the subject of criticism from the beginning but became intense after the disclosures of Abu Ghraib. Allegedly, it was at Guantánamo that some of the harsh treatment methods later employed at Abu Ghraib were developed. A number of released prisoners have recounted tales of serious torture and mistreatment of detainees.

David Hicks, an Australian who eventually pleaded guilty to material support charges and was returned to Australia, was released after completing his sentence on December 29, 2007. According to his father, Hicks pleaded guilty only to get out of Guantánamo and is concerned that other detainees are still being mistreated.

The most reputable watchdog groups monitoring the situation at Guantánamo are critical but guarded in their statements about conditions of confinement and treatment of the detainees. *Human Rights First*, http://www.humanrightsfirst.org. *Human Rights Watch*, http://www.hrw.org.

Meanwhile, criticisms of Guantánamo around the world have continued to build. The British Government has called the situation "unacceptable." "The historic tradition of the United States as a beacon of freedom, liberty and of justice deserves the removal of this symbol" *UK Told US Won't Shut Guantánamo*, BBC News, May 11, 2006, *available at* http://news.bbc.co.uk/1/hi/uk_politics/4760365.stm. The UN Committee against Torture, after criticizing the U.S. for aggressive interrogation methods, secret detentions, and extraordinary renditions, had this to say about Guantánamo:

> 22. The Committee, noting that detaining persons indefinitely without charge, constitutes per se a violation of the Convention, is concerned that detainees are held for protracted periods at Guantánamo Bay, without sufficient legal safeguards and without judicial assessment of the justification for their detention. (articles 2, 3, and 16) The State party should cease to detain any person at Guantánamo Bay and close this detention facility, permit access by the detainees to judicial process or release them as soon as possible, ensuring that they are not returned to any State where they could face a real risk of being tortured, in order to comply with its obligations under the Convention.

U.N. Doc #CAT/C/USA/CO/2 (18 May 2006), *available at* http://news.bbc.co.uk/2/shared/bsp/hi/pdfs/19_05_06_torture.pdf.

Colin Powell joined the chorus against Guantánamo in June 2007: "Essentially, we have shaken the belief the world had in America's justice system by keeping a place like Guantánamo open and creating things like the military commission. We don't need it and it is causing us far more damage than any good we get from it." *Colin Powell Says Guantánamo Should Be Closed*, REUTERS, June 10, 2007, *available at* http://www.reuters.com/article/topNews/idUSN1043646920070610?feedType=RSS.

It is a bit difficult to categorize the detainees at Guantánamo. Some of the detainees are there on what Senator Arlen Specter has called flimsy hearsay, while others are there as part of groups that were radicalized dissidents in places such as East Tajikstan. In September 2006, 14 "high value detainees" were transferred from CIA custody to Guantánamo.

In March 2007, the Department of Defense began releasing transcripts of hearings before the Combatant Status Review Tribunals (CSRT's). *See* http://www.defenselink.mil/news/Combatant_Tribunals.html.

One of the most interesting transcripts is that of Khalid Sheikh Mohammed (KSM), the alleged mastermind of 9/11 and the uncle of Ramzi Yousef. In his formal statement, KSM claimed responsibility for 31 separate plots and actions (he orally corrected the statement to say that he "shared" responsibility for one of the 31). All 31 statements began with the phrase "I was responsible for" except this one: "I decapitated with my blessed right hand the head of the American Jew, Daniel Pearl." After the formal recitation of his claims, he offered these comments orally:

> What I wrote here, is not I'm making myself hero, when I said I was responsible for this or that. But you're are military man. You know very well there are language for any war. So, there are, we are when I admitting these things I'm not saying I'm not did it. I did it but this the language of any war. If America they want to invade Iraq they will not send for Saddam roses or kisses they send for a bombardment. This is the best way if I want. If I'm fighting for anybody admit to them I'm American enemies. For sure, I'm American enemies. . . .
>
> So when we made any war against America we are jackals fighting in the nights. I consider myself, for what you are doing, a religious thing as you consider us fundamentalist. So, we derive from religious leading that we consider we and George Washington doing same thing. As consider George Washington as hero. . . .
>
> So when we say we are enemy combatant, that right. We are. But I'm asking you again to be fair with many Detainees which are not enemy combatant.

Because many of them have been unjustly arrested. Many, not one or two or three. . . .

But if you and me, two nations, will be together in war the others are victims. This is the way of the language. You know 40 million people were killed in World War One. Ten million kill in World War. You know that two million four hundred thousand be killed in the Korean War. So this language of the war. Any people who, when Usama bin Laden say I'm waging war because such such reason, now he declared it. But when you said I'm terrorist, I think it is deceiving peoples. Terrorists, enemy combatant. All these definitions as CIA you can make whatever you want. . . .

If now we were living in the Revolutionary War and George Washington he being arrested through Britain. For sure he, they would consider him enemy combatant. But American they consider him as hero. This right the any Revolutionary War they will be as George Washington or Britain. . . .

This is why the language of any war in the world is killing. I mean the language of the war is victims. I don't like to kill people. I feel very sorry they been killed kids in 9/11. What I will do? This is the language. Sometime I want to make great awakening between American to stop foreign policy in our land. . . .

Killing is prohibited in all what you call the people of the book, Jews, Judaism, Christianity, and Islam. You know the Ten Commandments very well. The Ten Commandments are shared between all of us. We all are serving one God. Then now kill you know it very well. But war language also we have language for the war. You have to kill. . . .

The American have human right. So, enemy combatant itself, it flexible word" So I think God knows that many who been arrested, they been unjustly arrested. Otherwise, military throughout history know very well. They don't want war will never stop. War start from Adam when Cain he killed Abel until now. It's never gonna stop killing people. . . .

The Defense Department provided a list in May 2006 of all detainees who had been through Guantánamo as of that time: http://www.dod.mil/pubs/foi/detainees/detaineesFOIArelease15May2006.pdf.

[B] Military Commissions and the Law of War

The trial before a military commission of a person for alleged "war crimes" raises the question of what law applies to a "non-state actor." Referring back to the concepts in Chapter 3, the "law of war" applies in time of "armed conflict." The Geneva Conventions deal with "combatants" who under Geneva III (GPW) and civilians under Geneva IV (GC). A person who meets the criteria for POW status under GPW article 4 should also have combat immunity for actions that did not violate the law of war. A civilian may be entitled to "protected status" under Geneva IV but may nevertheless be placed on trial for violent crimes committed in the absence of combat immunity. Both conventions depend on a state of armed conflict, but the assertion of criminal jurisdiction over an offender may exist completely apart from the law of war (as, for example, in occupied territory at the conclusion of hostilities). In that instance, one question would be what tribunal would have jurisdiction over the criminal charges.

HAMDAN v. RUMSFELD
548 U.S. 557 (2006)

JUSTICE STEVENS announced the judgment of the Court and delivered the opinion of the Court with respect to Parts I through IV, Parts VI through VI-D-iii, Part VI-D-v, and Part VII, and an opinion with respect to Parts V and VI-D-iv, in which JUSTICE SOUTER, JUSTICE GINSBURG, and JUSTICE BREYER join.

Petitioner Salim Ahmed Hamdan, a Yemeni national, is in custody at an American prison in Guantánamo Bay, Cuba. In November 2001, during hostilities between the United States and the Taliban (which then governed Afghanistan), Hamdan was captured by militia forces and turned over to the U.S. military. In June 2002, he was transported to Guantánamo Bay. Over a year later, the President deemed him eligible for trial by military commission for then-unspecified crimes. After another year had passed, Hamdan was charged with one count of conspiracy "to commit . . . offenses triable by military commission."

Hamdan filed petitions for writs of habeas corpus and mandamus to challenge the Executive Branch's intended means of prosecuting this charge. He concedes that a court-martial constituted in accordance with the Uniform Code of Military Justice (UCMJ), 10 U.S.C. § 801 *et seq.*, would have authority to try him. His objection is that the military commission the President has convened lacks such authority, for two principal reasons: First, neither congressional Act nor the common law of war supports trial by this commission for the crime of conspiracy — an offense that, Hamdan says, is not a violation of the law of war. Second, Hamdan contends, the procedures that the President has adopted to try him violate the most basic tenets of military and international law, including the principle that a defendant must be permitted to see and hear the evidence against him.

The District Court granted Hamdan's request for a writ of habeas corpus. 344 F. Supp. 2d 152 (DC 2004). The Court of Appeals for the District of Columbia Circuit reversed. 415 F.3d 33 (2005). Recognizing, as we did over a half-century ago, that trial by military commission is an extraordinary measure raising important questions about the balance of powers in our constitutional structure, *Ex parte Quirin*, 317 U.S. 1, 19 (1942), we granted certiorari.

For the reasons that follow, we conclude that the military commission convened to try Hamdan lacks power to proceed because its structure and procedures violate both the UCMJ and the Geneva Conventions. Four of us also conclude, see Part V, that the offense with which Hamdan has been charged is not an "offense that by . . . the law of war may be tried by military commissions." 10 U.S.C. § 821.

I

Congress responded [to 9/11] by adopting a Joint Resolution authorizing the President to "use all necessary and appropriate force against those nations, organizations, or persons he determines planned, authorized, committed, or aided the terrorist attacks . . . in order to prevent any future acts of international terrorism against the United States by such nations, organizations or persons." Authorization for Use of Military Force (AUMF). Acting pursuant to the AUMF, and having determined that the Taliban regime had supported al Qaeda, the President ordered the Armed Forces of the United States to invade Afghanistan. In the ensuing hostilities, hundreds of individuals, Hamdan among them, were captured and eventually detained at Guantánamo Bay.

On November 13, 2001, while the United States was still engaged in active combat with the Taliban, the President issued a comprehensive military order intended to govern the "Detention, Treatment, and Trial of Certain Non-Citizens in the War Against Terrorism," 66 Fed. Reg. 57833 (hereinafter November 13 Order or Order). Those subject to the November 13 Order include any noncitizen for whom the President determines "there is reason to believe" that he or she (1) "is or was" a member of al Qaeda or (2) has engaged or participated in terrorist activities aimed at or harmful to the United States. Any such individual "shall, when tried, be tried by military commission for any and all offenses triable by military commission that such individual is alleged to have committed, and may be punished in accordance with the penalties provided under applicable law, including imprisonment or death." The November 13 Order vested in the Secretary of Defense the power to appoint military commissions to try individuals subject to the Order, but that power has since been delegated to John D. Altenberg, Jr., a retired Army major general and longtime military lawyer who has been designated "Appointing Authority for Military Commissions."

On July 3, 2003, the President announced his determination that Hamdan and five other detainees at Guantánamo Bay were subject to the November 13 Order and thus triable by military commission. In December 2003, military counsel was appointed to represent Hamdan. Two months later, counsel filed demands for charges and for a speedy trial pursuant to Article 10 of the UCMJ, 10 U.S.C. § 810. On February 23, 2004, the legal adviser to the Appointing Authority denied the applications, ruling that Hamdan was not entitled to any of the protections of the UCMJ. Not until July 13, 2004, after Hamdan had commenced this action in the United States District Court for the Western District of Washington, did the Government finally charge him with the offense for which, a year earlier, he had been deemed eligible for trial by military commission.

The charging document, which is unsigned, contains 13 numbered paragraphs. Only the final two paragraphs, entitled "Charge: Conspiracy," contain allegations against Hamdan. Paragraph 12 charges that "from on or about February 1996 to on or about November 24, 2001," Hamdan "willfully and knowingly joined an enterprise of persons who shared a common criminal purpose and conspired and agreed with [named members of al Qaeda] to commit the following offenses triable by military commission: attacking civilians; attacking civilian objects; murder by an unprivileged belligerent; and terrorism." There is no allegation that Hamdan had any command responsibilities, played a leadership role, or participated in the planning of any activity.

Paragraph 13 lists four "overt acts" that Hamdan is alleged to have committed sometime between 1996 and November 2001 in furtherance of the "enterprise and conspiracy": (1) he acted as Osama bin Laden's "bodyguard and personal driver," "believing" all the while that bin Laden "and his associates were involved in" terrorist acts prior to and including the attacks of September 11, 2001; (2) he arranged for transportation of, and actually transported, weapons used by al Qaeda members and by bin Laden's bodyguards (Hamdan among them); (3) he "drove or accompanied Osama bin Laden to various al Qaida-sponsored training camps, press conferences, or lectures," at which bin Laden encouraged attacks against Americans; and (4) he received weapons training at al Qaeda-sponsored camps.

After this formal charge was filed, the United States District Court for the Western District of Washington transferred Hamdan's habeas and mandamus petitions to the United States District Court for the District of Columbia. Meanwhile, a Combatant Status Review Tribunal (CSRT) convened pursuant to a military order issued on July 7, 2004, decided that Hamdan's continued detention at Guantánamo Bay was warranted because he was an "enemy combatant."[13] Separately, proceedings before the military commission commenced.

On November 8, 2004, however, the District Court granted Hamdan's petition for habeas corpus and stayed the commission's proceedings. It concluded that the President's authority to establish military commissions extends only to "offenders or offenses triable by military [commission] under the law of war;" that the law of war includes the Geneva Convention (III) Relative to the Treatment of Prisoners of War; that Hamdan is entitled to the full protections of the Third Geneva Convention until adjudged, in compliance with that treaty, not to be a prisoner of war; and that, whether or not Hamdan is properly classified as a prisoner of war, the military commission

---

[13] [Court's Footnote 1] An "enemy combatant" is defined by the military order as "an individual who was part of or supporting Taliban or al Qaeda forces, or associated forces that are engaged in hostilities against the United States or its coalition partners." Memorandum from Deputy Secretary of Defense Paul Wolfowitz re: Order Establishing Combatant Status Review Tribunal § a (Jul. 7, 2004), http://www.defenselink.mil/news/Jul2004/d20040707review.pdf.

convened to try him was established in violation of both the UCMJ and Common Article 3 of the Third Geneva Convention because it had the power to convict based on evidence the accused would never see or hear.

The Court of Appeals for the District of Columbia Circuit reversed. [T]he panel rejected the District Court's conclusion that Hamdan was entitled to relief under the Third Geneva Convention. All three judges agreed that the Geneva Conventions were not "judicially enforceable," and two thought that the Conventions did not in any event apply to Hamdan. In other portions of its opinion, the court concluded that our decision in *Quirin* foreclosed any separation-of-powers objection to the military commission's jurisdiction, and held that Hamdan's trial before the contemplated commission would violate neither the UCMJ nor U.S. Armed Forces regulations intended to implement the Geneva Conventions. On November 7, 2005, we granted certiorari to decide whether the military commission convened to try Hamdan has authority to do so, and whether Hamdan may rely on the Geneva Conventions in these proceedings.

II

On February 13, 2006, the Government filed a motion to dismiss the writ of certiorari. The ground cited for dismissal was the recently enacted Detainee Treatment Act of 2005 (DTA), Pub. L. 109–148. We postponed our ruling on that motion pending argument on the merits and now deny it.

The DTA, which was signed into law on December 30, 2005, addresses a broad swath of subjects related to detainees. It places restrictions on the treatment and interrogation of detainees in U.S. custody, and it furnishes procedural protections for U.S. personnel accused of engaging in improper interrogation.

Subsection (e) of § 1005, which is entitled "JUDICIAL REVIEW OF DETENTION OF ENEMY COMBATANTS," supplies the basis for the Government's jurisdictional argument. The subsection contains three numbered paragraphs. The first paragraph amends the judicial code as follows:

> (1) IN GENERAL. — Section 2241 of title 28, United States Code, is amended by adding at the end the following:

> (e) Except as provided in section 1005 of the Detainee Treatment Act of 2005, no court, justice, or judge shall have jurisdiction to hear or consider

> (1) an application for a writ of habeas corpus filed by or on behalf of an alien detained by the Department of Defense at Guantánamo Bay, Cuba; or

> (2) any other action against the United States or its agents relating to any aspect of the detention by the Department of Defense of an alien at Guantánamo Bay, Cuba, who

> (A) is currently in military custody; or

> (B) has been determined by the United States Court of Appeals for the District of Columbia Circuit in accordance with the procedures set forth in section 1005(e) of the Detainee Treatment Act of 2005 to have been properly detained as an enemy combatant.

§ 1005(e)

Paragraph (2) of subsection (e) [of § 1005 — not subsection (e) of § 2241] vests in the Court of Appeals for the District of Columbia Circuit the "exclusive jurisdiction to determine the validity of any final decision of a [CSRT] that an alien is properly designated as an enemy combatant." Paragraph (2) also delimits the scope of that review.

Paragraph (3) mirrors paragraph (2) in structure, but governs judicial review of final decisions of military commissions, not CSRTs. It vests in the Court of Appeals for the District of Columbia Circuit "exclusive jurisdiction to determine the validity of any final decision rendered pursuant to Military Commission Order No. 1, dated August 31, 2005 (or any successor military order)."

Finally, § 1005 contains an "effective date" provision, which reads as follows:

(1) IN GENERAL. — This section shall take effect on the date of the enactment of this Act.

(2) REVIEW OF COMBATANT STATUS TRIBUNAL AND MILITARY COMMISSION DECISIONS. — Paragraphs (2) and (3) of subsection (e) shall apply with respect to any claim whose review is governed by one of such paragraphs and that is pending on or after the date of the enactment of this Act.

§ 1005(h)[14]

The Act is silent about whether paragraph (1) of subsection (e) "shall apply" to claims pending on the date of enactment.

The Government argues that §§ 1005(e)(1) and 1005(h) had the immediate effect, upon enactment, of repealing federal jurisdiction not just over detainee habeas actions yet to be filed but also over any such actions then pending in any federal court — including this Court. Accordingly, it argues, we lack jurisdiction to review the Court of Appeals' decision below.

Hamdan objects to this theory on both constitutional and statutory grounds. Principal among his constitutional arguments is that the Government's preferred reading raises grave questions about Congress' authority to impinge upon this Court's appellate jurisdiction, particularly in habeas cases. Hamdan also suggests that, if the Government's reading is correct, Congress has unconstitutionally suspended the writ of habeas corpus.

We find it unnecessary to reach either of these arguments. Ordinary principles of statutory construction suffice to rebut the Government's theory — at least insofar as this case, which was pending at the time the DTA was enacted, is concerned.

The Government acknowledges that only paragraphs (2) and (3) of subsection (e) are expressly made applicable to pending cases, but argues that the omission of paragraph (1) from the scope of that express statement is of no moment. This is so, we are told, because Congress' failure to expressly reserve federal courts' jurisdiction over pending cases erects a presumption against jurisdiction, and that presumption is rebutted by neither the text nor the legislative history of the DTA.

The first part of this argument is not entirely without support in our precedents. We have in the past "applied intervening statutes conferring or ousting jurisdiction, whether or not jurisdiction lay when the underlying conduct occurred or when the suit was filed." *Landgraf v. USI Film Products*, 511 U.S. 244, 274 (1994). But the "presumption" that these cases have applied is more accurately viewed as the nonapplication of another presumption — viz., the presumption against retroactivity — in certain limited circumstances. If a statutory provision "would operate retroactively" as applied to cases pending at the time the provision was enacted, then "our traditional presumption teaches that it does not govern absent clear congressional intent favoring such a result." We have explained, however, that, unlike other intervening changes in the law, a jurisdiction-conferring or jurisdiction-stripping statute usually "takes away no substantive right but simply changes the tribunal that is to hear the case." If that is truly all the statute does, no retroactivity problem arises because the change in the law does not "impair rights a party possessed when he acted, increase a party's liability for past conduct, or impose new duties with respect to transactions already completed." And if a new rule has no retroactive effect, the presumption against retroactivity will not

---

[14] [Court's Footnote 3] The penultimate subsections of § 1005 emphasize that the provision does not "confer any constitutional right on an alien detained as an enemy combatant outside the United States" and that the "United States" does not, for purposes of § 1005, include Guantánamo Bay. §§ 1005(f)–(g).

prevent its application to a case that was already pending when the new rule was enacted.

That does not mean, however, that all jurisdiction-stripping provisions — or even all such provisions that truly lack retroactive effect — must apply to cases pending at the time of their enactment. "Normal rules of construction," including a contextual reading of the statutory language, may dictate otherwise. *Lindh v. Murphy*, 521 U.S. 320, 326 (1997). A familiar principle of statutory construction, relevant both in *Lindh* and here, is that a negative inference may be drawn from the exclusion of language from one statutory provision that is included in other provisions of the same statute. The Court in *Lindh* relied on this reasoning to conclude that certain limitations on the availability of habeas relief imposed by AEDPA applied only to cases filed after that statute's effective date. Congress' failure to identify the temporal reach of those limitations, which governed noncapital cases, stood in contrast to its express command in the same legislation that new rules governing habeas petitions in capital cases "apply to cases pending on or after the date of enactment." That contrast, combined with the fact that the amendments at issue "affected substantive entitlement to relief," warranted drawing a negative inference.

A like inference follows a *fortiori* from *Lindh* in this case. "If . . . Congress was reasonably concerned to ensure that [§#xa7; 1005(e)(2) and (3)] be applied to pending cases, it should have been just as concerned about [§ 1005(e)(1)], unless it had the different intent that the latter [section] not be applied to the general run of pending cases." Here, Congress not only considered the respective temporal reaches of paragraphs (1), (2), and (3) of subsection (e) together at every stage, but omitted paragraph (1) from its directive that paragraphs (2) and (3) apply to pending cases only after having *rejected* earlier proposed versions of the statute that would have included what is now paragraph (1) within the scope of that directive. Congress' rejection of the very language that would have achieved the result the Government urges here weighs heavily against the Government's interpretation.

The Government's more general suggestion that Congress can have had no good reason for preserving habeas jurisdiction over cases that had been brought by detainees prior to enactment of the DTA not only is belied by the legislative history, but is otherwise without merit. There is nothing absurd about a scheme under which pending habeas actions — particularly those, like this one, that challenge the very legitimacy of the tribunals whose judgments Congress would like to have reviewed — are preserved, and more routine challenges to final decisions rendered by those tribunals are carefully channeled to a particular court and through a particular lens of review.

III

Relying on our decision in *Councilman*, 420 U.S. 738, the Government argues that, even if we have statutory jurisdiction, we should apply the "judge-made rule that civilian courts should await the final outcome of on-going military proceedings before entertaining an attack on those proceedings." Like the District Court and the Court of Appeals before us, we reject this argument.

In *Councilman*, an army officer on active duty was referred to a court-martial for trial on charges that he violated the UCMJ by selling, transferring, and possessing marijuana. Objecting that the alleged offenses were not " 'service connected,' " the officer filed suit in Federal District Court to enjoin the proceedings. He neither questioned the lawfulness of courts-martial or their procedures nor disputed that, as a serviceman, he was subject to court-martial jurisdiction. His sole argument was that the subject matter of his case did not fall within the scope of court-martial authority.

[N]either of the comity considerations identified in *Councilman* weighs in favor of abstention in this case. First, Hamdan is not a member of our Nation's Armed Forces, so concerns about military discipline do not apply. Second, the tribunal convened to try

Hamdan is not part of the integrated system of military courts, complete with independent review panels, that Congress has established. Unlike the officer in *Councilman*, Hamdan has no right to appeal any conviction to the civilian judges of the Court of Military Appeals (now called the United States Court of Appeals for the Armed Forces).

While we certainly do not foreclose the possibility that abstention may be appropriate in some cases seeking review of ongoing military commission proceedings (such as military commissions convened on the battlefield), the foregoing discussion makes clear that, under our precedent, abstention is not justified here. We therefore proceed to consider the merits of Hamdan's challenge.

IV

The military commission, a tribunal neither mentioned in the Constitution nor created by statute, was born of military necessity. *See* W. WINTHROP, MILITARY LAW AND PRECEDENTS 831 (rev. 2d ed. 1920) (hereinafter WINTHROP). Though foreshadowed in some respects by earlier tribunals like the Board of General Officers that General Washington convened to try British Major John Andre for spying during the Revolutionary War, the commission "as such" was inaugurated in 1847. *Id.*, at 832; G. DAVIS, A TREATISE ON THE MILITARY LAW OF THE UNITED STATES 308 (2d ed. 1909) (hereinafter *Davis*). As commander of occupied Mexican territory, and having available to him no other tribunal, General Winfield Scott that year ordered the establishment of both " '*military commissions*' " to try ordinary crimes committed in the occupied territory and a "*council of war*" to try offenses against the law of war. WINTHROP 832 (emphases in original).

When the exigencies of war next gave rise to a need for use of military commissions, during the Civil War, the dual system favored by General Scott was not adopted. Instead, a single tribunal often took jurisdiction over ordinary crimes, war crimes, and breaches of military orders alike. As further discussed below, each aspect of that seemingly broad jurisdiction was in fact supported by a separate military exigency. Generally, though, the need for military commissions during this period — as during the Mexican War — was driven largely by the then very limited jurisdiction of courts-martial: "The *occasion* for the military commission arises principally from the fact that the jurisdiction of the court-martial proper, in our law, is restricted by statute almost exclusively to members of the military force and to certain specific offences defined in a written code." *Id.*, at 831 (emphasis in original).

Exigency alone, of course, will not justify the establishment and use of penal tribunals not contemplated by Article I, § 8 and Article III, § 1 of the Constitution unless some other part of that document authorizes a response to the felt need. And that authority, if it exists, can derive only from the powers granted jointly to the President and Congress in time of war.

The Constitution makes the President the "Commander in Chief" of the Armed Forces, but vests in Congress the powers to "declare War . . . and make Rules concerning Captures on Land and Water," to "raise and support Armies," to "define and punish . . . Offences against the Law of Nations," and "To make Rules for the Government and Regulation of the land and naval Forces." The interplay between these powers was described by Chief Justice Chase in the seminal case of *Ex parte Milligan:*

> The power to make the necessary laws is in Congress; the power to execute in the President. Both powers imply many subordinate and auxiliary powers. Each includes all authorities essential to its due exercise. But neither can the President, in war more than in peace, intrude upon the proper authority of Congress, nor Congress upon the proper authority of the President . . . . Congress cannot direct the conduct of campaigns, nor can the President, or any commander under him, without the sanction of Congress, institute tribunals for

the trial and punishment of offences, either of soldiers or civilians, unless in cases of a controlling necessity, which justifies what it compels, or at least insures acts of indemnity from the justice of the legislature.

Whether Chief Justice Chase was correct in suggesting that the President may constitutionally convene military commissions "without the sanction of Congress" in cases of "controlling necessity" is a question this Court has not answered definitively, and need not answer today. For we held in *Quirin* that Congress had, through Article of War 15, sanctioned the use of military commissions in such circumstances. Article 21 of the UCMJ, the language of which is substantially identical to the old Article 15 and was preserved by Congress after World War II, reads as follows:

Jurisdiction of courts-martial not exclusive.

The provisions of this code conferring jurisdiction upon courts-martial shall not be construed as depriving military commissions, provost courts, or other military tribunals of concurrent jurisdiction in respect of offenders or offenses that by statute or by the law of war may be tried by such military commissions, provost courts, or other military tribunals.

We have no occasion to revisit *Quirin*'s controversial characterization of Article of War 15 as congressional authorization for military commissions. Contrary to the Government's assertion, however, even *Quirin* did not view the authorization as a sweeping mandate for the President to "invoke military commissions when he deems them necessary." Rather, the *Quirin* Court recognized that Congress had simply preserved what power, under the Constitution and the common law of war, the President had had before 1916 to convene military commissions — with the express condition that the President and those under his command comply with the law of war. That much is evidenced by the Court's inquiry, *following* its conclusion that Congress had authorized military commissions, into whether the law of war had indeed been complied with in that case.

The Government would have us dispense with the inquiry that the *Quirin* Court undertook and find in either the AUMF or the DTA specific, overriding authorization for the very commission that has been convened to try Hamdan. Neither of these congressional Acts, however, expands the President's authority to convene military commissions. First, while we assume that the AUMF activated the President's war powers, see *Hamdi v. Rumsfeld*, 542 U.S. 507 (2004) (plurality opinion), and that those powers include the authority to convene military commissions in appropriate circumstances, there is nothing in the text or legislative history of the AUMF even hinting that Congress intended to expand or alter the authorization set forth in Article 21 of the UCMJ.

Likewise, the DTA cannot be read to authorize this commission. Although the DTA, unlike either Article 21 or the AUMF, was enacted after the President had convened Hamdan's commission, it contains no language authorizing that tribunal or any other at Guantánamo Bay. The DTA obviously "recognizes" the existence of the Guantánamo Bay commissions in the weakest sense, because it references some of the military orders governing them and creates limited judicial review of their "final decisions." But the statute also pointedly reserves judgment on whether "the Constitution and laws of the United States are applicable" in reviewing such decisions and whether, if they are, the "standards and procedures" used to try Hamdan and other detainees actually violate the "Constitution and laws."

Together, the UCMJ, the AUMF, and the DTA at most acknowledge a general Presidential authority to convene military commissions in circumstances where justified under the "Constitution and laws," including the law of war. Absent a more specific congressional authorization, the task of this Court is, as it was in *Quirin*, to decide whether Hamdan's military commission is so justified. It is to that inquiry we now turn.

V

The common law governing military commissions may be gleaned from past practice and what sparse legal precedent exists. Commissions historically have been used in three situations. *See* Bradley & Goldsmith, *Congressional Authorization and the War on Terrorism*, 118 HARV. L. REV. 2048, 2132–2133 (2005); Winthrop 831–846. First, they have substituted for civilian courts at times and in places where martial law has been declared. Their use in these circumstances has raised constitutional questions, see *Duncan v. Kahanamoku*, 327 U.S. 304 (1946); *Milligan*, 4 Wall., at 121–122, but is well recognized. See WINTHROP 822, 836–839. Second, commissions have been established to try civilians "as part of a temporary military government over occupied enemy territory or territory regained from an enemy where civilian government cannot and does not function." *Duncan*, 327 U.S., at 314; see *Milligan*, 4 Wall., at 141–142 (Chase, C. J., concurring in judgment) (distinguishing "MARTIAL LAW PROPER" from "MILI-TARY GOVERNMENT" in occupied territory). Illustrative of this second kind of commission is the one that was established, with jurisdiction to apply the German Criminal Code, in occupied Germany following the end of World War II. See *Madsen v. Kinsella*, 343 U.S. 341, 356 (1952).

The third type of commission, convened as an "incident to the conduct of war" when there is a need "to seize and subject to disciplinary measures those enemies who in their attempt to thwart or impede our military effort have violated the law of war," *Quirin*, 317 U.S., at 28–29, has been described as "utterly different" from the other two. Not only is its jurisdiction limited to offenses cognizable during time of war, but its role is primarily a factfinding one — to determine, typically on the battlefield itself, whether the defendant has violated the law of war. The last time the U.S. Armed Forces used the law-of-war military commission was during World War II. In *Quirin*, this Court sanctioned President Roosevelt's use of such a tribunal to try Nazi saboteurs captured on American soil during the War. And in *Yamashita*, we held that a military commission had jurisdiction to try a Japanese commander for failing to prevent troops under his command from committing atrocities in the Philippines

Quirin is the model the Government invokes most frequently to defend the commission convened to try Hamdan. That is both appropriate and unsurprising. Since Guantánamo Bay is neither enemy-occupied territory nor under martial law, the law-of-war commission is the only model available. At the same time, no more robust model of executive power exists; *Quirin* represents the high-water mark of military power to try enemy combatants for war crimes.

The classic treatise penned by Colonel William Winthrop, whom we have called "the Blackstone of Military Law," describes at least four preconditions for exercise of jurisdiction by a tribunal of the type convened to try Hamdan. First, "[a] military commission, (except where otherwise authorized by statute), can legally assume jurisdiction only of offenses committed within the field of the command of the convening commander." Winthrop 836. The "field of command" in these circumstances means the "theatre of war." Second, the offense charged "must have been committed within the period of the war." No jurisdiction exists to try offenses "committed either before or after the war." Third, a military commission not established pursuant to martial law or an occupation may try only "individuals of the enemy's army who have been guilty of illegitimate warfare or other offences in violation of the laws of war" and members of one's own army "who, in time of war, become chargeable with crimes or offences not cognizable, or triable, by the criminal courts or under the Articles of war." Finally, a law-of-war commission has jurisdiction to try only two kinds of offense: "Violations of the laws and usages of war cognizable by military tribunals only," and "breaches of military orders or regulations for which offenders are not legally triable by court-martial under the Articles of war."

All parties agree that Colonel Winthrop's treatise accurately describes the common law governing military commissions, and that the jurisdictional limitations he identifies were incorporated in Article of War 15 and, later, Article 21 of the UCMJ. It also is undisputed that Hamdan's commission lacks jurisdiction to try him unless the charge "properly sets forth, not only the details of the act charged, but the circumstances conferring *jurisdiction.*" The question is whether the preconditions designed to ensure that a military necessity exists to justify the use of this extraordinary tribunal have been satisfied here.

The charge against Hamdan, described in detail in Part I, *supra,* alleges a conspiracy extending over a number of years, from 1996 to November 2001. All but two months of that more than 5-year-long period preceded the attacks of September 11, 2001, and the enactment of the AUMF — the Act of Congress on which the Government relies for exercise of its war powers and thus for its authority to convene military commissions.[15] Neither the purported agreement with Osama bin Laden and others to commit war crimes, nor a single overt act, is alleged to have occurred in a theater of war or on any specified date after September 11, 2001. None of the overt acts that Hamdan is alleged to have committed violates the law of war.

These facts alone cast doubt on the legality of the charge and, hence, the commission; as Winthrop makes plain, the offense alleged must have been committed both in a theater of war and *during,* not before, the relevant conflict. But the deficiencies in the time and place allegations also underscore — indeed are symptomatic of — the most serious defect of this charge: The offense it alleges is not triable by law-of-war military commission.

There is no suggestion that Congress has, in exercise of its constitutional authority to "define and punish . . . Offences against the Law of Nations," positively identified "conspiracy" as a war crime. As we explained in *Quirin,* that is not necessarily fatal to the Government's claim of authority to try the alleged offense by military commission; Congress, through Article 21 of the UCMJ, has "incorporated by reference" the common law of war, which may render triable by military commission certain offenses not defined by statute. When, however, neither the elements of the offense nor the range of permissible punishments is defined by statute or treaty, the precedent must be plain and unambiguous. To demand any less would be to risk concentrating in military hands a degree of adjudicative and punitive power in excess of that contemplated either by statute or by the Constitution.

This high standard was met in *Quirin;* the violation there alleged was, by "universal agreement and practice" both in this country and internationally, recognized as an offense against the law of war. Although the picture arguably was less clear in *Yamashita,* compare 327 U.S. at 16 (stating that the provisions of the Fourth Hague Convention of 1907 "plainly" required the defendant to control the troops under his command), with 327 U.S. at 35 (Murphy, J., dissenting), the disagreement between the majority and the dissenters in that case concerned whether the historic and textual evidence constituted clear precedent — not whether clear precedent was required to justify trial by law-of-war military commission.

At a minimum, the Government must make a substantial showing that the crime for which it seeks to try a defendant by military commission is acknowledged to be an offense against the law of war. That burden is far from satisfied here. The crime of "conspiracy" has rarely if ever been tried as such in this country by any law-of-war military commission not exercising some other form of jurisdiction, and does not appear in either the Geneva Conventions or the Hague Conventions — the major treaties on the law of war. Winthrop explains that under the common law governing military commis-

---

[15] [Court's Footnote 31] Justice Thomas would treat Osama bin Laden's 1996 declaration of jihad against Americans as the inception of the war. But even the Government does not go so far; although the United States had for some time prior to the attacks of September 11, 2001, been aggressively pursuing al Qaeda, neither in the charging document nor in submissions before this Court has the Government asserted that the President's war powers were activated prior to September 11, 2001.

sions, it is not enough to intend to violate the law of war and commit overt acts in furtherance of that intention unless the overt acts either are themselves offenses against the law of war or constitute steps sufficiently substantial to qualify as an attempt.

That the defendants in *Quirin* were charged with conspiracy is not persuasive, since the Court declined to address whether the offense actually qualified as a violation of the law of war — let alone one triable by military commission. If anything, *Quirin* supports Hamdan's argument that conspiracy is not a violation of the law of war. Not only did the Court pointedly omit any discussion of the conspiracy charge, but its analysis of [the charge of violation of the law of war] placed special emphasis on the *completion* of an offense; it took seriously the saboteurs' argument that there can be no violation of a law of war — at least not one triable by military commission — without the actual commission of or attempt to commit a "hostile and warlike act."

That limitation makes eminent sense when one considers the necessity from whence this kind of military commission grew: The need to dispense swift justice, often in the form of execution, to illegal belligerents captured on the battlefield. The same urgency would not have been felt vis-a-vis enemies who had done little more than agree to violate the laws of war. Cf. *31 Op. Atty. Gen.* 356, 357, 361 (1918) (opining that a German spy could not be tried by military commission because, having been apprehended before entering "any camp, fortification or other military premises of the United States," he had "committed [his offenses] outside of the field of military operations"). The *Quirin* Court acknowledged as much when it described the President's authority to use law-of-war military commissions as the power to "seize and subject to disciplinary measures those enemies *who in their attempt to thwart or impede our military effort* have violated the law of war."

[I]nternational sources confirm that the crime charged here is not a recognized violation of the law of war. As observed above, none of the major treaties governing the law of war identifies conspiracy as a violation thereof. And the only "conspiracy" crimes that have been recognized by international war crimes tribunals (whose jurisdiction often extends beyond war crimes proper to crimes against humanity and crimes against the peace) are conspiracy to commit genocide and common plan to wage aggressive war, which is a crime against the peace and requires for its commission actual participation in a "concrete plan to wage war." 1 Trial of the Major War Criminals Before the International Military Tribunal: Nuremberg, 14 November 1945-1 October 1946, p. 225 (1947). The International Military Tribunal at Nuremberg, over the prosecution's objections, pointedly refused to recognize as a violation of the law of war conspiracy to commit war crimes, and convicted only Hitler's most senior associates of conspiracy to wage aggressive war. As one prominent figure from the Nuremberg trials has explained, members of the Tribunal objected to recognition of conspiracy as a violation of the law of war on the ground that "the Anglo-American concept of conspiracy was not part of European legal systems and arguably not an element of the internationally recognized laws of war." T. Taylor, Anatomy of the Nuremberg Trials: A Personal Memoir 36 (1992).

In sum, the sources that the Government and Justice Thomas rely upon to show that conspiracy to violate the law of war is itself a violation of the law of war in fact demonstrate quite the opposite. Far from making the requisite substantial showing, the Government has failed even to offer a "merely colorable" case for inclusion of conspiracy among those offenses cognizable by law-of-war military commission. Because the charge does not support the commission's jurisdiction, the commission lacks authority to try Hamdan.

The charge's shortcomings are not merely formal, but are indicative of a broader inability on the Executive's part here to satisfy the most basic precondition — at least in the absence of specific congressional authorization — for establishment of military commissions: military necessity. Hamdan's tribunal was appointed not by a military commander in the field of battle, but by a retired major general stationed away from any active hostilities. Hamdan is charged not with an overt act for which he was caught redhanded in a theater of war and which military efficiency demands be tried expeditiously, but with an *agreement* the inception of which long predated the attacks of September 11, 2001 and the AUMF. That may well be a crime,[16] but it is not an offense that "by the law of war may be tried by military commission." None of the overt acts alleged to have been committed in furtherance of the agreement is itself a war crime, or even necessarily occurred during time of, or in a theater of, war. Any urgent need for imposition or execution of judgment is utterly belied by the record; Hamdan was arrested in November 2001 and he was not charged until mid-2004. These simply are not the circumstances in which, by any stretch of the historical evidence or this Court's precedents, a military commission established by Executive Order under the authority of Article 21 of the UCMJ may lawfully try a person and subject him to punishment.

VI

Whether or not the Government has charged Hamdan with an offense against the law of war cognizable by military commission, the commission lacks power to proceed. The UCMJ conditions the President's use of military commissions on compliance not only with the American common law of war, but also with the rest of the UCMJ itself, insofar as applicable, and with the "rules and precepts of the law of nations" — including, *inter alia*, the four Geneva Conventions signed in 1949. The procedures that the Government has decreed will govern Hamdan's trial by commission violate these laws.

A

The commission's procedures are set forth in Commission Order No. 1, which was amended most recently on August 31, 2005 — after Hamdan's trial had already begun. Every commission established pursuant to Commission Order No. 1 must have a presiding officer and at least three other members, all of whom must be commissioned officers. The presiding officer's job is to rule on questions of law and other evidentiary and interlocutory issues; the other members make findings and, if applicable, sentencing decisions. The accused is entitled to appointed military counsel and may hire civilian counsel at his own expense so long as such counsel is a U.S. citizen with security clearance "at the level SECRET or higher." The accused also is entitled to a copy of the charge(s) against him, both in English and his own language (if different), to a presumption of innocence, and to certain other rights typically afforded criminal defendants in civilian courts and courts-martial. These rights are subject, however, to one glaring condition: The accused and his civilian counsel may be excluded from, and precluded from ever learning what evidence was presented during, any part of the proceeding that either the Appointing Authority or the presiding officer decides to "close." Grounds for such closure "include the protection of information classified or classifiable . . . ; information protected by law or rule from unauthorized disclosure; the physical safety of participants in Commission proceedings, including prospective witnesses; intelligence and law enforcement sources, methods, or activities; and other national security interests." § 6(B)(3). Appointed military defense counsel must be privy to these closed sessions, but may, at the presiding officer's discretion, be forbidden to reveal to his or her client what took place therein.

Another striking feature of the rules governing Hamdan's commission is that they permit the admission of *any* evidence that, in the opinion of the presiding officer, "would have probative value to a reasonable person." § 6(D)(1). Under this test, not only is

---

[16] [Court's Footnote 41] Justice Thomas' suggestion that our conclusion precludes the Government from bringing to justice those who conspire to commit acts of terrorism is therefore wide of the mark. That conspiracy is not a violation of the law of war triable by military commission does not mean the Government may not, for example, prosecute by court-martial or in federal court those caught "plotting terrorist atrocities like the bombing of the Khobar Towers."

testimonial hearsay and evidence obtained through coercion fully admissible, but neither live testimony nor witnesses' written statements need be sworn. Moreover, the accused and his civilian counsel may be denied access to evidence in the form of "protected information" (which includes classified information as well as "information protected by law or rule from unauthorized disclosure" and "information concerning other national security interests," so long as the presiding officer concludes that the evidence is "probative" under § 6(D)(1) and that its admission without the accused's knowledge would not "result in the denial of a full and fair trial." Finally, a presiding officer's determination that evidence "would not have probative value to a reasonable person" may be overridden by a majority of the other commission members.

Once all the evidence is in, the commission members (not including the presiding officer) must vote on the accused's guilt. A two-thirds vote will suffice for both a verdict of guilty and for imposition of any sentence not including death (the imposition of which requires a unanimous vote). Any appeal is taken to a three-member review panel composed of military officers and designated by the Secretary of Defense, only one member of which need have experience as a judge. The review panel is directed to "disregard any variance from procedures specified in this Order or elsewhere that would not materially have affected the outcome of the trial before the Commission." Once the panel makes its recommendation to the Secretary of Defense, the Secretary can either remand for further proceedings or forward the record to the President with his recommendation as to final disposition. The President then, unless he has delegated the task to the Secretary, makes the "final decision." He may change the commission's findings or sentence only in a manner favorable to the accused.

B

Hamdan raises both general and particular objections to the procedures set forth in Commission Order No. 1. His general objection is that the procedures' admitted deviation from those governing courts-martial itself renders the commission illegal. Chief among his particular objections are that he may, under the Commission Order, be convicted based on evidence he has not seen or heard, and that any evidence admitted against him need not comply with the admissibility or relevance rules typically applicable in criminal trials and court-martial proceedings.

The Government objects to our consideration of any procedural challenge at this stage . . . . One of Hamdan's complaints is that he will be, and *indeed already has been*, excluded from his own trial. Under these circumstances, review of the procedures in advance of a "final decision" — the timing of which is left entirely to the discretion of the President under the DTA — is appropriate. We turn, then, to consider the merits of Hamdan's procedural challenge.

C

In part because the difference between military commissions and courts-martial originally was a difference of jurisdiction alone, and in part to protect against abuse and ensure evenhandedness under the pressures of war, the procedures governing trials by military commission historically have been the same as those governing courts-martial. Accounts of commentators from Winthrop through General Crowder — who drafted Article of War 15 and whose views have been deemed "authoritative" by this Court — confirm as much. As recently as the Korean and Vietnam wars, during which use of military commissions was contemplated but never made, the principle of procedural parity was espoused as a background assumption. See Paust, *Antiterrorism Military Commissions: Courting Illegality*, 23 MICH. J. INT'L L. 1, 3–5 (2001–2002).

There is a glaring historical exception to this general rule. The procedures and evidentiary rules used to try General Yamashita near the end of World War II deviated in significant respects from those then governing courts-martial. The force of that precedent, however, has been seriously undermined by post-World War II developments.

At least partially in response to subsequent criticism of General Yamashita's trial, the UCMJ's codification of the Articles of War after World War II expanded the category of persons subject thereto to include defendants in Yamashita's (and Hamdan's) position, and the Third Geneva Convention of 1949 extended prisoner-of-war protections to individuals tried for crimes committed before their capture. The most notorious exception to the principle of uniformity, then, has been stripped of its precedential value.

The uniformity principle is not an inflexible one; it does not preclude all departures from the procedures dictated for use by courts-martial. But any departure must be tailored to the exigency that necessitates it. That understanding is reflected in Article 36 of the UCMJ, which provides:

> (a) The procedure, including modes of proof, in cases before courts-martial, courts of inquiry, military commissions, and other military tribunals may be prescribed by the President by regulations which shall, so far as he considers practicable, apply the principles of law and the rules of evidence generally recognized in the trial of criminal cases in the United States district courts, but which may not be contrary to or inconsistent with this chapter.

> (b) All rules and regulations made under this article shall be uniform insofar as practicable and shall be reported to Congress.

Article 36 places two restrictions on the President's power to promulgate rules of procedure for courts-martial and military commissions alike. First, no procedural rule he adopts may be "contrary to or inconsistent with" the UCMJ — however practical it may seem. Second, the rules adopted must be "uniform insofar as practicable." That is, the rules applied to military commissions must be the same as those applied to courts-martial unless such uniformity proves impracticable.

Nothing in the record before us demonstrates that it would be impracticable to apply court-martial rules in this case. There is no suggestion, for example, of any logistical difficulty in securing properly sworn and authenticated evidence or in applying the usual principles of relevance and admissibility. Assuming *arguendo* that the reasons articulated in the President's Article 36(a) determination ought to be considered in evaluating the impracticability of applying court-martial rules, the only reason offered in support of that determination is the danger posed by international terrorism. Without for one moment underestimating that danger, it is not evident to us why it should require, in the case of Hamdan's trial, any variance from the rules that govern courts-martial.

The absence of any showing of impracticability is particularly disturbing when considered in light of the clear and admitted failure to apply one of the most fundamental protections afforded not just by the Manual for Courts-Martial but also by the UCMJ itself: the right to be present. Whether or not that departure technically is "contrary to or inconsistent with" the terms of the UCMJ, 10 U.S.C. § 836(a), the jettisoning of so basic a right cannot lightly be excused as "practicable."

Under the circumstances, then, the rules applicable in courts-martial must apply. Since it is undisputed that Commission Order No. 1 deviates in many significant respects from those rules, it necessarily violates Article 36(b).

D

The procedures adopted to try Hamdan also violate the Geneva Conventions. The Court of Appeals dismissed Hamdan's Geneva Convention challenge on three independent grounds: (1) the Geneva Conventions are not judicially enforceable; (2) Hamdan in any event is not entitled to their protections; and (3) even if he is entitled to their protections, *Councilman* abstention is appropriate. Judge Williams, concurring, rejected the second ground but agreed with the majority respecting the first and the last. As we explained in Part III, *supra*, the abstention rule applied in *Councilman*, is not applicable here. And for the reasons that follow, we hold that neither of the other grounds the Court of Appeals gave for its decision is persuasive.

i

The Court of Appeals relied on *Johnson v. Eisentrager*, 339 U.S. 763 (1950), to hold that Hamdan could not invoke the Geneva Conventions to challenge the Government's plan to prosecute him in accordance with Commission Order No. 1. *Eisentrager* involved a challenge by 21 German nationals to their 1945 convictions for war crimes by a military tribunal convened in Nanking, China, and to their subsequent imprisonment in occupied Germany. The petitioners argued, *inter alia*, that the 1929 Geneva Convention rendered illegal some of the procedures employed during their trials, which they said deviated impermissibly from the procedures used by courts-martial to try American soldiers. We rejected that claim on the merits because the petitioners (unlike Hamdan here) had failed to identify any prejudicial disparity "between the Commission that tried [them] and those that would try an offending soldier of the American forces of like rank," and in any event could claim no protection, under the 1929 Convention, during trials for crimes that occurred before their confinement as prisoners of war.

Buried in a footnote of the opinion, however, is this curious statement suggesting that the Court lacked power even to consider the merits of the Geneva Convention argument:

> We are not holding that these prisoners have no right which the military authorities are bound to respect. The United States, by the Geneva Convention of July 27, 1929, concluded with forty-six other countries, including the German Reich, an agreement upon the treatment to be accorded captives. These prisoners claim to be and are entitled to its protection. It is, however, the obvious scheme of the Agreement that responsibility for observance and enforcement of these rights is upon political and military authorities. Rights of alien enemies are vindicated under it only through protests and intervention of protecting powers as the rights of our citizens against foreign governments are vindicated only by Presidential intervention.

The Court of Appeals, on the strength of this footnote, held that "the 1949 Geneva Convention does not confer upon Hamdan a right to enforce its provisions in court."

Whatever else might be said about the *Eisentrager* footnote, it does not control this case. We may assume that "the obvious scheme" of the 1949 Conventions is identical in all relevant respects to that of the 1929 Convention, and even that that scheme would, absent some other provision of law, preclude Hamdan's invocation of the Convention's provisions as an independent source of law binding the Government's actions and furnishing petitioner with any enforceable right. For, regardless of the nature of the rights conferred on Hamdan, they are, as the Government does not dispute, part of the law of war. And compliance with the law of war is the condition upon which the authority set forth in Article 21 is granted.

ii

For the Court of Appeals, acknowledgment of that condition was no bar to Hamdan's trial by commission. As an alternative to its holding that Hamdan could not invoke the Geneva Conventions at all, the Court of Appeals concluded that the Conventions did not in any event apply to the armed conflict during which Hamdan was captured. The court accepted the Executive's assertions that Hamdan was captured in connection with the United States' war with al Qaeda and that that war is distinct from the war with the Taliban in Afghanistan. It further reasoned that the war with al Qaeda evades the reach of the Geneva Conventions. We, like Judge Williams, disagree with the latter conclusion.

The conflict with al Qaeda is not, according to the Government, a conflict to which the full protections afforded detainees under the 1949 Geneva Conventions apply because Article 2 of those Conventions (which appears in all four Conventions) renders the full protections applicable only to "all cases of declared war or of any other armed conflict which may arise between two or more of the High Contracting Parties.Since Hamdan was captured and detained incident to the conflict with al Qaeda and not the conflict with the Taliban, and since al Qaeda, unlike Afghanistan, is not a "High Contracting Party" — i.e., a signatory of the Conventions, the protections of those Conventions are not, it is argued, applicable to Hamdan.

We need not decide the merits of this argument because there is at least one provision of the Geneva Conventions that applies here even if the relevant conflict is not one between signatories.[17] Article 3, often referred to as Common Article 3 because, like Article 2, it appears in all four Geneva Conventions, provides that in a "conflict not of an international character occurring in the territory of one of the High Contracting Parties, each Party[18] to the conflict shall be bound to apply, as a minimum," certain provisions protecting "persons taking no active part in the hostilities, including members of armed forces who have laid down their arms and those placed *hors de combat* by . . . detention." One such provision prohibits "the passing of sentences and the carrying out of executions without previous judgment pronounced by a regularly constituted court affording all the judicial guarantees which are recognized as indispensable by civilized peoples."

The Court of Appeals thought, and the Government asserts, that Common Article 3 does not apply to Hamdan because the conflict with al Qaeda, being " 'international in scope,' " does not qualify as a " 'conflict not of an international character.' " That reasoning is erroneous. The term "conflict not of an international character" is used here in contradistinction to a conflict between nations. So much is demonstrated by the "fundamental logic [of] the Convention's provisions on its application." Common Article 2 provides that "the present Convention shall apply to all cases of declared war or of any other armed conflict which may arise between two or more of the High Contracting Parties." High Contracting Parties (signatories) also must abide by all terms of the Conventions vis-a-vis one another even if one party to the conflict is a nonsignatory "Power," and must so abide vis-a-vis the nonsignatory if "the latter accepts and applies" those terms. Common Article 3, by contrast, affords some minimal protection, falling short of full protection under the Conventions, to individuals associated with neither a signatory nor even a nonsignatory "Power" who are involved in a conflict "in the territory of" a signatory. The latter kind of conflict is distinguishable from the conflict described in Common Article 2 chiefly because it does not involve a clash between nations (whether signatories or not). In context, then, the phrase "not of an international character" bears its literal meaning.

Although the official commentaries accompanying Common Article 3 indicate that an important purpose of the provision was to furnish minimal protection to rebels involved in one kind of "conflict not of an international character," *i.e.*, a civil war, the commentaries also make clear "that the scope of the Article must be as wide as possible." In fact, limiting language that would have rendered Common Article 3 applicable "especially [to] cases of civil war, colonial conflicts, or wars of religion," was omitted from the final version of the Article, which coupled broader scope of application with a narrower range of rights than did earlier proposed iterations.

---

[17] [Court's Footnote 61] Hamdan observes that Article 5 of the Third Geneva Convention requires that if there be "any doubt" whether he is entitled to prisoner-of-war protections, he must be afforded those protections until his status is determined by a "competent tribunal." Because we hold that Hamdan may not, in any event, be tried by the military commission the President has convened pursuant to the November 13 Order and Commission Order No. 1, the question whether his potential status as a prisoner of war independently renders illegal his trial by military commission may be reserved.

[18] [Court's Footnote 62] The term "Party" here has the broadest possible meaning; a Party need neither be a signatory of the Convention nor "even represent a legal entity capable of undertaking international obligations." GCIII Commentary 37.

iii

Common Article 3, then, is applicable here and, as indicated above, requires that Hamdan be tried by a "regularly constituted court affording all the judicial guarantees which are recognized as indispensable by civilized peoples." While the term "regularly constituted court" is not specifically defined in either Common Article 3 or its accompanying commentary, other sources disclose its core meaning. The commentary accompanying a provision of the Fourth Geneva Convention, for example, defines " 'regularly constituted' " tribunals to include "ordinary military courts" and "definitely exclude all special tribunals." And one of the Red Cross' own treatises defines "regularly constituted court" as used in Common Article 3 to mean "established and organized in accordance with the laws and procedures already in force in a country."

The Government offers only a cursory defense of Hamdan's military commission in light of Common Article 3. As Justice Kennedy explains, that defense fails because "the regular military courts in our system are the courts-martial established by congressional statutes." At a minimum, a military commission "can be 'regularly constituted' by the standards of our military justice system only if somepractical need explains deviations from court-martial practice." As we have explained, see Part VI-C, *supra*, no such need has been demonstrated here.

iv

Inextricably intertwined with the question of regular constitution is the evaluation of the procedures governing the tribunal and whether they afford "all the judicial guarantees which are recognized as indispensable by civilized peoples." Like the phrase "regularly constituted court," this phrase is not defined in the text of the Geneva Conventions. But it must be understood to incorporate at least the barest of those trial protections that have been recognized by customary international law. Many of these are described in Article 75 of Protocol I to the Geneva Conventions of 1949, adopted in 1977 (Protocol I). Although the United States declined to ratify Protocol I, its objections were not to Article 75 thereof. Indeed, it appears that the Government "regards the provisions of Article 75 as an articulation of safeguards to which all persons in the hands of an enemy are entitled." Taft, *The Law of Armed Conflict After 9/11: Some Salient Features*, 28 Yale J. Int'l L. 319, 322 (2003). Among the rights set forth in Article 75 is the "right to be tried in [one's] presence."

We agree with Justice Kennedy that the procedures adopted to try Hamdan deviate from those governing courts-martial in ways not justified by any "evident practical need," and for that reason, at least, fail to afford the requisite guarantees. We add only that, as noted in Part VI-A, *supra*, various provisions of Commission Order No. 1 dispense with the principles, articulated in Article 75 and indisputably part of the customary international law, that an accused must, absent disruptive conduct or consent, be present for his trial and must be privy to the evidence against him.[19] That the Government has a compelling interest in denying Hamdan access to certain sensitive information is not doubted. But, at least absent express statutory provision to the contrary, information used to convict a person of a crime must be disclosed to him.

v

Common Article 3 obviously tolerates a great degree of flexibility in trying individuals captured during armed conflict; its requirements are general ones, crafted to accom-

---

[19] [Court's Footnote 67] The Government offers no defense of these procedures other than to observe that the defendant may not be barred from access to evidence if such action would deprive him of a "full and fair trial." But the Government suggests no circumstances in which it would be "fair" to convict the accused based on evidence he has not seen or heard.

modate a wide variety of legal systems. But *requirements* they are nonetheless. The commission that the President has convened to try Hamdan does not meet those requirements.

VII

We have assumed, as we must, that the allegations made in the Government's charge against Hamdan are true. We have assumed, moreover, the truth of the message implicit in that charge — viz., that Hamdan is a dangerous individual whose beliefs, if acted upon, would cause great harm and even death to innocent civilians, and who would act upon those beliefs if given the opportunity. It bears emphasizing that Hamdan does not challenge, and we do not today address, the Government's power to detain him for the duration of active hostilities in order to prevent such harm. But in undertaking to try Hamdan and subject him to criminal punishment, the Executive is bound to comply with the Rule of Law that prevails in this jurisdiction.

The judgment of the Court of Appeals is reversed, and the case is remanded for further proceedings.

THE CHIEF JUSTICE took no part in the consideration or decision of this case.

JUSTICE BREYER, with whom JUSTICE KENNEDY, JUSTICE SOUTER, and JUSTICE GINSBURG join, concurring.

The dissenters say that today's decision would "sorely hamper the President's ability to confront and defeat a new and deadly enemy." They suggest that it undermines our Nation's ability to "prevent future attacks" of the grievous sort that we have already suffered. That claim leads me to state briefly what I believe the majority sets forth both explicitly and implicitly at greater length. The Court's conclusion ultimately rests upon a single ground: Congress has not issued the Executive a "blank check." Indeed, Congress has denied the President the legislative authority to create military commissions of the kind at issue here. Nothing prevents the President from returning to Congress to seek the authority he believes necessary.

Where, as here, no emergency prevents consultation with Congress, judicial insistence upon that consultation does not weaken our Nation's ability to deal with danger. To the contrary, that insistence strengthens the Nation's ability to determine — through democratic means — how best to do so. The Constitution places its faith in those democratic means. Our Court today simply does the same.

JUSTICE KENNEDY, with whom JUSTICE SOUTER, JUSTICE GINSBURG, and JUSTICE BREYER join as to Parts I and II, concurring in part.

Military Commission Order No. 1, which governs the military commission established to try petitioner Salim Hamdan for war crimes, exceeds limits that certain statutes, duly enacted by Congress, have placed on the President's authority to convene military courts. This is not a case, then, where the Executive can assert some unilateral authority to fill a void left by congressional inaction. It is a case where Congress, in the proper exercise of its powers as an independent branch of government, and as part of a long tradition of legislative involvement in matters of military justice, has considered the subject of military tribunals and set limits on the President's authority.

I join the Court's opinion, save Parts V and VI-D-iv. To state my reasons for this reservation, and to show my agreement with the remainder of the Court's analysis by identifying particular deficiencies in the military commissions at issue, this separate opinion seems appropriate.

I

Trial by military commission raises separation-of-powers concerns of the highest order. Located within a single branch, these courts carry the risk that offenses will be defined, prosecuted, and adjudicated by executive officials without independent review.

Concentration of power puts personal liberty in peril of arbitrary action by officials, an incursion the Constitution's three-part system is designed to avoid. It is imperative, then, that when military tribunals are established, full and proper authority exists for the Presidential directive.

In § 821 Congress has addressed the possibility that special military commissions — criminal courts other than courts-martial — may at times be convened. At the same time, however, the President's authority to convene military commissions is limited: It extends only to "offenders or offenses" that "by statute or by the law of war may be tried by" such military commissions. The Government does not claim to base the charges against Hamdan on a statute; instead it invokes the law of war. If the military commission at issue is illegal under the law of war, then an offender cannot be tried "by the law of war" before that commission.

Assuming the President has authority to establish a special military commission to try Hamdan, the commission must satisfy Common Article 3's requirement of a "regularly constituted court affording all the judicial guarantees which are recognized as indispensable by civilized peoples." The terms of this general standard are yet to be elaborated and further defined, but Congress has required compliance with it by referring to the "law of war" in § 821. The Court correctly concludes that the military commission here does not comply with this provision.

II

As compared to the role of the convening authority in a court-martial, the greater powers of the Appointing Authority here — including even the resolution of dispositive issues in the middle of the trial — raise concerns that the commission's decisionmaking may not be neutral. If the differences are supported by some practical need beyond the goal of constant and ongoing supervision, that need is neither apparent from the record nor established by the Government's submissions.

As the Court explains, the Government has made no demonstration of practical need for these special rules and procedures, either in this particular case or as to the military commissions in general, nor is any such need self-evident. For all the Government's regulations and submissions reveal, it would be feasible for most, if not all, of the conventional military evidence rules and procedures to be followed.

III

I would not decide whether Common Article 3's standard — a "regularly constituted court affording all the judicial guarantees which are recognized as indispensable by civilized peoples" — necessarily requires that the accused have the right to be present at all stages of a criminal trial. There should be reluctance, furthermore, to reach unnecessarily the question whether, as the plurality seems to conclude, Article 75 of Protocol I to the Geneva Conventions is binding law notwithstanding the earlier decision by our Government not to accede to the Protocol. For all these reasons, and without detracting from the importance of the right of presence, I would rely on other deficiencies noted here and in the opinion by the Court — deficiencies that relate to the structure and procedure of the commission and that inevitably will affect the proceedings — as the basis for finding the military commissions lack authorization under 10 U.S.C. § 836 and fail to be regularly constituted under Common Article 3 and § 821.

I likewise see no need to address the validity of the conspiracy charge against Hamdan — an issue addressed at length in Part V of Justice Stevens' opinion. In light of the conclusion that the military commissions at issue are unauthorized Congress may choose to provide further guidance in this area. Congress, not the Court, is the branch in the better position to undertake the "sensitive task of establishing a principle not inconsistent with the national interest or international justice."

Finally, for the same reason, I express no view on the merits of other limitations on military commissions described as elements of the common law of war in Part V of Justice Stevens' opinion.

With these observations I join the Court's opinion with the exception of Parts V and VI-D-iv.

JUSTICE SCALIA, with whom JUSTICE THOMAS and JUSTICE ALITO join, dissenting.

On December 30, 2005, Congress enacted the Detainee Treatment Act (DTA). It unambiguously provides that, as of that date, "no court, justice, or judge" shall have jurisdiction to consider the habeas application of a Guantánamo Bay detainee. Notwithstanding this plain directive, the Court today concludes that, on what it calls the statute's *most natural* reading, *every* "court, justice, or judge" before whom such a habeas application was pending on December 30 has jurisdiction to hear, consider, and render judgment on it. This conclusion is patently erroneous. And even if it were not, the jurisdiction supposedly retained should, in an exercise of sound equitable discretion, not be exercised.

An ancient and unbroken line of authority attests that statutes ousting jurisdiction unambiguously apply to cases pending at their effective date. This venerable rule that statutes ousting jurisdiction terminate jurisdiction in pending cases is not, as today's opinion for the Court would have it, a judge-made "presumption against jurisdiction," that we have invented to resolve an ambiguity in the statutes. It is simple recognition of the reality that the *plain import* of a statute repealing jurisdiction is to eliminate the power to consider and render judgment — in an already pending case no less than in a case yet to be filed.

Even if Congress had not clearly and constitutionally eliminated jurisdiction over this case, neither this Court nor the lower courts ought to exercise it. Traditionally, equitable principles govern both the exercise of habeas jurisdiction and the granting of the injunctive relief sought by petitioner. In light of Congress's provision of an alternate avenue for petitioner's claims in § 1005(e)(3), those equitable principles counsel that we abstain from exercising jurisdiction in this case.

I would abstain from exercising our equity jurisdiction, as the Government requests.

JUSTICE THOMAS, with whom JUSTICE SCALIA joins, and with whom JUSTICE ALITO joins in all but Parts I, II-C-1, and III-B-2, dissenting.

For the reasons set forth in Justice Scalia's dissent, it is clear that this Court lacks jurisdiction to entertain petitioner's claims. The Court having concluded otherwise, it is appropriate to respond to the Court's resolution of the merits of petitioner's claims because its opinion openly flouts our well-established duty to respect the Executive's judgment in matters of military operations and foreign affairs. The Court's evident belief that *it* is qualified to pass on the "military necessity" of the Commander in Chief's decision to employ a particular form of force against our enemies is so antithetical to our constitutional structure that it simply cannot go unanswered. I respectfully dissent.

I

Our review of petitioner's claims arises in the context of the President's wartime exercise of his commander-in-chief authority in conjunction with the complete support of Congress. Accordingly, it is important to take measure of the respective roles the Constitution assigns to the three branches of our Government in the conduct of war.

II

In one key respect, the plurality departs from the proper framework for evaluating the adequacy of the charge against Hamdan under the laws of war. The plurality holds that where, as here, "neither the elements of the offense nor the range of permissible punishments is defined by statute or treaty, the precedent [establishing whether an offense is triable by military commission] must be plain and unambiguous." This is a pure contrivance, and a bad one at that. It is contrary to the presumption we acknowledged in *Quirin*, namely, that the actions of military commissions are "not to be set aside by the courts without the *clear conviction* that they are" unlawful. It is also contrary to *Yamashita*, which recognized the legitimacy of that military commission notwithstanding a substantial disagreement pertaining to whether Yamashita had been charged with a violation of the law of war. Nor does it find support from the separation of powers authority cited by the plurality.

The plurality's newly minted clear-statement rule is also fundamentally inconsistent with the nature of the common law which, by definition, evolves and develops over time and does not, in all cases, "say what may be done." Similarly, it is inconsistent with the nature of warfare, which also evolves and changes over time, and for which a flexible, evolutionary common-law system is uniquely appropriate. Though the charge against Hamdan easily satisfies even the plurality's manufactured rule, the plurality's inflexible approach has dangerous implications for the Executive's ability to discharge his duties as Commander in Chief in future cases. We should undertake to determine whether an unlawful combatant has been charged with an offense against the law of war with an understanding that the common law of war is flexible, responsive to the exigencies of the present conflict, and deferential to the judgment of military commanders.

For well over a century it has been established that "to unite with banditti, jayhawkers, guerillas, or any other unauthorized marauders is a high offence against the laws of war; *the offence is complete when the band is organized or joined. The atrocities committed by such a band do not constitute the offence, but make the reasons, and sufficient reasons they are, why such banditti are denounced by the laws of war.*" 11 Op. Atty. Gen., at 312 (emphasis added). In other words, unlawful combatants, such as Hamdan, violate the law of war merely by joining an organization, such as al Qaeda, whose principal purpose is the "killing [and] disabling . . . of peaceable citizens or soldiers." Winthrop 784; see also 11 Op. Atty. Gen., at 314 ("A bushwhacker, a jayhawker, a bandit, a war rebel, an assassin, being public enemies, may be tried, condemned, and executed as offenders against the laws of war"). This conclusion is unsurprising, as it is a "cardinal principle of the law of war . . . that the civilian population must enjoy complete immunity." 4 International Committee of Red Cross, Commentary: Geneva Convention Relative to the Protection of Civilian Persons in Time of War 3 (J. Pictet ed. 1958). "Numerous instances of trials, for 'Violation of the laws of war,' of offenders of this description, are published in the General Orders of the years 1862 to 1866." Winthrop 784, and n. 57. Accordingly, on this basis alone, "the allegations of [Hamdan's] charge, tested by any reasonable standard, adequately allege a violation of the law of war." *Yamashita*, 327 U.S., at 17.

The conclusion that membership in an organization whose purpose is to violate the laws of war is an offense triable by military commission is confirmed by the experience of the military tribunals convened by the United States at Nuremberg. Pursuant to Article 10 of the Charter of the International Military Tribunal (IMT), the United States convened military tribunals "to bring individuals to trial for membership" in "a group or organization . . . declared criminal by the [IMT]." The IMT designated various components of four Nazi groups — the Leadership Corps, Gestapo, SD, and SS — as criminal organizations. "[A] member of [such] an organization [could] be . . . convicted of the crime of membership and be punished for that crime by death." Under this authority, the United States Military Tribunal at Nuremberg convicted numerous individuals for the act of knowing and voluntary membership in these organizations.

Hamdan's military commission complies with the requirements of Common Article 3. It is plainly "regularly constituted" because such commissions have been employed throughout our history to try unlawful combatants for crimes against the law of war. The Court concludes Hamdan's commission fails to satisfy the requirements of Common Article 3 not because it differs from the practice of previous military commissions but because it "deviates from [the procedures] governing courts-martial." But there is neither a statutory nor historical requirement that military commissions conform to the structure and practice of courts-martial. A military commission is a different tribunal, serving a different function, and thus operates pursuant to different procedures. The 150-year pedigree of the military commission is itself sufficient to establish that such tribunals are "regularly constituted courts."

JUSTICE ALITO, with whom JUSTICES SCALIA and THOMAS join in Parts I-III, dissenting.

In order to determine whether a court has been properly appointed, set up, or established, it is necessary to refer to a body of law that governs such matters. I interpret Common Article 3 as looking to the domestic law of the appointing country because I am not aware of any international law standard regarding the way in which such a court must be appointed, set up, or established, and because different countries with different government structures handle this matter differently. Accordingly, "a regularly constituted court" is a court that has been appointed, set up, or established in accordance with the domestic law of the appointing country.

I see no basis for the Court's holding that a military commission cannot be regarded as "a regularly constituted court" unless it is similar in structure and composition to a regular military court or unless there is an "evident practical need" for the divergence. There is no reason why a court that differs in structure or composition from an ordinary military court must be viewed as having been improperly constituted. Tribunals that vary significantly in structure, composition, and procedures may all be "regularly" or "properly" constituted. Consider, for example, a municipal court, a state trial court of general jurisdiction, an Article I federal trial court, a federal district court, and an international court, such as the International Criminal Tribunal for the Former Yugoslavia. Although these courts are "differently constituted" and differ substantially in many other respects, they are all "regularly constituted."

NOTES AND QUESTIONS

1. What Law Applies? It is important in dealing with the military cases to determine what law applies so that we can determine whether Congress can change the law. If a holding is constitutional, then Congress cannot. If the holding relies on international law, then it will be necessary to know whether the Supreme Court has held that body of doctrine to be incorporated into the U.S. Constitution. With that in mind,

  a. what is the source of the majority's conclusion in Part V that "conspiracy" is not a valid charge before a military commission?

  b. what is the source of the majority's conclusion in Part VI(C) that the commissions are invalidly constituted?

  c. what is the basis of the majority's conclusions in Part VI(D) that the commissions violate Geneva Conventions?

2. The Significance of International Law. Perhaps now the connections with international law considered in Chapter 3 will be more clear. Recall the very extended treatment of Common Article 3 in the opinions of the International Criminal Tribunals for Yugoslavia and Rwanda. *See* Jordan J. Paust, *Antiterrorism Military Commissions: The Ad Hoc DOD Rules of Procedure*, 23 MICH. J. INT'L L. 677 (2002). Does the *Hamdan* majority hold that the Geneva Conventions create individual rights binding within U.S. law? If so, is that a holding that Congress can overrule, or is international law binding on the legislature?

Does a majority incorporate international law into domestic U.S. constitutional law? or does the Stevens opinion incorporate international law only to the extent that Congress has implicitly incorporated it into domestic law?

What is the basis of Justice Kennedy's refusal to concur in Part VI(D)(iv)? and what is the significance of a lack of a majority on that particular point?

In the District Court, Judge Robertson had pointed out that commissions can try only offenses against the "law of war." But what part of the law of war would a civilian unconnected to a national government or a belligerent group violate?

3. The Military Commission Act of 2006. The Bush Administration immediately took up the challenge put forward by the Supreme Court's opinion in *Hamdan* and began drafting legislation to authorize the use of military commissions. The effort hit a stumbling block when Republican Senators McCain, Graham, and Warner initially insisted upon language that would prevent cruel, inhumane or degrading treatment of detainees and would commit the U.S. to adherence to Common Article 3 in its handling of detainees. Ultimately, the White House and the Senators reached a "compromise" in which the Senators acceded to the White House that both the Torture Convention and GPW would be satisfied by a list of "war crimes" that would define the scope of the Conventions.

In brief, the Military Commissions Act of 2006 (MCA) does the following:

a. authorizes "the use of military commissions to try alien unlawful enemy combatants engaged in hostilities against the United States for violations of the law of war and other offenses triable by military commission"

b. defines an "unlawful enemy combatant" as "a person who has engaged in hostilities or who has purposefully and materially supported hostilities against the United States or its co-belligerents who is not a lawful enemy combatant"

c. provides a specific list of "war crimes" that may be tried by military commission, including conspiracy, torture, "cruel or inhuman treatment" (not degrading treatment or outrages upon personal dignity); performing biological experiments; murder; mutilation or maiming; intentionally causing great suffering or bodily injury; rape; sexual assault or abuse; and taking hostages

d. precludes habeas corpus review on behalf of any detainee classified as an "unlawful enemy combatant" (not just Guantánamo) and allows only D.C. Circuit review of the determinations by Combatant Status Review Tribunals (CSRTs)

e. provides that "no person in any habeas action or any other action may invoke the Geneva Conventions or any protocols thereto as a source of rights, whether directly or indirectly, for any purpose in any court of the United States"

4. Commission Jurisdiction. In proceedings at Guantánamo on June 4, 2007, Navy Capt. Keith Allred dismissed charges against Salim Hamdan (http://www.defenselink.mil/news/newsarticle.aspx?id=46288), while Army Colonel Peter Brownback dismissed charges against Omar Khadr (http://www.defenselink.mil/news/newsarticle.aspx?id=46281). In both cases, the judges ruled that the commissions had no jurisdiction over the defendants because their CSRT panels had merely found them to be "enemy combatants" rather than "unlawful enemy combatants." The MCA jurisdiction extends to crimes committed by "unlawful enemy combatants" and the judges held that this requires a prior determination of unlawfulness. These were puzzling rulings because they seemed to insist that some other tribunal would make findings of guilt or innocence as a precursor to jurisdiction of the tribunal charged with determining guilt or innocence. The purpose of the commission trial is to determine whether the defendant acted unlawfully and a finding to that effect by another tribunal would be either prejudicial or meaningless. In many situations, the jurisdictional facts for a tribunal are often intertwined with the merits and can be determined at the trial over which the tribunal has taken jurisdiction. Given these rather obvious arguments, the dismissals were taken by some observers as reflecting frustration by professional military judges over the entire course of proceedings. Six months later, Capt. Allred issued the following opinion.

UNITED STATES v. HAMDAN
United States Military Commission (12/19/07)

ON RECONSIDERATION — RULING ON MOTION TO DISMISS
FOR LACK OF JURISDICTION

After a hearing on 4 June 2007, the Commission granted a Defense Motion to Dismiss for Lack of Jurisdiction. Thereafter, the Government moved the Commission to reconsider that dismissal, and to hear evidence regarding the accused's activities that would make him subject to the jurisdiction of a military commission, *i.e.* the Government sought to show the Commission directly that the accused was an alien unlawful enemy combatant, as defined in the Military Commissions Act (M.C.A.) § 48a(I)(i). The Commission granted the Motion for Reconsideration, and a hearing was held at Guantánamo Bay on 5 and 6 December 2007, at which the Government presented testimonial evidence from Major Hank Smith, U.S. Army, FBI Special Agent George Crouch, and DoD Special Agent Robert McFadden. The Defense offered the testimony of Professor Brian Williams of the University of Massachusetts at Dartmouth, Mr. Said Boujaadia, a detainee being held at Guantánamo Bay, and the stipulated testimony of Mr. Nasser al Bahri of Sana'a, Yemen. Both sides offered documentary and photographic evidence. The Defense concedes that Mr. Hamdan is an "alien" for purposes of the Motion.

Having considered this evidence, the Commission finds that the following facts are true:

1. In 1996, the accused was recruited in Yemen to go to Tajikistan for jihad. As a result of difficulty crossing the border into Tajikistan, he remained in Afghanistan. Because of his experience driving vehicles, he soon came in contact with Osama bin-Ladin, and was offered work as a driver.

2. The accused began his work driving farm vehicles on bin-Ladin's farms, and after a probationary period, was invited to join the bin-Ladin security detail as a driver of one of the security caravan vehicles. With the passage of additional time, the accused became bin-Ladin's personal driver sometime in 1997, and continued in that capacity until the fall of 2001.

3. On occasion, the accused also served as a personal bodyguard to bin-Ladin. It was customary to rotate bodyguards as a security measure, and the accused engaged in this rotation. Bodyguards not actually protecting bin-Ladin would serve as fighters, receive training at al-Qaeda training camps, serve as emirs of al-Qaeda guesthouses, and perform other duties during their rotations away from body guarding duties.

4. During this period as bin-Ladin's personal driver and sometimes bodyguard, the accused pledged bayat, or "unquestioned allegiance" to bin-Ladin. The bayat extended to bin-Ladin's campaign to conduct jihad against Jews and crusaders, and to liberate the Arabian Peninsula from infidels, but the accused reserved the right to withdraw his bayat if bin-Ladin undertook a mission he did not agree with. The accused told investigators after his capture that there were some men in bin-Ladin's company who did not agree with everything bin-Ladin did or proposed to do.

5. The accused was aware of two of bin-Ladin's fatwas, including the 1998 fatwa issued by the International Islamic Front for Jihad against the Jews and Crusaders, and which called upon all Muslims to "kill Americans and their allies, both civilian and military . . . in any country where it is possible, to liberate Al-Agsa Mosque and the Holy Mosque from their grip, and to expel their armies from all Islamic territory."

6. During the years between 1997 and 2001, the accused's duties sometimes included the delivery of weapons to Taliban and other fighters at bin-Ladin's request. On these occasions, he would drive to a weapons warehouse, present a document that contained bin-Ladin's order, and his vehicle would be loaded with the required weapons. He then delivered the weapons to fighters or elsewhere as directed by bin-Ladin. On at least one

occasion, he took weapons to an al-Qaeda base in Kandahar.

7. As bin-Ladin's driver and bodyguard, the accused always carried a Russian handgun. It is not unusual for men in Afghanistan to carry weapons, and the accused had a Taliban-issued permit to carry weapons when he was apprehended. His duty in case of attack was to spirit bin-Ladin to safety, while the other vehicles in the convoy were to engage the attackers.

8. The accused received small arms and other training at al-Farouq training camp.

9. The accused became aware, after the al-Qaeda attacks on the U.S. embassies in Africa, and after the USS Cole attack, that bin-Ladin and al-Qaeda had planned and executed those attacks. No evidence was presented that the accused was aware of the attacks in advance, or that he helped plan or organize them.

10. Osama bin-Ladin told the accused that he wanted to demonstrate that he could threaten America, strike fear, and kill Americans anywhere. On hearing this declaration, the accused felt "uncontrollable enthusiasm."

11. In the days before 9/11, Osama bin-Ladin told the accused to get ready for an extended trip. After the 9/11 attacks, the accused drove bin-Ladin and his son on a ten-day jaunt around Afghanistan, visiting several cities, staying in different homes or camping in the desert, and otherwise helping bin-Ladin escape retaliation by the United States. During this period, he learned that bin-Ladin had been responsible for the attacks.

THE ANSAR BRIGADE

12. Between the early 1990's and the fall of 2001, there was in Afghanistan a bona fide military fighting force composed primarily of Arabs, known as the Ansars. This force engaged the Soviets during their occupation of Afghanistan. They were subject to a rigid command structure, were highly disciplined, usually wore a uniform (or uniform parts), and carried their arms openly. The Ansar uniforms usually consisted of either completely black attire or traditional military camouflage uniform parts.

13. Taliban leaders did not permit the Ansars to operate independently. As a result, the Ansars were integrated with, subject to the command of, and usually formed the elite fighting troops of, the Taliban army.

14. The Taliban had a conventional fighting force that may well be described as a traditional army. They possessed aged-but-functional battle tanks, helicopters, artillery pieces and fighter aircraft. The Ansars comprised up to 25% of the Taliban army.

15. Osama bin-Ladin contributed forces to the Ansars, and provided them with weapons, funding, propaganda and other support.

16. By 1997, al-Farouq training camp, and several other training camps, were under the symbolic control of bin-Ladin.

17. The Ansars were primarily motivated by the desire to expel the Soviets and other foreigners from Afghanistan, but also fought against the Northern Alliance. Some of the Ansar units rejected bin-Ladin's calls for war against America, and the attacks of 9/11.

18. During the U.S. invasion of Afghanistan in the fall of 2001, the Ansars were engaged in the defense of Kandahar.

24 NOVEMBER 2001

19. On 24 November 2001, U.S. forces were operating in the vicinity of Takta Pol, a small Afghan village astride Highway 4, which ran between Kandahar and the Pakistani border. Major Hank Smith had under his command a small number of Americans and six to eight hundred Afghanis he referred to as his Anti-Taliban Forces (ATF). Their mission was to capture Takta Pol from the Taliban and prevent arms and

supplies from Pakistan from entering Kandahar by means of Highway 4.

20. Highway 4 was the main, and perhaps the only, road between Kandahar and the Pakistan border. It was a significant supply route for people and materials transiting between Pakistan and Kandahar.

21. During the battle for control of Takta Pol and Highway 4, U.S. and coalition forces fought all night with the Taliban forces in the area. A U.S./ATF negotiating party attempting negotiations under a flag of truce was ambushed by Taliban forces, and the U.S. and coalition troops engaged the Taliban in combat, taking casualties. The Taliban forces engaged against coalition forces at Takta Pol did not wear uniforms or any distinctive insignia.

22. After an overnight battle on 23–24 November, the Taliban vacated the town, and coalition forces entered Takta Pol the morning of 24 November 2001. They swept and secured the town, and set up a road block south of town to intercept troops, munitions or other war materials, and explosive vehicles before they entered the town. The road block was also intended to prevent munitions and war materials from being carried toward Kandahar.

23. After capturing the town of Takta Pol, and while securing the town and establishing his road blocks, Major Smith and his ATF continued to receive rocket or mortar fire from outside the town.

24. At the same time, Kandahar to the north was occupied by a large number of Taliban forces. Coalition forces, including Major Smith's forces, were preparing to participate in a major battle for control of Kandahar, which was already under way.

25. During the late morning or early afternoon of 24 November, a vehicle stopped at the road block engaged Major Smith's ATF in gunfire. Two men, apparently Egyptians, from the vehicle were killed, and an occupant later identified as Mr. Said Boujaadia was captured.

26. On hearing the gunfire, Major Smith proceeded to the road block, arriving within 3–15 minutes of the firing. By the time he arrived, the accused, driving a different vehicle, had also been stopped at the roadblock. His vehicle carried two SA-7 missiles, suitable for engaging airborne aircraft. The missiles were in their carrying tubes, and did not have the launchers or firing mechanisms with them.

27. The accused was captured while driving north towards Kandahar from the direction of the Pakistani border. The vehicle carrying Mr. Boujaadia and the two Egyptian fighters was also traveling north, towards Kandahar when it was stopped.

28. The only operational aircraft then in the skies were U.S. and coalition aircraft providing close air support and other support for coalition troops on the ground.

29. Major Smith's ATF did not have any surface-to-air missiles in their inventory because the Taliban had no operational aircraft in the skies. There was no need for missiles that had no target.

30. After consulting with higher headquarters, Major Smith's forces photographed the two missiles on the tailgate of one of their vehicles, and destroyed the missiles to prevent them or their explosives from being used against Coalition forces.

31. Major Smith took control of the accused from the Afghan forces who, he feared, would kill the accused if he remained in their control. The accused was fed, protected and otherwise cared for while he was in U.S. custody. A Medic checked on him several times a day, and Major Smith visited him at least once a day until he was evacuated by helicopter a few days after his capture.

32. At the time of his capture, the accused was wearing traditional Afghan civilian clothes, and nothing suggestive of a uniform or distinctive emblem.

DISCUSSION OF LAW

The personal jurisdiction of a military commission is limited to those who are found to be "alien unlawful enemy combatants," defined in the M.C.A. as those who have "engaged in hostilities or who ha[ve] purposefully and materially supported hostilities against the United States or its co-belligerents, who [are] not a lawful enemy combatant[s]." M.C.A. § 948a(I)(i). Mr. Hamdan may only be tried by this Commission if he falls within this definition. The burden is on the Government to demonstrate jurisdiction over the accused by a preponderance of the evidence R.M.C. 905(c)(1). This Commission assumes that Congress intended to comply with the International Law of Armed Conflict when it enacted the Military Commissions Act and chose this definition of "unlawful enemy combatant."

International Law scholars and experts have long debated the exact meaning of Law of Armed Conflict terms such as "hostilities" and "direct participation." Professor Dinstein explains "It is not always easy to define what active participation in hostilities denotes. Usually, the reference is to 'direct' participation in hostilities. However, the adjective 'direct' does not shed much light on the extent of participation required. For instance, a driver delivering ammunition to combatants and a person who gathers military intelligence in enemy-controlled territory are commonly acknowledged to be actively taking part in hostilities." YORAM DINSTEIN, THE CONDUCT OF HOSTILITIES UNDER THE LAW OF INTERNATIONAL ARMED CONFLICT 27 (Oxford University Press 2004).

It is ironic that Professor Dinstein should have chosen the "driver delivering ammunition to combatants" as his example of someone who is obviously taking an active part in hostilities. Other scholars have debated the scenario of a driver delivering ammunition, and held that the issue of 'direct participation' should depend on how close the driver actually is to the ongoing hostilities. See International Committee of the Red Cross, Summary Report, Third Expert Meeting on the Notion of Direct Participation in Hostilities, Geneva, 32–33, (2005), where one expert argued that "a distinction had to be made between driving the same ammunition truck close to the front line, which would constitute 'direct' participation, and driving it thousands of miles in the rear, which would not." Even after making this distinction, it is widely acknowledged that driving "close to the front line" is direct participation.

Writing in the Chicago Journal of International Law, Professor Michael Schmitt acknowledges that the meaning of direct participation is "highly ambiguous." He concludes, however, that "The Commentary appears to support the premise of a high threshold: '[d]irect participation in hostilities implies a direct causal relationship between the activity engaged in and the harm done to the enemy at the time and the place where the activity takes place.' It also describes direct participation as 'acts which by their nature and purpose are intended to cause actual harm to the personnel and equipment of the armed forces' and defines hostilities as 'acts of war which are intended by their nature or their purpose to hit specifically the personnel and the materiel of the armed forces of the adverse Party.'" Michael N. Schmitt, *Direct Participation in Hostilities by Private Contractors or Civilian Employees*, CHICAGO J. INT'L LAW, 511, 531, 533 (2004).

Jean-Francois Quguiner, in a working paper sponsored by Harvard University's Program on Humanitarian Policy and Conflict Research, addresses the term "direct participation" as contained in Article 51 of Additional Protocol I to the Conventions, and notes that direct participation has been held to be broad enough to encompass "direct logistical support for units engaged directly in battle such as the delivery of ammunition to a firing position." Jean-Francois Quguiner, *Direct Participation in Hostilities Under International Humanitarian Law* 4 (2003), http://www.ihlresearch.org/ihl/pdfs/briefing3297.pdf.

Application and Conclusion

The Commission finds that "hostilities" were in progress on the 24th of November 2001 when the accused was captured with missiles in his car. Major Smith and his Anti-Taliban Forces were actively engaged in a firefight with Taliban forces on the night of 23–24 November, had taken casualties, and had been attacked while attempting to negotiate under a flag of truce. Even after capturing the town of Takta Pol and while securing it, they continued to receive mortar or rocket fire from troops in the distance. In addition, the Battle of Kandahar was already under way, with a larger contest expected in the near future, for control of the city. Both the local battle for control of Takta Pol and the ongoing battle for the more distant Kandahar amount to "hostilities."

The Commission also finds that the accused directly participated in those hostilities by driving a vehicle containing two surface-to-air missiles in both temporal and spatial proximity to both ongoing combat operations. The fact that U.S. and coalition forces had the only air assets against which the missiles might have been used supports a finding that the accused actively participated in hostilities against the United States and its coalition partners. Although Kandahar was a short distance away, the accused's past history of delivering munitions to Taliban and al Qaeda fighters, his possession of a vehicle containing surface to air missiles, and his capture while driving in the direction of a battle already underway, satisfies the requirement of "direct participation." If the two vehicles stopped within minutes of each other at Major Smith's road block were in fact traveling together, a point of dispute during the hearing, it is arguable that the accused was also traveling towards the battle in the company of enemy fighters. Taken together, the evidence presented at the hearing supports a finding that the accused "engaged in hostilities, or . . . purposefully and materially supported hostilities against the United States or its cobelligerents. M.C.A. § 948a(1)(i).

The Government also argues that the accused "purposefully and materially supported hostilities" by (1) serving as the personal driver and bodyguard of the al-Qaeda mastermind Osama bin-Ladin, (2) continuing to work for bin-Ladin after he became aware that bin-Ladin had planned and directed the USS Cole bombing, the attacks on the two U.S. Embassies in Africa, and the 9/11 attacks on the United States; and (3) by driving bin-Ladin around Afghanistan after the attacks of 9/11, in an effort to help him avoid detection and punishment by the United States. While these arguments may well provide grist for the debates of future generations of Law of Armed Conflict scholars, the Commission does not reach them here. Having found that the accused drove a vehicle to and towards the battle field, containing missiles that could only be used against the United States and its co-belligerents, the Commission finds that the accused meets the first half of the definition of unlawful enemy combatant.

The final element of M.C.A. § 948a.(I)(i)'s definition of alien unlawful enemy combatant is that the accused must not have been "a lawful combatant." The M.C.A. defines "lawful combatant" in § 948a(2) to include:

(A) a member of the regular forces of a State party engaged in hostilities against the United States;

(B) a member of a militia, volunteer corps, or organized resistance movement belonging to a State party engaged in such hostilities, which are under responsible command, wear a fixed distinctive sign recognizable at a distance, carry their arms openly, and abide by the law of war; or

(C) a member of a regular armed force who professes allegiance to a government engaged in such hostilities, but not recognized by the United States.

The Defense does not argue that the accused is entitled to lawful combatant status under any of these alternatives. After an examination of the evidence presented, the Commission agrees. Alternatively, the Defense has urged the Commission to find the accused entitled to lawful combatant/ Prisoner of War status under alternative definitions contained in the Third Geneva Convention.

ARTICLE 5 STATUS ISSUE

This Commission has elsewhere granted a Defense Motion to determine the accused's status under Article 5 of the Third Geneva Convention. The Defense has argued that the accused may have been a lawful combatant, and therefore entitled to Prisoner of War status, under any of the following subsections of Article 4.A of the Third Geneva Convention:

(1) Members of the armed forces of a Party to the conflict as well as members of militias or volunteer corps forming part of such armed forces.

(2) Members of other militias and members of volunteer corps, including those of organized resistance movements, belonging to a Party to the conflict and operating in or outside their own territory, even if this territory is occupied, provided that such militias or volunteer corps, including such organized resistance movements, fulfill the following conditions: [recitation of the conditions is omitted here].

(4) Persons who accompany the armed forces without actually being members thereof, such as civilian members of military aircraft crews, war correspondents, supply contractors, members of labor units or of services responsible for the welfare of the armed forces, provided that they have received authorization from the armed forces which they accompany, who shall provide them for that purpose with an identity card similar to the annexed model.

(5) Members of crews, including masters, pilots and apprentices, of the merchant marine and the crews of civil aircraft of the Parties to the conflict, who do not benefit by more favorable treatment under any other provisions of international law,

(6) Inhabitants of a non-occupied territory, who on the approach of the enemy spontaneously take up arms to resist the invading forces, without having had time to form themselves into regular armed units, provided they carry arms openly and respect the laws and customs of war.

The Commission has searched carefully through the evidence presented by the Defense, and finds nothing that would support a claim of entitlement to lawful combatant or Prisoner of War Status under options (1) or (2) above. While the Defense showed, through the testimony of Professor Williams, that the Ansars were "members of the armed forces of a Party" or members of a militia or volunteer corps "forming part of such armed forces" there is no evidence that the accused was a member of the Ansars or any other militia or volunteer corps.

Nor is there any evidence before this Commission suggesting that the accused qualifies for Prisoner of War status under option (4) a civilian accompanying the armed forces. He fails to fit into any of the suggested categories of civilians who might properly accompany the armed forces, or any similar categories of persons, there is no evidence that he "accompanied" such forces, or that he was properly identified as required by the rule. Indeed, it is clear that even civilians who fall into this category can forfeit their entitlement to prisoner of war status by directly participating in hostilities.

With respect to categories (5) and (6) above, there is likewise no evidence that the accused was a member of a merchant marine or civil aircraft crew, or that he engaged in the traditional levee-en-masse. The Commission is left to conclude that the accused has not presented any evidence from which it might find that he was a lawful combatant, or that he is entitled to Prisoner of War Status under any Geneva Convention Category. The Commission concludes, then, that he is an alien unlawful enemy combatant, and not a lawful combatant entitled to Prisoner of War protection. The accused is subject to the jurisdiction of this Commission.

Notwithstanding this finding of jurisdiction under the Military Commissions Act and the Law of International Armed Conflict, the Defense has raised three Constitutional objections to this Commission's exercise of jurisdiction over him. These are summarized briefly below:

Ex Post Facto: The Defense argued, in its May 2007 Motion to Dismiss, that it would be a violation of the Constitutional prohibition against ex post facto laws to give a Combat Status Review Tribunal (CSRT) determination "additional force after the fact," by making them determinative of the accused's status before a military commission.

The Court notes at the outset that the United States Court of Appeals for the D.C. Circuit has held that the Constitution of the United States does not protect detainees held at the U.S. Naval Base, Guantánamo Bay. *Boumediene v. Bush* 375 U.S. App. D.C. 48 (2007). In light of this current state of the law in the Circuit under which military commissions are reviewed, all of this accused's Constitutional arguments are deemed to be without merit.

Beyond this, the Commission finds that the ex post facto violations the Defense complains of have been cured by the Commission's refusal to accept the October 2004 CSRT finding as binding, and by holding its own hearing to determine whether the accused would be subject to the jurisdiction of a military commission. At that hearing, the accused was represented by no less than six counsel, had the benefits of an open and public proceeding before a military judge, and at which representatives of the world press, Human Rights groups, and organizations interested in the application of International Humanitarian Law were present. He confronted the witnesses against him, called and presented his own witnesses, and persuaded the Commission to hold open the receipt of evidence so an additional witness on his behalf could be heard.

Bill of Attainder: The Defense also argued, in its May 2007 Motion to Dismiss, that the Bill of Attainder Clause "prevents the MCA from authorizing a non-judicial finding of unlawful combatant status." This objection, in the Commission's view, is likewise mooted by the evidentiary hearing held in Guantánamo Bay on 5–6 December. There has been no "non-judicial" finding of unlawful combatant status.

Equal Protection: Because the jurisdiction of the military commission is limited to "alien" unlawful enemy combatants, the Defense challenges its Constitutionality as a violation of the equal protection clause of the United States Constitution. As before, the United States Court of Appeals for the D.C. Circuit, under which the review of military commissions falls, has expressly ruled that the United States Constitution does not protect detainees at Guantánamo Bay. The accused's challenge to the exercise of jurisdiction as a violation of the equal protection clause must likewise fail.

CONCLUSION

The Government has carried its burden of showing, by a preponderance of the evidence, that the accused is an alien unlawful enemy combatant, subject to the jurisdiction of a military commission. The Commission has separately conducted a status determination under Article 5 of the Third Geneva Convention, and determined by a preponderance of the evidence that he is not a lawful combatant or entitled to Prisoner of War Status. There being no Constitutional impediment to the Commission's exercise of jurisdiction over him, the Defense Motion to Dismiss for Lack of Jurisdiction is *DENIED*. The accused may be tried by military commission.

So Ordered this 19th day of December, 2007.

Keith J. Allred, Captain, JAGC, U.S. Navy Military Judge.

§ 8.05   MILITARY DETENTIONS REVISITED

[A]   Guantánamo Revisited

Following *Rasul*, most of the habeas corpus petitions that were pending in the D.C. District Court were consolidated before Judge Green, who issued a decision upholding some of the petitioners' claims in January 2005. *In re Guantánamo Detainee Cases*, 355 F. Supp. 2d 443 (D.D.C. 2005). Judge Leon retained his cases and issued a contrary decision 12 days before Judge Green released hers. Judge Leon concluded that due process did not apply to aliens detained outside the United States (relying on *Eisentrager*), that the Geneva Conventions were not self-executing, and that international law provided no cognizable rights to the detainees. *Khalid v. Bush*, 355 F. Supp. 2d 311 (D.D.C. 2005).

Judge Green, however, held

> that the petitioners have stated valid claims under the Fifth Amendment and that the CSRT procedures are unconstitutional for foiling to comport with the requirements of due process. Additionally, the Court holds that Taliban fighters who have not been specifically determined to be excluded from prisoner of war status by a competent Article 5 tribunal have also stated valid claims under the Third Geneva Convention. Finally, the Court concludes that the remaining claims of the petitioners must be denied.

Judge Green began by noting the lack of connection between many of the detainees and anything resembling a battlefield:

> In addition to belligerents captured during the heat of war in Afghanistan, the U.S. authorities are also detaining at Guantánamo Bay pursuant to the AUMF numerous individuals who were captured hundreds or thousands of miles from a battle zone in the traditional sense of that term. For example, detainees at Guantánamo Bay who are presently seeking habeas relief in the United States District Court for the District of Columbia include men who were taken into custody as far away from Afghanistan as Gambia, Zambia, Bosnia, and Thailand. Some have already been detained as long as three years while others have been captured as recently as September 2004. Although many of these individuals may never have been close to an actual battlefield and may never have raised conventional arms against the United States or its allies, the military nonetheless has deemed them detainable as "enemy combatants" based on conclusions that they have ties to al Qaeda or other terrorist organizations.

She also injected some levity into the difficulty that detainees would have in proving their innocence without knowing the evidence against them:

> Tribunal President: Mustafa, does that conclude your statement?
>
> Detainee: That is it, but I was hoping you had evidence that you can give me. If I was in your place — and I apologize in advance for these words — but if a supervisor came to me and showed me accusations like these, I would take these accusations and I would hit him in the face with them. Sorry about that.
>
> [Everyone in the Tribunal room laughs.]
>
> Tribunal President: We had to laugh, but it is okay.
>
> Detainee: Why? Because these are accusations that I can't even answer. I am not able to answer them. You tell me I am from Al Qaida, but I am not an Al Qaida. I don't have any proof to give you except to ask you to catch bin Laden and ask him if I am a part of Al Qaida. To tell me that I thought, I'll just tell you that I did not. I don't have proof regarding this. What should be done is you should give me evidence regarding these accusations because I am not able to give you any evidence. I can just tell you no, and that is it.

The laughter reflected in the transcript is understandable, and this exchange might have been truly humorous had the consequences of the detainee's "enemy combatant" status not been so terribly serious and had the detainee's criticism of the process not been so piercingly accurate.

The *Khalid* opinion dealt with the question of constitutional rights and habeas jurisdiction by separating the two, holding that *Rasul* did not impliedly overrule *Eisentrager*. By contrast, the *In re Detainees* opinion engages in an extensive review of cases before and after *Eisentrager* to determine that due process applies at least to aliens detained on soil under the exclusive control of the U.S.

For the Supreme Court to hold in *Rasul* that the courts have power to entertain the petition, did it necessarily hold that there must be some rights that pertain to the petitioners? How can there be jurisdiction in the absence of a claim of right? This is the conundrum presented by Justice Stevens' footnote 15. If *Khalid* is correct, then what is the point of *Rasul*?

Judge Leon held that detention was authorized by Congress but then found that the petitioners could not identify any rights protecting them under federal law. With regard to treaty law, they "conceded at oral argument that [the Geneva] Convention does not apply because these petitioners were not captured in the 'zone of hostilities . . . in and around Afghanistan.' " The combination of these two holdings seems to place the alleged terrorist within authorization to use executive force but outside the protection of any law other than international law. Of course, the Geneva Conventions are not the only source of international law but the petitioners seem to have made no arguments under international other than with respect to their conditions of confinement. Is the court correct to view allegations regarding conditions of confinement as failing to state a claim regarding the basis of confinement?

What about Professor Paust's argument that customary international law requires some level of judicial review to prevent "arbitrary" confinement? Do other countries have no interest in our imprisoning their citizens? Can the U.S. run around the world apprehending and detaining anyone we want with no controls?

Khalid raises what may be the ultimate question to which this course is addressed: what law applies in dealing with terrorists around the world. Is it permissible for U.S. agents to apprehend suspects wherever they may be found? without probable cause? to imprison them without due process? to shoot them?

The Supreme Court will take up these questions and probably issue an opinion in June 2008. The *al Odah* case and Judge Leon's *Khalid* case were decided by the D.C. Circuit under the heading of *Boumediene*.

BOUMEDIENE [& AL ODAH] v. BUSH
476 F.3d 981 (D.C. Cir. 2007),
cert denied 127 S. Ct. 1478 (April 2, 2007),
cert granted on rehearing, 127 S. Ct. 3078 (June 29, 2007)

RANDOLPH, CIRCUIT JUDGE.

Do federal courts have jurisdiction over petitions for writs of habeas corpus filed by aliens captured abroad and detained as enemy combatants at the Guantánamo Bay Naval Base in Cuba? The question has been the recurring subject of legislation and litigation. In these consolidated appeals, foreign nationals held at Guantánamo filed petitions for writs of habeas corpus alleging violations of the Constitution, treaties, statutes, regulations, the common law, and the law of nations. In the "Al Odah" cases, which consist of eleven cases involving fifty-six detainees, Judge Green denied the government's motion to dismiss with respect to the claims arising from alleged violations of the Fifth Amendment's Due Process Clause and the Third Geneva Convention, but dismissed all other claims. See *In re Guantánamo Detainee Cases*, 355 F. Supp. 2d 443 (D.D.C. 2005). After Judge Green certified the order for interlocutory appeal under 28 U.S.C. § 1292(b), the government appealed and the detainees cross-appealed. In the "Boumediene" cases — two cases involving seven detainees — Judge Leon granted the government's motion and dismissed the cases in their entirety. See *Khalid v. Bush*, 355 F. Supp. 2d 311 (D.D.C. 2005).

In the two years since the district court's decisions the law has undergone several changes. As a result, we have had two oral arguments and four rounds of briefing in these cases during that period. The developments that have brought us to this point are as follows.

In *Al Odah v. United States*, 355 U.S. App. D.C. 189, 321 F.3d 1134 (D.C. Cir. 2003), we affirmed the district court's dismissal of various claims — habeas and non-habeas — raised by Guantánamo detainees. With respect to the habeas claims, we held that "no court in this country has jurisdiction to grant habeas relief, under 28 U.S.C. § 2241, to the Guantánamo detainees." 321 F.3d at 1141. The habeas statute then stated that "Writs of habeas corpus may be granted by the Supreme Court, any justice thereof, the district courts and any circuit judge within their respective jurisdictions." 28 U.S.C. § 2241(a) (2004). Because Guantánamo Bay was not part of the sovereign territory of the United States, but rather land the United States leases from Cuba, we determined it was not within the "respective jurisdictions" of the district court or any other court in the United States. We therefore held that § 2241 did not provide statutory jurisdiction to consider habeas relief for any alien — enemy or not — held at Guantánamo.

The Supreme Court reversed in *Rasul v. Bush*, 542 U.S. 466 (2004), holding that the habeas statute extended to aliens at Guantánamo. Although the detainees themselves were beyond the district court's jurisdiction, the Court determined that the district court's jurisdiction over the detainees' custodians was sufficient to provide subject-matter jurisdiction under § 2241. The Court further held that the district court had jurisdiction over the detainees' non-habeas claims because nothing in the federal question statute or the Alien Tort Act categorically excluded aliens outside the United States from bringing such claims. The Court remanded the cases to us, and we remanded them to the district court.

In the meantime Congress responded with the Detainee Treatment Act of 2005, Pub. L. No. 109-148, 119 Stat. 2680 (2005) (DTA), which the President signed into law on December 30, 2005. The DTA added a subsection (e) to the habeas statute. This new provision stated that, "[e]xcept as provided in section 1005 of the [DTA], no court, justice, or judge" may exercise jurisdiction over

(1) an application for a writ of habeas corpus filed by or on behalf of an alien detained by the Department of Defense at Guantánamo Bay, Cuba; or

(2) any other action against the United States or its agents relating to any aspect of the detention by the Department of Defense of an alien at Guantánamo Bay, Cuba, who

(A) is currently in military custody; or

(B) has been determined by the United States Court of Appeals for the District of Columbia Circuit . . . to have been properly detained as an enemy combatant.

DTA § 1005(e)(1). The "except as provided" referred to subsections (e)(2) and (e)(3) of section 1005 of the DTA, which provided for exclusive judicial review of Combatant Status Review Tribunal determinations and military commission decisions in the D.C. Circuit. See DTA § 1005(e)(2), (e)(3).

The following June, the Supreme Court decided *Hamdan v. Rumsfeld*, 548 U.S. 557 (2006). Among other things, the Court held that the DTA did not strip federal courts of jurisdiction over habeas cases pending at the time of the DTA's enactment. The Court pointed to a provision of the DTA stating that subsections (e) (2) and (e)(3) of section 1005 "shall apply with respect to any claim . . . that is pending on or after the date of the enactment of this Act." DTA § 1005(h). In contrast, no provision of the DTA stated whether subsection (e)(1) applied to pending cases. Finding that Congress "chose not to so provide . . . after having been presented with the option," the Court concluded "[t]he omission [wa]s an integral part of the statutory scheme."

In response to *Hamdan*, Congress passed the Military Commissions Act of 2006, Pub. L. No. 109-366, 120 Stat. 2600 (2006) (MCA), which the President signed into law on October 17, 2006. Section 7 of the MCA is entitled "Habeas Corpus Matters." In subsection (a), Congress again amended § 2241(e). The new amendment reads:

> (1) No court, justice, or judge shall have jurisdiction to hear or consider an application for a writ of habeas corpus filed by or on behalf of an alien detained by the United States who has been determined by the United States to have been properly detained as an enemy combatant or is awaiting such determination.

> (2) Except as provided in [section 1005(e)(2) and (e)(3) of the DTA], no court, justice, or judge shall have jurisdiction to hear or consider any other action against the United States or its agents relating to any aspect of the detention, transfer, treatment, trial, or conditions of confinement of an alien who is or was detained by the United States and has been determined by the United States to have been properly detained as an enemy combatant or is awaiting such determination.

MCA § 7(a). Subsection (b) states:

> The amendment made by subsection (a) shall take effect on the date of the enactment of this Act, and shall apply to all cases, without exception, pending on or after the date of the enactment of this Act which relate to any aspect of the detention, transfer, treatment, trial, or conditions of detention of an alien detained by the United States since September 11, 2001.

MCA § 7(b).

The first question is whether the MCA applies to the detainees' habeas petitions. If the MCA does apply, the second question is whether the statute is an unconstitutional suspension of the writ of habeas corpus.

I.

As to the application of the MCA to these lawsuits, section 7(b) states that the amendment to the habeas corpus statute, 28 U.S.C. § 2241(e), "shall apply to all cases, without exception, pending on or after the date of the enactment" that relate to certain subjects. The detainees' lawsuits fall within the subject matter covered by the amended § 2241(e); each case relates to an "aspect" of detention and each deals with the detention of an "alien" after September 11, 2001. The MCA brings all such "cases, without exception" within the new law.

Everyone who has followed the interaction between Congress and the Supreme Court knows full well that one of the primary purposes of the MCA was to overrule Hamdan. Everyone, that is, except the detainees. Their cases, they argue, are not covered. The arguments are creative but not cogent. To accept them would be to defy the will of Congress. Section 7(b) could not be clearer. It states that "the amendment made by subsection (a)" — which repeals habeas jurisdiction — applies to "all cases, without exception" relating to any aspect of detention. It is almost as if the proponents of these words were slamming their fists on the table shouting "When we say 'all,' we mean all — **without exception!**"

The detainees of course do not see it that way. They say Congress should have expressly stated in section 7(b) that habeas cases were included among "all cases, without exception, pending on or after" the MCA became law. Otherwise, the MCA does not represent an "unambiguous statutory directive" to repeal habeas corpus jurisdiction. The detainees' argument means that Congress, in amending the habeas statute, specified an effective date only for non-habeas cases. Of course Congress did nothing of the sort. Habeas cases are simply a subset of cases dealing with detention.

II.

This brings us to the constitutional issue: whether the MCA, in depriving the courts of jurisdiction over the detainees' habeas petitions, violates the Suspension Clause of the Constitution, U.S. Const. art. I, § 9, cl. 2, which states that "The Privilege of the Writ of Habeas Corpus shall not be suspended, unless when in Cases of Rebellion or Invasion the public Safety may require it."

The Supreme Court has stated the Suspension Clause protects the writ "as it existed in 1789," when the first Judiciary Act created the federal courts and granted jurisdiction to issue writs of habeas corpus. The detainees rely mainly on three cases to claim that in 1789 the privilege of the writ extended to aliens outside the sovereign's territory. In Lockington's Case, Bright. (N.P.) 269 (Pa. 1813), a British resident of Philadelphia had been imprisoned after failing to comply with a federal marshal's order to relocate. The War of 1812 made Lockington an "enemy alien" under the Alien Enemies Act of 1798. Although he lost on the merits of his petition for habeas corpus before the Pennsylvania Supreme Court, two of three Pennsylvania justices held that he was entitled to review of his detention. In The Case of Three Spanish Sailors, 96 Eng. Rep. 775 (C.P. 1779), three Spanish seamen had boarded a merchant vessel bound for England with a promise of wages on arrival. After arriving in England, the English captain refused to pay their wages and turned them over to a warship as prisoners of war. The King's Bench denied the sailors' petitions because they were "alien enemies and prisoners of war, and therefore not entitled to any of the privileges of Englishmen; much less to be set at liberty on a habeas corpus." The detainees claim that, as in Lockington's Case, the King's Bench exercised jurisdiction and reached the merits. The third case — Rex v. Schiever, 97 Eng. Rep. 551 (K.B. 1759) — involved a citizen of Sweden intent on entering the English merchant trade. While at sea on an English merchant's ship, a French privateer took Schiever along with the rest of the crew as prisoners, transferred the crew to another French ship, and let the English prisoners go free. An English ship thereafter captured the French ship and its crew, and carried them to Liverpool where Schiever was imprisoned. From Liverpool Schiever petitioned for habeas corpus, claiming he was a citizen of Sweden and only by force entered the service of the French. The court denied him relief because it found ample evidence that he was a prisoner of war.

None of these cases involved an alien outside the territory of the sovereign. Lockington was a resident of Philadelphia. And the three Spanish sailors and Schiever were all held within English sovereign territory. The detainees cite no case and no historical treatise showing that the English common law writ of habeas corpus extended to aliens beyond the Crown's dominions. Our review shows the contrary. Robert Chambers, the successor to Blackstone at Oxford, wrote in his lectures that the writ of habeas corpus extended only to the King's dominions. Chambers cited Rex v. Cowle, 97 Eng. Rep. (2 Burr.) 587 (K.B. 1759), in which Lord Mansfield stated that "[t]o foreign dominions . . . this Court has no power to send any writ of any kind. We cannot send a habeas corpus to Scotland, or to the electorate; but to Ireland, the Isle of Man, the plantations [American colonies] . . . we may." Every territory that Mansfield, Blackstone, and Chambers cited as a jurisdiction to which the writ extended (e.g., Ireland, the Isle of Man, the colonies, the Cinque Ports, and Wales) was a sovereign territory of the Crown.

When agents of the Crown detained prisoners outside the Crown's dominions, it was understood that they were outside the jurisdiction of the writ. Even British citizens imprisoned in "remote islands, garrisons, and other places" were "prevent[ed] from the benefit of the law." Compliance with a writ from overseas was also completely impractical given the habeas law at the time. In Cowle, Lord Mansfield explained that even in the far off territories "annexed to the Crown," the Court would not send the writ, "notwithstanding the power." 97 Eng. Rep. at 600. This is doubtless because of the Habeas Corpus Act of 1679. The great innovation of this statute was in setting time limits for producing the prisoner and imposing fines on the custodian if those limits were not met. For a prisoner detained over 100 miles from the court, the detaining officer had twenty days after receiving the writ to produce the body before the court. If he did not produce the body, he incurred a fine. One can easily imagine the practical problems this would have entailed if the writ had run outside the sovereign territory of the Crown and reached British soldiers holding foreign prisoners in overseas conflicts, such as the War of 1812. The short of the matter is that given the history of the writ in England prior to the founding, habeas corpus would not have been available in 1789 to aliens without presence or property within the United States.

Johnson v. Eisentrager, 339 U.S. 763 (1950), ends any doubt about the scope of common law habeas. "We are cited to no instance where a court, in this or any other country where the writ is known, has issued it on behalf of an alien enemy who, at no relevant time and in no stage of his captivity, has been within its territorial jurisdiction. Nothing in the text of the Constitution extends such a right, nor does anything in our statutes." The detainees claim they are in a different position than the prisoners in *Eisentrager*, and that this difference is material for purposes of common law habeas. They point to dicta in *Rasul*, in which the Court discussed English habeas cases and the "historical reach of the writ." *Rasul* refers to several English and American cases involving varying combinations of territories of the Crown and relationships between the petitioner and the country in which the writ was sought. But as Judge Robertson found in *Hamdan*, "[n]ot one of the cases mentioned in *Rasul* held that an alien captured abroad and detained outside the United States — or in 'territory over which the United States exercises exclusive jurisdiction and control,' — had a common law or constitutionally protected right to the writ of habeas corpus." We are aware of no case prior to 1789 going the detainees' way, and we are convinced that the writ in 1789 would not have been available to aliens held at an overseas military base leased from a foreign government.

The detainees encounter another difficulty with their Suspension Clause claim. Precedent in this court and the Supreme Court holds that the Constitution does not confer rights on aliens without property or presence within the United States. As we explained in *Al Odah*, 321 F.3d at 1140–41, the controlling case is *Johnson v. Eisentrager*. There twenty-one German nationals confined in custody of the U.S. Army in Germany filed habeas corpus petitions. Although the German prisoners alleged they were civilian agents of the German government, a military commission convicted them of war crimes arising from military activity against the United States in China after Germany's surrender. They claimed their convictions and imprisonment violated various constitutional provisions and the Geneva Conventions. The Supreme Court rejected the proposition "that the Fifth Amendment confers rights upon all persons, whatever their nationality, wherever they are located and whatever their offenses." The Court continued: "If the Fifth Amendment confers its rights on all the world . . . [it] would mean that during military occupation irreconcilable enemy elements, guerrilla fighters, and 'werewolves' could require the American Judiciary to assure them freedoms of speech, press, and assembly as in the First Amendment, right to bear arms as in the Second, security against 'unreasonable' searches and seizures as in the Fourth, as well as rights to jury trial as in the Fifth and Sixth Amendments."

Later Supreme Court decisions have followed *Eisentrager*. In 1990, for instance, the Court stated that *Eisentrager* "rejected the claim that aliens are entitled to Fifth Amendment rights outside the sovereign territory of the United States." *United States v. Verdugo-Urquidez*, 494 U.S. 259, 269 (1990). After describing the facts of *Eisentrager* and quoting from the opinion, the Court concluded that with respect to aliens, "our rejection of extraterritorial application of the Fifth Amendment was emphatic." By analogy, the Court held that the Fourth Amendment did not protect nonresident aliens against unreasonable searches or seizures conducted outside the sovereign territory of the United States. Citing *Eisentrager* again, the Court explained that to extend the Fourth Amendment to aliens abroad "would have significant and deleterious consequences for the United States in conducting activities beyond its boundaries," particularly since the government "frequently employs Armed Forces outside this country." A decade after *Verdugo-Urquidez*, the Court — again citing *Eisentrager* — found it "well established that certain constitutional protections available to persons inside the United States are unavailable to aliens outside of our geographic borders." *Zadvydas v. Davis*, 533 U.S. 678, 693 (2001).[20]

Any distinction between the naval base at Guantánamo Bay and the prison in Landsberg, Germany, where the petitioners in Eisentrager were held, is immaterial to the application of the Suspension Clause. The United States occupies the Guantánamo Bay Naval Base under an indefinite lease it entered into in 1903. The text of the lease and decisions of circuit courts and the Supreme Court all make clear that Cuba — not the United States — has sovereignty over Guantánamo Bay.

As against this line of authority, the dissent offers the distinction that the Suspension Clause is a limitation on congressional power rather than a constitutional right. But this is no distinction at all. Constitutional rights are rights against the government and, as such, are restrictions on governmental power. *See H.P. Hood & Sons, Inc. v. Du Mond*, 336 U.S. 525, 534 (1949) ("Even the Bill of Rights amendments were framed only as a limitation upon the powers of Congress."). Consider the First Amendment. (In contrasting the Suspension Clause with provisions in the Bill of Rights, see Dissent at 3, the dissent is careful to ignore the First Amendment.) Like the Suspension Clause, the First Amendment is framed as a limitation on Congress: "Congress shall make no law . . . ." Yet no one would deny that the First Amendment protects the rights to free speech and religion and assembly.

The dissent's other arguments are also filled with holes. It is enough to point out three of the larger ones.

There is the notion that the Suspension Clause is different from the Fourth, Fifth, and Sixth Amendments because it does not mention individuals and those amendments do (respectively, "people," "person," and "the accused"). Why the dissent thinks this is significant eludes us. Is the point that if a provision does not mention individuals there is no constitutional right? That cannot be right. The First Amendment's guarantees of freedom of speech and free exercise of religion do not mention individuals; nor does the Eighth Amendment's prohibition on cruel and unusual punishment or the Seventh Amendment's guarantee of a civil jury. Of course it is fair to assume that these provisions apply to individuals, just as it is fair to assume that petitions for writs of habeas corpus are filed by individuals.

The dissent also looks to the Bill of Attainder and Ex Post Facto Clauses, both located next to the Suspension Clause in Article I, Section 9. We do not understand what the dissent is trying to make of this juxtaposition. The dissent's point cannot be that the Bill of Attainder Clause and the Ex Post Facto Clause do not protect individual rights.

Why is the dissent so fixated on how to characterize the Suspension Clause? The unstated assumption must be that the reasoning of our decisions and the Supreme Court's in denying constitutional rights to aliens outside the United States would not apply if a constitutional provision could be characterized as protecting something other than a "right." On this theory, for example, aliens outside the United States are entitled to the protection of the Separation of Powers because they have no individual rights under the Separation of Powers. Where the dissent gets this strange idea is a mystery, as is the reasoning behind it.

---

[20] [Court's Footnote 10] The *Rasul* decision, resting as it did on statutory interpretation, could not possibly have affected the constitutional holding of *Eisentrager*. Even if *Rasul* somehow calls *Eisen-trager's* constitutional holding into question, as the detainees suppose, we would be bound to follow *Eisentrager*.

III.

Federal courts have no jurisdiction in these case. In supplemental briefing after enactment of the DTA, the government asked us not only to decide the habeas jurisdiction question, but also to review the merits of the detainees' designation as enemy combatants by their Combatant Status Review Tribunals. The detainees objected to converting their habeas appeals to appeals from their Tribunals. In briefs filed after the DTA became law and after the Supreme Court decided *Hamdan*, they argued that we were without authority to do so. Even if we have authority to convert the habeas appeals over the petitioners' objections, the record does not have sufficient information to perform the review the DTA allows. Our only recourse is to vacate the district courts' decisions and dismiss the cases for lack of jurisdiction.

So ordered.

ROGERS, CIRCUIT JUDGE, dissenting.

I can join neither the reasoning of the court nor its conclusion that the federal courts lack power to consider the detainees' petitions. While I agree that Congress intended to withdraw federal jurisdiction through the Military Commissions Act of 2006 ("MCA"), the court's holding that the MCA is consistent with the Suspension Clause of Article I, section 9, of the Constitution does not withstand analysis. By concluding that this court must reject "the detainees' claims to constitutional rights," the court fundamentally misconstrues the nature of suspension: Far from conferring an individual right that might pertain only to persons substantially connected to the United States, the Suspension Clause is a limitation on the powers of Congress. Consequently, it is only by misreading the historical record and ignoring the Supreme Court's well-considered and binding dictum in *Rasul v. Bush*, that the writ at common law would have extended to the detainees, that the court can conclude that neither this court nor the district courts have jurisdiction to consider the detainees' habeas claims.

A review of the text and operation of the Suspension Clause shows that, by nature, it operates to constrain the powers of Congress. Prior to the enactment of the MCA, the Supreme Court acknowledged that the detainees held at Guantánamo had a statutory right to habeas corpus. The MCA purports to withdraw that right but does so in a manner that offends the constitutional constraint on suspension. The Suspension Clause limits the removal of habeas corpus, at least as the writ was understood at common law, to times of rebellion or invasion unless Congress provides an adequate alternative remedy. The writ would have reached the detainees at common law, and Congress has neither provided an adequate alternative remedy, through the Detainee Treatment Act of 2005 nor invoked the exception to the Clause by making the required findings to suspend the writ. The MCA is therefore void and does not deprive this court or the district courts of jurisdiction.

BOUMEDIENE v. BUSH
127 S. Ct. 1478 (2007)

[On June 29, 2007, the last day of the October 2006 Term, the Supreme Court granted certiorari in these cases. Some Justices had written opinions regarding the earlier denial of certiorari on April 2, 2007, and those opinions are reprinted here.]

OPINION

Petitions for writs of certiorari to the United States Court of Appeals for the District of Columbia Circuit denied.

Statement of JUSTICE STEVENS and JUSTICE KENNEDY respecting the denial of certiorari.

Despite the obvious importance of the issues raised in these cases, we are persuaded that traditional rules governing our decision of constitutional questions and our practice of requiring the exhaustion of available remedies as a precondition to accepting jurisdiction over applications for the writ of habeas corpus, make it appropriate to deny these petitions at this time. However, "this Court has frequently recognized that the policy underlying the exhaustion-of-remedies doctrine does not require the exhaustion of inadequate remedies." If petitioners later seek to establish that the Government has unreasonably delayed proceedings under the Detainee Treatment Act of 2005, or some other and ongoing injury, alternative means exist for us to consider our jurisdiction over the allegations made by petitioners before the Court of Appeals. Were the Government to take additional steps to prejudice the position of petitioners in seeking review in this Court, "courts of competent jurisdiction," including this Court, "should act promptly to ensure that the office and purposes of the writ of habeas corpus are not compromised." Padilla v. Hanft, 547 U.S. 1062, 1064 (2006) (Kennedy, J., concurring in denial of certiorari). And as always, denial of certiorari does not constitute an expression of any opinion on the merits.

JUSTICE BREYER, with whom JUSTICE SOUTER joins, and with whom JUSTICE GINSBURG joins as to Part I, dissenting from the denial of certiorari.

I would grant the petitions for certiorari and expedite argument in these cases.

I

Petitioners, foreign citizens imprisoned at Guantánamo Bay, Cuba, raise an important question: whether the Military Commissions Act of 2006 deprives courts of jurisdiction to consider their habeas claims, and, if so, whether that deprivation is constitutional. I believe these questions deserve this Court's immediate attention.

First, the "province" of the Great Writ, "shaped to guarantee the most fundamental of all rights, is to provide an effective *and speedy* instrument by which judicial inquiry may be had into the legality of the detention of a person." Yet, petitioners have been held for more than five years. They have not obtained judicial review of their habeas claims. If petitioners are right about the law, immediate review may avoid an additional year or more of imprisonment. If they are wrong, our review is nevertheless appropriate to help establish the boundaries of the constitutional provision for the writ of habeas corpus. Finally, whether petitioners are right or wrong, our prompt review will diminish the legal "uncertainty" that now "surrounds" the application to Guantánamo detainees of this "fundamental constitutional principle." Doing so will bring increased clarity that in turn will speed review in other cases.

Second, petitioners plausibly argue that the lower court's reasoning is contrary to this Court's precedent. This Court previously held that federal jurisdiction lay to consider petitioners' habeas claims. *Rasul v. Bush*, 542 U.S. 466, 485 (2004) (providing several of these petitioners with the right to habeas review under law as it then stood). Our analysis proceeded under the then-operative statute, but petitioners urge that our reasoning applies to the scope of the constitutional habeas right as well. In holding that the writ extended to the petitioners in *Rasul*, we said that Guantánamo was under the complete control and jurisdiction of the United States. We then observed that the writ at common law would have extended to petitioners:

> Application of the habeas statute to persons detained at the base is consistent with the historical reach of the writ of habeas corpus. At common law, courts exercised habeas jurisdiction over the claims of aliens detained within sovereign territory of the realm, as well as the claims of persons detained in the so-called exempt jurisdictions, where ordinary writs did not run, and all other dominions under the sovereign's control. . . . Even if a territory was no part of the realm, there was no doubt as to the court's power to issue writs of habeas corpus if the territory was under the subjection of the Crown.

Our reasoning may be applicable here. The lower court's holding, petitioners urge, disregards these statements and reasoning.

Further, petitioners in *Boumediene* are natives of Algeria, and citizens of Bosnia, seized in Bosnia. Other detainees, including several petitioners in *Al Odah*, also are citizens of friendly nations, including Australia, Canada, Kuwait, Turkey, and the United Kingdom; and many were seized outside of any theater of hostility, in places like Pakistan, Thailand, and Zambia. It is possible that these circumstances will make a difference in respect to our resolution of the constitutional questions presented. *Cf. Hamdi v. Rumsfeld*, 542 U.S. 507, 509, 514, 521 (2004) (plurality opinion of O'Connor, J., joined by Rehnquist, C. J., and Kennedy and Breyer, JJ.) (holding military had authority to detain United States citizen "enemy combatant," captured in a "*zone of active combat* in a foreign theater of conflict," specifically Afghanistan, and stressing, in a "narrow" holding, that "*active combat operations against Taliban fighters . . . [were] ongoing in Afghanistan*" (emphasis added)).

The Government, of course, contests petitioners' arguments on the merits. But I do not here say petitioners are correct; I say only that the questions presented are significant ones warranting our review. If petitioners have the right of access to habeas corpus in the federal courts, this Court would then have to consider whether Congress' provision in the Detainee Treatment Act of 2005 (DTA), providing for review in the Court of Appeals for the D. C. Circuit of those proceedings, is a constitutionally adequate substitute for habeas corpus. The Government argues that we should therefore wait for a case where, unlike petitioners here, the detainee seeking certiorari has actually sought and received review under these alternative means. Petitioners respond, however, that further proceedings in the Court of Appeals under the DTA could not possibly remedy a constitutional violation. The lower court expressly indicated that *no constitutional rights* (not merely the right to habeas) extend to the Guantánamo detainees. Therefore, it is irrelevant, to petitioners, that the DTA provides for review in the D. C. Circuit of any constitutional infirmities in the proceedings under that Act; the lower court has already rendered that provision a nullity.

Here, as in *Hamdan*, petitioners have a compelling interest in assuring in advance that the procedures to which they are subject are lawful. And here, *unlike Hamdan*, the military tribunals in Guantánamo have completed their work; all that remains are the appeals. For all these reasons, I would grant the petitions.

II

Moreover, I would expedite our consideration. In the past, this Court has expedited other cases where important issues and a need for speedy consideration were at stake. In *Ex parte Quirin*, 317 U.S. 1 (1942), the Court decided that it should grant expedited consideration, "in view of the public importance of the questions raised by [the] petitions and of the duty which rests on the courts, in time of war as well as in time of peace, to preserve unimpaired the constitutional safeguards of civil liberty, and because in our opinion the public interest required that we consider and decide those questions without any avoidable delay."

For these reasons, I would grant the petitions for certiorari and the motions to expedite the cases in accordance with the schedule deemed acceptable (in the alternative) by the Government.

NOTES AND QUESTIONS

1. The Reach of Habeas Corpus. The *Boumediene* arguments were held on December 5, 2007. Most observers heard little to suggest any shift from the five votes that have already been cast (in *Hamdan* and *Rasul*) for the position that habeas corpus extends to Guantánamo. The MCA and DTA do not by their terms suspend habeas corpus, and the Court is unlikely to find an implicit suspension.

2. Rights of the Detainees. If the above speculation is accurate, then the question will become what rights the detainees might have. It is rather clear that the MCA and

DTA establish the limit of statutory rights for detainees, and the most likely sources of additional rights would be constitutional or international law.

a.　With regard to constitutional rights, Judge Green held that the detainees have minimal due process rights and that CSRT hearings failed to satisfy due process because of the reliance on secret evidence undisclosed to the detainee. The imposition of due process in this context should not be confused with extending other constitutional rights to other contexts, such as requiring search warrants when DEA agents act in other countries. Nevertheless, there are institutional concerns with extending constitutional rights to government action outside the "sovereign territory" of the United States.

b.　With regard to international law, Part VI(D)(iv) of *Hamdan* deals with due process from the specific vantage point of the Geneva Conventions Common Article 3 applicable to situations of armed conflict. There are also provisions in the UDHR and ICCPR that protect against arbitrary detention. Those provisions could give rise to an argument for customary international law of due process that would apply to any tribunal responsible for determining the validity of detention.

The Supreme Court almost certainly will not resolve these issues without remanding to the D.C. Circuit for its views on the matters. Thus, the validity of the CSRT proceedings and the Guantánamo detentions are unlikely to be resolved before 2009. Given the chorus of calls for closing the facility, is it not likely that the issues will dissipate before the Supreme Court reaches finality on all of the questions involved?

3. Israeli Practice. An amicus brief filed with the Supreme Court in the *Boumediene* case on behalf of "Specialists in Israeli Military Law and Constitutional Law" makes the following points:

> Despite great danger and pressing needs for intelligence, Israel affords all detainees prompt, independent judicial review of their detention, protected by procedural safeguards and aided by access to counsel.

1.　Unlike the United States, Israel provides suspected unlawful combatants the right to judicial review of the basis for their detention within no more than 14 days of their seizure.

2.　Unlike the United States, Israel provides suspected unlawful combatants the right to judicial review in a tribunal independent from the executive.

3.　Unlike the United States, Israel limits detention to only those circumstances in which the suspected unlawful combatant poses a threat to State security and when no other means are available to neutralize the threat.

4.　Unlike the United States, Israel subjects the evidence and judgments supporting the detention of suspected unlawful combatants to searching judicial review.

5.　Unlike the United States, Israel prohibits all inhumane methods of interrogation and limits the use of coerced testimony against suspected unlawful combatants when assessing the basis for their detention.

6.　Unlike the United States, Israel requires judicial approval before limiting a suspected unlawful combatant's access to classified information offered in support of detention.

7.　Unlike the United States, Israel provides access to counsel within no more than 34 days.

8.　Unlike the United States, Israel provides for periodic review of detention at least once every 6 months, permitting the continuation of detention only upon a fresh judicial finding of dangerousness following a fully adversarial hearing.

4. Grounds for Detention. Notice particularly point #3 in the Israeli amicus brief, in which a standard for detention is set out. Compare the very broad definition of "unlawful enemy combatant" in the MCA: "a person who has engaged in hostilities or who has purposefully and materially supported hostilities against the United States or its co-belligerents who is not a lawful enemy combatant." Could you be an unlawful enemy combatant if you sent money to a Pakistani opposition group without knowing whether they might engage in violence against a government friendly to the U.S.? Perhaps you should be prevented from doing so, but should you not be entitled to a hearing to determine if indeed you had done so?

BISMULLAH v. GATES
503 F.3d 137 (D.C. Cir. 2007)
hearing en banc denied (Feb. 4, 2007)

GINSBURG, CHIEF JUDGE.

The petitioners are eight men detained at the Naval Station at Guantánamo Bay, Cuba. Each petitioner seeks review under the Detainee Treatment Act (DTA), of the determination by a Combatant Status Review Tribunal (CSRT or Tribunal) that he is an "enemy combatant." In our opinion of July 20, 2007, we addressed various procedural motions filed by the Government and the petitioners to govern our review of the merits of the detainees' petitions. The Government then petitioned for rehearing or, in the alternative, suggested rehearing *en banc*. The petition for rehearing addresses two distinct aspects of *Bismullah I*: the scope of the record on review before the court; and the extent to which the Government must disclose that record to the petitioners' counsel. We deny the Government's petition for rehearing for the reasons discussed below.

I. The Scope of the Record on Review.

As we explained in *Bismullah I*, the Secretary of Defense, in a July 2004 Memorandum for the Secretary of the Navy, established skeletal procedures for the conduct of a CSRT proceeding with respect to a foreign national held at Guantánamo to "review the detainee's status as an enemy combatant." The Secretary of the Navy then issued a memorandum elaborating upon those procedures in three enclosures (collectively, the DoD Regulations). The DoD Regulations provide that the Tribunal is "authorized," insofar as is relevant here, to

> [r]equest the production of such reasonably available information in the possession of the U.S. Government bearing on the issue of whether the detainee meets the criteria to be designated as an enemy combatant, including information generated in connection with the initial determination to hold the detainee as an enemy combatant and in any subsequent reviews of that determination, as well as any records, determinations, or reports generated in connection with such proceedings (cumulatively called hereinafter "Government Information").

The Recorder must collect the Government Information, examine it, and then decide which information to pass on to the Tribunal. The Recorder is required to

> present to the Tribunal such evidence in the Government Information as may be sufficient to support the detainee's classification as an enemy combatant-. . . (the evidence so presented shall constitute the "Government Evidence") . . . [and, in] the event the Government Information contains evidence to suggest that the detainee should not be designated as an enemy combatant, the Recorder shall also separately provide such evidence to the Tribunal.

In *Bismullah I* the Government argued that the record on review should consist solely of the Record of Proceedings, which, under the DoD Regulations, includes only such Government Information as the Recorder forwarded to the Tribunal. Taking the view that the record on review should consist of "all evidence reasonably available to the Government," the petitioners contended that the record should include all of the Government Information. We held the record on review must include all the Government Information because the DTA requires the court to review the CSRT determination to ensure it is "consistent with the standards and procedures specified by the Secretary of Defense (including the requirement that the conclusion of the Tribunal be supported by a preponderance of the evidence)."[21] Whether the Recorder selected to be put before the Tribunal all exculpatory Government Information, as required by the DoD Regulations, and whether the preponderance of the evidence supported the conclusion of the Tribunal, cannot be ascertained without consideration of all the Government Information.

In its petition for rehearing, the Government asserts that *Bismullah I* defined the record on review to include "a broad and amorphous class of material" out of "a desire to ensure that exculpatory information was properly considered."

[T]he Government argues that if *Bismullah I* "is allowed to stand, the Government will be required to undertake searches of all relevant Department of Defense components and all relevant federal agencies in an effort to recreate a 'record' that is entirely different from the record before the Tribunal that made the decision at issue in a DTA case." The burden of collecting all these materials, the Government says, would be so great that it would "divert limited resources and sidetrack the intelligence community from performing other critical national security duties during a time of war." For example, the Government reports that its searches of certain databases for relevant documents are yielding "tens of thousands, and in many cases hundreds of thousands, of documents" relating to a given detainee. According to Deputy Secretary of Defense Gordon England, two offices within the DoD have expended well over 2000 man-hours in a recent effort to collect material relating to six detainees who have petitioned for review of their status determination.

The Government, it seems, is overreading *Bismullah I* and underreading the DoD Regulations. Those regulations provide that "information in the possession of the U.S. Government bearing on the issue of whether the detainee meets the criteria to be designated as an enemy combatant" comes within the definition of Government Information only if it is "reasonably available." In its petition for rehearing, the Government adverts repeatedly to this limitation upon the scope of Government Information. Yet, the Government reports that it "is now conducting . . . entirely new searches of all relevant DoD components and all relevant federal agencies." A search for information without regard to whether it is "reasonably available" is clearly not required by *Bismullah I*.

Apparently, the Government is searching for all relevant information without regard to whether it is reasonably available because it did not retain all the Government Information that the Recorder collected.[22] The Government has consequently determined that it must now search for relevant information without regard to whether the information is reasonably available "because [it] can conceive of no other comprehensive method to ensure that [it] identif[ies] information that the Recorder could have examined." The Government explains that it did not retain all the Government Information because, "[a]t the time, Recorders had no reason to believe that DoD would be required to produce (or explain post hoc) what was *not* provided to the Tribunal." We note in the Government's defense that CSRTs made hundreds of status determinations, including those under review in the present cases, before the DTA was enacted in

---

[21] [Court's Footnote 2] We also held the record on review includes any evidence submitted to the Tribunal by the detainee or his Personal Representative, a matter not in dispute here. Nor is it disputed that any material requested by the Tribunal pursuant to the DoD Regulations is part of the record on review.

[22] [Court's Footnote 4] The Government tells us "there is no readily accessible set of Government Information for completed CSRTs" and that the Government Information is not "sitting in a file drawer." Thus, it seems that, having collected the Government Information and selected the Government Evidence for the Tribunal to see, the Recorder then did not retain that portion of the Government Information he did not forward to the Tribunal.

December 2005 and therefore without knowing what the Congress would later specify concerning the scope and nature of judicial review.

Be that as it may, if the Government cannot, within its resource constraints, produce the Government Information collected by the Recorder with respect to a particular detainee, then this court will be unable to confirm that the CSRT's determination was reached in compliance with the DoD Regulations and applicable law. The Government does have an alternative: It can abandon its present course of trying to reconstruct the Government Information by surveying all relevant information in its possession without regard to whether that information is reasonably available, and instead convene a new CSRT. If the Government elects to convene a new CSRT, it will have to collect only the Government Information specified by the DoD Regulations-that is, the relevant information in its possession that is then *reasonably available*.

In summary, the record on review must include all the Government Information, as defined by the DoD Regulations. If the Government did not preserve that entire body of information with respect to a particular petitioner, then it will have either to reassemble the Government Information it did collect or to convene a new CSRT, taking care this time to retain all the Government Information.

II. Access by the Petitioner's Counsel to Classified Government Information.

The Government also objects to *Bismullah I* insofar as it requires the Government to turn over Government Information to the petitioners' counsel. The Government sees two problems with this: The disclosure of classified Government Information "could seriously disrupt the Nation's intelligence gathering programs;" and the burden of reviewing all the Government Information to determine whether it must be turned over is so great that it will "divert limited resources and sidetrack the intelligence community from performing other critical national security duties during a time of war."

In *Bismullah I*, we dealt with the Government's concern about disclosure by providing, just as the Government urged, that it may withhold from the petitioners' counsel any Government Information that is either "highly sensitive information, or . . . pertain[s] to a highly sensitive source or to anyone other than the detainee."[23] The Government's need to review the Government Information in order to determine whether it fits within any of these three exceptions gives rise to the Government's present concern about the burden of complying with *Bismullah I*.

Although the Government represented in its brief and at oral argument in *Bismullah I* that it would need to withhold "only a small amount of information" from a detainee's counsel, the Government now indicates that a substantial amount of the Government Information comes within one or another of the three exceptions, thereby "exponentially increas[ing] the magnitude of" its review of Government Information to determine what to withhold. The Government's petition is unclear as to why it now anticipates so much more Government Information will be non-disclosable. Perhaps it is because, as discussed above, the Government has been searching for all relevant information without regard to whether it is reasonably available. According to the DoD Regulations, "[c]lassified information . . . which the originating agency declines to authorize for use in the CSRT process is not reasonably available." Consequently, if the Government convenes a new CSRT and the Recorder collects as Government Information only the information in its possession that is both relevant and "reasonably available," then the amount of information to be redacted may indeed be as small as the Government anticipated earlier. We note, however, that, according to the DoD Regulations, when an originating agency withholds relevant information, it must "provide either an acceptable substitute for the information requested or a certification to the Tribunal that none of

---

[23] [Court's Footnote 6] To the extent the Government now suggests that certain information may be too sensitive to disclose even to the court, we leave that issue for case-by-case determination upon ex parte motion filed by the Government.

the withheld information would support a determination that the detainee is not an enemy combatant."

In any event, the proportion of the Government Information that may be withheld from the petitioners' counsel should not affect to an appreciable degree the burden upon the Government of producing the Government Information to the petitioners' counsel. Regardless of how much ultimately may be withheld, the Government will have to conduct the same review of the Government Information in order to make that determination; so much was inherent in the Government's proposed standard for withholding information, which we adopted. Thus, the real import of the Government's argument seems to be that having to review the Government Information to determine whether it must be disclosed creates a substantial burden for the Government and therefore, because the Government obviously cannot indiscriminately turn over all of the Government Information to the petitioners' counsel, the only solution is to turn over none of it. As we explained in *Bismullah I*, however, entirely *ex parte* review of a CSRT determination is inconsistent with effective judicial review as required by the DTA and should be avoided to the extent consistent with safeguarding classified information.[24]

NOTE ON THE LAWYERS OF GUANTÁNAMO

Much has been written about the question of whether key lawyers in the crafting of interrogation and detention policies violated ethical norms by advising policymakers that it would be legally acceptable to ignore certain statutory and treaty obligations in pursuit of the President's executive powers. *See, e.g.*, Milan Markovic, *Can Lawyers Be War Criminals?* 20 GEO. J. LEGAL ETHICS 347 (2007). JACK GOLDSMITH, THE TERROR PRESIDENCY (2007) created further controversy first by disclosing his role in repudiating the "torture memo" and also by appearing to disclose conversations that could be argued to have been protected by attorney-client privilege.

In contrast, a number of military lawyers have come forward with criticisms of the processes of the military commissions and CSRTs.

Colonel Charles Swift, who was assigned to represent Salim Hamdan, pursued Hamdan's case to the rather clear detriment of his career. Swift took Hamdan's constitutional claims to the Supreme Court, gave an interview to *Vanity Fair*, was passed over for promotion, and is now Visiting Associate Professor and Acting Director, International Humanitarian Law Clinic, at Emory Law School from which base he continues to represent Hamdan.

See http://www.vanityfair.com/politics/features/2007/03/Guantánamo200703; http://www.law.emory.edu/faculty/faculty-profiles/ charles-d-swift.html.

Maj. Thomas Roughneen, Swift's replacement as Hamdan's lawyer, reportedly told the *Miami Herald*, "It's like the Titanic. You know someday the ship is going to sink. God almighty, let's get there already." http://www.andyworthington.co.uk/?p=97.

Lt. Col. Stephen Abraham is a lawyer and intelligence officer who was assigned to review files going before the CSRTs and to provide an assurance that other intelligence agencies did not possess exculpatory information for the detainee's benefit. He provided an affidavit that was attached to the petition for rehearing from denial of certiorari in *al-Odah*. In that affidavit, he described some problems with the chain of command and training of CSRT members. Specifically, he addressed the availability of information from intelligence agencies this way:

> I was specifically told on a number of occasions that the information provided
> to me was all that I would be shown, but I was never told that the information

---

[24] [Court's Footnote 7] Nonetheless, if it is true that most of the Government Information will come within an exception to the requirement that the petitioners' counsel be given access to the Government Information, then the practical effect of the exceptions may yet be that our review of a CSRT determination is in large part *ex parte*.

that was provided constituted all available information. On those occasions when I asked that a representative of the organization provide a written statement that there was no exculpatory evidence, the requests were summarily denied. At one point, following a review of information, I asked the Office of General Counsel of the intelligence organization that I was visiting for a statement that no exculpatory information had been withheld. I explained that I was tasked to review all available materials and to reach a conclusion regarding the non-existence of exculpatory information, and that I could not do so without knowing that I had seen all information. The request was denied, coupled with a refusal even to acknowledge whether there existed additional information that I was not permitted to review.

http://www.scotusblog.com/movabletype/archives/Al%20Odah%20reply%206-22-07.pdf.

Colonel Morris Davis had this to say about his experience:

I was the chief prosecutor for the military commissions at Guantánamo Bay, Cuba, until Oct. 4 [2007], the day I concluded that full, fair and open trials were not possible under the current system. I resigned on that day because I felt that the system had become deeply politicized and that I could no longer do my job effectively or responsibly.

AWOL Military Justice, Op-Ed Los Angeles Times, Dec. 15, 2007, *available at* http://www.latimes.com/news/opinion/la-oe-davis10dec10,0,2446661.story?coll=la-opinion-rightrail.

An unidentified legal officer filed an affidavit in the habeas corpus case of Adel Hamad. In his affidavit, this officer observed that many CSRT determinations were supported by mere conclusory statements from intelligence files, and that when CSRT panels found that a detainee was not an enemy combatant, the file would be sent back with instructions to make different findings but without any additional evidence. http://jurist.law.pitt.edu/pdf/TeesdaleCSRTofficerRedacted.pdf

[B]   Domestic Executive Detentions Revisited

AL-MARRI v. WRIGHT
487 F.3d 160 (4th Cir. 2007)

Diana Gribbon Motz, Circuit Judge.

For over two centuries of growth and struggle, peace and war, the Constitution has secured our freedom through the guarantee that, in the United States, no one will be deprived of liberty without due process of law. Yet more than four years ago military authorities seized an alien lawfully residing here. He has been held by the military ever since — without criminal charge or process. He has been so held despite the fact that he was initially taken from his home in Peoria, Illinois by civilian authorities, and indicted for purported domestic crimes. He has been so held although the Government has never alleged that he is a member of any nation's military, has fought alongside any nation's armed forces, or has borne arms against the United States anywhere in the world. And he has been so held, without acknowledgment of the protection afforded by the Constitution, solely because the Executive believes that his military detention is proper.

While criminal proceedings were underway against Ali Saleh Kahlah al-Marri, the President ordered the military to seize and detain him indefinitely as an enemy combatant. Since that order, issued in June of 2003, al-Marri has been imprisoned without charge in a military jail in South Carolina. Al-Marri petitions for a writ of habeas corpus to secure his release from military imprisonment. The Government defends this detention, asserting that al-Marri associated with al Qaeda and "prepar[ed] for acts of international terrorism." It maintains that the President has both statutory and inherent constitutional authority to subject al-Marri to indefinite military detention and, in any event, that a new statute — enacted years after al-Marri's seizure — strips federal courts of jurisdiction even to consider this habeas petition.

We hold that the new statute does not apply to al-Marri, and so we retain jurisdiction to consider his petition. Furthermore, we conclude that we must grant al-Marri habeas relief. Even assuming the truth of the Government's allegations, the President lacks power to order the military to seize and indefinitely detain al-Marri. If the Government accurately describes al-Marri's conduct, he has committed grave crimes. But we have found no authority for holding that the evidence offered by the Government affords a basis for treating al-Marri as an enemy combatant, or as anything other than a civilian.

This does not mean that al-Marri must be set free. Like others accused of terrorist activity in this country, from the Oklahoma City bombers to the surviving conspirator of the September 11th attacks, al-Marri can be returned to civilian prosecutors, tried on criminal charges, and, if convicted, punished severely. But the Government cannot subject al-Marri to indefinite military detention. For in the United States, the military cannot seize and imprison civilians — let alone imprison them indefinitely.

I.

Al-Marri, a citizen of Qatar, lawfully entered the United States with his wife and children on September 10, 2001, to pursue a master's degree at Bradley University in Peoria, Illinois, where he had obtained a bachelor's degree in 1991. The following day, terrorists hijacked four commercial airliners and used them to kill and inflict grievous injury on thousands of Americans. Three months later, on December 12, 2001, FBI agents arrested al-Marri at his home in Peoria as a material witness in the Government's investigation of the September 11th attacks. Al-Marri was imprisoned in civilian jails in Peoria and then New York City.

In February 2002, al-Marri was charged in the Southern District of New York with the possession of unauthorized or counterfeit credit-card numbers with the intent to defraud. A year later, in January 2003, he was charged in a second, six-count indictment, with two counts of making a false statement to the FBI, three counts of making a false statement on a bank application, and one count of using another person's identification for the purpose of influencing the action of a federally insured financial institution. Al-Marri pleaded not guilty to all of these charges. In May 2003, a federal district court in New York dismissed the charges against al-Marri for lack of venue.

The Government then returned al-Marri to Peoria and he was re-indicted in the Central District of Illinois on the same seven counts, to which he again pleaded not guilty. The district court set a July 21, 2003 trial date. On Friday, June 20, 2003, the court scheduled a hearing on pretrial motions, including a motion to suppress evidence against al-Marri assertedly obtained by torture. On the following Monday, June 23, before that hearing could be held, the Government moved *ex parte* to dismiss the indictment based on an order signed that morning by the President.

In the order, President George W. Bush stated that he "DETERMINE[D] for the United States of America that" al-Marri: (1) is an enemy combatant; (2) is closely associated with al Qaeda; (3) "engaged in conduct that constituted hostile and war-like acts, including conduct in preparation for acts of international terrorism;" (4) "possesses intelligence . . . that . . . would aid U.S. efforts to prevent attacks by al Qaeda;" and (5) "represents a continuing, present, and grave danger to the national security of the United States." The President determined that al-Marri's detention by the military was "necessary to prevent him from aiding al Qaeda" and thus ordered the Attorney General to surrender al-Marri to the Secretary of Defense, and the Secretary of Defense to "detain him as an enemy combatant."

The federal district court in Illinois granted the Government's motion to dismiss the criminal indictment against al-Marri. In accordance with the President's order, al-

Marri was then transferred to military custody and brought to the Naval Consolidated Brig in South Carolina.

Since that time (that is, for four years) the military has held al-Marri as an enemy combatant, without charge and without any indication when this confinement will end. For the first sixteen months of his military confinement, the Government did not permit al-Marri any communication with the outside world, including his attorneys, his wife, or his children. He alleges that he was denied basic necessities, interrogated through measures creating extreme sensory deprivation, and threatened with violence. A pending civil action challenges the "inhuman, degrading" and "abusive" conditions of his confinement.

On July 8, 2003, counsel for al-Marri petitioned on his behalf (because it was undisputed that he was unavailable to petition) for a writ of habeas corpus in the Central District of Illinois. The district court dismissed the petition for lack of venue. On July 8, 2004, al-Marri's counsel filed the present habeas petition on al-Marri's behalf in the District of South Carolina. On September 9, 2004, the Government answered al-Marri's petition, citing the Declaration of Jeffrey N. Rapp, Director of the Joint Intelligence Task Force for Combating Terrorism, as support for the President's order to detain al-Marri as an enemy combatant.

The Rapp Declaration asserts that al-Marri: (1) is "closely associated with al Qaeda, an international terrorist organization with which the United States is at war"; (2) trained at an al Qaeda terrorist training camp in Afghanistan sometime between 1996 and 1998; (3) in the summer of 2001, was introduced to Osama bin Laden by Khalid Shaykh Muhammed; (4) at that time, volunteered for a "martyr mission" on behalf of al Qaeda; (5) was ordered to enter the United States sometime before September 11, 2001, to serve as a "sleeper agent" to facilitate terrorist activities and explore disrupting this country's financial system through computer hacking; (6) in the summer of 2001, met with terrorist financier Mustafa Ahmed Al-Hawsawi, who gave al-Marri money, including funds to buy a laptop; (7) gathered technical information about poisonous chemicals on his laptop; (8) undertook efforts to obtain false identification, credit cards, and banking information, including stolen credit card numbers; (9) communicated with known terrorists, including Khalid Shaykh Muhammed and Al-Hawsawi, by phone and email; and (10) saved information about jihad, the September 11th attacks, and bin Laden on his laptop computer.

The Rapp Declaration does *not* assert that al-Marri: (1) is a citizen, or affiliate of the armed forces, of any nation at war with the United States; (2) was seized on or near a battlefield on which the armed forces of the United States or its allies were engaged in combat; (3) was ever in Afghanistan during the armed conflict between the United States and the Taliban there; or (4) directly participated in any hostilities against United States or allied armed forces.

On October 14, 2004, the Government permitted al-Marri access to his counsel for the first time since his initial confinement as an enemy combatant sixteen months before. Al-Marri then submitted a reply to the Government's evidence, contending that he is not an enemy combatant; he then moved for summary judgment. The district court denied the summary judgment motion and referred the case to a magistrate judge for consideration of the appropriate process to be afforded al-Marri in light of *Hamdi v. Rumsfeld*, 542 U.S. 507 (2004). The magistrate judge ruled that the Rapp Declaration provided al-Marri with sufficient notice of the basis of his detention as an enemy combatant and directed al-Marri to file rebuttal evidence.

In response to the magistrate's ruling, al-Marri again denied the Government's allegations, but filed no rebuttal evidence, contending that the Government had an initial burden to produce evidence that he was an enemy combatant and that the Rapp Declaration did not suffice. The magistrate judge recommended dismissal of al-Marri's habeas petition because al-Marri had failed to rebut the allegations in the Rapp Declaration. In August 2006, the district court adopted the magistrate judge's report and recommendation and dismissed al-Marri's habeas petition. A few days later, al-Marri noted this appeal.

II.

On November 13, 2006, three months after al-Marri noted his appeal, the Government moved to dismiss this case for lack of jurisdiction, citing section 7 of the recently enacted Military Commissions Act of 2006 (MCA).

A.

Section 7 of the MCA amends 28 U.S.C. § 2241(e) — a provision Congress added to the federal habeas corpus statute in the Detainee Treatment Act of 2005 (DTA). Congress enacted the DTA in response to the Supreme Court's holding, in *Rasul v. Bush*, 542 U.S. 466, 475–84 (2004), that the federal habeas corpus statute, 28 U.S.C. § 2241(a), (c), granted the federal courts jurisdiction over habeas petitions filed by aliens held at Guantánamo Bay.

In the DTA, Congress amended 28 U.S.C. § 2241 by adding a new subsection, 2241(e), which removed the statutory grant of federal jurisdiction over actions filed by alien enemy combatants held at Guantánamo Bay. DTA § 1005(e)(1). Through the DTA, Congress sought to replace the procedures that *Rasul* had upheld with a substitute remedy. In place of the statutory right to petition for habeas directly to a federal district court in § 2241(a), Guantánamo Bay detainees would receive a Combatant Status Review Tribunal (CSRT) conducted "pursuant to applicable procedures specified by the Secretary of Defense," followed by review by the United States Court of Appeals for the District of Columbia Circuit.

The Supreme Court considered the reach of the DTA in *Hamdan v. Rumsfeld*, 548 U.S. 557 (2006). It held that the DTA did not divest the federal courts of jurisdiction over § 2241 habeas actions filed by Guantánamo Bay detainees that were *pending* when the DTA was enacted in December 2005.

On October 17, 2006, in response to *Hamdan*, Congress enacted the MCA, in part to clarify that it wished to remove § 2241 jurisdiction over pending and future habeas cases from detainees whom it believed had only a "*statutory* right of habeas." Thus, section 7 of the MCA replaces the habeas provision added by the DTA and substitutes the following:

> (e)(1) No court, justice, or judge shall have jurisdiction to hear or consider an application for a writ of habeas corpus filed by or on behalf of an alien detained by the United States who has been determined by the United States to have been properly detained as an enemy combatant or is awaiting such determination.

> (2) Except as provided in paragraphs (2) and (3) of section 1005(e) of the [DTA], no court, justice, or judge shall have jurisdiction to hear or consider any other action against the United States or its agents relating to any aspect of the detention, transfer, treatment, trial, or conditions of confinement of an alien who is or was detained by the United States and has been determined by the United States to have been properly detained as an enemy combatant or is awaiting such determination.

The new statute expressly provides that this amendment to § 2241(e) "shall take effect on the date of the enactment of this Act [October 17, 2006], and shall apply to all cases, without exception, pending on or after the date of the enactment of this Act" MCA § 7(b).

B.

The Government asserts that the MCA divests federal courts of all subject matter jurisdiction over al-Marri's petition. Al-Marri maintains that the MCA, by its plain terms, does not apply to him and that if we were to hold it does, the MCA would be unconstitutional.

Al-Marri's constitutional claim is a serious one. As an alien captured and detained within the United States, he has a right to habeas corpus protected by the Constitution's Suspension Clause. The Supreme Court has explained that "at the absolute minimum, the Suspension Clause protects the writ as it existed in 1789," *INS v. St. Cyr*, 533 U.S. 289, 301 (2001), and "[a]t common law, courts exercised habeas jurisdiction over the claims of aliens detained within sovereign territory of the realm," *Rasul*, 542 U.S. at 481.

The Government seems to concede that al-Marri has a right to habeas corpus protected by the Suspension Clause, and acknowledges that "the touchstone of habeas corpus," and thus any substitute remedy, is "[j]udicial review of constitutional claims and questions of law." The Government asserts, however, that Congress has provided al-Marri a constitutionally adequate habeas substitute through the DTA and MCA scheme — an administrative determination by a CSRT followed by limited review of the CSRT's decision in the D.C. Circuit. Since al-Marri has never been afforded a CSRT and neither the DTA, the MCA, nor any other statute, regulation, or policy guarantees that he be granted one, it is not immediately apparent how this statutory arrangement could provide al-Marri a substitute remedy. Al-Marri has also raised substantial questions as to whether this statutory arrangement — were it available to him — would be constitutionally adequate.

We need not, however, resolve these difficult constitutional questions because we conclude that the MCA does not apply to al-Marri. The Supreme Court has instructed that when it is "fairly possible" to read a statute to avoid serious constitutional problems a court must do so. In this case, ordinary principles of statutory interpretation demonstrate that the MCA does not apply to al-Marri.

C.

The MCA eliminates habeas jurisdiction under § 2241 only for an alien who "has been determined by the United States to have been properly detained as an enemy combatant or is awaiting such determination." Thus, the MCA does not apply to al-Marri and the Government's jurisdictional argument fails *unless* al-Marri (1) "has been determined by the United States to have been properly detained as an enemy combatant," or (2) "is awaiting such determination."

The Government asserts that al-Marri "has been determined by the United States to have been properly detained" through the President's order of June 23, 2003, designating al-Marri an enemy combatant. Alternatively, the Government argues that because the Department of Defense claims that if this court dismisses his habeas action al-Marri will be provided with a CSRT, al-Marri is "awaiting" such a determination for the purposes of the MCA. We find neither argument persuasive.

The statute's use of the phrase "has been determined . . . to have been properly detained" requires a two-step process to remove § 2241 jurisdiction: (1) an initial decision to detain, followed by (2) a determination by the United States that the initial detention was proper. The President's June 23 order only constitutes an initial decision to detain. To read the statute as the Government proposes would eliminate the second step and render the statutory language "has been determined . . . to have been properly detained" superfluous — something courts are loathe to do.

Moreover, the DTA and MCA provisions establishing D.C. Circuit review of CSRT final decisions are entitled "Review of decisions of combatant status review tribunals of *propriety of detention*." These provisions allow for D.C. Circuit review only of a final decision of a "Combatant Status Review Tribunal that an alien is *properly detained* as an enemy combatant." These procedures reinforce the plain language of section 7 of the MCA. Congress intended to remove federal courts' § 2241 jurisdiction only when an individual has been detained *and* a CSRT (or similar Executive Branch tribunal) has made a subsequent determination that the detention is proper.>

Thus, the plain language of the MCA does not permit the Government's interpretation — i.e., that the President's initial order to detain al-Marri as an enemy combatant constitutes both a decision to detain al-Marri *and* a determination under the MCA that al-Marri *has been* properly detained as an enemy combatant. The MCA requires both to eliminate our jurisdiction.

The Government's remaining jurisdictional contention is that even if al-Marri has not yet "been determined by the United States to have been properly detained," the Government plans to provide him with a CSRT in the future, and so under the MCA he is "awaiting such determination."

Neither the DTA-MCA nor any other law or policy requires that al-Marri receive a CSRT, or even indicates that Congress believed he would be eligible for a CSRT and so could be "awaiting" one. At the same time, Congress did not expressly prohibit al-Marri from receiving a CSRT. To the extent that the plain language of the MCA does not clearly state who is "awaiting" a determination, its context and legislative history make clear that this phrase does not apply to persons, like al-Marri, captured and held within the United States.

Congress sought to eliminate the statutory grant of habeas jurisdiction for those aliens captured and held outside the United States who could not lay claim to constitutional protections, but to preserve the rights of aliens like al-Marri, lawfully residing within the country with substantial, voluntary connections to the United States, for whom Congress recognized that the Constitution protected the writ of habeas corpus.

In fact, notwithstanding its posture in this case, the Government has otherwise demonstrated that it shares this understanding of the scope of the MCA. On January 18, 2007, while al-Marri's appeal was pending, the Attorney General himself testified before Congress that the MCA did *not* affect any habeas rights historically protected by the Constitution. Citing *Eisentrager* in written testimony to the Senate Judiciary Committee, he explained: "The MCA's restrictions on habeas corpus petitions did not represent any break from the past. Indeed, it has been well-established since World War II that enemy combatants *captured abroad* have no constitutional right to habeas petitions in the United States courts."

If al-Marri is "awaiting" a CSRT it is only because he might, through the good graces of the Executive, some day receive one. But he might not. After all, the Government's primary jurisdictional argument in this case is that the President's initial order to detain al-Marri constitutes the sole "determination" that he is due. And so under the Government's view, al-Marri might well be "awaiting" a determination of the propriety of his detention for the rest of his life — a result Congress could not have countenanced for an individual it understood to have a constitutional right to habeas corpus.

In sum, the Government's interpretation of the MCA is not only contrary to legislative intent, but also requires reading the phrase "awaiting such determination" so broadly as to make it meaningless. We are not at liberty to interpret statutes so as to render them meaningless. The phrase "awaiting such determination" gains meaning only if it refers to alien detainees captured and held outside the United States — whom Congress both believed had no constitutional right to habeas and expected would receive a CSRT based on the larger DTA-MCA scheme. Al-Marri is not such a detainee; therefore he is not "awaiting such determination" within the terms of the MCA.

For these reasons, we must conclude that the MCA does not apply to al-Marri. He was not captured outside the United States, he is not being held at Guantánamo Bay or elsewhere outside the United States, he has not been afforded a CSRT, he has not been "determined by the United States to have been properly detained as an enemy combatant," and he is not "awaiting such determination." The MCA was not intended to, and does not, apply to aliens like al-Marri, who have legally entered, and are seized while legally residing in, the United States. Accordingly, the Government's jurisdictional argument fails and we turn to the merits of al-Marri's petition.

III.

Al-Marri premises his habeas claim on the Fifth Amendment's guarantee that no person living in this country can be deprived of liberty without due process of law. He maintains that even if he has committed the acts the Government alleges, he is not a combatant but a civilian protected by our Constitution, and thus is not subject to military detention. Al-Marri acknowledges that the Government can deport him or charge him with a crime, and if he is convicted in a civilian court, imprison him. But he insists that neither the Constitution nor any law permits the Government, on the basis of the evidence it has proffered to date — even assuming all of that evidence is true — to treat him as an enemy combatant and subject him to indefinite military detention, without criminal charge or process.

The Government contends that the district court properly denied habeas relief to al-Marri because the Constitution allows detention of enemy combatants by the military without criminal process, and according to the Government it has proffered evidence that al-Marri is a combatant.

A.

Each party grounds its case on well established legal doctrine. Moreover, important principles guiding our analysis seem undisputed. Before addressing the conflicting contentions of the parties, we note these fundamental principles, which we take to be common ground.

The Constitution guarantees that no "person" shall "be deprived of life, liberty, or property, without due process of law." The text of the Fifth Amendment affords this guarantee to "person[s]," not merely citizens, and so the constitutional right to freedom from deprivation of liberty without due process of law extends to all lawfully admitted aliens living within the United States.

"Freedom from imprisonment — from government custody, detention, or other forms of physical restraint — lies at the heart of the liberty that [the Due Process] Clause protects." *Zadvydas v. Davis*, 533 U.S. 678, 690 (2001). This concept dates back to Magna Carta, which guaranteed that "government would take neither life, liberty, nor property without a trial in accord with the law of the land." The "law of the land" at its core provides that "no man's life, liberty or property be forfeited as a punishment until there has been a charge fairly made and fairly tried in a public tribunal." Thus, the Supreme Court has recognized that, because of the Due Process Clause, it "may freely be conceded" that as a " 'general rule' . . . the government may not detain a person prior to a judgment of guilt in a criminal trial."

The Court, however, has permitted a limited number of specific exceptions to this general rule. Although some process is always required in order to detain an individual, in special situations detention based on process less than that attendant to a criminal conviction does not violate the Fifth Amendment. *See, e.g., Kansas v. Hendricks*, 521 U.S. 346 (1997) (civil commitment of mentally ill sex offenders); *United States v. Salerno*, 481 U.S. 739 (1987) (pretrial detention of dangerous adults); *Schall v. Martin*, 467 U.S. 253 (1984) (pretrial detention of dangerous juveniles); *Addington v. Texas*, 441 U.S. 418 (1979) (civil commitment of mentally ill); *Humphrey v. Smith*, 336 U.S. 695 (1949) (courts martial of American soldiers). Among these recognized exceptions is the one on which the Government grounds its principal argument in this case: Congress may constitutionally authorize the President to order military detention, without criminal process, of persons who "qualify as 'enemy combatants,'" that is, fit within that particular "legal category." *Hamdi v. Rumsfeld*, 542 U.S. 507, 516, 522 n.1 (2004) (plurality).[25]

The act of depriving a person of the liberty protected by our Constitution is a momentous one; thus, recognized exceptions to criminal process are narrow in scope, and generally permit only limited periods of detention. And, of course, the Government can never invoke an exception, and so detain a person without criminal process, if the individual does not fit within the narrow legal category of persons to whom the exception applies. For example, the Supreme Court has explained that the Constitution does not permit the Government to detain a predatory sex criminal through a civil commitment process simply by establishing that he is dangerous. The civil commitment process may only be substituted for criminal process for such a criminal if the Government's evidence establishes "proof of dangerousness" *and* "proof of some additional factor, such as a 'mental illness' or 'mental abnormality.'" *Hendricks*, 521 U.S. at 358.

In *Hamdi*, the plurality explained that precisely the same principles apply when the Government seeks to detain a person as an enemy combatant. Under the habeas procedure prescribed in *Hamdi*, if the Government asserts an exception to the usual criminal process by detaining as an enemy combatant an individual with constitutional rights, it must proffer evidence to demonstrate that the individual "qualif[ies]" for this exceptional treatment. Only *after* the Government has "put[] forth credible evidence that" an individual "meets the enemy-combatant criteria" does "the onus" shift to the individual to demonstrate "that he falls outside the [enemy combatant] criteria." For in this country, the military cannot seize and indefinitely detain an individual — particularly when the sole process leading to his detention is a determination by the Executive that the detention is necessary — unless the Government demonstrates that he "qualif[ies]" for this extraordinary treatment because he fits within the "legal category" of enemy combatants.

These principles thus form the legal framework for consideration of the issues before us. Both parties recognize that it does not violate the Due Process Clause for the President to order the military to seize and detain individuals who "qualify" as enemy combatants for the duration of a war. They disagree, however, as to whether the evidence the Government has proffered, even assuming its accuracy, establishes that al-Marri fits within the "legal category" of enemy combatants.

B.

Tellingly, the Government does *not* argue that the broad language of the AUMF authorizes the President to subject to indefinite military detention anyone he believes to have aided any "nation[], organization[], or person[]" related to the September 11th attacks. Such an interpretation would lead to absurd results that Congress could not have intended. Under that reading of the AUMF, the President would be able to subject to indefinite military detention anyone, including an American citizen, whom the President believed was associated with any organization that the President believed in some way "planned, authorized, committed, or aided" the September 11th attacks, so long as the President believed this to be "necessary and appropriate" to prevent future acts of terrorism.

Under such an interpretation of the AUMF, if some money from a nonprofit charity

---

[25] [Court's Footnote 5] Case law also establishes that during times of war Congress may constitutionally authorize the President to detain "enemy aliens," also known as "alien enemies," defined as "subject[s] of a foreign state at war with the United States." *Eisentrager*, 339 U.S. at 769 n.2. But, as the Government recognizes, the Alien Enemy Act, the statute the Court considered in *Eisentrager* and *Ludecke*, does not apply to al-Marri's case — in fact, al-Marri is not an "enemy alien" but a citizen of Qatar, with which the United States has friendly diplomatic relations.

that feeds Afghan orphans made its way to al Qaeda, the President could subject to indefinite military detention any donor to that charity. Similarly, this interpretation of the AUMF would allow the President to detain indefinitely any employee or shareholder of an American corporation that built equipment used by the September 11th terrorists; or allow the President to order the military seizure and detention of an American-citizen physician who treated a member of al Qaeda.

We need not here deal with the absurd results, . . [f]or the Government wisely limits its argument. The precedent interpreting the AUMF on which the Government relies for this argument consists of two cases: the Supreme Court's opinion in *Hamdi*, and our opinion in *Padilla v. Hanft*, 423 F.3d 386 (4th Cir. 2005). The "legal background" for the AUMF, which it cites, consists of two cases from earlier conflicts, *Ex Parte Quirin* (World War II), and *Ex Parte Milligan* (U.S. Civil War), as well as constitutional and law-of-war principles.

With respect to the latter, we note that American courts have often been reluctant to follow international law in resolving domestic disputes. In the present context, however, they, like the Government here, have relied on the law of war — treaty obligations including the Hague and Geneva Conventions and customary principles developed alongside them. The law of war provides clear rules for determining an individual's status during an international armed conflict, distinguishing between "combatants" (members of a nation's military, militia, or other armed forces, and those who fight alongside them) and "civilians" (all other persons).[26] *See, e.g.*, Geneva Convention Relative to the Treatment of Prisoners of War (Third Geneva Convention) arts. 2, 4, 5; Geneva Convention Relative to the Protection of Civilian Persons in Time of War (Fourth Geneva Convention) art. 4. American courts have repeatedly looked to these careful distinctions made in the law of war in identifying which individuals fit within the "legal category" of "enemy combatants" under our Constitution.

In *Hamdi*, the Supreme Court looked to precedent and the law of war to determine whether the AUMF authorized the President to detain as an enemy combatant an American citizen captured while engaging in battle against American and allied armed forces in Afghanistan as part of the Taliban. In support of that detention, the Government offered evidence that Yaser Esam Hamdi "affiliated with a Taliban military unit and received weapons training," "took up arms with the Taliban," "engaged in armed conflict against the United States" in Afghanistan, and when captured on the battlefield "surrender[ed] his Kalishnikov assault rifle." Hamdi's detention was upheld because in fighting against the United States on the battlefield in Afghanistan with the Taliban, the de facto government of Afghanistan at the time, Hamdi bore arms with the army of an enemy nation and so, under the law of war, was an enemy combatant.

In *Padilla*, we similarly held that the AUMF authorized the President to detain as an enemy combatant an American citizen who "was armed and present in a combat zone" in Afghanistan as part of Taliban forces during the conflict there with the United States. The Government had not been able to capture Jose Padilla until he came to the border of the United States, but because the Government presented evidence that Padilla "took up arms against United States forces in [Afghanistan] in the same way and to the same

---

26 [Court's Footnote 6] Thus, "civilian" is a term of art in the law of war, not signifying an innocent person but rather someone in a certain legal category, not subject to military seizure or detention. So too, a "combatant" is by no means always a wrongdoer, but rather a member of a different "legal category" who is subject to military seizure and detention. *Hamdi*, 542 U.S. at 522 n.1. For example, our brave soldiers fighting in Germany during World War II were "combatants" under the law of war, and viewed from Germany's perspective they were "enemy combatants." While civilians are subject to trial and punishment in civilian courts for all crimes committed during wartime in the country in which they are captured and held, combatant status protects an individual from trial and punishment by the capturing nation, unless the combatant has violated the laws of war. Nations in international conflicts can summarily remove the adversary's "combatants," i.e. the "enemy combatants," from the battlefield and detain them for the duration of such conflicts, but no such provision is made for "civilians."

extent as did Hamdi" we concluded that he "unquestionably qualifies as an 'enemy combatant' as that term was defined for the purposes of the controlling opinion in *Hamdi*." We too invoked the law of war, upholding Padilla's detention because we understood "the plurality's *reasoning* in *Hamdi* to be that the AUMF authorizes the president to detain all who qualify as 'enemy combatants' within the meaning of the laws of war." We also noted that Padilla's detention, like Hamdi's, was permissible "to prevent a *combatant's return to the battlefield* . . . a fundamental incident of waging war."[27]

Al-Marri urges us to ignore *Padilla* in light of its subsequent history. *See Padilla v. Hanft*, 432 F.3d 582, 583 (4th Cir. 2005) (noting that the Government's transfer of Padilla to civilian custody for criminal trial after arguing before this court that he was an enemy combatant created "an appearance that the government may be attempting to avoid consideration of our decision by the Supreme Court"). That history is troubling but we see no need to avoid *Padilla*'s narrow holding.

Supreme Court precedent offered substantial support for the narrow rulings in *Hamdi* and *Padilla*. In *Quirin*, which the *Hamdi* plurality characterized as the "most apposite precedent," the Supreme Court upheld the treatment, as enemy combatants, of men directed, outfitted, and paid by the German military to bring explosives into the United States to destroy American war industries during World War II. The *Quirin* Court concluded that even a petitioner claiming American citizenship had been properly classified as an enemy combatant because "[c]itizens who associate themselves with the military arm of the enemy government, and with its aid, guidance and direction enter this county bent on hostile acts, are enemy belligerents [combatants] within the meaning of . . . the law of war." The Court cited the Hague Convention "which defines the persons to whom belligerent [i.e. combatant] rights and duties attach," in support of its conclusion that the *Quirin* petitioners qualified as enemy combatants. Given the "declaration of war between the United States and the German Reich," and that all the *Quirin* petitioners, including one who claimed American citizenship, were directed and paid by the "military arm" of the German Reich, the Court held that the law of war classified them as enemy belligerents (or combatants) and so the Constitution permitted subjecting them to military jurisdiction.

Hamdi and *Padilla* ground their holdings on this central teaching from *Quirin*, i.e., enemy combatant status rests on an individual's affiliation during wartime with the "military arm of the enemy government." In *Quirin* that enemy government was the German Reich; in *Hamdi* and *Padilla*, it was the Taliban government of Afghanistan.

Hamdi and *Padilla* also rely on this principle from *Quirin* to distinguish (but not disavow) *Milligan*. In *Milligan*, the Court rejected the Government's impassioned contention that a presidential order and the "laws and usages of war," justified exercising military jurisdiction over Lamdin Milligan, an Indiana resident, during the Civil War. The Government alleged that Milligan had communicated with the enemy, had conspired to "seize munitions of war," and had "join[ed] and aid[ed] . . . a secret" enemy organization "for the purpose of overthrowing the Government and duly constituted authorities of the United States." The Court recognized that Milligan had committed "an enormous crime" during "a period of war" and at a place "within . . . the theatre of military operations, and which had been and was constantly threatened to be invaded by the enemy." But it found no support in the "laws and usages of war" for subjecting Milligan to military jurisdiction as a combatant, for although he was a "dangerous enem[y]" of the nation, he was a civilian, and had to be treated as such.

Quirin, *Hamdi*, and *Padilla* all emphasize that *Milligan's* teaching — that our

---

[27] [Court's Footnote 10] Although our opinion discussed Padilla's association with al Qaeda, we *held* that Padilla was an enemy combatant because of his association with Taliban forces, *i.e.* Afghanistan government forces, on the battlefield in Afghanistan during the time of the conflict between the United States and Afghanistan.

Constitution does not permit the Government to subject *civilians* within the United States to military jurisdiction — remains good law. In sum, the holdings of *Hamdi* and *Padilla* share two characteristics: (1) they look to law of war principles to determine who fits within the "legal category" of enemy combatant; and (2) following the law of war, they rest enemy combatant status on affiliation with the military arm of an enemy nation.

In view of the holdings in *Hamdi* and *Padilla*, we find it remarkable that the Government contends that they "compel the conclusion" that the President may detain al-Marri as an enemy combatant. For unlike *Hamdi* and *Padilla*, al-Marri is not alleged to have been part of a Taliban unit, not alleged to have stood alongside the Taliban or the armed forces of any other enemy nation, not alleged to have been on the battlefield during the war in Afghanistan, not alleged to have even been in Afghanistan during the armed conflict there, and not alleged to have engaged in combat with United States forces anywhere in the world. *See* Rapp Declaration (alleging none of these facts, but instead that "Al-Marri engaged in conduct in preparation for acts of international terrorism intended to cause injury or adverse effects on the United States").

[C]ontrary to the Government's apparent belief, no precedent and nothing in the "legal background against which the AUMF was enacted" permits a person to be classified as an enemy combatant because of his criminal conduct on behalf of an enemy organization. And, the AUMF itself neither classifies certain civilians as enemy combatants, nor otherwise authorizes the President to subject civilians to indefinite military detention.

Rather than supporting the Government's position, the Supreme Court's most recent terrorism case provides an additional reason for rejecting the contention that al-Marri is an enemy combatant. In *Hamdan*, the Court held that because the conflict between the United States and al Qaeda in Afghanistan is not "between nations," it is a " 'conflict not of an international character' " — and so is governed by Common Article 3 of the Geneva Conventions. Common Article 3 and other Geneva Convention provisions applying to non-international conflicts (in contrast to those applying to international conflicts, such as that with Afghanistan's Taliban government) simply do not recognize the "legal category" of enemy combatant. *See* Third Geneva Convention, art. 3, 6 U.S.T. at 3318. As the International Committee of the Red Cross — the official codifier of the Geneva Conventions — explains, "an 'enemy combatant' is a person who, either lawfully or unlawfully, engages in hostilities for the opposing side in an *international* armed conflict;" in contrast, "[i]n non-international armed conflict combatant status *does not exist*." Int'l Comm. of the Red Cross, *Official Statement: The Relevance of IHL in the Context of Terrorism*, at 1, 3 (Feb. 21, 2005), http://www.icrc.org/Web/Eng/siteeng0.nsf/htmlall/terrorismihl-210705 (emphasis added).[28]

Perhaps for this reason, the Government ignores *Hamdan*'s holding that the conflict with al Qaeda in Afghanistan is a non-international conflict, and ignores the fact that in

---

[28] [Court's Footnote 13] Notwithstanding this principle, we recognize that some commentators have suggested that "for such time as they take a direct part in hostilities," participants in non-international armed conflicts may, as a matter of customary international law, be placed in the formal legal category of "enemy combatant." *See, e.g.,* Curtis A. Bradley & Jack L. Goldsmith, *Congressional Authorization and the War on Terrorism*, 118 HARV. L. REV. 2047, 2115 & n.304 (2005) (internal quotation marks omitted). No precedent from the Supreme Court or this court endorses this view, and the Government itself has not advanced such an argument. This may be because even were a court to follow this approach in some cases, it would not assist the Government here. For the Government has proffered no evidence that al-Marri has taken a "direct part in hostilities." Moreover, the United States has elsewhere adopted a formal treaty understanding of the meaning of the term "direct part in hostilities," which plainly excludes al-Marri. *See* Message from the President of the United States Transmitting Two Optional Protocols to the Convention on the Rights of the Child, S. Treaty Doc. No. 106-37, at VII (2000) (distinguishing between "immediate and actual action on the battlefield" and "indirect participation," including gathering and transmitting military information, weapons, and supplies).

such conflicts the "legal category" of enemy combatant does not exist. Indeed, the Government's sole acknowledgment of *Hamdan* in its appellate brief is a short footnote, in which it asserts that "the Court took it as a given that Hamdan was subject to detention as an enemy combatant during ongoing hostilities." The weakness of this response is apparent. Not only does it avoid the holding in *Hamdan* that the conflict between the United States and al Qaeda is a non-international conflict, but also it suggests that the Supreme Court approved Hamdan's detention when the legality of that detention was not before the Court, and in fact, the legality of the detention of those like Hamdan, captured and detained in the conflict with al Qaeda *outside* the United States, is still being litigated. *See, e.g., Boumediene.*

The core assumption underlying the Government's position, notwithstanding *Hamdi, Padilla, Quirin, Milligan,* and *Hamdan,* seems to be that persons lawfully within this country, entitled to the protections of our Constitution, lose their civilian status and become "enemy combatants" if they have allegedly engaged in criminal conduct on behalf of an organization seeking to harm the United States. Of course, a person who commits a crime should be punished, but when a civilian protected by the *Due Process Clause* commits a crime he is subject to charge, trial, and punishment in a civilian court, *not* to seizure and confinement by military authorities.

We recognize the understandable instincts of those who wish to treat domestic terrorists as "combatants" in a "global war on terror." Allegations of criminal activity in association with a terrorist organization, however, do not permit the Government to transform a civilian into an enemy combatant subject to indefinite military detention, any more than allegations of murder in association with others while in military service permit the Government to transform a civilian into a soldier subject to trial by court martial.

To be sure, enemy combatants may commit crimes just as civilians may. When an enemy combatant violates the law of war, that conduct will render the person an "unlawful" enemy combatant, subject not only to detention but also to military trial and punishment. But merely engaging in unlawful behavior does not make one an enemy combatant. *Quirin* well illustrates this point. The *Quirin* petitioners were first enemy combatants — associating themselves with the military arm of the German government with which the United States was at war. They became unlawful enemy combatants when they violated the laws of war by "without uniform com[ing] secretly through the lines for the purpose of waging war." By doing so, in addition to being subject to military detention for the duration of the conflict as enemy combatants, they also became "subject to trial and punishment by military tribunals for acts which render their belligerency illegal." Had the *Quirin* petitioners never "secretly and without uniform" passed our "military lines," they still would have been enemy combatants, subject to military detention, but would not have been unlawful enemy combatants subject to military trial and punishment.

In sum, the Government has not offered, and although we have exhaustively searched, we have not found, any authority that permits us to hold that the AUMF empowers the president to detain al-Marri as an enemy combatant. If the Government's allegations are true, and we assume they are for present purposes, al-Marri, like Milligan, is a dangerous enemy of this nation who has committed serious crimes and associated with a secret enemy organization that has engaged in hostilities against us. But, like Milligan, al-Marri is still a civilian: he does not fit within the "permissible bounds of" "[t]he legal category of enemy combatant." Therefore, the AUMF provides the President no statutory authority to order the military to seize and indefinitely detain al-Marri.

C.

Accordingly, we turn to the Government's final contention. The Government summarily argues that even if the AUMF does not authorize al-Marri's seizure and indefinite detention as an enemy combatant, the President has "inherent constitutional authority" to order the military to seize and detain al-Marri. The Government maintains that the President's "war-making powers" granted him by Article II "include the authority to capture and detain individuals involved in hostilities against the United States." In other words, according to the Government, the President has "inherent" authority to subject persons legally residing in this country and protected by our Constitution to military arrest and detention, without the benefit of any criminal process, if the President believes these individuals have "engaged in conduct in preparation for acts of international terrorism." *See* Rapp Declaration. This is a breathtaking claim, for the Government nowhere represents that this "inherent" power to order indefinite military detention extends only to aliens or only to those who "qualify" within the "legal category" of enemy combatants.

To assess claims of presidential power, the Supreme Court has long recognized, as Justice Kennedy stated most recently, that courts look to the "framework" set forth by Justice Jackson in *Youngstown Sheet & Tube Co. v. Sawyer*, 343 U.S. 579, 635–38 (1952) (Jackson, J., concurring).

In . . . the Patriot Act, Congress carefully stated how it wished the Government to handle aliens believed to be terrorists who were seized and held within the United States. In contrast to the AUMF, which is silent on the detention of asserted alien terrorists captured and held within the United States, the Patriot Act, enacted shortly after the AUMF, provides the Executive with broad powers to deal with "terrorist aliens." But the Patriot Act *explicitly prohibits* their indefinite detention.

Section 412 of the Patriot Act, entitled "Mandatory Detention of Suspected Terrorists," permits the short-term "[d]etention of [t]errorist [a]liens." The statute authorizes the Attorney General to detain any alien whom he "has reasonable grounds to believe" is [engaged or intending to engage in a terrorist activity or is a member of a "terrorist organization" or has "received military-type training" from a terrorist organization].

Recognizing the breadth of this grant of power, however, Congress also imposed strict limits in the Patriot Act on the duration of the detention of such "terrorist aliens" within the United States. Thus, the Patriot Act expressly prohibits unlimited "indefinite detention;" instead it requires the Attorney General either to begin "removal proceedings" or to "charge the alien with a criminal offense" "not later than 7 days after the commencement of such detention."

In sum, Congress has carefully prescribed the process by which it wishes to permit detention of "terrorist aliens" within the United States, and has expressly prohibited the indefinite detention the President seeks here. The Government's argument that the President may indefinitely detain al-Marri is thus contrary to Congress's expressed will.

In light of the Patriot Act, therefore, we must "scrutinize[] with caution," the Executive's contention that the Constitution grants the President the power to capture and subject to indefinite military detention certain civilians lawfully residing within the United States. The Government nowhere suggests that the President's inherent constitutional power to detain does not extend to American citizens. Yet it grounds its argument that the President has constitutional power to detain al-Marri on his alien status. The Government apparently maintains that alien status eliminates the due process protection applicable to al-Marri, and for this reason permits the President to exercise special "peak" authority over him. The Government can so contend only by both ignoring the undisputed and relying on the inapposite.

It is undisputed that al-Marri had been legally admitted to the United States, attending an American university from which he had earlier received an undergraduate degree, and legally residing here (with his family) for several months before the Government arrested him at his home in Peoria. No case suggests that the President, by fiat, can eliminate the due process rights of such an alien.

Without even a mention of these undisputed facts and controlling legal principles, the

Government relies on two sorts of inapposite cases as assertedly establishing special presidential authority over aliens like al-Marri. The first of these, *Eisentrager* and *Ludecke* involves "enemy aliens." In those cases, the Supreme Court specifically defined "enemy aliens," but the Court did *not* define them as aliens who commit crimes against our country and so are enemies, as the Government seems to suggest. Rather, the Supreme Court defined "enemy aliens" as "subject[s] of a foreign state at war with the United States." Al-Marri plainly is *not* the "subject of a foreign state at war with the United States" and so is *not* an "enemy alien," but rather a citizen of Qatar, a country with which the United States has friendly relations. Thus *Eisentrager* and *Ludecke* provide no basis for asserting authority over al-Marri.

The other inapposite cases on which the Government relies involve *congressional* authority over aliens stemming from Congress's power over naturalization and immigration — not some special "inherent" constitutional authority enjoyed by the President over aliens. These cases do not speak to the powers of the President acting alone — let alone contrary to an Act of Congress — and certainly do not suggest that the President has the power to subject to indefinite military detention an alien lawfully residing in this country, like al-Marri.

In light of al-Marri's due process rights under our Constitution and Congress's express prohibition in the Patriot Act on the indefinite detention of those civilians arrested as "terrorist aliens" within this country, we can only conclude that in the case at hand, the President claims power that far exceeds that granted him by the Constitution.

We do not question the President's wartime authority over enemy combatants; but absent suspension of the writ of habeas corpus or declaration of martial law, the Constitution simply does not provide the President the power to exercise military authority over civilians within the United States.

Of course, this does not mean that the President lacks power to protect our national interests and defend our people, only that in doing so he must abide by the Constitution. We understand and do not in any way minimize the grave threat international terrorism poses to our country and our national security. But as *Milligan* teaches, "the government, within the Constitution, has all the powers granted to it, which are necessary to preserve its existence." Those words resound as clearly in the twenty-first century as they did in the nineteenth.

Thus, the President plainly has plenary authority to deploy our military against terrorist enemies overseas. Similarly, the Government remains free to defend our country against terrorist enemies within, using all the considerable powers "the well-stocked statutory arsenal" of domestic law affords.

In an address to Congress at the outset of the Civil War, President Lincoln defended his emergency suspension of the writ of habeas corpus to protect Union troops moving to defend the Capital. Lincoln famously asked: "[A]re all the laws, but one, to go unexecuted, and the government itself to go to pieces, lest that one be violated?" The authority the President seeks here turns Lincoln's formulation on its head. For the President does not acknowledge that the extraordinary power he seeks would result in the suspension of even one law and he does not contend that this power should be limited to dire emergencies that threaten the nation. Rather, he maintains that the authority to order the military to seize and detain certain civilians is an inherent power of the Presidency, which he and his successors may exercise as they please.

To sanction such presidential authority to order the military to seize and indefinitely detain civilians, even if the President calls them "enemy combatants," would have disastrous consequences for the Constitution — and the country. For a court to uphold a claim to such extraordinary power would do more than render lifeless the Suspension Clause, the Due Process Clause, and the rights to criminal process in the Fourth, Fifth, Sixth, and Eighth Amendments; it would effectively undermine all of the freedoms guaranteed by the Constitution. It is that power — were a court to recognize it — that could lead all our laws "to go unexecuted, and the government itself to go to pieces." We refuse to recognize a claim to power that would so alter the constitutional foundations of our Republic.

IV.

For the foregoing reasons, we reverse the judgment of the district court dismissing al-Marri's petition for a writ of habeas corpus. We remand the case to that court with instructions to issue a writ of habeas corpus directing the Secretary of Defense to release al-Marri from military custody within a reasonable period of time to be set by the district court. The Government can transfer al-Marri to civilian authorities to face criminal charges, initiate deportation proceedings against him, hold him as a material witness in connection with grand jury proceedings, or detain him for a limited time pursuant to the Patriot Act. But military detention of al-Marri must cease.

HUDSON, DISTRICT JUDGE, dissenting.

I regret that I am unable to concur in the majority opinion, except to the extent that I agree that this Court has jurisdiction over this appeal. Although I do not embrace all aspects of the majority's jurisdictional reasoning, I agree that Section 7 of the Military Commission Act of 2006 (MCA) does not divest this Court of its constitutional jurisdiction, under Article I, Section 9, to review habeas corpus decisions involving individual detainees within the United States. Beyond the jurisdictional question, the majority and I part company.

While I commend the majority on a thoroughly researched and impressively written opinion, I must conclude that their analysis flows from a faulty predicate. In my view, the appellant was properly designated as an enemy combatant by the President of the United States pursuant to the war powers vested in him by Articles I and II of the United States Constitution and by Congress under the Authorization to Use Military Force (AUMF). I am also of the opinion that al-Marri has received all due process entitlements prescribed by existing United States Supreme Court precedent. I would therefore vote to affirm the district court's dismissal of al-Marri's Petition for Writ of Habeas Corpus.

The wellspring of the majority's reasoning is the notion that a non-military person arrested on U.S. soil, outside the zone of battle, for providing active aid to the enemy at time of war, cannot be declared an enemy combatant and detained for the duration of the hostilities, but must be prosecuted in the civilian courts of the United States. In fact, the majority would even go further and find that the language of the AUMF does not include organizations, such as al Qaeda, that are not affiliated with recognized nation states. The clear congressional intent underlying the AUMF was to afford the President of the United States all the powers necessary to suppress those individuals or organizations responsible for the terrorist attack on September 11, 2001. This broad language would certainly seem to embrace surreptitious al Qaeda agents operating within the continental United States.

History has proven that al Qaeda, an international terrorist organization with which the United States is at war, falls squarely within that definition. Central to the majority's analysis is the locus of his arrest. Unlike the petitioners in *Hamdi v. Rumsfeld*, 542 U.S. 507 (2004), and *Hamdan v. Rumsfeld*, 548 U.S. 557 (2006), al-Marri is a lawful resident alien who was not taken into custody in a battle zone. He was arrested in Peoria, Illinois, where he was residing on a student visa. Despite powerful evidence of his connection to al Qaeda, the majority believe the President is without power to declare him an enemy combatant. They believe he must be indicted and tried for crimes against the United States. Although definitive precedent is admittedly sparse, in my opinion, this position is unsupported by the weight of persuasive authority.

In *Padilla v. Hanft*, 423 F.3d 386 (4th Cir. 2005), a panel of this Court unanimously rejected the argument that the locus of capture was relevant to the President's authority to detain an enemy combatant. A close associate of al Qaeda, Padilla had been "armed and present in a combat zone during armed conflict between al Qaeda/Taliban forces and the armed forces of the United States." Moreover, "Padilla met with Khalid Sheikh Mohammad, a senior al Qaeda operations planner, who directed Padilla to travel to the United States for the purpose of blowing up apartment buildings, in continued prosecution of al Qaeda's war of terror against the United States."

The only significant fact that distinguishes the justification for Padilla's detention from that of al-Marri is that Padilla at some previous point in time had been armed and present in a combat zone. There was no indication, however, that Padilla was ever a soldier in a formal sense, particularly while acting on U.S. soil.

Like Padilla, al-Marri, an identified al Qaeda associate, was dispatched to the United States by the September mastermind as a "sleeper agent" and to explore computer hacking methods to disrupt the United States' financial system. Moreover, al-Marri volunteered for a martyr mission on behalf of al Qaeda, received funding from a known terrorist financier, and communicated with known terrorists by phone and email. Decl. of Jeffrey N. Rapp, Director, Joint Intelligence Task Force for Combating Terrorism. It is also interesting to note that al-Marri arrived in the United States on September 10, 2001.

After upholding the power of the President to detain al-Marri under the AUMF, the district court, after providing him with all due process entitlements articulated in *Hamdi*, found that his continued detention as an enemy combatant was proper and dismissed his petition.

I believe the district court correctly concluded that the President had the authority to detain al-Marri as an enemy combatant or belligerent. Although al-Marri was not personally engaged in armed conflict with U.S. forces, he is the type of stealth warrior used by al Qaeda to perpetrate terrorist acts against the United States. Al-Marri's detention is authorized under the AUMF "to prevent any future acts of international terrorism against the United States." Furthermore, setting aside the amorphous distinction between an "enemy combatant" and an "enemy belligerent," there is little doubt from the evidence that al-Marri was present in the United States to aid and further the hostile and subversive activities of the organization responsible for the terrorist attacks that occurred on September 11, 2001.

NOTES AND QUESTIONS

1. Non-state Combatants and Congress. The majority seems to hold that the law of war does not allow for defining a civilian unaffiliated with an enemy nation to be a combatant. Is that a constitutional holding that would prevent Congress from adopting such a definition? Given the definition in the MCA, hasn't Congress attempted to do so? If the only problem with the MCA is that it applies only in Guantánamo, is there anything to prevent Congress from validating the President's determination with regard to al-Marri?

2. International and Domestic Law. The majority states that

> American courts have often been reluctant to follow international law in resolving domestic disputes. In the present context, however, they, like the Government here, have relied on the law of war — treaty obligations including the Hague and Geneva Conventions and customary principles developed alongside them. The law of war provides clear rules for determining an individual's status during an international armed conflict, distinguishing between "combatants" (members of a nation's military, militia, or other armed forces, and those who fight alongside them) and "civilians" (all other persons).

This passage takes us back to the discussions in the ICTY opinions regarding the control of paramilitary groups and individuals by a State. What is the relevance of "control by a State" to the question of whether an individual is a combatant? Again, the majority seems to hold that the law of war does not allow for defining a civilian unaffiliated with an enemy nation to be a combatant, but what about the insurgent group that commits atrocities without being affiliated with any nation-state? Is the answer that the group is subject to domestic law as armed criminals rather than subject to international law as combatants? at least, until the group reaches the level of "belligerent?"

3. "Hostilities." The status of "combatant" in this analysis now seems to turn on whether the events amount to "hostilities." Given the importance of this term, is it surprising that there does not seem to be much international law on when violence rises to the level of "armed conflict" or "hostilities." The ICJ addresses this question to some extent in the *Nicaragua* case, *supra* § 6.01[B]2.

NOTE ON THE EMERGENCE OF "PRIVATE MILITARY FIRMS"

A number of the persons alleged to have been involved in prisoner abuse, both in Iraq and Afghanistan, have been employed by private contractors. Some high-profile shootings of Iraqi civilians have been attributed to private security firms from the U.S., Britain, and Australia. To the extent that a contractor is a company working directly for the U.S. Government, application of basic federal criminal law might be enhanced by special provisions applying to federal contracts. But the Uniform Code of Military Justice would be of doubtful applicability to anyone not in the uniformed services. The UCMJ applies to "in time of war, persons serving with or accompanying an armed force in the field." A critical question, regardless of whether the UCMJ applies, is simply whether the private military operative is subject to the command structure of the U.S. military.

By some estimates, "private military firms" (PMF's) make up a $100 billion industry. In centuries past, many nations relied on mercenaries to fight their battles. With the Treaty of Westphalia in 1769 and the rise of the "nation-state," nations began to assemble armies from their own citizenry, wars were fought by soldiers who bore allegiance to the sovereign by virtue of their nationality and not just by oath, and military force became the exclusive province of the sovereign. As a corollary, it became possible to enforce distinctions between combatants and noncombatants more rigorously than had been the case, producing the 20th Century treaties such as the Geneva Conventions. In the emerging privatization of military force, these distinctions may once again become more blurred.

The Atlantic Monthly provided a list of the largest private military contracts as of August 2004, which included a number in Iraq such as:

- Creating a new Iraqi police force, $50 million for the first year (2003): DynCorp.

- Training a new Iraqi army, $48 million (2003): Vinnell Corp. The contract called for Vinnell to train nine battalions; more than half of the first completed battalion later abandoned the army.

- Protecting Iraq's oil pipeline, $39.2 million (2003–present): Erinys International. The job requires 14,500 guards.

- Providing interrogation services in Iraq, $19.9 million (2003–present): CACI Systems. At least two contractors, one from CACI and one from Titan Corp., have been implicated in the Abu Ghraib scandal.

Matthew Quirk, *Private Military Contractors: A buyer's Guide*, ATLANTIC MONTHLY ONLINE, Sept 2004, *available at* http://www.theatlantic.com/doc/prem/200409/quirk:

> While many of these firms initially found work in the disintegrating states of Africa, it is in Iraq that the private military industry has truly come into its own. The raid on the home of Ahmed Chalabi was overseen by armed civilians who work for DynCorp; two Americans suspected of committing abuses in Abu Ghraib prison were civilian contractors employed to assist interrogations; the four armed Americans murdered in Falluja in March worked for Blackwater

USA; Paul Bremer, the chief American administrator in Iraq, was guarded during his tenure not by military personnel but by a team of heavily armed commandos in civilian clothes, who also happened to work for Blackwater. Headline by headline, a picture has begun to take shape over the last year: our military is being privatized before our eyes.

Patrick Radden Keefe, *Iraq: America's Private Armies*, New York Review of Books, Aug. 12, 2004.

One particularly compelling story is that of the Sierra Leone government which was threatened with imminent overthrow by a rebel force and called on a private military company from South Africa. The PMF arrived replete with military aircraft and tanks, ran the rebels back into the hills, and destroyed their bases. P.W. Singer, Corporate Warriors: The Rise of the Privatized Military Industry (2004). Quirk reports that the private firm then engineered a coup and a new government even more sympathetic to their interests.

Among the factors often cited for the rise of privatized military forces are the need for experts to maintain and control highly sophisticated weapons systems, the scaling back of the uniformed services in the wake of the Cold War, and the resulting "stretched thin" configuration of the American military around the world. Given that this phenomenon is likely to increase unless specific action is taken to curtail it, we should consider some of the possible legal ramifications.

How close a connection to the U.S. Government will be required to make a "civilian" subject to federal laws on use of excessive force or abuse of power? For example, if A, a private construction company, has a contract from the U.S. to build a power plant in another country and employs B, a PMF, to guard its facilities and employees, are the agents of B to be considered federal agents for purposes of federal law?

It seems clear that employees of a PMF are not in the uniformed services for purposes of the Uniform Code of Military Justice. But should the uniformed officers who enter into these agreements be responsible for exercising discipline over these agents? In this regard, recall the *Yamashita* case. How can the military exert control and discipline over the PMF's?

The same questions need to be asked regarding the application of international conventions. The answer may be different for the Geneva Convention that it would be for the Convention on Torture.

Protocol I to the Geneva Convention of 1949 (1977) (to which the United States is not a Party) contains this language:

Art 47. Mercenaries

1. A mercenary shall not have the right to be a combatant or a prisoner of war.

2. A mercenary is any person who:

(a) is specially recruited locally or abroad in order to fight in an armed conflict;

(b) does, in fact, take a direct part in the hostilities;

(c) is motivated to take part in the hostilities essentially by the desire for private gain and, in fact, is promised, by or on behalf of a Party to the conflict, material compensation substantially in excess of that promised or paid to combatants of similar ranks and functions in the armed forces of that Party;

(d) is neither a national of a Party to the conflict nor a resident of territory controlled by a Party to the conflict;

(e) is not a member of the armed forces of a Party to the conflict; and

(f) has not been sent by a State which is not a Party to the conflict on official duty as a member of its armed forces.

§ 8.06 SELECTED READINGS

General Treatments of Military Action in Terrorism Context:

· PHILLIP B. HEYMANN, TERRORISM AND AMERICA (1998)

· PHILLIP B. HEYMANN, TERRORISM, FREEDOM, AND SECURITY (2004)

· SEYMOUR M. HERSH, CHAIN OF COMMAND (2004)

· THE BATTLE FOR HEARTS AND MINDS (Alexander T.J. Lennon ed., 2004)

· *Symposium on Terrorism, War, and Justice*, 114 ETHICS 647 (2004)

· Ronald J. Sievert, *War on Terrorism or Global Law Enforcement Operation?*, 78 NOTRE DAME L. REV. 307 (2003)

Critiques of the Military Commissions:

· A. Christopher Bryant & Carl Tobias, Quirin *Revisited*, 2003 WIS. L. REV. 309

· Christopher M. Evans, *Terrorism on Trial: The President's Constitutional Authority To Order the Prosecution of Suspected Terrorists by Military Commissions*, 51 DUKE L.J. 1831 (2002) (valid by constitution but against international law)

· Joan Fitzpatrick, *Jurisdiction of Military Commissions and the Ambiguous War on Terrorism*, 96 AM. J. INT'L L. 345 (2002) ("legally insupportable")

· Jack Goldsmith & Cass R. Sunstein, *Military Tribunals and Legal Culture: What a Difference Sixty Years Makes*, 19 CONST. COMMENT. 261 (2002) (commenting on the difference in reaction between 1942 and 2002)

· Phillip B. Heymann, *Civil Liberties and Human Rights in the Aftermath of September 11*, 25 HARV. J.L. & PUB. POL'Y 441 (2002) ("foolhardy disdain for American pride in, and foreign admiration of, the fairness of our courts")

· Neal K. Katyal & Laurence H. Tribe, *Waging War, Deciding Guilt: Trying the Military Tribunals*, 111 YALE L.J. 1259 (2002) ("flatly unconstitutional")

· Carl Tobias, *Detentions, Military Commissions, Terrorism, and Domestic Case Precedent*, 76 So. CAL. L. REV. 1371 (2003)

· Ruth Wedgwood, *Al Qaeda, Terrorism, and Military Commissions*, 96 AM. J. INT'L L. 328 (2002) (valid under both international and constitutional standards)

Chapter 9

INTERROGATION AND EMERGENCY POWERS

Many claims for extraordinary executive power have been made in the name of the "global war on terror." Some specific measures have involved extraordinary renditions (see Chapter 4), electronic surveillance (see Chapter 5), detentions without trial (see Chapter 8), and aggressive interrogation (and alleged torture). These claims share a general premise that exceptional times call for exceptions to the normal distribution and limits of power. Some writers argue that the exception tends to become the norm. "President . . . Bush is attempting to produce a situation in which the emergency becomes the rule, and the very distinction between peace and war (and between foreign and civil war) becomes impossible." GIORGIO AGAMBEN, STATE OF EXCEPTION 22 (2005).

Many of these arguments borrow heavily from the precedent of President Lincoln during the Civil War who justified his unilateral suspension of the writ of habeas corpus to allow military detentions with this famous statement to Congress: "Are all the laws but one to go unexecuted, and the Government itself go to pieces lest that one be violated?" Chief Justice Rehnquist had the foresight to conduct a thorough examination of the Lincoln precedent three years before 9/11. WILLIAM H. REHNQUIST, ALL THE LAWS BUT ONE (1998).

The U.S. is not alone in invoking the notion of emergency or necessity to depart from the usual limits on government power. Other nations have engaged in detention of suspected terrorists, aggressive interrogation, and even targeted killings. In this Chapter, we will examine the torture debate and then turn to questions of emergency powers by looking at some answers given by Canada, the United Kingdom, and Israel in the struggle with terrorism.

§ 9.01   INTERROGATION AND TORTURE

[A]   The General Parameters

As the torture debate has unfolded, some significant attention has been given to the question of whether harsh interrogation methods are even effective. Some interrogators take the position that a person in extreme pain or torment will say anything to relieve the pain, so the likelihood of getting reliable information is minimal. *See* Anne Applebaum, *The Torture Myth*, WASHINGTON POST, (Jan. 12, 2005, at A21; Center for the Victims of Torture, *Eight Lessons of Torture, available at* http://www.cvt.org. The effectiveness issue is beyond the scope of what we can accomplish in this Chapter, and it should be sufficient to say that some examples of both effective intelligence and misleading information can be found in the annals of torture. The best approach is to assume that we don't have a definitive answer that would apply in all cases.

As the Israeli Supreme Court points out in the opinion below, interrogation is inherently coercive but effective interrogation requires understanding of, if not active empathy with, the situation of the detainee.

> As the Abu Ghraib scandal reveals, some guards and interrogators can be sadistic ghouls; but many other interrogators could qualify as the most liberal people in the armed services since, for one thing, they have spent years studying the language and the history of their captives. As one Special Forces officer told me in Afghanistan, "In order to defeat the enemy you first have to love him, and his culture."

Robert D. Kaplan, *"The Interrogators" and "Torture": Hard Questions*, N.Y. TIMES, Jan. 23, 2005. Kaplan and the Israeli Court also agree that setting specific rules for interrogation in advance is not a productive exercise because the interrogator must constantly revise strategy in light of both how the detainee is feeling and what information is available from whatever source.

Caleb Carr, urging an approach of "limited progressive war," reminded us before the Iraqi invasion of Vattel's admonition that

> the rights founded on the state of war, . . . do not, externally and between mankind, depend on the justice of the cause, but on the legality of the means in themselves. . . . If you once open the door for continual accusation of outrageous excess in hostilities, you will only augment the number of complaints, and influence the minds of the contending parties with increasing animosity: fresh injuries will be perpetually springing up; and the sword will never be sheathed till one of the parties be utterly destroyed.

EMMERICH DE VATTEL, THE LAW OF NATIONS (1758), *as quoted by* CALEB CARR, THE LESSONS OF TERROR 106–07 (2002).

The House of Lords in the *Pinochet* case, *supra* § 6.02[D], discussed the ways in which prohibitions on official torture become part of the domestic law of an Anglo-American legal system. The U.S. has ratified the Convention on Torture and has implemented it through 18 U.S.C. § 2340. One interesting feature of the statute is that its scope is limited by § 2340A to actions "outside the United States." In theory, this should not be of any great significance because § 2340B points out that nothing "shall be construed as precluding the application of State or local laws on the same subject," and all federal laws prohibiting the use of excessive force by federal agents would also be applicable to actions taken within the U.S.

In the context of terrorism, the "ticking bomb scenario" was made famous in ALAN DERSHOWITZ, WHY TERRORISM SUCCEEDS (2000). The scenario posits that no sane person would refuse to torture a terrorist who knows the location of a bomb that is set to go off in a crowded location before protracted interrogation could be expected to produce results. Dershowitz contends that courts should provide oversight of torture by issuing a torture warrant rather than leaving the matter to be resolved either by prosecutorial discretion or the defense of necessity.

Further elaboration of interrogation techniques in the context of terrorism investigations was contained in Mark Bowden, *The Dark Art of Interrogation*, ATLANTIC MONTHLY (Oct. 2003), which described some of the "aggressive interrogation" techniques of investigators around the world. So far as Bowden had discovered at that time, no country sanctioned the use of these techniques, although many investigators admitted that they might be used on occasion in clandestine fashion. Bowden specifically stated that the Bush Administration took the view that these techniques would not be permitted. The principal techniques highlighted in the article were nakedness in cold conditions, sleep deprivation, playing on fears (such as personal fear of dogs or threats to family members), maintaining painful positions for extended periods of time, alternating terrible food with treats.

Professor Bassiouni describes the U.S. involvement with "aggressive interrogation" this way:

> The institutionalization of torture became a reality when President Bush authorized the establishment of Camp Delta at Guantánamo Bay, Cuba, concluded that the Geneva Conventions did not apply to combatants seized in Afghanistan (Taliban and Al Qaeda), approved the use of "enhanced interrogation techniques," issued an Executive Order that bypassed Congress, and unilaterally established a new parallel system of justice to deal with "terrorists" through Military Commissions. . . . The practices that followed this policy have resulted to date in the estimated deaths of over 200 detainees in U.S. custody, presumably as a result of torture; probably as many as several thousand persons have been tortured during interrogation at U.S.-controlled detention facilities and at foreign detention facilities where officials acting for

and on behalf of the U.S. have engaged in torture.

M. Cherif Bassiouni, *The Institutionalization of Torture under the Bush Administration*, 37 Case W. Res. J. Int'l L. 389 (2006).

[B] The Path to "Torture"

The Abu Ghraib prisoner abuse scandal began surfacing in public around the first of May, 2004. Prior to that time, Army investigations had already disclosed widespread abuses and resulted in some sanctions. *See* Seymour M. Hersh, Chain of Command (2004); *see also* Mark Danner, Torture and Truth: America, Abu Ghraib, and the War on Terror (2004); Karen Greenberg & Joshua Dratel, The Torture Papers: The Road to Abu Ghraib (2005).

The first Army investigation of the situation by Major General Antonio M. Taguba, prepared before the scandal became public, summarized the principal abuses this way:

> Breaking chemical lights and pouring the phosphoric liquid on detainees; pouring cold water on naked detainees; beating detainees with a broom handle and a chair; threatening male detainees with rape; allowing a military police guard to stitch the wound of a detainee who was injured after being slammed against the wall in his cell; sodomizing a detainee with a chemical light and perhaps a broom stick, and using military working dogs to frighten and intimidate detainees with threats of attack, and in one instance actually biting a detainee.

As journalists and investigators probed further, it appeared that many of the "interrogation" techniques were the subject of high-level analysis if not approval. The most controversial document was the "Torture Memorandum," signed by Jay Bybee (later appointed to the Ninth Circuit) and widely attributed to John Yoo, which described a very narrow reading of torture and outlined arguments by which torture or "inhumane or degrading treatment" of prisoners could be excused under U.S. law.

1. The Torture Memorandum

The Bybee-Yoo Memorandum is dated August 1, 2002 and headed "Standards of Conduct for Interrogation Under 18 U.S.C. §§ 2334–2340A." The Memorandum points out that the Convention on Torture (CAT) requires signatory nations to criminalize torture while merely committing to "undertake to prevent other acts of cruel, inhuman, or degrading treatment." Drawing on a variety of sources, the Memorandum concludes that torture consists of "severe" or "extreme" infliction of pain.

> The victim must experience intense pain or suffering of the kind that is equivalent to the pain that would be associated with serious physical injury so severe that death, organ failure, or permanent damage resulting in a loss of significant bodily function will likely result. If that pain or suffering is psychological, that suffering must result from one of the acts set forth in the statute. In addition, these acts must cause long-term mental harm.

> CAT not only defines torture as involving severe pain and suffering, but also it makes clear that such pain and suffering is at the extreme end of the spectrum of acts by reserving criminal penalties solely for torture. . . . [T]he treaty (and hence the statute) prohibits only the worst forms of cruel, inhuman, or degrading treatment or punishment.

After reviewing the *Ireland* case and cases in both U.S. and Israeli courts, the Memorandum emphasizes what it terms the torture/cruelty distinction:

> In sum, both the European Court on Human Rights and the Israeli Supreme Court have recognized a wide array of acts that constitute cruel, inhuman, or degrading treatment or punishment, but do not amount to torture. Thus they appear to permit, under international law, an aggressive interpretation as to

what amounts to torture, leaving that label to be applied only where extreme circumstances exist.

The next section of the Memorandum considers whether the President of the United States can insulate interrogators from criminal responsibility.

> Even if an interrogation method arguably were to violate Section 2340A, the statute would be unconstitutional if it impermissibly encroached on the President's constitutional power to conduct a military campaign. As Commander-in-Chief, the President has the constitutional authority to order interrogations of enemy combatants to gain intelligence information concerning the military plans of the enemy. The demands of the Commander-in-Chief power are especially pronounced in the middle of a war in which the nation has already suffered a direct attack. In such a case, the information gained from interrogations may prevent future attacks by foreign enemies. Any effort to apply Section 2340A in a manner that interferes with the President's direction of such core war matters as the detention and interrogation of enemy combatants thus would be unconstitutional.

> Congress can no more interfere with the President's conduct of the interrogation of enemy combatants than it can dictate strategic or tactical decisions on the battlefield. Just as statutes that order the President to conduct warfare in a certain manner or for specific goals would be unconstitutional, so too are laws that seek to prevent the President from gaining the intelligence he believes necessary to prevent attacks upon the United States.

Finally, the Memorandum attempts to set forth defenses under the headings of necessity and self-defense.

> Under the current circumstances, we believe that a defendant accused of violating Section 2340A could have, in certain circumstances, grounds to properly claim the defense of another. The threat of an impending terrorist attack threatens the lives of hundreds if not thousands of American citizens. If an attack appears increasingly likely, but our intelligence services and armed forces cannot prevent it without the information from the interrogation of a specific individual, then the more likely it will appear that the conduct in question will be seen as necessary.

> To be sure, this situation is different from the usual self-defense justification, and, indeed, it overlaps with elements of the necessity defense. Self-defense as usually discussed involves using force against an individual who is about to conduct the attack. In the current circumstances, however, an enemy combatant in detention does not himself present a threat of harm. He is not actually carrying out the attack; rather, he has participated in the planning and preparation for the attack, or merely has knowledge of the attack through his membership in the terrorist organization. Nonetheless, . . . even though a detained enemy combatant may not be the exact attacker — he is not planting the bomb, or piloting a hijacked plane to kill civilians — he still may be harmed in self-defense if he has knowledge of future attacks because he has assisted in their planning and execution.

2. Critiques and Consequences

One of the most biting critiques of the Bybee Memorandum was presented by Yale Law School Dean Harold Koh in January 2005 testimony regarding the nomination of Alberto Gonzales as Attorney General. Koh took the position that Gonzales, as Counsel to the President, should have been expected "to have immediately repudiated such an opinion."

> [I]n my professional opinion, the August 1, 2002 OLC Memorandum is perhaps the most clearly erroneous legal opinion I have ever read. The opinion

has five obvious failures. First, it asks which coercive interrogation tactics are permissible, never mentioning what President Bush correctly called every person's "inalienable human right" to be free from torture. The opinion's apparent purpose is to explore how U.S. officials can use tactics tantamount to torture against suspected terrorists, without being held criminally liable. Second, the opinion defines "torture" so narrowly that it flies in the face of the plain meaning of the term. For example, the memorandum would require that the interrogator have the precise objective of inflicting "physical pain . . . equivalent in intensity to the pain accompanying serious physical injury, such as organ failure, impairment of bodily function or even death." Under this absurdly narrow legal definition, many of the heinous acts committed by the Iraqi security services under Saddam Hussein would not be torture.

Third, the OLC memorandum grossly overreads the inherent power of the President under the Commander-in-Chief power in Article II of the Constitution. Fourth, the August 1 memorandum suggests that executive officials can escape prosecution for torture on the ground that "they were carrying out the President's Commander-in-Chief powers." The opinion asserts that this would preclude the application of a valid federal criminal statute "to punish officials for aiding the President in exercising his exclusive constitutional authorities." By adopting the doctrine of "just following orders" as a valid defense, the opinion undermines the very underpinnings of individual criminal responsibility. These principles were set forth in the landmark judgments at Nuremberg, and now embodied in the basic instruments of international criminal law.

Fifth and finally, the August 1 memorandum concludes that, for American officials, the International Convention *against* Torture and *Other Cruel, Inhuman or Degrading Treatment or Punishment* allows cruel, inhuman, or degrading treatment as permissible U.S. government interrogation tactics. In effect, the opinion gives the Executive Branch a license to dehumanize, degrade, and act cruelly, notwithstanding the Fifth Amendment's rejection of government acts that shock the conscience and the Eighth Amendment's rejection of any "cruel and unusual punishments."

The August 1 memorandum cannot be justified as a case of lawyers doing their job and setting out options for their client. If a client asks a lawyer how to break the law and escape liability, the lawyer's ethical duty is to say no. A lawyer has no obligation to aid, support, or justify the commission of an illegal act.

Other critiques have mentioned that both the European Court of Human Rights and the Israeli Supreme Court, on which the Memorandum relies for their definitions of torture, observed that the prohibition on torture cannot be derogated in time of emergency. Moreover, those opinions also recognized that cruel, inhuman, or degrading treatment is also prohibited under international conventions.

With regard to the executive power argument, if Congress were truly disabled for "interfer[ing] with the President's conduct of the interrogation of enemy combatants," then is the UCMJ, which establishes norms of behavior for military personnel, unconstitutional? The Constitution gives Congress the power to make rules and regulations for governance of the armed forces as well as to define crimes against the law of nations. And, as Dean Koh pointed out, the memorandum does not deal with the Supreme Court's upholding of congressional lawmaking power in *Youngstown Sheet & Tube*.

On the other hand, if, as Professor Dershowitz insists, anyone in the "ticking bomb" scenario will do whatever it takes to avoid mass casualties, what should be the legal system's response to this reality? If your child has been kidnaped and held under threat of death by terrorists, would you torture someone who knew the location and means of access to the child? If so, what would you expect the legal system to do with you after the safe return of your child? Is it really rational to expect our agents around the world to "play fair" in all the various settings in which they might have control over suspected terrorists with valuable knowledge?

As the scandal unfolded, it was learned that there were several memoranda of this type drafted in interaction among the White House, Justice Department, and Pentagon. The Pentagon responded with additional investigative reports, the most significant of which has been the Schlesinger Report from the "Independent Panel to Review DoD Detention Operations" chaired by James R. Schlesinger, a former Director of Central Intelligence and Secretary of Defense under Presidents Nixon and Ford. The Schlesinger Panel found "abuses occurred at the hands of both military police and military intelligence personnel. The pictured abuses, unacceptable even in wartime, were not part of authorized interrogations nor were they even aimed at intelligence targets. They represent deviant behavior and a failure of leadership and discipline."

With regard to the chain of command, the Report stated, "No approved procedures called for or allowed the kinds of abuse that occurred. There is no evidence of a policy of abuse promulgated by senior officials or military authorities. Still, the abuses were not just the failure of some individuals to follow known standards, and they are more than the failure of a few leaders to enforce proper discipline. There is institutional and personal responsibility at higher levels."

On December 29, 2004, the Justice Department released a memorandum "withdrawing" the 2002 memorandum. Primarily, the new memorandum states that "we disagree with statements in the August 2002 Memorandum limiting 'severe' pain under the statute to 'excruciating and agonizing' pain or to pain 'equivalent in intensity to the pain accompanying serious physical injury, such as organ failure, impairment of bodily function, or even death.' . . . Because the discussion in that memorandum concerning the President's Commander-in-Chief power and the potential defenses to liability was — and remains — unnecessary, it has been eliminated." The sequence of events leading to this statement is described by its author in JACK GOLDSMITH, THE TERROR PRESIDENCY (2007).

Some observers have asserted that it was unethical for lawyers Bybee and Yoo to advise the administration on methods of violating the law. Others have even gone so far as to accuse the authors of "war crimes." *See, e.g.*, Milan Markovic, *Can Lawyers Be War Criminals?* 20 GEO. J. LEGAL ETHICS 347 (2007). John Dean, former White House Counsel, has asked why Judge Bybee should not be impeached. *See* John W. Dean, *The Torture Memo By Judge Jay S. Bybee That Haunted Alberto Gonzales's Confirmation Hearings*, FINDLAW, Jan. 14, 2005, *available at* http://writ.news.findlaw.com/dean/20050114.html#continue. John Yoo has been haunted by accusations of war crimes and has been sued for damages by Jose Padilla.

The debate over interrogation techniques focused in late 2007 on whether "waterboarding" should be considered torture. CIA Director Hayden confirmed that waterboarding was used against Khalid Sheikh Mohammed, Abu Zubaydah, and Abd al-Rahim al-Nashiri. Attorney General Mukasey then said there would be no investigation into whether that constituted a crime because the CIA interrogators had relied on legal opinions that it would not be a crime. Meanwhile, Director of National Intelligence McConnell expressed the view that he would consider it torture if used on him.

Judge Wallach of the International Court of Trade has chronicled instances of war crimes prosecutions against Japanese prison camp officials and interrogators for "water cure" or "water torture" committed against American prisoners, as well as prosecutions of American military personnel and Philippine officials, and even one Texas sheriff for similar behavior.

If we remember what we said and did when our military personnel were victims, if we remember our response when they were perpetrators, how can our government possibly opine that the use of water torture is within the bounds of law? To do so is beneath contempt; it is beyond redemption; and it is a repudiation of the rule of law that in our origins was the core principle of governance which distinguished our nation from the crowned dictatorships of the European continent.

Evan Wallach, *Drop by Drop: Forgetting the History of Water Torture in U.S. Courts*, 45 COLUM. J. TRANSNAT'L L. 468 (2007).

EL-MASRI v. UNITED STATES
479 F.3d 296 (4th Cir. 2007)

KING, CIRCUIT JUDGE.

Khaled El-Masri appeals from the dismissal of his civil action against former Director of Central Intelligence George Tenet, three corporate defendants, ten unnamed employees of the Central Intelligence Agency (the "CIA"), and ten unnamed employees of the defendant corporations.

In his Complaint, El-Masri alleged that the defendants were involved in a CIA operation in which he was detained and interrogated in violation of his rights under the Constitution and international law. The United States intervened as a defendant in the district court, asserting that El-Masri's civil action could not proceed because it posed an unreasonable risk that privileged state secrets would be disclosed. By its Order of May 12, 2006, the district court agreed with the position of the United States and dismissed El-Masri's Complaint.

El-Masri, a German citizen of Lebanese descent, [alleges] in substance, as follows: on December 31, 2003, while traveling in Macedonia, he was detained by Macedonian law enforcement officials; after twenty-three days in Macedonian custody, he was handed over to CIA operatives, who flew him to a CIA-operated detention facility near Kabul, Afghanistan; he was held in this CIA facility until May 28, 2004, when he was transported to Albania and released in a remote area; and Albanian officials then picked him up and took him to an airport in Tirana, Albania, from which he traveled to his home in Germany.

The Complaint asserted that El-Masri had not only been held against his will, but had also been mistreated in a number of other ways during his detention, including being beaten, drugged, bound, and blindfolded during transport; confined in a small, unsanitary cell; interrogated several times; and consistently prevented from communicating with anyone outside the detention facility, including his family or the German government. El-Masri alleged that his detention and interrogation were carried out pursuant to an unlawful policy and practice devised and implemented by defendant Tenet known as "extraordinary rendition": the clandestine abduction and detention outside the United States of persons suspected of involvement in terrorist activities, and their subsequent interrogation using methods impermissible under U.S. and international laws.

According to the Complaint, the corporate defendants provided the CIA with an aircraft and crew to transport El-Masri to Afghanistan, pursuant to an agreement with Director Tenet, and they either knew or reasonably should have known that "Mr. El-Masri would be subjected to prolonged arbitrary detention, torture and cruel, inhuman, or degrading treatment in violation of federal and international laws during his transport to Afghanistan and while he was detained and interrogated there." El-Masri also alleges that CIA officials "believed early on that they had the wrong person," and that Director Tenet was notified in April 2004 that "the CIA had detained the wrong person" in El-Masri.

In the period after the district court's dismissal of El-Masri's Complaint, his alleged rendition — and the rendition operations of the United States generally — have remained subjects of public discussion. In El-Masri's view, two additions to the body of public information on these topics are especially significant in this appeal. First, on June 7, 2006, the Council of Europe released a draft report on alleged United States renditions and detentions involving the Council's member countries. This report concluded that El-Masri's account of his rendition and confinement was substantially accurate. Second, on September 6, 2006, in a White House address, President Bush publicly disclosed the existence of a CIA program in which suspected terrorists are detained and interrogated at locations outside the United States. The President declined, however, to reveal any of this CIA program's operational details, including the locations or other circumstances of its detainees' confinement.

El-Masri maintains on appeal that the district court misapplied the state secrets doctrine in dismissing his Complaint without requiring any responsive pleadings from the defendants or permitting any discovery to be conducted. Importantly, El-Masri does not contend that the state secrets privilege has no role in these proceedings. To the contrary, he acknowledges that at least some information important to his claims is likely to be privileged, and thus beyond his reach. But he challenges the court's determination that state secrets are so central to this matter that any attempt at further litigation would threaten their disclosure. As explained below, we conclude that the district court correctly assessed the centrality of state secrets in this dispute. We therefore affirm its Order and the dismissal of El-Masri's Complaint. Under the state secrets doctrine, the United States may prevent the disclosure of information in a judicial proceeding if "there is a reasonable danger" that such disclosure "will expose military matters which, in the interest of national security, should not be divulged." *United States v. Reynolds*, 345 U.S. 1, 10 (1953).

After information has been determined to be privileged under the state secrets doctrine, it is absolutely protected from disclosure — even for the purpose of in camera examination by the court. On this point, *Reynolds* could not be more specific: "When . . . the occasion for the privilege is appropriate, . . . the court should not jeopardize the security which the privilege is meant to protect by insisting upon an examination of the evidence, even by the judge alone, in chambers." 345 U.S. at 10. Moreover, no attempt is made to balance the need for secrecy of the privileged information against a party's need for the information's disclosure; a court's determination that a piece of evidence is a privileged state secret removes it from the proceedings entirely.

The effect of a successful interposition of the state secrets privilege by the United States will vary from case to case. If a proceeding involving state secrets can be fairly litigated without resort to the privileged information, it may continue. But if " 'the circumstances make clear that sensitive military secrets will be so central to the subject matter of the litigation that any attempt to proceed will threaten disclosure of the privileged matters,' dismissal is the proper remedy."

The controlling inquiry is not whether the general subject matter of an action can be described without resort to state secrets. Rather, we must ascertain whether an action can be litigated without threatening the disclosure of such state secrets.

If El-Masri's civil action were to proceed, the facts central to its resolution would be the roles, if any, that the defendants played in the events he alleges. To establish a prima facie case, he would be obliged to produce admissible evidence not only that he was detained and interrogated, but that the defendants were involved in his detention and interrogation in a manner that renders them personally liable to him. Such a showing could be made only with evidence that exposes how the CIA organizes, staffs, and supervises its most sensitive intelligence operations. With regard to Director Tenet, for example, El-Masri would be obliged to show in detail how the head of the CIA participates in such operations, and how information concerning their progress is relayed to him. With respect to the defendant corporations and their unnamed employees, El-Masri would have to demonstrate the existence and details of CIA espionage contracts, an endeavor practically indistinguishable from that categorically barred by *Totten* and *Tenet v. Doe. See Totten v. United States*, 92 U.S. 105, 107 (1875) (establishing absolute bar to enforcement of confidential agreements to conduct espionage, on ground that "public policy forbids the maintenance of any suit in a court of justice, the trial of which would inevitably lead to the disclosure of matters which the law itself regards as confidential"); *Tenet v. Doe*, 544 U.S. 1, 10–11 (2005) (reaffirming *Totten* in unanimous decision). Even marshalling the evidence necessary to make the requisite showings would implicate privileged state secrets, because El-Masri would need to rely on witnesses whose identities, and evidence the very existence of which, must remain confidential in the interest of national security. *See Sterling*, 416 F.3d at 347 ("[T]he very methods by which evidence would be gathered in this case are themselves problematic.").

Furthermore, if El-Masri were somehow able to make out a prima facie case despite the unavailability of state secrets, the defendants could not properly defend themselves without using privileged evidence. The main avenues of defense available in this matter are to show that El-Masri was not subject to the treatment that he alleges; that, if he was subject to such treatment, the defendants were not involved in it; or that, if they were involved, the nature of their involvement does not give rise to liability. Any of those three showings would require disclosure of information regarding the means and methods by which the CIA gathers intelligence.

El-Masri also contends that, instead of dismissing his Complaint, the district court should have employed some procedure under which state secrets would have been revealed to him, his counsel, and the court, but withheld from the public. Specifically, he suggests that the court ought to have received all the state secrets evidence in camera and under seal, provided his counsel access to it pursuant to a nondisclosure agreement (after arranging for necessary security clearances), and then conducted an in camera trial. We need not dwell long on El-Masri's proposal in this regard, for it is expressly foreclosed by Reynolds, the Supreme Court decision that controls this entire field of inquiry. Reynolds plainly held that when "the occasion for the privilege is appropriate, . . . the court should not jeopardize the security which the privilege is meant to protect by insisting upon an examination of the evidence, even by the judge alone, in chambers." 345 U.S. at 10.

In this matter, the reasons for the United States' claim of the state secrets privilege and its motion to dismiss were explained largely in the Classified Declaration, which sets forth in detail the nature of the information that the Executive seeks to protect and explains why its disclosure would be detrimental to national security. We have reviewed the Classified Declaration, as did the district court, and the extensive information it contains is crucial to our decision in this matter. El-Masri's contention that his Complaint was dismissed based on the Executive's "unilateral assert[ion] of a need for secrecy" is entirely unfounded. It is no doubt frustrating to El-Masri that many of the specific reasons for the dismissal of his Complaint are classified. An inherent feature of the state secrets privilege, however, is that the party against whom it is asserted will often not be privy to the information that the Executive seeks to protect. That El-Masri is unfamiliar with the Classified Declaration's explanation for the privilege claim does not imply, as he would have it, that no such explanation was required, or that the district court's ruling was simply an unthinking ratification of a conclusory demand by the executive branch.

It should be unnecessary for us to point out that the Executive's authority to protect confidential military and intelligence information is much broader in civil matters than in criminal prosecutions. The Supreme Court explained this principle in *Reynolds*, observing:

> Respondents have cited us to those cases in the criminal field, where it has been held that the Government can invoke its evidentiary privileges only at the price of letting the defendant go free. The rationale of the criminal cases is that, since the Government which prosecutes an accused also has the duty to see that justice is done, it is unconscionable to allow it to undertake prosecution and then invoke its governmental privileges to deprive the accused of anything which

might be material to his defense. Such rationale has no application in a civil forum where the Government is not the moving party, but is a defendant only on terms to which it has consented.

NOTES AND QUESTIONS

Rasul v. Myers, 2008 U.S. App. LEXIS 509 (D.C. Cir. Jan. 11, 2008). Rasul was repatriated to the United Kingdom from Guantánamo in 2004. He brought suit against a variety of federal officials, including Secretary of Defense Rumsfeld, for tortious mistreatment and religious discrimination. Rasul and two others alleged that they were in Afghanistan to provide humanitarian relief when they were captured by the Northern Alliance and handed over to western forces. Another co-plaintiff, al-Harith, alleged that he was actually kidnaped out of Pakistan by the Taliban, from whom he escaped before he was mistakenly detained by western forces. The D.C. Circuit held that

a.   their claims under the Alien Tort Act and international law were properly within the Federal Tort Claims Act, which has a specialized procedure that must be followed,

b.   the constitutional claims were unavailing because non-resident aliens outside the U.S. have no constitutional rights and because the claims would be barred by the good faith immunity of the defendants,

c.   their religious freedom claims were not cognizable under the Religious Freedom Restoration Act because the statute has no application to aliens located outside sovereign United States territory at the time their alleged RFRA claim arose.

ARAR v. ASHCROFT
414 F. Supp. 2d 250 (E.D.N.Y. 2006)

TRAGER, UNITED STATES DISTRICT JUDGE.

Plaintiff Maher Arar brings this action against defendants, U.S. officials, who allegedly held him virtually incommunicado for thirteen days at the U.S. border and then ordered his removal to Syria for the express purpose of detention and interrogation under torture by Syrian officials. He brings claims under the Torture Victim Prevention Act and the Fifth Amendment to the U.S. Constitution.

BACKGROUND

Plaintiff Maher Arar ("Arar" or "plaintiff") is a 33-year-old native of Syria who immigrated to Canada with his family when he was a teenager. He is a dual citizen of Syria and Canada and presently resides in Ottawa. In September 2002, while vacationing with family in Tunisia, he was called back to work by his employer to consult with a prospective client. He purchased a return ticket to Montreal with stops in Zurich and New York and left Tunisia on September 25, 2002.

On September 26, 2002, Arar arrived from Switzerland at John F. Kennedy Airport ("JFK Airport") in New York to catch a connecting flight to Montreal. Upon presenting his passport to an immigration inspector, he was identified as "the subject of a . . . lookout as being a member of a known terrorist organization." [He was incarcerated and eventually allowed one phone call, which he made to his mother in Canada, who then obtained counsel for him. He was held in custody and interrogated without being allowed to consult with counsel except for one occasion. After two weeks, he was transported to Jordan, where he was delivered to Syrian authorities.]

During his ten-month period of detention in Syria, Arar alleges that he was placed in a "grave" cell measuring six-feet long, seven feet high and three feet wide. The cell was located within the Palestine Branch of the Syrian Military Intelligence ("Palestine Branch"). The cell was damp and cold, contained very little light and was infested with rats, which would enter the cell through a small aperture in the ceiling. Cats would urinate on Arar through the aperture, and sanitary facilities were nonexistent. Arar was allowed to bathe himself in cold water once per week. He was prohibited from exercising and was provided barely edible food. Arar lost forty pounds during his ten-month period of detention in Syria.

During his first twelve days in Syrian detention, Arar was interrogated for eighteen hours per day and was physically and psychologically tortured. He was beaten on his palms, hips and lower back with a two-inch-thick electric cable. His captors also used their fists to beat him on his stomach, face and back of his neck. He was subjected to excruciating pain and pleaded with his captors to stop, but they would not. He was placed in a room where he could hear the screams of other detainees being tortured and was told that he, too, would be placed in a spine-breaking "chair," hung upside down in a "tire" for beatings and subjected to electric shocks. To lessen his exposure to the torture, Arar falsely confessed, among other things, to having trained with terrorists in Afghanistan, even though he had never been to Afghanistan and had never been involved in terrorist activity.

Arar alleges that his interrogation in Syria was coordinated and planned by U.S. officials, who sent the Syrians a dossier containing specific questions. As evidence of this, Arar notes that the interrogations in the U.S. and Syria contained identical questions, including a specific question about his relationship with a particular individual wanted for terrorism. In return, the Syrian officials supplied U.S. officials with all information extracted from Arar; plaintiff cites a statement by one Syrian official who has publicly stated that the Syrian government shared information with the U.S. that it extracted from Arar.

The Canadian Embassy contacted the Syrian government about Arar on October 20, 2002, and, the following day, Syrian officials confirmed that they were detaining him. At this point, the Syrian officials ceased interrogating and torturing Arar. Canadian officials visited Arar at the Palestine Branch five times during his ten-month detention. Prior to each visit, Arar was warned not to disclose that he was being mistreated. He complied but eventually broke down during the fifth visit, telling the Canadian consular official that he was being tortured and kept in a grave.

On October 5, 2003, Syria, without filing any charges against Arar, released him into the custody of Canadian Embassy officials in Damascus. He was flown to Ottawa the following day and reunited with his family.

The complaint alleges on information and belief that Arar was removed to Syria under a covert U.S. policy of "extraordinary rendition," according to which individuals are sent to foreign countries to undergo methods of interrogation not permitted in the United States. The extraordinary rendition policy involves the removal of "non-U.S. citizens detained in this country and elsewhere and suspected — reasonably or unreasonably — of terrorist activity to countries, including Syria, where interrogations under torture are routine." Arar alleges on information and belief that the United States sends individuals "to countries like Syria precisely because those countries can and do use methods of interrogation to obtain information from detainees that would not be morally acceptable or legal in the United States and other democracies." The complaint further alleges that "these officials have facilitated such human rights abuses, exchanging dossiers with intelligence officials in the countries to which non-U.S. citizens are removed." The complaint also alleges that the U.S. involves Syria in its extraordinary rendition program to extract counter-terrorism information.

DISCUSSION

Arar raises four claims for relief.

First, he alleges that defendants violated the Torture Victim Prevention Act by conspiring with and/or aiding and abetting Jordanian and Syrian officials to bring about his torture.

Second, Arar alleges that defendants violated his rights under the Fifth Amendment to the U.S. Constitution by knowingly and intentionally subjecting him to torture and coercive interrogation in Syria.

Third, Arar alleges that as a result of the actions of the defendants, he was subjected to arbitrary and indefinite detention in Syria, including the denial of access to counsel, the courts and his consulate, all of which also violated the Fifth Amendment.

Fourth, Arar alleges that he suffered outrageous, excessive, cruel, inhumane and degrading conditions of confinement in the United States, was subjected to coercive and involuntary custodial interrogation and deprived of access to lawyers and courts, in violation of the Fifth Amendment. Although Arar's complaint also alleges that defendants violated "treaty law," he appears to have abandoned any such claims in the subsequent briefing.

TORTURE VICTIM PROTECTION ACT

Section 3(b)(1) of the Torture Victim Protection Act further requires that a plaintiff be in the offender's "custody or physical control." Defendants argue that this element is lacking because the alleged torture occurred while Arar was in Syrian custody. However, according to the complaint, defendants orchestrated Arar's ordeal by sending him to Syria for the express purpose of being confined and questioned there under torture. Arar alleges that defendants provided the Syrians a dossier on him to be used during interrogations conducted under conditions of torture and that U.S. officials were supplied with information gained from those investigations.

The legislative history to the Torture Victim Protection Act explains that the statute, a statutory note to the ATCA, was intended to provide an explicit grant of a cause of action to victims of torture committed in foreign nations and to extend the remedy under the ATCA to U.S. citizens tortured abroad. In addition to enacting the Torture Victim Protection Act and creating a private cause of action for officially sanctioned torture, Congress implemented Article 3 of the CAT by enacting the Foreign Affairs Reform and Restructuring Act of 1988 ("FARRA")(codified as Note to 8 U.S.C. § 1231).

Under FARRA, "it shall be the policy of the United States not to expel, extradite, or otherwise effect the involuntary return of any person to a country in which there are substantial grounds for believing the person would be in danger of being subjected to torture. . . . " The Torture Victim Protection Act makes clear that individuals are liable only if they have committed torture or extrajudicial killing "under actual or apparent authority, or color of law, of any foreign nation." The Second Circuit has held that the "color of law" requirement of the TVPA is "intended to 'make[] clear that the plaintiff must establish some governmental involvement in the torture or killing to prove a claim,' and that the statute does not attempt to deal with torture or killing by purely private groups." *Kadic v. Karadzic*, 70 F.3d 232, 245 (2d Cir. 1995). Plaintiff argues that defendants operated under color of law of a foreign nation by conspiring with, or aiding and abetting, Syrian officials in their unlawful detention and torture of Arar.

Schneider v. Kissinger, 310 F. Supp. 2d. 251 (D.D.C. 2004), aff'd 366 U.S. App. D.C. 408, 412 F.3d 190 (D.C. Cir. 2005), held that a U.S. official acting under the directive of the President of the United States would *ipso facto* act only under auspices of U.S., not foreign, law. *Schneider* involved claims arising out of the CIA's alleged involvement in the anti-Allende coup in Chile. The survivors and personal representative of General Rene Schneider, who was killed during a botched kidnaping by plotters of the 1970 Chilean government coup, sued the United States and former national security advisor Henry A. Kissinger, alleging that President Nixon had ordered Kissinger, the CIA and others to do whatever would be necessary to prevent the election of Dr. Salvadore

Allende as Chile's first Socialist President and that Kissinger, apparently unconcerned with the risks involved, allocated $ 10 million to effect a military coup, leading to Schneider's death.

Plaintiff argues that *Schneider* is inapposite because, in that case, Kissinger was acting at the direction of the President, whereas, here, the defendants are not alleged to have acted at the behest of President Bush. However, Arar's complaint alleges unconstitutional conduct by some of the highest policy-making officials of this country, not low-level officers acting on their own. Thus, in this case, as in *Schneider*, the defendants' alleged conduct would have been taken pursuant to U.S., not Syrian, law. Although *Schneider* does not provide extensive analysis of the issue, its analysis would seem applicable here.

The issues federal officials confront when acting in the realm of foreign affairs may involve conduct and relationships of an entirely different order and policy-making on an entirely different plane. In the realm of foreign policy, U.S. officials deal with unique dangers not seen in domestic life and negotiate with foreign officials and individuals whose conduct is not controlled by the standards of our society. The negotiations are often more delicate and subtle than those occurring in the domestic sphere and may contain misrepresentations that would be unacceptable in a wholly domestic context. Thus, it is by no means a simple matter to equate actions taken under the color of state law in the domestic front to conduct undertaken under color of foreign law. That arena is animated by different interests and issues.

Due Process Claims for Detention and Torture in Syria

Counts 2 and 3 of plaintiff's complaint allege that defendants violated Arar's rights to substantive due process by removing him to Syria and subjecting him to both torture and coercive interrogation and arbitrary and indefinite detention. He seeks damages under *Bivens v. Six Unknown Fed. Narcotics Agents*, 403 U.S. 388 (1971), claiming deprivation of Fifth Amendment due process rights. *Bivens* establishes "that the victims of a constitutional violation by a federal agent have a right to recover damages against the official in federal court despite the absence of any statute conferring such a right."

Arar argues that the treatment he allegedly suffered unquestionably constitutes a violation of substantive due process. However, defendants question whether robust Fifth Amendment protections can extend to someone like Arar, who, for juridical purposes, never actually entered the United States. Moreover, they cite precedent rejecting extraterritorial Fifth Amendment protections to non-U.S. citizens.

Defendants argue that Arar's claims alleging torture and unlawful detention in Syria are *per se* foreclosed under *Johnson v. Eisentrager*, 339 U.S. 763 (1950), and its progeny. These cases, they claim, unequivocally establish that non-resident aliens subjected to constitutional violations on non-U.S. soil are prohibited from bringing claims under the Due Process clause.

In *Eisentrager*, the Supreme Court held that a federal district court lacked jurisdiction to issue a writ of habeas corpus to twenty-one German nationals who had been captured in China by U.S. forces, brought to trial and convicted before an American military commission in Nanking and placed in incarceration in occupied Germany. The Supreme Court ruled that non-U.S. citizens with absolutely no relationship to the United States, captured outside U.S. territory and tried before a military tribunal, could not avail themselves of the right of habeas corpus to prove their innocence before a U.S. court. The Court held that "in extending constitutional protections beyond the citizenry, the Court has been at pains to point out that it was the alien's presence within its territorial jurisdiction that gave the Judiciary power to act." Bereft of any established contacts with the United States, the *Eisentrager* petitioners could not avail themselves of U.S. courts.

Under *Eisentrager*, given that "the privilege of litigation has been extended to aliens, whether friendly or enemy, only because permitting their presence in the country implied protection," aliens outside the United States could not invoke the Constitution on their behalf. Consequently, the "nonresident enemy alien, especially one who has remained in the service of the enemy, does not have even this qualified access to our courts, for he neither has comparable claims upon our institutions nor could his use of them fail to be helpful to the enemy."

However, there are obvious distinctions between *Eisentrager* and the case at bar. The *Eisentrager* petitioners had a trial pursuant to the laws of war. Although that trial might not have afforded them the panoply of rights provided in the civilian context, one cannot say that the petitioners had no fair process. Moreover, the *Eisentrager* detainees had "never been or resided in the United States," were "captured outside of our territory and there held in military custody as prisoner[s] of war," were "tried by a Military Commission sitting outside the United States" and were "at all times imprisoned outside the United States." Arar, by contrast, was held virtually incommunicado — moreover, on U.S. soil — and denied access to counsel and process of any kind. Owing to these factual distinctions, *Eisentrager* is not squarely applicable to the case at bar.

Defendants also cite *United States v. Verdugo-Urquidez*, 494 U.S. 259 (1990), in which the Supreme Court revisited the question of the extraterritoriality of the U.S. Constitution to non-U.S. citizens. *Verdugo-Urquidez* involved a question regarding the extraterritoriality of the Fourth Amendment's protection against unreasonable searches and seizures. The Court held that a warrantless search and seizure of an alien's property in Mexico, even though orchestrated within the United States, did not constitute a Fourth Amendment violation. Although the illegal search was ordered by U.S. officials, it took place "solely in Mexico," which, the Court held, amounted to no Fourth Amendment violation.

However, *Verdugo-Urquidez*, which involved a search and seizure of a home in Mexico, can be distinguished from the case at bar. As Justice Kennedy observed in his concurring opinion, Mexico's different legal regime compounded (and perhaps created) the *Fourth Amendment* violations. "The absence of local judges or magistrates available to issue warrants, the differing and perhaps unascertainable conceptions of reasonableness and privacy that prevail abroad, and the need to cooperate with foreign officials all indicate that the Fourth Amendment's warrant requirement should not apply in Mexico as it does in this country."

After *Verdugo-Urquidez*, the Court of Appeals for the District of Columbia Circuit considered a case, more directly applicable to the facts at issue here, involving a Guatemalan citizen and high-ranking member of a Guatemalan rebel organization who was allegedly tortured in Guatemala at the behest of CIA officials, who had ordered and directed the torture and then engaged in an eighteen-month cover-up. *Harbury v. Deutch*, 344 U.S. App. D.C. 68, 233 F.3d 596 (D.C. Cir. 2000), *rev'd on other grounds sub nom., Christopher v. Harbury*, 536 U.S. 403 (2002). The constitutional violations at issue in *Harbury* included torture. Moreover, the torture was allegedly planned and orchestrated by U.S. officials acting within the United States. Thus, unlike *Eisentrager* and *Verdugo-Urquidez*, the factual background of *Harbury* is closely related to the case at bar.

The D.C. Circuit relied heavily on dicta in *Verdugo-Urquidez*, particularly its reading of *Eisentrager*, to ultimately hold that the decedent's wife (a U.S. citizen) could not bring a Fifth Amendment claim on his behalf for the torture he suffered in Guatemala. The D.C. Circuit noted, first, that *Verdugo-Urquidez* did not attach constitutional significance to the fact "that the search was both planned and ordered from within the United States. Instead, it focused on the location of the primary constitutionally significant conduct at issue: the search and seizure itself." Because of this, the D.C. Circuit found that "the primary constitutionally relevant conduct at issue here — [the deceased's] torture — occurred outside the United States."

The D.C. circuit further noted that *Verdugo-Urquidez* read *Eisentrager* to "emphatically" reject the notion of any extraterritorial application of the Fifth Amendment. That language, although "dicta . . . is firm and considered dicta that binds this court."

Still, the case at bar, unlike *Harbury,* presents a claim of torture by an alien apprehended at the U.S. border and held here pending removal; furthermore, the fact that Arar's alleged torture began with his removal from the territory of the United States makes this case factually different from *Harbury.* Nevertheless, by answering the question "whether the Fifth Amendment prohibits torture of non-resident foreign nationals living abroad" in the negative, *Harbury* appears to have important implications for the case at bar.

However, in *Rasul v. Bush,* 542 U.S. 466 (2004), the Supreme Court issued a ruling potentially favorable to Arar. *Rasul* considered the statutory habeas claims of two Australian and twelve Kuwaiti citizens captured abroad, who challenged the legality of their detention at the Guantánamo Bay Naval Base. The Supreme Court extended statutory habeas jurisdiction to the detainees, finding that they could challenge their detention in Guantánamo Bay, a territory over which "the United States . . . exercise[s] complete jurisdiction and control."

To be sure, there is no argument that the United States exercises the same control over the Syrian officials alleged to have detained and tortured Arar as it does in the case of Guantánamo Bay. Nevertheless, one might read *Rasul* as extending habeas jurisdiction to a group of aliens with even less of a connection to the United States than Arar.

Defendants reject that contention, arguing that, in light of the above-cited cases, the substantive due process violations asserted in Arar's complaint "are predicated upon a constitutional protection that has never been extended to arriving aliens, much less aliens whom the executive has determined pursuant to legislative authorization have terrorist connections."

Another difference between *Rasul* and the case at bar is that *Rasul* based its jurisdiction on the statutory habeas provision (28 U.S.C. § 2241), not the U.S. Constitution. Arar, by contrast, alleges substantive constitutional claims not addressed in *Rasul.*

At this juncture, the question whether the *Due Process Clause* vests Arar with substantive rights is unresolved. Assuming, without resolving, the existence of some substantive protection, Arar's claims are foreclosed under an exception to the *Bivens* doctrine.

SPECIAL FACTORS COUNSELING HESITATION

The substantive due process analysis notwithstanding, the Supreme Court's creation of a *Bivens* remedy for alleged constitutional violations by federal officials is subject to certain prudential limitations and exceptions. The Supreme Court has "expressly cautioned . . . that such a remedy will not be available when 'special factors counseling hesitation' are present." Those factors do not concern "the merits of the particular remedy [being] sought. Rather, they involve "the question of who should decide whether such a remedy should be provided." [C]ourts will refrain from extending a *Bivens* claim if doing so trammels upon matters best decided by coordinate branches of government.

Defendants argue that this court should decline to extend a *Bivens* remedy in light of the national-security concerns and foreign policy decisions at the heart of this case. Such determinations, they claim, are uniquely reserved to the political branches of government and counsel against the extension of a damages remedy here.

This case undoubtedly presents broad questions touching on the role of the Executive branch in combating terrorist forces — namely the prevention of future terrorist attacks within U.S. borders by capturing or containing members of those groups who seek to inflict damage on this country and its people. Success in these efforts requires coordination between law-enforcement and foreign-policy officials; complex relationships with foreign governments are also involved. In light of these factors, courts must proceed cautiously in reviewing constitutional and statutory claims in that arena, especially where they raise policy-making issues that are the prerogative of coordinate branches of government.

A number of considerations must be noted here. First, Article I, Section 8 of the U.S. Constitution places the regulation of aliens squarely within the authority of the Legislative branch. Congress has yet to take any affirmative position on federal-court review of renditions; indeed, by withholding any explicit grant of a private cause of action under the Torture Victim Protection Act to plaintiffs like Arar, the opposite is the more reasonable inference.

Second, this case raises crucial national-security and foreign policy considerations, implicating "the complicated multilateral negotiations concerning efforts to halt international terrorism." The propriety of these considerations, including supposed agreements between the United States and foreign governments regarding intelligence-gathering in the context of the efforts to combat terrorism, are most appropriately reserved to the Executive and Legislative branches of government. Moreover, the need for much secrecy can hardly be doubted. One need not have much imagination to contemplate the negative effect on our relations with Canada if discovery were to proceed in this case and were it to turn out that certain high Canadian officials had, despite public denials, acquiesced in Arar's removal to Syria. More generally, governments that do not wish to acknowledge publicly that they are assisting us would certainly hesitate to do so if our judicial discovery process could compromise them. Even a ruling sustaining state-secret-based objections to a request for interrogatories, discovery demand or questioning of a witness could be compromising. Depending on the context it could be construed as the equivalent of a public admission that the alleged conduct had occurred in the manner claimed — to the detriment of our relations with foreign countries, whether friendly or not. Hence, extending a *Bivens* remedy "could significantly disrupt the ability of the political branches to respond to foreign situations involving our national interest."

On a related point, despite plaintiff's counsel's contention to the contrary at oral argument, the qualified immunity defense, which works effectively in the domestic sphere to protect officials in the performance of their duties, is not a sufficient protection for officials operating in the national-security and foreign policy contexts. This is because the ability to define the line between appropriate and inappropriate conduct, in those areas, is not, as stated earlier, one in which judges possess any special competence. Moreover, it is an area in which the law has not been developed or specifically spelled out in legislation. Nor can we ignore the fact that an erroneous decision can have adverse consequences in the foreign realm not likely to occur in the domestic context. For example, a judge who, because of his or her experience living in the community, rejects a police claim that a certain demonstration is potentially violent and, as a result, allows the demonstration to proceed over the objections of these law-enforcement officials faces a much smaller risk that this decision will result in serious consequences even if, with the benefit of hindsight, his or her judgment turns out to be wrong. On the other hand, a judge who declares on his or her own Article III authority that the policy of extraordinary rendition is under all circumstances unconstitutional must acknowledge that such a ruling can have the most serious of consequences to our foreign relations or national security or both.

Accordingly, the task of balancing individual rights against national-security concerns is one that courts should not undertake without the guidance or the authority of the coordinate branches, in whom the Constitution imposes responsibility for our foreign affairs and national security. Those branches have the responsibility to determine whether judicial oversight is appropriate. Without explicit legislation, judges should be hesitant to fill an arena that, until now, has been left untouched — perhaps deliberately — by the Legislative and Executive branches. To do otherwise would threaten "our customary policy of deference to the President in matters of foreign affairs." In sum, whether the policy be seeking to undermine or overthrow foreign governments, or rendition, judges should not, in the absence of explicit direction by Congress, hold officials who carry out such policies liable for damages even if such conduct violates our treaty obligations or customary international law.

For these reasons, I conclude that a remedy under *Bivens* for Arar's alleged rendition to Syria is foreclosed. Accordingly, Counts 2 and 3 of the complaint are dismissed.

Detention Within the United States

Count 4 of Arar's complaint challenges his thirteen-day period of detention within the United States, during which time he alleges he was denied access to counsel and subjected to coercive and involuntary custodial interrogation. This included being placed in a cell at JFK Airport with lights remaining on all night, the denial of telephone privileges and adequate food, denial of access to his consulate and verbal attacks by interrogators. Arar's complaint further alleges that he was involuntarily subjected to coercive interrogation "for excessively long periods of time and at odd hours of the day and night" and was "placed in solitary confinement, shackled, chained, strip-searched and deprived of sleep and food for extended periods of time." The interrogation was "designed to overcome his will and compel incriminating statements from him.."

An individual in Arar's shoes, detained at the U.S. border and held pending removal, does not officially effect an "entry into the United States." Instead, such a person is " 'treated,' for constitutional purposes, 'as if stopped at the border.' "

Arar's rights in the U.S. are by no means nonexistent. The First Circuit, affirming a lower court denial of habeas petitions, noted various constitutional guarantees afforded excludable aliens. The court noted that excludable aliens "have *personal* constitutional protections against illegal government action of various kinds; the mere fact that one is an excludable alien would not permit a police officer savagely to beat him, or a court to impose a standardless death penalty as punishment for having committed a criminal offense." [The Fifth and Eleventh Circuits similarly noted constitutional protections against abuse of aliens present but not fully admitted to the U.S.]

In sum, Count 4, construed most favorably to plaintiff, alleges a possible "gross physical abuse" due process violation and perhaps a limited denial of access to counsel right (apart from the rendition aspect of the claim).

Having dismissed Counts 2 and 3 of the complaint under the special factors precluding *Bivens* relief, the only remaining question is whether Count 4, if still viable, is subject to a defense under the qualified immunity doctrine. Defendants argue that none of the claimed violations raised in Arar's complaint could have been deemed clearly established under law at the time the events took place.

"Government officials performing discretionary functions generally are shielded from liability for civil damages insofar as their conduct does not violate clearly established statutory or constitutional rights of which a reasonable person would have known." *Harlow v. Fitzgerald*, 457 U.S. 800 (1982). Excluding the rendition aspect of the claim, the alleged "gross physical abuse" in the United States in Count 4 involved deprivations that would appear to violate clearly established rights. Such treatment, if true, may well violate the basic standards for a detainee in *any* context — civil, criminal, immigration, or otherwise — and possibly constitute conduct that a defendant could reasonably foresee giving rise to liability for damages.

Defendants note, however, that the complaint lacks the requisite amount of personal involvement needed to bring a claim against them in their individual capacities or even to establish personal jurisdiction. Indeed, at this point, the allegations against the individually named defendants do not adequately detail which defendants directed, ordered and/or supervised the alleged violations of Arar's due process rights, as defined in section (5) of this opinion, or whether any of the defendants were otherwise aware, but failed to take action, while Arar was in U.S. custody. Accordingly, all claims against the individual defendants are dismissed without prejudice with leave for plaintiff to replead Count 4.

STATE-SECRETS PRIVILEGE

The United States, invoking the state-secrets privilege, has moved for summary judgment with respect to Counts 1, 2 and 3 of the complaint. The government has submitted declarations from former Deputy Attorney General James B. Comey and former Secretary of the U.S. Department of Homeland Security Tom Ridge, attesting that foreign affairs considerations are involved in this case. Certain defendants, noting the invocation of that privilege, argue that it constitutes yet a further reason warranting dismissal of any *Bivens* claim.

I determined that before addressing the state-secrets privilege, it would be more appropriate to resolve the motions to dismiss the statutory and constitutional claims because it was not clear how the confidentiality of such information could be maintained without prejudicing my ability to hear and fairly respond to plaintiff's arguments. Now that those Counts have been dismissed on other grounds, the issue involving state secrets is moot.

The United States does not seek to dismiss Count 4 on grounds of state-secrets privilege. The individual defendants, however, have asserted that all counts — including 4 — must be dismissed against them in light of the invocation of privilege by the United States. Because, as this court construes Count 4, the issue of state secrets is of little or no relevance, the individually named defendants' assertion that Count 4 must be dismissed with respect to them in light of the privilege is denied at this time. Should an amended complaint alter that picture, the issue can be addressed at that time.

CONCLUSION

1. [Because he is not likely to incur a similar experience in the future,] Arar lacks standing to bring a claim for declaratory relief against plaintiffs in their official capacities, and thus those claims are denied.

2. With respect to claims under the Torture Victim Protection Act against defendants in their personal capacities, plaintiff as a non-citizen is unable to demonstrate that he has a viable cause of action under that statute or that defendants were acting under "color of law, of any foreign nation." Accordingly, Count 1 is dismissed with prejudice.

3. With respect to claims alleging that defendants violated Arar's rights to substantive due process by removing him to Syria and subjecting him to torture, coercive interrogation and detention in Syria, the INA does not foreclose jurisdiction over plaintiff's claims. Nonetheless, no cause of action under *Bivens* can be extended given the national-security and foreign policy considerations at stake. Accordingly, Counts 2 and 3 are dismissed with prejudice.

4. With respect the claim that Arar was deprived of due process or other constitutional rights by the defendants during his period of domestic detention, prior cases holding that inadmissible aliens deserve little due process protection are inapplicable because Arar was not attempting to effect an entry into the United States; in any event, the circumstances and conditions of confinement to which Arar was

subjected while in U.S. custody may potentially raise *Bivens* claims. However, plaintiff must replead those claims without regard to any rendition claim and name those defendants that were personally involved in the alleged unconstitutional treatment. Count 4 is therefore, dismissed without prejudice.

5. Claims against all ten John Doe law enforcement agents named in connection with that Count 4 are dismissed without prejudice as well, with leave to replead.

NOTES AND QUESTIONS

1. *Wilson v. Libby*, 498 F. Supp. 2d 74 (D.D.C. 2007). The "state secrets" doctrine was employed to create an explicit exception to the Bivens doctrine in the suit by Valerie Plame against Scooter Libby based on his disclosure of her CIA employment to the press.

> Defendants argue that creating a private right of action for the disclosure of covert identity would "be inimical to" the Executive Branch's broad exercise of discretion to protect information pertaining to national security. The need to maintain Executive Branch discretion regarding the protection of national security information raises serious questions of justiciability with respect to a civil damages remedy for unauthorized disclosure of covert identity. In particular, the doctrine established in *Totten v. United States*, 92 U.S. 105 (1876), "prohibit[s] suits against the Government based on covert espionage agreements." *Tenet v. Doe*, 544 U.S. 1, 3 (2005). The *Totten* Court stated "as a general principle, that public policy forbids the maintenance of any suit in a court of justice, the trial of which would inevitably lead to the disclosure of matters which the law itself regards as confidential, and respecting which it will not allow the confidence to be violated." This broad prohibition applies to suits alleging constitutional violations: "No matter the clothing in which alleged spies dress their claims, Totten precludes judicial review in cases . . . where success depends upon the existence of their secret espionage relationship with the Government."

2. *In re Iraq and Afghanistan Detainees Litigation*, 479 F. Supp. 2d 85 (D.D.C. 2007). In what it described as a "lamentable case," complete with details of the despicable treatment to which some detainees were subjected in Abu Ghraib and Afghanistan, the D.C. District Court reached a similar conclusion. In addition to the "crucial national-security and foreign policy considerations" discussed by Judge Trager, the D.C. court engaged in a more extended discussion of Eisentrager and its progeny because the plaintiffs in these cases had never attempted to enter the U.S. and indeed were detained in areas of active hostilities.

> The plaintiffs, as well as *amici* [retired military officers], contest the notion that a *Bivens* remedy would impose judicial oversight over military decision-making and chill military effectiveness on the battlefield, arguing instead that "providing an effective remedy for the violation of Plaintiffs' constitutional rights would be wholly consonant with longstanding military laws and regulations and would not entangle the Court in any inappropriate inquiry." The Court cautions against the myopic approach advocated by the plaintiffs and amici, which essentially frames the issue as whether torture is universally prohibited and thereby warrants a judicially-created remedy under the circumstances. There is no getting around the fact that authorizing monetary damages remedies against military officials engaged in an active war would invite enemies to use our own federal courts to obstruct the Armed Forces' ability to act decisively and without hesitation in defense of our liberty and national interests, a prospect the Supreme Court found intolerable in *Eisentrager*.

3. *Padilla v. Yoo*. On January 4, 2008, Jose Padilla filed an action for nominal damages against John Yoo on the basis that Yoo's authorship of memos involving detention and torture had violated his constitutional rights. The Padilla complaint recites these theories of recovery:

Defendant Yoo proximately and foreseeably injured Mr. Padilla by violating numerous clearly established constitutional and statutory rights including, but not limited to, the following:

a. Denial of Access to Counsel. Acting under color of law and his authority as a federal officer, Defendant Yoo violated Mr. Padilla's right of access to legal counsel protected by the First, Fifth, and Sixth Amendments to the U.S. Constitution.

b. Denial of Access to Court. Acting under color of law and his authority as a federal officer, Defendant Yoo violated Mr. Padilla's right of access to court protected by the First and Fifth Amendments to the U.S. Constitution, Article III of the U.S. Constitution, and the Habeas Suspension Clause of the U.S. Constitution.

c. Unconstitutional Conditions of Confinement. Acting under color of law and his authority as a federal officer, Defendant Yoo subjected Mr. Padilla to illegal conditions of confinement and treatment that shocks the conscience in violation of Mr. Padilla's Fifth Amendment rights to procedural and substantive due process, as well as his Eighth Amendment right to be free of cruel and unusual punishment, including torture, outrages on personal dignity, and humiliating and degrading treatment.

d. Unconstitutional Interrogations. Acting under color of law and his authority as a federal officer, Defendant Yoo subjected Mr. Padilla to coercive and involuntary illegal interrogations, both directly and through unlawful conditions of confinement designed to aid the interrogation, all in violation of Mr. Padilla's Fifth Amendment rights to procedural due process, freedom from treatment that shocks the conscience, and freedom from self-incrimination, as well as his Eighth Amendment right to be free from cruel and unusual punishment, including torture, outrages on personal dignity, and humiliating and degrading treatment.

e. Denial of Freedom of Religion. Acting under color of law and his authority as a federal officer, Defendant Yoo violated Mr. Padilla's right to the free exercise of religion guaranteed under the First Amendment to the U.S. Constitution, as well as the Religious Freedom Restoration Act, 42 U.S.C. § 2000bb.

f. Denial of the Right to Information. Acting under color of law and his authority as federal officer, Defendant Yoo violated Mr. Padilla's right to information guaranteed under the First Amendment to the U.S. Constitution.

g. Denial of the Right to Association. Acting under color of law and his authority as a federal officer, Defendant Yoo violated Mr. Padilla's right to association with family and others guaranteed under the First Amendment to the U.S. Constitution.

h. Unconstitutional Military Detention. Acting under color of law and his authority as a federal officer, Defendant Yoo violated Mr. Padilla's right to be free from military detention guaranteed by the Fourth Amendment to the U.S. Constitution, the Due Process Clause of the Fifth Amendment to the U.S. Constitution, the Habeas Suspension and Treason Clauses of the U.S. Constitution, and Article III of the U.S. Constitution.

i. Denial of Due Process. Acting under color of law and his authority as a federal officer, Defendant Yoo violated Mr. Padilla's Fifth Amendment right not to be detained or subjected to the collateral effects of designation as an "enemy combatant" without due process of law.

Because Padilla was a U.S. citizen imprisoned and interrogated within the U.S., the

Eisentrager rationale does not apply. The principal questions will be whether the Government invokes the "state secrets" privilege and the extent of prosecutorial immunity. (To the extent that the suit alleges constitutional violations, 28 U.S.C. § 2679(b)(2) prevents it from being converted to a suit under the Federal Tort Claims Act.)

[C]   The International Scene

REPUBLIC OF IRELAND v. UNITED KINGDOM
European Court of Human Rights
(Series A, No 25) (1979–80) 2 EHRR 25

HEADNOTE:

The British Government, faced with serious acts of terrorism perpretrated by members of the Irish Republican Army (IRA) and Loyalist groups in Northern Ireland, introduced special powers of arrest and detention without trial, which were widely used, chiefly against the IRA. Notices of derogation under Article 15(1) were lodged with the Secretary-General of the Council of Europe in view of the ?public emergency threatening the life of the nation.' The Government of the Republic of Ireland brought an application before the Commission alleging, inter alia, (i) that the extrajudicial detention infringed Article 5 (right to liberty) and was not saved by Article 15; (ii) that various interrogation practices — in particular the so-called 'five techniques,' which included wall-standing, hooding and deprivation of sleep and food — and other practices to which suspects were subjected amounted to torture and inhuman or degrading treatment contrary to Article 3; and (iii) that the use of the special powers primarily against IRA members constituted discrimination in violation of Article 14. The Commission unanimously found that the five techniques did constitute a practice of torture and that other practices amounted to inhuman and degrading treatment; but that there was no infringement of Article 14, and the derogations from Article 5 were justified under Article 15. The applicant Government referred the case to the Court (although the offending practices had been discontinued and the respondent Government did not contest the allegations or the findings in connection with the five techniques), renewing its original submissions and asking the Court in addition to address a consequential order to the British Government requiring it to institute criminal and disciplinary proceedings against the particular persons responsible for the breaches of Article 3. The case was heard by the plenary Court.

FACTS:

11. The tragic and lasting crisis in Northern Ireland lies at the root of the present case. In order to combat what the respondent Government describes as 'the longest and most violent terrorist campaign witnessed in either part of the island of Ireland,' the authorities in Northern Ireland exercised from August 1971 until December 1975 a series of extrajudicial powers of arrest, detention and internment. The proceedings in this case concern the scope and the operation in practice of those measures as well as the alleged ill-treatment of persons thereby deprived of their liberty.

12. Up to March 1975, over 1,100 people had been killed, over 11,500 injured and more than £140,000,000 worth of property destroyed during the recent troubles in Northern Ireland. This violence found its expression in part in civil disorders, in part in terrorism, that is, organised violence for political ends.

34. It was against the background outlined above that on 9 August 1971 the Northern Ireland Government brought into operation extrajudicial measures of detention and internment of suspected terrorists. From then until 7 November 1972, when certain of the Special Powers Regulations were replaced, the authorities in

Northern Ireland in fact exercised four such extrajudicial powers: (i) arrest for interrogation purposes during 48 hours; (ii) arrest and remand in custody; (iii) detention of an arrested person; and (iv) internment.

96. Twelve persons arrested on 9 August 1971 and two persons arrested in October 1971 were singled out and taken to one or more unidentified centres. There, between 11 and 17 August and 11 to 18 October respectively, they were submitted to a form of 'interrogation in depth' which involved the combined application of five particular techniques. These methods, sometimes termed 'disorientation' or 'sensory deprivation' techniques, were not used in any cases other than the 14 so indicated above. The techniques consisted of the following:

(a) wall-standing: forcing the detainees to remain for periods of some hours in a 'stress position,' described by those who underwent it as being 'spreadeagled against the wall, with their fingers put high above the head against the wall, the legs spread apart and the feet back, causing them to stand on their toes with the weight of the body mainly on the fingers';

(b) hooding: putting a black or navy coloured bag over the detainees' heads and, at least initially, keeping it there all the time except during interrogation;

(c) subjection to noise: pending their interrogations, holding the detainees in a room where there was a continuous loud and hissing noise;

(d) deprivation of sleep: pending their interrogations, depriving the detainees of sleep;

(e) deprivation of food and drink: subjecting the detainees to a reduced diet during their stay at the centre and pending interrogations.

97. From the start, it has been conceded by the respondent Government that the use of the five techniques was authorised at 'high level.' Although never committed to writing or authorised in any official document, the techniques had been orally taught to members of the RUC by the English Intelligence Centre as at seminar held in April 1971.

98. The two operations of interrogation in depth by means of the five techniques led to the obtaining of a considerable quantity of intelligence information, including the identification of 700 members of both IRA factions and the discovery of individual responsibility for about 85 previously unexplained criminal incidents.

99. Reports alleging physical brutality and ill-treatment by the security forces were made public within a few days. A committee of enquiry under the chairmanship of Sir Edmund Compton was appointed by the United Kingdom Government on 31 August 1971 to investigate such allegations. Among the 40 cases this Committee examined were 11 cases of persons subjected to the five techniques in August 1971; its findings were that interrogation in depth by means of the techniques constituted physical ill-treatment but not physical brutality as it understood that term.

100. The Compton reports came under considerable criticism in the United Kingdom. On 16 November 1971, the British Home Secretary announced that a further Committee had been set up under the chairmanship of Lord Parker of Waddington to consider 'whether, and if so in what respects, the procedures currently authorised for interrogation of persons suspected of terrorism and for their custody while subject to interrogation require amendment.' The Parker report, adopted on 31 January 1972, contained a majority and a minority opinion. The majority report concluded that the application of the techniques, subject to recommended safeguards against excessive use, need not be ruled out on moral grounds. On the other hand, the minority report by Lord Gardiner disagreed that such interrogation procedures were morally justifiable, even in emergency terrorist conditions. Both the majority and the minority considered the methods to be illegal under domestic law, although the majority confined their view to English law and to 'some if not all the techniques.'

101. The Parker report was published on 2 March 1972. On the same day, the United

Kingdom Prime Minister stated in Parliament that the techniques would not be used in future as an aid to interrogation. As foreshadowed in the Prime Minister's statement, directives expressly prohibiting the use of the techniques, whether singly or in combination, were then issued to the security forces by the Government.

102. At the hearing before the Court on 8 February 1977, the United Kingdom Attorney-General declared that the 'five techniques' would not in any circumstances be reintroduced as an aid to interrogation.

The Commission found no physical injury to have resulted from the application of the five techniques as such, but loss of weight by the two case-witnesses and acute psychiatric symptoms developed by them during interrogation were recorded in the medical and other evidence. The Commission was unable to establish the exact degree of any psychiatric after-effects produced on T6 and T13, but on the general level it was satisfied that some psychiatric after-effects in certain of the 14 persons subjected to the techniques could not be excluded.

150. Article 3 provides that 'no one shall be subjected to torture or to inhuman or degrading treatment or punishment.'

The Merits

162. As was emphasised by the Commission, ill-treatment must attain a minimum level of severity if it is to fall within the scope of Article 3. The assessment of this minimum is, in the nature of things, relative; it depends on all the circumstances of the case, such as the duration of the treatment, its physical or mental effects and, in some cases, the sex, age and state of health of the victim, etc.

163. The Convention prohibits in absolute terms torture and inhuman or degrading treatment or punishment, irrespective of the victim's conduct. Unlike most of the substantive clauses of the Convention and of Protocols 1 and 4, Article 3 makes no provision for exceptions and, under Article 15(2), there can be no derogation therefrom even in the event of a public emergency threatening the life of the nation.

164. In the instant case, the only relevant concepts are 'torture' and 'inhuman or degrading treatment,' to the exclusion of 'inhuman or degrading punishment.'

(a) The 'five techniques'

165. The facts concerning the five techniques are summarised at paragraphs 96–104 and 106–107 above. In the Commission's estimation, those facts constituted a practice not only of inhuman and degrading treatment but also of torture. The applicant Government ask for confirmation of this opinion which is not contested before the Court by the respondent Government.

167. The five techniques were applied in combination, with premeditation and for hours at a stretch; they caused, if not actual bodily injury, at least intense physical and mental suffering to the persons subjected thereto and also led to acute psychiatric disturbances during interrogation. They accordingly fell into the category of inhuman treatment within the meaning of Article 3. The techniques were also degrading since they were such as to arouse in their victims feelings of fear, anguish and inferiority capable of humiliating and debasing them and possibly breaking their physical or moral resistance.

On these two points, the Court is of the same view as the Commission.

In order to determine whether the five techniques should also be qualified as torture, the Court must have regard to the distinction, embodied in Article 3, between this notion and that of inhuman or degrading treatment.

In the Court's view, this distinction derives principally from a difference in the intensity of the suffering inflicted.

The Court considers in fact that, whilst there exists on the one hand violence which is to be condemned both on moral grounds and also in most cases under the domestic law of the Contracting States but which does not fall within Article 3 of the Convention, it appears on the other hand that it was the intention that the Convention, with its distinction between 'torture' and 'inhuman or degrading treatment,' should by the first of these terms attach a special stigma to deliberate inhuman treatment causing very serious and cruel suffering.

Moreover, this seems to be the thinking lying behind Article 1 . . . of Resolution 3452 (XXX) adopted by the General Assembly of the United Nations on 9 December, 1975, which declares: 'Torture constitutes an aggravated and deliberate form of cruel, inhuman or degrading treatment or punishment.'

Although the five techniques, as applied in combination, undoubtedly amounted to inhuman and degrading treatment, although their object was the extraction of confessions, the naming of others and/or information and although they were used systematically, they did not occasion suffering of the particular intensity and cruelty implied by the word torture as so understood.

168. The Court concludes that recourse to the five techniques amounted to a practice of inhuman and degrading treatment, which practice was in breach of Article 3.

According to the applicant Government (Ireland), the violence in question should also be classified, in some cases, as torture.

On the basis of the data before it, the Court does not share this view. Admittedly, the acts complained of often occurred during interrogation and, to this extent, were aimed at extracting confessions, the naming of others and/or information, but the severity of the suffering that they were capable of causing did not attain the particular level inherent in the notion of torture as understood by the Court.

NOTES AND QUESTIONS

1. **Torture and Inhumane Treatment.** The ECHR draws a distinction between torture and inhumane treatment that will become important in the American prisoner abuse cases. Is there any significance to the distinction, however, in terms of the European Covenant?

The distinction is perhaps more important in applying the International Convention on Torture and Other Cruel, Inhuman or Degrading Treatment or Punishment, which carries this definition:

> Article 1. For purposes of this Convention, the term "torture" means any act by which severe pain or suffering, whether physical or mental, is intentionally inflicted on a person for such purposes as obtaining from him or a third person information or a confession, punishing him for an act he or a third person has committed or is suspected of having committed, or intimidating or coercing him or a third person, or for any reason based on discrimination of any kind, when such pain or suffering is inflicted by or at the instigation of or with the consent or acquiescence of a public official or other person acting in an official capacity.

In addition, in Article 16, signatory nations

> undertake to prevent in any territory under its jurisdiction other acts of cruel, inhuman or degrading treatment or punishment which do not amount to torture as defined in article 1.

Under the Convention, signatory nations commit to make torture a criminal offense, whereas they merely "undertake to prevent" inhumane treatment. Does that mean that practices short of torture are still "legal" in a signatory nation? under international law?

2. **TVPA.** U.S. cases dealing with torture have been brought under either the Torture Victims Protection Act, codified as a note to the Alien Tort Claims Act, 28 U.S.C. § 1350. *See Filartiga v. Pena-Irala*, 630 F.2d 876 (2d Cir. 1980) (holding that international law can be the basis of federal question jurisdiction under Article III); *Tel-Oren v. Libyan Arab Republic*, 726 F.2d 774 (D.C. Cir. 1984) (adopting similar conclusion over the

objection of Judge Bork that general incorporation of international law exceeds Congress' jurisdictional grants). Professor Bradley argues that federal jurisdiction for civil actions by aliens for torture committed by other aliens outside the U.S. is difficult to justify because there is no extraterritorial federal law for the courts to apply. By contrast, criminal actions can be brought within federal court jurisdiction because Congress can act to enforce international law under its power to "define and punish offenses against the law of nations." Curtis Bradley, *Universal Jurisdiction and U.S. Law*, 2001 U. CHI. LEGAL FORUM 323.

NOTE ON THE ISRAELI INTERROGATION EXPERIENCE

As a result of some highly publicized incidents involving Israeli interrogation of Palestinian suspects, in 1987 a Commission of Inquiry appointed by then-Justice Moshe Landau issued a report usually called the Landau Commission Report. The report recognized that some degree of coercion is inherent in any interrogation, even if it is nothing other than the presence and appearance of the interrogator. The Commission went on to decide that in the face of threats to public safety, a "moderate degree of pressure, including physical pressure, in order to obtain crucial information, is unavoidable under certain circumstances. Such circumstances include situations in which information sought from a detainee believed to be personally involved in serious terrorist activities can prevent imminent murder, or where the detainee possesses vital information on a terrorist organization which could not be uncovered by any other source (for example, location of arms or caches of explosives for planned acts of terrorism)."

The Landau Commission then attempted to outline guidelines for the use of force in interrogations.

(i) Disproportionate exertion of pressure on the suspect is not permissible — pressure must never reach the level of physical torture or maltreatment of the suspect, or grievous harm to his honour which deprives him of his human dignity.

(ii) The use of less serious measures must be weighed against the degree of anticipated danger, according to the information in the possession of the interrogator.

(iii) The physical and psychological means of pressure permitted for use by an interrogator must be defined and limited in advance, by issuing binding directives.

(iv) There must be strict supervision of the implementation in practice of the directives given to GSS interrogators.

(v) The interrogators' supervisors must react firmly and without hesitation to every deviation from the permissible, imposing disciplinary punishment, and in serious cases, causing criminal proceedings to be instituted against the offending interrogator.

In addition to the general guidelines, the Commission provided a detailed set of limits that were to be kept secret so that terrorists would not be able to train and prepare for interrogation knowing the limits to which they might be subjected.

The recommendations of the Commission were accepted by the Government and put into place as guidance for the General Security Service. Following the report, the Supreme Court received occasional petitions from counsel for prisoners seeking injunctions against the use of any physical pressure in their interrogation. In one controversial case, *Hamdan v. GSS* (HCJ 8049/96), the court first granted an injunction and then cancelled it on a showing by GSS that Hamdan likely had information that would be critical to disrupting a dangerous plot.

PUBLIC COMMITTEE AGAINST
TORTURE v. GENERAL SECURITY SERVICE
Israel Supreme Court HCJ No. 5100/94 (1999)

PRESIDENT A. BARAK.

The General Security Service [hereinafter the "GSS"] investigates individuals suspected of committing crimes against Israel's security. Authorization for these interrogations is granted by directives that regulate interrogation methods. These directives authorize investigators to apply physical means against those undergoing interrogation, including shaking the suspect and placing him in the "Shabach" position. These methods are permitted since they are seen as immediately necessary to save human lives. Are these interrogation practices legal? These are the issues before us.

Background

1. Ever since it was established, the State of Israel has been engaged in an unceasing struggle for its security — indeed, its very existence. Terrorist organizations have set Israel's annihilation as their goal. Terrorist acts and the general disruption of order are their means of choice. In employing such methods, these groups do not distinguish between civilian and military targets. They carry out terrorist attacks in which scores are murdered in public areas — in areas of public transportation, city squares and centers, theaters and coffee shops. They do not distinguish between men, women and children. They act out of cruelty and without mercy. (For an in depth description of this phenomenon see the Report of the Commission of Inquiry Regarding the Interrogation Practices of the GSS with Respect to Hostile Terrorist Activities headed by Justice (ret.) M. Landau, 1987 [hereinafter the Report of the Commission of Inquiry]. *See* 1 THE LANDAU BOOK 269, 276 (1995).

The facts before this Court reveal that 121 people died in terrorist attacks between January 1, 1996 and May 14, 1998. Seven hundred and seven people were injured. A large number of those killed and injured were victims of harrowing suicide bombings in the heart of Israel's cities. Many attacks — including suicide bombings, attempts to detonate car bombs, kidnappings of citizens and soldiers, attempts to highjack buses, murders, and the placing of explosives — were prevented due to daily measures taken by authorities responsible for fighting terrorist activities. The GSS is the main body responsible for fighting terrorism.

In order to fulfill this function, the GSS also investigates those suspected of hostile terrorist activities. The purpose of these interrogations includes the gathering of information regarding terrorists in order to prevent them from carrying out terrorist attacks. In the context of these interrogations, GSS investigators also make use of physical means.

The Petitions

2. These petitions are concerned with the interrogation methods of the GSS. They outline several of these methods in detail. Two of the petitions are of a public nature. One of these is brought by the Public Committee against Torture in Israel. It submits that GSS investigators are not authorized to investigate those suspected of hostile terrorist activities. Moreover, they claim that the GSS is not entitled to employ those methods approved by the Report of the Commission of Inquiry, such as "the application of non-violent psychological pressure" and of "a moderate degree of physical pressure." The second petition is brought by the Association for Civil Rights in Israel. It argues that the GSS should be ordered to cease shaking suspects during interrogations.

The five remaining petitions involve individual petitioners. They each petitioned the Court to hold that the methods used against them by the GSS are illegal.

3. [Two arrested persons] petitioned the Court for an order nisi prohibiting the use of physical force against them during their interrogation. The Court granted the order.

The two petitioners were released from custody prior to the hearing. As per their request, we have elected to continue hearing their case, in light of the importance of the issues they raise.

4. Petitioner Hat'm Abu Zayda . . . complained of the interrogation methods allegedly used against him, including sleep deprivation, shaking, beatings, and use of the "Shabach" position. We immediately ordered the petition be heard. The Court was then informed that petitioner's interrogation had ended. Petitioner was subsequently convicted of activities in the military branch of the Hamas terrorist organization. He was sentenced to 74 months in prison. During oral arguments, it was asserted that the information provided by petitioner during his interrogation led to the thwarting of a plan to carry out serious terrorist attacks, including the kidnapping of soldiers.

5. [Petitioner] Ganimat . . . claimed to have been tortured by his investigators, through use of the "Shabach" position, excessively tight handcuffs, and sleep deprivation. His interrogation revealed that he was involved in numerous terrorist activities, which resulted in the deaths of many Israeli citizens. He was instrumental in the kidnapping and murder of Sharon Edry, an IDF soldier. Additionally, he was involved in the bombing of Cafe "Appropo" in Tel Aviv, in which three women were murdered and thirty people were injured. He was charged with all these crimes and convicted at trial. He was sentenced to five consecutive life sentences plus an additional twenty years in prison.

Subsequent to the dismantling and interrogation of the terrorist cell to which petitioner belonged, a powerful explosive device, identical to the one detonated at Cafe "Appropo" in Tel Aviv, was found in Tzurif, petitioner's village. Uncovering this explosive device thwarted an attack like the one at Cafe "Appropo." According to GSS investigators, the petitioner possessed additional crucial information which he revealed only as a result of the interrogation. Revealing this information immediately was essential to safeguarding national and regional security and preventing danger to human life.

Physical Means

8. The GSS did not describe the physical means employed by GSS investigators. The State Attorney was prepared to present this information in camera. Petitioners opposed this proposal. As such, the information before the Court was provided by the petitioners and was not examined in each individual petition. This having been said, the state did not deny the use of these interrogation methods, and even offered justifications for these methods. This provided the Court with a picture of the interrogation practices of the GSS.

The decision to utilize physical means in a particular instance is based on internal regulations, which requires obtaining permission from the higher ranks of the GSS. The regulations themselves were approved by a special Ministerial Committee on GSS interrogations. Among other guidelines, the committee set forth directives regarding the rank required of an officer who was to authorize such interrogation practices. These directives were not examined by this Court. Different interrogation methods are employed in each situation, depending what is necessary in that situation and the likelihood of obtaining authorization. The GSS does not resort to every interrogation method at its disposal in each case.

Shaking

9. A number of petitioners claimed that they were subject to shaking. Among the investigation methods outlined in the GSS interrogation regulations, shaking is considered the harshest. The method is defined as the forceful and repeated shaking of the suspect's upper torso, in a manner which causes the neck and head to swing rapidly. According to an expert opinion, the shaking method is likely to cause serious brain

damage, harm the spinal cord, cause the suspect to lose consciousness, vomit and urinate uncontrollably and suffer serious headaches.

The state entered several opposing expert opinions into evidence. It admits the use of this method by the GSS. It contends, however, that shaking does not present an inherent danger to the life of the suspect, that the risk to life as a result of shaking is rare, that there is no evidence that shaking causes fatal damage, and that medical literature has not, to date, reported a case in which a person died as a direct result of having been shaken. In any event, they argue, doctors are present at all interrogation areas, and the possibility of medical injury is always investigated.

All agree that, in one particular case, the suspect expired after being shaken. According to the state, that case was a rare exception. Death was caused by an extremely rare complication which resulted in pulmonary edema. In addition, the state argues that the shaking method is only resorted to in very specific cases, and only as a last resort. The directives define the appropriate circumstances for its use, and the rank responsible for authorizing its use. The investigators were instructed that, in every case where they consider the use of shaking, they must examine the severity of the danger that the interrogation is intending to prevent, consider the urgency of uncovering the information presumably possessed by the suspect in question, and seek an alternative means of preventing the danger. Finally, the directives state that, in cases where this method is to be used, the investigator must first provide an evaluation of the suspect's health and ensure that no harm comes to him. According to the respondent, shaking is indispensable to fighting and winning the war on terrorism. It is not possible to prohibit its use without seriously harming the ability of the GSS to effectively thwart deadly terrorist attacks. Its use in the past has lead to the prevention of murderous attacks.

Waiting in the "Shabach" Position

10. This interrogation method arose in several petitions. As per petitioners' submission, a suspect investigated under the "Shabach" position has his hands tied behind his back. He is seated on a small and low chair, whose seat is tilted forward, towards the ground. One hand is tied behind the suspect, and placed inside the gap between the chair's seat and back support. His second hand is tied behind the chair, against its back support. The suspect's head is covered by a sack that falls down to his shoulders. Loud music is played in the room. According to the briefs submitted, suspects are detained in this position for a long period of time, awaiting interrogation.

Petitioners claim that prolonged sitting in this position causes serious muscle pain in the arms, the neck and headaches. The state did not deny the use of this method. It submits that both crucial security considerations and the safety of the investigators require the tying of the suspect's hands as he is being interrogated. The head covering is intended to prevent contact with other suspects. Loud music is played for the same reason.

The "Frog Crouch"

11. This interrogation method appeared in one of the petitions. According to the petition, the suspect was interrogated in a "frog crouch" position. This refers to consecutive, periodical crouches on the tips of one's toes, each lasting for five minute intervals. The state did not deny the use of this method, and the Court issued an order nisi in the petition. Prior to hearing the petition, however, this interrogation practice ceased.

Excessively Tight Handcuffs

12. In a number of petitions, several petitioners complained of excessively tight hand or leg cuffs. They contended that this practice results in serious injuries to the suspect's hands, arms and feet, due to the length of the interrogations. The petitioners contend

that particularly small cuffs were used. The state, for its part, denies the use of unusually small cuffs, arguing that those used were of standard issue and were properly applied. Even so, the state is prepared to admit that prolonged hand or foot cuffing is likely to cause injuries to the suspect's hands and feet. The state contends, however, that injuries of this nature are inherent to any lengthy interrogation.

Sleep Deprivation

13. In a number of petitions, petitioners complained of being deprived of sleep as a result of being tied in the "Shabach" position, while subject to the playing of loud music, or of being subjected to intense non-stop interrogations without sufficient rest breaks. They claim that the purpose of depriving them of sleep is to cause them to break from exhaustion. While the state agrees that suspects are at times deprived of regular sleep hours, it argues that this does not constitute an interrogation method aimed at causing exhaustion, but rather results from the long amount of time necessary for conducting the interrogation.

Petitioners' Arguments

14. All the petitions . . . argue that the physical means employed by GSS investigators not only infringe the human dignity of the suspect undergoing interrogation, but also constitute criminal offences. These methods, argue the petitioners, are in violation of international law as they constitute "torture." Furthermore, the "necessity defense" at most constitutes an exceptional post factum defense, exclusively confined to criminal proceedings against investigators.

We asked petitioners whether the "ticking bomb" rationale was sufficiently persuasive to justify the use of physical means. This rationale would apply in a situation where a bomb is known to have been placed in a public area and will cause human tragedy if its location is not revealed. This question elicited different responses from the petitioners. There are those convinced that physical means are not to be used under any circumstances; the prohibition on such methods, to their mind, is absolute, whatever the consequences may be. On the other hand, there are others who argue that, even if it is acceptable to employ physical means in the exceptional circumstances of the "ticking bomb," these methods are used even in absence of "ticking bomb" conditions. The very fact that the use of such means is illegal in most cases warrants banning their use altogether, even if doing so would include those rare cases in which physical coercion may have been justified. Whatever their individual views, all petitioners unanimously highlight the distinction between the post factum possibility of escaping criminal liability and the advance granting of permission to use physical means for interrogation purposes.

The State's Arguments

15. With respect to the physical means employed by the GSS, the state argues that these methods do not violate international law. Indeed, it is submitted that these methods cannot be described as "torture," as "cruel and inhuman treatment," or as "degrading treatment," which are all strictly prohibited under international law. The state further contends that the practices of the GSS do not cause pain and suffering.

Moreover, the state argues that these means are legal under domestic Israeli law. This is due to the "necessity defense" of article 34(11) of the Penal Law-1977. In the specific cases where the "necessity defense" would apply, GSS investigators are entitled to use "moderate physical pressure" as a last resort in order to prevent real injury to human life and well-being. Such "moderate physical pressure" may include shaking. Resort to such means is legal, and does not constitute a criminal offence. In any case, if a specific method is not deemed to be a criminal offence, there is no reason not to employ it, even for interrogation purposes. According to the state, there is no reason to prohibit a particular act if, in specific circumstances, it does not constitute a crime.

The Report of the Commission of Inquiry

16. The authority of the GSS to employ particular interrogation methods was examined by the Commission of Inquiry. The Commission, appointed by the government . . . concluded that, in cases where the saving of human lives requires obtaining certain information, the investigator is entitled to apply both psychological pressure and "a moderate degree of physical pressure." As such, an investigator who, in the face of such danger, applies a degree of physical pressure, which does not constitute abuse or torture of the suspect, but is proportionate to the danger to human life can, in the face of criminal liability, avail himself of the "necessity defense." The Commission was convinced that its conclusions were not in conflict with international law, but were rather consistent with both the rule of law and the need to effectively protect the security of Israel and its citizens.

The commission approved the use of "moderate degree of physical pressure." Such "moderate physical pressure" could be applied under stringent conditions. Directives to this effect were set out in the second, secret part of the report, and subject to the supervision of bodies both internal and external to the GSS. The commission's recommendations were approved by the government.

The Petitions

17. Until now, it was not possible for the Court to hear the sort of arguments that would provide a complete normative picture, in all its complexity. At this time, in contrast, a number of petitions have properly laid out complete arguments. For this we thank them.

Some of the petitions are rather general or theoretical while others are quite specific. Even so, we have decided to deal with all of them, since we seek to clarify the state of the law in this most complicated question. To this end, we shall . . . examine whether a general power to investigate could potentially sanction the use of physical means — including mental suffering — the likes of which the GSS employs. Finally, we shall examine circumstances where such methods are immediately necessary to rescue human lives and shall decide whether such circumstances justify granting GSS investigators the authority to employ physical interrogation methods.

The Authority to Interrogate

18. The term "interrogation" takes on various meanings in different contexts. For the purposes of these petitions, we refer to the asking of questions which seek to elicit a truthful answer, subject to the privilege against self-incrimination. Generally, the investigation of a suspect is conducted at the suspect's place of detention. Any interrogation inevitably infringes the suspect's freedom — including his human dignity and privacy — even if physical means are not used. In a country adhering to the rule of law, therefore, interrogations are not permitted in absence of clear statutory authorization, whether such authorization is through primary or secondary legislation.

The Means Employed for Interrogation Purposes

21. As we have seen, GSS investigators are endowed with the authority to conduct interrogations. What is the scope of these powers and do they include the use of physical means in the course of the interrogation? Can use be made of the physical means presently employed by GSS investigators — such as shaking, the "Shabach" position, and sleep deprivation — by virtue of the investigating powers given the GSS investigators? Let us note that the state did not argue before us that all the means employed by GSS investigators are permissible by virtue of the "law of interrogation."

Thus, for instance, the state did not make the argument that shaking is permitted simply because it is an "ordinary" method of investigation in Israel.

22. An interrogation, by its very nature, places the suspect in a difficult position. "The criminal's interrogation," wrote Justice Vitkon over twenty years ago, "is not a negotiation process between two open and honest merchants, conducting their affairs in mutual trust." An interrogation is a "competition of minds," in which the investigator attempts to penetrate the suspect's mind and elicit the information that the investigator seeks to obtain.

Indeed, the authority to conduct interrogations, like any administrative power, is designed for a specific purpose, and must be exercised in conformity with the basic principles of the democratic regime. In setting out the rules of interrogation, two values clash. On the one hand, lies the desire to uncover the truth, in accord with the public interest in exposing crime and preventing it. On the other hand is the need to protect the dignity and liberty of the individual being interrogated. This having been said, these values are not absolute. A democratic, freedom-loving society does not accept that investigators may use any means for the purpose of uncovering the truth. "The interrogation practices of the police in a given regime," noted Justice Landau, "are indicative of a regime's very character" At times, the price of truth is so high that a democratic society is not prepared to pay. To the same extent, however, a democratic society, desirous of liberty, seeks to fight crime and, to that end, is prepared to accept that an interrogation may infringe the human dignity and liberty of a suspect — provided that it is done for a proper purpose and that the harm does not exceed that which is necessary.

Our concern, therefore, lies in the clash of values and the balancing of conflicting values. The balancing process results in the rules for a "reasonable interrogation." These rules are based, on the one hand, on preserving the "human image" of the suspect, and on preserving the "purity of arms" used during the interrogation. On the other hand, these rules take into consideration the need to fight crime in general, and terrorist attacks in particular. These rules reflect "a degree of reasonableness, straight thinking, and fairness." The rules pertaining to investigations are important to a democratic state. They reflect its character. An illegal investigation harms the suspect's human dignity. It equally harms society's fabric.

23. Here we deal with the "law of interrogation" as a power of an administrative authority. The "law of interrogation" by its very nature, is intrinsically linked to the circumstances of each case. This having been said, a number of general principles are nonetheless worth noting.

First, a reasonable investigation is necessarily one free of torture, free of cruel, inhuman treatment, and free of any degrading conduct whatsoever. There is a prohibition on the use of "brutal or inhuman means" in the course of an investigation. Human dignity also includes the dignity of the suspect being interrogated. This conclusion is in accord with international treaties, to which Israel is a signatory, which prohibit the use of torture, "cruel, inhuman treatment" and "degrading treatment." *See* M. EVANS & R. MORGAN, PREVENTING TORTURE 61 (1998); N.S. RODLEY, THE TREATMENT OF PRISONERS UNDER INTERNATIONAL LAW 63 (1987). These prohibitions are "absolute." There are no exceptions to them and there is no room for balancing. Indeed, violence directed at a suspect's body or spirit does not constitute a reasonable investigation practice. The use of violence during investigations can lead to the investigator being held criminally liable.

Second, a reasonable investigation is likely to cause discomfort. It may result in insufficient sleep. The conditions under which it is conducted risk being unpleasant. Of course, it is possible to conduct an effective investigation without resorting to violence. Within the confines of the law, it is permitted to resort to various sophisticated techniques. Such techniques — accepted in the most progressive of societies — can be effective in achieving their goals. In the end result, the legality of an investigation is deduced from the propriety of its purpose and from its methods. Thus, for instance, sleep deprivation for a prolonged period, or sleep deprivation at night when this is not necessary to the investigation time-wise, may be deemed disproportionate.

From the General to the Particular

24. We shall now turn from the general to the particular. Clearly, shaking is a prohibited investigation method. It harms the suspect's body. It violates his dignity. It is a violent method which can not form part of a legal investigation. It surpasses that which is necessary. Even the state did not argue that shaking is an "ordinary" investigatory method which every investigator, whether in the GSS or the police, is permitted to employ. The argument before us was that the justification for shaking is found in the "necessity defense." That argument shall be dealt with below. In any event, there is no doubt that shaking is not to be resorted to in cases outside the bounds of "necessity" or as part of an "ordinary" investigation.

25. It was argued before the Court that one of the employed investigation methods consists of compelling the suspect to crouch on the tips of his toes for periods of five minutes. The state did not deny this practice. This is a prohibited investigation method. It does not serve any purpose inherent to an investigation. It is degrading and infringes an individual's human dignity.

26. The "Shabach" method is composed of several components: the cuffing of the suspect, seating him on a low chair, covering his head with a sack, and playing loud music in the area. [W]e accept that the suspect's cuffing, for the purpose of preserving the investigators' safety, is included in the general power to investigate. Even petitioners agree that it is permissible to cuff a suspect in such circumstances and that cuffing constitutes an integral part of an interrogation. The cuffing associated with the "Shabach" position, however, is unlike routine cuffing. The suspect is cuffed with his hands tied behind his back. One hand is placed inside the gap between the chair's seat and back support, while the other is tied behind him, against the chair's back support. This is a distorted and unnatural position. The investigators' safety does not require it. Similarly, there is no justification for handcuffing the suspect's hands with especially small handcuffs, if this is in fact the practice. The use of these methods is prohibited. As has been noted, "cuffing that causes pain is prohibited." Moreover, there are other ways of preventing the suspect from fleeing which do not involve causing pain and suffering.

27. The same applies to seating the suspect in question in the "Shabach" position. We accept that seating a man is inherent to the investigation. This is not the case, however, when the chair upon which he is seated is a very low one, tilted forward facing the ground, and when he is seated in this position for long hours. This sort of seating is not authorized by the general power to interrogate. Even if we suppose that the seating of the suspect on a chair lower than that of his investigator can potentially serve a legitimate investigation objective — for instance, to establish the "rules of the game" in the contest of wills between the parties, or to emphasize the investigator's superiority over the suspect — there is no inherent investigative need to seat the suspect on a chair so low and tilted forward towards the ground, in a manner that causes him real pain and suffering. Clearly, the general power to conduct interrogations does not authorize seating a suspect on a tilted chair, in a manner that applies pressure and causes pain to his back, all the more so when his hands are tied behind the chair, in the manner described. All these methods do not fall within the sphere of a "fair" interrogation. They are not reasonable. They infringe the suspect's dignity, his bodily integrity and his basic rights in an excessive manner. They are not to be deemed as included within the general power to conduct interrogations.

28. We accept that there are interrogation related concerns regarding preventing contact between the suspect under interrogation and other suspects, and perhaps even between the suspect and the interrogator. These concerns require means to prevent the said contact. The need to prevent contact may, for instance, flow from the need to

safeguard the investigators' security, or the security of the suspects and witnesses. It can also be part of the "mind game" which pits the information possessed by the suspect, against that found in the hands of his investigators. For this purpose, the power to interrogate — in principle and according to the circumstances of each particular case — may include the need to prevent eye contact with a given person or place. In the case at bar, this was the explanation provided by the state for covering the suspect's head with a sack, while he is seated in the "Shabach" position. From what was stated in the declarations before us, the suspect's head is covered with a sack throughout his "wait" in the "Shabach" position. It was argued that the head covering causes the suspect to suffocate. The sack is large, reaching the shoulders of the suspect. All these methods are not inherent to an interrogation. They are not necessary to prevent eye contact between the suspect being interrogated and other suspects. Indeed, even if such contact is prevented, what is the purpose of causing the suspect to suffocate? Employing this method is not related to the purpose of preventing the said contact and is consequently forbidden. Moreover, the statements clearly reveal that the suspect's head remains covered for several hours, throughout his wait. For these purposes, less harmful means must be employed, such as letting the suspect wait in a detention cell. Doing so will eliminate any need to cover the suspect's eyes. In the alternative, the suspect's eyes may be covered in a manner that does not cause him physical suffering. For it appears that, at present, the suspect's head covering — which covers his entire head, rather than eyes alone — for a prolonged period of time, with no essential link to the goal of preventing contact between the suspects under investigation, is not part of a fair interrogation. It harms the suspect and his dignity. It degrades him. It causes him to lose his sense of time and place. It suffocates him. All these things are not included in the general authority to investigate. In the cases before us, the State declared that it will make an effort to find a "ventilated" sack. This is not sufficient. The covering of the head in the circumstances described, as distinguished from the covering of the eyes, is outside the scope of authority and is prohibited.

29. Cutting off the suspect from his surroundings can also include preventing him from listening to what is going on around him. We are prepared to assume that the authority to investigate an individual may include preventing him from hearing other suspects under investigation or voices and sounds that, if heard by the suspect, risk impeding the interrogation's success. At the same time, however, we must examine whether the means employed to accomplish this fall within the scope of a fair and reasonable interrogation. In the case at bar, the detainee is placed in the "Shabach" position while very loud music is played. Do these methods fall within the scope or the general authority to conduct interrogations? Here too, the answer is in the negative. Being exposed to very loud music for a long period of time causes the suspect suffering. Furthermore, the entire time, the suspect is tied in an uncomfortable position with his head covered. This is prohibited. It does not fall within the scope of the authority to conduct a fair and effective interrogation. In the circumstances of the cases before us, the playing of loud music is a prohibited.

30. To the above, we must add that the "Shabach" position employs all the above methods simultaneously. This combination gives rise to pain and suffering. This is a harmful method, particularly when it is employed for a prolonged period of time. For these reasons, this method is not authorized by the powers of interrogation. It is an unacceptable method. "The duty to safeguard the detainee's dignity includes his right not to be degraded and not to be submitted to sub-human conditions in the course of his detention, of the sort likely to harm his health and potentially his dignity."

A similar — though not identical — combination of interrogation methods were discussed in the case of *Ireland v. United Kingdom*, 23 Eur. Ct. H.R. (ser. B) at 3 (1976). In that case, the Court examined five interrogation methods used by England to investigate detainees suspected of terrorist activities in Northern Ireland. The methods included protracted standing against a wall on the tip of one's toes, covering of the suspect's head throughout the detention (except during the actual interrogation), exposing the suspect to very loud noise for a prolonged period of time, and deprivation of sleep, food and drink. The Court held that these methods did not constitute "torture." However, since they subjected the suspect to "inhuman and degrading" treatment, they were nonetheless prohibited.

31. The interrogation of a person is likely to be lengthy, due to the suspect's failure to cooperate, the complexity of the information sought, or in light of the need to obtain information urgently and immediately. Indeed, a person undergoing interrogation cannot sleep like one who is not being interrogated. The suspect, subject to the investigators' questions for a prolonged period of time, is at times exhausted. This is often the inevitable result of an interrogation. This is part of the "discomfort" inherent to an interrogation. This being the case, depriving the suspect of sleep is, in our opinion, included in the general authority of the investigator. Justice Shamgar noted as much in Cr. A. 485/76 *Ben Loulou v. The State of Israel* (unreported decision):

> The interrogation of crimes and, in particular, murder or other serious crimes, cannot be accomplished within an ordinary work day. . . . The investigation of crime is essentially a game of mental resistance . . . For this reason, the interrogation is often carried out at frequent intervals. This, as noted, causes the investigation to drag on . . . and requires diligent insistence on its momentum and consecutiveness.

The above described situation is different from one in which sleep deprivation shifts from being a "side effect" of the interrogation to an end in itself. If the suspect is intentionally deprived of sleep for a prolonged period of time, for the purpose of tiring him out or "breaking" him, it is not part of the scope of a fair and reasonable investigation. Such means harm the rights and dignity of the suspect in a manner beyond what is necessary.

32. All these limitations on an interrogation, which flow from the requirement that an interrogation be fair and reasonable, is the law with respect to a regular police interrogation. The power to interrogate granted to the GSS investigator is the same power the law bestows upon the ordinary police investigator. The restrictions upon the police investigations are equally applicable to GSS investigations. There is no statute that grants GSS investigators special interrogating powers that are different or more significant than those granted the police investigator. From this we conclude that a GSS investigator, whose duty it is to conduct the interrogation according to the law, is subject to the same restrictions applicable to police interrogators.

Physical Means and the "Necessity" Defense

33. We have arrived at the conclusion that GSS personnel who have received permission to conduct interrogations, as per the Criminal Procedure Statute [Testimony], are authorized to do so. This authority — like that of the police investigator — does not include most of the physical means of interrogation in the petition before us. Can the authority to employ these methods be anchored in a legal source beyond the authority to conduct an interrogation? This question was answered by the state in the affirmative. As noted, our law does not contain an explicit authorization permitting the GSS to employ physical means. An authorization of this nature can, however, in the state's opinion, be obtained in specific cases by virtue of the criminal law defense of "necessity," as provided in section 34(1) of the Penal Law. The statute provides:

> A person will not bear criminal liability for committing any act immediately necessary for the purpose of saving the life, liberty, body or property, of either himself or his fellow person, from substantial danger of serious harm, in response to particular circumstances during a specific time, and absent alternative means for avoiding the harm.

The state's position is that by virtue of this defense against criminal liability, GSS investigators are authorized to apply physical means — such as shaking — in the appropriate circumstances and in the absence of other alternatives, in order to prevent serious harm to human life or limb. The state maintains that an act committed under conditions of "necessity" does not constitute a crime. Instead, the state sees such acts as worth committing in order to prevent serious harm to human life or limb. These are actions that society has an interest in encouraging, which should be seen as proper under the circumstances. In this, society is choosing the lesser evil. Not only is it legitimately permitted to engage in fighting terrorism, it is our moral duty to employ the means necessary for this purpose. This duty is particularly incumbent on the state authorities — and, for our purposes, on the GSS investigators — who carry the burden of safeguarding the public peace. As this is the case, there is no obstacle preventing the investigators' superiors from instructing and guiding them as to when the conditions of the "necessity" defense are fulfilled. This, the state contends, implies the legality of the use of physical means in GSS interrogations.

In the course of their argument, the state presented the "ticking bomb" argument. A given suspect is arrested by the GSS. He holds information regarding the location of a bomb that was set and will imminently explode. There is no way to diffuse the bomb without this information. If the information is obtained, the bomb may be neutralized. If the bomb is not neutralized, scores will be killed and injured. Is a GSS investigator authorized to employ physical means in order to obtain this information? The state answers in the affirmative. The use of physical means should not constitute a criminal offence, and their use should be sanctioned, according to the state, by the "necessity" defense.

34. We are prepared to assume, although this matter is open to debate, that the "necessity defense" is available to all, including an investigator, during an interrogation, acting in the capacity of the state. *See* A. Dershowitz, *Is it Necessary to Apply 'Physical Pressure' to Terrorists — And to Lie About It?*, 23 ISRAEL L. REV. 193 (1989); K. Bernsmann, *Private Self-Defense and Necessity in German Penal Law and in the Penal Law Proposal — Some Remarks*, 30 ISRAEL L. REV. 171, 208–10 (1998). Likewise, we are prepared to accept — although this matter is equally contentious — that the "necessity defense" can arise in instances of "ticking bombs," and that the phrase "immediate need" in the statute refers to the imminent nature of the act rather than that of the danger. Hence, the imminence criteria is satisfied even if the bomb is set to explode in a few days, or even in a few weeks, provided the danger is certain to materialize and there is no alternative means of preventing it.

Consequently we are prepared to presume, as was held by the Report of the Commission of Inquiry, that if a GSS investigator — who applied physical interrogation methods for the purpose of saving human life — is criminally indicted, the "necessity defense" is likely to be open to him in the appropriate circumstances.

35. Indeed, we are prepared to accept that, in the appropriate circumstances, GSS investigators may avail themselves of the "necessity defense" if criminally indicted. This, however, is not the issue before this Court. We are not dealing with the criminal liability of a GSS investigator who employed physical interrogation methods under circumstances of "necessity." Nor are we addressing the issue of the admissibility or probative value of evidence obtained as a result of a GSS investigator's application of physical means against a suspect. We are dealing with a different question. The question before us is whether it is possible, ex ante, to establish permanent directives setting out the physical interrogation means that may be used under conditions of "necessity." Moreover, we must decide whether the "necessity defense" can constitute a basis for the authority of a GSS investigator to investigate, in the performance of his duty. According to the state, it is possible to imply from the "necessity defense" — available post factum to an investigator indicted of a criminal offence — the ex ante legal authorization to allow the investigator to use physical interrogation methods. Is this position correct?

36. In the Court's opinion, the authority to establish directives respecting the use of physical means during the course of a GSS interrogation cannot be implied from the

"necessity defense." The "necessity defense" does not constitute a source of authority, which would allow GSS investigators to make use physical means during the course of interrogations. The reasoning underlying our position is anchored in the nature of the "necessity defense." The defense deals with cases involving an individual reacting to a given set of facts. It is an improvised reaction to an unpredictable event. Thus, the very nature of the defense does not allow it to serve as the source of authorization. Authorization of administrative authority is based on establishing general, forward looking criteria, as noted by Professor Enker:

> Necessity is an after-the-fact judgment based on a narrow set of consider-ations in which we are concerned with the immediate consequences, not far-reaching and long-range consequences, on the basis of a clearly established order of priorities of both means and ultimate values. . . . The defense of necessity does not define a code of primary normative behavior. Necessity is certainly not a basis for establishing a broad detailed code of behavior such as how one should go about conducting intelligence interrogations in security matters, when one may or may not use force, how much force may be used and the like.

See A. Enker, *The Use of Physical Force in Interrogations and the Necessity Defense*, in Israel and International Human Rights Law: The Issue of Torture 61, 62 (1995). In a similar vein, Kremnitzer and Segev note:

> The basic rationale underlying the necessity defense is the impossibility of establishing accurate rules of behavior in advance, appropriate in concrete emergency situations, whose circumstances are varied and unexpected. From this it follows, that the necessity defense is not well suited for the regulation of a general situation, the circumstances of which are known and may repeat themselves. In such cases, there is no reason for not setting out the rules of behavior in advance, in order that their content be determined in a thought out and well-planned manner, which would allow them to apply in a uniform manner to all.

The "necessity defense" has the effect of allowing one who acts under the circum-stances of "necessity" to escape criminal liability. The "necessity defense" does not possess any additional normative value. It can not authorize the use of physical means to allow investigators to execute their duties in circumstances of necessity. The very fact that a particular act does not constitute a criminal act — due to the "necessity defense" — does not in itself authorize the act and the concomitant infringement of human rights. The rule of law, both as a formal and as a substantive principle, requires that an infringement of human rights be prescribed by statute. The lifting of criminal responsibility does not imply authorization to infringe a human right.

37. In other words, general directives governing the use of physical means during interrogations must be rooted in an authorization prescribed by law and not in defenses to criminal liability. The principle of "necessity" cannot serve as a basis of authority. If the state wishes to enable GSS investigators to utilize physical means in interrogations, it must enact legislation for this purpose. This authorization would also free the investigator applying the physical means from criminal liability. This release would not flow from the "necessity defense," but rather from the "justification" defense. This defense is provided for in section 34(13) of the Penal Law, which states:

> A person shall not bear criminal liability for an act committed in one of the following cases:

> (1) He was obliged or authorized by law to commit it.

This "justification" defense to criminal liability is rooted in an area outside the criminal law. This "external" law serves as a defense to criminal liability. This defense does not rest upon "necessity," which is "internal" to the Penal Law itself. Thus, for instance, where the question of when an officer is authorized to apply deadly force in the course of detention arises, the answer is found in the laws of detention, which is external to the Penal Law. If a man is killed as a result of this application of force, the "justification" defense will likely come into play. The power to enact rules and to act according to them requires legislative authorization. In such legislation, the legislature, if it so desires, may express its views on the social, ethical and political problems of authorizing the use of physical means in an interrogation. Naturally, such considerations did not come before the legislature when the "necessity" defense was enacted. The "necessity" defense is not the appropriate place for laying out these considerations.

38. We conclude, therefore, that, according to the existing state of the law, neither the government nor the heads of the security services have the authority to establish directives regarding the use of physical means during the interrogation of suspects suspected of hostile terrorist activities, beyond the general rules which can be inferred from the very concept of an interrogation itself. Similarly, the individual GSS investigator — like any police officer — does not possess the authority to employ physical means that infringe a suspect's liberty during the interrogation, unless these means are inherent to the very essence of an interrogation and are both fair and reasonable.

An investigator who employs these methods exceeds his authority. His responsibility shall be fixed according to law. His potential criminal liability shall be examined in the context of the "necessity defense." Provided the conditions of the defense are met by the circumstances of the case, the investigator may find refuge under its wings. Just as the existence of the "necessity defense" does not bestow authority, the lack of authority does not negate the applicability of the necessity defense or of other defenses from criminal liability. The Attorney-General can establish guidelines regarding circumstances in which investigators shall not stand trial, if they claim to have acted from "necessity." A statutory provision is necessary to authorize the use of physical means during the course of an interrogation, beyond what is permitted by the ordinary "law of investigation," and in order to provide the individual GSS investigator with the authority to employ these methods. The "necessity defense" cannot serve as a basis for such authority.

A Final Word

39. This decision opened with a description of the difficult reality in which Israel finds herself. We conclude this judgment by revisiting that harsh reality. We are aware that this decision does make it easier to deal with that reality [sic- does not?]. This is the destiny of a democracy — it does not see all means as acceptable, and the ways of its enemies are not always open before it. A democracy must sometimes fight with one hand tied behind its back. Even so, a democracy has the upper hand. The rule of law and the liberty of an individual constitute important components in its understanding of security. At the end of the day, they strengthen its spirit and this strength allows it to overcome its difficulties.

This having been said, there are those who argue that Israel's security problems are too numerous, and require the authorization of physical means. Whether it is appropriate for Israel, in light of its security difficulties, to sanction physical means is an issue that must be decided by the legislative branch, which represents the people. We do not take any stand on this matter at this time. It is there that various considerations must be weighed. The debate must occur there. It is there that the required legislation may be passed, provided, of course, that the law "befit[s] the values of the State of Israel, is enacted for a proper purpose, and [infringes the suspect's liberty] to an extent no greater than required." See article 8 of the Basic Law: Human Dignity and Liberty.

40. Deciding these petitions weighed heavily on this Court. True, from the legal perspective, the road before us is smooth. We are, however, part of Israeli society. Its problems are known to us and we live its history. We are not isolated in an ivory tower. We live the life of this country. We are aware of the harsh reality of terrorism in which we are, at times, immersed. The possibility that this decision will hamper the ability to properly deal with terrorists and terrorism disturbs us. We are, however, judges. We

must decide according to the law. This is the standard that we set for ourselves. When we sit to judge, we ourselves are judged. Therefore, in deciding the law, we must act according to our purest conscience. We recall the words of Deputy President Landau, in HCJ 390/79 *Dawikat v. The State of Israel*, at 4:

> We possess proper sources upon which to construct our judgments and have no need — and, indeed, are forbidden — to allow our personal views as citizens to influence our decisions. Still, I fear that the Court will appear to have abandoned its proper role and to have descended into the whirlwind of public debate; that its decision will be acclaimed by certain segments of the public, while others will reject it absolutely. It is in this sense that I see myself as obligated to rule in accordance with the law on any matter properly brought before the Court. I am forced to rule in accordance with the law, in complete awareness that the public at large will not be interested in the legal reasoning behind our decision, but rather in the final result. Conceivably, the stature of the Court as an institution that stands above the arguments that divide the public will be damaged. But what can we do, for this is our role and our obligation as judges?

The Commission of Inquiry pointed to the "difficult dilemma between the imperative to safeguard the very existence of the State of Israel and the lives of its citizens, and between the need to preserve its character — a country subject to the rule of law and basic moral values." The commission rejected an approach that would consign our fight against terrorism to the twilight shadows of the law. The commission also rejected the "ways of the hypocrites, who remind us of their adherence to the rule of law, even as they remain willfully blind to reality." Instead, the Commission chose to follow "the way of truth and the rule of law." In so doing, the Commission of Inquiry outlined the dilemma faced by Israel in a manner open to examination to all of Israeli society.

Consequently, it is decided that the order nisi be made absolute. The GSS does not have the authority to "shake" a man, hold him in the "Shabach" position (which includes the combination of various methods, as mentioned in paragraph 30), force him into a "frog crouch" position, and deprive him of sleep in a manner other than that which is inherently required by the interrogation. Likewise, we declare that the "necessity defense," found in the Penal Law, cannot serve as a basis of authority for interrogation practices, or for directives to GSS investigators, allowing them to employ interrogation practices of this kind. Our decision does not negate the possibility that the "necessity defense" will be available to GSS investigators — either in the choice made by the Attorney-General in deciding whether to prosecute, or according to the discretion of the court if criminal charges are brought.

JUSTICE Y. KEDMI.

I accept the conclusion reached by my colleague, the President, that the use of exceptional interrogation methods, according to the directives of the Ministerial Committee, "has not been authorized, and is illegal." I am also of the opinion that the time has come for this issue to be regulated by explicit, clear, and unambiguous legislation.

Even so, it is difficult for me to accept that, due to the absence of explicit legislation, the state should be helpless in those rare emergencies defined as "ticking bombs," and that the state would not be authorized to order the use of exceptional interrogation methods in such circumstances. As far as I am concerned, authority does exist under such circumstances, a result of the basic obligation of the state — like all countries of the world — to defend its existence, its well-being, and to safeguard the lives of its citizens. It is clear that, in those circumstances, the state — as well as its agents — will have the natural right of "self-defense," in the broad meaning of the term, against terrorist organizations that seek to take its life and the lives of its citizens.

Against this background, and in order to prevent a situation where the state stands helpless while the "bomb ticks" before our eyes, I suggest that this judgment be suspended for one year. During that year, the GSS will be allowed to employ exceptional interrogative methods in those rare cases of "ticking bombs," on the condition that explicit authorization is granted by the Attorney-General.

Such a suspension would not limit our present ruling that the use of exceptional interrogation methods — those that rely on directives of the Ministerial Committee — are illegal. The suspension of the judgment would not constitute authorization to continue acting according to those directives, and the authorization of the Attorney-General would not legalize the performance of an illegal action. This suspension would only affect the employment of exceptional interrogation methods under the emergency circumstances of a "ticking bomb."

During such a suspension period, the Knesset would be given an opportunity to consider the issue of exceptional interrogation methods in security investigations, both in general and in times of emergency. The GSS would be given the opportunity to cope with emergency situations until the Knesset considers the issue. Meanwhile, the GSS would also have an opportunity to adapt, after a long period during which the directives of the Ministerial Committee have governed.

I therefore join the judgment of the President, subject to my proposal to suspend the judgment for a period of one year.

NOTES AND QUESTIONS

1. Advance Guidelines. Justice Kedmi would have the Court's judgment "suspended" for one year while the Knesset considers legislation, but he says that the suspension would not constitute authorization and would apply only under the circumstances of a "ticking bomb." But how would that differ from the very result the government wanted, which was advance authorization for interrogation methods under extreme circumstances?

2. Necessity and Justification. The distinction between "necessity" and "justification" is an extremely sophisticated and complex problem in most of criminal law. In this situation, however, it turns out to be a reasonably straightforward proposition — the difference between advance authorization and the hope for later exoneration from something that is illegal. In a sense, the difference is something like the converse of the doctrine of prior restraint in First Amendment law — the distinction between punishing someone for speaking without permission and punishing that person for the nature of the speech or its consequences. U.S. law does not allow prior restraints absent a sufficiently strong governmental interest but it does allow punishment for harmful speech.

§ 9.02 EMERGENCY POWERS AND CIVIL LIBERTIES

A fitting conclusion to our study comes from the various opinions of the House of Lords in a case falling somewhere between *Hamdi* and *Rasul*. Although the case is important on its own terms, the opinions address several matters of more general interest such as the relative roles of the three branches of government, the applicability of international law, and the significance of national emergency.

To set the stage for what should be a general discussion of emergency powers and civil liberties, consider this argument:

> The Extra-Legal Measures model proposed in this Article informs public officials that they may act extralegally when they believe that such action is necessary for protecting the nation and the public in the face of calamity, provided that they openly and publicly acknowledge the nature of their actions. It is then up to the people to decide . . . how to respond to such actions.

Oren Gross, *Chaos and Rules: Should Responses to Violent Crises Always Be Constitutional?* 112 YALE L.J. 1011, 1023 (2003). What happens to minority rights in this model? Does the model actually contemplate anything other than the normal political process in a democratic society?

> [I]t should not be a surprise that courts have all too often deferred to unfounded assertions of government power on issues of national security; when the executive claims that the fate of the nation is at stake, it takes real courage to stand up to that assertion and subject it to careful scrutiny. . . . At the same time, the conventional wisdom that courts have failed during times of crisis is itself overstated. . . . Judicial decisions, while rarely providing relief to the initial victims of a crisis mentality, have played a role in restricting the options available to the government in the next emergency.

David Cole, *Judging the next Emergency: Judicial Review and Individual Rights in Times of Crisis*, 101 MICH. L. REV. 2565, 2594 (2003).

As you read the House of Lords opinions, reflect on how they differ from the U.S. Supreme Court?s approach in *Hamdi*. The House of Lords is the highest appellate judicial tribunal in the United Kingdom. It acts through an Appellate Committee of appointed "Law Lords," a panel of which is chosen for each case. A proposal is pending to take the appellate judicial power out of the House of Lords and convert the Appellate Committee to a Supreme Court of the United Kingdom. In a way, that is the essence of the committee function at this time, but its opinions are still expressed as "speeches" to the House.

A v. SECRETARY OF STATE FOR THE HOME DEPARTMENT
[2004] UKHL 56, [2004] All ER (D) 271 (Dec 16, 2004)

PANEL: Lord Bingham of Cornhill, Lord Nicholls of Birkenhead, Lord Hoffmann, Lord Hope of Craighead, Lord Scott of Foscote, Lord Rodger of Earlsferry, Lord Walker of Gestingthorpe, Baroness Hale of Richmond and Lord Carswell

LORD BINGHAM OF CORNHILL.

My Lords,

[Nine aliens (Appellants) were detained as suspected terrorists or suspected of having links to terrorist organizations. The 2001 Anti-Terrorism Act contained in section 23 an authorization similar to section 412 of PATRIOT, allowing detention pursuant to a "Derogation Order" declaring a national emergency and derogating from certain provisions of the European Convention on Human Rights. Under a prior 1998 Human Rights Act, the UK courts had been given power to declare that a particular government action was "incompatible" with the ECHR.]

8. First, the Secretary of State might detain a non-British national pending the making of a deportation order against him. In *R. v Governor of Durham Prison, Ex parte Hardial Singh* [1984] 1 WLR 704 it was held, in a decision which has never been questioned, that such detention was permissible only for such time as was reasonably necessary for the process of deportation to be carried out. [ECHR] article 5(1) . . . guarantees the fundamental human right of personal freedom . . . [but] goes on to prescribe certain exceptions. One exception is crucial to these appeals:

> (1) Everyone has the right to liberty and security of person. No one shall be deprived of his liberty save in the following cases and in accordance with a procedure prescribed by law:

>> (f) the lawful arrest or detention of . . . a person against whom action is being taken with a view to deportation

Thus there is . . . no warrant for the long-term or indefinite detention of a non-UK national whom the Home Secretary wishes to remove. Such a person may be detained only during the process of deportation. Otherwise, the Convention is breached and the Convention rights of the detainee are violated.

9. Secondly, reference must be made to the important decision of the European Court

of Human Rights in *Chahal v United Kingdom* (1996) 23 EHRR 413. Mr Chahal was an Indian citizen who had been granted indefinite leave to remain in this country but whose activities as a Sikh separatist brought him to the notice of the authorities both in India and here. The Home Secretary of the day decided that he should be deported from this country because his continued presence here was not conducive to the public good for reasons of a political nature, namely the international fight against terrorism. He resisted deportation on the ground (among others) that, if returned to India, he faced a real risk of death, or of torture in custody contrary to article 3 of the European Convention, which provides that "No one shall be subjected to torture or to inhuman or degrading treatment or punishment." [The European Court] held that "Article 3 makes no provision for exceptions and no derogation from it is permissible under Article 15 even in the event of a public emergency threatening the life of the nation. Thus, whenever substantial grounds have been shown for believing that an individual would face a real risk of being subjected to treatment contrary to Article 3 if removed to another State, the responsibility of the Contracting State to safeguard him or her against such treatment is engaged in the event of expulsion."

In a case like Mr Chahal's, where deportation proceedings are precluded by article 3, article 5(1)(f) would not sanction detention because the non-national would not be "a person against whom action is being taken with a view to deportation." A person who commits a serious crime under the criminal law of this country may of course, whether a national or a non-national, be charged, tried and, if convicted, imprisoned. But a non-national who faces the prospect of torture or inhuman treatment if returned to his own country, and who cannot be deported to any third country and is not charged with any crime, may not under article 5(1)(f) of the Convention be detained here even if judged to be a threat to national security.

10. The European Convention gives member states a limited right to derogate from some articles of the Convention (including article 5, although not article 3).

ECHR article 15. Derogation in time of emergency

> 1. In time of war or other public emergency threatening the life of the nation any High Contracting Party may take measures derogating from its obligations under this Convention to the extent strictly required by the exigencies of the situation, provided that such measures are not inconsistent with its other obligations under international law.

A member state availing itself of the right of derogation must inform the Secretary General of the Council of Europe of the measures it has taken and the reasons for them. It was in exercise of his power under [the 1998 Act] that the Home Secretary, on 11 November 2001, made the Derogation Order, which came into force two days later.

15. The Act makes provision in section 25 for appeal to SIAC against certification by a certified suspected international terrorist.

Public Emergency

16. The appellants repeated before the House a contention rejected by both SIAC and the Court of Appeal, that there neither was nor is a "public emergency threatening the life of the nation" within the meaning of article 15(1). Thus, they contended, the threshold test for reliance on article 15 has not been satisfied.

17. The European Court considered the meaning of this provision in *Lawless v. Ireland* (No 3) (1961) 1 EHRR 15, a case concerned with very low-level IRA terrorist activity in Ireland and Northern Ireland between 1954 and 1957. The Irish Government derogated from article 5 in July 1957 in order to permit detention without charge or trial and the applicant was detained between July and December 1957. [EHR Court] ruled:

> 28. In the general context of Article 15 of the Convention, the natural and customary meaning of the words 'other public emergency threatening the life of the nation' is sufficiently clear; they refer to an exceptional situation of crisis or

emergency which affects the whole population and constitutes a threat to the organised life of the community of which the State is composed. The Court, after an examination, finds this to be the case; the existence at the time of a 'public emergency threatening the life of the nation' was reasonably deduced by the Irish Government from a combination of several factors, namely: in the first place, the existence in the territory of the Republic of Ireland of a secret army engaged in unconstitutional activities and using violence to attain its purposes; secondly, the fact that this army was also operating outside the territory of the State, thus seriously jeopardising the relations of the Republic of Ireland with its neighbour; thirdly, the steady and alarming increase in terrorist activities from the autumn of 1956 and throughout the first half of 1957.

28. The European Court decisions seem to me to be, with respect, clearly right. In each case the member state had actually experienced widespread loss of life caused by an armed body dedicated to destroying the territorial integrity of the state. To hold that the article 15 test was not satisfied in such circumstances, if a response beyond that provided by the ordinary course of law was required, would have been perverse.

29. I would accept that great weight should be given to the judgment of the Home Secretary, his colleagues and Parliament on this question, because they were called on to exercise a pre-eminently political judgment. It involved making a factual prediction of what various people around the world might or might not do, and when (if at all) they might do it, and what the consequences might be if they did. Any prediction about the future behaviour of human beings (as opposed to the phases of the moon or high water at London Bridge) is necessarily problematical. Reasonable and informed minds may differ, and a judgment is not shown to be wrong or unreasonable because that which is thought likely to happen does not happen. It would have been irresponsible not to err, if at all, on the side of safety. The more purely political (in a broad or narrow sense) a question is, the more appropriate it will be for political resolution and the less likely it is to be an appropriate matter for judicial decision. The smaller, therefore, will be the potential role of the court. It is the function of political and not judicial bodies to resolve political questions. Conversely, the greater the legal content of any issue, the greater the potential role of the court, because under our constitution and subject to the sovereign power of Parliament it is the function of the courts and not of political bodies to resolve legal questions. The present question seems to me to be very much at the political end of the spectrum. I conclude that the appellants have shown no ground strong enough to warrant displacing the Secretary of State's decision on this important threshold question.

Proportionality

31. The appellants' argument under this head can, I hope fairly, be summarised as involving the following steps:

(5) If the threat presented to the security of the United Kingdom by UK nationals suspected of being Al-Qaeda terrorists or their supporters could be addressed without infringing their right to personal liberty, it is not shown why similar measures could not adequately address the threat presented by foreign nationals.

(6) Since the right to personal liberty is among the most fundamental of the rights protected by the European Convention, any restriction of it must be closely scrutinised by the national court and such scrutiny involves no violation of democratic or constitutional principle.

36. In urging the fundamental importance of the right to personal freedom, as the sixth step in their proportionality argument, the appellants were able to draw on the long libertarian tradition of English law, dating back to chapter 39 of Magna Carta 1215, given effect in the ancient remedy of habeas corpus, declared in the Petition of Right

1628, upheld in a series of landmark decisions down the centuries and embodied in the substance and procedure of the law to our own day.

37. [T]he Attorney General . . . directed the weight of his submission to challenging the standard of judicial review for which the appellants contended in this sixth step. He submitted that as it was for Parliament and the executive to assess the threat facing the nation, so it was for those bodies and not the courts to judge the response necessary to protect the security of the public. These were matters of a political character calling for an exercise of political and not judicial judgment. Just as the European Court allowed a generous margin of appreciation to member states, recognising that they were better placed to understand and address local problems, so should national courts recognise, for the same reason, that matters of the kind in issue here fall within the discretionary area of judgment properly belonging to the democratic organs of the state. It was not for the courts to usurp authority properly belonging elsewhere.

39. While any decision made by a representative democratic body must of course command respect, the degree of respect will be conditioned by the nature of the decision. In *R v. Director of Public Prosecutions, Ex p Kebilene* [2000] 2 AC 326, 381, Lord Hope of Craighead said:

> It will be easier for such [a discretionary] area of judgment to be recognised where the Convention itself requires a balance to be struck, much less so where the right is stated in terms which are unqualified. It will be easier for it to be recognised where the issues involve questions of social or economic policy, much less so where the rights are of high constitutional importance or are of a kind where the courts are especially well placed to assess the need for protection.

In his dissenting judgment (cited with approval in *Libman*) in *RJR- MacDonald Inc v. Attorney General of Canada* [1995] 3 SCR 199, para 68, La Forest J, sitting in the same court, said:

> Courts are specialists in the protection of liberty and the interpretation of legislation and are, accordingly, well placed to subject criminal justice legislation to careful scrutiny. However, courts are not specialists in the realm of policy-making, nor should they be.

Jackson J, sitting in the Supreme Court of the United States in *West Virginia State Board of Education v. Barnette*, 319 U.S. 624 (1943), stated, speaking of course with reference to an entrenched constitution:

> The very purpose of a Bill of Rights was to withdraw certain subjects from the vicissitudes of political controversy, to place them beyond the reach of majorities and officials and to establish them as legal principles to be applied by the courts. . . . We cannot, because of modest estimates of our competence in such specialties as public education, withhold the judgment that history authenticates as the function of this Court when liberty is infringed.

42. It follows from this analysis that the appellants are in my opinion entitled to invite the courts to review, on proportionality grounds, the Derogation Order and the compatibility with the Convention of section 23 and the courts are not effectively precluded by any doctrine of deference from scrutinising the issues raised. It also follows that I do not accept the full breadth of the Attorney General's submissions. I do not in particular accept the distinction which he drew between democratic institutions and the courts. It is of course true that the judges in this country are not elected and are not answerable to Parliament. It is also of course true that Parliament, the executive and the courts have different functions. But the function of independent judges charged to interpret and apply the law is universally recognised as a cardinal feature of the modern democratic state, a cornerstone of the rule of law itself. The Attorney General is fully entitled to insist on the proper limits of judicial authority, but he is wrong to stigmatise judicial decision-making as in some way undemocratic. The effect is not, of course, to override the sovereign legislative authority of the Queen in Parliament, since if primary

legislation is declared to be incompatible the validity of the legislation is unaffected and the remedy lies with the appropriate minister, who is answerable to Parliament. The 1998 Act gives the courts a very specific, wholly democratic, mandate.

43. The appellants' proportionality challenge to the Order and section 23 is, in my opinion, sound . . . . [I agree with] the central complaint made by the appellants: that the choice of an immigration measure to address a security problem had the inevitable result of failing adequately to address that problem (by allowing non-UK suspected terrorists to leave the country with impunity and leaving British suspected terrorists at large) while imposing the severe penalty of indefinite detention on persons who, even if reasonably suspected of having links with Al-Qaeda, may harbour no hostile intentions towards the United Kingdom. The conclusion that the Order and section 23 are, in Convention terms, disproportionate is in my opinion irresistible.

73. I would allow the appeals. There will be a quashing order in respect of the [Derogation Order]. There will also be a declaration that section 23 of the Act 2001 is incompatible with articles 5 and 14 of the European Convention insofar as it is disproportionate and permits detention of suspected international terrorists in a way that discriminates on the ground of nationality or immigration status.

LORD NICHOLLS OF BIRKENHEAD.

My Lords,

74. Indefinite imprisonment without charge or trial is anathema in any country which observes the rule of law. It deprives the detained person of the protection a criminal trial is intended to afford. Wholly exceptional circumstances must exist before this extreme step can be justified.

75. The government contends that these post-9/11 days are wholly exceptional. The circumstances require and justify the indefinite detention of non-nationals suspected of being international terrorists.

76. The principal weakness in the government's case lies in the different treatment accorded to nationals and non-nationals. The extended power of detention conferred by [the 2001 Act] applies only to persons who are not British citizens. It is difficult to see how the extreme circumstances, which alone would justify such detention, can exist when lesser protective steps apparently suffice in the case of British citizens suspected of being international terrorists.

81. In the present case I see no escape from the conclusion that Parliament must be regarded as having attached insufficient weight to the human rights of non-nationals. The subject matter of the legislation is the needs of national security. This subject matter dictates that, in the ordinary course, substantial latitude should be accorded to the legislature. But the human right in question, the right to individual liberty, is one of the most fundamental of human rights. Indefinite detention without trial wholly negates that right for an indefinite period. With one exception all the individuals currently detained have been imprisoned now for three years and there is no prospect of imminent release. It is true that those detained may at any time walk away from their place of detention if they leave this country. Their prison, it is said, has only three walls. But this freedom is more theoretical than real. This is demonstrated by the continuing presence in Belmarsh of most of those detained. They prefer to stay in prison rather than face the prospect of ill treatment in any country willing to admit them.

LORD HOFFMANN.

My Lords,

86. This is one of the most important cases which the House has had to decide in recent years. It calls into question the very existence of an ancient liberty of which this country has until now been very proud: freedom from arbitrary arrest and detention. The power which the Home Secretary seeks to uphold is a power to detain people indefinitely without charge or trial. Nothing could be more antithetical to the instincts and traditions of the people of the United Kingdom.

88. The technical issue in this appeal is whether such a power can be justified on the ground that there exists a "war or other public emergency threatening the life of the nation" within the meaning of article 15 of the European Convention on Human Rights. But I would not like anyone to think that we are concerned with some special doctrine of European law. Freedom from arbitrary arrest and detention is a quintessentially British liberty, enjoyed by the inhabitants of this country when most of the population of Europe could be thrown into prison at the whim of their rulers. It was incorporated into the European Convention in order to entrench the same liberty in countries which had recently been under Nazi occupation. The United Kingdom subscribed to the Convention because it set out the rights which British subjects enjoyed under the common law.

89. The exceptional power to derogate from those rights also reflected British constitutional history. There have been times of great national emergency in which habeas corpus has been suspended and powers to detain on suspicion conferred on the government. It happened during the Napoleonic Wars and during both World Wars in the twentieth century. These powers were conferred with great misgiving and, in the sober light of retrospect after the emergency had passed, were often found to have been cruelly and unnecessarily exercised. But the necessity of draconian powers in moments of national crisis is recognised in our constitutional history. Article 15 of the Convention, when it speaks of "war or other public emergency threatening the life of the nation," accurately states the conditions in which such legislation has previously been thought necessary.

91. What is meant by "threatening the life of the nation"? The "nation" is a social organism, living in its territory (in this case, the United Kingdom) under its own form of government and subject to a system of laws which expresses its own political and moral values. When one speaks of a threat to the "life" of the nation, the word life is being used in a metaphorical sense. The life of the nation is not coterminous with the lives of its people. The nation, its institutions and values, endure through generations. In many important respects, England is the same nation as it was at the time of the first Elizabeth or the Glorious Revolution. The Armada threatened to destroy the life of the nation, not by loss of life in battle, but by subjecting English institutions to the rule of Spain and the Inquisition. The same was true of the threat posed to the United Kingdom by Nazi Germany in the Second World War.

94. The Home Secretary has adduced evidence, both open and secret, to show the existence of a threat of serious terrorist outrages. I am willing to accept that credible evidence of such plots exist. The events of 11 September 2001 in New York and Washington and 11 March 2003 in Madrid make it entirely likely that the threat of similar atrocities in the United Kingdom is a real one.

95. But the question is whether such a threat is a threat to the life of the nation. The Attorney General's submissions and the judgment of the Special Immigration Appeals Commission treated a threat of serious physical damage and loss of life as necessarily involving a threat to the life of the nation. But in my opinion this shows a misunderstanding of what is meant by "threatening the life of the nation." Of course the government has a duty to protect the lives and property of its citizens. But that is a duty which it owes all the time and which it must discharge without destroying our constitutional freedoms. There may be some nations too fragile or fissiparous to withstand a serious act of violence. But that is not the case in the United Kingdom. When Milton urged the government of his day not to censor the press even in time of civil war, he said:

> Lords and Commons of England, consider what nation it is whereof ye are, and whereof ye are the governours.

96. This is a nation which has been tested in adversity, which has survived physical destruction and catastrophic loss of life. I do not underestimate the ability of fanatical groups of terrorists to kill and destroy, but they do not threaten the life of the nation.

Whether we would survive Hitler hung in the balance, but there is no doubt that we shall survive Al-Qaeda. The Spanish people have not said that what happened in Madrid, hideous crime as it was, threatened the life of their nation. Their legendary pride would not allow it. Terrorist violence, serious as it is, does not threaten our institutions of government or our existence as a civil community.

97. For these reasons I think that the Special Immigration Appeals Commission made an error of law and that the appeal ought to be allowed. Others of your Lordships who are also in favour of allowing the appeal would do so, not because there is no emergency threatening the life of the nation, but on the ground that a power of detention confined to foreigners is irrational and discriminatory. I would prefer not to express a view on this point. I said that the power of detention is at present confined to foreigners and I would not like to give the impression that all that was necessary was to extend the power to United Kingdom citizens as well. In my opinion, such a power in any form is not compatible with our constitution. The real threat to the life of the nation, in the sense of a people living in accordance with its traditional laws and political values, comes not from terrorism but from laws such as these. That is the true measure of what terrorism may achieve. It is for Parliament to decide whether to give the terrorists such a victory. Lord Hope of Craighead.

Lord Hope of Craighead.

My Lords,

99. Although these appeals are concerned with general issues and not with the cases of each of the appellants individually, their importance to them is nevertheless very great. Two cardinal principles lie at the heart of the argument. It is the first responsibility of government in a democratic society to protect and safeguard the lives of its citizens. That is where the public interest lies. It is essential to the preservation of democracy, and it is the duty of the court to do all it can to respect and uphold that principle. But the court has another duty too. It is to protect and safeguard the rights of the individual. Among these rights is the individual's right to liberty.

100. It is impossible ever to overstate the importance of the right to liberty in a democracy. In the words of Baron Hume, Commentaries on the Law of Scotland Respecting Crimes, 4th ed (1844), vol 2, p 98:

> As indeed it is obvious, that, by its very constitution, every court of criminal justice must have the power of correcting the greatest and most dangerous of all abuses of the forms of law — that of the protracted imprisonment of the accused, untried, perhaps not intended ever to be tried, nay, it may be, not informed of the nature of the charge against him, or the name of the accuser.

These were not idle words. When Hume published the first edition of his Commentaries in 1797 grave abuses of the kind he described were within living memory. He knew the dangers that might lie in store for democracy itself if the courts were to allow individuals to be deprived of their right to liberty indefinitely and without charge on grounds of public interest by the executive. The risks are as great now in our time of heightened tension as they were then.

101. There is a third principle which the court must also recognise when it is called upon to perform its central function, which is to strike the balance between the public interest and the right to liberty. The basic principle is that the right belongs to everyone, whoever they may be and wherever they may have come from, who happen to be within the Contracting State's territory. Everyone enjoys this right. It is a right, not a privilege. And it is accorded to everyone within the jurisdiction, as article 1 of the Convention declares. It is not given just to British citizens and those who have the right of abode in this country — not just to "British nationals."

105. The Secretary of State was, of course, entitled to discriminate between British nationals on the one hand and foreign nationals on the other for all the purposes of immigration control, subject to the limitations established by the *Chahal* case. What he

was not entitled to do was to treat the right to liberty of foreign nationals as different in any respect from that enjoyed by British nationals.

114. [T]hat the European Court will accord a large margin of appreciation to the contracting states on the question whether the measures taken to interfere with the right to liberty do not exceed those strictly required by the exigencies of the situation cannot be taken as the last word on the matter so far as the domestic courts are concerned. Final responsibility for determining whether they do exceed these limits must lie with the courts.

The Public Emergency

115. The question whether there is a public emergency of the kind contemplated by article 15(1) requires the exercise of judgment. The primary meaning of the word is an occurrence that is sudden or unexpected. It has an extended meaning — a situation of pressing need. A patch of fog on the motorway or a storm which brings down power lines may create a situation of emergency without the life of the nation being under threat. It is a question of degree. The range of situations which may demonstrate such a threat will extend from the consequences of natural disasters of all kinds to the consequences of acts of terrorism. Few would doubt that it is for the executive, with all the resources at its disposal, to judge whether the consequences of such events amount to an emergency of that kind. But imminent emergencies arouse fear and, as has often been said, fear is democracy's worst enemy. So it would be dangerous to ignore the context in which the judgment is to be exercised. Its exercise needs to be watched very carefully if it is a preliminary to the invoking of emergency powers, especially if they involve actions which are incompatible with Convention rights.

116. I am content therefore to accept that the questions whether there is an emergency and whether it threatens the life of the nation are pre-eminently for the executive and for Parliament. The judgment that has to be formed on these issues lies outside the expertise of the courts. But in my opinion it is nevertheless open to the judiciary to examine the nature of the situation that has been identified by government as constituting the emergency, and to scrutinise the submission by the Attorney General that for the appellants to be deprived of their fundamental right to liberty does not exceed what is "strictly required" by the situation which it has identified. The use of the word "strictly" invites close scrutiny of the action that has been taken. Where the rights of the individual are in issue the nature of the emergency must first be identified, and then compared with the effects on the individual of depriving him of those rights. In my opinion it is the proper function of the judiciary to subject the government's reasoning on these matters in this case to very close analysis.

119. The picture which emerges clearly from these statements is of a current state of emergency. It is an emergency which is constituted by the threat that these attacks will be carried out. It threatens the life of the nation because of the appalling consequences that would affect us all if they were to occur here. But it cannot yet be said that these attacks are imminent. It has to be recognised that, as the attacks are likely to come without warning, it may not be possible to identify a stage when they can be said to be imminent. This is an important factor, and I do not leave it out of account. But the fact is that the stage when the nation has to face that kind of emergency, the emergency of imminent attack, has not been reached.

120. The distinction which is to be drawn between these two situations is important. The situation which is said to require the derogation is the situation which we face now, not the situation that might arise at some unknown time in the future. The life of the nation is said to be threatened. But do the exigencies of the situation which we face now require that the appellants be deprived of their right to liberty? All the factual material which may provide an answer to this question is in the hands of the Home Secretary. But has he asked himself the right question in his analysis of this material? And did SIAC ask itself the right question when it was examining the decision of the Home Secretary?

Strictly Required

121. In my opinion there were two questions that had to be addressed in order to determine whether or not the derogation that was proposed was strictly required. One was what its effects would be on the individuals who were to be affected by it. The other was whether, given those effects and the way British nationals who posed the same threat to the life of the nation were to be dealt with, derogating from the right to liberty of those individuals was strictly necessary. The second question is relevant to the discrimination issue, but I think that it also bears directly on the question whether the derogation went beyond what was strictly required.

129. The Attorney General, for understandable reasons, was not willing to elaborate on the measures that were being taken to contain the threat to the life of this nation from British nationals. But he said that a number of measures were in place for the protection of the public, and that those involved were being prosecuted where possible. He explained that any response which provided for the indefinite detention of those people would have had to have been a different response, as they were not subject to immigration control. The distinction which was drawn between their case and that of the foreign nationals was that the foreign nationals had no right to be here. For British nationals the measure would have had to have provided for a form of detention that had four walls. It would have had to have been more draconian. But that answer, while true, does not meet the objection that the indefinite detention without trial of foreign nationals cannot be said to be strictly required to meet the exigencies of the situation, if the indefinite detention without trial of those who present a threat to the life of the nation because they are suspected of involvement in international terrorism is not thought to be required in the case of British nationals.

132. I would hold that the indefinite detention of foreign nationals without trial has not been shown to be strictly required, as the same threat from British nationals whom the government is unable or unwilling to prosecute is being met by other measures which do not require them to be detained indefinitely without trial. The distinction which the government seeks to draw between these two groups — British nationals and foreign nationals — proceeds on the misconception that it is a sufficient answer to the question whether the derogation is strictly required that the two groups have different rights in the immigration context. So they do. But the derogation is from the right to liberty. The right to liberty is the same for each group. If derogation is not strictly required in the case of one group, it cannot be strictly required in the case of the other group that presents the same threat.

LORD SCOTT OF FOSCOTE.

My Lords,

142. It has not been suggested, nor could it be suggested, that the 2001 Act is otherwise than an effective enactment made by a sovereign legislature. It was passed by both Houses of Parliament and received the Royal Assent. Whether the terms of the 2001 Act are consistent with the terms of the European Convention on Human Rights ("the ECHR") is, so far as the courts of this country are concerned, relevant only to the question whether a declaration of incompatibility under section 4 of the Human Rights Act 1998 should be made. The making of such a declaration will not, however, affect in the least the validity under domestic law of the impugned statutory provision. The import of such a declaration is political not legal.

143. So what is the point of these proceedings and these appeals, with nine of your Lordships sitting in judgment, with intervention from the National Council of Civil Liberties and from Amnesty International and with avid attention from the media?

145. The normal and proper function of the courts of this country is to adjudicate on the rights and liabilities under domestic law of citizens (or of institutions with legal personality) or to adjudicate on the validity of executive actions or omissions that may affect those rights and liabilities. It is not, normally, the function of the courts to

entertain proceedings the purpose of which is to obtain a ruling as to whether an Act of Parliament is compatible with an international treaty obligation entered into by the executive. The executive cannot make laws for the United Kingdom otherwise than pursuant to and within the constraints imposed by an enabling Act of Parliament. The executive has extensive and varied prerogative powers that it can exercise in the name of the Crown but none that permit lawmaking. In being asked, therefore, to perform the function to which I have referred, the courts are, it seems to me, being asked to perform a function the consequences of which will be essentially political in character rather than legal. A ruling that an Act of Parliament is incompatible with the ECHR does not detract from the validity of the Act. It does not relieve citizens from the burdens imposed by the Act. It provides, of course, ammunition to those who disapprove of the Act and desire to agitate for its amendment or repeal.

160. For the reasons . . . given by my noble and learned friends I conclude that the Order is not compliant with article 15 of the ECHR. I understand the Attorney General to have accepted that this conclusion would require the Order to be quashed. I venture to repeat my doubts about this. In the circumstances, however, I too would make the Order suggested by Lord Bingham of Cornhill.

LORD RODGER OF EARLSFERRY.

My Lords,

189. My Lords, I have anxiously considered all the evidential and other material, as well as the arguments which the Attorney General advanced to justify the legislation. Proceeding on the same basis as the Government and Parliament, that detention of the British suspects is not strictly required to meet the threat that they pose to the life of the nation, I have come, however, to the conclusion that the detention of the foreign suspects cannot be strictly required, either, to meet the comparable threat that they pose. The second requirement of article 15(1) is accordingly not satisfied.

LORD WALKER OF GESTINGTHORPE.

My Lords,

191. As all your Lordships recognise, these are very important and difficult appeals. Your Lordships have to consider the balancing of one of the most fundamental human freedoms — freedom from imprisonment for an indefinite period, without indictment, trial or conviction on a criminal charge — with one of the state's most basic and imperative duties — the duty of safeguarding the lives and well-being of its citizens and others resident in the United Kingdom. It is unnecessary to repeat citations as to the importance of these two principles.

192. The detention without trial of terrorist suspects is therefore a crucial instance — probably the most crucial instance of all-of the problems of reconciling individual human rights with the interests of the community, and of determining the proper functions, in this process, of different arms of government.

207. In these appeals attention has of course focused on Part 4 of the 2001 Act, since it contains the only provisions in respect of which the British Government thought it necessary to make a derogation from the Convention. Those are the measures which must be shown to be strictly required by the exigencies of the situation. But it would be a mistake, in my view, to divorce them entirely from their context, that is as part of a major enactment most of whose provisions are aimed impartially at British nationals and non-nationals, and some of whose provisions (those creating offences committed overseas) are aimed exclusively at nationals.

209. I have the misfortune to differ from most of your Lordships as to whether the derogating measures are proportionate, rational and non-discriminatory, or are in the alternative disproportionate, irrational and offensively discriminatory. In the circumstances it would be inappropriate for me to add much to the already considerable volume of your Lordships' reasons; but it would also be inappropriate, in such an important case, not to set out briefly the reasons for my dissent. I hardly need add that having had the

great advantage of reading and considering in draft all your Lordships' speeches, it is only with great diffidence that I have arrived at, and I still maintain, a different opinion. I do so for three main reasons:

(1) When this country is faced, as it is, with imminent threats from enemies who make use of secrecy, deception and surprise, the need for anti-terrorist measures to be "strictly necessary" must be interpreted in accordance with the precautionary principle recognised by the Strasbourg Court in *Ireland v. United Kingdom*.

(2) I agree with the Court of Appeal, and very respectfully disagree with SIAC and the majority of the House, on the issue of discrimination.

(3) SIAC is an independent and impartial tribunal of unquestioned standing and expertise. It carefully considers any appeal by a suspected terrorist, and periodically reviews any of its decisions which have been adverse to a detained suspect. I would in no way dissent from condemning the odiousness of indefinite detention at the will of the Executive, but such a description cannot be applied to detention under Part 4 of the 2001 Act without so much qualification as to amount almost to contradiction.

215. In this case a power of interning British citizens without trial, and with no option of going abroad if they chose to do so, would be far more oppressive, and a graver affront to their human rights, than a power to detain in "a prison with three walls" a suspected terrorist who has no right of abode in the United Kingdom, and whom the government could and would deport but for the risk of torture if he were returned to his own country. Detention of non-national suspects is still a cause of grave concern, and I share the anxieties expressed by [others]. But in my view Part 4 of the 2001 Act is not offensively discriminatory, because there are sound, rational grounds for different treatment.

217. As I have said, the detention without trial of non-national suspected terrorists is a cause of grave concern. But the judgment of Parliament and of the Secretary of State is that these measures were necessary, and the 2001 Act contains several important safeguards against oppression. The exercise of the Secretary of State's powers is subject to judicial review by SIAC, an independent and impartial court, which under sections 25 and 26 of the 2001 Act has a wide jurisdiction to hear appeals, and must also review every certificate granted under section 21 at regular intervals. Moreover the legislation is temporary in nature. Any decision to prolong it is anxiously considered by the legislature. While it is in force there is detailed scrutiny of the operation of sections 21 to 23 by the individual appointed under section 28. There is also a wider review by the Committee of Privy Councillors appointed under section 122. All these safeguards seem to me to show a genuine determination that the 2001 Act should not be used to encroach on human rights any more than is strictly necessary.

218. I think it is also significant that in a period of nearly three years no more than seventeen individuals have been certified under section 21. Of course every single detention without trial is a matter of concern, but in the context of national security the number of persons actually detained (now significantly fewer than 17) is to my mind relevant to the issue of proportionality. [*Amicus*] in its written submissions appears to rely on the small number of certifications as evidence that there is not a sufficiently grave emergency. That is, I think, a striking illustration of the dilemma facing a democratic government in protecting national security. I would dismiss these appeals.

BARONESS HALE OF RICHMOND.

My Lords,

226. The courts' power to rule on the validity of the derogation is another of the safeguards enacted by Parliament in this carefully constructed package. It would be meaningless if we could only rubber-stamp what the Home Secretary and Parliament have done. But any sensible court, like any sensible person, recognises the limits of its expertise. Assessing the strength of a general threat to the life of the nation is, or should be, within the expertise of the Government and its advisers. If a Government were to declare a public emergency where patently there was no such thing, it would be the duty

of the court to say so. But we are here considering the immediate aftermath of the unforgettable events of 11 September 2001. The attacks launched on the United States on that date were clearly intended to threaten the life of that nation. SIAC were satisfied that the open and closed material before them justified the conclusion that there was also a public emergency threatening the life of this nation. I, for one, would not feel qualified or even inclined to disagree.

235. Are foreigners and nationals alike for this purpose? The Attorney General argued that they are not. The foreigners have no right to be here and we would expel them if we could. Hence, he argued, the true comparison is not with suspected international terrorists who are British nationals but with foreign suspected international terrorists who can be deported. This cannot be right. The foreigners who can be deported are not like the foreigners who cannot. These foreigners are only being detained because they cannot be deported. They are just like a British national who cannot be deported. The relevant circumstances making the two cases alike for this purpose are the same three which constitute the problem: a suspected international terrorist, who for a variety of reasons cannot be successfully prosecuted, and who for a variety of reasons cannot be deported or expelled.

237. Democracy values each person equally. In most respects, this means that the will of the majority must prevail. But valuing each person equally also means that the will of the majority cannot prevail if it is inconsistent with the equal rights of minorities. As Thomas Jefferson said in his inaugural address:

> Though the will of the majority is in all cases to prevail, that will to be rightful must be reasonable. . . . The minority possess their equal rights, which equal law must protect, and to violate would be oppression.

238. No one has the right to be an international terrorist. But substitute "black," "disabled," "female," "gay," or any other similar adjective for "foreign" before "suspected international terrorist" and ask whether it would be justifiable to take power to lock up that group but not the "white," "able-bodied," "male" or "straight" suspected international terrorists. The answer is clear.

LORD CARSWELL [concurred with LORD BINGHAM].

NOTES AND QUESTIONS

1. **Emergency and Judicial Review.** Is the presence of a national emergency a matter for political or judicial judgment? Compare the approaches and standards of review applied by Lord Bingham, Lord Hoffman, Lord Hope, and Baroness Hale. Then compare their approaches to the responses of the U.S. Justices when met with governmental claims for deference in the *Hamdi* and *Rasul* cases. When the next claim of emergency arises, which approach would you prefer to have in your bag of precedents?

On what basis does Lord Hoffman claim the power of judicial review over the findings of executive and legislative branches that an emergency exists in the UK?

2. **Equal Protection.** Lord Bingham articulates a vision of strict scrutiny that sounds familiar to students of U.S. equal protection and First Amendment law. The reason the statute fails, in his view, is that its lack of application to UK nationals shows that other measures could be found to meet the emergency. What would he be likely to do if Parliament extended the power of detention without trial to UK nationals?

3. **Deportation Options.** Lord Nicholls makes the point that most of the detainees could leave at any time but have chosen to remain in prison rather than go to any country that would have them. This is reminiscent of the dilemma faced in *Zadvydas*. What should a free society do about an alien who can't go home but who is a danger to the host country? Is monitoring that person's activities after release a sufficient answer? How long would it take to bankrupt a country, either economically or

psychologically, if it were trying to monitor the activities of millions of suspected terrorists within its borders?

4. House Arrest: *Secretary of State v. JJ, KK, et al.* **(QB 2007).** Following the opinion in *A v. Home Secretary*, the British Parliament adopted statutory measures allowing for a form of "house arrest" through "control orders" that could be issued by the Secretary. In a case consolidating challenges to several control orders, the appellate division of Queen's Bench ruled that the control orders amounted to a "deprivation of liberty" under the ECHR and thus were invalid executive detentions.

The court recognized a distinction between a "restriction on movement" and a "deprivation of liberty." In some instances, government may be able to prevent a person from entering certain locations (restriction) without confining that person to a certain location (deprivation). In this instance, the Government argued that restricting a person to a state-provided one-room apartment for 18 hours per day, allowing him out for six hours during the work day, was merely a restriction on movement. The appellate bench agreed with the trial judge's assessment of this argument:

> I have considered the cumulative impact of the obligations and therefore the extent to which they restrict the respondents' liberty in the six hours when they are allowed out of their residences, as well as the effect of the 18 hour curfew and the obligations imposed on the respondents whilst they have to remain within their residences during that period. If I had to assess the impact of the obligations individually, I would consider that house arrest for 18 hours each day, even if it was the only obligation (apart from obligations such as reporting and tagging to ensure that it was strictly observed) would be more realistically described as deprivation of liberty, and not as a restriction on liberty, if it prevented the individual from pursuing a normal "in at home/out at work" life cycle.

5. House Arrest: *Thomas v. Mowbray* **[2007] HCA 33 (High Court of Australia).** Mowbray had received training at an al Qaeda camp before returning home to Australia. He then was made the subject of a "control order" issued by a magistrate. "The order required the plaintiff to remain at his residence between midnight and 5 am each day unless he notified the Australian Federal Police of a change of address. It also required him to report to the police three times each week. It required him to submit to having his fingerprints taken. He was prohibited from leaving Australia without the permission of the police. He was prohibited from acquiring or manufacturing explosives, from communicating with certain named individuals, and from using certain communications technology. The order was made ex parte." The High Court held that control order were a valid exercise of government power because the issuing court was required to make findings that the measures were reasonably necessary to prevent a terrorist act of violence. Reasonableness would require balancing the governmental interest with personal liberty. "The level of risk of the occurrence of a terrorist act, and the level of danger to the public from an apprehended terrorist act, will vary according to international or local circumstances."

CHARKAOUI v. MINISTER OF CITIZENSHIP AND IMMIGRATION
2007 SCC 9 (Supreme Court of Canada 2007)

The judgment of the Court was delivered by THE CHIEF JUSTICE:

I. INTRODUCTION

One of the most fundamental responsibilities of a government is to ensure the security of its citizens. This may require it to act on information that it cannot disclose and to detain people who threaten national security. Yet in a constitutional democracy, governments must act accountably and in conformity with the Constitution and the rights and liberties it guarantees. These two propositions describe a tension that lies at the heart of modern democratic governance. It is a tension that must be resolved in a way that respects the imperatives both of security and of accountable constitutional governance.

In this case, we are confronted with a statute, the Immigration and Refugee Protection Act ("IRPA"), that attempts to resolve this tension in the immigration context by allowing the Minister of Citizenship and Immigration (the "Minister"), and the Minister of Public Safety and Emergency Preparedness (collectively "the ministers") to issue a certificate of inadmissibility leading to the detention of a permanent resident or foreign national deemed to be a threat to national security. The certificate and the detention are both subject to review by a judge, in a process that may deprive the person named in the certificate of some or all of the information on the basis of which the certificate was issued or the detention ordered. The question is whether the solution that Parliament has enacted conforms to the Constitution, and in particular the guarantees in the Canadian Charter of Rights and Freedoms that protect against unjustifiable intrusions on liberty, equality and the freedom from arbitrary detention and from cruel and unusual treatment.

I conclude that the IRPA unjustifiably violates § 7 of the Charter by allowing the issuance of a certificate of inadmissibility based on secret material without providing for an independent agent at the stage of judicial review to better protect the named person's interests. I also conclude that some of the time limits in the provisions for continuing detention of a foreign national violate §§ 9 and 10(c) because they are arbitrary. I find that § 12 has not been shown to be violated since a meaningful detention review process offers relief against the possibility of indefinite detention. Finally, I find that there is no breach of the § 15 equality right.

II. Background

The provisions of the IRPA at issue permit deportation on the basis of confidential information that is not to be disclosed to the person named in the certificate or anyone acting on the person's behalf or in his or her interest. The scheme was meant to "facilitat[e] the early removal of persons who are inadmissible on serious grounds, including persons posing a threat to the security of Canada." In reality, however, it may also lead to long periods of incarceration.

The IRPA requires the ministers to sign a certificate declaring that a foreign national or permanent resident is inadmissible to enter or remain in Canada on grounds of security, among others. A judge of the Federal Court then reviews the certificate to determine whether it is reasonable. If the state so requests, the review is conducted *in camera* and *ex parte*. The person named in the certificate has no right to see the material on the basis of which the certificate was issued. Non-sensitive material may be disclosed; sensitive or confidential material must not be disclosed if the government objects. The named person and his or her lawyer cannot see undisclosed material, although the ministers and the reviewing judge may rely on it. At the end of the day, the judge must provide the person with a summary of the case against him or her — a summary that does not disclose material that might compromise national security. If the judge determines that the certificate is reasonable, there is no appeal and no way to have the decision judicially reviewed.

The consequences of the issuance and confirmation of a certificate of inadmissibility vary, depending on whether the person is a permanent resident of Canada or a foreign national whose right to remain in Canada has not yet been confirmed. Permanent residents who the ministers have reasonable grounds to believe are a danger to national security *may* be held in detention. In order to detain them, the ministers must issue a warrant stating that the person is a threat to national security or to another person, or is unlikely to appear at a proceeding or for removal. Foreign nationals, meanwhile, *must* be detained once a certificate is issued — the detention is automatic. While the detention of a permanent resident must be reviewed within 48 hours, a foreign national, on the other hand, must apply for review, but may not do so until 120 days after a judge of the Federal Court determines the certificate to be reasonable. In both cases, if the judge finds the certificate to be reasonable, it becomes a removal order. Such an order deprives permanent residents of their status; their detention is then subject to review on the same basis as that of other foreign nationals.

III. Issues

The appellants argue that the IRPA's certificate scheme under which their detentions were ordered is unconstitutional. They argue that it violates five provisions of the Charter: the § 7 guarantee of life, liberty and security of the person; the § 9 guarantee against arbitrary detention; the § 10(c) guarantee of a prompt review of detention; the § 12 guarantee against cruel and unusual treatment; and the § 15 guarantee of equal protection and equal benefit of the law. They also allege violations of unwritten constitutional principles.

Section 7 of the Charter guarantees the right to life, liberty and security of the person, and the right not to be deprived thereof except in accordance with the principles of fundamental justice. If the claimant succeeds, the government bears the burden of justifying the deprivation under § 1, which provides that the rights guaranteed by the Charter are subject only to such reasonable limits prescribed by law as can be demonstrably justified in a free and democratic society.

The provisions at issue clearly deprive detainees such as the appellants of their liberty. Section 7 of the Charter requires that laws that interfere with life, liberty and security of the person conform to the principles of fundamental justice — the basic principles that underlie our notions of justice and fair process. These principles include a guarantee of procedural fairness, having regard to the circumstances and consequences of the intrusion on life, liberty or security.

Is the Judge Independent and Impartial?

The IRPA scheme provides for the certificate issued by the ministers to be reviewed by a "designated judge," a judge of the Federal Court of Canada. The question here is whether, from an institutional perspective, the role assigned to designated judges under the IRPA leads to a perception that independence and impartiality are compromised.

When reviewing the certificate, the judge sees all the material relied on by the government. But if the government claims confidentiality for certain material, the judge cannot share this material with the named person. The judge must make his or her decision without hearing any objections the named person might be able to make, were he or she granted access to the whole of the record. Part of the hearing may be held *in camera*, with only the judge and the government lawyers in the room. The named person is not there. His or her lawyer is not there. There is no one to speak for the person or to test the evidence put against him or her.

I conclude that, on its face, the IRPA process is designed to preserve the independence and impartiality of the designated judge, as required by § 7. Properly followed by judges committed to a searching review, it cannot be said to compromise the perceived independence and impartiality of the designated judge.

Is the Decision Based on the Facts and the Law?

To comply with § 7 of the Charter, the magistrate must make a decision based on the facts and the law. The IRPA process at issue seeks to meet this requirement by placing material before the judge for evaluation. As a practical matter, most if not all of the material that the judge considers is produced by the government and can be vetted for reliability and sufficiency only by the judge. The normal standards used to ensure the reliability of evidence in court do not apply. The named person may be shown little or none of the material relied on by the ministers and the judge, and may thus not be in a position to know or challenge the case against him or her. It follows that the judge's decision, while based on the evidence before him or her, may not be based on all of the evidence available.

There are two types of judicial systems, and they ensure that the full case is placed before the judge in two different ways. In inquisitorial systems, as in Continental Europe, the judge takes charge of the gathering of evidence in an independent and impartial way. By contrast, an adversarial system, which is the norm in Canada, relies on the parties — who are entitled to disclosure of the case to meet, and to full participation in open proceedings — to produce the relevant evidence. The designated judge under the IRPA does not possess the full and independent powers to gather evidence that exist in the inquisitorial process. At the same time, the named person is not given the disclosure and the right to participate in the proceedings that characterize the adversarial process. The result is a concern that the designated judge, despite his or her best efforts to get all the relevant evidence, may be obliged — perhaps unknowingly — to make the required decision based on only part of the relevant evidence.

Judges of the Federal Court have worked assiduously to overcome the difficulties inherent in the role the IRPA has assigned to them. To their credit, they have adopted a pseudo-inquisitorial role and sought to seriously test the protected documentation and information. But the role remains *pseudo*-inquisitorial. The judge is not afforded the power to independently investigate all relevant facts that true inquisitorial judges enjoy. At the same time, since the named person is not given a full picture of the case to meet, the judge cannot rely on the parties to present missing evidence. The result is that, at the end of the day, one cannot be sure that the judge has been exposed to the whole factual picture.

Similar concerns arise with respect to the requirement that the decision be based on the law. Without knowledge of the information put against him or her, the named person may not be in a position to raise legal objections relating to the evidence, or to develop legal arguments based on the evidence. The named person is, to be sure, permitted to make legal representations. But without disclosure and full participation throughout the process, he or she may not be in a position to put forward a full legal argument.

Is the "Case to Meet" Principle Satisfied?

Last but not least, a fair hearing requires that the affected person be informed of the case against him or her, and be permitted to respond to that case. This right is well established in immigration law. The question is whether the procedures "provide an adequate opportunity for [an affected person] to state his case and know the case he has to meet."

Where limited disclosure or *ex parte* hearings have been found to satisfy the principles of fundamental justice, the intrusion on liberty and security has typically been less serious than that effected by the IRPA. It is one thing to deprive a person of full information where fingerprinting is at stake, and quite another to deny him or her information where the consequences are removal from the country or indefinite detention. Moreover, even in the less intrusive situations, courts have insisted that disclosure be as specific and complete as possible.

In the context of national security, non-disclosure, which may be extensive, coupled with the grave intrusions on liberty imposed on a detainee, makes it difficult, if not impossible, to find substitute procedures that will satisfy § 7. Fundamental justice requires substantial compliance with the venerated principle that a person whose liberty is in jeopardy must be given an opportunity to know the case to meet, and an opportunity to meet the case. Yet the imperative of the protection of society may preclude this. Information may be obtained from other countries or from informers on condition that it not be disclosed. Or it may simply be so critical that it cannot be disclosed without risking public security. This is a reality of our modern world. If § 7 is to be satisfied, either the person must be given the necessary information, or a substantial substitute for that information must be found. Neither is the case here.

The only protection the IRPA accords the named person is a review by a designated judge to determine whether the certificate is reasonable. The ministers argue that this is adequate in that it maintains a "delicate balance" between the right to a fair hearing and the need to protect confidential security intelligence information. The appellants, on the other hand, argue that the judge's efforts, however conscientious, cannot provide an effective substitute for informed participation.

I agree with the appellants. The judge, working under the constraints imposed by the IRPA, simply cannot fill the vacuum left by the removal of the traditional guarantees of a fair hearing. The judge sees only what the ministers put before him or her. The judge, knowing nothing else about the case, is not in a position to identify errors, find omissions or assess the credibility and truthfulness of the information in the way the named person would be.

Is the Limit Justified under Section 1 of the Charter?

The Canadian Charter of Rights and Freedoms does not guarantee rights absolutely. The state is permitted to limit rights — including the § 7 guarantee of life, liberty and security — if it can establish that the limits are demonstrably justifiable in a free and democratic society.

This is not the first time Canada has had to reconcile the demands of national security with the procedural rights guaranteed by the Charter. In a number of legal contexts, Canadian government institutions have found ways to protect sensitive information while treating individuals fairly. In some situations, the solution has involved the use of special counsel, in a manner closely approximating an adversarial process.

The Security Intelligence Review Committee (SIRC) is an independent review body that monitors the activities of the Canadian Security Intelligence Service (CSIS). Established in 1984 under the Canadian Security Intelligence Service Act, S.C. 1984, SIRC is composed of three to five members of the Privy Council who are not currently serving in Parliament. Under the former Immigration Act, SIRC had the power to vet findings of inadmissibility based on alleged threats to national security; a ministerial certificate could not be issued without a SIRC investigation. Empowered to develop its own investigative procedures, SIRC established a formal adversarial process, with "a court-like hearing room" and "procedures that mirrored judicial proceedings as much as possible." The process also included an independent panel of lawyers with security clearances to act as counsel to SIRC. The non-citizen and his or her counsel would normally be present in the hearing room, except when sensitive national security evidence was tendered. (The presiding SIRC member would decide whether to exclude the non-citizen during certain testimony.) At such a juncture, independent, security-cleared SIRC counsel would act on behalf of the non-citizen. The SIRC counsel were instructed to cross-examine witnesses for CSIS "with as much vigour as one would expect from the complainant's counsel" At the end of this *ex parte* portion of the hearing, the excluded person would be brought back into the room and provided with a summary, which would include "the gist of the evidence, without disclosing the national security information." The SIRC counsel would negotiate the contents of the summary with CSIS, under the supervision of the presiding SIRC member. The affected person and his or her counsel would then be allowed to ask their own questions, and to cross-examine on the basis of the summary.

These procedures illustrate how special counsel can provide not only an effective substitute for informed participation, but can also help bolster actual informed participation by the affected person. Since the special counsel had a role in determining how much information would be included in the summary, disclosure was presumably more complete than would otherwise have been the case. Sensitive national security information was still protected, but the executive was required to justify the breadth of this protection.

The SIRC process is not the only example of the Canadian legal system striking a better balance between the protection of sensitive information and the procedural rights of individuals. A current example is found in the Canada Evidence Act ("CEA"), which permits the government to object to the disclosure of information on grounds of public interest, in proceedings to which the Act applies. Under the recent amendments to the CEA set out in the Anti-terrorism Act, a participant in a proceeding who is required to disclose or expects to disclose potentially injurious or sensitive information, or who believes that such information might be disclosed, must notify the Attorney General about the potential disclosure, and the Attorney General may then apply to the Federal Court for an order prohibiting the disclosure of the information. The judge enjoys considerable discretion in deciding whether the information should be disclosed. If the judge concludes that disclosure of the information would be injurious to international relations, national defence or national security, but that the public interest in disclosure outweighs in importance the public interest in non-disclosure, the judge may order the disclosure of all or part of the information, on such conditions as he or she sees fit. No similar residual discretion exists under the IRPA, which requires judges not to disclose information the disclosure of which would be injurious to national security or to the safety of any person.

Crown and defence counsel in the recent Air India trial (*R. v. Malik*, [2005] B.C.J. No. 521 (QL), 2005 BCSC 350) were faced with the task of managing security and intelligence information and attempting to protect procedural fairness. The Crown was in possession of the fruits of a 17-year-long investigation into the terrorist bombing of a passenger aircraft and a related explosion in Narita, Japan. It withheld material on the basis of relevance, national security privilege and litigation privilege. Crown and defence counsel came to an agreement under which defence counsel obtained consents from their clients to conduct a preliminary review of the withheld material, on written undertakings not to disclose the material to anyone, including the client. Disclosure in a specific trial, to a select group of counsel on undertakings, may not provide a working model for general deportation legislation that must deal with a wide variety of counsel in a host of cases. Nevertheless, the procedures adopted in the Air India trial suggest that a search should be made for a less intrusive solution than the one found in the IRPA.

The Arar Inquiry provides another example of the use of special counsel in Canada. The Commission had to examine confidential information related to the investigation of terrorism plots while preserving Mr. Arar's and the public's interest in disclosure. The Commission was governed by the CEA. To help assess claims for confidentiality, the Commissioner was assisted by independent security-cleared legal counsel with a background in security and intelligence, whose role was to act as *amicus curiae* on confidentiality applications. The scheme's aim was to ensure that only information that was rightly subject to national security confidentiality was kept from public view. There is no indication that these procedures increased the risk of disclosure of protected information.

Finally, I note the special advocate system employed by the Special Immigration Appeals Commission (SIAC) in the United Kingdom. SIAC and the special advocate system were created in response to *Chahal v. United Kingdom* (1996), 23 E.H.R.R. 413, in which the European Court of Human Rights had held that the procedure then in place was inadequate. The court in *Chahal* commented favourably on the idea of security-cleared counsel instructed by the court, identifying it as being Canadian in origin (perhaps referring to the procedure developed by SIRC).

Parliament is not required to use the *perfect*, or least restrictive, alternative to achieve its objective. However, bearing in mind the deference that is owed to Parliament in its legislative choices, the alternatives discussed demonstrate that the IRPA does not minimally impair the named person's rights.

Under the IRPA, the government effectively decides what can be disclosed to the named person. Not only is the named person not shown the information and not permitted to participate in proceedings involving it, but no one but the judge may look at the information with a view to protecting the named person's interests. Why the drafters of the legislation did not provide for special counsel to objectively review the material with a view to protecting the named person's interest, as was formerly done for the review of security certificates by SIRC and is presently done in the United Kingdom, has not been explained. The special counsel system may not be perfect from the named person's perspective, given that special counsel cannot reveal confidential material. But, without compromising security, it better protects the named person's § 7 interests.

I conclude that the IRPA's procedures for determining whether a certificate is reasonable and for detention review cannot be justified as minimal impairments of the individual's right to a judicial determination on the facts and the law and right to know and meet the case. Mechanisms developed in Canada and abroad illustrate that the government can do more to protect the individual while keeping critical information confidential than it has done in the IRPA. Precisely what more should be done is a matter for Parliament to decide. But it is clear that more must be done to meet the requirements of a free and democratic society.

[The Court proceeded to hold that the statutory scheme did not violate constitutional time limits on review of immigration decisions, did not constitute cruel and unusual punishment, and did not unjustifiably discriminate against foreign nationals.]

IV. CONCLUSION

[I]n order to give Parliament time to amend the law, I would suspend this declaration for one year from the date of this judgment. If the government chooses to go forward with the proceedings to have the reasonableness of Mr. Charkaoui's certificate determined during the one-year suspension period, the existing process under the IRPA will apply. If the government intends to employ a certificate after the one-year delay, it will need to seek a fresh determination of reasonableness under the new process devised by Parliament. Likewise, any detention review occurring after the delay will be subject to the new process.

PUBLIC COMMITTEE AGAINST TORTURE v. GOVERNMENT OF ISRAEL
(Targeted Killings Case)
HCJ 769/02 (Supreme Ct. Israel Dec. 11, 2005)

PRESIDENT BARAK.

The Government of Israel employs a policy of preventative strikes which cause the death of terrorists in Judea, Samaria, or the Gaza Strip. It fatally strikes these terrorists, who plan, launch, or commit terrorist attacks in Israel and in the area of Judea, Samaria, and the Gaza Strip, against both civilians and soldiers. These strikes at times also harm innocent civilians. Does the State thus act illegally? That is the question posed before us.

Petitioners' position is that the legal system applicable to the armed conflict between Israel and the terrorist organizations is not the laws of war, rather the legal system dealing with law enforcement in occupied territory. At first it was claimed that the laws of war deal primarily with international conflicts, whereas the armed conflict between

Israel and the Palestinians does not fit the definition of an international conflict. [Then] petitioners conceded that the conflict under discussion is an international conflict [but argued that in this setting] military acts to which the laws of war apply are not allowed. Against a civilian population under occupation there is no right to self defense; there is only the right to enforce the law in accordance with the laws of belligerent occupation. In any case, the laws applicable to the issue at hand are the laws of policing and law enforcement within the framework of the law of belligerent occupation, and not the laws of war. Within that framework, suspects are not to be killed without due process, or without arrest or trial. The targeted killings violate the basic right to life, and no defense or justification is to be found for that violation. The prohibition of arbitrary killing which is not necessary for self defense is entrenched in the customary norms of international law. Such a prohibition stems also from the duties of the force controlling occupied territory toward the members of the occupied population, who are protected persons according to IV Geneva.

Alternatively, petitioners claim that the targeted killings policy violates the rules of international law even if the laws applicable to the armed conflict between Israel and the Palestinians are the laws of war. These laws recognize only two statuses of people: combatants and civilians. Combatants are legitimate targets, but they also enjoy the rights granted in international law to combatants, including immunity from trial and the right to the status of prisoner of war. Civilians enjoy the protections and rights granted in international law to civilians during war. Inter alia, they are not a legitimate target for attack. Petitioners' stance is that this division between combatants and civilians is an exhaustive division. There is no intermediate status, and there is no third category of "unlawful combatants." Any person who is not a combatant, and any person about whom there is doubt, automatically has the status of civilian, and is entitled to the rights and protections granted to civilians at the time of war. Nor is a civilian participating in combat activities an "unlawful combatant"; he is a civilian criminal, and in any case he retains his status as a civilian. Petitioners thus reject the State's position that the members of terrorist organizations are unlawful combatants.

Petitioners note that a civilian participating in combat might lose part of the protections granted to civilians at a time of combat; but that is so only when such a person takes a direct part in combat, and only for such time as that direct participation continues. Thus, for example, from the time that the civilian returns to his house, and even if he intends to participate again later in hostilities, he is not a legitimate target for attack, although he can be arrested and tried for his participation in the combat. Petitioners claim that the targeted killings policy, as carried out in practice, and as respondents testify expressly, strays beyond those narrow boundaries. It harms civilians at times when they are not taking a direct part in combat or hostilities. The targeted killings are carried out under circumstances in which the conditions of immediacy and necessity — without which it is forbidden to harm civilians — are not fulfilled. Thus, it is an illegal policy which constitutes forbidden attack of civilian targets.

Respondents point out the security background which led to the targeted killings policy. Since late September 2000, acts of combat and terrorism are being committed against Israel. As a result of those acts, more than one thousand Israeli citizens have been killed during the period from 2000–2005. Thousands more have been wounded. The security forces take various steps in order to confront these acts of combat and terrorism. In light of the armed conflict, the laws applicable to these acts are the laws of war, or the laws of armed conflict, which are part of international law. Respondents' stance is that the argument that Israel is permitted to defend herself against terrorism only via means of law enforcement is to be rejected. Even if there is disagreement among experts regarding the question what constitutes an "armed attack," there can be no doubt that the assault of terrorism against Israel fits the definition of an armed attack. Thus, Israel is permitted to use military force against the terrorist organizations.

Respondents' position is that the laws of war apply not only to war in the classic sense, but also to other armed conflicts. International law does not include an unequivocal definition of the concept of "armed conflict." However, there is no longer any doubt that an armed conflict can exist between a state and groups and organizations which are not states. That is due, inter alia, to the military ability and means which such organizations have, as well as their willingness to use them. The current conflict between Israel and the terrorist organizations is an armed conflict, in the framework of which Israel is permitted to use military means. That is because according to all of the classifications, the laws of armed conflict will apply to the acts of the State. These laws allow striking at persons who are party to the armed conflict and take an active part in it, whether it is an international or non-international armed conflict, and even if it belongs to a new category of armed conflict which has been developing over the last decade in international law — a category of armed conflicts between states and terrorist organizations. According to each of these categories, a person who is party to the armed conflict and takes an active part in it is a combatant, and it is permissible to strike at him. Respondents' position is that the members of terrorist organizations are party to the armed conflict between Israel and the terrorist organizations, and they take an active part in the fighting. Thus, they are legal targets for attack for as long as the armed conflict continues. However, they are not entitled to the rights of combatants according to [IV] Geneva since they do not differentiate themselves from the civilian population, and since they do not obey the laws of war. In light of that complex reality, respondents' position is that a third category of persons — the category of unlawful combatants — should be recognized. Persons in that category are combatants, and thus they constitute legitimate targets for attack. However, they are not entitled to all the rights granted to legal combatants, as they themselves do not fulfill the requirements of the laws of war.

Alternatively, respondents' position is that the targeted killings policy is legal even if the Court should reject the argument that terrorist organization members are combatants and party to the armed conflict, and even if they are to be seen as having the status of civilians. That is because the laws of armed conflict allow harming civilians taking a direct part in hostilities. There is no prohibition on striking at the terrorist at any time and place, as long as he has not laid down his arms and exited the circle of violence. Respondents' position is that the very narrow interpretation proposed by petitioners for article 51(3) is unreasonable and angering. It appears from the stance of petitioners, as well as from the expert opinion on their behalf, that terrorists are granted immunity from harm for the entire time that they plan terrorist attacks, and that this immunity is removed for only a most short time, at the time of the actual execution of the terrorist attack. After the execution of the terrorist attack the immunity once again applies to the terrorists, even if it is clearly known that they are returning to their homes to plan and execute the next terrorist attack. This interpretation allows those who take an active part in hostilities to "change their hat" at will, between the hat of a combatant and the hat of a civilian. That result is unacceptable.

Our starting point is that the law that applies to the armed conflict between Israel and the terrorist organizations in the area is the international law dealing with armed conflicts. So this Court has viewed the character of the conflict in the past, and so we continue to view it in the petition before us. According to that view, the fact that the terrorist organizations and their members do not act in the name of a state does not turn the struggle against them into a purely internal state conflict. Indeed, in today's reality, a terrorist organization is likely to have considerable military capabilities. At times they have military capabilities that exceed those of states. Confrontation with those dangers cannot be restricted within the state and its penal law.

Customary international law regarding armed conflicts distinguishes between combatants and military targets, and non-combatants, in other words, civilians and civilian objectives. According to the basic principle of the distinction, the balancing point between the State's military need and the other side's combatants and military objectives is not the same as the balancing point between the state's military need and the other side's civilians and civilian objectives. In general, combatants and military objectives are legitimate targets for military attack. Their lives and bodies are endangered by the combat. They can be killed and wounded. However, not every act of combat against them is permissible, and not every military means is permissible. Thus, for example, they can be shot and killed. However, "treacherous killing" and "perfidy" are forbidden. Use of certain weapons is also forbidden.

In the oral and written arguments before us, the state asked us to recognize a third category of persons, that of unlawful combatants. These are people who take active and continuous part in an armed conflict, and therefore should be treated as combatants, in the sense that they are legitimate targets of attack, and they do not enjoy the protections granted to civilians. However, they are not entitled to the rights and privileges of combatants, since they do not differentiate themselves from the civilian population, and since they do not obey the laws of war. Thus, for example, they are not entitled to the status of prisoners of war. The state's position is that the terrorists who participate in the armed conflict between Israel and the terrorist organizations fall under this category of unlawful combatants.

We shall take no stance regarding the question whether it is desirable to recognize this third category. The question before us is not one of desirable law, rather one of existing law. In our opinion, as far as existing law goes, the data before us are not sufficient to recognize this third category. It is difficult for us to see how a third category can be recognized in the framework of the Hague and Geneva Conventions. It does not appear to us that we were presented with data sufficient to allow us to say, at the present time, that such a third category has been recognized in customary international law. However, new reality at times requires new interpretation. Rules developed against the background of a reality which has changed must take on dynamic interpretation which adapts them, in the framework of accepted interpretational rules, to the new reality. In the spirit of such interpretation, we shall now proceed to the customary international law dealing with the status of civilians who constitute unlawful combatants.

Civilians enjoy comprehensive protection of their lives, liberty, and property. "The protection of the lives of the civilian population is a central value in humanitarian law."As opposed to combatants, whom one can harm due to their status as combatants, civilians are not to be harmed, due to their status as civilians. A provision in this spirit is determined in article 51(2) of The First Protocol, which constitutes customary international law: "The civilian population as such, as well as individual civilians, shall not be the object of attack." Article 8(2)(b)(i)-(ii) of the Rome Statute of the International Criminal Court determines, in the same spirit, in defining a war crime, that if an order to attack civilians is given intentionally, that is a crime. That crime applies to those civilians who are "not taking direct part in hostilities." In addition, civilians are not to be harmed in an indiscriminate attack; in other words, in an attack which, inter alia, is not directed against a particular military objective. That protection is granted to all civilians, excepting those civilians taking a direct part in hostilities.

The basic principle is that the civilians taking a direct part in hostilities are not protected from attack upon them at such time as they are doing so. This principle is manifest in §51(3) of The First Protocol, which determines: "Civilians shall enjoy the protection afforded by this section, unless and for such time as they take a direct part in hostilities."

As is well known, Israel is not party to The First Protocol. Thus, it clearly was not enacted in internal Israeli legislation. Does the basic principle express customary international law? The position of The Red Cross is that it is a principle of customary international law. That position is acceptable to us. It fits the provision Common Article 3 of The Geneva Conventions, to which Israel is party and which, according to all, reflects customary international law, pursuant to which protection is granted to persons. "[T]aking no active part in the hostilities." The International Criminal Tribunal for the former Yugoslavia determined that article 51 of The First Protocol constitutes customary international law. In military manuals of many states, including England, France, Holland, Australia, Italy, Canada, Germany, the United States (Air Force), and New Zealand, the provision has been copied verbatim, or by adopting its essence, according to which civilians are not to be attacked, unless they are taking a (direct) part in the hostilities.

The basic approach is thus as follows: a civilian — that is, a person who does not fall into the category of combatant – must refrain from directly participating in hostilities. A civilian who violates that law and commits acts of combat does not lose his status as a civilian, but as long as he is taking a direct part in hostilities he does not enjoy — during that time — the protection granted to a civilian. He is subject to the risks of attack like those to which a combatant is subject, without enjoying the rights of a combatant, e.g., those granted to a prisoner of war. True, his status is that of a civilian, and he does not lose that status while he is directly participating in hostilities. However, he is a civilian performing the function of a combatant. As long as he performs that function, he is subject to the risks which that function entails and ceases to enjoy the protection granted to a civilian from attack.

The terrorists and their organizations, with which the State of Israel has an armed conflict of international character, do not fall into the category of combatants. They do not belong to the armed forces, and they do not belong to units to which international law grants status similar to that of combatants. Indeed, the terrorists and the organizations which send them to carry out attacks are unlawful combatants. They do not enjoy the status of prisoners of war. They can be tried for their participation in hostilities, judged, and punished.

Needless to say, unlawful combatants are not beyond the law. They are not "outlaws." God created them as well in his image; their human dignity as well is to be honored; they as well enjoy and are entitled to protection, even if most minimal, by customary international law

On the one hand, a civilian who took a direct part in hostilities once, or sporadically, but detached himself from them (entirely, or for a long period) is not to be harmed. On the other hand, the "revolving door" phenomenon, by which each terrorist has "horns of the alter" (1 Kings 1:50) to grasp or a "city of refuge" (Numbers 35:11) to flee to, to which he turns in order to rest and prepare while they grant him immunity from attack, is to be avoided. In the wide area between those two possibilities, one finds the "gray" cases, about which customary international law has not yet crystallized. There is thus no escaping examination of each and every case. In that context, the following four things should be said: first, well based information is needed before categorizing a civilian as falling into one of the discussed categories. Innocent civilians are not to be harmed. Information which has been most thoroughly verified is needed regarding the identity and activity of the civilian who is allegedly taking part in the hostilities.

Second, a civilian taking a direct part in hostilities cannot be attacked at such time as he is doing so, if a less harmful means can be employed. In our internal law, that rule is called for by the principle of proportionality. Indeed, among the military means, one must choose the means whose harm to the human rights of the harmed person is smallest. Thus, if a terrorist taking a direct part in hostilities can be arrested, interrogated, and tried, those are the means which should be employed. Trial is preferable to use of force. A rule-of-law state employs, to the extent possible, procedures of law and not procedures of force. That question arose in *McCann v. United Kingdom*, 21 E.H.R.R. 97 (1995). In that case, three terrorists from Northern Ireland who belonged to the IRA were shot to death. They were shot in the streets of Gibraltar, by English agents. The European Court of Human Rights determined that

England had illegally impinged upon their right to life (§ 2 of the European Convention on Human Rights). So wrote the court:

> [T]he use of lethal force would be rendered disproportionate if the authorities failed, whether deliberately or through lack of proper care, to take steps which would have avoided the deprivation of life of the suspects without putting the lives of others at risk.

Arrest, investigation, and trial are not means which can always be used. At times the possibility does not exist whatsoever; at times it involves a risk so great to the lives of the soldiers, that it is not required. However, it is a possibility which should always be considered.

Third, after an attack on a civilian suspected of taking an active part, at such time, in hostilities, a thorough investigation regarding the precision of the identification of the target and the circumstances of the attack upon him is to be performed (retroactively). That investigation must be independent. In appropriate cases it is appropriate to pay compensation as a result of harm caused to an innocent civilian.

Last, if the harm is not only to a civilian directly participating in the hostilities, rather also to innocent civilians nearby, the harm to them is collateral damage. That damage must withstand the proportionality test.

The examination of the "targeted killing" — and in our terms, the preventative strike causing the deaths of terrorists, and at times also of innocent civilians — has shown that the question of the legality of the preventative strike according to customary international law is complex. The result of that examination is not that such strikes are always permissible or that they are always forbidden. The approach of customary international law applying to armed conflicts of an international nature is that civilians are protected from attacks by the army. However, that protection does not exist regarding those civilians "for such time as they take a direct part in hostilities." Harming such civilians, even if the result is death, is permitted, on the condition that there is no other means which harms them less, and on the condition that innocent civilians nearby are not harmed. Harm to the latter must be proportional.

As we have seen, we cannot determine that a preventative strike is always legal, just as we cannot determine that it is always illegal. All depends upon the question whether the standards of customary international law regarding international armed conflict allow that preventative strike or not.

The question is not whether it is possible to defend ourselves against terrorism. Of course it is possible to do so, and at times it is even a duty to do so. The question is how we respond. On that issue, a balance is needed between security needs and individual rights. That balancing casts a heavy load upon those whose job is to provide security. Not every efficient means is also legal. The ends do not justify the means. The army must instruct itself according to the rules of the law.

Indeed, decision of the petition before us is not easy. [As stated in a prior case]:

> We are members of Israeli society. Although we are sometimes in an ivory tower, that tower is in the heart of Jerusalem, which is not infrequently hit by ruthless terrorism. We are aware of the killing and destruction wrought by the terrorism against the State and its citizens. As any other Israelis, we too recognize the need to defend the country and its citizens against terrorism's severe blow. We are aware that in the short term, this judgment will not make the State's struggle against those rising up against her easier. That knowledge is difficult for us. But we are judges. When we sit in trial, we stand trial. We act according to our best conscience and understanding. Regarding the State's struggle against the terror that rises up against her, we are convinced that at the end of the day, a struggle according to law (and while complying with the law) strengthens her and her spirit. There is no security without law. Satisfying the provisions of the law is a component of national security.

In one case we decided the question whether the state is permitted to order its interrogators to employ special methods of interrogation which involve the use of force against terrorists, in a "ticking bomb" situation. We answered that question in the negative. In my judgment, I described the difficult security situation in which Israel finds itself, and added:

> We are aware that this judgment of ours does not make confronting that reality any easier. That is the fate of democracy, in whose eyes not all means are permitted, and to whom not all the methods used by her enemies are open. At times democracy fights with one hand tied behind her back. Despite that, democracy has the upper hand, since preserving the rule of law and recognition of individual liberties constitute an important component of her security stance. At the end of the day, they strengthen her and her spirit, and allow her to overcome her difficulties.

Let it be so.

VICE-PRESIDENT RIVLIN, concurring:

The interpretation proposed by my colleague President Barak creates a new group, and rightly so. It can be derived from the combatant group ("unlawful combatants") and it can be derived from the civilian group. My colleague President Barak takes the second path. If we go his way, we should derive a group of international-law-breaking civilians, whom I would call "uncivilized civilians." In any case, there is no difference between the two paths in terms of the result, since the interpretation of the provisions of international law proposed by my colleague President Barak adapts the rules to the new reality. That interpretation is acceptable to me. It is a dynamic interpretation which overcomes the limitations of a black letter reading of the laws of war.

SOME CONCLUDING THOUGHTS AND QUESTIONS

This course could conclude by spending some time ruminating on what all this means to us today and could mean in the future. There are many articles on the internet regarding the general themes of civil liberties and terrorism. Within academic writing, much effort is being spent on what constitutes an emergency and what powers government should be given in time of emergency.

> Experience shows that when grave national crises are upon us, democratic nations tend to race to the bottom as far as the protection of human rights and civil liberties, indeed of basic and fundamental legal principles, is concerned. . . . Speaking in Jerusalem in 1987, Justice Brennan stated:

>> There is considerably less to be proud about, and a good deal to be embarrassed about, when one reflects on the shabby treatment civil liberties have received in the United States during times of war and perceived threats to its national security. . . . After each perceived security crisis ended, the United States has remorsefully realized that the abrogation of civil liberties was unnecessary. But it has proven unable to prevent itself from repeating the error when the next crisis came along.

Oren Gross, *Chaos and Rules: Should Responses to Violent Crises Always Be Constitutional?*, 112 YALE L.J. 1011 (2003).

The post-9/11 world epitomizes the constant need for law to assist in the elaboration of public policy issues. Toward that end, we should all be engaged in ongoing discussions of issues such as:

> 1. Do you dare take risks with the safety of your family given the avowed intent of some terrorists to kill Americans at any opportunity? Isn?t the first responsibility of government to keep us alive?

> 2. How do you feel about the use of military force against non-state actors?

> 3. What is the law regarding the capture or killing of known terrorists hiding

in other countries? Should we rethink our position on assassination of foreign persons in light of the difficulty of capture and prosecution?

　　4. Given threats to public safety, how important is the privacy of your

　　　　a. communications and reading habits?

　　　　b. bank accounts?

　　　　c. membership or affinity with organizations?

　　5. Do you trust your government without knowing all it does? Do you want to know

　　　　a. how many explosive devices and weapons have been confiscated at ports?

　　　　b. who has been killed or captured in foreign lands?

　　　　c. what communications have been recorded from satellite relays?

　　6. Do you trust the courts to protect your freedoms in time of crisis?

　　7. How important is it to you that we have the right to discuss these matters without fear of government reprisal?

§ 9.03　SELECTED READINGS

Interrogation and Torture:

- MARK DANNER, TORTURE AND TRUTH: AMERICA, ABU GHRAIB, AND THE WAR ON TERROR (2004)

- KAREN GREENBERG AND JOSHUA DRATEL, THE TORTURE PAPERS: THE ROAD TO ABU GHRAIB (2005)

- SEYMOUR HERSH, CHAIN OF COMMAND (2004)

- JOHN LANGBEIN, TORTURE AND THE LAW OF PROOF: EUROPE AND ENGLAND IN THE ANCIENT REGIME (1977)

- M. Cherif Bassiouni, *The Institutionalization of Torture under the Bush Administration*, 37 CASE W. RES. J. INT'L L. 389 (2006)

- Ian Brownlie, *Interrogation in Depth: The Compton and Parker Reports*, 35 MOD. L. REV. 501 (1972)

- Oren Gross, *Are Torture Warrants Warranted? Pragmatic Absolutism and Official Disobedience*, 88 MINN. L. REV. 1481 (2004)

- Dawn J. Miller, *Holding States to Their Convention Obligations: The United Nations Convention Against Torture and the Need for a Broad Interpretation of State Action*, 17 GEO. IMMIGR. L.J. 299 (2003)

- John T. Parry, *What Is Torture, Are We Doing It, and What If We Are?* 64 U. PITT. L. REV. 237 (2003)

Emergency Powers (in chronological order):

- PAUL L. MURPHY, THE CONSTITUTION IN CRISIS TIMES, 1918–1969 (1972)

- MARTHA CRENSHAW (ED.), TERRORISM, LEGITIMACY, AND POWER (1983)

- Pnina Lahav, *A Barrel Without Hoops: The Impact of Counterterrorism on Israel's Legal Culture*, 10 CARDOZO L. REV. 529 (1988)

- William J. Brennan, *The Quest To Develop a Jurisprudence of Civil Liberties in Times of Security Crisis*, 18 ISR. YB HUM. RTS. 11 (1988)

- Jules Lobel, *Emergency Power and the Decline of Liberalism*, 98 YALE L.J. 1385 (1989)

- Itzhak Zamir, *Human Rights and National Security*, 22 ISR. L. REV. 375 (1989)

·   MICHAEL LINFIELD, FREEDOM UNDER FIRE: U.S. CIVIL LIBERTIES IN TIMES OF WAR (1990)

·   Peter Rosenthal, *The New Emergencies Act: Four Times the War Measures Act*, 20 MAN. L.J. 563 (1991) (Canadian experience)

·   Oren Gross, *"Once More Unto the Breach:" The Systemic Failure of Applying the European Convention on Human Rights to Entrenched Emergencies*, 23 YALE J. INT'L L. 437 (1998)

·   WILLIAM H. REHNQUIST, ALL THE LAWS BUT ONE (1998)

    Keith E. Whittington, *Yet Another Constitutional Crisis?* 43 WM. & MARY L. REV. 2093 (2002)

·   Rodney A. Smolla, *Terrorism and the Bill of Rights*, 10 WM. & MARY BILL OF RTS. J. 551 (2002)

·   Oren Gross, *Chaos and Rules: Should Responses to Violent Crises Always Be Constitutional?* 112 YALE L.J. 1011, 1023 (2003)

·   David Cole, *Judging the Next Emergency: Judicial Review and Individual Rights in Times of Crisis*, 101 MICH. L. REV. 2565, 2594 (2003)

·   Oren Gross, *Providing for the Unexpected: Constitutional Emergency Provisions*, 33 ISR. Y.B. HUM. RTS. 13 (2003)

·   Eric A. Posner & Adrian Vermeule, *Accommodating Emergencies*, 56 STAN. L. REV. 605 (2003)

·   Bruce Ackerman, *The Emergency Constitution*, 113 YALE L.J. 1029 (2004).

·   David Cole, *The Priority of Morality: The Emergency Constitution's Blind Spot*, 113 YALE L.J. 1753 (2004)

·   Laurence H. Tribe & Patrick O. Gudridge, *The Anti-Emergency Constitution*, 113 YALE L.J. 1801 (2004)

Appendix

DOCUMENTS

A. U.S. STATUTES, RESOLUTIONS, AND ORDERS

1. General Federal Criminal Law

18 U.S.C. § 1111. Murder

(a)   Murder is the unlawful killing of a human being with malice aforethought. Every murder perpetrated by poison, lying in wait, or any other kind of willful, deliberate, malicious, and premeditated killing; or committed in the perpetration of, or attempt to perpetrate, any arson, escape, murder, kidnaping, treason, espionage, sabotage, aggravated sexual abuse or sexual abuse, child abuse, burglary, or robbery; or perpetrated as part of a pattern or practice of assault or torture against a child or children; or perpetrated from a premeditated design unlawfully and maliciously to effect the death of any human being other than him who is killed, is murder in the first degree.

Any other murder is murder in the second degree.

(b)   Within the special maritime and territorial jurisdiction of the United States,

Whoever is guilty of murder in the first degree shall be punished by death or by imprisonment for life;

Whoever is guilty of murder in the second degree, shall be imprisoned for any term of years or for life.

18 U.S.C. § 1114. Protection of officers and employees of the United States

Whoever kills or attempts to kill any officer or employee of the United States or of any agency in any branch of the United States Government (including any member of the uniformed services) while such officer or employee is engaged in or on account of the performance of official duties, or any person assisting such an officer or employee in the performance of such duties or on account of that assistance, shall be punished

(1)   in the case of murder, as provided under section 1111;

(2)   in the case of manslaughter, as provided under section 1112; or

(3)   in the case of attempted murder or manslaughter, as provided in section 1113.

18 U.S.C. § 1119. Foreign murder of United States nationals

(a)   Definition. In this section, "national of the United States" has the meaning stated in section 101(a)(22) of the Immigration and Nationality Act (8 U.S.C. 1101(a)(22)).

(b)   Offense. A person who, being a national of the United States, kills or attempts to kill a national of the United States while such national is outside the United States but within the jurisdiction of another country shall be punished as provided under sections 1111, 1112, and 1113.

(c)   Limitations on prosecution.

(1)   No prosecution may be instituted against any person under this section except upon the written approval of the Attorney General, the Deputy Attorney General, or an Assistant Attorney General, which function of approving prosecutions may not be delegated. No prosecution shall be approved if prosecution has been previously undertaken by a foreign country for the same conduct.

(2)   No prosecution shall be approved under this section unless the Attorney General, in consultation with the Secretary of State, determines that the conduct took

place in a country in which the person is no longer present, and the country lacks the ability to lawfully secure the person's return. A determination by the Attorney General under this paragraph is not subject to judicial review.

§ 956. Conspiracy to kill, kidnap, maim, or injure persons or damage property in a foreign country

(a)(1)   Whoever, within the jurisdiction of the United States, conspires with one or more other persons, regardless of where such other person or persons are located, to commit at any place outside the United States an act that would constitute the offense of murder, kidnapping, or maiming if committed in the special maritime and territorial jurisdiction of the United States shall, if any of the conspirators commits an act within the jurisdiction of the United States to effect any object of the conspiracy, be punished as provided in subsection (a)(2).

(2)   The punishment for an offense under subsection (a)(1) of this section is—

(A)   imprisonment for any term of years or for life if the offense is conspiracy to murder or kidnap; and

(B)   imprisonment for not more than 35 years if the offense is conspiracy to maim.

(b)   Whoever, within the jurisdiction of the United States, conspires with one or more persons, regardless of where such other person or persons are located, to damage or destroy specific property situated within a foreign country and belonging to a foreign government or to any political subdivision thereof with which the United States is at peace, or any railroad, canal, bridge, airport, airfield, or other public utility, public conveyance, or public structure, or any religious, educational, or cultural property so situated, shall, if any of the conspirators commits an act within the jurisdiction of the United States to effect any object of the conspiracy, be imprisoned not more than 25 years.

18 U.S.C. § 844   [Penalties for unlawful use of explosive materials]

(d)   Whoever transports or receives, or attempts to transport or receive, in interstate or foreign commerce any explosive with the knowledge or intent that it will be used to kill, injure, or intimidate any individual or unlawfully to damage or destroy any building, vehicle, or other real or personal property, shall be imprisoned for not more than ten years, or fined under this title, or both; and if personal injury results to any person, including any public safety officer performing duties as a direct or proximate result of conduct prohibited by this subsection, shall be imprisoned for not more than twenty years or fined under this title, or both; and if death results to any person, including any public safety officer performing duties as a direct or proximate result of conduct prohibited by this subsection, shall be subject to imprisonment for any term of years, or to the death penalty or to life imprisonment.

(e)   Whoever, through the use of the mail, telephone, telegraph, or other instrument of interstate or foreign commerce, or in or affecting interstate or foreign commerce, willfully makes any threat, or maliciously conveys false information knowing the same to be false, concerning an attempt or alleged attempt being made, or to be made, to kill, injure, or intimidate any individual or unlawfully to damage or destroy any building, vehicle, or other real or personal property by means of fire or an explosive shall be imprisoned for not more than 10 years or fined under this title, or both.

(f)(1)   Whoever maliciously damages or destroys, or attempts to damage or destroy, by means of fire or an explosive, any building, vehicle, or other personal or real property in whole or in part owned or possessed by, or leased to, the United States, or any department or agency thereof, or any institution or organization receiving Federal financial assistance, shall be imprisoned for not less than 5 years and not more than 20 years, fined under this title, or both.

(2) Whoever engages in conduct prohibited by this subsection, and as a result of such conduct, directly or proximately causes personal injury or creates a substantial risk of injury to any person, including any public safety officer performing duties, shall be imprisoned for not less than 7 years and not more than 40 years, fined under this title, or both.

(3) Whoever engages in conduct prohibited by this subsection, and as a result of such conduct directly or proximately causes the death of any person, including any public safety officer performing duties, shall be subject to the death penalty, or imprisoned for not less than 20 years or for life, fined under this title, or both.

2. Federal "Civil Rights" Statutes

18 U.S.C. § 241. Conspiracy against rights

If two or more persons conspire to injure, oppress, threaten, or intimidate any person in any State, Territory, Commonwealth, Possession, or District in the free exercise or enjoyment of any right or privilege secured to him by the Constitution or laws of the United States, or because of his having so exercised the same; or

If two or more persons go in disguise on the highway, or on the premises of another, with intent to prevent or hinder his free exercise or enjoyment of any right or privilege so secured;

They shall be fined under this title or imprisoned not more than ten years, or both; and if death results from the acts committed in violation of this section or if such acts include kidnapping or an attempt to kidnap, aggravated sexual abuse or an attempt to commit aggravated sexual abuse, or an attempt to kill, they shall be fined under this title or imprisoned for any term of years or for life, or both, or may be sentenced to death.

18 U.S.C. § 242. Deprivation of rights under color of law

Whoever, under color of any law, statute, ordinance, regulation, or custom, willfully subjects any person in [U.S. territory] to the deprivation of any rights, privileges, or immunities secured or protected by the Constitution or laws of the United States, . . . shall be fined under this title or imprisoned not more than one year, or both; and if bodily injury results from the acts committed in violation of this section or if such acts include the use, attempted use, or threatened use of a dangerous weapon, explosives, or fire, shall be fined under this title or imprisoned not more than ten years, or both; and if death results from the acts committed in violation of this section or if such acts include kidnaping or an attempt to kidnap, aggravated sexual abuse, or an attempt to commit aggravated sexual abuse, or an attempt to kill, shall be fined under this title, or imprisoned for any term of years or for life, or both, or may be sentenced to death.

18 U.S.C. § 245 Federally Protected Activities

(b) Whoever, whether or not acting under color of law, by force or threat of force willfully injures, intimidates or interferes with, or attempts to injure, intimidate or interfere with

(1) any person because he is or has been, or in order to intimidate such person or any other person or any class of persons from

(A) voting or qualifying to vote, qualifying or campaigning as a candidate for elective office, or qualifying or acting as a poll watcher, or any legally authorized election official, in any primary, special, or general election;

(B) participating in or enjoying any benefit, service, privilege, program, facility, or activity provided or administered by the United States; . . . or

(2) any person because of his race, color, religion or national origin and because he is or has been

(A) enrolling in or attending any public school or public college;

(B) participating in or enjoying any benefit, service, privilege, program, facility or activity provided or administered by any State or subdivision thereof; . . .

(E) traveling in or using any facility of interstate commerce, or using any vehicle, terminal, or facility of any common carrier by motor, rail, water, or air;

(F) enjoying the goods, services, facilities, privileges, advantages, or accommodations of any inn, hotel, motel, or other establishment which provides lodging to transient guests, or of any restaurant, cafeteria, lunchroom, lunch counter, soda fountain, or other facility which serves the public . . . or

. . .

shall be fined under this title, or imprisoned not more than one year, or both; and if bodily injury results from the acts committed in violation of this section or if such acts include the use, attempted use, or threatened use of a dangerous weapon, explosives, or fire shall be fined under this title, or imprisoned not more than ten years, or both; and if death results from the acts committed in violation of this section or if such acts include kidnapping or an attempt to kidnap, aggravated sexual abuse or an attempt to commit aggravated sexual abuse, or an attempt to kill, shall be fined under this title or imprisoned for any term of years or for life, or both, or may be sentenced to death.

3. U.S. Statutes Based on Extraterritoriality

18 U.S.C. § 7 (2002) Special maritime and territorial jurisdiction of the United States defined

The term "special maritime and territorial jurisdiction of the United States", as used in this title, includes:

(1) The high seas, any other waters within the admiralty and maritime jurisdiction of the United States and out of the jurisdiction of any particular State, and any vessel belonging in whole or in part to the United States or any citizen thereof, or to any corporation created by or under the laws of the United States, or of any State, Territory, District, or possession thereof, when such vessel is within the admiralty and maritime jurisdiction of the United States and out of the jurisdiction of any particular State.

(2) Any vessel registered, licensed, or enrolled under the laws of the United States, and being on a voyage upon the waters of any of the Great Lakes, or any of the waters connecting them, or upon the Saint Lawrence River where the same constitutes the International Boundary Line.

(3) Any lands reserved or acquired for the use of the United States, and under the exclusive or concurrent jurisdiction thereof, or any place purchased or otherwise acquired by the United States by consent of the legislature of the State in which the same shall be, for the erection of a fort, magazine, arsenal, dockyard, or other needful building.

(4) Any island, rock, or key containing deposits of guano, which may, at the discretion of the President, be considered as appertaining to the United States.

(5) Any aircraft belonging in whole or in part to the United States, or any citizen thereof, or to any corporation created by or under the laws of the United States, or any State, Territory, district, or possession thereof, while such aircraft is in flight over the high seas, or over any other waters within the admiralty and maritime jurisdiction

of the United States and out of the jurisdiction of any particular State.

(6)   Any vehicle used or designed for flight or navigation in space and on the registry of the United States pursuant to the Treaty on Principles Governing the Activities of States in the Exploration and Use of Outer Space, Including the Moon and Other Celestial Bodies and the Convention on Registration of Objects Launched into Outer Space, while that vehicle is in flight, which is from the moment when all external doors are closed on Earth following embarkation until the moment when one such door is opened on Earth for disembarkation or in the case of a forced landing, until the competent authorities take over the responsibility for the vehicle and for persons and property aboard.

(7)   Any place outside the jurisdiction of any nation with respect to an offense by or against a national of the United States.

(8)   To the extent permitted by international law, any foreign vessel during a voyage having a scheduled departure from or arrival in the United States with respect to an offense committed by or against a national of the United States.

(9)   With respect to offenses committed by or against a national of the United States as that term is used in section 101 of the Immigration and Nationality Act

(A)   the premises of United States diplomatic, consular, military or other United States Government missions or entities in foreign States, including the buildings, parts of buildings, and land appurtenant or ancillary thereto or used for purposes of those missions or entities, irrespective of ownership; and

(B)   residences in foreign States and the land appurtenant or ancillary thereto, irrespective of ownership, used for purposes of those missions or entities or used by United States personnel assigned to those missions or entities.

Nothing in this paragraph shall be deemed to supersede any treaty or international agreement with which this paragraph conflicts. This paragraph does not apply with respect to an offense committed by a person described in section 3261(a) of this title.

18 U.S.C. § 32.   Destruction of aircraft or aircraft facilities

(a)   Whoever willfully

(1)   sets fire to, damages, destroys, disables, or wrecks any aircraft in the special aircraft jurisdiction of the United States or any civil aircraft used, operated, or employed in interstate, overseas, or foreign air commerce;

(2)   places or causes to be placed a destructive device or substance in, upon, or in proximity to, or otherwise makes or causes to be made unworkable or unusable or hazardous to work or use, any such aircraft, or any part or other materials used or intended to be used in connection with the operation of such aircraft, if such placing or causing to be placed or such making or causing to be made is likely to endanger the safety of any such aircraft;

(3)   sets fire to, damages, destroys, or disables any air navigation facility, or interferes by force or violence with the operation of such facility, if such fire, damaging, destroying, disabling, or interfering is likely to endanger the safety of any such aircraft in flight;

(4)   with the intent to damage, destroy, or disable any such aircraft, sets fire to, damages, destroys, or disables or places a destructive device or substance in, upon, or in proximity to, any appliance or structure, ramp, landing area, property, machine, or apparatus, or any facility or other material used, or intended to be used, in connection with the operation, maintenance, loading, unloading or storage of any such aircraft or any cargo carried or intended to be carried on any such aircraft;

(5)   performs an act of violence against or incapacitates any individual on any such

aircraft, if such act of violence or incapacitation is likely to endanger the safety of such aircraft;

(6) communicates information, knowing the information to be false and under circumstances in which such information may reasonably be believed, thereby endangering the safety of any such aircraft in flight; or

(7) attempts or conspires to do anything prohibited under paragraphs (1) through (6) of this subsection;

shall be fined under this title or imprisoned not more than twenty years or both.

(b) Whoever willfully

(1) performs an act of violence against any individual on board any civil aircraft registered in a country other than the United States while such aircraft is in flight, if such act is likely to endanger the safety of that aircraft;

(2) destroys a civil aircraft registered in a country other than the United States while such aircraft is in service or causes damage to such an aircraft which renders that aircraft incapable of flight or which is likely to endanger that aircraft's safety in flight;

(3) places or causes to be placed on a civil aircraft registered in a country other than the United States while such aircraft is in service, a device or substance which is likely to destroy that aircraft, or to cause damage to that aircraft which renders that aircraft incapable of flight or which is likely to endanger that aircraft's safety in flight; or

(4) attempts or conspires to commit an offense described in paragraphs (1) through (3) of this subsection;

shall be fined under this title or imprisoned not more than twenty years, or both. There is jurisdiction over an offense under this subsection if a national of the United States was on board, or would have been on board, the aircraft; an offender is a national of the United States; or an offender is afterwards found in the United States. For purposes of this subsection, the term "national of the United States" has the meaning prescribed in section 101(a)(22) of the Immigration and Nationality Act [8 U.S.C. § 1101(a)(22)].

(c) Whoever willfully imparts or conveys any threat to do an act which would violate any of paragraphs (1) through (5) of subsection (a) or any of paragraphs (1) through (3) of subsection (b) of this section, with an apparent determination and will to carry the threat into execution shall be fined under this title or imprisoned not more than five years, or both.

18 U.S.C. § 2340. [Torture Act] Definitions

As used in this chapter

(1) "torture" means an act committed by a person acting under the color of law specifically intended to inflict severe physical or mental pain or suffering (other than pain or suffering incidental to lawful sanctions) upon another person within his custody or physical control;

(2) "severe mental pain or suffering" means the prolonged mental harm caused by or resulting from

(A) the intentional infliction or threatened infliction of severe physical pain or suffering;

(B) the administration or application, or threatened administration or application, of mind-altering substances or other procedures calculated to disrupt profoundly the senses or the personality;

(C) the threat of imminent death; or

(D) the threat that another person will imminently be subjected to death, severe physical pain or suffering, or the administration or application of mind-altering substances or other procedures calculated to disrupt profoundly the senses or personality; and

(3)   "United States" includes all areas under the jurisdiction of the United States including any of the places described in sections 5 and 7 of this title and section 46501(2) of title 49.

18 U.S.C. § 2340A.   Torture

(a)   Offense. Whoever outside the United States commits or attempts to commit torture shall be fined under this title or imprisoned not more than 20 years, or both, and if death results to any person from conduct prohibited by this subsection, shall be punished by death or imprisoned for any term of years or for life.

(b)   Jurisdiction. There is jurisdiction over the activity prohibited in subsection (a) if

(1)   the alleged offender is a national of the United States; or

(2)   the alleged offender is present in the United States, irrespective of the nationality of the victim or alleged offender.

4.   U.S. Statutes Referring to "Terrorism"

A.   Designation of Organizations by State Department

8 U.S.C. § 1189.   Designation of foreign terrorist organizations

(a)   Designation.

(1)   In general. The Secretary is authorized to designate an organization as a foreign terrorist organization in accordance with this subsection if the Secretary finds that

(A)   the organization is a foreign organization;

(B)   the organization engages in terrorist activity (as defined in [8 U.S.C. § 1182(a)(3)(B)]) or terrorism (as defined in [22 U.S.C. § 2656f(d)(2)]), or retains the capability and intent to engage in terrorist activity or terrorism; and

(C)   the terrorist activity or terrorism of the organization threatens the security of United States nationals or the national security of the United States.

(2)   Procedure.

(A)   Notice.

(i)   To congressional leaders. Seven days before making a designation under this subsection, the Secretary shall, by classified communication, notify the Speaker and Minority Leader of the House of Representatives, the President pro tempore, Majority Leader, and Minority Leader of the Senate, and the members of the relevant committees of the House of Representatives and the Senate, in writing, of the intent to designate an organization under this subsection, together with the findings made under paragraph (1) with respect to that organization, and the factual basis therefor.

(ii)   Publication in Federal Register. The Secretary shall publish the designation in the Federal Register seven days after providing the notification under clause (i).

(B)   Effect of designation.

(i)   For purposes of section 2339B of title 18, United States Code, a designation under this subsection shall take effect upon publication under subparagraph (A)(ii).

(ii)   Any designation under this subsection shall cease to have effect upon an Act of Congress disapproving such designation.

(C)   Freezing of assets. Upon notification under paragraph (2)(A)(i), the Secretary of the Treasury may require United States financial institutions possessing or controlling any assets of any foreign organization included in the notification to block all financial transactions involving those assets until further directive from either the Secretary of the Treasury, Act of Congress, or order of court.

(3)   Record.

(A)   In general. In making a designation under this subsection, the Secretary shall create an administrative record.

(B)   Classified information. The Secretary may consider classified information in making a designation under this subsection. Classified information shall not be subject to disclosure for such time as it remains classified, except that such information may be disclosed to a court ex parte and in camera for purposes of judicial review under subsection (b).

(4)   Period of designation.

(A)   In general. Subject to paragraphs (5) and (6), a designation under this subsection shall be effective for all purposes for a period of 2 years beginning on the effective date of the designation under paragraph (2)(B).

(B)   Redesignation. The Secretary may redesignate a foreign organization as a foreign terrorist organization for an additional 2-year period at the end of [any] 2-year period.

(5)   Revocation by Act of Congress. The Congress, by an Act of Congress, may block or revoke a designation made under paragraph (1).

(6)   Revocation based on change in circumstances.

(A)   In general. The Secretary may revoke a designation made under paragraph (1) or a redesignation made under paragraph (4)(B) if the Secretary finds that

(i)   the circumstances that were the basis for the designation or redesignation have changed in such a manner as to warrant revocation; or

(ii)   the national security of the United States warrants a revocation.

(B)   Procedure. The procedural requirements of paragraphs (2) and (3) shall apply to a revocation under this paragraph. Any revocation shall take effect on the date specified in the revocation or upon publication in the Federal Register if no effective date is specified.

(7)   Effect of revocation. The revocation of a designation under paragraph (5) or (6), or the revocation of a redesignation under paragraph (6), shall not affect any action or proceeding based on conduct committed prior to the effective date of such revocation.

(8)   Use of designation in trial or hearing. If a designation under this subsection has become effective . . . , a defendant in a criminal action or an alien in a removal proceeding shall not be permitted to raise any question concerning the validity of the issuance of such designation or redesignation as a defense or an objection at any trial or hearing.

(b)   Judicial review of designation.

(1)   In general. Not later than 30 days after publication of the designation in the Federal Register, an organization designated as a foreign terrorist organization may seek judicial review of the designation in the United States Court of Appeals for the District of Columbia Circuit.

(2)   Basis of review. Review under this subsection shall be based solely upon the administrative record, except that the Government may submit, for *ex parte* and *in camera* review, classified information used in making the designation.

(3)   Scope of review. The Court shall hold unlawful and set aside a designation the court finds to be

(A)   arbitrary, capricious, an abuse of discretion, or otherwise not in accordance with law;

(B)   contrary to constitutional right, power, privilege, or immunity;

(C)   in excess of statutory jurisdiction, authority, or limitation, or short of statutory right;

(D)   lacking substantial support in the administrative record taken as a whole or in classified information submitted to the court under paragraph (2), or

(E)   not in accord with the procedures required by law.

(4)   Judicial review invoked. The pendency of an action for judicial review of a designation shall not affect the application of this section, unless the court issues a final order setting aside the designation.

8 U.S.C. § 1182(a)(3).   Terrorist activity defined.

As used in [§ 1189], the term "terrorist activity" means any activity which is unlawful under the laws of the place where it is committed (or which, if it had been committed in the United States, would be unlawful under the laws of the United States or any State) and which involves any of the following:

(I)   The highjacking or sabotage of any conveyance (including an aircraft, vessel, or vehicle).

(II)   The seizing or detaining, and threatening to kill, injure, or continue to detain, another individual in order to compel a third person (including a governmental organization) to do or abstain from doing any act as an explicit or implicit condition for the release of the individual seized or detained.

(III)   A violent attack upon an internationally protected person (as defined in 18 U.S.C. § 1116(b)(4)) or upon the liberty of such a person.

(IV)   An assassination.

(V)   The use of any

(a)   biological agent, chemical agent, or nuclear weapon or device, or

(b)   explosive, firearm, or other weapon or dangerous device (other than for mere personal monetary gain), with intent to endanger, directly or indirectly, the safety of one or more individuals or to cause substantial damage to property.

(VI)   A threat, attempt, or conspiracy to do any of the foregoing.

22 U.S.C. § 2256f(d)   [definition of terrorism for purposes of designations]

(2)   the term "terrorism" means premeditated, politically motivated violence perpetrated against noncombatant targets by subnational groups or clandestine agents.

B.   Criminal Statutes Referring to Terrorism

18 U.S.C. § 2331.   Definitions

As used in this chapter [18 U.S.C. §§ 2331 et seq.]

(1)   the term "international terrorism" means activities that

(A)   involve violent acts or acts dangerous to human life that are a violation of the criminal laws of the United States or of any State, or that would be a criminal violation if committed within the jurisdiction of the United States or of any State;

(B)   appear to be intended

    (i)   to intimidate or coerce a civilian population;

    (ii)   to influence the policy of a government by intimidation or coercion; or

    (iii)   to affect the conduct of a government by mass destruction, assassination or kidnapping; and

    (C)   occur primarily outside the territorial jurisdiction of the United States, or transcend national boundaries in terms of the means by which they are accomplished, the persons they appear intended to intimidate or coerce, or the locale in which their perpetrators operate or seek asylum;

    (2)   the term "national of the United States" has the meaning given such term in section 101(a)(22) of the Immigration and Nationality Act [8 U.S.C.S § 1101(a)(22)];

    (3)   the term "person" means any individual or entity capable of holding a legal or beneficial interest in property;

    (4)   the term "act of war" means any act occurring in the course of

    (A)   declared war;

    (B)   armed conflict, whether or not war has been declared, between two or more nations; or

    (C)   armed conflict between military forces of any origin; and

    (5)   the term "domestic terrorism" means activities that

    (A)   involve acts dangerous to human life that are a violation of the criminal laws of the United States or of any State;

    (B)   appear to be intended

    (i)   to intimidate or coerce a civilian population;

    (ii)   to influence the policy of a government by intimidation or coercion; or

    (iii)   to affect the conduct of a government by mass destruction, assassination, or kidnapping; and

    (C)   occur primarily within the territorial jurisdiction of the United States.

18 U.S.C. § 2332. Criminal penalties

    (a) *Homicide.* Whoever kills a national of the United States, while such national is outside the United States, shall,

    (1)   if the killing is murder (as defined in section 1111(a)), be fined under this title, punished by death or imprisonment for any term of years or for life, or both;

    (2)   if the killing is a voluntary manslaughter as defined in section 1112(a) of this title, be fined under this title or imprisoned not more than ten years, or both; and

    (3)   if the killing is an involuntary manslaughter as defined in section 1112(a) of this title, be fined under this title or imprisoned not more than three years, or both.

    (b) *Attempt or conspiracy with respect to homicide.* Whoever outside the United States attempts to kill, or engages in a conspiracy to kill, a national of the United States shall

    (1)   in the case of an attempt to commit a killing that is a murder as defined in this chapter be fined under this title or imprisoned not more than 20 years, or both; and in the case of a conspiracy by two or more persons to commit a killing that is a murder as defined in section 1111(a) of this title, if one or more of such persons do any overt act to effect the object of the conspiracy, be fined under this title or imprisoned for any term of years or for life, or both so fined and so imprisoned.

    (c) *Other conduct.* Whoever outside the United States engages in physical violence

    (1)   with intent to cause serious bodily injury to a national of the United States; or

(2)   with the result that serious bodily injury is caused to a national of the United States;

shall be fined under this title or imprisoned not more that ten years, or both.

(d)   *Limitation on prosecution.*   No prosecution for any offense described in this section shall be undertaken by the United States except on written certification of the Attorney General or the highest ranking subordinate of the Attorney General with responsibility for criminal prosecutions that, in the judgment of the certifying official, such offense was intended to coerce, intimidate, or retaliate against a government or a civilian population.

18 U.S.C. § 2332b   Acts of terrorism transcending national boundaries

(a)   Prohibited acts.

(1)   Offenses. Whoever, involving conduct transcending national boundaries and in a circumstance described in subsection (b)

(A)   kills, kidnaps, maims, commits an assault resulting in serious bodily injury, or assaults with a dangerous weapon any person within the United States; or

(B)   creates a substantial risk of serious bodily injury to any other person by destroying or damaging any structure, conveyance, or other real or personal property within the United States or by attempting or conspiring to destroy or damage any structure, conveyance, or other real or personal property within the United States;

in violation of the laws of any State, or the United States, shall be punished as prescribed in subsection (c).

(2)   Treatment of threats, attempts and conspiracies. Whoever threatens to commit an offense under paragraph (1), or attempts or conspires to do so, shall be punished under subsection (c).

(b)   Jurisdictional bases.

(1)   Circumstances. The circumstances referred to in subsection (a) are

(A)   the mail or any facility of interstate or foreign commerce is used in furtherance of the offense;(B)the offense obstructs, delays, or affects interstate or foreign commerce, or would have so obstructed, delayed, or affected interstate or foreign commerce if the offense had been consummated;

(C)   the victim, or intended victim, is the United States Government, a member of the uniformed services, or any official, officer, employee, or agent of the legislative, executive, or judicial branches, or of any department or agency, of the United States;

(D)   the structure, conveyance, or other real or personal property is, in whole or in part, owned, possessed, or leased to the United States, or any department or agency of the United States;

(E)   the offense is committed in the territorial sea (including the airspace above and the seabed and subsoil below, and artificial islands and fixed structures erected thereon) of the United States; or

(F)   the offense is committed within the special maritime and territorial jurisdiction of the United States.

(2)   Co-conspirators and accessories after the fact. Jurisdiction shall exist over all principals and co-conspirators of an offense under this section, and accessories after the fact to any offense under this section, if at least one of the circumstances described in subparagraphs (A) through (F) of paragraph (1) is applicable to at least one offender.

(c)   Penalties.

(1)   Penalties. Whoever violates this section shall be punished

(A) for a killing, or if death results to any person from any other conduct prohibited by this section, by death, or by imprisonment for any term of years or for life;

(B) for kidnapping, by imprisonment for any term of years or for life;

(C) for maiming, by imprisonment for not more than 35 years;

(D) for assault with a dangerous weapon or assault resulting in serious bodily injury, by imprisonment for not more than 30 years;

(E) for destroying or damaging any structure, conveyance, or other real or personal property, by imprisonment for not more than 25 years;

(F) for attempting or conspiring to commit an offense, for any term of years up to the maximum punishment that would have applied had the offense been completed; and

(G) for threatening to commit an offense under this section, by imprisonment for not more than 10 years.

(2) Consecutive sentence. Notwithstanding any other provision of law, the court shall not place on probation any person convicted of a violation of this section; nor shall the term of imprisonment imposed under this section run concurrently with any other term of imprisonment.

(d) Proof requirements. The following shall apply to prosecutions under this section:

(1) Knowledge. The prosecution is not required to prove knowledge by any defendant of a jurisdictional base alleged in the indictment.

(2) State law. In a prosecution under this section that is based upon the adoption of State law, only the elements of the offense under State law, and not any provisions pertaining to criminal procedure or evidence, are adopted.

(e) Extraterritorial jurisdiction. There is extraterritorial Federal jurisdiction

(1) over any offense under subsection (a), including any threat, attempt, or conspiracy to commit such offense; and

(2) over conduct which, under section 3, renders any person an accessory after the fact to an offense under subsection (a).

(f) Investigative authority. In addition to any other investigative authority with respect to violations of this title, the Attorney General shall have primary investigative responsibility for all Federal crimes of terrorism, and any violation of section 351(e), 844(e), 844(f)(1), 956(b), 1361, 1366(b), 1366(c), 1751(e), 2152, or 2156 of this title, and the Secretary of the Treasury shall assist the Attorney General at the request of the Attorney General. Nothing in this section shall be construed to interfere with the authority of the United States Secret Service under section 3056.

(g) Definitions. As used in this section

(1) the term "conduct transcending national boundaries" means conduct occurring outside of the United States in addition to the conduct occurring in the United States;

(2) the term "facility of interstate or foreign commerce" has the meaning given that term in section 1958(b)(2);

(3) the term "serious bodily injury" has the meaning given that term in section 1365(g)(3);

(4) the term "territorial sea of the United States" means all waters extending seaward to 12 nautical miles from the baselines of the United States, determined in accordance with international law; and

(5) the term "Federal crime of terrorism" means an offense that

(A) is calculated to influence or affect the conduct of government by intimidation or coercion, or to retaliate against government conduct; and

(B)   is a violation of

(i)   section 32 (relating to destruction of aircraft or aircraft facilities), 37 (relating to violence at international airports), 81 (relating to arson within special maritime and territorial jurisdiction), 175 or 175b (relating to biological weapons), 229 (relating to chemical weapons), subsection (a), (b), (c), or (d) of section 351 (relating to congressional, cabinet, and Supreme Court assassination and kidnaping), 831 (relating to nuclear materials), 842(m) or (n) (relating to plastic explosives), 844(f)(2) or (3) (relating to arson and bombing of Government property risking or causing death), 844(i) (relating to arson and bombing of property used in interstate commerce), 930(c) (relating to killing or attempted killing during an attack on a Federal facility with a dangerous weapon), 956(a)(1) (relating to conspiracy to murder, kidnap, or maim persons abroad), 1030(a)(1) (relating to protection of computers), 1030(a)(5)(A)(i) resulting in damage as defined in 1030(a)(5)(B)(ii) through (v) (relating to protection of computers), 1114 (relating to killing or attempted killing of officers and employees of the United States), 1116 (relating to murder or manslaughter of foreign officials, official guests, or internationally protected persons), 1203 (relating to hostage taking), 1362 (relating to destruction of communication lines, stations, or systems), 1363 (relating to injury to buildings or property within special maritime and territorial jurisdiction of the United States), 1366(a) (relating to destruction of an energy facility), 1751(a), (b), (c), or (d) (relating to Presidential and Presidential staff assassination and kidnaping), 1992 (relating to wrecking trains), 1993 (relating to terrorist attacks and other acts of violence against mass transportation systems), 2155 (relating to destruction of national defense materials, premises, or utilities), 2280 (relating to violence against maritime navigation), 2281 (relating to violence against maritime fixed platforms), 2332 (relating to certain homicides and other violence against United States nationals occurring outside of the United States), 2332a (relating to use of weapons of mass destruction), 2332b (relating to acts of terrorism transcending national boundaries), 2332f (relating to bombing of public places and facilities), 2339 (relating to harboring terrorists), 2339A (relating to providing material support to terrorists), 2339B (relating to providing material support to terrorist organizations), 2339C (relating to financing of terrorism, or 2340A (relating to torture) of this title;

(ii)   section 236 (relating to sabotage of nuclear facilities or fuel) of the Atomic Energy Act of 1954 *(42 U.S.C. 2284)*; or

(iii)   section 46502 (relating to aircraft piracy), the second sentence of section 46504 (relating to assault on a flight crew with a dangerous weapon), section 46505(b)(3) or (c) (relating to explosive or incendiary devices, or endangerment of human life by means of weapons, on aircraft), section 46506 if homicide or attempted homicide is involved (relating to application of certain criminal laws to acts on aircraft), or section 60123(b) (relating to destruction of interstate gas or hazardous liquid pipeline facility) of title 49.

18 U.S.C. § 2332f.   Bombings of places of public use, government facilities, public transportation systems and infrastructure facilities

(a)   Offenses.

(1)   In general. Whoever unlawfully delivers, places, discharges, or detonates an explosive or other lethal device in, into, or against a place of public use, a state or government facility, a public transportation system, or an infrastructure facility

(A)   with the intent to cause death or serious bodily injury, or

(B)   with the intent to cause extensive destruction of such a place, facility, or system, where such destruction results in or is likely to result in major economic loss, shall be punished as prescribed in subsection (c).

(2) Attempts and conspiracies. Whoever attempts or conspires to commit an offense under paragraph (1) shall be punished as prescribed in subsection (c).

(b) Jurisdiction. There is jurisdiction over the offenses in subsection (a) if

(1) the offense takes place in the United States and

(A) the offense is committed against another state or a government facility of such state, including its embassy or other diplomatic or consular premises of that state;

(B) the offense is committed in an attempt to compel another state or the United States to do or abstain from doing any act;

(C) at the time the offense is committed, it is committed

(i) on board a vessel flying the flag of another state;

(ii) on board an aircraft which is registered under the laws of another state; or

(iii) on board an aircraft which is operated by the government of another state;

(D) a perpetrator is found outside the United States;

(E) a perpetrator is a national of another state or a stateless person; or

(F) a victim is a national of another state or a stateless person;

(2) the offense takes place outside the United States and

(A) a perpetrator is a national of the United States or is a stateless person whose habitual residence is in the United States;

(B) a victim is a national of the United States;

(C) a perpetrator is found in the United States;

(D) the offense is committed in an attempt to compel the United States to do or abstain from doing any act;

(E) the offense is committed against a state or government facility of the United States, including an embassy or other diplomatic or consular premises of the United States;

(F) the offense is committed on board a vessel flying the flag of the United States or an aircraft which is registered under the laws of the United States at the time the offense is committed; or

(G) the offense is committed on board an aircraft which is operated by the United States.

(c) Penalties. Whoever violates this section shall be punished as provided under section 2332a(a) of this title.

(d) Exemptions to jurisdiction. This section does not apply to

(1) the activities of armed forces during an armed conflict, as those terms are understood under the law of war, which are governed by that law,

(2) activities undertaken by military forces of a state in the exercise of their official duties; or

(3) offenses committed within the United States, where the alleged offender and the victims are United States citizens and the alleged offender is found in the United States, or where jurisdiction is predicated solely on the nationality of the victims or the alleged offender and the offense has no substantial effect on interstate or foreign commerce.

18 U.S.C. § 2339A.   Providing material support to terrorists

(a)   Offense. Whoever, within the United States, provides material support or resources or conceals or disguises the nature, location, source, or ownership of material support or resources, knowing or intending that they are to be used in preparation for, or in carrying out, a violation of [specified federal crimes], or in preparation for, or in carrying out, the concealment or an escape from the commission of any such violation, shall be fined under this title, imprisoned not more than 10 years, or both.

(b)   Definitions. As used in this section

(1)   the term "material support or resources" means any property, tangible or intangible, or service, including currency or monetary instruments or financial securities, financial services, lodging, training, expert advice or assistance, safehouses, false documentation or identification, communications equipment, facilities, weapons, lethal substances, explosives, personnel (1 or more individuals who may be or include oneself), and transportation, except medicine or religious materials;

(2)   the term "training" means instruction or teaching designed to impart a specific skill, as opposed to general knowledge; and

(3)   the term "expert advice or assistance" means advice or assistance derived from scientific, technical or other specialized knowledge.

[Prior to Dec. 17, 2004, subsection (b) read: In this section, the term "material support or resources" means currency or other financial securities, financial services, lodging, training, safehouses, false documentation or identification, communications equipment, facilities, weapons, lethal substances, explosives, personnel, transportation, and other physical assets, except medicine or religious materials.]

18 U.S.C. § 2339B.   Providing material support or resources to designated foreign terrorist organizations

(a)   Prohibited Activities.

(1)   Unlawful conduct. Whoever knowingly provides material support or resources to a foreign terrorist organization, or attempts or conspires to do so, shall be fined under this title or imprisoned not more than 10 years, or both. To violate this paragraph, a person must have knowledge that the organization is a designated terrorist organization (as defined in subsection (g)(6)), that the organization has engaged or engages in terrorist activity (as defined in 8 U.S.C. § 1182(a)(3)), or that the organization has engaged or engages in terrorism (as defined in 8 U.S.C. 2656f). [The last sentence was added by Pub. L. 108-458 Dec. 17, 2004]

(2)   Financial institutions. Except as authorized by the Secretary, any financial institution that becomes aware that it has possession of, or control over, any funds in which a foreign terrorist organization, or its agent, has an interest, shall

(A)   retain possession of, or maintain control over, such funds; and

(B)   report to the Secretary the existence of such funds in accordance with regulations issued by the Secretary

(b)   Civil Penalty. Any financial institution that knowingly fails to comply with subsection (a)(2) shall be subject to a civil penalty in an amount that is the greater of

(A) $50,000 per violation; or

(B)   twice the amount of which the financial institution was required under subsection (a)(2) to retain possession or control.

(c)   Injunction. Whenever it appears to the Secretary or the Attorney General that any person is engaged in, or is about to engage in, any act that constitutes, or would constitute, a violation of this section, the Attorney General may initiate civil action in a district court of the United States to enjoin such violation.

(d) Extraterritorial Jurisdiction.

(1) In general. There is jurisdiction over an offense under subsection (a) if

(A) an offender is a national of the United States or an alien lawfully admitted for permanent residence in the United States;

(B) an offender is a stateless person whose habitual residence is in the United States;

(C) after the conduct required for the offense occurs an offender is brought into or found in the United States, even if the conduct required for the offense occurs outside the United States;

(D) the offense occurs in whole or in part within the United States;

(E) the offense occurs in or affects interstate or foreign commerce; or

(F) an offender aids or abets any person over whom jurisdiction exists under this paragraph in committing an offense under subsection (a) or conspires with any person over whom jurisdiction exists under this paragraph to commit an offense under subsection (a).

(2) Extraterritorial jurisdiction. There is extraterritorial Federal jurisdiction over an offense under this section.

(e) Investigations.

(1) In general. The Attorney General shall conduct any investigation of a possible violation of this section, or of any license, order, or regulation issued pursuant to this section.

(2) Coordination with the department of the treasury. The Attorney General shall work in coordination with the Secretary in investigations relating to

(A) the compliance or noncompliance by a financial institution with the requirements of subsection (a)(2); and

(B) civil penalty proceedings authorized under subsection (b).

(3) Referral. Any evidence of a criminal violation of this section arising in the course of an investigation by the Secretary or any other Federal agency shall be referred immediately to the Attorney General for further investigation. The Attorney General shall timely notify the Secretary of any action taken on referrals from the Secretary, and may refer investigations to the Secretary for remedial licensing or civil penalty action.

(f) Classified Information in Civil Proceedings Brought by the United States.

(1) Discovery of classified information by defendants.

(A) Request by united states. — In any civil proceeding under this section, upon request made ex parte and in writing by the United States, a court, upon a sufficient showing, may authorize the United States to

(i) redact specified items of classified information from documents to be introduced into evidence or made available to the defendant through discovery under the Federal Rules of Civil Procedure;

(ii) substitute a summary of the information for such classified documents; or

(iii) substitute a statement admitting relevant facts that the classified information would tend to prove.

[omitted details on introduction of redacted classified information and interlocutory appeals]

(g) Definitions. As used in this section

. . . .

(4) the term "material support or resources" has the same meaning as in section 2339A;

. . . .

(6)   the term "terrorist organization" means an organization designated as a terrorist organization under [8 U.S.C. § 1189].

(h)   Provision of Personnel. No person may be prosecuted under this section in connection with the term "personnel" unless that person has knowingly provided, attempted to provide, or conspired to provide a foreign terrorist organization with 1 or more individuals (who may be or include himself) to work under that terrorist organization's direction or control or to organize, manage, supervise, or otherwise direct the operation of that organization. Individuals who act entirely independently of the foreign terrorist organization to advance its goals or objectives shall not be considered to be working under the foreign terrorist organization's direction and control. [added by Pub. L. 108-458, 12/17/04]

(i)   Rule of Construction. Nothing in this section shall be construed or applied so as to abridge the exercise of rights guaranteed under the First Amendment to the Constitution of the United States.

(j)   Exception. No person may be prosecuted under this section in connection with the term "personnel", "training", or "expert advice or assistance" if the provision of that material support or resources to a foreign terrorist organization was approved by the Secretary of State with the concurrence of the Attorney General.

18 U.S.C. § 2339D.   Receiving military-type training from a foreign terrorist organization

[added by Pub. L. 108-458, Dec. 17, 2004]

(a)   Offense. Whoever knowingly receives military-type training from or on behalf of any organization designated at the time of the training by the Secretary of State under section 219(a)(1) of the Immigration and Nationality Act as a foreign terrorist organization shall be fined under this title or imprisoned for ten years, or both. To violate this subsection, a person must have knowledge that the organization is a designated terrorist organization (as defined in subsection (c)(4)), that the organization has engaged or engages in terrorist activity (as defined in section 212 of the Immigration and Nationality Act), or that the organization has engaged or engages in terrorism (as defined in section 140(d)(2) of the Foreign Relations Authorization Act, Fiscal Years 1988 and 1989).

(b)   Extraterritorial Jurisdiction. There is extraterritorial Federal jurisdiction over an offense under this section. There is jurisdiction over an offense under subsection (a) if

(1)   an offender is a national of the United States (as defined in 101(a)(22) of the Immigration and Nationality Act) or an alien lawfully admitted for permanent residence in the United States (as defined in section 101(a)(20) of the Immigration and Nationality Act);

(2)   an offender is a stateless person whose habitual residence is in the United States;

(3)   after the conduct required for the offense occurs an offender is brought into or found in the United States, even if the conduct required for the offense occurs outside the United States;

(4)   the offense occurs in whole or in part within the United States;(5) the offense occurs in or affects interstate or foreign commerce; or

(6)   an offender aids or abets any person over whom jurisdiction exists under this paragraph in committing an offense under subsection (a) or conspires with any person over whom jurisdiction exists under this paragraph to commit an offense under subsection (a).

(c)   Definitions. As used in this section

(1)   the term "military-type training" includes training in means or methods that can cause death or serious bodily injury, destroy or damage property, or disrupt services to critical infrastructure, or training on the use, storage, production, or assembly of any explosive, firearm or other weapon, including any weapon of mass destruction.

5.   Statutes Providing for Civil Actions

A.   Damages for Terrorist Actions

18 U.S.C. § 2333.   Civil remedies

(a)   Action and jurisdiction. Any national of the United States injured in his or her person, property, or business by reason of an act of international terrorism, or his or her estate, survivors, or heirs, may sue therefor in any appropriate district court of the United States and shall recover threefold the damages he or she sustains and the cost of the suit, including attorney's fees.

(b)   Estoppel under United States law. A final judgment or decree rendered in favor of the United States in any criminal proceeding under [designated statutes] shall estop the defendant from denying the essential allegations of the criminal offense in any subsequent civil proceeding under this section.

(c)   Estoppel under foreign law. A final judgment or decree rendered in favor of any foreign state in any criminal proceeding shall, to the extent that such judgment or decree may be accorded full faith and credit under the law of the United States, estop the defendant from denying the essential allegations of the criminal offense in any subsequent civil proceeding under this section.

B.   Federal Tort Claims Act

28 U.S.C. § 2674.   Liability of United States

The United States shall be liable, respecting the provisions of this title relating to tort claims, in the same manner and to the same extent as a private individual under like circumstances, but shall not be liable for interest prior to judgment or for punitive damages.

With respect to any claim under this chapter, the United States shall be entitled to assert any defense based upon judicial or legislative immunity which otherwise would have been available to the employee of the United States whose act or omission gave rise to the claim, as well as any other defenses to which the United States is entitled.

28 U.S.C. § 2679   Exclusiveness of remedy

(b)(1)   The remedy against the United States provided by [the FTCA] is exclusive of any other civil action or proceeding for money damages by reason of the same subject matter against the employee whose act or omission gave rise to the claim or against the estate of such employee.

(2)   Paragraph (1) does not extend or apply to a civil action against an employee of the Government

(A)   which is brought for a violation of the Constitution of the United States, or
(B) which is brought for a violation of a statute of the United States under which such action against an individual is otherwise authorized.

(d)(1)   Upon certification by the Attorney General that the defendant employee was acting within the scope of his office or employment at the time of the incident out of which the claim arose, any civil action or proceeding commenced upon such claim in a United States district court shall be deemed an action against the United States under the provisions of this title and all references thereto, and the United States shall be substituted as the party defendant.

28 U.S.C. § 2680.   [FTCA] Exceptions

The provisions of [the Federal Tort Claims Act] shall not apply to—

(a)   Any claim based upon an act or omission of an employee of the Government, exercising due care, in the execution of a statute or regulation, whether or not such statute or regulation be valid, or based upon the exercise or performance or the failure to exercise or perform a discretionary function or duty on the part of a federal agency or an employee of the Government, whether or not the discretion involved be abused.

(h)   Any claim arising out of assault, battery, false imprisonment, false arrest, malicious prosecution, abuse of process, libel, slander, misrepresentation, deceit, or interference with contract rights: Provided, That, with regard to acts or omissions of investigative or law enforcement officers of the United States Government, the provisions of this chapter shall apply to any claim arising, on or after [March 16, 1974], out of assault, battery, false imprisonment, false arrest, abuse of process, or malicious prosecution. For the purpose of this subsection, "investigative or law enforcement officer" means any officer of the United States who is empowered by law to execute searches, to seize evidence, or to make arrests for violations of Federal law.

(j)   Any claim arising out of the combatant activities of the military or naval forces, or the Coast Guard, during time of war.

(k)   Any claim arising in a foreign country.

C.   Alien Tort Statute and Torture Victim Protection Act

28 U.S.C. § 1350   Alien's action for tort

The district courts shall have original jurisdiction of any civil action by an alien for a tort only, committed in violation of the law of nations or a treaty of the United States.

[The Torture Victim Protection Act is not separately codified. It appears as a "Note" to 28 U.S.C. § 1350.]

Note

Sec. 2. Establishment of civil action

(a)   Liability. An individual who, under actual or apparent authority, or color of law, of any foreign nation

(1)   subjects an individual to torture shall, in a civil action, be liable for damages to that individual; or

(2)   subjects an individual to extrajudicial killing shall, in a civil action, be liable for damages to the individual's legal representative, or to any person who may be a claimant in an action for wrongful death.

Sec. 3. Definitions

(a)   Extrajudicial killing. For the purposes of this Act, the term"extrajudicial killing" means a deliberated killing not authorized by a previous judgment pronounced by a regularly constituted court affording all the judicial guarantees which are recognized as indispensable by civilized peoples. Such term, however, does not include any such killing that, under international law, is lawfully carried out under the authority of a foreign nation.

(b)   Torture. For the purposes of this Act

(1)   the term "torture" means any act, directed against an individual in the offender's custody or physical control, by which severe pain or suffering (other than pain or suffering arising only from or inherent in, or incidental to, lawful sanctions), whether physical or mental, is intentionally inflicted on that individual for such purposes as obtaining from that individual or a third person information or a confession, punishing that individual for an act that individual or a third person has committed or is suspected of having committed, intimidating or coercing that individual or a third person, or for any reason based on discrimination of any kind; and

(2)   mental pain or suffering refers to prolonged mental harm caused by or resulting from

(A)   the intentional infliction or threatened infliction of severe physical pain or suffering;

(B)   the administration or application, or threatened administration or application, of mind altering substances or other procedures calculated to disrupt profoundly the senses or the personality;

(C)   the threat of imminent death; or

(D)   the threat that another individual will imminently be subjected to death, severe physical pain or suffering, or the administration or application of mind altering substances or other procedures calculated to disrupt profoundly the senses or personality.

D.   Foreign Sovereign Immunities Act

28 U.S.C. § 1603.   Definitions

For purposes of this chapter

(a)   A "foreign state", except as used in section 1608 of this title, includes a political subdivision of a foreign state or an agency or instrumentality of a foreign state as defined in subsection (b).

(b)   An "agency or instrumentality of a foreign state" means any entity

(1)   which is a separate legal person, corporate or otherwise, and

(2)   which is an organ of a foreign state or political subdivision thereof, or a majority of whose shares or other ownership interest is owned by a foreign state or political subdivision thereof, and

(3)   which is neither a citizen of a State of the United States . . . nor created under the laws of any third country.

(c)   The "United States" includes all territory and waters, continental or insular, subject to the jurisdiction of the United States.

(d)   A "commercial activity" means either a regular course of commercial conduct or a particular commercial transaction or act. The commercial character of an activity shall be determined by reference to the nature of the course of conduct or particular transaction or act, rather than by reference to its purpose.

(e)   A "commercial activity carried on in the United States by a foreign state" means commercial activity carried on by such state and having substantial contact with the United States.

§ 1605. General exceptions to the jurisdictional immunity of a foreign state

(a)   A foreign state shall not be immune from the jurisdiction of courts of the United States or of the States in any case

(1)   in which the foreign state has waived its immunity either explicitly or by implication, notwithstanding any withdrawal of the waiver which the foreign state may purport to effect except in accordance with the terms of the waiver;

(2)   in which the action is based upon a commercial activity carried on in the United States by the foreign state; or upon an act performed in the United States in connection with a commercial activity of the foreign state elsewhere; or upon an act outside the territory of the United States in connection with a commercial activity of the foreign state elsewhere and that act causes a direct effect in the United States;

(3)   in which rights in property taken in violation of international law are in issue and that property or any property exchanged for such property is present in the United States in connection with a commercial activity carried on in the United States by the foreign state; or that property or any property exchanged for such property is owned or operated by an agency or instrumentality of the foreign state and that agency or instrumentality is engaged in a commercial activity in the United States;

(4)   in which rights in property in the United States acquired by succession or gift or rights in immovable property situated in the United States are in issue;

(5)   not otherwise encompassed in paragraph (2) above, in which money damages are sought against a foreign state for personal injury or death, or damage to or loss of property, occurring in the United States and caused by the tortious act or omission of that foreign state or of any official or employee of that foreign state while acting within the scope of his office or employment; except this paragraph shall not apply to

(A)   any claim based upon the exercise or performance or the failure to exercise or perform a discretionary function regardless of whether the discretion be abused, or

(B)   any claim arising out of malicious prosecution, abuse of process, libel, slander, misrepresentation, deceit, or interference with contract rights;

(6)   in which the action is brought, either to enforce an agreement made by the foreign state with or for the benefit of a private party to submit to arbitration all or any differences which have arisen or which may arise between the parties with respect to a defined legal relationship, or

(7)   not otherwise covered by paragraph (2), in which money damages are sought against a foreign state for personal injury or death that was caused by an act of torture, extrajudicial killing, aircraft sabotage, hostage taking, or the provision of material support or resources (as defined in section 2339A of title 18) for such an act if such act or provision of material support is engaged in by an official, employee, or agent of such foreign state while acting within the scope of his or her office, employment, or agency, except that the court shall decline to hear a claim under this paragraph.

(A)   if the foreign state was not designated as a state sponsor of terrorism . . . at the time the act occurred, unless later so designated as a result of such act or the act is related to Case Number 1:00CV03110(EGS) in the United States District Court for the District of Columbia; and

(B)   even if the foreign state is or was so designated, if

(i)   the act occurred in the foreign state against which the claim has been brought and the claimant has not afforded the foreign state a reasonable opportunity to arbitrate the claim in accordance with accepted international rules of arbitration; or

(ii)   neither the claimant nor the victim was a national of the United States (as that term is defined in [8 U.S.C. § 1101(a)(22)]) when the act upon which the claim is based occurred.

(e) For purposes of paragraph (7) of subsection (a)

(1) the terms "torture" and "extrajudicial killing" have the meaning given those terms in section 3 of the Torture Victim Protection Act of 1991 [28 U.S.C. § 1350 note];

(2) the term "hostage taking" has the meaning given that term in Article 1 of the International Convention Against the Taking of Hostages; and

(3) the term "aircraft sabotage" has the meaning given that term in Article 1 of the Convention for the Suppression of Unlawful Acts Against the Safety of Civil Aviation.

6. Statutes Relating to Information and Investigations

A. Espionage and Spying Prohibitions

18 U.S.C. § 793. Gathering, transmitting, or losing defense information

(a) Whoever, for the purpose of obtaining information respecting the national defense with intent or reason to believe that the information is to be used to the injury of the United States, or to the advantage of any foreign nation, goes upon, enters, flies over, or otherwise obtains information concerning any vessel, aircraft, . . . canal, railroad, . . . factory, mine, . . . telephone, wireless, . . . building, office, . . . or other place connected with the national defense owned . . . or under the control of the United States, . . . or any prohibited place so designated by the President by proclamation in time of war or in case of national emergency; or

(b) Whoever, for the purpose aforesaid, and with like intent or reason to believe, copies, takes, makes, or obtains, . . . any sketch, photograph, . . . plan, map, . . . writing, or note of anything connected with the national defense; or

(f) Whoever, being entrusted with or having lawful possession or control of any document . . . or information, relating to the national defense, (1) through gross negligence permits the same to be removed from its proper place of custody or delivered to anyone in violation of his trust, or to be lost, stolen, abstracted, or destroyed, or (2) having knowledge that the same has been illegally removed from its proper place of custody or delivered to anyone in violation of his trust, or lost, or stolen, abstracted, or destroyed, and fails to make prompt report of such loss, theft, abstraction, or destruction to his superior officer

Shall be fined under this title or imprisoned not more than ten years, or both.

18 U.S.C. § 794. Gathering or delivering defense information to aid foreign government

(a) Whoever, with intent or reason to believe that it is to be used to the injury of the United States or to the advantage of a foreign nation, communicates, delivers, or transmits, or attempts to communicate, deliver, or transmit, to any foreign government, or to any faction or party or military or naval force within a foreign country, whether recognized or unrecognized by the United States, or to any representative, officer, agent, employee, subject, or citizen thereof, either directly or indirectly, any document, writing, code book, signal book, sketch, photograph, photographic negative, blueprint, plan, map, model, note, instrument, appliance, or information relating to the national defense, shall be punished by death or by imprisonment for any term of years or for life, except that the sentence of death shall not be imposed unless the jury or, if there is no jury, the court, further finds that the offense resulted in the identification by a foreign power (as defined in section 101(a) of the Foreign Intelligence Surveillance Act of 1978) of an individual acting as an agent of the United States and consequently in the death of that individual, or directly concerned nuclear weaponry, military spacecraft or satellites, early warning systems, or other means of defense or retaliation against large-scale attack; war plans; communications intelligence or cryptographic information; or any other major weapons system or major element of defense strategy.

(b)   Whoever, in time of war, with intent that the same shall be communicated to the enemy, collects, records, publishes, or communicates, or attempts to elicit any information with respect to the movement, numbers, description, condition, or disposition of any of the Armed Forces, ships, aircraft, or war materials of the United States, or with respect to the plans or conduct, or supposed plans or conduct of any naval or military operations, or with respect to any works or measures undertaken for or connected with, or intended for the fortification or defense of any place, or any other information relating to the public defense, which might be useful to the enemy, shall be punished by death or by imprisonment for any term of years or for life.

18 U.S.C. § 798.   Disclosure of classified information

(a)   Whoever knowingly and willfully communicates, furnishes, transmits, or otherwise makes available to an unauthorized person, or publishes, or uses in any manner prejudicial to the safety or interest of the United States or for the benefit of any foreign government to the detriment of the United States any classified information

(1)   concerning the nature, preparation, or use of any code, cipher, or cryptographic system of the United States or any foreign government; or

(2)   concerning the design, construction, use, maintenance, or repair of any device, apparatus, or appliance used or prepared or planned for use by the United States or any foreign government for cryptographic or communication intelligence purposes; or

(3)   concerning the communication intelligence activities of the United States or any foreign government; or

(4)   obtained by the processes of communication intelligence from the communications of any foreign government, knowing the same to have been obtained by such processes

Shall be fined under this title or imprisoned not more than ten years, or both.

(b)   As used in subsection (a) of this section

The term "classified information" means information which, at the time of a violation of this section, is, for reasons of national security, specifically designated by a United States Government Agency for limited or restricted dissemination or distribution;

The term "foreign government" includes in its meaning any person or persons acting or purporting to act for or on behalf of any faction, party, department, agency, bureau, or military force of or within a foreign country, . . . whether or not such government is recognized by the United States;

The term "communication intelligence" means all procedures and methods used in the interception of communications and the obtaining of information from such communications by other than the intended recipients; The term "unauthorized person" means any person who, or agency which, is not authorized to receive information of the categories set forth in subsection (a) of this section, by the President, or by the head of a department or agency of the United States Government which is expressly designated by the President to engage in communication intelligence activities for the United States.

B. Classified Information Procedures Act, 18 U.S.C. App

§ 1. Definitions

(a) "Classified information", as used in this Act, means any information or material that has been determined by the United States Government pursuant to an Executive order, statute, or regulation, to require protection against unauthorized disclosure for reasons of national security and any restricted data, as defined in paragraph r. of section 11 of the Atomic Energy Act of 1954.

(b) "National security", as used in this Act, means the national defense and foreign relations of the United States.

§ 3. Protective orders

Upon motion of the United States, the court shall issue an order to protect against the disclosure of any classified information disclosed by the United States to any defendant in any criminal case in a district court of the United States.

§ 4. Discovery of classified information by defendant

The court, upon a sufficient showing, may authorize the United States to delete specified items of classified information from documents to be made available to the defendant through discovery under the Federal Rules of Criminal Procedure, to substitute a summary of the information for such classified documents, or to substitute a statement admitting relevant facts that the classified information would tend to prove. The court may permit the United States to make a request for such authorization in the form of a written statement to be inspected by the court alone. If the court enters an order granting relief following such an ex parte showing, the entire text of the statement of the United States shall be sealed and preserved in the records of the court to be made available to the appellate court in the event of an appeal.

§ 5. Notice of defendant's intention to disclose classified information

(a) Notice by defendant. If a defendant reasonably expects to disclose or to cause the disclosure of classified information in any manner in connection with any trial or pretrial proceeding involving the criminal prosecution of such defendant, the defendant shall, within the time specified by the court or, where no time is specified, within thirty days prior to trial, notify the attorney for the United States and the court in writing. Such notice shall include a brief description of the classified information. Whenever a defendant learns of additional classified information he reasonably expects to disclose at any such proceeding, he shall notify the attorney for the United States and the court in writing as soon as possible thereafter and shall include a brief description of the classified information. No defendant shall disclose any information known or believed to be classified in connection with a trial or pretrial proceeding until notice has been given under this subsection and until the United States has been afforded a reasonable opportunity to seek a determination pursuant to the procedure set forth in section 6 of this Act, and until the time for the United States to appeal such determination under section 7 has expired or any appeal under section 7 by the United States is decided.

(b) Failure to comply. If the defendant fails to comply with the requirements of subsection (a) the court may preclude disclosure of any classified information not made the subject of notification and may prohibit the examination by the defendant of any witness with respect to any such information.

§ 6. Procedure for cases involving classified information

(a) Motion for hearing. Within the time specified by the court for the filing of a motion under this section, the United States may request the court to conduct a hearing to make all determinations concerning the use, relevance, or admissibility of classified information that would otherwise be made during the trial or pretrial proceeding. Upon such a request, the court shall conduct such a hearing. Any hearing held pursuant to this subsection (or any portion of such hearing specified in the request of the Attorney General) shall be held in camera if the Attorney General certifies to the court in such petition that a public proceeding may result in the disclosure of classified information. As to each item of classified information, the court shall set forth in writing the basis for its determination. Where the United States' motion under this subsection is filed prior to the trial or pretrial proceeding, the court shall rule prior to the commencement of the relevant proceeding.

(b) Notice.

(1) Before any hearing is conducted pursuant to a request by the United States under subsection (a), the United States shall provide the defendant with notice of the classified information that is at issue. Such notice shall identify the specific classified information at issue whenever that information previously has been made available to the defendant by the United States. When the United States has not previously made the information available to the defendant in connection with the case, the information may be described by generic category, in such form as the court may approve, rather than by identification of the specific information of concern to the United States.

(2) Whenever the United States requests a hearing under subsection (a), the court, upon request of the defendant, may order the United States to provide the defendant, prior to trial, such details as to the portion of the indictment or information at issue in the hearing as are needed to give the defendant fair notice to prepare for the hearing.

(c) Alternative procedure for disclosure of classified information.

(1) Upon any determination by the court authorizing the disclosure of specific classified information under the procedures established by this section, the United States may move that, in lieu of the disclosure of such specific classified information, the court order

(A) the substitution for such classified information of a statement admitting relevant facts that the specific classified information would tend to prove; or

(B) the substitution for such classified information of a summary of the specific classified information.

The court shall grant such a motion of the United States if it finds that the statement or summary will provide the defendant with substantially the same ability to make his defense as would disclosure of the specific classified information. The court shall hold a hearing on any motion under this section. Any such hearing shall be held in camera at the request of the Attorney General.

(2) The United States may, in connection with a motion under paragraph (1), submit to the court an affidavit of the Attorney General certifying that disclosure of classified information would cause identifiable damage to the national security of the United States and explaining the basis for the classification of such information. If so requested by the United States, the court shall examine such affidavit in camera and ex parte.

(d) Sealing of records of in camera hearings. If at the close of an in camera hearing under this Act (or any portion of a hearing under this Act that is held in camera) the court determines that the classified information at issue may not be disclosed or elicited at the trial or pretrial proceeding, the record of such in camera hearing shall be sealed and preserved by the court for use in the event of an appeal. The defendant may seek reconsideration of the court's determination prior to or during trial.

(e) Prohibition on disclosure of classified information by defendant, relief for defendant when United States opposes disclosure.

(1) Whenever the court denies a motion by the United States that it issue an order under subsection (c) and the United States files with the court an affidavit of the Attorney General objecting to disclosure of the classified information at issue, the court shall order that the defendant not disclose or cause the disclosure of such information.

(2) Whenever a defendant is prevented by an order under paragraph (1) from disclosing or causing the disclosure of classified information, the court shall dismiss the indictment or information; except that, when the court determines that the interests of justice would not be served by dismissal of the indictment or information, the court shall order such other action, in lieu of dismissing the indictment or information, as the court determines is appropriate. Such action may include, but need not be limited to

(A) dismissing specified counts of the indictment or information;

(B) finding against the United States on any issue as to which the excluded classified information relates; or

(C) striking or precluding all or part of the testimony of a witness.

An order under this paragraph shall not take effect until the court has afforded the United States an opportunity to appeal such order under section 7, and thereafter to withdraw its objection to the disclosure of the classified information at issue.

(f) Reciprocity. Whenever the court determines pursuant to subsection (a) that classified information may be disclosed in connection with a trial or pretrial proceeding, the court shall, unless the interests of fairness do not so require, order the United States to provide the defendant with the information it expects to use to rebut the classified information. The court may place the United States under a continuing duty to disclose such rebuttal information. If the United States fails to comply with its obligation under this subsection, the court may exclude any evidence not made the subject of a required disclosure and may prohibit the examination by the United States of any witness with respect to such information.

§ 7. Interlocutory appeal

(a) An interlocutory appeal by the United States taken before or after the defendant has been placed in jeopardy shall lie to a court of appeals from a decision or order of a district court in a criminal case authorizing the disclosure of classified information, imposing sanctions for nondisclosure of classified information, or refusing a protective order sought by the United States to prevent the disclosure of classified information.

(b) An appeal taken pursuant to this section either before or during trial shall be expedited by the court of appeals. Prior to trial, an appeal shall be taken within ten days after the decision or order appealed from and the trial shall not commence until the appeal is resolved. If an appeal is taken during trial, the trial court shall adjourn the trial until the appeal is resolved and the court of appeals (1) shall hear argument on such appeal within four days of the adjournment of the trial, (2) may dispense with written briefs other than the supporting materials previously submitted to the trial court, (3) shall render its decision within four days of argument on appeal, and (4) may dispense with the issuance of a written opinion in rendering its decision. Such appeal and decision shall not affect the right of the defendant, in a subsequent appeal from a judgment of conviction, to claim as error reversal by the trial court on remand of a ruling appealed from during trial.

C.   Foreign Intelligence Surveillance Act

[50 U.S.C. §§ 1801–1862, as amended by USA PATRIOT and again on March 9, 2006 — section 1861 is due to expire December 31, 2009]

§ 1801.   Definitions

As used in this title:

(a)   "Foreign power" means

(1)   a foreign government or any component thereof whether or not recognized by the United States;

(2)   a faction of a foreign nation or nations, not substantially composed of United States persons;

(3)   an entity that is openly acknowledged by a foreign government or governments to be directed and controlled by such foreign government or governments;

(4)   a group engaged in international terrorism or activities in preparation therefor;

(5)   a foreign-based political organization, not substantially composed of United States persons; or

(6)   an entity that is directed and controlled by a foreign government or governments.

(b)   "Agent of a foreign power" means

(1)   any person other than a United States person, who

(A)   acts in the United States as an officer or employee of a foreign power, or as a member of a foreign power as defined in subsection (a)(4);

(B)   acts for or on behalf of a foreign power which engages in clandestine intelligence activities in the United States contrary to the interests of the United States, when the circumstances of such person's presence in the United States indicate that such person may engage in such activities in the United States, or when such person knowingly aids or abets any person in the conduct of such activities or knowingly conspires with any person to engage in such activities; or

(C)   engages in international terrorism or activities in preparation therefor [paragraph (C) is scheduled to "sunset" on Dec. 31, 2009]; or

(2)   any person who

(A)   knowingly engages in clandestine intelligence gathering activities for or on behalf of a foreign power, which activities involve or may involve a violation of the criminal statutes of the United States;

(B)   pursuant to the direction of an intelligence service or network of a foreign power, knowingly engages in any other clandestine intelligence activities for or on behalf of such foreign power, which activities involve or are about to involve a violation of the criminal statues of the United States;

(C)   knowingly engages in sabotage or international terrorism, or activities that are in preparation therefor, for or on behalf of a foreign power;

(D)   knowingly enters the United States under a false or fraudulent identity for or on behalf of a foreign power or, while in the United States, knowingly assumes a false or fraudulent identity for or on behalf of a foreign power; or

(E)   knowingly aids or abets any person in the conduct of activities described in subparagraph (A), (B), or (C) or knowingly conspires with any person to engage in activities described in subparagraph (A), (B), or (C).

(c) "International terrorism" means activities that

(1) involve violent acts or acts dangerous to human life that are a violation of the criminal laws of the United States or of any State, or that would be a criminal violation if committed within the jurisdiction of the United States or any State;

(2) appear to be intended

(A) to intimidate or coerce a civilian population;

(B) to influence the policy of a government by intimidation or coercion; or

(C) to affect the conduct of a government by assassination or kidnapping; and

(3) occur totally outside the United States or transcend national boundaries in terms of the means by which they are accomplished, the persons they appear intended to coerce or intimidate, or the locale in which their perpetrators operate or seek asylum.

(d) "Sabotage" means activities that involve a violation of [18 U.S.C. §§ 2151 *et seq.*], or that would involve such a violation if committed against the United States.

(e) "Foreign intelligence information" means

(1) information that relates to, and if concerning a United States person is necessary to, the ability of the United States to protect against—

(A) actual or potential attack or other grave hostile acts of a foreign power or an agent of a foreign power;

(B) sabotage or international terrorism by a foreign power or an agent of a foreign power; or

(C) clandestine intelligence activities by an intelligence service or network of a foreign power or by an agent of a foreign power; or

(2) information with respect to a foreign power or foreign territory that relates to, and if concerning a United States person is necessary to

(A) the national defense or the security of the United States; or

(B) the conduct of the foreign affairs of the United States.

(f) "Electronic surveillance" means

(1) the acquisition by an electronic, mechanical, or other surveillance device of the contents of any wire or radio communication sent by or intended to be received by a particular, known United States person who is in the United States, if the contents are acquired by intentionally targeting that United States person, under circumstances in which a person has a reasonable expectation of privacy and a warrant would be required for law enforcement purposes;

(2) the acquisition by an electronic, mechanical, or other surveillance device of the contents of any wire communication to or from a person in the United States, without the consent of any party thereto, if such acquisition occurs in the United States, but does not include the acquisition of those communications of computer trespassers that would be permissible under 18 U.S.C. § 2511(2)(I) [Title III];

(3) the intentional acquisition by an electronic, mechanical, or other surveillance device of the contents of any radio communication, under circumstances in which a person has a reasonable expectation of privacy and a warrant would be required for law enforcement purposes, and if both the sender and all intended recipients are located within the United States; or

(4) the installation or use of an electronic, mechanical, or other surveillance device in the United States for monitoring to acquire information, other than from a wire or radio communication, under circumstances in which a person has a reasonable expectation of privacy and a warrant would be required for law enforcement purposes.

(h) "Minimization procedures", with respect to electronic surveillance, means

(1) specific procedures, which shall be adopted by the Attorney General, that are reasonably designed in light of the purpose and technique of the particular surveillance, to minimize the acquisition and retention, and prohibit the dissemination, of nonpublicly available information concerning unconsenting United States persons consistent with the need of the United States to obtain, produce, and disseminate foreign intelligence information;

(2) procedures that require that nonpublicly available information, which is not foreign intelligence information, as defined in subsection (e)(1), shall not be disseminated in a manner that identifies any United States person, without such person's consent, unless such person's identity is necessary to understand foreign intelligence information or assess its importance;

(3) notwithstanding paragraphs (1) and (2), procedures that allow for the retention and dissemination of information that is evidence of a crime which has been, is being, or is about to be committed and that is to be retained or disseminated for law enforcement purposes; and

(4) notwithstanding paragraphs (1), (2), and (3), with respect to any electronic surveillance approved pursuant to section 1802(a), procedures that require that no contents of any communication to which a United States person is a party shall be disclosed, disseminated, or used for any purpose or retained for longer than 72 hours unless a court order under section 1805 is obtained or unless the Attorney General determines that the information indicates a threat of death or serious bodily harm to any person.

(i) "United States person" means a citizen of the United States, an alien lawfully admitted for permanent residence, an unincorporated association a substantial number of members of which are citizens of the United States or aliens lawfully admitted for permanent residence, or a corporation which is incorporated in the United States, but does not include a corporation or an association which is a foreign power, as defined in subsection (a)(1), (2), or (3).

§ 1802. Electronic surveillance authorization without court order

(a)(1) Notwithstanding any other law, the President, through the Attorney General, may authorize electronic surveillance without a court order under this title to acquire foreign intelligence information for periods of up to one year if the Attorney General certifies in writing under oath that

(A) the electronic surveillance is solely directed at—

(i) the acquisition of the contents of communications transmitted by means of communications used exclusively between or among foreign powers; or

(ii) the acquisition of technical intelligence, other than the spoken communications of individuals, from property or premises under the open and exclusive control of a foreign power;

(B) there is no substantial likelihood that the surveillance will acquire the contents of any communication to which a United States person is a party; and

(C) the proposed minimization procedures with respect to such surveillance meet the definition of minimization procedures under section 1801(h); and if the Attorney General reports such minimization procedures and any changes thereto to the House Permanent Select Committee on Intelligence and the Senate Select Committee on Intelligence at least thirty days prior to their effective date, unless the Attorney General determines immediate action is required and notifies the committees immediately of such minimization procedures and the reason for their becoming effective immediately.

(2) An electronic surveillance authorized by this subsection may be conducted

only in accordance with the Attorney General's certification and the minimization procedures adopted by him. The Attorney General shall assess compliance with such procedures and shall report such assessments to the House Permanent Select Committee on Intelligence and the Senate Select Committee on Intelligence under the provisions of section 1808(a).

(3)   The Attorney General shall immediately transmit under seal to the court established under section 1803(a) a copy of his certification.

(4)   With respect to electronic surveillance authorized by this subsection, the Attorney General may direct a specified communication common carrier to

(A)   furnish all information, facilities, or technical assistance necessary to accomplish the electronic surveillance in such a manner as will protect its secrecy and produce a minimum of interference with the services that such carrier is providing its customers; and

(B)   maintain under security procedures approved by the Attorney General and the Director of National Intelligence any records concerning the surveillance or the aid furnished which such carrier wishes to retain. The Government shall compensate, at the prevailing rate, such carrier for furnishing such aid.

§ 1803.   Designation of judges

(a)   Court to hear applications and grant orders; record of denial; transmittal to court of review. The Chief Justice of the United States shall publicly designate 11 district court judges from seven of the United States judicial circuits of whom no fewer than 3 shall reside within 20 miles of the District of Columbia who shall constitute a court which shall have jurisdiction to hear applications for and grant orders approving electronic surveillance anywhere within the United States under the procedures set forth in this Act.

(b)   Court of review; record, transmittal to Supreme Court. The Chief Justice shall publicly designate three judges, one of whom shall be publicly designated as the presiding judge, from the United States district courts or courts of appeals who together shall comprise a court of review which shall have jurisdiction to review the denial of any application made under this Act.

(c)   Expeditious conduct of proceedings; security measures for maintenance of records. Proceedings under this Act shall be conducted as expeditiously as possible. The record of proceedings under this Act, including applications made and orders granted, shall be maintained under security measures established by the Chief Justice in consultation with the Attorney General and the Director of National Intelligence.

(d)   Tenure. Each judge designated under this section shall so serve for a maximum of seven years and shall not be eligible for redesignation.

(e)(1)   Three judges designated under subsection (a) who reside within 20 miles of the District of Columbia, or, if all of such judges are unavailable, other judges of the court established under subsection (a) as may be designated by the presiding judge of such court, shall comprise a petition review pool which shall have jurisdiction to review petitions filed pursuant to 50 U.S.C. § 1805b(h) or 1861(f)(1).

§ 1804.   Applications for court orders [for electronic surveillance — essentially the same procedures apply to searches under § 1823 by substituting "premises" for "target"]

(a)   Submission by Federal officer; approval of Attorney General; contents. Each application for an order approving electronic surveillance under this title shall be made by a Federal officer in writing upon oath or affirmation to a judge having jurisdiction under section 1803. Each application shall require the approval of the Attorney General based upon his finding that it satisfies the criteria and requirements of such application as set forth in this title. It shall include

(1)   the identity of the Federal officer making the application;

(2)   the authority conferred on the Attorney General by the President of the United States and the approval of the Attorney General to make the application;

(3)   the identity, if known, or a description of the target of the electronic surveillance;

(4)   a statement of the facts and circumstances relied upon by the applicant to justify his belief that—

(A)   the target of the electronic surveillance is a foreign power or an agent of a foreign power; and

(B)   each of the facilities or places at which the electronic surveillance is directed is being used, or is about to be used, by a foreign power or an agent of a foreign power;

(5)   a statement of the proposed minimization procedures;

(6)   a detailed description of the nature of the information sought and the type of communications or activities to be subjected to the surveillance;

(7)   a certification or certifications by the Assistant to the President for National Security Affairs or an executive branch official or officials designated by the President from among those executive officers employed in the area of national security or defense and appointed by the President with the advice and consent of the Senate—

(A)   that the certifying official deems the information sought to be foreign intelligence information;

(B)   that a significant purpose of the surveillance is to obtain foreign intelligence information;

(C)   that such information cannot reasonably be obtained by normal investigative techniques;

(D)   that designates the type of foreign intelligence information being sought according to the categories described in section 1801(e); and

(E)   including a statement of the basis for the certification that

(i)   the information sought is the type of foreign intelligence information designated; and

(ii)   such information cannot reasonably be obtained by normal investigative techniques;

(8)   a statement of the means by which the surveillance will be effected and a statement whether physical entry is required to effect the surveillance;

§ 1805.   Issuance of order

(a)   Necessary findings. Upon an application made pursuant to section 1804, the judge shall enter an ex parte order as requested or as modified approving the electronic surveillance if he finds that—

(3)   on the basis of the facts submitted by the applicant there is probable cause to believe that—

(A)   the target of the electronic surveillance is a foreign power or agent of a foreign power: *Provided,* That no United States person may be considered a foreign power or an agent of a foreign power solely upon the basis of activities protected by the first amendment to the Constitution of the United States; and

(B)   each of the facilities or places at which the electronic surveillance is directed is being used, or is about to be used, by a foreign power or an agent of a foreign power;

(4) the proposed minimization procedures meet the definition of minimization procedures under section 1804(h); and

(5) the application which has been filed contains all statements and certifications required by section 1804 and, if the target is a United States person, the certification or certifications are not clearly erroneous on the basis of the statement made under section 1804(a)(7)(E) and any other information furnished under section 1804(d).

§ 1805a. Clarification of electronic surveillance of persons outside the United States [expire Feb. 1, 2008]

Nothing in the definition of electronic surveillance under 50 U.S.C. § 1801(f)] shall be construed to encompass surveillance directed at a person reasonably believed to be located outside of the United States.

§ 1805b. Additional procedure for authorizing certain acquisitions concerning persons located outside the United States [expired Feb. 1, 2008]

(a) Notwithstanding any other law, the Director of National Intelligence and the Attorney General, may for periods of up to one year authorize the acquisition of foreign intelligence information concerning persons reasonably believed to be outside the United States if the Director of National Intelligence and the Attorney General determine, based on the information provided to them, that

(1) there are reasonable procedures in place for determining that the acquisition of foreign intelligence information under this section concerns persons reasonably believed to be located outside the United States, and such procedures will be subject to review of the Court pursuant to section 50 U.S.C. § 1805c;

(2) the acquisition does not constitute electronic surveillance;

(3) the acquisition involves obtaining the foreign intelligence information from or with the assistance of a communications service provider, custodian, or other person (including any officer, employee, agent, or other specified person of such service provider, custodian, or other person) who has access to communications, either as they are transmitted or while they are stored, or equipment that is being or may be used to transmit or store such communications;

(4) a significant purpose of the acquisition is to obtain foreign intelligence information; and

(5) the minimization procedures to be used with respect to such acquisition activity meet the definition of minimization procedures under 50 U.S.C. § 1801(h).

§ 1806. Use of information

(a) *Compliance with minimization procedures; privileged communications; lawful purposes.* Information acquired from an electronic surveillance conducted pursuant to this title concerning any United States person may be used and disclosed by Federal officers and employees without the consent of the United States person only in accordance with the minimization procedures required by this title. No otherwise privileged communication obtained in accordance with, or in violation of, the provisions of this title shall lose its privileged character. No information acquired from an electronic surveillance pursuant to this title may be used or disclosed by Federal officers or employees except for lawful purposes.

(b) *Statement for disclosure.* No information acquired pursuant to this title shall be disclosed for law enforcement purposes unless such disclosure is accompanied by a statement that such information, or any information derived therefrom, may only be used in a criminal proceeding with the advance authorization of the Attorney General.

(c) *Notification by United States.* Whenever the Government intends to enter into evidence or otherwise use or disclose in any trial, hearing, or other proceeding in or before any court, department, officer, agency, regulatory body, or other authority of the United States, against an aggrieved person, any information obtained or derived from an electronic surveillance of that aggrieved person pursuant to the authority of this title, the Government shall, prior to the trial, hearing, or other proceeding or at a reasonable time prior to an effort to so disclose or so use that information or submit it in evidence, notify the aggrieved person and the court or other authority in which the information is to be disclosed or used that the Government intends to so disclose or so use such information.

(e) *Motion to suppress.* Any person against whom evidence obtained or derived from an electronic surveillance to which he is an aggrieved person is to be, or has been, introduced or otherwise used or disclosed in any trial, hearing, or other proceeding in or before any court, department, officer, agency, regulatory body, or other authority of the United States, a State, or a political subdivision thereof, may move to suppress the evidence obtained or derived from such electronic surveillance on the grounds that

(1)　the information was unlawfully acquired; or

(2)　the surveillance was not made in conformity with an order of authorization or approval.

Such a motion shall be made before the trial, hearing, or other proceeding unless there was no opportunity to make such a motion or the person was not aware of the grounds of the motion.

(f) *In camera and ex parte review by district court.* Whenever a court or other authority is notified pursuant to subsection (c) or (d), or whenever a motion is made pursuant to subsection (e), or whenever any motion or request is made by an aggrieved person pursuant to any other statute or rule of the United States of any State before any court or other authority of the United States or any state to discover or obtain applications or orders or other materials relating to electronic surveillance or to discover, obtain, or suppress evidence or information obtained or derived from electronic surveillance under this Act, the United States district court or, where the motion is made before another authority, the United States district court in the same district as the authority, shall, notwithstanding any other law, if the Attorney General files an affidavit under oath that disclosure or an adversary hearing would harm the national security of the United States, review in camera and ex parte the application, order, and such other materials relating to the surveillance as may be necessary to determine whether the surveillance of the aggrieved person was lawfully authorized and conducted. In making this determination, the court may disclose to the aggrieved person, under appropriate security procedures and protective orders, portions of the application, order, or other materials relating to the surveillance only where such disclosure is necessary to make an accurate determination of the legality of the surveillance.

(k) *Coordination with law enforcement.*

(1)　Federal officers who conduct electronic surveillance to acquire foreign intelligence information under this title may consult with Federal law enforcement officers or law enforcement personnel of a State or political subdivision of a State (including the chief executive officer of that State or political subdivision who has the authority to appoint or direct the chief law enforcement officer of that State or political subdivision) to coordinate efforts to investigate or protect against

(A)　actual or potential attack or other grave hostile acts of a foreign power or an agent of a foreign power;

(B)　sabotage or international terrorism by a foreign power or an agent of a foreign power; or

C)　clandestine intelligence activities by an intelligence service or network of a foreign power or by an agent of a foreign power.

(2)   Coordination authorized under paragraph (1) shall not preclude the certification required by section 1804(a)(7)(B) or the entry of an order under section 1805.

§ 1861.   Access to certain business records for foreign intelligence and international terrorism investigations [expires December 31, 2009]

(a)   Application for order; conduct of investigation generally.

(1)   [T]he Director of the Federal Bureau of Investigation or a designee of the Director (whose rank shall be no lower than Assistant Special Agent in Charge) may make an application for an order requiring the production of any tangible things (including books, records, papers, documents, and other items) for an investigation to obtain foreign intelligence information not concerning a United States person or to protect against international terrorism or clandestine intelligence activities, provided that such investigation of a United States person is not conducted solely upon the basis of activities protected by the first amendment to the Constitution.

(3)   In the case of an application for an order requiring the production of library circulation records, library patron lists, book sales records, book customer lists, firearms sales records, tax return records, educational records, or medical records containing information that would identify a person, the Director of the Federal Bureau of Investigation may delegate the authority to make such application to either the Deputy Director of the Federal Bureau of Investigation or the Executive Assistant Director for National Security (or any successor position). The Deputy Director or the Executive Assistant Director may not further delegate such authority.

(b)   Recipient and contents of application. Each application under this section

(1)   shall be made to

(A)   a judge of the [FISA] court; or

(B)   a United States Magistrate Judge, who is publicly designated by the Chief Justice of the United States to have the power to hear applications and grant orders for the production of tangible things under this section on behalf of a judge of that court; and

(2)   shall include—

(A)   a statement of facts showing that there are reasonable grounds to believe that the tangible things sought are relevant to an authorized investigation . . . to obtain foreign intelligence information not concerning a United States person or to protect against international terrorism or clandestine intelligence activities, such things being presumptively relevant to an authorized investigation if the applicant shows in the statement of the facts that they pertain to—

(i)   a foreign power or an agent of a foreign power;

(ii)   the activities of a suspected agent of a foreign power who is the subject of such authorized investigation; or

(iii)   an individual in contact with, or known to, a suspected agent of a foreign power who is the subject of such authorized investigation; and

(B)   an enumeration of the minimization procedures adopted by the Attorney General under subsection (g) that are applicable to the retention and dissemination by the Federal Bureau of Investigation of any tangible things to be made available to the Federal Bureau of Investigation based on the order requested in such application.

(c)(1)   Upon an application made pursuant to this section, if the judge finds that the application meets the requirements of subsections (a) and (b), the judge shall enter an ex parte order as requested, or as modified, approving the release of tangible things. Such order shall direct that minimization procedures adopted pursuant to subsection (g) be followed.

(2)   An order under this subsection—

(A)   shall describe the tangible things that are ordered to be produced with sufficient particularity to permit them to be fairly identified;

(B)   shall include the date on which the tangible things must be provided, which shall allow a reasonable period of time within which the tangible things can be assembled and made available;

(C)   shall provide clear and conspicuous notice of the principles and procedures described in subsection (d);

(D)   may only require the production of a tangible thing if such thing can be obtained with a subpoena duces tecum issued by a court of the United States in aid of a grand jury investigation or with any other order issued by a court of the United States directing the production of records or tangible things; and

(E)   shall not disclose that such order is issued for purposes of an investigation described in subsection (a).

(d)(1)   No person shall disclose to any other person that the Federal Bureau of Investigation has sought or obtained tangible things pursuant to an order under this section, other than to—

(A)   those persons to whom disclosure is necessary to comply with such order;

(B)   an attorney to obtain legal advice or assistance with respect to the production of things in response to the order; or

(C)   other persons as permitted by the Director of the Federal Bureau of Investigation or the designee of the Director.

(e)   A person who, in good faith, produces tangible things under an order pursuant to this section shall not be liable to any other person for such production. Such production shall not be deemed to constitute a waiver of any privilege in any other proceeding or context.

(f)(1)   In this subsection—

(A)   the term "production order" means an order to produce any tangible thing under this section; and

(B)   the term "nondisclosure order" means an order imposed under subsection (d).

(2)(A)(i)   A person receiving a production order may challenge the legality of that order by filing a petition with the pool established by 50 U.S.C. § 1803(e)(1). Not less than 1 year after the date of the issuance of the production order, the recipient of a production order may challenge the nondisclosure order imposed in connection with such production order by filing a petition to modify or set aside such nondisclosure order.

(B)   A judge considering a petition to modify or set aside a production order may grant such petition only if the judge finds that such order does not meet the requirements of this section or is otherwise unlawful.

(C)(i)   A judge considering a petition to modify or set aside a nondisclosure order may grant such petition only if the judge finds that there is no reason to believe that disclosure may endanger the national security of the United States, interfere with a criminal, counterterrorism, or counterintelligence investigation, interfere with diplomatic relations, or endanger the life or physical safety of any person.

(ii)   If, upon filing of such a petition, the Attorney General, Deputy Attorney General, an Assistant Attorney General, or the Director of the Federal Bureau of Investigation certifies that disclosure may endanger the national security of the United States or interfere with diplomatic relations, such certification shall be treated as conclusive, unless the judge finds that the certification was made in bad faith.

(iii)   If the judge denies a petition to modify or set aside a nondisclosure order, the recipient of such order shall be precluded for a period of 1 year from filing another such petition with respect to such nondisclosure order.

(g)   Minimization procedures.

(1)   In general. The Attorney General shall adopt specific minimization procedures governing the retention and dissemination by the Federal Bureau of Investigation of any tangible things, or information therein, received by the Federal Bureau of Investigation in response to an order under this title.

(2)   Defined. In this section, the term "minimization procedures" means—

(A)   specific procedures that are reasonably designed in light of the purpose and technique of an order for the production of tangible things, to minimize the retention, and prohibit the dissemination, of nonpublicly available information concerning unconsenting United States persons consistent with the need of the United States to obtain, produce, and disseminate foreign intelligence information;

(B)   procedures that require that nonpublicly available information, which is not foreign intelligence information, shall not be disseminated in a manner that identifies any United States person, without such person's consent, unless such person's identity is necessary to understand foreign intelligence information or assess its importance; and

(C)   notwithstanding subparagraphs (A) and (B), procedures that allow for the retention and dissemination of information that is evidence of a crime which has been, is being, or is about to be committed and that is to be retained or disseminated for law enforcement purposes.

(h)   Use of information. Information acquired from tangible things received by the Federal Bureau of Investigation in response to an order under this title concerning any United States person may be used and disclosed by Federal officers and employees without the consent of the United States person only in accordance with the minimization procedures adopted pursuant to subsection (g).

D.   National Security Letters

18 U.S.C. § 2709.   Counterintelligence access to telephone toll and transactional records

(a)   Duty to provide. A wire or electronic communication service provider shall comply with a request for subscriber information and toll billing records information, or electronic communication transactional records in its custody or possession made by the Director of the Federal Bureau of Investigation [when certified to be relevant to an authorized investigation to protect against international terrorism or clandestine intelligence activities].

18 U.S.C. § 3511.   Judicial review of requests for information

(a)   The recipient of a request for records, a report, or other information under 18 U.S.C. § 2709, section 626(a) or (b) or 627(a) of the Fair Credit Reporting Act [15 U.S.C. § 1681u(a) or (b) or 1681v(a)], section 1114(a)(5)(A) of the Right to Financial Privacy Act [12 U.S.C. § 3414(a)(5)(A)], or section 802(a) of the National Security Act of 1947 [50 U.S.C. § 436(a)] may, in the United States district court for the district in which that person or entity does business or resides, petition for an order modifying or setting aside the request. The court may modify or set aside the request if compliance would be unreasonable, oppressive, or otherwise unlawful.

(b)(1)   The recipient of a request for records, a report, or other information . . . may petition any court described in subsection (a) for an order modifying or setting aside a nondisclosure requirement imposed in connection with such a request.

(2)   If the petition is filed within one year of the request for records, a report, or other information, the court may modify or set aside such a nondisclosure requirement if it finds that there is no reason to believe that disclosure may endanger the national security of the United States, interfere with a criminal, counterterrorism, or counterintelligence investigation, interfere with diplomatic relations, or endanger the life or physical safety of any person. If, at the time of the petition, the Attorney General, Deputy Attorney General, an Assistant Attorney General, or the Director of the Federal Bureau of Investigation, or in the case of a request by a department, agency, or instrumentality of the Federal Government other than the Department of Justice, the head or deputy head of such department, agency, or instrumentality, certifies that disclosure may endanger the national security of the United States or interfere with diplomatic relations, such certification shall be treated as conclusive unless the court finds that the certification was made in bad faith.

7.   Military Provisions

A.   Uniform Code of Military Justice

10 U.S.C. § 821   Jurisdiction of courts-martial not exclusive

The provisions of this chapter [10 U.S.C. §§ 801 *et seq.*] conferring jurisdiction upon courts-martial do not deprive military commissions, provost courts, or other military tribunals of concurrent jurisdiction with respect to offenders or offenses that by statute or by the law of war may be tried by military commissions, provost courts, or other military tribunals.

10 U.S.C. § 836   President may prescribe rules

(a)   Pretrial, trial, and post-trial procedures, including modes of proof, for cases arising under this chapter [10 U.S.C. §§ 801 *et seq.*] triable in courts-martial, military commissions and other military tribunals, and procedures for courts of inquiry, may be prescribed by the President by regulations which shall, so far as he considers practicable, apply the principles of law and the rules of evidence generally recognized in the trial of criminal cases in the United States district courts, but which may not be contrary to or inconsistent with this chapter.

(b)   All rules and regulations made under this article shall be uniform insofar as practicable.

B.   Resolutions and Orders

MILITARY ORDER #1
PUBLIC PAPERS OF THE PRESIDENTS (Volume 37 — Number 46, Nov. 19, 2001)
(Fed. Reg. Nov. 16, 2001)
November 13, 2001

By the authority vested in me as President and as Commander in Chief of the Armed Forces of the United States by the Constitution and the laws of the United States of America, including the Authorization for Use of Military Force Joint Resolution (Public Law 107-40, 115 Stat. 224) and sections 821 and 836 of title 10, United States Code, it is hereby ordered as follows:

Sec. 1. Findings.

(a) International terrorists, including members of al Qaida, have carried out attacks on United States diplomatic and military personnel and facilities abroad and on citizens and property within the United States on a scale that has created a state of armed conflict that requires the use of the United States Armed Forces.

(b) In light of grave acts of terrorism and threats of terrorism, including the terrorist attacks on September 11, 2001, on the headquarters of the United States Department of Defense in the national capital region, on the World Trade Center in New York, and on civilian aircraft such as in Pennsylvania, I proclaimed a national emergency on September 14, 2001 (Proc. 7463, Declaration of National Emergency by Reason of Certain Terrorist Attacks).

(e) To protect the United States and its citizens, and for the effective conduct of military operations and prevention of terrorist attacks, it is necessary for individuals subject to this order pursuant to section 2 hereof to be detained, and, when tried, to be tried for violations of the laws of war and other applicable laws by military tribunals.

(f) Given the danger to the safety of the United States and the nature of international terrorism, and to the extent provided by and under this order, I find consistent with section 836 of title 10, United States Code, that it is not practicable to apply in military commissions under this order the principles of law and the rules of evidence generally recognized in the trial of criminal cases in the United States district courts.

Sec. 2. Definition and Policy.

(a) The term "individual subject to this order" shall mean any individual who is not a United States citizen with respect to whom I determine from time to time in writing that:

(1) there is reason to believe that such individual, at the relevant times,

(i) is or was a member of the organization known as al Qaida;

(ii) has engaged in, aided or abetted, or conspired to commit, acts of international terrorism, or acts in preparation therefor, that have caused, threaten to cause, or have as their aim to cause, injury to or adverse effects on the United States, its citizens, national security, foreign policy, or economy; or

(iii) has knowingly harbored one or more individuals described in subparagraphs (i) or (ii) of subsection 2(a)(1) of this order; and

(2) it is in the interest of the United States that such individual be subject to this order.

(b) It is the policy of the United States that the Secretary of Defense shall take all necessary measures to ensure that any individual subject to this order is detained in accordance with section 3, and, if the individual is to be tried, that such individual is tried only in accordance with section 4.

(c) It is further the policy of the United States that any individual subject to this order who is not already under the control of the Secretary of Defense but who is under the control of any other officer or agent of the United States or any State shall, upon delivery of a copy of such written determination to such officer or agent, forthwith be placed under the control of the Secretary of Defense.

Sec. 3.   Detention Authority of the Secretary of Defense.

Any individual subject to this order shall be

(a)   detained at an appropriate location designated by the Secretary of Defense outside or within the United States;

(b)   treated humanely, without any adverse distinction based on race, color, religion, gender, birth, wealth, or any similar criteria;

(c)   afforded adequate food, drinking water, shelter, clothing, and medical treatment;

(d)   allowed the free exercise of religion consistent with the requirements of such detention; and

(e)   detained in accordance with such other conditions as the Secretary of Defense may prescribe.

Sec. 4.   Authority of the Secretary of Defense Regarding Trials of Individuals Subject to this Order.

(a)   Any individual subject to this order shall, when tried, be tried by military commission for any and all offenses triable by military commission that such individual is alleged to have committed, and may be punished in accordance with the penalties provided under applicable law, including life imprisonment or death.

(b)   As a military function and in light of the findings in section 1, including subsection (f) thereof, the Secretary of Defense shall issue such orders and regulations, including orders for the appointment of one or more military commissions, as may be necessary to carry out subsection (a) of this section.

(c)   Orders and regulations issued under subsection (b) of this section shall include, but not be limited to, rules for the conduct of the proceedings of military commissions, including pretrial, trial, and post-trial procedures, modes of proof, issuance of process, and qualifications of attorneys, which shall at a minimum provide for

(1)   military commissions to sit at any time and any place, consistent with such guidance regarding time and place as the Secretary of Defense may provide;

(2)   a full and fair trial, with the military commission sitting as the triers of both fact and law;

(3)   admission of such evidence as would, in the opinion of the presiding officer of the military commission (or instead, if any other member of the commission so requests at the time the presiding officer renders that opinion, the opinion of the commission rendered at that time by a majority of the commission), have probative value to a reasonable person;

(4)   in a manner consistent with the protection of information classified or classifiable under Executive Order 12958 of April 17, 1995, as amended, or any successor Executive Order, protected by statute or rule from unauthorized disclosure, or otherwise protected by law, (A) the handling of, admission into evidence of, and access to materials and information, and (B) the conduct, closure of, and access to proceedings;

(5)   conduct of the prosecution by one or more attorneys designated by the Secretary of Defense and conduct of the defense by attorneys for the individual subject to this order;

(6)   conviction only upon the concurrence of two-thirds of the members of the commission present at the time of the vote, a majority being present;

(7)   sentencing only upon the concurrence of two-thirds of the members of the commission present at the time of the vote, a majority being present; and

(8)   submission of the record of the trial, including any conviction or sentence, for

review and final decision by me or by the Secretary of Defense if so designated by me for that purpose.

Joint Resolution to authorize the use of United States Armed Forces against those responsible for the recent attacks launched against the United States
PUB. L. 107-40 [S.J. Res. 23] (Sept. 18, 2001)

Whereas, on September 11, 2001, acts of treacherous violence were committed against the United States and its citizens; and

Whereas, such acts render it both necessary and appropriate that the United States exercise its rights to self-defense and to protect United States citizens both at home and abroad; and

Whereas, in light of the threat to the national security and foreign policy of the United States posed by these grave acts of violence; and

Whereas, such acts continue to pose an unusual and extraordinary threat to the national security and foreign policy of the United States; and

Whereas, the President has authority under the Constitution to take action to deter and prevent acts of international terrorism against the United States: Now, therefore, be it

Resolved by the Senate and House of Representatives of the United States of America in Congress assembled,

Sec. 1.   Short Title.

This joint resolution may be cited as the "Authorization for Use of Military Force".

Sec. 2.   Authorization For Use of United States Armed Forces.

(a)   In General. That the President is authorized to use all necessary and appropriate force against those nations, organizations, or persons he determines planned, authorized, committed, or aided the terrorist attacks that occurred on September 11, 2001, or harbored such organizations or persons, in order to prevent any future acts of international terrorism against the United States by such nations, organizations or persons.

(b)   War Powers Resolution Requirements

(1)   Specific statutory authorization. Consistent with section 8(a)(1) of the War Powers Resolution, the Congress declares that this section is intended to constitute specific statutory authorization within the meaning of section 5(b) of the War Powers Resolution.

(2)   Applicability of other requirements. Nothing in this resolution supercedes any requirement of the War Powers Resolution.

Joint Resolution to authorize the use of United States Armed Forces against Iraq
PUB. L. 107-243 [H.J. Res. 114] (Oct. 16, 2002).

Whereas in 1990 in response to Iraq's war of aggression against and illegal occupation of Kuwait, the United States forged a coalition of nations to liberate Kuwait and its people in order to defend the national security of the United States and enforce United Nations Security Council resolutions relating to Iraq;

Whereas after the liberation of Kuwait in 1991, Iraq entered into a United Nations sponsored cease-fire agreement pursuant to which Iraq unequivocally agreed, among other things, to eliminate its nuclear, biological, and chemical weapons programs and the means to deliver and develop them, and to end its support for international terrorism;

Whereas the efforts of international weapons inspectors, United States intelligence agencies, and Iraqi defectors led to the discovery that Iraq had large stockpiles of chemical weapons and a large scale biological weapons program, and that Iraq had an advanced nuclear weapons development program that was much closer to producing a nuclear weapon than intelligence reporting had previously indicated;

Whereas Iraq, in direct and flagrant violation of the cease-fire, attempted to thwart the efforts of weapons inspectors to identify and destroy Iraq's weapons of mass destruction stockpiles and development capabilities, which finally resulted in the withdrawal of inspectors from Iraq on October 31, 1998;

. . . .

Whereas United Nations Security Council Resolution 678 (1990) authorizes the use of all necessary means to enforce United Nations Security Council Resolution 660 (1990) and subsequent relevant resolutions and to compel Iraq to cease certain activities that threaten international peace and security, including the development of weapons of mass destruction and refusal or obstruction of United Nations weapons inspections in violation of United Nations Security Council Resolution 687 (1991), repression of its civilian population in violation of United Nations Security Council Resolution 688 (1991), and threatening its neighbors or United Nations operations in Iraq in violation of United Nations Security Council Resolution 949 (1994);

. . . .

Sec. 3.   Authorization For Use of United States Armed Forces.

(a)   Authorization. The President is authorized to use the Armed Forces of the United States as he determines to be necessary and appropriate in order to

(1)   defend the national security of the United States against the continuing threat posed by Iraq; and

(2)   enforce all relevant United Nations Security Council resolutions regarding Iraq.

(b)   Presidential Determination. In connection with the exercise of the authority granted in subsection (a) to use force the President shall, prior to such exercise or as soon thereafter as may be feasible, but no later than 48 hours after exercising such authority, make available to the Speaker of the House of Representatives and the President pro tempore of the Senate his determination that

(1)   reliance by the United States on further diplomatic or other peaceful means alone either (A) will not adequately protect the national security of the United States against the continuing threat posed by Iraq or (B) is not likely to lead to enforcement of all relevant United Nations Security Council resolutions regarding Iraq; and

(2)   acting pursuant to this joint resolution is consistent with the United States and other countries continuing to take the necessary actions against international terrorist and terrorist organizations, including those nations, organizations, or persons who planned, authorized, committed or aided the terrorist attacks that occurred on September 11, 2001.

(c)   War Powers Resolution Requirements.

(1)   Specific statutory authorization. Consistent with section 8(a)(1) of the War Powers Resolution, the Congress declares that this section is intended to constitute specific statutory authorization within the meaning of section 5(b) of the War Powers Resolution.

(2)   Applicability of other requirements. Nothing in this joint resolution supersedes any requirement of the War Powers Resolution.

Sec. 4.   Reports to Congress.

(a)   Reports. The President shall, at least once every 60 days, submit to the Congress a report on matters relevant to this joint resolution, including actions taken pursuant to the exercise of authority granted in section 3 and the status of planning for efforts that are expected to be required after such actions are completed, including those actions described in section 7 of the Iraq Liberation Act of 1998 (Public Law 105-338).

(b)   Single Consolidated Report. To the extent that the submission of any report described in subsection (a) coincides with the submission of any other report on matters relevant to this joint resolution otherwise required to be submitted to Congress pursuant to the reporting requirements of the War Powers Resolution (Public Law 93-148), all such reports may be submitted as a single consolidated report to the Congress.

(c)   Rule of Construction. To the extent that the information required by section 3 of the Authorization for Use of Military Force Against Iraq Resolution (Public Law 102-1) is included in the report required by this section, such report shall be considered as meeting the requirements of section 3 of such resolution.

C.   Detainee Treatment Act of 2005

28 U.S.C. § 2241   [Habeas Corpus] Power to grant writ.

(e)(1)   No court, justice, or judge shall have jurisdiction to hear or consider an application for a writ of habeas corpus filed by or on behalf of an alien detained by the United States who has been determined by the United States to have been properly detained as an enemy combatant or is awaiting such determination.

(2)   Except as provided in paragraphs (2) and (3) of section 1005(e) of the Detainee Treatment Act of 2005, no court, justice, or judge shall have jurisdiction to hear or consider any other action against the United States or its agents relating to any aspect of the detention, transfer, treatment, trial, or conditions of confinement of an alien who is or was detained by the United States and has been determined by the United States to have been properly detained as an enemy combatant or is awaiting such determination.

[The remainder of the DTA is uncodified but printed at 10 U.S.C. § 801]:

Sec. 1002.   Uniform standards for the interrogation of persons under the detention of the Department of Defense.

(a)   In general. No person in the custody or under the effective control of the Department of Defense or under detention in a Department of Defense facility shall be subject to any treatment or technique of interrogation not authorized by and listed in the United States Army Field Manual on Intelligence Interrogation.

Sec. 1005.   Procedures for status review of detainees outside the United States.

(a)   Submittal of procedures for status review of detainees at Guantánamo Bay, Cuba, and in Afghanistan and Iraq.

(1)   In general. Not later than 180 days after the date of the enactment of this Act, the Secretary of Defense shall submit to the Committee on Armed Services and the Committee on the Judiciary of the Senate and the Committee on Armed Services and the Committee on the Judiciary of the House of Representatives a report setting forth

(A)   the procedures of the Combatant Status Review Tribunals and the Administrative Review Boards established by direction of the Secretary of Defense that are in operation at Guantánamo Bay, Cuba, for determining the status of the detainees held at Guantánamo Bay or to provide an annual review to determine the need to continue to detain an alien who is a detainee; and

(B)   the procedures in operation in Afghanistan and Iraq for a determination of the status of aliens detained in the custody or under the physical control of the Department of Defense in those countries.

(b)   Consideration of statements derived with coercion.

(1)   Assessment. The procedures submitted to Congress pursuant to subsection (a)(1)(A) shall ensure that a Combatant Status Review Tribunal or Administrative Review Board, or any similar or successor administrative tribunal or board, in making a determination of status or disposition of any detainee under such procedures, shall, to the extent practicable, assess—

(A)   whether any statement derived from or relating to such detainee was obtained as a result of coercion; and

(B)   the probative value (if any) of any such statement.

(2)   Applicability. Paragraph (1) applies with respect to any proceeding beginning on or after the date of the enactment of this Act.

(e)   Judicial review of detention of enemy combatants.

(1)   [this paragraph added 28 U.S.C. § 2241(e)]

(2)   Review of decisions of combatant status review tribunals of propriety of detention.

(A)   In general. Subject to subparagraphs (B), (C), and (D), the United States Court of Appeals for the District of Columbia Circuit shall have exclusive jurisdiction to determine the validity of any final decision of a Combatant Status Review Tribunal that an alien is properly detained as an enemy combatant.

(C)   Scope of review. The jurisdiction of the United States Court of Appeals for the District of Columbia Circuit on any claims with respect to an alien under this paragraph shall be limited to the consideration of—

(i)   whether the status determination of the Combatant Status Review Tribunal with regard to such alien was consistent with the standards and procedures specified by the Secretary of Defense for Combatant Status Review Tribunals (including the requirement that the conclusion of the Tribunal be supported by a preponderance of the evidence and allowing a rebuttable presumption in favor of the Government's evidence); and

(ii)   to the extent the Constitution and laws of the United States are applicable, whether the use of such standards and procedures to make the determination is consistent with the Constitution and laws of the United States.

(3)   Review of final decisions of military commissions.

(A)   In general. Subject to subparagraphs (B), (C), and (D), the United States Court of Appeals for the District of Columbia Circuit shall have exclusive jurisdiction to determine the validity of any final decision rendered by a military commission.

(B)   Grant of review. Review under this paragraph shall be as of right.

(D)   Scope of review. The jurisdiction of the United States Court of Appeals for the District of Columbia Circuit on an appeal of a final decision with respect to an alien under this paragraph shall be limited to the consideration of — (i) whether the final decision was consistent with the standards and procedures specified for a military commission referred to in subparagraph (A); and (ii) to the extent the Constitution and laws of the United States are applicable, whether the use of such standards and procedures to reach the final decision is consistent with the Constitution and laws of the United States.

(f)   Construction. Nothing in this section shall be construed to confer any constitutional right on an alien detained as an enemy combatant outside the United States.

(g)   United States defined. For purposes of this section, the term 'United States', when used in a geographic sense, is as defined in section 101(a)(38) of the Immigration and Nationality Act and, in particular, does not include the United States Naval Station, Guantánamo Bay, Cuba.

(h)   Effective date.

(1)   In general. This section shall take effect on the date of the enactment of this Act.

(2)   Review of combatant status tribunal and military commission decisions. Paragraphs (2) and (3) of subsection (e) shall apply with respect to any claim whose review is governed by one of such paragraphs and that is pending on or after the date of the enactment of this Act.

D.   Military Commission Act of 2006

10 U.S.C. § 948a.   Definitions

In this chapter

(1)   Unlawful enemy combatant.

(A)   The term "unlawful enemy combatant" means—

(i)   a person who has engaged in hostilities or who has purposefully and materially supported hostilities against the United States or its co-belligerents who is not a lawful enemy combatant (including a person who is part of the Taliban, al Qaeda, or associated forces); or

(ii)   a person who, before, on, or after the date of the enactment of the Military Commissions Act of 2006 [Oct. 17, 2006], has been determined to be an unlawful enemy combatant by a Combatant Status Review Tribunal or another competent tribunal established under the authority of the President or the Secretary of Defense.

(2)   Lawful enemy combatant. The term "lawful enemy combatant" means a person who is—

(A)   a member of the regular forces of a State party engaged in hostilities against the United States;

(B)   a member of a militia, volunteer corps, or organized resistance movement belonging to a State party engaged in such hostilities, which are under responsible command, wear a fixed distinctive sign recognizable at a distance, carry their arms openly, and abide by the law of war; or(C) a member of a regular armed force who professes allegiance to a government engaged in such hostilities, but not recognized by the United States.

10 U.S.C. § 948d.   Jurisdiction of military commissions

(a)   Jurisdiction. A military commission shall have jurisdiction to try any offense made punishable by this chapter or the law of war when committed by an alien unlawful enemy combatant before, on, or after September 11, 2001.

(b)   Lawful enemy combatants. Military commissions shall not have jurisdiction over lawful enemy combatants. Lawful enemy combatants who violate the law of war are subject to [courts-martial, 10 U.S.C. §§ 801 et seq.] Courts-martial established under that chapter shall have jurisdiction to try a lawful enemy combatant for any offense made punishable under this chapter.

(c) Determination of unlawful enemy combatant status dispositive. A finding, whether before, on, or after the date of the enactment of the Military Commissions Act of 2006 [enacted Oct. 17, 2006], by a Combatant Status Review Tribunal or another competent tribunal established under the authority of the President or the Secretary of Defense that a person is an unlawful enemy combatant is dispositive for purposes of jurisdiction for trial by military commission.

(d) Punishments. A military commission may, under such limitations as the Secretary of Defense may prescribe, adjudge any punishment not forbidden by this chapter, including the penalty of death when authorized under this chapter or the law of war.

10 U.S.C. § 950v.   Crimes triable by military commissions

(a) Definitions and construction. In this section:

(1) Military objective. The term "military objective" means

(A) combatants; and

(B) those objects during an armed conflict—

(i) which, by their nature, location, purpose, or use, effectively contribute to the opposing force's war-fighting or war-sustaining capability; and

(ii) the total or partial destruction, capture, or neutralization of which would constitute a definite military advantage to the attacker under the circumstances at the time of the attack.

(2) Protected person. The term "protected person" means any person entitled to protection under one or more of the Geneva Conventions, including

(A) civilians not taking an active part in hostilities;

(B) military personnel placed hors de combat by sickness, wounds, or detention; and

(C) military medical or religious personnel.

(b) Offenses. The following offenses shall be triable by military commission under this chapter at any time without limitation:

[28 offenses including murder of protected persons, hostage taking, attack of civilians, terrorism, material support of terrorism, spying, conspiracy to commit any of the other listed offenses]

E. CIA Detention and Interrogation

Executive Order: Interpretation of the Geneva Conventions Common Article 3 as Applied to a Program of Detention and Interrogation Operated by the Central Intelligence Agency
(July 20, 2007)

By the authority vested in me as President and Commander in Chief of the Armed Forces by the Constitution and the laws of the United States of America, including the Authorization for Use of Military Force (Public Law 107 40), the Military Commissions Act of 2006 (Public Law 109 366), and section 301 of title 3, United States Code, it is hereby ordered as follows:

Sec. 1. General Determinations.

(a) The United States is engaged in an armed conflict with al Qaeda, the Taliban, and associated forces. Members of al Qaeda were responsible for the attacks on the United States of September 11, 2001, and for many other terrorist attacks, including against the United States, its personnel, and its allies throughout the world. These forces continue to fight the United States and its allies in Afghanistan, Iraq, and elsewhere, and they continue to plan additional acts of terror throughout the world. On February 7, 2002, I determined for the United States that members of al Qaeda, the Taliban, and associated forces are unlawful enemy combatants who are not entitled to the protections that the Third Geneva Convention provides to prisoners of war. I hereby reaffirm that determination.

(b)   The Military Commissions Act defines certain prohibitions of Common Article 3 for United States law, and it reaffirms and reinforces the authority of the President to interpret the meaning and application of the Geneva Conventions.

Sec. 2.   Definitions.

As used in this order:

(a)   "Common Article 3" means Article 3 of the Geneva Conventions.

(b)   "Geneva Conventions" means:

(i)   the Convention for the Amelioration of the Condition of the Wounded and Sick in Armed Forces in the Field, done at Geneva August 12, 1949 (6 UST 3114);

(ii)   the Convention for the Amelioration of the Condition of Wounded, Sick and Shipwrecked Members of Armed Forces at Sea, done at Geneva August 12, 1949 (6 UST 3217);

(iii)   the Convention Relative to the Treatment of Prisoners of War, done at Geneva August 12, 1949 (6 UST 3316); and

(iv)   the Convention Relative to the Protection of Civilian Persons in Time of War, done at Geneva August 12, 1949 (6 UST 3516).

(c)   "Cruel, inhuman, or degrading treatment or punishment" means the cruel, unusual, and inhumane treatment or punishment prohibited by the Fifth, Eighth, and Fourteenth Amendments to the Constitution of the United States.

Sec. 3.   Compliance of a Central Intelligence Agency Detention and Interrogation Program with Common Article 3.

(a)   Pursuant to the authority of the President under the Constitution and the laws of the United States, including the Military Commissions Act of 2006, this order interprets the meaning and application of the text of Common Article 3 with respect to certain detentions and interrogations, and shall be treated as authoritative for all purposes as a matter of United States law, including satisfaction of the international obligations of the United States. I hereby determine that Common Article 3 shall apply to a program of detention and interrogation operated by the Central Intelligence Agency as set forth in this section. The requirements set forth in this section shall be applied with respect to detainees in such program without adverse distinction as to their race, color, religion or faith, sex, birth, or wealth.

(b)   I hereby determine that a program of detention and interrogation approved by the Director of the Central Intelligence Agency fully complies with the obligations of the United States under Common Article 3, provided that:

(i)   the conditions of confinement and interrogation practices of the program do not include:

(A)   torture, as defined in section 2340 of title 18, United States Code;

(B)   any of the acts prohibited by section 2441(d) of title 18, United States Code, including murder, torture, cruel or inhuman treatment, mutilation or maiming, intentionally causing serious bodily injury, rape, sexual assault or abuse, taking of hostages, or performing of biological experiments;

(C)   other acts of violence serious enough to be considered comparable to murder, torture, mutilation, and cruel or inhuman treatment, as defined in section 2441(d) of title 18, United States Code;

(D)　any other acts of cruel, inhuman, or degrading treatment or punishment prohibited by the Military Commissions Act (subsection 6(c) of Public Law 109 366) and the Detainee Treatment Act of 2005 (section 1003 of Public Law 109 148 and section 1403 of Public Law 109 163);

(E)　willful and outrageous acts of personal abuse done for the purpose of humiliating or degrading the individual in a manner so serious that any reasonable person, considering the circumstances, would deem the acts to be beyond the bounds of human decency, such as sexual or sexually indecent acts undertaken for the purpose of humiliation, forcing the individual to perform sexual acts or to pose sexually, threatening the individual with sexual mutilation, or using the individual as a human shield; or

(F)　acts intended to denigrate the religion, religious practices, or religious objects of the individual;

(ii)　the conditions of confinement and interrogation practices are to be used with an alien detainee who is determined by the Director of the Central Intelligence Agency:

(A)　to be a member or part of or supporting al Qaeda, the Taliban, or associated organizations; and

(B)　likely to be in possession of information that:

(1)　could assist in detecting, mitigating, or preventing terrorist attacks, such as attacks within the United States or against its Armed Forces or other personnel, citizens, or facilities, or against allies or other countries cooperating in the war on terror with the United States, or their armed forces or other personnel, citizens, or facilities; or

(2)　could assist in locating the senior leadership of al Qaeda, the Taliban, or associated forces;

(iii)　the interrogation practices are determined by the Director of the Central Intelligence Agency, based upon professional advice, to be safe for use with each detainee with whom they are used; and

(iv)　detainees in the program receive the basic necessities of life, including adequate food and water, shelter from the elements, necessary clothing, protection from extremes of heat and cold, and essential medical care.

(c)　The Director of the Central Intelligence Agency shall issue written policies to govern the program, including guidelines for Central Intelligence Agency personnel that implement paragraphs (i)(C), (E), and (F) of subsection 3(b) of this order, and including requirements to ensure:

(i)　safe and professional operation of the program;

(ii)　the development of an approved plan of interrogation tailored for each detainee in the program to be interrogated, consistent with subsection 3(b)(iv) of this order;

(iii)　appropriate training for interrogators and all personnel operating the program;

(iv)　effective monitoring of the program, including with respect to medical matters, to ensure the safety of those in the program; and

(v)　compliance with applicable law and this order.

Sec. 4. Assignment of Function.

With respect to the program addressed in this order, the function of the President under section 6(c)(3) of the Military Commissions Act of 2006 is assigned to the Director of National Intelligence.

Sec. 5. General Provisions.

(a) Subject to subsection (b) of this section, this order is not intended to, and does not, create any right or benefit, substantive or procedural, enforceable at law or in equity, against the United States, its departments, agencies, or other entities, its officers or employees, or any other person.

(b) Nothing in this order shall be construed to prevent or limit reliance upon this order in a civil, criminal, or administrative proceeding, or otherwise, by the Central Intelligence Agency or by any individual acting on behalf of the Central Intelligence Agency in connection with the program addressed in this order.

GEORGE W. BUSH

THE WHITE HOUSE,

July 20, 2007.

B. INTERNATIONAL CONVENTIONS

1. Geneva Conventions (1949)

[Note: There are four 1949 Geneva Conventions. Convention I deals with "Wounded and Sick Members of Armed Forces in the Field," II with "Wounded, Sick and Shipwrecked Members of Armed Forces at Sea," and IV with "Protection of Civilian Persons in Time of War." Convention IV is "Relative to the Treatment of Prisoners of War." Article 3 is identical in all four conventions and is known as "Common Article 3."]

III

Convention Relative to the Treatment of Prisoners of War

Article 2

In addition to the provisions which shall be implemented in peace time, the present Convention shall apply to all cases of declared war or of any other armed conflict which may arise between two or more of the High Contracting Parties, even if the state of war is not recognized by one of them.

The Convention shall also apply to all cases of partial or total occupation of the territory of a High Contracting Party, even if the said occupation meets with no armed resistance.

Although one of the Powers in conflict may not be a party to the present Convention, the Powers who are parties thereto shall remain bound by it in their mutual relations. They shall furthermore be bound by the Convention in relation to the said Power, if the latter accepts and applies the provisions thereof.

Article 3

In the case of armed conflict not of an international character occurring in the territory of one of the High Contracting Parties, each party to the conflict shall be bound to apply, as a minimum, the following provisions:

1. Persons taking no active part in the hostilities, including members of armed forces

who have laid down their arms and those placed hors de combat by sickness, wounds, detention, or any other cause, shall in all circumstances be treated humanely, without any adverse distinction founded on race, colour, religion or faith, sex, birth or wealth, or any other similar criteria.

To this end the following acts are and shall remain prohibited at any time and in any place whatsoever with respect to the above-mentioned persons:

(a)   Violence to life and person, in particular murder of all kinds, mutilation, cruel treatment and torture;

(b)   Taking of hostages;

(c)   Outrages upon personal dignity, in particular, humiliating and degrading treatment;

(d)   The passing of sentences and the carrying out of executions without previous judgment pronounced by a regularly constituted court affording all the judicial guarantees which are recognized as indispensable by civilized peoples.

2. The wounded and sick shall be collected and cared for.

An impartial humanitarian body, such as the International Committee of the Red Cross, may offer its services to the Parties to the conflict.

The Parties to the conflict should further endeavour to bring into force, by means of special agreements, all or part of the other provisions of the present Convention.

The application of the preceding provisions shall not affect the legal status of the Parties to the conflict.

Article 4

(A)   Prisoners of war, in the sense of the present Convention, are persons belonging to one of the following categories, who have fallen into the power of the enemy:

1.   Members of the armed forces of a Party to the conflict as well as members of militias or volunteer corps forming part of such armed forces.

2.   Members of other militias and members of other volunteer corps, including those of organized resistance movements, belonging to a Party to the conflict and operating in or outside their own territory, even if this territory is occupied, provided that such militias or volunteer corps, including such organized resistance movements, fulfil the following conditions:

(a)   That of being commanded by a person responsible for his subordinates;

(b)   That of having a fixed distinctive sign recognizable at a distance;

(c)   That of carrying arms openly;

(d)   That of conducting their operations in accordance with the laws and customs of war.

3.   Members of regular armed forces who profess allegiance to a government or an authority not recognized by the Detaining Power.

4.   Persons who accompany the armed forces without actually being members thereof, such as civilian members of military aircraft crews, war correspondents, supply contractors, members of labour units or of services responsible for the welfare of the armed forces, provided that they have received authorization from the armed forces which they accompany, who shall provide them for that purpose with an identity card similar to the annexed model.

5.   Members of crews, including masters, pilots and apprentices, of the merchant marine and the crews of civil aircraft of the Parties to the conflict, who do not benefit by more favourable treatment under any other provisions of international law.

6.   Inhabitants of a non-occupied territory, who on the approach of the enemy spontaneously take up arms to resist the invading forces, without having had time to

form themselves into regular armed units, provided they carry arms openly and respect the laws and customs of war.

(B)   The following shall likewise be treated as prisoners of war under the present Convention:

1.   Persons belonging, or having belonged, to the armed forces of the occupied country, if the occupying Power considers it necessary by reason of such allegiance to intern them, even though it has originally liberated them while hostilities were going on outside the territory it occupies, in particular where such persons have made an unsuccessful attempt to rejoin the armed forces to which they belong and which are engaged in combat, or where they fail to comply with a summons made to them with a view to internment.

2.   The persons belonging to one of the categories enumerated in the present Article, who have been received by neutral or non-belligerent Powers on their territory and whom these Powers are required to intern under international law, without prejudice to any more favourable treatment which these Powers may choose to give and with the exception of Articles 8, 10, 15, 30, fifth paragraph, 58–67, 92, 126 and, where diplomatic relations exist between the Parties to the conflict and the neutral or non-belligerent Power concerned, those Articles concerning the Protecting Power. Where such diplomatic relations exist, the Parties to a conflict on whom these persons depend shall be allowed to perform towards them the functions of a Protecting Power as provided in the present Convention, without prejudice to the functions which these Parties normally exercise in conformity with diplomatic and consular usage and treaties.

(C)   This Article shall in no way affect the status of medical personnel and chaplains as provided for in Article 33 of the present Convention.

Article 5

The present Convention shall apply to the persons referred to in Article 4 from t0he time they fall into the power of the enemy and until their final release and repatriation.

Should any doubt arise as to whether persons, having committed a belligerent act and having fallen into the hands of the enemy, belong to any of the categories enumerated in Article 4, such persons shall enjoy the protection of the present Convention until such time as their status has been determined by a competent tribunal.

Article 99

No prisoner of war may be tried or sentenced for an act which is not forbidden by the law of the Detaining Power or by international law, in force at the time the said act was committed.

No moral or physical coercion may be exerted on a prisoner of war in order to induce him to admit himself guilty of the act of which he is accused.

No prisoner of war may be convicted without having had an opportunity to present his defence and the assistance of a qualified advocate or counsel.

Article 100

Prisoners of war and the Protecting Powers shall be informed as soon as possible of the offences which are punishable by the death sentence under the laws of the Detaining Power.

Other offences shall not thereafter be made punishable by the death penalty without the concurrence of the Power upon which the prisoners of war depend.

The death sentence cannot be pronounced on a prisoner of war unless the attention of the court has, in accordance with Article 87, second paragraph, been particularly called to the fact that since the accused is not a national of the Detaining Power, he is not bound to it by any duty of allegiance, and that he is in its power as the result of circumstances independent of his own will.

Article 102

A prisoner of war can be validly sentenced only if the sentence has been pronounced by the same courts according to the same procedure as in the case of members of the armed forces of the Detaining Power, and if, furthermore, the provisions of the present Chapter have been observed.

Article 105

The prisoner of war shall be entitled to assistance by one of his prisoner comrades, to defence by a qualified advocate or counsel of his own choice, to the calling of witnesses and, if he deems necessary, to the services of a competent interpreter. He shall be advised of these rights by the Detaining Power in due time before the trial.

Failing a choice by the prisoner of war, the Protecting Power shall find him an advocate or counsel, and shall have at least one week at its disposal for the purpose. The Detaining Power shall deliver to the said Power, on request, a list of persons qualified to present the defence. Failing a choice of an advocate or counsel by the prisoner of war or the Protecting Power, the Detaining Power shall appoint a competent advocate or counsel to conduct the defence.

Article 118

Prisoners of war shall be released and repatriated without delay after the cessation of active hostilities.

IV

Convention Relative to the Protection of Civilian Persons in Time of War

Article 2

In addition to the provisions which shall be implemented in peace-time, the present Convention shall apply to all cases of declared war or of any other armed conflict which may arise between two or more of the High Contracting Parties, even if the state of war is not recognized by one of them.

The Convention shall also apply to all cases of partial or total occupation of the territory of a High Contracting Party, even if the said occupation meets with no armed resistance.

Article 3

In the case of armed conflict not of an international character occurring in the territory of one of the High Contracting Parties, each Party to the conflict shall be bound to apply, as a minimum, the following provisions:

(1) Persons taking no active part in the hostilities, including members of armed forces who have laid down their arms and those placed hors de combat by sickness, wounds, detention, or any other cause, shall in all circumstances be treated humanely, without any adverse distinction founded on race, colour, religion or faith, sex, birth or wealth, or any other similar criteria.

To this end the following acts are and shall remain prohibited at any time and in any place whatsoever with respect to the above-mentioned persons:

(a) violence to life and person, in particular murder of all kinds, mutilation, cruel treatment and torture;

(b) taking of hostages;

(c) outrages upon personal dignity, in particular humiliating and degrading treatment;

(d) the passing of sentences and the carrying out of executions without previous judgment pronounced by a regularly constituted court, affording all the judicial guarantees which are recognized as indispensable by civilized peoples.

Article 4

Persons protected by the Convention are those who, at a given moment and in any manner whatsoever, find themselves, in case of a conflict or occupation, in the hands of a Party to the conflict or Occupying Power of which they are not nationals.

Nationals of a State which is not bound by the Convention are not protected by it. Nationals of a neutral State who find themselves in the territory of a belligerent State, and nationals of a co-belligerent State, shall not be regarded as protected persons while the State of which they are nationals has normal diplomatic representation in the State in whose hands they are.

Article 5

Where in the territory of a Party to the conflict, the latter is satisfied that an individual protected person is definitely suspected of or engaged in activities hostile to the security of the State, such individual person shall not be entitled to claim such rights and privileges under the present Convention as would, if exercised in the favour of such individual person, be prejudicial to the security of such State.

Where in occupied territory an individual protected person is detained as a spy or saboteur, or as a person under definite suspicion of activity hostile to the security of the Occupying Power, such person shall, in those cases where absolute military security so requires, be regarded as having forfeited rights of communication under the present Convention.

In each case, such persons shall nevertheless be treated with humanity and, in case of trial, shall not be deprived of the rights of fair and regular trial prescribed by the present Convention. They shall also be granted the full rights and privileges of a protected person under the present Convention at the earliest date consistent with the security of the State or Occupying Power, as the case may be.

Section III. Occupied territories

Article 64

The penal laws of the occupied territory shall remain in force, with the exception that they may be repealed or suspended by the Occupying Power in cases where they constitute a threat to its security or an obstacle to the application of the present Convention.

Subject to the latter consideration and to the necessity for ensuring the effective administration of justice, the tribunals of the occupied territory shall continue to function in respect of all offences covered by the said laws.

The Occupying Power may, however, subject the population of the occupied territory to provisions which are essential to enable the Occupying Power to fulfil its obligations under the present Convention, to maintain the orderly government of the territory, and to ensure the security of the Occupying Power, of the members and property of the occupying forces or administration, and likewise of the establishments and lines of communication used by them.

Article 72

Accused persons shall have the right to present evidence necessary to their defence and may, in particular, call witnesses. They shall have the right to be assisted by a qualified advocate or counsel of their own choice, who shall be able to visit them freely and shall enjoy the necessary facilities for preparing the defence.

Failing a choice by the accused, the Protecting Power may provide him with an advocate or counsel. When an accused person has to meet a serious charge and the Protecting Power is not functioning, the Occupying Power, subject to the consent of the accused, shall provide an advocate or counsel.

2. Statutes of the International Criminal Tribunals

[Note: The two ICT's were established for slightly different circumstances. The assumption at the time seems to have been that Yugoslavia presented an "international armed conflict" while Rwanda was an "armed conflict not of an international character," thus producing slightly different statements of substantive law to be applied with respect to the Geneva Conventions.

[The four Geneva Conventions of 1949 separately protect Wounded or Sick Soldiers, Wounded or Shipwrecked at Sea, Prisoners of War, and Civilians. "Common Article 3" refers to an article in each Convention which states that "in the case of armed conflict not of an international character, . . . persons taking no active part in the hostilities, including members of armed forces who have laid down their arms, . . . shall be treated humanely without any adverse distinction founded on race, color, religion or faith, sex, birth or wealth, or any other similar criteria." The article then goes on to list prohibited acts in the same words as items (a), (c), (e), and (g) above. Notice that the Rwanda statute adds "collective punishments," "acts of terrorism," and "pillage" to the prohibited acts.

[The substantive law portions of the two statutes are rearranged for ease of comparison.]

STATUTE OF THE INTERNATIONAL CRIMINAL TRIBUNAL FOR YUGOSLAVIA

Article 1 Competence of the International Tribunal

The International Tribunal shall have the power to prosecute persons responsible for serious violations of international humanitarian law committed in the territory of the former Yugoslavia since 1991 in accordance with the provisions of the present Statute.

Article 2 Grave breaches of the Geneva Conventions of 1949

The International Tribunal shall have the power to prosecute persons committing or ordering to be committed grave breaches of the Geneva Conventions of 12 August 1949, namely the following acts against persons or property protected under the provisions of the relevant Geneva Convention:

    (a)   wilful killing;

    (b)   torture or inhuman treatment, including biological experiments;

    (c)   wilfully causing great suffering or serious injury to body or health;

    (d)   extensive destruction and appropriation of property, not justified by military necessity and carried out unlawfully and wantonly;

    (e)   compelling a prisoner of war or a civilian to serve in the forces of a hostile power;

    (f)   wilfully depriving a prisoner of war or a civilian of the rights of fair and regular trial;

    (g)   unlawful deportation or transfer or unlawful confinement of a civilian;

    (h)   taking civilians as hostages.

Article 3 Violations of the laws or customs of war

The International Tribunal shall have the power to prosecute persons violating the laws or customs of war. Such violations shall include, but not be limited to:

    (a)   employment of poisonous weapons or other weapons calculated to cause unnecessary suffering;

(b) wanton destruction of cities, towns or villages, or devastation not justified by military necessity;

(c) attack, or bombardment, by whatever means, of undefended towns, villages, dwellings, or buildings;

(d) seizure of, destruction or wilful damage done to institutions dedicated to religion, charity and education, the arts and sciences, historic monuments and works of art and science;

(e) plunder of public or private property.

Article 4 Genocide

1. The International Tribunal shall have the power to prosecute persons committing genocide as defined in paragraph 2 of this article or of committing any of the other acts enumerated in paragraph 3 of this article.

2. Genocide means any of the following acts committed with intent to destroy, in whole or in part, a national, ethnical, racial or religious group, as such:

(a) killing members of the group;

(b) causing serious bodily or mental harm to members of the group;

(c) deliberately inflicting on the group conditions of life calculated to bring about its physical destruction in whole or in part;

(d) imposing measures intended to prevent births within the group;

(e) forcibly transferring children of the group to another group.

3. The following acts shall be punishable:

(a) genocide;

(b) conspiracy to commit genocide;

(c) direct and public incitement to commit genocide;

(d) attempt to commit genocide;

(e) complicity in genocide.

Article 5 Crimes against humanity

The International Tribunal shall have the power to prosecute persons responsible for the following crimes when committed in armed conflict, whether international or internal in character, and directed against any civilian population:

(a) murder;

(b) extermination;

(c) enslavement;

(d) deportation;

(e) imprisonment;

(f) torture;

(g) rape;

(h) persecutions on political, racial and religious grounds;

(i) other inhumane acts.

STATUTE OF THE INTERNATIONAL CRIMINAL TRIBUNAL FOR RWANDA

Article 1: Competence of the International Tribunal for Rwanda

The International Tribunal for Rwanda shall have the power to prosecute persons responsible for serious violations of international humanitarian law committed in the territory of Rwanda and Rwandan citizens responsible for such violations committed in the territory of neighbouring States between 1 January 1994 and 31 December 1994, in accordance with the provisions of the present Statute.

Article 4: Violations of Article 3 Common to the Geneva Conventions and of Additional Protocol II

The International Tribunal for Rwanda shall have the power to prosecute persons committing or ordering to be committed serious violations of Article 3 common to the Geneva Conventions of 12 August 1949 for the Protection of War Victims, and of Additional Protocol II thereto of 8 June 1977. These violations shall include, but shall not be limited to:

(a)   Violence to life, health and physical or mental well-being of persons, in particular murder as well as cruel treatment such as torture, mutilation or any form of corporal punishment;

(b)   Collective punishments;

(c)   Taking of hostages;

(d)   Acts of terrorism;

(e)   Outrages upon personal dignity, in particular humiliating and degrading treatment, rape, enforced prostitution and any form of indecent assault;

(f)   Pillage;

(g)   The passing of sentences and the carrying out of executions without previous judgement pronounced by a regularly constituted court, affording all the judicial guarantees which are recognized as indispensable by civilised peoples;

(h)   Threats to commit any of the foregoing acts.

Article 2: Genocide

1.   The International Tribunal for Rwanda shall have the power to prosecute persons committing genocide as defined in paragraph 2 of this Article or of committing any of the other acts enumerated in paragraph 3 of this Article.

2.   Genocide means any of the following acts committed with intent to destroy, in whole or in part, a national, ethnical, racial or religious group, such as:

(a)   Killing members of the group;

(b)   Causing serious bodily or mental harm to members of the group;

(c)   Deliberately inflicting on the group conditions of life calculated to bring about its physical destruction in whole or in part;

(d)   Imposing measures intended to prevent births within the group;

(e)   Forcibly transferring children of the group to another group.

3.   The following acts shall be punishable:

(a)   Genocide;

(b)   Conspiracy to commit genocide;

(c)   Direct and public incitement to commit genocide;

(d)   Attempt to commit genocide;

(e)   Complicity in genocide.

Article 3: Crimes against Humanity

The International Tribunal for Rwanda shall have the power to prosecute persons responsible for the following crimes when committed as part of a widespread or systematic attack against any civilian population on national, political, ethnic, racial or religious grounds:

(a)   Murder;

(b)   Extermination;

(c)   Enslavement;

(d)   Deportation;

(e) Imprisonment;

(f) Torture;

(g) Rape;

(h) Persecutions on political, racial and religious grounds;

(i) Other inhumane acts.

3. Convention Against Torture and Other Cruel, Inhuman or Degrading Treatment or Punishment

Article 1

1. For the purposes of this Convention, torture means any act by which severe pain or suffering, whether physical or mental, is intentionally inflicted on a person for such purposes as obtaining from him or a third person information or a confession, punishing him for an act he or a third person has committed or is suspected of having committed, or intimidating or coercing him or a third person, or for any reason based on discrimination of any kind, when such pain or suffering is inflicted by or at the instigation of or with the consent or acquiescence of a public official or other person acting in an official capacity. It does not include pain or suffering arising only from, inherent in or incidental to lawful sanctions.

2. This article is without prejudice to any international instrument or national legislation which does or may contain provisions of wider application.

Article 2

1. Each State Party shall take effective legislative, administrative, judicial or other measures to prevent acts of torture in any territory under its jurisdiction.

2. No exceptional circumstances whatsoever, whether a state of war or a threat or war, internal political instability or any other public emergency, may be invoked as a justification of torture.

3. An order from a superior officer or a public authority may not be invoked as a justification of torture.

Article 3

1. No State Party shall expel, return ("refouler") or extradite a person to another State where there are substantial grounds for believing that he would be in danger of being subjected to torture.

2. For the purpose of determining whether there are such grounds, the competent authorities shall take into account all relevant considerations including, where applicable, the existence in the State concerned of a consistent pattern of gross, flagrant or mass violations of human rights.

Article 4

1. Each State Party shall ensure that all acts of torture are offences under its criminal law. The same shall apply to an attempt to commit torture and to an act by any person which constitutes complicity or participation in torture.

2. Each State Party shall make these offences punishable by appropriate penalties which take into account their grave nature.

Article 5

1.   Each State Party shall take such measures as may be necessary to establish its jurisdiction over the offences referred to in article 4 in the following cases:

When the offences are committed in any territory under its jurisdiction or on board a ship or aircraft registered in that State;

When the alleged offender is a national of that State;

When the victim was a national of that State if that State considers it appropriate.

2.   Each State Party shall likewise take such measures as may be necessary to establish its jurisdiction over such offences in cases where the alleged offender is present in any territory under its jurisdiction and it does not extradite him pursuant to article 8 to any of the States mentioned in Paragraph 1 of this article.

3.   This Convention does not exclude any criminal jurisdiction exercised in accordance with internal law.

Article 6

1.   Upon being satisfied, after an examination of information available to it, that the circumstances so warrant, any State Party in whose territory a person alleged to have committed any offence referred to in article 4 is present, shall take him into custody or take other legal measures to ensure his presence. The custody and other legal measures shall be as provided in the law of that State but may be continued only for such time as is necessary to enable any criminal or extradition proceedings to be instituted.

Article 7

1.   The State Party in territory under whose jurisdiction a person alleged to have committed any offence referred to in article 4 is found, shall in the cases contemplated in article 5, if it does not extradite him, submit the case to its competent authorities for the purpose of prosecution.

Article 8

1.   The offences referred to in article 4 shall be deemed to be included as extraditable offences in any extradition treaty existing between States Parties. States Parties undertake to include such offences as extraditable offences in every extradition treaty to be concluded between them.

4.   Such offences shall be treated, for the purpose of extradition between States Parties, as if they had been committed not only in the place in which they occurred but also in the territories of the States required to establish their jurisdiction in accordance with article 5, paragraph 1.

4.   International Convention for the Suppression of the Financing of Terrorism

Article 2

1.   Any person commits an offence within the meaning of this Convention if that person by any means, directly or indirectly, unlawfully and wilfully, provides or collects funds with the intention that they should be used or in the knowledge that they are to be used, in full or in part, in order to carry out:

(a)   An act which constitutes an offence within the scope of and as defined in one of the treaties listed in the annex; or

(b)   Any other act intended to cause death or serious bodily injury to a civilian, or to any other person not taking an active part in the hostilities in a situation of armed conflict, when the purpose of such act, by its nature or context, is to intimidate a population, or to compel a government or an international organization to do or to abstain from doing any act.

3. For an act to constitute an offence set forth in paragraph 1, it shall not be necessary that the funds were actually used to carry out an offence referred to in paragraph 1.

4. Any person also commits an offence if that person attempts to commit an offence as set forth in paragraph 1 of this article.

5. Any person also commits an offence if that person:

(a) Participates as an accomplice in an offence as set forth in paragraph 1 or 4 of this article;

(b) Organizes or directs others to commit an offence as set forth in paragraph 1 or 4of this article;

(c) Contributes to the commission of one or more offences as set forth in paragraphs 1 or 4 of this article by a group of persons acting with a common purpose. Such contribution shall be intentional and shall either:

(i) Be made with the aim of furthering the criminal activity or criminal purpose of the group, where such activity or purpose involves the commission of an offence as set forth in paragraph 1 of this article; or

(ii) Be made in the knowledge of the intention of the group to commit an offence as set forth in paragraph 1 of this article.

Article 3

This Convention shall not apply where the offence is committed within a single State, the alleged offender is a national of that State and is present in the territory of that State and no other State has a basis under article 7, paragraph 1, or article 7, paragraph 2, to exercise jurisdiction, except that the provisions of articles 12 to 18 shall, as appropriate, apply in those cases.

Article 4

Each State Party shall adopt such measures as may be necessary:

(a) To establish as criminal offences under its domestic law the offences set forth in article 2;

(b) To make those offences punishable by appropriate penalties which take into account the grave nature of the offences.

Article 5

1. Each State Party, in accordance with its domestic legal principles, shall take the necessary measures to enable a legal entity located in its territory or organized under its laws to be held liable when a person responsible for the management or control of that legal entity has, in that capacity, committed an offence set forth in article 2. Such liability may be criminal, civil or administrative.

2. Such liability is incurred without prejudice to the criminal liability of individuals having committed the offences.

3. Each State Party shall ensure, in particular, that legal entities liable in accordance with paragraph 1 above are subject to effective, proportionate and dissuasive criminal, civil or administrative sanctions. Such sanctions may include monetary sanctions.

Article 6

Each State Party shall adopt such measures as may be necessary, including, where appropriate, domestic legislation, to ensure that criminal acts within the scope of this

Convention are under no circumstances justifiable by considerations of a political, philosophical, ideological, racial, ethnic, religious or other similar nature.

Article 7

1.   Each State Party shall take such measures as may be necessary to establish its jurisdiction over the offences set forth in article 2 when:

(a)   The offence is committed in the territory of that State;

(b)   The offence is committed on board a vessel flying the flag of that State or an aircraft registered under the laws of that State at the time the offence is committed;

(c)   The offence is committed by a national of that State.

2.   A State Party may also establish its jurisdiction over any such offence when:

(a)   The offence was directed towards or resulted in the carrying out of an offence referred to in article 2, paragraph 1, subparagraph (a) or (b), in the territory of or against a national of that State;

(b)   The offence was directed towards or resulted in the carrying out of an offence referred to in article 2, paragraph 1, subparagraph (a) or (b), against a State or government facility of that State abroad, including diplomatic or consular premises of that State;

(c)   The offence was directed towards or resulted in an offence referred to in article 2, paragraph 1, subparagraph (a) or (b), committed in an attempt to compel that State to do or abstain from doing any act;

(d)   The offence is committed by a stateless person who has his or her habitual residence in the territory of that State;

(e)   The offence is committed on board an aircraft which is operated by the Government of that State.

[The "prosecute or extradite" provisions are essentially the same as in other Conventions, such as the Torture Convention.]

5.   UN Security Council Resolution 1373

Sept. 28, 2001

The Security Council,

Reaffirming its resolutions 1269 (1999) of 19 October 1999 and 1368 (2001) of 12 September 2001,

Reaffirming also its unequivocal condemnation of the terrorist attacks which took place in New York, Washington, D.C. and Pennsylvania on 11 September 2001, and expressing its determination to prevent all such acts,

Reaffirming further that such acts, like any act of international terrorism, constitute a threat to international peace and security,

Reaffirming the inherent right of individual or collective self-defence as recognized by the Charter of the United Nations as reiterated in resolution 1368 (2001),

Reaffirming the need to combat by all means, in accordance with the Charter of the United Nations, threats to international peace and security caused by terrorist acts,

Deeply concerned by the increase, in various regions of the world, of acts of terrorism motivated by intolerance or extremism,

Calling on States to work together urgently to prevent and suppress terrorist acts, including through increased cooperation and full implementation of the relevant international conventions relating to terrorism,

Recognizing the need for States to complement international cooperation by taking additional measures to prevent and suppress, in their territories through all lawful means, the financing and preparation of any acts of terrorism,

Reaffirming the principle established by the General Assembly in its declaration of October 1970 (resolution 2625 (XXV)) and reiterated by the Security Council in its resolution 1189 (1998) of 13 August 1998, namely that every State has the duty to refrain from organizing, instigating, assisting or participating in terrorist acts in another State or acquiescing in organized activities within its territory directed towards the commission of such acts,

Acting under Chapter VII of the Charter of the United Nations,

1. *Decides* that all States shall:

(a) Prevent and suppress the financing of terrorist acts;

(b) Criminalize the wilful provision or collection, by any means, directly or indirectly, of funds by their nationals or in their territories with the intention that the funds should be used, or in the knowledge that they are to be used, in order to carry out terrorist acts;

(c) Freeze without delay funds and other financial assets or economic resources of persons who commit, or attempt to commit, terrorist acts or participate in or facilitate the commission of terrorist acts; of entities owned or controlled directly or indirectly by such persons; and of persons and entities acting on behalf of, or at the direction of such persons and entities, including funds derived or generated from property owned or controlled directly or indirectly by such persons and associated persons and entities;

(d) Prohibit their nationals or any persons and entities within their territories from making any funds, financial assets or economic resources or financial or other related services available, directly or indirectly, for the benefit of persons who commit or attempt to commit or facilitate or participate in the commission of terrorist acts, of entities owned or controlled, directly or indirectly, by such persons and of persons and entities acting on behalf of or at the direction of such persons;

2. *Decides also* that all States shall:

(a) Refrain from providing any form of support, active or passive, to entities or persons involved in terrorist acts, including by suppressing recruitment of members of terrorist groups and eliminating the supply of weapons to terrorists;

(b) Take the necessary steps to prevent the commission of terrorist acts, including by provision of early warning to other States by exchange of information;

(c) Deny safe haven to those who finance, plan, support, or commit terrorist acts, or provide safe havens;

(d) Prevent those who finance, plan, facilitate or commit terrorist acts from using their respective territories for those purposes against other States or their citizens;

(e) Ensure that any person who participates in the financing, planning, preparation or perpetration of terrorist acts or in supporting terrorist acts is brought to justice and ensure that, in addition to any other measures against them, such terrorist acts are established as serious criminal offences in domestic laws and regulations and that the punishment duly reflects the seriousness of such terrorist acts;

(f) Afford one another the greatest measure of assistance in connection with criminal investigations or criminal proceedings relating to the financing or support of terrorist acts, including assistance in obtaining evidence in their possession necessary for the proceedings;

(g) Prevent the movement of terrorists or terrorist groups by effective border controls and controls on issuance of identity papers and travel documents, and through measures for preventing counterfeiting, forgery or fraudulent use of identity papers and travel documents;

3. *Calls* upon all States to:

(a) Find ways of intensifying and accelerating the exchange of operational information, especially regarding actions or movements of terrorist persons or networks; forged or falsified travel documents; traffic in arms, explosives or sensitive materials; use of communications technologies by terrorist groups; and the threat posed by the possession of weapons of mass destruction by terrorist groups;

(b) Exchange information in accordance with international and domestic law and cooperate on administrative and judicial matters to prevent the commission of terrorist acts;

(c) Cooperate, particularly through bilateral and multilateral arrangements and agreements, to prevent and suppress terrorist attacks and take action against perpetrators of such acts;

(d) Become parties as soon as possible to the relevant international conventions and protocols relating to terrorism, including the International Convention for the Suppression of the Financing of Terrorism of 9 December 1999;

(e) Increase cooperation and fully implement the relevant international conventions and protocols relating to terrorism and Security Council resolutions 1269 (1999) and 1368 (2001);

(f) Take appropriate measures in conformity with the relevant provisions of national and international law, including international standards of human rights, before granting refugee status, for the purpose of ensuring that the asylum-seeker has not planned, facilitated or participated in the commission of terrorist acts;

(g) Ensure, in conformity with international law, that refugee status is not abused by the perpetrators, organizers or facilitators of terrorist acts, and that claims of political motivation are not recognized as grounds for refusing requests for the extradition of alleged terrorists;

4. *Notes* with concern the close connection between international terrorism and transnational organized crime, illicit drugs, money-laundering, illegal armstrafficking, and illegal movement of nuclear, chemical, biological and other potentially deadly materials, and in this regard emphasizes the need to enhance coordination of efforts on national, subregional, regional and international levels in order to strengthen a global response to this serious challenge and threat to international security;

5. *Declares* that acts, methods, and practices of terrorism are contrary to the purposes and principles of the United Nations and that knowingly financing, planning and inciting terrorist acts are also contrary to the purposes and principles of the United Nations;

6. *Decides* to establish, in accordance with rule 28 of its provisional rules of procedure, a Committee of the Security Council, consisting of all the members of the Council, to monitor implementation of this resolution, with the assistance of appropriate expertise, and calls upon all States to report to the Committee, no later than 90 days from the date of adoption of this resolution and thereafter according to a timetable to be proposed by the Committee, on the steps they have taken to implement this resolution;

7. *Directs* the Committee to delineate its tasks, submit a work programme within 30 days of the adoption of this resolution, and to consider the support it requires, in consultation with the Secretary-General;

8. *Expresses* its determination to take all necessary steps in order to ensure the full implementation of this resolution, in accordance with its responsibilities under the Charter;

9. *Decides* to remain seized of this matter.

6. Draft Comprehensive Convention on International Terrorism

Article 1

For the purposes of this Convention:

1. "State or government facility" includes any permanent or temporary facility or conveyance that is used or occupied by representatives of a State, members of Government, the legislature or the judiciary or by officials or employees of a State or any other public authority or entity or by employees or officials of an intergovernmental organization in connection with their official duties.

2. "Military forces of a State" means the armed forces of a State which are organized, trained and equipped under its internal law for the primary purpose of national defence or security, and persons acting in support of those armed forces who are under their formal command, control and responsibility.

3. "Infrastructure facility" means any publicly or privately owned facility providing or distributing services for the benefit of the public, such as water, sewerage, energy, fuel or communications, and banking services, telecommunications and information networks.

4. "Place of public use" means those parts of any building, land, street, waterway or other location that are accessible or open to members of the public, whether continuously, periodically or occasionally, and encompasses any commercial, business, cultural, historical, educational, religious, governmental, entertainment, recreational or similar place that is so accessible or open to the public.

5. "Public transportation system" means all facilities, conveyances and instrumentalities, whether publicly or privately owned, that are used in or for publicly available services for the transportation of persons or cargo.

Article 2

1. Any person commits an offence within the meaning of this Convention if that person, by any means, unlawfully and intentionally, does an act intended to cause:

(a) Death or serious bodily injury to any person; or

(b) Serious damage to a State or government facility, a public transportation system, communication system or infrastructure facility with the intent to cause extensive destruction of such a place, facility or system, or where such destruction results or is likely to result in major economic loss;

when the purpose of such act, by its nature or context, is to intimidate a population, or to compel a Government or an international organization to do or abstain from doing any act. [In some versions of the draft, this last clause is printed at the end of, as if part of, subsection (b). If placed there, then (a) would stand alone without a requirement of political motivation and thus cover virtually any act of violence.]

2. Any person also commits an offence if that person attempts to commit an

offence or participates as an accomplice in an offence as set forth in paragraph 1.

3.   Any person also commits an offence if that person:

(a)   Organizes, directs or instigates others to commit an offence as set forth in paragraph 1 or 2; or

(b)   Aids, abets, facilitates or counsels the commission of such an offence; or

(c)   In any other way contributes to the commission of one or more offences referred to in paragraphs 1, 2 or 3(a) by a group of persons acting with a common purpose; such contribution shall be intentional and either be made with the aim of furthering the general criminal activity or purpose of the group or be made in the knowledge of the intention of the group to commit the offence or offences concerned.

Article 3

This Convention shall not apply where the offence is committed within a single State, the alleged offender is a national of that State and is present in the territory of that State and no other State has a basis under article 6, paragraph 1, or article 6, paragraph 2, to exercise jurisdiction, except that the provisions of articles 10 to 22 shall, as appropriate, apply in those cases.

Article 4

Each State Party shall adopt such measures as may be necessary:

(a)   To establish as criminal offences under its domestic law the offences set forth in article 2;

(b)   To make those offences punishable by appropriate penalties which take into account the grave nature of those offences.

Article 5

Each State Party shall adopt such measures as may be necessary, including, where appropriate, domestic legislation, to ensure that criminal acts within the scope of this Convention are under no circumstances justifiable by considerations of a political, philosophical, ideological, racial, ethnic, religious or other similar nature.

Article 6

1.   Each State Party shall take such measures as may be necessary to establish its jurisdiction over the offences referred to in article 2 in the following cases.

(a)   When the offence is committed in the territory of that State or on board a ship or aircraft registered in that State;

(b)   When the alleged offender is a national of that State or is a person who has his or her habitual residence in its territory;

(c)   When the offence is committed wholly or partially outside its territory, if the effects of the conduct or its intended effects constitute or result, within its territory, in the commission of an offence referred to in article 2.

2.   A State may also establish its jurisdiction over any such offence when it is committed:

(a)   By a stateless person whose habitual residence is in that State; or

(b)   With respect to a national of that State; or

(c)   Against a State or government facility of that State abroad, including an embassy or other diplomatic or consular premises of that State; or

(d)   In an attempt to compel that State to do or to abstain from doing any act;

(e)   On board a ship or aircraft which is operated by the Government of that State.

3.   Each State Party shall take such measures as may be necessary to establish

its jurisdiction over the offences referred to in article 2 in cases where the alleged offender is present in its territory and where it does not extradite such person to any of the States Parties that have established their jurisdiction in accordance with paragraphs 1 or 2.

4. When more than one State Party claims jurisdiction over the offences set forth in article 2, the relevant States Parties shall strive to coordinate their actions appropriately, in particular concerning the conditions for prosecution and the modalities for mutual legal assistance.

5. This Convention does not exclude any criminal jurisdiction exercised in accordance with national law.

Article 7

States Parties shall take appropriate measures, before granting asylum, for the purpose of ensuring that asylum is not granted to any person in respect of whom there are reasonable grounds indicating his involvement in any offence referred to in article 2.

Article 8

States Parties shall cooperate in the prevention of the offences set forth in article 2, particularly:

(a) By taking all practicable measures, including, if necessary, adapting their domestic legislation, to prevent and counter preparations in their respective territories for the commission, by whomsoever and in whatever manner, of those offences within or outside their territories, including:

(i) Measures to prohibit in their territories the establishment and operation of installations and training camps for the commission, within or outside their territories, of offences referred to in article 2; and

(ii) Measures to prohibit the illegal activities of persons, groups and organizations that encourage, instigate, organize, knowingly finance or engage in the commission, within or outside their territories, of offences referred to in article 2;

(b) By exchanging accurate and verified information in accordance with their national law, and coordinating administrative and other measures taken as appropriate to prevent the commission of offences as referred to in article 2.

Article 9

1. Each State Party, in accordance with its domestic legal principles, shall take the necessary measures to enable a legal entity located in its territory or organized under its laws to be held liable when a person responsible for the management or control of that legal entity has, in that capacity, committed an offence referred to in article 2. Such liability may be criminal, civil or administrative.

2. Such liability is incurred without prejudice to the criminal liability of individuals having committed the offences.

3. Each State Party shall ensure, in particular, that legal entities liable in accordance with paragraph (i) above are subject to effective, proportionate and dissuasive criminal, civil or administrative sanctions. Such sanctions may include monetary sanctions.

Article 10

1. Upon receiving information that a person who has committed or who is alleged to have committed an offence referred to in article 2 may be present in its territory, the State Party concerned shall take such measures as may be

necessary under its domestic law to investigate the facts contained in the information.

2.   Upon being satisfied that the circumstances so warrant, the State Party in whose territory the offender or alleged offender is present shall take the appropriate measures under its domestic law so as to ensure that person's presence for the purpose of prosecution or extradition.

6.   When a State Party, pursuant to the present article, has taken a person into custody, it shall immediately notify, directly or through the Secretary-General of the United Nations, the States Parties which have established jurisdiction in accordance with article 6, paragraph 1 or 2, and if it considers it advisable, any other interested States Parties, of the fact that such person is in custody and of the circumstances which warrant that person's detention. The State which makes the investigation contemplated in paragraph 1 shall promptly inform the said States Parties of its findings and shall indicate whether it intends to exercise jurisdiction.

Article 11

1.   The State Party in whose territory the alleged offender is found shall, if it does not extradite the person, be obliged, without exception whatsoever and whether or not the offence was committed in its territory, to submit the case to its competent authorities for the purpose of prosecution through proceedings in accordance with the laws of that State. Those authorities shall take their decision in the same manner as in the case of any ordinary offence of a grave nature under the law of that State.

2.   Whenever a State Party is permitted under its domestic law to extradite or otherwise surrender one of its nationals only upon the condition that the person will be returned to that State to serve the sentence imposed as a result of the trial or proceeding for which the extradition or surrender of the person was sought, and that State and the State seeking the extradition of the person agree with this option and other terms they may deem appropriate, such a conditional extradition or surrender shall be sufficient to discharge the obligation set forth in paragraph 1.

TABLE OF CASES

[References are to pages]

(Rel. 002 Pub.3211)

[References are to pages]

[References are to pages]

[References are to pages]

INDEX

[References are to page numbers.]

[References are to page numbers.]

[References are to page numbers.]